EDITION 9

Operations Management

Norman Gaither

Texas A&M University

Greg Frazier

The University of Texas at Arlington

SOUTH-WESTERN

THOMSON LEARNING

Australia · Canada · Mexico · Singapore · Spain · United Kingdom · United States

Operations Management, 9e
by Norman Gaither and Greg Frazier

VICE PRESIDENT/PUBLISHER: Dave Shaut
SENIOR ACQUISITIONS EDITOR: Charles McCormick, Jr.
SENIOR MARKETING MANAGER: Joseph A. Sabatino
SENIOR DEVELOPMENTAL EDITOR: Alice C. Denny
SENIOR PRODUCTION EDITOR: Kara ZumBahlen
MEDIA TECHNOLOGY EDITOR: Diane Van Bakel
MEDIA DEVELOPMENTAL EDITOR: Christine Wittmer
MEDIA PRODUCTION EDITOR: Robin K. Browning
MANUFACTURING COORDINATOR: Sandee Milewski
INTERNAL DESIGN: Ann Small, A Small Design Studio
PHOTO RESEARCH: Michelle Kunkler
COVER DESIGN: Liz Harasymczuk, Liz Harasymczuk Design
COVER ILLUSTRATION: Kevin Ghiglione, i2i Art, Inc.
COVER DESIGN MANAGER: Rick A. Moore
PRODUCTION HOUSE: Litten Editing and Production, Inc.
PRINTER: R.R. Donnelley

Printed in China by R.R. Donnelley
5 04

For more information contact South-Western, 5101 Madison Road, Cincinnati, Ohio, 45227 or find us on the Internet at http://www.swcollege.com

For permission to use material from this text or product, contact us by
• **telephone: 1-800-730-2214**
• **fax: 1-800-730-2215**
• **web: http://www.thomsonrights.com**

0-324-06685-6 (package, text and CDs)
0-324-06686-4 (text only)
0-324-06687-2 (CD with *POM Software Library*)
0-324-15092-X (CD with *Project 2000*)

Library of Congress Cataloging-in-Publication Data

Gaither, Norman.
     Operations management / Norman Gaither, Greg Frazier.—9th ed.
          p. cm.
     Rev. ed. of: Production and operations management. 8th ed. ©1999.
     Includes bibliographical references and index.
     ISBN 0-324-06685-6 (alk. paper)
     1. Production management.   I. Frazier, Greg   II. Title.
TS155.G17   2001
     658.5—dc21   2001034493

Brief Contents

PART 1

MANAGING OPERATIONS IN A GLOBAL ENVIRONMENT 2

Chapter 1
Introduction to Operations Management 5

Chapter 2
Operations Strategies in a Global Economy 26

PART 2

PLANNING THE STRATEGIC USE OF RESOURCES 60

Chapter 3
Demand Forecasting 62

Chapter 4
Product, Process, and Service Design 113

Chapter 5
Facility Capacity, Location, and Layout 163

Chapter 6
Operations Technologies 229

Chapter 7
Operations Quality Management 265

Chapter 8
Strategic Allocation of Resources 297

Chapter 9
Service Operations Planning and Scheduling 333

Chapter 10
Project Management 375

PART 3

MANAGING OPERATIONS IN THE SUPPLY CHAIN 422

Chapter 11
Supply Chain Management and E-Business 424

Chapter 12
Just-in-Time and Lean Manufacturing 462

Chapter 13
Production Planning 491

Chapter 14
Inventory Management 535

Chapter 15
Resource Requirements Planning: MRP and CRP 582

Chapter 16
Manufacturing Operations Scheduling 622

PART 4

MAINTAINING EFFECTIVE AND EFFICIENT OPERATIONS 660

Chapter 17
Quality Control 662

Chapter 18
Employee Productivity 696

Chapter 19
Maintenance Management 741

Appendices

A Normal Probability Distribution 774

B Student's t Probability Distribution 776

C Answers to Odd-Numbered Problems 778

D Glossary 783

Author Index 795

Subject Index 799

Photo Credits 813

Contents

PART 1

MANAGING OPERATIONS IN A GLOBAL ENVIRONMENT 2

Chapter 1
Introduction to Operations Management 5

Historical Milestones in POM 8
    The Industrial Revolution 8
    Post–Civil War Period 10
    Scientific Management 10
    Human Relations and Behavioralism 13
    Operations Research 13
    The Service Revolution 15
    The Computer Revolution 16

Factors Affecting Operations Management Today 16

Studying Operations Management 17
    Operations as a System 17
    Decision Making in POM 20

Business Snapshot:
1.1 Scientific Management at Ford's Rouge Plant 12

Chapter 2
Operations Strategies in a Global Economy 26

Today's Global Business Conditions 29
    Reality of Global Competition 29
    Quality, Customer Service, and Cost Challenges 35
    Advanced Technologies 37
    Continued Growth of the Service Sector 37
    Scarcity of Operations Resources 38
    Social-Responsibility Issues 39

Operations Strategy 43
    Competitive Priorities 45
    Elements of Operations Strategy 46
    Operations Strategy in Services 50

Forming Operations Strategies 52
    Evolution of Positioning Strategies 52
    Linking Operations and Marketing Strategies 52
    A Variety of Strategies Can Be Successful 53

Business Snapshots:
2.1 Opening China's Markets to Foreign Firms 31
2.2 Strategic Alliances 33
2.3 GM's New Brazilian Auto Complex 36
2.4 Cleaning Up Medical Waste 40
2.5 Recycling and Conservation in Industry 41
2.6 Environmental Efforts at Compaq 42

PART 2

PLANNING THE STRATEGIC USE OF RESOURCES 60

Chapter 3
Demand Forecasting 62

Qualitative Forecasting Methods 66

Quantitative Forecasting Models 67
    Forecast Accuracy 67
    Long-Range Forecasts 68
    Short-Range Forecasts 81

How to Have a Successful Forecasting System 92
    How to Select a Forecasting Method 92
    How to Monitor and Control a Forecasting Model 95

Computer Software for Forecasting 97

Forecasting in Small Businesses and Start-Up Ventures 97

Business Snapshots:
3.1 Forecasting Telephone Calls at L. L. Bean 79
3.2 Using a Forecasting Expert System at Xerox 93
3.3 Forecasting Flare Sales at Olin Corporation 94
3.4 Focus Forecasting at American Hardware Supply 95

Chapter 4
Product, Process, and Service Design 113

Designing and Developing Products and Services 114
    Sources of Product Innovation 115
    Developing New Products 115
    Getting New Products to Market Faster 116
    Improving the Designs of Existing Products 119
    Designing for Ease of Production 119
    Designing for Quality 120
    Designing and Developing New Services 120

Process Planning and Design 121

Major Factors Affecting Process Design
Decisions 122
Nature of Product/Service Demand 122
Degree of Vertical Integration 123
Production Flexibility 123
Degree of Automation 124
Product/Service Quality 125

Types of Process Designs 125
Product-Focused 125
Process-Focused 127
Group Technology/Cellular Manufacturing 128

Interrelationships among Product Design, Process
Design, and Inventory Policy 131

Process Design in Services 132

Deciding among Processing Alternatives 134
Batch Size and Product Variety 134
Capital Requirements for Process Designs 136
Economic Analysis 136
Assembly Charts 140
Process Charts 140

Plant Tours 140
A Product-Focused, Dedicated Factory: Safety
Products Corporation, Richmond, Virginia 140
A Process-Focused Factory: R. R. Donnelley &
Sons, Willard, Ohio 147
A Service Operation: Wal-Mart Regional
Distribution Center, New Braunfels, Texas 150

Business Snapshots:
4.1 Applied Research Pays Off with Cool Sound 115
4.2 Developing the Prodigy at Ford 117
4.3 Virtual Reality Simulations in the Product Design
Process at Boeing 118
4.4 Strategic Outsourcing—From Vertical to Virtual
Integration 124
4.5 Compaq Changes to Produce-to-Order 132

Chapter 5
Facility Capacity, Location, and Layout 163

Long-Range Capacity Planning 165
Definition of Production Capacity 165
Measurements of Capacity 166
Forecasting Capacity Demand 166
Ways of Changing Capacity 168
Economies of Scale 168
Analyzing Capacity-Planning Decisions 173
Decision Tree Analysis 174

Facility Location 176
Factors Affecting Location Decisions 177
Types of Facilities and Their Dominant Locational
Factors 177
Data, Politics, Incentives, and Preemptive Tactics 182
Analyzing Retailing and Other Service
Locations 184
Analyzing Industrial Facility Locations 184
Integrating Quantitative and Qualitative Factors into
Location Decisions 185

Facility Layout 186

Manufacturing Facility Layouts 187
Materials Handling 187
Process Layouts 188
Product Layouts 189
Cellular Manufacturing Layouts 190
Fixed-Position Layouts 191
Hybrid Layouts 192
New Trends in Manufacturing Layouts 192

Analyzing Manufacturing Facility Layouts 194
Software for Analyzing Facility Layouts 194
Planning Process and Warehouse Layouts 194
Planning Product Layouts 195
Planning Cellular Manufacturing Layouts 204

Service Facility Layouts 207
Types of Service Facility Layouts 207
Analyzing Service Facility Layouts 208

Business Snapshots:
5.1 Automakers Facing Overcapacity in Asia 167
5.2 Too Little and Too Much Capacity 169
5.3 Intel Delays Opening of New Plant 170
5.4 Outsourcing Provides Additional Capacity 173
5.5 Global Facility Location at DEC 179
5.6 Texas Incentives Not Enough for Intel 183
5.7 Boeing Factory Saves Space 193

Chapter 6
Operations Technologies 229

Types of Manufacturing Automation 231
Machine Attachments 232
Numerically Controlled Machines 232
Robots 233
Automated Quality Control Inspection 234
Automatic Identification Systems 235
Automated Process Controls 235

Automated Production Systems 235
Automated Flow Lines 236
Automated Assembly Systems 236

Flexible Manufacturing Systems 237
Automated Storage and Retrieval Systems 238

Software Systems for Automation 239
CAD/CAM 239
Computer-Integrated Manufacturing 240
Enterprise Resource Planning 240

Automation in Services 242

Automation Issues 246
Use of Automation 246
Building Manufacturing Flexibility 247
Justifying Automation Projects 248
Managing Technological Change 248
Worker Displacement, Training, and Retraining 249

Deciding among Automation Alternatives 250
Rating Scale Approach 251
Relative-Aggregate-Scores Approach 252

Business Snapshots:
6.1 Northrop Grumman Searches for New Production Technology 231
6.2 One of the First N/C Machines 233
6.3 ASRS in Hospital Pharmacies 239
6.4 Managing a Company with SAP's ERP Software 241
6.5 Automated Checkout at Kroger Grocery Store 244
6.6 Communications Technology Demolishes Time and Distance 245
6.7 Automated Technologies at Countrywide 245

Chapter 7
Operations Quality Management 265

Nature of Quality 267
Dimensions of Quality 267
Determinants of Quality 267
Costs of Quality 268

Traditional Quality Management 269

Modern Quality Management 270
Quality Gurus 270
Quality Drives the Productivity Machine 272
Other Aspects of the Quality Picture 273

Quality Management Recognition 274
Malcolm Baldrige National Quality Award 274
The Deming Prize 275
ISO 9000 Standards 277

Total Quality Management (TQM) Programs 277
Top Management Commitment and Involvement 278

Customer Involvement 278
Designing Products for Quality 279
Designing and Controlling Production Processes 283
Developing Supplier Partnerships 284
Customer Service, Distribution, and Installation 285
Building Teams of Empowered Employees 285
Benchmarking and Continuous Improvement 288

Quality Management in Services 289

Business Snapshots:
7.1 Deming's 14 Points 271
7.2 The Malcolm Baldrige National Quality Award 275
7.3 Radio and Laser Technology Improves Steel Operations 286
7.4 Empowered Work Teams at Square D Corporation 287
7.5 Benchmarking at Sprint 289
7.6 Examples of TQM in Services 291

Chapter 8
Strategic Allocation of Resources 297

Recognizing LP Problems 302

Formulating LP Problems 303

Solving LP Problems 307
Graphical LP Solutions 307
Overview of Other LP Solution Methods 312

Real LP Problems 318

Interpreting Computer Solutions of LP Problems 320

Business Snapshots:
8.1 Operations Research in U.S. Corporations 299
8.2 Linear Programming Cutting Costs at American Airlines 301

Chapter 9
Service Operations Planning and Scheduling 333
Nature of Services Revisited 334
Operations Strategies for Services 336
Types of Service Operations 337
Scheduling Challenges in Services 337

Scheduling Quasi-Manufacturing Service Operations 340
Product-Focused Operations 340
Process-Focused Operations 340
Work-Shift Scheduling in Service Operations 341

Scheduling Customer-as-Participant Service
Operations 345
Nature of These Operations 345
Waiting Lines in Service Operations 346

Scheduling Customer-as-Product Service
Operations 355
Nature of These Operations 356
Using Computer Simulation in Service
Operations 358

Business Snapshot:
9.1 Taco Bell Uses Simulation to Develop Employee
Schedules 358

Chapter 10
Project Management 375

Project Management 376

Project-Planning and Control Techniques 379
Scheduling and Control Charts 379
Critical Path Method (CPM) 384
Program Evaluation and Review Technique (PERT)
394
Project Cost Control Systems 398
CPM/PERT in Practice 400

Computer Software for Project Management 404

An Evaluation of CPM/PERT 406

Business Snapshot:
10.1 Project Management Professionals 380

PART 3

MANAGING OPERATIONS IN THE SUPPLY
CHAIN 422

Chapter 11
Supply Chain Management and E-Business 424

Supply Chain Management 425

Purchasing 427
Importance of Purchasing Today 428
Mission of Purchasing 429
What Purchasing Managers Do 430
Purchasing Departments in Organizations 430
Purchasing Processes 431
Buyers and Their Duties 433
Make-or-Buy Analysis 433
Ethics in Buying 435
Purchasing: The International Frontier 436

Logistics 437
Production Control: Movement of Materials within
Factories 437
Shipments to and from Factories 438
Innovations in Logistics 440

Warehousing 441
Warehousing Operations 441
Methods of Inventory Accounting 443
Contemporary Developments in Warehousing 445

Expediting 446

Benchmarking the Performance of Materials
Managers 446

Third-Party Logistics Management Providers 447

E-Business and Supply Chain Management 448

Business Snapshots:
11.1 Allegations of Improper Behavior by Buyers 435
11.2 Guidelines for Ethical Behavior in Purchasing 436
11.3 Trucking on the Web 441
11.4 Top-Selling Supply Chain Management
Software 442

Chapter 12
Just-in-Time and Lean Manufacturing 462

The Just-in-Time Manufacturing Philosophy 464

Prerequisites for JIT Manufacturing 468

Elements of JIT Manufacturing 470
Eliminating Waste 470
Enforced Problem Solving and Continuous
Improvement 471
People Make JIT Work 472
Total Quality Management 472
Parallel Processing 472
Kanban Production Control 473
JIT Purchasing 476
E-Commerce and JIT Purchasing 477
Reducing Inventories through Setup Reduction 478
Working toward Repetitive Manufacturing 480

Benefits of JIT Manufacturing 481

Success and JIT Manufacturing 482

JIT in Service Companies 484

Business Snapshots:
12.1 Using Queuing Theory to Achieve Time-Based
Competition 467
12.2 JIT Purchasing at Waterville TG, Inc. 477

12.3 JIT at Perlos 481
12.4 Maturing JIT Implementation at Amadas 483

Chapter 13
Production Planning 491

Production-Planning Hierarchy 492

Aggregate Planning 493
Aggregate Demand 494
Dimensions of Production Capacity 495
Sources of Medium-Range Production Capacity 497
Some Traditional Aggregate Plans 497
Criteria for Selecting Aggregate Plans 504
Aggregate Plans for Services 506
Mathematical Models for Aggregate Planning 508
Preemptive Tactics 510

Master Production Scheduling 511
Objectives of Master Production Scheduling 511
Time Fences in Master Production Schedules 511
Procedures for Developing Master Production
Schedules 512
Demand Management 516
Weekly Updating of the MPS 516
MPS in Produce-to-Stock and Produce-to-Order
Firms 517
Length of Planning Horizons 518
Computerized MPS 518

Types of Production-Planning and Control
Systems 520
Pond-Draining Systems 520
Push Systems 521
Pull Systems 522
Focusing on Bottlenecks 523

Business Snapshot:
13.1 Aggregate Planning at Sherman-Brown Chemical
Company 495

Chapter 14
Inventory Management 535

Opposing Views of Inventories 536
Why We Want to Hold Inventories 536
Why We Do Not Want to Hold Inventories 537

Nature of Inventories 539

Fixed Order Quantity Systems 540
Determining Order Quantities 541
Determining Order Points 550

Fixed Order Period Systems 559

Other Inventory Models 561
Hybrid Inventory Models 561
Single-Period Inventory Models 562

Some Realities of Inventory Planning 565
ABC Classification of Materials 565
EOQ and Uncertainty 567
Dynamics of Inventory Planning 568
Other Factors Affecting Inventory Planning 568
Vendor-Managed Inventories 568
Computers and Inventory Planning 569

Business Snapshots:
14.1 Improved Inventory Management at 3M 569
14.2 Computer Manufacturers Adopt Produce-to-Order
Strategies 572

Chapter 15
Resource Requirements Planning: MRP and
CRP 582

Material Requirements Planning (MRP) 584
Objectives of MRP 586
Elements of MRP 588
Green Thumb Water Sprinkler Company 591
Lot-Sizing in MRP 598
Issues in MRP 600
From MRP I to MRP II to ERP 602
How MRP Adapts to Change 603
Evaluation of MRP 604

Capacity Requirements Planning (CRP) 605
Load Schedules 607

Business Snapshot:
15.1 Green Thumb Water Sprinkler Company 591

Chapter 16
Manufacturing Operations Scheduling 622

Scheduling Process-Focused Manufacturing 623
Shop-Floor Planning and Control 626
Order-Sequencing Problems 630
Assignment Problems 638

Scheduling Product-Focused Manufacturing 638
Batch Scheduling 639
Delivery Schedules: Line-of-Balance Method 642

Computerized Scheduling Systems 645

Business Snapshots:
16.1 Input–Output Control at Boeing 628
16.2 Finite Loading at SMC 630
16.3 One Company's Experience with *OPT* Software
646
16.4 *OPT*—The Logical Solution 647

PART 4

MAINTAINING EFFECTIVE AND EFFICIENT
OPERATIONS 660

Chapter 17
Quality Control 662

Statistical Concepts in Quality Control 665
Sampling 665
Central Limit Theorem and Quality Control 666

Control Charts 666
Control Charts for Attributes 667
Control Charts for Variables 670

Acceptance Plans 673
Single, Double, and Sequential Samples 674
Single-Sample Acceptance Plans for Attributes 675
Estimating Acceptance Criteria 680
Single-Sample Acceptance Plans for Variables 685

Computers in Quality Control 686

Quality Control in Services 687

Business Snapshot:
17.1 SPC at Georgia-Pacific 668

Chapter 18
Employee Productivity 696

Productivity and Human Behavior 698
Multifactor Approach to Measuring Productivity 699
Labor Productivity 701

Designing Workers' Jobs 705

Empowering Workers 707

Work Methods Analysis 708
How to Do Methods Analysis 708

Work Measurement 712
Labor Standards 712
Time Study 713
Work Sampling 714
Predetermined Time Standards 717

Learning Curves 720
Arithmetic Analysis 722
Logarithmic Analysis 722
Learning-Curve Tables 723
Selecting a Learning Rate 725
Uses and Limitations of Learning Curves 725

Employees' Health and Safety 726

Business Snapshots:
18.1 Productivity Improvements in the United States 701
18.2 Smarter and Better-Trained Employees 703
18.3 Dramatic Safety Improvements at Georgia-Pacific 728

Chapter 19
Maintenance Management 741

Repair Programs 745
Repair Crews, Standby Machines, and Repair Shops 746
Breakdowns Trigger Repairs and Corrective Actions 747
Early Parts-Replacement Policies 748
Letting Workers Repair Their Own Machines 748

Preventive Maintenance (PM) Programs 752
PM and Operations Strategies 752
Automation and the Prominence of PM 752
Scheduling PM Activities 752
PM Database Requirements 753
Modern Approaches to PM 753

Machine Reliability 760

Secondary Maintenance Department Responsibilities 760

Trends in Maintenance 760

Maintenance Issues in Service Organizations 761

Business Snapshots:
19.1 Total Productive Maintenance at Asten, Inc. 754
19.2 Decision Support System for Aircraft Maintenance Planning at American Airlines 762

Appendices

A Normal Probability Distribution 774

B Student's t Probability Distribution 776

C Answers to Odd-Numbered Problems 778

D Glossary 783

Author Index 795

Subject Index 799

Photo Credits 813

Leading organizations today are leaner and more agile than in the past, and they take advantage of technology whenever possible. To maintain this competitive stance, these organizations rely on their operations functions to be dependable and efficient. Effective operations management is the key to business success that integrates other functional areas, which together enable an organization to excel in the marketplace. The successful integrated organization will meet global competition with quality outputs, outstanding customer service, and effective control of costs.

OPERATIONS MANAGEMENT, 9e, will introduce students to the many operations topics and issues faced by leading organizations, both in services and in manufacturing. In revising this edition, we address new developments in the field of operations management and new information resources available, such as the Internet, while retaining a strong focus on the fundamental concepts. The goal of this text is to help students gain an understanding of what operations management involves, how it relates to other functional areas in an organization, the types of problems that are faced by operations managers, and common decision-making approaches.

As with previous editions, courses in college algebra and introductory statistics are considered prerequisites to OM courses using this textbook. Although the mathematical and statistical concepts in this text are not complex, students with a basic background in these topics tend to perform better.

WHAT'S NEW IN THE NINTH EDITION?

While the basic premise of *OPERATIONS MANAGEMENT* has not changed, the new edition contains a number of important changes and revisions. Many of the Business Snapshot features within the text are new or updated. Examples, tables, references, and suggested readings lists throughout the book have been updated. New features and topical coverage include:

- **Reorganization of chapters.** Several chapters have been moved earlier in the text to reflect the stronger emphasis they often receive in business and course content. Operations Quality Management is now Chapter 7; Service Operations Planning and Scheduling is now Chapter 9; Project Management is now Chapter 10; and Supply Chain Management and E-Business is now Chapter 11.
- **New problems and cases.** Over 150 new problems and cases are included. Where relevant, these new materials encourage use of spreadsheet applications.
- **Operations management in services.** Service operations are emphasized in this edition. The application of operations strategy, process planning, automation, and quality to service operations is specifically discussed. Examples, problems, and cases are cast in the setting of transportation, retailing and wholesaling, banking, and other service industries. Chapter 9 addresses many of the operational decisions in services.
- **Supply chain management.** Chapter 11 introduces students to the concept of managing a supply chain. Topics such as purchasing, logistics, and warehousing are presented from the perspective of managing the flow of materials from raw material suppliers to final consumers of finished goods.

- **E-business.** The impact of E-business on business operations is discussed specifically in Chapter 11 and noted elsewhere throughout the text.
- **Internet assignments.** Internet assignments have been updated for every chapter. These give students the opportunity to search the vast resources of the Internet for information relevant to topics covered in each chapter. Some of the assignments require written answers that encourage critical thinking and communications skills.

FEATURES FOR TEACHING AND LEARNING

Distinctive features of the ninth edition include:

- **A comprehensive, practical, balanced, and nontheoretical approach to operations management.** The text places the student squarely in the operations function in a variety of situations: manufacturing and services, small businesses and large corporations, quantitative and managerial approaches, start-up and established businesses, and high-tech and traditional businesses. Many of the problems and examples in the text have been abstracted from actual situations in industry.
- **A problem-solving and decision-making approach.** Each chapter includes examples of operations management problems with complete solutions. The step-by-step approach allows readers to follow every detail of the solutions. A strength of the text is its problem sets and cases, which are numerous and can be worked directly from the information provided in the chapters. The problems become progressively more difficult as one proceeds through a set. In a continuing effort to keep the problem sets current and effective, over 150 problems and cases are new in this edition.

  The chapter framework encourages learning by students. Students can move from concepts, solved examples, odd-numbered problem assignments with answers, and finally to even-numbered problem assignments without the assistance of answers. This process builds students' understanding and confidence.

- **An ongoing emphasis on contemporary topics.** This includes:

  Global competition, quality management, and customer service. The ever-increasing role of global competition and environmental forces in operations strategy is highlighted in Chapter 2, and their influences are discussed throughout the text. Chapter 7, Operations Quality Management, and Chapter 17, Quality Control, present the overall philosophy and methods of managing quality.

  Just-in-Time (JIT) and lean manufacturing. Chapter 12 discusses the philosophy and methods of planning and controlling manufacturing operations. The ways that JIT affects purchasing and materials management, human resources practices, quality control, customer service, and other concepts are integrated throughout the text.

  Advanced production technology. Chapter 1 introduces automation and related concepts. Chapter 2 discusses the strategic implications of high-tech manufacturing. Chapter 6 discusses the types of automated machines and production systems from the perspective of the operations manager and how they affect the strategic performance of operations.

- **Business Snapshots.** Special accounts of service and manufacturing applications are featured in every chapter, including many new ones in the ninth edition. When possible, these Business Snapshots include the names of real companies and people and their actual situations to demonstrate the relevance of what we teach in operations management courses.

- **Web addresses.** Where relevant throughout the text and boxed features, web site URLs are provided for companies and organizations that are discussed. This allows students to further research operations management topics in particular organizations.
- **Wrap-Up: What World-Class Companies Do.** This unique feature at the end of each chapter replaces a conventional summary. The discussions apply chapter concepts to the explanations of what the world's best-managed companies are doing in globally competitive markets. By this means, the latest and most advanced thinking about structuring, analyzing, and managing operations systems is integrated throughout the text.

ANCILLARY TEACHING AND LEARNING MATERIALS

Several excellent ancillaries accompany the new edition of *OPERATIONS MANAGEMENT*. Two software products are included within the textbook itself:

- The **POM Software Library** includes updated Microsoft® Windows based software for solving OM problems and cases provided in the text. A software icon in the margin identifies these items.
- **Microsoft® Project 2000 software (Trial version)** is also included inside the textbook.

New to the ninth edition are learning materials that may be purchased directly by students:

- The **Study Guide** provides the student with significant supplementary study materials. Prepared by John Loucks of St. Edward's University, it contains an outline of key concepts, review materials, examples with step-by-step solutions, exercises with answers, and a series of self-test questions with answers.
- **WebTutor™**, a brand new electronic ancillary, is available with the new edition of *OPERATIONS MANAGEMENT*. There are two main formats for this product:
  - WebTutor is used by an entire class under the direction of the instructor. It provides web-based learning resources to students as well as powerful communication and other course management tools including course calendar, chat, and email for instructors. WebTutor is available for use on WebCT and Blackboard. See http://webtutor.thomsonlearning.com for more information.
  - Personal WebTutor provides the learning resources for individual students to purchase and use for study and review. See http://pwt.swcollege.com for more information about this product.

The following instructor support materials are available to adopters from the Thomson Learning™ Academic Resource Center at 800-423-0563 or through **www.swcollege.com:**

- **Instructor's Resource Kit on CD-ROM** (ISBN: 0-324-06688-0). All instructor ancillaries are provided on a single CD-ROM. Included in this convenient format are:
  - **Solutions Manual.** The Solutions Manual, prepared by Greg Frazier, includes solutions for all problems in the text.
  - **PowerPoint™ Presentation Slides.** Prepared also by John Loucks, the presentation slides incorporate color and graphics to help instructors create even more stimulating lectures. The PowerPoint 97 slides may be adapted using PowerPoint software to facilitate classroom use.
  - **Test Bank** and **ExamView™.** The Test Bank includes true/false and problem-based multiple-choice questions for each chapter. Examview Pro is a fully in-

tegrated software suite of test creation, delivery, and classroom management tools.
- **Videos** (ISBN: 0-324-06689-9). Video segments taken from real companies as well as business features shown on CNN, the cable business news network, were chosen to reinforce coverage of various topical areas in the text.

ACKNOWLEDGEMENTS

As this edition is completed, numerous persons deserve special recognition for their contributions to the project. Academic colleagues who have contributed to both formal and informal reviews of the text manuscript deserve special recognition:

Sal Agnihothri, *State University of New York, Binghamton*
F. J. Brewerton, *University of Texas—Pan American*
George D. Brower, *Moravian College*
Russel A. Chambers, *Urbana University*
Dinesh S. Dave, *Appalachian State University*
Abe Feinberg, *California State University, Northridge*
Jorge Haddock, *Rensselaer Institute of Technology*
Raymond Jacobs, *Ashland University*
Jeffrey B. Kaufmann, *Saint Mary's University*
Roger C. Schoenfeldt, *Murray State University*
Arijit K. Sengupta, *New Jersey Institute of Technology*
Lori Seward, *University of Colorado—Boulder*
Jeffrey F. Sherlock, *Huntington College*
John B. Washbush, *University of Wisconsin—Whitewater*
K. Paul Yoon, *Fairleigh Dickinson University*
Amy Zeng, *Worcester Institute of Technology*

Last, but not least, we also acknowledge the efforts of the members of the Decision Sciences Team at South-Western/Thomson Learning who worked with us on the revision. Our senior acquisitions editor, Charles McCormick, Jr., Senior developmental editor Alice Denny, senior production editor Kara ZumBahlen, media production editor Robin Browning, and senior marketing manager Joe Sabatino should be mentioned in particular. The attractive and useful layout of the new text resulted from the work of designer Rick Moore and Michelle Kunkler's supervision of photo research.

Norman Gaither
Greg Frazier

Norman Gaither

Norman Gaither is Professor Emeritus of Business Analysis and Research at Texas A&M University. He received his Ph.D. and MBA from the University of Oklahoma and his B.S.I.E. from Oklahoma State University. Prior to teaching, Professor Gaither worked at Olin Corporation, where he held the positions of chief industrial engineer, plant manager, and director of a multiplant operation, and at B.F. Goodrich Company as senior industrial engineer.

Professor Gaither's writings on a wide range of operations management topics have appeared in *Management Science, Decision Sciences, Academy of Management Journal, Academy of Management Review, Simulation, Journal of Purchasing and Materials Management, IIE Transactions, Journal of Cost Analysis,* and *International Journal of Operations and Production Management.*

Dr. Gaither has served on the editorial boards of several highly respected journals in the operations management field. He is also an AACSB Federal Faculty Fellow.

Greg Frazier

Greg Frazier is Associate Professor of Operations Management in the Department of Information Systems and Operations Management at The University of Texas at Arlington. He is an APICS Certified Fellow in Production and Inventory Management (CFPIM) and has served as a Faculty Fellow at The Boeing Company. Other teaching experience includes Texas A&M University, University of Oregon, and Harvard Summer School at Harvard University.

Professor Frazier received a BS in mechanical engineering and an MBA from Texas A&M University. His Ph.D. in production and operations management is also from Texas A&M, where Norman Gaither chaired his dissertation research.

Dr. Frazier's long association with Norman Gaither has resulted in co-authored publications in several journals, including *Journal of Operations Management, International Journal of Production Research,* and *Production and Inventory Management Journal.* He has also published in journals such as *International Journal of Production Economics, Journal of Productivity Analysis, IIE Transactions,* and *Business Horizons.*

For her extraordinary patience and support, this book is dedicated to:

Angela Kay Frazier

Operations Management

Managing Operations in a Global Environment

CHAPTER

1 Introduction to Operations Management

2 Operations Strategies in a Global Economy

Part 1: Managing Operations in a Global Environment

1. An overview of the operations management field—its history and challenges, and the preparations ready to shape the operations of tomorrow's products/companies.

Operations management in the twenty-first century is a more exciting area to study than ever before. The computer and information technology revolution during the past two decades has led to rapid changes in the ways that organizations manage their operations. New communications technologies and integrated enterprise software systems have greatly increased the speed at which firms make decisions. Automation investments in service and manufacturing industries have improved the quality of services and products. The Internet has created a brand-new outlet from which firms can market and sell their goods and services. The enormous amount of information that is now available to consumers on the Internet is mind-boggling. And consumer expectations for quick response and high quality have escalated in recent years. In this new business environment, companies that do not keep up with the information age will wither to extinction. This indeed is a very exciting time for the field of operations management.

Improvements in communication technologies have also led to increased globalization of businesses. Most major companies in the world today conduct business in many countries. More and more countries are relaxing trade barriers to encourage global trade. Without question, international business has become the norm. When the Japanese stock market hiccups, the entire world feels some impact. Today we truly live in a global economy. And managing business operations in this global economy has forced companies to overcome many obstacles in order to compete effectively with global competitors.

Whether you have or choose a career in operations management or some other business field such as accounting, finance, engineering, human resources, information systems, or marketing, what you study in this course on operations management will be important to you because you will interact with others in your organization's operations areas. By better understanding the challenges and issues facing operations managers, you will be more effective as you cooperate and work together to achieve what is in the best interest of your organization.

This text is divided into four parts. Part 1 introduces the field of operations management and addresses operations strategies. Part 2 deals with the strategic use of resources. Part 3 presents a number of topics involved in managing operations within a supply chain. Part 4 addresses methods of maintaining operations in an efficient and effective manner.

To begin our study of operations management, Part 1 of the text provides the following:

1. An overview of the operations management field—its history and challenges and the major factors likely to shape the structure of tomorrow's production systems

2. Different frameworks for studying operations management—production as a system, production/operations as an organizational function, and decision making in operations management are useful ways of viewing POM

3. A study of business strategy and operations strategy necessary for competing in global markets

Introduction to Operations Management

Introduction

Historical Milestones in POM
The Industrial Revolution
Post–Civil War Period
Scientific Management
Human Relations and Behavioralism
Operations Research
The Service Revolution
The Computer Revolution

Factors Affecting Operations Management Today

Studying Operations Management
Operations as a System
Decision Making in POM

Wrap-Up: What World-Class Companies Do

Review and Discussion Questions

Internet Assignments

Endnotes

Selected Bibliography

ADDING VALUE BY IMPROVING OPERATIONS MANAGEMENT

Better management of a company's operations can add substantial value to the company by improving its competitiveness and long-term profitability. Consider the following examples of important operations decisions at a few companies: Intel needs to construct a new multibillion-dollar fabrication plant to produce its next generation of computer chips. Where should it build the factory? American Airlines needs to allocate the necessary resources to meet all of its customer demand for air travel next month. How should it assign different-sized aircraft to flight routes, pilots to aircraft, and flight attendants to flights? Hewlett-Packard needs to increase output for one model of printer ink cartridges on a production line that is already running at full capacity. What is the most cost-effective way to redesign the production line to increase the output? The manager of Chicago's 911 emergency call center wants to better utilize the call answering staff and avoid long waits for 911 callers by improving forecast accuracy. What method should be used to forecast the number of 911 calls received during each work shift?

These examples are just a small sample of the types of problems faced by operations managers. Poor operations decisions can hurt a company's competitive position and increase its costs. Good operations decisions can improve the value of the company by increasing profitability and growth. Understanding the fundamental concepts of operations management and being able to use a variety of common decision-making tools and problem-solving approaches is key to making better operations decisions.

As the preceding paragraphs suggest, operations management is an important discipline in the struggle to remain competitive in an ever-changing global marketplace.

Of the many functions in business, there are three primary functions: operations, marketing, and finance/accounting. This book is about operations management.

An earlier name for this activity was production and operations management (POM), which has now been shortened to operations management. Throughout this chapter we will use these two names interchangeably as we discuss historical and current issues in this field. As a quick history, the management approaches and tools addressed in this book were originally applied primarily in manufacturing companies, where the focus was on production management. These approaches and tools later were also applied to service organizations, where the focus was on managing an organization's operations. But most manufacturers have service activities as well as production activities, so the study of this discipline was then referred to as production and operations management. Some organizations have only a production manager, some have only an operations manager, and some have both a production manager and an operations manager. Today this discipline is generally referred to simply as operations management, but includes both the management of production activities and the management of other operations.

Operations management is the management of an organization's productive resources or its production system, which converts inputs into the organization's products and services.

A **production system** takes inputs—raw materials, personnel, machines, buildings, technology, cash, information, and other resources—and converts them into outputs—products and services. This conversion process is the heart of what is called operations or production and is the predominant activity of a production system. Because managers in POM, whom we shall simply call **operations managers,** manage the production system, their primary concern is with the activities of the conversion process or production.

Managers in the marketing function are responsible for creating a demand for an organization's products and services. Managers in the finance/accounting function are responsible for achieving the financial objectives of the firm. Businesses cannot succeed without operations, marketing, or finance. Without operations, no products or services could be produced; without marketing, no products or services could be sold; and without finance/accounting, financial failure would surely result. Whereas production, marketing, and finance act independently to achieve their individual functional goals, they act together to achieve the organization's goals. Achievement of the organizational goals of profitability, survival, and growth in a dynamic business climate requires cooperative teamwork among these primary business functions. While managers in production, marketing, and finance have much in common, the decisions that they make can be distinctly different. In this study of operations management, we shall pay particular attention to the decisions that operations managers make and how they make them.

Career opportunities abound in the field of operations management. Table 1.1 illustrates some of the entry-level jobs available today. These entry-level positions can lead to mid-career jobs such as manufacturing manager, operations manager, plant manager, factory manager, production control manager, inventory manager, manager of production analysis, and quality control manager and eventually to executive positions

| Table 1.1 | Some Entry-Level Jobs in Operations Management |

Manufacturing Industry: Job Title	Line/Staff	Job Description/Duties	Service Industry: Similar Job Title
Production supervisor	Line	Supervises employees as products or services are produced. Responsible for cost, quality, and schedule performance.	Department supervisor
Purchasing planner/buyer	Staff	Buys products or services to support operations. Responsible for supplier performance.	Purchasing agent
Inventory analyst	Staff	Oversees all aspects of inventories. Responsible for inventory levels, audits, record accuracy, authorizing orders, and expediting.	Inventory analyst
Production controller	Staff	Authorizes production of orders, develops production schedules and plans, and expedites orders. Responsible for meeting customer due dates and efficient shop loading.	Staff scheduler Shipping scheduler
Production analyst	Staff	Analyzes production problems, develops forecasts, plans for new products, and carries out other special projects.	Operations analyst
Quality specialist	Staff	Oversees acceptance sampling, process control, and quality management. Responsible for product quality from suppliers and from production.	Quality specialist

such as vice-president of manufacturing, vice-president for materials management, vice-president of operations, and even president or chief operating officer. Large corporations such as Wal-Mart, Motorola, Eastman Kodak, General Foods, Chase Manhattan, Johnson & Johnson, Texaco, Trane, Ford, General Electric, and Procter & Gamble and many smaller companies are beating paths to the doors of colleges and universities to hire creative persons to enter career paths in manufacturing and service operations.

Why would you want to consider a career in operations management? We have asked many operations managers what they liked about their jobs, and their answers are interesting. One operations manager's answer from Motorola was particularly graphic:

> *In my job, I'm doing the main job of business—making products for customers. Being involved in the process of producing products and services is something tangible that I can grab on to and understand. Every day is interesting because there is such a variety of things that I do, from solving problems related to quality to installing a new robotic machine. And there are plenty of opportunities for dealing with people, from suppliers, to our personnel, to customers. After being here, I don't think that I could handle a job that deals only in intangibles like debits and credits.*

Interesting and challenging work, opportunities for advancement, and high salaries are the key reasons given by operations managers for liking their work.

How does one qualify for a career in production and operations management? Understanding the concepts in this course is a first step. A college degree in operations management or another business discipline can qualify you for the company training programs that lead to entry-level positions, and then you're on your way. Is a challenging and interesting career in operations management in your future? A good source of information about jobs in small and large companies is the College Edition of the *National Business Employment Weekly: Managing Your Career,* which is published each fall by The Wall Street Journal, Dow Jones & Company.

Operations management has evolved to its present form by adapting to the challenges of each new era. Figure 1.1 illustrates that POM today is an interesting blend of time-tested practices from the past and of a search for new ways to manage production systems. This introductory study of POM will explore both the historical developments in POM and today's challenges in operations management.

HISTORICAL MILESTONES IN POM

A number of historical developments have impacted the evolution of POM. To gain insights into the background of this field, we will briefly examine several of these developments: the Industrial Revolution, the post–Civil War period, scientific management, human relations and behavioralism, operations research, the service revolution, and the computer revolution.

The Industrial Revolution

There have always been production systems. The Egyptian pyramids, the Greek Parthenon, the Great Wall of China, and the aqueducts and roads of the Roman Empire attest to the industry of the peoples of ancient times. But the ways in which these ancient peoples produced products were quite different from the production methods of today. Production systems prior to the 1700s are often referred to as **cottage systems,**

| Figure 1.1 | The Evolution of POM |

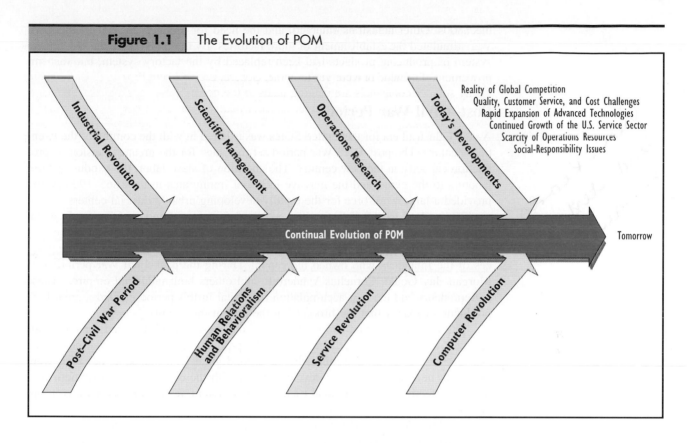

Industrial Revolution

Scientific Management

Operations Research

Today's Developments

Reality of Global Competition
Quality, Customer Service, and Cost Challenges
Rapid Expansion of Advanced Technologies
Continued Growth of the U.S. Service Sector
Scarcity of Operations Resources
Social-Responsibility Issues

Continual Evolution of POM

Tomorrow

Post-Civil War Period

Human Relations and Behavioralism

Service Revolution

Computer Revolution

because the production of products took place in homes or cottages where craftsmen directed apprentices in performing handwork on products.

In England in the 1700s, a development occurred that we refer to as the Industrial Revolution. This advancement involved two principal elements: the widespread substitution of **machine power** *for human and water power and the establishment of the factory system.* The steam engine, invented by James Watt in 1764, provided machine power for factories and stimulated other inventions of the time. The availability of the steam engine and production machines made practical the gathering of workers into factories away from rivers. The large number of workers congregated into factories created the need for organizing them in logical ways to produce products. The publication of Adam Smith's *The Wealth of Nations* in 1776 touted the economic benefits of the **division of labor**, also referred to as the **specialization of labor,** which broke the production of products into small, specialized tasks that were assigned to workers along production lines. Thus the factories of the late 1700s had developed not only production machinery but also ways of planning and controlling the work of production workers.

The Industrial Revolution spread from England to other European countries and to the United States. In 1790 Eli Whitney, an American inventor, developed the concept of **interchangeable parts.** Whitney designed rifles to be manufactured for the U.S. government on an assembly line such that parts were produced to tolerances allowing every part to fit right the first time. This method of production displaced the old method of either sorting through parts to find one that fit or modifying a part so that it would fit.

The first great industry in the United States was the textile industry. By the War of 1812, there were almost 200 textile mills in New England. The Industrial Revolution was advanced further by the development of the gasoline engine and electricity in

Eli Whitney cotton gin

the 1800s. Other industries emerged, and the need for products to support the Civil War stimulated the establishment of more factories. By the mid-1800s, the old cottage system of producing products had been replaced by the factory system, but vast improvements to factories were yet to come.

Post–Civil War Period

A new industrial era for the United States was ushered in with the coming of the twentieth century. The post–Civil War period set the stage for the great expansion of production capacity in the new century. The abolition of slave labor, the exodus of farm laborers to the cities, and the massive influx of immigrants in the 1865–1900 period provided a large workforce for the rapidly developing urban industrial centers.

The end of the Civil War witnessed the beginning of modern forms of capital through the establishment of joint stock companies. This development led to the separation of the capitalist from the employer, with managers becoming salaried employees of the financiers who owned the capital. During the post–Civil War period, J. P. Morgan, Jay Gould, Cornelius Vanderbilt, and others built industrial empires. These entrepreneurs and the vast accumulation of capital in this period created a great U.S. production capacity that mushroomed at the turn of the century.

The rapid exploration and settlement of the West created the need for numerous products and a means to deliver them to the product-hungry settlers. The post–Civil War period produced large railroads, the second great U.S. industry. Rail lines were extended; new territories were developed; and with the coming of the twentieth century, an effective and economical transportation system, national in scope, was in operation.

By 1900 all of these developments—increased capital and production capacity, the expanded urban workforce, new Western markets, and an effective national transportation system—set the stage for the great production explosion of the early twentieth century.

Scientific Management

The economic and social environments of the new century formed the crucible in which scientific management was formulated. The one missing link was management—the ability to develop this great production machine to satisfy the massive markets of the day. A nucleus of engineers, business executives, consultants, educators, and researchers developed the methods and philosophy called **scientific management**. Table 1.2 presents the main characters of the scientific management era.

Frederick Winslow Taylor is known as the father of scientific management. He studied the factory problems of his day scientifically and popularized the notion of efficiency—getting the desired result with the least waste of time, effort, and materials.

In the late 1800s after attending preparatory school and then an apprentice program for machinists, Taylor worked for six years at Midvale Steel Company in Pennsylvania. During these years he rapidly advanced from laborer to machinist, to foreman, to master mechanic of maintenance, and finally to chief engineer, while at the same time attending school to earn a degree in mechanical engineering. It was during this time that Taylor found an interest in using scientific investigation and experimentation to improve manufacturing operations. At Midvale Steel, his scientific investigations led to improvements in worker efficiency that resulted in great savings in labor costs.

Taylor's **shop system**, a systematic approach to improving worker efficiency, employed the following steps:

[handwritten: main characters of the scientific mgt era.]

Table 1.2	Scientific Management: The Players and Their Parts

Contributor	Life Span	Contributions
Frederick Winslow Taylor	1856–1915	Scientific management principles, exception principle, time study, methods analysis, standards, planning, control
Frank B. Gilbreth	1868–1934	Motion study, methods, therbligs, construction contracting, consulting
Lillian M. Gilbreth	1878–1973	Fatigue studies, human factor in work, employee selection and training
Henry L. Gantt	1861–1919	Gantt charts, incentive pay systems, humanistic approach to labor, training
Carl G. Barth	1860–1939	Mathematical analysis, slide rule, feeds and speeds studies, consulting to automobile industry
Harrington Emerson	1885–1931	Principles of efficiency, million-dollars-a-day savings in railroads, methods of control
Morris L. Cooke	1872–1960	Scientific management application to education and government

[handwritten left margin: father of scientific mgt. father of industrial engineering; Motion studies, Put motion into models, manufactured symmetrical, added valuable steel, non valuable effort; diner Electric, lives $50,000 in 1884, Christmas bonus, Walthorton Steel, $3000 a quarter, non-union shops, only steel company, quality! company maker!]

1. Skill, strength, and learning ability were determined for each worker so that individuals could be placed in jobs for which they were best suited.
2. Stopwatch studies were used to precisely set standard output per worker on each task. The expected output on each job was used for planning and scheduling work and for comparing different methods of performing tasks.
3. Instruction cards, routing sequences, and materials specifications were used to coordinate and organize the shop so that work methods and work flow could be standardized and labor output standards could be met.
4. Supervision was improved through careful selection and training. Taylor frequently indicated that management was negligent in performing its functions. He believed that management had to accept planning, organizing, controlling, and methods determination responsibilities, rather than leave these important functions to the workers.
5. Incentive pay systems were initiated to increase efficiency and to relieve foremen of their traditional responsibility of driving the workers.

In 1893 Taylor left Midvale to form a private consulting practice in order to apply his system to a broader range of situations. Those analysts who followed Taylor were known as **efficiency experts, efficiency engineers,** and, finally, **industrial engineers.** In addition to the title of father of scientific management, Taylor is known as the father of industrial engineering.

[handwritten right margin: test question]

The other scientific management pioneers listed in Table 1.2 rallied to spread the gospel of efficiency. Each of these individuals contributed valuable techniques and approaches that eventually shaped scientific management into a powerful force to facilitate mass production.

The high-water mark of scientific management occurred at the Ford Motor Company early in the twentieth century. Henry Ford (1863–1947) designed the "Model T" Ford automobile to be built on assembly lines. Ford's assembly lines embodied the chief elements of scientific management—standardized product designs, mass production, low manufacturing costs, mechanized assembly lines, specialization of labor, and interchangeable parts. Business Snapshot 1.1 describes Ford's massive Rouge plant in

[handwritten bottom: one can black - single product & works well.]

BUSINESS SNAPSHOT 1.1

Scientific Management at Ford's Rouge Plant

In 1908 Ford hired an industrial efficiency expert named Walter Flanders to reorganize his factory for producing Model T cars. The factory was made to operate like "a river and its tributaries." Each section of the factory was mechanized and speeded up. Model T parts flowed into straight-line production with little pieces becoming steadily larger. Starting with the magneto-coil assembly department and spreading through the entire factory to the final assembly department, parts and assemblies were moved by automatic conveyor belts and every work task was broken into smaller pieces and speeded up.

The results were astounding. Where it had previously taken a worker 728 hours to assemble a Model T, it now took only 93 minutes. This increased speed of production greatly reduced the cost of each Model T, increased Ford's cash balance from $2 million to $673 million, and allowed the reduction of the price of the Model T from $780 to $360. The world had never seen anything remotely like it. The cars simply poured off the line.

At its maturity in the mid-1920s, the Rouge, located just outside Detroit, dwarfed all other industrial complexes. It was a mile and a half long and three-quarters of a mile wide. Its 1,100 acres contained 93 buildings, 23 of them major. There were 93 miles of railroad track on it and 27 miles of conveyor belts. Some 75,000 men worked there, 5,000 of them doing nothing but keeping it clean, using 86 tons of soap and wearing out 5,000 mops each month. The Rouge had its own steel mill and glass plant right on site.

Source: Halberstam, David. *The Reckoning,* pp. 79–82, 87. New York: Morrow, 1986.

the 1920s. The technology of assembly lines, refined to an art at the Rouge plant, expanded and grew throughout the buildup of production capacity during World War II.

Although Ford did not invent many of the production methods that he used, he did, perhaps more than any other industrial leader of his time, incorporate into his factories the best of that period's efficient production methods. In fact, he was responsible in large measure for popularizing assembly lines as the way to produce large volumes of low-cost products. Ford was not only concerned with mass production, he was also concerned for his workers. He paid his workers more than the going wage of the day so that they could afford to buy his cars, and he established "sociological departments" that became the forerunners of today's personnel departments. The following excerpt from Henry Ford's 1926 book entitled *Today and Tomorrow* describes Ford's view of how his approach to mass production had impacted society.

Take just one idea—a little idea in itself—an idea that any one might have had, but which fell to me to develop that of making a small, strong, simple automobile, to make it cheaply, and pay high wages in its making. On October 1, 1908, we made the first of our present type of small cars. On June 4, 1924, we made the ten millionth. Now, in 1926, we are in our thirteenth million.

That is interesting but perhaps not important. What is important is that, from a mere handful of men employed in a shop, we have grown into a large industry directly employing more than two hundred thousand men, not one of whom receives less than six dollars a day. Our dealers and service stations employ another two hundred thousand men. But by no means do we manufacture all that we use. Roughly we buy twice as much as we manufacture, and it is safe to say that two hundred thousand men are employed on our work in outside factories. This gives a rough total of six hundred thousand em-

ployees, direct and indirect, which means that about three million men, women, and children get their livings out of a single idea put into effect only eighteen years ago. And this does not take into account the great number of people who in some way or other assist in the distribution or the maintenance of those cars. And this one idea is only in its infancy.[1]

Scientific management's thrust was at the lower level of the organization's hierarchy—the shop floor, workers, foremen, superintendents, and lower middle management. The pioneers of scientific management concentrated on the shop level because it was here that most management problems of the day were found. What was needed was **mass production** and **efficiency** while focusing on the details of operations. Scientific management methods met that challenge.

Human Relations and Behavioralism

Factory workers of the Industrial Revolution were uneducated, unskilled, undisciplined, and fresh off the farms. Although these workers had a basic dislike for factory work, factory jobs were all that stood between them and starvation. Factory managers developed rigid controls to force them to work hard. This legacy of rigid controls carried over into the 1800s and early 1900s. Basic to this management method was the assumption that workers had to be placed in jobs designed to ensure that they would work hard and efficiently.

Between World War I and World War II, however, there began to emerge in the United States a philosophy among managers that workers were human beings and should be treated with dignity while on the job. The human relations movement began in Illinois with the work of Elton Mayo, F. J. Roethlisberger, T. N. Whitehead, and W. J. Dickson at the Hawthorne, Illinois, plant of the Western Electric Company in the 1927–1932 period. These **Hawthorne studies** were initially begun by industrial engineers and were aimed at determining the optimal level of lighting to get the most production from workers. When these studies produced confusing results about the relationship between physical environment and worker efficiency, the researchers realized that human factors must be affecting production. This was perhaps the first time that researchers and managers alike recognized that psychological and sociological factors affected not only human motivation and attitude but production as well.

These early human relations studies and experiments soon gave way to a broad range of research into the behavior of workers in their job environments. *The work and writings of Chester Barnard, Abraham Maslow, Frederick Herzberg, Douglas McGregor, Peter Drucker, and others disseminated to industrial managers a basic understanding of workers and their attitudes toward their work. From the efforts of these **behavioralists**, as they would soon be known, came a gradual change in the way managers thought about and treated workers.* We are still learning how to utilize the great potential present in industrial workers today. Succeeding in today's global business environment depends more than ever on tapping the underutilized capabilities of employees. Operations managers must therefore attempt to create an organizational climate that encourages employees to devote their energy, ingenuity, and skill to the achievement of organizational objectives.

Operations Research

The European campaign of World War II used enormous quantities of manpower, supplies, planes, ships, materials, and other resources that had to be deployed in an extremely hectic environment. Perhaps never before had organizations faced such complex management decisions. Because of this complexity, operations research teams were formed in all branches of the military services. These teams utilized many of the academic disciplines of the time. The concepts of a **total systems approach** and of **interdisciplinary teams** and the utilization of **complex mathematical techniques** evolved as a result of the chaotic conditions existing in the huge military organizations involved in World War II.

After World War II, military operations researchers and their approaches found their way back to universities, industry, government agencies, and consulting firms. These researchers introduced operations research into the curricula of colleges and universities, developed consulting firms that specialized in operations research, and formed operations research societies. As time passed, the characteristics of operations research (shown in Table 1.3) became those that we know today.

During the postwar era, operations research has been, and perhaps today still is, known chiefly for its quantitative techniques, such as linear programming, PERT/CPM, and forecasting models. As firms become larger and use higher levels of technology, adoption of the techniques is more intense. Operations research helps operations managers make decisions when problems are complex and when the cost of a wrong decision is high and long lasting. Problems such as the following are commonly analyzed by using operations research techniques:

1. A company has 12 manufacturing plants that ship products to 48 warehouses nationwide. To maximize profits, how many units of each product should be shipped from each plant to each warehouse each month?
2. A firm contemplates building a $157 million production facility. The project involves company resources, 2 prime contractors, and 75 subcontractors over a four-year period. How can the company plan the completion of each activity of the project and the use of workers, materials, and contractors so that the cost and the duration of the project are minimized?

Operations research, like scientific management, seeks to replace intuitive decision making for large complex problems with an approach that identifies the optimal, or best, alternative through analysis. Operations managers, like managers in marketing, finance, and other management specialties, have adopted the approaches and techniques of operations research to improve their decision making.

Table 1.3	Characteristics of Operations Research (OR)

1. OR approaches problem solving and decision making from the total system's perspective.
2. OR does not necessarily use interdisciplinary teams, but it is interdisciplinary; it draws on techniques from sciences such as biology, physics, chemistry, mathematics, and economics and applies the appropriate techniques from each field to the system being studied.
3. OR does not experiment with the system itself but constructs a model of the system on which to conduct experiments.
4. Model building and mathematical manipulation provide the methodology that has perhaps been the key contribution of OR.
5. The primary focus is on decision making.
6. Computers are used extensively.

Service can't survive w/o manufacturing

Wal-Mart, McDonald's, and Kroger are just three of the top 1,000 companies in the rapidly growing service industry that rely on continuous improvement of operations to maintain their competitive edge.

The Service Revolution

Losing manufacturing base ... strong base to lose

One important development of our time is the mushrooming of services in the U.S. economy. The creation of service organizations accelerated sharply after World War II and is still expanding today. *More than two-thirds of the U.S. workforce is employed in services and more than one-half of these workers are in white-collar jobs, roughly two-thirds of the gross domestic product (GDP) is produced by services, there is a huge trade surplus in services, and investment per office worker now exceeds the investment per factory worker.* Consider the diversity of the private service industries and their companies listed in Table 1.4. Furthermore, this table does not include the local, state, and federal government agencies that exist to provide public services.

not a mfg ... no machine in service industry

The impact of this explosion of service organizations on operations management has been enormous. Frequently throughout the text, we will explore some of the difficulties and opportunities in managing these many private and public services.

Table 1.4	Some Service Industries and Service Companies

Service Industries	Representative Companies
Airlines	AMR, UAL, Delta Air Lines, Northwest Airlines
Commercial banks	Citicorp, BankAmerica, J.P. Morgan & Co.
Computer and data services	Dun & Bradstreet, ACNielsen, America Online
Diversified financials	Fannie Mae, American Express, Countrywide
Entertainment	Walt Disney, Viacom, Time Warner
Food and drug stores	Kroger, Safeway, Albertson's, Walgreen
Food services	Starbucks, McDonald's, Outback Steakhouse, Wendy's
General merchandisers	Wal-Mart, Sears Roebuck, Kmart, Nordstrom
Health care	Columbia/HCA, Aetna, Humana
Hotels, casinos, resorts	Marriott, Hilton Hotels, Harrah's Entertainment
Insurance	Prudential, New York Life, Allstate, State Farm
Mail, package, and freight delivery	United Parcel Service, FedEx, Airborne Freight
Publishing, printing	Gannett, Times Mirror, McGraw-Hill, Knight-Ridder
Railroads	CSX, Union Pacific, Norfolk Southern
Savings institutions	Golden State Bancorp, Washington Mutual
Specialist retailers	Costco, Home Depot, Toys-R-Us, The Limited
Telecommunications	AT&T, GTE, BellSouth, MCI Worldcom, Sprint
Temporary help	Manpower, Olsten, Kelly Services
Trucking	CNF, Landstar System, Roadway Express, J.B. Hunt
Utilities, gas, and electric	Southern Co., PG&E, Edison, Entergy
Waste management	Allied Waste, Republic Services
Wholesalers	Fleming, Supervalu, McKesson, SYSCO

Source: From 2000 Fortune 500 Industry List top companies; **http://www.fortune.com**.

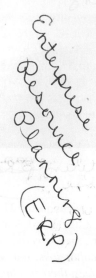

Enterprise Resource Planning (ERP)

The Computer Revolution

Another important development of our time is the explosive growth of computer and communication technologies. Computers and software have had a significant impact on the ways organizations manage their operations. Today many operations decisions are made more quickly because of easy access to information and the availability of more information. And many operations activities can be performed more quickly because of advances in computer technologies and software applications. For example, popular Enterprise Resource Planning (ERP) software such as *SAP, PeopleSoft,* and *Oracle* allows operations managers to obtain near-real-time information about inventory levels, customer orders, current workloads, orders to vendors, and so on. This improved information allows for more timely and better decisions than ever before.

Advances in communications technologies have allowed firms to more easily manage international operations and to work on projects in globally dispersed teams. The widespread use of e-mail today allows employees to quickly and cheaply communicate with vendors and customers as well as with coworkers. This also results in faster decisions and improved operational performance.

The Internet is having a particularly strong impact on the way many organizations do business and is even leading to the creation of new industries. More and more firms have become involved in e-business using the Internet, and they must adapt their operations to this new way of doing business. Consumers have come to expect organizations to have a presence on the Internet, and these expectations are increasing.

All of these new technologies are forcing organizations to change the ways they do business and conduct their operations. This in turn has created additional challenges for operations managers.

A recent supplement to the *Harvard Business Review* listed the following developments that have impacted POM in the 1980s and 1990s:

- Robotics and numerical control
- Computer-assisted design
- Statistical process control for quality (total quality management)
- Lean (just-in-time) manufacturing
- Benchmarking
- ISO standards
- Time-based competition
- Process reengineering
- Outsourcing
- Supply chain management
- "Virtual" organization[2]

These and other factors are continuing to combine with historical developments to shape the ways in which we manage production systems.

FACTORS AFFECTING OPERATIONS MANAGEMENT TODAY

Best value
— best price
— best quality
— best service

have to have all three to be Best value

Of the many factors affecting operations management today, six have had a major impact:

1. Reality of global competition
2. Quality, customer service, and cost challenges
3. Rapid expansion of advanced technologies
4. Continued growth of the service sector
5. Scarcity of operations resources
6. Social-responsibility issues

A key impact of these factors on operations managers is that a country's borders no longer provide protection from foreign imports. Competition has become intense and is increasing. *To succeed in global competition, companies must make a commitment to customer responsiveness and continuous improvement toward the goal of quickly developing innovative products and services that have the best combination of exceptional quality, fast and on-time delivery, and low prices and costs.* And this competition dictates that operations managers use more sophisticated methods made possible by rapidly expanding advanced technologies.

And as if the challenges of global competition were not enough, operations managers' jobs are complicated by the need for more effective management of the expanding service sector; scarcity of capital, materials, and other resources for operations; and the need for operations managers to exercise more social responsibility. Given these factors, how can operations managers cope and succeed today? How operations managers can develop long-range game plans for succeeding in an atmosphere characterized by these factors is what Chapter 2, Operations Strategies in a Global Economy, is all about.

These factors do indeed create an interesting and challenging opportunity for operations managers and others studying this field.

STUDYING OPERATIONS MANAGEMENT

The study of operations management can be approached in different ways. One particularly effective approach is to view a firm's operations as a system and then focus on operations decision making.

Operations as a System

Russell Ackoff, a pioneer in systems theory, describes a system: *"A system is a whole that cannot be taken apart without loss of its essential characteristics, and hence it must be studied as a whole. Now, instead of explaining a whole in terms of its parts, parts began to be explained in terms of the whole."*[3] The concepts from the field of systems theory are helpful in understanding production as a system.

An **operations** or **production system** receives inputs in the form of materials, personnel, capital, utilities, and information. These inputs are changed in a conversion subsystem into the desired products and services, which are called outputs. A portion of the output is monitored in the control subsystem to determine if it is acceptable in terms of quantity, cost, and quality. If the output is acceptable, no changes are required in the system; if the output is not acceptable, managerial corrective action is required. The control subsystem ensures system performance by providing feedback so that corrective action can be taken by managers.

Figure 1.2 illustrates a production system model. Inputs are classified into three general categories—external, market, and primary resources. **External inputs** generally are informational in character and tend to provide operations managers with knowledge about conditions outside the production system. Legal or political inputs may establish constraints within which the system must operate. Social and economic inputs allow operations managers to sense trends that may affect the system. Technological inputs may come from trade journals, government bulletins, trade association newsletters, suppliers, and other sources. This information provides managers with knowledge of important breakthroughs in technology that affect machinery, tools, or processes.

Like external inputs, **market inputs** tend to be informational in character. Information concerning competition, product design, customer desires, and other aspects of the market is essential if the system is to respond to the needs of the market. Inputs that directly support the production and delivery of goods and services are referred to

| **Figure 1.2** | A Production System Model |

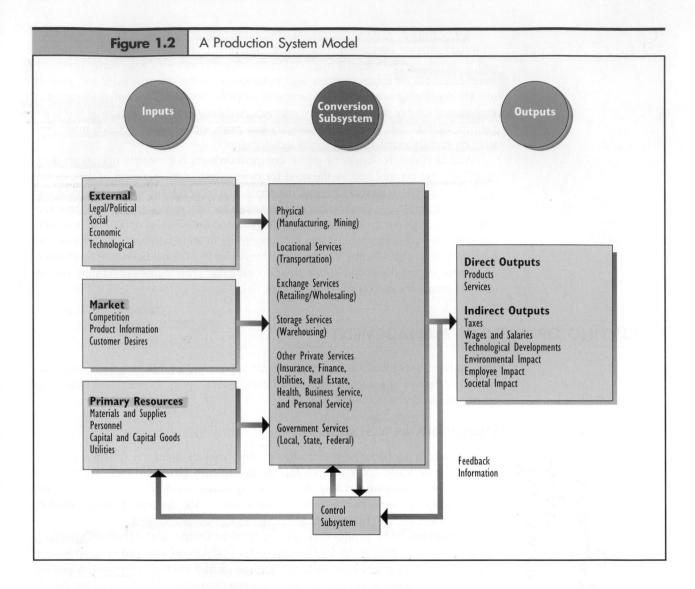

as **primary resources.** These are materials and supplies, personnel, capital and capital goods, and utilities (water, gas, oil, coal, electricity).

The **direct outputs** of production systems are usually of two forms, tangible or intangible. An enormous array of **tangible goods** or products is produced each day—automobiles, hair dryers, toothpicks, calculators, rubber bands, clothes, tractors, cakes, typewriters, and soap. Similarly, services—the **intangible outputs** that pour from production systems—seem inexhaustible: education, trash hauling, haircuts, tax accounting, hospitals, government agencies, banking, insurance, lodging, and transportation.

Interestingly, we often overlook **indirect outputs** of production systems. Taxes, waste and pollution, technological advances, wages and salaries, and community outreach activities are examples of indirect outputs. Although they do not receive the same attention as the goods and services outputs that generate the revenues which perpetuate the systems, these indirect outputs are a cause of both concern and pride.

All organizations have at least one production system. A wide variety of these systems exist, several examples of which are shown in Table 1.5.

| Table 1.5 | Some Typical Production or Operations Systems |

Production System	Primary Inputs	Conversion Subsystem	Outputs
Department store	Buildings, displays, shopping carts, machines, stock goods, personnel, supplies, utilities, customers	Attracts customers, stores goods, sells products (exchange)	Marketed goods
Public accounting firm	Supplies, personnel, information, computers, buildings, office furniture, machines, utilities	Attracts customers, compiles data, supplies management information, computes taxes (private service)	Management information, tax services, and audited financial statements
Pet food factory	Grain, water, fish meal, personnel, tools, machines, paper bags, cans, buildings, utilities	Converts raw materials into finished goods (physical)	Pet food products
Hamburger stand	Meat, bread, vegetables, spices, supplies, personnel, utilities, machines, cartons, napkins, buildings, hungry customers	Transforms raw materials into fast-food products and packages (physical)	Satisfied customers and fast-food products
Automobile factory	Purchased parts, raw materials, supplies, paints, tools, equipment, personnel, buildings, utilities	Transforms raw materials into finished automobiles through fabrication and assembly operations (physical)	Automobiles
Trucking firm	Trucks, personnel, buildings, fuel, goods to be shipped, packaging supplies, truck parts, utilities	Packages and transports goods from sources to destinations (locational)	Delivered goods
Automobile body shop	Damaged autos, paints, supplies, machines, tools, buildings, personnel, utilities	Transforms damaged auto bodies into facsimiles of the originals (private service)	Repaired automobile bodies
College or university	Students, books, supplies, personnel, buildings, utilities	Transmits information and develops skills and knowledge (private/public service)	Educated persons
County sheriff's department	Supplies, personnel, equipment, automobiles, office furniture, buildings, utilities	Detects crimes, brings criminals to justice, keeps the peace (public service)	Acceptable crime rates and peaceful communities
National Marine Fisheries Service	Supplies, personnel, ships, computers, aircraft, utilities, office furniture, equipment	Detects offenders of federal fishery laws, brings them to justice, preserves fishery resources (public service)	Optimal stock of fish resources

This supervisor on an automobile assembly line is performing an important production function.

© PABLO CORRAL V/CORBIS

The core of a production system is its conversion subsystem, wherein workers, materials, and machines are used to convert inputs into products and services. *The process of conversion is at the heart of production and operations management and is present in some form in all organizations.* Where this conversion process is carried out and what we call the department or function where it is located vary greatly among organizations.

Table 1.6 compares the jobs and names of the production or operations function departments of three different types of firms. This table shows the typical job titles given to the line and staff jobs within this function, the name of the department where the function is housed, and the jobs in other departments that are also a part of the larger system but not directly assigned to the production function. Notice that services such as retailing and trucking tend to use the word *operations* rather than *production* for the name of the production function department, and also that the types of jobs considered line jobs tend to depend on the purpose of the organization.

There is a consensus that in today's world of global competition and technological expansion, U.S. companies cannot compete with marketing, finance, accounting, and engineering alone. Increasingly, we focus on POM as we think of global competitiveness, because that is where the vast majority of a firm's workers, capital assets, and expenses reside. And it is in POM that the ability to produce low-cost products and services of superior quality in a timely manner resides. We need new products, competent marketing, and shrewd finance, but we must also have a strong operations function teaming with the other organization functions if we are to succeed in international competition.

Decision Making in POM

Earlier in this chapter we defined POM in terms of what operations managers do. They manage all activities of the operations systems, which convert inputs into the organization's products and services. This definition states in very general terms *what* POM does, but *how* operations managers manage may be more important to an understand-

| Table 1.6 | Production and Operations Functions and Jobs in Diverse Organizations |

	PRODUCTION FUNCTION DEPARTMENTS AND JOBS		Name of Production Function Department	Some Production System Activities in Other Departments (Jobs—Department)
Type of Firm	**Some Line Jobs**	**Some Staff Jobs**		
Manufacturing	V.P. manufacturing Plant manager Production manager Superintendent Foreman Team leader Crew chief	Manufacturing engineer Industrial engineer Quality control manager Quality control engineer Materials manager Inventory analyst Production scheduler	Manufacturing	Purchasing agent—purchasing Buyer—purchasing Personnel specialist—personnel Product designer—marketing or engineering Budget analyst—accounting Shipping specialist—shipping
Retailing	V.P. operations Store manager Operations manager Departmental supervisor Sales clerk Stocking clerk	Customer service manager Security manager Maintenance manager Supplies specialist Warehouse manager	Operations	Purchasing agent—merchandising Buyer—merchandising Merchandise control analyst—merchandising Budget analyst—accounting Inspector—merchandising
Trucking	Owner V.P. operations Branch manager Dock supervisor Truck operations manager Driver Dockworker	Rates specialist Maintenance director Truck scheduler Repair mechanic Dispatcher	Operations	Personnel manager—personnel Stores manager—administrative services Budget analyst—accounting Systems analyst—accounting Purchasing manager—administrative services

ing of POM. *Perhaps no other approach helps us understand how operations managers manage than the examination of the decisions in POM, because, in large part, operations managers manage by making decisions about all the activities of production systems.*

Strategic, Operating, and Control Decisions

Classifying operations decisions is difficult, but in our experience as operations managers, decisions tended to fall into three general categories:

- **Strategic decisions:** Decisions about products, processes, and facilities. These decisions are of strategic importance and have long-term significance for the organization.
- **Operating decisions:** Decisions about planning production to meet demand. These decisions are necessary if the ongoing production of goods and services is to satisfy the demands of the market and provide profits for the company.
- **Control decisions:** Decisions about planning and controlling operations. These decisions concern the day-to-day activities of workers, quality of products and services, production and overhead costs, and maintenance of equipment.

Strategic decisions concern operations strategies and the long-range game plan for the firm. These decisions are so important that typically people from production or operations, personnel, engineering, marketing, and finance get together to study the business opportunities carefully and to arrive at a decision that puts the organization in the best position for achieving its long-term goals. Examples of this type of planning decision are:

- Deciding whether to launch a new-product development project
- Deciding on the design for a production process for a new product
- Deciding how to allocate scarce materials, utilities, capacity, and personnel among new and existing business opportunities
- Deciding what new facilities are needed and where to locate them

Operating decisions must resolve the issues concerned with planning production to meet customers' demands for products and services. The principal responsibility of operations is to take the orders for products and services from customers, which the marketing function has generated, and deliver products and services in such a way that there are *satisfied customers* at reasonable costs. In carrying out this responsibility, numerous decisions are made. Examples of this type of decision are:

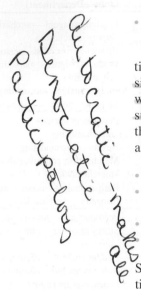

- Deciding how much finished-goods inventory to carry for each product
- Deciding what products and how much of each to include in next month's production schedule
- Deciding how many temporary employees to hire next week
- Deciding how much to purchase from each vendor next month

Such decisions are fundamental to the success of the production function and the entire organization.

Control decisions are concerned with a variety of problems in operations. The facts of life for operations managers are that their workers do not always perform as expected, product quality can vary, and production equipment can break down and usually does so when it is least expected. Operations managers engage in planning, analyzing, and controlling activities so that poor worker performance, inferior product quality, and excessive equipment breakdowns do not interfere with the profitable operation of the production system. Examples of this type of decision are:

- Deciding what to do about a department's failure to meet the planned labor cost target
- Developing labor cost standards for a revised product design that is about to go into production
- Deciding what the new quality control acceptance criteria should be for a product that has had a change in design
- Deciding how often to perform preventive maintenance on a key piece of equipment

The day-to-day decisions about workers, product quality, and equipment, when taken together, may be the most pervasive aspect of an operations manager's job.

This book is generally organized around these three types of decision making in operations management: strategic decisions, operating decisions, and control decisions. In the early portion of the book we focus on strategic decisions necessary to plan and manage resources. These decisions have long-lasting impacts on the operations system. Then we move on to operating decisions, which are more routine in nature and are necessary to manage resources and operations in the short to medium term. Finally, we progress to control decisions, which are necessary to maintain the operations system at its top level of performance.

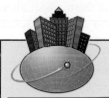

Wrap-Up

WHAT WORLD-CLASS COMPANIES DO

In this chapter we have discussed the emergence of POM, defined POM, discussed historical and contemporary developments in POM, and presented a way of studying POM. The Industrial Revolution, post–Civil War period, scientific management, human relations and behavioralism, operations research, the service revolution, and the computer revolution represent important historical developments in POM. Today, global competition, computers and advanced production technology, and social-responsibility issues are providing challenges for POM and are shaping the nature of production systems for the future.

We discussed studying operations as a system and decision making in POM. Production systems convert inputs such as materials, labor, capital, and utilities into outputs that are the organization's products and services. Understanding system concepts (inputs, conversion subsystems, and outputs) leads to improved management of these systems. All organizations, regardless of their purpose, have operations functions—departments in which the conversion process actually occurs.

Studying decision making in POM demonstrates how operations managers go about their jobs. Analyzing strategic decisions (planning products, processes, and facilities), operating decisions (planning production to meet demand), and control decisions (planning and controlling operations) has been described as a helpful way to view decision making in POM.

As we proceed through the chapters of this text, it will be important to understand what the best-managed companies in the world are doing relative to their competititors. We call such organizations **world-class companies.** *Focusing on these companies will give us insight into the most advanced approaches to structuring, analyzing, and managing production and operations systems. To assist us in this task, as we complete each chapter in this text, we shall present the most advanced ideas about the topics discussed in the chapter in one section,* **Wrap-Up: What World-Class Companies Do.** *This summary will allow a thorough integration of the latest thinking about the important issues that operations managers face today.*

REVIEW AND DISCUSSION QUESTIONS

1. Define *operations management.*
2. Name and describe three entry-level positions in POM. What are the pros and cons of a career in POM?
3. What was the Industrial Revolution? When did it occur?
4. What role did the settlement of the American West play in the development of factories in the post–Civil War period?
5. Describe Frederick Winslow Taylor's shop management approach.
6. Who were the foremost pioneers in scientific management, and what were their contributions?
7. What was Henry Ford's approach to mass production?
8. Who were the investigators of the Hawthorne studies? Explain the impact of human relations and behavioralism on today's production systems. pg 13
9. What are the characteristics of operations research?
10. To what extent are operations research techniques used in today's business organizations?
11. Explain what is meant by the term *service revolution.* Name five service industries. What approximate percentage of U.S. employment and GDP originate in the service sector?
12. What are the most important factors affecting operations management today?
13. Define *production system.* How does the concept of a production system help in the understanding of POM?

14. What are the inputs to production systems? How can they be classified?
15. Define *conversion subsystems*. How can they be classified?
16. What are the outputs of production systems?
17. Define *control subsystems*. Do all organizations have them? Describe some of them. What do they control?
18. Describe the primary inputs, outputs, and conversion subsystems of the following organizations: (a) dry-cleaning business, (b) factory making computers, (c) medical clinic, (d) fire station, and (e) public employment office.
19. Name two organizations that have no production functions. Defend your answer.
20. What are the probable job titles of the top operations managers at a retailing firm and a manufacturing firm? Compare and contrast the nature of these jobs.
21. Define *strategic decision*. Give an example of a strategic decision for: (a) a retailer, (b) a manufacturer, and (c) a government agency.
22. Define *operating decision*. Give an example of an operating decision for: (a) a computer center, (b) a university, and (c) a manufacturer.
23. Define *control decision*. Give an example of a control decision for: (a) a museum, (b) a ship, and (c) a hot-dog stand.
24. Define *world-class company*.

INTERNET ASSIGNMENTS

1. More and more companies are posting job openings on their Internet pages. On the Internet, find two companies with entry-level job listings related to the production and operations management function.
2. On the Internet, visit the web site of *Fortune* magazine (**http://www.fortune.com**) and locate the *Fortune* 500 web pages. Find three service companies that are not listed in Table 1.4. In which industry category is each company, and what is the current *Fortune* ranking for each company?
3. The Institute for Operations Research and Management Sciences (INFORMS) is a professional organization for people from industry and academics who are interested in operations research. Visit the group's web site (**http://www.informs.org**) and locate the web pages for jobs. Describe two jobs that sound interesting to you.

ENDNOTES

1. Ford, Henry. *Today and Tomorrow*. pp. 1–2. London: William Heinemann, Ltd., 1926.
2. Sibbet, David. "75 Years of Management Ideas and Practice, 1922–1997." Supplement to the *Harvard Business Review* 75 (September–October 1997).
3. Ackoff, Russell L. "A Note on Systems Science." *Interfaces* 2 (August 1972): 40.

SELECTED BIBLIOGRAPHY

Ackoff, Russell L. "A Note on Systems Science." *Interfaces* 2 (August 1972): 40.

Anderson, David R., Dennis J. Sweeney, and Thomas A. Williams. *An Introduction to Management Science*. Cincinnati, OH: South-Western College Publishing, 2000.

Andrew, C. G., et al. "The Critical Importance of Production and Operations Management." *Academy of Management Review* 7 (January 1982): 143–147.

Chase, Richard B., and Eric L. Prentis. "Operations Management: A Field Rediscovered." *Journal of Management* 13, no. 2 (October 1987): 351–366.

Copely, F. B. *Frederick W. Taylor*, vol. 2. New York: Harper, 1923.

Drucker, Peter F., Esther Dyson, Charles Handy, Paul Saffo, and Peter M. Senge. "Looking Ahead: Implications of the Present." *Harvard Business Review* 75 (September–October 1997): 18–32.

Etienne-Hamilton, E. C. *Managing World-Class Service Business.* Cincinnati, OH: South-Western College Publishing, 1998.

Ford, Henry. *Today and Tomorrow.* London: William Heinemann, Ltd., 1926.

Halberstam, David. *The Reckoning.* New York: Morrow, 1986.

Hayes, Robert H. "Towards a 'New Architecture' for POM." *Production and Operations Management* 9, no. 2 (Summer 2000): 105–110.

Schmenner, Roger W. *Service Operations Management.* Upper Saddle River, NJ: Prentice Hall, 1995.

Schonberger, Richard J. *World Class Manufacturing: The Next Decade.* New York: The Free Press, 1996.

Skinner, Wickham, "What Matters to Manufacturing." *Harvard Business Review* (January–February 1988): 10.

Taha, Hamdy A. *Operations Research: An Introduction.* Upper Saddle River, NJ: Prentice Hall, 1997.

Taylor, Frederick Winslow. *Shop Management.* New York: Harper, 1911.

———. *The Principles of Scientific Management.* New York: Harper, 1923.

Witt, Chris, and Alan Muhlemann. *Service Operations Management: Strategy, Design and Delivery.* Upper Saddle River, NJ: Prentice Hall, 1997.

Operations Strategies in a Global Economy

Introduction

Today's Global Business Conditions
Reality of Global Competition
Quality, Customer Service, and Cost Challenges
Advanced Technologies
Continued Growth of the Service Sector
Scarcity of Operations Resources
Social-Responsibility Issues

Operations Strategy
Competitive Priorities
Elements of Operations Strategy
Operations Strategy in Services

Forming Operations Strategies
Evolution of Positioning Strategies
Linking Operations and Marketing Strategies
A Variety of Strategies Can Be Successful

Wrap-Up: What World-Class Companies Do

Review and Discussion Questions

Internet Assignments

Cases
Operations Strategy for Globaltel in Asia
Holiday Candle Company

Endnotes

Selected Bibliography

STRATEGIES AT THE U.S. POSTAL SERVICE AND DELL

All organizations need plans that describe how they will achieve their business goals and successfully compete for customers. Although the United States Postal Service and Dell Computers are very different organizations, notice in the following excerpts from their web sites how they both have a strong focus on satisfying the customer.

The United States Postal Service's fundamental goals are to satisfy the customer, improve employee and organizational effectiveness, and improve financial performance. The Postal Service shall have as its basic function the obligation to provide postal services to bind the Nation together through the personal, educational, literary, and business correspondence of the people. It shall provide prompt, reliable, and efficient services to patrons in all areas and shall render postal services to all communities.

We are the United States Postal Service. Our goal is to evolve into a premier provider of 21st-century postal communications by providing postal products and services of such quality that they will be recognized as the best value in America. To grow through the creation of unique value represents an explicit choice. It demands discipline, priorities, and a focus on customer requirements. Four core strategies drive the growth principle—commit to customer service excellence; practice aggressive cost management; become a 21st-century growth company; and create unique customer value.

The Postal Service's five-year strategic plan, which commences with the 1998 fiscal year, reflects a process of data gathering, analysis, and decision-making that has taken place within the most challenging environment the United States Postal Service has experienced since its inception. Sophisticated competition, substitute technologies, globalization, and heightened customer expectations have led us to direct the Postal Service onto a transformational path of process improvement, greater productivity, and a commitment to product and service innovation. Only by traveling such a path—one that will take us to both revenue growth and cost containment—will the Postal Service's ability to achieve its historic mission of reliable, efficient universal postal delivery service be ensured.[1]

Dell Computer Corporation was founded in 1984 with a bold plan: bring the right computers directly to our customers at the lowest possible price. Doing business directly does more than lower prices by eliminating reseller markup. It provides an unprecedented relationship between the customer and the manufacturer, a relationship that extends throughout the life cycle of the product. Whether you are purchasing a computer system for yourself, your company, or your organization, Dell offers a customized solution to meet your needs. Each computer is built to your specifications and supported by superior service throughout its life.

Dell emphasizes customer satisfaction by effectively integrating all operations. Through cooperative R&D, the company benefits from the expertise of its leading technology partners. Dell partners benefit from feedback received by the sales and tech support groups as well as the tens of thousands of calls Dell receives daily. A build-to-order business philosophy combines an in-depth knowledge of customer demand with the latest technology offerings. Dell's infinitely flexible manufacturing structure and superior inventory management enables the company to swiftly fulfill unique customer orders of any size and complexity.

Dell believes no approach is better suited to understanding and meeting the needs of different customer segments than its direct-relationship business model. The company will continue to work to secure its position among the industry's leaders through its direct relationships with its customers, its proven distribution strategy, and its focus on operating efficiently.[2]

All organizations must have business goals and strategies that guide their strategic decisions. In today's high-tech, global economy, organizations have had to adapt their strategies in order to compete effectively.

From the early 1900s through the 1970s American manufacturing emphasized mass markets, standard product designs, and high-volume production. In the late 1970s and 1980s Japanese companies began offering consumer products of superior quality, reliability, and durability at a lower cost than U.S. manufacturers could offer. The Japanese companies' ability to avoid the long-perceived trade-off between product cost and product quality was attributed to their manufacturing strategy.

As U.S. companies lost market share to Japanese counterparts in many industries during the 1980s, there was a frantic effort in the United States to imitate Japanese manufacturing practices. U.S. companies sent managers and executives to visit Japanese factories and observe their manufacturing practices. Statistical process control, just-in-time, quality at the source, kanbans, quality circles, flexible employees, and setup reductions are a few of the Japanese practices adopted in the United States during the 1980s. This was part of a nationwide effort by American companies to "catch up" to the new manufacturing performance standards set by the Japanese.

As some companies later discovered, merely copying the operational tactics of other companies is not enough to succeed in a competitive industry. Although many of these improvement efforts in the United States were successful, many others were not. And even when Japanese practices were implemented successfully by American companies, increased profitability did not always result. According to well-known Harvard Business School author Michael Porter, "The root problem is the failure to distinguish between operational effectiveness and strategy."[3] **Operational effectiveness** is the ability to perform similar operations activities better than competitors. In the 1980s Japanese companies were far ahead of their U.S. counterparts in operational effectiveness.

To achieve superior business performance, both operational effectiveness and a good strategy are essential. Although Porter points out that companies must continuously improve their operational effectiveness to achieve superior profitability, he also stresses that it is very difficult for companies to compete successfully in the long run based just on operational effectiveness. "Competitors can quickly imitate management techniques, new technologies, input improvements, and superior ways of meeting customers' needs."[4] As companies in the United States and other countries adopted Japanese manufacturing practices, the competitive advantage of superior operational effectiveness in Japanese companies all but disappeared during the 1990s for many products. And many U.S. companies adopted competitive strategies that allowed them to catch up to and surpass their Japanese counterparts.

Simply stated, a company's competitive strategy is its plan for how the company will compete in the marketplace. An effective strategy is critical in competitive markets. To sustain a competitive advantage, companies must decide how to differentiate themselves from competitors, which Porter describes as the "essence of strategy." *The challenge for operations managers is not just to improve their companies' operations to achieve operational effectiveness, but also to determine how operational effectiveness can be used to achieve a sustainable competitive advantage.*

Today's competitive business environment changes much faster than it did 20 years ago, primarily because of advances in technologies. To remain competitive, companies today must be flexible and be able to respond quickly to changes in their environment and changes in customer demands.[5] In our fast moving, global environment, managing operations effectively is more important to competitive success than ever. Developing a competitive strategy that exploits the strengths of a company's operations can create a powerful competitive advantage. But before developing a competitive strategy that will be effective, it is necessary to consider present and future global business conditions.

TODAY'S GLOBAL BUSINESS CONDITIONS

The starting point for developing business strategy—a long-range game plan for achieving the corporate mission—is to study today's business conditions as a basis for predicting those of tomorrow. Table 2.1 lists some of the developments affecting business conditions today.

Reality of Global Competition

What follows is a discussion of the changing nature of world business, international companies, strategic alliances and production sharing, and fluctuation of international financial conditions.

Changing Nature of World Business

The U.S. gross domestic product (GDP), the amount spent each year for goods and services, is more than $10 trillion and is the largest in the world (**http://www.bea.doc.gov**). This makes U.S. markets a big target for foreign products/services. *Companies all over the globe are aggressively exporting their products/services to the United States. Partly because of this increased competition at home, many U.S. companies are looking to foreign markets to shore up profits.*

Communications, transportation, and relatively friendly global-trade policies have made exporting easier for U.S. companies. And recent political and economic developments have made many foreign markets attractive. Representatives from 108 nations worked to develop the General Agreement of Tariffs and Trade (GATT) aimed at easing world trade across national borders (**http://trading.wmw.com**). Countries in Eastern Europe and the former Soviet Union are trying to move toward market-driven economies, and this is creating appealing markets. The rapid GDP growth of countries such as Brazil, Mexico, Malaysia, South Korea, China, and Taiwan is higher than in the United States, and their growing markets are targets for U.S. products/services. Table 2.2 illustrates the extent of this increase in exports by U.S. companies.

Table 2.1	Factors Affecting Today's Global Business Conditions
	1. Reality of global competition
	2. Quality, customer service, and cost challenges
	3. Rapid expansion of advanced technologies
	4. Continued growth of the service sector
	5. Scarcity of operations resources
	6. Social-responsibility issues

*All of this international trade has resulted in a global economy that interconnects the economies of all nations into what has been termed the **global village.** Economic events in one country affect the economies of all countries. For example, a recession in one country affects all other countries, and one country's recession can become a global recession.*

The formation of trading blocks is sure to affect world trade. The European Union (EU) of Western Europe allows nearly all goods to flow across EU borders unimpeded, EU–wide product standards have been adopted, and value-added taxes have been standardized (**http://www.europa.eu.int**). The North American Free Trade Agreement (NAFTA) links Canada, the United States, and Mexico into one large trading block that has increased trade across these national borders (**http://www.nafta-sec-alena.org**). Trade within and across these blocks will never be the same. Companies will be forced to restructure and streamline to compete on a block rather than a national scale to survive. While many details are still being ironed out on these agreements, they are the wave of the future and are certain to increase world trade opportunities.

One of the most important new markets for the world's international producers and service providers is China. Having the world's largest population of 1.2 billion people, China's potential as a major importer of foreign goods and services is tremendous. For example, consider this statement: "China represents the largest commercial airplane market in the world and is expected to order 1,900 planes worth $140 billion over the next 20 years."[6] General Motors Corporation predicts China's market in 25 years will rival the 15 million new vehicles sold each year in the United States.[7]

Slowly but surely, China is allowing more foreign companies to compete in its previously closed markets. China's future impact on global trade cannot be ignored. "China is just irresistible," says Randy Yeh, head of Lucent Technologies in China. "If you want to be a global player, you have to be here."[8] Business Snapshot 2.1 discusses probable impacts on U.S. companies if China opens its markets to outsiders.

International Companies

Such market dynamics create the need for international companies, those whose scope of operations spans the globe as they buy, produce, and sell in world markets. Table 2.3 lists the world's 20 largest corporations. In 1999 U.S. manufacturers directly invested a whopping $46 billion in foreign operations, a 72 percent increase over the previous year.[9]

In the changing nature of global competition, international companies from around the world search out opportunities for profits relatively unencumbered by national

Table 2.2	U.S. Export Growth				
Country	**1998 Exports ($ billions)**	**% Increase Since 1994**	**Country**	**1998 Exports ($ billions)**	**% Increase Since 1994**
Canada	156.6	37	Hong Kong	12.9	13
Mexico	78.8	55	Australia	11.9	22
Japan	57.8	8	Saudi Arabia	10.5	75
United Kingdom	39.0	45	Italy	9.0	25
Germany	26.7	39	Malaysia	9.0	29
Netherlands	19.0	40	Switzerland	7.2	29
Taiwan	18.2	6	Israel	7.0	40
France	17.7	30	Philippines	6.7	73
Republic of Korea	16.5	−8	Venezuela	6.5	61
Singapore	15.7	21	Argentina	5.9	32
Brazil	15.1	86	Spain	5.5	18
China	14.2	53	Thailand	5.2	8
Belgium	13.9	28			

BUSINESS SNAPSHOT 2.1

Opening China's Markets to Foreign Firms

Companies around the world are considering the possible impacts that would result if China joins the World Trade Organization (WTO) and plays by the rules that govern commerce in the rest of the world. China's entry into the 137-nation WTO, likely not far away, could do what two decades of economic reform have not: unlock the world's largest market. Here are some of the anticipated impacts for U.S. firms.

- U.S. products would become cheaper, some overnight, others gradually over periods of up to 15 years.
- Many goods, particularly meat and other farm products, could be sold in China for the first time.
- Entire industries now shut off to foreigners or restricted to a few handpicked companies could be pried open as import quotas, licensing requirements, and other barriers fall. The sectors likely to benefit most include telecommunications, insurance, films and TV, banking, retailing, and securities.
- Cumbersome restrictions that shield Chinese producers from competition and fill government coffers with fee revenue would begin to fall away.
- U.S. companies would be free to set prices for their own products and sell directly to consumers, businesses, and other customers. Now they must go through Chinese distributors and other middlemen.

Source: James Cox, "The Push to Open China: World Trade Status Would Benefit Foreign Firms." *USA Today*, Oct. 27, 1997, 5B; **http:// www.wto.org**.

Table 2.3 | World's 20 Largest Corporations

Company	Home Country	Annual Revenues ($ billions)
General Motors	U.S.	177
Wal-Mart Stores	U.S.	167
Exxon Mobil	U.S.	164
Ford Motor	U.S.	163
DaimlerChrysler	Germany	160
Mitsui	Japan	119
Mitsubishi	Japan	118
Toyota Motor	Japan	116
General Electric	U.S.	112
Itochu	Japan	109
Royal Dutch/Shell Group	Netherlands	105
Sumitomo	Japan	96
Nippon Telegraph & Telephone	Japan	94
Marubeni	Japan	92
AXA	France	88
International Business Machines	U.S.	88
BP Amoco	United Kingdom	84
Citigroup	U.S.	82
Volkswagen	Germany	80
Nippon Life Insurance	Japan	79

Source: 2000 *Fortune* Global 500, **http://www.fortune.com**.

boundaries. This global expansion has a great impact on operations managers who must coordinate geographically dispersed operations.

Strategic Alliances and Production Sharing

In the face of world free-trade agreements and the formation of regional trading blocks, the scope of a firm's operations tends to shift from national to global. *Such shifts create the need for the formation of strategic alliances, which are joint ventures among international companies to exploit global business opportunities.* While reasons for strategic alliances may differ, they often are motivated by product or production technology, market access, production capability, or pooling of capital and the belief that a joint venture will be more successful than if individual companies go it on their own. Business Snapshot 2.2 describes some strategic alliances among companies around the world. Such ventures are expected to increase in the future.

It would appear that U.S. antitrust laws today are being interpreted more liberally to allow increased cooperation among U.S. companies in the face of global competition. Japanese companies have long practiced **keiretsu,** the linking of companies into industrial groups. A financial keiretsu links companies together with cross-holding of shares, sales and purchases within the group, and consultations. A production keiretsu, exemplified by Toyota Motor Corporation, is a web of interlocking long-term relationships between a big manufacturer and its suppliers.

Production sharing, a term coined by Peter Drucker, means that a product may be designed and financed by one country, raw materials may be produced in many countries and shipped to other countries for further processing, parts may be shipped to yet another country for assembly, and the product may be sold throughout world markets. The country that is the highest-quality and least-cost producer for a particular activity would perform that portion of the production of the product.

Expanding globally has both advantages and disadvantages for companies and people. Table 2.4 describes the pros and cons of globalization. Since many companies today do operate all over the world, they must deal with widely varying financial and economic issues in different countries.

Fluctuation of International Financial Conditions

Inflation, fluctuating currency exchange rates, turbulent interest rates, volatility of international stock markets, huge national debts of many countries, and enormous trade

This woman works on a computer board in Maquilladora, Mexico. How does NAFTA affect the operations of U.S. companies?

© SUSAN VAN ETTEN

BUSINESS SNAPSHOT 2.2

Strategic Alliances

- General Motors Corp., unable to crack the difficult South Korean market on its own, is in talks with South Korea's automakers to find a local partner to help GM sell and market its cars in South Korea without creating an entirely new distribution system. Kia Motor Corp. has been rumored as a likely partner.[a] GM is also planning a joint venture in Shenyang in northeastern China with a local partner, First Auto Works, to develop a truck-based vehicle.[b]
- Renault SA of France signed a letter of intent with the city of Moscow to manufacture as many as 120,000 vehicles annually at the AO Moskvich car factory just outside the Russian capital. The French intend to take a 50 percent stake in the joint venture and invest $350 million.[c]
- Sino Aerospace Investment Corp. of Taiwan is partnering with Swearingen Aircraft Co. of San Antonio to form the Texas-based Sino Swearingen Aircraft Co. The new company will produce business jets that will fly higher and faster and be less expensive to operate than other business jets on the market.[d]
- German automaker giant Daimler-Benz merged with Chrysler, the smallest but most efficient U.S. automaker, to form DaimlerChrysler, with headquarters in Stuttgart, Germany. The objective of the merger was to build a new kind of car company that would boast global economies of scale.[e]
- The forest bureau of China's southwestern Sichuan province has joined with Singapore philanthropist Laurence Moh and American Daniel Spitzer in a joint venture to create Plantation Timber Products (PTP). PTP has built a new $65 million state-of-the-art fiberboard factory in Sichuan, which produces 4 million cubic feet a year of fiberboard for the China market.[f]

Sources:

[a]"GM Seeks Partnership with a South Korean Auto Maker." *Wall Street Journal*, October 2, 1997, B4.

[b]"Auto Giants Build a Glut of Asian Plants, Just as Demand Falls." *New York Times*, November 5, 1997, C1, C8.

[c]"Renault Plans Auto-Manufacturing Venture in Moscow." *Wall Street Journal*, November 3, 1997, A17.

[d]"Sky's the Limit: Executive Jet Unveiled in San Antonio." *Arlington Star Telegram*, July 18, 2000, 2C.

[e]"The Merger That Can't Get in Gear." *Business Week*, July 31, 2000, 16–17.

[f]"Where the Future Is Made of Wood." *Business Week*, May 15, 2000, 180.

imbalances among international trading partners have created complex financial conditions for global businesses.

Consider the effects of currency exchange rate changes. The United States, Germany, and Japan are the top three world exporters. Table 2.5 illustrates the great variation in currency exchange rates among these three trading partners. The significance of the fall in the value of the U.S. dollar in the 1975–2000 period is astounding. For example, *if we take into account only the effects of shifts in exchange rates,* a product produced and sold in the United States for $1 would have sold in Japan for 210 yen in 1985 and 135 yen in 1990, a price decrease of 36 percent:

$$1990 \text{ price} = 1985 \text{ price} \times \frac{1990 \text{ exchange rate}}{1985 \text{ exchange rate}}$$

$$= 1985 \text{ price} \times \frac{135}{210} = 1985 \text{ price} \times 0.643$$

On the other hand, a product that was produced and sold in Japan for 210 yen in 1985 and sold for $1 in the United States would have sold in the United States for $1.56 in 1990, a 56 percent price increase:

Table 2.4	The Pros and Cons of Globalization

Pluses

- Productivity grows more quickly when countries produce goods and services in which they have a comparative advantage. Living standards can go up faster.
- Global competition and cheap imports keep a lid on prices, so inflation is less likely to derail economic growth.
- An open economy spurs innovation with fresh ideas from abroad.
- Export jobs often pay more than other jobs.
- Unfettered capital flows give the U.S. access to foreign investment and keep interest rates low.

Minuses

- Millions of Americans have lost jobs due to imports or production shifts abroad. Most find new jobs—that pay less.
- Millions of others fear losing their jobs, especially at those companies operating under competitive pressure.
- Workers face pay-cut demands from employers, which often threaten to export jobs.
- Service and white-collar jobs are increasingly vulnerable to operations moving overseas.
- U.S. employees can lose their comparative advantage when companies build advanced factories in low-wage countries, making them as productive as those at home.

Source: "Backlash: Behind the Anxiety over Globalization." *Business Week*, April 24, 2000, 38–46.

$$1990 \text{ price} = 1985 \text{ price} \times \frac{1985 \text{ exchange rate}}{1990 \text{ exchange rate}}$$

$$= 1985 \text{ price} \times \frac{210}{135} = 1985 \text{ price} \times 1.56$$

And the volatility between the U.S. dollar and the German mark over the same period was almost as great.

The fall in the value of the dollar over two decades had long-term and short-term effects on both U.S. and foreign producers. In the short term, prices of U.S. products/services abroad fell and demand increased. On the other hand, the prices of Japanese products in the United States increased, but not by as much as expected because smaller profit margins were accepted in an attempt to maintain market share. Two noteworthy effects resulted:

Table 2.5	The Dollar versus the Yen and the Mark

Year	Yen per Dollar	Mark per Dollar
1975	305	2.7
1980	215	2.0
1985	210	2.4
1990	135	1.6
1995	85	1.4
2000	108	2.2

1. Combined with a *growing fear of increased U.S. import quotas*, foreign companies, particularly Japanese, bought or built factories in North America to supply their products/services to U.S. markets. The automobile industry was acutely affected by this development. By the 1990s, Japanese manufacturers supplied about 40 to 50 percent of U.S. autos including imports, transplants, joint ventures, and parts.

2. Japanese manufacturers moved upscale toward higher-priced products, creating opportunities for companies from South Korea and other countries to fill the gap in the U.S. market for low-priced consumer durables.

An important lesson was learned: *U.S. manufacturers must develop business strategies with built-in flexibility and with an eye to world financial markets. They must be ready to move quickly to shift strategies as world financial conditions change.* Some strategic decisions, such as building a factory on foreign soil, are difficult to change quickly. But opportunities are usually available to reduce risk. Smaller and more flexible factories can be built, or foreign suppliers can be used to supply materials, parts, or products. Also, careful planning and forecasting must be integral parts of strategic planning so that as many changes as possible can be anticipated and accounted for in long-range plans. Business Snapshot 2.3 describes GM's new plant in Brazil and the implications of fluctuating financial conditions.

Quality, Customer Service, and Cost Challenges

Some companies are particularly vulnerable in today's global competition because of product quality, customer service, and production costs.

In the 1980s, when the quality of U.S. goods and services was thought to be inferior, many U.S. companies took a hard look at themselves. They determined that global competition in the 1990s and beyond would be based primarily on product and service quality. They decided that the lip service and slogans of the past would no longer be enough to survive. The goal of **adequate quality** had to be replaced with the objective of **perfect product and service quality.**

Today, many small and large companies alike focus on managing their quality as a way of life. This causes a company to focus on the customer's needs and structure the organization to deliver on those needs. Fundamental changes in the ways that businesses operate had to be achieved before this could be effective. The entire organizational culture had to change so that every activity of the organization could be redirected and committed to the ideal of perfect quality. The people who made the products and delivered the services had to be empowered so that they could achieve the objective of perfect quality. And the objective of perfect quality had to take precedence over all other objectives. The commitment to continuous improvement of the quality of products and services had to be organization-wide. The good news is that today the quality of many U.S. products and services either equals or exceeds that of their foreign competitors.

To succeed in global competition in the twenty-first century, companies must quickly develop innovative products and respond quickly to customers' needs. The old bureaucratic organizational forms that were designed to provide stability are incompatible with the ever-changing nature of today's global business. Companies like General Motors and International Business Machines have spun off whole business units, making them entrepreneurial autonomous businesses so that they could compete with smaller, more aggressive competitors. In other companies such as Xerox, Motorola, Ford, General Electric, and AT&T, organizational structures were changed to accommodate successful innovations. Old vertical organizational structures were made more

BUSINESS SNAPSHOT 2.3

GM's New Brazilian Auto Complex

General Motors Corp. (GM) opened a new automotive plant in Gravataí, Brazil, in summer 2000. The new complex is actually a collection of 17 plants, 16 of which are occupied by suppliers, including Delphi, Lear, and Goodyear. The suppliers deliver preassembled modules to GM's production line workers, who then piece the cars together in record time. Suppliers also had a hand in designing the new Celta car as well as the Gravataí complex.

According to Roberto Tinoco, the Brazilian GM executive in charge of the complex, the facility will be "possibly the most productive in the world." While other carmakers are content with 30 to 50 vehicles per worker per hour, GM is shooting for 100. GM plans to roll out 120,000 cars per year using two shifts.

The new cars will not only be sold in Brazil, but also in Asia, Eastern Europe, and South Africa, and will carry a price tag of less than $8,000. Total vehicle produc-

tion in Brazil by all automakers is expected to soar from 1.6 million vehicles in 1995 to 2.8 million in 2005. Unfortunately, the recent devaluation of the Brazil *real* (its currency) knocked vehicle sales down to 1.2 million in 1999, and industry analysts expect that a surplus of vehicles will linger for years to come. "Manufacturers invested heavily right ahead of the downturn, and there's no sign of anyone pulling back," says analyst Nicholas Lobaccaro at Lehman Brothers in New York.

Source: "Super Factory—or Super Headache." Business Week, July 31, 2000, 66.

horizontal by eliminating whole layers of management. Multidisciplined teams were empowered with decision-making authority to design, develop, and introduce new products, saving time and money and responding better to the marketplace.

In the 1980s, several developments combined to put great pressure on U.S. manufacturers to reduce the costs and prices of their products. An important impact was that Asian producers marketed lower-priced products in U.S. markets. For example, it cost the big three U.S. automakers $1,500 more per auto for labor in 1980 than it cost the Japanese automakers. By the 1990s, American automakers had all but erased the cost advantage enjoyed by Japanese automakers such as Toyota and Honda. Today, U.S. automakers are leading the way in production automation and productivity gains.

Another development in the 1980s and 1990s was to have dramatic effects on prices and costs of U.S. products. Giant retailers such as Wal-Mart, Kmart, Home Depot, Target, Circuit City, Costco, Toys-R-Us, and others squeezed weaker competitors out of the market. These retailers represent such a huge market that they have great leverage on manufacturer suppliers to streamline their operations and to reduce costs and prices. Losing a supply contract to Wal-Mart because a competitor quotes a lower price is an enormous incentive to continuously reduce costs. Many suppliers responded to these challenges by attempting to reduce overhead and labor costs.

During the 1990s many U.S. companies eliminated jobs in an effort to be more efficient and competitive. Between 1990 and 1997 General Motors cut 107,000 jobs, and by the year 2002 GM plans to lay off an additional 42,000 employees as it streamlines and automates its key factories and closes older plants.[10] Other companies such as Eastman Kodak, Raytheon, Levi Strauss, Boeing, Citicorp, Xerox, AT&T, IBM, Johnson & Johnson, and Westinghouse announced layoffs and plant closures during the 1990s. This downsizing of our largest corporations was aimed at reducing overhead costs and improving the bottom line, but also at shedding whole business units so that they would become more flexible, entrepreneurial, and responsive to customer needs in their core businesses. Another reason for downsizing is the increase in automation of processes, both in manufacturing and service activities. Advances in computer technologies and software applications have allowed for the automation of many business processes that used to be manual, such as processing of customer orders, compiling accounting reports, and inspecting product quality.

To reduce labor costs, most firms focus on labor rates, labor productivity, and process automation. Firms from Germany, Canada, the United States, and Japan have substantially higher labor rates than South Korea, Taiwan, and Mexico. *How do high–labor-cost countries compete? Three approaches are common: Move production to low–labor-cost countries, negotiate lower labor rates with unions/workers, and automate operations to reduce the number of workers.* In the last three decades, companies from Japan and the United States moved much production to Taiwan, South Korea, Mexico, and other low–labor-cost countries. This was particularly true for operations that were labor intensive—that had a high labor cost relative to other costs. Many firms have invested heavily in automated processes. As we will discuss later, automation not only reduces labor cost and increases labor productivity but also can improve product quality and speed up the introduction of new products.

Advanced Technologies

The use of automation is one of the most far-reaching developments to affect manufacturing and services in the past century. For small and large organizations alike, these automation systems are revolutionizing many factories and service operations in countries around the globe. *Although the initial cost of these assets is high, the benefits go far beyond a reduction in labor costs. Increased product/service quality, reduced scrap and material costs, faster responses to customer needs, and faster introduction of new products and services are a few of their benefits.*

One type of automation that is affecting the operations of many organizations is advanced computer technologies and software applications. Computer automation is replacing many labor-intensive processes in service organizations as well as in manufacturing companies. For example, most large companies today have computerized their payroll systems, billing systems, sales order processing systems, inventory control systems, and maintenance management systems. Large, integrated Enterprise Resource Planning (ERP) software systems provide near-real-time information to operations managers so that many decisions can be made much quicker than before.

Automation systems are available to any company in the world today, at a price. This means that U.S. factories and service operations cannot use automated production technology as a *long-term* competitive advantage, because foreign competitors also have access to this technology. But not investing in this technology can put U.S. factories and service operations at a distinct long-term competitive disadvantage, and delaying could be disastrous.

For some manufacturers, these high-tech systems may form an important part of their business strategy to remain competitive in the high-stakes game of global competition. For others, the cost of admission to the game may be prohibitive. We will study more about these advanced automation systems in Chapter 6, Operations Technologies.

Continued Growth of the Service Sector

The emergence of a variety of private and public organizations to supply services to our growing population is one of the most compelling facts about the U.S. economy today. As we focus on our burgeoning service sector, however, let us recognize that a growing service sector does not necessarily mean an unhealthy manufacturing sector.

And it is important to recognize the interrelationships between the manufacturing and service sectors.

The U.S. manufacturing sector held steady at about 20 to 21 percent of the U.S. gross domestic product during the past three decades while the percentage of total employment in manufacturing dropped from about 20 percent and is working its way toward about 15 percent. Some speculate that the manufacturing sector in the United States is on its way to looking a lot like the U.S. agriculture sector, which employs only 3 percent of the total U.S. workers but produces so much food that the government pays some farmers not to produce. *While the number of jobs in manufacturing is declining, this results from greater productivity by doing things better, not declining outputs. This is precisely what the U.S. manufacturing sector has had to do to survive the competitive wars, and the U.S. service sector must also streamline and improve its operations if it is to survive.*

Many service companies exist only because the manufacturing sector buys their services; thus a strong and vigorous manufacturing sector is necessary to support the service sector. Service companies in such industries as construction, industrial distribution, pollution control, printing and advertising, broadcasting, publishing, business services, financial services, insurance, lodging, health care, banking, telecommunications, utilities, railroads, trucking, and e-business could not survive if it were not for a healthy manufacturing sector. In their book, *Manufacturing Matters: The Myth of the Post-Industrial Economy*, Stephen Cohen and John Zysman contend that manufacturing-linked service jobs raise the percentage of employment dependent on manufacturing from about 20 percent to between 40 and 60 percent in the United States.[11]

Similarly, many manufacturing companies sell some of their products to service companies; thus a robust service sector helps support the manufacturing sector. Also, many technological innovations were first developed in manufacturing and have proven crucial to keeping services competitive. *This network of interrelationships between services and manufacturing calls into question the phrase* **service economy**, *because many services clearly could not exist without a strong manufacturing sector, and the reverse is undoubtedly true.* And yet we must recognize the service sector as a large and growing presence in the U.S. economy. If the U.S. service sector is to prosper, however, like manufacturing, it must continue to improve quality, flexibility, and cost. U.S. service companies are not immune to foreign competition. Among the 10 largest banks in the world, only 2 are U.S. banks. There are far too many examples of poor service quality. "Your shirt comes back from the laundry with a broken button. Within a week of paying an outrageous repair bill, that ominous rattle reappears in your car's engine. A customer service representative says he'll get back to you and doesn't. An automatic teller swallows your card."[12] These reminders that all is not perfect in service operations motivate us to develop more effective ways of managing service operations.

What is needed in services, perhaps more than anything else, is a more effective way of developing operations strategies. This will be discussed later in this chapter.

Scarcity of Operations Resources

The scarcity of funds, employees, and other operations resources will always cause headaches for operations managers. Certain raw materials like titanium and nickel, personnel skills, coal, natural gas, water, petroleum products, and other resources are periodically unavailable or in short supply and probably will become scarcer in the future. Given the finite supply of these scarce resources to firms and given an ever-increasing demand, an important issue in the formation of business strategy is how to allocate these resources among business opportunities. We will study more about these allocation decisions in Chapter 8, Strategic Allocation of Resources.

Social-Responsibility Issues

The attitudes in U.S. corporate boardrooms toward social responsibility have evolved from doing what companies have a legal right to do, to doing what is right. While the reasons for this evolution are varied and complex, these factors are thought to be important:

1. **Consumer attitudes.** There is increasing evidence that consumers and consumer groups are influencing companies to act responsibly. This influence is felt through such things as resolutions presented at stockholder meetings, consumer preference for particular socially responsible products/services, product liability suits, and political/lobbying activities.

2. **Government regulation.** Local, state, and federal agencies and laws are a growing force in controlling the behavior of U.S. businesses. The EPA (Environmental Protection Agency), OSHA (Occupational Safety & Health Act), Clean Air Act of 1990, state and federal product safety regulations, and the Family Leave Act of 1993 are only a few of the many societal constraints imposed on businesses.

3. **Self-interests.** Companies are changing the way they behave regarding social issues because they perceive that long-term profits will be greater if they act responsibly.

Three important categories of social-responsibility issues will be discussed: environmental impacts, safety impacts, and employee impacts.

Environmental Impact

Concerns about the global environment abound: ozone layer, rain forests, global warming, and acid rain; petroleum and chemical spills, toxic and radioactive waste disposal, and air, ground, water, light, and sound pollution; and energy conservation, landfill waste reduction, and recycling of paper, glass, aluminum, and steel. Business Snapshots 2.4, 2.5, and 2.6 describe what some companies are doing to protect the global environment and conserve natural resources. Some companies have seen these developments as business opportunities. Entirely new industries have been created in the

Companies must consider the environmental impact of all of their operations, to protect themselves both legally and ethically.

Handwritten margin notes: "Consumers control companies buy products" and "most important"

© CORBIS

BUSINESS SNAPSHOT 2.4

Cleaning Up Medical Waste

Among the array of impressive machinery in a hospital operating room sits an innocuous and relatively cheap red can bearing a biohazardous waste symbol. This can holds a small piece of some of the most regulated and expensive trash in the country and is part of the fast-growing $1.4 billion industry of handling and disposing of medical waste.

The size of the medical waste industry has doubled in the past decade and is expected to expand at a faster rate in the coming decade, as regulations become more stringent and the demand for health services booms with the aging population.

Most medical waste starts with a doctor or nurse and a patient in the exam room, operating room, or emergency room. Human tissue is disposed of in one place. Anything with more than three ounces of blood is disposed of in another place. Needles and other sharp objects are disposed of in still another place. And anything exposed to radiation is destined for yet another container. Extensive training is provided to janitorial staff on how to handle the various types of waste.

After the waste is bagged, it is shipped to treatment centers around the country or burned in an incinerator. Doctors and hospitals pay medical waste disposal services 25 to 50 cents per pound to haul the waste away. In the past, many hospitals have used their own incinerators to burn most medical waste. But new Environmental Protection Agency rules could cause as many as 80 percent of the 2,400 incinerators in the country to be shut down for good. The new rules place emission limits on nine pollutants including mercury, lead, dioxins, and carbon monoxide. This is steering more medical waste to outside treatment plants.

Stericycle, a medical waste treatment company in Illinois, uses Electro-Thermal-Deactivation (ETD), a patented process using low-frequency radiowaves, to destroy everything from viruses to yeast without melting plastics as incineration and autoclaving does. This allows some of the plastic to be recycled into disposal containers for needles and blades. The company is also working on a way to use the nonplastic waste treated with the ETD process as a replacement for fossil fuels in heating cement kilns.

Source: "Dangerous Disposables: New Laws and Changing Demographics Fuel Medical Waste Industry's Growth." *San Antonio Express-News,* February 27, 2000, 1J, 3J.

United States to supply products/services related to the environment. These industries provide products that range from smokestack scrubbers for cleaning polluted air to equipment for cleaning oil spills to consulting services offering advice about the environment.

With the trend toward international firms and production sharing, the need for standardizing government regulations of the environment seems obvious; otherwise, firms will tend to gravitate to the less-regulated countries. A case in point exists along the U.S.–Mexico border. Unless environmental regulations between the United States and Mexico can be standardized through the NAFTA agreement, the environment is sure to suffer in this region. There has been some progress in multinational agreements, as evidenced by such things as international conferences on protecting the environment, multinational agreements regulating the release of industrial chlorofluorocarbons (CFCs), and multinational agreements on curtailing the catches of whales and dolphins.

 The International Organization for Standardization has developed a set of environmental guidelines called ISO 14000 (**http://www.iso.ch**). These guidelines help companies develop ways to better manage and control the impact of their activities, products, and services on the environment, with a focus on prevention and continuous improvement. If a company follows the ISO 14000 guidelines and criteria, it can ap-

BUSINESS SNAPSHOT 2.5

Recycling and Conservation in Industry

- McDonald's is building a new restaurant in Westland, Michigan, that will incorporate a geothermal heating and cooling system using the earth's constant natural temperatures underground.[a]
- Although many adhesives cause problems in paper recycling mills, the 3M Company designed a unique adhesive on its Post-It notes that disperses in water and is washed away in the early stages of the recycling process.[b]
- A number of companies have found interesting ways to recycle the world's second most used plastic material, polyvinyl chloride (PVC). Collins & Aikman Floorcoverings, based in Georgia, takes old carpet from its installation sites, reprocesses the plastic, and transforms it into recycled carpet backing, industrial flooring, highway sound

barriers, and marine bulkheads.[c]
- DuPont has codeveloped 3GT, a bioengineered polyester fabric made from cornstarch that is lower in cost than oil-based polyester and can be recycled indefinitely.
- Sonoco has created a rectangular "paper can" for Lipton Iced Tea that is 70 percent recyclable.
- 3M has developed a plastic coating for the Navy to replace paint on trucks, ships, and trains. It's lighter than paint—which leads to greater fuel efficiency.
- S. C. Johnson reformulated Raid roach killer, converting it * ter-based formula.
- Toyota is introducing a hybrid car that gets 66 mph on a combination of gasoline and electricity.[d]
- Xerox Corp. has taken several steps to cut factory waste

and reuse or recycle more parts. Designers have cut the number of chemicals used in printer cartridges from 500 to 50 to facilitate recycling. Print and toner cartridges now come with prepaid return labels, boosting reuse rates to as much as 60 percent. The efforts have saved Xerox an estimated $200 million a year or more.[e]
- Massachusetts instituted the nation's first ban on the disposal of computer screens, TV sets, and other glass picture tubes in landfills and incinerators. They set up six collection centers around the state to handle the items, and cities and towns must transport the items to those centers.[f]
- A Massachusetts company has developed a pothole filler that can be made with the plastic recovered from discarded computers.[g]

Sources:
[a]"Michigan McDonald's Will Have Geothermal Power." *Houston Chronicle*, October 19, 1997, 11E.
[b]"Paper Recyclers Unable to Lick Sticky Problem." *USA Today*, October 7, 1997, 3A; "Post-Its Don't Cause Problems for Recycling Mills." *USA Today*, October 22, 1997, 14A.
[c]"Demand Increases: Reprocessed PVC Products Create a New Market." *Dallas Morning News*, October 10, 1997, 5G.
[d]"Loading the Way to Eco-Friendly Profits." *Business Week*, November 10, 1997, 99.
[e]"A Society That Reuses Almost Everything." *Business Week*, November 10, 1997, 106.
[f]"Massachusetts Prohibits Flood of Electronic Junk." *San Antonio Express-News*, April 1, 2000, 1D, 8D.
[g]"Recyclers Take On Old Technology." *Arlington Star-Telegram*, May 5, 2000, 2C.

ply to be ISO 14000 certified. The number of firms becoming ISO 14000 certified is fast increasing. In fact, General Motors is requiring all of its suppliers to be ISO 14000 certified by 2002. And Ford is requiring all of its suppliers to be ISO 14000 certified by 2003, which affects about 5,000 suppliers.[13]

Safety Impact

Product safety for customers or consumers is of great concern to companies and governments. Harm to people or animals that results from poor product design damages a

BUSINESS SNAPSHOT 2.6

Environmental Efforts at Compaq

Compaq is committed to conducting business in a manner that is compatible with the environment and protecting the quality of the communities in which the company operates. Compaq has taken a leadership role in developing company programs focused on energy efficiency in products and buildings, recycling, design for environment, waste reduction, and environmental auditing. Compaq's operations minimize manufacturing by-products, and the company has implemented extensive recycling programs for various materials, including office paper, aluminum cans, and electronic scrap.

In June 1997, Compaq was awarded the 1997 World Environment Center's Gold Medal for International Corporate Environmental Achievement. The company was recognized for its performance and commitment to environmental, health, and safety leadership. In March 1997, for the second year in a row, the U.S. Environmental Protection Agency named Compaq "PC Partner of the Year." The award recognizes Compaq's outstanding efforts to advance environmental features in its products, promote the Energy Star Program, and offer Energy Star–compliant computer products. Compaq also participates in several programs including the Green Lights program for energy-efficient lighting, and the Energy Star Program to develop energy-efficient computers.

Energy Efficiency

As part of the EPA's Energy Star Computer Program, Compaq participates in a voluntary effort to design energy efficiency into computer products, in addition to educating customers and employees in methods that can be used to reduce energy consumption. In 1995, 100 percent of Compaq's portable computers and desktop monitors were Energy Star compliant and the company has incorporated energy-saving features into 100 percent of its desktop PCs.

Recycling

Compaq engineering teams are actively evaluating alternatives for product designs that will ease the disassembly and recycling process at the end of a product's life cycle. The company calls this effort "Design for Environment" (DFE) and is expanding the program to encompass all new product designs. The DFE program includes elements such as energy usage, recyclability of materials, use of recycled materials, ease of disassembly, and ease of recycling, to reduce the environmental impact at every stage of product life.

Waste Disposal

Compaq has also developed and implemented a comprehensive waste disposal, and recycling vendor review process that includes an on-site review and audit of commercial waste treatment, storage, disposal, and recycling facilities prior to use. The goal of this program is to ensure that Compaq identifies and uses waste treatment facilities that operate in a safe, environmentally responsible manner.

Auditing

Compaq continually monitors the improvement of its environmental programs through formal audits, as well as through its International Standards Organization (ISO) certification requirements (ISO 14000).

Source: **http://www.compaq.com**.

company's reputation, requires a large expense to remedy, and causes governments to impose more regulations. Companies in today's highly competitive global environment are torn between rushing new products to market as quickly as possible and spending a sufficient amount of time to analyze all the safety implications of new product designs.

When products are sold that later turn out to have design problems and result in harm to humans or animals, companies may have to recall, replace, or repair the products. Consider the following examples. Reckitt & Colman, Inc., the manufacturer of Easy-Off oven cleaner, voluntarily recalled 50,000 cans of the product after receiving reports that a faulty spray valve had caused skin and eye burns.[14] Kia Motors Corp. voluntarily recalled about 103,000 Sephia compact sedans in the United States to replace the fuel pump connectors, which sometimes caused the fuel pump to stop operating, resulting in the engine stalling.[15] Bridgestone/Firestone voluntarily recalled 6.5 million tires on sport-utility vehicles and light trucks because the treads were sometimes peeling off the tires. The National Highway Traffic Safety Administration said 174 deaths were linked to the tires. The company said the recall, expected to cost hundreds of millions of dollars, will be in phases because it cannot make enough tires to do all U.S. states at once.[16] Companies usually choose to voluntarily take corrective action on product safety issues to avoid governments stepping in and forcing corrective action.

Employee Impact

Labor shortages, societal and consumer pressure, ethics, and local, state, and federal laws all work together to cause companies to develop policies governing the fair treatment of employees. Employee safety and health programs; fair hiring and promotion practices with regard to age, race, color, gender, religious preference, and disabilities; benefit programs including health care for employees' families, day-care programs for children of working parents, pregnancy leaves, elder-care programs for dependents of employees, retirement plans; and other policies are provided for by U.S. companies. Some programs are mandated by law and are supervised and enforced by governmental agencies. Other programs are undertaken voluntarily. Special-interest groups have lodged boycotts against the products/services of companies believed to be engaged in unfair treatment of employees.

Such programs are costly. But employee morale and productivity, recruitment and retention of employees, turnover of personnel, consumer demand for a company's products, and cost of defending against lawsuits and boycotts are all affected by employee policies. And ethics, the code of company behavior that is considered to be morally right or wrong, also plays a part. Employee benefits and company employee policies are all of strategic importance because long-term profitability is acutely affected.

As our society and global marketplace evolve, more and more companies have formally stated their intention to be socially responsible. Consider Boeing's commitment to good corporate citizenship: "We will provide a safe workplace and protect the environment. We will promote the health and well-being of Boeing people and their families. We will work with our communities by volunteering and financially supporting education and other worthy causes." Boeing's slogan for its corporate vision wraps up nicely the view that today's leading multinational corporations have of their business approaches: "People working together as one global company for aerospace leadership."[17]

Important!

OPERATIONS STRATEGY

forecasting is an example. (LT levels we should know

Given the many factors a company must consider, both internally and externally, it must develop operations strategies that will achieve its business strategies and corporate mission. Figure 2.1 shows that operations strategies are derived directly from the corporate mission and business strategy.

A *corporate mission* is a set of long-range goals unique to each organization and including statements about the kind of business the company wants to be in, who its customers are, its basic beliefs about business, and its goals of survival, growth, and profitability. *Business strategy is a long-range game plan of an organization and provides a road map of how to achieve the corporate mission.* These strategies are embodied in the company's business plan, which includes a plan for each functional area

Figure 2.1	Developing Operations Strategy

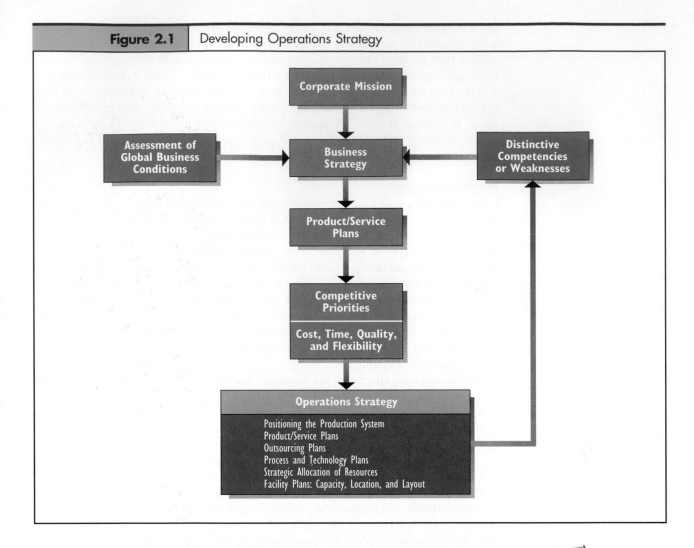

of the business, including production/operations, marketing, and finance. Business strategy is developed while considering an assessment of global business conditions and the distinctive competencies or weaknesses of the company's business units. Global business conditions include such factors as an analysis of markets, analysis of competition in those markets, and economic, political, technological, and social developments. **Distinctive competencies** or weaknesses represent great competitive advantages or disadvantages in capturing markets. They could include things like automated production technology, a skilled and dedicated workforce, an ability to quickly bring new products into production, a talented sales force, or worn-out production equipment. The central focus in forming business strategy is finding ways to capitalize on a firm's distinctive competencies and developing new ones so that market shares can be developed or increased.

Operations strategy is a long-range game plan for the production of a company's products/services and provides a road map for what the production or operations function must do if business strategies are to be achieved. Operations strategies include decisions on such issues as what new products or services must be developed and when they must be introduced into production, what new facilities are required and when they are needed, what new technologies and processes must be developed and when they are needed, and what production schemes will be followed to produce products/services.

A better understanding of competitive priorities will help us grasp the scope of operations strategy.

Competitive Priorities

Table 2.6 lists some competitive priorities. These can be thought of as the things that customers want from products/services; thus, they can be used as tools to capture market share. But all of these competitive priorities cannot ordinarily be used for a single product. For example, a company may not be able to provide great flexibility and at the same time provide very low cost production, although many companies today are improving both. Business strategy determines the mix of these priorities that is appropriate for each product or service. *Once the competitive priorities are set for a product or service, operations strategy must then determine the required production system needed to provide the priorities for the product or service.*

As an example of a company changing its operations strategies to be more competitive, consider the case of Apple Computer, Inc., after Steve Jobs returned to the company as CEO. Apple's lineup of 15 product families was cut back to just a handful that share common components. The company tries to use consistent technologies in its new products. It focuses on a few key features in new products instead of many bells and whistles like some competitors. It focuses strongly on meeting new product deadlines, which are usually within a year.

The most striking change since CEO Jobs took over has been in operations. When Jobs returned, Apple had about 70 days' worth of finished-goods inventory at the end of each quarter, a $500 million-plus drag on profits that was the worst in the industry. Jobs decided to outsource manufacturing of half of Apple's products to contractors who

Table 2.6	Competitive Priorities		
	Competitive Priority	**Definition**	**Some Ways of Creating**
	Low production costs	Unit cost of each product/service, including labor, material, and overhead costs	Redesign of products/services New technology Increase in production rates Reduction of scrap or waste Reduction of inventories
	Delivery performance	Fast delivery	Larger finished-goods inventories Faster production rates Quicker shipping methods
		On-time delivery	More realistic promises Better control of production of orders Better information systems
	High-quality products/services	Customers' perceptions of degree of excellence exhibited by products/services	Improve product/services': Appearance Malfunction or defect rates Performance and function Wear, endurance ability After-sales service
	Customer service and flexibility	Ability to quickly change production to other products/services, customer responsiveness	Change in type of processes used Use of advanced technologies Reduction of amount of work in process through lean manufacturing Increase in capacity

could do it far more efficiently. That decreased finished-goods inventory to about 30 days' worth within a year. As a result, 10 warehouses for finished products were closed, leaving 9 regional warehouses. According to Apple executive Thomas Cook, "With fewer places for stuff to sit, the less stuff there would be. If you have closets, you'll fill them up." The company also began outsourcing the printed circuit cards used in its products, simplifying Apple's manufacturing function. Simplicity was the key to Apple's operations strategies.

Apple's list of key suppliers was trimmed from more than 100 to just 24. That further eased the job of keeping track of all the parts used in Apple's products. And since it meant more business for each supplier, Apple wielded more influence with each— resulting in better prices. Finally, the company scrapped an off-the-shelf software program for managing manufacturing and inventories that had been limping along. Instead, it devised its own build-to-order system for handling on-line purchases. Apple began shipping 75 percent of on-line orders the day they were placed, compared with only 5 percent previously. Apple's parts inventory was reduced to less than one day's worth, obliterating the record in an industry where weeks or even months was the norm. The company also persuaded key suppliers to set up shop close to Apple facilities, for just-in-time deliveries.[18]

Let us now examine operations strategy in more detail.

Elements of Operations Strategy

Operations strategy is discussed in the following sections: (1) positioning the production system, (2) product/service plans, (3) outsourcing plans, (4) process and technology plans, (5) strategic allocation of resources, and (6) facility plans: capacity, location, and layout.

Positioning the Production System

Positioning the production system means selecting the type of product design, type of production processing system, and type of finished-goods inventory policy for each product group in the business strategy.

The two basic types of product design are custom and standard. **Custom products** are designed according to the needs of individual customers. The choice of this type of product design results in many different products, each being produced in small batches. Flexibility and on-time delivery are usually needed for this type of product. A luxury cruise ship and a supercomputer are examples of this type of product. The choice of **standard products** results in only a few product models that are typically produced either continuously or in very large batches. Fast delivery and low production costs are usually needed for this type of product. A television set is an example of a standard product.

The two classic types of production processes are product-focused and process-focused. **Product-focused production** is also called line flow production, production lines, and assembly lines. In this approach, the machines and workers needed to produce a product are grouped together. This type of production is usually best if there are only a few standard products, each with a high volume. Assembly lines such as in auto manufacturing typify these systems. Today's auto assembly lines can produce 30 to 60 vehicles per hour. Because such systems are usually difficult and expensive to change to other product designs and production volumes, they are not very flexible. **Process-focused production** is usually best when producing many unique products, each with a relatively low volume. Each production department ordinarily performs only one type of process, such as painting. All products that need to be painted would be transported to the painting department. Custom products usually require this form of production be-

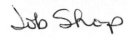
Job Shop

cause process-focused systems are relatively easy and inexpensive to change to other products and volumes, thereby offering great flexibility. If a business strategy calls for custom products whose market strategy requires the competitive priorities of flexibility and on-time delivery, then process-focused production is usually preferred.

There are two basic types of finished-goods inventory policies: produce-to-stock and produce-to-order. In the **produce-to-stock** policy, products are produced ahead of time and placed in inventory. Then when orders for the products are received, the products are shipped immediately from inventory. In the **produce-to-order** policy, operations managers wait until they have the customers' orders in hand before they produce the products. If fast delivery of products is important, then produce-to-stock is usually preferred because the products can be shipped directly from finished-goods inventory. McDonald's uses a produce-to-stock policy, although this has begun to change, and Burger King ("Have it your way") uses a produce-to-order policy.

Once the type of product design, production process, and finished-goods inventory policy has been selected for a product, much of the structure required of the production system has been established. To further explore factory structure, let us consider the scope of a factory's operations.

Product/Service Plans

An important part of business strategy is to plan for new products and services to be designed, developed, and introduced. Operations strategy is directly influenced by product/service plans for these reasons:

1. As products are designed, all the detailed characteristics of each product are established.
2. Each product characteristic directly affects how the product can be made or produced.
3. How the product is made determines the design of the production system, and the design of the production system is the heart of operations strategy.

Figure 2.2 illustrates the concept of a product life cycle. As a product is designed and developed, it enters the **introduction** stage of its life cycle. In this stage, sales begin, production and marketing are developing, and profits are negative. Successful products move on to the **growth** stage when sales grow dramatically, marketing efforts intensify, production concentrates on expanding capacity fast enough to keep up with demand, and profits begin. Next comes the **maturity** stage when production concentrates on high-volume production, efficiency, and low costs; marketing shifts to competitive sales promotion aimed at increasing or maintaining market share; and profits are at their peak. Finally, the product enters the **decline** stage of its life cycle, which is characterized by declining profits and sales. Eventually the product may be dropped by the firm or replaced by improved products.

There is a trend toward shortened product life cycles, particularly in industries such as computers and consumer goods. Shortened product life cycles have three important effects:

1. The amount of spending on product design and development is increased.
2. Production systems tend to be whipsawed by continuously changing product models. This creates the need for flexible production systems that can be easily changed to other products.
3. Operations strategies emphasize the ability to bring new product designs on stream quickly. Computer-aided design and manufacturing (CAD/CAM), described in Chapter 6, is allowing some companies to respond faster to designing and redesigning products and launching them into production quickly.

| **Figure 2.2** | Stages in a Product's Life Cycle |

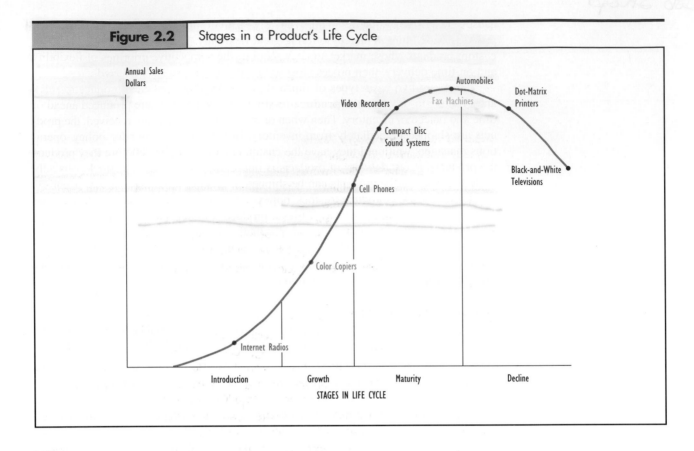

We will study more about these strategic issues in Chapter 4, Product, Process, and Service Design.

Outsourcing Plans

One important part of operations strategy is how much work will be outsourced. **Outsourcing** refers to hiring out or subcontracting some of the work that a company needs to do. Today this operations strategy is being increasingly used as companies strive to operate more efficiently. Outsourcing has many advantages and disadvantages, and companies try to determine the best level of outsourcing to achieve their operations and business goals. More outsourcing usually means a company needs fewer employees, so outsourcing is understandably a sensitive issue for labor unions. Some large companies, such as Boeing, must negotiate with their labor unions before increasing the amount of outsourcing.

At one extreme, a company could design a new product, purchase all the basic raw materials, and then process all of the subcomponents, subassemblies, major assemblies, and finished products. This would require the company to have more equipment, more employees, and a larger facility to do all the work itself, but the company would have more control over quality and other production issues. At the other extreme, a company could design a new product, outsource all the production of the product to one or more subcontractors, and then distribute the product under its own brand name. The company could even outsource the technical design work and the distribution function. This strategy requires much less capital investment, but the company loses some control over quality and production and may incur a higher cost per product unit. Many companies today even outsource some service functions such as payroll, billing, order

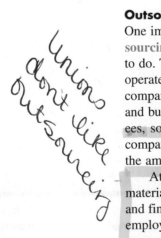

processing, developing and maintaining a web site, finding and interviewing potential employees, facility maintenance, and computer maintenance.

Outsourcing is an integral part of a company's supply chain, and better supply chain management has become an important part of many companies' operations strategies. Chapter 11, Supply Chain Management and E-Business, addresses this topic in more detail.

Process and Technology Plans

An essential part of operations strategy is the determination of how products and services will be produced. This involves planning every detail of production processes and facilities. The range of technologies available to produce both products and services is great and is continuously increasing. Combining high-technology equipment with conventional equipment and devising effective overall production schemes are indeed challenges. Automated technology is an important strength to be used as companies strive to capture shares of global markets. Chapter 4, Product, Process, and Service Design, and Chapter 6, Operations Technologies, contain the important concepts and issues related to these topics.

Strategic Allocation of Resources

All companies today have limited resources available for operations. Cash and capital funds, capacity, research labs, workers, engineers, machines, materials, and other resources are scarce in varying degrees for each firm. Because for most companies the vast majority of the firm's resources are used in production/operations, shortages of these resources impact most severely on their production systems. These resources must be divided among, or allocated to, products, business units, projects, or profit opportunities in ways that maximize the achievement of the objectives of operations. Allocation decisions, which are constrained by the availability of resources, constitute a common type of strategic decision to be made by operations managers today. These decisions are so important that Chapter 8, Strategic Allocation of Resources, is devoted to them.

Facility Plans: Capacity, Location, and Layout *Chapter 5*

How to provide the long-range capacity to produce the products/services for a firm is a critical part of setting the operations strategy. Enormous capital investment is required to make production capacity available. Land may need to be purchased, specialized technologies may have to be developed, new equipment may need to be made or purchased and installed, and new facilities may need to be located and built. The decisions involved have long-lasting effects and are subject to great risk. If poor decisions are made or if circumstances change after the company has committed to a choice of alternatives, companies will live with the results of these decisions for many years. The internal arrangement of workers, production processes, and departments within facilities is a crucial part of the positioning strategy that affects the ability to provide the desired volume, quality, and cost of products and services. Chapter 5, Facility Location, Capacity, and Layout, is devoted to these decisions.

If we have learned anything from our foreign competitors, it is that paying attention to the details of production can be of strategic importance. Effectively planning the workforce, maintaining good working relations with labor unions, managing personnel, making on-time deliveries, keeping on top of the management of product and service quality, and keeping the production machinery in excellent working condition can, when taken together, equal in importance any of the strategic decisions discussed in this section. These issues are discussed in later chapters of this text.

Operations Strategy in Services

Most of what has been discussed about the elements of operations strategy in this section applies equally well to both manufacturing and services. But there are some differences.

Characteristics of Services and Manufactured Products

Table 2.7 describes the characteristics of services and manufactured products, but this table really describes the polar extremes of a continuum because while some service organizations are strikingly different from manufacturers, other service firms may be very much like manufacturers. Also, both manufacturing and service firms can provide both tangible products and intangible services. For example, a service organization like a restaurant provides food, a tangible good, for customers. A manufacturer like a computer producer may provide customer services such as technical advice, credit, and field repairs.

Manufactured products are **tangible goods**—they have physical form, they can be seen and touched, and they ordinarily must be shipped to customers. Services, however, are **intangible**—they are usually without physical form. Their consumption is often simultaneous with their production.

Because manufactured products are tangible, customer demand can be anticipated and products may often be produced, transported, and held in inventory until customers need them. This allows manufacturers flexibility in deciding when to produce products. Inventory can be used as a buffer between a stable production capacity and a highly variable customer demand. This means that when production levels are held constant, in periods of low demand inventory levels of finished goods will climb, and in periods of peak demand inventory levels of finished goods will fall. This is not to say that all manufacturers inventory finished goods, because some manufacturers choose to wait until products are demanded, then produce the products and ship them directly to customers. *Services cannot ordinarily be produced in advance of customer demand and must be delivered to customers at the time of demand or later. This means that service operations must ordinarily plan production levels to approximately equal customer demand.*

With manufactured products, customers do not ordinarily intrude into the manufacturing process. In fact, customers have little contact with the manufacturing system in most cases. In service operations, however, customers are routinely involved in the production of many services. In hospitals, restaurants, and banks, customers enter the production process, are routed to the necessary service operations, and exit from the service system. In almost all services, operations personnel need training in people skills because the key element of quality control is the way in which operations personnel conduct their transactions with customers.

Table 2.7	Characteristics of Services and Manufactured Products	
	Services	**Manufactured Products**
	Intangible outputs	Tangible products
	Outputs cannot be inventoried	Products can be inventoried
	Extensive customer contact	Little customer contact
	Short lead times	Long lead times
	Labor intensive	Capital intensive
	Service quality subjectively determined	Product quality objectively determined

In manufacturing, determining the quality level of products is ordinarily based on objective evidence. A Gallup survey of purchasers of automobiles indicated that customers were interested in product performance, durability, ease of repair, customer service, and customer satisfaction. The first three of these elements of product quality can be measured, because objective evidence can be presented to determine the quality level of products. It is the last two factors, customer service and customer satisfaction, that are difficult to measure, and it is on factors such as these that service organizations must base much of the determination of the quality of their services. Pleasant surroundings, friendly and courteous personnel, speed of performing the service, craftsmanship of the person doing the repair, skill of the physician, soundness of the financial planner's advice, and other factors are difficult to measure, but they affect the perception of quality of services.

Given these differences between manufactured products and services, let us now discuss the kinds of competitive priorities available to services.

Competitive Priorities for Services

Table 2.6 listed these competitive priorities for firms: low production costs, fast delivery and on-time delivery, high-quality products/services, and customer service. All the priorities in Table 2.6 are also available to service firms. Service companies can seldom provide all the priorities simultaneously to customers, and for each service a set of priorities must be chosen that will provide the greatest market advantage. The trade-off between cost and service quality is perhaps the most obvious. A small retailer that emphasizes close personal contact with customers may have high-quality services, but its cost may be higher than the cost of its high-volume discount competitors.

Positioning Strategies for Services

A positioning strategy in manufacturing includes the type of finished-goods inventory policy (produce-to-stock or produce-to-order), type of product design (standard or custom), and type of production process (product-focused or process-focused). Such a positioning strategy would not be possible for services because of the differences listed in Table 2.7. These differences dictate that a positioning strategy for services includes:

1. **Type of service design,** with several interesting dimensions—standard or custom services, amount of customer contact, and the mix of physical goods and intangible services
2. **Type of production process**—quasi-manufacturing; customer-as-participant; and customer-as-product

As you can see, the type of service design and the type of production process are very much different from manufacturing counterparts. McDonald's has a very successful positioning strategy as evidenced by its long-term profitability. It has chosen to provide customers with a service design that is highly standardized, with a low amount of customer contact, and with physical goods dominating intangible services. Its back-room production process is a quasi-manufacturing approach.

Just as in manufacturing, the positioning strategy of the service firm determines the structure of the production system. This structure is crucial to the success of service organizations. We further discuss the design of the production system for services in Chapter 4, Product, Process, and Service Design.

Now that we have examined the elements of operations strategy, let us consider how we go about integrating these elements into a comprehensive operations strategy.

FORMING OPERATIONS STRATEGIES

Forming operations strategy follows the procedure in Figure 2.1. The core of operations strategy is the formation of positioning strategies (custom or standard products, product-focused or process-focused production, and produce-to-stock or produce-to-order inventory), because this sets the fundamental structure and capability of the production/operations system. *It is crucial that the structure of operations determined by the positioning strategy be linked to product/service plans and competitive priorities defined in business strategy.* This linkage ensures not only that operations strategy supports the business strategy but also that production/operations takes on a proactive role and can then be used as a competitive weapon in the struggle to capture market share in global markets.[19]

In this section we discuss the evolution of positioning strategies for products, linking operations and marketing strategies, and diversity of operations strategies.

Evolution of Positioning Strategies

Robert Hayes and Steven Wheelwright suggested that the characteristics of production systems tend to evolve as products move through their product life cycles.[20] Figure 2.3 illustrates this evolution. In the early stages of such a product's life cycle, it will typically be custom designed and produced in very small batches in a process-focused, produce-to-order factory. As the market demand for the product grows, the batch size and volume of the product increases, and we see the positioning strategy shift to one of a standard product design, produced in product-focused, produce-to-stock factories. Finally, when market demand for the product reaches its maturity, the highly standard product is produced continuously at very high volume in dedicated product-focused, produce-to-stock factories.

The concept illustrated in Figure 2.3 applies to new traditional products with long product life cycles. Redesigned products usually do not begin their product life cycles at the introduction stage; rather, they reenter the cycle at approximately the stage of the old product that is being replaced. Products with particularly short product life cycles may not precisely follow the evolution illustrated in Figure 2.3. For example, Motorola's cellular telephone reached the maturity stage so fast that the production system had to be designed for the maturity stage soon after introduction of the product.

The pattern of change illustrated in Figure 2.3 has important implications for operations strategy. *Operations strategies must include plans for modifying production systems to a changing set of competitive priorities as products mature, and the capital and production technology required to support these changes must be provided.*

Linking Operations and Marketing Strategies

Two positioning strategies that are combinations of type of product, type of production process, and finished-goods inventory policy that commonly occur together are standard-product/product-focused/produce-to-stock and custom-product/process-focused/produce-to-order. These are often referred to as **pure positioning strategies.** Other combinations are called **mixed positioning strategies.**

Table 2.8 presents a range of positioning strategies. An important principle is suggested in this table: *All elements of operations strategy (positioning strategies, product plans, outsourcing plans, process and technology plans, strategic allocation of resources, and facility plans) must be carefully linked. Most important, the positioning strategy must be linked with the market strategy.* In the 1970s and 1980s, many foreign manufacturers developed pure positioning strategies (highly standard products,

Figure 2.3 | Evolution of Positioning Strategies for a Product Life Cycle

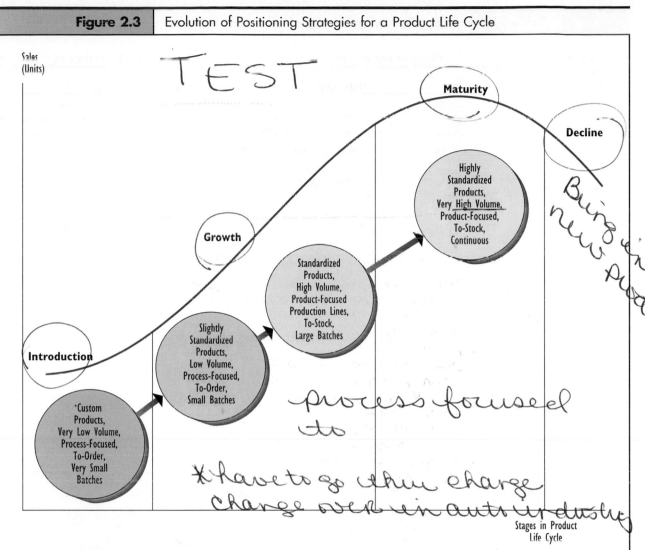

product-focused production, and produce-to-stock inventory) for mass-produced consumer durables. This positioning strategy meshed perfectly with their market strategy, which was based on low price, fast product delivery, and high product quality. At the same time, some U.S. firms had business strategies requiring their production functions to be all things to all people and did not take into account the structure of the production system and their positioning strategies. These U.S. business strategies may not have allowed the production systems to develop pure positioning strategies that could compete with their foreign counterparts on either cost or product quality.

A Variety of Strategies Can Be Successful

As indicated in Figure 2.1, operations strategy must be derived from an assessment of global business conditions, the competitive priorities required to capture market segments, and the distinctive competencies or weaknesses of a company. The appropriate operations strategy can depend on a firm's strengths and weaknesses. Two companies,

Table 2.8	Linking Positioning Strategies with Market Strategies

Some Common Positioning Strategies	CUSTOM PRODUCTS		STANDARDIZED PRODUCTS	
	Low Volume	High Volume	Low Volume	High Volume
Product-focused, to-stock				*Market Strategy:* Competition based largely on production cost, fast delivery of products, and quality; *example:* TV sets
Product-focused, to-order			*Market Strategy:* Competition based largely on production cost, keeping delivery promises, and quality; *example:* school buses	
Process-focused, to-stock		*Market Strategy:* Competition based largely on flexibility, quality, and fast delivery of products; *example:* medical instruments		
Process-focused, to-order	*Market Strategy:* Competition based largely on keeping delivery promises, quality, and flexibility; *example:* large supercomputers			

each with different strengths and weaknesses, can develop different operations strategies in the same market, and surprisingly, both can be successful.

In addition to a firm's strengths and weaknesses, the appropriate operations strategy can also depend on the nature of a firm's products and its industry. We have already discussed how competitive priorities and positioning strategies for services tend to differ from manufacturing because of the characteristics of services and their operations. Likewise, a small business, a start-up business, and a high-tech business ordinarily will develop operations strategies different from those of their counterparts.

Small businesses are almost always short of everything from capital to employee skills to production capacity. Start-up and small manufacturers usually prefer positioning strategies with custom products, process-focused production, and produce-to-order policies because these systems are more flexible and less capital is required. As their products move through their product life cycles, production systems usually mature toward standard products, product-focused production, and produce-to-stock policies if they are to compete with larger corporations.

Small services can successfully compete with large corporations by carving out a specialty niche and emphasizing high customer contact to develop a loyal customer base. For example, when Wal-Mart comes to town, the surviving small retailers usually develop specialty product outlets where price is not the principal competitive priority and close, personal customer service is emphasized.

For companies in industries that are technology intensive, product life cycles tend to be short and production systems tend to be capital intensive. This means that production systems must be capable of producing new products and services in high volumes soon after introduction. Production systems in these industries must be very flexible and capable of quickly introducing new products. Such companies must have two key strengths if they are to be successful: highly capable technical people and sufficient capital.

As businesses in the United States and other countries continue to increase their global operations, they must develop effective operations strategies that exploit their strengths and allow them to successfully compete in this global economy. We have discussed many factors that are included in operations strategies. No one operations strategy exists that is best for all companies or even for all companies within the same industry. An organization must develop its own operations strategy so as to best achieve its business strategies and its corporate mission.

Wrap-Up

WHAT WORLD-CLASS COMPANIES DO

World-class companies excel in developing business and operations strategies for capturing increasing shares of global markets. A broad cross section of their personnel contribute to the development of these long-range business plans. No single organization function dominates business planning. The long-range business plan represents the best thinking and analysis about what must be done to capture shares of global markets. Because of the soundness of their long-range planning process, world-class producers confidently invest in all areas of their business for the long haul: personnel training and education, market development, new product/service development, factories and advanced high-tech production processes, and research and development. These investments position them to exploit the opportunities in their business plans.

In particular, world-class producers:

- Put customers first. Are responsive to needs of customers, willing to customize products and expedite or change customer orders.

- Get new products/services to market fast.
- Are high-quality producers. They are known for the quality of their products/services; quality is emphasized from the top to the bottom of their organizations.
- Have high labor productivity and low production costs, matching or beating their competition.
- Carry little excess inventory.
- Think globally in general; market products globally and shop globally for supplies.
- Quickly adopt and develop new technologies and implement proven technologies.
- Trim organizations to be lean and flexible in adapting to rapidly changing world conditions.
- Are not resistant to strategic alliances and joint ventures to exploit global opportunities.
- Consider relevant social issues when setting strategies.

REVIEW AND DISCUSSION QUESTIONS

1. Explain what *operational effectiveness* is.
2. Arrange the developments listed in Table 2.1 in order of their importance (in your opinion). Defend your choice.
3. What are the top three countries for U.S. exports?
4. Why is China so important for potential U.S. exports in the future?
5. What is ISO 14000?

6. Define, describe, and give an example of production sharing.

7. Discuss the pros and cons of U.S. companies using advanced production technology to combat foreign competition.

8. What are the pros and cons of globalization?

9. Assume that a dollar could buy 125 yen and two years later a dollar could buy 150 yen. If the only factor considered was the change in exchange rates, would the price of a Japanese product sold in the United States go up or down in this period? By what percentage would the price change?

10. What advice would you give managers today about developing business strategy, given that international financial conditions are changing rapidly? Defend your advice.

11. Give evidence of the prominence of service systems in the U.S. economy.

12. What are some reasons why companies are concerned about the safety impacts of their products?

13. Define corporate mission, business strategy, and operations strategy.

14. How is operations strategy related to business strategy? How does operations strategy impact business strategy?

15. Name and describe four competitive priorities. Discuss how these priorities are created.

16. Define and describe: (a) positioning of the production system in manufacturing and in services, (b) outsourcing, (c) process and technology plans, (d) strategic allocation of resources, (e) facility planning.

17. Define and describe the concept of a product life cycle. For each stage of the product life cycle, give an example of a product that is in that stage.

18. Explain what is meant by "evolution of positioning strategies for products." What is the significance of this concept to operations strategy?

19. What are the advantages of a "product-focused, standardized-product, produce-to-stock" positioning strategy?

20. Define, describe, and give an example of pure positioning strategy and mixed positioning strategy.

21. Explain these statements: (a) "All of the elements of positioning strategy must be perfectly matched to market strategy." (b) "The operations strategy must be linked to product/service plans and competitive priorities."

22. Summarize what world-class companies do relative to business and operations strategy.

INTERNET ASSIGNMENTS

1. Search the Internet for a recent development in or impact from the North American Free Trade Agreement (NAFTA). Write a brief summary of the development or impact.

2. Search the Internet to find a U.S. company with operations in China. Describe the type of operations the company has in China.

3. Search the Internet to find a description of the ISO 14000 components. Summarize these components.

4. Find an example of a company that is using its Internet web site to let the public know about its position or actions concerning environmental or social responsibility.

5. Look through the McDonald's web site (**http://www.mcdonalds.com**) to find the number of countries in which it has restaurants. How many restaurants does McDonald's have in the entire world?

CASES

Operations Strategy for GlobalTel in Asia

GlobalTel, Inc., is a U.S. telecommunications company that has developed a new type of low-cost cellular telephone system technology. The technology has the potential to provide widespread access to telephone service at a very reasonable cost to users.

GlobalTel is planning to design and engineer the telephone systems in the United States, manufacture most of the components in Mexico and Taiwan, assemble the finished products in South Korea, and initially sell the products in China and India. GlobalTel plans to establish joint ventures with manufacturers in Mexico, Taiwan, and South Korea, and to contract with local distributors in China and India.

Assignments

1. Write a list of elements that should be included in an operations strategy for GlobalTel.
2. Briefly list the information you would need to know before an operations strategy could be developed for GlobalTel.
3. For each of the items of information included on your list in Assignment 2, suggest ways in which the necessary information could be obtained.
4. Briefly describe a positioning strategy for GlobalTel. State any assumptions that you make about the company, its products, and its customers.
5. Discuss the importance of linking the product plans, competitive priorities, and operations strategy of GlobalTel.
6. Discuss the importance of linking the market plans of local distributors and the positioning strategy of GlobalTel.

Holiday Candle Company

Bob Venture is the owner of Holiday Candle Company and would like to expand his company's operations. For the past two years Bob has sold candles via the Internet, but sales have steadily grown beyond his ability to produce the candles alone from his garage workshop. Because future sales growth looks very promising, Bob has decided to open a small manufacturing plant to produce the candles. Sales have primarily been to customers in the United States with occasional orders from other countries. In addition to selling via the Internet, Bob would like to start selling his candles to specialty stores in the United States. With the new plant, he would also like to consider expanding the products he offers in the near future.

Assignments

1. Discuss what you think should be Bob's competitive priorities.
2. Referring to the elements of operations strategy in this chapter, discuss different aspects of the operations strategy that you think Bob needs to develop.

ENDNOTES

1. **http://www.usps.gov**.
2. **http://www.dell.com**.
3. Porter, Michael E. "What Is Strategy?" *Harvard Business Review* 74 (November–December 1996): 61–78.
4. *Ibid.*
5. Hayes, Robert H., and Gary P. Pisano. "Beyond World-Class: The New Manufacturing Strategy." *Harvard Business Review* 72 (January–February 1994): 77–86.
6. "Boeing Finally Seals Deal to Sell China 50 Planes." *Houston Chronicle*, October 31, 1997, 3C.
7. "GM Set to Build Buicks in China." *Arlington Morning News*, October 23, 1997, 1B.
8. "Motorola Stands by China: Patience Is Key to Telecom's Fastest-Growing Market." *USA Today*, November 3, 1997, 1B, 2B.
9. "U.S. Manufacturers Set Record for Investments in Other Nations." *Chicago Tribune*, Business section, January 6, 2000.
10. "GM Plans to Unload Plants, 42,000 Jobs." *USA Today*, November 17, 1997, 1B.
11. Cohen, Stephen S., and John Zysman. *Manufacturing Matters: The Myth of the Post-Industrial Economy*. New York: Basic Books, 1987.

12. Shostack, G. Lynn. "Designing Services That Deliver." *Harvard Business Review* (January–February 1984): 133.
13. "Automakers Issue New Mandate." *Industry Week*, October 18, 1999, 19–21.
14. "Company Recalls Oven Cleaner." *Boston Globe*, January 12, 2000, Business section.
15. "Jim Mateja's Transportation Notebook." *Chicago Tribune*, January 2, 2000, Auto section.
16. "6.5M Tires Recalled: Firestone Plans Action in Phases." *USA Today*, August 10, 2000, 1A.; "NHTSA: Death Toll Linked to Firestone Tires Climbs 26 to 174." *USA Today*, February 7, 2001, 2B.
17. **www.boeing.com**.
18. Burrows, Peter. "Apple." *Business Week*, July 31, 2000, 102–113.
19. Wheelwright, Steven C., and Robert H. Hayes. "Competing Through Manufacturing." *Harvard Business Review* (January–February 1995): 99–109.
20. Hayes, Robert H., and Steven C. Wheelwright. "Link Manufacturing Process and Product Life Cycles." *Harvard Business Review* (January–February 1979): 133–140.

SELECTED BIBLIOGRAPHY

Cannon, Terry. *China's Economic Growth: The Impacts on Regions, Migration and the Environment*. New York: St. Martin's Press, 2000.

Cattanach, Robert E., Jake M. Holdreith, Daniel P. Reinke, and Larry K. Sibik. *The Handbook of Environmentally Conscious Manufacturing*. Chicago: Irwin Professional Publishing, 1995.

"China's Wealth Gap." *Business Week*, May 15, 2000, 172–180.

Etienne-Hamilton, E. C. *Managing World-Class Service Business*. Cincinnati, OH: South-Western College Publishing, 1998.

Ferrell, O. C., John Fraedrich, and Linda Ferrell. *Business Ethics: Ethical Decision Making and Cases*, 4th ed. Boston: Houghton Mifflin College, 2000.

Fitzsimmons, James A., and Mona J. Fitzsimmons. *Service Management: Operations, Strategy, and Information Technology*. Boston: Irwin/McGraw-Hill, 2000.

Flattery, M. Thérèse. *Global Operations Management*. New York: McGraw-Hill, 1996.

Hart, Stuart L. "Beyond Greening: Strategies for a Sustainable World." *Harvard Business Review* 75 (January–February 1997): 66–76.

Hayes, Robert H., and Gary P. Pisano. "Beyond World-Class: The New Manufacturing Strategy." *Harvard Business Review* 72 (January–February 1994): 77–86.

Hayes, Robert H., and Steven C. Wheelwright. "Link Manufacturing Process and Product Life Cycles." *Harvard Business Review* 57 (January–February 1979): 133–140.

Long, Frederick J., and Matthew B. Arnold. *The Power of Environmental Partnerships*. Fort Worth, TX: The Dryden Press, 1995.

Lovelock, Christopher H., and George S. Yip. "Developing Global Strategies for Service Businesses." *California Management Review* 38, no. 2 (Winter 1996): 64–86.

Porter, Michael E. "What Is Strategy?" *Harvard Business Review* 74 (November–December 1996): 61–78.

Sayre, Don. *Inside ISO 14000*. Boca Raton, FL: St. Lucie Press, 1996.

Schmenner, Roger W. *Service Operations Management*. Upper Saddle River, NJ: Prentice Hall, 1995.

Schonberger, Richard J. *World Class Manufacturing: The Next Decade*. New York: The Free Press, 1996.

Van Biema, Michael, and Bruce Greenwald. "Managing Our Way to Higher Service-Sector Productivity." *Harvard Business Review* 75 (July–August 1997): 87–95.

Walley, Noah, and Bradley Whitehead. "It's Not Easy Being Green." *Harvard Business Review* 72 (May–June 1994): 46–52.

"When Green Begets Green." *Business Week*, November 10, 1997, 98–106.

Witt, Chris, and Alan Muhlemann. *Service Operations Management: Strategy, Design, and Delivery*. Upper Saddle River, NJ: Prentice Hall, 1997.

PART **2**

Planning the Strategic Use of Resources

CHAPTER

3 Demand Forecasting

4 Product, Process, and Service Design

5 Facility Capacity, Location, and Layout

6 Operations Technologies

7 Operations Quality Management

8 Strategic Allocation of Resources

9 Service Operations Planning and Scheduling

10 Project Management

© PHOTODISC, INC.

In Chapter 2 of this book we discussed operations strategy, which is embodied in the long-range operations/production plan. This plan specifies positioning strategies; product, process, and technology plans; strategic allocation of resources; and facility planning. Once these issues have been decided and set in place, the fundamental structure of the operations function is established.

In Part 2 of this book we discuss many issues related to the strategic planning of how resources are used. Before resources can be planned, it is critical to estimate or forecast long-range and short-range demand for products and services. These forecasts guide the strategic allocation of resources. Based on the expected levels of demand, decisions are made concerning product, process, and service designs; facility capacity, location, and layout; operations technologies; and allocation of operations resources. Other issues involving the strategic allocation of resources include managing quality, planning service operations, and managing projects.

Chapter 3 covers a variety of issues and common techniques in forecasting demand. Chapter 4 discusses product, process, and service design. Chapter 5 addresses facility capacity, location, and layout decisions. Chapter 6 discusses modern operations and production technologies. Chapter 7 presents a number of issues related to managing the quality of operations. Chapter 8 focuses specifically on allocating limited resources in the best way. Chapter 9 covers the planning and scheduling of service operations. Chapter 10 covers project management.

Demand Forecasting

Introduction

Qualitative Forecasting Methods

Quantitative Forecasting Models
Forecast Accuracy
Long-Range Forecasts
Short-Range Forecasts

How to Have a Successful Forecasting System
How to Select a Forecasting Method
How to Monitor and Control a Forecasting Model

Computer Software for Forecasting

Forecasting in Small Businesses and Start-Up Ventures

Wrap-Up: What World-Class Companies Do

Review and Discussion Questions

Internet Assignments

Problems

Cases
San Diego Retailers
Chasewood Apartments
Sundance Chemical Company
XYZ Inc.

Endnote

Selected Bibliography

FORECASTING MEALS ON AIRLINE FLIGHTS

Providing in flight meals to airline passengers is big business. Northwest Air lines' and Continental's food budgets are each around $300 million per year. Delta serves about 135,000 meals per day. American Airlines spends around $800 million each year on food, with each meal averaging $8.20. With these huge expenses for meals, airlines are very interested in accurately forecasting the number of meals that will be needed on each flight.

Factors that make airline meal forecasting difficult include passenger no-shows, passengers purchasing tickets just before a flight, and cancelled flights. To further complicate matters, some passengers decide not to have meals, children can request a kid's meal, some passengers request special-diet meals, and first-class passengers receive different meals than economy-class passengers and may have two or more choices of meals. Some flights may be only 60 percent full while others may be 100 percent full. And sometimes, an airline gate agent must decide between getting a flight out on time or waiting until extra meals arrive.

If an airline orders too many meals for a flight, the extra meals must be thrown away, although some items such as boxed cereal might be given to charity. If it does not order enough meals, then hungry passengers may be upset and may not fly on that airline in the future, even if they receive meal vouchers, frequent-flier coupons, or free mixed drinks. The stakes are indeed high to accurately forecast the number of meals needed.

In the entire airline industry, meal shortages run around 1 percent. Last year Continental had an average meal shortage of 0.6 percent and had excess meals that averaged 3.5 percent at outlying hubs and 5 percent at its home base in Houston. To help ensure that first-class passengers are satisfied with their choice of meals, Northwest raised the ratio of meals on board to passengers boarded in first class from 100 percent to as much as 125 percent.

"People expect to be fed," says Linda Zane, senior director of dining services at Continental. "Good food is something we take very seriously."[1] Accurate demand forecasting is critical to providing good customer service in a cost-efficient manner.

It is imperative that companies have effective approaches to forecasting and that forecasting be an integral part of business planning. When managers plan, they determine in the present what courses of action they will take in the future. *The first step in planning is therefore forecasting, or estimating the future demand for products and services and the resources necessary to produce these outputs.* Estimates of the future demand for products and services are commonly called **sales forecasts,** which are the starting point for all the other planning in operations management.

Operations managers need long-range forecasts to make strategic decisions about products, processes, and facilities. They also need short-range forecasts to assist them in making decisions about operations issues that span only the next few days or weeks. Table 3.1 summarizes some of the reasons why operations managers must develop forecasts. Table 3.2 cites some examples of things that are commonly forecasted. Long-range forecasts usually span a year or longer and estimate demand for entire product lines such as lawn products. Medium-range forecasts usually span several months and group products into product families such as lawn mowers. Short-range forecasts usually span a few weeks and focus on specific products such as lawn mower model #3559.

Table 3.1	Some Reasons Why Forecasting Is Essential in Operations Management

1. **New facility planning.** It can take as long as five years to design and build a new factory or design and implement a new production process. Such strategic activities in POM require long-range forecasts of demand for existing and new products so that operations managers can have the necessary lead time to build factories and install processes to produce the products and services when needed.

2. **Production planning.** Demands for products and services vary from month to month. Production and service rates must be scaled up or down to meet these demands. It can take several months to change the capacities of production processes. Operations managers need medium-range forecasts so that they can have the lead time necessary to provide the production capacity to produce these variable monthly demands.

3. **Workforce scheduling.** Demands for products and services vary from week to week. The workforce must be scaled up or down to meet these demands by using reassignment, overtime, layoffs, or hiring. Operations managers need short-range forecasts so that they can have the lead time necessary to provide workforce changes to produce the weekly demands.

Table 3.2	Some Examples of Things That Must Be Forecasted in POM

Forecast Horizon	Time Span	Examples of Things That Must Be Forecasted	Some Typical Units of Forecasts
Long range	Years	New product lines	Dollars
		Old product lines	Dollars
		Factory capacities	Gallons, hours, pounds, units, or customers per time period
		Capital funds	Dollars
		Facility needs	Space, volume
Medium range	Months	Product groups	Units
		Departmental capacities	Hours, strokes, pounds, gallons, units, or customers per time period
		Workforce	Workers, hours
		Purchased materials	Units, pounds, gallons
		Inventories	Units, dollars
Short range	Weeks	Specific products	Units
		Labor-skill classes	Workers, hours
		Machine capacities	Units, hours, gallons, strokes, pounds, or customers per time period
		Cash	Dollars
		Inventories	Units, dollars

Figure 3.1 illustrates that forecasting is an integral part of business planning. The inputs are processed through forecasting models or methods to develop demand estimates. *These demand estimates are not the sales forecasts; rather, they are the starting point for management teams to develop sales forecasts.* The sales forecasts become inputs to both business strategy and production resource forecasts.

The forecasting methods or models may be either qualitative or quantitative in nature.

Figure 3.1	Forecasting as an Integral Part of Business Planning

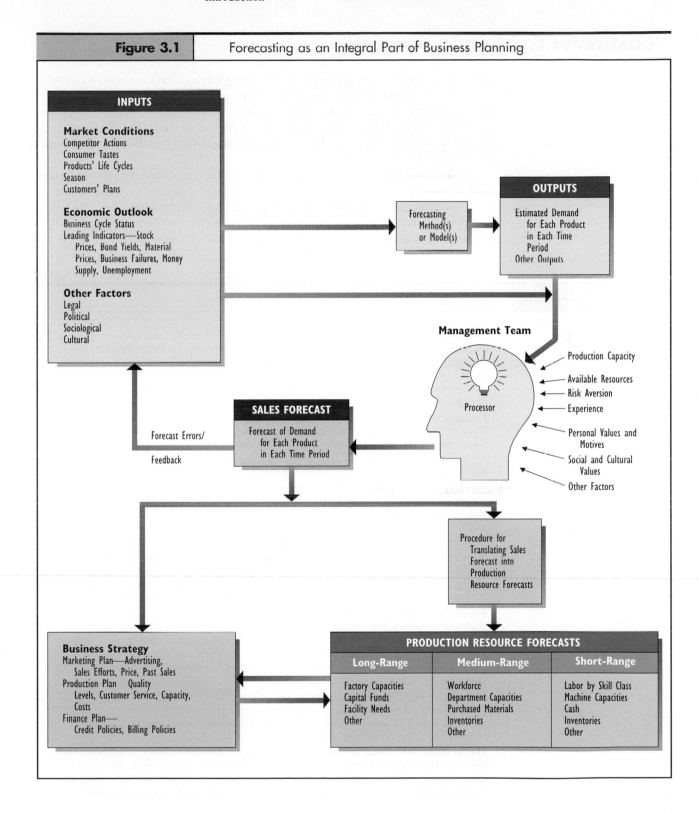

INPUTS

Market Conditions
Competitor Actions
Consumer Tastes
Products' Life Cycles
Season
Customers' Plans

Economic Outlook
Business Cycle Status
Leading Indicators—Stock
   Prices, Bond Yields, Material
   Prices, Business Failures, Money
   Supply, Unemployment

Other Factors
Legal
Political
Sociological
Cultural

Forecasting
Method(s)
or Model(s)

OUTPUTS
Estimated Demand
for Each Product
in Each Time
Period
Other Outputs

Management Team

Processor

Production Capacity
Available Resources
Risk Aversion
Experience
Personal Values and
   Motives
Social and Cultural
   Values
Other Factors

SALES FORECAST
Forecast of Demand
for Each Product
in Each Time Period

Forecast Errors/

Feedback

Procedure for
Translating Sales
Forecast into
Production
Resource Forecasts

Business Strategy
Marketing Plan—Advertising,
   Sales Efforts, Price, Past Sales
Production Plan   Quality
   Levels, Customer Service, Capacity,
   Costs
Finance Plan—
   Credit Policies, Billing Policies

PRODUCTION RESOURCE FORECASTS		
Long-Range	**Medium-Range**	**Short-Range**
Factory Capacities	Workforce	Labor by Skill Class
Capital Funds	Department Capacities	Machine Capacities
Facility Needs	Purchased Materials	Cash
Other	Inventories	Inventories
	Other	Other

QUALITATIVE FORECASTING METHODS

Table 3.3 describes several qualitative forecasting methods that are used to develop sales forecasts. These methods are usually based on judgments about the causal factors that underlie the sales of particular products or services and on opinions about the relative likelihood of those causal factors being present in the future. These methods may involve several levels of sophistication, from scientifically conducted opinion surveys to intuitive hunches about future events.

An **educated guess** is made when one person uses his or her intuition and experience to estimate a forecast. It is most often used when the cost of forecast inaccuracy is low. **Executive committee consensus** and the **Delphi method** describe procedures for assimilating information within a committee for the purpose of generating a sales forecast and are useful for either existing or new products and services. On the

Table 3.3	Qualitative Forecasting Methods

1. **Educated guess.** This is made when one person uses his or her best judgment, based on experience and intuition, to estimate a sales forecast. This approach is often used for shorter-term forecasts when the cost of forecast inaccuracy is low. For example, the owner of a small convenience store might use her experience and intuition to decide how many cases of canned corn to order for next week to meet demand. Since this type of forecasting occurs so frequently, an educated guess is the most common approach to forecasting.

2. **Executive committee consensus.** Knowledgeable executives from various departments within the organization form a committee charged with the responsibility of developing a sales forecast. The committee may use many inputs from all parts of the organization and may have staff analysts provide analyses as needed. Such forecasts tend to be compromise forecasts, not reflecting the extremes that could be present had they been prepared by individuals.

3. **Delphi method.** This method is used to achieve consensus within a committee. In this method, executives anonymously answer a series of questions on successive rounds. Each response is fed back to all participants on each round, and the process is then repeated. As many as six rounds may be required before consensus is reached on the forecast. This method can result in forecasts that most participants have ultimately agreed to in spite of their initial disagreement.

4. **Survey of sales force.** Estimates of future regional sales are obtained from individual members of the sales force. These estimates are combined to form an estimate of sales for all regions. Managers must then transform this estimate into a sales forecast to ensure realistic estimates. This is a popular forecasting method for companies that have a good communication system in place and that have salespeople who sell directly to customers.

5. **Survey of customers.** Estimates of future sales are obtained directly from customers. Individual customers are surveyed to determine what quantities of the firm's products they intend to purchase in each future time period. A sales forecast is determined by combining individual customers' responses. This method may be preferred by companies that have relatively few customers, such as automobile industry suppliers and defense contractors.

6. **Historical analogy.** This method ties the estimate of future sales of a product to knowledge of a similar product's sales. Knowledge of one product's sales during various stages of its product life cycle is applied to the estimate of sales for a similar product. This method may be particularly useful in forecasting sales of new products.

7. **Market research.** In market surveys, mail questionnaires, telephone interviews, or field interviews form the basis for testing hypotheses about real markets. In market tests, products marketed in target regions or outlets are statistically extrapolated to total markets. These methods are ordinarily preferred for new products or for existing products to be introduced into new market segments.

Qualatator

TEST

other hand, the **survey of sales force** and **survey of customers** describe methods that are primarily used for existing products and services. **Historical analogy** and **market surveys** and tests describe procedures that are useful for new products and services. The forecasting method that is appropriate, therefore, depends on a product's life cycle stage.

QUANTITATIVE FORECASTING MODELS

Quantitative forecasting models are mathematical models based on historical data. Such models assume that past data are relevant to the future. Some relevant data can almost always be found. Here, we discuss several quantitative models, forecast accuracy, long-range forecasts, and short-range forecasts.

Table 3.4 exhibits the quantitative forecasting models that we are going to study in this chapter. Although many more quantitative forecasting models exist, the models in Table 3.4 provide a useful introduction to forecasting in POM. All of these models can be used with times series. A *time series* is a set of observed values measured over successive time periods, such as monthly sales for the last two years.

successive periods of time

no forecast is ever correct

Forecast Accuracy

Forecast accuracy refers to how close forecasts come to actual data. Because forecasts are made *before* actual data become known, the accuracy of forecasts can be determined

Table 3.4	Some Quantitative Forecasting Models

1. **Linear regression.** A model that uses what is called the least-squares method to identify the relationship between a dependent variable and one or more independent variables that are present in a set of historical observations. In simple regression there is only one independent variable. In multiple regression there is more than one independent variable. If the historical data set is a time series, the independent variable is the time period and the dependent variable in sales forecasting is sales. A regression model does not have to be based on a time series; in such cases the knowledge of future values of the independent variable (which may also be referred to as the *causal variable*) is used to predict future values of the dependent variable. Linear regression is ordinarily used in long-range forecasting, but if care is used in selecting the number of periods included in the historical data and that data set is projected only a few periods into the future, regression may also be appropriately used in short-range forecasting.

2. **Moving average.** A short-range time series type of forecasting model that forecasts sales for the next time period. In this model the arithmetic average of the actual sales for a specific number of most recent past time periods is the forecast for the next time period.

3. **Weighted moving average.** This model is like the moving average model described above except that instead of an arithmetic average of past sales, a weighted average of past sales is the forecast for the next time period. Typically, more weight would be placed on the most recent time periods.

4. **Exponential smoothing.** Also a short-range time series forecasting model that forecasts sales for the next time period. In this method the forecasted sales for the last period is modified by information about the forecast error of the last period. This modification of the last period's forecast is the forecast for the next time period.

5. **Exponential smoothing with trend.** The exponential smoothing model described above but modified to accommodate data with a trend pattern. Such patterns can be present in medium-range data. Also called **double exponential smoothing,** both the estimate for the average and the estimate for the trend are smoothed, two smoothing constants being used.

only after the passage of time. If forecasts are very close to the actual data, we say that they have **high accuracy** and that the **forecast error** is low. We determine the accuracy of forecasting models by keeping a running tally of how far forecasts have missed the actual data points over time. If the accuracy of a model is low, we modify the method or select a new one. We discuss ways of measuring and monitoring forecasting model performance later in the chapter.

Long-Range Forecasts

Long-range forecasting means estimating future conditions over time spans that are usually greater than one year. Long-range forecasts are necessary in POM to support strategic decisions about planning products, processes, technologies, and facilities. Such decisions are so important to the long-term success of production and operations systems that intense organizational effort is applied to developing these forecasts. Activities such as purchasing and building new machines and buildings and developing new sources of materials take time, and long-range forecasts give managers the time to develop plans for these activities.

Cycles, Trends, and Seasonality

Although long-range data may look erratic, if we look beyond this surface appearance, we usually can identify rather simple underlying data patterns. Figure 3.2 shows how historical sales data tend to be made up of several components. Among these components are trends, cycles, seasonality, and random fluctuation or noise. Long-range **trends** are illustrated by an upward- or downward-sloping line. A **cycle** is a data pattern that may cover several years before it repeats itself again. **Random fluctuation,** or **noise,** is a pattern resulting from random variation or unexplained causes. **Seasonality** is a data pattern that repeats itself after a period of time, usually one year. Seasons such as autumn, winter, spring, and summer are well known, but seasonal patterns such as the following can also occur:

Length of Time before Pattern Is Repeated	Length of Season	Number of Seasons in Pattern
Year	Quarter	4
Year	Month	12
Year	Week	52
Month	Day	29–31
Week	Day	7

Whenever long-range forecasts are to be made using historical time series data, plotting the data is often helpful in deciding which forecasting methods to consider. Patterns such as trend or seasonality may be obvious from viewing the historical data on a graph. Changes in historical patterns and unusual observations may also be obvious from the graph. Popular spreadsheet and forecasting software makes it easy to create these graphs.

In Figure 3.2, six years of historical sales data are plotted on the top graph. Long-range forecasts could be developed by graphically fitting a line through these past data and extending it forward into the future. The sales forecasts for Periods 7 and 8 could then be read off the graph. This graphical approach to long-range forecasts is used in practice, but its principal drawback is the inability to accurately fit a line through the past data. Regression analysis provides a more accurate way to develop trend line forecasts.

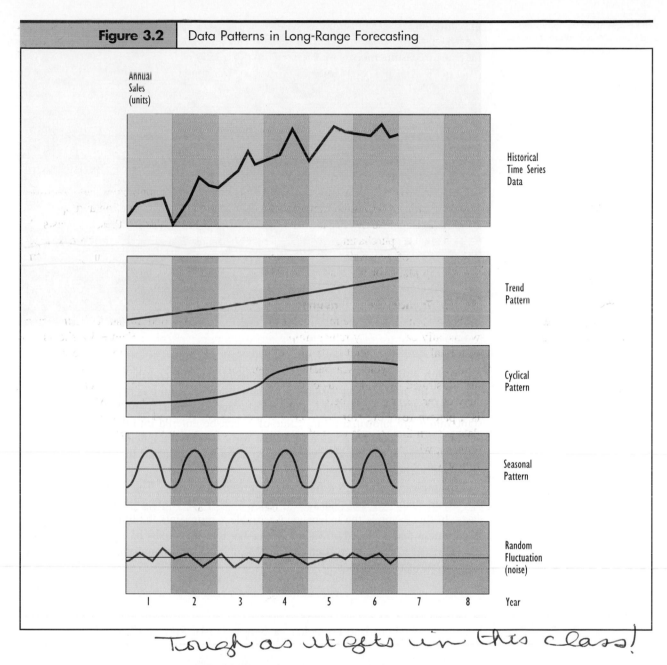

Figure 3.2 | Data Patterns in Long-Range Forecasting

Annual Sales (units)

Historical Time Series Data

Trend Pattern

Cyclical Pattern

Seasonal Pattern

Random Fluctuation (noise)

1   2   3   4   5   6   7   8   Year

Tough as it gets in this class!

Linear Regression and Correlation

Linear regression analysis is a forecasting model that establishes a relationship between a dependent variable and one or more independent variables. We use our knowledge about that relationship and about the future values of the independent variables to forecast the future values of the dependent variable. In **simple linear regression analysis** there is only one independent variable. If the data are a time series, the independent variable is the time period, and the dependent variable is usually sales, or whatever we wish to forecast.

Table 3.5 displays the variables, variable definitions, and formulas for simple linear regression analysis. This model is of the form $Y = a + bX$, which is called the

© R.W. JONES/CORBIS

regression equation, where Y is the dependent variable and the variable to be forecast, X is the independent variable, a is the y intercept, and b is the slope of the trend line. The formulas in Table 3.5 allow us to compute values a and b. Once these constant values are known, a future value of X can be entered into the regression equation and a corresponding value of Y (the forecast) can be calculated. Conceptually, this procedure is the same as graphically extending the trend line in Figure 3.2, as discussed earlier.

Example 3.1 develops a forecast from time series data. The example shows how operations managers can plan facility capacities by developing long-range sales forecasts. In this example the independent variable x represents the time period. The only requirement that is placed on values of x is that its values must be equally spaced; thus the values of x could have been 1993, 1994, . . . , 2002 or any other meaningful representation of time periods.

Table 3.5	Variable Definitions and Formulas for Simple Linear Regression Analysis

x = independent variable values	Y = values of y that lie on the
y = dependent variable values	trend line Y = a + bX
n = number of observations	X = values of x that lie on the
a = vertical axis intercept	trend line
b = slope of the regression line	r = coefficient of correlation
$\bar{y}$ = mean value of the dependent variable	r^2 = coefficient of determination
$a = \dfrac{\sum x^2 \sum y - \sum x \sum xy}{n\sum x^2 - (\sum x)^2}$	$Y = a + bX$
$b = \dfrac{n\sum xy - \sum x \sum y}{n\sum x^2 - (\sum x)^2}$	$r = \dfrac{n\sum xy - \sum x \sum y}{\sqrt{[n\sum x^2 - (\sum x)^2][n\sum y^2 - (\sum y)^2]}}$

| **Example 3.1** | Simple Linear Regression Analysis: A Time Series |

AromaDrip Coffee Inc. produces commercial coffee machines that are sold all over the world. The company's production facility has operated at near capacity for over a year now. Wayne Conners, the plant manager, thinks that sales growth will continue, and he wants to develop long-range forecasts to help plan facility requirements for the next 3 years. Sales records for the past 10 years have been compiled:

Year	Annual Sales (thousands of units)	Year	Annual Sales (thousands of units)
1	1,000	6	2,000
2	1,300	7	2,200
3	1,800	8	2,600
4	2,000	9	2,900
5	2,000	10	3,200

We study the formulas and variable definitions in Table 3.5, and then we construct the following table to establish the values to use in the formulas. (It is helpful to use a spreadsheet such as *Microsoft Excel* to perform many of the calculations.)

Year	Annual Sales (thousands of units) (y)	Time Period (x)	x^2	xy
1	1,000	1	1	1,000
2	1,300	2	4	2,600
3	1,800	3	9	5,400
4	2,000	4	16	8,000
5	2,000	5	25	10,000
6	2,000	6	36	12,000
7	2,200	7	49	15,400
8	2,600	8	64	20,800
9	2,900	9	81	26,100
10	3,200	10	100	32,000
Totals	$\sum y = 21{,}000$	$\sum x = 55$	$\sum x^2 = 385$	$\sum xy = 133{,}300$

Solution

1. Let us now solve for the a and b values:

$$a = \frac{\sum x^2 \sum y - \sum x \sum xy}{n \sum x^2 - (\sum x)^2} = \frac{(385)(21{,}000) - (55)(133{,}300)}{10(385) - (55)^2}$$

$$= \frac{8{,}085{,}000 - 7{,}331{,}500}{3{,}850 - 3{,}025} = \frac{753{,}500}{825} = 913.333$$

$$b = \frac{n\sum xy - \sum x\sum y}{n\sum x^2 - (\sum x)^2} = \frac{(10)(133,300) - (55)(21,000)}{825}$$

$$= \frac{1,333,000 - 1,155,000}{825} = \frac{178,000}{825} = 215.758$$

2. Now that we know the values of a and b, the regression equation can be used to forecast future years' sales:

$$Y = a + bX = 913.333 + 215.758X$$

3. If we wish to forecast sales in thousands of units for the next three years, we would substitute 11, 12, and 13, the next three values for x, into the regression equation for X:

$$Y_{11} = 913.333 + 215.758(11) = 3,286.7, \text{ or } 3,290 \text{ thousand units}$$
$$Y_{12} = 913.333 + 215.758(12) = 3,502.4, \text{ or } 3,500 \text{ thousand units}$$
$$Y_{13} = 913.333 + 215.758(13) = 3,718.2, \text{ or } 3,720 \text{ thousand units}$$

The forecasts are rounded to one significant digit more than the original data. Notice that the sales data contain only two significant digits; the forecasts are carried to three.

Simple linear regression can also be used when the independent variable x represents a variable other than time. In this case, linear regression is representative of a class of forecasting models called **causal forecasting models**. These models develop forecasts after establishing and measuring an association between the dependent variable and one or more independent variables. This class of models is excellent at predicting **turning points** in sales.

Example 3.2 uses the amount of regional construction as the independent variable x to forecast a company's sales y, the dependent variable. In this example, a long-range sales forecast is needed to assist the manager in planning the number of engineers and facilities for the next year. This example also explains how the coefficient of correlation and the coefficient of determination can be used to evaluate the forecasting model developed through linear regression analysis.

Example 3.2	Simple Linear Regression Analysis

Jack Weis, the general manager of Precision Engineering Corporation, thinks that his firm's engineering services supplied to highway construction firms are directly related to the amount of highway construction contracts let in his geographic area. He wonders if this is really so and if it is, can this information help him plan his operations better? Jack asked Maria Cortez, one of his engineers, to perform a simple linear regression analysis on historical data. Maria plans to do the following: **a.** Develop a regression equation for predicting the level of demand of Precision's services. **b.** Use the regression equation to predict the level of demand for the next four quarters. **c.** Determine how closely demand is related to the amount of construction contracts released.

Solution

a. Develop a regression equation:
   1. Maria goes back through local, state, and federal records to gather the dollar amount of contracts released in the geographic area for two years by quarters.

2. She examines the demand for her firm's services over the same period.
3. The following data are prepared:

Year	Quarter	Sales of Precision Engineering Services (thousands of dollars)	Total Amount of Contracts Released (thousands of dollars)
1	Q_1	8	150
	Q_2	10	170
	Q_3	15	190
	Q_4	9	170
2	Q_1	12	180
	Q_2	13	190
	Q_3	12	200
	Q_4	16	220

4. Maria now develops the totals required to perform the regression analysis. The formulas and variable definitions are found in Table 3.5. (It is helpful to use a spreadsheet to perform many of the calculations.)

Time Period	Sales (y)	Contracts (x)	x^2	xy	y^2
1	8	150	22,500	1,200	64
2	10	170	28,900	1,700	100
3	15	190	36,100	2,850	225
4	9	170	28,900	1,530	81
5	12	180	32,400	2,160	144
6	13	190	36,100	2,470	169
7	12	200	40,000	2,400	144
8	16	220	48,400	3,520	256
Totals	$\sum y = 95$	$\sum x = 1,470$	$\sum x^2 = 273,300$	$\sum xy = 17,830$	$\sum y^2 = 1,183$

5. Use these values in the formulas in Table 3.5 to compute a and b:

$$a = \frac{\sum x^2 \sum y - \sum x \sum xy}{n \sum x^2 - (\sum x)^2} = \frac{(273,300)(95) - (1,470)(17,830)}{8(273,300) - (1,470)^2}$$

$$= \frac{25,963,500 - 26,210,100}{2,186,400 - 2,160,900} = \frac{-246,600}{25,500} = -9.671$$

$$b = \frac{n \sum xy - \sum x \sum y}{n \sum x^2 - (\sum x)^2} = \frac{(8)(17,830) - (1,470)(95)}{25,500} = \frac{142,640 - 139,650}{25,500}$$

$$= \frac{2,990}{25,500} = 0.1173$$

6. The regression equation is therefore $Y = -9.671 + 0.1173X$.

b. Forecast the level of demand for the next four quarters:
 1. Maria calls representatives of the contracting agencies and prepares estimates of the quarterly contracts for the next four quarters in thousands of dollars. These were 260, 290, 300, and 270.
 2. Next, Maria forecasts the demand for Precision's engineering services (in thousands of dollars) for the next four quarters by using the regression equation $Y = -9.671 + 0.1173X$:

$$Y_1 = -9.671 + .1173(260) \qquad Y_2 = -9.671 + .1173(290)$$
$$= -9.671 + 30.498 \qquad\qquad = -9.671 + 34.017$$
$$= 20.827 \qquad\qquad\qquad = 24.346$$

$$Y_3 = -9.671 + .1173(300) \qquad Y_4 = -9.671 + .1173(270)$$
$$= -9.671 + 35.190 \qquad\qquad = -9.671 + 31.671$$
$$= 25.519 \qquad\qquad\qquad = 22.000$$

The total forecast (in thousands of dollars) for the next year is the total of the four quarter forecasts:

$$20.827 + 24.346 + 25.519 + 22.000 = \$92.7$$

Notice that the forecast is rounded to one significant digit more than the original data.

c. Evaluate how closely demand is related to the amount of the construction contracts released:

$$r = \frac{n\sum xy - \sum x\sum y}{\sqrt{[n\sum x^2 - (\sum x)^2][n\sum y^2 - (\sum y)^2]}} = \frac{2{,}990}{\sqrt{[25{,}550][8(1{,}183) - (95)^2]}}$$

$$= \frac{2{,}990}{\sqrt{[25{,}500][9{,}464 - 9{,}025]}} = \frac{2{,}990}{\sqrt{(25{,}500)(439)}} = \frac{2{,}990}{\sqrt{11{,}194{,}500}}$$

$$= \frac{2{,}990}{3{,}345.8} = .894$$

$$r^2 = 0.799$$

The amount of contracts released explains approximately 80 percent ($r^2 = 0.799$) of the observed variation in quarterly demand for Precision's services.

The coefficient of correlation (r) explains the relative importance of the relationship between y and x; the sign of r shows the direction of the relationship, and the absolute value of r shows the strength of the relationship. r can take any value between -1 to $+1$. The sign of r is always the same as the sign of b. A negative r indicates that the values of y and x tend to move in opposite directions, and a positive r indicates that the values of y and x move in the same direction. Here are the meanings of several values of r:

-1 A perfect negative relationship; as y goes up, x goes down unit for unit and vice versa.

$+1$ A perfect positive relationship; as y goes up, x goes up unit for unit and vice versa.

0 No relationship exists between y and x.

$+0.3$ A weak positive relationship.

-0.9 A strong negative relationship.

In Example 3.2, r = +0.894. This means that there is a strong positive relationship between demand for engineering services and amount of contracts released.

Although the coefficient of correlation is helpful in measuring the relationship between x and y, terms such as *strong, moderate,* and *weak* are not very specific measures of relationship. The coefficient of determination (r^2) is the square of the coefficient of correlation. The seemingly insignificant modification of r to r^2 allows us to shift from subjective measures of relationship to a more specific measure. There are three types of variation in y: total, explained, and unexplained:

$$\text{Total variation} = \text{Explained variation} + \text{Unexplained variation}$$
$$\Sigma(y - \bar{y})^2 \qquad \Sigma(Y - \bar{y})^2 \qquad \Sigma(y - Y)^2$$

Figure 3.3 illustrates these sources of variation. The **total variation** is the sum of the squared deviations of each value of y from its mean $\bar{y}$. The **explained variation** is the sum of the squared deviations of Y values that lie on the trend line from $\bar{y}$. The **unexplained variation,** or the variation from random or unidentified sources, is the sum of the squared deviations of y from the Y values on the trend line.

The **coefficient of determination** is determined by the ratio of explained variation to total variation:

$$r^2 = \frac{\Sigma(Y - \bar{y})^2}{\Sigma(y - \bar{y})^2}$$

The coefficient of determination, therefore, illustrates how much of the total variation in the dependent variable y is explained by x or the trend line. If $r^2 = 80$ percent, as in Example 3.2, we can say that the amount of contracts released (x) explains 80 percent of the variation in sales of engineering services (y). Twenty percent of the variation in sales of engineering services is not explained by the amount of contracts released and thus is attributed to other variables or to chance variation.

Figure 3.3	Variation of Dependent Variable (y)

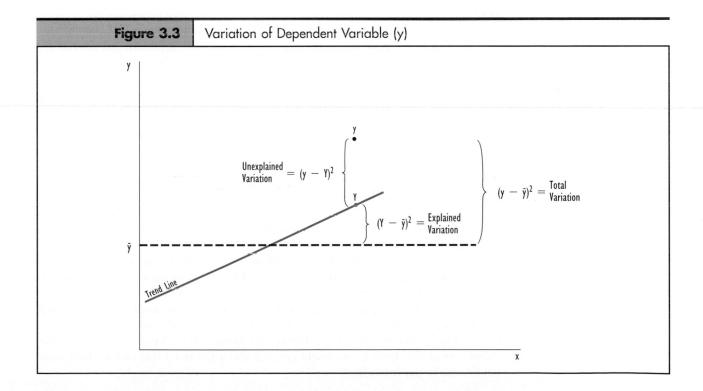

Both the coefficients of correlation and determination are helpful measures of the strength of the relationship between dependent and independent variables and thus of the value of regression equations as forecasting models. The stronger the relationship, the more accurate the forecasts resulting from the regression equations are likely to be.

Simple linear regression analysis has its limitations in developing forecasts with high accuracy in the real worlds of government and business. Although there are instances where one independent variable explains enough of the dependent variable variation to provide sufficient accuracy, more sophisticated models may be required. While the formulas are more complex and beyond the scope of this discussion, **multiple regression analysis** is used when there are two or more independent variables. An example of a multiple regression equation is:

$$Y = 15.5 + 2.9X_1 + 12.8X_2 - 1.2X_3 + 8.5X_4$$

where:

$$Y = \text{next quarter's sales in thousands of units}$$
$$X_1 = \text{prior quarter's national freight car loadings in millions}$$
$$X_2 = \text{percent GDP growth} \times \text{ten thousands}$$
$$X_3 = \text{unemployment rate in region} \times \text{ten thousands}$$
$$X_4 = \text{population in county in thousands}$$

Such an equation is used just like the simple linear regression equation ($Y = a + bX$): The estimated values of the independent variables (X_1, X_2, X_3, and X_4) are substituted into the regression equation to calculate the value of the dependent variable (Y).

Notice in the multiple regression equation above that the variable X_1 is *prior* quarter's national freight car loadings. This data is used to forecast *next* quarter's sales. In this case, freight car loadings lead sales by one quarter. We call X_1 a **leading indicator** because its value is *known* before sales occur. *It is always desirable to find leading indicators in forecasting because it avoids the necessity of estimating the values of the independent variables,* as we did in Step b.1 of Example 3.2.

Nonlinear multiple regression analysis, stepwise regression, and **partial** and **multiple correlation coefficients** are also part of the family of techniques known as regression and correlation analysis, but these are beyond the scope of this text. However, the concepts presented here generally apply to these more sophisticated techniques, and Y, X, a, b, and r all have their counterparts in the more complex models.

Ranging Forecasts

When linear regression analysis generates forecasts for future periods, these are only estimates and are subject to error. The presence of forecasting errors or chance variations is a fact of life for forecasters; forecasting is a process permeated with uncertainty. One way to deal with this uncertainty is to develop confidence intervals for forecasts.

Figure 3.4 shows graphically how confidence intervals might be set for forecasts. Ten periods of data are used to develop a trend line. By extending the trend line forward to Period 12, a forecast of 2,400 units is obtained. By drawing upper and lower limits through the data parallel to the trend line such that actual annual sales only rarely exceed the limits, upper and lower limits can be extended to Period 12 to obtain an upper limit of 3,300 units and a lower limit of 1,500 units. If the limits are close together, the historical data have been closely grouped about the trend line and we have more confidence in our forecasts.

| **Figure 3.4** | Errors in Forecasting |

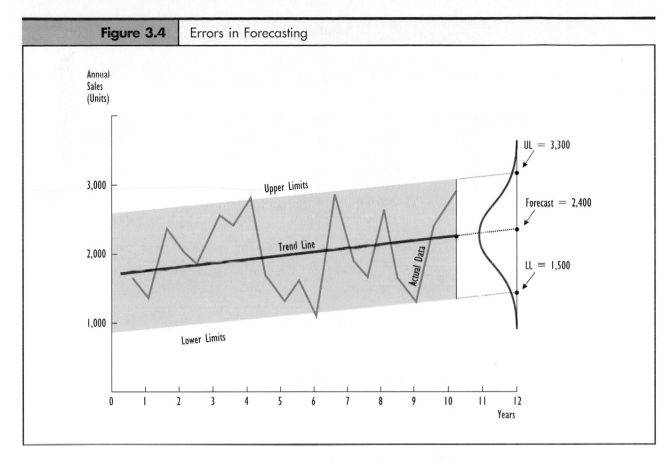

Although this graphical approach is sometimes used to set upper and lower limits or ranges of forecasts, a more precise method is available. Example 3.3 uses the following formula to estimate ranges for a forecast:

$$s_{yx} = \sqrt{\frac{\sum y^2 - a\sum y - b\sum xy}{n - 2}}$$

The expression s_{yx} is referred to as the **standard error of the forecast** or the **standard deviation of the forecast,** and is a measure of how historical data points have been dispersed about the trend line. If s_{yx} is small relative to the forecast, past data points have been tightly grouped about the trend line and the upper and lower limits are close together.

Forecast ranging allows analysts to deal with the uncertainty that surrounds their forecasts by developing best-estimate forecasts and the ranges within which the actual data are likely to fall.

| **Example 3.3** | Ranging Time Series Forecasts |

The annual sales data of AromaDrip Coffee Inc. from Example 3.1 are used here. The distribution of forecast values for a future time period has a standard deviation (s_{yx}), which is a relative measure of how the distribution is dispersed about its expected value (Y). Distribution of all future time periods' forecast values are assumed to be Student's t distributions.

Solution

1.   From Example 3.1 we have computed all of these values: $\sum y = 21,000$; $\sum x = 55$; $\sum x^2 = 385$; $\sum xy = 133,300$; $n = 10$; $\bar{x} = 5.5$; $\bar{y} = 2,100$. Let us now compute $\sum y^2$:

Year	y (thousands of units)	y^2	Year	y (thousands of units)	y^2
1	1,000	1,000,000	6	2,000	4,000,000
2	1,300	1,690,000	7	2,200	4,840,000
3	1,800	3,240,000	8	2,600	6,760,000
4	2,000	4,000,000	9	2,900	8,410,000
5	2,000	4,000,000	10	3,200	10,240,000
				Total	$\sum y^2 = 48,180,000$

2.   Now let us compute the value of s_{yx}:

$$s_{yx} = \sqrt{\frac{\sum y^2 - a\sum y - b\sum xy}{n-2}}$$

$$= \sqrt{\frac{48,180,000 - 913.333(21,000) - 215.758(133,300)}{10-2}}$$

$$= \sqrt{\frac{48,180,000 - 19,179,993 - 28,760,541.4}{8}} = \sqrt{\frac{239,465.6}{8}} = \sqrt{29,933.2}$$

$$= 173.0 \text{ thousand units}$$

3.   Now that we have the value of s_{yx}, let us compute the upper and lower limits of the forecast for Time Period 11*:

$$\text{Upper limit} = Y_{11} + t\, s_{yx}$$
$$\text{Lower limit} = Y_{11} - t\, s_{yx}$$

where t is the number of standard deviations out from the mean of the distribution to provide a given probability of exceeding these upper and lower limits through chance. Say, for example, that we wish to set the limits so that there is only a 10 percent probability (5 percent in either tail) of exceeding the limits by chance. Appendix B lists t values. Since the degrees of freedom (d.f.) = $n - 2$ for a simple regression analysis and the level of significance is 0.10, the t value equals 1.860 and:

$$\text{Upper limit} = 3,286.7 + 1.86(173) = 3,608.5, \text{ or } 3,610 \text{ thousand units}$$
$$\text{Lower limit} = 3,286.7 - 1.86(173) = 2,964.9, \text{ or } 2,960 \text{ thousand units}$$

Notice that the limits are rounded to one significant digit more than the original data.

4.   Now we can describe to Wayne Conners what we have: There is a 90 percent probability that our annual sales for next year will be between 3,610 and 2,960 thousand units. There is only a 10 percent probability that our sales will fall outside these limits. Our best estimate is 3,290 thousand units.

*Another expression of the upper and lower limits of the forecast Y is sometimes used when the point of the forecast is far removed from the original data: Limits = $Y \pm t(s_f)$, where $s_f = s_{yx}\sqrt{1 + 1/n + [(X_0 - \bar{X})^2/\sum(X - \bar{X})^2]}$, and X_0 is the value of X for which a value of Y is being forecast.

BUSINESS SNAPSHOT 3.1

Forecasting Telephone Calls at L. L. Bean

L. L. Bean is a widely known retailer of high-quality outdoor goods and apparel. Roughly 10 percent of its sales are derived through retail stores, 20 percent through mail orders, and 70 percent through telephone orders at the company's call center. Customers call one of two toll-free numbers to place orders or to contact customer service. Customer service agents are specially trained to handle a wide variety of customer issues, whereas sales agents are trained primarily to take orders.

To plan its staffing needs effectively, it is important for L. L. Bean to forecast accurately the number of daily telephone calls for sales and for customer service. Staffing schedulers use the forecasts to create weekly employee schedules

for the coming three weeks. Inaccurate forecasts are very costly to L. L. Bean. Forecasting too high results in excess direct labor cost. Forecasting too low results in understaffing, which causes dissatisfied customers, lost sales, and high telephone-connect charges from longer waits. Further complicating the forecasting and staffing challenge is the erratic nature and extreme seasonality of L. L. Bean's business. The company receives nearly 20 percent of its annual calls in the three weeks before Christmas, during which time it usually doubles the number of agents and quadruples the quantity of telephone lines.

In an effort to improve forecasting accuracy, new forecasting models were developed using the autoregressive integrated moving

average (ARIMA or Box–Jenkins) methodology. The improvements were substantial. One L. L. Bean manager described the improvements as follows: "We have been using the new forecasting system to make our call-center staffing schedules for about five months now and have benefited greatly from its improved precision. In the past, we forecasted call volumes using a less statistically sophisticated approach which was based primarily on order forecasts provided by marketing.

"The recurring annual savings derived from switching to the new forecasting system is estimated to be $300,000. This does not include the substantial ongoing savings derived from greatly reducing the labor required to prepare the forecasts every week."

Source: Andrews, Bruce H., and Shawn M. Cunningham. "L. L. Bean Improves Call-Center Forecasting." *Interfaces* 25, no. 6 (November–December 1995): 1–13.

Seasonality in Time Series Forecasts

Seasonal patterns are usually fluctuations that take place within one year and tend to be repeated annually. These seasons can be caused or determined by weather, holidays, paydays, school events, or other phenomena. Business Snapshot 3.1 describes the experience of L. L. Bean in forecasting seasonal patterns.

Example 3.4 demonstrates how to develop forecasts with linear regression analysis when seasonality is present in time series data. The example follows these steps:

1. Select a representative historical data set.
2. Develop a seasonal index for each season (i.e., month or quarter).
3. Use the seasonal indexes to deseasonalize the data; in other words, remove the seasonal patterns.
4. Perform a linear regression analysis on the deseasonalized data. This will result in a regression equation in the form: $Y = a + bX$.
5. Use the regression equation to compute the forecasts for the future.
6. Use the seasonal indexes to reapply the seasonal patterns to the forecasts.

When we develop seasonalized forecasts using linear regression analysis, as in Example 3.4, and we wish to range these forecasts, the procedure is straightforward. The deseasonalized forecasts would be ranged and then these forecasts, along with their upper and lower limits, would be seasonalized by multiplying them by their seasonal indexes.

| Example 3.4 | Seasonalized Time Series Forecasts |

Wayne Conners, the plant manager of AromaDrip Coffee Inc., is trying to plan cash, personnel, and materials and supplies requirements for each quarter of next year. The quarterly sales data for the past three years seem to reflect fairly the seasonal output pattern that should be expected in the future. If Wayne could estimate quarterly sales for next year, the cash, personnel, and materials and supplies needs could be determined. (It is helpful to use a spreadsheet to perform many of the calculations.)

Solution

1. First, we compute the seasonal indexes:

		Quarterly Sales (thousands of units)				Annual
	Year	Q_1	Q_2	Q_3	Q_4	Total
	8	520	730	820	530	2,600
	9	590	810	900	600	2,900
	10	650	900	1,000	650	3,200
Totals		1,760	2,440	2,720	1,780	8,700
Quarter average		$586\frac{2}{3}$	$813\frac{2}{3}$	$906\frac{2}{3}$	$593\frac{1}{3}$	725*
Seasonal index (S.I.)**		0.809	1.122	1.251	0.818	

*Overall quarter average = 8700/12 = 725.
**S.I. = Quarter average/Overall quarter average.

2. Next, we deseasonalize the data by dividing each quarterly value by its S.I. (seasonal index). For instance, $520 \div 0.809 = 642.8$, $730 \div 1.122 = 650.6$, and so on.

			Deseasonalized	
			Adjusted Quarterly Data	
Year	Q_1	Q_2	Q_3	Q_4
8	642.8	650.6	655.5	647.9
9	729.3	721.9	719.4	733.5
10	803.5	802.1	799.4	794.6

3. Next, we perform a regression analysis on the deseasonalized data (12 quarters) and forecast for the next 4 quarters:

Time Period	x	y	y^2	x^2	xy
Year 8, Q_1	1	642.8	413,191.84	1	642.8
Year 8, Q_2	2	650.6	423,280.36	4	1,301.2
Year 8, Q_3	3	655.5	429,680.25	9	1,966.5
Year 8, Q_4	4	647.9	419,774.41	16	2,591.6

Time Period	x	y	y^2	x^2	xy
Year 9, Q_1	5	729.3	531,878.49	25	3,646.5
Year 9, Q_2	6	721.9	521,139.61	36	4,331.4
Year 9, Q_3	7	719.4	517,536.36	49	5,035.8
Year 9, Q_4	8	733.5	538,022.25	64	5,868.0
Year 10, Q_1	9	803.5	645,612.25	81	7,231.5
Year 10, Q_2	10	802.1	643,364.41	100	8,021.0
Year 10, Q_3	11	799.4	639,040.36	121	8,793.4
Year 10, Q_4	12	794.6	631,389.16	144	9,535.2
Totals	$\sum x = 78$	$\sum y = 8,700.5$	$\sum y^2 = 6,353,909.75$	$\sum x^2 = 650$	$\sum xy = 58,964.9$

4. Now we use these values to substitute into the formulas found in Table 3.5:

$$a = \frac{\sum x^2 \sum y - \sum x \sum xy}{n \sum x^2 - (\sum x)^2} = \frac{650(8,700.5) - 78(58,964.9)}{12(650) - (78)^2} = 615.421$$

$$b = \frac{n \sum xy - \sum x \sum y}{n \sum x^2 - (\sum x)^2} = \frac{12(58,964.9) - 78(8,700.5)}{12(650) - (78)^2} = 16.865$$

$$Y = a + bX = 615.421 + 16.865X$$

5. Now we substitute the values 13, 14, 15, and 16—the next four values for x—into the regression equation. These are the deseasonalized forecasts, in thousands of units, for the next four quarters.

$$Y_{13} = 615.421 + 16.865(13) = 834.666 \qquad Y_{15} = 615.421 + 16.865(15) = 868.396$$
$$Y_{14} = 615.421 + 16.865(14) = 851.531 \qquad Y_{16} = 615.421 + 16.865(16) = 885.261$$

6. Now we use the seasonal indexes (S.I.) to seasonalize the forecasts:

Quarter	S.I.	Deseasonalized Forecasts	Seasonalized Forecasts [S.I. × deseasonalized forecasts] (thousands of units)
Q_1	0.809	834.666	675
Q_2	1.122	851.531	955
Q_3	1.251	868.396	1,086
Q_4	0.818	885.261	724

Notice that the forecasts are rounded to one significant digit more than the original data.

Short-Range Forecasts

Short-range forecasts are usually estimates of future conditions over time spans that range from a few days to several weeks. *These forecasts may span such short periods of time that cycles, seasonality, and trend patterns have little effect.* The main data pattern affecting these forecasts is random fluctuation.

Short-range forecasts provide operations managers with information to make such decisions as these:

*   How much inventory of a particular product should be carried next month?
*   How much of each product should be scheduled for production next week?

- How much of each raw material should be ordered for delivery next week?
- How many workers should be scheduled to work on a straight-time and overtime basis next week?

Evaluating Forecasting Model Performance

Short-range forecasting models are evaluated on the basis of three characteristics: impulse response, noise-dampening ability, and accuracy.

Impulse Response versus Noise-Dampening Ability   Short-range forecasting involves taking historical data from the past and projecting the estimated values for these data one or more periods into the future. Forecasts that reflect every little happenstance fluctuation in the past data are said to include random variation, or **noise.** Such forecasts are erratic from period to period. If, on the other hand, forecasts have little period-to-period fluctuation, the forecasts are said to be **noise dampening.**

Forecasts that respond very fast to changes in historical data are described as having a **high impulse response.** On the other hand, when forecasts reflect few of the changes in historical data, these forecasts are said to have a **low impulse response.** It is usually desirable to have short-range forecasts that have both high impulse response and high noise-dampening ability, but this is not possible. A forecasting system that responds very fast to changes in the data necessarily picks up a great deal of noise. Forecasters, therefore, must ordinarily choose which characteristic—high impulse response or high noise-dampening ability—has more value as they select forecasting models for particular applications.

Measures of Forecast Accuracy   The accuracy of a forecasting model refers to how close actual data follow forecasts. Three measures of forecast accuracy are commonly used: (1) standard error of the forecast (s_{yx}), which was discussed earlier, (2) mean squared error (MSE), which is simply $(s_{yx})^2$, and (3) mean absolute deviation (MAD), which is computed with the formulas below:

$$MAD = \frac{\text{Sum of absolute deviation for n periods}}{n}$$

$$MAD = \frac{\sum_{i=1}^{n} \left|\text{Actual demand} - \text{Forecast demand}\right|_i}{n}$$

Like s_{yx} and MSE, if MAD is small, the actual data closely follow forecasts of the dependent variable and the forecasting model is providing accurate forecasts. When the forecast errors are normally distributed, the values of MAD and s_{yx} are related by the expression:

$$S_{yx} = 1.25MAD$$

MAD, s_{yx}, and MSE are used to measure the *after-the-fact* accuracy of both long-range and short-range forecasting models. In the case of short-range forecasting models, however, MAD can also be used to determine good values of the parameters of the forecasting models *before* the models are applied.

Naive Forecasts

Naive forecasting models are those that are quick and easy to use, have virtually no cost, and are easy to understand. Examples of naive forecasts are (1) using yesterday's sales as tomorrow's sales forecast and (2) using the sales for the same date last year for tomorrow's sales forecast. The main objection to using such naive approaches to short-range forecasting is that they are so simplistic they are likely to result in substantial forecast error. There are some applications, however, in which naive approaches are as accurate as more complex models or forecast error is not costly enough to justify more expensive forecasting models.

Moving Average Method

The **moving average method** averages the data from a few recent periods, and this average becomes the forecast for the next period. Example 3.5 demonstrates how to use the moving average method. Of particular importance is the number of periods (AP) of data to include in the average.

| Example 3.5 | Moving Average Short-Range Forecasting |

Shirley Johnson, an inventory manager, wants to develop a short-range forecasting system to estimate the amount of inventory flowing out of her warehouse each week. She thinks that the demand for inventory has been generally steady with some slight week-to-week random fluctuations. An analyst from company headquarters suggested that she use a 3-, 5-, or 7-week moving average. Before selecting one of these, Shirley decides to compare the accuracy of each for the most recent 10-week period.

Solution

1. Compute the 3-, 5-, and 7-week moving average forecasts:

Week	Actual Inventory Demand (thousands of dollars)	Forecasts		
		AP = 3 Weeks	AP = 5 Weeks	AP = 7 Weeks
1	100			
2	125			
3	90			
4	110			
5	105			
6	130			
7	85			
8	102	106.7	104.0	106.4
9	110	105.7	106.4	106.7
10	90	99.0	106.4	104.6
11	105	100.7	103.4	104.6
12	95	101.7	98.4	103.9
13	115	96.7	100.4	102.4
14	120	105.0	103.0	100.3
15	80	110.0	105.0	105.3
16	95	105.0	103.0	102.1
17	100	98.3	101.0	100.0

Notice that the forecasts are rounded to one significant digit more than the original data. Sample computations—forecasts for the 10th week:

$$F_3 = \frac{85 + 1032 + 110}{3} = 99.0$$

$$F_5 = \frac{105 + 130 + 85 + 102 + 110}{5} = 106.4$$

$$F_7 = \frac{90 + 110 + 105 + 130 + 85 + 102 + 110}{7} = 104.6$$

Note: To forecast for the 10th week, remember that the only historical weekly actual inventory demand data you have to work with is Weeks 1–9. Therefore you cannot include the actual data for the 10th week in computing the 10th-week forecasts.

2. Next, compute the mean absolute deviation (MAD) for the three forecasts:

Week	Actual Inventory Demand (thousands of dollars)	AP = 3 Weeks Forecasts	AP = 3 Weeks Absolute Deviation	AP = 5 Weeks Forecasts	AP = 5 Weeks Absolute Deviation	AP = 7 Weeks Forecasts	AP = 7 Weeks Absolute Deviation
8	102	106.7	4.7	104.0	2.0	106.4	4.4
9	110	105.7	4.3	106.4	3.6	106.7	3.3
10	90	99.0	9.0	106.4	16.4	104.6	14.6
11	105	100.7	4.3	103.4	1.6	104.6	0.4
12	95	101.7	6.7	98.4	3.4	103.9	8.9
13	115	96.7	18.3	100.4	14.6	102.4	12.6
14	120	105.0	15.0	103.0	17.0	100.3	19.7
15	80	110.0	30.0	105.0	25.0	105.3	25.3
16	95	105.0	10.0	103.0	8.0	102.1	7.1
17	100	98.3	1.7	101.0	1.0	100.0	0.0
Total absolute deviation			104.0		92.6		96.3
Mean absolute deviation (MAD)			10.40		9.26		9.63

3. The accuracy of the AP = 5 forecast is the best because its MAD tends to be less than with 3 or 7 weeks. The accuracy of the 7-week average period forecast is very close to the 5-week one; therefore future checking is recommended.

4. She now uses an AP of 5 weeks to forecast the cash demand for the next week, the 18th:

$$\text{Forecast} = \frac{115 + 120 + 80 + 95 + 100}{5} = 102, \text{ or } \$102,000$$

Figure 3.5 plots the three moving average forecasts against the actual data in Example 3.5. Notice that *the larger the AP is, the greater is the noise-dampening ability and the lower impulse response of the forecast and vice versa:* The AP = 7 forecast has a slightly higher noise-dampening ability and a slightly lower impulse response than the other two forecasts because its curve exhibits less period-to-period variation. The AP that is the most accurate tends to vary with the unique characteristics of each data set. The AP must therefore be determined by experimentation, as in Example 3.5.

The selection of an AP will depend on the criteria of accuracy, impulse response, and noise-dampening ability. Which is more desirable, high impulse response or high noise-dampening ability, and how much accuracy can be given up to achieve either of these two characteristics? In the final analysis, the AP selected will depend on a complete knowledge of the intended use of the forecasts and on the nature of the forecasting situation.

Weighted Moving Average Method

The moving average method discussed earlier weights the historical data equally in developing a forecast. In some situations, it may be desirable to apply unequal weights to the historical data. For example, if more recent data are believed to be more relevant to a forecast, larger weights could be applied to these data as below:

Week	Actual Data	Weight
7	85	.20
8	102	.30
9	110	.50

$$\text{Forecast}_{10} = 0.2(85) + 0.3(102) + 0.5(110) = 102.6, \text{ or } \$102,600$$

This simple modification to the moving average method allows forecasters to specify the relative importance of each past period of data.

| **Figure 3.5** | Moving Average Forecasts versus Actual Cash Demand in Example 3.5 |

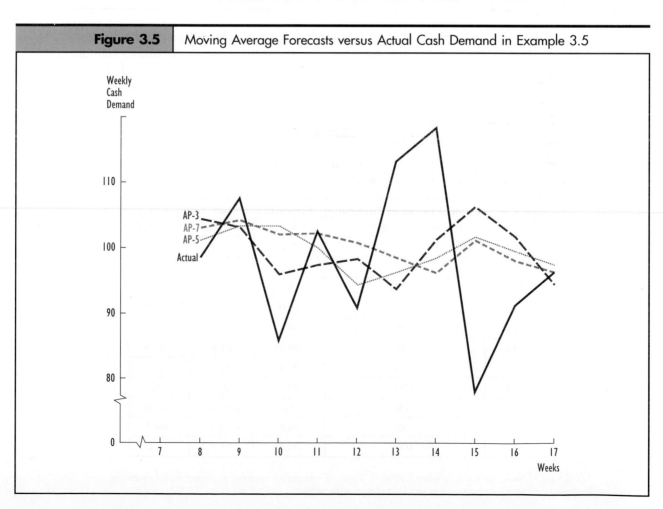

Table 3.6	Formulas and Variable Definitions for Exponential Smoothing Forecasts

F_t = forecast for period t, the next period
F_{t-1} = forecast for period t − 1, the prior period
A_{t-1} = actual data for period t − 1, the prior period
α = smoothing constant, from 0 to 1

$F_t = F_{t-1} + \alpha(A_{t-1} - F_{t-1})$, which can also be expressed as:
$F_t = \alpha A_{t-1} + (1 - \alpha)F_{t-1}$

Exponential Smoothing Method

The variables, the variable definitions, and the formulas for exponential smoothing forecasts are found in Table 3.6. **Exponential smoothing** takes the forecast for the prior period and adds an adjustment to obtain the forecast for the next period. This adjustment is a proportion of the forecast error in the prior period and is computed by multiplying the forecast error in the prior period by a constant that is between zero and one. This constant alpha (α) is called the **smoothing constant.** Example 3.6 demonstrates how to use exponential smoothing to develop forecasts.

Example 3.6	Exponential Smoothing Short-Range Forecast

Shirley Johnson, from Example 3.5, talks to an analyst at company headquarters about forecasting weekly demand for inventory from her warehouse. The analyst suggests that Shirley consider using exponential smoothing with smoothing constants of 0.1, 0.2, and 0.3. Shirley decides to compare the accuracy of the smoothing constants for the most recent 10-week period.

Solution

1. First, we study the formulas and variable definitions in Table 3.6. We compute the weekly forecasts for the 8th through the 17th weeks:

Week	Actual Inventory Demand (thousands of dollars)	Forecasts $\alpha = 0.1$	$\alpha = 0.2$	$\alpha = 0.3$
7	85	85.0*	85.0	85.0
8	102	85.0	85.0	85.0
9	110	86.7	88.4	90.1
10	90	89.0	92.7	96.1
11	105	89.1	92.2	94.3
12	95	90.7	94.8	97.5
13	115	91.1	94.8	96.8
14	120	93.5	98.8	102.3
15	80	96.2	103.0	107.6
16	95	94.6	98.4	99.3
17	100	94.6	97.7	98.0

*All of these 7th-week forecasts were selected arbitrarily. Beginning forecasts are necessary to use exponential smoothing. Traditionally, we set these forecasts equal to the actual data of the period.

Notice that the forecasts are rounded to one significant digit more than the original data. Here are sample calculations for the 10th-week forecasts:

$$F_{10} = F_9 + \alpha(A_9 - F_9)$$
$$\alpha = 0.1: F_{10} = 86.7 + 0.1(110 - 86.7) = 89.0$$
$$\alpha = 0.2: F_{10} = 88.4 + 0.2(110 - 88.4) = 92.7$$
$$\alpha = 0.3: F_{10} = 90.1 + 0.3(110 - 90.1) = 96.1$$

Note: When the 10th-week forecasts are made, the only historical data available are through the 9th week. Only the 9th-week actual data and the 9th-week forecasts are used to compute the 10th-week forecasts.

2. Next, we compute the mean absolute deviation (MAD) for the three forecasts:

Week	Actual Inventory Demand (thousands of dollars)	Forecast					
		$\alpha = 0.1$		$\alpha = 0.2$		$\alpha = 0.3$	
		Forecasts	Absolute Deviation	Forecasts	Absolute Deviation	Forecasts	Absolute Deviation
8	102	85.0	17.0	85.0	17.0	85.0	17.0
9	110	86.7	23.3	88.4	21.6	90.1	19.9
10	90	89.0	1.0	92.7	2.7	96.1	6.1
11	105	89.1	15.9	92.2	12.8	94.3	10.7
12	95	90.7	4.3	94.8	0.2	97.5	2.5
13	115	91.1	23.9	94.8	20.2	96.8	18.2
14	120	93.5	26.5	98.8	21.2	102.3	17.7
15	80	96.2	16.2	103.0	23.0	107.6	27.6
16	95	94.6	0.4	98.4	3.4	99.3	4.3
17	100	94.6	5.4	97.7	2.3	98.0	2.0
Total absolute deviation			133.9		124.4		126.0
Mean absolute deviation (MAD)			13.39		12.44		12.60

3. The smoothing constant $\alpha = 0.2$ gives slightly better accuracy when compared with $\alpha = 0.1$ and $\alpha = 0.3$.

4. Next, using $\alpha = 0.2$, compute the forecast (in thousands of dollars) for the 18th week:

$$F_{18} = F_{17} + 0.2(A_{17} - F_{17})$$
$$= 97.7 + 0.2(100 - 97.7) = 97.7 + 0.2(2.3) = 97.7 + 0.46 = 98.2, \text{ or } \$98,200$$

Forecasters select values for α based on the criteria of accuracy, impulse response, and noise-dampening ability. As can be seen from Example 3.6, higher levels of α do not always result in more accurate forecasts. Each data set tends to have unique qualities so that experimentation with different α levels is advised in order to obtain forecast accuracy. Figure 3.6 plots the exponential smoothing forecasts ($\alpha = 0.1$, 0.2, and 0.3) against the actual weekly demand for inventory from Example 3.6. Notice that *the higher α is, the higher its impulse response and the lower its noise-dampening ability and vice versa:* When $\alpha = 0.3$, the forecast exhibits slightly higher impulse response and slightly lower noise-dampening ability because its curve exhibits greater period-to-period variation.

An earlier term for exponential smoothing was **exponentially weighted moving average.** This term reminds us that *exponential smoothing, like the moving average*

Figure 3.6	Exponential Smoothing Forecasts versus Actual Cash Demand in Example 3.6

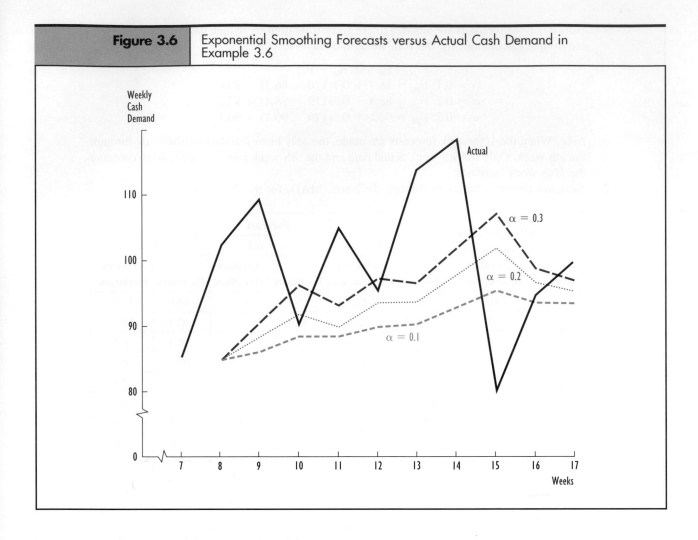

and the weighted moving average models, develops forecasts that effectively are averages. *Exponential smoothing weights data from recent periods heavier than data from more distant periods.* Figure 3.7 illustrates the weights for some smoothing constants.

Exponential Smoothing with Trend

We ordinarily consider short-range planning to cover such short spans of time that seasonality and trend are not important factors in short-range forecasting. As we move from short-range forecasts toward medium-range forecasts, however, seasonality and trend become more important. Incorporating a trend component into exponentially smoothed forecasts is called **double exponential smoothing,** because the estimate for the average and the estimate for the trend are both smoothed. Both α, the smoothing constant for the average, and β, the smoothing constant for the trend, are used in this model. Table 3.7 (on page 90) exhibits formulas for incorporating a trend component into exponential smoothing forecasts, and Example 3.7 illustrates the use of the formulas.

The forecast with trend in Month 7 is computed this way:

$$FT_t = S_{t-1} \qquad\quad + T_{t-1}$$
$$FT_7 = S_6 \qquad\qquad + T_6$$
$$= 149.28 + 3.81 = 153.09, \text{ or } \$153.1 \text{ thousand}$$

| Figure 3.7 | Weighting of Past Data in Exponential Smoothing |

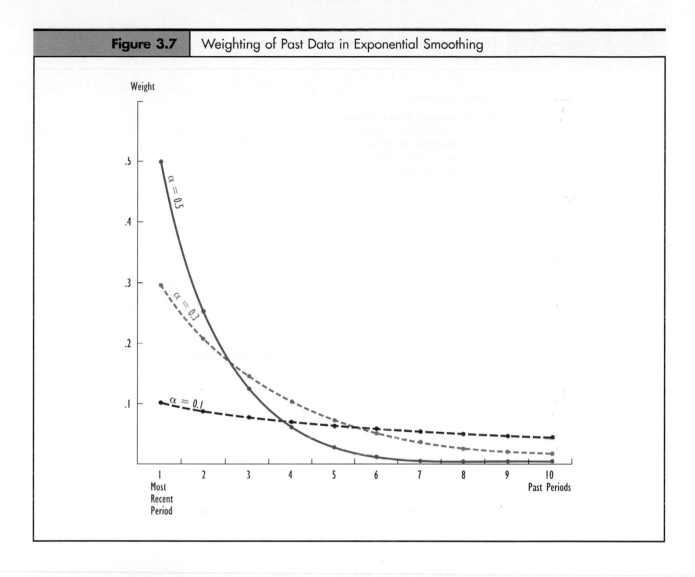

Weight

α = 0.5
α = 0.3
α = 0.1

| Example 3.7 | Exponential Smoothing with Trend Forecasts |

Ann Hickman must forecast the sales of her expanding trucking firm so that she can plan cash, personnel, and fuel needs in the future. She believes that the sales during the past six-month period should be representative of future sales. Develop an exponential smoothing forecast with trend for sales in Month 7 if $\alpha = 0.2$, $\beta = 0.3$, and past sales, in thousands of dollars, were:

Month (t)	Sales (thousands of dollars) (A_t)
1	130
2	136
3	134
4	140
5	146
6	150

Table 3.7	Formulas, Variable Definitions, and Procedure for Exponential Smoothing Forecasts with Trend

Variable Definitions

S_t = smoothed forecast in period t
T_t = trend estimate in period t
A_t = actual data in period t
t   = the next time period
t − 1 = the prior time period
FT_t = forecast with trend in period t
α = smoothing constant for the average, from 0 to 1
β = smoothing constant for the trend, from 0 to 1

Formulas
$FT_t = S_{t-1} + T_{t-1}$
$S_t = FT_t + \alpha(A_t - FT_t)$
$T_t = T_{t-1} + \beta(FT_t - FT_{t-1} - T_{t-1})$

Procedure
If we want to complete the exponential smoothing forecast with trend for Week 7, we would follow this procedure:

1. To begin, we need to know values of α and β. The values of the smoothing constants α and β are between 0 and 1 and must be estimated or experimentally derived.
2. S_6 and T_6 would have been computed earlier.
3. Compute: $FT_7 = S_6 + T_6$. This is the exponential smoothing forecast with trend for Week 7.
4. In preparation for computing the forecast for the next week, we compute S_7 and T_7. Knowing the values of FT_7, FT_6, α, β, and T_6, and after the value of A_7 is known, compute:
   $S_7 = FT_7 + \alpha(A_7 - FT_7)$
   $T_7 = T_6 + \beta(FT_7 - FT_6 - T_6)$

Solution

1. We estimate a starting forecast for Month 1: A naive forecast for Month 1 would be the actual sales in Month 1, or 130.

$$FT_1 = A_1 = 130$$

2. We estimate a starting trend component. One way to estimate the trend component is to subtract the actual sales in Month 1 from the actual sales in Month 6 and then divide by 5 the number of periods between 1 and 6:

$$T_1 = \frac{A_6 - A_1}{5} = \frac{150 - 130}{5} = 4$$

3. Next, using the starting forecast and starting trend component from Steps 1 and 2, above, we compute a forecast for sales in each of the months leading to the forecast for Month 7:

Month (t)	Sales (thousands of dollars) (A_t)	FT_t	+	$\alpha(A_t$	$-$	$FT_t)$	$-$	S_t
1	130	130	+	0.2 (130	−	130)	=	130.00
2	136	134	+	0.2 (136	−	134)	=	134.40
3	134	138.40	+	0.2 (134	−	138.40)	=	137.52
4	140	141.64	+	0.2 (140	−	141.64)	=	141.31
5	146	145.17	+	0.2 (146	−	145.17)	=	145.34
6	150	149.10	+	0.2 (150	−	149.10)	=	149.28

Month (t)	Sales (thousands of dollars) (A_t)	T_{t-1}	+	$\beta(FT_t$	$-$	FT_{t-1}	$-$	$T_{t-1})$	=	T_t
1	130							given	=	4.00
2	136	4.00	+	0.3 (134	−	130	−	4.00)	=	4.00
3	134	4.00	+	0.3 (138.40	−	134	−	4.00)	=	4.12
4	140	4.12	+	0.3 (141.64	−	138.40	−	4.12)	=	3.86
5	146	3.86	+	0.3 (145.17	−	141.64	−	3.86)	=	3.76
6	150	3.76	+	0.3 (149.10	−	145.17	−	3.76)	=	3.81

Month (t)	Sales (thousands of dollars) (A_t)	S_{t-1}	+	T_{t-1}	=	FT_t
1	130			given	=	130.00
2	136	130	+	4.00	=	134.00
3	134	134.40	+	4.00	=	138.40
4	140	137.52	+	4.12	=	141.64
5	146	141.31	+	3.86	=	145.17
6	150	145.34	+	3.76	=	149.10
7	—	149.28	+	3.81	=	153.09

Example 3.7 could have incorporated a seasonality component into the forecasts, just as was done in Example 3.4. Seasonal indexes would have been developed for each season, the indexes would have been used to deseasonalize the data, the formulas in Table 3.7 would have been used to develop deseasonalized forecasts, and then the indexes would have been used to put the seasonal patterns on the forecasts. As an alternative for dealing with seasonality and trend, a modification of exponential smoothing is available in many software packages. Often called *Winters exponential smoothing*, three smoothing constants are required: one for smoothing the average, one for smoothing the trend, and one for smoothing the seasonality.

Exponential smoothing is a special case of the *Box–Jenkins model*, the autocorrelation methods of which examine the actual historical data points and fit a mathematical function to these data. The mathematical function then becomes the forecasting model for future estimates. Available in many standard computer forecasting packages, this method is reported to be the most accurate of all the short-range forecasting methods. However, about 60 data points are required, some time is required to get forecast results, and the model is moderately expensive to use. These and other developments in exponential smoothing forecasting make it a powerful force in short-range forecasting.

Now that we have examined some forecasting methods and issues, we conclude the chapter by considering how to have a successful forecasting system and by discussing the types of computer software available for forecasting.

HOW TO HAVE A SUCCESSFUL FORECASTING SYSTEM

Figure 3.1 illustrated the role of forecasting in business planning. Some of the reasons for ineffective forecasting are found in Table 3.8. Of particular importance is to consider how to select the forecasting method and how to control the forecasting model.

How to Select a Forecasting Method

Several factors should be considered in the selection of a forecasting method: (1) cost, (2) accuracy, (3) data available, (4) time span, (5) nature of products and services, and (6) impulse response and noise dampening.

Cost and Accuracy

In choosing a forecasting method, a trade-off may result between cost and accuracy; in other words, more forecast accuracy can be obtained at a cost. High-accuracy approaches use more data, the data are ordinarily more difficult to obtain, and the models are more costly to design, implement, and operate. Such methods as statistical models, historical analogies, and executive committee consensus tend to be of low or moderate cost, whereas complex econometric models, Delphi, and market research tend to be high cost and take longer to use. Each organization must make the cost and accuracy trade-off that is appropriate to its own situation.

Business Snapshots 3.2, 3.3, and 3.4 contrast three different approaches to forecasting. The first describes an expensive and complex forecasting system, the second describes an inexpensive and simple forecasting system, and the third describes a dynamic system for selecting forecasting models. That all three organizations appear to

Table 3.8	Some Reasons for Ineffective Forecasting

1. Failure of the organization to involve a broad cross section of people in forecasting. Individual effort is important, but the need to involve everyone who has pertinent information and who will need to implement the forecast is also important.

2. Failure to recognize that forecasting is integral to business planning (see Figure 3.1).

3. Failure to recognize that forecasts will always be wrong. Estimates of future demand are bound to be subject to error, and the magnitude of error tends to be greater for forecasts that cover very long spans of time. When operations managers have unrealistic expectations of forecasts, the fact that the forecasts were not on the nose is often used as an excuse for poor performance in operations.

4. Failure to forecast the right things. Organizations may forecast the demand for raw materials that go into finished products. The demand for raw materials need not be forecast because these demands can be computed from the forecasts for the finished products. Forecasting too many things can overload the forecasting system and cause it to be too expensive and time consuming.

5. Failure to select an appropriate forecasting method.

6. Failure to track the performance of the forecasting models so that the forecast accuracy can be improved. The forecasting models can be modified as needed to control the performance of the forecasts.

BUSINESS SNAPSHOT 3.2

Using a Forecasting Expert System at Xerox

They've changed the way they do forecasting at the Xerox Corporation. In the old way of developing sales forecasts, seven analysts used a patchwork of forecasting models and methods. At one extreme, they graphed historical data and extrapolated it forward into the future for the many types of copying machines in their product line. These graphs were then passed around to all interested and contributing parties within the corporation. At the other extreme, some analysts used computer spreadsheets. This array of methods and laborious approach to developing forecasts took so long that the forecasting team would start to work on next year's forecast in the middle of the current year, and they only had enough time to develop forecasts for 12 months into the future. This approach was so laborious and the forecasts were so inaccurate that Xerox organized an effort to develop an expert system to do much of the forecasting.

It took two years to develop the expert system, but now analysts can wait until October to start developing the sales forecasts for the next year. The new system now develops forecasts three years out, which gives the company a longer-range view of the future for business planning. And this is not all; the system continuously monitors its own performance and updates its parameters so that forecast accuracy is constantly being refined. The time saved by using the expert system allows the forecasting team to consider the impacts of such things as inflation and competitor activity on Xerox's future sales.

Source: "Software Even a CFO Could Love." *Business Week,* November 2, 1992, 132–135.

be pleased with the accuracy and cost of their forecasting system demonstrates that no single forecasting approach is appropriate for all situations. In many situations, simple and low-cost forecasting methods tend to provide forecasts that are as accurate as more complex and high-cost forecasting methods.

Data Available

The data that are available and relevant for forecasts is an important factor in choosing a forecasting method. For example, if the attitudes and intentions of customers are a relevant factor in forecasts and if the data can be economically obtained from customers about their attitudes and intentions, then a survey of customers may be an appropriate method for developing demand estimates. On the other hand, if the requirement is to forecast sales of a new product, then a survey of customers may not be a practical way to develop a forecast; historical analogy, market research, executive committee consensus, or some other method may have to be used.

Time Span

The choice of an appropriate forecasting method is affected by the nature of the production resource that is to be forecasted. Workers, cash, inventories, and machine schedules are short range in nature and can be forecasted with moving average or exponential smoothing models. Long-range production resource needs such as factory capacities and capital funds can be estimated by regression, executive committee consensus, market research, or other methods that are appropriate for long-range forecasts.

Nature of Products and Services

Managers are advised to use different forecasting methods for different products. Such factors as whether a product is high volume and high cost, whether the product is a manufactured good or a service, whether product demand demonstrates seasonal fluctuations or growth or decline, and where the product is in its life cycle all affect the choice of a forecasting method.

BUSINESS SNAPSHOT 3.3

Forecasting Flare Sales at Olin Corporation

At the Morgan Hill Works of the Olin Corporation, located in Morgan Hill, California, plant manager Perry Spangler is planning the schedule for the production of railroad flares in the first quarter of next year. These products are sold to every major railroad in the United States and are used for signaling purposes. Mr. Spangler knows that sales forecasts need to be close to actual sales, but because the railroad flare is a produce-to-stock item, ample inventory is ordinarily on hand to ship to customers in case of minor inaccuracies in the forecasts.

For several quarters now, Mr. Spangler has been forecasting

railroad flare sales using a simple graphing technique (Figure 3.8). On one side of the graph he plots the millions of national freight car loadings in each quarter, which is information that he finds in a U.S. Department of Commerce publication at his local library. On the other side of the graph he plots Olin's railroad flare sales in thousands of gross (a gross equals 144 flares). He has noticed a very close relationship between the previous quarter's national freight car loadings and the current quarter's sales of railroad flares: The national freight car loadings in millions in the previous quarter times 0.3 approxi-

mately equal the railroad flare sales in thousands of gross in the current quarter.

Accordingly, Mr. Spangler estimates the sales of railroad flares in the first quarter of next year will be:

Sales = 0.3 × 55 million fourth-quarter loadings
      = 16.5, or 16,500 gross

He believes that this relationship is logical because railroad flare sales should be directly related to the number of railroad cars placed in service. He is pleased with the accuracy of the forecasts and the ease of preparing them.

Figure 3.8 | Olin Corporation's Railroad Flare Sales

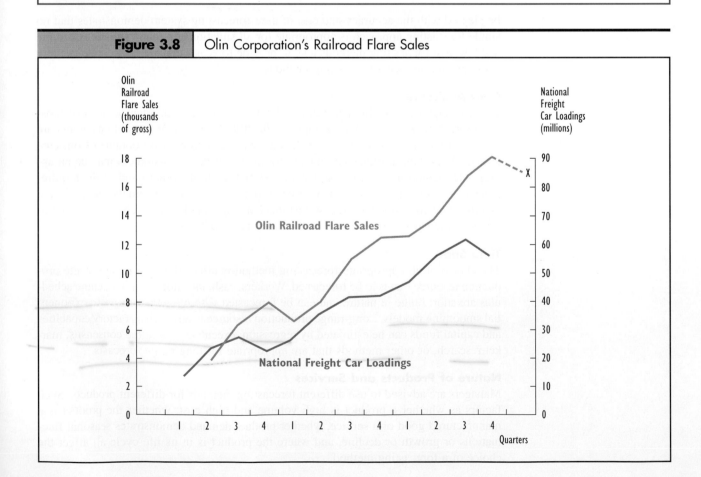

BUSINESS SNAPSHOT 3.4

Focus Forecasting at American Hardware Supply

Bernard Smith at American Hardware Supply developed a system for selecting forecasting methods. He called his approach *focus forecasting,* and it was based on two principles: (1) More sophisticated and expensive forecasting methods do not always provide better forecasts, and (2) there is no single forecasting technique that should be used for all products and services.

The forecasting system at American Hardware Supply had to forecast purchase quantities for about 100,000 items purchased by the company's buyers. The buyers tended not to use the old exponential smoothing forecasting model to predict the purchase quantities because they did not understand or trust the model. Instead, they used very simple forecasting approaches, such as using an item's demand figure from the prior period for the next period. Mr. Smith selected seven forecasting methods, including the simple ones that

were used by the buyers, the old exponential smoothing model, and some new statistical forecasting methods. Each month every model was used to forecast the demand for each item. The model that provided the best forecast for an item was used to forecast the demand for that item for the next month.

Although buyers could override the forecasts from focus forecasting, the approach is said to be providing excellent forecasts for American Hardware Supply.

Source: Bernard Smith. *Focus Forecasting: Computer Techniques for Inventory Control.* Essex Junction, VT: O. Wight Limited Publications, 1984.

Impulse Response and Noise Dampening

As pointed out earlier in our discussion of short-range forecasting, how responsive we want the forecasting model to be to changes in the actual demand data must be balanced against our desire to suppress undesirable chance variation or noise in the data. Each forecasting model differs in its impulse response and noise-dampening abilities, and the model selected must fit the forecasting situation.

Once managers have selected the forecasting model to use, the performance of the model must be tracked.

How to Monitor and Control a Forecasting Model

Forecasts can be monitored and controlled by setting upper and lower limits on how much the performance characteristics of a model can deteriorate before we change the parameters of the model. One common way that we can track the performance of forecasting models is to use what is called a **tracking signal**:

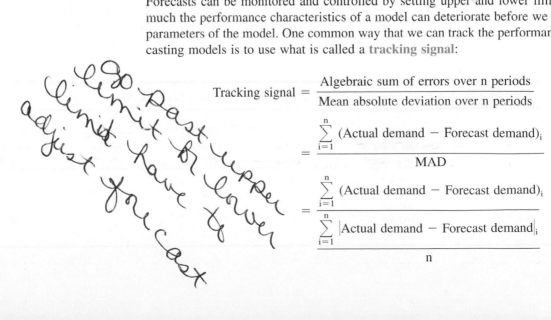

$$\text{Tracking signal} = \frac{\text{Algebraic sum of errors over n periods}}{\text{Mean absolute deviation over n periods}}$$

$$= \frac{\sum_{i=1}^{n} (\text{Actual demand} - \text{Forecast demand})_i}{\text{MAD}}$$

$$= \frac{\sum_{i=1}^{n} (\text{Actual demand} - \text{Forecast demand})_i}{\dfrac{\sum_{i=1}^{n} |\text{Actual demand} - \text{Forecast demand}|_i}{n}}$$

Using accurate forecasting methods can help to maintain an appropriate inventory of merchandise on hand, as in this hardware store.

© SUSAN VAN ETTEN

The tracking signal measures the cumulative forecast error over n periods in terms of MAD. For example, if the algebraic sum of errors for 12 periods has been a positive 1,000 units and the MAD in these same 12 periods is 250 units, then the tracking signal is +4, which is very high. This indicates that actual data have been greater than the forecasts a total of +4 MADs over the 12 periods, which is about $5s_{yx}$ because of the relationship $S_{yx} = 1.25$ MAD. If the algebraic sum of errors for 12 periods has been a minus 1,250 units and the MAD in these same 12 periods is 250 units, then the tracking signal is −5, which is very low. This indicates that the actual data have been less than the forecasts a total of −5 MADs over the 12 periods. If the forecasting model is performing well, the tracking signal should be around zero, which would indicate that there have been about as many actual data points above the forecasts as below. The ability of the tracking signal to indicate the direction of the forecasting error is very helpful because whether forecasts should be reduced or increased is indicated: If the tracking signal is positive, increase the forecasts; if it is negative, reduce the forecasts.

The value of the tracking signal can be used to automatically trigger new parameter values of models, thereby correcting model performance. For instance, rules like

Table 3.9	One Company's Rules for Changing the Smoothing Constant (α)			
Limits for Absolute Value of Tracking Signal	Do Not Change	Slight: Increase α by 0.1	Moderate: Increase α by 0.3	Panic: Increase α by 0.5
0–2.4	✓			
2.5–2.9		✓		
3.0–3.9			✓	
Over 4.0				✓

those found in Table 3.9 could be used to change the parameters of the forecasting model. But we must not assume that α is always increased to reduce error, because this depends on the data. There are no universal rules; rather, the rules must be custom designed by each firm to fit its data through experimentation. If the limits for the tracking signal are set too low, then a forecasting model's parameters will need to be revised too often. But if the limits for the tracking signal are set too high, then a forecasting model's parameters will not be changed often enough and the accuracy of the forecasts will suffer.

COMPUTER SOFTWARE FOR FORECASTING

Forecasters in the real world of government and industry use computers to do most of their calculations. Numerous standard computer programs based on the forecasting models presented in this chapter are readily available to do these calculations.

The computer software packages in the following list are examples of software that provides forecasting capabilities. The first three are primarily for forecasting, and the last four have forecasting modules included.

- *Forecast Pro*
- *Autobox*
- *SmartForecasts for Windows*
- *SAS*
- *SPSS*
- *SAP*
- *POM Software Library* (accompanies this text); includes moving average, weighted moving average, exponential smoothing, exponential smoothing with trend, time series regression with ranging, seasonalized time series regression with ranging, simple linear regression with ranging, and multiple linear regression

FORECASTING IN SMALL BUSINESSES AND START-UP VENTURES

One characteristic of small businesses and start-up businesses is that they are typically short on everything from capital to floor space to specialty skills. This is particularly true of forecasting capability. This is not to say that such businesses do not do forecasting, because they must. But they may not have the critical mass of people to participate in forecasting, enough personnel with the time to do forecasting studies, or in some cases the necessary skills to develop good forecasts.

Most of the forecasting methods in this chapter probably would be within their capability. Almost certainly, they could use some of these methods—executive committee consensus, survey of sales force, survey of customers, simple time series regression, and moving average methods. But forecasting in these businesses is difficult for these reasons:

1. Such businesses are not data-rich environments.
2. There may not be a long history of data.
3. Forecasting for new products is always difficult, and these companies may not have much experience with new products or forecasting successes and failures.

But all is not lost—help is available to these and other companies with particular forecasting needs. Much information and data are available from sources outside of the companies. Government agencies at the local, regional, state, and federal levels can be a source of forecasting data. From the U.S. Department of Commerce, the U.S. Department of Labor, and the Office of the President, much information is available concerning historical and expected future industry and regional economic activity. Table 3.10 lists some sources of data available. At the local level, many chambers of commerce have developed a great deal of data regarding economic activity in their areas. Such information and data can provide small and start-up companies with industry and regional economic data that can be combined with their own data as the bases for forecasts.

An enormous amount of information and data about economic activity is also available from industry associations. The National Home Builders Association, the American Manufacturers Association, the American Bar Association, the Conference Board, and other nonprofit associations provide a rich information and data resource for their membership. These associations provide a good place for small and start-up businesses to begin developing information and data for forecasting.

Another source of forecasting help is private consulting companies. Management consultants like Booz, Allen & Hamilton and Andersen Consulting can do in-depth cross-sectional studies of new products and estimate their sales potential. Such services are used by small businesses, start-up businesses, and large corporations alike. This is particularly true for new products for which companies have little or no experience. Consultants from large national consulting firms can obtain data from sources not available to the client. For example, because of their network of clients, these consultants have entree to many firms with competing or similar products. Although expensive for small and start-up businesses, management consultants provide one source of sales-forecasting services.

Table 3.10	Sources of Forecasting Data

- **Auto Sales:** Every 10 days by major automakers.
- **Consumer Confidence Index:** Monthly by the Conference Board.
- **Consumer Price Index:** Monthly by the Labor Department, retail inflation.
- **Durable Goods:** Monthly by the Commerce Department, new orders for long-lasting manufactured goods.
- **Employment:** Monthly by the Labor Department, jobless rate and number of jobs available.
- **Factory Orders:** Monthly by the Commerce Department, orders for durable and nondurable goods.
- **Gross Domestic Product:** Quarterly by the Commerce Department, goods and services in the U.S.
- **Housing Starts:** Monthly by the Commerce Department.
- **Index of Leading Economic Indicators:** Monthly by the Commerce Department, a basket of forward-looking indicators designed to predict the economy's strength 6 to 9 months in advance.
- **Industrial Production:** Monthly by the Federal Reserve, output of U.S. factories, mines, and utilities.
- **Merchandise Trade:** Monthly by the Commerce Department, output of goods the U.S. sells or buys overseas.
- **Personal Income and Consumption:** Monthly by the Commerce Department, growth in personal income and consumption.
- **Producer Price Index:** Monthly by the Labor Department, inflation at the wholesale level.
- **Purchasing Manager's Index:** Monthly by the National Association of Purchasing Management, strength of U.S. manufacturing economy.
- **Retail Sales:** Monthly by the Commerce Department, consumer spending.

Source: "Which Indicators Are Truly Indicative of Economy's Health?" Houston Chronicle, August 8, 1993, 10E.

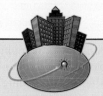

Wrap Up

WHAT WORLD-CLASS COMPANIES DO

Forecasting in POM is estimating the future demand for products and services and the resources necessary to produce them. Forecasting is integral to business planning. Long-range survival, growth, and profitability as well as short-range efficiency and effectiveness depend on accurate forecasts.

Long-range forecasts usually span one year or longer, medium-range forecasts several months, and short-range forecasts only a few weeks. Educated guess, executive committee consensus, Delphi, survey of sales force, survey of customers, historical analogy, and market research are examples of qualitative forecasting methods. Quantitative forecasting models of linear regression and correlation analysis, seasonalized linear regression, moving averages, weighted moving averages, exponential smoothing, and exponential smoothing with trend are demonstrated in the chapter.

World class companies, large or small, are predisposed to have effective methods of forecasting because they have exceptional long-range business planning systems in place, and forecasting is integral to these plans. Long-range business plans permeate the entire organization and affect all facets of the business. These plans are updated often because the firms have a built-in, forward-looking, long-range perspective that continuously generates business opportunities and needed actions. These plans are developed by involving a broad cross section of personnel from many organization functions. It is literally everyone's job to do long-range business planning, and everyone is affected by long-range forecasts.

Because forecasting is integral to long-range business planning, world-class companies have a formal forecasting effort. Staff specialists maintain sophisticated computer software capable of incorporating great quantities of data. These specialists also subscribe to forecasting and data sources outside their firms from many locations throughout the world. Banking system research groups, industry trade association research centers, university research, government agency publications, and other sources are used. This effort is aimed at providing the best long-range estimates of sales of new and existing products and services in global markets, thus allowing the firms' business plans to include actions for capturing market share.

World-class companies develop methods to monitor the performance of their forecasting models. Because business plans are updated often, it is crucial that they reflect any significant departures of actual data from forecasts. This effort not only results in business plans that reflect the latest thinking and information, but the forecasting models evolve to be the most accurate ones available for their type of applications.

While world-class companies may have a long-range bias, this does not mean that they overlook the short run. What they really have is a planning and control bias, and this leads them to develop excellent short-range forecasts as well. This is particularly true in production. The effective forecasting of production capacity, size of workforce, quantity of purchased materials, inventory levels, and cash drives a closely managed production planning system. This system ensures the timely production of products and services of the highest quality, at the least cost, with little inventory while remaining responsive to customers' needs.

REVIEW AND DISCUSSION QUESTIONS

1. What is forecasting?
2. Name three underlying reasons why operations managers must forecast.
3. Name and describe three qualitative forecasting methods used in business today. Which qualitative forecasting methods would be appropriate for new products?
4. Describe how forecasting is integral to business planning.
5. Describe briefly the steps in linear regression analysis.
6. Linear regression analysis is based on identifying independent variables and gathering historical data for these variables. Name some independent variables to forecast these dependent variables: (a) demand for hospital services, (b) students entering colleges of business, (c) local hamburger-stand sales, (d) county sheriff's department services.
7. Name the four components or data patterns of long-range demand in forecasting.
8. Explain what is meant by *ranging a forecast*.
9. Define and describe the *coefficient of correlation* and the *coefficient of determination*.
10. What are the three types of variation of the dependent variable y in linear regression analysis? How are the three types of variation related? How are they calculated?
11. What is multiple regression analysis? How is multiple regression different from simple linear regression?
12. What are impulse response and noise dampening? How are they related?
13. What inputs are required in linear regression analysis? What are the outputs from this analysis?
14. What are the key advantages of moving averages and exponential smoothing? What are the disadvantages?
15. Explain how the moving averages method is different from the weighted moving averages method. Does AP = 3 or AP = 5 have the higher impulse response? Explain.
16. Are exponential smoothing forecasts weighted averages? Explain.
17. How is exponential smoothing different from exponential smoothing with trend? Why is exponential smoothing with trend called *double exponential smoothing?*
18. What is s_{yx}? How is it calculated? What are its uses? What is MSE? How is it calculated?
19. What is mean absolute deviation (MAD)? How is it calculated? What are its uses?
20. Name three common reasons why forecasting systems fail.
21. What is the tracking signal? How is it calculated? How is it used?

INTERNET ASSIGNMENTS

1. Search the Internet for a consulting company that offers assistance with business forecasting. What services does it offer?
2. Go to the web site for *Forecast Pro* software (**http://www.forecastpro.com**). Describe some of the features of this software.
3. Visit the web site for the *Institute of Business Forecasting* (**http://www.ibf.org**) and locate the web page for "Jobs in Forecasting." Make a brief list of companies and job position titles. Which job would you be most interested in, and why?

PROBLEMS

Simple Regression

1. RCB manufacturers black-and-white television sets for overseas markets. Annual exports in thousands of units are shown below for the past six years. Given this long-term decline in exports, forecast the expected number of units to be exported next year.

Year	Exports	Year	Exports
1	33	4	26
2	32	5	27
3	29	6	24

2. A small hospital is planning for future needs in its maternity wing. The data below show the number of births in each of the past eight years.

Year	Births	Year	Births
1	565	5	615
2	590	6	611
3	583	7	610
4	597	8	623

   a. Use simple linear regression to forecast the annual number of births for each of the next three years.

   b. Determine the correlation coefficient for the data and interpret its meaning.

   c. Find the coefficient of determination for the data and interpret its meaning.

3. Suregrip Calculator Company (SCC) needs to estimate its sales for next year. The most recent six years of revenue data for the company's popular line of calculators are given below:

Year	Sales Revenues (millions of dollars)	Year	Sales Revenues (millions of dollars)
1	46.7	4	77.9
2	59.3	5	85.1
3	74.2	6	98.0

   a. Assuming that the sales data above are representative of sales expected next year, use time series regression analysis to forecast next year's (Year 7's) sales revenues.

   b. Determine the correlation coefficient for the data and interpret its meaning.

   c. Find the coefficient of determination for the data and interpret its meaning.

4. A firm needs to develop a sales forecast for next year for its RV sales. It believes that its annual sales are related to the sales of its industry. It has prepared these historical data:

Industry Sales (millions of dollars)	Firm's Annual Sales (number of RVs)
536	98
791	137
650	112
813	145
702	120
575	103
684	116

If estimates of industry sales next year are $725 million, use simple linear regression to forecast annual demand for the firm's RVs for next year.

5. In Problem 3, SCC wonders if time series regression analysis is the best way to forecast next year's sales. It is examining the following industry data:

Year	SCC Sales Revenues (millions of dollars)	All Industry Calculator Sales Revenues (billions of dollars)
1	46.7	6.1
2	59.3	11.4
3	74.2	12.8
4	77.9	10.5
5	85.1	15.3
6	98.0	14.4

a.   Perform a regression analysis between the annual sales revenues of SCC's calculators and all industry calculator annual sales revenues. What is the forecast for next year's (Year 7's) sales revenues for SCC's calculators if the estimate of next year's industry calculator sales revenues is $14.8 billion?

b.   Which forecast—the time series forecast from Problem 3 or the forecast from this problem—seems to be "better"? Why is it better?

6. Finley Heaters Inc. is a mid-sized manufacturer of residential water heaters. Sales have grown during the last several years, and the company's production capacity needs to be increased. The company's management wonders if national housing starts might be a good indicator of the company's sales:

Year	National Housing Starts (millions)	Finley Heaters' Annual Sales (millions of dollars)
1	6.2	57
2	5.1	59
3	6.5	65
4	7.9	78
5	6.3	72
6	7.4	80
7	7.0	86

a.   Develop a simple linear regression analysis between Finley Heaters' sales and national housing starts. Forecast Finley Heaters' sales for the next two years. The National Home Builders Association estimates that national housing starts will be 7.1 million and 8.0 million for the next two years.

b.   What percentage of variation in Finley Heaters' sales is explained by national housing starts?

c.   Would you recommend that Finley Heaters management use the forecast from Part a to plan facility expansion? Why or why not? What could be done to improve the forecast?

7. Chasewood Apartments is a 300-unit complex near Fairway University that attracts mostly university students. Manager Joan Newman suspects that the number of units leased during each semester is impacted by the number of students enrolled at the university. The university enrollment and number of apartment units leased during the past eight semesters is:

Semester	University Enrollment (thousands)	Number of Units Leased
1	7.2	291
2	6.3	228

(continued)

Semester	University Enrollment (thousands)	Number of Units Leased
3	6.7	252
4	7.0	265
5	6.9	270
6	6.4	240
7	7.1	288
8	6.7	246

a. Use a simple regression analysis to develop a model to forecast the number of apartment units leased, based on university enrollment. If the enrollment for next semester is expected to be 6,600 students, forecast the number of apartment units that will be leased.

b. What percent of variation in apartment units leased is explained by university enrollment?

c. How useful do you think university enrollment is for forecasting the number of apartment units leased?

Moving Averages

8. IPC's plant estimates weekly demand for its many materials held in inventory. One such part, the CTR 5922, is being studied. The most recent 12 weeks of demand for the CTR 5922 are:

Week	Demand (units)	Week	Demand (units)	Week	Demand (units)	Week	Demand (units)
1	169	4	171	7	213	10	158
2	227	5	163	8	175	11	188
3	176	6	157	9	178	12	169

Use the moving average method of short-range forecasting with an averaging period of three weeks to develop a forecast of the demand for the CTR 5922 component in Week 13.

9. A large health maintenance organization (HMO) was created as a result of a corporate merger two years ago. Cindy Belle, the operations manager, needs to develop a staffing plan for the legal department. She wants to use the two years of historical lawsuit data given below to forecast the number of lawsuits filed against the company for one month ahead.

Month	Number of Lawsuits	Month	Number of Lawsuits	Month	Number of Lawsuits
1	16	9	51	17	63
2	25	10	56	18	57
3	16	11	67	19	48
4	24	12	45	20	55
5	38	13	53	21	61
6	46	14	61	22	51
7	54	15	55	23	56
8	52	16	69	24	53

a. Develop moving average forecasts for the past 10 months (Months 15–24) for AP = 2, 4, 6, and 8 months.

   b.   Which AP results in the lowest mean absolute forecasting error? Which AP would you recommend? Why?

   c.   Using your recommended AP, forecast the number of lawsuits expected for next month (Month 25).

10. Cindy Belle, the operations manager for the HMO in Problem 9, wonders if recent past data are more important than older data. She wants to use a five-month weighted moving average and has decided to try the weights .45, .25, .15, .10, .05 (i.e., .45 is for the most recent period of past data).

   a.   Use this weighted moving average approach to forecast Months 15–24 using the data from Problem 9.

   b.   Compute the mean absolute deviation (MAD) for Months 15–24.

   c.   Forecast the number of lawsuits expected for Month 25.

11. The number of Texas tax auditors needed by the Internal Revenue Service varies from quarter to quarter. The past 12 quarters of data are shown below:

Year	Quarter	Auditors
1	1	132
	2	139
	3	136
	4	140
2	1	134
	2	142
	3	140
	4	139
3	1	135
	2	137
	3	139
	4	141

   a.   Use moving averages to forecast the number of auditors needed next quarter if AP = 2, AP = 4, and AP = 6.

   b.   Which of these forecasts exhibits the best forecast accuracy over the past six quarters of historical data based on mean absolute deviation?

12. Using the data in Problem 2, determine if an averaging period of AP = 1, AP = 2, or AP = 4 should be used to develop moving average forecasts so that MAD over the past four periods is minimized. Considering the pattern of the past data, why might one expect that this value for AP would provide greater forecast accuracy?

Exponential Smoothing

13. A toy company buys large quantities of plastic pellets for use in the manufacture of its products. Production manager Josh Kang wants to develop a forecasting system for plastic pellet prices. The price per pound of plastic pellets has varied as shown:

Month	Plastic Pellets Price/Pound	Month	Plastic Pellets Price/Pound
1	$0.39	9	$0.35
2	0.41	10	0.38
3	0.45	11	0.39
4	0.44	12	0.43

(continued)

Month	Plastic Pellets Price/Pound	Month	Plastic Pellets Price/Pound
5	$0.40	13	$0.37
6	0.41	14	0.38
7	0.38	15	0.36
8	0.36	16	0.39

a.   Use exponential smoothing to forecast monthly plastic pellet prices. Compute what the forecasts would have been for all the months of historical data for $\alpha = 0.1$, $\alpha = 0.3$, and $\alpha = 0.5$ if the assumed forecast for all α's in the first month is $0.39.

b.   Which alpha value results in the least mean absolute deviation for Months 7–16?

c.   Use the best alpha value from Part b to compute the forecasted plastic pellets price for Month 17.

14. Josh Kang would like to compare two forecasting systems to forecast plastic pellet prices from the data in Problem 13: moving averages ($AP = 3$) and exponential smoothing ($\alpha = 0.1$).

a.   Compute the two sets of monthly forecasts for the past 10 months (Months 7–16). The assumed forecast for Month 1 for exponential smoothing is $0.39.

b.   Plot on a graph the two forecasts for each of the past 10 months against the actual plastic pellet prices. What conclusions can you reach about the graph?

c.   Select the best system and forecast the plastic pellets price for the next month (Month 17).

15. In Problem 8, if a smoothing constant of 0.25 is used and the exponential smoothing forecast for Week 11 was 170.76 units, what is the exponential smoothing forecast for Week 13?

16. In Problems 8 and 15, which forecasting method is preferred—the $AP = 3$ moving average method or the $\alpha = 0.25$ exponential smoothing method? The criterion for choosing between the methods is mean absolute deviation (MAD) over the most recent nine weeks. Assume that the exponential smoothing forecast for Week 3 is the same as the actual demand.

17. Using the data in Problem 2, determine if a smoothing constant of $\alpha = 0.1$, $\alpha = 0.5$, or $\alpha = 0.9$ should be used to develop exponential smoothing forecasts so that MAD over the eight periods is minimized. Assume that the forecast in the first period is 565. Why might one have anticipated that this value for α would result in the best forecast accuracy?

18. Use the data in Problem 2 to develop a forecast for Year 9 using the exponential smoothing with trend model. Begin your analysis in Year 4: $FT4 = 597$, $T4 = 7$, $\alpha = 0.4$, and $\beta = 0.3$.

19. Use the data in Problem 3 to develop a forecast for Year 7 using the exponential smoothing with trend model. Begin your analysis in Year 1 and assume that $\alpha = 0.1$ and $\beta = 0.2$. Estimate FT_1 and T_1 as in Example 3.7.

Multiple Regression

20. Cougill and Cox (C&C) is a law firm that specializes in providing legal services to small manufacturers. Julie Nemeth, an operations analyst for C&C, has developed a linear regression model from historical data that estimates the number of billing hours per year for a client. Her model takes the following form:

$$Y = 76.4 - 35.4X_1 + 268X_2 + 3.5X_3 + 67X_4$$

where:

Y = expected number of billing hours per year for a client
X_1 = number of years the manufacturing company has been a client of C&C
X_2 = number of C&C attorneys assigned to the client for the year
X_3 = number of client's employees
X_4 = number of client's manufacturing plants
r^2 = 0.81 (coefficient of determination based on past data)

a. Estimate the number of billing hours next year for a manufacturer that has been a C&C client for seven years, will have four C&C attorneys assigned to it, has 378 employees, and has nine manufacturing plants.

b. Explain the meaning of $r^2 = 0.81$.

21. Omega Engineering of Omaha, Nebraska, changes its staff size of engineers each quarter depending on demand. In the past, the number of engineers needed has been related to the number of commercial building permits issued by the city, the number of manufacturing companies in the area, and the U.S. gross domestic product. Omega has developed this multiple regression forecasting model for the number of engineers it needs each quarter:

$$Y = -96.651 + 0.228X_1 + 0.094X_2 + 13.077X_3$$

where:

Y = number of engineers needed next quarter
X_1 = number of commercial building permits issued last quarter
X_2 = number of manufacturing companies in the area
X_3 = most recent quarterly U.S. gross domestic product (trillions of dollars)

It is now time for Omega to plan for its staffing needs next quarter. City records show that 81 commercial building permits were issued last quarter and 212 manufacturing companies currently are located in the area. The most recent quarterly U.S. gross domestic product was $6.27 trillion.

a. Use the multiple regression forecasting model to develop a forecast for the number of engineers needed next quarter.

b. Explain the assumptions implied in your forecast.

22. The Burling Company has noticed that its monthly sales appear to be related to the number of salespeople it hires, the amount spent on advertising, and the price of its product. A multiple regression sales forecasting model has been developed:

$$Y = 12,348 + 657X_1 + 0.469X_2 - 240X_3$$

where:

Y = number of units sold in a month
X_1 = number of salespeople hired
X_2 = dollar amount spent on advertising in a month
X_3 = price charged for one unit of the product

Burling's sales manager would like a sales forecast for next month if 17 salespeople are used, $21,000 is spent on advertising, and the price is set at $31.99.

a. Use the multiple regression forecasting model to develop a forecast for the number of units of the product to be sold next month.

b. Explain the assumptions implied in your forecast.

Forecast Ranging

23. From the data in Problem 2:
    a. Compute the standard error of the forecast.
    b. Determine what upper and lower confidence limits can be estimated for the Year 11 forecast if a significance level of 0.01 is used.

24. From the data in Problem 3, what is the range of the forecast for next year if a 95 percent confidence interval is used?

25. From the data in Problem 5:
    a. If you have not already done so, compute the forecast of SCC's sales revenues for next year.
    b. What is the range of the forecast of SCC's sales revenues for next year if a significance level of 0.02 percent (confidence interval of 98 percent) is used?

26. From the data in Problem 7:
    a. Compute the forecast of apartment units leased next semester if university enrollment is expected to be 6,600 students.
    b. Determine the range of the forecast of next semester's apartment units leased if a significance level of 10 percent is used (confidence interval of 90 percent).
    c. Determine the probability that the actual number of apartment units leased next semester will be within 10 units of your forecast. What is the probability within 5 units?

Seasonalized Forecasts

27. A computer manufacturer wants to develop next year's quarterly forecasts of sales revenues for its line of personal computers. The company believes that the most recent eight quarters of sales should be representative of next year's sales:

Year	Quarter	Sales (millions of dollars)	Year	Quarter	Sales (millions of dollars)
1	1	9.2	2	1	10.3
1	2	5.4	2	2	6.4
1	3	4.3	2	3	5.4
1	4	14.1	2	4	16.0

Use seasonalized time series regression analysis to develop a forecast of next year's quarterly sales revenues for the line of personal computers.

28. A tractor dealer has been in business for three-and-a-half years and needs to estimate sales for next year. Sales in past years have tended to be seasonal, as shown below:

Year	Quarterly Sales (number of products)			
	Q_1	Q_2	Q_3	Q_4
1				32
2	49	72	114	41
3	55	88	135	44
4	60	93	149	49
5	63			

    a. Develop forecasts for the next four quarters.
    b. Develop a 90 percent confidence interval for each of your forecasts.

29. AirLite Inc. manufacturers high-quality tennis racquets. The production manager wants to develop a forecasting system to use for future production resource planning. Quarterly demand data for the past four years is given below:

Year	Quarter	Demand (thousands of racquets)	Year	Quarter	Demand (thousands of racquets)
1	Summer	66	3	Summer	48
1	Fall	41	3	Fall	32
2	Winter	29	4	Winter	14
2	Spring	65	4	Spring	55
2	Summer	56	4	Summer	52
2	Fall	45	4	Fall	25
3	Winter	23	5	Winter	19
3	Spring	57	5	Spring	47

a. Use seasonalized time series regression analysis to forecast inventory levels for each of the next eight quarters beginning with Summer of Year 5.

b. Interpret the meaning of the four seasonal indices.

c. Compute upper and lower forecast range limits for Winter of Year 6 using an 80 percent confidence level.

30. From the data in Problem 11:

a. Use moving averages to forecast the number of auditors required in the first quarter of next year if AP = 4 and AP = 8.

b. Do these forecasts reflect a seasonal pattern? Why or why not?

c. Develop quarterly seasonal indexes from the original data. Apply the appropriate seasonal index to your forecasts from Part a.

CASES

San Diego Retailers

The chief operating officer of San Diego Retailers is looking over the most recent sales information for the company. She has called a meeting of all salespersons in the region for one week from today, and she is attempting to estimate the sales levels that should be expected for their company during the next three months. She needs to have this information so that sales quotas can be set for the individual salespersons. Her staff has accumulated these historical sales data:

Year 1	Sales (millions of dollars)	Year 2	Sales (millions of dollars)	Year 3	Sales (millions of dollars)
Jan.	4.1	Jan.	4.6	Jan.	4.7
Feb.	5.1	Feb.	5.4	Feb.	5.6
Mar.	3.5	Mar.	3.6	Mar.	4.1
Apr.	2.4	Apr.	3.1	Apr.	2.8
May	4.2	May	4.3	May	4.6
June	8.3	June	8.8	June	9.1
July	9.6	July	10.5	July	11.9
Aug.	10.1	Aug.	12.2	Aug.	13.1
Sept.	8.0	Sept.	8.5	Sept.	9.0
Oct.	5.4	Oct.	5.6	Oct.	6.1
Nov.	3.2	Nov.	3.8	Nov.	4.1
Dec.	4.2	Dec.	3.9	Dec.	4.4

These sales patterns and trends are expected to continue.

Assignment

1. Plot the sales data on a graph and examine the data.
2. From your graph in Part 1, what patterns are present? Which forecasting models would be appropriate for short-range forecasts from these data?
3. Use the *POM Software Library,* which accompanies this book, and determine, if the exponential smoothing with trend model were applied to these data, which values of alpha and beta result in the least value of mean absolute deviation (MAD) over the last 12 months of these data.
4. Use the *POM Software Library* and seasonalized time series regression analysis to develop a forecast for the next three months' sales. How confident are you of these forecasts? Develop a statistical statement about next month's forecast (Year 4, January) that reflects your level of confidence if you use a 95 percent confidence interval.
5. Based on your findings in Parts 3 and 4, would you recommend that the company use exponential smoothing with trend, or seasonalized time series regression analysis? What are the pros and cons of each method in this case?

Chasewood Apartments

In Problem 7, Joan Newman has just completed a simple regression analysis of the relationship between university enrollment and the number of apartment units leased. Ms. Newman suspects that the number of units leased might also be affected by the average apartment lease price charged. She has collected the following information:

Semester	University Enrollment (thousands)	Average Lease Price ($)	Number of Units Leased
1	7.2	450	291
2	6.3	460	228
3	6.7	450	252
4	7.0	470	265
5	6.9	440	270
6	6.4	430	240
7	7.1	460	288
8	6.7	440	246

Assignment

Use the *POM Software Library*, which accompanies this book, to help you answer these questions:

1. If you have not done so in Problem 7, perform a simple regression analysis to forecast the number of apartment units leased, based only on university enrollment. What is your forecast if enrollment is expected to be 6,600 students? What percentage of variation in number of units leased is explained by university enrollment? Evaluate the goodness of this forecasting model.
2. Perform a simple regression analysis to forecast the number of apartment units leased, based only on average lease price. What is your forecast if the average lease price is to be $455? What percentage of variation in number of units leased is explained by average lease price? Evaluate the goodness of this forecasting model.
3. Perform a multiple regression analysis to forecast the number of apartment units leased, based both on university enrollment and average lease price. What is your forecast if university enrollment is expected to be 6,500 students and the average

lease price is to be $465? What percentage of variation in number of units leased is explained by this model? Evaluate the goodness of this forecasting model.

4. Which forecasting model above would you recommend to Joan Newman? Why?
5. Based on your multiple regression model and forecast from Part 3, what would be the net financial impact if the apartment lease price were increased by $6? What is your recommendation on setting apartment lease prices?

Sundance Chemical Company

Tyler Jones has just been hired as the new production manager at the Sundance Chemical Company (SCC). He believes his first action should be to develop his own sales forecasts for the company's primary chemical product. Mr. Jones asked his assistant to collect quarterly sales data for the past 10 years, as shown below:

	Quarterly Sales (thousands of gallons)			
Year	Q_1	Q_2	Q_3	Q_4
1	594	570	560	565
2	540	531	515	498
3	485	479	463	456
4	319	324	336	340
5	348	355	354	367
6	375	379	385	396
7	404	416	422	430
8	436	439	450	459
9	470	475	485	489
10	505	513	516	518

The president of SCC has been disappointed in recent years by the previous production manager's poor forecasting accuracy. To make a good impression with top management, Tyler Jones intends to perform a thorough forecasting analysis to forecast sales for the next four quarters.

Assignment

Use the *POM Software Library*, which accompanies this book, to help you answer these questions:
1. Graph the data. What kinds of patterns do you observe?
2. Decide how much of the past data should be used to develop a forecasting model. Provide an explanation that justifies your decision.
3. Which forecasting methods from the chapter would be most appropriate to evaluate? Why?
4. Using only the data you decided on in Part 2, decide whether time series regression or exponential smoothing with trend ($\alpha = 0.4$, $\beta = 0.4$, beginning forecast $= 319$, initial trend $= 7$) should be used, based on MAD computed over the last four years.
5. Using the forecasting method you recommended in Part 4, forecast sales for next quarter.

XYZ Inc.

Susan Romero is an investment analyst for a financial planning business in Santa Rosa, California. She has been asked to select a forecasting approach to predict the next-day closing price of XYZ Inc. common stock. Ms. Romero has obtained the closing stock prices for the past 40 days, which are shown below:

Day	Price	Day	Price	Day	Price	Day	Price
1	43.50	11	41.25	21	44.50	31	45.00
2	42.75	12	42.00	22	44.50	32	44.00
3	42.75	13	42.00	23	43.75	33	43.75
4	42.00	14	42.75	24	44.75	34	44.00
5	42.25	15	43.00	25	45.25	35	43.25
6	42.50	16	43.50	26	45.25	36	43.75
7	41.50	17	42.75	27	45.00	37	43.00
8	41.25	18	43.00	28	45.50	38	42.00
9	41.75	19	44.25	29	45.75	39	42.25
10	41.25	20	44.00	30	44.75	40	41.75

Assignment

Use the *POM Software Library* or spreadsheet software such as *Excel* to help you with the forecasting analysis.

1. Plot the data on a graph.
2. Forecast Days 4 through 40 using these forecasting approaches:
    a. Moving average with $AP = 1$.
    b. Moving average with $AP = 3$.
    c. Exponential smoothing with $\alpha = 0.4$ ($F_1 = 43.00$).
    d. Exponential smoothing with $\alpha = 0.8$ ($F_1 = 43.00$).
3. Use MAD values based on Days 4 through 40 to decide which forecasting approach to choose. Forecast Day 41 with this approach.
4. Explain why one might expect forecast methods with a higher impulse response to be more accurate than methods with a lower impulse response in forecasting day-to-day stock prices.

ENDNOTE

1. Blank, Dennis. "Meal Shortfalls Still Gnaw at Some Airlines." *USA Today*, February 22, 2000, 5B.

SELECTED BIBLIOGRAPHY

Box, George E. P., Gwilym M. Jenkins, and Gregory C. Reinsel. *Time Series Analysis: Forecasting and Control.* Englewood Cliffs, NJ: Prentice Hall, 1994.

Chambers, J. C., et al. "How to Choose the Right Forecasting Technique." *Harvard Business Review* 49, no. 4 (July–August 1971): 45–74.

DeLurgio, Stephen A. *Forecasting Principles and Applications.* Boston: Irwin/McGraw-Hill, 1998.

Fisher, Marshall L., Janice H. Hammond, Walter R. Obermeyer, and Ananth Raman. "Making Supply Meet Demand in an Uncertain World." *Harvard Business Review* 72, no. 3 (May–June 1994): 83–89.

Galbraith, Craig S., and Gregory B. Merrill. "Politics of Forecasting: Managing the Truth." *California Management Review* 38, no. 2 (1996): 29–43.

Gardner, Everette S. "Exponential Smoothing: The State of the Art." *Journal of Forecasting* 4 (March 1984): 1–28.

Georgoff, David M., and Robert G. Murdick. "Manager's Guide to Forecasting." *Harvard Business Review* 64 (January–February 1986): 110–123.

Jain, Chaman L., ed. *A Managerial Guide to Judgmental Forecasting.* Flushing, NY: Graceway Publishing Co., 1987.

Lewis, Colin D. *Demand Forecasting and Inventory Control: A Computer Aided Learning Approach.* New York: Wiley, 1998.

Makridakis, Spyros G. "Accuracy Measures: Theoretical and Practical Concerns." *International Journal of Forecasting* 9, no. 4 (1993): 527–529.

Makridakis, Spyros. "The Art and Science of Forecasting." *International Journal of Forecasting* 2 (1986): 15–39.

Makridakis, Spyros G., Steven C. Wheelwright, and Rob J. Hyndman. *Forecasting: Methods and Applications,* 3rd ed. New York: Wiley, 1998.

Sanders, Nada R. "Measuring Forecast Accuracy: Some Practical Suggestions." *Production and Inventory Management Journal* 38, no. 1 (1997): 43–46.

Sanders, Nada R. "The Status of Forecasting in Manufacturing Firms." *Production and Inventory Management Journal* 38, no. 2 (1997): 32–36.

Shim, Jae K. *Strategic Business Forecasting: The Complete Guide to Forecasting Real World Company Performance.* Boca Raton, FL: St. Lucie Press, 2000.

Smith, Bernard T. *Focus Forecasting: Computer Techniques for Inventory Control.* Essex Junction, VT: O. Wight Limited Publications, 1984.

Tryfos, Peter. *Methods for Business Analysis and Forecasting: Text and Cases.* New York: Wiley, 1998.

Product, Process, and Service Design

Introduction

Designing and Developing Products and Services
Sources of Product Innovation
Developing New Products
Getting New Products to Market Faster
Improving the Designs of Existing Products
Designing for Ease of Production
Designing for Quality
Designing and Developing New Services

Process Planning and Design

Major Factors Affecting Process Design Decisions
Nature of Product/Service Demand
Degree of Vertical Integration
Production Flexibility
Degree of Automation
Product/Service Quality

Types of Process Designs
Product-Focused
Process-Focused
Group Technology/Cellular Manufacturing

Interrelationships among Product Design, Process Design, and Inventory Policy

Process Design in Services

Deciding among Processing Alternatives
Batch Size and Product Variety
Capital Requirements for Process Designs
Economic Analysis
Assembly Charts
Process Charts

Plant Tours
A Product-Focused, Dedicated Factory: Safety Products Corporation, Richmond, Virginia
A Process-Focused Factory: R. R. Donnelley & Sons, Willard, Ohio
A Service Operation: Wal-Mart Regional Distribution Center, New Braunfels, Texas

Wrap-Up: What World-Class Companies Do

Review and Discussion Questions

Internet Assignments

Problems

Cases

Endnotes

Selected Bibliography

WINNING OPERATIONS STRATEGIES FOR THE TWENTY-FIRST CENTURY

Succeeding in the twenty-first century requires that firms build an infrastructure that allows them to accomplish the following:

1. Quickly develop and design new innovative products and services of superior quality and commit to a policy of continuous improvement.
2. Build flexible production systems capable of quickly producing products of near-perfect quality and low cost that can be quickly changed to accommodate customer needs.

Achievement of these goals requires fundamental changes in the way firms design and develop products and production processes. Though expensive and time consuming, these actions promise to dramatically change not only the appearance of industry organizations but the ways they act and behave as well.

Increasingly, U.S. and foreign companies have reorganized their product design and development efforts. Autonomous work teams made up of research and development engineers and marketing, production, and financial personnel are given more freedom and responsibility for the entire design and development effort. Using the latest design technology, these teams save huge amounts of time and money in bringing new products to market.

Many companies today are on the forefront of installing systems of production processes called lean production systems. These systems are smaller and more compact. Workers are organized in work teams, and parts and tools are positioned close to where they are needed. Assembly lines use robots and other automated, computer-driven machines. Production and orders for materials are so closely coordinated with customer demand that little inventory is needed. The results can be astounding. Customer orders are quickly shipped with products of superior quality with far fewer workers and much lower costs.

As the above account indicates, designing and developing products and production processes are key elements in successful strategies in today's global economy. Let us begin our study of these important topics.

DESIGNING AND DEVELOPING PRODUCTS AND SERVICES

In Chapter 2, we discussed the importance of product design in operations strategy. It was stressed that when products are designed:

1. The detailed characteristics of each product are established.
2. The characteristics of a product directly affect how a product can be produced.
3. How the product is produced determines the design of the production system.

Additionally, *product design directly affects product quality, production costs, and customer satisfaction. The design of products and services is therefore crucial to success in today's global competition.*

In this discussion of product design, we will consider the sources of product innovation, developing new products, getting new products to market faster, improving the designs of existing products, designing products for ease of production, designing products for quality, and designing and developing new services.

Sources of Product Innovation

New product and service ideas can come from many sources: customers, managers, marketing, production, and engineering. Large corporations have formal research and development departments. These departments:

1. Take what can be learned from **basic research** (general scientific knowledge with no commercial uses).
2. Engage in **applied research** (specific scientific knowledge that may have commercial uses).
3. Work toward the design and development of new products and services and production processes.

Business Snapshot 4.1 illustrates the results of applied research. The resulting product idea appears to have many potential commercial applications. Now let us more closely explore the activities related to new product development.

Developing New Products

Figure 4.1 shows some of the important steps in designing and developing new products. Once a new-product opportunity has been recognized, initial **technical and economic feasibility studies** determine the advisability of establishing a project for developing the product. If initial feasibility studies are favorable, engineers prepare an initial **prototype design**. This prototype design should exhibit the basic form, fit, and function of the final product, but it will not necessarily be identical to the production model. Performance testing and redesign of the prototype continues until this design–test–redesign process produces a satisfactorily performing prototype. Next, **market sensing**

BUSINESS SNAPSHOT 4.1

Applied Research Pays Off with Cool Sound

Compressors are the ungainly guts of air conditioners, refrigerators, and industrial cooling systems. Because pistons, crankshafts, and other moving parts are essential, compressors guzzle electricity while pumping refrigerants through cooling pipes. But not for long, if MacroSonix Corp. in Richmond, Va., has its way. President Tim S. Lucas has invented an energy-stingy compressor that requires no moving parts. He recently showed a prototype to a meeting of acoustical engineers in San Diego.

The compressor's secret: super-powerful sound waves. Energy transmitted by sound is already used by ultrasonic welding to melt plastics. Beyond a certain amplitude, though, sound energy dissipates as shock waves. Lucas discovered he could thwart this dissipation by precisely shaping the sound waves inside special containers called resonators. These can generate sound waves that pack 1,600 times more energy than ever before and create pressures reaching 500 pounds per square inch. "It's one of the most exciting things to come along in acoustics in several years," says Gregory W. Swift, an acoustics expert at the Los Alamos National Laboratory.

Source: Gross, Neil. "Cool Air: A Sound Approach." *Business Week,* December 15, 1997, 108. Reprinted from December 15, 1997, issue of *Business Week* by special permission, copyright © 1997 by The McGraw-Hill Companies, Inc.

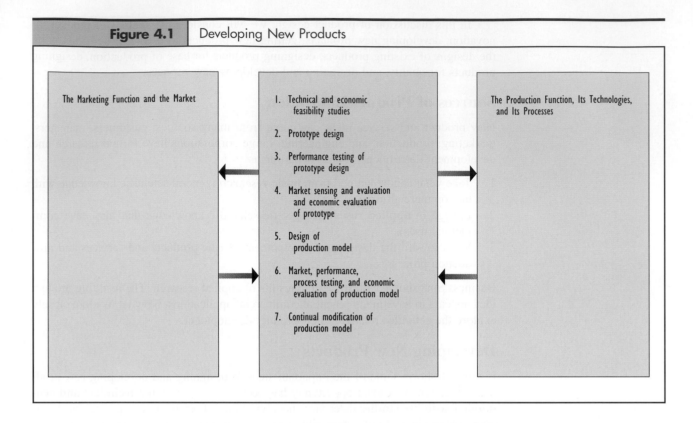

| **Figure 4.1** | Developing New Products |

The Marketing Function and the Market

1. Technical and economic feasibility studies

2. Prototype design

3. Performance testing of prototype design

4. Market sensing and evaluation and economic evaluation of prototype

5. Design of production model

6. Market, performance, process testing, and economic evaluation of production model

7. Continual modification of production model

The Production Function, Its Technologies, and Its Processes

and evaluation is accomplished by demonstrations to potential customers, market tests, or market surveys. If the response to the prototype is favorable, **economic evaluation of the prototype design** is performed to estimate production volume, costs, and profits for the product. If satisfactory, the project will enter the production design phase.

The **production design** will evolve through performance testing, production trials and testing, market testing, and economic studies. It will exhibit low cost, reliable quality, superior performance, and the ability to be produced in the desired quantities on the intended production equipment. Production designs are continuously modified to adapt to changing market conditions and changing production technology and to allow for manufacturing improvements. Business Snapshot 4.2 illustrates how Ford has designed and redesigned a new vehicle.

About 5 percent of all new-product ideas survive to production, and only about one in ten of these is successful. It is best to cancel unpromising new-product/service development projects early so that human effort and development money can be directed toward more promising projects. This is easier said than done, because managers, engineers, and marketers become emotionally caught up in their projects and are reluctant to dispose of them. This fact justifies the need for impartial management review boards for periodic reviews of the progress of new-product/service projects.

Getting New Products to Market Faster

To succeed in global competition, companies must design, develop, and introduce products faster. One approach to speeding up new-product design and introduction is with the use of autonomous design and development teams. At companies like General Motors, IBM, Xerox, Motorola, General Electric, Toyota, Nissan, Honda, and AT&T, design teams are given decision-making responsibility and more freedom to design and

BUSINESS SNAPSHOT 4.2

Developing the Prodigy at Ford

New product development is sometimes undertaken in response to government directives. In 1993 the U.S. government directed U.S. automakers to dramatically improve the fuel efficiency of their vehicles during the next decade. By 2000 Ford Motor Co. had built a test car, the Prodigy, with the space and convenience of a Taurus sedan that gets more than 70 miles per gallon (mpg) thanks to a long list of high-tech improvements.

The Prodigy was developed under the Partnership for a New Generation of Vehicles (PNGV), a joint effort by automakers and the federal government to design and build a prototype five-passenger car that gets 80 mpg by 2004 without compromising passenger needs. The U.S. government spent $240 million on PNGV development in 1999, much of it for research at government and university laboratories. Ford estimated that it, along with General Motors and DaimlerChrysler, spent $980 million that year on their various PNGV projects.

To achieve 60 mpg with the Prodigy, Ford developed a small turbocharged diesel engine and an electric motor with a battery pack in the trunk of its early prototype. To achieve 70 mpg, Ford's engineers designed a slippery new exterior that uses video cameras in place of rearview mirrors, a smooth underbody, special wheel covers, and vents in the front grille that open only when the engine needs extra air. The Prodigy is built mostly of aluminum, with some magnesium and titanium components, weighing in at 2,387 pounds—about a thousand pounds less than other midsize sedans.

Although the objective of 80 mpg has yet to be achieved, Ford continues to refine the Prodigy's design and is confident that it is closing in on the government's goal.

Source: "Ford Announces 70-M.P.G. Prodigy." *Chicago Tribune,* January 2, 2000, Transportation Section.

---

introduce new products. The results have been dramatic. The time required to get new products designed, developed, and introduced into the market has been slashed, and enormous sums of money have been saved. The source of these savings is that these teams do not have to deal with the bureaucratic red tape ordinarily required to obtain the necessary approvals to everything from design details to pricing to advertising spending.

Another tool in achieving the goal of faster introduction of new products is with the use of computer-aided design/computer-aided manufacturing (CAD/CAM). Engineers can sit at computer workstations, generate many views of parts and assemblies, rotate images, magnify views, and check for interference between parts. Designs can be stored in a database, compared with other designs, and stored for use on other products. When it is time for manufacturing, the product design information in the database is translated into a language that production machinery understands. The production system can then be automatically set up to run the new products.

Traditionally, designing products and designing the production processes to produce the products have been two separate activities. Companies would go through all the steps to design products, and then these designs would be *thrown over the wall* to production people to design the production processes. But this approach took too much time to get new products to the market. Figure 4.2 illustrates the concept of **simultaneous engineering** or **concurrent engineering**, which means that product/service design proceeds at the same time as process design with continuous interaction. *The concept of simultaneous engineering has significantly compressed the design, production, and introduction cycle of new products.* Business Snapshot 4.3 illustrates how Boeing uses computer simulation to speed up the product development process.

| Figure 4.2 | Simultaneous Engineering: Process and Product/Service Design |

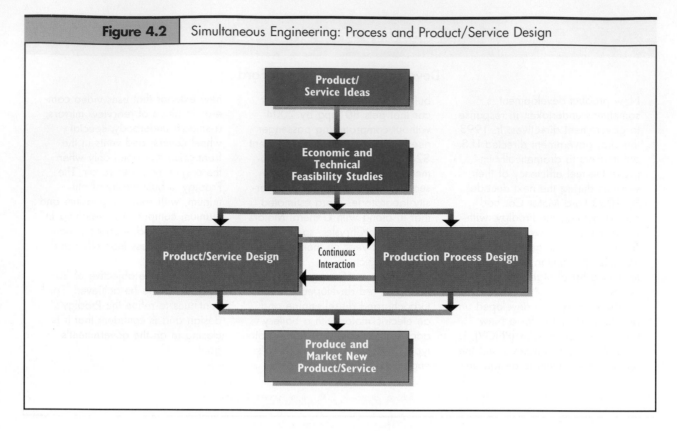

The activities in production, marketing, finance, and engineering related to product/service design and development are intense as new products/services are developed. As products/services move through the later stages of their life cycles, these efforts shift to concerns about improving the designs of existing products.

BUSINESS SNAPSHOT 4.3

Virtual Reality Simulations in the Product Design Process at Boeing

As computer software continues to advance, computer simulations are being developed that can speed up the design process by making sure that many parts and systems will all fit together properly within a product. Boeing uses a computer simulation that can be considered a form of virtual reality to help design engineers integrate many of the component systems within its airplanes. For example, different groups of engineers design the freshwater plumbing, electrical, and air circulation systems independently, using CAD software. The simulation software then reads all of the CAD files for the different systems and integrates or combines them three dimensionally. Boeing engineers can use the computer simulation to perform an *animated virtual fly-through* to view the airplane's plumbing, electrical, and air circulation systems. The computer simulates a video camera traveling along the pipes and cables within the plane. The user controls the speed and direction of the virtual camera as it moves along.

The simulation allows the designers of one system to check for design interference with the airplane structure and with other systems. The use of virtual fly-throughs to check for design problems has resulted in fewer engineering changes, which in turn speeds up the product development process and reduces design and development costs.

Improving the Designs of Existing Products

Companies are putting more and more effort into modifying and improving existing products. The focus of this effort is to improve performance, quality, and cost with the objective of maintaining or improving market share of maturing products. And little changes can be significant. For instance, at Toyota a continuous program was undertaken to refine product designs to reduce production costs. Products were redesigned so that taillights could be hooked up with a single connector instead of two, savings = $0.42; the plastic clip that anchors the body's weather-stripping was made smaller, savings = $1.05; and the underside of a car was undercoated only where it was needed, savings = $2.00.[1] Such improvements are often referred to as **value analysis.** By emphasizing *continuous* product design improvements, these small steady improvements have added up to huge long-term improvements in product quality and production costs.

Designing for Ease of Production

Product quality, production cost, number of suppliers, and levels of inventories can be affected by product design. *Designing products for ease of production is a key way for U.S. manufacturers to be competitive with foreign manufacturers.*

Three concepts are closely related to designing for ease of production: specifications, standardization, and simplification.

A specification is a detailed description of a material, part, or product, including such measures as viscosity, surface finish, pH rating, and physical dimensions. These specifications provide production departments with precise information about the characteristics of the product to be produced. Eli Whitney's **system of interchangeable parts** required each part of a rifle to be manufactured to specific tolerances. Tolerances are stated as a minimum and maximum for each dimension of a product. For example, a minimum of 3.999 inches and a maximum of 4.001 inches could be specified as 4.000 ± 0.001 inch. Specifications, including tolerances, are needed to allow both ease of assembly and effective functioning of the finished products. Generally speaking, parts produced to tighter tolerances (smaller deviations from the target dimension) will fit together better, but may cost more to produce if more accurate and expensive equipment is required or if extra processing time is needed to achieve the desired precision.

Standardization refers to the design activity that reduces variety among a group of products or parts. For example, if a product group having 20 models were redesigned to have only 10 models, we would refer to the new group as more standardized. Standardization of groups of products or parts usually results in higher volume for each product or part model, which can lead to lower production costs, higher product quality, greater ease of automation, and lower inventory investment.

Simplification of product design is the elimination of the complex features so that the intended function is performed but with reduced costs, higher quality, or more customer satisfaction. Customer satisfaction may be increased by making a product easier to recognize, buy, install, maintain, or use. Costs can be reduced through easier assembly, eliminated operations, less expensive substitute materials, and when less material is wasted as scrap.

The concepts of specifications, tolerances, standardization, and simplification are all important in designing products for ease of production. Of particular importance is that products must be designed to accommodate automated equipment. This topic will be discussed in more detail in Chapter 6, Operations Technologies.

Designing for Quality

A crucial element of product design is its impact on quality. Whether products of superior quality are received by customers is ultimately determined in large part to the extent that products are designed for quality. *Building product quality into the product designs is the first step in producing products of superior quality.* Quality is determined by the customer's *perception* of the degree of excellence of the characteristics of products or services.

We will study the principles of designing products for quality in Chapter 7, Operations Quality Management.

Designing and Developing New Services

In Chapter 2, we discussed positioning strategies for services—the type of product design, custom or standard; the type of process design, product-focused or process-focused; and the amount of customer contact, high or low. It must be apparent by now that classifying service designs into neat and simple categories is not easy. Perhaps the most obvious thing about service designs is their diversity, but there are three general dimensions of service design:

1. *The degree of standardization of a service.* Is the nature of the service custom-fashioned for particular customers or classes of customers, or is the nature of the service the same for all customers?
2. *The degree of customer contact in delivering the service.* Is there a high level of customer contact as in a dress boutique or a low level of customer contact as in a fast-food restaurant?
3. *The mix of physical goods and intangible services.* Is the mix dominated by intangible services as in a university or by physical goods as in a tailored suit?

There are both advantages and disadvantages to the amount of each of these dimensions to include in a service design. For example, services that are standardized with a low degree of customer contact are usually less expensive and quicker to deliver and may be more appropriate for the strategies of some services. On the other hand, custom services with a high degree of customer contact may be appropriate for the strategies of other services. All of these dimensions come together as service designs are established, and the final choice of designs must be based on the desired competitive priorities of the business strategies employed as illustrated in Figure 2.1 in Chapter 2.

Consider the dimensions discussed above about service designs—degree of standardization, degree of customer contact, and mix of physical goods and intangible services. Because of the intangible nature of some services, it is almost impossible to separate consideration of the nature of the service and the production process to generate and deliver the service. For example, the degree of customer contact says as much about the production process of the service as about its nature. This is one thing about design of services that is distinctly different from design of products. We will discuss more about designing production processes for services later in this chapter.

How we go about developing new services is similar to the development of new products illustrated in Figure 4.1. But there are some important differences. Unless services are dominated by physical goods, their development usually does not require the engineering, testing, and prototype building of product design. And because many service businesses involve intangible services, market sensing tends to be more by surveys rather than from market tests and demonstrations.

Next, we study how to plan and design the processes that must *produce* the products and services of operations.

PROCESS PLANNING AND DESIGN

In designing production processes, we delineate and describe the specific *processes* to be used in production. Table 4.1 lists some common production processes. Process planning is intense for new products and services, but replanning can also occur as capacity needs change, business or market conditions change, or technologically superior machines become available. *The type of production processes to be selected must necessarily follow directly from the operations strategies* that were discussed in Chapter 2. The design of products and the design of production processes are interrelated. Figure 4.2 illustrated the concept of **simultaneous engineering,** which means that product/service design proceeds at the same time as process design with continuous interaction.

Figure 4.3 illustrates the elements of process planning and design and its inputs and outputs. Knowledge about operations strategies, product/service designs, technologies of the production system, and markets are used to develop a detailed plan for producing products/services. The outputs of these studies are a complete determination of the individual technological process steps to be used and the linkages among the steps; the selection of equipment, design of buildings, and layout of facilities; and the number of personnel required, their skill levels, and their supervision requirements.

Once process planning has been completed, the fundamental structure and character of the operations function is set. This important activity determines in large measure the details of how products/services will be produced, and it positions production to be used by the business to capture world markets.

Who does process planning? Several departments such as manufacturing engineering, plant engineering, tool engineering, purchasing, industrial engineering, design

Table 4.1	Some Production Processes

SOME METALWORKING PROCESSES

Assembly	Casting and Molding	Cutting	Forming	Finishing
Braze	Cast:	Broach	Draw	Blast
Cement	die, sand,	Drill	Extrude	Buff
Fasten	investment	Grind	Punch	Clean
Press-fit	Mold:	Hone	Roll	Debur
Shrink-fit	injection	Mill	Trim	Heat treat
Solder	powdered metal	Shape	Swage	Paint
Weld	permanent mold	Turn	Spin	Polish

SOME NONMETALWORKING PROCESSES

Chemicals	Food	Mining	Textiles	Lumber
Crack	Can	Dry	Braid	Debark
Cook	Cook	Crush	Knit	Cure
Cure	Crush	Excavate	Polish	Joint
Distill	Freeze	Extract	Shrink	Kiln
Evaporate	Pasteurize	Load	Spin	Plane
Grind	Press	Screen	Wash	Saw
Screen	Sterilize	Smelt	Weave	Turn

Figure 4.3	The Process Planning and Design System

INPUTS	PROCESS PLANNING AND DESIGN	OUTPUTS

1. Product/Service Information
Product/Service Demand
Prices/Volumes
Patterns
Competitive Environment
Consumer Wants/Needs
Desired Product Characteristics
 	
2. Production System Information
Resource Availability
Production Economics
Known Technologies
Technology That Can Be
    Acquired
Predominant Strengths
Weaknesses
 	
3. Operations Strategy
Positioning Strategies
Competitive Weapons Needed
Outsourcing Plans
Allocation of Resources
	1. Select Process Type
	Coordinated with Strategies
	
	2. Vertical Integration Studies
	Vendor Capabilities
	Acquisition Decisions
	Make-or-Buy Decisions
	
	3. Process/Product Studies
	Major Technological Steps
	Minor Technological Steps
	Product Simplification
	Product Standardization
	Product Design for Producibility
	
	4. Equipment Studies
	Level of Automation
	Linkages of Machines
	Equipment Selection
	Tooling
	
	5. Production Procedures Studies
	Production Sequence
	Materials Specifications
	Personnel Requirements
	
	6. Facilities Studies
	Building Designs
	Layout of Facilities
		1. Technological Processes
		Design of Specific Processes
		Linkages among Processes
		
		2. Facilities
		Building Design
		Layout of Facilities
		Selection of Equipment
		
		3. Personnel Estimates
		Skill Level Requirements
		Number of Employees
		Training/Retraining
		    Requirements
		Supervision Requirements

engineering, and, of course, production may be involved. Engineers are involved because the very nature of process planning is inseparable from the technology of production. For example, in the electronics industry, terms such as flow soldering, component autoinsertion, and printed circuit (pc) acid baths are part of the everyday language of process planning.

MAJOR FACTORS AFFECTING PROCESS DESIGN DECISIONS

Table 4.2 lists the major factors affecting process design decisions, each of which is discussed in the following subsections.

Nature of Product/Service Demand

First, production processes must have adequate capacity to produce the volume of the products/services that customers want. And provision must be made for expanding or contracting capacity to keep pace with the demand patterns of sales. Some types of processes can be more easily expanded or contracted than others, and the choice of the type of production process will be affected by the forecasted product/service demand.

Table 4.2	Major Factors Affecting Choice of Process Designs
	1. Nature of product/service demand, patterns of demand and price–volume relationships
	2. Degree of vertical integration: forward and backward integration
	3. Production flexibility: product and volume flexibility
	4. Degree of automation
	5. Product/service quality

Business plans set the prices of products and services. Prices affect sales volume, product design, and the required production capacity and costs. Therefore the choice of price and the choice of the design of production processes must be synchronized.

Degree of Vertical Integration

One of the first issues to resolve when developing production processing designs is determining how much of the production of products/services a company should bring under its own roof. A firm's outsourcing plans, which should be part of its operations strategy, should help guide these decisions. **Vertical integration** is the amount of the production and distribution chain, from suppliers of components to the delivery of products/services to customers, that is brought under the ownership of a company. The degree to which a company decides to be vertically integrated determines how many production processes need to be planned and designed.

Because of shortages of both capital and production capacity, small businesses and start-up ventures ordinarily choose to have a very low degree of vertical integration. In the beginning, when products or services are being introduced to the market, as much of the production of products as practical will be contracted to suppliers. Likewise, distribution of products will be contracted to shipping and distributor firms. As the businesses grow and products mature, however, more and more of the production and distribution of products typically will be brought back in-house as the companies seek more ways to reduce costs and consolidate their businesses.

The decision of whether to make components (or perform services) or buy them from suppliers (outsourcing) is not simple. One issue is whether the cost of making components is less than that of buying them from suppliers. Other issues are also important, such as availability of investment capital to expand production capacity, technological capability, and whether the necessary production processes are proprietary.

In industry today there appears to be a trend toward strategic outsourcing. **Strategic outsourcing** is the outsourcing of processes for the primary purpose of being able to react more quickly to changes in customer demands, competitor actions, and new technologies. Business Snapshot 4.4 discusses the concept of strategic outsourcing.

Production Flexibility

Production flexibility means being able to respond fast to customers' needs. Flexibility is of two forms, product flexibility and volume flexibility, both of which are determined in large part when production processes are designed. **Product flexibility** means the ability of the production system to quickly change from producing one product/service to producing another. Product flexibility is required when business strategies call for many custom-designed products/services, each with rather small volumes, or when new products must be introduced quickly. In such cases, production

BUSINESS SNAPSHOT 4.4

Strategic Outsourcing—From Vertical to Virtual Integration

Strategic outsourcing is emerging as one of the fastest-growing management tools of the decade. Traditionally, outsourcing assisted companies in cutting costs, improving business focus, and freeing management from some of its day-to-day operations. And it still does. But today companies are using outsourcing to gain long-term flexibility, consistent best practices, and new skills.

Strategic outsourcing offers businesses innovative ways to enter or create new markets rapidly without a significant upfront invest-ment of resources. It provides a modular environment in which it is possible to scale up and ramp down depending on seasonal forces and production needs.

As the pace of change accelerates, few companies can excel on all fronts. Nor can they afford to be saddled with the responsibility of building and maintaining an infrastructure for essential—but non-core—parts of their business, such as telephones, mailrooms, credit collections, computer networks, or help-desk services. Outsourcing noncritical processes allows a company to focus better on what it does best, its core business processes.

On the back of strategic out-sourcing, leading companies are successfully riding the waves of globalization, the advent of advanced communications and computer technologies, and increasing complexity and hypercompetition. They are also using communications and networking technologies to provide a vital link to their suppliers and partners, resulting in what could be called virtual integration.

Source: "Outsourcing: From Vertical to Virtual—The Race to Change." *Business Week,* December 15, 1997, 72–76.

processes must be designed to include general-purpose equipment and cross-trained employees who can be easily changed from one product/service to another. Also, new forms of flexible automation allow great product flexibility.

Volume flexibility means the ability to quickly increase or reduce the volume of products/services produced. Volume flexibility is needed when demand is subject to peaks and valleys and when it is impractical to inventory products in anticipation of customer demand. In these cases, production processes must be designed with production capacities that can be quickly and inexpensively expanded and contracted. Manufacturing operations are ordinarily **capital intensive**, which simply means that the predominant resource used is capital rather than labor. Thus, in the presence of variable product demand, capital equipment in production processes must be designed with production capacities that are near the peak levels of demand.

Degree of Automation

A key issue in designing production processes is determining how much automation to integrate into the production system. Because automated equipment is very expensive and managing the integration of automation into existing or new operations is difficult, automation projects are not undertaken lightly. Automation can reduce labor and related costs, but in many applications the huge investment required by automation projects cannot be justified on labor savings alone. Increasingly, it is the goals of improving product quality and product flexibility that motivate companies to make the huge investments in automation projects. As with other factors affecting the design of production processes, the degree of automation appropriate for production of a product/service must be driven by the operations strategies of the firm. If those strategies call for high product quality and product flexibility, automation can be an important element of operations strategy.

Product/Service Quality

In today's competitive environment, product quality has become an important weapon in the battle for world markets of mass-produced products. In earlier times, it was thought that the only way to produce products of high quality was to produce products in small quantities by expert craftsmen performing painstaking hand work. Mercedes and Rolls-Royce are examples of automobiles that were produced with this approach. In recent times, many mass-produced products, such as Japan's Toyota automobiles, are considered to be of very high quality. The choice of design of production processes is certainly affected by the need for superior product quality. At every step of process design, product quality enters into most of the major decisions. For many firms, the issue of how much product quality is required is directly related to the degree of automation integrated into the production processes, because automated machines can produce products of incredible uniformity.

We have now discussed what process planning and design is, how it is achieved, and what factors affect it. Now let us study the major types of process designs we find in practice.

TYPES OF PROCESS DESIGNS

At the earliest stages of process planning, we must decide on the basic type of production processing organization to use in producing each major product. The common types of production processing organizations are product-focused, process-focused, and group technology/cellular manufacturing.

Product-Focused

*The term **product-focused** is used to describe a form of production processing organization in which production departments are organized according to the type of product/service being produced.* In other words, all of the production operations required to produce a product/service are ordinarily grouped into one production department.

Product-focused production is also sometimes called **production line** or **continuous production**. Both of these terms describe the nature of the routes that products follow through production. Products/services tend to follow direct linear paths without backtracking or sidetracking. In continuous production, products/services tend to proceed through production without stopping. Figure 4.4 illustrates the rather direct linear and continuous paths that raw materials, components, subassemblies, assemblies, and finished products follow in the product-focused production of a product.

Product-focused organization is applied to two general forms of production: discrete unit manufacturing and process manufacturing. **Discrete unit manufacturing** refers to the manufacture of distinct or separate products such as automobiles or dishwashers. Such products may be produced in batches, requiring the system to be changed over to other products between batches. Or a system may be dedicated to only one product, in which case the system is almost never changed over to other products. In discrete unit manufacturing, the term product-focused is also sometimes used synonymously with the term **production line** or **assembly line,** as in the case of automobile assembly plants.

In **process manufacturing,** flows of materials are moved between production operations such as screening, grinding, cooking, mixing, separating, blending, cracking, fermenting, evaporating, reducing, and distilling. This form of production is common in the food, brewing, chemical, petroleum refining, petrochemicals, plastics, paper, and

The production process is where raw materials are turned into products for the consumer.

© PAUL A. SOUDERS/CORBIS

cement industries. As in discrete unit manufacturing, product-focused production in process manufacturing can also be referred to as continuous production. It is called continuous production because materials tend to move through production in a linear fashion without much stopping and because the term describes the nature of the materials, which are nondiscrete or without form, as in liquids or powders.

Compared to other types of production, product-focused systems in manufacturing usually require higher initial investment levels. This increased investment stems from (1) the use of more expensive, fixed-position materials-handling equipment,

Figure 4.4	Product-Focused Production

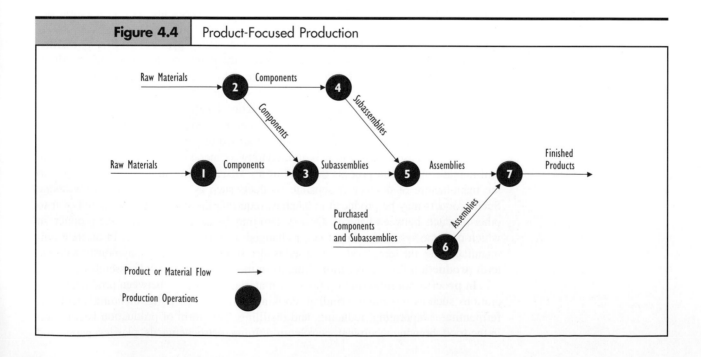

such as overhead conveyors, and (2) the use of equipment that is specialized to a particular product/service, such as automatic welding machines specially designed and tooled for only one product. Additionally, the product flexibility of these systems tends to be rather low because they are ordinarily difficult to change over to other products/services. Offsetting these drawbacks are the advantages of lower labor-skill requirements, reduced worker training, reduced supervision, and ease of planning and controlling production.

This arrangement of equipment and personnel was, until after World War I, uniquely American. Since World War II, product-focused production systems have been used in every industrialized country in the world. The main reason for the extensive use of this type of production is simple: It offers what most operations managers relish most—high-volume production, low unit costs, and ease of planning and controlling production.

Process-Focused

The term process-focused *is used to describe a form of production in which production operations are grouped according to type of processes.* In other words, all production operations that have similar technological processes are grouped together to form a production department. For example, all production operations throughout a factory that involve painting are grouped together in one location to form a painting department.

Process-focused systems are also sometimes referred to as **intermittent production** because production is performed on products intermittently, that is, on a start-and-stop basis. Process-focused systems are also commonly referred to as **job shops** because products move from department to department in batches (jobs) that are usually determined by customer orders. Figure 4.5 illustrates the routes of two hypothetical products through a job shop.

As we can see in Figure 4.5, in job shops, products follow highly irregular stop-and-go, zigzag-type routes with sidetracking and backtracking. In this figure, Job X

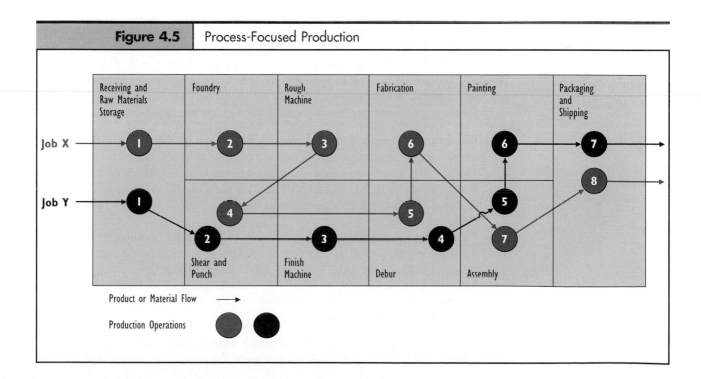

Figure 4.5 | Process-Focused Production

and Job Y represent two distinctly different product designs. Because of their different designs, they require different production operations and must be routed through different production departments and in different sequences. Notice that in Figure 4.5 at times both Job X and Job Y must be processed through the same department, for example, the assembly department. Let us say that the assembly department does not have enough production capacity to work on both of these jobs simultaneously. This means that one of the jobs must wait its turn. This is the fundamental nature of job shops. Jobs spend the large majority of their time *waiting* to be processed in production departments.

Process-focused production systems include hospitals, automobile repair shops, machine shops, and some manufacturing plants. The key advantage of these systems is their product flexibility—the ability to produce small batches of a wide variety of products. Additionally, they usually require less initial investment since they typically use general-purpose equipment and mobile materials-handling equipment, which are usually less expensive. These systems do, however, require greater employee skill, more employee training, more supervision, more technically trained supervision, and more complex production planning and control.

Product-focused and process-focused systems represent two traditional approaches to organizing production. In practice, we also find blends and hybrids of these two approaches.

Group Technology/Cellular Manufacturing

Group technology/cellular manufacturing (GT/CM) is a form of production that has become popular in the last two decades. It is reported to have been used first in the Soviet Union in the late 1940s by Mitrofanov and Sokolovskii.[2] Since the end of World War II, it has been studied and applied in most of Eastern and Western Europe, and in India, Hong Kong, Japan, and the United States. Most of the early applications of this form of production were in metalworking.

Cellular manufacturing is a subset of the broader group technology concept. In **group technology**, a coding system is developed for the parts made in a factory. Each part receives a multidigit code that describes the physical characteristics of the part. For example, let us say that a part is cylindrical, 6 inches long, 1 inch in diameter, and made of stainless steel. The part's code would indicate these physical characteristics. Figure 4.6 shows an example of a GT code for such a part. By the use of a coding system for parts, production activities are simplified in the following ways:

1. It is easier to determine how to route parts through production because the production steps required to make a part are obvious from its code.
2. The number of part designs can be reduced because of part standardization. When new parts are designed, the codes of existing parts can be accessed in a computer database to identify similar parts in the database. New designs can be made like the existing ones.
3. Parts with similar characteristics can be grouped into **part families.** Because parts with similar characteristics are made in similar ways, the parts in a part family are typically made on the same machines with similar tooling.
4. Some part families can be assigned to manufacturing cells for production, usually one part family to a cell. The organization of the shop floor into cells is referred to as **cellular manufacturing**.

In metalworking job shops, parts are made on equipment such as lathes, boring mills, drills, and grinders. Job shops make a great variety of part designs that are pro-

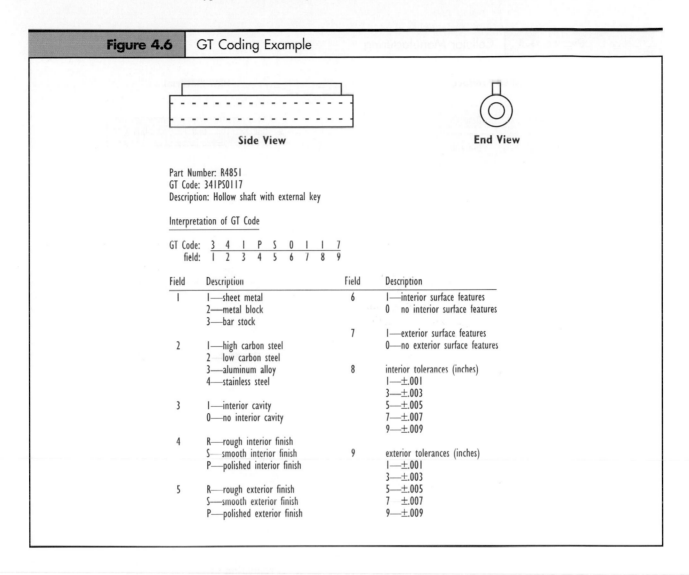

Figure 4.6 | GT Coding Example

Side View   **End View**

Part Number: R4851
GT Code: 341PS0117
Description: Hollow shaft with external key

Interpretation of GT Code

GT Code: 3 4 1 P S 0 1 1 7
    field: 1 2 3 4 5 6 7 8 9

Field	Description	Field	Description
1	1—sheet metal	6	1—interior surface features
	2—metal block		0 no interior surface features
	3—bar stock		
		7	1—exterior surface features
2	1—high carbon steel		0—no exterior surface features
	2 low carbon steel		
	3—aluminum alloy	8	interior tolerances (inches)
	4—stainless steel		1—±.001
			3—±.003
3	1—interior cavity		5—±.005
	0—no interior cavity		7—±.007
			9—±.009
4	R—rough interior finish		
	S—smooth interior finish	9	exterior tolerances (inches)
	P—polished interior finish		1—±.001
			3—±.003
5	R—rough exterior finish		5—±.005
	S—smooth exterior finish		7 ±.007
	P—polished exterior finish		9—±.009

duced infrequently and in small batches. Through group technology, some part designs become more standardized, which tends to increase their batch sizes and requires that they be produced more often. Part families with parts that need to be produced more often in moderate batch sizes become candidates for cellular manufacturing.

Figure 4.7 illustrates how one production cell might be created within a job shop. In this example, the parts in one part family require the following processing steps in order: cutting on a saw, turning on a lathe, grinding, drilling, milling, and deburring. One of each machine type is taken out of each processing department in the job shop and moved to an area within the shop to create a cell. The machines with dashed lines in Figure 4.7 (Saw 2, Lathe 3, Grinder 3, Drill 1, Mill 1, Debur 3) are the ones taken to create the cell. Machines in a cell are most often arranged in a U-shape as shown at the bottom of the figure, so the parts in the part family can flow through the cell in an efficient manner. We can see clearly how the part flow has been simplified. In the top figure, the dashed line shows the previous flow of these parts through the job shop. In the bottom figure, the solid line shows the new flow through the cell. The remaining job shop retains the flexibility to produce a wide variety of part designs.

Figure 4.7	Cellular Manufacturing

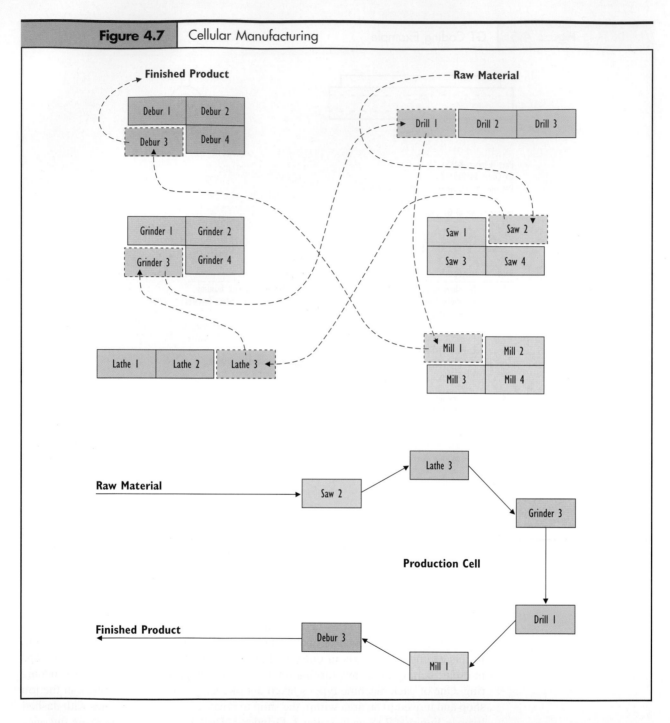

Two key features differentiate cellular manufacturing islands from the larger surrounding job shop: There is a greater degree of similarity among parts within cells, and the flow of parts within cells tends to be more like product-focused systems.

The advantages claimed for cellular manufacturing over job shops are many.[3] Because the parts within a family in a cell require the same machines with similar tooling and require similar production operations:

1. Machine changeovers between batches of parts are simplified, thereby reducing costs of changeovers and increasing production capacity.

2. Variability of tasks on a particular machine is reduced, and training periods for workers are shortened.
3. There are more direct routes through production, allowing parts to be made faster and shipped quicker.
4. Parts spend less time waiting, and in-process inventory levels are reduced.
5. Because parts are made under conditions of less part-design variability by workers who are more specifically trained for the parts, quality control is improved.
6. With shorter, more direct routes through production and with reduction of materials-handling costs, production planning and control is simpler.
7. As a result of reduced part variety and similarity of tooling and machines within cells, automation of cells is simplified. The formation of cells may therefore be viewed as an intermediate step in the automation of job shops.

As you would expect, GT/CM also has some disadvantages. For example, duplicate pieces of equipment may be needed so that parts do not have to be transported between cells. Also, because not all parts from a job shop can be made in the GT/CM cells, producing the remaining parts in a job shop may not be as efficient once GT/CM cells have been established. As we will discuss later, only job shops that have a degree of parts standardization and moderate batch sizes are candidates for GT/CM.

INTERRELATIONSHIPS AMONG PRODUCT DESIGN, PROCESS DESIGN, AND INVENTORY POLICY

In Chapter 2, we discussed the concept of positioning strategy for manufacturers. Positioning requires that managers select a basic type of production design such as product-focused, process-focused, or GT/CM, as we discussed earlier. Of equal importance in positioning decisions, however, are two interrelated decisions about each business:

1. Determining the type of product design—custom or standard
2. Deciding the finished-goods inventory policy—produce-to-stock or produce-to-order

These two decisions are closely interrelated, because deciding between custom or standard designs necessarily affects the type of finished-goods inventory policy that is either practical or possible.

Standard product designs are usually linked with produce-to-stock finished-goods inventory systems. With this approach, customer orders are typically filled and shipped as soon as they are received, using inventory in stock in the finished-goods warehouse. Sales forecasts give inventory control departments estimates of demand for particular products in future weeks and months. If inventory shortages appear likely, a production order is created. Raw materials, components, subassemblies, and assemblies are ordered from suppliers, and the order is scheduled for production. After the materials from suppliers are received and after the order has been produced, it is sent to replenish the finished-goods warehouse.

Custom product designs are usually linked with produce-to-order finished-goods inventory systems. With this approach, products are not produced until after customer orders have been received. If a product is new, then either the customer provides the product design or the company's engineers create the product design to meet the customer's specifications. The production planners must develop a processing plan for the product—a description of the specific processing steps needed to produce the product. The technical designing of products and the development of processing plans are referred to as **preproduction planning** in job shops.

If the product has been previously produced for the customer, then the product designs and process plans would be retrieved, and a production order would be released to the production department. After the customer's order has been scheduled for production, the customer has been notified of the promised delivery date, and the materials have been ordered from suppliers, the order waits in an **order backlog** until it is produced and shipped to the customer.

Do not assume that companies follow only pure positioning strategies, as discussed in Chapter 2. We also find mixed positioning strategies in practice. As an example of a product-focused, produce-to-order production system, let us say that a firm has a few basic product designs that are highly standardized but have options or accessories that can be added to suit individual customers. Components can be produced ahead of time and inventoried in advance of customers' orders; then products may be assembled at the last minute according to customers' specifications. Some automobile manufacturers have this form of process design and can build an automobile to a customer's order on an assembly line. As Business Snapshot 4.5 illustrates, Compaq Computer Corporation changed the assembly of its computers from a produce-to-stock to a produce-to-order system. The standardization of components, the standardization of the basic product design, and a very good information and communication system make this combination feasible.

On the other hand, a furniture manufacturer may use a process-focused, produce-to-stock production system. Because of the nature of the technology of wood preparation, sanding and surface preparation, painting, upholstering, and packaging, these operations are more compatible with a process-focused system. But because of the standardized product designs, a produce-to-stock finished-goods inventory policy is used.

PROCESS DESIGN IN SERVICES

As discussed earlier, the dimensions of service design are degree of standardization, degree of customer contact, and the mix of physical goods and intangible services. The

---

BUSINESS SNAPSHOT 4.5

Compaq Changes to Produce-to-Order

Compaq Computer Corporation has scrapped its long assembly lines and now makes its personal computers with three-person cells that assemble the computers produce-to-order. In this arrangement, the three-person team looks at the next customer's order on a monitor to see the attributes of the computer to be assembled (accessories, type of drives, etc.) and assembles the computer specifically for that customer. In the three-person cells, one person prepares all the subassemblies that go into a computer. The second person installs these into the computer's frame. The third person performs all the tests to make sure the circuits are connected properly. In this method of production, parts and subassemblies are inventoried before customer orders are received, but finished products are not; final assembly occurs only after receipt of orders. This allows Compaq to match production to customer orders and reduces the cost of every step of production—inventory, handling, freight, and unsold goods. Shifting to a produce-to-order system also decreases Compaq's dependence on market forecasts. Compaq says that the output of each employee in the three-person cell increased 23 percent and output per square foot of factory floor space increased 16 percent compared to produce-to-stock assembly lines.

Source: "Compaq Storms the PC Heights from Its Factory Floor." *The New York Times,* November 13, 1994, 1.

ultimate design of a service will establish each of these dimensions and will be driven by the firm's business strategy. Operations strategy that follows from business strategy also requires a plan for producing the services.

Much of the discussion about designing production processes for producing products also applies to designing production processes for services. Some of the factors important in process design for products are also important in services and are not explained again here. These are the nature of customer demand (both level and pattern), degree of vertical integration, production flexibility, degree of automation, and service quality. Volume flexibility is of particular importance in many services. The fundamental nature of many services, as illustrated in Table 2.7, creates the need for volume flexibility, the ability to quickly increase or reduce the volume of products produced. This need stems from the inability of many services to store finished services in anticipation of customer demand. For some services, this inability requires that production processes be designed to generate and deliver services when demanded by customers, or lose sales.

Another way design of production processes for services is like that for products is that the techniques used to decide among processing alternatives for products would also apply to services. But the types of production processes for services are much different from those for products.

To better understand production processes for services, it helps to think about three different schemes for producing and delivering services:

1. **Quasi-manufacturing**. An example of this approach would be in the back rooms of fast-food outlets like McDonald's. Either product focused or process-focused production could be appropriate depending on the nature of the goods or services to be produced. Here, physical goods are dominant over intangible services and there is little customer contact. *The distinguishing feature of this scheme is that production of goods takes place along a production line with almost no customer involvement in production.*

2. **Customer-as-participant**. Examples of this approach are automated teller machines, retailing, self-serve gas stations, and salad bars. Physical goods may be a significant part of the service, and services may be either standardized or custom. *The distinguishing characteristic of this approach is the high degree of customer involvement in the process of generating the service.*

3. **Customer-as-product**. Examples of this approach are medical clinics and hair salons. Such schemes provide customized service and a high degree of customer contact. *The distinguishing feature of this approach is that the service is provided through personal attention to the customer.* This scheme can provide a perception of high quality.

In examining these types of processes for producing services, the degree of customer contact is particularly relevant to process design. At one extreme, the customer-as-product services of barbershops, hair salons, and medical clinics, the service is actually performed *on* the customer. The customer becomes the central focus of the design of production processes. Every element of the equipment, employee training, and buildings must be designed with the customer in mind. Also, courteous attention and comfortable surroundings must be provided to receive, hold, process, and release customers. At the other extreme, quasi-manufacturing services, as in back-room operations of banks, there is no customer contact and these operations can be highly automated to achieve low cost and speed with little regard for customer relations.

There is a tendency of managers of service operations to leave the design of production processes for services at the verbal and subjective level. G. Lynn Shostack, a senior vice-president in charge of the Private Clients Group at Bankers Trust Company, urges managers to develop a more quantifiable and objective approach to designing service processes. He suggests the following steps:

1. *Identify processes.* Develop flowcharts or diagrams that connect the production steps in the overall production system. Include steps that the customer does not see, such as purchasing supplies.
2. *Isolate fail points.* Once the process is diagrammed, determine the decision points where the production system might fail. Build in corrective steps that avoid the consequences of possible errors.
3. *Establish time frame.* Estimate the amount of time that each step of the service should require. These time estimates become standards against which to measure performance of the system. If services are provided in more time than the standards, productivity and profitability will be lower than should be expected.
4. *Analyze profitability.* Continuously monitor the profitability of the service. This monitoring allows unprofitability to be avoided, productivity to be measured, uniformity to be maintained, and quality to be controlled.[4]

Such approaches as these are needed to improve the competitiveness of services.

Another popular concept related to process design is **process reengineering**. Process reengineering is the concept of *drastically* changing an existing process design, as though you were designing it from scratch on a blank piece of paper, instead of merely making marginal improvements to the process. Because a correctly reengineered process should be more efficient, a smaller labor force is often a result of process reengineering.

We have now discussed the different types of process designs, but how do we decide among the different types of process designs?

DECIDING AMONG PROCESSING ALTERNATIVES

In choosing a production process, several factors must be considered. Among these are batch size and product variety, capital requirements, and economic analysis.

Batch Size and Product Variety

Figure 4.8 illustrates that the type of process design that is appropriate depends on the number of product designs and the size of the batches to be produced in a production system.

As we move from Point A to Point D in Figure 4.8, the production cost per unit and product flexibility increase. At Point A, there is a single product, and the demand for the product is very large. In this extreme case, a product-focused organization that is dedicated to only that product would be appropriate. Production costs per unit are very low, but this type of production organization is very inflexible because equipment specialized to the product and the specific training of the employees make it impractical to change to the production of other products. As the number of product designs increases and as the batch size of the products decreases, at some point, say Point B, a product-focused, batch system becomes appropriate. Although this system is relatively inflexible, employees are trained to shift to the production of other products, and equipment is designed to be changed to other products, but with some difficulty.

At the other extreme, Point D represents the production of many one-of-a-kind products. In this case, a job shop producing unique products in batches of a single item would be appropriate. This form of production is the ultimate in product flexibility. As

| **Figure 4.8** | Type of Process Design Depends on Product Diversity and Batch Size |

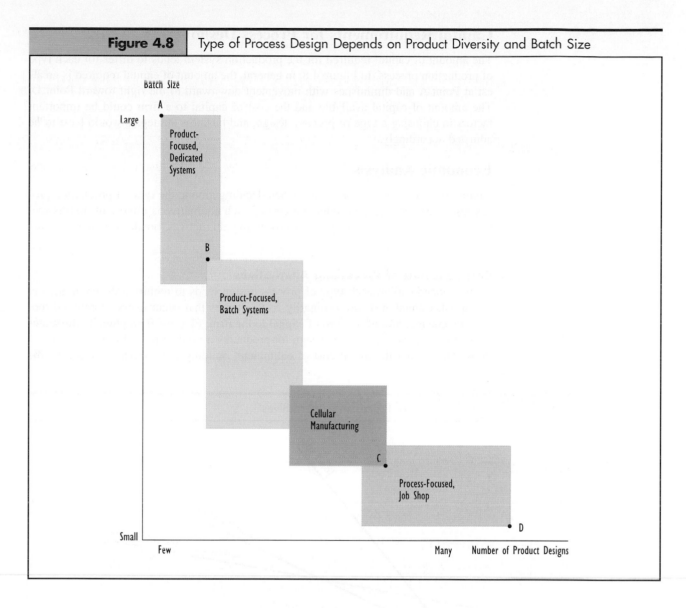

the number of products decreases and as the batch size of the products increases from this extreme, at some point, say Point C, cellular manufacturing for some of the production of parts within a job shop becomes appropriate.

It would now be helpful to refer to Figure 2.3 in Chapter 2. In this figure, the concept of a **process life cycle** was introduced. Simply put, production systems tend to evolve as products move through their **product life cycles**. Two principles are fundamental to the concept of process life cycles. Product life cycles and process life cycles are interdependent; each affects the other. The production processes affect production costs, quality, and production capacity, which in turn affects the volume of products that can be sold. Similarly, the volume of products that are sold affects the type of production processes that can be justified.

Thus, *as business strategies are developed for each major product line, the determination of the volume of demand expected for each product and the number of product models necessary to appeal to the market is an important factor in choosing the type of process design.* Other factors also have some impact on this decision.

Capital Requirements for Process Designs

The amount of capital required for the production system tends to differ for each type of production process. In Figure 4.8, in general, the amount of capital required is greatest at Point A and diminishes with movement downward to the right toward Point D. The amount of capital available and the cost of capital to a firm could be important factors in choosing a type of process design, and business strategies would have to be adjusted accordingly.

Economic Analysis

Among the factors to be considered when deciding among the type of production processing organizations, the production cost of each alternative is important. In this section, we discuss the cost functions of processing alternatives, break-even analysis, and financial analysis.

Cost Functions of Processing Alternatives

As mentioned earlier, each type of process design tends to require a different amount of capital. Capital costs are ordinarily fixed charges that occur every month and represent some measure of the cost of capital to the firm. Figure 4.9 graphically illustrates that different forms of process design for producing a product have different cost functions. The greater the initial cost of equipment, buildings, and other fixed assets, the

| Figure 4.9 | Cost Functions of Processing Alternatives |

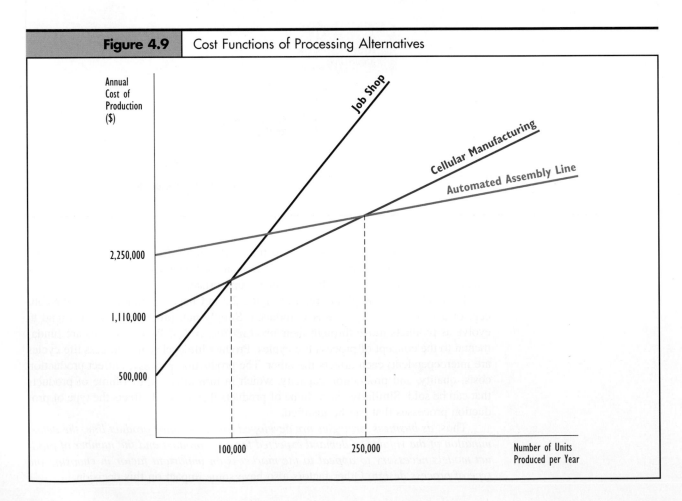

greater are the fixed costs. Also, different forms of production organizations have different variable costs—those costs that vary with the volume of products produced in each month.

As can be seen in Figure 4.9, the automated assembly line alternative has annual fixed costs of $2,250,000. Fixed costs are the annual costs when the volume of the product produced is zero. These costs are related to the very expensive robotics, computer controls, and material-handling equipment required for an automated assembly line. Also, it can be seen from Figure 4.9 that the variable costs (labor, material, and variable overhead) for the automated assembly line are very low relative to the other forms of process design, because the slope (rise over run) of its cost function is very flat. This means that annual costs do not climb very fast as annual volume of production grows. The cost function of a job shop usually exhibits very low fixed costs and very high variable costs. The fixed and variable costs of cellular manufacturing are usually intermediate to those of the other two process designs.

An important conclusion from Figure 4.9 is this: *If capital availability is not a factor and annual production costs are the predominant consideration, the process design that is preferred depends on the production volume of the product.* In the example of Figure 4.9, if annual production volume is less than 100,000 units, a job shop would be preferred. If production volume of between 100,000 and 250,000 units is expected, cellular manufacturing would be preferred. And if production volume of greater than 250,000 units is expected, an automated assembly line would be preferred.

Break-Even Analysis

Break-even analysis is commonly used to help choose between processing alternatives. Here we work our way through an example to refresh your memory of break-even concepts and to demonstrate how break-even analysis can be used to compare production processing alternatives.

Table 4.3 contains the variable definitions and formulas for straight-line break-even analysis. Example 4.1 compares the cost functions of three production processing alternatives.

Table 4.3	Variable Definitions and Formulas for Break-Even Analysis

p = selling price per unit	Q = number of units produced and sold per period
v = variable cost per unit	P = pretax profits per period
FC = total fixed cost per period	TR = total revenue per period
TVC = total variable cost per period	TC = total cost period
C = contribution per period	c = contribution per unit

	At break-even (P = 0):
1. $TR = pQ$	8. $FC = pQ - vQ = Q(p - v)$
2. $c = p - v$	9. $Q = FC/(p - v)$
3. $C = Q(p - v) = TR - vQ = FC + P$	10. $TVC = TR - FC = pQ - FC$
4. $TC = FC + TVC$	11. $v = \dfrac{TR - FC}{Q} = \dfrac{pQ - FC}{Q} = p - \dfrac{FC}{Q}$
5. $TVC = vQ$	
6. $P = TR - TC = pQ - (FC + vQ)$	12. $TR = FC + TVC = FC + vQ$
7. $Q = (P + FC)/(p - v)$	13. $p = (FC + vQ)/Q = FC/Q + v$

| **Example 4.1** | Break-Even Analysis: Selecting a Production Process |

Three production processes—automated (A), cellular manufacturing (C), and job shop (J)—have the following cost structure:

Process	Fixed Cost per Year	Variable Cost per Unit
A	$110,000	$2
C	80,000	4
J	75,000	5

a.   What is the most economical process for a volume of 10,000 units per year?
b.   At what volume would each of the processes be preferred?
c.   What is the annual break-even quantity for the automated process (A) if the selling price of the product is $14 per unit?

Solution

a.
$$TC = FC + v(Q)$$
$$TC_A = FCA + v_A(10,000) = \$110,000 + \$2(10,000) = \$130,000$$
$$TC_C = FC_C + v_C(10,000) = \$80,000 + \$4(10,000) = \$120,000$$
$$TC_J = FC_J + v_J(10,000) = \$75,000 + \$5(10,000) = \$125,000$$

The cellular manufacturing production process has the lowest cost when Q = 10,000 units.

b.
$$TC_J = TC_C$$
$$FC_J + v_J(Q) = FC_C + v_C(Q)$$
$$\$75,000 + \$5(Q) = \$80,000 + \$4(Q)$$
$$Q = 5,000 \text{ units}$$
$$TC_C = TC_A$$
$$FC_C + v_C(Q) = FC_A + v_A(Q)$$
$$\$80,000 + \$4(Q) = \$110,000 + \$2(Q)$$
$$\$2Q = \$30,000$$
$$Q = 15,000 \text{ units}$$

The job shop process would be preferred in the annual volume range of 0–5,000 units, cellular manufacturing would be preferred in the 5,000–15,000 range, and the automated process would be preferred at 15,000 units or above. We would be indifferent between the job shop process and cellular manufacturing and the automated process at 15,000 units.

c.
$$P = 0 = TR - TC = p(Q) - [FC + v(Q)]$$
$$0 = \$16(Q) - [\$110,000 + \$2(Q)]$$
$$\$14(Q) = \$110,000$$
$$Q = 7,857 \text{ units}$$

A positive annual profit would be made with the automated process if more than 7,857 units are sold. If less than 7,857 units are sold, a loss would result with this process. We would be indifferent between the job shop process and cellular manufacturing at 5,000 units, and indifferent between cellular manufacturing and the automated process at 15,000 units.

Break-even analysis is widely used to analyze and compare decision alternatives. It does have some weaknesses, however, when compared to other methods. A primary weakness is the technique's inability to deal in a direct way with uncertainty. All the costs, volumes, and other information used in the technique must be assumed to be known with certainty. Another disadvantage of the tool is that the costs are assumed to hold over the entire range of possible volumes. Additionally, break-even analysis does not take into account the time value of money.

Break-even analysis can be displayed either algebraically as in Example 4.1, or graphically as in Figure 4.10. In either form, the results are easily explained. This is an important advantage, because *managers would often rather live with a problem they can't solve than implement a solution they don't understand.*

It is important to analyze the cost functions graphically. In Figure 4.10, suppose that the annual fixed cost for Process C were $100,000 instead of $80,000. The line for Process C would shift upward by $20,000, keeping the same slope. In this case the line for Process C would be above the intersection of the lines for Process A and Process J ($Q = 11,667$: the quantity where $TC_A = TC_J$). Now Process J would be preferred in the annual volume range of 0–11,667, Process A would be preferred in the annual volume range of 11,667 and above, and Process C would not be preferred at any annual volume range.

| Figure 4.10 | Graphical Approach to Break-Even Analysis |

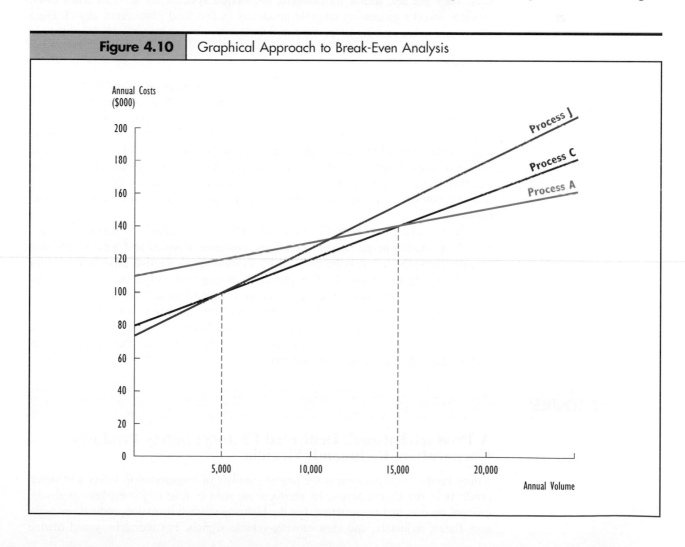

Financial Analysis

The great amount of money to be invested in production processing alternatives and the length of time these assets are expected to last make the time value of money an important concept. The payback period, net present value, internal rate of return, and profitability index are methods used to analyze POM problems involving long periods of time. Although beyond the scope of this course, these techniques are valuable tools for comparing processing alternatives.

Assembly Charts

Assembly charts are typically used to provide an overall macroview of how materials and subassemblies are united to form finished products. These charts list all major materials, components, subassembly operations, inspections, and assembly operations. Figure 4.11 is an assembly chart that shows the major steps in assembling a calculator. Follow through these steps and try to visualize the actual operations for producing this familiar product.

Assembly charts, sometimes called **gozinto charts** (from the words *goes into*), are ideal for getting a bird's-eye view of the process for producing most assembled products. They are also useful for planning production systems for services when those services involve processing tangible goods, as in fast-food restaurants, dry-cleaning shops, and quick tune-up shops for automobiles.

Process Charts

Process charts provide more detail for process planners than do assembly charts. Figure 4.12 shows the individual steps required to process 1,500 pounds of prepared materials through a mixing operation. This chart is a detailed analysis of only one of the operations required to produce aspirin tablets. This planning tool breaks down the mixing operation into 14 elemental steps and segregates them into five classes—operation, transport, inspect, delay, and store. The frequency of occurrence of each class, distance traveled, and description and time for each step are recorded. When the heading of the chart is completed, the method of performing this mixing operation is thoroughly documented.

Process charts can be used to compare alternative methods of performing individual operations or groups of operations. Distance traveled and time to produce products/services can thus be reduced by examining alternative process charts for different production methods. This process-planning tool can be used for products/services that are produced in either continuous or intermittent production systems. Additionally, it is equally valuable for process planning when new products/services are being planned or when existing operations are being analyzed for improvement. Process charts will surface again in Chapter 18 when we study the analysis of human performance in production systems.

PLANT TOURS

A Product-Focused, Dedicated Factory: Safety Products Corporation, Richmond, Virginia

Safety Products Corporation is the largest supplier of transportation safety and signal products in the United States. Its products are sold in four major markets: highway, railway, marine, and construction. For the highway market, its major products are highway flares, reflectors, and slow-moving-vehicle signals. For the railway and marine

Figure 4.11 Assembly Chart for OK-20 Calculator

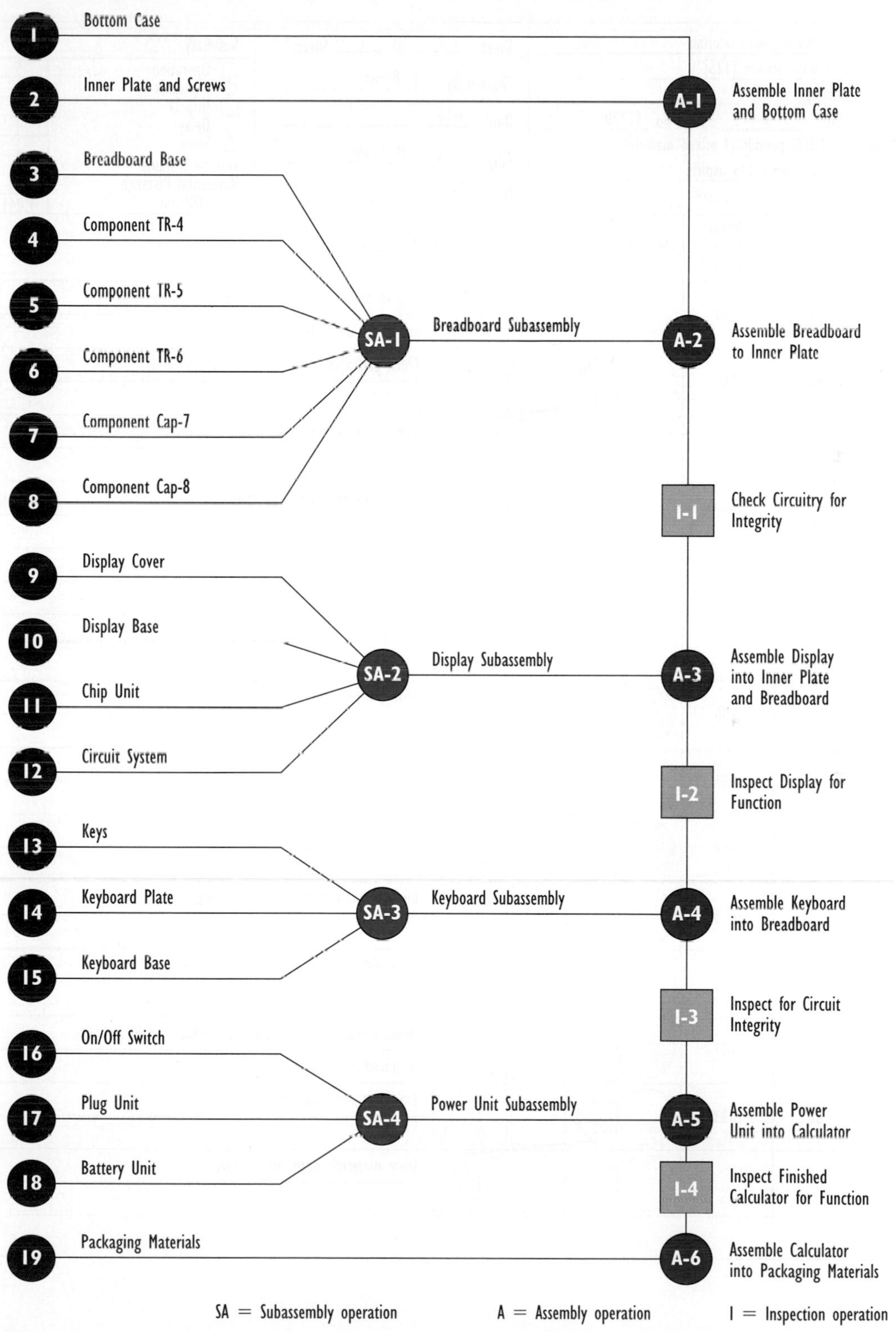

1 — Bottom Case

2 — Inner Plate and Screws — A-1 Assemble Inner Plate and Bottom Case

3 — Breadboard Base

4 — Component TR-4

5 — Component TR-5

6 — Component TR-6 — SA-1 Breadboard Subassembly — A-2 Assemble Breadboard to Inner Plate

7 — Component Cap-7

8 — Component Cap-8

I-1 Check Circuitry for Integrity

9 — Display Cover

10 — Display Base

11 — Chip Unit — SA-2 Display Subassembly — A-3 Assemble Display into Inner Plate and Breadboard

12 — Circuit System

I-2 Inspect Display for Function

13 — Keys

14 — Keyboard Plate — SA-3 Keyboard Subassembly — A-4 Assemble Keyboard into Breadboard

15 — Keyboard Base

I-3 Inspect for Circuit Integrity

16 — On/Off Switch

17 — Plug Unit — SA-4 Power Unit Subassembly — A-5 Assemble Power Unit into Calculator

18 — Battery Unit

I-4 Inspect Finished Calculator for Function

19 — Packaging Materials — A-6 Assemble Calculator into Packaging Materials

SA = Subassembly operation   A = Assembly operation   I = Inspection operation

| **Figure 4.12** | Process Chart for Mixing Aspirin |

Operation	Mix aspirin materials
Product	Pronto aspirin (325)
Depts.	Mixing
Drawing No.	——— Part No. 42200
Quantity	1,500 pounds of mixed materials
	for Pronto 325 aspirin
Present	X Proposed ———

Sheet	1 of 1 Sheets
Charted By	B. Brown
Date	3-16
Approved By	M. Sharp
Date	3-17

Summary	
○ Operation	5
⇨ Transport	5
☐ Inspect	1
D Delay	1
△ Store	2
Vertical Distance	—
Horizontal Distance	212
Time (Hours)	1.041

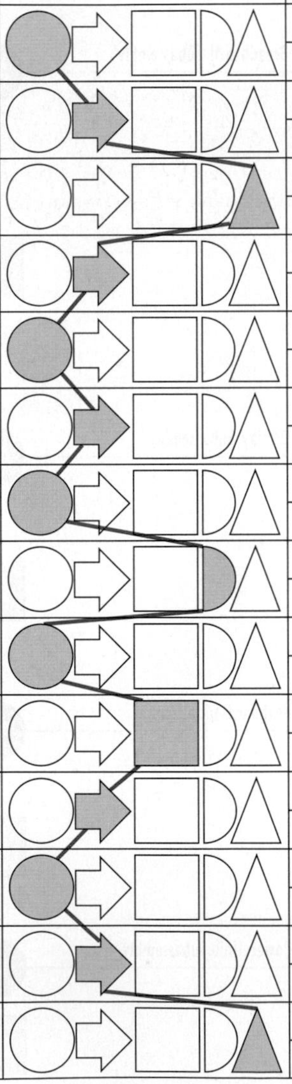

No.	Dist. Moved (Feet)	Worker Time (Hours)	Symbols	Description
1	15	.200	○⇨☐D△	Unload packages of material from truck to dock and place on pallet.
2	42	.033	○⇨☐D△	Truck packages of material to storage area.
3			○⇨☐D△	Store materials until needed.
4	25	.025	○⇨☐D△	Move packages to charge chute.
5		.330	○⇨☐D△	Unpackage materials and pour into charge chute.
6	20	.030	○⇨☐D△	Transport charge to mixer.
7		.100	○⇨☐D△	Charge mixer and begin mixing cycle.
8		.083	○⇨☐D△	Wait until mixer completes cycle.
9		.017	○⇨☐D△	Dump mixer charge into receiving vehicle.
10		.020	○⇨☐D△	Inspect materials for proper mixing.
11	50	.033	○⇨☐D△	Transport vehicle to weighing and packaging station.
12		.167	○⇨☐D△	Operate machine to weigh and package 1,500 pounds of mixed material.
13	60	.033	○⇨☐D△	Transport materials to dock.
14			○⇨☐D△	Store materials until truck arrives.

Safety Products Corporation is a major supplier of highway flares, such as these used by stranded motorists.

© DOUG WILSON/CORBIS

markets, the company supplies a variety of flares for signaling purposes. For the construction market, it produces a wide range of warning signs and signaling devices.

The company began in 1938 and soon became the principal supplier of flares for the nation's railroads. Since that time, highway traffic has dwarfed railway traffic, and the company has gradually added safety and signal products for this growing market. Among all of its products, highway flares account for about 60 percent of the firm's sales revenue. Highway flares are used as signal devices when highway emergencies require the warning of oncoming traffic. They can be easily seen by oncoming motorists both at night and in daytime, as well as in adverse weather conditions such as rain or snow. Municipalities and state law enforcement agencies account for a large part of this product's sales. But sales of highway flares to auto parts stores, hardware stores, and other outlets catering to individual private motorists are increasing. The growth of sales of highway flares was so great that three new factories were built in Richmond, Virginia, Salinas, California, and Des Moines, Iowa.

Business Strategy

The Richmond, Virginia, factory was built as a key element of the business strategy for the highway flare product. This strategy stresses low manufacturing costs through automation, low shipping costs, and technological superiority of the product. Manufacturing and shipping costs are of strategic importance because law enforcement agencies buy about 75 percent of the product, and winning this business depends on the ability of the company to submit low-priced competitive bids.

The location of the factory is of strategic importance in keeping shipping costs low. The East Coast location is an excellent choice for controlling incoming raw material shipping costs because paper from the northeastern United States and Canada and chemicals from Europe are the major materials received at the factory. Outbound shipping costs for finished products are kept low because of the factory's proximity to the population centers of the northeastern United States.

The technological superiority of the company's highway flares has been established through superior chemical formulations, extensive research and development programs, and technical service to customers. The company has built a valuable reputation as the oldest supplier of railroad flares with a tradition of strict safety and performance standards. Extensive research and development programs have resulted in robust product designs, those that perform as expected even when manufacturing or field conditions depart from the ordinary. The company encourages major law enforcement agencies to perform tests of competing products and has supplied testing equipment and manuals to support these tests. As a consequence of these activities, law enforcement agencies have refined their performance criteria for highway flares to favor the higher performing products.

The Product

Figure 4.13 illustrates a 15-minute highway flare. This product is made of a rolled-paper tube filled with a mix of chemicals called the *flame mix*, tipped with a mix of chemicals called the *ignitor button*, and fitted with a cap, one end of which is a surface covered with a mix of chemicals called the *scratch mix*. The flare is lit by removing the scratch cover from the cap and the cap from the flare body, holding the

| Figure 4.13 | A 15-Minute Highway Flare |

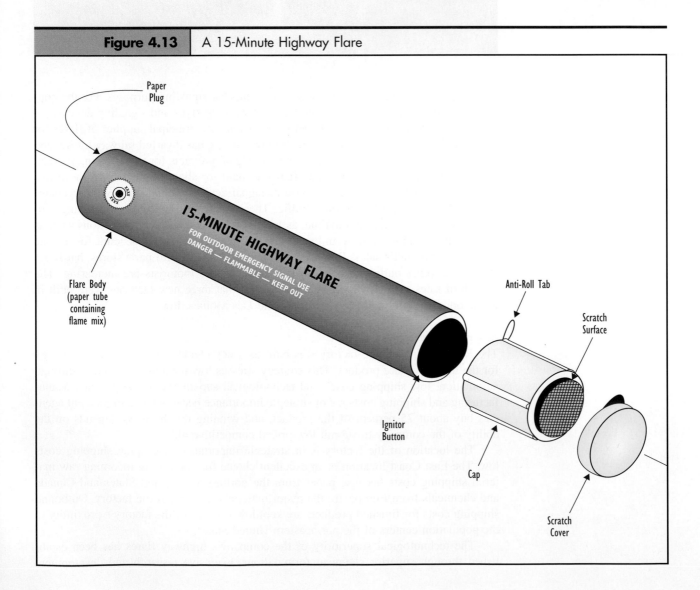

flare body in one hand, the cap in the other hand, and lightly striking the scratch surface across the ignitor button. Safety and use instructions are printed on the flare body.

The Factory

Safety Products Corporation's factory in Richmond, Virginia, ships 15 minute highway flares to 15 states along the Eastern seaboard. The factory cost approximately $50 million to build, and its annual sales are approximately $25 million. The factory is referred to as a **dedicated factory.** This means that the factory is dedicated to just one product, a 15-minute highway flare, which is produced continuously on the factory's equipment without the need to change over to other products. There are 10 highly automated production operations through which products flow without stopping. The only significant work-in-process inventory consists of the products on the continuously moving conveyor that runs through the entire factory. Materials are scheduled to flow in from suppliers to approximately match the production rates of the factory. Although demand for the product is seasonal, employment levels at the factory are kept rather uniform by allowing finished-goods inventory to build during periods of low market demand and to fall during periods of high market demand. Two complete eight-hour shifts are worked each day by the workforce year-round. Overtime labor is used during very high market demand periods. Such a production plan requires careful forecasting of sales demand.

The workforce at the factory is made up of approximately 150 hourly employees. A division of a well-known national transportation union represents the employees. Each employee is given a one-week training program that includes an explanation of company programs and policies, courses in product safety and product quality, and on-the-job training. There are 16 salaried employees at the factory: a plant manager, five office personnel, a production superintendent, six production shift foremen, two engineering and maintenance employees, and a quality control specialist.

Figure 4.14 illustrates how highway flares are manufactured. Raw materials are received into the raw materials warehouse from either commercial trucks or railroad cars. Raw materials are moved from the warehouse in small quantities to the production line as needed. Finished goods are moved from the production line to the finished-goods warehouse and held for shipment to customers by commercial trucks.

Each of the major production operations is described below.

Roll Tubes Great rolls of red-colored paper are positioned on *tube-rolling machines*. These machines continuously and automatically pull the paper from the rolls, cut it to the length of a flare, apply paste to one side, roll the pasted paper into the shape of a tube, and place it into a holding tray for drying. Each tray holds 144 tubes, or a gross. Operators at this operation, like the operators at all of the factory's operations, monitor the equipment, make machine adjustments as necessary, clean the machines and work area, and start up and shut down the machines as required.

Plug and Crimp Tubes Trays of dried paper tubes are pulled into *plugging and crimping machines*. These machines automatically grasp the paper tubes, insert paper plugs into the ends of the tubes, crimp the tubes around the plugs that close the bottom ends of the tubes, and place the trays back on the conveyor.

Mixing Flame, Scratch, and Ignitor Mixes Chemicals are combined in a proprietary formulation for each of the three mixes for the product: the flame mix, the ignitor mix, and the scratch mix. Operators carefully follow prescribed safety and quality procedures to ensure safe operation and product performance. Materials are removed from their shipping containers and placed into *mixing machines*, and preprogrammed mixing instructions are coded into the machines. After the mixes are complete, they are moved by conveyors into the production line areas. The key responsibility of the operators is

Figure 4.14 | Product Flow at Safety Products Corporation

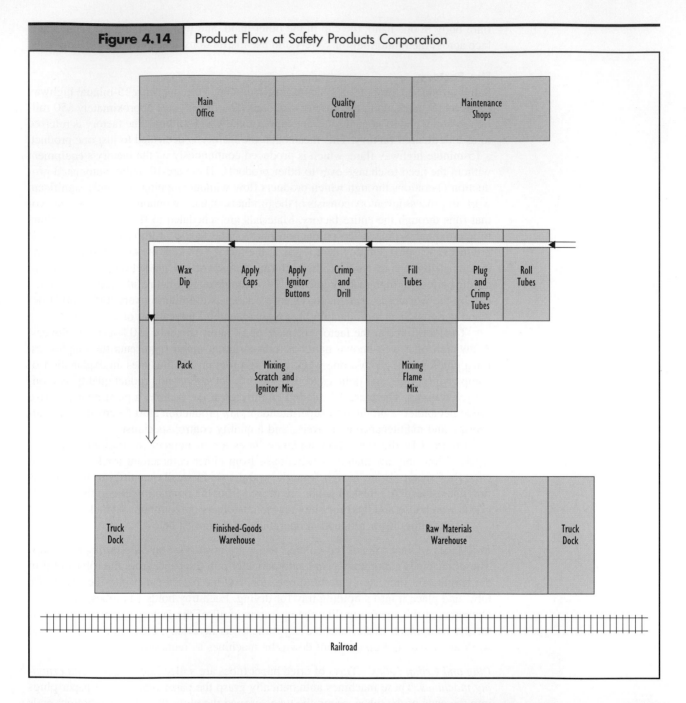

to maintain safe working conditions by strictly following the printed operating procedures and keeping the mixing areas meticulously clean. Additionally, operators must rigidly follow the prescribed chemical formulations for the product.

Fill Tubes   Trays of paper tubes are automatically pulled into *filling machines* that fill the 144 paper tubes with flame mix, tamp the column of mix to the desired density, and place the trays back on the conveyor.

Crimp and Drill   Trays of filled paper tubes move along conveyors to *crimp and drill machines*. These machines position the trays, crimp the tops of the flare bodies, drill holes into the tops of the flare bodies into which the ignitor mix will later be placed, and push the trays, each holding a gross of flare bodies, back onto the conveyor.

Apply Ignitor Buttons Trays of flare bodies are automatically placed into *ignitor-dispensing machines*. These machines automatically dispense a prescribed amount of the thick liquid ignitor mix into the cavities created at the crimp and drill operation and place the trays back on the conveyor.

Apply Caps Fully automated *capping machines* pull trays of flare bodies into position, place plastic cap assemblies on the flare bodies, and place the trays back on the conveyor.

Wax Dip Trays of flares are automatically conveyed through a hot wax dip to ensure long-term protection against moisture and water intrusion.

Pack Flares are automatically removed from trays and placed in corrugated shipping cartons containing one gross, or 144 flares. The cartons are automatically sealed, palletized, and unitized with shrink wrap. Pallets are disposable base frames that allow forklift trucks to place their forks under the loads for transporting, and shrink wrap is a plastic film that is wrapped around an entire load. Each pallet holds 72 cartons. The unitized loads are transported to shipping where they are entered into inventory or labeled for immediate shipping.

The Richmond factory has performed beyond the expectations of Safety Products Corporation. Shipping and production costs have been so low that the firm has achieved a commanding position in competitive bids for the regional law enforcement agency business. Additionally, the quality and technological superiority of the company's products have been dominant factors in its increased market share.

A Process-Focused Factory: R. R. Donnelley & Sons, Willard, Ohio

R. R. Donnelley & Sons is the world's largest book manufacturer. One of its factories is located in Willard, Ohio, in rural north central Ohio about equidistant from Columbus, Cleveland, and Toledo. The Willard factory has been in operation for about 45 years and benefits from being adjacent to the main line of the Baltimore & Ohio Railroad and near an abundant local workforce. R. R. Donnelley contracts with publishing companies to print hardcover books, softcover books, and software documentation products. There are many domestic and foreign competitors, and the business strategy of R. R. Donnelley is to provide custom production of book products with superior product quality, on-time deliveries, competitive prices, and manufacturing flexibility.

Superior quality is achieved by many means. First, top management has created an environment in which the attitude is "close is not good enough." A separate quality control department oversees the overall quality program at the factory. Strict material specifications are adhered to on all purchased materials. Teams of employees study and find solutions to quality-related production problems throughout the production process. Extremely high quality standards are applied to products at every step in the production process, and employees are conscientious in seeing that each product adheres to the standards. Employees seem sincerely dedicated to the company's quality control program.

The factory contains over 1 million square feet of floor space and has more than 1,400 employees. Toward the goals of providing on-time deliveries and competitive prices, customers' orders for books are carefully planned, produced, shipped, and controlled as single batches or jobs. For example, if South-Western College Publishing placed an order for 5,000 of Gaither and Frazier's *Operations Management* book, the entire order would ordinarily be produced as a single batch flowing from department to department through the factory. This arrangement is often referred to as a *job shop* because customers' orders are treated as jobs that flow through the factory, and jobs become the focus of production planning and control.

Because enormous variety exists among the jobs that must be produced by the factory, great manufacturing flexibility is required. This means that in any particular production department, the employees, production machinery, and materials must be flexible enough to be quickly changed from one job to another. Employee flexibility is aided by cross-training among several jobs, training in the technical aspects of jobs, and rewards for employee initiative. Production machines must be designed so that they are general-purpose machines that can be quickly changed to other jobs to accommodate the great product variety. Because the myriad of materials necessary to produce the enormous variety of jobs must be ordered in large amounts from distant suppliers that require up to three months for delivery, large quantities of materials are warehoused until needed.

The factory is like all other job shops in that production is planned and controlled by focusing on customers' jobs. In one respect, though, the factory is unusual when compared to other job shops: All jobs take the same basic route through the production departments—plate making, print, slitting and collating, and binding. In most other job shops, jobs take a great number and variety of routes through production departments to the degree that to the unknowing eye, routings seem almost random. Some routing differences do exist among jobs, however, because jobs can be assigned to several different work centers and individual machines within the production departments.

The production processes at the factory are illustrated in Figure 4.15. The major production steps are (1) receiving, (2) plate making, (3) plate proofing, (4) printing, (5) drying, (6) slitting and collating, (7) binding, and (8) shipping.

Figure 4.15	Flow of Printing Jobs at R. R. Donnelley & Sons

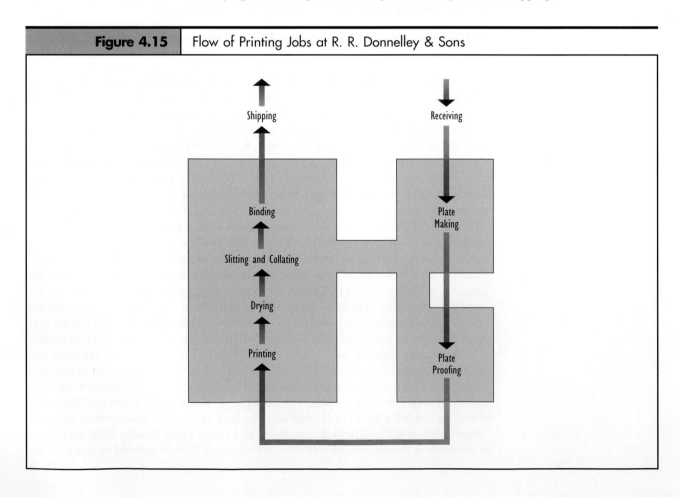

Receiving

Materials are received at the factory from suppliers that may be as near as the Ohio region or as far away as Seattle, Washington. These materials are paper stocks and inks, as well as maintenance, production, and office supplies. The material with the most weight and greatest storage needs, however, is paper, which comes in large heavy rolls. The factory uses 200 million pounds of paper each year, and it receives hundreds of different types of paper from over 25 different paper mills. Picture, if you can, the amount of warehouse space that would be needed to store such amounts of paper. Each material that is received must be checked by quality control personnel to determine if it meets the prescribed specifications and quality standards. Only after materials pass these inspections can they be placed in the warehouse to be made ready for use.

Plate Making

This operation makes the plates that are used in printing presses to print the books. These plates are produced by a photographic process in which a photographic image of an original page that is supplied by the publisher is transferred to a "plate." A plate is a sheet of metal with raised letters such that when ink is applied to the letters and pressed onto paper, the intended page of the book is transferred to the paper. The equipment used in this process is computerized for better quality control. Very highly skilled labor is required in this production step, and in spite of computerization of the equipment, plate making remains labor intensive.

Plate Proofing

This operation involves verifying that the images on the plates are exact duplications of the original pages supplied by the publisher. The original pages contain type text, line drawings, tables, photographs, mathematical equations, and all manner of material that you see in books today. Plate proofing of such material is painstakingly exacting, and microscopes are commonly used to inspect and compare the plates to the original pages. This operation is therefore also labor intensive and requires employees who are dedicated to the highest standards of product quality.

Printing and Drying

Depending on its size, a job is routed to one of three different types of printing presses: a large press, a smaller automated press, or a sheetfed press. These presses incorporate the latest printing technology, with continuous computerized monitoring of paper stock, automated handling of rolls of paper stock, optical scanners, and computerized control of machine adjustments. Running sheets of paper through presses as wide as 10 feet at speeds of 1,500 feet per minute results in enormous production rates of printed pages. The printed paper stock is then run over a series of heated and cooled rollers until dry. The drying equipment requires a large amount of floor and overhead space. This production step, rather than labor intensive, is very capital intensive.

Slitting and Collating

Slitting involves cutting the sheets of printed paper stock into page-size sheets. Large shearing machines are used to slit stacks of sheets into successively smaller sheets. After slitting, pages are sorted into sequence and glued into small bundles of 16 sheets or 32 pages, which are called *signatures*. The signatures are briefly exposed to an open flame to remove any excess scrap paper particles, and sets of signatures for each book are then gathered for binding.

Binding

Hard covers are assembled in a separate process. Back and front covers are printed on a single sheet, glued to a cardboard backing, and folded to fit. Soft covers are printed directly on the paper stock of the cover. In binding, casing-in equipment is used to wrap covers around preglued packages of signatures to form finished books.

Shipping

Finished books are placed either in boxes and then on pallets or directly on pallets. Pallets are wooden, paper, plastic, or fiberglass frames onto which products are stacked. Plastic shrink wrap is then wrapped around each pallet load to form a unitized load. Pallets of books are transported by forklift trucks from the shipping department to trucks or railroad cars for shipment to publishers' regional warehouses.

R. R. Donnelley's strategy is to provide its customers with superior product quality, on-time deliveries, and competitive prices. The design, layout, and operation of its factory in Willard, Ohio, seem well suited to provide these distinctive competencies.

A Service Operation: Wal-Mart Regional Distribution Center, New Braunfels, Texas

Wal-Mart Stores Inc. is a retail discount chain operating in all 50 states and around the world, with headquarters in Bentonville, Arkansas. The stores offer one-stop family shopping with a wide range of merchandise, including electronics, toys, fabric and craft supplies, automotive supplies, lawn and patio equipment, sporting goods, jewelry, and shoes. Wal-Mart's stated merchandising philosophy is to offer name brand, quality merchandise at everyday low prices, not just during sales.

The first Wal-Mart store was opened in Rogers, Arkansas, in 1962 by Sam and Bud Walton. Its stock was first traded on the New York Stock Exchange in 1972. Today in the United States Wal-Mart has around 3,000 retail stores, over 35 regional distribution centers, around 900,000 employees (or *associates*, as Wal-Mart calls them), one of the largest private fleets of trucks in the United States, more than 100,000 U.S. suppliers, and annual sales of more than $150 billion.[5]

Wal-Mart uses regional distribution centers to receive shipments of merchandise from suppliers, receive orders for merchandise from its stores, make up orders for the stores, and load and ship orders to the stores. The regional distribution center in New Braunfels, Texas, was built in 1988 and presently serves stores scattered throughout central and south Texas. After reaching its capacity, it was expected to serve approximately 180 stores and employ about 800 associates.

It is difficult to imagine the size of this facility by reading about it in an account such as this, but consider these facts:

- The facility has over 1 million square feet of floor space under one roof. This is the rough equivalent of 23 football fields, or more than 23 acres of floor space.
- The facility has 96 dock doors for loading and unloading truck trailers.
- The facility has 5.62 miles of conveyors for moving merchandise from incoming trucks, to and from storage, and to outgoing trucks.
- The facility has 43.6 miles of rack width and 83,980 different address locations or rack slots within the warehouse where merchandise can be stored. The racks alone weigh 3.6 million pounds.
- The site contains over 1,200 parking spaces for truck trailers, 110 parking spaces for trucks, and 700 parking spaces for associates.

The facility is organized according to functions such as quality assurance, maintenance, traffic, distribution, loss prevention, data processing, and personnel. Quality assurance receives great emphasis at the center. Its main purpose is to make sure that the right quantity and type of merchandise has been received, that the merchandise has not been damaged in shipment, and that the right quantity and type of merchandise has been shipped to the stores. The traffic department is concerned primarily with scheduling and coordinating common-carrier trucks inbound from suppliers. The distribution department is concerned with scheduling and coordinating company-owned trucks outbound to the stores. The loss prevention department is responsible for security and safety.

Figure 4.16 illustrates the general layout of the center. The following operations of the facility will be discussed below: orders from the stores, inbound merchandise, order filling, conveyor/sort system, and outbound merchandise.

Orders from the Stores

Each Wal-Mart store has a direct computer connection with headquarters in Bentonville, Arkansas. At the end of every workday, associates at each store send in a list of merchandise orders over a computer terminal to Bentonville. The computer system at headquarters breaks down the list of orders and assigns the orders to regional distribution centers. Although most of the merchandise will be shipped from the nearest regional distribution center, certain specialty goods are stocked by only a few of the centers. A computer system at each of the regional distribution centers receives the orders by the next morning and prints the labels for the orders.

The labels play a crucial part in the operation of the center. Each package of merchandise that is to be shipped to a store must have a preprinted adhesive label attached.

| **Figure 4.16** | Wal-Mart Regional Distribution Center |

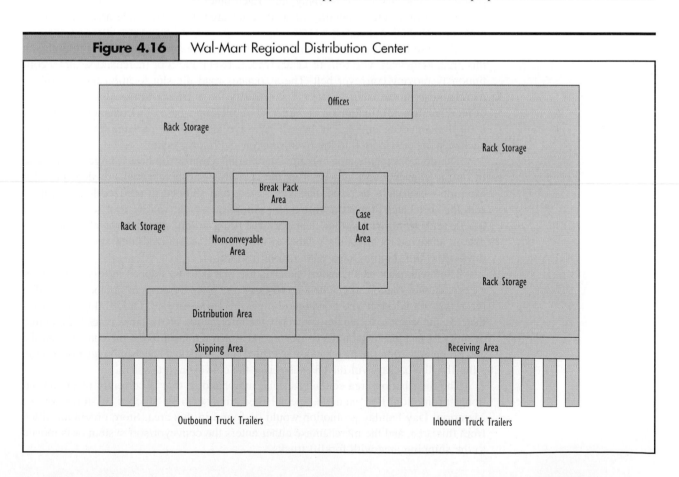

These labels are in bar-code form so that they can be read by optical scanning equipment and in printed form so that they can be easily read by associates. A label represents the authorization to ship the merchandise and contains all the information relating to the order: store destination, name of merchandise, quantity of merchandise, name of supplier, and warehouse location or slot.

Inbound Merchandise

The purchasing department at the Bentonville, Arkansas, headquarters buys merchandise from suppliers on long-term contracts. The purchasing department keeps the traffic departments at the regional distribution centers informed about which supplier is to supply each type of merchandise. Almost all merchandise is made in the United States and literally comes from every region in the nation. As merchandise is shipped from regional distribution centers, inventory records are perpetually reviewed so that the traffic department will know when shipments of each type of merchandise are needed from suppliers. The traffic department then schedules shipments from suppliers to arrive before the regional distribution centers run out of each type of merchandise. Perhaps equally important, merchandise does not arrive at the distribution centers too early, thereby keeping inventory levels low and inventory investment controlled.

Order Filling

Order filling involves using the preprinted labels to locate within the warehouse each package of merchandise on a store order, attaching the label to the package, and transporting the package to the shipping area. Each label to be shipped each day is sent to one of four areas on the facility floor: case lot area, nonconveyable area, break pack area, or distribution area.

The case lot area contains merchandise that is shipped in whole-case multiples. In this area, associates with rolls of labels walk between racks of merchandise and a continuously moving conveyor belt. The associates read the slot location number of the merchandise on the label, locate the slot, verify the accuracy of the quantity and type of merchandise information on the order label, pick up a case of merchandise and place it on the conveyor, and attach the self-adhesive label to the package. From there the packages are transported to the overhead conveyor/sort system.

The nonconveyable area contains merchandise that is too heavy, large, or bulky to fit on the conveyor/sort system. This merchandise—50-pound sacks of dog food, for example—is usually received, handled, stored, and shipped in unitized loads. A unitized load is a batch of merchandise that is placed on a pallet (a four-foot-square wooden frame) and shrink-wrapped in clear plastic. Filling orders of nonconveyable merchandise is achieved by attaching a label to the top of the unitized load and transporting the load to the shipping area with a forklift truck.

The break pack area contains merchandise that is to be shipped in less than whole-case quantities. Associates cut the tops off cases and place the cases in slot locations within racks that are adjacent to a continuously moving conveyor belt. Order-filling associates then use the labels to locate the slot, verify the information on the label, place the required quantity of merchandise on the conveyor, and attach the label to the merchandise. At the end of the conveyor, the merchandise is loaded into cases and checked by quality control. After this the packages of merchandise enter the conveyor/sort system.

The distribution area contains special merchandise that is currently receiving national promotion. For example, special merchandise to be stocked at stores for the Memorial Day holiday promotion would be found in this area. Store orders are filled from this area, and the merchandise either enters the conveyor/sort system or is moved to the shipping area with forklift trucks.

Conveyor/Sort System

The conveyor/sort system is used to transport packages from the storage areas of the warehouse, move them to the shipping area, and sort them to the appropriate loading bay. The conveyor/sort system is a network of conveyors, optical scanners, and package-diverting equipment. Packages are transported from the order-filling areas in the warehouse floor to an overhead conveyor system, which is approximately three stories high and just under the ceiling of the warehouse. Here the packages are turned so that their labels are facing upward, and they are then channeled through optical scanners. These scanners read all of the information from the bar codes on the labels, send the information to the inventory record system, and send to the package-diverting equipment information about which shipping bay should receive each package. The package-diverting equipment pushes packages off the main conveyor onto side conveyors that are bound for particular cargo bays in the shipping area.

Outbound Merchandise

Packages of merchandise exit the conveyor/sort system on apron conveyors that extend into outbound trucks. Associates scan each label with handheld optical scanner wands to verify the information from the optical scanners of the conveyor/sort system. Packages from the conveyor/sort system are placed by hand in the outbound trucks, and unitized loads of nonconveyable merchandise are placed in the outbound trucks with forklift trucks. The facility has the capacity of shipping to stores about 200 fully loaded trucks per day.

This regional facility, in combination with the computer information system at the stores and at the Bentonville headquarters, delivers orders to the stores no later than 48 hours after the orders have been placed. The breakdown of this 48-hour lead time is as follows:

1. Orders are transmitted from the stores to headquarters at the end of the workday.
2. Orders are assigned to regional distribution centers and labels are printed by the next morning.
3. Orders are filled, loaded into trucks, and shipped during the same day.
4. Orders are transported to the stores on company-owned trucks and arrive no later than the next day, depending on the distance between the store and regional distribution center.

Because the stores do not have warehouses, the orders of merchandise go directly from the trucks to the shelves on the stores' display floors. This system of fast delivery of merchandise from regional distribution centers allows the stores to operate without warehouses. Also, stores can wait until merchandise on the shelves is almost gone before ordering, thereby permitting lower shelf inventories. This all translates into lower operating costs, higher productivity, and better customer service.

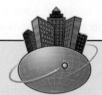

Wrap-Up

WHAT WORLD-CLASS COMPANIES DO

World-class companies plan and design products, services, and production processes so that production systems can be used as competitive weapons in capturing shares of world markets. This requires that production processes be planned and designed with specific capabilities that are matched with the competitive priorities of their business strategies. Toward this end, world-class companies are doing the following:

- Getting products to market faster by using simultaneous engineering, new computer technologies, and autonomous new-product-development teams.
- Designing products for ease of production and for quality so that production systems can be used as weapons to compete in global markets and improving product designs with continuous programs aimed at steady small improvements.
- Refining forecasting efforts so that the capabilities of production processes actually fit the needs of markets.
- Becoming less vertically integrated by concentrating on their core businesses, thus becoming less vulnerable to smaller and more specialized competitors, and by developing a supplier network in which suppliers are treated more as partners than adversaries.
- Reducing production costs and becoming more flexible by adopting the concept of *lean production*, using highly trained employees at every

stage and taking a painstaking approach to every detail of production. This concept is vastly different from conventional mass production, which simplifies each task to mindless routine while relying on armies of supervisors to control costs and limit defects.
- Improving flexibility by replacing some manual production lines and *hard automation* (automatic machinery that is difficult to change to other products) with *flexible automation* (computer-driven automated machines that are easily reprogrammed for other products).
- Improving flexibility by redesigning production processes to speed the flow of products through production and by reducing in-process inventories.
- Modifying some job shops to include some cellular manufacturing to improve production costs, product quality, and speed production.
- Installing improved computerized production control systems to better plan and track customer orders, thus providing better customer service, reduced costs, and improved flexibility.

REVIEW AND DISCUSSION QUESTIONS

1. Name and describe the steps in developing new products. What are the key differences between a *prototype* and a *production design?*
2. Explain three ways that U.S. companies are getting new products to market faster.
3. Explain the meaning of designing products for ease of production. Why is this important?
4. Explain the meaning of designing products for quality. Why is this important?
5. Compare developing new products and developing new services. How are they alike? How are they different?
6. Why might positioning strategies for products change over time? What is the significance of this concept to operations strategy?
7. Discuss the role of process design in operations strategy.
8. Describe the relationship between process design and product design. What is *simultaneous engineering?* What are its advantages?
9. What are the steps in process design? What inputs are required for process design? What are the outputs of process design?
10. Explain how these factors affect process-design decisions: (a) nature of product demand, (b) degree of vertical integration, (c) product and volume flexibility, (d) degree of automation, (e) product quality.
11. Explain why product-focused systems are sometimes called: (a) continuous production, (b) production lines or assembly lines. Explain the difference between: (a) discrete unit manufacturing and process manufacturing, (b) process-focused production and process manufacturing.
12. Explain why process-focused production is sometimes called: (a) intermittent production, (b) job shops.
13. Under what conditions would a manager want to form manufacturing cells in a job shop? What is a *family of parts?*
14. As the number of product designs increases and as the batch sizes decrease, explain what happens to: (a) production cost per unit, (b) product flexibility. Give some reasons why this relationship exists.
15. Briefly explain how you would decide between two different process designs. What factors would you consider? What analysis tools would you use?

16. Explain what is meant by *annual break-even quantity* for a process. How is this related to risk?
17. Describe an assembly chart and a process chart. How are they different? Explain how they are used in process design.
18. Name and describe three classes of production processes for services. Give an example for each class.

19. What steps can be taken in designing production processes for services that would make this activity more quantifiable and more objective? Discuss the difficulties that could be encountered in following these steps.

INTERNET ASSIGNMENTS

1. More companies today are allowing customers to select design features of their products using the Internet. Visit the web site of Ford Motor Company (**http://www.ford.com**) and find the web page that allows you to build and price a Ford Mustang. Select all the design options you would like. What is the price you would pay for your new Mustang?
2. AutoCAD is the most popular CAD software for designing new products. Visit the AutoCAD web site (**http://www.autocad.com**) and discuss some of the new features in the latest version of AutoCAD.
3. Search the Internet for information describing the processes used to produce steel. A good place to start is **http://www.steelnet.org**. Describe how steel is produced.
4. Search the Internet for a restaurant consultant. Describe what services are offered related to the design and operations of a restaurant.

PROBLEMS

Assembly Charts

1. Select a simple assembled product with only a few parts such as a stapler, Scotch tape dispenser, pair of scissors, pair of eyeglasses, or postage scale. Prepare an assembly chart for the product.

2. Select an assembled product with at least six parts. Prepare an assembly chart for the product.

3. Susan Stemelski, a production analyst for Thermoquick, has prepared the following information for the production of a new outdoor digital thermometer. Prepare an assembly chart for the product.

Component List for Model 245B Thermometer

Component Description	Component Code	Predecessor Component Code*	Inspection Required after Component Is Installed?
1. Base	544	—	N
2. Circuitry	520	544	N
3. Wiring harness	623	520	Y
4. Display assembly	715	623	N
5. Outer casing	571	571	Y
6. Packaging	475	475	N

*The code of the component that must immediately precede this component.

4. Ken Chang, a production analyst for SharpEase Company, has prepared the following information for the production of a new electric pencil sharpener. Prepare an assembly chart for the product.

Component List for Model D-41 Sharpener

Component Description	Component Code	Predecessor(s) Component Code(s)*	Inspection Required after Component Is Installed?
1. Motor	318	—	N
2. Grinding assembly	290	318	N
3. Base	256	290	N
4. Housing	155	—	N
5. Electric cord	310	155	N
6. Screws (3)	199	256, 310	N
7. Rubber feet (4)	175	199	N
8. Shavings tray	225	175	Y
9. Packaging	110	225	N

*The code or codes of the component or components that must immediately precede this component.

5. Prepare a process chart for brushing your teeth.

6. Select an activity with which you are familiar that has at least six steps—for example, changing the oil in your auto, refilling a stapler, or turning on and accessing a program on your personal computer. Prepare a process chart for the activity.

7. a. Prepare a process chart from the information below.
   b. Explain how such a process chart could be used.

Assembly Tasks for Model 245B Thermometer

Task Description	Distance Moved (in.)	Time Required (min.)
1. Get base, orient to correct position.	24	0.08
2. Get circuitry, attach to base.	18	0.06
3. Get wiring harness, connect to base and circuitry.	20	0.17
4. Position unit, connect to circuit test.	12	0.10
5. Wait for circuit test, stop if unit fails and sound alarm.	—	0.15
6. Get display assembly, attach to base.	18	0.06
7. Attach wiring harness to display assembly.	—	0.05
8. Get outer casing, attach to base unit.	20	0.08
9. Position unit, connect to final test.	12	0.10
10. Wait for final test, stop if unit fails and sound alarm.	—	0.20
11. Place unit in package, close package, place in chute.	24	0.13

8. a. Prepare a process chart from the information below.
   b. Explain how such a process chart could be used.

Assembly Tasks for Model D-41 Sharpener

Task Description	Distance Moved (in.)	Time Required (min.)
1. Get motor and hold.	20	0.05
2. Get grinding assembly, attach to motor.	24	0.08
3. Get base, attach motor and grinding assembly to base.	24	0.12
4. Get housing, position correctly.	18	0.05
5. Get electric cord, insert into housing.	12	0.07
6. Place housing unit beside base unit, connect electric cord to motor.	6	0.10
7. Attach housing unit to base unit using three screws.	12	0.25
8. Attach four rubber feet to base.	15	0.15
9. Get shavings tray, insert into unit.	20	0.06
10. Position unit, connect to electrical test.	12	0.08
11. Wait for test, stop if unit fails and sound alarm.	—	0.07
12. Place unit in package, close package, place in chute.	24	0.16

Economic Analysis

9. A company is considering the purchase of a machine to use for producing a new product. The selling price of the new product will be $47 per unit. The annual demand for the new product is still very uncertain at this point. Three different machines that could produce the product are being considered. Machine A would have an annual fixed cost of $28,750 and a variable cost per unit of $25. Machine B would have an annual fixed cost of $34,500 and a variable cost per unit of $23. Machine C would have an annual fixed cost of $26,250 and a variable cost per unit of $27. Compute the annual break-even quantity for each machine.

10. A company needs to replace an old machine that is used to produce its primary product. The selling price of the product will be $219 per unit. Two different machines that could produce the product are being considered. Machine A would have an annual fixed cost of $9,500 and a variable cost per unit of $119. Machine B would have an annual fixed cost of $7,900 and a variable cost per unit of $128.
    a. Compute the annual break-even quantity for each machine.
    b. Based on annual cost, at what annual volume would the company be indifferent to purchasing Machine A or B?

11. A company is trying to decide whether to buy a part from a supplier, produce the part while using manual assembly, or produce the part with an automated assembly system. The company expects an annual volume of 185,000 parts. Here are the cost data for each alternative:

	Buy	Produce–Manual Assembly	Produce–Automated Assembly
Fixed cost per year	$0	$260,000	$875,000
Variable cost per part	$18.60	$16.75	$16.25

   a.   Based on these data, which alternative is best?

   b.   At what annual volume of the part would the company be indifferent between buying the part and producing the part with automated assembly?

   c.   At what annual volume of the part would the company be indifferent between producing the part with manual assembly and with automated assembly?

   d.   What other considerations should be important in the decision?

12. Joe Bordoli, office manager at a large accounting firm, wants to purchase a new copying machine. Two brands of machines are being considered, Zenon and Matrox. The Zenon copier would provide an annual fixed cost of $2,760 and a variable cost of $0.061 per copy. The Matrox copier would provide an annual fixed cost of $4,135 and a variable cost of $0.052 per copy.

   a.   If Mr. Bordoli expects 125,000 copies to be made annually, which copier should be purchased based on annual cost?

   b.   If Mr. Bordoli expects 165,000 copies to be made annually, which copier should be purchased based on annual cost?

   c.   Based on annual cost, at what annual copy volume would Mr. Bordoli be indifferent to purchasing the Zenon or Matrox machine?

   d.   For what range of annual copy volume would each machine be preferred?

   e.   What factors other than annual cost should be considered in selecting a copier?

13. Bundey's Mfg. is a small manufacturer that makes metal parts based on customers' engineering drawings. Some parts are one of a kind, but others are repeat orders from long-time customers for medium-sized quantities. For a new family of part types it has decided to start making, Bundey's management is considering the creation of either a low-tech production line or a high-tech manufacturing cell. Because the family of parts is new for Bundey's, management is very uncertain about what annual production volumes to expect. The production approach it selects will partly depend on the economics of each approach:

	Low-Tech Prod. Line	High-Tech Mfg. Cell
Annual fixed cost	$55,000	$87,000
Variable cost per part	$62.50	$48.25

   a.   Which alternative is best?

   b.   At what annual production volume would management be indifferent between the two approaches?

   c.   For what range of annual production volumes would each approach be preferred?

   d.   What other considerations should be important in the decision?

14. Look back at Problem 12. Joe Bordoli now wants to consider a Cantrell copier as well as the Zenon and Matrox copiers. The Cantrell copier would provide an annual fixed cost of $4,865 and a variable cost of $0.043 per copy.

   a.   If Mr. Bordoli expects 125,000 copies to be made annually, which copier should be purchased based on annual cost?

   b.   If Mr. Bordoli expects 165,000 copies to be made annually, which copier should be purchased based on annual cost?

   c.   Based on annual cost, at what annual copy volumes would Mr. Bordoli be indifferent between alternatives Zenon versus Matrox, between Matrox versus Cantrell, and between Zenon versus Cantrell?

   d.   For what range of annual copy volume would each machine be preferred?

   e.   What factors other than annual cost should be considered in selecting a copier?

15. A city is considering changing the way it bills customers for their electricity use. Rather than billing them based on monthly meter readings, the new proposal would bill them for a flat monthly rate of $300. Without the flat rate, customers' monthly cost of service is normally distributed, with a mean of $270 and a standard deviation of $40.
    a. What is the probability that customers will pay more than the flat rate?
    b. What is the expected monthly profit per customer from the proposal?

16. A furniture manufacturer buys a product from a supplier and stocks it for resale to its customers. The supply contract between the manufacturer and the supplier stipulates the following information:

Year	Number of Products/Year	Price/Product	Tooling Charges
1	1,000	$350	$10,000
2	1,500	375	20,000
3	2,500	395	30,000
4	3,500	420	35,000
5	4,500	450	50,000

The supplier has informed the company that it cannot honor its previous supply agreements past the first year. The manufacturer believes that another supplier can be obtained to fulfill the remainder of the supplier contract, but it also wants to consider making the product in-house. It has developed two plans for producing the product in-house, an automation process and a conventional process. The two plans have these costs:

	Automation Process			Conventional Process		
Year	First Cost	Tooling Charges	Cost/ Unit	First Cost	Tooling Charges	Cost/ Unit
2	$1,000,000	$20,000	$125	$250,000	$30,000	$275
3		30,000	145		40,000	290
4		35,000	150		45,000	310
5		50,000	200		60,000	360

Assume that the number of products per year will be the same as projected in the previous supply contract.
    a. Draw a vertical bar chart showing the annual costs for Years 2 through 5 for these three alternatives: Supplier, Automation, and Conventional. How do the three alternatives compare on annual costs?
    b. Draw a graph showing the cumulative costs for the three alternatives for Years 2 through 5. During what years would the automation process begin to show a cost advantage over the supplier and conventional design alternatives?
    c. If the company follows your recommendation in Part b, how much money will be saved over what would have been paid to the supplier over the four-year period?

CASES

Sweet Sound Speakers Company

The Sweet Sound Speakers Company (SSS) manufactures a variety of speakers for other companies that package the speakers with their audio products. One product made by

SSS is K33 headphone speakers that are sold for use with portable radios and CD players. The production process involves assembling purchased components and subassemblies. Dave Johnson, a production analyst at SSS, is analyzing the production process for the K33 headphones to try to identify ways to produce the product more efficiently. Dave intends to draw an assembly chart and a process chart to show the current K33 production process. He hopes these charts will help him to better understand the current production process and to develop improvement ideas. The two tables below list the required components and the assembly steps to produce one unit of K33.

Component List for K33:

Component Description	Component Code	Predecessor Component Code(s)	Quantity Required
1. Left speaker frame	P14L	—	1
2. Right speaker frame	P14R	—	1
3. Speaker	S37	P14L, P14R	2
4. Wire assembly	W25	S37	1
5. Faceplate	F12	W25	2
6. Foam earpiece cover	C44	F12	2
7. Metal center connector	M11	C44	1

Assembly Tasks for K33 Headphone Speakers:

Task Description	Distance Moved (feet)	Worker Time (minutes)
1. Get components kit.	12	0.2
2. Inspect that kit contains all parts.	—	0.1
3. Insert one speaker into left frame.	3	0.1
4. Insert one speaker into right frame.	—	0.1
5. Attach wire to left speaker.	4	0.1
6. Attach wire to right speaker.	—	0.1
7. Inspect wire connections.	4	0.1
8. Test sound quality.	—	0.1
9. Snap faceplate on each frame.	4	0.2
10. Put foam cover over each earpiece.	4	0.2
11. Insert connector into both frames.	4	0.2
12. Final inspection.	4	0.2

Assignment

1. Prepare an assembly chart for the K33 headphone assembly.
2. Prepare a process chart for the K33 headphone assembly.
3. How might an assembly chart and process chart be helpful in identifying improvements?

Infinity Printing Company

Jenny O'Connell is the production manager at Infinity Printing Company, a medium-sized printing business in eastern Connecticut. Recently an increasing number of customers have complained about the quality of the bindings on their books. After a meeting of Infinity's top managers, blame for the problem was placed on the company's 30-year-old binding machine. A decision was made to replace the binding machine with one that should last the next 10 years. Jenny O'Connell was assigned the task of evaluating different binding machines and making a recommendation to top management on which machine to purchase.

After an initial analysis, Ms. O'Connell narrowed the candidates down to two binding machines, a Gunderson model 76-C and a Matsunita model 1203B. As part of her evaluation, she wants to compare the annual cost of each machine. For the Gunderson machine, the annual fixed cost would be $64,550 and the average variable cost per book would be $1.35. For the Matsunita machine, the annual fixed cost would be $78,750 and the average variable cost per book would be $1.20. Last year Infinity printed and bound 81,300 books, and that volume is expected to increase by 5 percent each year.

Assignment

1. Forecast annual book volume for each of the next 10 years, based on the expected growth over last year's volume.
2. With the volume expected next year only, which machine would be preferred based on annual cost?
3. With the volume expected in Year 10 only, which machine would be preferred?
4. Based on annual cost, at what annual volume would the company be indifferent to the purchase of either machine?
5. In each of the 10 years, which machine would be preferred based on annual cost?
6. Which machine should Jenny O'Connell recommend on the basis of annual cost alone?
7. What factors other than annual cost should be considered in this decision?

Airsoft Athletic Shoes Company

Hernandez Mendoza is the production manager at Airsoft Athletic Shoes, a manufacturer of high-end running shoes. Mr. Mendoza would like to automate the process of gluing the rubber soles onto shoe uppers, a process currently being performed manually. Five companies offer automated machines that perform this process, but they vary in initial cost and operating cost. Due to ever-changing competition in the running shoe industry, Airsoft's sales vary substantially from year to year and are difficult to forecast accurately.

Mr. Mendoza feels that part of his machine selection analysis should be to evaluate the annual cost of each machine. The uncertainty of annual sales volume has made the comparison of annual cost more difficult than he anticipated. Mr. Mendoza has decided that it would be most useful to obtain a range of annual volumes in which each machine would be the preferred alternative. The annual fixed cost and the variable cost per shoe for each machine are shown below:

	Annual Fixed Cost	Variable Cost/Shoe
Machine A	$20,500	$0.83
Machine B	28,200	0.59
Machine C	21,100	0.85
Machine D	11,900	0.99
Machine E	29,600	0.68

Assignment

1. Rearrange the machine cost information in order of increasing annual fixed cost. Are any machines clearly inferior to any other machines? If so, eliminate them from further analysis.
2. Draw a graph with annual total cost on the vertical axis and annual quantity or volume on the horizontal axis. Plot the total cost line for each remaining machine.

To plot the line for each machine, arbitrarily pick any two values for annual quantity (such as Q = 0 and Q = 70,000) and compute the total cost with each quantity. Then connect these two points on your graph.

3. For what range of annual volumes is each machine the preferred alternative, based only on annual cost? (Compute only those points of indifference that are necessary to answer the question.)

4. What factors other than annual cost should be considered in selecting the machine?

ENDNOTES

1. "Overhaul in Japan." *Business Week*, December 21, 1991, 82.
2. Mitrofanov, S. P. *Scientific Principles of Group Technology*, 1958, translated by E. Harris. England: National Lending Library for Science and Technology, 1966.
3. Frazier, Gregory V., and Mark T. Spriggs. "Achieving Competitive Advantage through Group Technology." *Business Horizons* (May–June 1996): 83–90.
4. Shostack, G. Lynn. "Designing Services That Deliver." *Harvard Business Review* (January–February 1984): 135.
5. **http://www.wal-mart.com**.

SELECTED BIBLIOGRAPHY

Carr, David K., and Henry J. Johansson. *Best Practices in Reengineering: What Works and What Doesn't in the Reengineering Process.* New York: McGraw-Hill, 1995.

Cashin, Jerry. *Reengineering Business for Success in the Internet Age.* Charleston, SC: Computer Technology Research Corp., 2000.

Cox, James F., III, and John H. Blackstone, Jr., eds. *APICS Dictionary,* 9th ed. Falls Church, VA: APICS—The Educational Society for Resource Management, 1998.

Feitzinger, Edward, and Hau L. Lee. "Mass Customization at Hewlett-Packard: The Power of Postponement." *Harvard Business Review* 75 (January–February 1997): 116–21.

Frazier, Gregory V., and Mark T. Spriggs. "Achieving Competitive Advantage through Group Technology." *Business Horizons* 39, no. 3 (May–June 1996): 83–90.

Gaither, N., Gregory V. Frazier, and Jerry C. Wei. "From Job Shops to Manufacturing Cells." *Production and Inventory Management Journal* 31, no. 4 (Fourth Quarter 1990): 33–36.

Gilmore, James H., and B. Joseph Pine II. "The Four Faces of Mass Customization." *Harvard Business Review* 75 (January–February 1997): 91–101.

Haksever, Cengiz, Barry Render, Roberta S. Russell, and Robert G. Murdick. *Service Management and Operations,* 2nd ed. Upper Saddle River, NJ: Prentice Hall, 2000.

Halvey, John K., and Barbara M. Melby. *Business Process Outsourcing: Process, Strategies, and Contracts.* New York: Wiley, 2000.

Hammer, Michael. *Beyond Reengineering: How the Process-Centered Organization Is Changing Our Work and Our Lives.* New York: HarperCollins, 1997.

Hayes, Robert H., and Steven C. Wheelwright. "Link Manufacturing Process and Product Life Cycles." *Harvard Business Review* 57 (January–February 1979): 133–140.

Hope, Christine, Alan Muhlemann, and Christine Witt. *Service Operations Management: Strategy, Design, and Delivery.* Upper Saddle River, NJ: Prentice Hall, 1997.

Hyer, N. L., and U. Wemmerlov. "Group Technology and Productivity." *Harvard Business Review* 62 (July–August 1984): 140–149.

Lacity, Mary C., and Leslie Willcocks. *Global Information Technology Outsourcing: In Search of Business Advantage.* New York: Wiley, 2001.

Lampel, Joseph, and Henry Mintzberg. "Customizing Customization." *Sloan Management Review* 38, no. 1 (Fall 1996): 21–30.

Levitt, T. "The Industrialization of Services." *Harvard Business Review* 54 (1976): 41–52.

Mitrofanov, S. P. *Scientific Principles of Group Technology,* 1958, translated by E. Harris. England: National Lending Library for Science and Technology, 1966.

Prasad, Biren. *Concurrent Engineering Fundamentals: Integrated Product and Process Organization.* Upper Saddle River, NJ: Prentice Hall, 1996.

Ramaswamy, Rohit. *Design and Management of Service Processes: Keeping Customers for Life.* Reading, MA: Addison-Wesley, 1996.

Ribbens, Jack. *Simultaneous Engineering for New Product Development: Manufacturing Applications.* New York: Wiley, 2000.

Upton, David M., and Stephen E. Macadam. "Why (and How) to Take a Plant Tour." *Harvard Business Review* 75 (May–June 1997): 97–106.

5

Facility Capacity, Location, and Layout

Introduction

Long-Range Capacity Planning
Definition of Production Capacity
Measurements of Capacity
Forecasting Capacity Demand
Ways of Changing Capacity
Economies of Scale
Analyzing Capacity-Planning Decisions
Decision Tree Analysis

Facility Location
Factors Affecting Location Decisions
Types of Facilities and Their Dominant Locational
    Factors
Data, Politics, Incentives, and Preemptive Tactics
Analyzing Retailing and Other Service Locations
Analyzing Industrial Facility Locations
Integrating Quantitative and Qualitative Factors
    into Location Decisions

Facility Layout

Manufacturing Facility Layouts
Materials Handling
Process Layouts
Product Layouts
Cellular Manufacturing Layouts

Fixed-Position Layouts
Hybrid Layouts
New Trends in Manufacturing Layouts

Analyzing Manufacturing Facility Layouts
Software for Analyzing Facility Layouts
Planning Process and Warehouse Layouts
Planning Product Layouts
Planning Cellular Manufacturing Layouts

Service Facility Layouts
Types of Service Facility Layouts
Analyzing Service Facility Layouts

Wrap-Up: What World-Class Companies Do

Review and Discussion Questions

Internet Assignments

Problems

Cases
Blue Powder Company
Power Byte Computers
Integrated Products Corporation
Mexibell Telephones Incorporated
Precision Machine Works

Endnotes

Selected Bibliography

© RONNEN ESHEL/CORBIS

NEW YORK STOCK EXCHANGE AND A HOG FARM?

What could the New York Stock Exchange possibly have in common with a hog farm? Answer: They both need to increase their long-range production or operations capacity. The following two accounts describe how two very different organizations, one a service organization and the other a meat producer, must plan how to expand their capacity to meet their needs for the next several years.

Like the four-minute mile, the recent billion-share trading day was an achievement that had been long anticipated but not fully expected. The previous record of 750 million shares traded was shattered as volume exceeded 1.2 billion shares. And now, the events of recent weeks are causing Wall Street executives to accelerate their plans to increase the capacity of their computer systems.

"If you asked me before last week, I would have said that three years out we will need capacity to handle three and a half, maybe four and a quarter billion shares," said Richard A. Grasso, chairman and chief executive of the New York Stock Exchange. "Now I think it's closer to five or five and a half billion. We want the capacity to handle five times our average daily volume. If you assume that we will be averaging a billion shares a day in three years, and that may be a little aggressive, we need to be able to handle five billion shares." This year, average daily volume has been 520 million shares, and the stated capacity is 2.5 billion shares a day.[1]

Japan's Nippon Meat Packers Inc. is moving to double its original plans for a giant hog production farm near Perryton, Texas, and now hopes to raise 1.1 million animals a year. Nippon disclosed recently in Tokyo that it will invest a total of $240 million to build 175 hog barns, a feed mill, and a slaughterhouse. The operation, known as Texas Farm Inc. plans to produce 55,000 tons of pork annually for shipment to Japan, where demand for the meat is rising amid dwindling supplies.

Texas Farm has acquired 10,000 acres of land south of Perryton, in the northern Texas Panhandle, and plans production with 55,000 sows. Each long metal hog barn can turn out hundreds of uniform animals, closely confined and fed with automatic feeders. These types of operations have proliferated in the Southeast and Midwest but have only entered Texas in the last few years.

As of this writing, Texas Farms has 70 barns completed, with between 6,000 and 7,000 sows, and employs 135 workers. The company so far has invested about $47 million in land and facilities. It has filed four permits for expansion with the Texas Natural Resource Conservation Commission and is awaiting approval of three of them.[2]

The preceding accounts emphasize the importance of facility-planning decisions in a company's strategy for competing in world markets. *Facility planning includes determining how much long-range production capacity is needed, when additional capacity is needed, where the production facilities should be located, and the layout and characteristics of the facilities.* Facility planning is based on the long-range strategic plan for the firm that delineates the product lines to be produced in each time period of the plan. For many firms, long-range capacity and facility location plans are the most important strategic decisions that are made.

These decisions are crucial because, first, the capital investment in machinery, technology, land, and buildings for manufacturing and services is enormous. Once a firm has sunk millions of dollars into a facility, it lives with the decision for a long time.

These decisions therefore receive intense study and are made at the firm's highest level. Second, the long-range strategies are embodied in a firm's facility plans. Such issues as what product lines are to be produced, where they will be sold, and what technologies will be employed reflect the strategic plans of the firm, and these issues are also resolved at the firm's highest level. Third, the operating efficiency of operations is dependent on the capacity of the facilities. Maintenance costs, ease of scheduling, and economy of scale are among the factors affected by the capacity of facilities. Fourth, the capacity of facilities becomes a constraint on many other POM decisions. How much of a product can be economically produced in a specific time period is a limiting factor in short-range production planning.

In this chapter we develop a framework for planning long-range facility capacities, explore some of the important issues in capacity planning today, study some of the methods used to analyze facility location decisions, and examine a variety of issues concerning facility layouts.

LONG-RANGE CAPACITY PLANNING

Capacity-planning decisions usually involve these activities:

1. Estimating the capacities of the present facilities
2. Forecasting the long-range future capacity needs for all products and services
3. Identifying and analyzing sources of capacity to meet future capacity needs
4. Selecting from among the alternative sources of capacity

Definition of Production Capacity

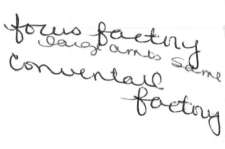

In general, **production capacity** is the maximum production rate of an organization. Several factors underlying the concept of capacity make its use and understanding somewhat complex. First, day-to-day variations such as employee absences, equipment breakdowns, vacations, and material-delivery delays combine to make the output rate of facilities uncertain. Second, the production rates of different products and services are not the same. Thus 50,000 A's or 20,000 B's may be produced per month, or some mix of A's and B's may be produced. The product mix must therefore be taken into account when capacity is estimated. Third, what level of capacity are we talking about? The maximum possible, the capacity based on a five-day–week work schedule, the practical capacity based on the use of existing facilities without the need to activate mothballed facilities, or some other level? Should the capacity level include overtime usage, temporary workers, or outsourcing usage?

The Federal Reserve Board measures and tracks industrial production and capacity in the United States (**http://www.bog.frb.fed.us**). It defines **sustainable practical capacity** as "the greatest level of output that a plant can maintain within the framework of a realistic work schedule, taking account of normal downtime, and assuming sufficient availability of inputs to operate the machinery and equipment in place."[3]

In service organizations, capacity is just as important an issue as in manufacturing. Sustainable practical capacity in service organizations can be defined as the greatest level of output that can be provided with a given level of resources under sustainable operating conditions. These resources include employees, facilities, equipment, materials, and funds. Sustainable operating conditions refer to such things as hours of operation and promotional activities. For example, if a clothing retail store puts on a big sales promotion with all items 30 percent off the regular price, output will increase (more clothes will be sold) but the store may not be able to profitably sustain this operating condition for very long.

*When we
have a focus
plant*

Measurements of Capacity

For firms that produce only a single product or a few homogeneous products, the units used to measure output rate capacity are straightforward: Automobiles per month, tons of coal per day, and barrels of beer per quarter are examples of such measures. When a mix consisting of such products as lawn mowers, grass seed, and lawn furniture is produced from a facility, however, the diversity of the products presents a problem in measuring capacity. In such cases, an aggregate unit of capacity must be established. This aggregate measure of capacity must allow the output rates of the various products to be converted to a common unit of output measure. For example, such measures as tons per hour and sales dollars per month are often used as aggregate measures of capacity among diverse products.

In capacity planning for services, output measures are particularly difficult. In these cases, input rate capacity measures may be used. For example, airlines use available-seat-miles per month, hospitals use available beds per month, tax services use available accountant-days per month, and engineering service firms use labor-hours per month.

"U.S. factory use grew to 85 percent of capacity in December, the highest rate since 1985": What does this mean? Capacity utilization percentage relates output measures to inputs available. For example, a tax service that had 10,000 labor-hours available during March used only 8,200 labor-hours to meet the demands of its customers. We divide the actual labor-hours used by the maximum labor-hours available during a normal schedule to arrive at the percentage of capacity utilization, or 82 percent in this example. Other commonly used capacity utilization calculations are actual automobiles produced per quarter divided by the quarterly automobile production capacity, and occupied airline seats per month divided by the monthly airline seat capacity.

Forecasting Capacity Demand

Providing long-range capacity means making production facilities available—land, buildings, machines, tools, materials, personnel, and utilities. The planning, buying, building, starting up, and training required for a new production facility could take 5 to 10 years, and then such a facility would ordinarily be expected to remain economically productive for another 15 to 20 years. Forecasting demand for the products or services that such a facility is to produce, therefore, must necessarily cover from 10 to 30 years. Forecasts covering these long periods of time are difficult because fundamental changes in the economy, changes in consumer preferences, technological developments, demographic shifts, changes in government regulations, political and military events, and other developments can occur.

Because of the relatively long life of a production facility, product life cycles (introduction, growth, maturity, and decline) will have to be considered. As a product moves through its product life cycle, production capacity needed will also have to change and provisions must be made for expanding or contracting capacity. Technological developments must be anticipated and integrated into facility planning because they can dramatically affect the way that a product is produced, and this affects capacity.

Forecasting production capacity for a product or service usually involves four steps. First, the total demand for a particular product or service from all producers is estimated. Second, the market share (percentage of total demand) for a single company is estimated. Third, the market share is multiplied times the total demand to obtain estimated demand for a single company. Finally, product or service demand is translated into capacity needs. Once a company has obtained its best estimates of demand for its products and services, it must determine how much production capacity should be provided for each product and service.

There are several reasons why the production capacity to be provided does not necessarily equal the amount of products and services expected to be demanded. First, enough capital and other resources may not be economically available to satisfy all the demand. Second, because of the uncertainty of forecasts and the need to link production capacity to operations strategies in terms of competitive priorities, a capacity cushion may be provided. A **capacity cushion** is an additional amount of production capacity added onto the expected demand to allow:

- Extra capacity in case more demand than expected occurs.
- The ability to satisfy demand during peak demand seasons.
- Lower production costs; production facilities operated too close to capacity experience higher costs.
- Product and volume flexibility; responding to customers' needs for different products and higher volumes is possible because of the extra capacity.
- Improved quality of products and services; production facilities operated too close to capacity experience deteriorating quality.

Another important consideration in determining how much long-range capacity for products and services that a single company should provide is how much capacity its competitors are likely to add. If competitors have added or are expected to add capacity that will create an overcapacity situation in an industry, a company should rethink how much capacity, if any, it should add. Videotapes, polyethylene film, semiconductors, automobiles, and personal computers are examples of how excess industry capacity can lead to depressed prices and unprofitability. Business Snapshot 5.1 discusses the excess capacity in the automobile industry in Asia.

BUSINESS SNAPSHOT 5.1

Automakers Facing Overcapacity in Asia

Demand for new Japanese and American import cars has sagged sharply in Southeast Asia as currencies and stock markets in Thailand, Malaysia, and Indonesia have plunged. Despite the economic crisis in the region, the world's giant automakers have continued their expansion push in Southeast Asia.

Even though some industry experts insist they should pull back, General Motors and Ford Motor are busy building huge new assembly plants in Thailand and preparing to open up more factories in Southeast Asia and China. Ford is even opening a new plant in Vietnam. General Motors, Ford,

Chrysler, Toyota, and Honda already operate more than 20 factories in the region.

The giant automakers are betting that the future potential in Southeast Asia is worth the risk. "You have to roll the dice," says J. T. Battenberg III, president of General Motors' auto parts division. However, some Wall Street analysts are concerned about the expansion in Southeast Asia. "This industry is suicidal," says Maryann N. Keller, an auto analyst with Furman Selz, a New York investment banking and brokerage firm. She is concerned because the auto industry already has more worldwide capacity

than it needs and more factories continue to be built. "They should just stop it. This isn't going to be a 12-month problem in Thailand," Ms. Keller says. According to Nariman Behravesh, chief international economist at Standard & Poor's DRI, "There is going to have to be some shake-out in the auto industry in Asia sometime in the next three to five years."

In light of the auto industry capacity expansion occurring in Asia, Chrysler dropped its plans to open a new factory in Vietnam. It decided to focus its capacity expansion plans on South America instead of East Asia.

Sources: Meredith, Robyn. "Auto Giants Build a Glut of Asian Plants, Just as Demand Falls." *New York Times*, November 5, 1997, C1, C8; "Despite Slowdown in Asia, Auto Makers Keep Building." *New York Times*, November 5, 1997, A1.

Table 5.1	Ways of Changing Long-Range Capacity

Type of Capacity Change	Ways of Accommodating Long-Range Capacity Changes
Expansion	1. Subcontract with other companies to become suppliers of the expanding firm's components or entire products. 2. Acquire other companies, facilities, or resources. 3. Develop sites, build buildings, buy equipment. 4. Expand, update, or modify existing facilities. 5. Reactivate facilities on standby status.
Reduction	1. Sell off existing facilities, sell inventories, and lay off or transfer employees. 2. Mothball facilities and place on standby status, sell inventories, and lay off or transfer employees. 3. Develop and phase in new products as other products decline.

Ways of Changing Capacity

Once the long-range capacity needs are estimated through long-range forecasts, many avenues exist to provide for the capacity. Firms may either find themselves in a capacity shortage situation, where present capacity is insufficient to meet the forecast demand for their products and services, or they may have present capacity in excess of the expected future needs. Table 5.1 lists some of the ways in which managers can accommodate the changing long-range capacity needs of organizations. Business Snapshot 5.2 illustrates how companies sometimes face a shortage or a surplus of capacity.

One avenue usually preferred by operations managers to maintain high levels of facility utilization in spite of declining long-range demand for their present products and services is the phasing-in of new products to replace older and declining ones. Figure 5.1 shows how a firm might design and develop new products as old ones decline over time. This time-phasing may be a key motivating force behind the development of new products and services.

If operations managers decide on building new facilities as the best alternative source of additional capacity, how to time-phase in the capacity remains an important issue. Business Snapshot 5.3 illustrates how one company tries to time-phase the opening of its new facilities to match demand.

Economies of Scale

For a given production facility, there is an annual volume of outputs that results in the least average unit cost. This level of output is called the facility's **best operating level.** Figure 5.2 illustrates this concept. Notice that as the annual volume of outputs increases outward from zero in a particular production facility, average unit costs fall. These declining costs result from fixed costs being spread over more and more units, longer production runs that result in a smaller proportion of labor being allocated to setups and machine changeovers, proportionally less material scrap, and other economies. Such savings, which are called economies of scale, continue to accrue as the volume of outputs increases to the best operating level for that particular facility.

Past this point, however, additional volume of outputs results in ever-increasing average unit costs. These increasing costs arise from increased congestion of materials and workers, which contributes to increasing inefficiency, difficulty in scheduling, damaged goods, reduced morale, increased use of overtime, and other diseconomies.

BUSINESS SNAPSHOT 5.2

Too Little and Too Much Capacity

The following accounts of Boeing and automakers in Brazil illustrate how companies sometimes scramble to increase capacity and other times scramble to decrease capacity.

Business is so good at Boeing that it's losing money. Just three years ago The Boeing Co., the world's largest manufacturer of commercial jets, reduced its production capacity and cut employment by 12,000 people because of slow sales. Now Boeing has been blindsided by a sudden turnaround in orders and has recently hired 32,000 more people, with plans to hire even more.

Ironically, the recent doubling of jet orders is going to cost Boeing $2.6 billion in the coming year, news that caused its stock price to tumble more than 7 percent. In an effort to meet all the new orders, Boeing more than doubled its rate of production from 18 planes a month to 43. It tried to increase capacity as quickly as possible. Unfortunately, the poor capacity planning for the higher rate of production caused many problems, such as a lack of skilled labor, parts shortages, a snarled assembly line, and late aircraft deliveries. To try to unscramble the problems, Boeing has had to suspend production of some jetliner models and slow production of others. It estimates that six to nine months may be needed to get all the problems straightened out.

The world's automakers, hit hard by Brazil's recent economic crisis, are responding quickly. Until the economic crisis, Brazilian auto sales were expected to boom in the coming year. General Motors, Ford, Daimler-Chrysler, Toyota, Fiat, Honda, Renault, and Mercedes all have new plants in the works. But now, auto sales are expected to plummet.

In response, the automakers have quickly tried to cut back production and capacity. General Motors is slicing production 25 percent. Ford shut its Brazilian plant for two weeks. Volkswagen began cutting the workweek at two of its plants in São Paulo, operating only three days a week instead of five. Analysts say the automaker's quick moves are wise, given the past volatility of Brazil's economy.

Sources: "Boeing Hitting Turbulence: 747 Production to Halt 20 Days; 737 Slowdown." *Houston Chronicle,* October 4, 1997, 2C; "Boeing Victimized by Success." *Houston Chronicle,* October 23, 1997, 3C; Maynard, Micheline. "Auto Industry Reacts Quickly." *USA Today,* November 17, 1997, 3B; "Super Factory—Or Super Headache." *Business Week,* July 31, 2000, 66.

Figure 5.1 | Effects of Time-Phasing Products on Facility Capacity Utilization

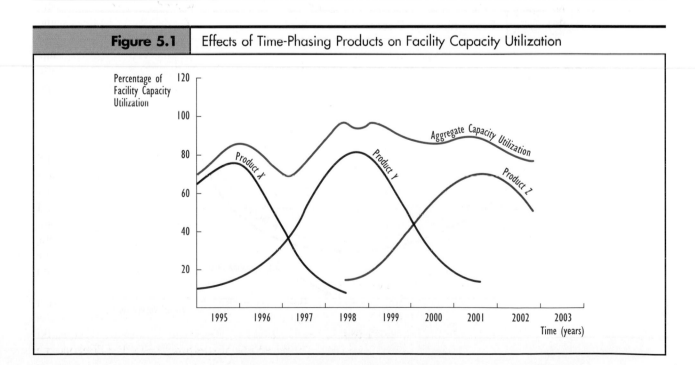

BUSINESS SNAPSHOT 5.3

Intel Delays Opening of New Plant

In 1996 Intel announced that it would build a new $1.3 billion computer chip plant near the Alliance Airport in Fort Worth, Texas. The plant was to produce the current logic memory chips, the "brain" of most computers. Intel began construction in July 1997 on the new facility, and planned to initially hire 800 to 1,000 employees, thinking that number might grow to more than 5,000 employees over five years.

About this same time a sudden downturn in the market for flash memory chips, caused by increased competition and oversupply, caused Intel to switch its production plans. Another new plant in Israel had been scheduled to produce a different kind of chip, a flash memory chip, but with the market downturn Intel decided to produce the logic memory chips in Israel instead of Fort Worth. To avoid building unneeded capacity, Intel announced in late 1997 that it would postpone the opening of the Fort Worth plant for a year.

In early 1998, after already investing $70 million in the Fort Worth site construction, Intel announced that it would further postpone the opening of the Fort Worth site until late 2002 or early 2003, at which time the factory would produce the next genera-

tion of logic memory chips. Because the chip market was still down, Intel said that it did not need the extra capacity yet.

In 1999 the chip market rebounded strongly, and in 2000 Intel expected to make about $5 billion of capital expenditures worldwide, mainly to expand capacity. In early 2000 Intel had 12 chip-making plants around the world. Unfortunately for Fort Worth, Intel chose to expand its manufacturing plant in Chandler, Arizona, to produce the chips that had been planned for Fort Worth. As of late 2000, the partially completed Fort Worth facility was still on hold.

Sources: Goldstein, Alan. "Intel Delays FW Plan Production." *Dallas Morning News,* October 24, 1997, 1D, 11D; Piller, Dan. "Intel Plant Delayed by One Year." *Fort Worth Star-Telegram,* October 24, 1997, 1A, 21A; Ahles, Andrea. "Intel Puts Fort Worth Plant on Indefinite Hold." *Fort Worth Star-Telegram,* January 26, 2000, 1A, 6A.

| **Figure 5.2** | Economies and Diseconomies of Scale |

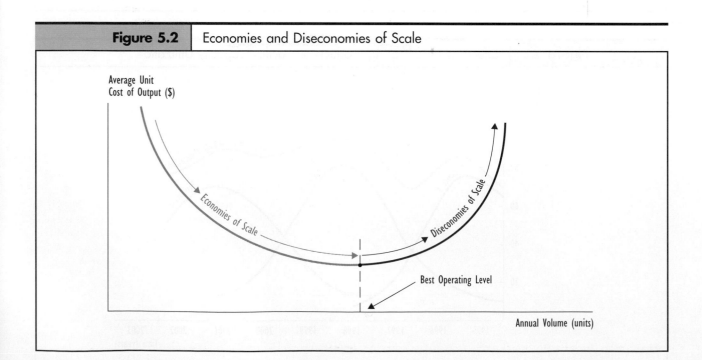

The impact of such factors, which are called diseconomies of scale, increases at an accelerating rate past the best operating level for the facility.

Because each facility has its own unique best operating level and, all other things being equal, facilities with higher best operating levels require greater investments, operations managers must decide between two general approaches to expanding long-range capacity:

1. Invest heavily in one large facility that requires a big initial investment, but one that will have a higher best operating level and that ultimately will fulfill the capacity needs of the firm. In other words, build the ultimate facility now and grow into it.
2. Plan to invest in an initial facility design now and expand or modify that facility as needed to raise the best operating levels to meet the long-range demand for products and services. In other words, expand long range capacity incrementally as needed to match future capacity demands.

Figure 5.3 compares these strategies. Notice that Designs A, B, and C exhibit best operating levels at 240,000, 450,000, and 640,000 annual volume, respectively. Let us suppose, for example, that our long-range capacity needs were estimated to be 640,000 annual volume 10 years from now. How do we best provide for this long-range capacity, incrementally or all at once?

As shown in Figure 5.3, the strategy of initially selecting Design A and subsequently modifying that design to Design B and then to Design C would seem to make sense because the average unit cost tends to be the lowest. Additionally, this incremental approach may be less risky because if our forecast capacity needs do not

Figure 5.3 Increases in Incremental Facility Capacity

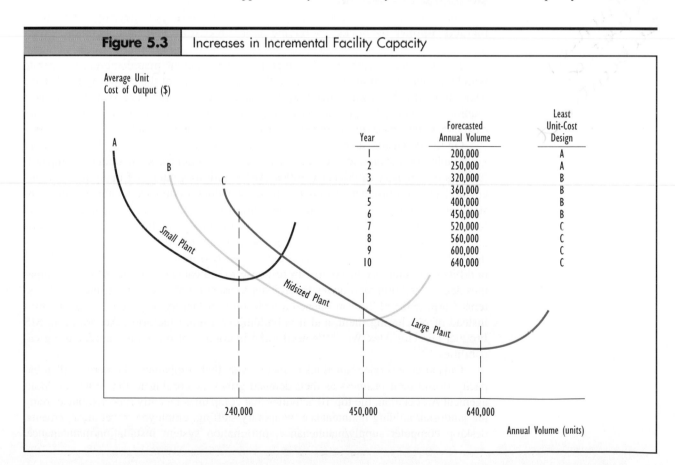

materialize, then the expansion program could be stopped in time to avoid unnecessary investment in unneeded expansion. On the other hand, one large construction project is likely to involve less investment and costs than several smaller projects because there would be no redundant construction work or interruptions of production. Because of inflation, construction costs may be less if we build all the needed capacity now. Furthermore, we avoid the risk of having to turn down future business if our long-range forecast turns out to be too low and our capacity is inadequate. *But one of the major causes of industry overcapacity is the argument for larger facilities to achieve greater economies of scale.* A major concern about building the big facility now is because funds will be tied up in excess capacity on which no return will be realized for several years. This results either in great additional interest expense or in income forgone owing to not having the funds committed to other types of investments that would generate revenue.

Choosing between expanding capacity all at once or incrementally is not a clearcut choice for most firms. In cases of mature products with stable and predictable demand patterns, firms are more receptive to building the ultimate facility now. With new products, however, firms lean more toward an incremental expansion strategy because of the riskiness of forecasts and the unpredictable nature of their long-range demands. The eventual choice will differ from firm to firm because of the nature of their products, the availability of investment funds, their attitude toward risk, and other factors.

Subcontractor Networks

A viable alternative to larger capacity production facilities is to develop **subcontractor and supplier networks**. By relying on less backward vertical integration, parent manufacturers develop long-range contractual relationships with suppliers of parts, components, and assemblies. This approach allows parent manufacturers to operate with less capacity within their own facilities because much of their capacity needs have been "farmed out," or outsourced, to their suppliers. Not only does such an approach require less capital for production facilities, but parent manufacturers can also more easily vary their capacity during slack or peak periods of demand.

On the downside, a company that increases its use of outsourcing becomes more vulnerable to subcontractors' capacity shortages. Consider the semiconductor chip (silicon wafer) industry in the early 2000s. An operations strategy of many manufacturers of electronics products is to purchase semiconductor chips from subcontractors instead of producing the chips themselves. Unfortunately for these companies, demand for semiconductor chips had been booming worldwide, which caused a severe shortage of chips. For example, Taiwan electronics manufacturer Universal Scientific Industrial Co. had been able to obtain only about two-thirds of the chips it needed to build its computer circuit boards. In response to the capacity shortage, some companies decided to build their own silicon-wafer fabrication plants. Silicon Integrated Systems Corp. (SIS) of Taiwan opened a $340 million factory to produce its own chips instead of purchasing them, and it is building two more factories. According to SIS Product Director Alex Wu, "We need to be in control of our own manufacturing capabilities."[4]

Outsourcing service functions is another way that companies can increase their capacity to run their business as their demand grows. According to the American Management Association, the top 10 activities that companies recently reported outsourcing are janitorial/building maintenance, temporary staffing, employee travel arrangements, desktop computer supply/maintenance, information system installation/maintenance, component manufacturing, moving/storage, delivery, advertising, and payroll. Some activities that companies expect to outsource more in the future are customer service, bookkeeping, telemarketing, mailroom, product design, data processing, sales representation, and benefits administration.[5] Business Snapshot 5.4 describes a typical outsourcing company.

Economies of Scope

Another important concept that must be taken into account as we consider economies of scale is **economies of scope.** Economies of scope refer to the ability to produce many product models in one highly flexible production facility more cheaply than in separate production facilities. Traditional thinking has assumed that as capital investment, mechanization, and automation are increased, product flexibility must decrease and that automated production can be justified only for high-volume products because of economies of scale. But technological breakthroughs in the development of programmable automation, described in Chapter 6, have overturned this way of thinking. Now, highly flexible and programmable automation allows production systems to change to other products quickly and inexpensively, with the result that economies are created by spreading the cost of automated facilities over many product lines.

Analyzing Capacity-Planning Decisions

Facility-planning decisions can be analyzed using several different approaches. **Break-even analysis,** discussed in Chapter 4, is commonly used to compare the cost functions of two or more facility alternatives. **Present-value analysis** is also particularly useful in long-range capacity planning. **Computer simulation** and **waiting line analysis,** illustrated in Chapter 9, can also be used to analyze capacity-planning decisions. **Linear programming,** discussed in Chapter 8, is also used in these decisions.

BUSINESS SNAPSHOT 5.4

Outsourcing Provides Additional Capacity

Loan Link Lending Center in Grand Prairie, Texas, is a young outsourcing company. Established in 1996, the 55-employee company handles loan applications and approves or denies loans for nearly 100 clients, mostly credit unions.

When a credit union or bank customer calls a toll-free number, a Loan Link employee can answer with the institution's name, thanks to a caller-ID system. With the stroke of a key, the lender's standards for making a loan appear on a computer monitor. As the employee enters data such as income, debt, and loan amount, a request for a credit report flashes to a credit bureau and is returned within seconds. Using this and other information, the employee can inform the customer institution about how well the potential borrower meets the institution's standards for receiving a loan.

"I thought everyone would sign up for nights and weekends only" (when banks and credit unions typically have few employees working), says Loan Link President Brett Christiansen, referring to his firm's 24-hours-a-day, seven-days-a-week service. "But 95 percent of them also use us for backup" when the institution's own employees are swamped and it needs more capacity to process loans. Loan Link's use of the latest technologies and its operations design allows it to provide services cheaper and faster than can many of its customer institutions. To its customers, Loan Link is able to provide instant additional capacity on demand.

Source: Fuquay, Jim. "Outsourcing Helps Businesses Get More Done for Less." *Arlington Star-Telegram,* April 24, 2000, Tarrant Business Section, 16–17.

In addition to these techniques, decision trees are particularly helpful in analyzing facility-planning decisions.

Decision Tree Analysis

Decisions about facility planning are complex. They often are difficult to organize because they are **multiphase decisions,** those that involve several interdependent decisions that must be made in a sequence. Decision trees were developed for multiphase decisions as aids to analysts who must see clearly what decisions must be made, in what sequence the decisions must occur, and the interdependence of the decisions. This ability to structure the way we think about multiphase decisions simplifies the analysis.

Example 5.1 demonstrates the essentials of decision tree analysis. This form of analysis gives managers:

- A way of structuring complex multiphase decisions by mapping decisions from the present to the future
- A direct way of dealing with uncertain events
- An objective way of determining the relative value of each decision alternative

A note of caution should be observed in regard to the interpretation of expected value (EV) in decision tree analysis. One error that we might make is to interpret the EV for each decision literally and absolutely. The EVs are only **relative measures** of value and not **absolute measures.** Consider the profits (losses) in Example 5.1. These are possible outcomes to the study alternative: $30,000, $490,000, ($110,000), or $2,000. Only one of these values will ultimately be returned to the decision maker. The EV of $66,000 will never be returned to the firm. The EV is only a measure of value of this alternative relative to the other alternatives.

Expected value as a decision criterion varies in effectiveness depending on the decision situation. With a one-time decision, which is usually the case with facility-planning decisions, expected value is at best only a relative measure of value.

But even if expected values or probabilities are not included in decision trees, the value of decision trees as a useful way of organizing the way we think about complex multiphase decisions must be recognized. This tool allows decision makers to see clearly what decisions must be made, in what sequence they must occur, and their interdependence. Expected value, if interpreted correctly, is a fringe benefit.

Regardless of the specific techniques employed to analyze long-range capacity-planning decisions, you may be assured that these decisions are among the most analyzed decisions that involve operations managers. The reasons for this involvement reside in the importance that these decisions hold for these managers, as we discussed early in the chapter.

When existing facility capacities are inadequate to meet the long-range capacity needs and new facilities are to be built, rented, or purchased, an important issue that must be resolved is where to locate the new facilities.

Example 5.1	Decision Tree: To Manufacture or Not to Manufacture?

Biltmore Manufacturing has developed a promising new product. The firm's management faces three choices: It can sell the idea for the new product to a company for $20,000, it can hire a consultant to study the market and then make a decision, or it can arrange financing for building a factory and then manufacture and market the product.

The study will cost Biltmore $10,000, and its management believes that there is about a 50–50 chance that a favorable market will be found. If the study is unfavorable, management figures that it can still sell the idea for $12,000. If the study is favorable, it figures that it can sell the idea for $40,000. But even if a favorable market is found, the chance of an ultimately successful product is about 2 out of 5. A successful product will return $500,000. Even with an unfavorable study, a successful product can be expected about once in every ten new-product introductions. If Biltmore's management decides to manufacture the product without a study, it figures there is only a 1-in-4 chance of its being successful. A product failure costs $100,000. What should Biltmore do?

Solution

1. Draw a tree from left to right with squares (□) for decisions and circles (○) for chance events. These decisions and chance events are often called **nodes** or **forks.** Write the outcome values (profits or losses) in the right margin, and write the probability of chance events in parentheses on the branches to the right of the circles.

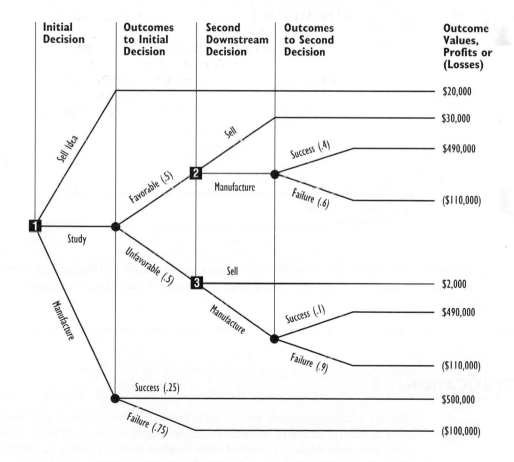

2. Working from right to left, compute the expected value (EV) at each circle for chance events to the second downstream decisions. Write the EVs to the right of each circle. For example, the EV of the chance events to manufacture—decision ② —is computed: EV = 0.4($490,000) + 0.6(−$110,000) = $130,000. Continuing to work from right to left, decide which

alternative of the second downstream decisions (② and ③) has the highest EV. Write the selected EV to the right of the decision boxes and prune (–/ /–) all other branches. Continue working from right to left as before, and compute the EV for the initial decision. For example, the EV for the study alternative is computed: EV = 0.5($130,000) + 0.5($2,000) = $66,000.

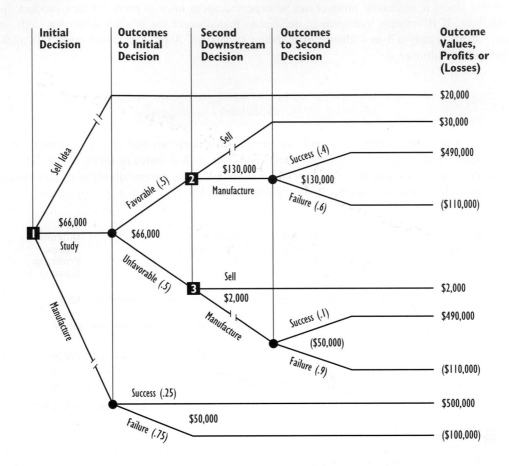

| Initial Decision | Outcomes to Initial Decision | Second Downstream Decision | Outcomes to Second Decision | Outcome Values, Profits or (Losses) |

3. The EV for the initial decision is $66,000. The sequence of decisions is deduced by following the unpruned branches of the tree from left to right: study, if favorable, manufacture; if unfavorable, sell.

FACILITY LOCATION

Facility location decisions are not made lightly. On the contrary, they usually involve long and costly studies of alternative locations before the eventual site is selected. Those who have been through several of these location studies generally conclude that there is no clear-cut best location, but rather that there are several good locations. If one site is clearly superior to all others in all respects, the location decision is an easy one. Typically, however, several site candidates, each with its strengths and weaknesses, emerge as good choices; and the location decision becomes a **trade-off decision:** You can gain

domestically or internation
what region

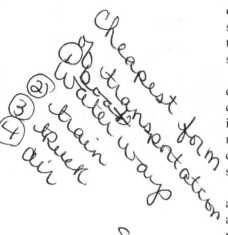

one type of benefit only by giving up another. These trade-off decisions among sites can be agonizing and are usually resolved only after long and careful weighing of the pros and cons of each location.

Location decisions can be better understood by examining the factors that commonly affect the final selection of facility locations.

Factors Affecting Location Decisions

Selecting a facility location usually involves a sequence of decisions. This sequence can include a national decision, a regional decision, a community decision, and a site decision. Figure 5.4 shows this location decision sequence.

First, management must decide whether the facility will be located *internationally* or *domestically*. Not many years ago, this choice would have received only minor consideration. Today, however, with the internationalization of business, managers are routinely considering *where in the world* their facilities should be located. Business Snapshot 5.5 illustrates how facility location decisions transcend national boundaries.

Once the international-versus-domestic issue has been resolved, management must decide the general geographic region within the country where the facility is to be located. This **regional decision** may involve choosing among a few national regions, as in Figure 5.4, or among several regions within a much smaller geographic area. Figure 5.5 illustrates the ranking of U.S. regions and states as desirable manufacturing locations, prepared by a Chicago-based international accounting and management consulting company.

Once the geographic region decision has been made, management must decide among several communities within the region. Figure 5.4 also lists some of the factors affecting the community decision. Most of the factors taken into consideration in the regional decision are also present in the community decision.

The **community decision** has some additional factors affecting the location choice. Community services and taxes, attitudes and incentives toward new facility locations, availability and costs of sites, environmental impact, banking services, and management preferences are important inputs in deciding among communities.

Finally, once a community has been selected, a site within that community must be chosen. Some additional factors emerge in **site selection:** size and cost of each site, proximity to transportation systems and related industries or services, availability of utilities and materials and supplies, and zoning restrictions.

Types of Facilities and Their Dominant Locational Factors

Have you wondered why:

- Many automobile manufacturers are in Detroit,
- Many high-tech computer R&D firms are in Silicon Valley in Northern California,
- Several personal computer and chip manufacturers are in Austin, Texas,
- Several mass-merchandising mail-order houses are in Chicago, and yet,
- Small convenience grocery stores seem to be on about every other corner in your town?

Are there reasons why one type of company is located near its raw materials while another is located near its customers? And why would companies that are obvious competitors locate right next door to one another? These questions suggest that each type of company has a few dominant factors that ultimately determine its facility location decisions.

Figure 5.4   The Facility Location Decision

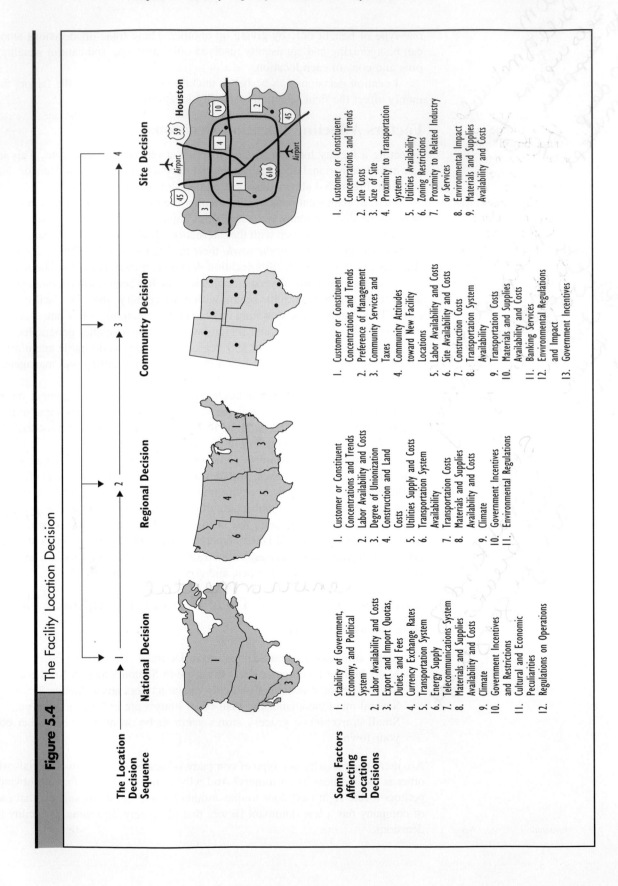

The Location Decision Sequence

1 → **National Decision**

2 → **Regional Decision**

3 → **Community Decision**

4 → **Site Decision**

Some Factors Affecting Location Decisions

National Decision
1. Stability of Government, Economy, and Political System
2. Labor Availability and Costs
3. Export and Import Quotas, Duties, and Fees
4. Currency Exchange Rates
5. Transportation System
6. Energy Supply
7. Telecommunications System
8. Materials and Supplies Availability and Costs
9. Climate
10. Government Incentives and Restrictions
11. Cultural and Economic Peculiarities
12. Regulations on Operations

Regional Decision
1. Customer or Constituent Concentrations and Trends
2. Labor Availability and Costs
3. Degree of Unionization
4. Construction and Land Costs
5. Utilities Supply and Costs
6. Transportation System Availability
7. Transportation Costs
8. Materials and Supplies Availability and Costs
9. Climate
10. Government Incentives
11. Environmental Regulations

Community Decision
1. Customer or Constituent Concentrations and Trends
2. Preference of Management
3. Community Services and Taxes
4. Community Attitudes toward New Facility Locations
5. Labor Availability and Costs
6. Site Availability and Costs
7. Construction Costs
8. Transportation System Availability
9. Transportation Costs
10. Materials and Supplies Availability and Costs
11. Banking Services
12. Environmental Regulations and Impact
13. Government Incentives

Site Decision
1. Customer or Constituent Concentrations and Trends
2. Site Costs
3. Size of Site
4. Proximity to Transportation Systems
5. Utilities Availability
6. Zoning Restrictions
7. Proximity to Related Industry or Services
8. Environmental Impact
9. Materials and Supplies Availability and Costs

BUSINESS SNAPSHOT 5.5

Global Facility Location at DEC

Digital Equipment Corporation (DEC) is a large computer manufacturer based in the United States. More than half of its revenues comes from over 80 countries outside the United States, principally Europe. DEC has operated over 30 plants in more than a dozen countries.

In deciding on the international locations of new manufacturing plants and distribution centers, DEC considers a number of factors:

- Location of customers and suppliers
- Location and availability of inexpensive skilled labor
- Length of material pipeline in distance and time
- Transit time and cost of various transportation modes
- Cost of materials in different nations
- Significance and location of tax havens (tax-free trade zones)
- Offset trade (value of goods and services purchased in a

country to balance the sale of products in that country)
- Local content targets (percentage of components, by value, for a product)
- Export regulations, duty rates, and drawback policies

Based on these factors, DEC uses a linear programming–based approach to develop 18-month and five-year plans for facility locations, capacity plans, and sourcing strategies around the world.

Source: Arntzen, Bruce C., Gerald G. Brown, Terry P. Harrison, and Linda L. Trafton. "Global Supply Chain Management at Digital Equipment Corporation." *Interfaces* 25, no. 1 (January–February 1995): 69–93.

| **Figure 5.5** | Rankings of U.S. Regions and States as Desirable Manufacturing Locations |

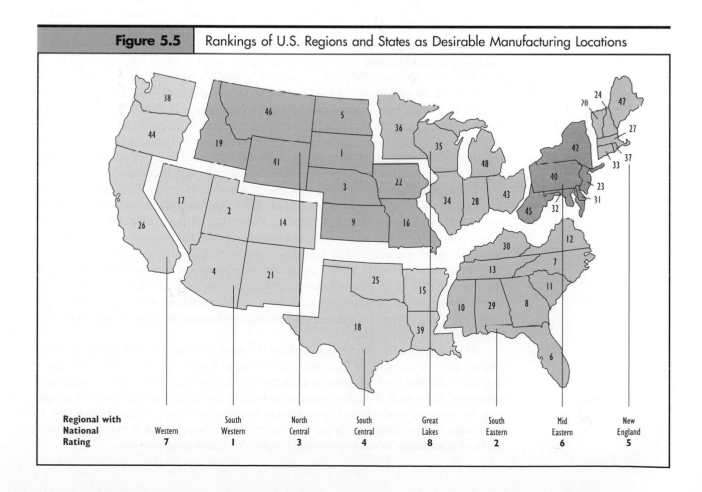

Why do some industries cluster together by location, and some do business in widespread areas? Convenience stores such as this one can be found very near their competitors.

Table 5.2 rates the relative importance of some of the factors affecting location decisions for different types of facilities. Mining, quarrying, and heavy manufacturing have **capital-intensive** facilities that are expensive to build, cover large geographic areas, and use great quantities of heavy and bulky raw materials. Additionally, their production processes discard large amounts of wastes, total finished outputs weigh much less than total raw material inputs, enormous quantities of utilities are absorbed, and products are shipped to only a few customers. These facilities consequently tend to be located near their raw material sources rather than near their markets so as to minimize the total transportation costs of inputs and outputs. Additionally, they tend to select sites where land and construction costs are relatively inexpensive and where waste disposal is not expected to harm the environment. The availability of an abundant supply of utilities and the proximity of railroad service are also necessary.

Light manufacturing facilities make such items as electronic components, small mechanical parts, and assembled products. These facilities do not necessarily locate near either raw material sources or markets. Rather, they strike a balance between transportation costs of inputs and outputs, and other locational factors therefore tend to dominate the location decision. The availability and cost of labor is important in the location decisions of these facilities, whereas transportation cost is of lesser importance. If the trend toward more factory automation increases as expected, labor cost could become less important in factory location decisions in the future. The trend could be toward more dispersed, decentralized production systems with many small plants that utilize flexible automation.

The location of warehouses is perhaps the most straightforward location decision among the various types of facilities. The dominant factors are those affecting incoming and outgoing transportation costs. Although it is desirable and indeed frequently necessary to be near enough to markets to both communicate effectively with recipients of outgoing products and react quickly to customer orders, transportation cost is the paramount locational factor for warehouses. These facilities are therefore often subjects of quantitative economic evaluations such as linear programming.

Table 5.2	Relative Importance of Locational Factors in Types of Facilities

Factor Affecting Location Decision	Mining, Quarrying, Heavy Manufacturing	Light Manufacturing	R&D and High-Tech Manufacturing	Warehousing	Retailing	Customer Services for Profit	Local Government Services	Health and Emergency Services
1. Proximity to concentrations of customers or constituents	C	C	B	B	A	A	A	A
2. Labor availability and costs	B	A	B	B	B	A	B	B
3. Attractiveness of community for recruiting professionals	C	B	A	C	C	C	C	C
4. Degree of unionization	A	A	C	B	B	B	C	B
5. Construction and land costs	A	B	B	B	B	B	B	B
6. Proximity to transportation facilities	A	B	C	A	B	C	C	C
7. Incoming transportation costs	A	B	C	A	B	C	C	C
8. Outgoing transportation costs	B	B	C	A	C	C	C	C
9. Utilities availability and costs	A	B	C	C	C	C	C	C
10. Proximity to raw materials and supplies	A	B	C	C	C	C	C	C
11. Zoning restrictions and environmental impact	A	B	C	C	C	B	C	C

Note: A = very important, B = important, C = less important.

The success and survival of R&D and high-tech manufacturing companies depend in large measure on their ability to recruit and retain scientists, engineers, and other professionals. The attractiveness of community lifestyle and proximity to universities are predominant factors in recruiting these employees. And when several companies with similar technology interests locate near one another, a community of scientific associations and a better trained community workforce benefit all. For these reasons we see communities like these being attractive:

- Telecom Corridor, telecommunications in Richardson, Texas
- Laser Lane, lasers and electro-optics in Orlando, Florida

- Silicon Prairie, software development in Champaign/Urbana, Illinois
- Medical Alley, medical instruments, health care in Minneapolis/St. Paul, Minnesota
- Biomed Mountains, medical devices, artificial organs in Salt Lake City, Utah

Retailing facilities and customer services for profit are located near concentrations of target customers. All other locational factors are subordinate to this single factor. The studies of these facility locations typically involve the identification of target customer residential concentrations, traffic data on nearby streets, growth trends of communities and suburbs, discretionary spending levels of nearby neighborhoods, and other demographic information. Because some service facilities such as dry cleaners, medical clinics, and photo processors can discard large quantities of waste paper, chemicals, and spent supplies, zoning restrictions and environmental impact can play more important roles than in retailing location decisions.

Local government service facilities also are usually located near concentrations of their constituents. Local government services are often grouped together so that constituents can economize in their time, effort, and transportation costs by making multiple calls with one trip. Additionally, these services are grouped in order to allow interagency interactions. For example, county jails tend to be located near county court buildings so as to minimize the transportation of prisoners between the jails and the courts.

Health and emergency services are traditionally located near concentrations of constituents because the key consideration in selecting locations is that such locations result in the lowest overall response times between the constituents and the services. The minimizing of property loss and loss of life is the overriding consideration in these locations. Fire stations are typically located near concentrations of residential constituents to minimize the time it takes for fire engines to arrive at fire scenes. Ambulance services are similarly located near these community neighborhood population centers to minimize the time required to transport patients to hospitals and health clinics. Hospitals are usually located near the centers of community population density concentrations.

The type of facility, the nature of its products and services, and the nature of its daily activities affect the importance that each locational factor plays in location decisions. Each location decision is unique because the nature of each facility and its daily operation is unique. The understanding of the factors that affect these decisions and of their relative importance in locating several classes of facilities provides a useful framework for analysis.

Data, Politics, Incentives, and Preemptive Tactics

The amount of data needed to compare facility location alternatives can be immense, and the sources of these data are numerous. One source is the *Business Site/Construction Planner* published by *Dun's Review*. Other valuable sources of location data are the chambers of commerce of the cities under consideration. Another surefire way for a firm to be inundated with facility location data is to prepare a press release to the news media announcing its intention of locating a new facility that will employ 500 people and have an annual payroll of $20 million.

Once governments, chambers of commerce, and communities get wind of a new facility being planned, the political aspects of facility location decisions become apparent. There seems to be no end to the extremes to which government and civic organizations will go to woo new facilities to their communities. For example, when Chrysler-Mitsubishi was looking for a facility location for its Diamond-Star automobile assembly plant, the news media provided almost day-by-day and blow-by-blow accounts of where the research team was visiting, which communities had made presentations to the company, and which state politicians had visited the corporate offices. Community after community rolled out the red carpet for the visiting team, and the list of incentives offered to the company grew. The facility was finally located in Bloomington, Illinois. This account illustrates that economic incentives in the form of reduced income tax, property tax, and other taxes; free or discounted land, buildings, utilities, roads, parking lots; and other freebies are powerful factors in facility location decisions. Business Snapshot 5.6 illustrates how government incentives can persuade companies about where they locate new facilities.

Once a firm announces that it intends to locate a facility somewhere, conversations begin at the various headquarters of the firm's competitors. Such an announcement is the first step in a **preemptive tactic,** and it usually has at least two effects. First, if competitors had been contemplating expanding their capacity, they may fear overcapacity within the industry and be scared off. Second, if a specific location choice is announced, competitors may be dissuaded from locating in the region of the announced location. Such a preemptive tactic is thus aimed at deterring competition.

Location decisions are very complex. So many variables are related in complicated ways and so much uncertainty is present that it is difficult to mentally juggle all the information simultaneously. Because of this complexity, analysis techniques tend to analyze only part of the relevant information in sometimes rather simple ways; thus,

---

BUSINESS SNAPSHOT 5.6

Texas Incentives Not Enough for Intel

In the late 1990s Intel decided that it needed to build another computer chip manufacturing plant, at an estimated cost of $1.3 billion. After much negotiation and analysis, Intel chose Fort Worth, Texas, as the site for its new plant. As mentioned in Business Snapshot 5.3, after investing $70 million in the initial construction of the plant, a downturn in the computer chip market caused Intel to halt construction.

About a year later, Intel reconsidered its choice of where to locate its new chip plant: in Fort Worth or in Chandler, Arizona, where it had an existing facility.

Intel finally chose Arizona over Texas in large part because of the differences in government incentive packages.

Arizona was willing to provide the tax incentives that Intel requested, according to Intel's government relations manager Diana Daggett, whereas Texas lawmakers were not willing to change the tax laws to allow those incentive levels. Two tax changes that were requested by Intel from Texas were one that would give companies tax breaks from local school districts for expansion project investments exceeding $500 million and another that

would allow a tax break on the state's franchise tax for high-dollar investments. Texas law prohibits making a tax deal with just one company, so any tax system change must apply to all companies in the state.

On the other hand, Arizona allowed Intel to build in a foreign trade zone that allows property and capital to be taxed at a different rate from other parts of the state. Says economist Ray Perryman, president of Perryman Group, locating in Texas would have cost Intel around $80 million more in taxes over the life of the plant, compared with Arizona.

Sources: Moritz, John. "Intel's Tax Break Was Too Costly for Texas, Lawmakers Say." *Fort Worth Star-Telegram,* January 26, 2000, 7A; Ahles, Andrea. "Intel Puts Fort Worth Plant on Indefinite Hold." *Fort Worth Star-Telegram,* January 26, 2000, 1A, 6A.

in making the decision, the decision maker is left the task of intelligently integrating the results of the analysis with the remainder of the information. The analysis techniques that are presented in the following sections should be viewed with this perspective: They provide an orderly way of analyzing part of the relevant information present in a location decision. It is up to management to use the results of the analysis along with other information to make the final location decision.

Analyzing Retailing and Other Service Locations

Table 5.2 showed that the dominant factor in location decisions for some facilities is proximity to concentrations of customers. Facilities such as retailing, customer services for profit, and health and emergency services are types of facilities that attempt to locate near their customers/constituents.

Retailing and other service organizations typically perform empirically based studies of alternative facility locations. Table 5.3 shows the basic steps in these studies. First, an organization's management must understand why customers buy its products and services. Next, market research must be performed to determine target customer characteristics. When large concentrations of target customers are identified, alternative locations near these concentrations can be considered. Enormous data-gathering activities can occur at this point in the study. Traffic patterns, local spending and income data, competition, and projected growth trends are estimated for each location. Revenues and operating costs are projected for each location. The projected profits based on empirical data become the basis for comparing the location alternatives under consideration.

Analyzing Industrial Facility Locations

Proximity to concentrations of customers is a less dominant factor in locating industrial facilities. Factors such as transportation costs, labor cost and availability, materials cost and availability, and utilities cost tend to dominate the location decision.

Industrial facility location decisions can range from the simpler problem of where in the United States to locate one warehouse to the more complex decision of where throughout the world to locate five manufacturing plants. One fairly simple approach to analyze alternative locations for a single facility is **conventional cost analysis.** Table 5.4 shows a cost analysis for three alternative locations for a new steel mill. The advantage of this type of cost analysis is its ease of communication

Table 5.3	Steps in Analyzing Service Facility Location Decisions

1. **Consumer behavior research:** Why do customers buy our products and services?
2. **Market research:** Who are our customers, and what are their characteristics?
3. **Data gathering for each location alternative:** Where are concentrations of target customers? What are their traffic and spending patterns? What are the growth trends and degree of present and projected competition?
4. **Revenue projections for each location alternative:** What are the relevant economic projections, discretionary spending projections, competition activity, and time-phased location revenue?
5. **Profit projections for each location alternative:** What are the projected revenues less time-phased operating costs?

Table 5.4	Cost Comparisons: Three Alternative Manufacturing Locations for a Steel Mill								
	ST. LOUIS, MISSOURI			CLEVELAND, OHIO			MILWAUKEE, WISCONSIN		
Cost Element	Year 1	Year 5	Year 10	Year 1	Year 5	Year 10	Year 1	Year 5	Year 10
Transportation in	$18.5	$22.9	$28.4	$17.4	$21.5	$26.8	$16.4	$19.9	$24.6
Transportation out	6.1	7.6	10.2	6.0	7.6	10.0	6.1	7.6	10.1
Labor	14.7	19.4	26.2	18.6	22.7	30.5	21.5	25.4	33.9
Raw materials	30.3	39.4	57.1	29.5	39.1	56.3	28.9	38.6	55.2
Supplies	4.2	4.5	5.9	4.4	4.9	5.9	4.6	4.9	6.2
Utilities	6.0	9.2	18.5	8.4	12.6	29.2	10.1	16.3	32.1
Variable overhead	5.9	6.8	7.5	6.1	7.2	8.2	6.0	7.6	8.6
Fixed overhead	9.6	10.5	14.2	10.2	11.6	14.9	10.4	12.3	15.3
Total Operating Cost	95.3	120.3	168.0	100.6	127.2	181.8	104.0	132.6	186.0
Projected Volume	1,201	1,489	2,001	1,201	1,489	2,001	1,201	1,489	2,001
Unit Production Cost ($/ton)	$79.4	$80.8	$84.0	$83.8	$85.4	$90.85	$86.6	$89.1	$93.0

Note: Costs are in millions of dollars, and volume is in millions of tons.

and understanding. Note from Table 5.4 that one disadvantage of this approach is that costs from 1, 5, and 10 years in the future are being compared without considering the time value of money. Note also that relevant qualitative factors are not considered in this analysis.

When a company is deciding where to locate multiple facilities, more sophisticated analytical techniques are often used. These include linear programming, which is discussed in Chapter 8 of this book, computer simulation, network analysis, and others. Marc Schniederjans presents a number of analytical techniques used in facility location problems for both domestic and international location decisions.[6]

Integrating Quantitative and Qualitative Factors into Location Decisions

Managers who make location decisions know that in many cases qualitative factors can be dominant when compared to quantitative ones. Some of these qualitative factors are housing, cost of living, availability of labor, climate, community activities, education and health services, recreation, churches, union activities, local transportation systems, proximity of similar industrial facilities, and community attitudes. These factors all work together with quantitative factors such as annual operations costs to determine the acceptability of a particular location.

Managers often wrestle with the task of trading off qualitative factors against quantitative ones. Methods for systematically displaying the relative advantages and disadvantages of each location alternative, both quantitative and qualitative, have evolved. Table 5.5 illustrates the relative-aggregate-scores approach. Approaches such as this can be helpful in comparing location alternatives, particularly when qualitative factors are important in the location decisions.

The concepts, locational factors, and analysis techniques for approaching facility location decisions presented in this chapter do not exhaust the subject. What is presented here serves only as an introduction to a large topic.

Table 5.5	Relative-Aggregate-Scores Approach to Comparing Alternative Locations for a Steel Mill

Relevant Locational Factor	Weight of Factor	ST. LOUIS, MISSOURI			CLEVELAND, OHIO			MILWAUKEE, WISCONSIN		
		Economic Data	Score	Weighted Score	Economic Data	Score	Weighted Score	Economic Data	Score	Weighted Score
Production cost/ton	0.60	$79.40	1.000*	0.600	$83.80	0.948*	0.569	$86.60	0.917*	0.550
Cost of living	0.05		0.600†	0.030		0.650	0.033		0.500	0.025
Labor availability	0.20		0.650	0.130		0.600	0.120		0.950	0.190
Union activities	0.10		0.700	0.070		0.700	0.070		0.650	0.065
Proximity to similar industry	0.03		0.600	0.018		0.650	0.020		0.850	0.026
Local transporation	0.02		0.600	0.012		0.700	0.014		0.700	0.014
Total Location Score				0.860			0.826			0.870

*These scores are determined by dividing the lowest cost/ton by the actual cost per ton:

$$\frac{79.40}{79.40} = 1.000 \qquad \frac{79.40}{83.80} = 0.947 \qquad \frac{79.40}{86.60} = 0.917$$

†Qualitative factor scores are estimated based on a maximum score of 1.000.

FACILITY LAYOUT

Facility layout means planning for the location of all machines, utilities, employee workstations, customer service areas, material storage areas, aisles, rest rooms, lunchrooms, drinking fountains, internal walls, offices, and computer rooms, and for the flow patterns of materials and people around, into, and within buildings. Facility layout planning should be viewed as a natural extension of the discussion of process planning in Chapter 4. In process planning, we select or design processing machinery; in conjunction with product design, we determine the characteristics of the materials in the products, and we introduce new technology into operations. Through facility layouts, the physical arrangement of these processes within and around buildings, the space necessary for the operation of these processes, and the space required for support functions are provided. As process planning and facility layout planning proceed, there is a continuous interchange of information between these two planning activities, because each affects the other.

Table 5.6 lists some objectives of facility layouts for manufacturing, warehouse, service, and office operations. The table is organized to show first the objectives for manufacturing operations, which also apply to warehouse, service, and office operations. Then the additional objectives for warehouse, service, and office operations are shown.

A thoughtful reading of the objectives for facility layouts in Table 5.6 should suggest that facility layout planning must be linked with operations strategy. Remember from Chapter 2, Operations Strategies in a Global Economy, that the mix of competitive priorities the operations function can provide are low production costs, fast and on-time deliveries, high-quality products and services, and product and volume flexibility. The objectives in Table 5.6 that drive our facility layouts must reflect an appropriate mix of these competitive priorities that are embodied in our operations strategy. *Operations strategy drives facility layout planning, and facility layouts serve as a means of achieving operations strategies.*

Table 5.6	Some Objectives of Facility Layouts

Objectives for Manufacturing Operation Layouts

Provide enough production capacity
Reduce materials-handling costs
Conform to site and building constraints
Allow space for production machines
Allow high labor, machine, and space utilization and productivity
Provide for volume and product flexibility
Provide space for rest rooms, cafeterias, and other personal-care needs of employees
Provide for employee safety and health
Allow ease of supervision
Allow ease of maintenance
Achieve objectives with least capital investment

Additional Objectives for Warehouse Operation Layouts

Promote efficient loading and unloading of shipping vehicles
Provide for effective stock picking, order filling, and unit loading
Allow ease of inventory counts
Promote accurate inventory record keeping

Additional Objectives for Service Operation Layouts

Provide for customer comfort and convenience
Provide appealing setting for customers
Allow attractive display of merchandise
Reduce travel of personnel or customers
Provide for privacy in work areas
Promote communication between work areas
Provide for stock rotation for shelf life

Additional Objectives for Office Operation Layouts

Reinforce organization structure
Reduce travel of personnel or customers
Provide for privacy in work areas
Promote communication between work areas

MANUFACTURING FACILITY LAYOUTS

Among the many objectives of facility layouts, the central focus of most manufacturing layouts is to minimize the cost of processing, transporting, and storing materials throughout the production system.

Materials Handling

The materials used in manufacturing are many: raw materials, purchased components, materials-in-process, finished goods, packaging materials, maintenance and other supplies, and scrap and waste. These materials vary greatly in size, shape, chemical properties, and special features.

Most of this variety in material characteristics is determined by product design decisions. The layout of facilities is directly affected by the nature of these materials. Large and bulky materials, heavy materials, fluids, solids, flexible and inflexible materials, and materials requiring special handling to protect them from conditions such as heat, cold, humidity, light, dust, flame, and vibration—all affect the layout of facilities for handling, storing, and processing these materials.

A materials-handling system is the entire network of transportation that receives materials, stores materials in inventories, moves them about between processing points within and between buildings, and finally deposits the finished products into vehicles that will deliver them to customers.

The design and layout of buildings must be integrated with the design of the materials-handling system. For example, if overhead conveyors are to be used, the structure of the building must be strong enough to support the operation of these devices. Similarly, if heavy loads are to be transported on trucks, floors must have adequate support to withstand the constant stress of day-to-day pounding from these loads. Additionally, aisles must be wide enough to accommodate forklift trucks or other devices that will travel through the areas. Fixed-position devices such as conveyors must also be provided floor space.

Certain principles have evolved to guide facility layout to ensure the efficient handling of materials. Table 5.7 summarizes some of these fundamentals. Table 5.8 describes some materials-handling devices. Each of these devices has its own unique characteristics and advantages and disadvantages. Conveyors, for instance, are expensive to purchase, typically do not require operators, follow fixed routes, and serve as temporary storage and holding devices. Trucks, on the other hand, are relatively inexpensive to purchase, follow no fixed routes, and provide the greatest materials-handling flexibility.

The four basic types of layouts for manufacturing facilities are process, product, cellular manufacturing (CM), and fixed position.

Process Layouts

Process layouts, functional layouts, or job shops as they are sometimes called, are designed to accommodate variety in product designs and processing steps. See Figure 4.5 in Chapter 4. *If a manufacturing facility produces a variety of custom products in relatively small batches, the facility probably will use a process layout.* Process layouts typically use general-purpose machines that can be changed over rapidly to new operations for different product designs. These machines are usually

Table 5.7	Materials-Handling Principles

1. Materials should move through the facility in direct flow patterns, minimizing zigzagging or backtracking.
2. Related production processes should be arranged to provide for direct material flows.
3. Mechanical materials-handling devices should be designed and located and material storage locations should be selected so that human effort expended through bending, reaching, lifting, and walking is minimized.
4. Heavy or bulky materials should be moved the shortest distance through locating processes that use them near receiving and shipping areas.
5. The number of times each material is moved should be minimized.
6. Systems flexibility should allow for unexpected situations such as materials-handling equipment breakdowns, changes in production system technology, and future expansion of production capacities.
7. Mobile equipment should carry full loads at all times; empty and partial loads should be avoided.

Table 5.8	Materials-Handling Equipment

Automatic transfer devices—Machines that automatically grasp materials, hold them firmly while operations are being performed, and move them to other locations.

Containers and manual devices
Hand carts—Unpowered wagons, dollies, and trucks pushed about by workers.
Pallets—Base structures on which materials are stacked and moved about by materials-handling vehicles.
Tote boxes—Containers for holding loose parts or materials for storage and movement between operations.
Wire bins—Containers for storing loose parts of materials in inventory.

Conveyors
Belt—Motor-driven belt, usually made from rubberized fabric or metal fabric on a rigid frame.
Chain—Motor-driven chain that drags materials along a metal slide base.
Pneumatic—High volume of air flows through a tube, carrying materials along with the air flow.
Roller—Boxes, large parts, or unitized loads roll atop a series of rollers mounted on a rigid frame. The rollers can be either powered or unpowered.
Tube—Chain with circular scraper blades drags materials along inside a tube.

Cranes—Hoists mounted on overhead rails or ground-level wheels or rails; they lift, swing, and transport large and heavy materials.

Elevators—A type of crane that, while in a fixed position, lifts materials—usually between floors of buildings.

Pipelines—Closed tubes that transport liquids by means of pumps or gravity.

Turntables—Devices that hold, index, and rotate materials or parts from operation to operation.

Trucks—Electric, diesel, gasoline, or liquefied petroleum gas–powered vehicles equipped with beds, forks, arms, or other holding devices.

Automated guided vehicle systems (AGVS)—Driverless trains, pallet trucks, and unit load carriers. (See Chapter 6 of this book.)

arranged according to the type of process being performed. For example, all machining would be in one department, all assembly in another department, and all painting in another department. The materials-handling equipment generally consists of forklift trucks and other mobile vehicles that allow for the variety of paths followed through the facility by the products produced. The workers in process layouts must change and adapt quickly to the multitude of operations to be performed on each unique batch of products being produced. These workers must be highly skilled and require intensive job instructions and technical supervision. Process layouts require ongoing planning, scheduling, and controlling functions to ensure an optimum amount of work in each department and each workstation. The products are in the production system for relatively long periods of time, and large in-process inventories usually are present.

Product Layouts

Product layouts, often called production lines or assembly lines, are designed to accommodate only a few product designs. See Figure 4.4 in Chapter 4. Such layouts are designed to allow a direct material flow through the facility for products. Auto-manufacturing plants are good examples of facilities that use a product layout.

Product layouts typically use specialized machines that are set up once to perform a specific operation for a long period of time on one product. To change over these machines to a new product design requires great expense and long down times.

Companies that produce only a few product types often set up a different production line for each product type. The facility layout would allow for the different product lines to be separated from each other.

Workers in product layouts repeatedly perform a narrow range of activities on only a few product designs. The amount of skill, training, and supervision required is small. Although the planning and scheduling activities associated with these layouts are complex, they are not ongoing. Rather, planning and scheduling tend to be done intermittently as product changeovers occur.

Cellular Manufacturing Layouts

In **cellular manufacturing (CM)***, machines are grouped into cells, and the cells function somewhat like a product layout island within a larger job shop or process layout.* Figure 4.7 in Chapter 4 illustrates a CM layout. Each cell in a CM layout is formed to produce a single **parts family**—a few parts all with common characteristics, which usually means that they require the same machines and have similar machine settings.

Although the layout of a cell can take on many different forms, the flow of parts tends to be more like a product layout than a job shop. A CM layout would be attempted for these reasons:

not a job shop
not an assembly line

Consolidated Papers' facility at Wisconsin Rapids, Wisconsin, cost $495 million and can produce 212,000 tons of coated printing papers for annual reports, brochures, advertising circulars, magazine inserts, and other commercial printing applications. The plant facility is the company's largest, measuring five city blocks long and two city blocks wide. The highest points of the complex are the finished goods and roll storage facilities that reach a height of nine stories.

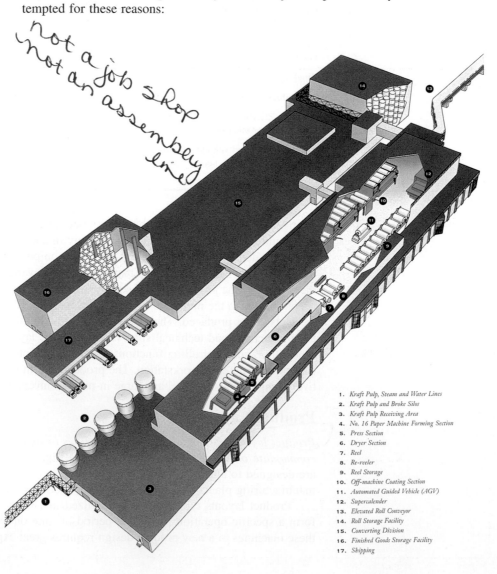

1. *Kraft Pulp, Steam and Water Lines*
2. *Kraft Pulp and Broke Silos*
3. *Kraft Pulp Receiving Area*
4. *No. 16 Paper Machine Forming Section*
5. *Press Section*
6. *Dryer Section*
7. *Reel*
8. *Re-reeler*
9. *Reel Storage*
10. *Off-machine Coating Section*
11. *Automated Guided Vehicle (AGV)*
12. *Supercalender*
13. *Elevated Roll Conveyor*
14. *Roll Storage Facility*
15. *Converting Division*
16. *Finished Goods Storage Facility*
17. *Shipping*

- Machine changeovers are simplified.
- Training periods for workers are shortened.
- Materials-handling costs are reduced.
- Parts can be made faster and shipped more quickly.
- Less in-process inventory is required.
- Production is easier to automate.

In developing a CM layout, the first step is the **cell formation decision,** the initial decision about which production machines and which parts to group into a cell. Next, the machines are arranged within each cell.

Fixed-Position Layouts

Some manufacturing and construction firms use a layout for arranging work that locates the product in a fixed position and transports workers, materials, machines, and subcontractors to and from the product. Figure 5.6 demonstrates this type of layout. Missile assembly, large aircraft assembly, ship construction, and bridge construction are examples of fixed-position layouts. Fixed-position layouts are used when a product is very bulky, large, heavy, or fragile. The fixed-position nature of the layout minimizes the amount of product movement required.

| **Figure 5.6** | Fixed-Position Layout |

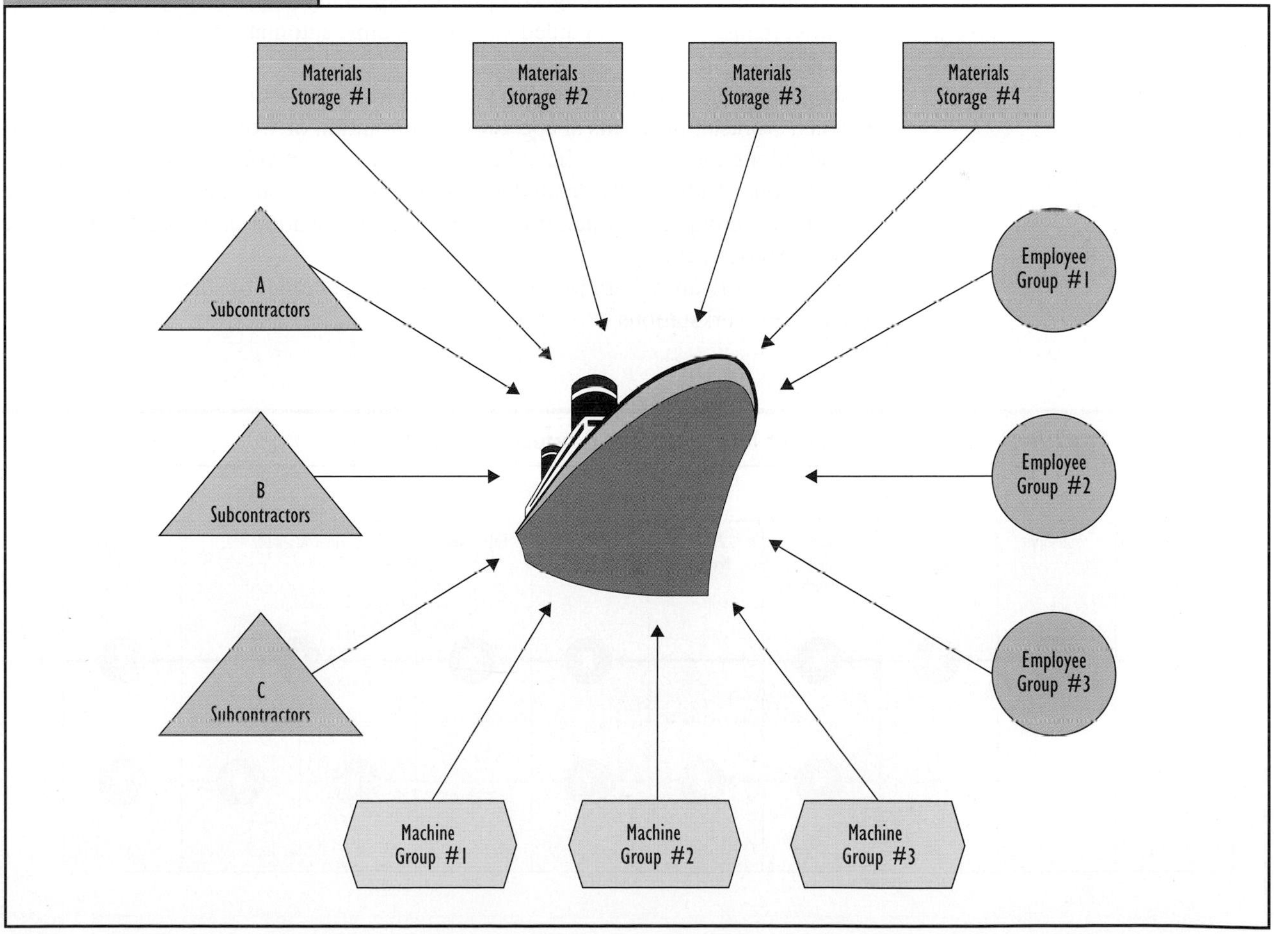

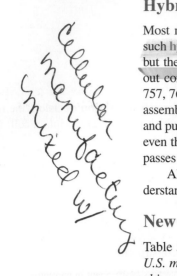

Hybrid Layouts

Most manufacturing facilities use a combination of layout types. Figure 5.7 shows one such hybrid layout where the departments are arranged according to the types of processes but the products flow through on a product layout. As another example of a hybrid layout consider the final assembly of Boeing's commercial aircraft (i.e., models 737, 747, 757, 767, and 777). During final assembly, each aircraft unit is located in a fixed-position assembly bay. However, every two or three days each aircraft unit is rolled out of its bay and pushed into the next assembly bay, where different assembly tasks are performed. So, even though an aircraft is assembled for two or three days at a time in a fixed position, it passes through six or eight different assembly bays in a product layout fashion.

Although hybrids make the identification of layout types fuzzy, it is important to understand the characteristics, advantages, and disadvantages of each basic type of layout.

New Trends in Manufacturing Layouts

Table 5.9 compares and contrasts traditional layouts with modern layouts. *In general, U.S. manufacturers' layouts have been traditionally designed for high worker and machine utilization, whereas modern layouts are designed for quality and flexibility, the ability to quickly shift to different product models or to different production rates.*

As U.S. facilities move toward modern layouts, these trends in layouts can be observed:

- Cellular manufacturing layouts within larger process layouts.
- Automated materials-handling equipment, especially automated storage and retrieval systems, automated guided vehicle systems, automatic transfer devices, and turntables.
- U-shaped production lines that allow workers to see the entire line and easily travel between workstations. This shape allows the rotation of workers among the workstations along the lines to relieve boredom and relieve work imbalances between workstations. Additionally, teamwork and improved morale tend to result because workers are grouped in smaller areas and communication and social contact are thereby encouraged.
- More open work areas with fewer walls, partitions, or other obstacles to clear views of adjacent workstations.

| Figure 5.7 | Hybrid Layout for Producing Products X and Y |

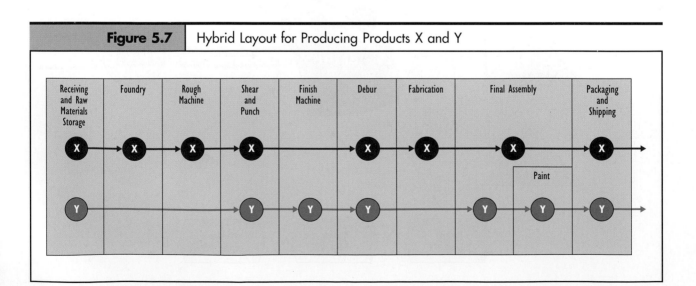

Table 5.9	Traditional Facility Layouts versus Modern Layouts

Characteristics of Traditional Layouts

Chief objective: High machine and worker utilization.

Means of achieving objective: Long production runs, fixed job assignments for workers in order to realize specialization-of-labor benefits, inventory to guard against machine breakdowns, constant production rates and with defects set aside for later rework, and large production machines that are kept fully utilized.

Appearance of layouts: Very large manufacturing-plant floor plans, extensive areas reserved for inventory, much space used for long conveyors and other materials-handling devices, large production machines requiring much floor space, L-shaped or linear production lines, and generally underutilized floor space.

Characteristics of Modern Layouts

Chief objective: Product quality and flexibility, the ability to modify production rates quickly and to change to different product models.

Means of achieving objective: Workers trained at many jobs, heavy investment in preventive maintenance, small machines easily changed over to different product models, workers encouraged to exercise initiative in solving quality and other production problems as they occur, workers and machines shifted as needed to solve production problems, production lines slowed down and machine breakdown or quality problems solved as they occur, little inventory carried, and workstations placed close together.

Appearance of layouts: Relatively small manufacturing-plant floor plans, compact and tightly packed layouts, large percentage of floor space used for production, less floor space occupied by inventory or materials-handling devices, and U-shaped production lines.

- Smaller and more compact factory layouts. With more automation such as robots, less space needs to be provided for workers. Machines can be placed closer to each other, and materials and products travel shorter distances.
- Less space provided for storage of inventories throughout the layout.

Business Snapshot 5.7 describes how one company saved floor space by converting to a modern factory layout.

BUSINESS SNAPSHOT 5.7

Boeing Factory Saves Space

The Boeing Company operates a manufacturing plant in Spokane, Washington, that produces primarily floor panels and air ducts for its commercial jets. In 1996 Boeing made substantial changes to the process designs and facility layout at this plant. As part of a company-wide transformation to modern production approaches and facility layouts, the Spokane plant was converted to a lean manufacturing facility. Much of the work-in-process inventory was eliminated, the part flows were redesigned, and machines were moved closer together.

In addition to shorter lead times and lower operating costs, one result was freed-up floor space in the building. Before the conversion to lean manufacturing, the entire building was utilized. After the conversion, about half of the manufacturing floor space was freed up. Six months later half of the building was still empty and was posing an interesting dilemma to the plant manager and to Boeing: what to do with the empty space.

ANALYZING MANUFACTURING FACILITY LAYOUTS

When the facility layout design is selected for a new manufacturing facility, materials-handling equipment is installed, storage areas are built, and machines and other equipment are moved in and installed. In heavy manufacturing, some concrete floor areas must be reinforced to handle the heavy loads and reduce vibration. In most manufacturing environments, the facility layout design will be used for at least a few years with only minor changes. However, in some high-tech industries where product life cycles are very short, such as computer-related products, the facility layout may be changed more than once a year. Advances in computer software have allowed for faster and better decisions about facility layout designs.

Software for Analyzing Facility Layouts

During the last 10 years the biggest development in analyzing manufacturing facility layouts has been the advancement and availability of software tools to help with this task. Although these software tools have seen the greatest use in manufacturing and industrial applications, they are also helpful in analyzing service facility layouts. Two categories of software tools are most helpful in analyzing facility layouts: computer-aided design (CAD) software and computer simulation software.

CAD software was initially developed to assist design engineers in designing new products, but recent applications have spread to designing new facilities as well. The use of architectural CAD software has become the standard approach in designing facilities. Modern CAD software allows three-dimensional (3D) views of facility designs in full color. The more advanced software also allows virtual walk-throughs to obtain a realistic sense of the new facility design. On the computer screen the user can freely move through the facility and look up, down, and all around with the click of the mouse. Some of the more common CAD software packages include *AutoSketch, AutoCAD Architectural Desktop, S8 Architectural and Building Design Software* (**http://www.autodesk.com**), and *ArchiCAD* (**http://www.graphisoft.com**).

Computer simulation software is particularly helpful in designing manufacturing facility layouts. Computer models of proposed layouts of equipment and product flows can easily be developed with the software. The manufacturing operation can then be simulated and the performance of the production system can be recorded. Different proposed layouts can be analyzed, and the best-performing layout can be identified. Potential changes in machine locations, materials-handling systems, product flow routings, number of workers, and storage locations can be easily evaluated. Examples of a few common simulation software packages are *SIMPROCESS* (**http://www.simprocess.com**), *ProModel* (**http://www.promodel.com**), and *VisFactory* (**http://www.cimtech.com**). The more advanced simulation software can even help to optimize facility layouts. For example, *VisFactory* allows the user to display 3D views of factory layouts; analyze, compare, and improve layouts with respect to material flow; create dynamic simulation models; and optimize the floor plans. It can include qualitative factors such as noise, dirt, shared utilities, aisle congestion, and safety issues, and can help to reduce part travel distances, lot sizes, and inventory levels, and improve communication and the throughput of parts. *VisFactory* uses up to 256 algorithms to find the most optimal layout and generates layouts using actual space requirements information for the facility.

Planning Process and Warehouse Layouts

In planning process layouts, the primary focus is on the efficient flow of materials. Computer simulation software is the most helpful tool for this purpose. It can be used to help decide where each process department should be located to minimize the travel distance of materials through the facility. The best locations for work-in-process inventory storage areas can be determined, and ample space for materials-handling vehicle travel can be provided. Because process (process-focused) layouts can have a wide variety of product routings through the facility, the power of computer simulation is crucial in considering all of the different material flows.

Computer simulation software is also helpful in analyzing warehouse layouts. Warehouse layouts are usually designed for fast storage and retrieval of inventory items, as well as efficient use of space. Warehouse layouts must be designed around the type of materials-handling equipment to be used. If forklift trucks will be used, then sufficiently wide aisles must be designed, and the storage shelves must not be taller than the forklift trucks can reach. If an automated storage and retrieval system will be used, then the aisles can be much narrower and the shelves can be as tall as the equipment can reach. Quality inspection areas for materials would be located near the receiving docks to minimize the travel of materials.

Various types of warehouse management software are available to help manage where materials are stored in a warehouse. As with warehouse layout decisions, inventory location decisions are made to facilitate fast storage and retrieval of materials. For instance, more frequently used materials would be stored on lower shelves so that they can be retrieved faster.

Planning Product Layouts

The analysis of production lines is the central focus of the analysis of product layouts. The product design and the market demand for products ultimately determine the technological process steps and the required production capacity of production lines. The number of workers, attended and unattended machines, and tools required to provide the market demand must then be determined. This information is provided by line balancing.

Line Balancing

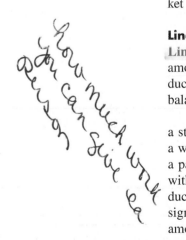

Line balancing is an analysis process that tries to equally divide the work to be done among workstations so that the number of workers or workstations required on a production line is minimized. Table 5.10 summarizes some of the terms often used in line balancing, and Table 5.11 describes the line-balancing procedure.

Production lines have workstations and work centers arranged in sequence along a straight or curved line. A workstation is a physical area where a worker with tools, a worker with one or more machines, or an unattended machine like a robot performs a particular set of tasks. A work center is a small grouping of identical workstations, with each work station performing the same set of tasks. The goal of analysis of production lines is to determine how many workstations to have and which tasks to assign to each work station so that the minimum number of workers and the minimum amount of machines are used to provide the required amount of capacity.

Let us say that we need a product to come off the end of a production line every 5 minutes; then the cycle time is 5 minutes. This means that there must be a product coming out of every workstation every 5 minutes or less. If the time required to do the tasks at a workstation were 10 minutes, then two workstations would be combined into a work center such that two products would be coming out of the center every 10 minutes, or the equivalent of one every 5 minutes. On the other hand, if the amount of work assigned to a workstation is only 4 minutes, that workstation would work 4 minutes and be idle 1 minute. It is practically impossible to assign tasks to workstations such that each one produces a product in exactly 5 minutes. In line balancing, our objective is to assign tasks to workstations such that there is little idle time. This means

Table 5.10	Terminology of Production Line Analysis

Tasks—Elements of work. *Grasp pencil, position pencil on paper to write, and write the number 4* is an example of a task.

Task precedence—The sequence or order in which tasks must be performed. Precedence for each task is known from a listing of the tasks that must immediately precede it.

Task times—The amount of time required for a well-trained worker or unattended machine to perform a task. Task times are usually expressed in minutes.

Cycle time—The time in minutes between products coming off the end of a production line.

Productive time per hour—The number of minutes in each hour that a workstation is working on the average. A workstation may not be working because of such things as lunch, personal time, breakdowns, start-ups, and shutdowns.

Workstation—Physical location where a particular set of tasks is performed. Workstations are usually of two types: a manned workstation containing one worker who operates machines and/or tools, and an unmanned workstation containing unattended machines like robots.

Work center—A physical location where two or more identical workstations are located. If more than one workstation is required to provide enough production capacity, they are combined to form a work center.

Number of workstations working—The amount of work to be done at a work center expressed in number of workstations. Twenty-eight hours of work at a work center during an 8-hour shift would be equivalent to 28/8, or 3.5, workstations working.

Minimum number of workstations—The least number of workstations that can provide the required production, calculated by:

$$\frac{\text{Sum of all task times}}{\text{Cycle time}} = \frac{\text{Sum of all task times} \times \text{Demand per hour}}{\text{Productive time per hour}}$$

Actual number of workstations—The total number of workstations required on the entire production line, calculated as the next higher integer value of the number of workstations working.

Utilization—The percentage of time that a production line is working. This is usually calculated by:

$$\frac{\text{Minimum number of workstations}}{\text{Actual number of workstations}} \times 100$$

Table 5.11	Line-Balancing Procedure

1. Determine which tasks must be performed to complete one unit of a particular product.
2. Determine the order or sequence in which the tasks must be performed.
3. Draw a precedence diagram. This is a flowchart wherein circles represent tasks and connecting arrows represent precedence.
4. Estimate task times.
5. Calculate the cycle time.
6. Calculate the minimum number of workstations.
7. Use one of the heuristics to assign tasks to workstations so that the production line is balanced.

assigning tasks to workstations and work centers such that a finished product is completed very close to but not exceeding the cycle time.

Line-Balancing Heuristics Researchers have used linear programming, dynamic programming, and other mathematical models to study line-balancing problems. But these methods are beyond the scope of this text, and they are usually not helpful in solving large problems. Heuristic methods, or methods based on simple rules, have been used to develop good solutions to these problems—not optimal solutions, but very good solutions. Among these methods are the incremental utilization (IU) heuristic and the longest-task-time (LTT) heuristic.

The **incremental utilization heuristic** simply adds tasks to a workstation in order of task precedence one at a time until utilization is 100 percent or is observed to fall. Then this procedure is repeated at the next workstation for the remaining tasks. Figure 5.8 illustrates the steps in the incremental utilization heuristic, and Example 5.2 uses this heuristic to balance a production line that assembles handheld calculators. *The incremental utilization heuristic is appropriate when one or more task times is equal to or greater than the cycle time. An important advantage of this heuristic is that it is capable of solving line-balancing problems regardless of the length of task times relative to the cycle time.* Under certain circumstances, however, this heuristic creates the need for extra tools and equipment. If the primary focus of the analysis is to minimize the number of workstations or if the tools and equipment used in the production line are either plentiful or inexpensive, this heuristic is appropriate.

The **longest-task-time heuristic** adds tasks to a workstation one at a time in the order of task precedence. If a choice must be made between two or more tasks, the one with the longest task time is added. This has the effect of assigning as quickly as possible the tasks that are the most difficult to fit into a station. Tasks with shorter times are then saved for fine-tuning the solution. This heuristic follows the steps in Table 5.12, and Example 5.3 uses this heuristic to balance a production line.

The conditions of the longest-task-time heuristic's use are:

1. It can be used only when each and every task time is less than or equal to the cycle time.
2. There can be no duplicate workstations.

Because there are no duplicate workstations, the amount of tools and equipment required is low. This restriction also reduces flexibility, however. *If each and every task time is less than or equal to the cycle time, and if the primary focus of the analysis of production lines is minimizing the number of workstations and the amount of tools and equipment required, then this heuristic would be appropriate.* Fortunately, there are modifications of this heuristic that allow task times to be greater than the cycle time. For example, the *POM Software Library*, which accompanies this book, allows the use of a modified longest-task-time heuristic that permits task times to be as much as twice the cycle time.

The two line-balancing heuristics discussed here are representative of a large group of such heuristics. So which one should you use in analyzing a particular line-balancing problem? In some circumstances, you may not have a choice because only one heuristic may accommodate the conditions that fit your line-balancing problem. For example, if one or more task times are equal to or greater than the cycle time, you may have to choose the incremental utilization heuristic. At other times, if the use of more than one heuristic seems appropriate, you would be advised to use several line-balancing heuristics on the same problem to determine which one yields the best solution.

| Figure 5.8 | Steps in the Incremental Utilization* Heuristic |

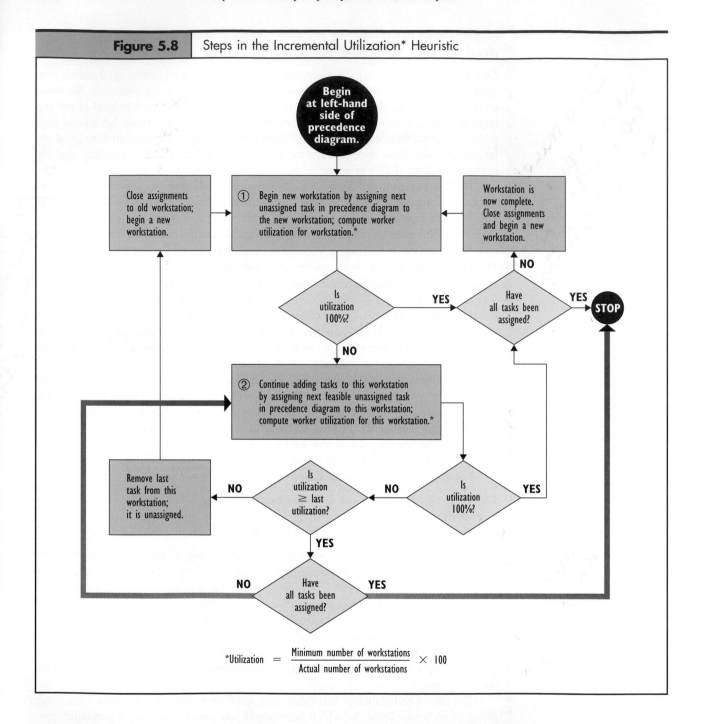

$$^*\text{Utilization} = \frac{\text{Minimum number of workstations}}{\text{Actual number of workstations}} \times 100$$

| Example 5.2 | Line Balancing with the Incremental Utilization Heuristic |

Textech, a large electronics manufacturer, assembles model AT75 handheld calculators at its Midland, Texas, plant. The assembly tasks that must be performed on each calculator are shown below. The parts used in this assembly line are supplied by materials-handling personnel to parts bins used in each task. The assemblies are moved along by belt conveyors between workstations.

Textech wants this assembly line to produce 540 calculators per hour: **a.** Compute the cycle time per calculator in minutes. **b.** Compute the minimum number of workstations. **c.** How would you combine the tasks into workstations to minimize idle time? Evaluate your proposal.

Task	Tasks That Must Immediately Precede	Time to Perform Task (minutes)
A. Place circuit frame on jig.		0.18
B. Place Circuit #1 into frame.	A	0.12
C. Place Circuit #2 into frame.	A	0.32
D. Place Circuit #3 into frame.	A	0.45
E. Attach circuits to frame.	B,C,D	0.51
F. Solder circuit connections to central circuit control.	E	0.55
G. Place circuit assembly in calculator inner frame.	F	0.38
H. Attach circuit assembly to calculator inner frame.	G	0.42
I. Place and attach display to inner frame.	H	0.30
J. Place and attach keyboard to inner frame.	I	0.18
K. Place and attach top body of calculator to inner frame.	J	0.36
L. Place and attach power assembly to inner frame.	J	0.42
M. Place and attach bottom body of calculator to inner frame.	K,L	0.48
N. Test circuit integrity.	M	0.30
O. Place calculator and printed matter in box.	N	0.39
	Total	5.36

Solution

a. Compute the cycle time per calculator:

$$\text{Cycle time} = \frac{\text{Productive time/hour*}}{\text{Demand/hour}} = \frac{54 \text{ minutes/hour}}{540 \text{ calculators/hour}} = 0.100 \text{ minute/calculator}$$

b. Compute the minimum number of workstations:

$$\begin{array}{l}\text{Minimum number}\\\text{of workstations}\end{array} = \frac{\text{Sum of task times} \times \text{Demand per hour}}{\text{Productive time per hour}}$$

$$= \frac{5.36 \text{ minutes/calculator} \times 540 \text{ calculators/hour}}{54 \text{ minutes/hour}}$$

$$= 53.60 \text{ workstations}$$

c. Balance the line:
  1. First, draw a precedence diagram for the production line. This diagram uses circles for tasks and arrows to show precedence relationships.

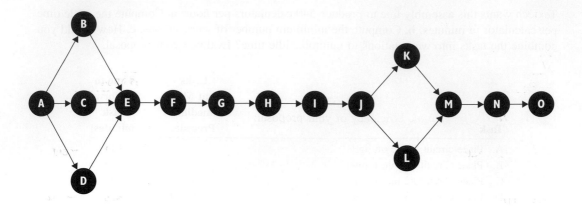

2. Next, assign tasks to work centers. This is done by strictly following the sequence of tasks (D must follow A, G must follow F, and so on), and the incremental utilization heuristic is used to group the tasks into work centers. In this method, tasks are combined in sequence until the utilization of the work center is 100 percent or until the utilization of the work center is observed to fall, and then a new work center is started. Look at Work Center 1 and note that we first consider Task A alone [(1.8 ÷ 2.0) × 100 = 90%]; next we consider Task A and Task B together [(3.0 ÷ 3.0) × 100 = 100%]. Because this combination has a 100 percent utilization, Tasks A and B are combined into Work Center 1 and we now move to Work Center 2. In Work Center 2, as Tasks C, D, and E are combined one task at a time, the work center utilization increases from 80 percent to 96.3 percent and to 98.5 percent; but, when Task F is added to C, D, and E, utilization falls to 96.3 percent. Work Center 2 therefore includes Tasks C, D, and E, and we go on to Work Center 3.

(1) Work Center	(2) Tasks	(3) Minutes/Calculator	(4) Number of Workstations Working [(3) ÷ cycle time]	(5) Actual Number of Workstations Required	(6) Utilization of Workstations [(4) ÷ (5)] × 100
1	A	.18	1.8	2	90.0%
	A,B	.18 + .12 = .30	3.0	3	100.0
2	C	.32	3.2	4	80.0
2	C,D	.32 + .45 = .77	7.7	8	96.3
2	C,D,E	.32 + .45 + .51 = 1.28	12.8	13	98.5
2	C,D,E,F	.32 + .45 + .51 + .55 = 1.83	18.3	19	96.3
3	F	.55	5.5	6	91.7
3	F,G	.55 + .38 = .93	9.3	10	93.0
3	F,G,H	.55 + .38 + .42 = 1.35	13.5	14	96.4
3	F,G,H,I	.55 + .38 + .42 + .30 = 1.65	16.5	17	97.0
3	F,G,H,I,J	.55 + .38 + .42 + .30 + .18 = 1.83	18.3	19	96.3
4	J	.18	1.8	2	90.0
4	J,K	.18 + .36 = .54	5.4	6	90.0
4	J,K,L	.18 + .36 + .42 = .96	9.6	10	96.0
4	J,K,L,M	.18 + .36 + .42 + .48 = 1.44	14.4	15	96.0
4	J,K,L,M,N	.18 + .36 + .42 + .48 + .30 = 1.74	17.4	18	96.7
4	J,K,L,M,N,O	.18 + .36 + .42 + .48 + .30 + .39 = 2.13	21.3	22	96.8
		Total		55	

3. Summarize the assignment of tasks to workstations on the production line:

Tasks in work centers	A,B	C,D,E	F,G,H,I	J,K,L,M,N,O	
Work centers	→ ① →	② →	③ →	④	
Actual number of workstations	3.0	13.0	17.0	22.0	55.0 Total

4. Next, compute the efficiency of your proposal:

$$\text{Utilization} = \frac{\text{Minimum number of workstations}}{\text{Actual number of workstations}} = \frac{53.6}{55} = 0.975, \text{ or } 97.5 \text{ percent}$$

*An average of six minutes per hour in this example is not productive because of lunch, personal time, machine breakdown, and start up and shutdown time.

Table 5.12	Steps in the Longest-Task-Time Heuristic

1. Let i = 1, where i is the number of the workstation being formed.

2. Make a list of all tasks that are candidates for assignment to this workstation. For a task to be on this list, it must satisfy all of these conditions:
   a. It cannot have been previously assigned to this or any previous workstation.
   b. Its immediate predecessors must have been assigned to this or a previous workstation.
   c. The sum of its task time and all other times of tasks already assigned to the workstation must be less than or equal to the cycle time. If no candidates can be found, go to Step 4.

3. Assign the task from the list with the longest task time to the workstation. Go back to Step 2.

4. Close the assignment of tasks to Workstation i. This can occur in two ways. If there are no tasks on the candidate list for the workstation but there are still tasks to be assigned, set i = i + 1 and go back to Step 2. If there are no more unassigned tasks, the procedure is complete.

Example 5.3	Line Balancing with the Longest-Task-Time Heuristic

Task	Immediate Predecessor	Task Time (minutes)
a	—	0.9
b	a	0.4
c	b	0.6
d	c	0.2
e	c	0.3
f	d,e	0.4
g	f	0.7
h	g	1.1
	Total	4.6

Using the information in the table above:

a. Draw a precedence diagram.
b. Assuming that 55 minutes per hour are productive, compute the cycle time needed to obtain 50 units per hour.

c. Determine the minimum number of workstations.

d. Assign tasks to workstations using the longest-task-time heuristic.

e. Calculate the utilization of the solution in Part d.

Solution

a. Draw a precedence diagram:

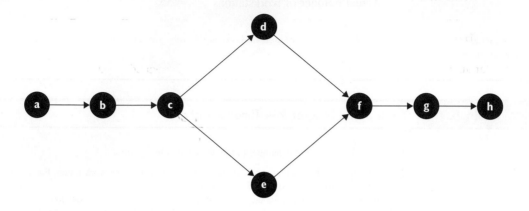

b. Assuming that 55 minutes per hour are productive, compute the cycle time needed to obtain 50 units per hour:

$$\text{Cycle time} = \frac{\text{Productive time per hour}}{\text{Demand per hour}} = \frac{55 \text{ minutes per hour}}{50 \text{ products per hour}}$$

$$= 1.1 \text{ minutes per product}$$

c. Determine the minimum number of workstations:

$$\frac{\text{Minimum number}}{\text{of workstations}} = \frac{\text{Sum of all task times} \times \text{Demand per hour}}{\text{Productive time per hour}}$$

$$= \frac{4.6 \text{ minutes/product} \times 50 \text{ products/hour}}{55 \text{ minutes/hour}}$$

$$= 4.2 \text{ workstations}$$

d. Assign tasks to workstations using the longest-task-time heuristic:

(1) Workstation	(2) Candidate List	(3) Assigned Task	(4) Task Time	(5) Sum of Task Times	(6) Unassigned Task Time at Workstation [1.1 − (5)]
1	a	a	0.9	0.9	0.2
2	b	b	0.4	0.4	0.7
2	c	c	0.6	1.0	0.1

(1) Workstation	(2) Candidate List	(3) Assigned Task	(4) Task Time	(5) Sum of Task Times	(6) Unassigned Task Time at Workstation $[1.1 - (5)]$
3	d,e*	e	0.3	0.3	0.8
3	d	d	0.2	0.5	0.6
3	f	f	0.4	0.9	0.2
4	g	g	0.7	0.7	0.4
5	h	h	1.1	1.1	0

*Task e is chosen over Task d because its task time is longer.

Summarize the assignment of tasks to workstations on the production line:

Tasks In Workstations	Workstation
a	1
b,c	2
e,d,f	3
g	4
h	5

e.   Calculate the utilization of the solution in Part d:

$$\text{Utilization} = \frac{\text{Minimum number of workstations}}{\text{Actual number of workstations}} \times 100$$

$$= \frac{4.2}{5} \times 100$$

$$= 84\%$$

Line-Balancing Issues   In earlier years, production lines were designed so that conveyor belts paced the speed of the employees' work. Research and common sense have shown that workers do not like such arrangements. They tend to be more irritable on the job, are absent more often from work, produce products of lower quality, and are less healthy on and off the job. Few companies today knowingly place workers under the control of machines; the workers must be in control.

Varying the cycle time can have important results in line balancing. A longer cycle time—the same thing as a lower production rate—may result in fewer workstations and less tooling and machinery, which may lead to lower production costs. Such a tactic may require carrying larger finished-goods inventories, which can be drawn down during peak demand seasons. A shorter cycle time—the same thing as a higher production rate—could conceivably lead to less idle time and lower production costs. Thus, experimentation with different lengths of cycle time is advised so that low production costs and less capital investment in machines and tools will result.

Changes in product demand, machine modifications, variations in employee learning and training, and other changes can lead to production lines being out of balance

FALSE! —

— cannot change unless there is a charge over

— or there is a change in technology

or having insufficient or excess capacity. In all of these cases, production lines must be rebalanced. **Rebalancing a production line** is a common occurrence in industry because change is a fact of life. Most production lines are rebalanced several times a year. Such rebalancing means a certain amount of disruption to production because layouts and worker jobs are affected. But to continue operating an out-of-date and out-of-balance production line with the incorrect capacity can cause high production costs, poor customer service, and excess inventories.

Planning Cellular Manufacturing Layouts

As discussed earlier in this chapter, the initial issue that must be resolved in CM layouts is the cell formation decision: Which machines are assigned to manufacturing cells, and which parts will be produced in each cell? If the advantages claimed in Chapter 4 for cellular manufacturing are to materialize, this initial decision is crucial. Example 5.4 illustrates the essential elements of such decisions.

Example 5.4	Cell Formation Decisions in Cellular Manufacturing Layouts

The Acme Machine Shop produces machined parts in a job shop. Acme has recently implemented a group technology (GT) program in its shop, and it is now ready to develop manufacturing cells on the shop floor. Production analysts have identified five parts that seem to meet the requirements of parts appropriate for CM: moderate batch sizes, stable demand, and common physical characteristics. The parts–machines matrix below identifies the five parts (1 through 5) and the machines (A through E) on which the parts are presently produced in the job shop. The Xs in the body of the matrix indicate the machines on which the parts must be produced. For example, Part 1 requires machine operations on Machines A and D.

Parts

		1	2	3	4	5
	A	X		X		X
	B		X		X	X
Machines	**C**		X		X	X
	D	X		X		
	E		X		X	X

Acme wishes to assign the machines (and the parts that the machines make) to cells such that if a part is assigned to a cell, all the machines required to make the part are also in the same cell. For example, if Part 1 is assigned to a cell, Machines A and D must also be assigned to that cell. Arrange the machines and the parts into cells.

Solution

1. **Rearrange the rows.** First, place the machines that produce the same parts in adjacent rows. Notice that Machines A and D are required by Parts 1 and 3; put these two machines in the first two rows. Also notice that Machines B, C, and E are required by Parts 2, 4, and 5; put these three machines in the next three rows.

Parts

Machines		1	2	3	4	5
	A	X		X		X
	D	X		X		
	B		X		X	X
	C		X		X	X
	E		X		X	X

2. **Rearrange the columns.** Next rearrange the columns such that parts requiring the same machines are put in adjacent columns. Notice that Parts 1 and 3 require Machines A and D; put these two parts in the first two columns. Also notice that Parts 2, 4, and 5 require Machines B, C, and E; put these three parts in the next three columns.

Parts

Machines		1	2	3	4	5*
	A	X	X			X
	D	X	X			
	B			X	X	X
	C			X	X	X
	E			X	X	X

This parts–machines matrix contains the solution to this cell formation problem. Parts 1 and 3 are to be produced in Cell 1 on Machines A and D. Parts 2 and 4 are to be produced in Cell 2 on Machines B, C, and E. Part 5* is called an exceptional part because it cannot be produced within a single cell: It requires Machine A, which is in Cell 1, and Machines B, C, and E, which are in Cell 2.

There are two fundamental requirements for parts to be made in cells:

1. The demand for the parts must be high enough and stable enough that moderate batch sizes of the parts can be produced periodically.
2. The parts being considered must be capable of being grouped into parts families. Within a parts family, the parts must have similar physical characteristics and thus require similar production operations.

In Example 5.4, we assume that the five parts have undergone close scrutiny such that the nature of their demand complies with the first requirement above. Also, parts are assumed to have been chosen such that they require similar production operations. Requiring the same machines is perhaps the strongest indication that parts have similar production operations.

The solution in Example 5.4 would result in four of the parts and five of the machines being assigned to two cells. One of the parts, Part 5, is an exceptional part, which means that it cannot be made entirely within a single cell. The alternatives for producing this part are:

1. **Produce Part 5 by transporting batches of the part between the two cells.** The advantage of this alternative would be that the machine utilization (the percentage of time that the machines operate) of the cells would be higher. The disadvantages of this alternative are the additional materials-handling cost and the additional complexity in coordinating the scheduling of production between the cells.
2. **Subcontract the production of Part 5 to suppliers outside the company.** The advantage of this alternative is that it avoids the additional materials-handling cost and scheduling complexity caused by transporting batches of the part between the cells. The disadvantage is that this subcontracting may cost more than making the part in-house.
3. **Produce Part 5 back in the job shop, outside the CM cells.** The advantage of this alternative is that it avoids the additional materials-handling cost and scheduling complexity caused by transporting batches of the part between the cells and any additional cost of subcontracting. The main disadvantage of this alternative is that the machines on which Part 5 is made (A, B, C, and E) are already in use in the cells of the CM layout. If Part 5 is now to be sent back to the job shop for production, additional machines may have to be purchased.
4. **Purchase an additional Machine A to produce Part 5 in the second cell.** This alternative would assign Machines A and D and Parts 1 and 2 to the first cell and Machines A, B, C, and E and Parts 3, 4, and 5 to the second cell. The advantage of this alternative is that the additional materials-handling cost and scheduling complexity of transporting batches of Part 5 between cells are avoided. The disadvantage is the additional cost of purchasing another Machine A.

The cell formation decision that is analyzed in Example 5.4 is not very complex, but many real problems in industry are solved in much the same way as in this example. For example, the Defense Systems Division of Texas Instruments in Dallas, Texas, has several cells in its machine shop that were formed in much the same way as in Example 5.4. In more complex problems, such issues as the following must be resolved:

1. If all the parts cannot be cleanly divided between cells and we must choose from among several parts the ones that are to be exceptional parts, how will we decide? In practice, the part that has the least additional cost of subcontracting or the least additional cost of producing it in the job shop is chosen.

2. If inadequate production capacity is available to produce all the parts in cells, which parts should be made outside the cells? Generally, the ones that require the least capacity and require the greatest additional cost to either subcontract or make in the job shop are chosen to remain in the cells.

We have discussed developing layouts for manufacturing operations. Let us now consider how we approach layouts for service operations.

SERVICE FACILITY LAYOUTS

In Chapter 2, Operations Strategies in a Global Economy, and Chapter 4, Product, Process, and Service Design, we discussed the characteristics of services and the processes used to produce services. Three points summarize these previous discussions:

1. Perhaps the most distinct characteristic of services is their diversity.
2. There are three dimensions to the type of service—standard or custom design, amount of customer contact, and the mix of physical goods and intangible services.
3. There are three types of service operations—quasi-manufacturing, customer-as-participant, and customer-as-product.

Understanding these three points prepares us for a discussion of the types of layouts for service facilities.

Types of Service Facility Layouts

Consider the nature of the service and how these businesses deliver or convey their services—airlines, banks, retailers, hospitals, restaurants, insurance, real estate, trucking, entertainment, telephones, and utilities. Because there is so much diversity among such services, there also tends to be wide variety in the kinds of layouts for service facilities.

For most service businesses, one characteristic makes at least part of their operations different from most manufacturing operations: The encounter between the customer and the service must be provided for. This encounter can be intense because the customer actually becomes a part of the production process, as in hospitals where the service is actually performed on the customer. Or the encounter can be less intense, as in retailing where customers choose, pay for, and carry out physical goods. But regardless of the nature and intensity of this encounter, service facility layouts are dramatically affected.

Service facility layouts must ordinarily provide for easy entrance to these properties from freeways and busy thoroughfares. And large, well-organized, and amply lighted parking areas or garages are typically provided. Additionally, these facilities usually have wide, well-designed walkways to carry people to and from the parking areas. Entryways and exits are typically well marked, conveniently located, and designed to accommodate large numbers of customers during peak hours. Powered doors and escalators are often provided to ease the physical effort of opening doors and climbing stairs when armloads of merchandise must be transported. Lobbies or other receiving or holding areas for customers, customer waiting lines, service counters, cash registers, employee workstations, merchandise displays, aisleways, and attractive decor and lighting must be provided.

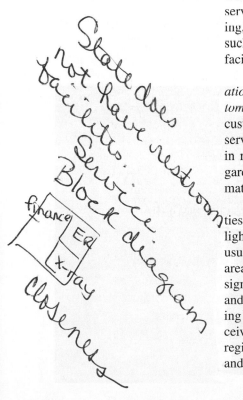

The degree to which service facilities must provide these customer-related facility features varies directly with the amount of involvement and customer contact inherent in the service. At one extreme is the front-room operations of a bank where the entire facility layout must be designed around customers—parking, easy entering and exiting, convenient and pleasant waiting areas, waiting lines for standardized customer servicing, teller windows and tellers, and individualized areas for customer savings account and loan customer servicing. At another extreme is the back-room operations of a bank where the facility layout must be designed only for the activities of processing financial transactions, updating account records, and generating statements and reports where the central focus is on the technologies or physical materials processing and production efficiency. This is a quasi-manufacturing service operation.

These two extremes in service facility layouts are near the endpoints of a continuum. Other service facilities blend the characteristics of these two layouts. Layouts of exclusive restaurants, for example, typically emphasize customer receiving and individualized servicing perhaps more than the processing and preparation of food products. On the other hand, fast-food restaurant layouts tend to emphasize the processing and preparation of food instead of customer receiving and individual servicing. The mix of customer or technology emphasis, physical materials processing, and production efficiency emphases varies according to the type of service offered and the operating strategies of each particular organization.

Analyzing Service Facility Layouts

For many service facilities, the techniques for the layout of manufacturing facilities that we have studied in this chapter can be directly applied. For services that are of the quasi-manufacturing type such as fast-food restaurants, back-room operations of banks, maintenance operations of airlines, warehousing operations of retailers, and electric generating facilities, these previously discussed topics are particularly relevant:

• The principles of materials handling and materials-handling equipment, for all types of services where the handling of physical goods is significant

Operations managers can greatly affect production costs by their decisions about manufacturing layouts in facilities such as this aircraft plant.

- The use of CAD software and computer simulation software to develop building floor plans for all kinds of services
- The use of line balancing for service operations with product-focused production

For many services of all types, an important element of facility layout is providing for customer waiting lines. Of particular importance is the amount of space required for service counters and waiting customers and fitting waiting lines into the overall facility layouts. These issues are of crucial importance to the layouts of service facilities. We will study these and other issues related to waiting lines in Chapter 9, Service Operations Planning and Scheduling.

For many other service operations, facility layouts are very much like process layouts in manufacturing because they must allow customers to follow a variety of paths through the facilities. Hospital layouts, for instance, typically allow great variety in the steps that patients follow—surgery, radiology, laboratory testing, physical therapy, intensive care, doctors' offices, pharmacy, emergency room, patients' rooms, and administration. The departments of hospitals are grouped and located according to their processes in much the same way that a custom machine shop would lay out its machines and workstations to minimize travel distance or cost of materials handling among departments.

In many services, the reasons for having departments near one another are more complex than this, and they are often multiple objective and subjective. In a hospital, for instance, we would want radiology near the emergency room to allow fast diagnosis of emergency cases, and we would want the pharmacy near the patients' rooms to allow for prompt dispensing of drugs to patients. Similarly, using the same equipment or personnel, ease of communicating, logical movement of customers, speed, safety, contamination, or other factors could be legitimate reasons for wanting two departments near or far from one another. In such cases, closeness ratings are used to reflect the desirability of having one department near another. Trial-and-error analysis could then use the closeness ratings to develop good facility layouts. In using these approaches, several objectives can be established: minimize the sum of pairs of closeness ratings, minimize the total distance between departments as weighted by the inverse of closeness ratings, and so on.

Example 5.5 illustrates the use of closeness ratings to develop a facility layout. The method employed in this example is explained in Table 5.13.

Example 5.5	Using Closeness Ratings to Develop Service Facility Layouts

These closeness ratings are used for the purpose of indicating the desirability of having departments near one another:

Closeness Rating	Meaning of Rating
1	Necessary
2	Very important
3	Important
4	Slightly important
5	Unimportant
6	Undesirable

Here are six departments and their closeness ratings. The closeness rating between a pair of departments is found at their intersections on the grid below.

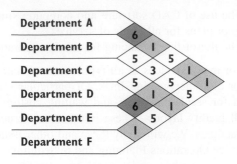

Use the method from Table 5.13 to lay out the six departments in a rectangular building two departments deep and three departments wide.

Solution

First, notice that the pairs of departments with closeness ratings of 1 (necessary) are A-C, A-E, A-F, C-E, C-F, and E-F. A must touch C, E, and F; C must touch E and F; and E must touch F. As a first trial, try a layout with A, C, E, and F all touching. The layout below satisfies all the pairings of departments with 1 closeness ratings.

A	C	
E	F	

Next, notice that the pairs of departments with closeness ratings of 6 (undesirable) are A-B and D-E. A must not touch B, and D must not touch E. By placing departments D and E in the two remaining spaces, the layout below satisfies all the pairings of departments with 6 closeness ratings.

A	C	B
E	F	D

Note that in this last step, satisfying the closeness ratings of 6 simultaneously satisfied the closeness ratings of 1. Problems may not always be this simple, and some additional rounds of juggling of departments may be required to see if improvements can be made.

Table 5.13	Procedure for Using Closeness Ratings

1. m = 1 and n = 6.
2. Identify pairs of departments with closeness ratings of m.
3. Develop a trial layout with the pairs of departments identified in Step 1 adjacent to one another.
4. Identify pairs of departments with closeness ratings of n.
5. Fit the pairs of departments identified in Step 4 into the trial layout from Step 3.
6. Examine the trial layout in Step 5. If any closeness ratings of pairs of departments are violated, rearrange departments to comply with all closeness ratings.
7. Does m = 3 and n = 4? If yes, go to Step 8. If no, m = m + 1 and n = n − 1, go to Step 2.
8. Quit.

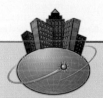

Wrap-Up

WHAT WORLD-CLASS COMPANIES DO

World-class companies recognize that long-range capacity decisions and facility location decisions are among the most important of their strategic decisions. Capital investment in production facilities is enormous, and the ability of production to be used as a competitive weapon in capturing world markets hangs in the balance. Capacity planning covers such long periods of time that fundamental changes can occur in the economy, consumer preferences, technology, demographics, and government regulations. Such planning is therefore subject to great uncertainty and risk.

World-class companies justify enormous investments in production facilities less on how much they save and on other conventional financial formulas of returns, and more on how such facilities position their companies to capitalize on strategic opportunities to capture shares of world markets. Reducing vertical integration through the development of an effective subcontractor network can lead to improved production technology, reduced capital investment, increased flexibility and capacity, and more stable employment levels. This means that production facilities in general tend to be smaller, more widely dispersed, and located closer to customers.

Facility location decisions at world-class companies increasingly involve a worldwide search for sites. National boundaries present less of an obstacle than in the past. A multitude of factors are considered in location decisions, and the importance of these factors varies with the type of facility. The type of facility—from heavy manufacturing to health services—has its own set of factors that must be carefully matched with those provided by potential site locations. The incentives offered by the governments of communities under consideration are important to the eventual choice of location. The eventual choice of facility location will involve the need to simultaneously consider many economic and qualitative factors.

Facility layout greatly affects the performance of production systems. World-class companies pour great effort into developing layouts designed to achieve the competitive priorities for products in their business plans. Manufacturing, warehouse operations, service operations, and office operations share many layout objectives. Chief among these are provision for enough production capacity, low materials-handling costs, provision for the personal and safety needs of workers, low capital investment, and low production costs.

World-class companies strive for flexibility in their layouts, allowing them to change production rates and to change to other product models quickly. To achieve this objective, these firms have intensive, multijob training of workers, sophisticated preventive-maintenance programs, small flexible machines, self-starting workers who are trained at problem solving, little unnecessary inventory, and workstations placed close to one another. Their layouts are relatively small, compact, and tightly packed, with a larger percentage of floor space used for production and a smaller percentage for inventory. World-class companies are using more cellular manufacturing layouts, more automated materials-handling equipment such as automated warehouses and automated guided vehicle systems, more U-shaped production lines that allow more interaction and job rotation of workers, and more open areas with fewer walls and clear views of adjacent workstations.

World-class producers of services are designing layouts for back-room operations in much the same way as world-class manufacturers. Here the technologies of production, processing of physical materials, production costs, and flexibility guide the development of layouts. Additionally, as they compete for customers, service producers design their facility layouts with their customers in mind. Customer parking, receiving, comfort, and waiting lines guide the development of service layouts.

World-class companies use consultants, computer programs, and in-house staff experts to develop facility layouts. Many major corporations have departments at their corporate headquarters that supply facility design, construction, location, and layout assistance to all divisions in the companies. Computer software such as *ArchiCAD* and *VisFactory* is used to analyze facility layouts.

REVIEW AND DISCUSSION QUESTIONS

1. Name four activities usually involved in any long-range capacity-planning decision.
2. Define *production capacity*. How does the Federal Reserve Board define *sustainable practical capacity?*
3. Define these terms: *output rate capacity, aggregate unit of capacity, input rate capacity, capacity utilization percentage, capacity cushion.*
4. Name three ways that firms can reduce long-range capacity. Name five ways that firms can expand long-range capacity.
5. Define these terms: *best operating level, economies of scale, diseconomies of scale, economies of scope, supplier networks.*
6. What factors affect national location decisions?
7. What factors affect community location decisions?
8. What factors affect site location decisions?
9. Name five steps in analyzing retailing and service facility locations.
10. Name five qualitative factors commonly considered in facility location decisions.
11. Describe how managers may simultaneously consider both quantitative and qualitative factors in facility location analysis.

12. Define *facility layout.*
13. Name three objectives for these types of layouts:
    a. Manufacturing operations
    b. Warehouse operations
    c. Service operations
    d. Office operations
14. Name four principles of materials handling.
15. Name and describe five types of materials-handling devices.
16. Name and describe four types of layouts for manufacturing operations.
17. What are the principal decisions that must be made in a CM layout? Define and describe the cell formation problem.
18. What are the objectives of cell formation decisions? Describe how cell formation problems are analyzed. What is an exceptional part? What is done with exceptional parts?
19. Compare and contrast the layout of a bank with the layout of a hospital. How are they alike and how are they different?
20. Explain why we balance production lines. Describe the general procedure of line balancing.
21. Name five trends in manufacturing layouts.

INTERNET ASSIGNMENTS

1. The office of System Capacity is a department within the U.S. Federal Aviation Administration. Visit and explore the web site for the Office of System Capacity (**http://www.faa.gov/ats/asc**). What is the purpose or role of this department? (That is, what does the department do?)
2. The Federal Reserve Board issues frequent reports on "Industrial Production and Capacity Utilization" in the United States. Find the most recent report on the web site **http://www.bog.frb.fed.us**. Summarize the recent changes in industrial production and output and in capacity utilization. What are the capacity utilizations for total industry and for manufacturing in the most recent month and what was the capacity growth percentage in the most recent year?
3. The Economic Development Commission of Mid-Florida provides facility location information for the Orlando area at the web site **http://www.business-orlando. org**. Based on information from the web site, summarize some of the reasons why Orlando is an attractive location for businesses. Find information on construction costs versus leasing costs per square foot for different types of facilities.
4. Search the Internet for a company that provides conveyor systems to industrial customers. Describe some of the conveyor systems the company can provide.
5. Crown Equipment Corporation (**http://www.crown.com**) manufactures heavy-duty electric lift trucks used in transporting materials and goods in warehouses and

distribution centers throughout the world. Provide details for three different trucks in Crown's product line.

6. Visit the web site of Boeing's commercial jets (**http://www.boeing.com/commercial**). What is the role in the marketplace of Boeing's new Model 717 jet? Select one of Boeing's other commercial jet models (737, 747, 757, 767, or 777) and find a diagram of the seating layout. Find the price range for this model.

PROBLEMS

Long-Range Facility-Planning Decisions

1. The Hardhead Lids Company plans to produce motorcycle helmets. The annual fixed cost for the production process is expected to be $185,000. The variable cost per helmet is expected to be $76. The company expects to sell the helmets for $99 each.
   a. How many helmets must be sold each year to break even?
   b. How much annual revenue is required to break even?
   c. If 15,000 helmets are sold in one year, how much profit will be earned?
   d. If annual sales are expected to be 15,000 helmets, what would the selling price need to be in order to earn a profit of $300,000?

2. A manufacturer needs to add more production capacity. Two alternatives are now being studied—automated and manual. The information below is important to this decision:

	Automated Process	Manual Process
Annual fixed cost	$545,000	$123,000
Variable cost per product	$15.66	$17.69
Estimated annual production		
(in number of products): Year 1	120,000	120,000
Year 5	150,000	150,000
Year 10	220,000	220,000

   a. Which alternative would be the least-cost alternative in Years 1, 5, and 10?
   b. How much would the variable cost per unit have to be in Year 5 for the automated alternative to justify the additional annual fixed cost of the automated alternative over the manual alternative?

3. A home products discount store is considering expanding its capacity to meet a growing demand for its products. The alternatives are to build a new store at a site nearby, expand and refurbish the old store, or do nothing. Economists have projected the regional economic outlook: a 50 percent probability that the economy will remain unchanged, a 20 percent probability of an economic upturn, and a 30 percent probability of an economic downturn. The following estimates of annual returns have been prepared (in millions of dollars):

	Market Downturn	Stable Market	Market Upturn
Build new store	$(0.8)	$0.5	$2.1
Expand old store	(0.4)	0.8	1.4
Do nothing	(0.1)	0.2	0.5

Note: ( ) means a negative annual return.

   a. Use a decision tree to analyze these decision alternatives.
   b. What should the company do based on your decision tree analysis?
   c. What returns will accrue to the company if your recommendation is followed?

4. A company has formalized a new-product concept and must now decide whether to provide for long-range production capacity in its five-year plan. The company has three opportunities for profiting from the new product: sell the idea outright now to another company, lease the concept for a royalty, or develop the product in-house. If the concept is sold outright, it will bring $1,500,000. A consulting firm has surveyed the potential markets for the idea. If the concept is leased for royalty, two companies have submitted proposals and this information applies:

Size of Market	Probability	Payoffs
Company A		
Large	0.5	$2,800,000
Marginal	0.5	2,200,000
Company B		
Large	0.5	2,600,000
Marginal	0.5	2,300,000

If the company develops the concept into a new product, it can sell the rights to the product. If this alternative is selected this information applies:

Size of Market	Probability	Payoffs
Large	0.5	$2,500,000
Marginal	0.5	2,200,000

If the company develops the new product and then produces and markets it, this information applies:

Size of Market	Probability	Payoffs
Large	0.5	$3,000,000
Marginal	0.5	1,800,000

   a. Use a decision tree analysis and recommend a course of action for this new-product idea.
   b. If the company follows your recommendation, what returns should the company expect to receive?

5. The SuperStorage Optical Media Company has developed a new storage device for computers and must now decide what to do with the idea. The expected life of the product is eight years. One possibility is to immediately license the product rights to another company that will market and sell the product. The best estimate for this alternative is a payoff of $5.5 million in licensing fees. Two other possibilities are to build a large manufacturing plant now to produce the product or build a small plant now to produce the product with the option of expanding the plant in three years. The expected payoff from producing the product depends on the market acceptance of the product during the first three years and during the last five years. If the market acceptance in the first three years is low, SuperStorage will stop production and cut its losses at that point. Analysts at SuperStorage have estimated a 70 percent probability of high market acceptance in the first three years.

If the market acceptance is high in the first three years, they believe the probability of a high market acceptance in the next five years to be 60 percent. The following tables give the net payoff estimates (in $ millions) for producing the product.

Market Acceptance		Large	Small Plant	Small Plant
First 3 Years	Next 5 Years	Plant	Don't Expand	Expand
High	High	$15	$10	$12
High	Low	4	6	4
Low	—	(2)	3	—

Note: ( ) means a negative payoff.

Using these estimates, analyze which decision SuperStorage should make:
a. Perform a complete decision tree analysis.
b. Recommend a strategy to SuperStorage.
c. Determine what payoffs will result from your recommendation.

6. A company manufactures stamped steel products. Increasingly, foreign producers are undercutting the company's prices for these stampings, and the company is studying the technology of its production capacity to determine if it should be upgraded to become competitive with the foreign firms. If the production processes are automated, the net present value of the returns (net present value means that the returns are expressed in terms of today's dollars) to the company is dependent on the market for the plant's products:

Process	Market Level	Likelihood	Return
Automated	High	0.1	$4,000,000
	Med	0.5	2,600,000
	Low	0.4	1,500,000

If the company decides to do nothing now and review the situation in five years, two alternatives will probably be present then—continue operating with the existing production processes or shut the plant down and liquidate its assets. If the plant continues to be operated in its existing condition after five years, the net present value of the returns is dependent on the market for the plant's products at that time:

Alternative	Market Level	Likelihood	Return
Do nothing now, continue operating	High	0.3	$3,000,000
in existing condition	Med	0.4	2,500,000
	Low	0.3	2,000,000

If the company shuts the plant down and liquidates its assets after five years, the net present value of the returns is estimated to be $2,000,000.
a. Use a decision tree analysis and recommend a course of action for the company.
b. What returns should the company actually expect from following your recommendation?

7. The Swing Time Golf Company manufactures golf clubs, primarily for large department store chains. Demand has been stable for the past several years and is expected to remain stable for the foreseeable future. Management is considering expanding the capabilities of the maintenance department by purchasing equipment

that would allow the department to perform certain types of machine maintenance that had previously been outsourced. The purchase cost of the new equipment would be $795,000, and the expected annual cost savings for machine maintenance is $215,000. Disregard the effects of taxes and monetary discount rates.

a. Would purchasing the new maintenance equipment increase the capacity of the maintenance department? Why or why not?

b. What would be the payback period for this investment in new equipment?

8. A U.S. manufacturer would like to build a manufacturing plant in East Asia to produce a new product that will be sold globally. The expected life of the plant is 20 years. Two locations are being considered: one in Singapore and one in Taiwan. Information on construction cost, annual fixed cost (excluding construction cost), variable cost, demand, and sales price has been gathered for the analysis:

	Singapore	**Taiwan**
Initial construction cost	$68,000,000	$53,000,000
Annual fixed cost	$2,800,000	$1,600,000
Variable cost per product	$130	$155
Annual demand (units)	250,000	250,000
Sales price per product	$210	$210

a. What is the payback period for the construction cost of each location?

b. What variable cost per product for Taiwan would make it equally attractive as Singapore in terms of annual profit?

c. What other factors should be considered in the location decision?

9. A national grocery store chain would like to open a store in Tulsa, Oklahoma. The company is considering two alternatives for the new store: construct a new building or lease an existing building left by another grocery store that was closed as the result of a merger. The economic life of the store is planned to be 30 years. The owner of the existing building has offered a 30-year lease agreement and has offered to remodel the building at no cost to the company. The monthly lease amount would be $11,000. Here is the information affecting the analysis:

	Build	**Lease**
Initial building cost	$4,200,000	—
Annual depreciation	$140,000	—
Annual lease payment	—	$132,000
Tax rate	40%	40%

a. Consider the after-tax savings of building a new store compared with leasing the existing building and compute the payback period for the initial building cost.

b. Do you recommend that the company build or lease? Why?

10. A distribution company is considering two locations for the construction of a new automated warehouse: Chicago and Dallas. Two types of automation are also being considered: bar coding and RF/ID (radio-frequency identification). The annual operating costs for each type of automation at the two locations are:

	Bar Coding		**RF/ID**	
Location	**Fixed Cost**	**Variable Cost per 1,000 Units**	**Fixed Cost**	**Variable Cost per 1,000 Units**
Chicago	$1,800,000	$12.30	$2,700,000	$9.70
Dallas	1,500,000	13.10	2,300,000	9.40

For what range of annual product volume handled would each location and type of automation be preferred?

11. A company is studying three locations for a new production facility for producing bar code scanners. The company has developed these estimates for the three locations:

Location Alternative	Annual Fixed Costs (millions)	Variable Cost per Bar Code Scanner
Dallas	$4.9	$2,400
San Antonio	3.6	2,700
Houston	4.1	2,500

The company estimates that sales for the bar code scanners will be 5,000 scanners in the first year, 10,000 in the third year, and 15,000 in the fifth year.
   a. Use break-even analysis to determine which location would be preferred in Years 1, 3, and 5.
   b. For what range of production capacity would each of the locations be preferred?

12. A company is evaluating Kansas City and Atlanta as alternative locations for a new plant to manufacture small-business computers. The following rating factors and scores have been prepared:

Locational Factor	Factor Weight	Location Kansas City	Atlanta
Cost per computer	0.60	$3,900	$4,300
Cost of living	0.10	0.60	0.60
Labor availability	0.10	0.70	0.70
Union activities	0.15	0.40	0.60
Proximity to similar industry	0.10	0.70	0.50
Local transportation systems	0.05	0.70	0.70

Use the relative–aggregate-scores approach to compare the two alternative locations. Which location would you recommend? Why?

13. East Coast Manufacturing Inc. plans to locate a new production facility in Hartford, Philadelphia, or Baltimore. Six location factors are important: cost per product unit, labor availability, union activities, local transportation, proximity to similar industry, and proximity to raw materials. The weighting of these factors and the scores for each location are shown below:

Location Factor	Weight	Hartford	Philadelphia	Baltimore
Cost per product unit	0.55	$48	$59	$52
Labor availability	0.15	0.5	0.8	0.8
Union activities	0.10	0.9	0.6	0.3
Local transportation	0.10	0.4	0.8	0.8
Proximity to similar industry	0.05	0.5	1.0	0.7
Proximity to raw materials	0.05	0.7	0.6	0.4

Note: Qualitative scores are based on a maximum of 1.00 as the best possible.

Use the relative-aggregate-scores approach to compare the three alternative locations. Which location is preferred?

14. The Comet Manufacturing Company needs to design a production line to manufacture a new product. The production analyst has determined that nine tasks need

to be performed to produce the product, and task times have been estimated. The desired rate of production is 25 units per hour. Employees are productive an average of 50 minutes each hour. The activity task times are given below. How many employees will be needed on the production line?

Task	Task Time (minutes per part)	Task	Task Time (minutes per part)
A	4	F	6
B	3	G	1
C	8	H	8
D	6	I	5
E	2		

15. A company assembles and mails advertising packages for customers on a contract basis. One such contract has just been signed and the company is developing a layout for the assembly line. These tasks, their predecessor tasks, and task times have been identified and estimated, as shown below. The contract specifies that 50,000 mailers must be processed in five working days, the company works only one 8-hour shift per day, and employees are allowed two 15-minute coffee breaks per shift.
    a. Draw the diagram of the precedence relationships.
    b. Compute the cycle time in minutes.
    c. Compute the minimum number of workstations for the contract.

Task	Tasks That Immediately Precede	Task Time (minutes/mailer)
A. Inspect materials for quality.	—	0.30
B. Prepare kits for assembly.	A	0.20
C. Assemble and glue envelopes.	B	0.15
D. Get and fold circular.	B	0.10
E. Attach address to envelope.	C	0.10
F. Place circular in envelope and seal envelope.	D,E	0.15
G. Prepare plastic sleeve to fit over envelope.	F	0.05
H. Seal package into plastic sleeve.	G	0.15
I. Process addressed mailers through postage machine.	H	0.15
J. Deliver mailers to mail bin.	I	0.05

16. In Problem 15, combine the tasks into workstations to minimize idle time by using the incremental utilization heuristic. Evaluate your solution. Could you use the longest-task-time heuristic? Why or why not?

17. The back-room operations of a fast-food restaurant have these tasks:

Task	Tasks That Immediately Precede	Time to Perform Task (minutes)	Task	Tasks That Immediately Precede	Time to Perform Task (minutes)
A	—	0.39	H	—	0.90
B	—	0.25	I	—	0.60
C	—	0.40	J	H,I,G	0.40
D	—	0.05	K	J	0.30
E	A,B	0.49	L	K	0.25
F	C,D	0.65			Total 5.07
G	E,F	0.39			

If 100 burgers per hour must be prepared by the crew and 50 minutes per hour are productive:

a.   Draw a diagram of the precedence relationships.

b.   Compute the cycle time per burger in minutes.

c.   Compute the minimum number of workstations required.

d.   How would you combine tasks into workstations to minimize idle time? Use the incremental utilization heuristic. Evaluate your proposal. Could you use the longest-task-time heuristic? Why or why not?

18. The time to perform each task and the tasks that must immediately precede are shown below:

Task	Tasks That Immediately Precede	Time to Perform Task (minutes)
A	—	0.25
B	A	0.08
C	B	0.12
D	B	0.17
E	C,D	0.06
F	E	0.05
G	E	0.09
H	E	0.11
I	F,G,H	0.16
J	I	0.08

If 150 products are needed per hour and 50 minutes per hour are productive:

a.   Draw a diagram of the precedence relationships.

b.   Compute the cycle time per unit in minutes.

c.   Compute the minimum number of workstations required.

d.   Use the longest-task-time heuristic to balance the production line. Evaluate your solution.

19. The time to perform each task and the tasks that must immediately precede are shown below:

Task	Tasks That Immediately Precede	Time to Perform Task (minutes)
A	—	0.07
B	—	0.15
C	A,B	0.08
D	C	0.05
E	C	0.18
F	—	0.12
G	—	0.06
H	F,G	0.10
I	D,E	0.15
J	H,I	0.11
K	J	0.06
L	K	0.19

If 220 products are needed per hour and 55 minutes per hour are productive:

a.   Draw a diagram of the precedence relationships.

b. Compute the cycle time per unit in minutes.
c. Compute the minimum number of workstations required.
d. Use the longest-task-time heuristic to balance the production line. Evaluate your solution.

20. From the information in Problem 15, use the *POM Software Library* that accompanies this book to balance the production line.
a. Use the incremental utilization heuristic to balance the production line. Explain and evaluate this solution.
b. Use the longest-task-time heuristic to balance the production line.
c. Use the modified longest-task-time heuristic to balance the production line. Explain and evaluate this solution.

21. From the information in Problem 19, use the *POM Software Library* to balance the production line.
a. Use the incremental utilization heuristic to balance the production line. Explain and evaluate this solution.
b. Use the longest-task-time heuristic to balance the production line.
c. Compare the solutions obtained in Parts a and b. What are the pros and cons of each solution?

22. A manufacturer is interested in creating a cellular manufacturing layout with its current machines. The chart below shows the machines required by each part. Organize the machines and parts into two production cells that minimize the number of exceptional parts.

		Parts				
	1	2	3	4	5	6
A			X		X	
B	X					X
Machines C		X	X		X	
D	X			X		X
E		X			X	

23. A manufacturer is interested in creating a cellular manufacturing layout with its current machines. The chart below shows the machines required by each part. Organize the machines and parts into two production cells that minimize the number of exceptional parts.

		Parts				
	1	2	3	4	5	6
A					X	X
B	X		X	X		
Machines C	X			X		
D		X			X	X
E	X		X			
F		X			X	

24. A manufacturer is interested in creating a cellular manufacturing layout with its current machines. The chart below shows the machines required by each part. Organize the machines and parts into two production cells that minimize the number of exceptional parts.

Parts

Machines	1	2	3	4	5	6
A	X	X			X	
B			X	X		
C	X	X				
D			X	X		X
E	X				X	
F				X		X

25. A manufacturer is interested in creating a cellular manufacturing layout with its current machines. The chart below shows the machines required by each part. Organize the machines and parts into three similar-sized production cells that minimize the number of exceptional parts.

Parts

Machines	1	2	3	4	5	6	7	8
A		X					X	
B			X		X			
C			X		X			X
D	X			X				
E		X				X		
F			X			X		X
G				X				
H		X				X	X	
I	X			X				

26. These closeness ratings are used for the purpose of indicating the desirability of having departments near one another:

Closeness Rating	Meaning of Rating
1	Necessary
2	Very important
3	Important
4	Slightly important
5	Unimportant
6	Undesirable

Here are six departments and their closeness ratings. The closeness rating between a pair of departments is found at their intersections on the grid below.

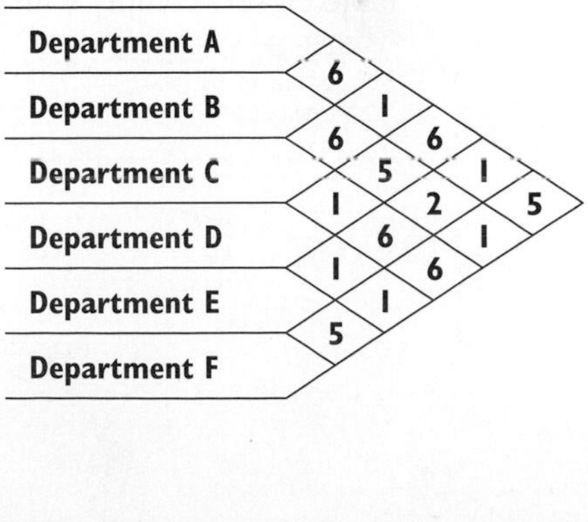

Here is a layout of the six departments. Suggest ways to improve the layout to more closely comply with the closeness ratings above.

C	D	F
E	A	B

27. These closeness ratings are used for the purpose of indicating the desirability of having departments near one another:

Closeness Rating	Meaning of Rating
1	Necessary
2	Very important
3	Important
4	Slightly important
5	Unimportant
6	Undesirable

Here are nine departments and their closeness ratings. The closeness rating between a pair of departments is found at their intersections on the grid below.

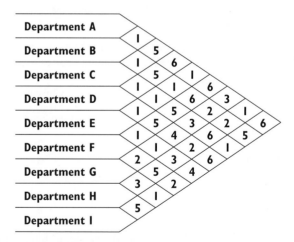

Here is a layout of the nine departments. Suggest ways to improve the layout to more closely comply with the closeness ratings above.

A	C	H
D	B	I
F	G	E

CASES

Blue Powder Company

The Blue Powder Company produces powder for shotgun shells in its only plant, which is in Cleveland, Ohio. The plant was originally built in 1861, but with the growing environmental pressures from being located in a large city, the company is considering three new location alternatives for its central offices and manufacturing plant: Las Vegas, Santa Fe, and Yuma. The production processes at Blue Powder require about 300 production workers and 200 engineering and management personnel, large amounts of water and other utilities, large expanses of land, large volumes of materials to be shipped in and out of the plant, and fire and explosion tolerant areas.

The three locations under consideration have been analyzed by the company's staff, and these operating costs have been developed for each location:

	Las Vegas	Santa Fe	Yuma
Annual fixed costs	$3,000,000	$2,700,000	$2,200,000
Variable cost/pound	$0.0500	$0.0700	$0.1100

These costs reflect all relocation costs, production costs, overhead costs, transportation costs, and so on. The company has produced 100 million pounds of powder this year, and sales are expected to increase by about 10 million pounds per year. The company does not think that sales volume or sales price will be affected by the location of the plant.

Assignment

1. What major factors should be considered in choosing one of the three location alternatives?
2. How would you weight the factors that you developed in No. 1 for Blue Powder's plant? Which ones are more important and which ones should not be weighted heavily? Discuss and defend your answer.
3. Analyze the factors listed in No. 1, and recommend a course of action for Blue Powder.

Power Byte Computers

Chang Yung Chong is considering whether to open a new computer store called Power Byte Computers in West Lafayette, Indiana. Mr. Chong wants to proceed cautiously since the market potential for another computer store is uncertain. He can either open a small store now, open a large store now, drop the idea now, or else have a market potential study conducted and then decide whether to open a small or large store or do nothing. A marketing research firm has offered to conduct a market potential survey for $5,000. The survey would suggest either a favorable or unfavorable market for a new computer store.

Based on Mr. Chong's calculations, he believes that if a small store is opened he would earn a first-year profit of $30,000 in a favorable market, but would lose $10,000 the first year in an unfavorable market. If a large store is opened he believes he would earn $60,000 the first year in a favorable market, but lose $35,000 the first year in an unfavorable market. Without the insight from a market potential survey, Mr. Chong believes there is a 50 percent chance that the market will be favorable.

In initial discussions with the marketing research firm, the marketing analyst guessed that there was a 60 percent chance that a survey would suggest a favorable market. Reluctantly, the analyst admitted that marketing surveys do not always assess markets correctly. Upon further prodding by Mr. Chong, the analyst estimated that if the survey suggested a favorable market then the chance of the market actually being favorable was 90 percent. But if the survey suggested an unfavorable market, there would still be a 15 percent chance that the market would actually be favorable. Mr. Chong is feeling rather perplexed by this time.

Assignment

1. Why do you think the decision of what to do seems difficult to Mr. Chong?
2. Construct a decision tree representing all possible actions, events, and payoffs.
3. Analyze your decision tree, computing all the expected values, and recommend what Mr. Chong should do (explain completely).
4. With your recommendation in No. 3, what is the best-case and worst-case first-year net financial result to which Mr. Chong would be exposed?
5. Mr. Chong has now decided that he does not want to be exposed to any first-year net loss over $25,000. This means he no longer wants to consider opening a large store. What would you recommend to Mr. Chong now?

Integrated Products Corporation

A methods analyst at Integrated Products Corporation (IPC) has been studying the assembly line that produces bar code scanners. The objective of the analysis is to reduce worker idle time on the assembly line to reduce the labor cost of the scanners. This information applies:

Task	Tasks That Must Immediately Precede	Task Time (minutes)
A. Kit the purchased assemblies.	—	1.35
B. Inspect the kitted assemblies.	A	2.20
C. Process controller board through auto-insertion equipment line.	—	1.90
D. Process controller board through soldering equipment line.	C	2.39
E. Trim and finish controller board.	D	1.75
F. Assemble power unit into chassis.	B	1.25
G. Assemble reader unit into chassis.	F	0.90
H. Assemble controller board into chassis.	E,G	2.49
I. Assemble display unit into chassis.	H	2.19
J. Inspect and test finished scanner.	I	2.40
K. Package finished scanner.	J	0.69
		Total 19.51

Twenty bar code scanners must be produced by the production line per hour. An average of 50 minutes per hour are productive because of personal time, machine breakdown, and start-up and shutdown times. Because the union contract restricts the kinds of tasks that can be combined into workstations, tasks can be grouped only within these compatibility groups:

Compatibility Group	Tasks
Group I	A,B
Group II	C
Group III	D
Group IV	E
Group V	F,G,H,I,J,K

For example, Tasks F and G could be combined into one workstation, but Tasks E and F could not. Tasks within compatibility groups may be combined while observing the precedence relationships; in other words, adjacent tasks along the network diagram may be combined. Group I work is essentially hand work requiring only inexpensive and plentiful tools.

Assignment

1. Draw a diagram of the precedence relationships.
2. Compute the cycle time per bar code scanner.
3. Compute the minimum number of workstations required.
4. Use the *POM Software Library* to solve this line-balancing problem.
5. Compare and explain the solutions of the incremental utilization heuristic and the longest-task-time heuristic.
6. Discuss how you would implement your solution in a real manufacturing setting. What obstacles would you expect to encounter? How would you overcome these obstacles?

Mexibell Telephones Incorporated

Mexibell Telephones Incorporated (MTI) manufacturers telephones that are sold primarily to large businesses and government organizations. MTI has just been awarded a large contract to supply telephones to the Canadian government, with deliveries to be spread over the next three years. The company has decided to set up a new production line at one of its maquiladora plants across the Mexican border from Laredo, Texas. This location would provide easy access to Interstate Highway 35 for direct shipments to Canada. Maria Garcia is the senior production analyst at the MTI plant and has the responsibility for designing the production line.

MTI must supply 260,000 telephones annually, with routine shipments throughout the year. The company operates 8 hours per day, 250 days per year. Because of employee breaks, maintenance and other reasons, about 80 minutes of each 8-hour workday are actually nonproductive. Ms. Garcia has identified all of the necessary tasks, the predecessor tasks, and the estimated task times for making a telephone.

Task	Tasks That Immediately Precede	Time to Perform Task (minutes)
A. Inspect parts kit for completeness.	—	0.23
B. Attach two bells to bell mount.	A	0.29
C. Attach feet to base.	A	0.40
D. Test base circuitry.	A	0.12
E. Attach keypad module to keypad mount.	A	0.15
F. Install loudness control knob on bell mount.	B	0.08
G. Rivet base circuitry to base.	C,D	0.20
H. Attach bell mount to base with screws.	F,G	0.14

(continued)

Task	Tasks That Immediately Precede	Time to Perform Task (minutes)
I. Snap keys onto keypad module.	E	0.37
J. Attach hangup buttons and spring to keypad mount.	I	0.09
K. Rivet keypad mount to base.	H,J	0.22
L. Connect wires between circuitry, keypad module, and bell mount.	K	0.06
M. Insert cable through handset.	A	0.08
N. Connect and insert earpiece module into handset.	M	0.05
O. Connect and insert mouthpiece module into handset.	N	0.05
P. Screw earpiece and mouthpiece covers onto handset.	O	0.13
Q. Connect handset cable to base circuitry.	L,P	0.07
R. Connect external cable to base circuitry.	Q	0.08
S. Attach top housing to base with screws.	R	0.14
T. Attach keypad face plate onto unit.	S	0.06
U. Test the finished unit.	T	0.18
V. Package for shipment.	U	0.28

Because it would be illogical for certain tasks to be performed by the same employee, compatibility restrictions exist. Tasks can only be grouped together if they are within the same compatibility group. Four compatibility groups have been created, with many tasks residing in more than one compatibility group:

Compatibility Group	Task
Group I	A,B,F,H,K,L,Q,R,S,T,U,V
Group II	A,C,D,G,H,K,L,Q,R,S,T,U,V
Group III	A,E,I,J,K,L,Q,R,S,T,U,V
Group IV	A,M,N,O,P,Q,R,S,T,U,V

For example, Tasks B and F can be grouped together into one workstation, but Tasks B and M cannot.

Assignment

1. Draw a diagram of the precedence relationships.
2. Compute the cycle time per telephone in minutes.
3. Compute the minimum number of workstations required.
4. Use the *POM Software Library* to design an assembly line for the telephones. Which heuristic has the highest utilization of labor and equipment?
5. What factors other than utilization should be considered in designing the production line?
6. Describe your recommended solution. Which tasks are combined into workstations? How many workstations are in each work center?
7. Discuss how you would implement your solution in a real manufacturing setting. What obstacles would you expect to encounter? How would you overcome these obstacles?

Precision Machine Works

Precision Machine Works (PMW) in Frankfurt, Germany, manufacturers aluminum parts for a variety of companies throughout Europe. PMW has decided to build a new manufacturing plant to replace its current facility, which it has outgrown. Franz Beckler, the production manager, is in charge of developing the production area layout within the new plant. Mr. Beckler has already decided that the production equipment should be organized into nine departments. With the help of his staff, Mr. Beckler has also developed closeness rating scores that represent the desirability level of having any two departments adjacent to each other. The volume of part flow between each pair of departments as well as certain technological restrictions have been considered in developing the closeness ratings. Below are shown the closeness rating between each pair of departments and the meaning of each rating:

Closeness Rating	Meaning of Rating
1	Necessary
2	Very important
3	Important
4	Slightly important
5	Unimportant
6	Undesirable

Department A								
	4							
Department B		6						
	5		5					
Department C		1		5				
	6		1		1			
Department D		1		5		5		
	6		6		4		1	
Department E		3		6		3		6
	5		2		6		1	
Department F		6		6		2		
	6		3		4			
Department G		5		5				
	6		6					
Department H		4						
	6							
Department I								

Here is a template of the plant floor space to represent the layout of the nine departments.

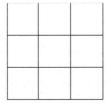

Assignment

1. Use trial and error to develop a layout of the nine departments that attempts to minimize the sum of the closeness ratings of adjacent departments. Two departments are considered adjacent if they share a common side (not a corner).

2. Besides the volume of part flow between each pair of departments, what other factors should be considered in deciding on the plant layout?

ENDNOTES

1. Hansell, Saul. "Wall St. Plans for Trading by the Billions." *New York Times,* November 3, 1997, C1, C8.
2. Lee, Steven H. "Hog Farm Will Double Production." *The Dallas Morning News,* November 20, 1997, 6D.
3. "Industrial Production and Capacity Utilization." Federal Reserve Statistical Release G.17, released August 15, 2000.
4. "The Chips Are Down. Way Down." *Business Week,* August 7, 2000, 58.
5. "Outsourcing Helps Businesses Get More Done for Less." *Arlington Star-Telegram,* April 24, 2000, Tarrant Business Section, 16–17.
6. Schniederjans, Marc J. *International Facility Acquisition and Location Analysis.* Westport, CT: Quorum, 1999.

SELECTED BIBLIOGRAPHY

Blackstone, William H., Jr. *Capacity Management.* Cincinnati, OH: South-Western, College Publishing, 1989.

Brandon, John A. *Cellular Manufacturing: Integrating Technology and Management.* New York: John Wiley & Sons, 1996.

Brausch, John M., and Thomas C. Taylor. "Who Is Accounting for the Cost of Capacity?" *Management Accounting* 78, no. 8 (February 1997): 44–50.

Canary, Patrick H. "International Transportation Factors in Site Selection." *Site Selection* (October 1988): 1217–1219.

Chan, Yupo. *Location Theory and Decision Analysis with Facility-Location & Land-Use Models.* Cincinnati, OH: South-Western College Publishing, 2001.

Domanski, Bernard. "A Look at Capacity Planning in Distributed Environments." *Capacity Management Review* 25, no. 4 (April 1997): 1–21.

Frazier, Gregory V., and Mark T. Spriggs. "Achieving Competitive Advantage through Group Technology." *Business Horizons* 39, no. 3 (May–June 1996): 83–90.

Gaither, N., G. V. Frazier, and J. C. Wei. "From Job Shops to Manufacturing Cells." *Production and Inventory Management Journal* 31, no. 4 (Fourth Quarter 1990): 33–36.

Haksever, Cengiz, Robert G. Murdick, Barry Render, and Roberta S. Russell. *Service Management and Operations,* 2nd ed. Englewood Cliffs, NJ: Prentice Hall, 2000.

Houshyar, Azim, and Bob White. "Comparison of Solution Procedures to the Facility Location Problem." *Computers & Industrial Engineering* 32, no. 1 (January 1997): 77–87.

Hurter, Arthur P., Jr., and Joseph S. Martinich. *Facility Location and the Theory of Production.* Boston: Kluwer Academic Publishers, 1989.

Hyer, Nancy Lea, and U. Wemmerlov. "Group Technology and Productivity." *Harvard Business Review* 62 (July–August 1984): 140–149.

Jackson, Harry K., and Normand L. Frigon. *A Practical Guide to Capacity Planning and Management.* New York: John Wiley & Sons, 1998.

Klammer, Thomas P. *Capacity Measurement & Improvement: A Manager's Guide to Evaluating and Optimizing Capacity Productivity.* Chicago: Irwin Professional Publishing, 1996.

McGregor, Wes, and Danny Shiem-Shin Then. *Facilities Management and the Business of Space.* New York: John Wiley & Sons, 1999.

McMahon, Chris, and Jimmie Browne. *CAD/CAM: Principles, Practice, and Manufacturing Management,* 2nd ed. Englewood Cliffs, NJ: Prentice Hall, 1998.

Meller, Russell D., and Kai-Yin Gau. "The Facility Layout Problem: Recent and Emerging Trends and Perspectives." *Journal of Manufacturing Systems* 15, no. 5 (1996): 351–366.

Meyers, Fred E., and Matthew P. Stephens. *Manufacturing Facilities Design and Material Handling,* 2nd ed. Englewood Cliffs, NJ: Prentice Hall, 2000.

Schniederjans, Marc J. *International Facility Acquisition and Location Analysis.* Westport, CT: Quorum, 1999.

Suresh, Nallan C., and John M. Kay, eds. *Group Technology and Cellular Manufacturing: A State-of-the-Art Synthesis of Research and Practice.* Boston: Kluwer Academic Publishers, 1997.

Swamidass, P. M. "A Comparison of the Plant Location Strategies of Foreign and Domestic Manufacturers in the U.S." *Journal of International Business Studies* 21, no. 2 (Second Quarter 1990): 301–317.

Winarchick, Charles, and Ronald D. Caldwell. "Physical Interactive Simulation: A Hands-On Approach to Facilities Improvements." *IIE Solutions* 29, no. 5 (May 1997): 34–42.

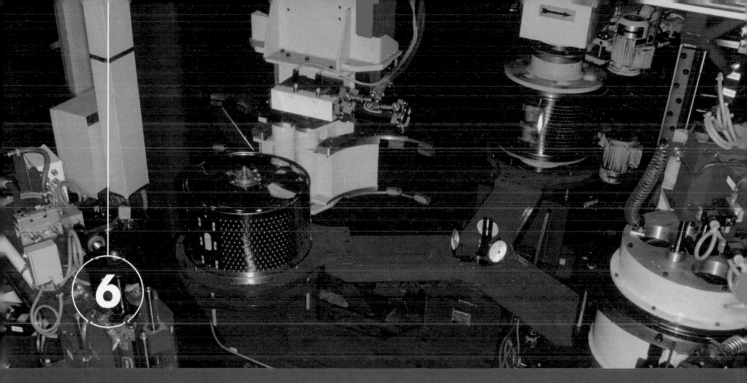

Operations Technologies

Introduction

Types of Manufacturing Automation
Machine Attachments
Numerically Controlled Machines
Robots
Automated Quality Control Inspection
Automatic Identification Systems
Automated Process Controls

Automated Production Systems
Automated Flow Lines
Automated Assembly Systems
Flexible Manufacturing Systems
Automated Storage and Retrieval Systems

Software Systems for Automation
CAD/CAM
Computer-Integrated Manufacturing
Enterprise Resource Planning

Automation in Services

Automation Issues
Use of Automation

Building Manufacturing Flexibility
Justifying Automation Projects
Managing Technological Change
Worker Displacement, Training, and Retraining

Deciding among Automation Alternatives
Rating Scale Approach
Relative-Aggregate-Scores Approach

Wrap-Up: What World-Class Companies Do

Review and Discussion Questions

Internet Assignments

Problems

Cases
Golden Kernel Processing Company I and II
Western Arizona University

Endnotes

Selected Bibliography

STRATEGIC USE OF TECHNOLOGY AT NABISCO

Karen Mattke, manager of logistics productivity at the snack giant Nabisco, is responsible for helping to streamline the company's distribution process by making sure Oreos and other cracker and cookie products move from bakery to store shelf as efficiently as possible. Mattke knew that technology must play a key part in helping the company to stay competitive, particularly at the company's nearly 100 small warehouses that serve as the final stopover before products reach the stores.

Although the mini-warehouses were serving Nabisco well, company management decided that these facilities needed to migrate from paper-based stock picking systems (to retrieve or pick items from warehouse shelves) to more efficient automated systems. The change was scheduled to coincide with the rollout of Nabisco's new SAP R/3 enterprise resource planning system, a highly integrated computer information system. Nabisco also changed from using in-house–developed inventory management systems to a more robust warehouse management system, a computer software system for managing warehouse inventories.

According to Mattke, economics played an important role in evaluating which processes to automate. After conducting an activity-based costing analysis, Nabisco discovered that stock picking had the highest cost per unit. Management decided that some form of automation was the answer, and the technology choices were whittled down to speech recognition or pick-to-light systems. In the end, the speech recognition technology won out due to its flexibility compared to the more static pick-to-light systems.

With the new voice recognition system, workers wear headsets and move about the warehouses listening to their order fulfillment instructions and responding to computer-generated tasks. Orders are generated by the SAP software system and sent to individual workers (stock pickers). The picker is then directed to a location on the conveyor line and told by the computer to pick a given amount of product. If the location contains the necessary amount of product, the worker says "Got it" to the computer and moves to the next location. If there is not enough product to fill the order, the worker verbally responds to the computer with this information.

The new system allows for hands-free and eyes-free operation for the workers, which has improved stock picking performance. Says Mattke, "We've seen some increase in the speed of fulfilling orders, but the key for us was to improve picking accuracy." Improved accuracy means better customer service. Also, because the workers do not have to spend extra time customizing the unit to their individual speech patterns, they begin to feel comfortable after just an hour of training. Nabisco is now looking to extend automation to other stages of the warehousing process.[1]

Today is truly an exciting time to study operations management. The changes brought about by new technologies keep operations managers on their toes, and require them to stay up-to-date on the latest developments in operations technologies. Advances in computer technologies and software applications have had broad-reaching impacts across all industries. To stay competitive, manufacturers as well as service organizations must adopt new technologies. And they must make their technology-adoption plans part of their operations strategies.

BUSINESS SNAPSHOT 6.1

Northrop Grumman Searches for New Production Technology

Northrop Grumman is a military aircraft manufacturer in the United States. Aircraft assembly is an expensive operation because of the labor intensity and sporadic quality problems involved in drilling millions of holes each year. More than 70,000 holes are manually drilled and fastened per shipset in each of Northrop Grumman's military airframes, accounting for nearly 44 percent of the total assembly costs.

The current method of hole drilling and countersinking for fastener installation uses unique drill fixtures for each assembly and subassembly processed, at an average cost of $50,000 each. Well over 900 conventional drill fixtures are required for airframe assembly on each program. Each drill fixture is constructed through a laborious process. Variation exists in the quality of drilled holes because each drill operator controls the drilling speed and feed as a hole is made with an air-powered, handheld drill.

Northrop Grumman is very interested in finding new production technologies to modernize its manufacturing operations, particularly its hole drilling process. The objective of its modernization effort is to identify automation opportunities for its assembly lines that will increase flexibility while simultaneously reducing direct labor costs and improving quality. In addition, to increase the quality and efficiency of assembly processes, areas must be identified where automation will eliminate the need for many of the assembly fixtures and drill templates currently in use, thereby reducing recurring and nonrecurring tooling costs.

Source: Bullen, George N. "The Mechanization/Automation of Major Aircraft Assembly Tools." *Production and Inventory Management Journal* 38, no. 3 (1997): 84–87.

Advanced technology refers to the application of the latest scientific or engineering discoveries to the design of operations and production processes. Today, new technology almost always means that information technology and automation have been integrated into the processes.

In the distant past, automation meant the replacement of human effort with machine effort, to save labor cost. Today's technologies, however, have far surpassed this older concept. The use of the term **automation** today refers to the integration of a full range of advanced information and engineering discoveries into operations processes for strategic purposes. Today, automation projects are initiated not only for labor-cost savings but also for improved quality, faster production and delivery of products and services, and increased flexibility. Business Snapshot 6.1 describes one company's search for new technologies for its production processes.

In this chapter we will study a variety of new technologies used in manufacturing and services, and we will discuss a number of issues that are important when adopting automation.

TYPES OF MANUFACTURING AUTOMATION

The enormous growth in the field of industrial automation has brought a myriad of automated machines with diverse features. These types of automation are particularly noteworthy: machine attachments, numerically controlled machines, robots, automated quality control inspection, automatic identification systems, and automated process controls. Table 6.1 describes each of these types and gives examples of each type.

Table 6.1	Types of Manufacturing Automation

Types of Machines	Description	Examples
Machine attachments	Machines that replace human effort with machine effort and typically perform from one to a few simple operations	Magazine feed attachments, quick centering and grasping devices for lathes, strip feeders for stamping machines, vibrating hoppers with scales that drop charges of chemicals into waiting containers
Numerically controlled (N/C) machines	Machines with control systems that read instructions and translate them into machine operations	Lathes, boring mills, tire-building machines, curing machines, weaving machines
Robots	General-purpose, reprogrammable, multifunction manipulators that possess some humanlike physiological characteristics	Machines that weld, paint, assemble, inspect for quality, grasp, transport, and store
Automated quality control inspection	Automated machines that perform part or all of the inspection process	Electronic circuit checks, computer-driven function checks, weighing robots, flexible inspection systems
Automatic identification systems (AIS)	Technologies used in automatic acquisition of product data for entry into a computer	Barcoding systems, inventory counting, data entry for shop-floor control, systems for adjusting settings of production machines
Automated process controls	Computer systems that receive data on the production process and send adjustments to process settings	Control systems for rolling mills in tire manufacturing, calenders in plastic film processing, cracking units in oil refineries

Machine Attachments

Machine attachments are usually relatively inexpensive add-ons to machines that reduce the amount of human effort and time required to perform an operation. These appendages represent the oldest technology in automation and are commonly found in all production systems.

Numerically Controlled Machines

Numerically controlled (N/C) machines were the heroes among automatic machines in the 1950–1980 period as a broad range of applications were developed for this important technological achievement. Today, these machines are programmed through computers to perform a cycle of operations repeatedly. The machines have a control system that reads the instructions and then translates them into machine operations. Machine settings are achieved by the control system rather than by human beings. Business Snapshot 6.2 describes an early experiment with N/C machines.

Over the years N/C machines have evolved. Early N/C machines used paper tape with punched holes representing machine instructions. Later some N/C machines incorporated automatic tool changing. With the advances in computing came computer numerically controlled machines (CN/C). As computing sophistication continued to increase, direct numerically controlled machines (DN/C), were developed that placed several machines under the control of a single computer.

BUSINESS SNAPSHOT 6.2

One of the First N/C Machines

One of the first demonstrations of a numerically controlled machine took place at MIT in the early 1950s. It was a Cincinnati vertical milling machine that had been modified at the servomechanism laboratory of MIT to operate from a punched tape input. At the time, it was machining a wingroot fitting for a B47. The fitting was machined from a solid block of mag-

nesium. The finished block was so complex that it weighed only 10 percent of the original block. The operator simply pushed a button to start the cycle. The machine then performed the roughing-cut cycle by operating in three planes simultaneously. When the cycle was completed, a bell rang to attract the operator's attention. The operator then brushed some chips

away and pressed the button for the finishing-cut cycle, which the machine quickly completed. The only operations the operator performed were to place the part in the machine, start it, brush away some chips, and remove the finished part. The operator, incidentally, was a law student from Harvard. This was the first machine tool he had ever operated.

Source: Maynard, H. B. *Industrial Engineering Handbook*, p. 1/101. New York: McGraw-Hill, 1963.

N/C machines are important automated machines in their own right. When their programs are efficiently produced and when their tools are effectively designed, they have great flexibility in being changed to other products and are therefore used extensively in process-focused job shops. Also, numerically controlled machines represent an important evolutionary stage in the advance toward the ultimate in automated machines—robots.

Robots

Joseph Engleberger, who is internationally acclaimed as the father of the industrial robot, developed the first robot for industrial use. It was installed in 1959 to unload a die-casting machine in a General Motors factory.[2] Today **robotry** is a fast-developing field in which humanlike machines perform production tasks. The Robotic Institute of America defines a **robot** as follows: *An industrial robot is a reprogrammable, multifunctional manipulator designed to move materials, parts, tools, or specialized devices through variable programmed motions for the performance of a variety of tasks.* The brain of these machines is a microcomputer that when programmed guides the machine through its predetermined operations.

The variety of robots available from suppliers today is impressive. And the kinds of things that robots can do are truly amazing. Such robots can move their arms in vertical, radial, and horizontal axes and hold tools such as spot-welding guns, arc-welding tools, spray-painting guns, rotating spindles for metal-cutting machines, screwdrivers, heating torches, and water-jet cutting tools.

Robots have grippers at the end of their arms that are vacuum, magnetized, or adhesive devices. Robots also have sensors that allow the grippers and arms to be positioned at precise locations as they perform their work. The common types of sensors follow:

1. **Tactile sensors** are of two kinds: *touch* and *force*. Touch sensors indicate whether contact has been made. Force sensors indicate the magnitude of the force of the contact made with the object.

Robots can operate in conditions unfavorable to humans, such as extreme heat, noise, or darkness.

© CHARLES O'REAR/CORBIS

2. **Proximity sensors** indicate when an object is close to the sensor.
3. **Machine vision and optical sensors:** *Machine vision sensors* are used for inspection, parts identification, guidance, and other uses; *optical sensors* are used to detect the presence of objects.

Robots can operate in environments that are hostile to humans. Heat, noise, dust, skin irritants, darkness, and other conditions pose no threat to robots. Also, in many applications, robots can produce products of a quality higher than is possible with human beings because robots are more predictable and perform the same operations precisely and repeatedly without fatigue.

Because robots are controlled by computers, they can be easily programmed and reprogrammed to perform a variety of tasks. This allows great flexibility in switching between different products and tasks. Robots are the basic building blocks for the automated production systems that we will discuss later.

Automated Quality Control Inspection

Automated quality control inspection systems are machines that have been integrated into the inspection of products for quality control purposes. These systems perform a wide range of tests and inspections and are found in many industries. They can be used to take physical dimensions of parts, compare the measurements to standards, and determine whether the parts meet quality specifications. Similarly, these machines can be used to check the performance of electronic circuits. For example, in the computer industry, computers are checked by software that tests every function the computers must perform.

As we discuss further in Chapter 17, Quality Control, as quality control inspections are performed increasingly by automated machines, 100 percent inspection is becoming economically feasible for many products. This trend should lead to improved product quality and reduced quality control inspection costs.

Automatic Identification Systems

Automatic identification systems (AIS) use bar codes, radio frequencies, magnetic stripes, optical character recognition, and machine vision to sense and input data into computers. Data are read from products, documents, parts, and containers without the need for workers to read or interpret the data. A good example of these systems is in checkout counters at grocery stores. The clerk passes the bar code on an item across the scanner. The system reads the identification number from the bar code on the item, accesses a computer database and sends the price of the item to the cash register, describes the item to the customer through a speaker, and inputs the item identification number to the inventory system for the purpose of adjusting inventory counts. AIS are becoming more commonplace in warehouses, shop floors of factories, retailing and wholesaling, and a variety of other applications.

Automated Process Controls

Automated process controls use sensors to obtain measures of the performance of industrial processes; they compare these measures to standards within stored computer software programs; and when the performance varies significantly from standards, they send signals that change the settings of the processes. Such systems have been in use for many years in the chemical processing, petroleum refining, and paper industries.

One example of automated process controls was recently observed in the paper industry. A large calender presses wood pulp between rolls to form a continuous sheet of paper. A large optical scanner is mounted above the paper sheet to monitor paper thickness and density. The readings from the optical scanner are fed into an expert system of a computer, which is a rule-based logical algorithm. This expert system decides whether the paper thickness and density are within tolerances. If they are not, the system decides what changes should be made and sends new machine settings to the calender machine, thus altering the paper thickness and density.

With the increasing use of computer-aided design and computer-aided manufacturing (CAD/CAM) systems, automated process controls have become important in other industries as well. Even in discrete-unit manufacturing, the settings of individual machines and groups of machines can now be sensed and changed as necessary to provide products of uniform dimensions and other characteristics.

As with other automated machinery, when automated process controls are installed, some flexibility is lost until software can be developed to accommodate different product characteristics. Also, although the initial cost of the hardware of these systems may not be very high, the cost of developing the supporting software and integrating the system with the remainder of the production system can be very costly. Nevertheless, the product quality necessary to support the business strategy may make such costs acceptable.

The automated machines described in this section are impressive, but the ultimate benefits from automation may not be achieved until the individual machines are integrated into entire automated production systems.

AUTOMATED PRODUCTION SYSTEMS

As the technology of automation has become more sophisticated, the focus has shifted away from individual machines and toward a broader concept. Today, whole systems of automated machines linked for broader purposes are becoming more common. We shall discuss four general categories of these systems: automated flow lines, automated assembly systems, flexible manufacturing systems, and automated storage and retrieval systems.

Automated Flow Lines

An **automated flow line** includes several automated machines that are linked by automated parts transfer and handling machines. The individual machines on the line use automated raw material feeders and automatically carry out their operations without the need for human attendance. As each machine completes its operations, partially completed parts are automatically transferred to the next machine on the line in a fixed sequence until the work of the line is finished. These systems are ordinarily used to produce an entire major component, for example, rear axle housings for trucks. They are common in the automobile industry.

These systems are often referred to as **fixed automation** or **hard automation**, which means that the flow lines are designed to produce one type of component or product. Because of the very high initial investment required and the difficulty of changing over to other products, these systems are used when product demand is high, stable, and extending well into the future. If these conditions are met, the production cost per unit is very low. But because of shortened product life cycles and shifts in production technology, the popularity of fixed automation may be declining. Production systems are increasingly favoring production equipment that provides greater product flexibility. We discuss this trend later in this section when we discuss flexible manufacturing systems.

Automated Assembly Systems

An **automated assembly system** is a system of automated assembly machines that are linked together by automated materials-handling equipment. Materials are automatically fed to each machine, which is ordinarily some type of robot such as a robotic welder or a component insertion unit, which joins one or more materials, parts, or assemblies. Then the partially completed work is automatically transferred to the next assembly machine. This process is repeated until the whole assembly is completed. The purpose of these systems is to produce major assemblies or even completed products.

For an automated assembly system to be successful, major product design modifications are necessary. The product design appropriate for assembly by human hands cannot be directly applied to an automated assembly system because the capabilities of human beings cannot always be duplicated by robots. For example, a worker can use a screw, lock washer, and nut to fasten two parts together, but in automated assembly new fastening procedures and modified product designs are necessary.

Principles such as the following are applied when redesigning products for automated assembly:

1. **Reduce the amount of assembly required.** For example, use one plastic molded part instead of two sheet metal parts that must be fastened together.
2. **Reduce the number of fasteners required.** For example, design parts that snap together or can be welded together rather than being fastened together by screws, nuts, and bolts.
3. **Design components to be automatically delivered and positioned.** This means designing parts so that they can be fed and oriented for delivery from parts hoppers, slotted chutes, vibratory bowls, and other continuous part-feeding mechanisms.
4. **Design products for layered assembly and vertical insertion of parts.** Products generally should be assembled from a base upward in layers to the top of the product. Parts should be designed so that they can be inserted vertically into the assembly.

5. **Design parts so that they are self-aligning.** Parts should have features like shoulders or protrusions that slide into matching features on adjacent parts that automatically position and align the parts as they are inserted into assemblies.

6. **Design products into major modules for production.** An automated assembly system would then be used to assemble each module. By breaking the assembly of the whole product into several assembly modules, downtime of the system is reduced.

7. **Increase the quality of components.** Components of high quality avoid jams in the feeding and assembly mechanisms.[3]

Automated assembly systems can provide manufacturers with low per-unit production costs, improved product quality, and greater product flexibility. Because some of the machines in these systems tend to be standard robots that are available from several suppliers today, the initial investment in equipment is not as high as we might imagine. Therefore, these systems are not limited to products of very high demand. Also, increasingly, these robots can be reprogrammed to other products and operations, thereby reducing the need for product demand to be stable and to extend well into the future.

Flexible Manufacturing Systems

Flexible manufacturing systems (FMS) are groups of production machines, arranged in a sequence, connected by automated materials-handling and transferring machines, and integrated by a computer system. Figure 6.1 illustrates such a system.

In these systems, which are also sometimes called *flexible machining systems*, kits of materials and parts for a product are loaded on the automated materials-handling system. A code is then entered into the computer system identifying the product to be produced and the location of the product in the sequence. As partially completed products finish at one production machine, they are automatically passed to the next production

| Figure 6.1 | A Flexible Manufacturing System |

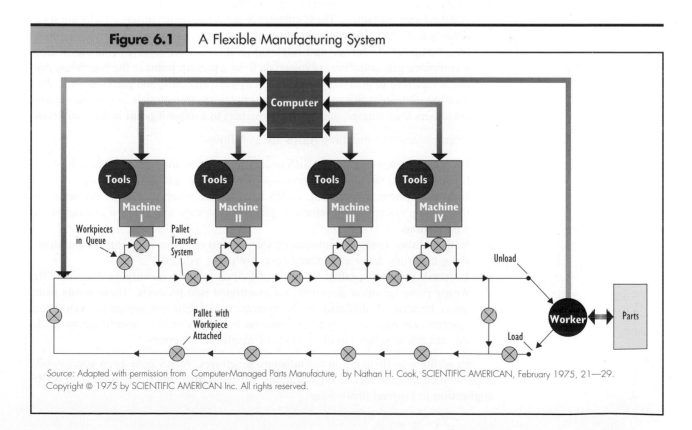

machine. Each production machine receives its settings and instructions from the computer, automatically loads and unloads tools as required, and completes its work without the need for workers to attend its operations.

Although the initial cost of these systems is high, per-unit production costs are low, quality of products is high, and product flexibility is high. FMS are growing in importance and many companies are now installing them.

Automated Storage and Retrieval Systems

Automated storage and retrieval systems (ASRS) are systems for receiving orders for materials from anywhere in operations, collecting the materials from locations within a warehouse, and delivering the materials to workstations in operations. There are three major elements of ASRS:

1. **Computers and communication systems.** These systems are used for placing orders for materials, locating the materials in storage, giving commands for delivery of the materials to locations in operations, and adjusting inventory records showing the amount and location of materials.
2. **Automated materials-handling and delivery systems.** These systems are automatically loaded with containers of materials from operations, which they deliver to the warehouse. Similarly, they are automatically loaded with orders of materials at the warehouse, which they deliver to workstations in operations. Powered and computer-controlled conveyors of several types are sometimes used, but **automated guided vehicle systems (AGVS)** are now being used in greater numbers for this purpose. AGVS are usually driverless trains, pallet trucks, and unit load carriers. AGVS usually follow either embedded guide wires or paint strips through operations until their destinations are reached.
3. **Storage and retrieval systems in warehouses.** Warehouses store materials in standard-size containers. These containers are arranged according to a location address scheme that allows the location of each material to be precisely determined by a computer. A **storage and retrieval (S/R) machine** receives commands from a computer, gets containers of materials from a **pickup point** in the warehouse, delivers materials to their assigned location in the warehouse, and places them in their location. Similarly, S/R machines locate containers of materials in storage, remove containers from storage, and deliver containers to a **deposit point** in the warehouse.

The main purposes of installing ASRS are as follows:

1. **Increase storage capacity.** ASRS ordinarily increase the storage density in warehouses; that is, the total maximum number of items that can be stored.
2. **Increase system throughput.** ASRS increase the number of loads per hour that the storage system can receive and place into storage and retrieve and deliver to workstations.
3. **Reduce labor costs.** By automating the systems of retrieving, storage, and delivering materials, labor and related costs are often reduced.
4. **Improve product quality.** Because of human error in identifying materials, the wrong parts are often delivered and assembled into products. These errors often occur because of similarity in the appearance of different materials. Automated systems that must identify parts based on bar codes or other identification methods are not as subject to these kinds of identification errors.

In addition to their use in manufacturing settings, ASRS have been successfully implemented in some service organizations. Business Snapshot 6.3 illustrates an ASRS application in hospital pharmacies.

BUSINESS SNAPSHOT 6.3

ASRS in Hospital Pharmacies

It stocks shelves. It fills prescriptions. It even bills patients automatically. But the one thing it won't do is talk back to the boss.

This automatic storage and retrieval system (ASRS) is finding its way into hospitals around the country. Dubbed the "Pharmacy Robot," this new, high-tech computer system can stock and retrieve drugs flawlessly in record time.

In an age of managed health care companies' never-ending efforts to be more efficient, the idea of an automated prescription-filling system immediately caught on in the 1990s. Hospitals were interested in ensuring accuracy and reducing the possibility of human error. Out of the 30 million prescriptions the "robots" have

filled so far, there have been zero errors.

Pittsburgh's Mercy Hospital got its ASRS in September 1994, one of the first hospitals in the country to install such a system. After one year the ASRS was responsible for filling 85 percent of the hospital's prescriptions. The Pharmacy Robot is not allowed to handle controlled and dangerous substances, refrigerated drugs, and doses that are larger than the five-inch bags used with the system.

The ASRS is connected to the hospital's computer system and recognizes any possible drug interaction problems or allergies. It can stock 1,000 doses of medications in just 20 minutes. The Pharmacy Robot looks more like a video camera on a pole than the

typical robots in movies. It sits in a 35-foot-long glass tunnel and hydraulic air pumps whoosh it back and forth on a metal rail. An infrared eye passes over bar codes on little bags of medication just as they are sucked off racks with suction cups, to be deposited in labeled bins taken to patients' bedsides. The size of each robot varies from hospital to hospital, depending on space and needs.

The Pharmacy Robot has seen great success so far and will most certainly continue to do so. In just a few seconds, it can process information that may have taken pharmacists hours or even days. And it frees pharmacists from nominal tasks so they can do more counseling for their patients.

Source: "Robot Eases Life of Hospital Pharmacists." San Antonio Express News, January 14, 1996, 5J.

We have now discussed several automated production systems that are in common use today. What are production systems going to be like in the future?

SOFTWARE SYSTEMS FOR AUTOMATION

To comprehend the nature of production that is likely to prevail in the future, we must understand three rather complex computer-based systems: computer-aided design and computer-aided manufacturing, (CAD/CAM), computer-integrated manufacturing, and enterprise resource planning (ERP).

CAD/CAM

CAD and CAM were discussed in Chapter 2. These CAD/CAM terms are defined:

- **CAD:** The use of computers in interactive engineering drawing and storage of designs. Programs complete the layout, geometric transformations, projections, rotations, magnifications, and interval (cross-section) views of a part and its relationship with other parts.
- **CAM:** Use of computers to program, direct, and control production equipment in the fabrication of manufactured items.[4]

CAD is concerned with the automation of certain phases of product design, and its use is growing as more and more powerful product design software is being developed. The increased availability of these engineering-design workstations is revolutionizing the way products are designed. CAD systems are installed to increase the productivity of designers, improve the quality of the designs, improve product standardization and design documentation, and create a manufacturing database. The most widely used CAD software is AutoCAD, which can run on personal computers.

It is currently in release 2000i and produced by Autodesk Inc. (**http://www.autodesk. com**). First introduced in 1982, more than 2 million copies of AutoCAD have been shipped to more than 160 countries, making Autodesk one of the largest PC software companies in the world.

CAM is concerned with automating the planning and control of production. It is coming along more slowly than CAD, but it is progressing. The ability to plan production, prepare product routings, generate N/C programs, fix the settings of production machinery, prepare production schedules, and control the operation of production processes with computers—all will undoubtedly continue to expand as computer software becomes more sophisticated. But it is the combination of these CAD and CAM systems into CAD/CAM that provides a vision of future production systems.

CAD/CAM implies a merger of CAD and CAM and an interaction between the two systems. The important result of this merger is the automation of the transition from product design to manufacturing. New products can be designed quickly as market demands change. And because these new product designs are stored in a common database, through CAM the new products can be introduced into production much more quickly and with less expense. Thus CAD/CAM promises great product flexibility, low production costs, and improved product quality.

Computer-Integrated Manufacturing

Computer-integrated manufacturing (CIM) is defined as "the application of a computer to bridge and connect various computerized systems and connect them into a coherent, integrated whole." With CIM, "budgeting, CAD/CAM, process controls, group technology systems, MRP II, financial reporting systems, etc., would be linked and interfaced."[5] As we can tell from this definition, CIM has a broader application than CAD/CAM.

> *The CIM concept is that all of the firm's operations related to the production function [are] incorporated in an integrated computer system to assist, augment, and/or automate the operations. The computer system is pervasive throughout the firm, touching all activities that support manufacturing. In this integrated computer system, the output of one activity serves as the input to the next activity, through the chain of events that starts with the sales order and culminates with the shipment of the product.*[6]

As is clear from this description, computer software is a critical component of new manufacturing technologies and automation. One of the most popular types of software packages in recent years is enterprise resource planning systems.

Enterprise Resource Planning

Enterprise resource planning (ERP) systems are the latest comprehensive software packages that companies are using to help automate a variety of business processes. These sophisticated software systems integrate most of the business functions in an organization. "ERP systems automate manufacturing processes, organize accountants' books, streamline corporate departments like human resources, and a whole lot more—they are the software applications that made reengineering possible."[7]

An ERP system is a complex set of software programs that can take several years and many millions of dollars to implement. For large companies with many locations around the world, buying and nurturing an ERP system can cost hundreds of millions of dollars. Chevron spent around $160 million over five years during the 1990s to get its ERP system up and running.

The five leading ERP software companies are SAP, Oracle, J.D. Edwards, PeopleSoft, and Baan. The granddaddy of ERP is the German software giant SAP, founded in 1972 by five former IBM engineers. With the largest market share, SAP's ERP software is called *R/3*. Initially *R/3* was focused on making manufacturing and accounting processes more efficient, but today SAP offers *R/3* modules for many other business functions, such as logistics and human resources. Business Snapshot 6.4 illustrates the integrative nature of SAP's *R/3* software.

The latest development in ERP systems has been the integration of e-business capabilities. *E-business is the use of the Internet to conduct or facilitate business transactions, such as sales, purchasing, communication, inventory management, customer*

BUSINESS SNAPSHOT 6.4

Managing a Company with SAP's ERP Software

SAP is the market leader in enterprise resource planning (ERP) software. Its R/3 software allows a company to integrate and better manage most of its business and operations functions. The following description of how R/3 works illustrates how a customer order triggers a chain reaction of events throughout a hypothetical shoe company.

1. **Ordering:** A sales rep from the shoe company takes an order for 1,000 blue tennis shoes from a Brazilian retailer. From her portable PC, the sales rep taps into the R/3 sales module back at the U.S. headquarters, which checks the price, including any discounts the retailer is eligible for, and looks up the retailer's credit history.

2. **Availability:** Simultaneously, R/3's inventory software checks the stock situation and notifies the sales rep that half the order can be filled immediately from a Brazilian warehouse. The remaining shoes in the order will be delivered in five days direct from the company's factory in Taiwan.

3. **Production:** R/3's manufacturing software schedules the production of the sneakers at the Taiwan factory, meanwhile alerting the company's warehouse manager in Brazil to go ahead and ship the 500 shoes to the retailer. An invoice gets printed up—in Portuguese.

4. **Manpower:** That's when R/3's human resources module identifies a shortage of workers at the Taiwan factory to handle the order and alerts the personnel manager of the need for temporary workers.

5. **Purchasing:** R/3's materials-planning module notifies the purchasing manager that it's time to reorder blue dye, rubber, and shoelaces.

6. **Order Tracking:** The customer logs on to the shoe company's R/3 system through the Internet and sees that 250 of the 500 shoes coming from Taiwan have been made and dyed. The customer also sees there are 500 red tennis shoes in stock and places a follow-up order on the Internet.

7. **Planning:** Based on data from R/3's forecasting and financial modules, the CEO sees that colored tennis shoes are not only in hot demand but are also highly profitable. He decides to add a line of fluorescent footwear.

Source: "Silicon Valley on the Rhine." *Business Week,* November 3, 1997, 162–166. Reprinted from November 3, 1997, issue of *Business Week* by special permission, copyright © 1997 by The McGraw-Hill Companies, Inc.

service, submitting orders, and checking the status of orders. As more and more companies use the Internet for different business purposes, ERP software companies have added features and functionality to their ERP software packages to facilitate e-business. SAP has even created a Web site (**http://www.mysap.com**) to help different companies coordinate their e-business activities.

Let us now consider the use of automation in the burgeoning service sector.

AUTOMATION IN SERVICES

When we consider the wide range of services supplied by companies in the following industries, the opportunities for applying automation are overwhelming: insurance, real estate, savings and loans and banks, trucking, airlines and air freight, construction, retailing and wholesaling, printing and publishing, advertising and broadcasting, business services, stock brokerages and financial services, health care, lodging and entertainment, communications, railroads, and utilities.

Business Snapshot 6.3 illustrated one example of the growth of advanced technology in services. Table 6.2 gives some examples of automation in four service industries. Perhaps no other service industry is so dominated by the use of computers and automated equipment as is the banking industry. Automatic teller machines, electronic funds transfer systems, and computerized bank statements are only the tip of the iceberg. This entire industry is so dependent on computers and related equipment for its day-to-day operations that it literally could not operate without them.

As more and more advanced technology equipment and systems are integrated into service operations, an interesting trend toward more standardized services and less customer contact could be developing. Because automated equipment cannot possibly operate in an environment subject to the amount of variety and change that is present in some services, reducing and standardizing the variety of services offered allows the introduction of automated equipment. This standardization, however, brings trade-offs.

Advances in automation technologies have revolutionized the banking industry, fostering the development of ATM machines, telephone banking, and on-line transactions.

© PHOTODISC, INC.

| Table 6.2 | Some Examples of Automation in Services |

Service Industries	Examples of Automation
Airlines	Air traffic control systems
	Autopilot systems
	Reservation systems, such as SABRE
	Cargo containerization
Banks, savings and loans, and financial services	Automatic teller machines (ATMs)
	Electronic funds transfer
	Magnetic-ink character recognition codes (MICR)
	Optical scanners
	Computerized bank statements
	Telephone and on-line banking
Retailing/wholesaling	Point-of-sale terminals
	Bar code systems
	Optical scanners
	Automated warehouses
	Automated photo booths
	Automated payment systems at service stations
Health care	AGVS for waste disposal
	CAT scanners
	Magnetic resonance imaging (MRI) systems
	Automated patient monitoring
	Bedside terminals
	Home and hospital robots

On the one hand, from the customers' perspective, standardized services may not be as appealing because the service is not specifically custom-designed for each customer. On the other hand, the cost of operations and the prices of services either are reduced or do not rise as rapidly, and they may be more convenient for customers. Consider, for instance, the proliferation of automated teller machines (ATMs), which are located in grocery stores, in shopping centers, and at drive-in branch bank facilities. Banking customers cannot obtain as wide a range of banking services at ATMs, but their locations are convenient, their service is prompt, and they are open 24 hours a day.

Generally speaking, where there is a large amount of customer contact in services, there tends to be less use of all types of equipment, including automated equipment. Figure 6.2 illustrates the relationship between the degree of customer contact and the amount of capital intensity. Capital intensity increases as we move from manual to mechanized to automated equipment. This figure suggests that automated equipment may not be appropriate for some service operations that have a high degree of customer contact. But as we discussed earlier, some service operations can be automated because of improved convenience and reduced costs. Also, services typically do not have a high amount of customer contact in all parts of their organization. For example, back-room operations at banks, where customers seldom go, are prime candidates for automation. Business Snapshot 6.5 describes how a grocery store is automating customer checkout services.

The operations of many service companies are improving because of advancing communications technologies, the Internet, and internal company intranets. Business Snapshot 6.6 describes how one company is using the Internet to shorten the lead time required to develop new software. Business Snapshot 6.7 illustrates how a mortgage lender has greatly increased its productivity through automation.

Figure 6.2 | Degree of Customer Contact in Services and the Use of Automated Equipment

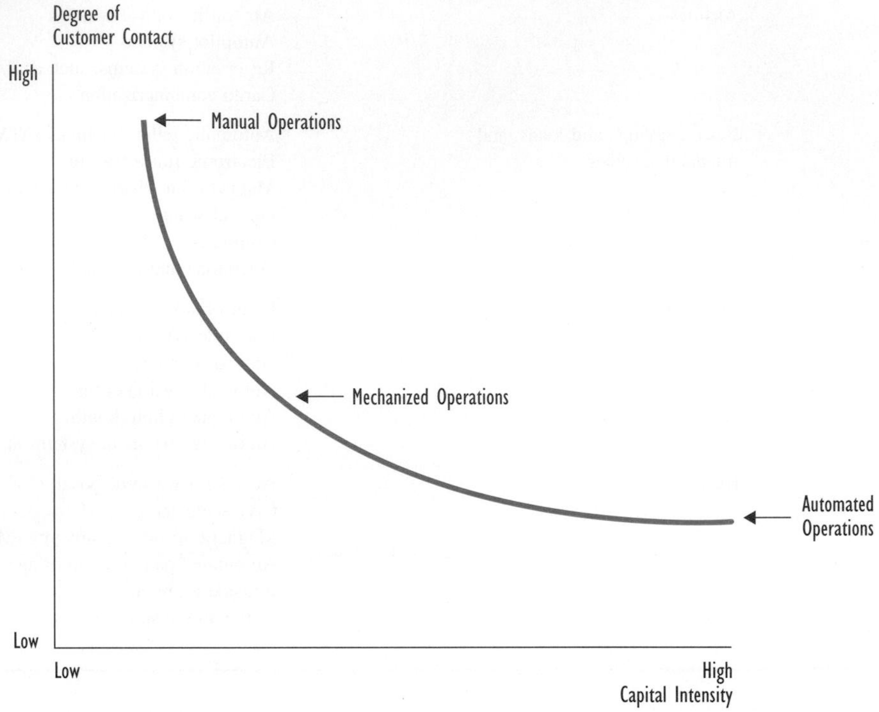

Degree of
Customer Contact

High

Manual Operations

Mechanized Operations

Automated
Operations

Low

Low   High
                                                        Capital Intensity

---

BUSINESS SNAPSHOT 6.5

Automated Checkout at Kroger Grocery Store

The Kroger Company is the largest retail food company in the United States, with close to 2,300 grocery stores in 31 states. The customer checkout process at its stores has been partly automated for many years with the use of laser scanning technologies and UPC bar codes. But now, Kroger is beginning to automate even more of the checkout process at some of its stores.

At one of its Kroger grocery stores in Arlington, Texas, four checkout stations were recently re-moved and replaced with four au-tomated, self-service checkout sta-tions. After a customer has found all the groceries he wants, he can take his basket of items to a self-service checkout station. The cus-tomer scans each item using the laser scanning system and places the item in a bag on a weigh table that keeps track of the weight of all items for verification purposes. A computer display shows the name and price of each item scanned. Any coupons the customer wishes to use are also scanned. After all items have been scanned the customer selects the type of payment desired: cash, credit card, or check. Cash (both coins and bills) are inserted into the machine and the correct change is returned by the ma-chine. Credit cards are swiped in a card reader. Customers bag their own groceries and are on their way.

One employee monitors all four self-service checkout stations, verifies identification for check-writing customers, checks the cus-tomer's ID if beer has been pur-chased, and handles any questions or problems that cus-tomers have. For those customers who are uncomfortable using the automated, self-service checkout system, the store still has many traditional checkout stations with one employee at each station.

BUSINESS SNAPSHOT 6.6

Communications Technology Demolishes Time and Distance

A group of computer programmers at Tsinghua University in Beijing is writing software using Java technology. They work for IBM. At the end of each day, they send their work over the Internet to an IBM facility in Seattle. There, programmers build on it and use the Internet to zap it 5,222 miles to the Institute of Computer Science in Belarus and Software House Group in Latvia. From there, the work is sent east to India's Tata Group, which passes the software back to Tsinghua by morning in Beijing, back to Seattle, and so on in a great global relay that never ceases until the project is done.

"We call it Java Around the Clock," says John Patrick, vice-president of Internet technology for IBM. "It's like we've created a 48-hour day through the Internet." The Internet and computer networks enable companies to work globally in ways they never could before.

Source: Maney, Kevin. "Technology Is 'Demolishing' Time, Distance." *USA Today,* April 24, 1997, 1–2B.

BUSINESS SNAPSHOT 6.7

Automated Technologies at Countrywide

Countrywide Home Loans, Inc., is the leading independent residential mortgage lender and servicer in the United States. Not so long ago, Countrywide needed an army of customer service reps to field the 20,000 calls that streamed into its offices every day. Each inquiry—ranging from payment problems to tax questions—cost the lender about $4.

Today, almost half of those calls are handled by an automated system, which identifies the caller from the incoming phone number, scans the homeowner's account, then automatically supplies the information it thinks the customer is seeking. Average cost per call: 60 cents. The mind-reading technology is not perfect, but it saves Countrywide about $6 million a year and frees up 86 full-time employees to work on more complex customer problems.

Employees used to spend weeks gathering paperwork needed to approve loans. Today, on-line computers use artificial intelligence to make decisions in 30 seconds. Mortgage payments mailed without preprinted coupons once sat for 24 hours before employees could process them by hand, costing the company lost interest revenue. Today, almost one-fifth of the company's 2.5 million borrowers have been coaxed to make payments electronically, which costs Countrywide less than 5 cents per transaction—one-fourth the cost of mailed payments.

"Ten years ago, I don't think we would have imagined that we would be able to process and underwrite loans as fast as we can today," said Richard Jones, chief technology officer at Countrywide. Ten years ago, Countrywide originated 51 loans per employee annually. Now that number has nearly doubled due to new technologies.

Processing insurance bills from dozens of companies was another challenge. Countrywide workers used to do all the paperwork by hand. Now the documents are scanned into a computer that can distinguish an Allstate renewal notice from a State Farm change of address form. Today the same number of workers as before handle almost twice the amount of mail.

All of the automation at Countrywide has eliminated many manual jobs, but it has not resulted in significant layoffs because the enhanced productivity has helped the company expand its business. In fact, the company's overall workforce has doubled in size during the last four years.

Source: Sanders, Edmund. "Tech-Driven Efficiency Spurs Economic Boom." *Los Angeles Times,* February 22, 2000, A1.

The wide dissemination of automated systems in manufacturing and service industries has created many issues that require examination.

AUTOMATION ISSUES

Of the important automation issues to be considered, we discuss these: use of automation; building manufacturing flexibility; justifying automation projects; managing technological change; and worker displacement, training, and retraining.

Use of Automation

We can find examples of very successful companies that utilize the oldest known manual technology. We can also find examples of companies that are failing despite having the latest advanced technology. But we must not jump to the conclusion that the production technology used by a company is unrelated to its profitability or to other measures of success. Careful thought on this issue should lead us to these conclusions:

1. **Not all automation projects are successful.** Companies that launch major automation projects may poorly manage the implementation of the automated machinery. The result can be that they are worse off after automation than they were with their former production technology. And automating a poorly designed process only makes it easier to do the work poorly.
2. **Automation cannot make up for poor management.** Even if implementation of the automated production machinery goes well, the company may be so poorly managed that it fails anyway.
3. **Economic analysis cannot justify automation of some operations.** For example, if labor cost is very low and automated equipment is very costly, the extra cost of automating may not be sufficiently offset by product quality and other improvements. This is the reason we find so many garment factories on both sides of the Mexico–U.S. border.
4. **It is not technically feasible to automate some operations.** In the garment industry, for example, the cloth that must be processed is so stretchable, flexible, and flimsy that certain production operations like cutting, assembling, and sewing are not yet automated. In these operations, the chief obstacle to automation is imprecise positioning of the cloth relative to cutters, sewing heads, and other mechanical devices.
5. **Automation projects may have to wait in small and start-up businesses.** Because of shortages of capital and technical and engineering skills, some of the production and distribution of products may be contracted to supplier, shipping, and distribution companies. As products mature, these businesses typically take production and/or shipping back in-house, but automation probably is not yet in the picture. Eventually, the production processes may be automated as the products mature and the companies acquire engineering and technological capabilities to design, install, and integrate automation projects. But not all automation expertise must reside inside a company, because there is a long list of companies that provide turnkey automation services to small and large companies alike. While expensive for small and start-up businesses, companies like Advanced Automation, Allen-Bradley, Automation Tooling Systems, Evana Automation Specialists, and JOT Automation Group are examples of such automation service companies.

Some production operations have not been automated, and undoubtedly some never will be automated. But for companies that are committed to long-term growth, survival, and profitability, the main reason for not automating cannot be because they have a closed mind on the subject. *The truth is that all companies must keep their production processes updated as production technology advances. To do otherwise would put their companies' future in jeopardy, because they must assume that their competitors will seize the strategic advantages offered by switching to advanced technology.* For many companies today, the question is not whether they will automate their operations. Rather, the questions are: Which operations will be automated? In what sequence will the operations be automated? When will the operations be automated?

Building Manufacturing Flexibility

The term flexible automation means the opposite of the term **fixed manufacturing systems** or **hard automation,** as in automated flow lines or conventional production lines. In recent years, this use of the term has grown to refer to all types of equipment and production systems that provide the ability to respond to changing market needs. **Manufacturing flexibility** is the ability to improve or maintain market share because of the following:

1. Customer orders can be delivered soon after receipt of the orders. Sometimes this means modifying production schedules to respond to a customer's extraordinary request for a quick delivery.
2. Production can quickly be shifted from product to product because in a particular week customers may order relatively small batches of many product models.
3. Production capacity can be increased rapidly to respond to peaking market demands in a particular week.
4. New products can be developed and introduced into production quickly and inexpensively in response to shifting market needs.

As we have previously noted, manufacturing flexibility is of two general types, volume flexibility and product flexibility. Volume flexibility is usually provided by the use of overtime, extra finished-goods inventory, and designing production processes with either **variable production rates** or **excess capacity**. As production systems have become more responsive to market demands, however, what used to be excess capacity is now considered to be only *enough capacity to respond to peak market demands.* But perhaps the more important form of manufacturing flexibility is product flexibility—the ability to quickly and inexpensively change the production system to other products.

As we discussed earlier in this chapter, process-focused production systems offer great product flexibility, although unit production costs can be high. Historically, the number of process-focused production systems has far exceeded that of other forms of production. But many manufacturers today are looking for alternatives to job shops because these process-focused production systems will not allow them to compete with their foreign competitors on unit production costs. Owing to improved production technology, however, there are other ways to achieve product flexibility and still obtain low unit production costs.

Here are some machines or production systems that are understood to provide product flexibility:

- N/C machines
- Programmable and reprogrammable robots
- Automated quality control inspection
- Automatic identification systems
- Automated process controls
- Automated assembly systems

- Flexible manufacturing systems
- Automated storage and retrieval systems
- Computer-aided design and computer-aided manufacturing
- Computer-integrated manufacturing

These machines and production systems represent the core of what is referred to as *flexible automation*. Perhaps the most significant thing about them is their ability to produce products at low unit costs and simultaneously offer great product flexibility. *Manufacturing flexibility has become the cornerstone of operations strategy in the 2000s, and production processes being designed today are increasingly being anchored to this cornerstone.*

Flexible automation and other forms of automation require large investments, however, and it is becoming increasingly apparent that the traditional approaches to justifying these huge investments are inadequate.

Justifying Automation Projects

There is growing evidence that for several decades U.S. management policies and capital-budgeting approaches have led to only small improvements to existing products and production processes.

The turnover rate of our managers has been so high that long-term product improvement and production process changes have been avoided. It often takes five years or longer to drastically modify product designs and automate factories. There has not been much incentive for managers who plan to be with a company for only a few years to commit to these long-term projects.

The payback period, net present value, internal rate of return, and other conventional capital-budgeting approaches may, when taken alone, be inadequate tools on which to base major product and process design and redesign decisions. These tools have tended to lead managers to expand present facilities with existing technology, rather than build new facilities with new production technology. Carrying this approach to its extreme, companies end up with huge, unwieldy, highly centralized production facilities based on outdated production technology.

Investment in product and process technology innovation must be taken out of the context of project-by-project investment decisions. Rather, investing in product and process technology must be seen as a long-term strategic choice for the company. These choices, like other major strategic business decisions, cannot be based solely on a simple payback formula. *Although returns on investment will continue to be an important criterion for these investment decisions, the term **returns** will take on new and expanded meaning. Improved product quality, faster delivery of customer orders, increased product and volume flexibility, reduced production costs, increased market share, and other advantages will have to be factored into future capital-budgeting decisions.* Investment in product and process technology must be seen as a strategic choice to change the factory into a competitive weapon that assists the corporation in capturing market share.

Managing Technological Change

Companies that have attempted ambitious automation projects have learned that implementing large automation projects is much more difficult and complex than they had anticipated. Automation projects almost always take longer and cost more than originally expected.

Given the difficulty of managing changes in production technology, what have we learned about how to manage the implementation of major automation projects? These suggestions are offered:

1. **Have a master plan for automation.** The plan should indicate what operations to automate, when and in what sequence to automate each area of the business, and how the organization and its products, marketing, and other business units will have to change because of automation.

2. **Recognize the risks in automating.** There are risks associated with every automation project. Among those that must be considered are the risk of radical obsolescence, the danger that new technologies cannot be protected and will be easily transferred to competitors, and the possibility that a new production technology cannot be successfully developed.

3. **Establish a new production technology department.** This unit will disseminate information about new technology, become an advocate for new-technology adoption, lead the way in educating and training others about new technology, and provide the technical assistance necessary for the installation and implementation of advanced-technology equipment.

4. **Allow plenty of time for the completion of automation projects.** Enough time must be allowed for learning how to install, tool, debug, program, and otherwise get an automated machine up to production speed. There is much to learn, and it always takes longer than expected. One automation expert recently suggested: "Estimate how long you expect it to take, then triple it." The key point: *What one learns about implementing one automation project is to be applied to the next one. There is a new technology associated with the implementation of automation projects, and it is best learned a little at a time.*

5. **Do not try to automate everything at once.** Glitches in automated equipment are inevitable. Try to phase in projects so that what is learned from one project can be applied to another project. By allowing plenty of time, the frequency of missed schedule dates, organization frustration, and pressure to compress the schedule are reduced. By phasing in projects, an organization's resources can be more tightly focused on one or two projects at a time, thereby increasing the likelihood of success.

6. **People are the key to making automation projects successful.** If automation is being planned at the strategic level, the training and education of everyone in the organization about advanced production technology must be an ongoing activity. Frequent and intensive participation by all involved personnel must accompany automation projects. Union representatives must be brought into an active role in automation. Unions are particularly interested in advance notice of affected jobs, retraining and reassignment of displaced workers, and layoff policies associated with automation.

7. **If companies move too slowly in adopting new production technology, they may get left behind.** Being deliberate and careful as it moves from automation project to automation project does not give a company license to drag its feet. Doing so may mean that it will be beaten by the competition.

Worker Displacement, Training, and Retraining

One consequence of industrial automation is the elimination of workers' jobs. For example, one worker may monitor three welding robots, where previously four workers did the welding. And in an office, one secretary can now do the work of three because of word processing, spreadsheet, and database software. Some economists say that in the long run, the number of jobs eliminated in factories and offices because of automation is outnumbered by the newly created jobs in engineering, manufacturing, programming, selling, and servicing the new-technology products. While this may be true, what about the short run—what happens to the factory and office workers who lose their jobs to automation? The answer is rather obvious: They transfer to other jobs within their company, or go to jobs in other companies, or become unemployed. None of these alternatives are pleasant.

Many companies have developed in-house training programs to deal with these issues, whereas others rely on outside sources for training. In the past decade as many thousands of automation projects have been implemented around the United States, more and more companies feel they cannot afford not to train or retrain their current employees.

With a strong economy, less need for low-skilled workers, and a shortage of higher-skilled manufacturing employees trained in newer production technologies, companies are providing more custom training for their workers than ever before. Northeast Tool & Manufacturing Co., a small tool-and-die shop outside Charlotte, North Carolina, has all of its employees take aptitude exams that measure everything from math and mechanical skills to leadership and adaptability. These employee tests are used to develop customized training for each worker. Based on the results, some employees enroll in courses at a nearby community college and others take remote courses through computers set up at the plant. Still others attend afternoon classes for which professors are brought right into the factory.[8]

Some white-collar and blue-collar workers will lose their jobs and find themselves job searching because not all companies provide for retention and retraining of displaced workers. For some of these workers, government training programs may provide retraining. The Small Business Administration, the U.S. Department of Labor, and the U.S. Department of Commerce have such training and retraining programs, which are administered through local businesses. Unfortunately, there may not be enough of these programs, and some workers will face the choice of taking minimum-wage unskilled jobs in service industries or being unemployed. But more U.S. government subsidized and sponsored training programs are promised. One proposal requires companies to spend 1.5 percent of their payroll on training programs each year. Even then, U.S. companies would trail our industrial trading partners. For example, German companies spend an average of 4 percent of payroll costs each year in training.[9]

As technology intensifies in the coming years, employee training and retraining will become an unavoidable responsibility and increasing burden in U.S. companies.

With the preceding discussion as a background, let us study some ways of deciding among automation alternatives.

DECIDING AMONG AUTOMATION ALTERNATIVES

As managers consider automation decisions, ordinarily several automation alternatives must be evaluated. Economic analysis will always be an important—if not a predominant—factor in choosing among automation alternatives. But other factors are also important. Managers who make automation decisions know that the following factors must be considered:

1. **Economic factors.** These factors provide managers with some idea of the *direct* impact of automation alternatives on profitability. Although the focus may be on cash flows, annual fixed costs, variable cost per unit, average production cost per unit, or total annual production costs at the forecasted production levels, the intent is to determine the direct impact on profitability. Break-even analysis and financial analysis are frequently used for this purpose.

2. **Effect on market share.** How are automation alternatives likely to affect market share? Some alternatives require product redesign and product specialization, which can affect sales. Although some alternatives allow more product variety and

greater customer appeal, the net effect of such changes on market share is a difficult measure to obtain. Nevertheless, the effects are there and must be taken into account in such decisions.

3. **Effect on product quality.** How are automation alternatives likely to affect product quality? Measuring this effect is not easy. Scrap rates, market share changes, production costs, and other measures represent efforts to *indirectly* tie changes in product quality resulting from automation alternatives to profitability.

4. **Effect on manufacturing flexibility.** How are automation alternatives likely to affect product and volume flexibility? This factor is increasing in importance as product life cycles shorten and as competing organizations provide consumers with opportunities to order products with characteristics custom-designed for them. Measures of manufacturing flexibility are extremely difficult to develop. Cost of machine changeovers, overtime labor costs, and market share changes are measures that can be used to evaluate the effect of automation alternatives on manufacturing flexibility.

5. **Effect on labor relations.** How are automation alternatives likely to affect workers, their union, and the relationship between management and the workforce? The number of workers that must be laid off, the amount of training and retraining required, and the availability of workers with the skills required to operate automated equipment are factors affecting the choice of automation alternatives.

6. **The amount of time required for implementation.** How much time will automation alternatives require to implement the automated machines and systems? Alternatives may have different time requirements for implementation because the alternatives have different levels of technology, organizational personnel may be unfamiliar with some types of technology, and alternatives require different kinds of changes in the rest of the production system.

7. **Effect of automation implementation on ongoing production.** If automation is to replace existing production operations, or if automation must share facilities with existing operations, how will automation alternatives affect existing production? It is a fact of life that production must go on in spite of automation projects. Products must be shipped, for customers will not wait just because of automation projects. Some automation alternatives affect existing operations less because they are to be installed in a different location, they do not require the use of existing production equipment, or they otherwise do not interact with existing production.

8. **Amount of capital required.** What is the amount of capital required for each automation alternative? If capital is in short supply, as it almost always is, this factor can be the predominant consideration in automation decisions.

Rating Scale Approach

Given that factors such as those just listed could all be important in deciding among automation alternatives, how can managers simultaneously consider all of these factors? Table 6.3 illustrates how the rating scale approach can be used as a manager analyzes two automation alternatives.

We can see in Table 6.3 that if only economic factors were taken into account, the automated flow line would be preferred. But if other factors are considered, the choice is not so clear. The flexible manufacturing system rates better on product flexibility, implementation time, and capital requirements, and the automated flow line rates better on economic factors, market share, and volume flexibility. In such cases where no alternative is clearly superior on all factors, the appropriate choice will depend on which of the factors is of greater importance to the managers who must make the decision.

The rating scale approach requires decision makers to weigh the factors for each alternative, process this information through their unique mental calculus, and arrive

Table 6.3	Rating Scale Approach to Comparing Automation Alternatives		
Automation Factors		**Automated Flow Line**	**Flexible Manufacturing System**
Economic factors			
Annual operating costs		$4,955,900	$5,258,100
Per-unit production costs		$59.40	$63.02
Other factors			
Market share		5	4
Product quality		4	4
Product flexibility		2	4
Volume flexibility		4	2
Labor relations		3	3
Implementation time		3	4
Existing operations		5	5
Capital requirements		3	4

Note: A five-point rating scale is used: 5 = excellent, 4 = good, 3 = average, 2 = below average, and 1 = poor.

at an overall rating of each automation alternative. Let us now consider another approach that directly develops the overall rating of each alternative.

Relative-Aggregate-Scores Approach

Table 6.4 illustrates the **relative-aggregate-scores** approach to the same decision depicted in Table 6.3. But in this approach the overall aggregate scores for each automation alternative are developed as a part of the analysis.

We can see from Table 6.4 that the flexible manufacturing system appears to be a slightly better choice, 0.818 versus 0.770. This approach requires that managers state

Table 6.4	Relative-Aggregate-Scores Approach to Comparing Automation Alternatives						
Automation Factors	**Factor Weights**	**AUTOMATED FLOW LINE**			**FLEXIBLE MANUFACTURING SYSTEM**		
		Economic Data	**Scores**	**Weighted Scores**	**Economic Data**	**Scores**	**Weighted Scores**
Unit production costs	0.30	$59.40	1.000*	0.300	$63.02	0.943*	0.283
Market share	0.10		1.000	0.100		0.800	0.080
Product quality	0.10		0.800	0.080		0.800	0.080
Product flexibility	0.20		0.400	0.080		0.800	0.160
Volume flexibility	0.05		0.800	0.040		0.400	0.020
Labor relations	0.05		0.600	0.030		0.600	0.030
Implementation time	0.10		0.600	0.060		0.800	0.080
Existing operations	0.05		1.000	0.050		1.000	0.050
Capital requirements	0.05		0.600	0.030		0.700	0.035
Total aggregate scores				0.770			0.818

*These scores are determined by dividing the lowest unit production cost by the actual unit production costs: $59.40/$59.40 = 1.000, and $59.40/$63.02 = 0.943; all other factor scores are estimated based on a maximum score of 1.000, where higher is better.

the factors that will be considered in the decision and the weights of each factor *before the decision is made*. Such considerations represent a decision structure imposed on decision makers that should be inherently superior to a purely subjective weighting of alternatives. It is assumed that each alternative included in the analysis has been required to meet certain qualifications. For example, if an alternative requires so much capital that it is impractical to consider it, that alternative should not be included in the analysis. In other words, all alternatives surviving to this point in the analysis are fundamentally sound and feasible, and in this approach we are attempting to determine which alternative is superior to the others.

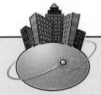

Wrap-Up
WHAT WORLD-CLASS COMPANIES DO

World-class companies view advanced technology as a competitive weapon that can be used to capture shares of world markets. U.S. producers use automation to further enhance their strengths of product quality and customer service and to make their production systems more competitive in flexibility and costs. Toward this end, large and small world-class companies are:

- Designing products to be *automation friendly:* reducing the amount of assembly, reducing the number of fasteners, allowing vertical insertion, self-aligning parts, and increasing quality of components.
- Using CAD/CAM for designing products and introducing products into production. The cost and time required to design and introduce products are greatly reduced.
- Selectively adopting automated production systems as soon as automation projects can be carefully planned and carried out: FMS, ASRS, and automated assembly systems. Also, advanced automated machines are integrated with traditional production: automated machining centers, groups of welding robots, and automated painting.
- Converting *hard automation* systems to more flexible automation.
- Challenging the long-held belief that high-volume runs of identical products are needed to achieve low cost, and moving toward the ideal of flexible production systems capable of producing small batches of products tailored to special customer requirements on short notice.

- Adopting a comprehensive CIM system. All phases of the business are integrated from a common database.
- Adopting ERP systems to help automate various business processes.
- Enjoying many of the performance characteristics of automated factories: high product quality, high flexibility, fast delivery of customer orders, and computer-driven and computer-integrated systems.
- Improving computerized production control systems to better plan and track customer orders, thus providing enhanced customer service, reduced costs, and improved flexibility.
- Operating from a plan for automation: recognizing the risks of automation, having a production technology department, allowing plenty of time for completion of automation projects, not trying to automate everything or everything at once, recognizing that people make automation projects successful, and not moving too slowly in adopting new production technology.
- Justifying automation projects based on multiple factors. Economics, market share, quality, flexibility, labor relations, time required, effect on ongoing production, and amount of capital required can all be important.
- Training and building teams of people capable of conceptualizing, designing, and using new production technology, and fostering the management ability to develop and implement new production processes.

REVIEW AND DISCUSSION QUESTIONS

1. Automation has traditionally meant the replacement of human effort with machine effort. Critique this traditional view of automation.
2. What benefits should be expected from automation projects? Discuss the overall impact on organizations from labor savings through automation.
3. What are the differences between N/C, CN/C, and DN/C machines?
4. Describe the conditions that would support the installation of an automobile painting robot.
5. Describe and give an example of each of these types of automated machines: (a) automatic attachments, (b) numerically controlled (N/C), (c) robots, (d) automated quality control inspection, (e) automatic identification systems, and (f) automated process controls.
6. Describe and give an example of each of these types of automated production systems: (a) automated flow lines, (b) automated assembly systems, (c) flexible manufacturing systems, and (d) automated storage and retrieval systems.
7. What is meant by the term *hard automation?* Explain the difference between hard automation and *flexible automation*.
8. Explain why products must usually be redesigned if automated assembly systems are to be used in production.
9. Define and describe: (a) CAD, (b) CAM, (c) CAD/CAM, (d) CIM, and (e) ERP.
10. Which companies are the leading producers of ERP software?
11. Give three examples of the use of automation in services that you know about from your personal experience.
12. What is meant by the term *flexible automation?* What are four reasons that market share can be increased because of *manufacturing flexibility?* Name three machines or production systems that provide product flexibility.
13. Explain the difficulties of implementing automation projects in small and start-up businesses. How can the difficulties be overcome?
14. If you could give managers who are considering automation projects advice on how to justify these projects, what would you tell them?
15. Give seven suggestions on how to better manage the implementation of major automation projects.
16. Define *worker displacement*, *training*, and *retraining* in the context of automation. Describe company-sponsored training programs, and explain their content and how they work.
17. Name and describe two ways of analyzing automation alternatives.
18. What are the strengths and weaknesses of each of the two ways of analyzing automation alternatives presented in this chapter?

INTERNET ASSIGNMENTS

1. Search the Internet for a manufacturer of robots. Describe the company's robot product line.
2. Search the Internet for a company that specializes in helping manufacturers with factory automation. Describe the company's products or services.
3. Visit the web site of Autodesk, the company that produces AutoCAD software (**http://www.autodesk.com**). Explore the site to find the company's news or press release pages. Find and summarize an interesting press release from the recent months. Give the title and date of the press release.
4. Visit the web site of German software producer SAP (**http://www.sap.com**). Explore the site for information about the latest version of its ERP software system. Briefly describe some of the new features.
5. Provia Software Inc. provides automated storage and retrieval systems (ASRS). Visit Provia's web site at **http://www.proviasoftware.com**. Describe the types of ASRS offered by Provia.

PROBLEMS

Field Projects

1. Visit a manufacturing company that has automated equipment. List the types of automated production technologies you observe. Find out which is the most recent piece of automated equipment that is currently in operation. Obtain the answers to these questions: What were the company's main reasons or justification for automating the process? Has this piece of automated equipment met the company's performance and cost expectations? Were any difficulties encountered when installing this equipment and making it operational? How long did it take to install and get the equipment operational? Were any employees displaced because of the automation and, if so, were they reassigned?

2. Visit a service company that has automated equipment or processes. List the types of automated technologies or processes you observe. Find out which is the most recent piece of automated equipment or automated process that is currently in operation. Obtain the answers to these questions: What were the company's main reasons or justification for automating the process? Has this process automation met the company's performance and cost expectations? Were there any difficulties in implementing the automation? How long did it take to implement the automation? Were any employees displaced because of the automation and, if so, were they reassigned?

3. Visit your university's library. Inquire about a process that has been recently automated (or will soon be automated). Obtain the answers to these questions: What were the main reasons or justifications for automating the process? Were there any difficulties in implementing the automation? How long did it take to implement the automation? Were any employees displaced because of the automation and, if so, were they reassigned?

Economic Analysis

4. The EasyPush Wheelbarrow Company needs a new riveting machine to replace its old riveting machine, which has become too expensive to maintain. The company needs to decide between a semiautomated riveting machine and a fully automated riveting machine. The semiautomated machine would have an annual fixed cost of $6,400 and a variable cost per rivet of $0.21. The fully automated machine would have an annual fixed cost of $17,300 and a variable cost per rivet of $0.17.
   a. For what range of number of rivets annually would each machine be preferred, based only on annual cost?
   b. What other factors should be considered when making this decision?

5. Great State Bank needs a new check sorting machine and is considering two brands, Vandine and Murcheck. The Vandine machine is highly automated and would have an annual fixed cost of $8,500 and a variable cost of $35 per sort. The Murcheck machine is less automated, requiring more employee time, with an annual fixed cost of $7,000 and a variable cost of $55 per sort. The bank performs only one sort per day, and operates 248 days each year. Use break-even analysis to analyze this problem.
   a. Compute the total annual cost for each machine. Based only on annual cost, which machine is preferred?
   b. For how many sorts per year would the bank be indifferent between the two machines?
   c. What other factors should be considered when making this decision?

6. KinderRead Inc. produces educational materials to help parents teach their kindergarten-age children to read. The company's printing press can no longer handle the current production volume, which is expected to grow. Two new machines are being considered. Machine A is more automated than Machine B and also costs more initially. The annual fixed cost is $7,500 for Machine A and $5,000 for Machine B. The variable cost per unit packaged is $1.70 with Machine A and $1.90 with Machine B.

   a. If annual production volume is 8,000 units, which machine would be preferred based only on annual costs?
   b. For what range of annual production volumes would each machine be preferred, based only on annual costs?
   c. If annual production volume is expected to be 9,000 units, how should the company decide which machine to purchase?

7. Two processing options are available to produce a new product, a semiautomated option and a fully automated option. The semiautomated option would have an annual fixed cost of $450,000 and a variable cost per unit of $580. The fully automated option would have an annual fixed cost of $800,000 and a variable cost per unit of $375. The selling price of the product will be $875 per unit. The demand forecasts for the new product are not yet available.

   a. Based only on annual cost, for what range of annual volume produced would each processing option be preferable?
   b. What is the break-even quantity for the fully automated option?
   c. What would be the annual profit for the semiautomated option if 2,150 units were produced and sold next year? What would be the annual profit for the fully automated option?

8. Prestige Machine Works manufactures parts for the aircraft industry. To become more competitive, the company has decided to upgrade its production technology. Three alternative technologies are being considered: cellular manufacturing (CM), numerically controlled machines (N/C), and a flexible manufacturing system (FMS). Annual production volume is expected to be at least 65,000 units per year during the next several years, but could be as high as 85,000 units per year. The costs for the three alternatives are:

	CM	N/C	FMS
Annual fixed cost ($)	85,000	230,000	410,000
Variable cost per unit ($)	42.50	40.30	39.10

   a. Based on annual cost, at what annual volume would the company be indifferent between the CM and N/C alternatives? Between the N/C and FMS alternatives?
   b. Determine the total annual cost for each alternative if annual volume is 65,000 and if annual volume is 85,000.
   c. Based only on the information provided, which production technology would you recommend to the company? Why?
   d. What other factors should be considered when making this decision?

9. The Crystal Machining Company produces titanium components for satellites. Because of increased competition the company has decided to modernize its production facility. Three alternative production technologies are being considered: cellular manufacturing (CM), numerically controlled machines (N/C), and a flex-

ible manufacturing system (FMS). Annual production volume is expected to be anywhere between 15,000 and 20,000 units per year during the next several years. Costs for the three alternatives are:

	CM	N/C	FMS
Annual fixed cost ($)	58,000	113,000	250,000
Variable cost per unit ($)	189	175	168

a. Based on annual cost, at what annual volume would the company be indifferent between the CM and N/C alternatives? Between the N/C and FMS alternatives?

b. Determine the total annual cost for each alternative if annual volume is 15,000 and if annual volume is 20,000.

c. Based only on the information provided, which production technology would you recommend to the company? Why?

d. What other factors should be considered when making this decision?

10. Sungchul Kim is the operations manager for a South Korean recycling company. He needs to decide between two alternative technologies for upgrading the company's sorting machinery. Alternative A would cost the company $300,000 initially and would save the company $70,000 per year compared with the current technology. Alternative B would cost the company $750,000 and would save the company $200,000 per year. The expected life of the technologies is 10 years. (All estimates are after-tax and discounted. You may want to review the payback method from a finance text or another source before attempting this problem.)

a. Compute the payback period for each technology alternative.

b. During the next 10 years, what would be the total net savings to the company with each technology alternative?

c. What other factors should be considered when making this decision?

11. Henry Hughes is the operations manager at a health clinic. Henry is trying to decide which of two blood testing machines to purchase. Model A performs blood tests faster with less employee involvement. Model B is less automated and requires more employee time to perform blood tests. Each machine has an expected life of five years. Machine A would initially cost $8,000, and Machine B would initially cost $5,000. The cost savings to the clinic are shown below for each machine in each year. (All estimates are after-tax and discounted. You may want to review the payback method from a finance text or another source before attempting this problem.)

	Annual Savings	
Year	Machine A	Machine B
1	$3,000	$2,000
2	2,300	1,800
3	2,000	1,300
4	1,800	1,000
5	1,600	600

a. Compute the payback period for each machine.

b. During the next five years, what would be the total net savings to the company with each machine?

c. Based only on this economic analysis, which machine would you recommend? Why?

d. What other factors should be considered when making this decision?

12. José Rodriguez is in charge of selecting a new high-output page printer for his company. Two available printers, each using a different technology, could meet the company's needs. Each printer has an expected life of six years. The Alpha printer would initially cost $20,000, and the Beta printer would initially cost $30,000. The discounted after-tax cost savings over the current printer are shown below for each printer in each year. (You may want to review the payback method from a finance text or another source before attempting this problem.)

	Annual Savings	
Year	**Alpha**	**Beta**
1	$7,500	$8,100
2	6,000	6,400
3	5,000	5,500
4	4,000	4,300
5	3,000	3,200
6	2,000	2,100

a. Compute the payback period for each printer.
b. During the next six years, what would be the total net savings to the company with each printer?
c. Based only on this economic analysis, which machine would you recommend? Why?
d. What other factors should be considered when making this decision?

Rating Scale Approach

13. The Weston Flyrod Company manufactures fishing rods for the U.S. and European markets. The company wants to upgrade its graphite wrapping process. LaTonya Johnson is a production analyst who has been tasked with recommending one of two alternative technologies for applying graphite. Each technology has its strengths and weaknesses. The following information has been prepared to help in the comparison:

Factors	Alternative 1	Alternative 2
Economic factor:		
Annual operating cost	$85,000	$125,000
Other factors:		
Product quality	4	5
Product flexibility	2	5
Volume flexibility	4	3
Maintenance requirements	5	2
Training requirements	4	2
Implementation time	5	2

Note: A five-point rating scale is used: 5 = excellent, 4 = good, 3 = average, 2 = below average, and 1 = poor.

Which technology alternative do you think Ms. Johnson should recommend? Why?

14. The Missoula Steel Company cuts customer-designed parts from plate steel. The company's current technology allows it to cut steel plates up to 1/4-inch thick. The company would like to purchase a new cutting machine using a different technology that would allow it to cut steel plates up to 1/2-inch thick. Carl Lefleur, production manager, has narrowed the decision down to two alternatives: a flame-based technology and a plasma-based technology. Each technology has its own strengths and weaknesses. The following information has been prepared to help in the evaluation:

Factors	Flame-Based	Plasma-Based
Economic factor:		
Annual operating cost	$110,000	$215,000
Other factors:		
Product quality	3	5
Product flexibility	4	5
Market share	4	5
Volume flexibility	5	2
Maintenance requirements	5	3
Training requirements	4	3
Implementation time	4	2
Capital requirements	4	2

Note: A five-point rating scale is used: 5 = excellent, 4 = good, 3 = average, 2 = below average, and 1 = poor.

Which technology alternative do you think Mr. Lefleur should recommend? Why?

Relative-Aggregate-Scores Approach

15. The Superior Insurance Company has decided to replace its outdated telephone voice mail system with a modern system. Sally Billings, vice-president of operations, has narrowed the choices to two voice mail systems: Gamma and Omega. The Gamma system is very basic and allows employees to retrieve their voice mail only from their offices. The Omega system is more technologically advanced, providing more message options to callers and allowing employees to retrieve their voice mail from any touchtone telephone. The Omega system also provides remote paging capabilities. To help with the evaluation, Ms. Billings has had the following information prepared:

Factors	Factor Weight	Scores	
		Gamma	Omega
Economic factor:			
Annual operating cost	0.15	$30,000	$50,000
Other factors:			
Perceived quality of system	0.10	0.6	1.0
System features	0.30	0.4	1.0
Ease of use	0.05	1.0	0.6
Message storage capacity	0.10	0.6	1.0
Training requirements	0.05	1.0	0.4
Implementation time	0.05	0.8	0.6
Capital requirements	0.20	0.8	0.6

Note: A higher score is better.

Use the relative-aggregate-scores approach to compare the two automation alternatives. Which alternative would you recommend to Ms. Billings? Why?

16. Modemcom Inc. manufactures circuit boards for the cable modem industry. Chris Jaegar, a production analyst at Modemcom, is trying to decide which circuit board assembly technology to recommend for a new product model. Chris is faced with two viable options for attaching electronic components to circuit boards: manual surface-mount technology and automated straight-down insertion technology. To help with the analysis, he has prepared the following information:

Factors	Factor Weight	Scores Manual	Scores Automated
Economic factor:			
Production cost per board	0.20	$22	$16
Other factors:			
Product quality	0.10	0.7	1.0
Product flexibility	0.15	1.0	0.5
Labor relations	0.10	1.0	0.6
Production speed	0.05	0.5	1.0
Training requirements	0.10	0.4	0.8
Implementation time	0.05	0.9	0.6
Capital requirements	0.25	0.7	0.4

Note: A higher score is better.

Use the relative-aggregate-scores approach to compare the two technology alternatives. Which alternative would you recommend to Mr. Jaegar? Why?

17. LaTonya Johnson, production analyst at the Weston Flyrod Company in Problem 13, has decided to use the relative-aggregate-scores approach to compare the two graphite application technologies. To use this approach, Ms. Johnson has prepared the following information:

Factors	Factor Weight	Scores Alternative 1	Scores Alternative 2
Economic factor:			
Annual operating cost	0.30	$85,000	$125,000
Other factors:			
Product quality	0.20	0.8	1.0
Product flexibility	0.20	0.4	1.0
Volume flexibility	0.05	0.8	0.6
Maintenance requirements	0.10	1.0	0.4
Training requirements	0.10	0.8	0.4
Implementation time	0.05	1.0	0.4

Note: A higher score is better.

Use the relative-aggregate-scores approach to compare the two technology alternatives. Which alternative would you recommend to Ms. Johnson? Why?

18. Carl Lefleur, production manager at the Missoula Steel Company in Problem 14, has decided to use the relative-aggregate-scores approach to compare the two steel-cutting technologies. To use this approach, Mr. Lefleur has prepared the following information:

	Factor	Scores	
Factors	Weight	Flame-Based	Plasma-Based
Economic factor:			
Annual operating cost	0.10	$110,000	$215,000
Other factors:			
Product quality	0.30	0.6	1.0
Product flexibility	0.10	0.8	1.0
Market share	0.20	0.8	1.0
Volume flexibility	0.05	1.0	0.4
Maintenance requirements	0.05	1.0	0.6
Training requirements	0.05	0.8	0.6
Implementation time	0.05	0.8	0.4
Capital requirements	0.10	0.8	0.4

Note: A higher score is better.

Use the relative-aggregate-scores approach to compare the two technology alternatives. Which alternative would you recommend to Mr. Lefleur? Why?

CASES

Golden Kernel Processing Company I

Delana Lightfoot is a production analyst at the Golden Kernel processing plant, which processes whole-kernel cut corn. Delana's current project is to evaluate different levels of automation for quality control inspection of corn kernels. Option 1 is to assign a number of employees along the conveyor belt to inspect the corn kernels manually as they go by and pick out small and off-color kernels. Option 2 involves using fewer employees who only check for off-color kernels and then running the corn over a screen that filters out the small kernels. Option 3 is to purchase a state-of-the-art, fully automated machine that uses video cameras, a computer workstation, and small bursts of air. This new machine can automatically inspect individual kernels of corn for size and color as the conveyer belt moves the kernels in a single layer by the machine. Inferior kernels are removed by a precisely placed small burst of air as the kernels pass over a perforated air tube.

As Delana expected, the initial costs of the options vary subtantially. She investigated the cost of each option and has summarized the information in the following table:

	Option 1	Option 2	Option 3
Annual fixed cost	$2,500	$4,500	$27,000
Variable cost per thousand pounds	100	80	20

Assignment

1. Based on annual cost, determine the annual volume (in thousands of pounds) at which the company would be indifferent between Option 1 and Option 2; between Option 2 and Option 3; and between Option 1 and Option 3.
2. Create a table showing the total annual cost of each option if annual volume (in thousands of pounds) is 50, 200, 350, and 500. Circle the lowest cost at each annual volume.

3. Based only on annual cost, for what range of annual volumes would each option be preferred?
4. What factors other than annual cost should be considered when making this decision?

Golden Kernel Processing Company II

Refer to the previous case (Golden Kernal Processing Company I) for a description of the technology alternatives. After initially analyzing the annual costs of the three technology alternatives, Delana Lightfoot discovered that a mistake had been made. The annual fixed cost for Option 2 should have been $10,500 instead of $4,500. Delana must now repeat the analysis using the correct value. The complete, corrected information is:

	Option 1	Option 2	Option 3
Annual fixed cost	$2,500	$10,500	$27,000
Variable cost per thousand pounds	100	80	20

Assignment

1. Based on annual cost, determine the annual volume (in thousands of pounds) at which the company would be indifferent between Option 1 and Option 2; between Option 2 and Option 3; and between Option 1 and Option 3.
2. Create a table showing the total annual cost of each option if annual volume (in thousands of pounds) is 50, 300, 350, and 500. Circle the lowest cost at each annual volume.
3. Based only on annual cost, for what range of annual volumes would each option be preferred?
4. What factors other than annual cost should be considered when making this decision?

Western Arizona University

Dr. Anne Gonzalez is the director of computing resources at Western Arizona University (WAU). The state legislature has recently allocated a pool of money for computing enhancements at WAU. The funds are to be used to upgrade the computer network infrastructure at WAU and to purchase additional computer lab equipment. The legislature's intent is to provide fast network access to all university offices, classrooms, labs, and dormitory rooms. Dr. Gonzalez is responsible for recommending which computer network technology would be best for the university.

Dr. Gonzalez feels that only two network technology alternatives would be suitable, but the decision of which one is best has been difficult. The two technology alternatives are a fiber-optic cable network and a wireless technology network. A fiber-optic cable network would initially cost $1.3 million and would require an annual maintenance expenditure of $140,000. A wireless technology network would initially cost $1.9 million and require an annual maintenance expenditure of $90,000.

Many other factors are important in choosing the type of network technology. Each technology has different strengths that would benefit students and faculty. Following Dr. Gonzalez's direction, a graduate assistant prepared the following information to help with the decision:

Factors	Factor Weight	Scores Fiber-Optic	Scores Wireless
Economic factors:			
Initial cost	0.10	$1,300,000	$1,900,000
Annual maintenance cost	0.25	$140,000	$90,000
Other factors:			
Data signal quality	0.15	1.0	0.7
Connection convenience	0.10	0.6	1.0
Data transmission speed	0.10	0.8	0.6
Data bandwidth	0.10	0.8	0.7
Future upgradability	0.10	0.6	0.8
Training effort	0.05	0.8	0.6
Implementation time	0.05	0.4	0.8

Note: A higher score is better.

Assignment

1. Use the relative-aggregate-scores approach to compare the technologies.
2. Which technology would you advise Dr. Gonzalez to use? Why?
3. What other factors should be considered in this decision?

ENDNOTES

1. Gurin, Rick. "Nabisco Reaps Sweet Rewards." *Frontline Solutions,* January 2000, 26.
2. "Invasion of the Robots." *Business Week,* March 3, 1997, 74–75.
3. Groover, Mikell P. *Automation, Production Systems, and Computer Integrated Manufacturing,* p. 171. Englewood Cliffs, NJ: Prentice Hall, 1987.
4. Cox, James F., III, and John H. Blackstone, eds. *APICS Dictionary,* 9th ed., pp. 14–15. Falls Church, VA: APICS—The Educational Society for Resource Management, 1998.
5. *Ibid.*
6. Groover, Mikell P. *Automation, Production Systems, and Computer Integrated Manufacturing,* pp. 721–722. Englewood Cliffs, NJ: Prentice Hall, 1987.
7. Brown, Eryn. "The Best Software Business Bill Gates Doesn't Own." *Fortune,* December 19, 1997, 242–250.
8. "The New Factory Worker." *Business Week,* September 30, 1996, 59–68.
9. "Carpet Firm Sets Up an In-House School to Stay Competitive." *Wall Street Journal,* October 5, 1992, A1; "Old Mill Pioneers Workers Education." *New York Times,* January 18, 1993, A10.

SELECTED BIBLIOGRAPHY

Brown, Eryn. "The Best Software Business Bill Gates Doesn't Own." *Fortune,* December 29, 1997, 242–250.

Cohen, Morris A., and Uday M. Apte. *Manufacturing Automation.* Chicago: Irwin, 1997.

Cohn, David S. *AutoCAD 2000: The Complete Reference.* Berkeley, CA: Osborne McGraw-Hill, 2000.

Cox, James F., III, and John H. Blackstone, Jr., eds. *APICS Dictionary,* 9th ed. Falls Church, VA: APICS—The Educational Society for Resource Management, 1998.

Dell, Kris A. *AutoCAD Management: A Guide to Maximizing Efficiency.* Stamford, CT: Thomson Learning, 2001.

Fitzsimmons, James A., and Mona J. Fitzsimmons. *Service Management: Operations, Strategy, and Information Technology.* New York: McGraw-Hill, 2001.

Groover, Mikell P. *Automation, Production Systems, and Computer Integrated Manufacturing,* 2nd ed. Englewood Cliffs, NJ: Prentice Hall, 2000.

Jacobs, F. Robert, and D. Clay Whybark. *Why ERP? A Primer on SAP Implementation.* Boston: Irwin/McGraw-Hill, 2000.

MacHover, Carl, ed. *The CAD/CAM Handbook.* New York: McGraw-Hill, 1996.

Monroe, Joseph. "Strategic Use of Technology." *California Management Review* (Summer 1989): 91–110.

Narayanan, V. K. *Managing Technology and Innovation for Competitive Advantage.* Upper Saddle River, NJ: Prentice Hall, 2000.

Palmer, Roger C. *The Bar Code Book: Reading, Printing, and Specification of Bar Code Symbols.* Peterborough, NH: Helmers Publishing, 1995.

Price, Robert M. "Technology and Strategic Advantage." *California Management Review* 38, no. 3 (Spring 1996): 38–56.

Rehg, James A., and Henry W. Kraebber. *Computer-Integrated Manufacturing,* 2nd ed. Upper Saddle River, NJ: Prentice Hall, 2001.

Shell, Richard L., and Ernest L. Hall, eds. *Handbook of Industrial Automation.* New York: Marcel Dekker, 2000.

Teufel, Thomas, Jurgen Robricht, and Peter Willems. *SAP Processes: Planning Procurement and Production.* Reading, MA: Addison-Wesley-Longman, 2001.

"The New Factory Worker." *Business Week,* September 30, 1996, 59–68.

Operations Quality Management

Introduction

Nature of Quality
Dimensions of Quality
Determinants of Quality
Costs of Quality

Traditional Quality Management

Modern Quality Management
Quality Gurus
Quality Drives the Productivity Machine
Other Aspects of the Quality Picture

Quality Management Recognition
Malcolm Baldrige National Quality Award
The Deming Prize
ISO 9000 Standards

Total Quality Management (TQM) Programs
Top Management Commitment and Involvement

Customer Involvement
Designing Products for Quality
Designing and Controlling Production Processes
Developing Supplier Partnerships
Customer Service, Distribution, and Installation
Building Teams of Empowered Employees
Benchmarking and Continuous Improvement

Quality Management in Services

Wrap-Up: What World-Class Companies Do

Review and Discussion Questions

Internet Assignments

Problems

Case
Integrated Switches Corporation

Endnotes

Selected Bibliography

QUALITY MANAGEMENT AT KFC

Managing the quality of service operations is just as critical as managing the quality of manufacturing operations. In service organizations, not only is the quality of the services and products provided important, but also important is the quality of the way services are provided.

Kentucky Fried Chicken (KFC) Corporation is a large chain of fast-food restaurants owned by Pepsico, with more than 5,000 franchised or company-owned restaurants. Recognizing the importance of managing the quality of foods and services in its restaurants, KFC adopted a company-wide quality management program with the hope of improving productivity as well as quality. Its quality management program consisted of two components for measuring quality: (1) a quality, service, and cleanliness (QSC) program for judging the quality of services and foods provided, from the perspective of a customer, and (2) an operations facility review (OFR) program for measuring a restaurant's process implementation performance against KFC's process specifications.

As part of the QSC program, "mystery shoppers" contracted by KFC evaluate the quality, service, and cleanliness of individual restaurants twice a month. The mystery shoppers fill out a standard QSC form as they evaluate each restaurant, so that evaluations are objective, accurate, and consistent. In addition, customer surveys and complaint cards are used to help evaluate quality at individual restaurants.

The objective of the OFR program is to help KFC ensure the consistency of high-quality products and services that customers have come to expect across all KFC restaurants. The OFR evaluation program measures a restaurant's operating performance against KFC's operating standards. The general manager at each restaurant completes a weekly standardized OFR evaluation form. Managers must also run training programs for restaurant employees and maintain facilities, equipment, and premises in accordance with KFC's operating standards.

In addition to the QSC and OFR programs, other quality control tools, such as Pareto charts, fishbone diagrams, and control charts, are sometimes used at KFC to help improve the quality of certain processes. In fact, many process improvements have resulted from KFC's quality management program, and these improvement ideas have been disseminated to all its restaurants.[1]

As the preceding account discusses, the management of quality is just as important for service organizations as it is for manufacturing organizations. For most companies today, superior quality is at the core of their business strategy. For these companies, attaining near-perfect product quality is seen as a principal means of capturing market share in global competition. The prominence of product quality in business strategy for many firms has come from the painful knowledge that *you may lose business to lower-priced products, but you win it back with superior product quality.* Achieving superior product quality within a business requires a long-term process of changing the fundamental culture of the organization. This chapter is about *quality management*, which is the process of redirecting organization cultures toward superior product and service quality.

NATURE OF QUALITY

What is quality? Basically, the quality of products and services is not defined or determined by the producing companies; it is determined by customers. *The quality of a product or service is a customer's perception of the degree to which the product or service meets his or her expectations.* To better understand the nature of quality, we discuss the dimensions, determinants, and costs of quality.

Dimensions of Quality

As customers evaluate quality, they consider several different aspects of products and services. Table 7.1 describes some of the dimensions of quality that customers use to evaluate quality. These dimensions of quality have important implications. Companies have to look to customers as they set standards for measuring quality. Customer surveys and suggestions can be used to obtain inputs from customers about quality. Customer expectations of quality are affected by many factors including competitors' products and are likely to change over time. Products and services must therefore be improved with time to meet the changing expectations of customers.

Customers' expectations of quality are not the same for different **grades** or **classes** of products. For example, customers do not ordinarily expect construction nails to be masterpieces that are designed and produced to the same exacting standards of excellence as Rolls-Royce automobiles. But nails should serve their intended purpose and be better than the competition. This point is an important one. It is the objective of many companies today to become what is called a world-class company. *Becoming a world-class company in terms of quality means that each product and service would be considered best-in-class by its customers.* Best-in-class quality means being the best product or service in a particular class of products or services.

Determinants of Quality

A key issue is how to achieve quality. Several activities or accomplishments are necessary:

Quality of design. After first identifying who its customers are, a company must determine what its customers want from its products and services. Then products and services are designed to exhibit the attributes necessary to meet its customers' expectations.

Table 7.1	Some Dimensions of Product Quality

- **Performance.** How well the product or service performs the customer's intended use. For example, the speed of a laser printer.
- **Features.** The special characteristics that appeal to customers. For example, power seats on an automobile.
- **Reliability.** The likelihood of breakdowns, malfunctions, or the need for repairs.
- **Serviceability.** The speed, cost, and convenience of repairs and maintenance.
- **Durability.** The length of time or amount of use before needing to be repaired or replaced.
- **Appearance.** The effects on human senses—the look, feel, taste, smell, or sound.
- **Customer service.** The treatment received by customers before, during, and after the sale.
- **Safety.** How well the product protects users before, during, and after use.

One quality control method, such as the use of this pressure tester to check fruit, traditionally used is a rigorous system of inspection. Many companies today are adopting a different approach, however.

© ED YOUNG/CORBIS

- **Quality capability of production processes.** Production processes must be designed and built that have the capability of producing products with the attributes wanted by customers.
- **Quality of conformance.** Production facilities must then be operated to produce products and services that meet design and performance specifications aimed at the quality expectations of customers.
- **Quality of customer service.** All contacts between customers and companies must be managed so that customers perceive that they have been treated fairly and courteously with their needs attended to promptly and with care and concern.
- **Organization quality culture.** The entire organization must become energized to doing what is necessary to design, produce, and service products and services that meet customers' expectations. Mechanisms must be in place to continuously improve every facet of the organization toward the objective of building ever-increasing levels of customer satisfaction.

[handwritten margin notes: deteriorate]

[handwritten margin notes: Jack Nasser didn't support #1 Quality Job #. he wanted # + quality diver. Bill is now pushing for quality.]

[handwritten note across text: Ford used to have a good quality job is #1 dictated from the top + was accepted by workers]

Costs of Quality

There are costs associated with product and service quality. Some costs are associated with preventing poor quality, and some costs occur after poor quality occurs. These costs include:

- **Scrap and rework.** When products are found to be defective while in production, they must be either scrapped or repaired. The costs include the costs of producing the items that are scrapped; the cost of repairing, reworking, and retesting defective products; and all the costs of delays, paperwork, rescheduling, and other hassles caused by defective products.
- **Defective products in the hands of customers.** When products are shipped to customers, the costs can be enormous and difficult to measure. These costs can in-

[handwritten note: major quality problem]

Quality products are made in clean environment

Idea of Quality area. Inspectors are costly. People that make the product need to inspect the product.

– Keep area clear

clude warranty costs, product liability suits or settlements, the cost of returns or recalls, and lost business and goodwill.

Detecting defects. The cost of all the activities aimed at finding products and services that do not conform to specifications before they are shipped to customers. This includes the cost of inspection, testing, and other quality control activities.

Preventing defects. The cost of training, charting of quality performance to study trends, revising product designs, making changes to production processes, working with suppliers, and other activities aimed at improving quality and preventing defects.

Costs

While each of these costs can be high, it is a generally accepted fact that the first three of these costs, the cost of finding and dealing with defective products, may account for as much as 25 percent of the cost of sales in many companies. Emphasizing the activities of finding and dealing with defects has been the traditional approach to quality management.

TRADITIONAL QUALITY MANAGEMENT

Do it right the first time
3, Perf × time
We believe in US
We can expect Quality

A factor keeping some U.S. companies from overtaking their foreign competitors is their traditional view of quality control. In this view, the way to ensure that customers receive quality products and services is to have a rigorous system of inspection. The idea is that if there is enough inspection, the defective products will be identified and discarded, leaving only good products to be shipped to customers. In this approach, the main decision is how many products to inspect, and this decision is largely a question of economics. Figure 7.1 demonstrates this traditional view: As more and more outputs are inspected, the costs of scrap, rework, and detecting defects increase while the costs of defective products to customers decline. At some level of inspection, an optimal trade-off is achieved where total quality control costs are minimized. Operations managers are somehow supposed to balance these costs in deciding how many products to inspect.

What is fundamentally wrong with this traditional view of quality management is that it implies quality can be inspected into products. In other words, acceptable product quality can be achieved by discarding defective products that are found in inspection while continuing to produce shoddy products with sloppy production practices. Enlightened operations managers today know that superior product quality is not attained through more inspection. They know that manufacturers must go back to production and make fundamental changes in the way that they design and produce products and *do it right the first time.* That way, products of superior quality will be coming out of production and inspection's job will shift from discarding bad products to preventing defects and providing feedback on how production can continue to improve product quality.

And besides, rigorous inspection does not guarantee that only good products and services go to customers. One story is told over and over about the human frailty of inspectors. A supervisor who wanted to check out the inspection skills of his inspectors purposely placed 100 defects in a batch of parts without telling his inspectors. The inspectors found only 68 of the defects on the first pass. Determined that the inspectors should be able to find the defects, the supervisor again put the batch with 32 defects through inspection. This time the inspectors found many of the defects, but not all. After this process was repeated for the third, fourth, and fifth times, 98 defects were found. The other 2 defects were never found. They went to a customer. Another version of this same story had the inspectors finding 110 defects.

More and more U.S. companies are abandoning this traditional view of quality management and have adopted a different approach.

Figure 7.1	Traditional View of How Much to Inspect

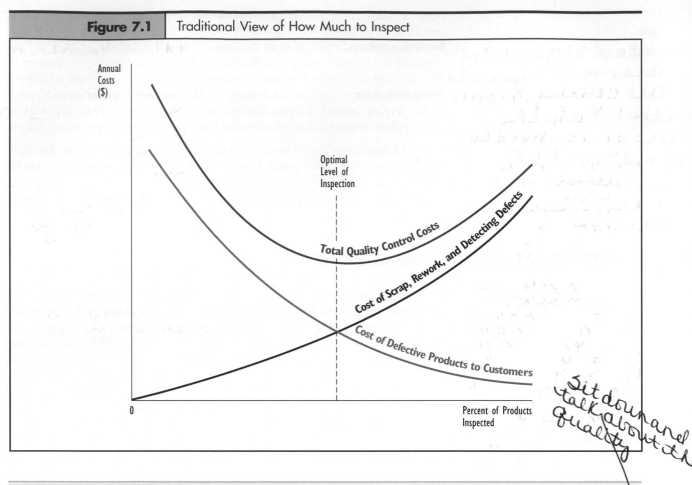

MODERN QUALITY MANAGEMENT

The modern approach to quality is reflected in the following discussions of quality gurus, the idea that quality drives the productivity machine, other aspects of the quality picture, and quality management recognition.

Quality Gurus

The modern era of quality management was heralded by a few new thinkers. Among these, Deming, Crosby, Feigenbaum, Ishikawa, Juran, and Taguchi are noteworthy. These educators, authors, and consultants worked with industry to start companies on their way to the development of quality improvement programs.

W. Edwards Deming, a professor at New York University, traveled to Japan after World War II at the request of the Japanese government to assist its industries in improving productivity and quality. Dr. Deming, a statistician and consultant, was so successful in his mission that in 1951 the Japanese government established the Deming Prize for innovation in quality management to be awarded annually to a company that had distinguished itself in quality management programs. Business Snapshot 7.1 discusses Deming's philosophy and approach to quality.

Deming also introduced to Japanese companies the **plan–do–check–act (PDCA) cycle**, which was originally developed by Walter Shewart. The PDCA cycle, shown in Figure 7.2, represents the concept of continuous improvement as an endless cycle of

BUSINESS SNAPSHOT 7.1

Deming's 14 Points

W. Edwards Deming is known as the father of quality control in Japan, but his recognition in his own country, the United States, was a long time coming. He taught the Japanese that higher quality meant lower cost, but the idea was so foreign to U.S. managers that they failed to listen until it was almost too late. Deming's ideas are embodied in his 14 points for managers:

1. Create constancy of purpose toward product quality to achieve organizational goals.
2. Refuse to allow commonly accepted levels of poor quality.
3. Stop depending on inspection to achieve quality.
4. Use fewer suppliers, selected based on quality and dependability instead of price.

5. Instill programs for continuous improvement of costs, quality, service, and productivity.
6. Train all employees on quality concepts.
7. Focus supervision on helping people to do a better job.
8. Eliminate fear, create trust, and encourage two-way communications between workers and management.
9. Eliminate barriers between departments and encourage joint problem solving.
10. Eliminate the use of numerical goals and slogans to make workers work harder.
11. Use statistical methods for continuous improvement of quality and productivity instead of numerical quotas.
12. Remove barriers to pride of workmanship.

13. Encourage education and self-improvement for everyone.
14. Clearly define management's permanent commitment to quality and productivity.

Permeating these points is a philosophy based on the belief in the worker's desire to do a good job. Workers are taught statistics so that they can keep control charts on their progress toward improved quality. Everyone in the organization, from board members to janitors, receives training in quality control concepts and statistics, and everyone is encouraged to suggest ideas for improvement.

| Figure 7.2 | PDCA Cycle |

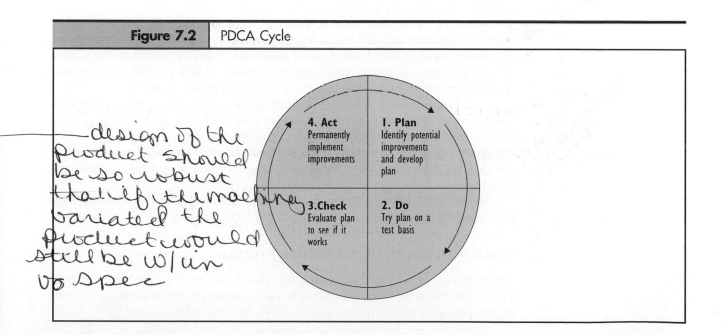

4. Act Permanently implement improvements

1. Plan Identify potential improvements and develop plan

3. Check Evaluate plan to see if it works

2. Do Try plan on a test basis

[handwritten note in margin:] design of the product should be so robust that if the machine variated the product would still be w/in vo spec

actions. In the first step—*Plan*—a process is studied, potential improvements are identified, and a plan is developed to implement the improvements. In the second step—*Do*—the plan is tried on a test basis and results are documented. In the third step—*Check*—the plan is thoroughly evaluated based on the testing to see if it improves the process. In the fourth step—*Act*—the plan is permanently implemented as part of the normal operation. The PDCA cycle then starts over with the first step again.

Philip B. Crosby wrote *Quality Is Free* in 1979 and set traditional thinking about "acceptable levels of defects" on its ear.[2] Crosby contended that any level of defects is too high and companies should put programs into place that will move them continuously toward the goal of **zero defects.** The main idea behind free quality is that the traditional trade-off between the costs of improving quality and the costs of poor quality is erroneous. The costs of poor quality should include all the costs of not doing the job right the first time: scrap, rework, lost labor-hours and machine-hours, the hidden costs of customer ill will and lost sales, and warranty costs. He states that the cost of poor quality is so understated that unlimited amounts can be profitably spent on improving quality.

Armand V. Feigenbaum developed the concept of **total quality control (TQC)** in his 1983 book.[3] Feigenbaum contended that the responsibility for quality must rest with the persons who do the work. This concept is referred to as quality at the source and means that every worker, secretary, engineer, and salesperson must be responsible for performing his or her work with perfect quality. In TQC, where product quality is more important than production rates, workers are given the authority to stop production whenever quality problems occur.

Kaoru Ishikawa not only had a direct impact on quality improvement in his work with industry, but his book *Guide to Quality Control* may have influenced later quality gurus.[4] He is credited with the concept of **quality circles,** which we discuss later in this chapter. He also suggested the use of fishbone diagrams, which are used to trace back customer complaints about quality problems to the responsible production operations. Figure 7.3 is a fishbone diagram used for finding the causes of tread blisters on automobile tires. Ishikawa contends that in U.S. companies responsibility for product and service quality is delegated to a few staff personnel, but that Japanese managers are totally committed to quality.

Joseph M. Juran, like Deming, was discovered late by U.S. companies. Juran played an important and early role in teaching Japanese manufacturers how to improve their product quality. His *Quality Control Handbook* argues for top management commitment to improved product quality, quality planning, statistics to identify discrepancies, and continuous improvement of every aspect of product quality.[5]

Genichi Taguchi has consulted with leading companies such as Ford and IBM to assist them in developing improved statistical control of their production processes. Taguchi contends that constant adjustment of production machines to achieve consistent product quality is not effective and that, instead, products should be designed so that they are **robust** enough to function satisfactorily despite variations on the production line or in the field.

The thinking of these quality gurus has, individually and collectively, permanently influenced the management of U.S. product and service quality.

Quality Drives the Productivity Machine

The traditional view of quality control was that it cost more to get higher product quality. But this is no longer the prevalent view. Japanese manufacturers are credited with popularizing the notion that *quality drives the productivity machine.* This means

Figure 7.3	Fishbone Diagram for Tread Blisters on Automobile Tires

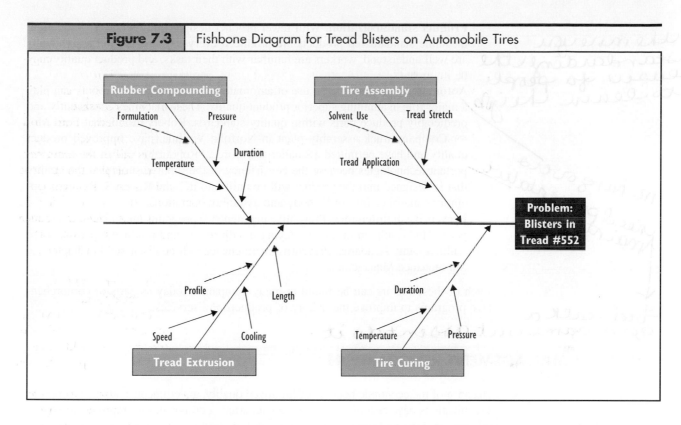

that if production does it right the first time and produces products and services that are defect free, waste is eliminated and costs are reduced. In this new way of thinking, when operations managers work to eliminate defects, the quality of products and services is improved and at the same time productivity also improves. Costs are reduced as product quality improves because there are fewer products lost to scrap, fewer products returned for warranty work, and fewer interruptions to production. It has been estimated that 20 to 25 percent of the overall cost of goods sold in the United States is spent on finding and correcting errors.[6] *Quality management programs today are, therefore, viewed by many companies as productivity improvement programs.*

Other Aspects of the Quality Picture

Other factors have also contributed to the improvement of the quality of products and services today:

- **Just-in-time (JIT) and lean manufacturing.** JIT has been called a system of enforced problem solving. Because in-process inventories are drastically reduced by cutting lot sizes, any interruption causes production to stop until the problem causing the interruption has been solved. This tends to improve product quality in several ways. Because only a few parts are in process inventory, if a quality problem does occur, fewer defective parts are produced before they are discovered. And, because production is stopped until the problem is corrected, everyone's attention is on solving the quality problem so that the problem will not be repeated. Further, the teamwork necessary for JIT contributes to increased pride in product quality and improved quality performance.

the more you standardize the easier for people to learn the job

no hangovers need preventative maintenance

did talk a good game, but absent do it.

- **Product standardization.** With fewer product designs and repetitive production, the same standardized products are produced every day, worker job assignments are well understood, workers are familiar with their tasks, and product quality may be improved.

Automated equipment. The use of automated equipment such as robots can play a major role in attaining superior product quality. These machines consistently and predictably produce parts within quality standards. Robots installed at Ford Motor Company truck assembly plant in Norfolk, Virginia, have improved product quality and have permitted a smaller workforce. "Robotics is one of the most important technologies because the consistency of the robot ensures that the quality that is designed into the product will be built into it," said Robert S. Rennard, operations manager for Ford's body and assembly operations.[7]

- **Preventive maintenance.** Preventive maintenance programs minimize machine repairs. This results in machines staying in adjustment and producing parts that are within quality standards. Preventive maintenance will be discussed in Chapter 19, Maintenance Management.

Each of these factors can be found in many companies today as parts of comprehensive programs to improve the quality of products and services.

QUALITY MANAGEMENT RECOGNITION

Because of the economic benefits of improved quality, governments and other nonprofit organizations have become interested in encouraging companies to improve the quality of their products and services. Many awards and certifications now exist that recognize superior quality management by companies. Three of these are particularly noteworthy: the Malcolm Baldrige National Quality Award, the Deming Prize, and ISO 9000.

know mission statement

Malcolm Baldrige National Quality Award

There is broad support in the United States for improved product and service quality, not only among consumers but also among and within companies. Perhaps nothing reflects the newfound U.S. desire for improved product and service quality as the *Malcolm Baldrige National Quality Award.* The award is administered by the National Institute of Standards and Technology, and only U.S. businesses are eligible (**http://www.quality.nist.gov**).

Business Snapshot 7.2 discusses this award. Business results are the heaviest weighted factor in the award. Winners of this prestigious award read like a who's who of U.S. industry. Table 7.2 shows all the past winners in each category. All applicants receive a written summary of the examiners' findings including the strengths and weaknesses of the quality programs and suggestions for improvements so that winning is not the greatest benefit from trying for the award. Participants say that going through the application process forces a company to examine the role of product and service quality in its business and to determine how things could be changed for improvement. BI won the 1999 Malcolm Baldrige National Quality Award in the service category after applying for the award for 10 consecutive years. Like many other companies, BI applied the award criteria to its operations year after year to improve and learn, not to win the award, according to company owner Guy Schoenecker. Along the way, BI also won the Baldrige-based Minnesota Quality Award in 1994.

The Baldrige award has great significance in and of itself, but perhaps more important, it reflects the growing commitment in the United States to the need for preeminence in product and service quality. Two new categories were recently added to

BUSINESS SNAPSHOT 7.2

The Malcolm Baldrige National Quality Award

The Malcolm Baldrige National Quality Award was established in 1987 and named for a former secretary of commerce. Its purpose is to recognize U.S. companies that attain preeminent quality leadership, encourage other U.S. companies to improve their quality programs, develop and publish award criteria that serve as quality improvement guidelines, and disseminate nonproprietary information about the quality strategies of the award recipients. Up to two awards may be issued annually in three categories: large manufacturers, large services, and small businesses. To be eligible, a company must be incorporated and located in the United States, and it must submit a 75-page application package. A board of examiners reviews and evaluates the applications.

High-scoring applications receive site examinations. Criteria for selection are:

1. **Leadership.** The company's leadership system, values, expectations, and public responsibilities.
2. **Strategic planning.** The effectiveness of strategic and business planning and deployment of plans, with a strong focus on customer and operational performance requirements.
3. **Customer and market focus.** How the company determines customer and market requirements and expectations, enhances relationships with customers, and determines their satisfaction.
4. **Information and analysis.** The effectiveness of information collection and analysis to support customer-driven performance excellence and marketplace success.
5. **Human resource focus.** The success of efforts to realize the full potential of the workforce to create a high-performance organization.
6. **Process management.** The effectiveness of systems and processes for assuring the quality of products and services.
7. **Business results.** Performance results, trends, and comparison to competitors in key business areas—customer satisfaction, financial and marketplace, human resources, suppliers and partners, and operations.

Source: 2000 Criteria for Performance Excellence, Malcolm Baldrige National Quality Award, U.S. Department of Commerce, National Institute of Standards and Technology (**http://www.quality.nist.gov**)

the Baldrige award program: education and health care. These additions attest to the growing recognition of the importance of managing quality in service organizations.

And most states in the United States are getting into the act. Nearly all states now have their own quality award programs, which are styled after the Baldrige quality award program.

As more firms compete for this valued award, our collective quality consciousness is raised and, in some cases, great progress is made toward achieving superior quality of products and services. And the criteria for receiving these awards are becoming etched into our thinking as standards of excellence in quality management.

The Deming Prize

The Deming Prize, named after W. Edwards Deming who was mentioned earlier, was established in 1951. The prize is awarded by the Union of Japanese Scientists and Engineers to companies that have demonstrated successful quality improvement programs (**http://www.deming.org** and **http://www.juse.or.jp**). Although all firms are eligible to apply, the first non-Japanese firm to win the prize was Florida Power and Light in 1991. Other well-known companies that have won the prize are Toyota Motors, NEC, and Kansai Electric Power. The emphasis of the prize has traditionally been on statistical quality control as a means of improving quality. But most winners also have well-

Table 7.2	Malcolm Baldrige National Quality Award Recipients

Manufacturing

Dana Corporation—Spicer Driveshaft Division (2000)
KARLEE Company, Inc. (2000)
STMicroelectronics, Inc.—Region Americas (1999)
Boeing Airlift and Tanker Programs (1998)
Solar Turbines Incorporated (1998)
3M Dental Products Division (1997)
Solectron Corporation (1997)
ADAC Laboratories (1996)
Armstrong World Industries, Building Products Operations (1995)
Corning Incorporated, Telecommunications Products Division (1995)
Eastman Chemical Company (1993)
Texas Instruments Incorporated Defense Systems & Electronics Group (1992) (now part of Raytheon Systems Company)
AT&T Network Systems Group Transmission Systems Business Unit (1992) (now part of Lucent Technologies, Inc., Optical Networking Group)
Solectron Corporation (1991)
Zytec Corporation (1991) (now Artesyn Technologies)
IBM Rochester, AS/400 Division (1990)
Cadillac Motor Car Company (1990)
Milliken & Company (1989)
Xerox Corporation Business Products and Systems (1989)
Motorola, Inc. (1988)
Westinghouse Electric Corporation Commercial Nuclear Fuel Division (1988)

Service

Operations Management International, Inc. (2000)
The Ritz-Carlton Hotel Company, LLC (1999)
BI (1999)
Merrill Lynch Credit Corporation (1997)
Xerox Business Services (1997)
Dana Commercial Credit Corporation (1996)
GTE Directories Corporation (1994)
AT&T Consumer Communications Services (1994) (now part of AT&T Consumer Markets Division)
The Ritz-Carlton Hotel Company (1992) (now part of Marriott International)
AT&T Universal Card Services (1992) (now part of Citigroup)
Federal Express Corporation (1990)

Small Business

Los Alamos National Bank (2000)
Sunny Fresh Foods (1999)
Texas Nameplate Company, Inc. (1998)
Custom Research, Inc. (1996)
Trident Precision Manufacturing, Inc. (1996)
Wainwright Industries, Inc. (1994)
Ames Rubber Corporation (1993)
Granite Rock Company (1992)
Marlow Industries, Inc. (1991)
Wallace Company, Inc. (1990)
Globe Metallurgical, Inc. (1988)

communicated and detailed programs that have set quality goals to be achieved over several years. Top management commitment and involvement in the programs is also emphasized. Four top-quality management activities are recognized: senior management activities, customer satisfaction activity, employee involvement activity, and training activity.

This prize was very early in the international movement to recognize, reward, and encourage progress toward improving the quality of products and services. As such, it was very important in the move toward elevating excellence in quality to the strategic level in organizations around the globe.

ISO 9000 Standards

The International Organization for Standardization (**http://www.iso.ch**), headquartered in Geneva, Switzerland, developed guidelines for quality management that were initially adopted in Europe. Since their initial publication in 1987, the ISO 9000 standards have now been adopted by companies all over the world.

Not important

The ISO 9000 standards were revised in 2000 to include these four groups:

- ISO 9000, Quality management systems—Fundamentals and vocabulary
- ISO 9001, Quality management systems—Requirements
- ISO 9004, Quality management systems—Guidelines for performance improvements
- ISO 19011, Guidelines on quality and environmental auditing

These standards are based on eight quality management principles that reflect best management practices:

- Customer-focused organization
- Leadership
- Involvement of people
- Process approach
- System approach to management
- Continual improvement
- Factual approach to decision making
- Mutually beneficial supplier relationship

The ISO 9000 family of standards provides guidelines for companies to better manage their quality, but it does not provide any levels of quality that must be attained. Companies can become ISO 9000 certified by applying to third-party providers that are authorized by each country to provide this certification service and that assess the level of conformity to the ISO 9000 standards. More than 300,000 companies worldwide have become ISO 9000 certified. In the United States, the American Society for Quality (**http://www.asq.org**) is charged with administering the ISO 9000 standards by the American National Standards Institute.

A closely related set of quality management standards adopted by the U.S. big three automakers (General Motors, Ford, and Daimler-Chrysler) is QS-9000. QS-9000 is based on the ISO 9000 standards but contains additional requirements that are particular to the automotive industry.

As our quality consciousness continues to rise, it is inevitable that the need for commonly agreed-to quality standards should also grow. This development should bring more firms into the new age of emphasizing the strategic importance of product and service quality.

TOTAL QUALITY MANAGEMENT (TQM) PROGRAMS

Many U.S. manufacturers have overhauled the structure of their organizations, changed their organization climates, and redirected their product quality programs toward becoming global quality leaders. Such efforts are often referred to as **total quality management (TQM)**. At Motorola it is called *Six Sigma*; at Xerox it is called *Leadership*

starts @ the top then it will flow throught organization.

Table 7.3	The Elements of Total Quality Management (TQM)

- **Top management commitment and involvement.** Top management gets involved and stays involved from setting business strategy based on using product quality as a weapon to capturing global market share to rewarding employees for achieving excellence in product quality.
- **Customer involvement.** Customer wants drive the TQM system. The characteristics that they value most are built into products from design to after-sale service.
- **Design products for quality.** What customers want sets the basic attributes of product design. Excellence in performance, features, reliability, serviceability, durability, appearance, and service are critically affected by design.
- **Design production processes for quality.** Production machinery and workers form a system of production that should be designed to produce products with the dimensions of quality that customers want.
- **Control production processes for quality.** As products and services are produced, the quality performance of production is monitored and managed to ensure that only products and services of superior quality are produced.
- **Developing supplier partnerships.** Selecting and developing suppliers that fit into the TQM system is an important priority. Long-term relationships are cultivated so that suppliers deliver parts of perfect quality.
- **Customer service, distribution, and installation.** Packaging, shipping, installation, and customer service can be crucially important to customers' perceptions of quality.
- **Building teams of empowered employees.** Making TQM work rests in the end with employees. They must be trained, organized, motivated, and empowered to produce and service products and services of perfect quality.
- **Benchmarking and continuous improvement.** Standards used to measure progress are taken from the performance of other world-class companies. Then these standards become the basis for long-term continuous improvement.

through *Quality;* at Intel it is called *(PDQ)²,* or *Perfect Design Quality, Pretty Darn Quick;* and at Hewlett-Packard it is called *Total Quality Control.*[8] Table 7.3 lists the important elements of TQM. We will study these elements in this section.

The objective of TQM programs is to build an organization that produces products and services that are considered best-in-class by its customers. This means that to achieve best-in-class in quality, every piece of the business must be done right the first time and every piece of the business must continue to improve.

Top Management Commitment and Involvement

TQM begins with top management commitment and involvement. Unless there is genuine top management support, TQM programs will be seen as just another fad that will pass into oblivion like so many other slogans and acronyms. Building superior product quality into business strategy forms the basis for building an organization to achieve TQM. Fundamental changes must occur in the culture of organizations if TQM is to succeed. Customer involvement, driving the design of products and production processes by customer needs, developing suppliers as partners, building teams of empowered employees, and benchmarking are revolutionary concepts to most organizations. Such changes are not easy, but they are impossible without top management commitment and involvement.

Customer Involvement

Mechanisms must be found to involve customers in organizations. *Focus groups are groups of customers brought together to discuss and evaluate quality with executives and engineers.* These groups can be useful in learning what customers want from products before products and services are designed. Market surveys, customer questionnaires, and market research programs can also provide valuable information. When automakers sent assembly line workers to dealerships to visit with customers about auto defects, useful information about customer needs and wants was carried back to the companies. Because in TQM customers drive much of the efforts toward quality, specific, practical, and tangible means must be found to bring about customer involvement.

Quality function deployment (QFD) is a formal system for identifying customer wants and eliminating wasteful product features and activities that do not contribute. QFD has its origins at Bridgestone Tire Corporation and Mitsubishi Heavy Industries, Ltd. in the late 1960s. Professor Yoji Akao of Tamagawa University and Shigeru Mizuno in the late 1970s gave QFD its name and popularized the concept of formalizing customer inputs into product design. In QFD every possible customer expectation is listed for a product. These expectations are then broken down into more and more specific product features. For example, if customers want a pencil that is easy to hold, this can be broken down into product features like length, diameter, weight, surface finish, and other functional characteristics. QFD also involves a weighting of customer demands and a customer rating of a product's functional characteristics compared with those of competitors' products. The aim of QFD is to identify product characteristics that need improvement. The QFD process is repeated until customer satisfaction with product designs can no longer identify product characteristics that can be improved.[9]

Designing Products for Quality

If products and services are to be of superior quality, it all begins with design. Three aspects of design are particularly important: robust designs, design for production, and design for reliability.

Designing for Robustness

It is not enough that products perform as intended when they are produced and used under ideal conditions. Customers want products to perform satisfactorily when used in all kinds of field conditions. And it is a fact of life that production conditions are almost never ideal, something is always occurring out of the ordinary. *A robust design is one that will perform as intended even if undesirable conditions occur either in production or in the field.* Robustness can be designed into products by assuming less than desirable field conditions when considering such things as heat, cold, humidity, nature of use, and other conditions. Likewise, assuming less than ideal production conditions when considering such things as employee skills, material characteristics and specifications, and machine capabilities can lead to more robust product designs.

Genichi Taguchi emphasized the importance of robust designs. In his approach, he stressed **parameter design**, determining product specifications and production process settings that will permit satisfactory product performance in spite of undesirable production and field conditions. Central to this approach is identifying *controllable factors* and *uncontrollable factors* in production and then setting the best levels of the controllable factors.[10]

Designing for Production

In Chapter 4, Product, Process, and Service Design, we discussed how product quality can be improved by designing products for ease of production. And in Chapter 6, Operations Technologies, we discussed the principles of designing products for automated assembly. When products are designed accordingly, products typically have fewer parts and can be assembled quickly and easily. Designing products for production can vastly reduce the sources of error and improve overall product quality.

Designing for Reliability

Each part of a product is designed for a given level of *component reliability, the probability that a type of part will not fail in a given time period or number of trials under ordinary conditions of use.* Component reliability is usually measured by: reliability (CR), failure rates (FR and FR_n), and mean time between failures (MTBF):

$$CR = (1 - FR)$$

where:

$$FR = \frac{\text{Number of failures}}{\text{Number tested}}$$

$$FR_n = \frac{\text{Number of failures}}{\text{Unit-hours of operation}}$$

$$MTBF = \frac{\text{Unit-hours of operation}}{\text{Number of failures}} \text{ or } \frac{1}{FR_n}$$

For instance, for a particular type of automobile tire with an expected life of 30,000 miles, if only 1 percent of the tires fail within the 30,000-mile span, we would say that a tire has a reliability level of 0.99.

When component parts are combined into a product, the combined reliability of all the components forms the basis for product or system reliability (SR). When independent critical components—those that can directly cause the product to fail—are combined into a product, the system reliability is determined by multiplying the reliabilities of all the interacting critical components. For example, four automobile tires, each with a reliability of 0.99, would have a system reliability of:

$$SR = CR_1 \times CR_2 \times CR_3 \times CR_4 = 0.99 \times 0.99 \times 0.99 \times 0.99 = 0.961$$

The concept of system reliability is further demonstrated in Figure 7.4. If the critical components of a system have a reliability of 90 percent, the system reliability is almost zero if there are more than 50 critical component parts. Similarly, when component parts have a 99.5 percent reliability, system reliability falls to 60.6 percent when there are 100 critical component parts.

Considering the concept of system reliability, what are some of the ways in which operations managers can increase the reliability of products? There are three practical ways. First, overdesign of component parts to improve reliability may be a viable strategy in holding product reliability at acceptable levels. *Overdesign means enhancing a design to avoid a particular type of failure.* Let us say that if a part tends to corrode, overdesigning the part could mean machining the part out of stainless steel to reduce corrosion. Or if a part tends to wear over time, making the part out of forged steel that has been hardened could improve its wearing quality. Similarly, manufacturing parts to closer tolerances may improve fit of the parts during assembly and reduce the likelihood of improper meshing of parts during use.

When products are relatively simple (have only a few critical interacting component parts), overdesign may be a reasonable alternative for improving system reliability. But when products are complex (have many critical component parts), overdesign of component parts may not significantly improve system reliability. Even if overdesign of critical component parts warrants consideration, the cost of designing, testing, and producing overdesigned parts may be exorbitant. Thus other alternatives must often be considered.

Second, *design simplification, the reduction of the number of interacting parts in a product,* will ordinarily improve system reliability. There are many examples of how

Figure 7.4	System Reliability as a Function of Component Part Reliability and Number of Component Parts

System Reliability (percent)

CR = 99.5%

CR = 98%

CR = 90%

Number of Component Parts in System

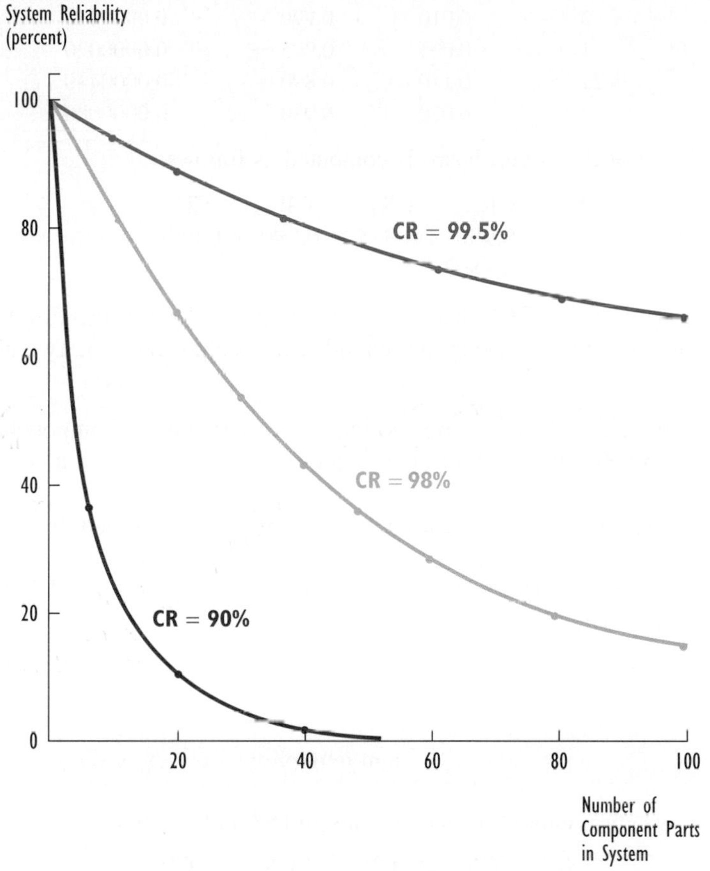

companies have redesigned products to have fewer parts. This is often done to reduce production costs, but another benefit is increased system reliability.

Third, another practical approach to improving product reliability is to provide **redundant components**. In this approach, *a component with low reliability may have a backup built right into the system; thus, if the first component fails, its backup is automatically substituted.* The electronics industry commonly employs this approach. Example 7.1 illustrates the overdesign and redundancy approaches to improving product reliability.

Example 7.1	Improving Product Reliability with Overdesign and Redundancy

Tennessee Component Systems (TCS) has experienced an excessive number of failures of an electrical circuit board. Two hundred of each of the four critical components in the circuit board were subjected to simulated accelerated operations tests. These tests have been proven to be the equivalent of 2,500 hours of normal operation, which is the advertised expected life of the components. The following data resulted from these tests:

	(1)	(2)	(3) CR	(4)	(5) MTBF
Component	Number of Failures	FR $[(1)/200]$	$(1 - FR)$ $[1 - (2)]$	FR_n $[(1)/(200 \times 2,500)]$	$1/FR_n$ $[1/(4)]$
155	2	0.010	0.990	0.0000040	250,000
175	1	0.005	0.995	0.0000020	500,000
205	22	0.110	0.890	0.0000440	22,727
315	4	0.020	0.980	0.0000080	125,000

The system reliability of the circuit board is computed as follows:

$$
\begin{aligned}
SR &= CR_{155} \times CR_{175} \times CR_{205} \times CR_{315} \\
&= 0.990 \times 0.995 \times 0.890 \times 0.980 \\
&= 0.8592
\end{aligned}
$$

It was clear to the managers at TCS that something had to be done to increase the system reliability of the circuit board by improving the reliability of Component 205. Two alternatives were suggested:

• Redesign, develop, and test a new overdesigned configuration of Component 205 at an estimated cost of $50,000. It is believed that this project would result in a component reliability for Component 205 of about 0.960.

• Modify the circuit board such that a backup Component 205 is automatically placed into service if the primary Component 205 fails. This use of redundancy in design is estimated to cost only $10,000, but TCS wonders what the system reliability of the circuit board will be with this alternative.

Compute the system reliability of the alternatives, and recommend a course of action for TCS.

Solution

1. Compute the system reliability of the overdesign (SR_o) alternative:

$$
\begin{aligned}
SR_o &= CR_{155} \times CR_{175} \times CR_{205} \times CR_{315} \\
&= 0.990 \times 0.995 \times 0.960 \times 0.980 \\
&= 0.9267
\end{aligned}
$$

2. Compute the reliability of Component 205 in the redundancy alternative. What is the combined reliability of the two components working together?

$$
CR_{205} = \begin{pmatrix} \text{Probability} \\ \text{of primary} \\ \text{component} \\ \text{working} \end{pmatrix} + \begin{pmatrix} \text{Probability} \\ \text{of backup} \\ \text{component} \\ \text{working} \end{pmatrix} \times \begin{pmatrix} \text{Probability} \\ \text{of needing} \\ \text{backup} \\ \text{component} \end{pmatrix}
$$

$$
\begin{aligned}
&= 0.890 \quad\;\; + \quad [0.890 \times (1 - 0.890)] \\
&= 0.9879
\end{aligned}
$$

3. Compute the system reliability of the redundancy (SR_r) alternative:

$$
\begin{aligned}
SR_r &= CR_{155} \times CR_{175} \times CR_{205} \times CR_{315} \\
&= 0.990 \times 0.995 \times 0.9879 \times 0.980 \\
&= 0.9537
\end{aligned}
$$

4. Because the system reliability is increased more with the redundancy alternative and at lower cost, the redundancy alternative is recommended.

Many U.S. manufacturers today have set goals of producing products of near-perfect quality. In the achievement of such goals, the concepts of simplification, overdesign, and redundancy are particularly relevant. Our knowledge of system reliability is also helpful in other areas of POM. We will study more about reliability in Chapter 19, Maintenance Management.

Designing and Controlling Production Processes

We discussed the design and development of production processes in Chapter 4. As Table 7.3 indicates, production processes must be designed with the customer in mind because production processes must be capable of producing products with characteristics that customers want. Once production processes are in place, they must be operated so that products conform to customer requirements. Production organizations must be totally committed to producing products and services of perfect quality. But more than this, there must be a commitment to strive relentlessly for improvement in product quality. The idea of perfect quality should apply to every facet of the production system, from every raw material at suppliers to every worker in production to every warehouse worker. The responsibility for *producing* products of high quality does not rest with quality control personnel; on the contrary, the workers who produce the products are responsible. Every worker is expected to pass on to the next operation products that are of perfect quality. In this sense, the next production operation is to be considered as an internal customer.

Product variation can be an obstacle to producing products that are acceptable to customers. Two types of factors can introduce variation in production processes: controllable factors and uncontrollable factors. *The effects of controllable factors, such things as machine malfunctions, bad materials, and incorrect work methods, can be reduced with diligence from workers and management. The effects of uncontrollable factors, such things as temperature, friction, vibration, chance variation, and other natural causes, can be reduced only by redesigning or replacing existing production processes.* Every production process has a built-in set of uncontrollable factors that

Production processes, such as this assembly line, can be designed to reduce variation in quality due to controllable factors.

cause product variation, and if this variation is too high, the resulting product quality may not measure up to customer expectations.

Process capability is a production process's ability to produce products within the desired expectations of customers. The **process capability index (PCI)** is useful for determining if a production process has the ability to produce products within the desired expectations of customers. If we assume that process variation due to uncontrollable factors is normally distributed:

$$\text{PCI} = \frac{\text{UL} - \text{LL}}{6\sigma} \text{, where}$$

UL = the upper limit of a product characteristic that
can be allowed within customer expectations

LL = the lower limit of a product characteristic that can be
allowed within customer expectations

σ = the standard deviation of a product characteristic
from a production process, a measure of the long-term
variation of a product characteristic from a production process

While the PCI can take on any positive value, these values of the PCI have these meanings:

PCI ≥ 1.00   the production process has the capability of
producing products that meet customer
expectations

PCI < 1.00   the production process does not have the
capability of producing products that meet
customer expectations

Figure 7.5 illustrates how the PCI could be used to determine if a production process is capable of producing products that meet customer expectations. If a production process does not have the capability of producing products that meet customer expectations, the production process must be redesigned, modified, or replaced with one with less product variation (σ).

Once production processes are in place that have the capability of producing products within customer expectations, the processes must be operated to produce products that meet customer expectations. This means that the controllable factors must be managed. In Chapter 17, Quality Control, we will explore the ways that we can ensure conformance of product quality to customer expectations. Control charts, process capability, and acceptance sampling are all used to achieve this objective.

In addition to improving the quality of production processes, the quality of other operations processes must be managed so they meet customer expectations. Business Snapshot 7.3 describes how a steel manufacturer used advanced technology to improve the quality of inventory operations.

Developing Supplier Partnerships   *part of TQM*

In Chapter 11, Supply Chain Management and E-Business, we discuss the modern approach to selection and development of suppliers. To ensure that materials from suppliers are of the highest quality, suppliers must be brought into a company's TQM program. Ford Motor Company is a good example of how this should work. At Ford the initial selection of suppliers is based on how well suppliers can interface with Ford's TQM program. Ford has about 300 suppliers on its *Q-1 list, a list of suppliers with which Ford is willing to have long-term (usually three-year) supply contracts in order to achieve*

Figure 7.5	Three Examples of the Process Capability Index (PCI)

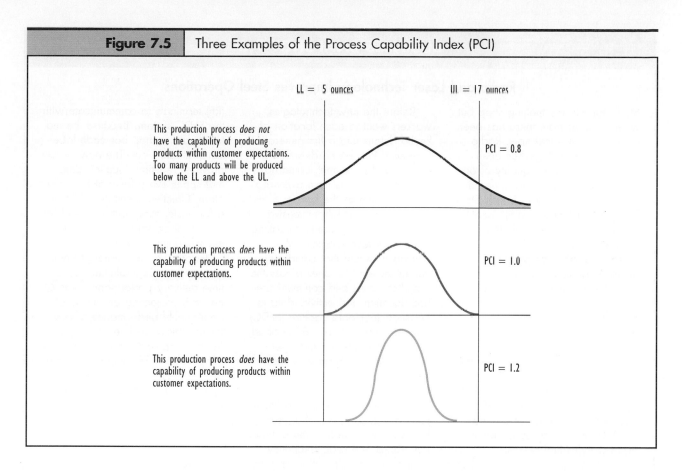

LL = 5 ounces   UL = 17 ounces

This production process *does not* have the capability of producing products within customer expectations. Too many products will be produced below the LL and above the UL.

PCI = 0.8

This production process *does* have the capability of producing products within customer expectations.

PCI = 1.0

This production process *does* have the capability of producing products within customer expectations.

PCI = 1.2

highest quality at competitive costs. Because Q-1 suppliers participate in the design of new Ford products, the designs reflect the suppliers' ability to produce high-quality materials. And suppliers participate in Ford's quality training programs; thus, suppliers' employees are capable of making TQM work within the suppliers' organizations.

Customer Service, Distribution, and Installation

Packaging, shipping, and installation must be included in TQM because poor product performance is equated with poor product quality by consumers, even if the product was damaged in shipment or was improperly installed. This means that warehousing, marketing, and the distribution function also have to be committed to perfect quality. And every contact between companies, their products, and customers must be planned and managed to provide satisfied customers.

Building Teams of Empowered Employees

There are several aspects to team building and empowerment: employee training, work teams, empowerment, quality at the source, and quality circles.

Employee Training Programs

Toward implementing the TQM philosophy, all employees—from the shop floor to the boardroom—as well as suppliers and customers should participate in a comprehensive training program. At Ford Motor Company, for example, over 6,000 people attended 59 different courses in a two-year period, and over 1,000 suppliers sent their employees to

BUSINESS SNAPSHOT 7.3

Radio and Laser Technology Improves Steel Operations

Steel starts in the melting shop but where it goes from there has been difficult to tell—until now. Radio and laser technology has been used to improve the quality of operations and improve on-time deliveries substantially at British Steel Engineering Steels (BSES), located at Stocksbridge, near Sheffield, United Kingdom.

The Stocksbridge plant produces alloy, stainless, and remelted steels for industries including aerospace, automotive, and offshore oil and gas. Production is geared to special section sizes and small order quantities. Tracking products had been a challenge because the premilled material is hot, and it gets turned into thousands of small and medium-sized orders. BSES operates with a stock of around 30,000 tons, made up of about 60,000 individual pieces.

Before the new technologies, workers went to each location and keyed details into a first-generation computer. Process cards would be issued, and personnel would have to extract products from awkward locations such as the bottom of a rack. This was a labor-intensive and error-prone process. Speaking of the new technologies, "We wanted a system that could plot the movement of cranes across the shop-floor area and communicate both location and activity data to our shop-floor data capture (SFDC) software system," says Brian Short, BSES's billet finishing manager. "The biggest problem was knowing where anything is at any one time."

The company decided to implement a rugged system that uses lasers to track the location of loading cranes and radio-frequency

(RF) terminals to communicate with the SFDC system. Because the materials are so hot, bar code labeling was ruled out. The new system provides real-time location data that spans every facet of the operation. Effective scheduling is now a far easier task, with no need for individual personnel to supervise the scheduling process.

Before the new material tracking system was implemented, on-time delivery performance was 65 percent, projecting an image of poor-quality performance to customers. Now on-time delivery is 90 percent, and the next target is 95 percent. BSES expects the cost of investment in the new technology to be recouped in less than two years.

Source: Excerpted with permission from "Tracking Steel That's Too Hot to Handle." *Frontline Solutions*, September 2000, p. 20. Copyright © 2001 Advanstar Communications, Inc. Advanstar Communications, Inc. retains all rights to this material.

Ford for training programs on quality control methods. These programs were aimed not only at statistical quality control techniques but also at the broader concepts of quality management.

In today's competitive environment, many companies are aggressively increasing their employee training efforts. No area in business is receiving more training attention than product quality. While many companies do all of their own training, a growing list of companies plan and conduct TQM programs for a fee. Training and educational materials are also available from these quality control societies: the American Society for Quality, the Association for Quality and Participation, the Quality & Productivity Management Association, and the American Productivity & Quality Center.

Work Teams and Empowerment

In Chapter 18, Employee Productivity, we discuss the importance of building work teams and empowering employees. For U.S. companies to achieve superior product quality, it is mandatory that they draw out and apply all the ability and energy of their employees. Employees—blue-collar workers, office workers, managers, engineers, and scientists—form the core resource which is the power for achieving excellence in superior product quality. Employees must step forward and accept responsibility for every facet of production. But managers must first give employees the authority to act, which is what worker empowerment is all about.

BUSINESS SNAPSHOT 7.4

Empowered Work Teams at Square D Corporation

At the Square D Corporation's Lexington, Kentucky, plant, about 800 workers have been reorganized into work teams of from 20 to 30 workers to assemble electrical control panels, switches, and transformers. Before the creation of work teams, employees would spend all day working on a single part over and over again, never seeing the end product. Now the plant has a new layout with each team operating a **factory-within-a-factory.** Each team does all the work on an entire product from start to finish and works like it is operating its own business. The company used to spend more on painting buildings than on training, but now it spends about 4 percent of payroll costs on training. Managers have also empowered the workers by giving them the authority to make decisions on the shop floor about all phases of production. Employees are trained to operate like a team, and it shows. They work together to fix machines when they break. They work together to make decisions about how to solve production problems when they occur. They are also trained to improve product quality, and it is working. Employees meet at the beginning of each shift to examine their quality performance. Each employee charts his or her accuracy every 30 minutes. The number of defects has been reduced by 75 percent, and the time it takes to get out customer orders has been reduced from six weeks to three days.

Source: Jennings, Peter, and Linda Patillo. "ABC Evening News." February 24, 1993.

Empowering workers is management's way of unleashing a powerful force for continuously working toward excellence in the quality of products and services. Business Snapshot 7.4 illustrates the power of empowered work teams at Square D Corporation.

Quality at the Source

The concept of quality at the source aims to put the production worker in the driver's seat in controlling product quality. Toward the goal of having each worker produce parts that are of perfect quality, quality at the source follows these principles:

ee can stop assembly

- Every worker's job becomes a quality control station. Workers are responsible for inspecting their own work, identifying any defects and reworking them into non-defectives, and correcting any causes of defects.
- Statistical quality control techniques are used to monitor the quality of parts produced at each workstation, and easy-to-understand charts and graphs are used to communicate progress to workers and managers.
- Each worker is given the right to stop the production line to avoid producing defective parts.

no one uses them anymore

- Workers and managers are organized into **quality circles**, or **QC circles**, *small groups of employees who analyze quality problems, work to solve the problems, and implement programs to improve product quality.*

This set of arrangements does four things: First, it assigns responsibility for product quality to production workers and the production function, where it belongs. Second, it can lead to production workers who are more committed to high product quality. Third, rather than checking on others, quality control personnel can do work that has a direct impact on producing products of high quality: working with production personnel to remove the causes of defects, training workers in quality control, and working with suppliers to improve their product quality. Fourth, it removes an obstacle to cooperation between quality control personnel and production workers so that they can better work together for higher product quality.

Quality Circles

A quality circle, or QC circle, is a small group of employees—the average number is nine—who volunteer to meet regularly to undertake work-related projects designed to advance the company, improve working conditions, and spur mutual self-development, all by using quality control concepts. QC circles are encouraged by Japanese companies and receive substantial training in quality control concepts and techniques. These groups often meet away from the job and combine their meetings with social or athletic activities. They tend to select their own projects for investigation and can generally count on the support of management in implementing their recommendations. The types of projects are varied and may extend beyond quality to such areas as productivity, tool design, safety, maintenance, and environmental protection. Membership in QC circles is voluntary, and there are no direct cash incentives. Members give the principal reasons for belonging to the groups as personal satisfaction from achievement and from recognition given at regional and national meetings. Their use is expanding to the United States, Britain, Brazil, Indonesia, South Korea, and other countries.

Despite the cultural differences between Japan and the United States, QC circles have been organized in companies such as Motorola, Minnesota Mining and Manufacturing (3M), NationsBank, and Schlumberger. For these programs to succeed, a sincere trust and loyalty must exist between the workers and management. U.S. companies in growing numbers are recognizing the importance of drawing their workers into the mainstream of their quality management programs. This effort is sure to contribute to an overall elevation of quality management in the workers' consciousness, to result in unique and innovative solutions to quality problems, and to improve the likelihood of the workers cooperating in the implementation of programs to improve product quality.

Benchmarking and Continuous Improvement

Companies like AT&T, Compaq, Ford, IBM, Motorola, Milliken & Company, Texas Instruments, and the Xerox Corporation engage in benchmarking, *the practice of establishing internal standards of performance by looking to how world-class companies run their businesses.* Benchmarking at Company A in an area like customer service would involve these activities:

- Examine companies like L. L. Bean, FedEx, and Xerox. These companies are thought to be among the very best at building customer satisfaction.
- Find out how these companies achieve customer service. This includes the minute details of their present practices relative to customer service.
- Predict how these best customer service practices are likely to change in the future.
- Develop strategies for changing Company A's present practices to what the best probably will be in the future.

Business Snapshot 7.5 gives examples of benchmarking at Sprint. Benchmarking may become easier in the future. The *International Benchmarking Clearinghouse (IBC),* which is housed at Houston's American Productivity & Quality Center (**http://www.apqc.org**), has built a database of best practices. The database is available on an electronic bulletin board that can be accessed by IBC members. The bulletin board allows members to share information and ask for benchmarking information from other members. More than 500 companies are IBC members.

Once benchmarks have been set and a plan has been developed to move companies toward best practices, an essential element of TQM is set in motion—the need for **continuous improvement**. This concept allows companies to accept modest beginnings and make small incremental improvements toward excellence. Such an approach

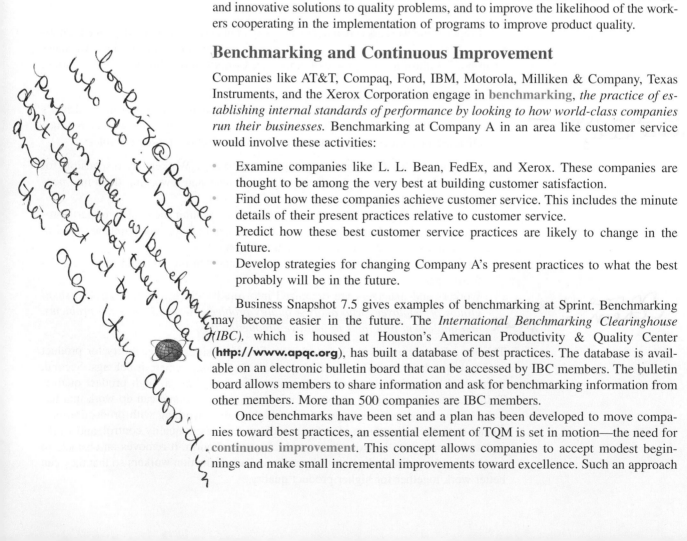

BUSINESS SNAPSHOT 7.5

Benchmarking at Sprint

Sprint is a large U.S. telecommunications company that strives to be at the forefront of good business practices. "At Sprint, we put benchmarking in the framework of total quality and process improvement—it is not seen as a stand-alone savior," says Jeff Amen, benchmarking manager. Sprint believes benchmarking should be used as a tool within strategic business process improvement and reengineering. According to Amen, benchmarking is the process of understanding what the organization does and what the critical components are.

Benchmarking is an outgrowth of Sprint's total quality framework, Sprint Quality, which started in the early 1990s. Sprint Quality's three phases include teamwork, strategic integration, and continuous quality improvement. The organization determined that benchmarking was needed in the strategic integration phase to understand what affects the customer and, therefore, be able to focus work groups on key areas.

Sprint developed a benchmarking training module and adopted the just-in-time approach to spreading the word. When management sees a need for it, teams are trained in benchmarking. That way, knowledge is not lost while employees wait to begin their first benchmarking study.

After numerous benchmarking studies at Sprint, several lessons have been learned. One lesson is to look internally first for new ideas before going outside Sprint. Because of the large size of Sprint, they now do internal benchmarking before going outside the company. Sprint also has learned the importance of controlling the scope of benchmarking projects. Employees are more willing to participate if the scope is narrow.

Another lesson learned from many benchmarking studies at Sprint is to work with executives and with the process owners at the outset of any benchmarking study, rather than lower-level employees who have been delegated to participate. Finally, a key factor that has enabled benchmarking to be successful at Sprint has been top management support.

Source: Powers, Vicki J. "Sprint Corp.: Blending in Benchmarking with Quality." American Productivity & Quality Center web site (**http://www.apqc.org**); appeared in January 1995 issue of *Continuous Journey* magazine from APQC.

has many advantages. First, because changes are gradual, frustration and abandonment are avoided. Also, gradual and continuous progress through incremental improvements means that companies can never accept that where they are is the best that they will ever be. Company practice is, therefore, never good enough. This results in companies, even world-class companies, struggling for even higher levels of performance. This result is essential in the competitive wars of global competition.

QUALITY MANAGEMENT IN SERVICES

The former chancellor of the University of Wisconsin, Donna Shalala, a Clinton administration cabinet appointee, stated on national television that TQM approaches would be applied to the agencies of the U.S. government. She said that what universities had learned from TQM about improving customer service, productivity, and cost effectiveness could be profitably used in the government. It is clear that every kind of organization can profit from the TQM approach, even government agencies.

Applying TQM in services is not without its difficulties. Many services are intangible, and by their very nature it is difficult to determine their quality. Take, for example, the problem that airlines face when they try to determine the quality of the performance of flight attendants. The things about a flight attendant's performance that affect the customer's perceptions of quality are difficult to identify and measure, and in most cases standards for measuring the performance do not exist. Rather, customers set their own standards, comparing the service they receive with the service they wished to receive.

Another complicating factor is that the perceived quality of some services is affected by the surroundings. Quiet, soft music, pleasant decor, comfortable furniture, convenient parking, friendly servers, cleanliness of facilities, and other features can determine the perceived quality of services more than the actual quality of the service. Hospitals, banks, and restaurants, for example, all invest heavily in designing and maintaining facilities that develop particular feelings in their customers and leave them with specific impressions.

Because many services tend to be labor intensive and workers tend to come in direct contact with customers, the performance of service employees determines in large part the quality of the services. Yet, because services tend to be highly decentralized and geographically dispersed, direct supervision of employees can be difficult. Recognizing this difficulty, many service organizations make an intensive continuing education and training program for their employees the cornerstone of quality management. McDonald's Hamburger University and Holiday Inn's University are examples of this development.

The difficulties in establishing quality management programs for services are not insurmountable obstacles. Service organizations do develop sophisticated quality control programs, and some of their features are very much like those found in manufacturing. Other aspects of their programs, however, are dramatically different.

Business Snapshot 7.6 gives several examples of TQM in services. These examples suggest the presence of quality management programs that have broad and far-reaching impacts on the management of the firms. For most services, the competitive weapon of choice is perceived service quality, because price, flexibility, and speed of delivery may not be much different from the competition. Service quality thus becomes the primary focus of operations strategy.

Business Snapshot 7.6 describes an important element of many quality programs in services, the use of **customer surveys**. This technique allows customers to fill out survey questionnaires or participate in interviews that are aimed at determining the customers' perceptions about several quality-related issues. Another way of gauging the quality of services is with the use of **mystery shoppers**, employees who pretend to be customers but who actually monitor the quality of services. For example, at American Express about 250 quality control personnel monitor the quality of services worldwide, and an important element of this program is the use of mystery shoppers. Also, as in other service organizations, American Express uses **statistical control charts** to monitor such things as the amount of time required to process a customer's application for an American Express card. Similarly, statistical control charts, using data gathered from customer surveys, are employed to track several measures of customer satisfaction. The diversity of such measures emphasizes the flexibility of control charts in controlling the quality of services as well as the cost and other dimensions of organization performance. We will study more about statistical quality control and control charts in Chapter 17, Quality Control.

Another important issue in managing quality of services is that of dealing with customers who are dissatisfied with the service they received. *Service recovery involves all actions taken to resolve problems, alter negative attitudes, and ultimately to retain customers who are dissatisfied with the quality of service they received.* Examples of service recovery actions include refunds for the service provided, performing the service again free of charge, coupons for free service in the future, telephone calls from managers, letters of apology from top management, and other free products. Customer loyalty is particularly important to service organizations, and a company's approach to service recovery is a key factor in a customer's decision to remain loyal.

BUSINESS SNAPSHOT 7.6

Examples of TQM in Services

Type of Organization	Example
Bank	Customers are surveyed every three months to determine how satisfactory the bank's services are to customers. Areas of deficiency are identified, policies are reviewed, and corrective actions are taken to change operations and modify the nature of the services delivered. Charts monitor the accuracy of customers' accounts and are updated weekly to show trends. Operating procedures are reviewed and corrected to bring deficiencies into an acceptable range.
Hospital	Here are examples of hospitals that use TQM: the Community Health Systems, which manages 15 hospitals in eight states, and Memorial Healthcare Systems, St. Joseph's Hospital, Hermann Hospital, and M. D. Anderson Hospital, all in Houston, Texas. Such hospitals are forming quality teams, giving employees quality training, and surveying their patients about the quality of their services. The purpose of the surveys is to determine the perceptions of patients regarding quality of food, promptness of service, friendliness, competency of personnel, costs, comfort factors, and other quality-related issues. This information is used to revise policies and operations at the hospital as needed. Charts are used extensively to monitor such things as billing accuracy, lab test accuracy, pharmacy prescription accuracy, and personnel absenteeism. Feedback is provided to the departments involved, and follow-up audits are conducted in areas that are trending out of control. Suggestion boxes are provided at several locations in the hospital to provide patients, visitors, and personnel with on-the-spot opportunities to report on both satisfactory and unsatisfactory incidents and to make recommendations for improvements. This mechanism provides an overall check of service quality, but it requires diligence and interpretation to be effective.[a]
University	In some experimental classes at Carnegie Mellon University, students are considered customers. Students participate in the planning of courses, determining what is taught, designing the syllabus, and assigning grades. The TQM motto in education is: Learn what the students need and constantly improve the educational processes to deliver it consistently. Some claim that students become better thinkers, problem solvers, and team members. At dozens of schools like the University of Wisconsin at Madison, University of Wyoming, Columbia University, and Oregon State University, TQM is applied to the administrative side of organizations.[b]
Law office	Applying TQM that emphasizes customer service and employee teamwork to improve products to a business in which the goods they sell are smarts, skill, and judgment is not without its challenges. The essence of quality in this setting is the intelligence and vigor that a lawyer brings to an assignment, and it's hard to formalize that. In a survey of Fortune 500 firms, 71% said that they would prefer law firms with TQM programs, 4% of law firms actually have TQM programs, 20% of law firms were in the process of starting TQM, and 46% of law firms were planning to start TQM. The term **client-focused quality (CFQ)** is being used by some law firms and consultants. At TQM firms, phones are answered by the second ring; the accuracy, timing, and formats of bills are improved; and software is developed to help lawyers manage their time.[c]
Insurance company	The American Family Insurance Group with headquarters in Madison, Wisconsin, is the 10th largest auto insurer and the 18th largest property insurer in the United States. The company's TQM program applies these concepts: customer focused, process oriented, team approach, eliminate complexity, reduce process variation, prevent errors, data-based improvement, maintain improvements, and continuous improvement.[d]

Sources:

[a]"Getting Better." *Houston Chronicle*, May 28, 1992, 4B.

[b]"Academe Gets Lessons from Big Business." *Wall Street Journal*, December 15, 1992, B1.

[c]"Grudgingly, Lawyers Try Total Quality." *Wall Street Journal*, February 12, 1992, B1.

[d]Presentation by St. Vincent, Jim. "Total Quality at American Family Insurance: A Practical Example." At the Seventh Annual Conference on Making Statistics More Effective in Schools of Business, Knoxville, Tenn., June 1992.

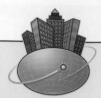

Wrap-Up

WHAT WORLD-CLASS COMPANIES DO

Product and service quality begins when business strategy is formulated. For each product or service, a plan is developed that aims at distinguishing it from its competitors. For many products and services today, quality is the weapon of choice to capture global markets. For world-class companies, preeminent product and service quality is the number one distinctive competency for which they are striving.

World-class companies do not differentiate between productivity improvement and quality improvement—for them they are the same thing. Quality drives the productivity machine for these companies. Perhaps most important of all, world-class companies have stopped depending on inspection to catch defects; rather, they are concentrating every organizational effort on doing everything right the first time. They are striving to find and fix their quality problems, not to have inspection programs aimed at catching defects while sloppy production methods continue. And world-class companies employ JIT manufacturing, product standardization, automated equipment, and preventive maintenance not just to reduce costs but also for their impact on quality and customer service.

World-class companies are committing tremendous resources to put in place total quality management (TQM) programs aimed at continuous quality improvement. At Motorola it is Six Sigma, at Xerox it is Leadership through Quality, at Intel it is $(PDQ)^2$, and at Hewlett-Packard it is Total Quality Control. Which companies aspire to world-class status? One way to answer this question is to watch which companies apply for the Malcolm Baldrige National Quality Award and the Deming Prize and qualify for the ISO 9000 standards in the coming years. Total quality management (TQM) programs often include these elements:

- Top management commitment and involvement
- Customer involvement
- Design products for quality
- Design production processes for quality
- Control production processes for quality
- Develop supplier partnerships
- Customer service, distribution, and installation
- Build teams of empowered workers
- Benchmarking and continuous improvement

A growing list of universities, banks, insurance companies, law offices, hospitals, and other service businesses have TQM programs. And there are glowing reports of growing numbers of successful TQM programs in manufacturing. But some companies have been unsuccessful in attempting TQM because their programs are too vague and unspecific, try to do too many things at once, and do not involve customers or enough employees, and their senior managers are not rewarded for quality performance.

REVIEW AND DISCUSSION QUESTIONS

1. Explain the role of product and service quality in business strategy.
2. State and briefly describe the *dimensions of quality.*
3. State and briefly describe the *determinants of quality,* the activities necessary to achieve quality products and services.
4. What are the *costs of quality?* Briefly explain each one.

5. The traditional view of quality control is to have rigorous inspections to find and discard defectives so that only nondefectives leave inspection. What is fundamentally wrong with this approach? Explain the meaning of this statement: "You cannot inspect quality into products."
6. Explain the meaning of this statement: "Quality drives the productivity machine."

7. Summarize the contributions of these people to quality management: (a) W. Edwards Deming, (b) Philip B. Crosby, (c) Armand V. Feigenbaum, (d) Kaoru Ishikawa, (e) Joseph M. Juran, (f) Genichi Taguchi.

8. Define, describe, and explain the use of *fishbone diagrams.*

9. Explain how these factors affect product quality: (a) just-in-time (JIT) manufacturing, (b) preventive maintenance.

10. Regarding the Malcolm Baldrige National Quality Award: (a) Which companies are eligible? (b) Name five criteria for selection. (c) What categories receive awards? (d) Name five recent winners.

11. Describe the Deming Prize. Explain its significance to quality management.

12. What are the ISO 9000 standards? Explain their significance.

13. Define a *total quality management (TQM) program.* What are some of the names used by companies for their TQM programs?

14. What are the important elements of total quality management? Explain how each contributes to products and services of superior quality.

15. Explain the meaning of: (a) *robust designs,* (b) *design for production,* (c) *design for reliability.*

16. What is the meaning of the term *quality at the source?*

17. What is the purpose of *quality circles?* How do they work? What factors must be present for them to be successful? What benefits do companies enjoy from them?

18. Explain what is meant by *service recovery.* Why is service recovery important to quality management in services?

19. Discuss quality management in services. What factors make quality management more difficult in services than in manufacturing? What approaches have been developed to mitigate the effects of these difficulties? What quality management strategy have service systems devised to deal with the fact that services tend to be labor intensive and geographically dispersed?

20. Describe a TQM program for these service businesses: (a) bank, (b) hospital, (c) university, (d) law office, (e) insurance company.

INTERNET ASSIGNMENTS

1. Visit and explore the Internet site of the American Society for Quality (ASQ) at **http://www.asq.org**. Locate information about QS-9000. Explain what QS-9000 is and who it involves.

2. Visit and explore the Internet site of the International Organization for Standardization (ISO) at **http://www.iso.ch**. What was the first standard published by ISO, and when? Why is international standardization needed?

3. Visit and explore the Internet site for the Malcolm Baldrige National Quality Award at **http://www.quality.nist.gov**. Briefly summarize the background of this award, describing its purposes. What companies won the award for the most recent year?

4. Search the Internet for a consulting company that specializes in helping companies with quality management or TQM. Describe some of the relevant services offered by the consulting company.

5. Visit and explore the Internet site for the Shingo Prize at **http://www.shingoprize.org**. Briefly describe the background and purpose of the Shingo Prize. Which organizations won the prize in the most recent year?

PROBLEMS

Reliability

1. A product has four critical interacting parts. Each has a 0.007 probability of failing during its usable life.
   a. What is the reliability of each part?
   b. What is the reliability of the product?

2. One-hundred-fifty units of a machine component are tested for 1,000 hours, and nine units of the component fail.
   a. What is the reliability of the component?
   b. What is the mean time between failures for the component?
   c. How would you explain to a manager the meaning of your answers to Parts a and b?

3. A machine has four critical component parts. If any of these components fails, the machine cannot operate. The four component reliabilities are 0.97, 0.99, 0.92 and 0.98.
   a. Compute the system reliability of the machine.
   b. If the machine could be redesigned to allow redundancy for the part that presently has a reliability of 0.92, what would be the new system reliability of the machine?

4. A product has three critical interacting parts. The reliability of the three parts is $CR_a = 0.998$, $CR_b = 0.980$, and $CR_c = 0.940$. Three alternatives are being considered to improve the reliability of Part c:
   • Simplify the design by combining Parts b and c into a single Part d with $CR_d = 0.965$.
   • Overdesign Part c such that the new $CR_c = 0.970$.
   • Provide a redundant design by using two Part c's, one a backup to be used if the primary Part c fails.
   a. What is the present reliability of the product?
   b. If the cost of the alternatives is not a factor, which alternative would you recommend?

Process Capability

5. If PCI = 0.9:
   a. Do the production processes have the capability of meeting customer expectations? Why or why not?
   b. What must be changed so that its production processes have the capability of producing products within customer expectations?

6. UL = 1.006 inch, LL = 0.994 inch, $\sigma = 0.0017$ inch: Does the production process have the capability of meeting customer expectations? Why or why not?

7. A company is going to introduce a new cell phone. Customers have been surveyed, and they expect the phone to weigh between 5 and 5.5 ounces. The company is now examining alternative process designs and wonders how much uncontrollable product variation can be allowed and still meet customer expectations. What value of σ is required to yield a PCI ≥ 1.00?

8. A company has just surveyed its customers and found that they expect its product to weigh between 1.2 and 1.3 kilograms. The company believes that the long-term variation of its products from its present production processes is $\sigma = 0.022$ kilogram.
   a. Compute the process capability of the production process.
   b. Does the production process have the capability of meeting customer expectations? Why or why not?
   c. What must be changed so that its production process has the capability of producing products within customer expectations?
   d. What new level of σ would make PCI ≥ 1.00?

CASE

Integrated Switches Corporation

The U.S. Army is about to award a contract for an electrical switching device to Integrated Switches Corporation (ISC) of Phoenix, Arizona. The switch will be used on the next version of infantry carrier vehicles. One obstacle that remains to be resolved, however, is that the Army requires a reliability of 0.995 for the device. ISC is studying its test data to determine if there is a practical way that its product can be made to meet the Army's reliability requirement. The switching device has four critical interacting component parts with the following test data:

Component Part	Number of Parts Tested	Number of Hours of Testing	Number of Failures
B13	400	2,500	2
X9	650	3,800	1
M22	275	1,750	0
R5	1,600	4,200	3

Assignment

1. What is the present system reliability of the switch? Does the switch meet the Army's system reliability requirement?
2. The Army has suggested redundancy in design of the switch. Determine the reliability of the switch with each component as a candidate for redundancy. Can the Army's suggestion meet the system reliability requirement?
3. One of ISC's engineers has suggested to the Army that it buy ISC's switching device as it is now and use two of the devices in parallel, one as the primary device and one as a backup device. Evaluate this proposal as a means of meeting the Army's system reliability requirement.
4. Which alternative would you recommend for meeting the Army's system reliability requirement? Why?
5. Discuss the concept of component redundancy as a practical means of increasing system reliability. What are the advantages and disadvantages of this approach?

ENDNOTES

1. Apte, Uday M., and Charles C. Reynolds. "Quality Management at Kentucky Fried Chicken." *Interfaces* 25, no. 3 (May–June 1995): 6–21.
2. Crosby, Philip B. *Quality Is Free.* New York: McGraw-Hill, 1979.
3. Feigenbaum, A. V. *Total Quality Control: Engineering and Management,* 3rd ed. New York: McGraw-Hill, 1983.
4. Ishikawa, Kaoru. *Guide to Quality Control.* Tokyo: Asian Productivity Organization, 1972.
5. Juran, Joseph M. *Quality Control Handbook,* 5th ed. New York: McGraw-Hill, 1999.
6. Johansson, Henry J. "Factories, Services, and Speed." *New York Times,* January 17, 1988, C1.
7. "Ford Says Robots Improve Quality of Truck Products." *Houston Chronicle,* August 21, 1982, sec. 2, p. 3.
8. Gill, Mark Stuart. "Stalking Six Sigma." *Business Month,* January 1990, 42.
9. ReVelle, Jack B., John W. Moran, and Charles A. Cox. *The QFD Handbook.* New York: John Wiley & Sons, 1998.
10. "A Design Master's End Run around Trial and Error." *Business Week/Quality,* October 25, 1991, 24.

SELECTED BIBLIOGRAPHY

Abromovitz, Hedy, and Les Abromovitz. *Insuring Quality: How to Improve Quality, Compliance, Customer Service, and Ethics in the Insurance Industry.* Boca Raton, FL: St. Lucie Press, 1998.

Arditi, David, and H. Murat Gunaydin. "Total Quality Management in the Construction Process." *International Journal of Project Management* 15, no. 4 (August 1997): 235–243.

Berry, Leonard L. *On Great Service: A Framework for Action.* New York: The Free Press, 1995.

Berry, Leonard L., and A. Parasuraman. *Marketing Services: Competing through Quality.* New York: The Free Press, 1991.

Crosby, Philip B. *Quality Is Free: The Art of Making Quality.* New York: McGraw-Hill, 1979.

Deming, W. Edwards. *Out of Crisis.* Cambridge, MA: Center for Advanced Engineering Study, 1986.

Feeney, Anne-Marie, and Mohamed Zairi. "TQM in Healthcare." *Journal of General Management* 22, no. 1 (Autumn 1996): 35–47.

Feigenbaum, Armand V. *Total Quality Control,* 3rd ed. New York: McGraw Hill, 1986.

Hauser, John R., and Don Clausing. "The House of Quality." *Harvard Business Review* 66, no. 3 (May–June 1988): 63–70.

Hendricks, Kevin B., and Vinod R. Singhal. "Does Implementing an Effective TQM Program Actually Improve Operating Performance? Empirical Evidence from Firms That Have Won Quality Awards." *Management Science* 43, no. 9 (September 1997): 1258–1274.

Huffman, Jack L. *Beyond TQM: Tools and Techniques for High Improvement.* Sunnyvale, CA: Lanchester Press, 1997.

Ishikawa, Kaoru. *What Is Total Quality Control?* Translated by David J. Lu. Englewood Cliffs, NJ: Prentice Hall, 1985.

Juran, Joseph M. *Juran on Planning for Quality.* New York: The Free Press, 1988.

Juran, Joseph M., and A. Blanton Godfrey, eds. *Juran's Quality Control Handbook.* 5th ed. New York: McGraw Hill, 1999.

Kessler, Sheila. *Total Quality Service: A Simplified Approach to Using the Baldrige Award Criteria.* Milwaukee, WI: ASQC Quality Press, 1995.

Knouse, Stephen B., ed. *Human Resource Management Perspectives on TQM: Concepts and Practices.* Milwaukee, WI: ASQC Quality Press, 1996.

Koehler, Jerry W. *Quality Government: Designing, Developing, and Implementing TQM.* Boca Raton, FL: Saint Lucie Press, 1996.

Mahoney, Francis X. and Carl G. Thor. *The TQM Trilogy: Using ISO 9000, the Deming Prize, and the Baldrige Award to Establish a System for Total Quality Management.* New York: American Management Association, 1994.

Milakovich, Michael E. *Improving Service Quality: Achieving High Performance in the Public and Private Sectors.* Boca Raton, FL: Saint Lucie Press, 1995.

Milas, Gene H. *Teambuilding and Total Quality: A Guidebook to TQM Success.* Norcross, GA: Engineering & Management Press, 1997.

Miller, Janis L., Christopher W. Craighead, and Kirk R. Karwan. "Service Recovery: A Framework and Emperical Investigation." *Journal of Operations Management* 18, no. 4 (June 2000): 387–400.

Reider, Rob. *Benchmarking Strategies: A Tool for Profit Improvement.* New York: John Wiley & Sons, 2000.

Roy, Ranjit K. *Design of Experiments Using the Taguchi Approach: 16 Steps to Product and Process Improvement.* New York: John Wiley & Sons, 2000.

Saylor, James H. *TQM Simplified: A Practical Guide.* New York: McGraw Hill, 1996.

Schmele, June A., ed. *Quality Management in Nursing and Health Care.* Albany, NY: Delmar Publishing, 1995.

Silos, Irene M. "Employee Involvement—A Component of Total Quality Management." *Production and Inventory Management Journal* 40, no. 1 (1999): 56–65.

Stamatis, Dean H. *Total Quality Service: Principles, Practices, and Implementation.* Boca Raton, FL: Saint Lucie Press, 1995.

Townsend, Patrick L., and Joan E. Gebhardt. *Quality Is Everybody's Business.* Boca Raton, FL: St. Lucie Press, 2000.

Wilkinson, Adrian, Graham Godfrey, and Mick Marchington. "Bouquets, Brickbats and Blinkers: Total Quality Management and Employee Involvement in Practice." *Organization Studies* 18, no. 5 (1997): 799–819.

Wilson, Darryl D., and David A. Collier. "An Empirical Investigation of the Malcolm Baldrige National Quality Award Causal Model." *Decision Sciences* 31, no. 2 (Spring 2000): 361–390.

Wu, Yuin, and Alan Wu. *Taguchi Methods for Robust Design.* New York: ASME Press, 2000.

Zeithaml, Valarie A., A. Parasuraman, and Leonard L. Berry. *Delivering Quality Service: Balancing Customer Perceptions and Expectations.* New York: The Free Press, 1990.

8

Strategic Allocation of Resources

Introduction
Recognizing LP Problems
Formulating LP Problems
Solving LP Problems
    Graphical LP Solutions
    Overview of Other LP Solution Methods
Real LP Problems
Interpreting Computer Solutions of LP Problems

Wrap-Up: What World-Class Companies Do
Review and Discussion Questions
Internet Assignments
Problems
Cases
    Quality Pixels Inc.
    Integrated Products Corporation
    Jane Deere Company
Selected Bibliography

EFFICIENT USE OF RESOURCES AT TRISTAR

TriStar Pet Food Company is a manufacturer of dog food, with headquarters in Knoxville, Tennessee. TriStar sell its pet food products to many grocery stores and pet stores throughout the eastern United States. The company has six manufacturing plants that supply its 14 regional warehouses. Using modern forecasting approaches, TriStar has been able to fairly accurately forecast demand at its regional warehouses.

Helen McPhearson is the distribution manager at TriStar's headquarters and is responsible for making sure that sufficient supplies of the company's products are delivered to its regional warehouses from its manufacturing plants. Each manufacturing plant has a maximum weekly capacity, and the weekly forecasted demand at each regional warehouse is also known. Each manufacturing plant is capable of shipping products to any of the warehouses, but the shipping cost varies according to the distance between the plant and each warehouse. Shipping costs are a substantial part of TriStar's total costs of providing its products to customers, so Ms. McPearson is under pressure from upper management to minimize these transportation expenses.

Ms. McPearson must develop an approach to decide how much product to ship from each of the manufacturing plants to each of the regional warehouses in order to minimize the total shipping costs for TriStar. The weekly capacity of each manufacturing plant must not be exceeded, and the forecasted demand at each warehouse must be supplied each week.

Like the distribution manager in the preceding account, all operations managers must use as few of their resources as necessary to accomplish as much of their operations strategies as possible. This is what managers mean by "getting the most bang for the buck." As operations managers develop operations strategies, they make decisions about positioning the production system, focusing the factories, designing products and developing production processes, determining production capacity and facility location, and facility layout. In these decisions they inevitably face up to the reality of limited resources.

When we refer to *resources,* we are talking about all the things that are required for production and operations. Included in this term are personnel, machines and equipment, cash and capital funds, materials and supplies, utilities, floor space, time, and other resources. These are the means of production, and one or more may be scarce to each operations manager's particular situation. The dominant question for the users of these resources is: Can we get the quantities of what we need when we need them?

Resource scarcities can cause hectic shifts in operations strategies to meet objectives; additionally, many resource prices are skyrocketing. The limited quantity of resources available and their high prices act as a double-barreled incentive to use them to the greatest advantage. Today, perhaps as never before, operations managers understand that operations strategies must be accomplished within constraints imposed on their organizations by the shortage of resources.

One approach used by many leading companies in recent years to make the most of their limited resources is operations research. **Operations research** refers to the application of quantitative methods and techniques to business problems in order to best utilize a company's resources. Operations researchers possess the knowledge and skills

BUSINESS SNAPSHOT 8.1

Operations Research in U.S. Corporations

Many U.S. companies have had great success in recent years using operations research (OR) tools such as linear programming, simulation, and decision analysis to reduce costs and improve their operations. The following examples reflect the wide use of OR techniques in modern companies.

Sears, Roebuck and Company manages a fleet of more than 1,000 delivery vehicles and 12,500 service vehicles in the United States. These vehicles make 4 million deliveries and 15 million service calls per year. Operations researchers at Sears have designed a planning system using OR techniques that automatically schedules vehicles in such a way as to (1) provide accurate and convenient time windows for Sears customers, (2) minimize costs, and (3) maximize certain objective measures of task performance, including customer satisfaction. This system generated a one-time cost savings of $9 million

as well as ongoing savings of $42 million per year.

The Procter and Gamble Company (P&G) makes and markets more than 300 brands of consumer goods in over 140 countries. In an effort to become more competitive, P&G's operations researchers applied OR techniques to streamline work processes, drive out non-value-added costs, eliminate duplication, and rationalize manufacturing and distribution. This effort involved such OR approaches as integer programming, network optimization models, and geographic information systems, which led to a reduction of nearly 20 percent in the number of North American plants and a savings of more than $200 million per year. P&G now requires that all sourcing decisions be based on operations research models.

Hewlett-Packard Corporation found itself unable to meet its production goals in the manufacture

of ink-jet printers. To address this problem, its operations researchers used OR methods to predict capacity and to determine the size and location of inventory buffers designed to increase that capacity at a cost of only minor increases in inventory. This work yielded incremental revenues of about $280 million as well as productivity gains around 50 percent.

Taco Bell Corporation has approximately 6,500 stores and annual sales of about $4.6 billion. The company developed and used an integrated set of operations research models, including forecasting to predict customer arrivals, simulation to determine the optimum manpower levels required to provide desired customer service levels, and optimization models to schedule and allocate crew members efficiently. This effort, among other accomplishments, saved $53 million in labor cost in just a few years.

Source: Pringle, Lew. "Operations Research: The Productivity Engine." *OR/MS Today,* June 2000, 28–31.

to analyze business problems and apply different quantitative tools to improve operations. They use a variety of computer software packages in these efforts. Business Snapshot 8.1 illustrates how operations research approaches are used in leading companies.

One of the ways that operations managers determine how best to allocate their scarce resources is with the use of **linear programming (LP)**. Five common types of LP problems are encountered by operations managers: product mix, ingredient mix, transportation, production plan, and assignment. Table 8.1 describes each problem type by posing three questions about each problem: What is the single management objective? What information do we need to achieve our objective? What factors restrain us from achieving our objective? The problem types listed in Table 8.1 are directly or indirectly of strategic importance to POM. Product mix and assignment problems may be of direct strategic importance because they can be integral to the development of long-run business strategy. But as Business Snapshot 8.2 shows, medium- and short-range decisions can also be of indirect strategic importance to firms in extremely competitive industries, as is American Airlines.

| **Table 8.1** | Five Common Types of LP Problems in POM—Typical Features |

Decision Type	Objective (What Is the Single Management Objective?)	Decision Variables (What Information Do We Need to Achieve Our Objective?)	Constraints (What Factors Restrain Us from Achieving Our Objective?)
1. Product mix	To select the mix of products or services that results in maximum profits for the planning period.	How much to produce and market of each product or service for the planning period.	*Market*—maximum amount of each product or service demanded and minimum amount policy will allow. *Capacity*—maximum amount of resources available (personnel, materials, machines, utilities, cash, floor space).
2. Ingredient mix	To select the mix of major ingredients going into final products that results in minimum operating costs for the planning period.	How much of each major raw material or ingredient to use in the planning period.	*Market*—amount of final products demanded. *Technology*—relationship among ingredients and final products. *Capacity*—maximum amount of ingredients and production capacity available.
3. Transportation	To select the distribution plan from sources to destinations that results in minimum shipping costs for the planning period.	How much product to ship from each source to each destination for the planning period.	*Destination requirements*—minimum or exact amount of products required at each destination. *Source capacity*—exact or maximum amount of products available at each source.
4. Production plan	To select the amount of products or services to be produced on both straight-time and overtime labor during each month of the year to minimize costs of labor and carrying inventory.	How much to produce on straight-time labor and overtime labor during each month of the year.	*Market*—amount of products demanded in each month. *Capacity*—maximum amount of products that can be produced with straight-time and overtime labor and machinery in each month. *Inventory space*—maximum storage capacity in each month.
5. Assignment	To assign projects to teams so that the total cost for all projects is minimized during the planning period.	To which team each project is assigned.	Each project must be assigned to a team, and each team must be assigned a project.

Such real-world decisions often involve hundreds or even thousands of constraints, large quantities of data, many products and services, many time periods, numerous decision alternatives, and other complications. The complexity of these constrained decisions prompted the development of linear programming methods. LP is a powerful

BUSINESS SNAPSHOT 8.2

Linear Programming Cutting Costs at American Airlines

American Airlines has slashed the penalty payments it must make to flight crews when scheduling snags leave employees sitting in airports, wasting time. Airline officials credit linear programming as the biggest single factor saving them an estimated $20 million a year.

Designing telephone networks, routing airplanes, and scheduling petroleum refinery production are just a few problems solved by linear programming. The technique, which mathematicians started developing during World War II to help military leaders find the most efficient deployment of men and weapons, attacks problems that have hundreds or even thousands of variables and constraints. It discerns patterns within extremely complex problems, selecting and

analyzing a large but manageable number of solutions that appear likely to offer the best answers. The alternative is to approach the enormously large set of all possible solutions by trial and error.

Airline scheduling is a powerful example of linear programming. At American Airlines there are 25,000 flight-crew members based in several cities who fly in eight different kinds of airplanes. Legal requirements and contractual agreements limit each crew member's working time and impose several other scheduling constraints. Crew members who fly American's MD-80 jets are based in San Francisco, Los Angeles, Chicago, Dallas, and Washington. The trick is to pick up each crew in its home city, then use the

plane to serve the many destinations in smaller towns and get the crew back to its home city in three days. The airline also wants to use its biggest planes for flights that draw the most passengers and smaller planes for less-traveled flights to minimize fuel costs. Route popularity can vary at different times of day.

The company solves the problem by addressing parts of it, solving each on a computer with linear programming software, and putting these solutions together to make up its monthly flight schedule. To improve on this piecemeal solution, American Airlines and Sabre are currently working together to develop a problem-solving approach that integrates scheduling, pricing, and yield management.

Sources: "Advances in Higher Math Cutting Costs for Business." *Bryan-College Station Eagle,* August 19, 1990, C1, C3; Jacobs, Timothy L., Richard M. Ratliff, and Barry C. Smith. "Soaring with Synchronized Systems." *OR/MS Today,* August 2000, 36–44.

Airline scheduling is one area in which linear programming can be a powerful tool.

tool in POM—powerful because of the variety of uses to which it is put by operations managers. This chapter is about LP: recognizing LP problems, formulating LP problems, solving LP problems, and interpreting LP solutions (what information do you have after you are finished?). The ability to think in terms of optimizing an objective within a set of constraints in real POM decision situations will definitely set a manager apart. This thinking is at the heart of linear programming.

The first step is recognizing problems that are appropriate for LP solutions.

RECOGNIZING LP PROBLEMS

This section is perhaps the most important part of this chapter. Being able to recognize problems for which LP solutions are appropriate is fundamental—the very least that you should master and retain from this chapter.

What are the characteristics of problems suitable for LP solutions? Table 8.2 outlines briefly the four basic problem characteristics. When all of these requirements are met, LP can be a suitable tool of analysis.

Examples 8.1 and 8.2 are examples of problems appropriate for LP solutions in POM. Follow through these examples carefully and see if you can recognize the objective, the alternatives available, and the nature of the constraints (the first three characteristics of LP problems). Don't worry about the mathematical requirements just yet.

Once we have the feel for what an LP problem is and is not, the next step is to formulate the problem in the LP format.

Table 8.2	Characteristics of LP Problems in POM

1. A well-defined single objective must be stated.
2. There must be alternative courses of action.
3. The total achievement of the objective must be constrained by scarce resources or other restraints.
4. The objective and each of the constraints must be expressed as linear mathematical functions.

Example 8.1	LP-1: Recognizing a Product Mix LP Problem

As a part of its strategic planning process, Precision Manufacturing Company must determine the mix of its products to be manufactured next year. The company produces two principal product lines for the commercial construction industry, a line of powerful portable circular saws and a line of precision table saws. The two product lines share the same production capacity and are sold through the same sales channels. Although some product variety does exist within each product line, the average profit is $900 for each circular saw and $600 for each table saw. The production capacity is constrained in two ways, fabrication and assembly capacity. A maximum of 4,000 hours of fabrication capacity is available per month, and each circular saw requires 2 hours and each table saw requires 1 hour. A maximum of 5,000 hours of assembly capacity is available per month, and each circular saw requires 1 hour and each table saw requires 2 hours. The marketing department estimates that there is a maximum market demand next year of 3,500 saws per month for both product lines combined. How many circular saws and how many table saws should be produced monthly next year to maximize profits?

1. Is there a single managerial objective?
    Yes. The objective is to maximize profits for the year.
2. Are there alternative courses of managerial action?
    Yes. Management can decide to produce all circular saws or all table saws or any mix of the two product lines during the year.
3. Is the total achievement of the objective constrained by scarce resources or other restraints? If so, what is the nature of the constraints?
    Yes. Profits are constrained by the maximum amount of fabrication hours available per month, the maximum amount of assembly hours available per month, and the maximum amount of market demand per month.

Example 8.2	LP-2: Recognizing an Ingredient Mix LP Problem

The Gulf Coast Foundry is developing a long-range strategic plan for buying scrap metal for its foundry operations. The foundry can buy scrap metal in unlimited quantities from two sources, Atlanta (A) and Birmingham (B), and it receives the scrap daily in railroad cars. The scrap is melted down, and lead and copper are extracted for use in the foundry processes. Each railroad car of scrap from Source A yields 1 ton of copper and 1 ton of lead and costs $10,000. Each railroad car of scrap from Source B yields 1 ton of copper and 2 tons of lead and costs $15,000. If the foundry needs at least 2.5 tons of copper and at least 4 tons of lead per day for the foreseeable future, how many railroad cars of scrap should be purchased per day from Source A and Source B to minimize the long-range scrap metal cost?

1. Is there a single managerial objective?
    Yes. Management wishes to minimize the daily costs of buying scrap metal from which copper and lead can be extracted.
2. Are there alternative courses of managerial action?
    Yes. Management can buy all of its scrap from either Source A or Source B, or it can buy any combination of amounts of scrap from both sources.
3. Is the total achievement of the objective constrained by scarce resources or other constraints? If so, what is the nature of the constraints?
    Yes. Daily costs are constrained by the minimum amount of copper and lead needed daily.

FORMULATING LP PROBLEMS

Although both recognition and formulation of LP problems tend to become intuitive after we gain experience, in the beginning a method to follow helps us to formulate them more effectively. Table 8.3 lists the steps to follow in formulating LP problems. These steps structure problems in a way that helps us better understand the problems with which we are dealing. Additionally, the problems are then in a form necessary for LP solutions.

Example 8.3 follows the LP formulating steps and sets up Problem LP-1, which was discussed in Example 8.1. Read Example 8.1 again and follow through the example carefully to make sure that you understand the procedures for formulating LP problems.

Table 8.3	Steps in Formulating LP Problems

1. Define the objective.
2. Define the decision variables.
3. Write the mathematical function for the objective (objective function).
4. Write a one- or two-word description of each constraint.
5. Write the right-hand side (RHS) of each constraint, including the units of measure.
6. Write $\leq$, $=$, or $\geq$ for each constraint.
7. Write all the decision variables on the left-hand side of each constraint.
8. Write the coefficient for each decision variable in each constraint.

Example 8.3	Formulating LP-1

You may find it helpful to study Figure 8.1 as you work through this example.

1. **Define the objective.** Precision Manufacturing Company seeks to maximize monthly profits. The problem is therefore a *maximization problem.*

2. **Define the decision variables.** What specific decisions does Precision need to make to maximize profits? The company needs to decide how many circular saws and table saws to manufacture each month. Therefore let:

   X_1 = number of circular saws to manufacture each month
   X_2 = number of table saws to manufacture each month

   X_1 and X_2 are the decision variables. When we know their values, the problem will be solved.

3. **Write the mathematical objective function.** Let Z equal the monthly profits; Z is a function of X_1 and X_2. In other words, the monthly profits depend on how many circular saws (X_1) and table saws (X_2) are manufactured each month. $Z = C_1X_1 + C_2X_2$, where C_1 and C_2 are the respective profits for each circular saw and table saw. C_1 = \$900 for each circular saw, C_2 = \$600 for each table saw, and $Z = 900X_1 + 600X_2$, where Z = total monthly profits, $900X_1$ = monthly profits for circular saws, and $600X_2$ = monthly profits for table saws. The objective function is therefore $Z = 900X_1 + 600X_2$ and suggests that we should select values of the decision variables X_1 and X_2 that result in the maximum value of Z. Were it not for production capacity and market constraints, Z monthly profits would be infinitely large.

4. **Write a one- or two-word description of each constraint.** There are three factors that constrain Precision from having infinite profits—fabrication hours available per month, assembly hours available per month, and market demand for saws per month. Therefore fabrication, assembly, and market are terms that describe each constraint.

5. **Write the right-hand side of each constraint.** The right-hand side (RHS) of each constraint is the maximum amount ($\leq$), exact amount ($=$), or minimum amount ($\geq$) of each constraint. Here the maximum amount of fabrication capacity is 4,000 hours per month, the maximum amount of assembly capacity is 5,000 hours per month, and the maximum market demand is 3,500 saws per month.

6. **Write $\subseteq$, $=$, $\supseteq$ for each constraint.** Because all the constraints in this problem are maximum amounts, all the constraints are the $\leq$ type. In other words, the amount of fabrication capacity that X_1 and X_2 use must be less than or equal to 4,000 hours per month, the amount

of assembly capacity that X_1 and X_2 use must be less than or equal to 5,000 hours per month, and the amount of saws sold to the market must be less than or equal to 3,500 per month.

7. **Write all the decision variables on the left-hand side of each constraint.** In this problem there are only two decision variables—X_1 and X_2. If there were more X's, they would be written in with enough space between them to allow us to write in their coefficients in the next step. If a particular decision variable does not appear in a constraint, this is taken care of in the next step by assigning a zero coefficient to that decision variable in that constraint.

8. **Write the coefficient for each decision variable in each constraint.** Consider the first constraint, fabrication. What is the coefficient of X_1 in this constraint? It is the amount of fabrication hours per unit of X_1. In other words, it is the amount of fabrication hours used in manufacturing each circular saw, or 2 hours. Similarly, the coefficient of X_2 in this first constraint is the amount of fabrication hours used in manufacturing each table saw, or 1 hour. The coefficients of X_1 and X_2 in the assembly constraint are 1 and 2, and the coefficients of X_1 and X_2 in the market demand constraint are 1 and 1.

Figure 8.1	Formulation of Problem LP-1

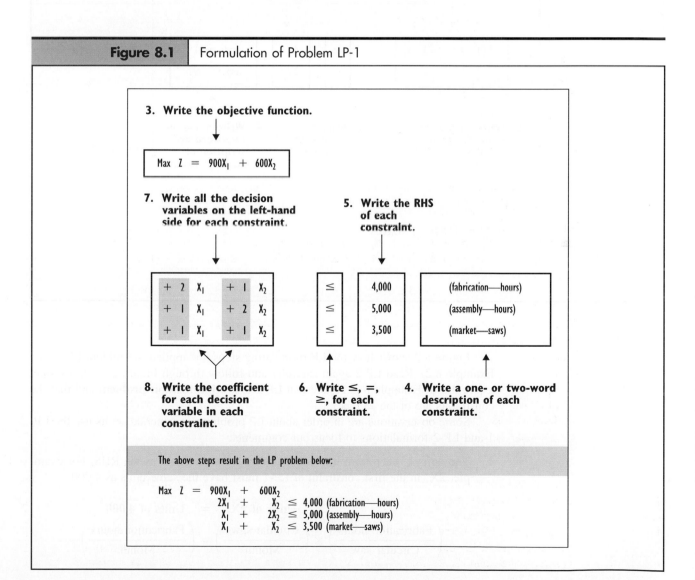

Figure 8.2 | Formulation of Problem LP-2

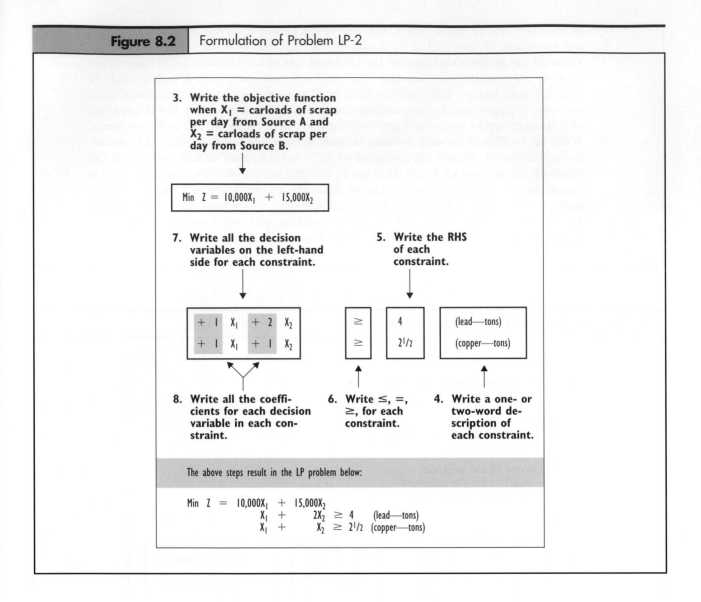

3. Write the objective function when X_1 = carloads of scrap per day from Source A and X_2 = carloads of scrap per day from Source B.

$$\text{Min } Z = 10{,}000X_1 + 15{,}000X_2$$

7. Write all the decision variables on the left-hand side for each constraint.

5. Write the RHS of each constraint.

| $+ 1 X_1 + 2 X_2$ |
| $+ 1 X_1 + 1 X_2$ |

| $\geq$ | 4 |
| $\geq$ | $2^{1}/_2$ |

| (lead—tons) |
| (copper—tons) |

8. Write all the coefficients for each decision variable in each constraint.

6. Write $\leq$, $=$, $\geq$, for each constraint.

4. Write a one- or two-word description of each constraint.

The above steps result in the LP problem below:

$$\text{Min } Z = 10{,}000X_1 + 15{,}000X_2$$
$$X_1 + 2X_2 \geq 4 \quad \text{(lead—tons)}$$
$$X_1 + X_2 \geq 2^{1}/_2 \quad \text{(copper—tons)}$$

Figure 8.2 shows how the LP-formulating steps are applied to Problem LP-2 (see Example 8.2). Read LP-2 again carefully and follow through Figure 8.2 step by step, as we did in Example 8.3. Notice that LP-2 is a **minimization problem** and that the constraints are of the $\geq$ type.

Some observations are in order about LP problems in general. Let us use the LP-1 and LP-2 formulations to focus our comments:

1. The units of each term in a constraint must be the same as the RHS. For example, $2X_1$ in the first constraint of LP-1 must have the same units as 4,000:

$$\textbf{Units of } 2X_1 \quad = \quad \textbf{Units of 4,000}$$

$$\left(\frac{\text{Fabrication hours}}{\text{Circular saw}}\right) \times \left(\frac{\text{Circular saws}}{\text{Month}}\right) = \left(\frac{\text{Fabrication hours}}{\text{Month}}\right)$$

2. The units of each term in the objective function must be the same as Z. For example, 15,000X$_2$ in LP-2 must be the same units as Z:

$$\textbf{Units of 15,000X}_2 = \textbf{ Units of Z}$$

$$\left(\frac{\$}{\text{Carload}}\right) \times \left(\frac{\text{Carloads}}{\text{Day}}\right) = \left(\frac{\$}{\text{Day}}\right)$$

3. The units *between* constraints do not *have* to be the same. For example, in LP-1, 4,000 fabrication hours and 3,500 saws per month are different units. The units *may* be the same between constraints, as LP-2 demonstrates, but they do not *have* to be.

4. An LP problem can have a mixture of constraint types. For example, minimization problems may have ≥, =, and ≤ constraints, and maximization problems may also have ≥, =, and ≤ constraints. However, maximization problems usually have more ≤ constraints, and minimization problems usually have more ≥ constraints.

Now that you have a grasp of how to recognize LP problems and how to formulate LP problems, you are ready to examine how LP problems are solved.

SOLVING LP PROBLEMS

Constrained operational decisions have been recognized and structured for analysis for several decades. In the 1930s W. W. Leontief developed his input–output economic analyses that were structured similarly to today's LP format. In the 1930s and 1940s F. L. Hitchcock and T. C. Koopsmans developed a method for structuring *and* solving transportation-type LP problems. In 1947 George Dantzig developed the simplex method of linear programming. Dantzig's simplex method was probably the beginning of the development of the present-day field of **mathematical programming.**

An early LP solution method was developed to solve facility location problems in POM. A physical model was built over a map of the geographic areas under examination. A string was threaded through a hole in the map over each proposed location, and a weight proportional to the location's total cost was tied to the end of the string. All the strings were then connected on the top surface of the map by a sliding knot apparatus. When all the weights were dropped simultaneously, the knot was pulled to a location point that minimized the total costs. While this "drop the string" method is archaic by today's standards, the time and effort plowed into these early methods emphasize the importance that managers place on the need for LP solution techniques.

The **graphical solution** approach conceptually demonstrates the process of LP solutions to those who have no experience with LP. Graphical solutions are therefore intended as a teaching tool to assist you in understanding the process of LP solutions. The simplex, transportation, and assignment methods are the practical LP solution tools.

Graphical LP Solutions

Table 8.4 outlines the steps in the graphical method of solving LP problems. These steps are demonstrated in Example 8.4, a maximization problem, and Example 8.5, a minimization problem. Study these two examples and make sure you understand the basics of these solutions: plotting the constraint equations, outlining the feasible solution space, circling the solution points, and, finally, selecting the optimal solution.

Delivery service companies, such as FedEx, may use an LP-based computer system to select delivery routes that reduce costs and turnaround times (e.g., by consolidating customer loads, etc.).

© AFP/CORBIS

Table 8.4	Steps in the Graphical Solution Method

1. Formulate the objective and constraint functions.
2. Draw a graph with one variable on the horizontal axis and one on the vertical axis.
3. Plot each of the constraints as if they were lines or equalities.
4. Outline the feasible solution space.
5. Circle the potential solution points. These are the intersections of the constraints or axes on the inner (minimization) or outer (maximization) perimeter of the feasible solution space.
6. Substitute each of the potential solution point values of the two decision variables into the objective function and solve for Z.
7. Select the solution point that optimizes Z.

Example 8.4	Graphical Solution of LP-1

Problem LP-1 is used to demonstrate the steps of the graphical solution of a maximization problem. Read LP-1 again (Example 8.1) and Table 8.4 before beginning this example.

1. **Formulate the objective and constraint functions.** When LP-1 was formulated in Example 8.3, the decision variables were X_1 = number of circular saws to manufacture per month and X_2 = number of table saws to manufacture per month. The objective and constraint functions were:

$$\text{Max } Z = 900X_1 + 600X_2$$
$$2X_1 + X_2 \leq 4{,}000 \text{ (fabrication—hours)}$$
$$X_1 + 2X_2 \leq 5{,}000 \text{ (assembly—hours)}$$
$$X_1 + X_2 \leq 3{,}500 \text{ (market—saws)}$$

2. **Draw a graph.**
3. **Plot the constraint functions.**
4. **Outline the feasible solution space.**
5. **Circle the potential solution points on the perimeter of the feasible solution space (see Figure 8.3).**

   Note that the constraints are plotted by treating each constraint as an equality or a line. For each constraint line, let $X_1 = 0$ and solve for X_2, then let $X_2 = 0$ and solve for X_1; this gives two sets of X_1 and X_2 values or points. Connect each pair of points with a straight line. This process is repeated for each constraint.

   Note that all values of X_1 and X_2 must fall inside all constraints (toward the origin) because the constraints are $\leq$. Points D and E are not feasible because they both violate the first constraint. *While any point within the feasible solution space satisfies all the constraints, only Points A, B, and C are candidates for the optimal solution because they are at the intersections of constraints or axes and lie on the outer perimeter of the feasible solution space.*

   Note also that Points A and C are formed by the intersection of a constraint and one of the axes. This is possible because the axes are implied constraints. In other words, X_1 cannot be negative; therefore the vertical axis $X_1 = 0$ is treated as a constraint. Similarly, $X_2 = 0$, the horizontal axis, is also treated as a constraint.

   The values of X_1 and X_2 at Points A, B, and C are three potential solutions to Problem LP-1:

$$\textbf{A: } X_1 = 0 \text{ and } X_2 = 2{,}500 \qquad \textbf{B: } X_1 = 1{,}000 \text{ and } X_2 = 2{,}000$$
$$\textbf{C: } X_1 = 2{,}000 \text{ and } X_2 = 0$$

How do we determine Point B accurately? If the coordinates cannot be read precisely, the two constraint equations can be solved simultaneously for X_1 and X_2:

The two equations that intersect at Point B:	Multiply the first equation by -2 and add the two equations together:	Substitute the value for X_1 back into either equation and solve for X_2:
$2X_1 + X_2 = 4{,}000$ $X_1 + 2X_2 = 5{,}000$	$-4X_1 - 2X_2 = -8{,}000$ $\underline{+ \ (X_1 + 2X_2 = 5{,}000)}$ $-3X_1 = -3{,}000$ or $ X_1 = 1{,}000$	$2(1{,}000) + X_2 = 4{,}000$ $2{,}000 + X_2 = 4{,}000$ $X_2 = 2{,}000$

The intersection of the two constraints is therefore $X_1 = 1{,}000$ and $X_2 = 2{,}000$. Points A, B, and C are potential solutions to Problem LP-1. Which one is optimal?

6. **Substitute the solution point values of the decision variables into the objective function and solve for Z:**

Point A:	**Point B:**	**Point C:**
$X_1 = 0$ and $X_2 = 2{,}500$	$X_1 = 1{,}000$ and $X_2 = 2{,}000$	$X_1 = 2{,}000$ and $X_2 = 0$
$Z = 900X_1 + 600X_2$	$Z = 900X_1 + 600X_2$	$Z = 900X_1 + 600X_2$
$= 900(0) + 600(2{,}500)$	$= 900(1{,}000) + 600(2{,}000)$	$= 900(2{,}000) + 600(0)$
$= 1{,}500{,}000$	$= 2{,}100{,}000$	$= 1{,}800{,}000$

7. **Select the solution that optimizes Z.** To maximize Z, the optimal solution is Point B, where $X_1 = 1{,}000$ circular saws per month, $X_2 = 2{,}000$ table saws per month, and $Z = \$2{,}100{,}000$ profits per month.

| Figure 8.3 | Graphical Solution of LP-1 |

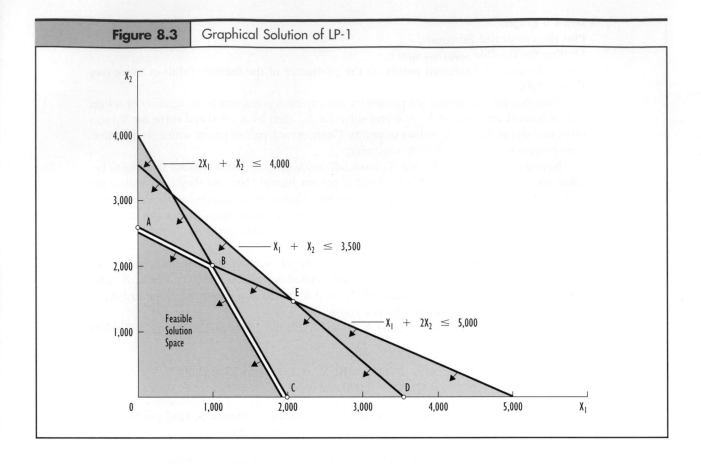

| Example 8.5 | Graphical Solution of LP-2 |

Problem LP-2 is used to demonstrate the steps of the graphical solution of a minimization LP problem. Read LP-2 again (Example 8.2).

1. **Formulate the objective and constraint functions.** Recall that LP-2 was formulated in Figure 8.2 with these decision variables:

    X_1 = carloads of scrap purchased from Source A per day
    X_2 = carloads of scrap purchased from Source B per day

    The objective and constraint functions were:

$$\text{Min } Z = 10{,}000X_1 + 15{,}000X_2$$
$$X_1 + \quad\quad 2X_2 \geq 4 \text{ (lead—tons)}$$
$$X_1 + \quad\quad X_2 \geq 2\tfrac{1}{2} \text{ (copper—tons)}$$

2. **Draw a graph.**
3. **Plot the constraint functions.**
4. **Outline the feasible solution space.**
5. **Circle the potential solution points on the perimeter of the feasible solution space (see Figure 8.4).**

Note that since both constraints are $\geq$, all possible values of X_1 and X_2 must lie outside both constraints, away from the origin. Point D is not possible because it violates the first constraint. Similarly, Point E violates the second constraint. *While any point within the feasible solution space satisfies all the constraints, only Points A, B, and C are candidates for the optimal solution because they are at the intersections of constraints or axes and lie on the inner perimeter of the feasible solution space.*

Points A, B, and C are three potential optimal solutions to Problem LP-2:

$$\textbf{A: } X_1 = 0 \text{ and } X_2 = 2.5 \qquad \textbf{B: } X_1 = 1 \text{ and } X_2 = 1.5 \qquad \textbf{C: } X_1 = 4 \text{ and } X_2 = 0$$

6. **Substitute the solution point values of the two decision variables into the objective function and solve for Z:**

Point A:
$X_1 = 0$ and $X_2 = 2.5$

$Z = 10{,}000X_1 + 15{,}000X_2$
$= 10{,}000(0) + 15{,}000(2.5)$
$= 37{,}500$

Point B:
$X_1 = 1$ and $X_2 = 1.5$

$Z - 10{,}000X_1 + 15{,}000X_2$
$= 10{,}000(1) + 15{,}000(1.5)$
$= 32{,}500$

Point C:
$X_1 = 4$ and $X_2 = 0$

$Z = 10{,}000X_1 + 15{,}000X_2$
$= 10{,}000(4) + 15{,}000(0)$
$= 40{,}000$

7. **Select the solution that optimizes Z.** To minimize Z, the optimal solution is Point B, where $X_1 = 1$ carload of scrap from Source A per day, $X_2 = 1.5$ carloads of scrap from Source B per day, and $Z = \$32{,}500$ total scrap cost per day.

Figure 8.4	Graphical Solution of LP-2

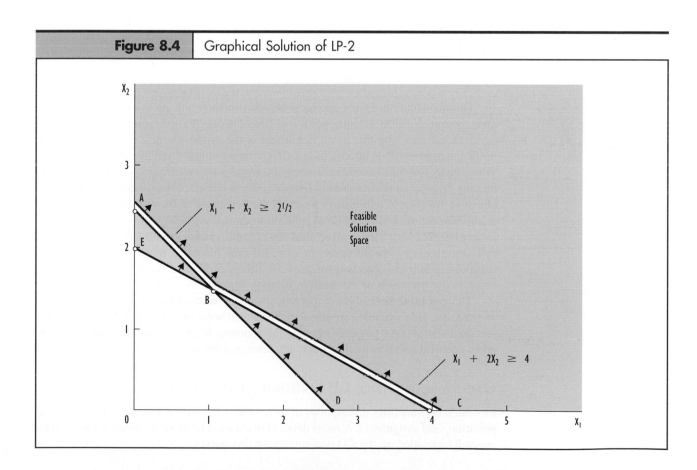

Figure 8.5	Isoprofit Lines in LP-1 Graphical Solution

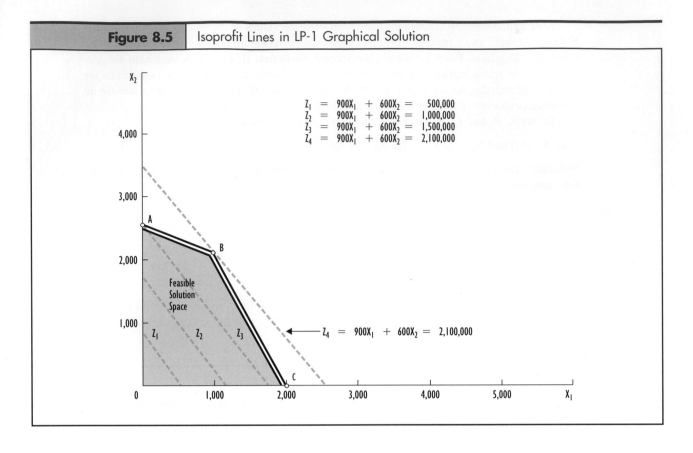

Optimal solutions in the graphical solution method will lie at intersections on the inner perimeter (min) or outer perimeter (max) of the feasible solution space. Figure 8.5 demonstrates why this is so. Beginning at the origin where $Z = 0$, we let Z, the profit function in LP-1, take on progressively larger values from 500,000 to 2,100,000. When these isoprofit functions, as they are sometimes called, are plotted, we can see that the *greatest* isoprofit function intersects the feasible solution space at Point B. The objective function Z will always intersect the perimeter of the feasible solution space at an intersection, and the optimal solution to the LP problem will be found at this intersection. Knowing this, we can find the optimal solution to an LP problem graphically by plotting isoprofit (max) or isocost (min) functions rather than algebraically substituting into the objective function the values of X_1 and X_2 at all of the intersections on the perimeter of the feasible solution space.

The graphical method is not a practical solution method because only two, or three at most, decision variables are allowed. Graphical solutions are a good place to begin solving LP problems, however, because the concepts learned are directly applied to the other practical solution methods that are described below.

Overview of Other LP Solution Methods

Presented here are brief descriptions of three other LP solution methods: simplex, transportation, and assignment. A more detailed discussion of these methods is found in the appendix included on the CD accompanying this book.

Simplex Method

The simplex method is the most common analytic tool for solving linear programming models. Although use of the simplex method by hand to solve LPs is tedious and error prone, enough standard LP computer programs are available for this task that real LP problems are always solved on computers. A few examples of such computer software are IBM's *Optimization Solutions and Library* (**http://www.ibm.com**), *GAMS* (**http://www.gams.com**), *MPL for Windows* (**http://www.maximal-usa.com**), and the LP program in the *POM Software Library* that accompanies this text. *Solver,* a software tool for solving LP models, is available within common spreadsheet packages such as *Excel, Lotus 1-2-3,* and *Quattro Pro.* Also, third-party software vendors offer software add-ons to common spreadsheet packages; *What's Best!* (**http://www.lindo.com**) and Frontline Systems' *Premium Solver* (**http://www.frontsys.com**), an enhanced version of the *Solver* program in spreadsheet packages, are just two of them.

Figures 8.6 through 8.11 illustrate how the *Solver* tool within Microsoft *Excel* can be used to solve Problem LP-1. Figure 8.6 shows the initial spreadsheet with formulas.

| **Figure 8.6** | Initial Spreadsheet for Problem LP-1 |

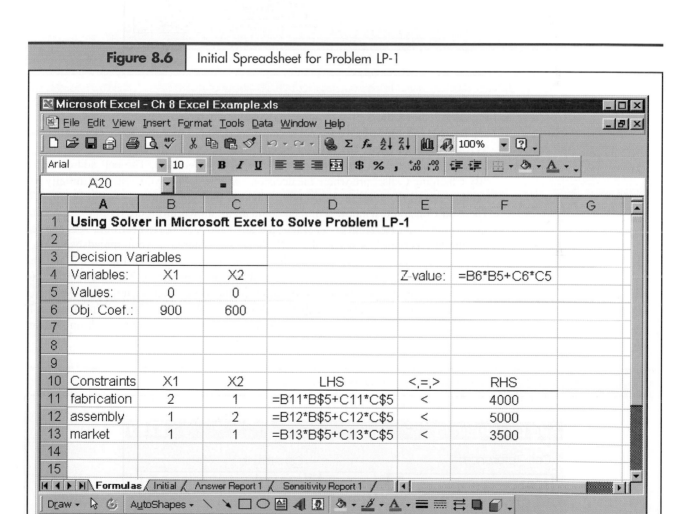

| **Figure 8.7** | *Solver* Parameters Window |

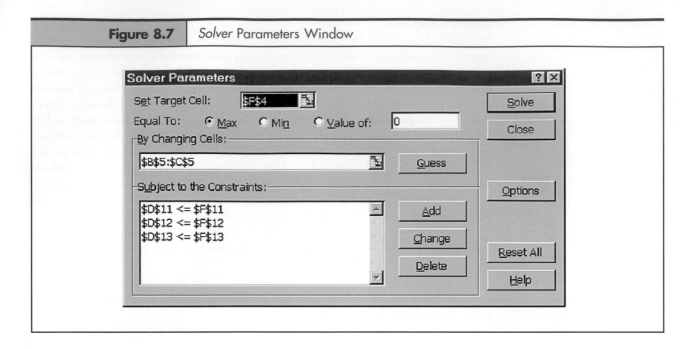

Figure 8.7 shows the *Solver* Parameters window when *Solver* is selected from the Excel Tools menu. (If *Solver* does not show as an option under the Tools menu, then select Add-Ins and check the box for Solver Add-in.) The cell address for "Set Target Cell:" is where the objective function Z formula was entered. The cell addresses for "By Changing Cells:" are where the decision variable values were entered (initially entered as zeros). To enter the constraints, click on the Add button shown in Figure 8.7. The Add Constraint window will then come up as shown in Figure 8.8. For each constraint, the "Cell Reference:" is where the left-hand side (LHS) formula was entered and the "Constraint:" is where the RHS value was entered in your spreadsheet. After all constraints are entered, click on the Options button shown in Figure 8.7 and the Solver Options window will come up as shown in Figure 8.9. The only options to change are checking the boxes for Assume Linear Model and Assume Non-Negative. After these have been checked, then click on the Solve button shown in Figure 8.7. When *Solver* has found the solution, another window will come up; click on Answer

| **Figure 8.8** | *Solver* Add Constraint Window |

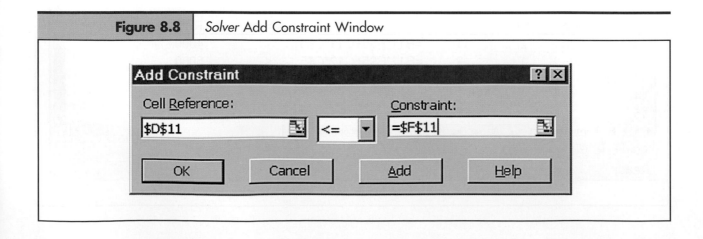

| Figure 8.9 | *Solver* Options Window |

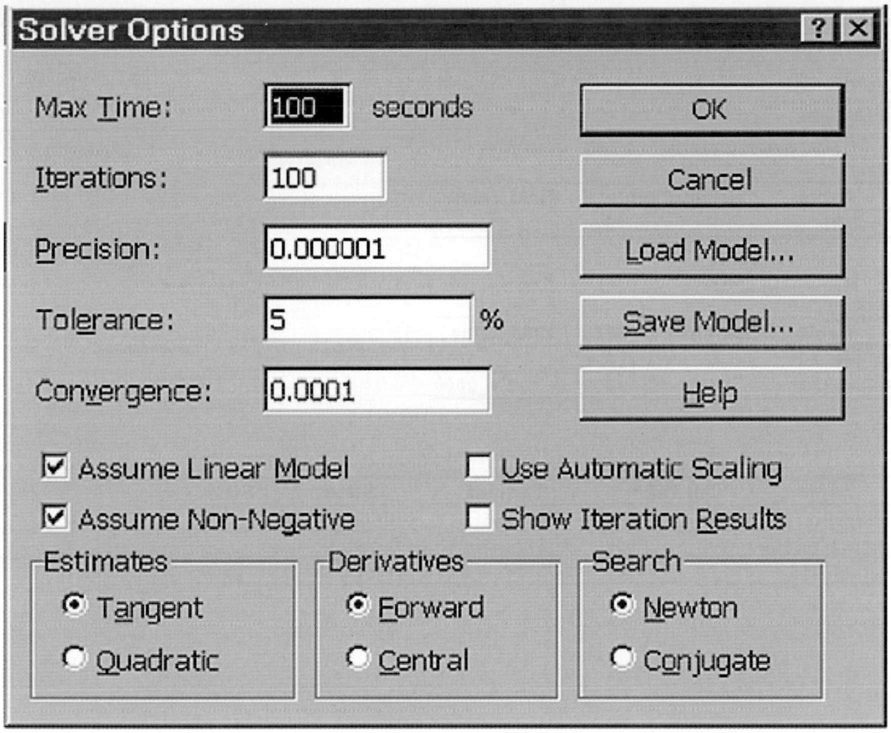

Report and Sensitivity Report to generate these two reports. Figure 8.10 shows the Answer Report, and Figure 8.11 shows the Sensitivity Report.

Transportation Method

One of the earliest LP solution methods was the transportation method. This method can solve only a special form of LP problem, those with m sources and n destinations and with these characteristics:

1. Number of variables is m $\times$ n.
2. Number of constraints is m $+$ n.
3. Costs appear only in objective function.
4. Coefficients of decision variables in the constraints are either 0 or 1.

The simplex method can solve any LP problem that the transportation method can solve, but not vice versa.

A **transportation LP problem** is of a special form where the objective is usually to minimize the cost of shipping products from several sources to several destinations. The constraints are for source capacity and destination demand. Example 8.6 is an LP problem of this form. Note that the coefficients of the decision variables in the constraints are either 0 or 1. Additionally, the pattern of the appearance of the decision variables in the constraints in the example is characteristic of transportation problems. The vignette at the beginning of this chapter is about a transportation problem.

| Figure 8.10 | *Solver* Answer Report |

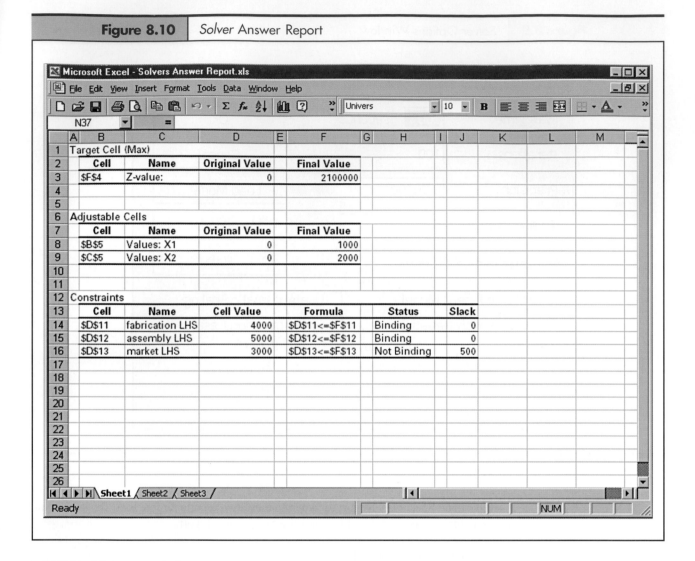

Example 8.6 | A Transportation LP Problem

The Green Up Fertilizer Company ships fertilizer from two plants to three customers. The shipping cost per ton of fertilizer from each plant to each customer is:

| | **Customer** | | |
Plant	A	B	C
1	$15	$30	$20
2	20	25	15

Plant 1 has a monthly capacity of 1,000 tons, and Plant 2 has a monthly capacity of 2,000 tons. The monthly customer demand is A = 500 tons, B = 1,500 tons, and C = 1,000 tons. Formulate an LP problem to determine how much fertilizer should be shipped from each plant to each customer per month to minimize monthly shipping costs.

1. **Define the objective.** Minimize the monthly shipping costs.
2. **Define the decision variables.** Notice that there are m × n (2 × 3 = 6) decision variables.

Figure 8.11	*Solver* Sensitivity Report

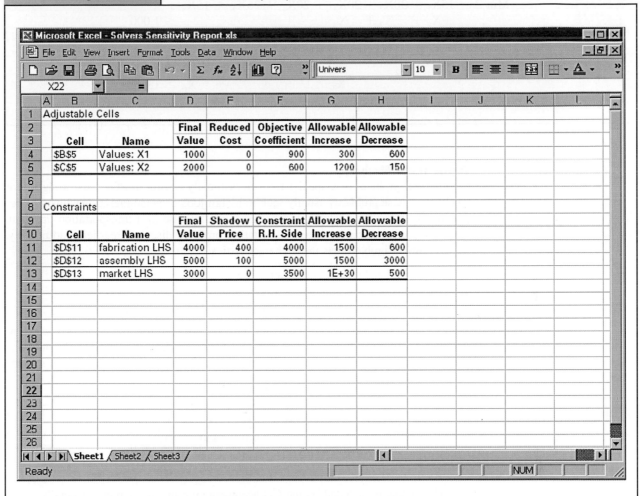

X22 | ▼ | = |

Adjustable Cells

Cell	Name	Final Value	Reduced Cost	Objective Coefficient	Allowable Increase	Allowable Decrease
B5	Values: X1	1000	0	900	300	600
C5	Values: X2	2000	0	600	1200	150

Constraints

Cell	Name	Final Value	Shadow Price	Constraint R.H. Side	Allowable Increase	Allowable Decrease
D11	fabrication LHS	4000	400	4000	1500	600
D12	assembly LHS	5000	100	5000	1500	3000
D13	market LHS	3000	0	3500	1E+30	500

X_1 = tons of fertilizer to be shipped from 1 to A per month
X_2 = tons of fertilizer to be shipped from 1 to B per month
X_3 = tons of fertilizer to be shipped from 1 to C per month
X_4 = tons of fertilizer to be shipped from 2 to A per month
X_5 = tons of fertilizer to be shipped from 2 to B per month
X_6 = tons of fertilizer to be shipped from 2 to C per month

3. **Write the mathematical function for the objective:**

$$\text{Min } Z = 15X_1 + 30X_2 + 20X_3 + 20X_4 + 25X_5 + 15X_6$$

4. **Write the constraints.** Notice that there are m + n (2 + 3 = 5) constraints.

$$
\begin{aligned}
X_1 + X_2 + X_3 &\leq 1{,}000 \text{ (Plant 1 capacity in tons)} \\
X_4 + X_5 + X_6 &\leq 2{,}000 \text{ (Plant 2 capacity in tons)} \\
X_1 \qquad + X_4 \qquad &\geq 500 \text{ (Customer A demand in tons)} \\
X_2 \qquad + X_5 \qquad &\geq 1{,}500 \text{ (Customer B demand in tons)} \\
X_3 \qquad + X_6 &\geq 1{,}000 \text{ (Customer C demand in tons)}
\end{aligned}
$$

The resultant LP problem is:

$$\text{Min } Z = 15X_1 + 30X_2 + 20X_3 + 20X_4 + 25X_5 + 15X_6$$

$$
\begin{array}{l}
X_1 + X_2 + X_3 \leq 1{,}000 \\
\qquad\qquad\quad X_4 + X_5 + X_6 \leq 2{,}000 \\
X_1 \qquad\qquad + X_4 \qquad\qquad \geq 500 \\
\qquad X_2 \qquad\qquad + X_5 \qquad \geq 1{,}500 \\
\qquad\qquad X_3 \qquad\qquad + X_6 \geq 1{,}000
\end{array}
$$

Assignment Method

Another LP problem of a special form occasionally occurs in POM: the **assignment problem.** These problems usually seek to assign jobs or personnel to machines or departments. An assignment problem is just a special case of a transportation problem, having the characteristics of a transportation problem discussed earlier. Additionally, an assignment problem has these characteristics:

1. The right-hand sides of constraints are all 1.
2. The signs of constraints are = rather than ≤ or ≥.
3. The value of all decision variables is either 0 or 1.

For example, suppose that three persons must be assigned to three projects, each project must be assigned to only one person, and each person must be assigned to only one project. The costs are shown below. The objective is to determine an assignment scheme that minimizes costs.

	Project		
Person	**A**	**B**	**C**
1	$20	$30	$10
2	40	30	40
3	30	20	30

The appendix included on the CD accompanying this book presents details of using the simplex method to solve LP problems, using the transportation method to solve transportation problems, and using the assignment method to solve assignment problems.

REAL LP PROBLEMS

Real LP problems in POM typically have numerous variables, numerous constraints, and other complex characteristics. The real LP problem in POM presented and formulated in Example 8.7 will deepen your comprehension of LP in POM.

Example 8.7 | Oklahoma Crude Oil Company

An oil refinery in Oklahoma buys domestic crude oil from five sources: Oklahoma, Texas, Kansas, New Mexico, and Colorado. Six end products are produced: regular gasoline, premium gasoline, low-lead gasoline, diesel fuel, heating oil, and lubricating oil base. The accompanying table shows the crude oil distribution to each end product, the crude oil costs, and the market requirements for each end product.

Product	Crude Oil Source					Monthly Market Requirement (thousands of gallons)
	Oklahoma	Texas	Kansas	New Mexico	Colorado	
Regular gasoline	40%	30%	30%	20%	30%	5,000
Premium gasoline	20	30	40	30	20	3,000
Low-lead gasoline	20	10	—	30	10	3,000
Diesel fuel	10	10	10	—	20	2,000
Heating oil	—	10	10	20	10	1,000
Lubricating oil base	10	10	10	—	10	2,000
Totals	100%	100%	100%	100%	100%	16,000
Delivered Cost/Gallon	$.20	$.14	$.15	$.18	$.12	

The sources of crude oil are captive within the company, and any quantity of each of the crudes can be purchased to satisfy the needs of this refinery up to these maximums:

Crude Source	Maximum Monthly Supply (thousands of gallons)	Crude Source	Maximum Monthly Supply (thousands of gallons)
Oklahoma crude	8,000	New Mexico crude	3,000
Texas crude	4,000	Colorado crude	6,000
Kansas crude	5,000		

How much crude oil should be purchased from each source to at least satisfy the market and to minimize crude oil costs?

1. **Define the decision variables:**

X_1 = thousands of gallons of Oklahoma crude to be purchased per month
X_2 = thousands of gallons of Texas crude to be purchased per month
X_3 = thousands of gallons of Kansas crude to be purchased per month
X_4 = thousands of gallons of New Mexico crude to be purchased per month
X_5 = thousands of gallons of Colorado crude to be purchased per month

2. **Formulate the LP problem:**

$\text{Min } Z = 200X_1 + 140X_2 + 150X_3 + 180X_4 + 120X_5$

$.4X_1 + .3X_2 + .3X_3 + .2X_4 + .3X_5 \geq 5,000$ (regular gasoline market requirement*)

$.2X_1 + .3X_2 + .4X_3 + .3X_4 + .2X_5 \geq 3,000$ (premium gasoline market requirement*)

$.2X_1 + .1X_2 + .3X_4 + .1X_5 \geq 3,000$ (low-lead gasoline market requirement*)

$.1X_1 + .1X_2 + .1X_3 + .2X_5 \geq 2,000$ (diesel fuel market requirement*)

$.1X_2 + .1X_3 + .2X_4 + .1X_5 \geq 1,000$ (heating oil market requirement*)

$.1X_1 + .1X_2 + .1X_3 + .1X_5 \geq 2,000$ (lubricating oil base market requirement*)

$$X_1 \qquad\qquad\qquad\qquad\qquad \le 8,000 \quad \text{(Oklahoma crude supply*)}$$
$$X_2 \qquad\qquad\qquad\qquad \le 4,000 \quad \text{(Texas crude supply*)}$$
$$X_3 \qquad\qquad\qquad \le 5,000 \quad \text{(Kansas crude supply*)}$$
$$X_4 \qquad\qquad \le 3,000 \quad \text{(New Mexico crude supply*)}$$
$$X_5 \le 6,000 \quad \text{(Colorado crude supply*)}$$

Solving this LP problem results in a minimum total cost of $3,420,000.

*In thousands of gallons.

INTERPRETING COMPUTER SOLUTIONS OF LP PROBLEMS

In this section we explain how to interpret the meaning of the printout of a solution of an LP problem from the *POM Software Library* that accompanies this text. Figure 8.12 exhibits the solution to Problem LP-1 that was formulated and solved graphically earlier in this chapter. It may be helpful to review Examples 8.3 and 8.4 before you read this section. In Figure 8.12 the first thing we notice is the formulation of the LP-1 problem—two decision variables and three $\le$ constraints. In the next section of the printout, we find the solution that was accomplished in three iterations or simplex tables. The solution is deduced from the variables that appear in the variable mix column, which is also called the solution column or **basis:** $X_1 = 1,000$; $X_2 = 2,000$; Slack 3 $= 500$; Z $= \$2,100,000$; and all other variables not in the basis equal zero.

The meaning of the decision variables (the X's) and Z were discussed earlier in this chapter. The meaning of Slack 3, or S_3, a **slack variable,** however, requires some explanation. The slack variable S_3 is associated with the third constraint, which is indicated by the subscript 3. The third constraint of LP-1 is $X_1 + X_2 \le 3,500$, which limits the total number of circular saws (X_1) and the table saws (X_2) that can be sold in each month to a maximum of 3,500. S_3 allows us to convert the third constraint from a $\le$ to an $=$:

$$X_1 + X_2 \qquad\quad \le 3,500$$
$$X_1 + X_2 + S_3 = 3,500$$

As such, S_3 represents the amount of unused market per month that is not satisfied by the sales of X_1 and X_2 saws. Because $S_3 = 500$, we would have 500 saws of unused market per month if we produce and sell 1,000 circular saws and 2,000 table saws. Similarly, Slack 1 or S_1 represents the amount of unused hours of fabrication capacity per month and Slack 2 or S_2 represents the amount of unused hours of assembly capacity per month (the subscripts 1 and 2 refer to the first and second constraints). Because both S_1 and $S_2 = 0$ (because they did not appear in the basis or variable mix column), all available fabrication and assembly capacity hours would be used in each month.

Now let us turn to the Sensitivity Analysis section of Figure 8.12. For constraints, the shadow prices indicate the impact on Z if the RHSs of the constraints are changed. For example, in the first constraint, which is a $\le$ constraint representing fabrication hours, if the RHS were changed by 1 hour, Z would change by $400. This information

| Figure 8.12 | Computer Printout for Problem LP-1 from the *POM Software Library* |

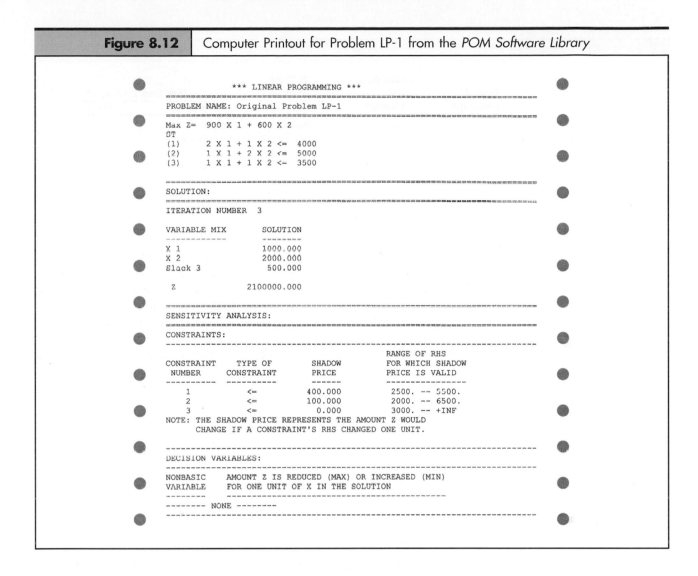

```
                    *** LINEAR PROGRAMMING ***
        ===============================================================
        PROBLEM NAME: Original Problem LP-1
        ===============================================================
        Max Z=   900 X 1 + 600 X 2
        ST
        (1)      2 X 1 + 1 X 2 <=  4000
        (2)      1 X 1 + 2 X 2 <=  5000
        (3)      1 X 1 + 1 X 2 <=  3500

        ===============================================================
        SOLUTION:
        ===============================================================
        ITERATION NUMBER   3

        VARIABLE MIX        SOLUTION
        -------------       ---------
        X 1                 1000.000
        X 2                 2000.000
        Slack 3              500.000

        Z                2100000.000

        ===============================================================
        SENSITIVITY ANALYSIS:
        ===============================================================
        CONSTRAINTS:
        ----------------------------------------------------------------
                                            RANGE OF RHS
        CONSTRAINT   TYPE OF      SHADOW     FOR WHICH SHADOW
          NUMBER     CONSTRAINT   PRICE      PRICE IS VALID
        ----------  ----------   ------    ----------------
            1          <=         400.000    2500. -- 5500.
            2          <=         100.000    2000. -- 6500.
            3          <=           0.000    3000. -- +INF
        NOTE: THE SHADOW PRICE REPRESENTS THE AMOUNT Z WOULD
              CHANGE IF A CONSTRAINT'S RHS CHANGED ONE UNIT.

        ----------------------------------------------------------------
        DECISION VARIABLES:
        ----------------------------------------------------------------
        NONBASIC     AMOUNT Z IS REDUCED (MAX) OR INCREASED (MIN)
        VARIABLE     FOR ONE UNIT OF X IN THE SOLUTION
        --------     ----------------------------------------------
        -------- NONE --------
        ----------------------------------------------------------------
```

allows us to answer such questions as: How would profits be affected if we could find a way to make more fabrication hours available? Z would change by $400 for each 1-hour change in the RHS, but does Z go up or down when the RHS goes up? Table 8.5 provides rules that indicate how Z changes with changes in the RHS.

Because the first constraint is a $\leq$ constraint, there is no slack on the constraint because $S_1 = 0$, and it is a maximization problem: Z would go up if the RHS goes up and Z would go down if the RHS goes down. If more fabrication hours were available, Z would go up by $400 for each additional hour of fabrication made available. If the RHS were reduced by 1 hour, Z would go down by $400. But this explanation is valid only if the RHS remains in the 2,500 to 5,500 range. If the RHS is outside this range, the impact on Z cannot be deduced, and we would have to reformulate the problem again with the new RHS and solve the problem again.

The explanation of the shadow price for the second constraint is similarly deduced. Z would increase by $100 for each 1-hour increase in the RHS of 5,000 assembly hours,

Table 8.5	Changes in Z with Changes in the RHS

Type of Constraint	How Does RHS Change?	Is There Slack on Constraint?	How Does Z Change?	
			Max Z	Min Z
$\leq$	Up	No	Up	Down
$\leq$	Down	No	Down	Up
$\leq$	Up or down	Yes	No change	No change
$\geq$	Up	No	Down	Up
$\geq$	Down	No	Up	Down
$\geq$	Up or down	Yes	No change	No change

or Z would decrease by \$100 for each 1-hour decrease in the RHS of 5,000 assembly hours. This explanation is valid only if the RHS remains in the 2,000 to 6,500 range.

The shadow price of the third constraint is zero, which means that Z will not change with upward (3,000 to + infinity) changes to the RHS of the third constraint. This follows because $S_3 = 500$, which means that we have unused market and increasing the market will not change Z.

For decision variables, the shadow prices indicate the change in Z if one unit of a nonbasic decision variable (an X variable that is not in the variable mix column or basis) is forced into the solution. Because both decision variables (X_1 and X_2) are in the basis above, there are no other decision variables to force into the solution. If there were, because Z is optimal, introducing any other X variable into the solution would cause Z to become less optimal (profits would fall or costs would increase) by the amount of the shadow price for each unit introduced in the solution.

LP-1 had only $\leq$ constraints. You may wonder how we would interpret a computer solution of an LP problem with $\geq$ constraints. Consider the first constraint of LP-2 from Example 8.2:

$$X_1 + 2X_2 \geq 4$$

This constraint represents the minimum daily number of tons of lead that must be provided. This constraint is converted to an equality by the introduction of S_1, where once again the subscript 1 refers to the first constraint:

$$X_1 + 2X_2 \qquad \geq 4$$
$$X_1 + 2X_2 \qquad = 4 + S_1$$
$$X_1 + 2X_2 - S_1 = 4$$

Notice that S_1 is added to the smaller side of the expression, which is the right side, to convert the expression to an equality. Also, note that S_1 is then subtracted from both sides to allow all the variables to appear on the left-hand side. By looking at the middle expression above, we can see that S_1 represents the tons of lead that are provided above the minimum of 4 tons. If the minimum of 4 tons is provided, $S_1 = 0$. As S_1 is allowed to take on larger values, a surplus of lead is provided above the 4-ton minimum. Thus, when a constraint is of the $\geq$ type, a slack variable represents the amount of the constraint that is provided above the minimum. If the RHS of the first constraint of LP-2 increased and $S_1 = 0$, because it is a $\geq$ constraint and LP-2 is a minimization problem Table 8.5 indicates that Z would go up by the amount of its shadow price. Similarly, if its RHS decreased, Z would go down by the amount of its shadow price.

In some computer solutions, artificial variables (A1) may appear. They have no interpretive value within the scope of this book.

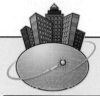

Wrap-Up

WHAT WORLD-CLASS COMPANIES DO

Today, perhaps more than ever before, operations managers understand that most decisions must be made and objectives achieved within constraints imposed on organizations. Customer demand for products and services, limited production resources, government regulations, quality requirements, and technological limitations are examples of constraints in POM. Within these and other constraints, managers seek to accomplish their operations strategies. At world-class companies, managers at all levels use the power of linear programming and other analysis tools to solve complex, constrained business problems. But we see some variation in the ways that managers choose to employ these versatile tools.

For some companies, formal departments are established that may be called *operations research, management science,* or *operations analysis departments.* These departments are staffed with analysts who have a special knowledge of LP and other mathematical techniques and the ability to apply them to organizational problems.

Another way that world-class companies may choose to use LP is to employ consultants to advise them on how best to approach their constrained decisions and how to design their computer hardware and software. A few resident analysts may be dispersed throughout the organization in functional departments. This organizational arrangement provides a sparse *network of analysts* to analyze LP problems as needed. Computer software may be purchased and used with only minor modifications by these analysts to solve recurring-type LP problems. Consultants may be needed from time to time to assist the analysts in formulating and solving LP problems to support strategic management decisions. Many petroleum refineries choose to use this organizational arrangement.

LP is applied to both strategic, one-of-a-kind, long-range decisions and short-range, recurring decisions. Both types can be of strategic importance in equipping a company for competition in a highly competitive industry. Deciding how to allocate scarce production capacity and capital among new products in a five-year plan and deciding where to locate a new production facility are examples of how LP can be used in long-range strategic decisions. The use of LP in medium- or short-range planning can also be of strategic importance because of its huge savings. Some examples of its use are American Airlines' monthly scheduling of airplanes in Business Snapshot 8.2, determining the right mix of ingredients in petroleum refining, finding the best shipping plan between factories and warehouses, formulating a production plan for a manufacturer, and assigning research teams to new-product development projects.

Whether a formal department or a network of analysts is chosen, the cost can be significant. For example, the group within American Airlines includes about 150 analysts. But the cost of not having such a group is just too great, for if timely and near-optimal solutions to constrained problems cannot be obtained, it is only a short distance between being a world-class company and being an also-ran in the race to capture world markets.

REVIEW AND DISCUSSION QUESTIONS

1. What are production system resources?
2. What effects do scarce resources have on POM today?
3. Name five common types of constrained decisions in POM. Briefly describe each.
4. Define *objective function, constraint function, decision variable, objective function value, maximization LP problem, and minimization LP problem.*
5. Name four characteristics of LP problems.
6. Name eight steps in formulating, or setting up, LP problems.
7. Name four solution methods to LP problems.
8. Describe the elements of a transportation LP problem.
9. Which LP solution method is used most often in POM? Why?
10. Why is the graphical method almost never used for real LP problems in POM?

INTERNET ASSIGNMENTS

1. Search the Internet to find a software package not mentioned in this chapter that will solve linear programming problems. Describe the features of this software.
2. The Institute for Operations Research and the Management Sciences (INFORMS) maintains a web site at **http://www.informs.org**. Locate the web page for professional opportunities or jobs. Find an operations research–related position announcement that you would be interested in and summarize this.
3. Frontline Systems Inc. produces the *Solver* software module within Microsoft Excel. Go to Frontline Systems' web site at **http://www.frontsys.com** and describe the features of the latest version of *Premium Solver.*
4. Search the Internet for a consulting company that specializes in operations research, management science, or operations analysis tools. Describe the services it provides.

PROBLEMS

LP-A. Montana Wood Products manufacturers two high-quality products, chairs and bookshelf units. Its profit is $15 per chair and $21 per bookshelf unit. Next week's production will be constrained by two limited resources, labor and wood. The labor available next week is expected to be 920 labor hours, and the amount of wood available is expected to be 2,400 board feet. Each chair requires 4 labor hours and 8 board feet of wood. Each bookshelf unit requires 3 labor hours and 12 board feet of wood. Management would like to produce at least 100 units of each product.

     a.   To maximize total profit, how many chairs and bookshelf units should be produced next week?

     b.   How much profit will result?

LP-B. The Ohio Creek Ice Cream Company is planning its production output for next week. Demand for Ohio Creek premium and light ice cream continues to outpace the company's production capacities. Ohio Creek earns a profit of $100 per hundred gallons of premium and $100 per hundred gallons of light ice cream. Two resources used in ice cream production are in short supply for next week: the capacity of the mixing machine and the amount of high-grade milk. After accounting for required maintenance time, the mixing machine will be available 140 hours next week. One hundred gallons of premium ice cream requires 0.3 hour of mixing, and one hundred gallons of light ice cream requires 0.5 hour of mixing. Only 28,000 gallons of high-grade milk will be available for next week. One hundred gallons of premium ice cream requires 90 gallons of milk, and one hundred gallons of light ice cream requires 70 gallons of milk.

a. To maximize total profit next week, how many hundreds of gallons of premium and light ice cream should Ohio Creek produce during that period?

b. How much profit will result?

LP-C. Harkin Electronics is planning its production next quarter for its two product lines, relays and capacitors. The profit contribution is $250 for a case of relays and $200 for a case of capacitors. Three resources limit how much of each product the company can produce: labor, stamping capacity, and testing capacity. Next quarter 80,000 labor hours will be available; a case of relays requires 200 labor hours and a case of capacitors requires 150. The stamping machine will be available for 1,200 hours next quarter, and a case of relays requires 4 hours on the stamping machine and a case of capacitors requires 2 hours. Relays require 3 hours of testing per case and capacitors require 5. The testing machine will be available for 2,000 hours next quarter.

a. To maximize total profit next quarter, how many cases of relays and capacitors should Harkin Electronics produce during that period?

b. How much profit will result?

LP-D. The Sureset Concrete Company produces concrete in a continuous process. Two ingredients in the concrete are sand, which Sureset purchases for $6 per ton, and gravel, which costs $8 per ton. Sand and gravel together must make up exactly 75 percent of the weight of the concrete. Furthermore, no more than 40 percent of the concrete can be sand, and at least 30 percent of the concrete must be gravel. Each day 2,000 tons of concrete are produced.

a. How many tons of sand and gravel should Sureset plan on purchasing each day so that the total cost is minimized?

b. What will be the total cost of sand and gravel each day?

LP-E. Nutrifeed, a hog feedlot operation near Omaha, Nebraska, blends ingredients to make low-cost feeds for its hogs. Oats and corn are the principal ingredients of the hog feed. The current costs for oats and corn are 12 and 7 cents per pound, respectively. Nutrifeed requires a minimum of 3,000 mineral units, 4,000 calories, and 2,000 units of vitamins per day for each hog. Each pound of oats supplies 200 mineral units, 200 calories, and 100 units of vitamins. Each pound of corn supplies 100 mineral units, 300 calories, and 200 units of vitamins. How many pounds of oats and corn should be fed to each hog per day to minimize feed cost?

LP-F. EcoPaper, Ltd., a Canadian manufacturer of environmentally friendly toilet paper, produces cases of its product at three paper mills and ships the product to four warehouses across Canada. The shipping cost per case, the monthly warehouse requirements, and the monthly mill production levels are:

		Destination			Monthly Mill Production (cases)
	A	**B**	**C**	**D**	
Mill 1	$7.90	$4.70	$3.20	$8.30	32,000
Mill 2	6.10	8.70	4.50	7.60	40,000
Mill 3	5.40	6.60	7.10	5.00	25,000
Monthly Warehouse Requirement (cases)	30,000	18,000	22,000	27,000	

How many cases of toilet paper should be shipped per month from each mill to each warehouse to minimize monthly shipping costs?

LP-G.   Staplex, a small manufacturer that produces staples, is planning its production for next month. Staplex has two products, staples for office use (Product A) and staples for construction use (Product B). Profit for Product A is $64 per case, and profit for Product B is $87 per case. The three main departments at the manufacturing plant are cutting, trimming, and coating. In the production process, metal wire is first cut to the proper length, then trimmed to the desired angle, then coated with corrosive protection. Each production department works two 8-hour shifts, 5 days per week. The production rates for staples in each production department are shown below.

	Production Rates of Production Departments (cases per shift)		
	Cutting	**Trimming**	**Coating**
Product A	3.2	2.0	0
Product B	2.5	4.0	1.0

How many of each product should be produced per week to maximize profits?

LP-H.   The Safari Company manufactures motor homes for the recreational vehicle market. Safari manufactures two product lines: Brave and Chief motor homes. The company is developing a production plan for next year and needs to know the number of each product to produce next year. This decision will be affected by (1) the profitability of each product, (2) the amount of scarce production capacity that each product line requires, and (3) the amount of each product line that the market will demand. After studying the decision, the analyst summed up by saying, "We want to produce the product mix that maximizes profits for the period within the production capacity and market constraints." The average contribution per product is $9,000 for each Brave and $15,000 for each Chief. The production capacity is constrained by two factors—labor and machine capacity. Because of labor agreements with the workforce, a maximum of 240,000 labor hours is available next year to manufacture the two product lines. Each Brave requires an average of 80 labor hours to manufacture, and each Chief requires an average of 100 labor hours. A maximum of 95,000 machine hours is available next year in the body molding process, the manufacturing operation that controls the maximum number of products that can be produced. Each Brave requires an average of 25 hours of machine time, and each Chief requires an average of 50 machine hours of machine time. The marketing department estimates that there is a maximum market demand next year of 2,500 motor homes for the Brave and Chief product lines combined. How many motor homes of each type should be produced next year?

LP-I.   The Superior Chemical Company manufactures carpenter's glue. The company wants to plan for the mix of ingredients that should go into the glue next year. The following information is important to this decision:

Ingredient	Cost/Pound	Mixing Instructions/Requirements
Carrier	$0.50	No more than 5 pounds can be used for each pound of adhesive agent.
Filler % Color	0.40	Maximum of 100,000 pounds is available per year from sole source supplier.
Adhesive	0.80	At least 1 pound must be used for every 5 pounds of carrier.

How much of each ingredient will provide at least 700,000 pounds of glue next year at the minimum cost?

LP-J.   The Integrated Products Corporation (IPC) is developing a monthly shipping plan for its computer systems. The following information affects this plan:

Plant	Monthly Capacity (Systems)	Warehouse	Monthly Requirements (Systems)
Atlanta	1,600	Chicago	500
El Paso	2,400	Dallas	1,000
		Denver	800
		New York	1,200
		San Jose	500

Plant	Warehouse	Shipping Cost ($/computer)	Plant	Warehouse	Shipping Cost ($/computer)
Atlanta	Chicago	$ 45	El Paso	Chicago	$ 60
	Dallas	50		Dallas	40
	Denver	70		Denver	45
	New York	55		New York	105
	San Jose	100		San Jose	50

a.   What shipping plan will minimize monthly shipping costs?
b.   What will be the monthly shipping costs of the optimal shipping plan from Part a?

Recognizing LP Problems

1. Confidence Air is a new airline company that wants to purchase a total of 35 new jets. Two types of jets are being considered, and the company's top management team must decide how many of each type to purchase. Because passenger ticket revenues and fuel costs are both important to the company's profitability, the top management team wants to choose the mix of jet types that provides the most seating capacity and that provides the lowest fuel cost. The two types of jets under consideration are the Boeing 787 and the Airbus 347. The Boeing 787 seats 165 passengers and uses 3.8 gallons of jet fuel per mile. The Airbus 347 seats 140 passengers and uses 2.9 gallons of jet fuel per mile. Total seating capacity of all jets should be at least 5,100 seats. How many of each type jet should be purchased?

a.   Review the characteristics of an LP problem listed in Table 8.2, and determine if this problem meets each characteristic.

b.   Is LP appropriate to use in this problem?

2.   GlideEasy Inc. manufacturers two models of automated wheelchairs, Model A and Model B. Demand for the two wheelchair models has increased dramatically in the past year, and future demand looks even greater. The production manager must decide how many of each model to produce next month. The profit of Model A is $136 per unit, and the profit of Model B is $179 per unit. Each Model A requires 14 labor hours and 19 pounds of steel alloy. Each Model B requires 26 labor hours and 28 pounds of steel alloy. How many units of each model should be produced next month in order to maximize total profit?

a.   Review the characteristics of an LP problem listed in Table 8.2, and determine if this problem meets each characteristic.

b.   Is LP appropriate to use in this problem?

Formulating LP Problems

3.   Formulate the objective function and constraint functions for Problem LP-A of this section. Define the decision variables.

4.   Formulate the objective function and constraint functions for Problem LP-B of this section. Define the decision variables.

5.   Formulate the objective function and constraint functions for Problem LP-C of this section. Define the decision variables.

6.   Formulate the objective function and constraint functions for Problem LP-D of this section. Define the decision variables.

7.   Formulate the objective function and constraint functions for Problem LP-E of this section. Define the decision variables.

8.   Formulate the objective function and constraint functions for Problem LP-F of this section. Define the decision variables.

9.   Formulate the objective function and constraint functions for Problem LP-G of this section. Define the decision variables.

10.   Formulate the objective function and constraint functions for Problem LP-H of this section. Define the decision variables.

11.   Formulate the objective function and constraint functions for Problem LP-I of this section. Define the decision variables.

12.   Formulate the objective function and constraint functions for Problem LP-J of this section. Define the decision variables.

Solving LP Problems Graphically

13.   Solve Problem LP-A graphically. What is the optimal solution? Explain what the solution means in terms of the original problem.

14.   Solve Problem LP-B graphically. What is the optimal solution? Explain what the solution means in terms of the original problem.

15.   Solve Problem LP-C graphically. What is the optimal solution? Explain what the solution means in terms of the original problem.

16. Solve Problem LP-D graphically. What is the optimal solution? Explain what the solution means in terms of the original problem.

17. Solve Problem LP-E graphically. What is the optimal solution? Explain what the solution means in terms of the original problem.

18. Solve Problem LP-G graphically. What is the optimal solution? Explain what the solution means in terms of the original problem.

19. Solve Problem LP-H graphically. What is the optimal solution? Explain what the solution means in terms of the original problem.

Solving LP Problems with a Computer

20. Use the *POM Software Library* or another computer software package to solve the LP problems listed below. A description of how to interpret computer solutions of LP problems can be found in this chapter. Explain the meaning of each solution in managerial language. Explain the meaning of the constraint and nonbasic variable shadow prices.

a.	LP-A	d.	LP-D	g.	LP-G	i.	LP-I
b.	LP-B	e.	LP-E	h.	LP-H	j.	LP-J
c.	LP-C	f.	LP-F				

CASES

Quality Pixels Inc.

Quality Pixels Inc. (QPI) manufactures high-end digital monitors for computers. QPI is a global company with manufacturing plants in Mexico City, Seoul, Hong Kong, and Warsaw, and warehouses in Bangkok, Shanghai, São Paulo, Dallas, Madrid, and Cairo. The table below shows the transportation cost per pallet of monitors from each plant to each warehouse, the maximum and minimum annual warehouse requirements, and the maximum annual capacity of each plant (all in pallets). QPI wishes to ship all of its plant capacity to the regional warehouses so that both the maximum and minimum annual warehouse requirements are satisfied and the annual total transportation cost is minimized.

| | Warehouse | | | | | | Maximum Annual |
Plants	Bangkok	Shanghai	São Paulo	Dallas	Madrid	Cairo	Capacity
Mexico City	$180	$160	$ 60	$ 40	$120	$150	30,000
Seoul	90	30	150	130	190	140	20,000
Hong Kong	40	35	160	150	110	125	40,000
Warsaw	80	105	95	125	60	50	50,000
Minimum Annual Warehouse Requirement	15,000	15,000	15,000	20,000	20,000	15,000	
Maximum Annual Warehouse Requirement	30,000	25,000	25,000	40,000	35,000	25,000	

Assignment

1. Formulate the information in this case into an LP format. Define the decision variables, write the objective function, and write the constraint functions.

2. Using *Excel Solver* or the LP module in the *POM Software Library* that accompanies this book, solve the problem that you have formulated in No. 1.

3. Fully interpret the meaning of the solution that you obtained in No. 2. In other words, what should QPI do? Fully explain the meaning of the slack variable values.

4. From examining the computer solution, how would costs change if the capacity of the Mexico City plant decreased to 26,000 pallets? Increased to 36,000 pallets?

5. From examining the computer solution, how would costs change if the minimum annual requirements at the Dallas warehouse decreased to 14,000 pallets? Increased to 24,000 pallets?

6. Explain the caution that must be observed in answering Nos. 4 and 5.

Integrated Products Corporation

The new-product development department of the Integrated Products Corporation (IPC) is planning next year's projects. Five new products have been selected to be developed next year. Each of the new-product projects will be assigned to a development team. Five such teams have just completed other development projects and are now ready to accept their new assignments. Because each team is made up of persons with unique abilities and experiences, and because each project requires persons with unique abilities and experiences, certain teams are better suited for assignment to certain projects. While every team could complete all the projects, certain team–project matchups will be less efficient, take longer, and cost more money. Here is the estimated cost of each team completing each project:

| | **New-Product Development Team** | | | | |
Project	1 ($000)	2 ($000)	3 ($000)	4 ($000)	5 ($000)
A	152	120	165	139	169
B	49	65	55	50	60
C	65	55	60	45	65
D	75	85	69	81	79
E	120	122	125	136	119

Which project should be assigned to each team to minimize the total cost of next year's new-product development budget?

Assignment

1. Formulate this case into an LP problem. Define the decision variables, write the objective function, and write the constraint functions.

2. Using the LP computer program in the *POM Software Library* that accompanies this book, solve the problem that you formulated in No. 1.

3. Fully interpret the meaning of the solution that you obtained in No. 2. In other words, what should management at IPC do?

4. How would the solution change if further analysis resulted in increasing the development cost of Project C by Team 2 from $55,000 to $65,000? With the new information, to which teams would the projects be assigned?

5. Explain the caution that must be observed in answering No. 4.

Jane Deere Company

The Jane Deere Company manufactures tractors in Provo, Utah. Jeremiah Goldstein, the production planner, is scheduling tractor production for the next three months. Factors that Mr. Goldstein must consider include sales forecasts, straight-time and overtime labor hours available, labor cost, storage capacity, and carrying cost. The marketing department has forecast that the number of tractors shipped during the next three months will be 250, 305, and 350. Each tractor requires 100 labor hours to produce. In each month 29,000 straight-time labor hours will be available, and company policy prohibits overtime hours from exceeding 10% of straight-time hours. Straight-time labor cost rate is $20 per hour, including benefits. The overtime labor cost rate is 150% (time and a half) of the straight-time rate. Excess production capacity during a month may be used to produce tractors that will be stored and sold during a later month. However, the amount of storage space can accommodate only 40 tractors. A carrying cost of $600 is charged for each month a tractor is stored (if not shipped during the month it was produced). Currently, no tractors are in storage.

How many tractors should be produced in each month using straight time and using overtime in order to minimize total labor cost and carrying cost? Sales forecasts, straight-time and overtime labor capacities, and storage capacity must be adhered to (*Tip:* During each month, all "sources" of tractors must exactly equal "uses" of tractors.)

Assignment

1. Formulate the information in this case into an LP model. Define the decision variables, write the objective function, and write the constraint functions.

2. Use the LP computer program in the *POM Software Library* to solve this problem.

3. Fully interpret the meaning of the solution you obtained in No. 2. In other words, explain in simple terms what Mr. Goldstein should recommend. Fully explain the meaning of the slack variable values.

(Answer Nos. 4, 5, and 6 from your computer printout of the original problem.)

4. If the demand forecast for Month 1 was 260 instead of 250, by how much would total cost change?

5. If the storage capacity at the end of the second month was 35 instead of 40, by how much would total cost change?

6. If the available straight-time labor hours in Month 2 were 28,200 instead of 29,000, by how much would total cost change? If they were 29,800 instead of 29,000?

7. Explain the caution that must be observed in answering Nos. 4, 5, and 6.

SELECTED BIBLIOGRAPHY

Al-Shammari, Minwir, and Isaam Dawood. "Linear Programming Applied to a Production Blending Problem: A Spreadsheet Modeling Approach." *Production & Inventory Management Journal* 38, no. 1 (1997): 1–7.

Ambs, Ken, Sebastian Cwilich, Mei Deng, and David J. Houck. "Optimizing Restoration Capacity in the AT&T Network." *Interfaces* 30, no. 1 (2000): 26–44.

Anderson, David R., Dennis J. Sweeney, and Thomas A. Williams. *An Introduction to Management Science: Quantitative Approaches to Decision Making,* 9th ed. Cincinnati, OH: South-Western College Publishing, 2000.

Anderson, Randy I., Robert Fok, and John Scott. "Hotel Industry Efficiency: An Advanced Linear Programming Examination." *American Business Review* 18, no. 1 (January 2000): 40–48.

Camm, Jeff, and James R. Evans. *Management Science and Decision Technology.* Cincinnati, OH: South-Western College Publishing, 2000.

Chakravarti, Nilotpal. "Tea Company Steeped in OR." *OR/MS Today* 27, no. 2 (April 2000): 32–34.

Gotlob, David, James S. Moore, and Kim S. Moore. "Optimizing Internal Audit Resources: A Linear Programming Perspective." *Internal Auditing* 13, no. 2 (Fall 1997): 20–30.

Guven, S., and E. Persentili. "A Linear Programming Model for Bank Balance Sheet Management." *Omega* 25, no. 4 (August 1997): 449–459.

Hillier, Frederick S., and Gerald J. Lieberman. *Introduction to Operations Research.* New York: McGraw-Hill, 2001.

Hooker, J. N. "Karmarkar's Linear Programming Algorithm." *Interfaces* 16, no. 4 (1986): 75–90.

Kolman, Bernard, and Robert E. Beck. *Elementary Linear Programming with Applications,* 2nd ed. San Diego: Academic Press, 1995.

Mason, Richard O., James L. McKenney, Walter Carlson, and Duncan Copeland. "Absolutely, Positively Operations Research: The Federal Express Story." *Interfaces* 27, no. 2 (March–April 1997): 17–36.

Moore, Jeffrey H., and Larry R. Weatherford. *Decision Modeling with Microsoft Excel,* 6th ed. Upper Saddle River, NJ: Prentice Hall, 2001.

Ragsdale, Cliff. *Spreadsheet Modeling and Decision Analysis,* 3rd ed. Cincinnati, OH: South-Western College Publishing, 2001.

Vanderbei, Robert J. "Linear Programming: A Modern Integrated Analysis." *Interfaces* 27, no. 2 (March–April 1997): 120–122.

© SUSAN VAN ETTEN

Service Operations Planning and Scheduling

Introduction
Nature of Services Revisited
Operations Strategies for Services
Types of Service Operations
Scheduling Challenges in Services

Scheduling Quasi-Manufacturing Service Operations
Product-Focused Operations
Process-Focused Operations
Work-Shift Scheduling in Service Operations

Scheduling Customer-as-Participant Service Operations
Nature of These Operations
Waiting Lines in Service Operations

Scheduling Customer-as-Product Service Operations
Nature of These Operations
Using Computer Simulation in Service Operations

Wrap-Up: What World-Class Companies Do

Review and Discussion Questions

Internet Assignments

Problems

Cases
Precision Calibration Services Company
Cincinnati Trucking Inc.

Selected Bibliography

EMPLOYEE SCHEDULING AT TEXAS GROCERY

The Texas Grocery store is located in northwest Houston, Texas. The store employs a total of 235 personnel to provide 24-hour service to its customers. The store is a complete superstore with departments ranging from bakery goods to pharmacy to nonfood items. There are personnel associates for operating cash registers at checkout counters, sacking groceries, stocking shelves, driving forklift trucks in the warehouse, counting inventories, ordering stock, dispensing pharmaceuticals, greeting customers, carrying out customers' purchases, cleaning, maintenance, managing departments, accounting, working on special projects, baking, and other duties.

Scheduling of personnel to work shifts during the week is complicated by two main factors: nonuniform demand and employee preferences. The volume of customer traffic is not uniform. Demand varies by day of the week, hour of the day, and even day of the month, with the days leading up to holidays being particularly busy. Demand tends to be heaviest on Friday, Saturday, and Sunday and lightest on Wednesday. The hours around 8:00 a.m. and 4:00 p.m. tend to be heaviest during the week, and midmorning, around lunchtime, and early evening tend to be heaviest on weekends.

The company has several policies that affect personnel shift scheduling. (1) Each employee shall work five 8-hour shifts during each week. (2) Each employee shall have two consecutive days off during each week. (3) Each employee shall rotate from day to evening to night shifts on a monthly basis. (4) Employee preference for shifts will be honored. If conflicts occur, pay grade and time in grade will be used to allocate preferred shifts.

Considering the nonuniform demand and the company policies, the store manager and assistant manager must develop work-shift schedules for the 235 employees for next month.

The preceding account illustrates some of the complexity present in scheduling service operations. In earlier chapters we studied service operations alongside manufacturing as we examined a variety of topics and decisions in POM. We took such an approach because it was thought to be the best way to understand the similarities and differences of manufacturing and services. In this chapter, however, we confine our study to the planning, scheduling, and controlling of service operations. By focusing only on service operations, we provide a more in-depth understanding of the unique properties of managing service operations.

Nature of Services Revisited

Before studying the planning and controlling of service operations, let us summarize some of what we have learned about services. This will allow us to better understand the nature of scheduling these diverse operations.

In Table 2.7 in Chapter 2, the nature of services was summarized and compared with manufacturing. Services were described as operations with:

- Intangible outputs that cannot be inventoried
- Close customer contact
- Short lead times

- High labor costs relative to capital costs; that is, labor intensive
- Subjectively determined quality

The discussion surrounding Table 2.7 emphasized that while the summary is accurate for many services, as often as not, the great diversity among services makes such a summary misleading. What is worse, such a summary can lead to misconceptions about services. Table 9.1 lists some misconceptions about services.

The number of service jobs has been steadily increasing during the past two decades. In the United States, a clear shift is occurring in the types of jobs available. Table 9.2 shows this shift from manufacturing to service jobs, based on data from the Bureau of Labor Statistics (**http://stats.bls.gov**).

Some of the largest corporations in the United States are service businesses. AT&T, Wal-Mart, Citigroup, State Farm, SBC Communications, and Sears, Roebuck & Company, to name a few, all rank in the top 20 U.S. corporations. These huge, global, publicly owned companies span the spectrum of service businesses—airlines, banking, retailing, health care, trucking, entertainment, insurance, real estate, telephone, utilities, and so on. Service industries export around $300 billion of services annually with a growing annual trade surplus of about $80 billion. Well, you get the picture; they are big, global, and diverse. And many of them are capital intensive and use automation and high technology extensively. In fact, the capital investment per employee for office workers now exceeds that of workers in manufacturing. And many employees in services are highly paid and technically trained; over one-half of service employees have white-collar jobs. With 5 times as many employees as in manufacturing, the average hourly wage of service employees is only 10 percent less than in goods-producing industries. The high-technology nature of such service businesses as telecommunications,

Table 9.1	Some Common Misconceptions about Services

- Service businesses are one-owner mom and pop neighborhood businesses.
- Service businesses are retail or fast-food drive-ins.
- Services are labor intensive and require little capital investment.
- Automation and new technologies do not affect services as much as manufacturing.
- Employees in services flip hamburgers, bus tables, or wait on customers, and they earn the minimum wage.
- Employees who work in services need a pleasant personality and need training only in selling and interpersonal relations.
- Few engineers, scientists, and other technically trained persons work in services.
- The U.S. service sector is highly profitable, and the downsizing and cutbacks in manufacturing in recent years have not been experienced in services.

Table 9.2	Percentage of Manufacturing and Service Jobs in the U.S.

	PERCENTAGE OF U.S. JOBS		
	1988	**1998**	**2008 (projected)**
Manufacturing jobs	16.1%	13.4%	11.6%
Service jobs	66.2	70.8	73.9

airlines, and utilities creates the need for engineers, scientists, and other technically trained employees.

A list of things to remember when thinking of service businesses follows.

- There is enormous diversity among services.
- Service businesses can be huge, tiny, or anywhere in between, just as in manufacturing.
- There are more than twice as many nonretail service businesses as there are retail service businesses.
- Although interpersonal relations abilities are important in services (or in manufacturing, for that matter), the fact is that technical training, computers, automation, and technology play an important part in most services.

Incorrect Alie ⎯⎯⟶
- Most workers in services are well paid relative to those in manufacturing.
- Service businesses need better planning, controlling, and management to ward off competition to survive and prosper.

No clear, clean line separates manufacturing on one side and services on the other. Customer service dominates some manufacturing businesses, and some service businesses behave and are managed just like manufacturing. Every business, whether manufacturing or services, has a mix of customer service on the one hand and materials, transportation, warehousing, technology, and production on the other. Therefore, manufacturing has a lot to learn from services that excel in customer service, and services have a lot to learn from manufacturers that excel in production.

The demarcation between manufacturing and services is fuzzy in many cases. If we are to better plan, control, and manage services, it is important that we develop logical paradigms, guidelines that structure the way we think about these diverse service operations. Product-focused and process-focused operations from manufacturing combine with quasi-manufacturing, customer-as-participant, and customer-as-product service operations to form a useful paradigm for planning and controlling production operations. If the U.S. service sector is to continue to prosper, like manufacturing, it must continue to improve quality, cost, and customer service. The day-to-day planning and controlling of operations is crucial to this improvement.

With this background discussion about the nature of services, let us now review operations strategy in services, because strategy drives the day-to-day planning and controlling of operations.

Operations Strategies for Services

In Chapter 2, we discussed positioning strategies for services, those long-term plans for capturing market share. Positioning strategies for services contain two elements, type of service design and type of production process.

already talked about
1. **Type of service design,** with three dimensions—standard or custom, amount of customer contact, and the mix of physical goods and intangible services.
2. **Type of production process**—quasi-manufacturing, customer-as-participant, and customer-as-product.

A firm's business strategy determines the type of service design, and the type of service design determines the type of production process. The ways that companies plan, schedule, and control service operations depend on the type of production process. Therefore, the discussion of scheduling service operations in this chapter is built around these types of service operations.

Types of Service Operations

There are three types of service operations—quasi-manufacturing, customer-as-participant, and customer-as-product.

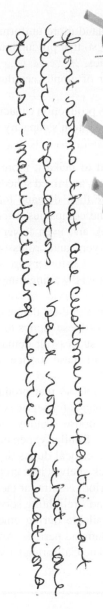

1. **Quasi-manufacturing.** In this type of service operation, production occurs much as in manufacturing. The emphasis is on production costs, technology, physical materials and products, product quality, and prompt delivery. Physical goods are dominant over intangible services, products may be either standard or custom, and there is little customer contact or involvement. The back-room operations at banks, industrial heat-treating services, and aircraft maintenance operations are examples of this type of service operation.

2. **Customer-as-participant.** There is a high degree of customer involvement in this type of service operation. Physical goods may or may not be a significant part of the service, and the services may be either custom or standard. Retailing is an example of this type of service operation.

3. **Customer-as-product.** In this type of service operation, customers are so involved that the service is actually performed on the customer. Physical goods may or may not be a significant part of the service, and the services are usually custom. Examples of this type of service operation are hair salons, medical clinics and hospitals, and tailors.

It is important to understand that these classifications of service operations are not mutually exclusive. It is not uncommon to find all three types of operations within one company. We frequently find two of the three types in one company. For instance, a McDonald's restaurant will have a quasi-manufacturing operation in the back room and a customer-as-participant operation in the front room. Banks, stock brokerages, restaurants, libraries, auto repair shops, and laundries also have front rooms that are customer-as-participant service operations and back rooms that are quasi-manufacturing service operations. And just as a manufacturing business can have a product-focused operation and a process-focused operation working side-by-side, one or more of these types of service operations can also be found within manufacturing businesses.

The occurrence of these types of service operations is so widespread that learning how to better plan and control these operations can have a great impact.

Scheduling Challenges in Services

Two predominant characteristics of service operations make planning and controlling day-to-day activities challenging:

1. Services are produced and delivered by people—men, women, teenagers, persons, workers, employees, personnel, or human resources, whichever term you prefer.
2. The pattern of demand for services is nonuniform.

Because the demand for services varies from hour to hour, day to day, and week to week throughout the year, the key challenge is to vary production capacity to satisfy this changing pattern of demand. For most service businesses, varying the size of the work force becomes the key way to rapidly change production capacity. Operations managers strive to vary the size of the workforce to meet nonuniform demand so that there is a reasonable balance between the costs of production and customer satisfaction. If too many employees are scheduled to work during any time period, costs are too high. If too few employees are scheduled, customer satisfaction suffers.

[handwritten margin notes: "Pre-emptive Packets", "example airlines raise price during peak time", "Bank- do this"]

Dealing with Nonuniform Demand

Because services cannot ordinarily be inventoried during low demand periods to be used in peak demand periods, service operations have developed other tactics to deal with nonuniform demand. Some of these approaches are:

- Develop preemptive actions that attempt to make demand more uniform.
- Use tactics that make service operations more flexible so that production capacity can be quickly increased or decreased as demand varies.
- Anticipate demand patterns and schedule the number of employees during each time period to meet the anticipated demand.
- Let waiting lines form when customer demand exceeds production capacity. In this approach, waiting lines level out demand and allow a system's capacity to be relatively uniform.

Several tactics have been used to manipulate demand to make it more uniform. Among these are off-peak incentives, appointment schedules, and fixed schedules. Off-peak incentives are offered to motivate customers to move their demand for services from peak hours to off-peak hours. For instance, telephone companies offer reduced rates for calls made after working hours during the week and even lower rates are charged for calls made on weekends. Doctors, dentists, lawyers, and professors require customers to make advance appointments for their services. Customers are scheduled for appointments with the dual objectives of reducing customers' waiting time and helping the service maintain a uniform production capacity. Other service operations, such as airlines, have fixed departure schedules. Customers arrange their demand patterns to fit the schedules or they do not fly with the airline. All of these tactics to make demand for services more uniform have been only partially successful; demand is less volatile but, nonetheless, still nonuniform. In the end, all of these service operations must devise ways of dealing with nonuniform demand.

There are ways of making service systems more flexible so that production capacity can be quickly increased or reduced as customer demands for services vary. One way is to use part-time personnel, subcontractors, and in-house standby facilities to augment production capacity during peak demand periods. Similarly, personnel ordinarily assigned to one duty can be assigned to other, more critical duties during peak demand periods. For instance, workers who ordinarily stock shelves in a grocery store could sack and carry out groceries during peak demand periods. A similar tactic is also used in emergency service operations such as ambulance and firefighting services. Full crews are scheduled round-the-clock so that they are available during emergencies. Then the crews perform nonemergency work during low demand periods. An example of this approach is illustrated in Figure 9.1 and Table 9.3. The California City Fire De-

Figure 9.1	Crew Schedules of California City Fire Department

JULY	S	M	T	W	T	F	S	S	M	T	W	T	F	S	S	M	T	W	T	F	S	S	M	T	W	T	F	S	S	M	T
	1	2	3	4	5	6	7	8	9	10	11	12	13	14	15	16	17	18	19	20	21	22	23	24	25	26	27	28	29	30	31
Crew A																															
Crew B																															
Crew C																															

Note: Shaded squares indicate a 24-hour shift.

Table 9.3	California City Fire Department Monthly Activity Schedule—July

			STATION 1		STATION 2		STATION 3		STATION 4		STATION 5	
Day	Cmdr.	Shift	AM	PM	AM	PM	AM	PM	AM	PM	AM	PM
SUN 01	C2	B	SM	SM	SM	SM	SM	SM	SM	SM	SM	FB
MON 02	C5	A	FM	FM	FM	FM	FM	FM	FM	FM	FM	FM
TUE 03	C2	B	HM	HM	HM	HM	HM	HM	HM	HM	HM	HM
WED 04	C3	C	PC	PC	PC	PC	PC	PC	PC	PC	PC	PC
THU 05	C2	B	FP	FP	FP	FP	FP	FP	FP	FP	FP	FP
FRI 06	C3	C	DS	DS	CD	CD	DS	DS	FP	FP	FP	FP
SAT 07	C2	B	EM	EM	EM	EM	EM	EM	EM	EM	EM	FB
SUN 08	C3	C	SD	SM	SD	SM	SD	SM	SD	SM	FB	SM
MON 09	C5	A	FP	FP	FP	FP	FP	FP	FP	FP	FP	FP
TUE 10	C3	C	FP	FP	DS	DS	CD	CD	DS	DS	CD	CD
WED 11	C5	A	SM	SM	SM	SM	SM	SM	SM	SM	SM	SM
THU 12	C2	B	FP	FP	FP	FP	HM	HM	HM	HM	FP	FP
FRI 13	C5	A	SD	SD	HM	HM	SD	SD	CD	CD	SD	SD
SAT 14	C2	B	PC	PC	PC	PC	PC	PC	PC	PC	PC	PC
SUN 15	C5	A	CD	CD	SD	SD	CD	CD	SD	SD	FB	FB
MON 16	C2	B	PC	PC	PC	PC	PC	PC	PC	PC	PC	PC
TUE 17	C3	C	HM	HM	FP	FP	HM	HM	HM	HM	DS	DS
WED 18	C2	B	EM	EM	EM	EM	EM	EM	EM	EM	DS	DS
THU 19	C3	C	SD	SD	SD	SD	SD	SD	SD	SD	SD	SD
FRI 20	C5	A	HM	HM	CD	CD	EM	EM	EM	EM	CD	CD
SAT 21	C3	C	PC	PC	EM	EM	EM	EM	PC	PC	PC	PC
SUN 22	C5	A	SD	SM	SD	SM	SD	SM	SD	SM	FB	SM
MON 23	C3	C	FP	FP	FP	FP	FP	FP	FP	FP	FP	FP
TUE 24	C5	A	CD	CD	FB	FB	CD	CD	HM	HM	HM	HM
WED 25	C2	B	FP	FP	FP	FP	FP	CD	FP	CD	FP	FP
THU 26	C5	A	FP	FP	FP	FP	HM	HM	HM	HM	FP	FP
FRI 27	C2	B	DS	DS	SD	SD	HM	HM	DS	DS	SD	SD
SAT 28	C3	C	EM	EM	EM	EM	EM	EM	EM	EM	EM	EM
SUN 29	C2	B	SM	SM	SM	SM	SM	SM	SM	SM	SM	FB
MON 30	C3	C	CD	CD	CD	CD	CD	CD	CD	CD	CD	CD
TUE 31	C2	B	SD	SD	DS	DS	DS	DS	SD	SD	SD	SD

AD—Administrative duties
CD—Captain's discretion
DS—Drill site training
FB—Fire boat training and maintenance
FH—Fire hydrants
HT—Hose testing
PC—Platoon commander's discretion
PP—Prefire plans
RT—Reserve training
ST—Simulator training

AM—Apparatus maintenance—monthly
CR—Certification training/testing
EM—Equipment maintenance
FP—Fire prevention
HM—Hydrant maintenance/service
PH—Paint/color-code hydrants
PI—Prefire inspection
PT—Pumper test
SD—Station drill
SM—Station/grounds maintenance

partment has five stations that work a total of 21 firefighting personnel in providing round-the-clock fire protection. Figure 9.1 shows how the three crews, A, B, and C, are scheduled to work 24-hour shifts. During low demand periods, the firefighters are scheduled to perform nonemergency tasks. Table 9.3 schedules some nonemergency tasks on every 24-hour shift.

In spite of attempts to manipulate customer demand to make demand more uniform, nonuniform demand persists in most service operations. To deal with this situation, many service operations attempt to plan work-shift schedules that approximately match the demand from hour to hour during business hours. And many companies allow waiting lines to form when demand exceeds production capacity. We discuss how companies use both of these approaches later in this chapter.

Now we address scheduling these types of service operations—quasi-manufacturing, customer-as-participant, and customer-as-product.

SCHEDULING QUASI-MANUFACTURING SERVICE OPERATIONS

The thing about these operations that makes them different from other service operations is that there is no involvement of customers in production. For this reason, quasi-manufacturing service operations for all practical purposes are manufacturing operations. They are designed, planned, controlled, analyzed, scheduled, and managed in the same ways as manufacturing operations. This type of service operation can be either product-focused or process-focused.

Product-Focused Operations

Some service operations resemble product-focused production lines in manufacturing. For instance, think about the back-room operations at a McDonald's restaurant. The building, machines, and workstations are designed and laid out as in a manufacturing operation. The assembly line is balanced just as in manufacturing. Issues of automation and technology are considered and evaluated just as in manufacturing. Customer demand is forecast and production capacity decisions are made just as in manufacturing. Employees are hired, trained, and supervised just as in manufacturing. Paper cartons, produce, hamburger buns, patties, and other materials are purchased, ordered for delivery, and inventoried while costs and demand patterns are considered, just as in manufacturing. High volumes of standardized products are routinely produced on a combination produce-to-stock and produce-to-order basis. Management objectives are identical to those in manufacturing—control of production costs, product quality, and prompt delivery of physical goods. And progress toward achieving these objectives can be objectively measured and evaluated just as in manufacturing. The primary scheduling concern is having the right amount of materials and personnel to produce enough products to meet the highly variable hour-to-hour customer demand. In Chapter 14, Inventory Management, we address ordering policies for such operations. Scheduling personnel to work shifts will be discussed later in this section.

Other service operations are also product-focused quasi-manufacturing service operations. For instance, consider the life insurance policy-writing process at the company headquarters of an insurance company. The customer's application for a life insurance policy is routed to several employee workstations at the company where payment is recorded, data are entered into the computer system, medical exam and history is checked, underwriters approve the policy, a policy is prepared, and finally the policy is mailed. When compared to the McDonald's back-room example above, this office service operation involves fewer physical goods and more white-collar work. But the planning, analyzing, controlling, scheduling, and managing of the operation is so familiar to manufacturing that most of what we have learned and will learn about manufacturing also applies here.

Process-Focused Operations

Just as the majority of manufacturing operations are of the process-focused type, so also are most quasi-manufacturing service operations. Consider, for instance, an industrial metallurgical service company that receives products from customers and subjects the products to metallurgical tests, treatments, and procedures. A variety of procedures are available—deep hardening, surface hardening, annealing, stress relief, radiological tests, surface crack analysis, metallurgical analyses, and so on. Each customer order specifies the nature of the service requested. Based on the customer's order, the job is routed to the appropriate departments within the company until the job is finished. The jobs are then packaged and shipped back to the customer.

Process-focused quasi-manufacturing service operations such as this are so much like job shops that they are planned, controlled, analyzed, scheduled, and managed just like job shops in manufacturing. They use forecasts to strategically design operations for production capacity, flexibility, advanced technology, and product quality. The facility layout decisions are based on the approaches discussed in Chapter 5, Facility Capacity, Location, and Layout; the principles of materials handling and materials-handling equipment, the use of templates and physical models to develop building floor plans, and analyzing layouts with computers are particularly relevant.

Ordering decisions are made according to the discussions in Chapter 14, Inventory Management, and Chapter 15, Resource Requirements Planning: MRP and CRP. And they use the same scheduling methods as we will discuss in Chapter 16:

1. Input–output control is important to balance capacity between operations. This is achieved by analyzing input–output reports.
2. Gantt charts are used to coordinate flows of jobs within and between departments.
3. Effective sequence of jobs at work centers is achieved by considering sequencing rules, changeover costs, and flow times.

All production operations, whether manufacturing or any type of service operation, must schedule personnel to work shifts.

Work-Shift Scheduling in Service Operations

One thing that all service operations have in common is that the principal means of performing services is through personnel. Three difficulties may be encountered in scheduling personnel in services: demand variability, service time variability, and availability of personnel when they are needed. Consider, for example, how many attendants you would schedule to work during each hour of each day of the week in a health club. Figure 9.2 illustrates that the number of members at the club varies drastically both throughout the day and throughout the week and that the hourly pattern of the number of members at the club varies among the days of the week. If attendants are required to assist members in their exercises, provide guidance in their exercise programs, hand out supplies, and perform other duties, the number of attendants needed in each hour of the week depends on the number of members at the club.

Because of the peaks and valleys in customer demand, operations managers often use two tactics to develop work schedules for employees. The first approach is to use full-time employees exclusively. With this arrangement, overstaffing will result in employee idle time in low demand periods. In periods of high demand, understaffing will require the use of overtime to increase capacity. These periods of overstaffing and understaffing result from the inability of managers to develop work schedules that exactly match anticipated customer demand.

When full-time employees want work schedules based on five consecutive days and eight consecutive hours per day, such situations can arise.

The other approach to developing work schedules for service systems is to use some full-time employees to form a base; then additional part-time employees are used to staff the system during peak demand periods. If the part-time employees can be

Figure 9.2 | Customer Demand Patterns for a Health Club

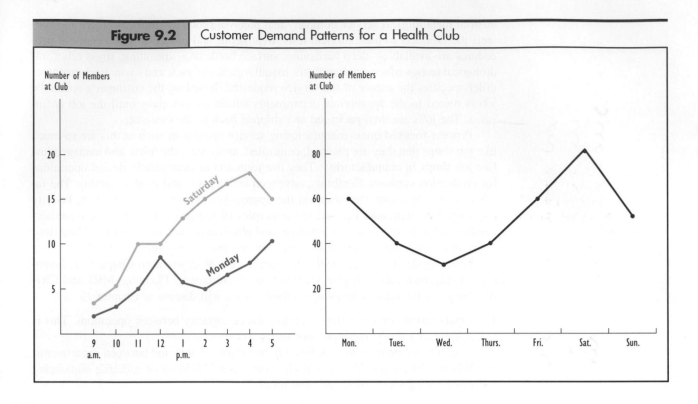

called in to work on short notice, so much the better. This approach avoids much of the planned overstaffing and understaffing in work-shift schedules, and the use of part-time employees avoids the use of overtime and waiting lines during peak demand periods. However, companies usually experience a higher turnover of part-time employees, so more effort and expense is required to hire and train new employees.

In some services, the use of appointment schedules and other efforts at leveling demand are not entirely feasible; indeed, in some cases they may be undesirable. Although it is true that leveling demand does simplify scheduling personnel, the nature of the service may dictate how much customer demand can or should be controlled. In Example 9.1, the health club that we discussed earlier is used to illustrate how appointment schedules can be used to make customer demand conform to patterns that are more conducive to personnel scheduling, even if the resulting demand pattern is not entirely uniform. In this example, we reshape the customer demand into a more manageable pattern through appointment schedules; next we determine the number of attendants required on each day of the week; and then we schedule individual workers to work shifts.

Example 9.1 | Scheduling Employees

Jose Ferdinand is studying the membership attendance records in Figure 9.2 with a view to scheduling his attendants to work shifts at the Fitness Health Club. The membership has recently voted to establish a system of appointments at the club to avoid overcrowding during certain hours of the week and to avoid the extra cost of attendant overtime that has recently been used to excess at the club. Jose knows that the number of members at the club throughout the day tends to be low in the mornings and higher in the afternoons. In spite of this hour-to-hour pattern, Jose believes that the workload on the attendants is usually uniform throughout the day because members who attend in the mornings tend to be on formal exercise programs and to require more assistance. Members who attend in the afternoons tend to participate in recreation activities and to require less assistance. Therefore, the hourly workload for attendants is approximately uniform.

Jose must now develop appointment and work-shift schedules for the attendants.

1. First, Jose converts the usage information in Figure 9.2 to the number of attendants required daily. This conversion is shown in Figure 9.3 in two ways: without appointments and with appointments.
2. Next, Jose develops the number of attendants required daily with the appointment system:

Mon.	Tues.	Wed.	Thurs.	Fri.	Sat.	Sun.	Weekly Attendant Work Shifts
6	6	6	6	10	10	10	54

Figure 9.3 | Requirements for Attendants at the Fitness Health Club

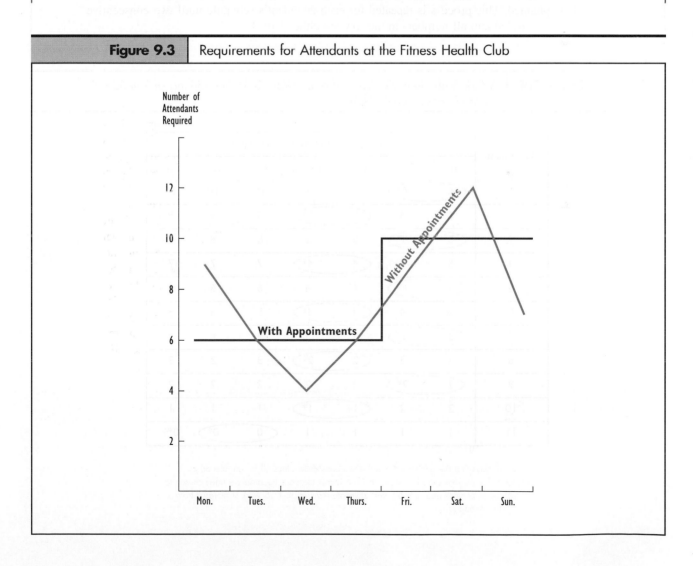

From this information Jose knows that with each attendant working five shifts per week, he will need a minimum of 11 attendants. *Minimum* means that this number may not actually be attained in practice because of the five-consecutive-workdays, two-consecutive-days-off, and eight-consecutive-hours-per-day constraint:

$$\text{Minimum number of attendants} = \frac{\text{Total number of attendant work shifts per week}}{\text{Number of work shifts per week per attendant}}$$

$$= 54/5 = 10.8, \text{ or } 11 \text{ attendants}$$

3. Next, Jose develops a work-shift schedule for the attendants. Figure 9.4 shows the procedure used to develop the work-shift schedule. This procedure uses the *work-shift heuristic rule* to determine days off for each worker:

Work-shift heuristic rule: *Choose two consecutive days with the least total number of work shifts required. In the case of ties, arbitrarily select a pair and continue.*

The number of attendant work shifts required each day when Attendant 1's schedule is planned is taken from Figure 9.3. One work shift is subtracted from Attendant 1's work shifts (Wed.–Sun.) to yield the remaining attendant work shifts required when Attendant 2's schedule is planned. This process is repeated for each attendant's schedule until two consecutive zeros are circled and all numbers in the row are either 1 or 0.

| **Figure 9.4** | Work-Shift Heuristic Procedure for Work-Shift Scheduling of Attendants at the Fitness Health Club |

Attendant	Number of Attendant Work Shifts						
	Mon.	Tues.	Wed.	Thurs.	Fri.	Sat.	Sun.
1	6	6*	6	6	10	10	10
2	6	6	5	5*	9	9	9
3	5	5*	5	5	8	8	8
4	5	5	4	4*	7	7	7
5	4	4*	4	4	6	6	6
6	4	4	3	3*	5	5	5
7	3	3*	3	3	4	4	4
8	3	3	2	2*	3	3	3
9	2	2*	2	2	2	2	2
10	2	2	1	1*	1	1	1
11	1	1	1	1	0	0*	0**

*The pairs of days that are circled indicate the two consecutive days off for an attendant.

**This day will have one extra attendant. This is unavoidable slack because we have chosen to use all full-time employees and only 54 work shifts are required, but 55 work shifts result from employing 11 attendants.

4. Next, from Figure 9.4 Jose can now determine the shifts that each attendant will be scheduled to work during each week:

Attendant	Workdays	Days Off	Attendant	Workdays	Days Off
1	Wed.–Sun.	Mon.–Tues.	7	Wed.–Sun.	Mon.–Tues.
2	Fri.–Tues.	Wed.–Thurs.	8	Fri.–Tues.	Wed.–Thurs.
3	Wed.–Sun.	Mon.–Tues.	9	Wed.–Sun.	Mon.–Tues.
4	Fri.–Tues.	Wed.–Thurs.	10	Fri.–Tues.	Wed.–Thurs.
5	Wed.–Sun.	Mon.–Tues.	11	Sun.–Thurs.	Fri.–Sat.
6	Fri.–Tues.	Wed.–Thurs.			

Although the work-shift heuristic procedure used does not guarantee optimal results, which means that the work-shift schedule requires the least number of attendants possible, Jose knows that it does result in schedules with very little slack time. Additionally, Jose knows that other schedules may exist that are equally as good as the one developed by this heuristic procedure. He also knows that the work-shift heuristic procedure may be used with or without appointment schedules.

Let us now consider scheduling another type of service operation.

SCHEDULING CUSTOMER-AS-PARTICIPANT SERVICE OPERATIONS

In this type of service operation, there is a high degree of customer involvement. Because customers actually participate in operations, the design, planning, controlling, analyzing, and managing of these operations are dramatically affected.

Nature of These Operations

Retailing, where customers shop, choose, pay for, and carry out physical goods, is an example of this type of service operation. Because customers participate in these operations, facility designs must necessarily accommodate customer needs. For instance, these features are usually provided:

- Easy access from freeways and busy thoroughfares
- Large, well-organized, and amply lighted parking areas or garages
- Wide, well-designed walkways to carry people to and from the parking areas; easily located entryways designed to accommodate large numbers of customers during peak hours
- Powered doors and escalators to ease the physical effort of opening doors and climbing stairs when armloads of merchandise must be transported
- Lobbies or other receiving or holding areas for customers and customer waiting lines
- Rest rooms, drinking fountains, credit departments, return stations, and information desks
- Service counters, cash registers, and employee workstations
- Merchandise displays, aisleways, and attractive decor and lighting

The degree to which these features must be provided varies with the amount of customer involvement in operations. Consider, for example, the front-room operations of a bank where the entire facility must be designed around customers—parking, easy entering and exiting, convenient and pleasant waiting areas, waiting lines for standardized customer servicing, teller windows and tellers, and individualized areas for customer savings account and loan customer servicing. The front room at a McDonald's restaurant and retail department stores such as Wal-Mart, Foley's, or Dillard's are examples of customer-as-participant service operations.

The layout and management of these operations requires the close cooperation and blending of the operations and marketing functions. Inventory planning and control, product quality of physical goods, scheduling of personnel, planning for waiting lines, facilities maintenance, warehousing, shipping, purchasing, and materials management are the domain of operations managers. And what we have learned about planning, controlling, analyzing, scheduling, and managing manufacturing operations directly applies here. But these issues are critically affected by merchandising strategies and tactics. For instance, the layout of these operations must display products so that customers can easily locate them and be motivated to buy them. The use of angular aisles to focus customers' attention on items located off main aisles, diamond and circular walking patterns, placement of high-profit items on the floor's perimeter shelves, placement of sale items at the ends of aisles, and other merchandising tactics are used to promote the sale of the organization's products. Also, competitive pricing policies, on-site and off-site advertising, buying, and other facets of retailing necessarily are the domain of marketing and merchandising. Operations management and merchandising are intertwined into the planning, controlling, and management of these service operations.

The objectives of these operations are dominated by customer satisfaction and product quality. All facets of operations management are acutely affected. Forecasting, facility layout, evaluation of automation and computers in operations, capacity planning, inventory ordering and stocking policies, and personnel scheduling are all driven by the need to maximize customer satisfaction. And because these operations usually have a strong element of physical goods, superior product quality is extremely important.

Because services occur at face-to-face encounters between employees and customers, employee performance is crucial in achieving customer satisfaction. Careful selection, hiring, training, supervising, evaluating, and rewarding of personnel is perhaps the number one factor in maintaining or increasing market share through increased customer satisfaction. We will discuss more about the importance of personnel in achieving customer satisfaction later in this chapter.

In these customer-as-participant service operations, customer waiting lines are an important concern for operations managers and customers alike.

Waiting Lines in Service Operations

As customers, you know how exasperating it can be to get hung up in long waiting lines. With the proliferation of service operations in recent years, customer waiting lines have become so prevalent that we wonder if long waiting lines are a necessary part of services.

Fundamentally, customer waiting lines form because managers have not provided enough production capacity to avoid waiting lines. Not enough personnel or equipment has been provided to immediately provide customer services when demanded. Excess capacity could be provided in the form of an abundance of personnel, facilities, and equipment, but operating costs would skyrocket. On the other hand, if not enough production capacity is provided and customers wait too long, they may not come back to a particular store and the resulting costs in lost profits would be great. Operations managers ordinarily attempt to strike a balance between providing enough personnel and equipment to keep waiting lines relatively short so that customer satisfaction is high, but not so short that operating costs are excessive.

Operations managers must balance the high cost of eliminating waiting lines with the possible effects of customer frustration with long lines.

© MARK RICHARDS/PHOTOEDIT

Waiting-line analysis has evolved to assist managers in answering questions such as these:

- How many customer service channels should be staffed during each hour of the day?
- How much time will customers wait on the average if we staff six customer service channels during each hour of the day?
- How many customers will be in waiting lines on the average if we staff six customer service channels during each hour of the day?

most important How many square feet of floor space will we need for waiting lines if we staff six customer service channels?

Waiting lines can form in many different kinds of operations: Computer printing jobs are waiting to be processed at a color laser printer. Workers are waiting to "clock in" at the company gate. Customers are waiting to be served at a bank teller's window. Parts are waiting to be processed at a manufacturing operation. Machines are waiting to be repaired at a maintenance shop. Customers are waiting to buy tickets at an airline ticket counter. Trucks are waiting to unload their cargo at an unloading dock. What causes waiting lines to form? When customers, parts, machines, printing jobs, or trucks are arriving at service centers irregularly and the capacity of service centers cannot be expanded or contracted to exactly meet the needs of these arrivals, waiting lines will always result. Even if managers *could* quickly expand service center capacities, the pattern of demand is often so unpredictable that managers can't respond fast enough to expand service center capacities; therefore, waiting lines form.

To further complicate the analysis of waiting lines, we don't usually know with certainty how long it will take to service each arrival. In banks, for example, some customers may take only about a minute to be served because they may only want to cash a small check or make a deposit. Other customers may require 15 to 20 minutes to service, particularly if they have a whole moneybag full of commercial transactions to complete.

Characteristics of Waiting Lines

Waiting lines typically have these characteristics:

1. Arrival patterns are irregular or random. Although we may know the average number of arrivals per hour to expect, we don't know for certain the number of arrivals in any specific hour.
2. Service times vary among arrivals. Although we may know the average time required to service an arrival, we don't know in advance how long it will take to service each arrival.

Some managers plan service center capacities to meet the average condition plus a safety factor. For example, if a bank manager knows that about 50 customers per hour on the average must be serviced at teller windows, enough tellers, cash, supplies, open teller windows, and waiting areas would be provided to service an average of about 70 customers per hour. This safety factor approach is based on the fact that, although 50 customers per hour arrive on the average, as few as 20 or as many as 90 customers can arrive in any one hour just through chance. Because arrival patterns are irregular or random, 20 minutes may go by without any customers and then 15 customers may flood through the doors.

Although the safety factor approach described above is observed in practice, more precise analysis techniques have evolved that provide managers with better information to plan waiting-line service center capacities. The first recorded systematic study of waiting lines was performed by A. K. Erlang, a Danish mathematician working for the Copenhagen Telephone Company in 1917. Erlang's early work has been expanded until today much is known about the behavior of waiting lines.

Terminology and Structures of Queuing Systems

This body of knowledge about waiting lines is often referred to today as **queuing theory,** and waiting lines are called **queues.** Before we examine the concepts of queuing theory and its analysis techniques, study the terminology of queues in Table 9.4. Figure 9.5 shows four common queuing system structures.

What information do managers usually need to know about waiting lines?

1. Given that a service system has been designed to service a certain number of arrivals per hour on the average:
   a. What is the average number of units waiting?
   b. What is the average time each unit spends waiting?
   c. What is the average number of units waiting and being served—in other words, in the system?
   d. What is the average time each unit spends in the system?
   e. What percentage of time is the system empty?
   f. What is the probability that n units will be in the system?
2. Or, given that management sets policies that limit the average number of units waiting, average number of units in the system, average time each unit waits, average time each unit is in the system, or the percentage of time that the system is empty, what service center capacity is necessary to comply with these management policies?

Four Queuing Models and Their Formulas

We present here four models that have been used to study particular queuing systems. Tables 9.5 and 9.6 show the definitions of variables, characteristics of these queuing systems, and the formulas for analyzing them.

Model 1: Single Channel, Single Phase   Waiting lines that are single channel, single phase can usually be analyzed by Model 1. When the arrival rate (λ) and service rate

Table 9.4	Terminology of Queues

Arrival—One unit of the arrival rate distribution. Occurs when one person, machine, part, etc., arrives and demands service. Each unit may continue to be called an arrival while in the service system.

Arrival Rate (λ)—The rate at which things or persons arrive, in arrivals per unit of time (e.g., persons per hour). Arrival rate is usually normal or Poisson distributed.

Channels—The number of waiting lines in a service system. A single-channel system has only one line, and a multichannel system has two or more lines.

Queue—A waiting line.

Queue discipline—The rules that determine the order in which arrivals are sequenced through service systems. Some common queue disciplines are first-come first-served, shortest processing time, critical ratio, and most valuable customers served first.

Queue length—The number of arrivals waiting to be serviced.

Service phases—The number of steps in servicing arrivals. A single-phase service system has only one service step, whereas a multiphase system has two or more service steps.

Service rate (μ)—The rate that arrivals are serviced, in arrivals per unit of time (e.g., per hour). Service rate is usually constant, normal, or Poisson distributed.

Service time ($1/\mu$)—The time it takes to service an arrival, expressed in minutes (or hours, days, etc.) per arrival. The measure does not include waiting time.

Time in system—The total time that arrivals spend in the system, including both waiting time and service time.

Utilization (P_n)—The degree to which any part of a service system is occupied by an arrival. Usually expressed as the probability that n arrivals are in the system.

Waiting time—The amount of time an arrival spends in queue.

(μ) are known, then the average number of arrivals in the line ($\bar{n}_l$), average number of arrivals in the system ($\bar{n}_s$), average time each arrival waits ($\bar{t}_l$), average time each arrival is in the system ($\bar{t}_s$), and the probability of exactly n arrivals being in the system (P_n) can all be computed. Example 9.2 demonstrates how the formulas of this model are applied.

Figure 9.5	Queuing System Structures

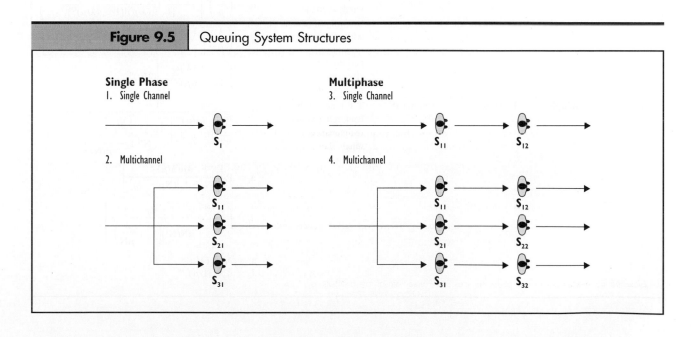

Table 9.5	Definitions of Variables for Queuing Models

λ = arrival rate—average number of arrivals per unit of time

μ = service rate—average number of arrivals that can be serviced per unit of time per channel

n = number of arrivals in the system

$\bar{n}_1$ = average number of arrivals waiting

$\bar{n}_s$ = average number of arrivals in the system

N = number of channels in multichannel system

P_n = probability that there are exactly n arrivals in the system

Q = maximum number of arrivals that can be in the system (sum of arrivals being served and waiting)

$\bar{t}_1$ = average time arrivals wait

$\bar{t}_s$ = average time arrivals are in the system

[handwritten: If all 4 models use a Poisson distribution — TEST answer NO]

Table 9.6	Four Queuing Models and Their Formulas

CHARACTERISTICS OF QUEUING SYSTEM

Model Number	Number of Channels	Service Rate Distribution	Maximum Queue Length	Examples	Formulas
1	Single	Poisson	Unlimited	Single-booth theater ticket sales, maintenance repair center	$\bar{n}_1 = \dfrac{\lambda^2}{\mu(\mu - \lambda)}$ $\quad$ $\bar{t}_1 = \dfrac{\lambda}{\mu(\mu - \lambda)}$ $\bar{n}_s = \dfrac{\lambda}{\mu - \lambda}$ $\quad$ $\bar{t}_s = \dfrac{1}{\mu - \lambda}$ $P_n = [1 - (\lambda/\mu)](\lambda/\mu)^n$
2	Single	Constant	Unlimited	Machine-controlled manufacturing operation, automatic car wash	$\bar{n}_1 = \dfrac{\lambda^2}{2\mu(\mu - \lambda)}$ $\quad$ $\bar{t}_1 = \dfrac{\lambda}{2\mu(\mu - \lambda)}$ $\bar{n}_s = \bar{n}_1 + \dfrac{\lambda}{\mu}$ $\quad$ $\bar{t}_s = \bar{t}_1 + \dfrac{1}{\mu}$
3	Single	Poisson	Limited	Bank drive-in window, manufacturing operation with in-process inventories, parking lot of retail store, maintenance repair center	$\bar{n}_1 = \left(\dfrac{\lambda}{\mu}\right)^2 \left[\dfrac{1 - Q(\lambda/\mu)^{Q-1} + (Q-1)(\lambda/\mu)^Q}{[1 - (\lambda/\mu)][1 - (\lambda/\mu)^Q]} \right]$ $\bar{n}_s = \left(\dfrac{\lambda}{\mu}\right) \left[\dfrac{1 - (Q+1)(\lambda/\mu)^Q + Q(\lambda/\mu)^{Q+1}}{[1 - (\lambda/\mu)][1 - (\lambda/\mu)^{Q+1}]} \right]$ $P_n = \left[\dfrac{1 - (\lambda/\mu)}{1 - (\lambda/\mu)^{Q+1}} \right](\lambda/\mu)^n$
4	Multiple	Poisson	Unlimited	Toll road pay booth, bank teller window, maintenance repair shop	$P_0 = \dfrac{1}{\displaystyle\sum_{n=0}^{N-1}\left[\dfrac{(\lambda/\mu)^n}{n!}\right] + \dfrac{(\lambda/\mu)^N}{N!\left(1 - \dfrac{\lambda}{\mu(N)}\right)}}$ $\bar{n}_1 = P_0\left[\dfrac{\lambda\mu(\lambda/\mu)^N}{(N-1)!(N\mu - \lambda)^2} \right]$ $\bar{t}_1 = \left(\dfrac{\lambda}{\mu}\right)^N \left[\dfrac{P_0}{\mu N(N!)\left(1 - \dfrac{\lambda}{\mu N}\right)^2} \right]$ $\bar{n}_s = \bar{n}_1 + (\lambda/\mu)$ $\bar{t}_s = \bar{t}_1 + (1/\mu)$

Note: All four models have single-phase services and Poisson arrival rate distributions.

Example 9.2	Analyzing Waiting Lines at DMV Express

The Oregon Department of Motor Vehicles (DMV) has a DMV Express station in the Valley River Mall in Eugene, Oregon. The DMV Express has only one customer service window and provides only one service: renewing Oregon driver's licenses. This information about customer arrivals and customer service is known:

$$\lambda = 50 \text{ customers per hour arrive on the average}$$
$$\mu = 75 \text{ customers per hour can be serviced on the average}$$

The arrival and service rates are considered to be Poisson distributed, the system is single phase and single channel, and the maximum queue length is unlimited. **a.** Compute the average queue length. **b.** Compute the average number of customers in the service system. **c.** Compute the average time that customers wait. **d.** Compute the average time that customers are in the system. **e.** Compute the probability that one or more customers are in the system.

Solution

a. Compute the average queue length (use the formula for Model 1):

$$\bar{n}_l = \frac{\lambda^2}{\mu(\mu - \lambda)} = \frac{(50)^2}{75(75 - 50)} = \frac{2{,}500}{75(25)} = \frac{2{,}500}{1{,}875} = 1.33 \text{ customers}$$

b. Compute the average number of customers in the system:

$$\bar{n}_s = \frac{\lambda}{(\mu - \lambda)} = \frac{50}{75 - 50} = \frac{50}{25} = 2.00 \text{ customers}$$

c. Compute the average time that customers wait:

$$\bar{t}_l = \frac{\lambda}{\mu(\mu - \lambda)} = \frac{50}{75(75 - 50)} = \frac{50}{75(25)} = \frac{50}{1{,}875} = 0.0267 \text{ hour} = 1.6 \text{ minutes}$$

d. Compute the average time that customers are in the system:

$$\bar{t}_s = \frac{1}{(\mu - \lambda)} = \frac{1}{75 - 50} = \frac{1}{25} = 0.040 \text{ hour} = 2.4 \text{ minutes}$$

e. Compute the probability that one or more customers are in the system.
First, compute the probability that the system is empty:

$$P_n = \left(1 - \frac{\lambda}{\mu}\right)\left(\frac{\lambda}{\mu}\right)^n, \text{ where } n = 0$$

$$P_0 = \left(1 - \frac{50}{75}\right)\left(\frac{50}{75}\right)^0 = \left(1 - \frac{50}{75}\right)(1) = 1 - \frac{50}{75} = 1 - 0.667 = 0.333$$

Next, because P_0 is the probability that the system is empty, $1 - P_0$ is the probability that one or more customers are in the system:

$$1 - P_0 = 1 - 0.333 = 0.667$$

Model 2: Single Channel, Single Phase, and Constant Service Times   When single-channel, single-phase waiting lines have constant service times, as in the case of an automatic car wash, an automatic coffee machine in an office building, or a machine-controlled manufacturing operation, Model 2 is usually appropriate for studying these systems. The $\bar{n}_l$, $\bar{n}_s$, $\bar{t}_l$, and $\bar{t}_s$ measures are also computed from the formulas of this model. Note that these values are always less than in Model 1. Constant service times are therefore usually preferred over random service times. Example 9.3 demonstrates the use of Model 2 formulas.

Example 9.3	Changing the DMV Express to a Constant Service Rate

The DMV Express in Example 9.2 is being considered as the first site for a new, automated driver's license renewal machine. A customer would insert his or her current driver's license, which contains a magnetic strip on the back, into the machine along with a credit card. The machine would then exchange information with a central computer in Salem, Oregon, and with the customer's credit card company. If no driving violations or arrest warrants are outstanding and the credit card company approves the charge, then the magnetic strip on the license is updated and the license, credit card, and a receipt are returned to the customer. Demonstrations have shown that total processing takes exactly 48 seconds for each customer, so 75 customers per hour can be serviced.

Use queuing Model 2 to compute: **a.** the average queue length, **b.** the average number of customers in the system, **c.** the average time that customers wait, and **d.** the average time that customers are in the system.

Solution

a.   Compute the average queue length:

$$\bar{n}_l = \frac{\lambda^2}{2\mu(\mu - \lambda)} = \frac{(50)^2}{2(75)(75 - 50)} = \frac{2{,}500}{3{,}750} = 0.667 \text{ customer}$$

b.   Compute the average number of customers in the system:

$$\bar{n}_s = \bar{n}_l + \frac{\lambda}{\mu} = \frac{\lambda^2}{2\mu(\mu - \lambda)} + \frac{\lambda}{\mu} = \frac{(50)^2}{2(75)(75 - 50)} + \frac{50}{75} = \frac{2{,}500}{3{,}750} + \frac{50}{75} = 0.6667 + 0.6667$$

$$= 1.333 \text{ customers}$$

c.   Compute the average time that customers wait:

$$\bar{t}_l = \frac{\lambda}{2\mu(\mu - \lambda)} = \frac{50}{2(75)(75 - 50)} = \frac{50}{3{,}750} = 0.0133 \text{ hour} = 0.8 \text{ minute}$$

d.   Compute the average time that customers are in the system:

$$\bar{t}_s = \bar{t}_l + \frac{1}{\mu} = \frac{\lambda}{2\mu(\mu - \lambda)} + \frac{1}{\mu} = \frac{50}{2(75)(75 - 50)} + \frac{1}{75} = \frac{50}{3{,}750} + \frac{1}{75} = 0.01333 + 0.01333$$

$$= 0.0267 \text{ hour} = 1.6 \text{ minutes}$$

Model 3: Single Channel, Single Phase, and Limited Waiting-Line Length When single-channel, single-phase waiting lines are limited in the maximum length that they can have, Model 3 usually can be used. Waiting-line lengths may be limited by such factors as waiting-room area, size of parking lots, and size of conveyors holding parts waiting to be processed at manufacturing operations. Example 9.4 demonstrates how the formulas of this model are used.

Example 9.4	The Shiny Car Wash

The Shiny Car Wash provides a variety of car care services for its customers. About six cars per hour arrive at the car wash, and employees can service about eight cars per hour. If the building and driveway will allow a maximum of only four cars ($Q = 4$), compute: **a.** $\bar{n}_l$, **b.** $\bar{n}_s$, and **c.** the probability that the car wash and its driveway will be full.

Solution

a. Compute $\bar{n}_l$:

$$\bar{n}_l = \left(\frac{\lambda}{\mu}\right)^2 \left[\frac{1 - Q(\lambda/\mu)^{Q-1} + (Q - 1)(\lambda/\mu)^Q}{[1 - (\lambda/\mu)][1 - (\lambda/\mu)^Q]}\right]$$

$$= \left(\frac{6}{8}\right)^2 \left[\frac{1 - 4(6/8)^{4-1} + (4 - 1)(6/8)^4}{[1 - (6/8)][1 - (6/8)^4]}\right]$$

$$= \left(\frac{6}{8}\right)^2 \left[\frac{1 - 4(6/8)^3 + (3)(6/8)^4}{[1 - (6/8)][1 - (6/8)^4]}\right] = 0.5625 \left[\frac{1 - 1.6875 + 0.9492}{0.25(0.6836)}\right]$$

$$= 0.5625 \left(\frac{0.2617}{0.1709}\right) = 0.861$$

b. Compute $\bar{n}_s$:

$$\bar{n}_s = \left(\frac{\lambda}{\mu}\right) \left[\frac{1 - (Q + 1)(\lambda/\mu)^Q + Q(\lambda/\mu)^{Q+1}}{[1 - (\lambda/\mu)][1 - (\lambda/\mu)^{Q+1}]}\right]$$

$$= \left(\frac{6}{8}\right) \left[\frac{1 - (4 + 1)(6/8)^4 + 4(6/8)^{4+1}}{[1 - (6/8)][1 - (6/8)^{4+1}]}\right]$$

$$= \left(\frac{6}{8}\right) \left[\frac{1 - (5)(6/8)^4 + 4(6/8)^5}{[1 - (6/8)][1 - (6/8)^5]}\right] = 0.75 \left[\frac{1 - 1.5820 + 0.9492}{0.25(0.7627)}\right]$$

$$= 0.75 \left(\frac{0.3672}{0.1907}\right) = 1.444$$

c. Compute the probability that the car wash and its driveway will be full:

$$P_n = \left[\frac{1 - (\lambda/\mu)}{1 - (\lambda/\mu)^{Q+1}}\right](\lambda/\mu)^n$$

$$P_4 = \left[\frac{1 - (6/8)}{1 - (6/8)^{4+1}}\right](6/8)^4 = \left[\frac{1 - (6/8)}{1 - (6/8)^5}\right](6/8)^4 = \left(\frac{0.25}{0.7627}\right)0.3164 = 0.104$$

Model 4: Multichannel, Single Phase   When more than one waiting line is used and services are single phase, Model 4 can usually be used to provide managers with information about these systems. As in Model 3, however, the formulas of Model 4 are also more complex to use and apply. Computer programs such as those in the *POM Software Library,* which accompanies this text, have greatly simplified the application of this model. Analysts supply the computer with arrival rates, service rates, and number of waiting lines. The computer then performs the necessary calculations to supply analysts with P_n, $\bar{n}_l$, $\bar{n}_s$, $\bar{t}_l$, and $\bar{t}_s$. Example 9.5 illustrates the application of Model 4.

Example 9.5	The Shiny Car Wash Expands

The Shiny Car Wash in Example 9.4 has received numerous complaints from its customers that they cannot get service because the car wash is full. Shiny's owner can buy the property next door and expand the car wash by duplicating its present facility (number of channels N = 2). About six cars per hour are still expected to arrive at the car wash, and employees could service about eight cars per hour in each of the two car washes. Shiny's owner wonders how the average number of cars waiting and in the system would change and what would be the probability that the two facilities would be empty.

Solution

a.   First, compute P_0, the probability that the system would be empty:

$$P_0 = \cfrac{1}{\sum_{n=0}^{N-1}\left[\cfrac{(\lambda/\mu)^n}{n!}\right] + \cfrac{(\lambda/\mu)^N}{N!\left(1 - \cfrac{\lambda}{\mu(N)}\right)}} = \cfrac{1}{\sum_{n=0}^{1}\left[\cfrac{(6/8)^n}{n!}\right] + \cfrac{(6/8)^2}{2!\left[1 - \cfrac{6}{8(2)}\right]}}$$

$$= \cfrac{1}{\left[\cfrac{(6/8)^0}{0!} + \cfrac{(6/8)^1}{1!}\right] + \cfrac{0.5625}{2[1 - (6/16)]}} = \cfrac{1}{\left[\cfrac{1}{1} + \cfrac{6/8}{1}\right] + \cfrac{0.5625}{2(0.625)}}$$

$$= \cfrac{1}{(1 + 0.75 + 0.45)} = \cfrac{1}{2.2} = 0.4545$$

b.   Compute $\bar{n}_l$:

$$\bar{n}_l = P_0\left[\cfrac{\lambda\mu(\lambda/\mu)^N}{(N-1)!(N\mu - \lambda)^2}\right] = 0.4545\left[\cfrac{(6)(8)(6/8)^2}{(2-1)![(2)(8)-6]^2}\right]$$

$$= 0.4545\left[\cfrac{27}{1(100)}\right] = 0.4545(0.27) = 0.1227$$

c.   Compute $\bar{n}_s$:

$$\bar{n}_s = \bar{n}_l + (\lambda/\mu) = 0.1227 + (6/8) = 0.1227 + 0.75 = 0.8727$$

An Evaluation of Waiting-Line Analysis in POM

An important benefit from understanding the models presented in Table 9.6 is the insight into the behavior of waiting lines that is gained through the use of these relatively simple models. For instance, look at the formula for $\bar{n}_1$ in Model 1. What happens to the length of the waiting line as the arrival rate (λ) approaches the service rate (μ)? The answer is that the waiting line becomes very large. The implication to operations managers of this finding is that service center capacities (service rates) must always be somewhat larger by a safe margin than the levels of customer demand (arrival rates). This somewhat simplistic finding is at the center of a new paradigm in POM. Traditionally, operations managers have attempted to keep production capacity as low as possible so that high utilization of personnel and facilities could be achieved. It was thought that this approach was more efficient since less capacity was being used to produce more goods and services. Now, however, *with the new paradigm of time-based competition (TBC), operations managers see the importance of having extra capacity so that waiting lines for products and services are shortened and production occurs more quickly. This new paradigm is seen as a key way of achieving greater customer satisfaction.* We will discuss more about this important concept in Chapter 12, Just-in-Time and Lean Manufacturing.

The use of these models is limited by the following factors:

1. Multiphase services may not be analyzed by the use of these formulas.
2. Arrival rates and service rates that are not from infinite Poisson distributions may not be analyzed by these formulas.
3. First-come first-served (FCFS) queue discipline is assumed. Other disciplines known to be commonly used in practice are shortest processing time, critical ratio, and most valued customers served first.
4. Line switching is not allowed in multichannel systems.

While these assumptions seem restrictive, do not be alarmed. It is comforting to know that a surprising number of single-phase queuing systems occur in operations, much research has verified that most arrival rates and service rates are Poisson distributed, and the FCFS queue discipline is prevalent in services and many manufacturing operations.

Let us say that an operations manager uses these models to staff and design a waiting-line system to comply with a policy of having no more than ten customers waiting on the average. What can be done if waiting lines grow beyond ten customers? All is not lost. The queuing models can assist in the design of queuing systems, but it is up to the operations manager to *manage* the queuing system on a day-to-day basis. As discussed earlier in this chapter, workers who ordinarily perform other duties can be called to activate additional channels or to speed up operating channels that have excessively long lines. Part-time workers who are on call, standby equipment, and other contingency measures to avoid excessive line lengths and excessive waiting times are also commonly used in services.

Waiting lines can occur in all types of service and manufacturing operations. Let us continue our discussion of service operations by examining customer-as-product service operations.

SCHEDULING CUSTOMER-AS-PRODUCT SERVICE OPERATIONS

In customer-as-product service operations, customers become so involved in operations that the service is actually performed on the customer—the customer becomes

This manicurist's salon is an example of a customer-as-product sevice operation.

© PHOTODISC, INC.

the product. Examples of this type of service operation are hair salons, medical clinics and hospitals, and tailors.

Nature of These Operations

A wide range of complexity is represented in this class of service operations. An example of the less complex customer-as-product service operation is a hair salon. Customers enter the system, are seated in the waiting area, and begin reading a magazine. After waiting, they are given a choice of several services—shampoo and hairset, conditioning treatments, haircuts, permanents, manicures, and other services. After receiving the service, they pay and exit the system. Every facet of these service operations is designed around the customer. These operations are designed, planned, controlled, analyzed, and managed with one paramount singular objective—satisfied customers.

Many factors combine to create satisfied customers. Some of these factors are:

- Extrinsic quality of the services. The extent to which the service itself achieves the results expected by the customer.
- The facilities. The comfort, convenience, and atmosphere created by the facility.
- The chemistry between customer and people in the service system. The friendliness and courtesy of the personnel and other customers.
- The skill, competence, and professionalism of the personnel.
- The value of the service. The cost of the services relative to the quantity of benefits received.

In simple customer-as-product service systems such as hair salons, the principal means of satisfying customers on a day-to-day basis is personnel. They are hired, trained, supervised, evaluated, and rewarded with care. An important part of having a

[handwritten margin notes: "Most Important", "What happen when you come out of th Salon"]

workforce that is effective in achieving high levels of customer service is through methods of acquiring feedback from customers about the perceived quality of services. Airlines, hotels, restaurants, and other services routinely provide customers with questionnaires to be filled out and returned to companies. From such feedback, two objectives are achieved. First, customers feel that companies care about what they think and want satisfied customers. Second, valuable information is provided for continuous improvement of operations. *If you could choose one factor on which the success and survival of these service operations depend, a highly trained, motivated, and effective workforce would be number one.* Of course, facilities, quality of materials used, prices, fast service, and other factors also affect customer satisfaction.

Waiting-line analysis can be helpful in determining the appropriate number of personnel to schedule during each hour of the day in these operations. In other, more complex operations, more comprehensive planning and scheduling methods are needed. An example of the more complex customer-as-product service operation is a hospital. While hospitals provide for receiving patients, settling accounts, and releasing patients, the dominant consideration in designing, planning, controlling, analyzing, and managing these service operations is the application of medical skills and technologies. Because the cases of patients are so different, hospitals must be flexible enough to accommodate a great variety of types and sequences of treatments for patients. For this reason, surgery, radiology, laboratory and testing, physical therapy, intensive care, emergency room, doctors' offices, patients' rooms, nursing stations, cafeteria, pharmacy, administration, and other departments are arranged in a process layout. The machinery, human work areas, and medical departments of hospitals are grouped and located according to their processing technologies in much the same way that a custom machine shop would lay out its machines and workstations. The facilities are designed to accommodate a variety of patient flow patterns through the facilities while grouping employee skills and machinery logically according to the technical processes performed.

While hospitals have objectives of cost effectiveness, friendly and courteous relations with patients, and other goals, the predominant objective of hospitals is to provide effective medical treatments and procedures for patients, which should lead to greater customer satisfaction. As hospitals are designed and planned, therefore, the main focus is on medical technological effectiveness. Because hospitals and other complex customer-as-product service operations use process layouts, the appropriate techniques discussed in Chapter 5, Facility Capacity, Location, and Layout, can be applied. Such an approach could attempt to minimize the total distance traveled monthly by patients, customers, or materials among departments or the monthly cost of materials handling among departments. In many services, the reasons for having departments near one another are more complex than this and they are often multiple objective and subjective. In a hospital, for instance, we would want radiology near the emergency room to allow fast diagnosis of emergency cases and we would want the pharmacy near the patients' rooms to allow for prompt dispensing of drugs to patients. Similarly, using the same equipment or personnel, ease of communicating, logical movement of customers, speed, safety, contamination, or other factors could be legitimate reasons for wanting two departments near or far from one another. In such cases, **closeness ratings** are used to reflect the desirability of having one department near another.

When it comes to scheduling customer-as-product service operations with process layouts, the appropriate approaches in Chapter 16, Manufacturing Operations Scheduling, can be used. Input–output control, Gantt charts, order sequencing rules, changeover costs, and minimizing flow time approaches can be particularly helpful. Can you see the similarities in scheduling a hospital and scheduling a job shop? For instance, consider that setting priorities among patients in a hospital and setting priorities among jobs in a machine shop, though obviously based on different criteria, follow the same general procedure. Job shops might use a first-come first-served criterion, whereas a hospital might use a most-critical-need criterion.

We find sophistication extremes in scheduling these services. Small services, such as doctors' offices, may use almost no formal scheduling systems. Instead, such devices as appointment schedules, take-a-number systems, or first-come first-served rules are often used to assign priorities among customers. Part-time workers, standby equipment, and patient referrals are also used during periods of peak demand. At the other extreme, some service systems such as hospitals have developed scheduling systems that often surpass the sophistication of scheduling in job-shop manufacturing. Because these services are produce-to-order systems with no finished-goods inventories, capacities must be variable to meet wide variations in customer demand levels. Because customer demand is highly variable from week to week and because medical services must often be provided on short notice, these scheduling systems tend to work on a rather short planning horizon; it is not uncommon to observe schedules in these systems for only one week into the future.

In complex service operations, computer simulation is a helpful tool in scheduling personnel and other resources.

Using Computer Simulation in Service Operations

Business Snapshot 9.1 illustrates the use of computer simulation to help make staffing and scheduling decisions in fast-food restaurants. The flexibility of computer simula-

---

BUSINESS SNAPSHOT 9.1

Taco Bell Uses Simulation to Develop Employee Schedules

In the competitive fast-food industry, any means of improving operations to achieve lower operating costs and better customer service are highly sought after. In an effort to better utilize its employees and ensure that customers do not have to wait in line longer than three to five minutes, Taco Bell Corporation developed its own decision support software. Its SMART (Scheduling Management And Restaurant Tool) Labor Management System consists of three models: a forecasting model, a simulation model, and an integer programming model.

Taco Bell's forecasting model is used to predict the number of customer arrivals at different times throughout each day. Because of

demand spikes at certain times of the day, particularly 11:30 a.m. and 12:30 p.m., forecasts are made for every 15-minute time interval during the day.

These customer arrival forecasts are then input into a computer simulation. The simulation model is used to analyze how many employees are needed at different times during the day. Besides the customer arrival forecasts, the computer simulation takes into account the size and configuration of a particular Taco Bell restaurant (e.g., whether there is a drive-through window), the variety of menu items offered, and the food preparation time.

Using the results of the computer simulation model, an integer

programming model then develops employee schedules that cover the customer service needs while minimizing labor cost. This scheduling model takes into account the number of employees needed throughout each day, the different customer service–related responsibilities (from preparing food to checking the customer's order to making change), and other tasks such as cleaning, maintenance, money drops, and drawer counts.

The SMART Labor Management System software is being used in all company-owned Taco Bell stores and in most franchised-based stores. Feedback from employees has been positive, and other fast-food competitors would like to follow Taco Bell's lead.

Source: Bistritz, Nancy. "Taco Bell Finds Recipe for Success." *OR/MS Today*, October 1997, 20–21.

tion in analyzing a variety of POM problems is perhaps its greatest virtue. These diverse problems share certain characteristics.

Characteristics of Computer Simulation Problems

Table 9.7 lists six of these important characteristics. When these features are present, computer simulation can be an effective tool to support decision making in POM.

To demonstrate the use of computer simulation, we shall identify the key steps in performing a computer simulation, work through a case study of a manual simulation analysis, and finally evaluate the usefulness of the technique in POM.

Procedures of Computer Simulation

Performing a computer simulation is not usually mathematically complex. Table 9.8 lists the procedures for developing a computer simulation analysis. After the problem under consideration has been defined, the central activity of simulation is performed: building the mathematical model. Model building begins with determining which variables and parameters of the problem are important to its solution. Elements subject to variation when the real system operates are allowed to take on values that vary randomly in the model and are called variables. Elements that are constant in the operation of the real system (either because of management policies or for technological reasons) are assigned constant values and are called parameters. In most simulations, the goal of the analysis is to provide a good set of parameter values (management policies) as the model simulates the operation of the real system.

Next, the decision rules of the model are specified. These rules answer questions such as this: If this happens, then what? For example, if an arrival enters a multichannel queuing system, which line does it go to—the shortest one, the quickest-moving one, or the nearest one? These decision rules guide the operation of models and allow them to simulate how the real system operates.

Data gathering allows analysts to specify the frequency distributions of the variables and the constant values of the parameters. Next is a key part of the model, specifying the time-incrementing procedures. A simulation analysis is a series (usually a long series) of snapshots (usually a thousand or more) of the model operating as time passes between the snapshots. The time-incrementing procedure sets the time interval

Table 9.7	Characteristics of POM Problems That Are Appropriate for Computer Simulation Analysis
	1. Experimentation with the real system is impossible, impractical, or uneconomical. 2. The system being analyzed is so complex that mathematical formulas cannot be developed. 3. The problem under consideration usually involves the passage of time. For example, policies are set and then executed as time passes. Although this characteristic is not absolutely mandatory, it is usually present.	4. The values of the variables of the problem are not known with certainty; rather, their values vary randomly through chance. We may know their average values and the degree of their variation, but their exact values at any point in time are not known in advance. 5. The severity of the problem justifies the expense of computer-based analysis. 6. The time available for analysis is long enough to permit computer-based analysis.

Table 9.8	Procedures of Computer Simulation

1. Thoroughly define the problem under consideration—its nature, scope, and importance.
2. Build a mathematical model of the problem. This usually involves these activities:
   a. Identify the variables and parameters.
   b. Specify the decision rules.
   c. Gather data so that variables and parameters can be assigned realistic values.
   d. Specify the probability distributions for each variable and the values of the parameters.
   e. Specify the time-incrementing procedures.
   f. Specify a procedure for summarizing the results of the simulation.
3. Write a computer program of the model and the summary procedures.
4. Process the program on the computer.
5. Evaluate the results of the computer simulation, modify parameter values, and rerun the program until a full range of parameter values has been evaluated.
6. Recommend a course of management action on the problem.

between these snapshots and the general rules for determining when a snapshot will be taken. At each snapshot each variable is randomly assigned a value, the decision rules are followed, and the results are recorded. The model is complete after a method of summarizing the results of all the snapshots is specified.

 When the model has been written in a computer language such as *Visual Basic* (**http://www.microsoft.com**) or a special computer simulation language such as *Arena* (**http://www.sm.com**), *ProModel, ServiceModel* (**http://www.promodel.com**), *SIMSCRIPT,* or *SIMPROCESS* (**http://www.cacisl.com**), and then processed on a computer, the results are evaluated. If other values of the parameters are to be analyzed, a new set of parameter values is established, the simulation is run again, and its results are again evaluated. When a full range of parameter values have been evaluated, the best set—those values that are recommended management policies to solve the problem—is selected. Example 9.6 illustrates these procedures in a computer simulation of an outpatient clinic.

Example 9.6	Computer Simulation of an Outpatient Clinic

An outpatient clinic serves patients who arrive randomly. The number of patients arriving varies between 6 and 10 per hour while the clinic is open. The clinic's daily schedule is from 8 a.m. to 5 p.m. Any patients who are waiting for doctors inside are served before the clinic closes. It takes between 6 and 30 minutes for a doctor to serve each patient, depending on the nature of the patient's medical problem.

Two doctors presently serve on the staff of the clinic. But lately both patients and doctors have been complaining about the service. Patients complain about excessive waiting times before being served, and doctors complain about being overworked, not having any time between patients to rest or perform other duties such as charting, and not being able to leave work promptly at 5 p.m. The director of the clinic wonders how much patient waiting time and doctor idle time is being experienced now and how much things would improve if a third doctor were added to the staff.

A simulation will now be developed to analyze the director's staffing problem.

Define the Problem

What does the director of the clinic need to know in order to solve the problem? He or she needs to know how much patient waiting time and doctor idle time result when two and three doctors are on the clinic's staff. Then the director can decide which staffing arrangement is best.

Build a Model

A mathematical model of the clinic is developed by following the procedures of Step 2 in Table 9.8.

Identify the Variables and Parameters.

The key variables of the model are the number of patients arriving each hour, the number of minutes required for a doctor to serve each patient, the time patients must wait before being served, and the time doctors are idle. The key parameter is the number of doctors on the clinic's staff.

Specify the Decision Rules.

These rules will guide our simulation:

1. Patients are assumed to arrive uniformly throughout each hour. (Patients do not wait and doctors are not idle because of irregular arrivals *within* each hour.)
2. Doctors are assumed to serve patients on a first-come, first-served basis. Any patients held over from previous periods are processed first before newly arriving patients are served.
3. Patient arrival patterns are assumed to be about the same for all hours of the day.
4. Patient waiting time or doctor idle time is computed hourly from this formula:

$$T_n = t_i - (60N - W_{n-1})$$

where:

T_n = either patient waiting time or doctor idle time in Time Period n (if T_n is positive, it represents patient waiting time; if T_n is negative, it represents doctor idle time)

t_i = service times for the ith patient arriving in Time Period n

N = number of doctors on the staff

W_{n-1} = patient waiting time in last period or Time Period n − 1

Gather Data and Specify Variables and Parameters.

The simulation will compare two staffing arrangements: N = 2 and N = 3, the number of doctors on the staff. Records at the front desk of the clinic yield the historical information about patient arrivals and service times found in Figure 9.6.

Specify Time-Incrementing Procedures.

Each time increment will be one hour, and enough time intervals will be simulated to cover one operating day from 8:00 a.m. to 5:00 p.m.

Specify Summarizing Procedures.

The patient waiting time and doctor idle time will be totaled across all time intervals of the simulation. Averages will then be computed for patient service time, patient waiting time, and doctor idle time.

Figure 9.6	Historical Data for Arrivals per Hour and Service Times

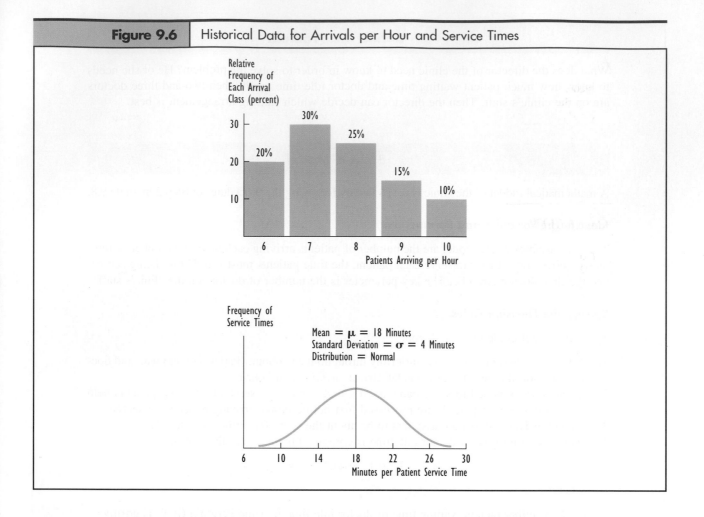

Process the Simulation

Because this simulation example will be processed manually, no computer program needs to be written as would ordinarily be the case. What follows in this section would be the output of such a computer program. The essential elements in this simulation are determining how many patients arrive in each hour and how many minutes are required to service each patient.

Monte Carlo Arrivals.

Monte Carlo is a technique for generating random values from discrete distributions, such as the discrete distribution of patients arriving per hour in the first part of Figure 9.6. Monte Carlo uses uniform random numbers (*uniform* meaning that each number has an equal chance of being drawn) to randomly select the number of patients arriving during any hour. First, in Table 9.9, we set up ranges of random numbers that correspond to the relative frequency of each class of the patient arrivals distribution.

Under this scheme the range of random numbers allocated to each class exactly equals the relative frequency of that class. Thus, 100 two-digit random numbers (0 to 99) are used to select one of the classes of patients arriving per hour from the distribution.

Table 9.10 is a table of uniformly distributed random numbers. This means that any of the digits from 0 to 9 all occur with equal frequency. They are not arranged in any order, and thus they

Table 9.9		Establishing Random Number Ranges for Each Class in Discrete Arrival Distribution for Monte Carlo			
Patients Arriving per Hour	Relative Frequency (percent)	Random Number Range	Patients Arriving per Hour	Relative Frequency (percent)	Random Number Range
6	20%	0–19	9	15%	75–89
7	30	20–49	10	10	90–99
8	25	50–74			

Table 9.10	Table of Uniformly Distributed Random Numbers

6351	8348	2924	2414	8168	7280	0164	5466
1322	8739	0532	4546	2482	3980	1543	3442
6763	9603	6748	4061	3636	5266	8868	5817
5091	8188	3314	6192	7322	8207	3347	6218
7182	7128	8132	4638	4643	6119	4925	4476
2533	4910	6664	5793	4777	6530	6187	8349
4415	1347	8346	7957	2627	4151	1266	0237
0028	8040	7986	5559	1479	8844	9750	8901
5661	3854	2177	8376	0663	8592	5586	6187
6844	5383	0699	5749	8201	7467	0991	8737
3509	2418	2928	5803	8471	8598	5349	4714
0141	8418	9238	9667	4857	2140	9129	5517
0939	5977	7415	0690	7409	8244	2783	2502
9969	7295	4053	8663	5499	5024	0652	8698
6321	9644	0971	9037	5476	1527	9879	5530
4268	5837	6611	7137	3323	5702	4309	4533
8417	9699	2447	7390	2312	7368	3398	4075
3869	6536	4393	7533	5664	6182	6118	1073
1377	8599	9206	7842	4198	4608	9864	7713
7495	5559	5896	5344	8997	5889	4361	3166
9744	9971	2129	3036	9055	7011	0568	0312
6759	7744	5634	4107	3940	6674	4587	7455
3451	3612	0610	1156	1445	8261	6565	5042
1163	1599	9134	0409	0248	7807	4608	7382
2822	0493	7563	0939	7569	6966	3677	9366
3100	4307	7942	8883	1821	0982	9504	8185
3570	7757	4412	6664	0271	1656	7491	0047
2857	6721	4616	7207	1696	5314	6621	1898
1800	3717	6102	3159	4036	5780	8360	8142
3607	8366	7733	1108	7052	2340	0569	2354
9008	2860	6091	0800	9986	2712	6403	4006
6416	2438	6883	9360	4209	1018	8223	0181
7079	0844	1351	0508	0886	0747	6502	2293
5241	0807	7674	8782	3627	2728	3727	7805
3291	9499	7374	8751	6143	8100	3308	6951
1928	9013	6726	9241	4907	6275	3487	4448
5310	1826	3163	2545	6803	7911	6237	6225
1215	1270	6680	8651	1790	2881	1176	1130
6195	6999	6240	4452	0552	3239	4469	7658
5731	5461	1187	7973	7158	1193	2734	5666

are random. To use the table to select random numbers from 0 to 99, as we want to do here, just pick a starting point anywhere in the table. For our purposes, begin at Row 8 and read from left to right: 00, 28, 80, 40, 79, 86, 55, 59, and 14 are nine random numbers (RN) that will be used to establish the number of patient arrivals during the nine daily operating hours of our simulation.

Table 9.11 uses these random numbers to set the number of patient arrivals for each hour of the simulation. The first RN = 00 falls in the 0–19 range of the random numbers in Table 9.9; this sets six arrivals for the first hour. RN = 28 falls in the 20–49 range for seven arrivals; RN = 80 falls in the 75–89 range of numbers for nine arrivals; and so on. This procedure is used to set the number of arrivals in all nine hours of the simulation. Remember that you can read uniformly distributed random numbers from Table 9.10 in any sequence from any starting point in the table: up, down, right, or left—but be consistent.

Normally Distributed Service Times.

Now we need to set the service times for our patients. But we cannot use Monte Carlo because our service times from Figure 9.6 are normally distributed with a mean of 18 minutes and a standard deviation of 4 minutes. Table 9.12 is a table of normally distributed random numbers that are **Z scores**—the number of standard deviations each service time is from the mean. This formula is used to compute the service time for each patient:

$$t_i = \mu + Z_i(\sigma) \quad \text{or} \quad t_i = 18 + Z_i(4)$$

Table 9.11	Using Monte Carlo to Determine Number of Patient Arrivals for Each Hour of Simulation							
Hour	Uniform Random Number (RN)	Patient Arrivals	Hour	Uniform Random Number (RN)	Patient Arrivals	Hour	Uniform Random Number (RN)	Patient Arrivals
1	00	6	4	40	7	7	55	8
2	28	7	5	79	9	8	59	8
3	80	9	6	86	9	9	14	6

Note: Number of arrivals is determined by fitting RN into one of the random number ranges from Table 9.9.

Table 9.12	Normally Distributed Z Scores						
1.21	−21.31	−1.12	1.32	0.86	0.31	−0.77	1.90
0.40	−0.11	−1.63	−0.75	0.92	−0.81	−1.12	1.28
1.40	−0.49	0.56	0.10	−1.05	0.48	1.00	−0.35
−0.04	1.21	1.80	−0.21	−1.58	0.15	−2.75	0.45
0.47	−0.28	2.02	3.00	1.14	−0.54	1.72	0.60
0.11	0.77	1.14	0.46	1.01	0.04	−1.05	−0.11
0.22	1.94	−0.11	1.02	−0.79	−0.24	0.52	1.66
−1.80	0.97	−0.76	0.31	1.27	0.81	−0.17	−0.28
0.09	−0.60	−0.63	0.56	0.09	1.08	−0.60	2.10
1.66	−2.26	0.10	1.66	−0.85	−0.34	0.02	0.73

Note: These numbers are not in any order and are normally distributed about a mean of zero.

Z is determined for each patient by selecting any starting point in Table 9.12. For our purposes, let us begin at the upper left-hand corner and read from left to right: 1.21, -1.31, -1.12, 1.32, 0.86, and 0.31 are our Z scores for the six patients in the first hour of our simulation. Therefore, we can now compute the service times for these patients:

$$
\begin{array}{ll}
t_1 = 18 + 1.21(4) = 22.84 \text{ minutes} & t_4 = 18 + 1.32(4) = 23.28 \text{ minutes} \\
t_2 = 18 - 1.31(4) = 12.76 \text{ minutes} & t_5 = 18 + 0.86(4) = 21.44 \text{ minutes} \\
t_3 = 18 - 1.12(4) = 13.52 \text{ minutes} & t_6 = 18 + 0.31(4) = \underline{19.24 \text{ minutes}} \\
& \text{Total} \qquad 113.08 \text{ minutes}
\end{array}
$$

By repeating this procedure, we can compute the service times for all patients and total these service times for each hour of the simulation: 113.1, 135.1, 160.6, 112.8, 197.1, 180.3, 154.7, 159.2, and 98.8. Using a computer spreadsheet such as Microsoft's *Excel* simplifies this task.

Performing the Simulation.

Now we are ready to perform the simulation. Table 9.13 lists the number of patients arriving and the total service time for each hour of the simulation. The patient waiting time and doctor idle time are computed for each hour for the two staffing arrangements. For example, in Hour 4:

Two doctors:

$$T_n = t_i - (60N - W_{n-1}) \qquad T_4 = 112.8 - (120 - 55.7) = 112.8 - 64.3 = 48.5$$

Because T_4 is positive, it represents patient waiting time.

Three doctors:

$$T_n = t_i - (60N - W_{n-1}) \qquad T_4 = 112.8 - (180 - 0) = -67.2$$

Because T_4 is negative, it represents doctor idle time.

Table 9.13 | Summary of Outpatient Clinic Simulation

| | | | TWO-DOCTOR STAFF | | THREE-DOCTOR STAFF | |
| | Number of | Total Service | Patient Waiting | Doctor Idle | Patient Waiting | Doctor Idle |
Hour	Patients Arriving	Time (minutes)	Time (minutes)	Time (minutes)	Time (minutes)	Time (minutes)
1	6	113.1	0	6.9	0	66.9
2	7	135.1	15.1	0	0	44.9
3	9	160.6	55.7	0	0	19.4
4	7	112.8	48.5	0	0	67.2
5	9	197.1	125.6	0	17.1	0
6	9	180.3	185.9	0	17.4	0
7	8	154.7	220.6	0	0	7.9
8	8	159.2	259.8	0	0	20.8
9	6	98.8	238.6	0	0	81.2
Totals 69		1,311.7	1,149.8	6.9	34.5	308.3
Average per Patient		19.0	16.7	0.1	0.5	4.5

After all the patient waiting times and doctor idle times have been similarly computed for all hours of the simulation, the totals and averages are computed. This summary information results:

	Two Doctors	Three Doctors
Average service time per patient	19.0 minutes	19.0 minutes
Average waiting time per patient	16.7 minutes	0.5 minute
Average doctor idle time between patients	0.1 minute	4.5 minutes

The director agrees with the patients—too much patient waiting time results with a two-doctor clinic staff. The doctors also presently are probably overworked. The three-doctor staffing arrangement alleviates both problems, but at a cost.

Example 9.6 demonstrates the essential steps in developing a computer simulation without overpowering you with complex calculations. You should realize, however, that this example is simple compared to most computer simulations on at least three points: (1) Most simulated systems are far more complex than a two- or three-doctor outpatient clinic. (2) Decision rules are seldom as simple as those of this example. (3) The number of random variables and their patterns of randomness are usually more extensive. Poisson, exponential, and other distributions frequently must be represented in addition to the discrete and normal distributions of this example. But despite the simplicity of our example, its procedures are similar in most respects to its real-world counterparts.

An Evaluation of Computer Simulation

Computer simulation deserves our attention on at least three counts:

1. It is perhaps one of the most flexible analytical tools in that it can be applied to a variety of POM problems.
2. It is frequently used in industry. Thus, the likelihood of encountering it in your future employment is relatively high.
3. It is not highly mathematical and complex; rather, it uses a relatively simple experimental approach to analyzing problems.

Computer simulation does not always yield best, or optimal, answers, but good workable solutions can be developed by comparing alternative management policies. Although it is true that the technique requires well-trained staff specialists and an effective computer system, these elements are increasingly assumed in most organizations today.

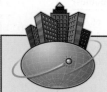

Wrap-Up

WHAT WORLD-CLASS COMPANIES DO

Managing service businesses presents many challenges. The fact that their outputs may not be inventoried, the involvement of customers in operations, short lead times, subjectively determined quality, and nonuniform demand can create difficulties. But some of our largest and most successful U.S. corporations are service businesses, so these difficulties can be overcome. Companies like

AT&T, Wal-Mart, Citigroup, American Airlines, and American Express from telecommunications, mass merchandising, banking, air transportation, and financial services have done two fundamental things to successfully manage their operations:

1. Where appropriate, they have adapted advanced and well-known planning, analyzing, and controlling approaches that were first developed in manufacturing.
2. They have recognized the unique properties of service operations and developed novel management approaches for these operations.

This is facilitated by classifying service operations into these types: quasi-manufacturing, customer-as-participant, and customer-as-product. The properties of these types of service operations provide an analytical framework for adapting existing approaches and developing new ones for these operations.

Almost every service business has one or more departments, groups of departments, or whole operations that are quasi-manufacturing. For all practical purposes, these operations are managed the same way as in manufacturing. Such activities as forecasting, designing production processes, selecting and managing production technology, capacity planning, facility layout, purchasing, inventory planning, and scheduling are conducted as in manufacturing. While some might say that these operations are driven more by the need to provide superior customer satisfaction than manufacturing, world-class manufacturers would disagree.

Customer-as-participant service operations are perhaps best epitomized by retailing. Here on the shopping floor, operations management and merchandising management are blended for the effective management of operations—achieving greater market share and profitability through increased customer satisfaction. While all elements of operations affect customer satisfaction, the encounter between personnel and the customer as services are provided is crucial. For this reason, employees are selected, hired, trained, supervised, evaluated, and rewarded with customer satisfaction as the supreme goal.

Customer-as-product service operations have an even closer contact between the customer and operations personnel because the service is actually performed on the customer. Recognizing the complexity of building customer satisfaction in this setting, employees become a critical means for achieving greater market share and profitability.

For many companies, effective scheduling of these service operations is achieved through personnel scheduling. Such techniques as work-shift scheduling, waiting-line analysis, and computer simulation are used to plan and control these service operations.

REVIEW AND DISCUSSION QUESTIONS

1. Name and explain four properties of services.
2. What are some of the misconceptions about services?
3. Name and explain five things that describe the nature of services.
4. Name and describe three types of service operations. Give an example of each.
5. What are the characteristics of services that make scheduling them difficult?
6. What are four approaches to dealing with nonuniform demand for services?
7. Describe a quasi-manufacturing service operation and give an example.
8. Describe how quasi-manufacturing service operations are planned, controlled, analyzed, scheduled, and managed.
9. Briefly explain and describe work-shift scheduling in service operations.
10. Describe a customer-as-participant service operation and give an example.
11. Describe how customer-as-participant service operations are planned, controlled, analyzed, scheduled, and managed.
12. Briefly explain and describe waiting-line analysis in service operations.
13. Give five examples of waiting lines in operations systems.
14. Explain why waiting lines form.
15. What are the assumptions of these queuing models? a. Model 1, b. Model 2, c. Model 3, d. Model 4
16. Describe some ways that managers can vary production capacities to avoid excessive waiting lines.

17. Describe a customer-as-product service operation, and give an example.
18. Describe how customer-as-product service operations are planned, controlled, analyzed, scheduled, and managed.
19. Briefly explain and describe computer simulation in service operations.
20. Name six characteristics of problems appropriate for computer simulation analysis.
21. Name six principal steps in computer simulation.
22. Name six activities in building a model for computer simulation.
23. Define *Monte Carlo.*
24. Define *uniformly distributed random numbers.*
25. Define *normally distributed random numbers.*

INTERNET ASSIGNMENTS

1. Visit the web site of ProModel Corporation at **http://www.promodel.com** and find the web pages for the *ServiceModel* simulation software. Describe the features and typical applications of the *ServiceModel* software.
2. Atlas Business Solutions, Inc., produces staff scheduling software. Visit the company's web site at **http://www.abs-usa.com** and find the web pages for its *Visual Staff Scheduler* software. Describe the features of this software.
3. Tempus Software, Inc., is the leading U.S. developer of enterprise-wide patient and resource scheduling software for the health care industry. Visit the company's web site at **http://www.tempus.com** and find the web pages for its *ENCOMPASS* scheduling software. Describe the features of this scheduling software.
4. HVS International provides consulting services for the hospitality industry. Visit the company's web site at **http://www.hvsinternational.com** and find the company's web pages for operational and management strategy development. Describe the services offered related to employee productivity and service efficiency.

PROBLEMS

1. A bank has cashiers who work eight hours per day Monday through Saturday. The number of daily work shifts required for cashiers is:

	Mon.	Tues.	Wed.	Thurs.	Fri.	Sat.	Total
Cashier work shifts	10	8	6	7	8	10	49

All of the cashiers are full-time employees and according to company policy must be provided four consecutive days of work and two consecutive days off each week.
a. What is the minimum number of cashiers required?
b. Use the work-shift heuristic procedure to develop weekly work-shift schedules for the cashiers.
c. How many cashier work shifts of slack per week are present in your proposed schedules? How could this slack be avoided? Are your schedules optimal?

2. The required number of work shifts for clerks at a food retailer is:

	Mon.	Tues.	Wed.	Thurs.	Fri.	Sat.	Sun.	Total
Day shift	8	6	5	6	9	12	7	53
Evening shift	6	5	4	5	7	8	5	40

The shifts are scheduled independently, the clerks' union contract calls for weekly schedules based on five consecutive days and eight hours per day, and only full-time clerks are employed.

a. What is the minimum number of clerks required on both the day and evening shifts?

b. Use the work-shift heuristic procedure to develop work-shift schedules for the clerks for both the day and evening shifts.

c. How many clerk work shifts of slack per week are present in your day and evening shift schedules? How could this slack be avoided? Is your solution optimal?

3. Given: Model 1, $\lambda = 7$ per hour, and $\mu = 10$ per hour. Required:
a. $\bar{n}_l$, b. $\bar{n}_s$, c. $\bar{t}_l$, d. $\bar{t}_s$, e. P_0.

4. If customers arrive at a single drive-in window at a local bank one every four minutes on the average, and if you can serve customers in three minutes on the average:
a. How long should customers expect to be at the bank facility on the average?
b. How many cars would we expect to be in the drive-in facility on the average? (Assume one customer per car.)
c. What is the probability that four or more cars will be in the drive-in facility?

5. The athletic department at a university has been ordered to verify students' identification before selling them tickets at its booth. The average arrival rate of students to the single waiting line is expected to remain at 30 students per hour, but the average time required to receive payment and provide tickets is expected to increase from 0.5 minute to 1.4 minutes at the single ticket booth. If the waiting line area is sufficient to accommodate the additional students, what changes will this cause in the average number of students in line, the average waiting time of students in line, and the proportion of the time that the staff will be at the window?

6. The maintenance repair shop of a manufacturer has a policy of 8 hours as the average time that each production machine to be repaired should be out of production. If it takes 12 hours on the average for a repair worker to repair a machine, two machines per hour on the average are failing, and Model 1 applies (assume that two workers can repair a machine in 6 hours, four workers can repair a machine in 3 hours, etc.):
a. How many repair workers are needed in the repair shop?
b. If each machine requires 10 square feet of floor space, how much area should be provided on the average for the repair facility? (Assume that repaired machines leave immediately.)

7. Given: Model 2, $\lambda = 20$ per hour, and $\mu = $ a constant 25 per hour. Required:
a. $\bar{n}_l$, b. $\bar{n}_s$, c. $\bar{t}_l$, d. $\bar{t}_s$.

8. Debbie Franz owns and operates Debbie's Automatic Car Wash. The automatic washing mechanism takes exactly 7 minutes to wash each car. During weekdays the average arrival rate of cars is 6 per hour, and on weekends the rate is 7.5 per hour. Each car takes approximately 20 feet of driveway length.
a. How much driveway length will be required on the average for cars waiting to be washed?
b. For what length of time will each customer be at the car wash on the average?

9. A manufacturer is studying a proposal to install an automatic device at one of its production operations. The device would perform the operation in exactly 0.5 minute. The arrival rate is 50 products per hour and the present service rate of the single-channel manual operation is 60 per hour. If the device costs $10,000, 1,500

products are produced a year, and each minute saved per product at the operation is worth $2, should the device be installed?

10. A bank would like to design an automatic teller. The bank's board has set a policy of no more than one customer waiting to be served on the average. If 20 customers per hour arrive on the average:
    a.   In how many minutes should the automatic teller be designed to process each customer?
    b.   How many minutes will each customer be at the bank on the average?

    Hint: The formula for the quadratic equation is $X = \left[-b \pm \sqrt{b^2 - 4ac} \right]/2a$.

11. Given: Model 3, $\lambda = 20$ per hour, $\mu = 25$ per hour, and Q = maximum of 5 units in the system. Required: $\bar{n}_s$.

12. A student organization is planning a car wash. A shopping center has granted permission to use a portion of its parking lot with the understanding that no more than 75 feet of driveway length will be used. The students expect the 25-foot-long cars to arrive at the car wash one every 10 minutes on the average, and the car-washing team believes that it can wash a car in 5 minutes on the average.
    a.   What proportion of the time will the students be able to rest?
    b.   How many cars will be waiting in line at the car wash on the average?

13. Given: Model 4, $\lambda = 15$ units per hour, $\mu = 7$ units per hour, and N = 3 channels. Required:
    a. P_0, b. $\bar{n}_l$.

14. A food store has an average of 220 customers arriving per hour during peak shopping hours. During these peak periods all eight checkout counters will be open and operating with a capacity of serving an average of 35 customers per hour per counter. All checkout counters are identical.
    a.   What proportion of the time would all of the checkout counters and waiting lines be empty of customers?
    b.   How long would customers wait in line on the average?
    c.   How many customers would be waiting in each line on the average?

15. The Financial Aid Center at Rhode Island State University would like to improve its responsiveness to students who come to the center for assistance. One idea is to hire additional financial aid counselors. A recent study of students using the Financial Aid Center found that an average of 17 students come to the center each hour. The study also found that each of the center's three financial aid counselors saw 4 students per hour on average. Use the *POM Software Library* to determine how many total counselors it would take so that the average waiting time for students before they see a counselor is less than 10 minutes.

16. Bubba Jones, the owner of Big Bubba's Bar, recently purchased six video poker machines. The new machines have been quite popular and some customers have complained that Big Bubba needs more machines. Over the last several evenings, Mr. Jones has closely observed the usage of the video poker machines. He found that an average of 30 customers per hour walk up to play video poker. If all the machines are in use, most customers will wait up to 2 minutes for an open machine before walking away. When customers start playing video poker, they stay at the machine an average of 12 minutes. Mr. Jones would like to have enough machines such that the average wait time per customer is less than 1 minute. Use

the *POM Software Library* to determine how many additional video poker machines he should purchase.

17. A professor keeps office hours between 10 a.m. and 12 noon one day per week. The number of students who come during these periods is given in this relative frequency distribution:

Number of Students (n)	Relative Frequency $F(n)$ (percent)	Number of Students (n)	Relative Frequency $F(n)$ (percent)
3	10%	5	40%
4	30	6	20

The amount of time per student is approximated by a normal distribution with a mean of 10 minutes and a standard deviation of 2 minutes. Use these uniform random numbers to establish the number of students arriving in five office-hours periods: 5, 1, 3, 9, and 7. Use the normally distributed Z scores in Table 9.12 to establish service times per student. (Begin in the upper left-hand corner of the table and read horizontally across the first line, return to the left margin, go down to the next line, and repeat until completed.) Follow the procedures of the outpatient clinic case in this chapter to determine:

a. The number of students arriving in each office-hours period for five periods.

b. The total number of minutes required to assist students during each of the five office-hours periods.

18. A newsstand sells a national daily newspaper. Its daily demand follows this pattern:

Newspapers Demanded	Relative Frequency (percent)	Newspapers Demanded	Relative Frequency (percent)
100	10%	160	20%
120	20	180	15
140	30	200	5

The newsstand buys newspapers in 20-paper bundles at a cost of $4 per bundle and charges its customers $0.50 per paper. Any leftover newspapers per day can be sold for scrap for $1 per bundle. The newsstand wants to compare two rules for ordering newspapers: (1) Order the quantity demanded today for tomorrow's sales. (Today's demand was 7 bundles.) (2) Order a constant 7 bundles per day. Use Monte Carlo to conduct a 7-day manual simulation to compare the average daily profit for the two decision rules. (These seven uniformly distributed random numbers are read downward from the upper right-hand corner of Table 9.10: 66, 42, 17, 18, 76, 49, and 37.)

CASES

Precision Calibration Services Company

The Precision Calibration Services Company provides on-site calibration services for electronic medical equipment. When a customer calls Precision for service, a calibrator travels to the customer's medical center, observes operation of the equipment, and calibrates the equipment. Calibration means a precise measurement and adjustment of the electronic characteristics of the equipment so that it gives precise performance. Quick and dependable service has been the cornerstone of Precision's growth and success.

Precision has had a few complaints about the time required for calibrators to respond to customers' calls. At a recent staff meeting, the calibrators said that they were working as hard and fast as humanly possible, but that on some days of the week the number of calls for service was so great that it could take a few days to get to some of these requests. All calibrators now work five days per week, 8 hours per day, Monday through Friday. A different scheduling arrangement is being considered for the calibrators so that they would be available to respond to calls six days per week. Each calibrator would work four days per week and 10 hours per day, and have two consecutive days off per week not including Sunday (Sunday is never worked). Such an arrangement would allow the number of adjustors available to answer requests to better match the daily pattern of the volume of requests.

These averages seem to be reasonable estimates of the number of daily calls for service for the next several weeks:

	Mon.	Tues.	Wed.	Thurs.	Fri.	Sat.	Total
Number of requests	29	25	19	30	33	40	176

Each request is expected to require an average of about 2 hours of a calibrator's time. Precision wants to plan work shifts for the calibrators to approximately match the requests for service, but is concerned about how this will affect the utilization of calibrators, group morale, and the time required to perform customer service.

Assignment

1. What is the minimum number of calibrators required?
2. Use the work-shift heuristic procedure to develop work-shift schedules for the calibrators.
3. How much slack per week is present in your work-shift schedules?
4. What ways could be used to reduce the amount of slack in your work-shift schedules?
5. What factors should be considered in changes in work-shift schedules such as the one under consideration at Precision? Which of these factors is most important? Can you suggest how Precision should go about making the schedule changes being considered?

Cincinnati Trucking Inc.

Scenario #1

Cincinnati Trucking Inc. (CTI) ships personal and small-business computers by company trucks to regional warehouses in the eastern half of the United States. Trucks return from the warehouses to the plant for loading on the average of five per eight-hour day. The plant uses one loading crew in the shipping department that assembles customers' orders for personal and small-business computers and loads outgoing orders onto the trucks. The loading crew does warehouse work when no outgoing trucks are at the plant and loads the outgoing trucks on a first-come, first-served basis. The loading crew can load seven trucks per eight-hour day on the average. Each truck occupies about 280 square feet of parking space, each truck driver is paid $30 per hour including fringe benefits, and the loading crew is paid a total of $200 per hour including fringe benefits. CTI's union contract with its truck drivers does not allow drivers to assist in loading or unloading trucks.

a. On the average, how much parking space should be necessary for trucks waiting to be loaded?
b. How much does the union contract clause barring drivers from doing loading work cost CTI per year if the Atlanta plant works 250 days per year and if we assume that drivers' idle time could be put to a use that would be of equal value to their present pay?

Scenario #2

The warehouse manager at CTI has established a policy that requires truck drivers to take their trucks to be serviced at the plant's maintenance center if one truck is waiting to be loaded, but each truck may be serviced a maximum of once per trip. Assume that the serviced trucks do not affect the arrival rate of five trucks per eight-hour day and that the truck-loading terminal operates much like a single-channel, limited–queue-length waiting-line system. If each truck makes a trip every 10 days on the average, how often will the trucks be serviced?

Scenario #3

The truck-loading dock described above has this arrival distribution:

(1) Trucks Arriving in an 8-Hour Day	(2) Minutes between Arriving Trucks [1/(1) × 480]	(3) Relative Frequency (percent)
1	480	5%
2	240	10
3	160	15
4	120	20
5	96	25
6	80	15
7	69	10

The time that it takes the single loading crew to load the trucks is normally distributed with a mean of 69 minutes and a standard deviation of 15 minutes. Use these uniform random numbers to establish the number of trucks arriving in 10 eight-hour days: 73, 22, 51, 45, 37, 59, 82, 08, 60, and 00. Use the normally distributed Z scores in Table 9.12 to establish loading times for each truck. (Begin in the third row of the table.) Follow the procedures of the outpatient clinic case in Example 9.6 to determine:

a. The number of trucks arriving in each day for 10 days.
b. The number of minutes required to load trucks in each day and the total for the 10 days.
c. The number of minutes of driver idle time in each day and the total for the 10 days.
d. The amount of loading crew idle time in each day and the total for the 10 days.

Scenario #4

Because of a large increase in sales, CTI has doubled the number of trucks that are hauling personal and small-business computers to regional warehouses. The trucks are now arriving at the rate of 10 trucks per eight-hour day on the average. A second loading crew has been added, and the two crews work separate loading docks and each can load 7 trucks per eight-hour day on the average. With the extra trucks, should the drivers expect to spend more time at the plant now than previously?

SELECTED BIBLIOGRAPHY

Aviel, David. "Cutting Queues Reduces Costs and Generates Cash." *IIE Solutions* 28, no. 12 (December 1996): 16–17.

Banks, Jerry, John S. Carson, Barry L. Nelson, and David Nicol. *Discrete-Event System Simulation.* Upper Saddle River, NJ: Prentice Hall, 2000.

Browne, Jim. "Scheduling Employees for Around-the-Clock Operations." *IIE Solutions* 32, no. 2 (February 2000): 30–33.

Carey, M., and S. Carville. "Testing Schedule Performance and Reliability for Train Stations." *Journal of the Operations Research Society,* 51, no. 6 (June 2000): 666–682.

Colley, John L. *Case Studies in Service Operations.* Belmont, CA: Wadsworth, 1996.

Dillon, Jeffrey E., and Spyros Kontogiorgis. "U.S. Airways Optimizes the Scheduling of Reserve Flight Crews." *Interfaces* 29, no. 5 (September/October 1999): 123–131.

Fitzsimmons, James A., and Mona J. Fitzsimmons. *Service Management: Operations, Strategy, and Information Technology,* 3rd ed. New York: McGraw-Hill, 2001.

Friedman, Hershey H., and Linda W. Friedman. "Reducing the 'Wait' in Waiting-Line Systems: Waiting Line Segmentation." *Business Horizons* 40, no. 4 (July–August 1997): 54–58.

Garcia, Luis. "Choosing a Staff Scheduling System." *Health Management Technology* 21, no. 8 (August 2000): 22.

Haksever, Cengiz, Barry Render, Roberta S. Russell, and Robert G. Murdick. *Service Management and Operations,* 2nd ed. Upper Saddle River, NJ: Prentice Hall, 2000.

Hall, Randolph W. *Queuing Methods: For Services and Manufacturing.* Upper Saddle River, NJ: Prentice Hall, 1997.

Kelton, David, Randall Sadowski, and Deborah Sadowski. *Simulation with Arena.* Boston: McGraw-Hill, 2001.

Klafehn, Keith, Jay Weinroth, and Jess Boronico. *Computer Simulation in Operations Management.* Westport, CT: Quorum, 1996.

Law, A. M., and W. D. Kelton. *Simulation Modeling and Analysis,* 3rd ed. Boston: McGraw-Hill, 2000.

Lesaint, David, Christos Voudouris, and Nader Asarmi. "Dynamic Workforce Scheduling for British Telecommunications PLC." *Interfaces* 30, no. 1 (January/February 2000): 45–56.

Ninemeier, Jack D. *Management of Food and Beverage Operations,* 3rd ed. Lansing, MI: Educational Institute, 2000.

Prabhu, N. U. *Foundations of Queuing Theory.* Boston: Kluwer Academic, 1997.

Pritsker, A. Alan B. Pritsker, Jean J. O'Reilly, and David K. LaVal. *Simulation and Visual SLAM and AweSim.* New York: John Wiley & Sons, 1997.

Robertazzi, Thomas G. *Computer Networks and Systems: Queueing Theory and Performance Evaluation,* 3rd ed. New York: Springer, 2000.

Schmenner, Roger W. *Service Operations Management.* Upper Saddle River, NJ: Prentice Hall, 1995.

Swain, James J. "Imagine New Worlds; 1999 Simulation Software Survey." *OR/MS Today* 26, no. 1 (February 1999): 38–51.

Winston, Wayne L. *Simulation Modeling Using @RISK.* Belmont, CA: Duxbury Press, 2001.

Project Management

Introduction

Project Management

Project-Planning and Control Techniques
Scheduling and Control Charts
Critical Path Method (CPM)
Program Evaluation and Review Technique (PERT)
Project Cost Control Systems
CPM/PERT in Practice

Computer Software for Project Management

An Evaluation of CPM/PERT

Wrap-Up: What World-Class Companies Do

Review and Discussion Questions

Internet Assignments

Problems

Cases
Baxter Construction Company
Advanced Aerospace Corporation

Selected Bibliography

MANAGING THE RATS PROJECT

Bill Williams, manager of the Power Systems plant in Marion, Illinois, received a telephone call from Ivor Kaney, vice-president of marketing at divisional headquarters. Ivor inquired if Bill wanted to bid on a new product that could more than double the annual sales at the plant from $9.5 million to $20.6 million. The new product, called Rocket Aerial Target System (RATS), was an expendable, low-cost, rocket-propelled, aerial target that would be shot down on U.S. military gunnery ranges by heat-seeking missiles. The project would require putting together a technical proposal, submitting a budget proposal, building 10 prototype rockets, and flying 3 rockets for the U.S. Army. And all of this had to be done in 4½ months. After a meeting with the division's marketing staff and U.S. Army representatives, Bill decided to put together a project team at his plant to respond to the proposal and development project. Bill appointed to the project team a project manager, a flight engineer, a system design specialist, a production engineer, a safety and security officer, and a cost analyst. These persons were among his best personnel from various departments at the plant. The project members would be assigned to the team for the duration of the project, which was expected to take no longer than 5 months. The project manager would report directly to the plant manager and would be responsible for the performance of the team in staying within budgets, meeting timetables, and successfully carrying out the objectives of the project team. The team had to quickly develop a plan for completing the activities of the project and then execute the plan.

As the preceding account illustrates, project teams must often be formed to achieve key organizational initiatives. Such projects as developing new products, automating production operations, implementing just-in-time (JIT) manufacturing, and starting a total quality management (TQM) program are crucial to success in global competition today. And all of these activities require that employees work together as teams. Chances are that you will have the opportunity to work on such teams early in your career. You will find that working in teams is a challenge because teams must ordinarily work on tight time schedules, adhere to strict budgets, be temporarily removed from their regular jobs, and really work at cooperating with one another. While their project work is proceeding, the remainder of the organization must continue to produce the organization's products. Because of the difficulty of simultaneously managing such projects and producing an organization's products and services, new approaches to planning and controlling projects have developed.

PROJECT MANAGEMENT

New organization forms have been developed to ensure both continuity of the production system in its day-to-day activities and the successful completion of projects. Foremost among these new organization forms is the **project organization**. Figure 10.1 shows that project teams are drawn from organizations' departments and temporarily assigned, full- or part-time, to project teams.

Figure 10.1	Project Organization

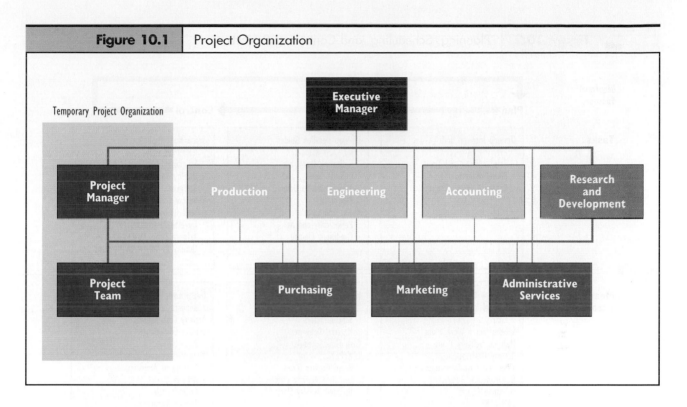

A project manager is usually appointed to head the team, coordinate its activities, coordinate other departments' activities on the project, and report directly to the top of the organization. This executive management exposure gives the project high visibility within the organization, ensures the attention of the functional departments to the project, and encourages cooperation between the project team and other organizational units.

The project organization is usually established well in advance of beginning the projects so that the project plan can be developed. Figure 10.2 shows the interrelationships among the planning, scheduling, and controlling functions of the project. Notice that the project plan is established before project activities begin and is modified as conditions change throughout the project. The plan is the blueprint and overall guide for achieving the successful completion of the project.

The scheduling and controlling functions of the project occur as the project proceeds. These ongoing functions ensure timely performance of the project's activities within cost and quality standards. The periodic generation of updated charts, reports, and schedules keeps all parties to the project informed about their particular work, when each activity must be done, corrective actions required, and particular problems to watch for.

The key ingredient in scheduling and controlling the project is the project team. Figure 10.3 shows that the project team is the hub around which the project rotates. The project team supplies updated changes to the project plan and project schedules through the management information system. The project team sends periodic time, cost, and quality performance reports to the project's internal and external resources. The project team receives back from its resources information about progress on the project. This process continues throughout the project.

| **Figure 10.2** | Planning, Scheduling, and Controlling Projects |

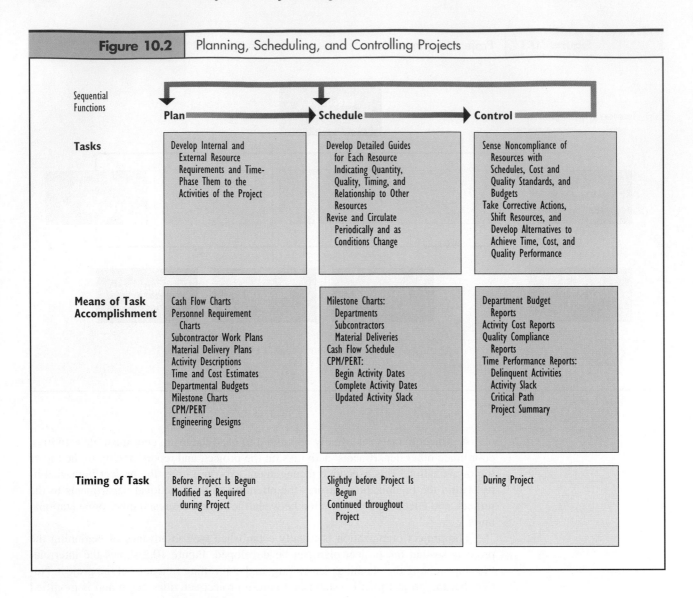

One rather interesting development concerns the permanent institutionalization of the project organization form in organizations that predominantly depend on products best managed as projects. Aerospace firms, construction firms, computer firms, and other types of firms have used the project organization form for so long that it has become a permanent part of their organizational structures. Project managers, project team members, and the project management information system continue to change and adapt to new project assignments. Business Snapshot 10.1 discusses the field of project management as a profession.

New techniques have evolved to facilitate the timely completion of project activities within time, cost, and quality standards of the project plan. Some of the most often used scheduling and control techniques are presented here.

Figure 10.3	Scheduling and Controlling Projects with Project Teams

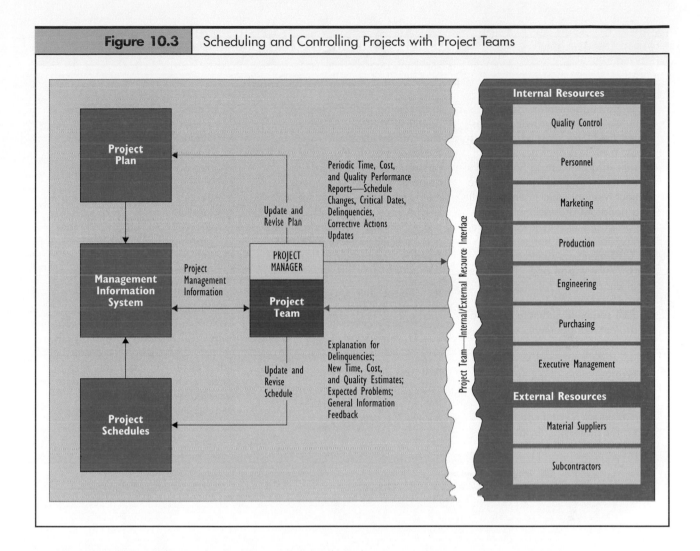

PROJECT-PLANNING AND CONTROL TECHNIQUES

Table 10.1 presents definitions of the terms used in project planning and control. *These terms are the language of project management.* Additionally, we use them to explain the use of scheduling and control charts, CPM, PERT, and project cost control systems.

Scheduling and Control Charts

Scheduling and control charts are the tools most frequently used to manage projects. Each chart first plans and schedules some particular part of the project—what must be done and when it must be done. Second, as the project proceeds, each chart is updated to indicate how much of the plan has been accomplished. In this way, project managers can compare actual project work accomplishment with planned project progress.

BUSINESS SNAPSHOT 10.1

Project Management Professionals

Project management is increasingly viewed as a growing professional field. Like most other professions, a professional association has been organized to help lead this growth. Founded in 1969, the Project Management Institute (PMI) is a nonprofit professional organization based in Newtown Square, Pennsylvania, and has more than 75,000 members worldwide (**http://www.pmi.org**). There are local chapters of PMI in more than 45 countries.

PMI serves to promote the field of project management, to encourage continued education in project management, and to disseminate information about the latest project management tools and approaches. Since 1984, PMI has administered a certification program for professionals interested

in becoming PMP (Project Management Professional) certified. The PMP certification is seen as evidence that an individual has passed industry standards for demonstrating project management knowledge and competency.

The body of knowledge that project management professionals are expected to learn and understand is grouped by PMI into five categories:

- Project initiation
- Project planning
- Project execution
- Project control
- Project closure

PMI alternatively categorizes this body of knowledge into the following *project management knowledge areas:*

- Project integration management
- Project scope management
- Project time management
- Project cost management
- Project quality management
- Project human resources management
- Project communications management
- Project risk management
- Project procurement management

Managing projects is an unavoidable activity in all organizations in all industries. Treating this field as a profession increases the status of project managers and leads to employees that are more knowledgeable, which clearly benefits the organization.

Source: Reprinted from **http://www.pmi.org** with permission of the Project Management Institute Headquarters, Four Campus Boulevard, Newton Square, PA 19073-3299, a worldwide organization dedicated to advancing the state-of-the-art in project management. Phone (610) 356-4600; Fax (610) 356-4647. © 2001 Project Management Institute, Inc. All rights reserved.

This procedure allows rational changes in management's use of resources to complete the project within time, cost, and quality targets.

Perhaps the most frequently used chart is the horizontal bar chart. These charts are applications of Gantt charts. One particularly useful horizontal bar chart is depicted in Figure 10.4. This chart is prepared in advance of the project to plan and schedule the activities of the project. Horizontal bars are drawn for each activity or group of activities along a time dimension. The letters at the beginning of each bar (left) indicate the activities that must be completed before that activity can begin.

After the bar chart is initially prepared, managers can be assured that all the activities of the project are planned for, the order in which the activities must be performed is taken into account, the time estimates for completing each activity are included, and finally, the overall estimated time for completing the project is developed. The horizontal bar chart becomes the overall plan for the project.

As the project proceeds and activities are completed, actual progress is recorded by shading in the horizontal bars. How much of an activity bar to shade in is determined from estimates of the percentage of completion of work involved in each activity. If an activity is estimated to be one-third completed, for example, then one-third of the horizontal bar is shaded in.

Table 10.1	Terms Used in Project Management

Activity—A certain amount of work or a task required in the project.

Activity duration—In CPM, the best estimate of the time to complete an activity. In PERT, the expected time or average time to complete an activity.

Critical activity—An activity that has no room for schedule slippage; if it slips, the entire project completion will slip. An activity with zero slack.

Critical path—The chain of critical activities for the project. The longest path through the network.

Dummy activity—An activity that consumes no time but shows precedence among activities.

Earliest finish (EF)—The earliest that an activity can finish, from the beginning of the project.

Earliest start (ES)—The earliest that an activity can start, from the beginning of the project.

Event—A beginning, completion point, or milestone accomplishment within the project. An activity begins and ends with events.

Latest finish (LF)—The latest that an activity can finish, from the beginning of the project, without causing a delay in the completion of the project.

Latest start (LS)—The latest that an activity can start, from the beginning of the project, without causing a delay in the completion of the project.

Most likely time (t_m)—The time for completing an activity that is the consensus best estimate; used in PERT.

Optimistic time (t_o)—The time for completing an activity if all goes well; used in PERT.

Pessimistic time (t_p)—The time for completing an activity if bad luck is encountered; used in PERT.

Predecessor activity—An activity that must occur before another activity.

Slack—The amount of time that an activity or a group of activities can slip without causing a delay in the completion of the project.

Successor activity—An activity that must occur after another activity.

Periodically, these charts are updated and distributed to all project participants. A vertical line is drawn on the chart corresponding to the date of the status report. Activity progress can be compared to the status date. In Figure 10.4, for example, Activity g, Flight System Design Modifications, can be observed to be on schedule because the horizontal bar is shaded up to the status date vertical line. Activity j, Materials and Components Costs, is approximately one week behind schedule, because its horizontal bar is shaded to a point about one week behind the status date. Similarly, Activity k, Labor and Overhead Costs, is approximately one week ahead of schedule.

These status reports allow managers to observe the progress of the project's activities, identify problem areas, and develop corrective action to bring the project back on target. These reports can be used alone or in conjunction with other techniques. When projects are not very complex, costly, or long lasting, horizontal bar charts can be used alone to plan and control the timely completion of the project. On the other hand, on more complex and costly projects, the charts may be used as a summary of project status even though other, more detailed techniques are also used.

The key advantages of horizontal bar charts are their ease of understanding, ease of modification, and low cost. Their chief disadvantages are that on complex projects the number of activities may require either unwieldy charts or aggregation of activities, and the charts may not adequately indicate the degree of interrelationship among the project's activities.

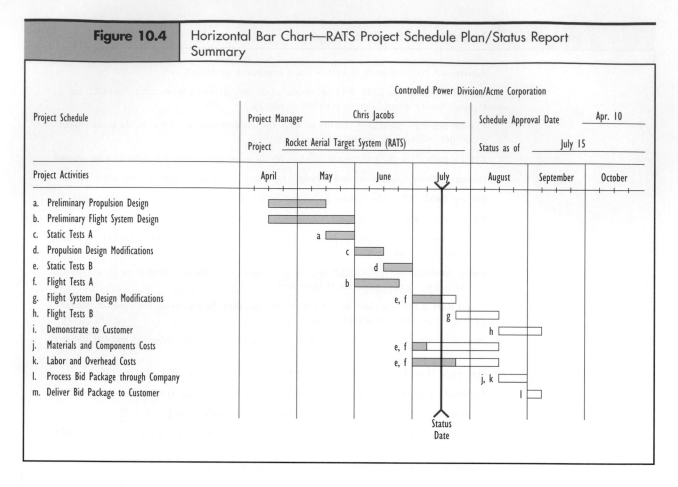

Figure 10.4 | Horizontal Bar Chart—RATS Project Schedule Plan/Status Report Summary

Other charts are used to plan and control the acquisition and use of resources such as cash, personnel, and materials. Figure 10.5 shows one example of a chart used to plan and control expenditures accumulated through June and a projection of expenditures over the remainder of the project.

Managers typically seek answers to these questions from the charts:

- Are we on our spending targets now?
- Do we expect to be on our spending targets at the end of the project?
- If we do not expect to be on our spending targets at the end of the project, should management corrective action begin in order to bring spending in on target?

The delivery of materials, components, and subcontracted parts presents special planning and control problems to project managers. First, the short duration and the unique nonrecurring nature of most projects rule out making components and parts in-house; therefore many materials, components, and parts are purchased from suppliers. Second, projects typically need the materials "yesterday," as the saying goes, because of severe time pressures. Third, materials for projects can be sufficiently different from the organization's other purchased materials that regular suppliers may be passed over in favor of new, untried suppliers specializing in these new materials.

In spite of the uncertainty associated with finding new suppliers and severe time pressures, organizations have learned to successfully manage the acquisition of projects' materials, components, and subcontracted parts. Figure 10.6 shows one chart approach to planning and controlling the acquisition of materials for the RATS project.

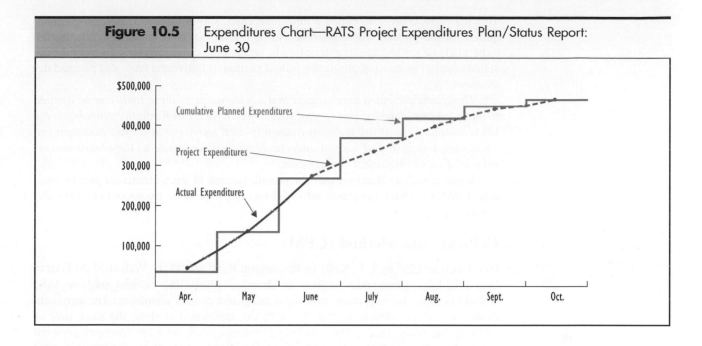

Figure 10.5 Expenditures Chart—RATS Project Expenditures Plan/Status Report: June 30

Figure 10.6 Materials Chart—RATS Project Key Materials Acquisition Plan/Status Report

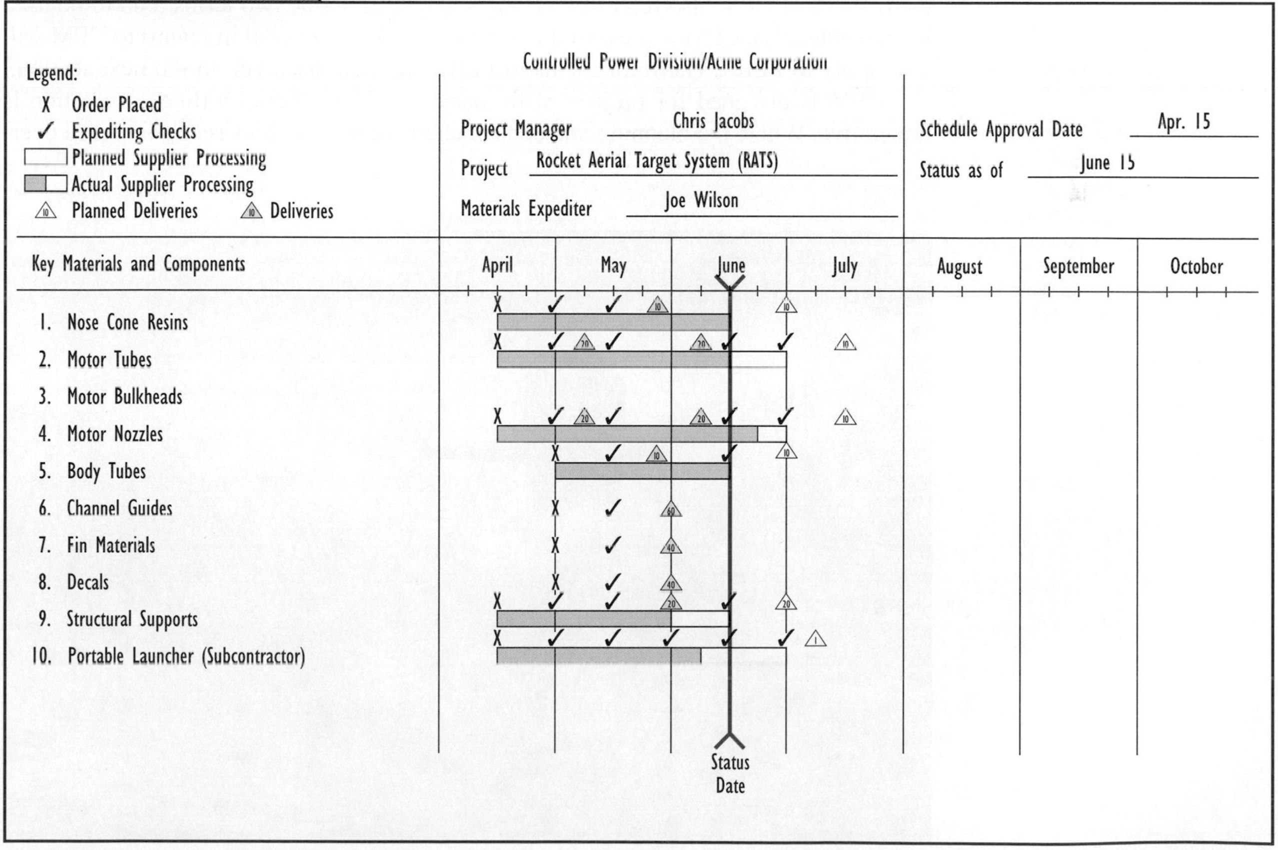

This materials chart, also called a milestone chart, shows the key materials to be acquired for the project, when orders are to be placed (x), when expediting checks are to be made (✓), when the supplier plans to process the order (an open horizontal bar), actual supplier processing progress (colored portion of horizontal bar), and planned deliveries (△).

The charts presented here suggest that a wide range of these tools can be applied to many project-planning and control situations. In fact, this flexibility probably is the key reason that charts are the most frequently used technique in project management. Flexibility, low cost, and ease of understanding—all contribute to the almost universal use of charts in project management.

Some complex situations call for minute control of each elemental part of projects. CPM and PERT have evolved to fill this need for close microcontrol of the duration of projects.

Critical Path Method (CPM)

Developed in 1957 by J. E. Kelly of Remington Rand and M. R. Walker of du Pont to help schedule maintenance projects in chemical plants, the **critical path method (CPM)** is today an important project-planning and control technique. The **program evaluation and review technique (PERT)** was developed at about the same time as CPM by the Navy Special Projects Office in cooperation with the management consulting firm Booz, Allen & Hamilton to plan and control the Polaris atomic-powered submarine and its intercontinental ballistic missile systems. PERT and CPM are alike in most respects, except for a few extra refinements incorporated into PERT that are not found in CPM. Because of the great similarity of the two methods and because many users of CPM also refer to their method as PERT (the two terms tend to be used interchangeably), CPM is presented first and everything covered in regard to CPM will also apply to PERT. The refinements in PERT are then discussed in the next section.

CPM is designed for projects with many activities where on-time completion is imperative. Where the planning and control charts of the previous section offered over-

The PERT technique was developed in response to the need for micromanaging project control for such complicated ventures as manufacturing atomic-powered submarines.

© CORBIS

all macrocontrol, CPM is designed to provide intense microcontrol. In its original form, time performance was considered paramount; in other words, the legacy from government's use of CPM was the implicit assumption of unlimited funds. The federal government was racing to complete the Polaris program to avoid a possible Russian-imposed nuclear blackmail on the United States. Under this critical time pressure, it is no small wonder that unlimited funding was assumed.

CPM today is typically combined with other project cost control systems such as the charts of the previous section. The combination of macrocontrol from control charts and microcontrol from CPM offers management both the big picture and minute detailed control.

Figure 10.7 shows a manager's view of CPM: What information must I supply CPM, and what project management information do I receive in return?

CPM is not a scheduling and controlling system that is done once, set on the shelf, and never used again. Conversely, the system is dynamic. CPM continues to provide management with periodic reports as the project progresses. As Figure 10.8 shows, project managers update their original time estimates for completing each activity as time passes and the computerized CPM system supplies management with current project management information: new estimates of project duration, a new list of critical activities, new activity estimates, and exception reports (e.g., new delinquent activities and compressed activities).

A series of examples now demonstrates the inner workings of CPM. Table 10.2 lists the steps that are followed in a CPM analysis. Examples 10.1 through 10.5 illustrate these steps.

In Example 10.1 the RAMOV project is described and a CPM network for the project is developed. Table 10.3 lists the activities and events for the project, the immediate predecessor activities, and the activity durations. *An activity is a task or a certain amount of work required in the project, and an event just signals the beginning or ending of an activity.* Activities require time to complete; events do not. Activities are represented by straight (not curved) arrows. Events are represented by circles. The first event of a project is always "the project is begun," and the last event of a project is always "the project is ended." The first activities (arrows) of a project are always drawn from the first event (circle), and the last activities of a project are always drawn to end in the last event. This convention avoids dangling arrows at the start and finish of CPM networks. The Immediate Predecessor Activities column in Table 10.3 indicates the order in which the activities must be performed. The activity durations are estimates of how much time will be required to complete each activity.

Figure 10.7	A Manager's View of CPM

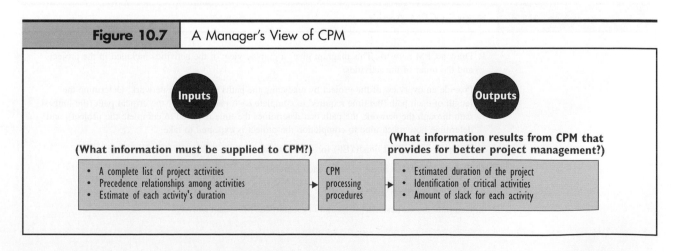

Inputs

(What information must be supplied to CPM?)

- A complete list of project activities
- Precedence relationships among activities
- Estimate of each activity's duration

CPM processing procedures

Outputs

(What information results from CPM that provides for better project management?)

- Estimated duration of the project
- Identification of critical activities
- Amount of slack for each activity

Figure 10.8 | The CPM Management Information System

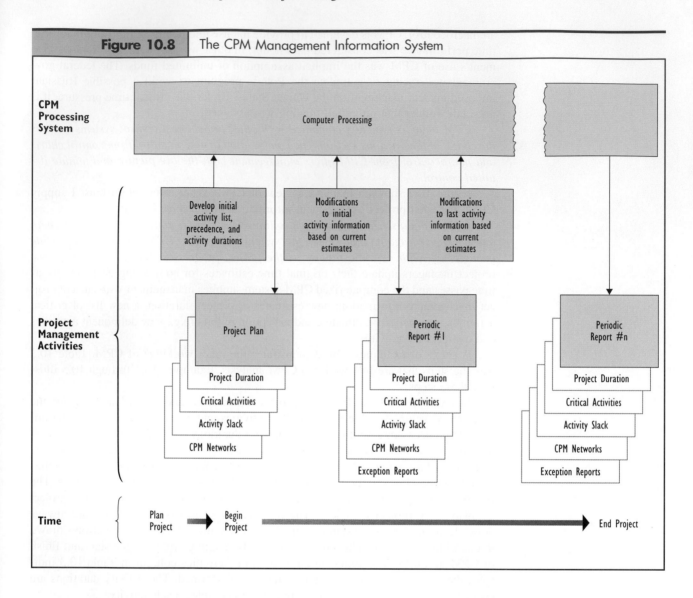

Table 10.2 | Steps in CPM Analysis

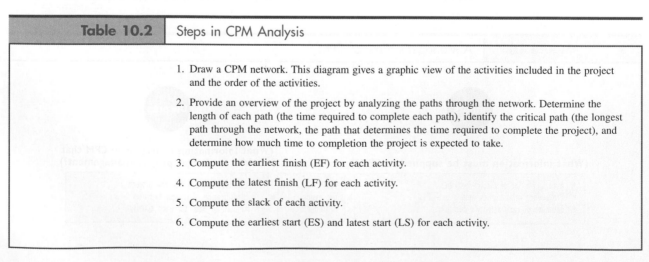

1. Draw a CPM network. This diagram gives a graphic view of the activities included in the project and the order of the activities.

2. Provide an overview of the project by analyzing the paths through the network. Determine the length of each path (the time required to complete each path), identify the critical path (the longest path through the network, the path that determines the time required to complete the project), and determine how much time to completion the project is expected to take.

3. Compute the earliest finish (EF) for each activity.

4. Compute the latest finish (LF) for each activity.

5. Compute the slack of each activity.

6. Compute the earliest start (ES) and latest start (LS) for each activity.

| Example 10.1 | Drawing the CPM Network of the RAMOV Project |

A project team has been organized at Manufacturing Technology Inc. (MTI) to design and develop a slightly different version of one of the firm's industrial robots. The new robot is called the Random Access Mobile Orthogonal Vision (RAMOV) robot. RAMOV is mobile, has visual capabilities, is multiaxial, and is programmable on the shop floor. One of MTI's most important customers, a large automobile manufacturer, plans to replace a bank of machines with the new robots on its assembly lines in five factories. The customer wants to see a demonstration of the robot, a technical proposal, and a cost proposal in two months. The first thing that the project team did was list and describe the project's activities, determine the order of the activities, and estimate how much time each activity would take. This information about the activities and events of the project is presented in Table 10.3. Prepare a CPM diagram from the information in Table 10.3.

| Table 10.3 | Activities and Events of the RAMOV Project |

Activity	Immediate Predecessor Activities	Activity Duration (days)
a. Design RAMOV	—	20
b. Build prototype units	a	10
c. Perform tests of prototypes	b	8
d. Estimate material costs	a	11
e. Refine RAMOV design	c,d	7
f. Demonstrate RAMOV to customer	e	6
g. Estimate labor costs	d	12
h. Prepare technical proposal	e	13
i. Deliver proposal to customer	g,h	5

Event

1. The project is begun.
2. The RAMOV design is completed.
3. The prototype units have been built.
4. The prototype tests are completed.
5. The material cost estimates are completed.
6. The RAMOV design refinement is completed.
7. The technical proposal and the labor cost estimates are completed.
8. The RAMOV units have been demonstrated and the proposal has been delivered to the customer. The project is ended.

| Solution |

1. First, look at Figure 10.9. This figure contains the conventions that are followed in drawing CPM networks.
2. Next, start with the activity and event information in Table 10.3. Activities are tasks or work that must be done as the project progresses and are represented by straight arrows. Events are the beginning or ending of activities and are represented by circles. The project begins

with Event 1, which is followed by Activity a. The order of the activities is found in the Immediate Predecessor Activities column of Table 10.3 and indicates which activity or activities must be completed just before each activity can begin. For instance, Activity b's immediate predecessor activity is Activity a. This means that Activity a must be completed before Activity b can begin.

3. Draw the CPM network and place each activity's letter under its arrow:

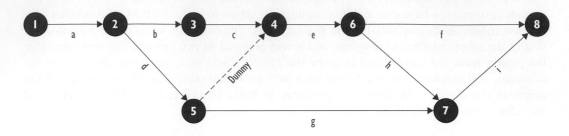

Note that both Activity c and Activity d are immediate predecessors to Activity e. To show that Activity d must be completed before beginning Activity e, a dummy activity is used. A **dummy activity** involves no work and no time; it simply shows the precedence relationship, or the order of the activities.

Study the conventions for drawing CPM networks in Figure 10.9 first, and then follow through Example 10.1. Notice that Conventions 6 and 7 in Figure 10.9 use a dummy activity. A dummy activity indicates only precedence relationships, or the order in which activities must be performed. Dummy activities do not require any time or effort. Once we have a CPM network, we have a graphic view of the activities that have to be completed in the project, the order in which the activities must be performed, and the interrelationships among the activities. To draw such networks, you are advised to first sketch a rough draft of the network on a sheet of paper. Then determine if the immediate predecessor activity information for the project fits your draft. If it does not, revise the draft and transfer it in its finished form to another sheet of paper.

Example 10.2 provides an overview of the RAMOV project by performing an analysis of the project's paths. In this example, the activity durations of each of the five paths are totaled to determine how much time each path is estimated to require. Notice that path a–b–c–e–h–i is estimated to require 63 days and that this is the longest path, or the critical path. All other paths are estimated to require less than 63 days. If the critical path were to be delayed for any reason, the project would also be delayed by the same amount of time.

Example 10.2	Providing an Overview of the RAMOV Project: Analyzing Its Paths

Now that the network diagram for the RAMOV project has been developed in Example 10.1, analyze the paths through the network. Determine which path is the critical path and how long the completion of the project is expected to take.

| Figure 10.9 | CPM Network Conventions |

Network Representation | **Interpretation**

1. Activity a must be completed before Activity b can begin.

2. Activities b and c can occur concurrently, but Activity a must be completed before either Activity b or c can begin.

3. Activities a and b can occur concurrently, but Activity c cannot begin until both a and b are completed.

4. Activities a and b, c and d can occur concurrently, but both Activities a and b must be completed before either Activity c or d can begin.

5. Activity a must be completed before Activity b can begin, and Activity c must be completed before Activity d can begin, but path a–b is independent of path c–d.

6. Activity a must be completed before either Activity b or c can begin. Activities b and c must both be completed before Activity d can begin. The dashed arrow is a dummy activity. Dummy activities have zero duration and show only precedence relationships.

7. Activities a and b, c and d can occur concurrently, but both Activities a and b must be completed before Activity c can begin and Activity b must be completed before Activity d can begin. The dashed arrow is a dummy activity. Dummy activities have zero time duration and show only precedence relationships.

Solution

1. First, write the duration of each activity below its arrow. For instance, a = 20 is written below a's arrow:

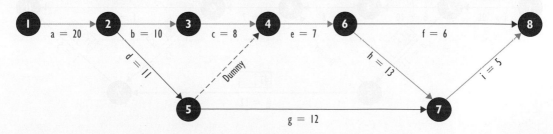

2. Next, identify the paths and compute the length of each path:

Paths	Length of Paths (days)
a–b–c–e–f	20 + 10 + 8 + 7 + 6 = 51
a–b–c–e–h–i	20 + 10 + 8 + 7 + 13 + 5 = 63*
a–d–e–f	20 + 11 + 7 + 6 = 44
a–d–e–h–i	20 + 11 + 7 + 13 + 5 = 56
a–d–g–i	20 + 11 + 12 + 5 = 48

*Critical path.

The longest path is 63 days, and it is the critical path. The critical path determines the length of the project; therefore, the project is expected to take 63 days to complete.

Example 10.3 illustrates how the **earliest finish (EF)** values are computed for each activity in the RAMOV project. EF is the earliest elapsed time from the beginning of the project that we can finish an activity. By following along the CPM network *from left to right,* the EF values are written in the left-hand part of the box over each activity's arrow. Activities that begin a project always have EFs equal to their durations (D). If an activity has more than one immediate predecessor activity, its EF is computed by using the largest EF among the immediate predecessor activities. The expected project completion time is the largest EF of all those activities that end at the very last event. This largest EF represents the length of the critical path.

Example 10.3	Computing Earliest Finish (EF) for the RAMOV Project's Activities

From the network in Example 10.1 compute the earliest finish (EF) for each activity. Write the EF for each activity in the left-hand part of the box over its arrow. Begin at Event 1 and move *from left to right* across the network and determine the EF value for each activity. EF represents the earliest elapsed time from the beginning of the project that we can finish an activity. *For all activities that begin a project, their EFs are their durations.* For instance, the EF of Activity a is 20, which is its duration, because it begins the project. *For all other activities, an activity's EF is the EF of its immediate predecessor activity plus its duration (D).* Let us compute the EF values:

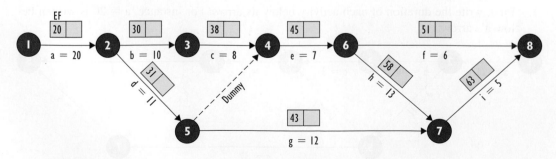

$$EF_a = 20$$
$$EF_b = EF_a + D_b = 20 + 10 = 30$$
$$EF_c = EF_b + D_c = 30 + 8 = 38$$
$$EF_d = EF_a + D_d = 20 + 11 = 31$$
$$EF_e = EF_c + D_e = 38 + 7 = 45$$
$$EF_f = EF_e + D_f = 45 + 6 = 51$$
$$EF_g = EF_d + D_g = 31 + 12 = 43$$
$$EF_h = EF_e + D_h = 45 + 13 = 58$$
$$EF_i = EF_h + D_i = 58 + 5 = 63$$

*Note that when an activity has two or more immediate predecessor activities, the **largest EF** among the immediate predecessor activities must be used in computing its EF.* For instance, Activity i has two immediate predecessor activities—h and g. Because $EF_h = 58$ is larger than $EF_g = 43$, EF_h must be used to compute EF_i:

$$EF_i = EF_h + D_i = 58 + 5 = 63$$

Similarly, Activity e has two predecessors—c and d. Because $EF_c = 38$ is larger than $EF_d = 31$, EF_c must be used to compute EF_e:

$$EF_e = EF_c + D_e = 38 + 7 = 45$$

The largest EF of the activities ending at Event 8 represents the expected project completion time and the length of the critical path. In this example, the largest EF is $EF_i = 63$, so the RAMOV project is expected to be completed 63 days after it is started.

Example 10.4 illustrates how the latest finish (LF) and slack (S) values are computed for each activity in the RAMOV project. LF is the latest elapsed time from the beginning of the project that we can finish an activity without delaying project completion. By following along the CPM network from *right to left*, the LF values are written in the right-hand part of the box over each activity's arrow. Activities that end in the last event of a project always have LFs equal to the largest EF among the activities of the project. If an activity has more than one immediate successor activity, its LF is the smallest LF − D among its immediate successor activities. The slack (S) value for an activity is computed by subtracting its EF from its LF and entering the value in the top part of the box over its arrow.

Example 10.4	Computing Latest Finish (LF) and Slack (S) for the RAMOV Project's Activities

In Example 10.3, by means of a left-to-right pass through the network, the earliest finishes (EF) for all the activities in the project have been completed. Now compute the latest finish (LF) and slack (S) for each activity.

Solution

1. Compute the LF for each activity:

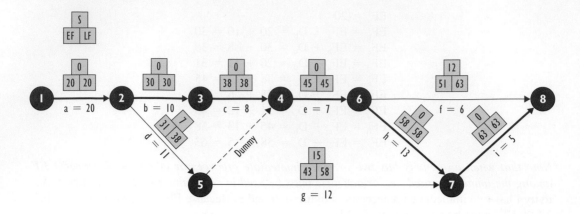

Begin at Event 8 at the far right-hand side of the diagram and move *from right to left* through the network. Write the LF for each activity in the right-hand part of the box over its arrow. *LF represents the latest elapsed time from the beginning of the project that we can finish an activity. The LF for all activities that end in the last event will always be the greatest EF of the project.* The LF of Activities f and i is therefore 63 days, the same as EF_i, which is the greatest EF of all the activities:

$$LF_i = EF_i = 63$$
$$LF_f = EF_i = 63$$

The LF for any other activity is computed by subtracting the immediate successor activity's (the activity to its immediate right in the network) duration (D) from the immediate successor activity's latest finish (LF). The latest finishes for the activities in the project are computed as follows:

$$LF_h = LF_i - D_i = 63 - 5 = 58$$
$$LF_g = LF_i - D_i = 63 - 5 = 58$$
$$LF_e = LF_h - D_h = 58 - 13 = 45*$$
$$LF_d = LF_e - D_e = 45 - 7 = 38*$$
$$LF_c = LF_e - D_e = 45 - 7 = 38$$
$$LF_b = LF_c - D_c = 38 - 8 = 30$$
$$LF_a = LF_b - D_b = 30 - 10 = 20*$$

*Note that when an activity has more than one immediate succeeding activity (activities to its immediate right in the network), its LF is computed by comparing the values of LF − D for all the immediate succeeding activities. The **smallest LF − D** value is then used as its LF.* For instance, Activities e, d, and a above have an asterisk (*) to indicate that these activities have more than one succeeding activity. Take Activity e, for instance: Both Activities f and h succeed Activity e. LF_e is computed thus:

$$LF_e = LF_f - D_f = 63 - 6 = 57 \quad \text{or} \quad LF_e = LF_h - D_h = 58 - 13 = 45$$

Therefore, $LF_e = 45$.

2. Compute the slack (S) for each activity:
    For each activity, $S = LF - EF$. For each activity, subtract its EF from its LF and write the value of S in the top part of the box over its arrow. The slack for all the activities in the network is computed as follows:

$$S_i = LF_i - EF_i = 63 - 63 = 0^*$$
$$S_h = LF_h - EF_h = 58 - 58 = 0^*$$
$$S_g = LF_g - EF_g = 58 - 43 = 15$$
$$S_f = LF_f - EF_f = 63 - 51 = 12$$
$$S_e = LF_e - EF_e = 45 - 45 = 0^*$$
$$S_d = LF_d - EF_d = 38 - 31 = 7$$
$$S_c = LF_c - EF_c = 38 - 38 = 0^*$$
$$S_b = LF_b - EF_b = 30 - 30 = 0^*$$
$$S_a = LF_a - EF_a = 20 - 20 = 0^*$$

Notice that the asterisked activities above have zero slack. These **critical activities** are on the critical path a–b–c–e–h–i, which is denoted by the bold-faced arrows through the network.

Adjacent activities on sections of paths share slack. For instance, consider path a d g i in the CPM network. Activity d has 7 days of slack, and Activity g has 15 days of slack. But the sum of activity durations along the path is 48 days. This means that there is a *total* of $63 - 48 = 15$ days of slack along the path. Therefore, 7 days of slack are shared between Activities d and g.

Example 10.5 completes the CPM analysis of the RAMOV project. In this example, the EF, LF, and S values are transferred from the network in Example 10.4 to the table. Then the **earliest start (ES)** and **latest start (LS)** values for each activity are computed using these formulas and entered into the table:

$$ES = EF - D$$
$$LS = LF - D$$

The table in Example 10.5 is typical of the outputs of CPM computer programs. The slack (S) values for each activity indicate how much an activity can be delayed without the completion time of the project being delayed. *The activities with zero slack are the activities on the critical path. If any activities on the critical path are delayed, the project completion time will also be delayed by the same amount of time.*

Example 10.5	Computing Earliest Start (ES) and Latest Start (LS) for the RAMOV Project's Activities

Solution

From the network in Example 10.4, compute the earliest start (ES) and latest start (LS) for each activity.

Obtain the EF, LF, and S values for each activity in Example 10.4, and place them in the table on the next page. Then compute the ES and LS values for each activity with these formulas:

$$ES = EF - D$$
$$LS = LF - D$$

Activity	Activity Duration (D)	Earliest Start (ES)	Earliest Finish (EF)	Latest Start (LS)	Latest Finish (LF)	Slack (S)
a	20	0	20	0	20	0
b	10	20	30	20	30	0
c	8	30	38	30	38	0
d	11	20	31	27	38	7
e	7	38	45	38	45	0
f	6	45	51	57	63	12
g	12	31	43	46	58	15
h	13	45	58	45	58	0
i	5	58	63	58	63	0

We have now demonstrated how CPM analysis develops information for management—project duration, critical activities, and activity slack. These computations are developed in the beginning of the project and modified when new estimates are provided as the project proceeds. Figure 10.8 illustrated how this updating of CPM takes place. These updates result in new periodic reports that are sent to project managers. CPM exception reports, delinquent activities reports, and compressed activities reports are examples of reports that provide project managers with current information about the details of the project, thus allowing close control of the activities.

Now that we have studied CPM, let us turn to PERT.

Program Evaluation and Review Technique (PERT)

PERT is almost identical to CPM in regard to its functions, network diagrams, internal calculations, and resulting project management reports. The minor exceptions surround the activity time estimates.*

In CPM an activity's duration is based on a single time estimate. In PERT three time estimates are made for each activity: pessimistic time (t_p), if bad luck were encountered; most likely time (t_m), the consensus best estimate; and optimistic time (t_o), if all goes well. From these three time estimates a mean (t_e) and variance (V_t) are computed for each activity:

$$t_e = (t_o + 4t_m + t_p)/6 \qquad \text{and} \qquad V_t = [(t_p - t_o)/6]^2$$

Why does PERT use multiple activity time estimates? Because we are *uncertain* about the duration of the activities. By estimating a pessimistic time and an optimistic time, a likely range of the duration is provided. The most likely time is our best estimate of the duration. Three time estimates allow the development of an average duration and a variance for each path in the network, thus totally defining the paths' duration distributions. The mean duration of a path is equal to the sum of its activity mean durations, and the variance of the path is equal to the sum of its activity variances. When the duration distribution of a path is assumed to be normal and its mean and variance have been computed, we can make probabilistic statements about the path. For example: (1) There is only a 10 percent probability that the critical path will be greater than 35 weeks. (2) There is a 35 percent probability that the project can be completed in less than 50 weeks. The ability to make probabilistic statements about

*Note to instructors: For simplicity of presentation, the activity-on-arrow (AOA) convention is used for both CPM and PERT.

Project managers have a variety of techniques to estimate cost and time requirements. What technique would best help the manager of this construction project?

© SUSAN VAN ET-EN

project path durations is the only difference between CPM and PERT. PERT uses t_e for activity durations, whereas CPM uses a single time estimate for activity durations; all other calculations of the two methods are identical.

Example 10.6 illustrates how PERT would be used to analyze the RAMOV project.

Example 10.6 | A PERT Analysis of the RAMOV Project

Refer to the description of the RAMOV project in Example 10.1. The project team has been asked by the customer to estimate the probability that the project could be completed within 65 days. To answer this question, the team developed three time estimates for each of the project's activities. Develop a PERT analysis of the project, and answer the customer's question.

Solution

1. First, compute the mean and variance for each activity:

Activity	Optimistic Time (t_o)	Most Likely Time (t_m)	Pessimistic Time (t_p)	Mean Duration $t_e = (t_o + 4t_m + t_p)/6$	Variance $V_t = [(t_p - t_o)/6]^2$
a	18	20	22	20.00	.44
b	8	10	14	10.33	1.00
c	5	8	9	7.67	.44
d	10	11	12	11.00	.11
e	7	7	7	7.00	0
f	4	6	7	5.83	.25
g	10	12	14	12.00	.44
h	12	13	15	13.17	.25
i	5	5	5	5.00	0

2. Next, draw the PERT network and compute the earliest finish (EF), latest finish (LF), and slack (S) for each activity. Determine the critical path.

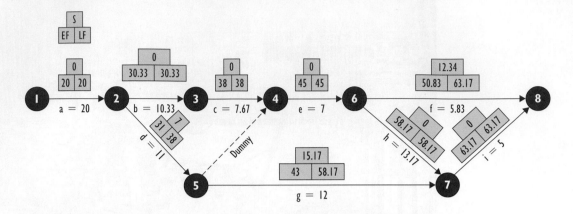

As we can see from the network above, the a–b–c–e–h–i path is the critical path and is expected to take 63.17 days.

3. Next, compute the standard deviation of the critical path:

Sum the variances of the activities along the critical path a–b–c–e–h–i:

$$V_{path} = V_a + V_b + V_c + V_e + V_h + V_i = 0.44 + 1.0 + 0.44 + 0 + 0.25 + 0 = 2.13$$

$$\sigma_{path} = \sqrt{\text{Variance of Path a–b–c–e–h–i}} = \sqrt{2.13} = 1.46 \text{ days}$$

4. Next, compute the probability of completing the project within 65 days:

Assuming that the distribution of the a–b–c–e–h–i path's completion time is normal with a mean of 63.17 days and a standard deviation of 1.46 days:

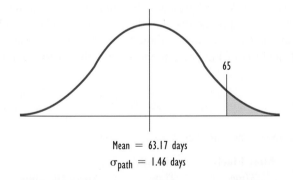

Mean $= 63.17$ days
$\sigma_{path} = 1.46$ days

Find how many standard deviations 65 days is from the mean:

$$Z = \frac{65 - 63.17}{\sigma_{path}} = \frac{65 - 63.17}{1.46} = 1.25$$

In Appendix A at the end of this book, locate $Z = 1.25$ in the left-hand margin of the table. The probability that the project will be completed in less than 65 days is 0.89435 (about 89.4 percent), but that is the good news. The bad news is that there is a 0.10565 (about 10.6 percent) probability that the project will take longer than 65 days.

We must use some care when interpreting the meaning of a critical path in a PERT analysis. The critical path in a PERT analysis is simply the path with the longest *expected* duration. The critical path in Example 10.6 was Path a–b–c–e–h–i, which had an expected duration of 63.17 days, and there was a probability of 10.6 percent that this path could take longer than 65 days. There could be one or more paths in the RAMOV network that could have smaller expected durations but which are subject to great uncertainty. Such *noncritical paths* could actually have a greater probability than Path a–b–c–e–h–i of taking longer than 65 days to complete. In such cases, the variance of the critical path understates the actual variance of the project duration. The significance of this point is that when PERT is used, analysts should pay attention to the critical path and any other paths with expected durations close to the critical path when determining the probability of exceeding some particular project completion date. Example 10.7 illustrates this concept.

| **Example 10.7** | A Closer Look at PERT Critical Paths |

Given these two PERT paths, which one offers the greatest probability of exceeding a 20-week target (T) project duration?

$$\textbf{Path 1: } \Sigma t_e = 19.34 \text{ weeks, } \sigma_t = 0.780 \text{ week (critical path)}$$
$$\textbf{Path 2: } \Sigma t_e = 19.17 \text{ weeks, } \sigma_t = 1.170 \text{ weeks (noncritical path)}$$

Solution

1. Compare the two paths' duration distributions:

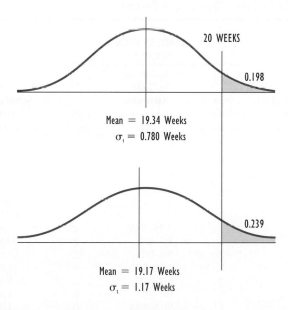

2. Compute the probability of each path's duration taking longer than 20 weeks. Compute the Z value for each path, use the Z values and look up the probability of each path's duration (D) taking less than 20 weeks in Appendix A, then compute the probability of each path's duration (D) taking longer than 20 weeks:

$$Z_1 = (T - \Sigma t_e)/\sigma_t = (20 - 19.34)/0.780 = 0.846$$

From Appendix A, $P(D_1 < 20 \text{ weeks}) = 0.80234$.

$$P(D_1 > 20 \text{ weeks}) = 1 - 0.80234 = 0.198$$

$$Z_2 = (T - \Sigma t_e)/\sigma_t = (20 - 19.17)/1.170 = 0.709$$

From Appendix A, $P(D_2 < 20 \text{ weeks}) = 0.76115$.

$$P(D_1 > 20 \text{ weeks}) = 1 - 0.76115 = 0.239$$

3. The duration of Path 2 (a noncritical path) actually has a higher probability of exceeding the 20-week target than Path 1 (the critical path).

Project Cost Control Systems

CPM and PERT are designed to offer project managers planning, scheduling, and control aimed at only one project performance dimension—time performance. Most organizations today, whether goods producing or service producing, private industry or government, must also plan and control for another project performance dimension—cost or project expenditures.

PERT/Cost was devised by the Department of Defense (DOD) and the National Aeronautics and Space Administration (NASA) in 1962 to tie together time and cost performance on government contracts. The term **PERT/Cost** is often used as a description of the general class of project time/cost planning and control systems.

One common PERT/Cost report is depicted in Table 10.4: the RATS Time/Cost Status Report. These computerized reports periodically show actual time and cost sta-

Table 10.4	RATS Time/Cost Status Report

ACTIVITY			TIME STATUS (WEEKS)			COST STATUS (THOUSANDS OF DOLLARS)		
Activity	Account Number	Scheduled Activity Duration	New Estimated Duration	Estimated vs. Latest Allowable Completion Date	Activity Slack	Scheduled Activity Cost	Actual Cost to Date	Estimated Cost (Over) or Under to Complete Activity
a	R-100	4	4	*		36.5	40.0	(3.5)
b	R-101	5	5	*		60.0	66.0	(6.0)
c	R-102	2	2	*		35.0	30.5	4.5
d	R-103	2	2	*		28.5	28.5	—
e	R-104	2	2	*		42.0	40.0	2.0
f	R-105	3	3	*		67.5	65.0	2.5
g	R-106	3	3	7/15–7/15	2	52.0	31.0	5.0
h	R-107	3	3	8/7–8/7	2	39.5	—	—
i	R-108	2	2	9/1–9/1	2	63.5	—	—
j	R-109	6	7	8/22–8/22	0	14.0	4.5	(4.0)
k	R-110	6	5	8/7–8/22	2	9.5	5.0	2.0
l	R-111	2	2	9/7–9/7	0	1.0	—	—
m	R-112	1	1	9/15–9/15	0	1.0	—	—
							Total	2.5

*Activity is complete.

tus compared to scheduled status for each activity of the project. For example, Activity c can be evaluated as follows: (1) The activity is completed. (2) The actual duration of the activity was the same as the scheduled duration. (3) An amount of $4,500 less than scheduled cost was actually expended on the activity. Similarly, Activity j can be evaluated as follows: (1) The activity is incomplete. (2) The activity duration has slipped from six weeks as scheduled to an estimated seven weeks. (3) The estimated completion date and the latest allowable completion date are the same—August 22. (4) There is zero slack for the activity. If the activity duration slips beyond the estimated seven weeks, the entire project will also slip by an equal amount of time. (5) Although the actual activity cost is well below the scheduled activity cost, the activity is estimated to be overspent by $4,000 at the completion of the activity. These evaluations of the project's activities give project managers information to better manage the project's activities. These and similar reports can be designed to offer much more refined exhibition of costs. The cost status of Table 10.4 could, for example, be broken into labor, materials, and overhead, or any other meaningful division of costs for each activity.

Charts and other visual devices are used to assess simultaneously the cost and time status of projects. Figure 10.10 is an example of a chart that summarizes a project's actual time and cost status compared to the project schedule. It shows that the RATS project on July 15 is about one week behind schedule and approximately $30,000 overspent. Expenditures are projected to be about the same as scheduled at the end of the project.

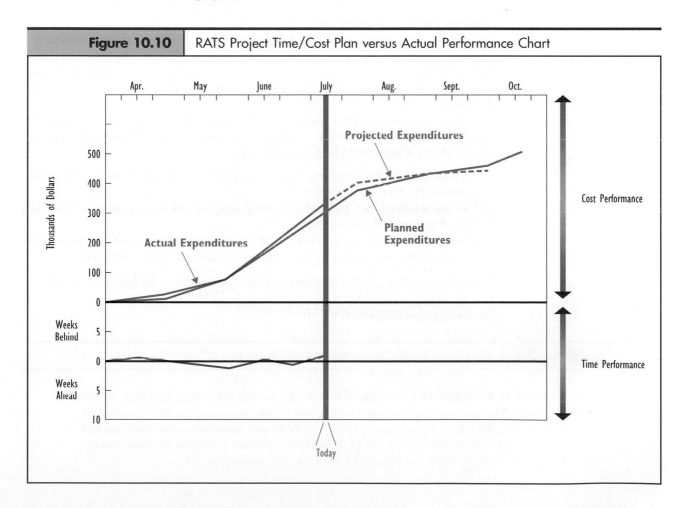

| **Figure 10.10** | RATS Project Time/Cost Plan versus Actual Performance Chart |

Regardless of the format for time/cost status reports for projects, cost performance and time performance are both critically important elements of project management.

CPM/PERT in Practice

CPM/PERT is widely used across a great variety of organizations. But it tends to be used across a narrow range of applications. Project planning and control dominate all other applications, while production planning and control and maintenance planning and control account for the remainder of the uses of PERT/CPM.

Target Slack versus Project Slack

Example 10.4, the RAMOV project, computes the slack for each activity—the amount of time that an activity can slip without causing a delay in the project completion. The slack is based on the duration of the critical path, which is 63 days. If the customer requirement were 65 days even if any critical activity slipped 2 days, the customer requirement would still be met. Each of the activities, then, in reality has 2 additional days of slack if the standard is the customer requirement. Some organizations add this additional slack on to the project slack of each activity; thus, activity slack is based on a target project duration rather than critical path duration.

Activity Cost–Time Trade-Offs

Project managers occasionally may have the option of *crashing*, or **accelerating,** activities—spending extra money to compress an activity's duration by using overtime, subcontracting, expediting materials, and so on. If projects are in danger of running over the allowable project duration, managers often consider crashing as a viable alternative.

Given that managers have several activities in the project that can be crashed or accelerated, how does one decide which activities not to crash, which activities to crash, if any, and in what order? The general rules are:

1. Crash only critical activities—activities on the critical path, those activities with zero slack.
2. Crash activities with the lowest crashing cost per unit of time first until the desired project duration is achieved.
3. When parallel critical paths exist, each of the parallel paths must be compressed. Accelerating only one of the paths will not reduce the project duration.

Example 10.8 illustrates the application of these principles in the RAMOV project.

Example 10.8	Cost–Time Trade-Offs in the RAMOV Project

MTI's customer in Examples 10.1 through 10.5 wants to shorten the completion time of the RAMOV project. The customer has indicated willingness to discuss paying for MTI's additional costs for shortening the length of the project. The RAMOV project team knows that overtime and other means can be used to accelerate some of the activities. Toward preparing for these discussions, the RAMOV project team has prepared these cost–time trade-offs:

Activity	Present Duration (days)	Accelerated Duration (days)	Present Cost	Accelerated Cost
a	20	18	$10,000	$14,000
b	10	5	12,000	16,500
c	8	3	6,000	11,000
d	11	9	4,000	5,600
e	7*	—	—	—
f	6*	—	—	—
g	12	9	9,000	11,000
h	13	12	12,000	13,500
i	5*	—	—	—

*These activities cannot be accelerated.

If the goal is to reduce the completion time of the project as much as possible, in what order and by how much would you accelerate the activities of the RAMOV project, and what would be the cost of accelerating the activities?

Solution

1. First, develop a CPM network for the project without accelerating any of the activities. This CPM network was developed in Example 10.4:

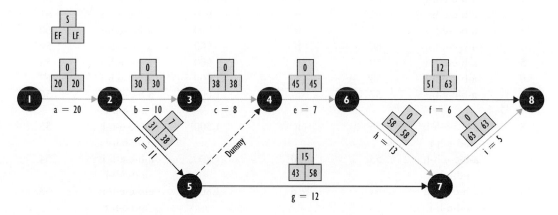

2. Next, compute the cost per day of accelerating each activity that could be accelerated:

	(1)	(2) Maximum Amount of Acceleration (days)	(3) Additional Cost of Acceleration	(4) Acceleration Cost per Day [$/day = (3)/(2)]
	Activity			
	a	2	$4,000	$2,000
	b	5	4,500	900
	c	5	5,000	1,000
	d	2	1,600	800
	g	3	2,000	667
	h	1	1,500	1,500

3. Next, develop the steps in accelerating the project. We assume that an activity's present duration can be partially accelerated by any number of days, but it cannot be below its minimum "accelerated duration." We also make the simplifying assumption that the acceleration cost per day that was computed above applies to each additional day that an activity is accelerated. (In practice, some activities may cost increasingly more for each additional day they are accelerated.)

    The acceleration process follows these steps:

Step 1.   Identify the current critical path(s).

Step 2.   Identify all possible alternative combinations of activities on the critical paths that could be accelerated by one day and would result in the project duration being shortened by one day. If there are no alternatives, then the project has been accelerated as much as possible.

Step 3.   Compute the cost of each alternative activity or set of activities.

Step 4.   Select the least-cost alternative and accelerate the activity or activities by one day. Keep track of the current duration of each activity in the project.

Step 5.   Go back to Step 1 and repeat all steps.

The table below summarizes all the iterations of the project acceleration process.

Iteration	Current Critical Path(s)	Project Duration (days)	Activities to Accelerate by One Day	Additional Acceleration Cost	New Critical Path(s)	New Project Duration (days)
1	a-b-c-e-h-i	63	b	$ 900	a-b-c-e-h-i	62
2	a-b-c-e-h-i	62	b	900	a-b-c-e-h-i	61
3	a-b-c-e-h-i	61	b	900	a-b-c-e-h-i	60
4	a-b-c-e-h-i	60	b	900	a-b-c-e-h-i	59
5	a-b-c-e-h-i	59	b	900	a-b-c-e-h-i	58
6	a-b-c-e-h-i	58	c	1,000	a-b-c-e-h-i	57
7	a-b-c-e-h-i	57	c	1,000	a-b-c-e-h-i; a-d-e-h-i	56
8	a-b-c-e-h-i; a-d-e-h-i	56	h	1,500	a-b-c-e-h-i; a-d-e-h-i	55
9	a-b-c-e-h-i; a-d-e-h-i	55	c,d	1,800	a-b-c-e-h-i; a-d-e-h-i	54
10	a-b-c-e-h-i; a-d-e-h-i	54	c,d	1,800	a-b-c-e-h-i; a-d-e-h-i	53
11	a-b-c-e-h-i; a-d-e-h-i	53	a	2,000	a-b-c-e-h-i; a-d-e-h-i	52
12	a-b-c-e-h-i; a-d-e-h-i	52	a	2,000	a-b-c-e-h-i; a-d-e-h-i	51*

*Every activity on critical path a-d-e-h-i has been accelerated to its minimum accelerated duration, so the project has been accelerated as much as possible.

Iteration I

Step 1:   The initial critical path is a–b–c–e–h–i, and the initial project duration is 63 days.

Steps 2 and 3:   The alternative activities on the critical path that could be accelerated by one day and would result in the project duration being one day shorter are:

Activity	Additional Cost of Acceleration
a	$2,000
b	900
c	1,000
h	1,500

Step 4:   Activity b is the least-cost alternative, so it is selected and its activity duration is accelerated from 10 days down to 9 days at an additional cost of $900. This results in a new project duration of 62 days.

Iterations 2, 3, 4, and 5

Activity b would also be selected in Iterations 2 through 5. After Iteration 5, Activity b is at its minimum accelerated duration, the project duration is 58 days, and the critical path is still a–b–c–e–h–i.

Iteration 6

Step 1:   The current critical path is a–b–c–e–h–i, and the current project duration is 58 days.

Steps 2 and 3:   The alternative activities on the critical path that could be accelerated by one day and would result in the project duration being one day shorter are:

Activity	Additional Cost of Acceleration
a	$2,000
c	1,000
h	1,500

Step 4:   Activity c is the least-cost alternative, so it is selected and its activity duration is accelerated from 8 days down to 7 days at an additional cost of $1,000. This results in a new project duration of 57 days.

Iteration 7

Activity c is also selected in Iteration 7, and the new project duration is 56 days. However, now there are two critical paths: a–b–c–e–h–i and a–d–e–h–i.

Iteration 8

Step 1:   The current critical paths are a–b–c–e–h–i and a–d–e–h–i, and the current project duration is 56 days.

Steps 2 and 3:   The alternative activities or combinations of activities that could be accelerated by one day and would result in both critical paths being one day shorter are:

Activity	Additional Cost of Acceleration
a	$2,000
c and d	1,800
h	1,500

Step 4:   Activity h is the least-cost alternative, so it is selected and its activity duration is accelerated from 13 days down to 12 days at an additional cost of $1,500. This results in a new project duration of 55 days. Activity h is now at its minimum accelerated duration.

Iteration 9

Step 1:   The current critical paths are a–b–c–e–h–i and a–d–e–h–i.

Steps 2 and 3:   The alternative activities or combinations of activities that could be accelerated by one day and would result in both critical paths being one day shorter are:

Activity	Additional Cost of Acceleration
a	$2,000
c and d	1,800

Step 4:   Activities c and d together are the least-cost alternative, so they are selected and their activity durations are each accelerated by one day at an additional cost of $1,800. This results in a new project duration of 54 days.

Iteration 10

Activities c and d are also selected in Iteration 10. Activity d is now at its minimum accelerated duration, but Activity c is not.

Iterations 11 and 12

Step 1:   The current critical paths are a–b–c–e–h–i and a–d–e–h–i.

Steps 2 and 3:   Activity a is the only alternative that would shorten both critical paths. Although Activity c could still be accelerated by one more day, doing so would not shorten critical path a–d–e–h–i.

After Iteration 12, Activity a is at its minimum accelerated duration. Also, every activity on critical path a–d–e–h–i has been shortened to its minimum accelerated duration, so the project has now been accelerated as much as possible. The resulting minimum project duration is 51 days and the total additional cost to accelerate the project from 63 days to 51 days is the sum of the additional acceleration cost in each iteration, or $15,600.

COMPUTER SOFTWARE FOR PROJECT MANAGEMENT

Most project management applications today use computers extensively. Although our PERT/CPM calculations in this chapter have been performed manually, such applications are almost never calculated without computers.

The *POM Software Library* that accompanies this book has both CPM and PERT modules. The user inputs activity time estimates and precedence information, and the programs output slack for each activity, duration and variance for critical paths, and other useful project management information. A few of the common software packages are:

- *AMS REALTIME Projects,* Advanced Management Solutions (**http://www.amsrealtime.com**)
- *Artemis Views,* Artemis Management Systems (**http://www.artemispm.com**)
- *FastTrack Schedule,* AEC Software Inc. (**http://www.aecsoft.com**)

- *GlobaLogic Projects,* GlobaLogic Inc. (**http://www.globalogicinc.com**)
- *Microsoft Project,* Microsoft Corp. (**http://www.microsoft.com**)
- *Oracle Projects,* Oracle Corporation (**http://www.oracle.com**)
- *PowerProject,* ASTA Development Inc. (**http://www.astaus.com**)
- *Primavera Project Planner,* Primavera Systems Inc. (**http://www.primavera.com**)
- *SuperProject,* Computer Associates International (**http://www.ca.com**)
- *TurboProject,* IMSI (**http://www.imsisoft.com**)

In recent years, *Microsoft Project* has become the most commonly used project management software in industry. This software is part of the *Microsoft Office* family of products and is relatively easy to use for project scheduling and cost management. Figure 10.11 shows how the RAMOV project information is entered into *Microsoft Project.* First the name of each activity or task is entered, along with the activity duration. The immediate predecessor of each activity is entered using the task ID numbers located on the left side of the table. For example, in Figure 10.11, Activity e Refine RAMOV design (ID #5) has two predecessor activities: c—Perform tests of prototypes (ID #3) and d—Estimate material costs (ID #4). The start date of the project is entered in the Project Information window by clicking on the Project menu at the top of the screen. All of the other start and finish dates shown in Figure 10.11 are automatically determined by *Microsoft Project.*

Figure 10.12 shows the Gantt chart created by *Microsoft Project* for the RAMOV project. The duration of each activity is shown inside each horizontal bar (one of many

| **Figure 10.11** | Microsoft Project Data Entry for the RAMOV Project |

Microsoft Project - RAMOV Project.mpp

File Edit View Insert Format Tools Project Window Help

a--Design RAMOV

	Task Name	Duration	Start	Finish	Predecessors	Resource Names
1	a--Design RAMOV	20 days	Mon 1/3/00	Fri 1/28/00		
2	b--Build prototype units	10 days	Mon 1/31/00	Fri 2/11/00	1	
3	c--Perform tests of prototypes	0 days	Mon 2/14/00	Wed 2/23/00	2	
4	d--Estimate material costs	11 days	Mon 1/31/00	Mon 2/14/00	1	
5	e--Refine RAMOV design	7 days	Thu 2/24/00	Fri 3/3/00	3,4	
6	f--Demonstrate RAMOV to cust.	6 days	Mon 3/6/00	Mon 3/13/00	5	
7	g--Estimate labor costs	12 days	Tue 2/15/00	Wed 3/1/00	4	
8	h--Prepare technical proposal	13 days	Mon 3/6/00	Wed 3/22/00	5	
9	I--Deliver proposal to customer	5 days	Thu 3/23/00	Wed 3/29/00	7,8	

Calendar

Gantt Chart

PERT Chart

Task Usage

Ready

Figure 10.12	Microsoft Project Gantt Chart for the RAMOV Project

display options that can be set). The project network diagram that was created by *Microsoft Project* is shown in Figure 10.13. Notice that the network is an activity-on-node representation of the project (instead of the activity-on-arrow representation presented in this chapter). Activity-on-node networks eliminate the need for dummy activities and are usually easier to draw. Each node represents an activity, and each arrow shows a precedence relationship and represents an event. The critical path is indicated by bold arrows in Figure 10.13.

Although not shown in these figures, *Microsoft Project* alternatively allows three PERT activity durations to be entered. It will then compute the expected duration for each activity. Cost information and resource requirements can also be entered for each activity.

Microsoft Project (120-day trial edition) is on one of the CDs that comes with this book. It can be used to solve many of the end-of-chapter problems.

AN EVALUATION OF CPM/PERT

As the use of CPM and PERT has grown, certain criticisms of these techniques have appeared. Among these criticisms are the following:

1. CPM/PERT assumes that the activities of the project are independent. In practice, we know that in some circumstances the duration of one activity is dependent on difficulties encountered in the performance of other, related activities. In these cases, the duration of one activity is dependent on the duration of one or more other activities.

| Figure 10.13 | Microsoft Project Network Diagram for the RAMOV Project |

2. CPM/PERT assumes that there are precise breaking points where one activity ends and another begins. In practice, one activity may begin before a preceding activity is completed as long as some of the preparatory work has been performed.

3. CPM/PERT focuses too much on activities on the critical path. In practice, an activity that is not on the critical path early in the project may encounter difficulty and delays. Such an activity may not receive the attention that it deserves until it appears on the critical path. By that time it may be too late to take corrective action to prevent delay of the project.

4. Activity time estimates can reflect behavioral issues that may diminish the usefulness of CPM/PERT. For instance, personnel who supply the activity time estimates, by being too optimistic or engaging in what is referred to as "blue sky" estimates, may develop activity times that are too short. On the other hand, they may be sandbagging, or developing activity times that are too long, thus giving themselves a cushion or fudge factor.

5. PERT has often been criticized because: (a) It may be unrealistic to expect three accurate time estimates from personnel. (b) It may be too much to expect personnel to understand its statistical underpinnings. (c) The assumptions of PERT concerning the probability distributions of activities and paths have been shown to cause errors in PERT's results. (d) The extra cost of PERT over CPM is not justified by the value of the additional information provided.

6. CPM/PERT is applied to too many projects, an overkill legacy from the government and the aerospace industry. In many of these applications, the cost of CPM/PERT cannot be justified by the value of the information provided when compared to other project management techniques such as project charts.

In spite of these criticisms, CPM/PERT forms a family of techniques that are used widely in organizations today. These techniques help operations managers to structure projects so that it is understood what activities must be done and when they must be done, to identify corrective actions that must be taken, to assign responsibilities for activities, to control costs, and to plan and control time performance. The bottom line is that they work and work well for operations managers in spite of their shortcomings, and that is the reason they are used so widely. The fact that so many low-cost CPM/PERT computer software packages are available today also supports their continued use.

Wrap-Up

WHAT WORLD-CLASS COMPANIES DO

World-class companies position themselves to capitalize on global business opportunities. They develop organization forms that are flexible enough to produce their products and services for world markets, and that at the same time have the ability to respond aggressively to business opportunities. Conventional organization forms based solely on functional departments have not proven to be flexible enough to exploit quickly developing opportunities. Foremost among these new forms is the project organization. Project teams are formed from personnel drawn from functional departments to manage and coordinate the activities of projects. The best personnel are drawn from departments and assigned to projects so that the needed expertise can be brought to bear on rapidly developing business opportunities. World-class companies select and train personnel to be flexible enough to move from department to department and project to project as needed. Flexibility is the key to being a world-class company today, and project teams in a project organization provide some of this needed flexibility.

New-product introductions, new-product development projects, construction projects, new-venture investigations, communication and information systems implementation projects, specialized training and education projects, facility location studies, factory automation projects, just-in-time program implementation projects, supplier improvement programs, quality improvement projects, and cost reduction programs are examples of projects that must be managed by world-class companies. And the more world class a company is, the more intense is the need to manage these kinds of projects. Continuously striving to be the best creates the need for these kinds of projects.

The need for effective planning and control of time and cost performance has motivated world-class companies to develop project management techniques. Scheduling and control charts are frequently used because of their simplicity, flexibility, low cost, and ability to be used as effective communication devices. CPM, PERT, and PERT/Cost are also used to provide computerized activity-by-activity planning control. Periodic status reports go to all interested parties with updated project duration, critical activities, activity slack, network diagrams, and exception reports from which to determine what must be done to ensure successful project completion.

New approaches to planning and controlling projects are still being developed. For example, the graphical evaluation and review technique (GERT) was developed to accommodate needs such as these: Activities may not be needed, some activities may fail and this affects activities that follow, and activities may loop back. Such refinements to existing techniques are likely to continue as project management continues to evolve.

REVIEW AND DISCUSSION QUESTIONS

1. Define *project management.*
2. Why is the management of projects a challenge for most managers in production systems? How do these managers meet this challenge?
3. What tasks must the project team perform before the project begins?
4. What tasks must the project team perform as the project progresses?
5. Why are the planning, scheduling, and controlling of materials, supplies, and subcontractors on projects more difficult than with these resources in production of the organization's usual goods and services?
6. Define these terms: *activity, event, critical activity, critical path, activity duration, slack.*

7. Define these terms: *predecessor activity, dummy activity, earliest start, earliest finish, latest finish, latest start.*
8. Define these terms: *most likely time (t_m), optimistic time (t_o), pessimistic time (t_p).*
9. How does the activity duration differ between CPM and PERT?
10. Horizontal bar charts and other charting techniques offer operations managers macrocontrol of projects, whereas CPM and PERT offer microcontrol. Explain.
11. What are the inputs (information supplied) and outputs (information returned) of CPM?
12. Name three steps in CPM processing.
13. What are the three principles of crashing projects?

INTERNET ASSIGNMENTS

1. Visit and explore the Internet site of the Project Management Institute (PMI) (**http://www.pmi.org**). PMI maintains a list of job postings for positions related to project management. Find two positions that seem interesting to you. Describe these positions and responsibilities.
2. Visit the web site of Primavera Systems Inc. at **http://www.primavera.com**. Find a companion software product for *Primavera Project Planner.* Describe the features of this companion product.
3. Visit Microsoft's Internet site at **http://www.microsoft.com**. Locate the web pages for *Microsoft Project.* Find and summarize some of the new enhancements in the latest version of *Microsoft Project.*
4. Brown & Root Services is a division of Halliburton Company that specializes in large construction projects. Visit Halliburton's web site at **http://www.halliburton. com** and describe the project management services offered by Brown & Root.
5. Search the Internet for a consulting company that specializes in project management. Describe the services it can provide.

PROBLEMS

Scheduling and Control Charts

1. From Figure 10.14, describe fully the status of Stratophonic's new-product development project as of March 1.

2. From Figure 10.15, describe fully the spending status of Stratophonic's new-product development project as of March 1.

3. From Figure 10.16, describe fully the status of key materials deliveries of Stratophonic's new-product development project as of March 15.

4. The Buildrite Construction Company is developing plans to build a new medical building in downtown Denver, Colorado. Buildrite has established these project activities, their precedence relationships, and their estimated activity durations:

Figure 10.14	Project Schedule—New Product Development Project: Stratophonic Sound Inc.

Project Schedule: Statrophonic Sound Inc.

Project: __New Low-Frequency Amplifier__   Scheduled Approval Date: __May 1__

Project Activities	June	July	Aug.	Sept.	Oct.	Nov.	Dec.	Jan.	Feb.	Mar.	Apr.	May	June
a. Market Survey													
b. Preliminary Design		a											
c. Prototype Design		a											
d. Laboratory Test			b										
e. Prototype Redesign					c,d								
f. Field Test									e				
g. Production Design									e				
h. Final Test										g			

Now

Figure 10.15	Expenditures Chart—New Product Development Project: Stratophonic Sound Inc.

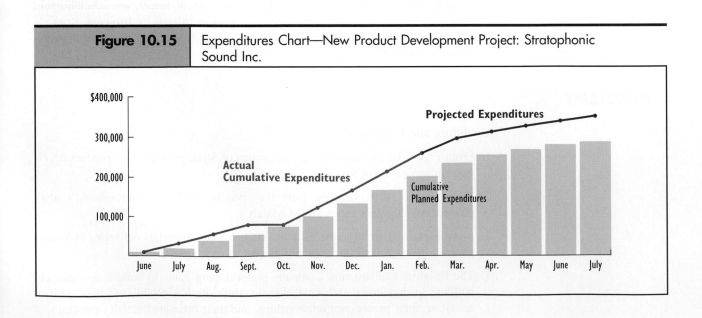

Projected Expenditures

Actual Cumulative Expenditures

Cumulative Planned Expenditures

$400,000

300,000

200,000

100,000

June July Aug. Sept. Oct. Nov. Dec. Jan. Feb. Mar. Apr. May June July

Figure 10.16	Materials Chart—New Product Development Project: Stratophonic Sound Inc.

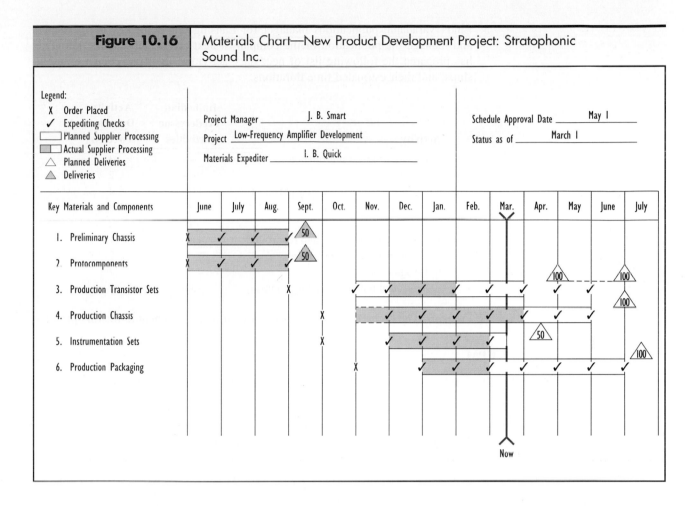

Activity	Precedence Relationship (immediate predecessor activities)	Estimated Activity Duration (weeks)
a. Demolition of present structures	—	3
b. Excavation and filling of site	a	2
c. Forming and pouring of footings and foundation	b	2
d. Construction of structural steel skeleton	c	3
e. Construction of concrete structure	c	2
f. Construction of exterior skin	d,e	1
g. Installation of plumbing system	e	3
h. Installation of electrical system	d,e	3
i. Installation of heating/cooling system	d,e,f	3
j. Construction of interior partitions	i	3
k. Installation of lighting fixtures, and finish work	j	2

Prepare a horizontal bar chart to plan the schedule for this construction project.

5. Linda Varadahn, publications manager for Lansing Oil Company, needs to plan and manage the publication of the company's next annual report. Ms. Varadahn has prepared the following list of necessary activities, their precedence relationships, and their estimated time durations.

Activity	Immediate Predecessor Activities	Activity Duration (weeks)
a. Collect financial information	—	3
b. Develop rough layout	—	2
c. Obtain letter from Lansing president	—	4
d. Write draft of text body	b	3
e. Collect artwork	b	2
f. Combine components into report draft	c,d,e	1
g. Get feedback from executives	f	2
h. Design cover	f	1
i. Send final report to printing company	g,h	2

Prepare a Gantt chart (horizontal bar chart) to plan the schedule for this project.

CPM

6. A project has these activities, precedence relationships, and activity durations:

Activity	Immediate Predecessor Activities	Activity Duration (days)	Activity	Immediate Predecessor Activities	Activity Duration (days)
a	—	5	f	b	4
b	—	7	g	c	6
c	a	5	h	d,e	7
d	a	6	i	f	5
e	b	3			

a. Draw a CPM network for the project.
b. Provide an overview for the project by computing the duration for each path.
c. What is the critical path? What is the project's estimated duration?

7. A project has these activities, precedence relationships, and activity durations:

Activity	Immediate Predecessor Activities	Activity Duration (days)	Activity	Immediate Predecessor Activities	Activity Duration (days)
a	—	3	g	d,e	5
b	—	6	h	d,e	4
c	a	8	i	c,g	3
d	a	4	j	f,h	7
e	b	4	k	i,j	9
f	b	6			

a. Draw a CPM network for the project.
b. Provide an overview for the project by computing the duration for each path.
c. What is the critical path? What is the project's estimated duration?

8. In Problem 7:
   a. Draw a CPM network for the project.
   b. Compute the EF, LF, and slack for each activity. Write the values on the CPM network.
   c. What is the critical path and its duration?

9. A company is about to begin a project to design a production process for producing a new product. Management has estimated that the project should require about 45 days to complete. Although 45 days seemed very short to the process engineers at first, after some discussion it was concluded that they probably could meet the deadline because the product and its processes were so similar to the present processing technologies in use at their plant. These activities, their precedence relationships, and their durations were estimated by the engineers:

Activities	Activity Duration (days)	Immediate Predecessor Activities
a. Initial study of the product design	12	—
b. Preliminary process technologies study	10	—
c. Vendor capability survey	8	—
d. Modification of facility for product redesign	14	b
e. Intermediate facility redesign	6	c
f. Intermediate product redesign	18	b,a
g. Specific process machinery design	11	d,e
h. Vendor involvement and integration	21	c
i. Final facility, product, process design	7	f,g

   a. Construct a CPM network for the design project.
   b. Compute the EF, LF, and slack for each activity. Write the values on the CPM network.
   c. Compute the ES and LS for all activities. Display the ES, EF, LS, LF, and slack values in a table.
   d. What is the critical path? What is the project's estimated duration?

10. A project has these activities, precedence relationships, and activity durations.

Activity	Immediate Predecessor Activities	Activity Duration (days)	Activity	Immediate Predecessor Activities	Activity Duration (days)
a	—	7	f	c	14
b	a	9	g	d	16
c	a	6	h	c,b	16
d	a	12	i	h	12
e	b,c	11	j	e,f,g	18

   a. Construct a CPM network for the project.
   b. Compute the EF, LF, and slack for each activity. Write the values on the CPM network.
   c. Compute the ES and LS for all activities. Display the ES, EF, LS, LF, and slack values in a table.
   d. What is the critical path and its duration?

11. A plant engineering group is responsible for setting up the assembly line to manufacture a new product. The production processes have already been designed by the process-engineering group, and the machinery has been delivered to the plant from vendors. Because the facility has been redesigned to contain the assembly line and because the machinery is already on site, the assembly line must be ready for a dry run in one month. The plant engineering group has identified these activities, determined their precedence relationships, and estimated their durations:

Activity	Activity Duration (days)	Immediate Predecessor Activities
a. Assemble process design package	3	—
b. Organize machinery layout team	5	—
c. Organize facility modification team	7	b
d. Meet with production personnel	4	b
e. Design personnel jobs	3	a,c
f. Set machinery in place	9	d
g. Connect utilities to machines	5	e,f
h. Modify overhead conveyor	6	d
i. Train personnel	3	e,f
j. Paint and clean up	5	g,h
k. Run pilot lot of products	4	i,j

   a.   Construct a CPM network for the project.
   b.   Compute the EF, LF, and slack for each activity. Write the values on the CPM network.
   c.   Compute the ES and LS for all activities. Display the ES, EF, LS, LF, and slack values in a table.
   d.   What is the critical path? What is the project's estimated duration?

PERT

12. An activity in a project has three time estimates: optimistic time (t_o) = 18 days, most likely time (t_m) = 22 days, and pessimistic time (t_p) = 27 days.
   a.   Compute the activity's expected time or duration (t_e).
   b.   Compute the activity's variance (V_t).
   c.   Compute the activity's standard deviation (σ_t).

13. An activity in a PERT network has these estimates: t_o = 11, t_m = 14, t_p = 18.
   a.   Compute the activity's expected time (t_e).
   b.   Compute the activity's variance (V_t).

14. Project path a–d–f–k has these activity time estimates in days:

Activity	Optimistic Time (t_o)	Most Likely Time (t_m)	Pessimistic Time (t_p)
a	3	4	5
d	9	12	14
f	12	15	20
k	7	9	9

   a.   Compute the expected time or duration (t_e) for each activity.
   b.   Compute the variance (V_t) for each activity.
   c.   Compute the expected duration and variance for the path.

15. A path in a PERT network has these activity time estimates in days:

Activity	Optimistic Time (t_o)	Most Likely Time (t_m)	Pessimistic Time (t_p)
a	8	11	13
b	10	12	14
k	15	15	17
l	13	15	20

Compute the mean path duration and the path variance.

16. A project has the following activities, precedence relationships, and time estimates in days:

Activity	Immediate Predecessor Activities	Optimistic Time (t_o)	Most Likely Time (t_m)	Pessimistic Time (t_p)
a	—	6	7	8
b	a	4	4	4
c	a	5	6	8
d	b	8	10	10
e	b	7	10	15
f	c	9	9	13
g	c	7	7	7
h	d	4	6	8
i	e,f	6	9	11
j	g	8	9	10
k	h,i,j	3	5	6

a. Compute the duration (expected time) and variances for each activity.
b. Draw a PERT network.
c. Compute the EF, LF, and slack for each activity. Write the values on the PERT network.
d. Compute the ES and LS for all activities. Display the ES, EF, LF, and slack values in a table.
e. What is the critical path?
f. What is the probability that the project will take longer than 38 days?

17. In Problem 9, the design team was asked how confident it was about completing the project in 45 days. To answer this question, these estimated time durations in days for the project were developed:

Activity	Predecessor Activities	Optimistic Time (t_o)	Most Likely Time (t_m)	Pessimistic Time (t_p)
a	—	10	12	14
b	—	10	10	10
c	—	6	8	10
d	b	11	14	16
e	c	5	6	8
f	a,b	14	18	22
g	d,e	10	11	13
h	c	18	21	24
i	f,g	5	7	9

a. Compute the duration (expected time) and variance for each activity.
b. Construct a PERT network for the project.

c. Compute the EF, LF, and slack for each activity. Write the values on the PERT network.
d. Compute the ES and LS for all activities. Display the ES, EF, LS, LF, and slack values in a table.
e. What is the critical path and its duration?
f. What is the probability that the project will take longer than 45 days? How confident are you that the team can complete the project within 45 days?

18. Three paths of a PERT network have these mean durations and variances in weeks:

Path	Mean Duration (Σt_e)	Variance (ΣV_t)
1	65	2.85
2	64	5.40
3	66	1.50

Which path offers the greatest risk of overrunning a contract deadline of 69 weeks?

19. Two paths of a PERT network have these mean durations and variances in days:

Path	Mean Duration (Σt_e)	Variance (ΣV_t)
1	45.1	2.75
2	44.5	5.50

Which path offers the greater risk of taking longer than 46 days?

Time/Cost and Cost–Time Trade-Offs

20. Here is a time/cost status report for a project:

	Time Status (weeks)				Cost Status (thousands of dollars)		
Activity	**Slack (S)**	**Duration (D)**	**New (D)**	**Old/New Completion Date**	**Target Cost**	**Cost to Date**	**Estimated Cost over/under Target to Completion**
a	—	8	8	*	12.5	10.5	2.0
b	—	10	10	*	10.0	13.5	(3.5)
c	0	9	10	9/15–9/22	11.0	10.0	(3.5)
d	0	14	17	12/15–1/7	19.0	7.5	(6.0)
e	3	9	7	9/1–8/15	7.5	0.0	1.0
f	2	6	6	10/1–10/1	5.0	0.0	1.0

*Activity is complete.

Describe fully the status of time and cost performance of the project's activities.

21. From Problem 9:
a. If you have not already done so, construct a CPM network for the project, compute EF, LF, and slack for each activity, and write their values on the CPM network. What is the critical path and its duration?
b. Given the costs of crashing the activities of the project below, develop a cost–time trade-off analysis. Detail the steps that you would use to accelerate or crash the project so that it could be completed in no more than 38 days. What are the new cost and duration of the project?

Activity	Present Duration (days)	Accelerated Duration (days)	Present Cost	Accelerated Cost
a	12	12*	$20,000	$20,000
b	10	8	18,000	20,000
c	8	6	20,000	24,000
d	14	14*	12,000	12,000
e	6	4	4,000	5,600
f	18	18*	19,000	19,000
g	11	10	24,000	25,500
h	21	20	34,000	34,700
i	7	6	31,000	32,800

*These activities cannot be accelerated.

22. From Problem 10:
   a. If you have not already done so, construct a CPM network for the project, compute EF, LF, and the slack for each activity, and write their values on the CPM network. What is the critical path and its duration?
   b. Given the costs of crashing the activities of the project below, develop a cost–time trade-off analysis. Detail the steps that you would use to accelerate or crash the project so that it could be completed in no more than 41 days. What are the new cost and duration of the project?

Activity	Present Duration (days)	Accelerated Duration (days)	Present Cost	Accelerated Cost
a	7	5	$14,000	$14,800
b	9	7	18,000	24,000
c	6	4	20,000	30,000
d	12	8	10,000	12,000
e	11	10	13,000	15,000
f	14	13	15,000	19,000
g	16	10	25,000	31,000
h	16	15	23,000	25,700
i	12	10	27,000	31,000
j	18	18*	29,000	29,000

*These activities cannot be accelerated.

CASES

Baxter Construction Company

The Baxter Construction Company is a large company that specializes in industrial and government construction projects. The company bids on only the largest projects at premium prices and tends to get its fair share because it has gained a reputation for doing work of outstanding quality within the time constraints of its contracts. Baxter is now in the process of bidding on the construction of an addition to the Northeast State University football stadium, a project that will go for about $90 million. The only problem is that the project falls at a time when Baxter has won several other large contracts and does not want to overextend itself and spread its resources too thin. If the project could be completed within 63 weeks of the beginning of the project, the company would feel confident in pursuing the contract. The cost estimator for Baxter has developed the estimates of activity durations and their precedence relationships that are shown in the table below.

Activity	Precedence Relationship (immediate predecessor activities)	Estimated Activity Duration (weeks)
a. Demolish and salvage existing structures	—	2
b. Excavate and grade site	a	3
c. Pour concrete footings and foundation	b	3
d. Install in-ground plumbing	b	4
e. Install underground electrical service	b	2
f. Preassemble mid-level steel skeleton	b	5
g. Construct and pour concrete substructure	c,d,e	4
h. Pour lower-level concrete floors	g	3
i. Erect mid-level steel skeleton	f,h	2
j. Erect mid-level concrete columns and cross beams	i	5
k. Install above-ground phase 2 plumbing	j	4
l. Install above-ground phase 2 electrical service	j	3
m. Pour mid-level concrete floors	k,l	5
n. Preassemble top-level steel skeleton	i	3
o. Erect top-level steel skeleton	m,n	5
p. Erect top-level concrete columns and cross beams	o	8
q. Pour top-level floors	p	7
r. Construct press box complex	q	9
s. Erect field lights	p	3
t. Construct restrooms	m,n	10
u. Install seats	q	4
v Paint and finish walls, floors, and ceilings	u	3
w. Clean up structure and grounds	v	1

Assignment

1. Draw a CPM network diagram of the project.

2. Develop a horizontal bar chart that summarizes the plan for the project. Each activity should be "mapped out" on this chart. Discuss how this chart would be used as the project proceeds and how it would be used in the planning phases of the project.

3. Use the CPM computer program in the *POM Software Library* to develop a CPM analysis of the project. What is the estimated duration of the project? What activities are on the critical path? How much can Activity u slip without affecting the project completion date?

4. Discuss how the CPM analysis results compare with your chart in No. 2. What are the advantages and disadvantages of CPM as a planning and controlling technique when compared with the project chart or horizontal bar chart?

5. Should the Baxter Construction Company bid on the project? Does the project require more time than Baxter has available?

Advanced Aerospace Corporation

A news release has just announced that a government contract will be awarded later this year to the company that successfully demonstrates a space signaling system, called the SS System. Bill Green, general manager at Advanced Aerospace Corporation (AAC), called a staff meeting to get staff's ideas on whether AAC should pursue the project. It was generally agreed that this was a piece of business the operation should pursue. The question was: How could the operation go after this new business and still successfully produce and deliver its other products? The corporate controller, Jane Glassner, informed Green that Corporate was so impressed with the prospects of the SS System that the operation had Corporate's approval to spend up to a half-million dollars in securing the contract, a very high-trust, high-priority allotment. All the department heads agreed that some sacrifice would have to be made by them to succeed in this new effort. Each of them would be asked to give up one or two key employees to serve on the project team. Green decided to commit the operation to an all-out effort on the project.

The next day the project team was announced. The project manager would be Cris Jacobs, an MBA with an undergraduate degree in management. She was selected because she was perhaps the best administrator in the operation and she had great rapport with the other units of the company. Also on the team were: Jim Sherry, flight engineer; Roberto Mendez, design engineer; Jim Dawson, production manager of the electronics department; Inez Thompson, director of loss prevention; and Wallace Potter, industrial engineer.

These individuals would be assigned to the project full-time for its duration. If the contract was won, all of them would carry their knowledge about the SS System back to their home departments, thus aiding in the conversion from development to production.

The team developed the following list of project activities, time estimates, and precedence relationships as part of the project plan:

Activity	Immediate Predecessor Activities	Estimated Time to Complete Activity (weeks)
a. Preliminary product design		4
b. Preliminary flight system design	a	3
c. Static tests A	a	2
d. Flight tests A	b	2
e. Static tests B	c	2
f. Flight system design modifications	d,e	3
g. Product design modifications	d,e	4
h. Material and component cost estimates	d,e	4
i. Labor and overhead cost estimates	d,e	2
j. Process bid package through company	h,i	2
k. Flight tests B	f,g	3
l. Delivery of bid package to customer	j	1
m. Demonstration to customer	k,l	1

Assignment

1. Draw a CPM network for the project.

2. Use the CPM computer program in the *POM Software Library* to develop a CPM analysis of the project. What is the estimated duration of the project? What activities are on the critical path?

3. How long would the project take to complete if Activity c were delayed 1 week? How long would the project take to complete if Activity e were delayed 1 week? How long would the project take to complete if both Activities c and e were delayed 1 week? Discuss the care that must be taken in interpreting the meaning of the activity slack values.

4. Explain how the assumptions and criticisms of CPM should cause us to modify our interpretation of our analysis of the SS System Project.

SELECTED BIBLIOGRAPHY

Bennatan, Edwin M. *On Time within Budget: Software Project Management Practices and Techniques.* New York: John Wiley & Sons, 2000.

Cameron, Bonnie. "Software Buyer's Guide: Project Management." *IIE Solutions* 32, no. 3 (March 2000): 48–51.

Chatfield, Carl, and Tim Johnson. *Microsoft Project 2000.* Redmond, WA: Microsoft Press, 2000.

Chen, Mark T. "Simplified Project Economic Evaluation." *Cost Engineering* 40, no. 1 (January 1998): 31–35.

Duncan, William R. *A Guide to the Project Management Body of Knowledge.* Upper Darby, PA: Project Management Institute Publications, 1996.

Edum-Fotwe, F. T., and R. McCaffer. "Developing Project Management Competency: Perspectives from the Construction Industry." *International Journal of Project Management* 18, no. 2 (April 2000): 111–124.

Gido, Jack, and James P. Clements. *Successful Project Management.* Cincinnati, OH: South-Western College Publishing, 1999.

Goldratt, Eliyahu M. *Critical Chain.* Croton-on-Hudson, NY: North River Press, 1997.

Graham, Robert J., and Randall L. Englund. *Creating an Environment for Successful Projects: The Quest to Manage Project Management.* San Francisco: Jossey-Bass Publishing, 1997.

Gray, Clifford F., and Erik W. Larson. *Project Management: The Managerial Process.* Boston: Irwin–McGraw-Hill, 2000.

Hallows, Jolyon E. *Information Systems Project Management: How to Deliver Function and Value in Information Technology Projects.* New York: AMACOM, 1998.

Kerzner, Harold. *Project Management: A Systems Approach to Planning, Scheduling, and Controlling,* 6th ed. New York: John Wiley & Sons, 1998.

Kruglianskas, Isak, and Hans J. Thamhain. "Managing Technology-Based Projects in Multinational Environments." *IEEE Transactions on Engineering Management* 47, no. 1 (February 2000): 55–64.

Lewis, James P. *Mastering Project Management: Applying Advanced Concepts of Project Planning, Control, & Evaluation.* New York: McGraw-Hill, 1998.

Lock, Dennis. "Making It Happen: A Non-Technical Guide to Project Management." *International Journal of Project Management* 18, no. 2 (April 2000): 150–151.

Marchman, David A. *Construction Scheduling with Primavera Project Planner.* New York: Delmar Publishing, 1998.

Meredith, Jack R., and Samuel J. Mantel, Jr. *Project Management: A Managerial Approach,* 4th ed. New York: John Wiley & Sons, 2000.

Michalski, Liz. "Effective Communication Equals Successful Project Management." *Pharmaceutical Technology* 24, no. 5 (May 2000): 84–88.

Naylor, Henry F.W. *Construction Project Management: Planning and Scheduling.* New York: Delmar Publishing, 1995.

Newmark, Henry R. "Auditing Construction Projects." *The Internal Auditor* 54, no. 6 (December 1997): 36–41.

Nicholas, John M. *Project Management for Business and Technology.* Upper Saddle River, NJ: Prentice Hall, 2001.

PERT, Program Evaluation Research Task, Phase I Summary Report, 646–669. Washington, DC: Special Projects Office, Bureau of Ordnance, 7, Department of the Navy, July 1958.

Purba, Sanjiv, and Bharat Shah. *How to Manage a Successful Software Project with Microsoft Project 2000.* New York: John Wiley & Sons, 2000.

Royer, Paul S. "Risk Management: The Undiscovered Dimension of Project Management." *Project Management Journal* 31, no. 1 (March 2000): 6–13.

Urli, Bruno, and Didier Urli. "Project Management in North America, Stability of the Concepts." *Project Management Journal* 31, no. 3 (September 2000): 33–43.

Verma, Vijay K., and Hans J. Thamhain. *Human Resource Skills for the Project Manager: The Human Aspects of Project Management.* Upper Darby, PA: Project Management Institute Publications, 1997.

Yasin, Mahmoud M., and James Martin. "An Empirical Investigation of International Project Management Practices: The Role of International Experience." *Project Management Journal* 31, no. 2 (June 2000): 20–30.

PART **3**

Managing Operations in the Supply Chain

CHAPTER

11 Supply Chain Management and E-Business

12 Just-in-Time and Lean Manufacturing

13 Production Planning

14 Inventory Management

15 Resource Requirements Planning: MRP and CRP

16 Manufacturing Operations Scheduling

In Part 2 of this text we explored how operations managers approach, analyze, and plan the strategic use of resources. Forecasting demand, designing and developing production processes, planning for long-range capacity and facility needs, planning and implementing new operations technologies, managing the quality of operations, allocating scarce resources to business units, planning service operations, and managing projects are so important that great attention and notoriety are focused on them. As important as these strategic decisions are, however, we must not allow them to overshadow other ongoing decisions in operations management that under certain conditions can be of equal importance.

To satisfy the final consumers of products or services, the efficient operations of an organization depend on the efficient supply of materials from its suppliers and its suppliers' suppliers as well as the efficient distribution of goods or services to the organization's customers and on to the ultimate consumer. This comprises what is referred to as the supply chain. Supply chain management involves not only managing materials and production within an organization, but also coordinating the flow of products and services with suppliers and customers from the beginning, when the goods and services are merely basic raw materials or ideas, to their final consumption.

When we visit with operations managers, they say that the greatest source of pressure and tension in their jobs is the constant push to produce high-quality products and services to meet delivery promises to customers and at the same time keep the lid on costs. Products and services must be delivered on time and within cost budgets. Toward this end, operations managers engage in planning activities such as these:

1. Plan for the purchase, storage, and shipment of materials so that the right materials of the right quality are available in the right quantity at the right time to support production schedules.

2. Establish production-planning systems to guide organizations toward keeping delivery promises to customers, meeting inventory targets, and maintaining low production costs.

3. Develop aggregate capacity plans that usually cover from 6 to 18 months. These medium-range plans should provide the production capacity necessary to meet customers' demand for products and services.

4. Provide sufficient inventory of finished products to meet the dual objectives of low operating costs and prompt delivery of products to customers.

5. Schedule the production of products and services necessary to meet customer deliveries and to load the production facilities such that production costs are low.

Part 3 of this text explores these and other related issues.

TM

e-vailability

the power underneath

11

Supply Chain Management and E-Business

Introduction

Supply Chain Management

Purchasing
Importance of Purchasing Today
Mission of Purchasing
What Purchasing Managers Do
Purchasing Departments in Organizations
Purchasing Processes
Buyers and Their Duties
Make-or-Buy Analysis
Ethics in Buying
Purchasing: The International Frontier

Logistics
Production Control: Movement of Materials within
    Factories
Shipments to and from Factories
Innovations in Logistics

Warehousing
Warehousing Operations
Methods of Inventory Accounting
Contemporary Developments in Warehousing

Expediting

**Benchmarking the Performance of
Materials Managers**

**Third-Party Logistics Management
Providers**

E-Business and Supply Chain Management

Wrap-Up: What World-Class Companies Do

Review and Discussion Questions

Internet Assignments

Field Projects in Materials Management

Problems

Cases
Primo Clothing Manufacturing
Acme Manufacturing

Endnote

Selected Bibliography

CENTRALIZED SUPPLY CHAIN MANAGEMENT AT MOTOARC

Motoarc is an electronics, aerospace, electrical machinery, semiconductor, and computer products company. Its annual sales are $16.7 billion, it has manufacturing plants in 17 states and 12 foreign countries, and it employs 284,000 people worldwide. While Motoarc's operations had expanded, its purchasing, warehousing, and shipping functions had lagged behind its other business units in effectiveness. Although a JIT system had been installed, problems with materials remained because no one seemed to be accountable when difficulties arose. For example, a recent order from a supplier arrived late at Motoarc's Indianapolis plant. Purchasing blamed the warehouse and shipping. The warehouse blamed production control. Production control blamed warehousing and purchasing. Shipping claimed that the motor carrier lost the order for several days in Chicago, thus delaying delivery. Each function pointed an accusing finger at the other functions. Because of such difficulties, Motoarc has recently reorganized all the materials management functions under a vice-president of supply chain management, who is responsible for all purchasing, logistics, warehousing, and expediting of materials in all divisions. Now the buck stops at the desk of the vice-president of supply chain management when any difficulties related to materials arise in any division of the company.

As the preceding account illustrates, some companies today have reorganized their materials management functions under a top-level executive who is responsible for all activities related to the flow of materials through the company. Such organizational changes focus management's attention on this function and underscore the importance of managing the flow of materials.

Materials are any commodities used directly or indirectly in producing a product or service, such as raw materials, component parts, assemblies, and supplies. *Management of materials in most companies is crucial to their success because the cost of buying, storing, moving, and shipping materials accounts for over half of a product's cost. Productivity basically means driving down the cost of doing business, and doing the job of materials management better is increasingly seen as the key to higher productivity in many U.S. firms today.* Operations managers are working hard to develop better ways of managing materials so that on-time deliveries, quality, and costs can be improved so that their companies can survive in an increasingly competitive world.

In this chapter we will first study supply chain management, including purchasing, logistics, warehousing, and related issues. We will then examine e-business and the impacts that e-business is having on supply chain management.

SUPPLY CHAIN MANAGEMENT

Consider how materials might flow from a company's suppliers, through the company's operations, and then on to its customers. An increasingly popular perspective today is to view the flow of materials from suppliers all the way to consumers as a system to be managed. This perspective is commonly referred to as *supply chain management*.

In its broadest sense, a **supply chain** refers to the way that materials flow through different organizations, starting with basic raw materials and ending with finished products delivered to the ultimate consumer. For example, consider the steel used in an automobile door. A mining company first excavates dirt containing iron ore, and then extracts only the iron ore from the dirt. The iron ore is then sold to a steel mill, where it is processed with other materials to form large steel ingots. The steel ingots are sold to another steel company, where they are heated, rolled into long, thin sheets, and annealed. These rolls of sheet metal are then sold to an automotive supplier that specializes in making doors. The sheet metal is cut and stamped, and used with other materials to make a completed car door. The door is then sold to the automobile manufacturer, where it is assembled with other components to produce a completed automobile. The automobile is then sold to a car dealership, which performs some final preparation work, such as adding pinstripes to the sides of the car. Finally, the ultimate consumer purchases the car from the dealership, the last link in the supply chain. Figure 11.1 illustrates this complete supply chain. Notice that the supply chain includes both manufacturing companies and a service company, the car dealership.

Supply chains can form complex networks involving many companies and materials. A raw material can be used in many different finished products produced by numerous companies, and a finished product is usually made from many different raw materials from numerous suppliers. Coordination of all companies involved in a supply chain, including effective communication, is crucial to providing high-quality finished products in a timely manner at the lowest cost possible. From an operations management perspective for a particular company that is in the middle of a supply chain, only a portion of the supply chain is of particular interest and must be managed carefully by the company. So for most companies, the most relevant aspects of *supply chain management* involve all management functions related to the flow of materials from the company's direct suppliers to its direct customers, including purchasing, warehousing, inspection, production, materials handling, and shipping and distribution. Figure 11.2 illustrates the supply chain management activities in a manufacturing plant.

Studying material flows—the acquisition, storage, movement, and processing of raw materials, components, assemblies, and supplies—is a good way to understand manufacturing. Also, services such as retailing, warehousing, and transportation companies can be viewed as systems of material flows. In these systems, all organizational functions are critically affected by the planning and control of the materials system.

Materials management and **logistics management** are two alternative names sometimes used to refer to supply chain management within a single company. Figure 11.3 illustrates how the supply chain management function fits into many organizations today. Some organizations have centralized their diverse materials management functions under one department headed by a **materials manager, supply chain manager, or vice-president of materials.** This executive position coordinates all the activities of supply chain management and bears total responsibility for the continuous supply of materials of low cost and specified quality when and where operating departments and customers require them. The responsibility of the materials manager is immense, a reality underscored by their typically high salaries, which rank with those of the highest industry positions.

Four important activities in materials management, or supply chain management, are purchasing, logistics, warehousing, and expediting. These activities form the framework for studying the nature and scope of materials management.

| Figure 11.1 | Supply Chain for Steel in an Automobile Door |

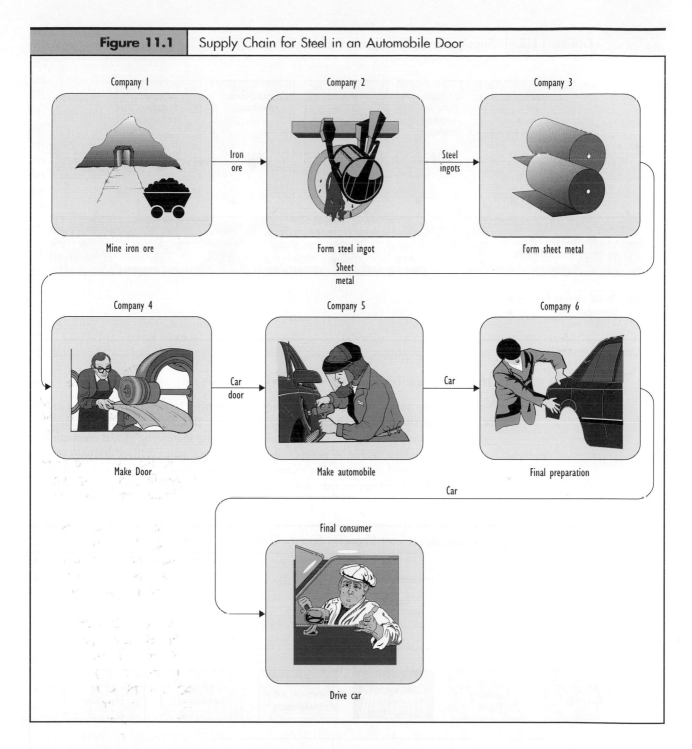

PURCHASING

Purchasing departments buy the raw materials, purchased parts, machinery, supplies, and all other goods and services used in production systems—from paper clips to steel to computers.

Figure 11.2 | Supply Chain Management in Manufacturing

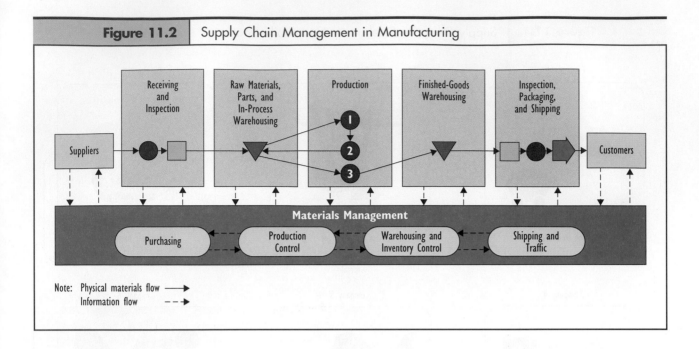

Note: Physical materials flow ——→
       Information flow   – – –→

Importance of Purchasing Today

Several factors are increasing the importance of purchasing today: the tremendous impact of material costs on profits, the increasing prominence of automated manufacturing, the growth of business-to-business Internet transactions, and increasing global competition.

On the average, about 60 percent of manufacturers' sales dollars are paid to suppliers for purchased materials. For example, automobile manufacturers spend about 60 percent of their revenues on material purchases, farm-implement manufacturers spend

Figure 11.3 | Organization Chart Showing Supply Chain Management

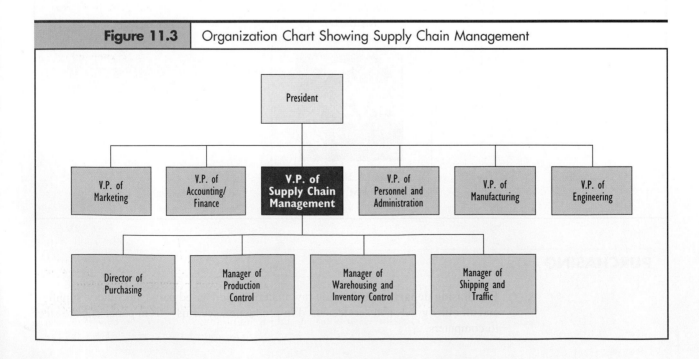

about 65 percent, food processors spend about 70 percent, and oil refineries spend about 80 percent. And these percentages are going up.

As the automation of manufacturing continues, two developments enhance the importance of purchasing. First, it has been estimated that labor costs represent only about 10 to 15 percent of production costs in many mass production industries today. Some observers estimate that labor costs will decline to about 5 percent of production costs in the near future. It is thought, therefore, that in some industries material costs will become the central focus in the control of production costs. Second, automation requires rigid control of design, delivery schedules, and quality of purchased materials. In this setting, purchasing must establish and maintain vendor relations to ensure that materials of the right design and of perfect quality are delivered in the right quantities at the right times. Purchasing could be a key organization function affecting the success of automated manufacturing.

As the Internet continues to develop and grow, *business-to-business (B2B) transactions* over the Internet between companies have become increasingly popular. This development is having dramatic impacts on the purchasing function in companies. Purchasing personnel can now search for sources of materials, purchase materials, request bids for materials, and participate in on-line auctions for materials by using the Internet. A number of material buying and selling auction-style web sites have recently been implemented for different industries. One result of this technological advance is that purchasers now have more information at their fingertips about material cost and availability more quickly than ever before. Purchase orders can be submitted to supplier Web sites and the status of orders can be checked via the Internet, reducing the purchasing department's operating costs and speeding up the purchase lead time.

With the increase in global competition for world markets, all manufacturers are working hard to reduce production costs. One of the most lucrative areas for this effort is in reducing materials costs. As the scope of business has expanded to global proportions, so the purchase of materials has moved to the world stage. Increasingly, materials are bought worldwide, transported to domestic and offshore manufacturing sites, and then shipped to markets throughout the world. This stretched out supply chain has become necessary to offset increased competition for scarce materials. But the increased scope of supply has created an environment where materials are more subject to uncertain supply. This has also increased the importance of purchasing functions today.

Across the totality of our country's economy, the amount of annual expenditures for purchased materials is indeed staggering. Yet purchasing department employees represent less than 1 percent of the total employees of organizations. Can you think of a more influential group of employees whose performance is so critical to organizational success?

Mission of Purchasing *to get best value*

The purchasing department is a key player in the achievement of a company's strategic objectives. It can affect fast delivery of products/services, on-time deliveries, production costs, and product/service quality, all of which are key elements in operations strategy. *The mission of purchasing is to sense the competitive priorities necessary for each major product/service (low production costs, fast and on-time deliveries, high-quality products/services, and flexibility) and to develop purchasing plans for each major product/service that are consistent with operations strategies.* One material, for example, may go into a product whose operations strategy calls for high volume, produce-to-stock production, and low production costs. For such a material, purchasing must emphasize developing suppliers that can produce the material at very low cost and in large quantities. On the other hand, another material may go into a product whose operations strategy calls for low volume, fast deliveries, high quality, and produce-to-order production. For this material, purchasing must emphasize fast response times by suppliers, very high quality, and dependable shipping schedules.

What Purchasing Managers Do

Purchasing engages in these activities as it buys materials:

1. **Maintain a database of available suppliers.** This database includes information about the kinds of products that suppliers produce or are capable of producing, information about the quality of their products, and information about their costs or prices. An important aspect of maintaining this database is the need to run periodic supplier surveys. These surveys may include actual plant tours to assess the supplier's ability to meet on-time delivery, quantity, quality, and cost requirements.
2. **Select suppliers to supply each material.** This selection will ordinarily be based on several criteria. Price is important, of course, but quality, quantity, and promptness of deliveries may be of equal or greater importance.
3. **Negotiate supply contracts with suppliers.** This activity pins down the specific conditions that suppliers must adhere to as the materials are supplied. Such things as price, payment of freight charges, delivery schedule, quality standards, product specifications or performance standards, and payment terms are usually included in these contracts.
4. **Act as the interface between the company and its suppliers.** When production, engineering, accounting, production control, or quality control needs to communicate with a supplier, such communications must ordinarily go through purchasing. Similarly, all suppliers communicate with the company through purchasing.

Purchasing engages in these activities in most organizations, but the location of the purchasing department in organizations varies widely.

Purchasing Departments in Organizations

The **manager of purchasing** or the **purchasing agent** may report to the president, vice-president of materials, vice-president of operations, plant manager, materials manager, or anyone in between. It is difficult to generalize about where purchasing will be assigned in the organization, except to say that its reporting level is generally directly related to the importance of its mission. In other words, if purchasing is critical to an organization's success, then we would expect to see the purchasing department report to a vice-president of materials, vice-president of operations, or even to the president. At General Motors, the vice-president of global purchasing reports to the CEO.

Organizations tend to go through cycles of decentralization and centralization, and purchasing has been caught up in these cycles. The tendency toward centralization of purchasing today is probably encouraged by the advances both in communication among plants and divisions of companies and in the information-processing capabilities of computers. Among the advantages of centralization are:

- Buying in larger quantities, which can mean better prices.
- More clout with suppliers when materials are scarce, orders are delayed, or other supply difficulties are encountered. This clout translates into greater supply continuity.
- Larger purchasing departments that can afford greater specialization of employees. For example, one buyer may specialize in buying only copper. This can lead to greater purchasing competence and lower material costs.
- Combining small orders and thereby reducing duplication of orders, which can reduce costs.

Purchasing functions can be vital components in keeping quality high and costs low in production systems.

© CHARLES O'REAR/CORBIS

- Reduction of transportation costs by combining orders and shipping larger quantities.
- Better overall control and consistency of financial transactions.

Regardless of its organizational location, purchasing follows certain buying processes to acquire materials.

Purchasing Processes

Figure 11.4 illustrates the process of acquiring materials in production systems. The figure emphasizes the interaction of the production departments, purchasing department, and suppliers. Some variation of these procedures exists among organizations and among different types of goods.

Basic Purchasing Instruments

The daily stock-in-trade of purchasing departments consists of material specifications, purchase requisitions, requests for quotation, and purchase orders. These instruments are fundamental to purchasing processes.

For every good to be purchased, the purchasing department must have a detailed description of that material. This detailed description is called a **material specification**. These instruments can include such descriptions as engineering drawings, chemical analyses, physical characteristics, and other details depending on the nature of the material. A material specification originates with the department requesting the material in its operations. Material specifications are the fundamental means of communicating what materials production wants purchasing to buy and what purchasing authorizes suppliers to supply.

Purchase requisitions originate with the departments that will use the materials. They authorize purchasing to buy the goods or services. The requisitions usually include identification of what is to be purchased, amount to be purchased, requested delivery date or schedule, account to which the purchase cost is to be charged, where the purchased goods or services are to be delivered, and approval by the manager charged with authority to approve the purchase.

Figure 11.4	Process of Acquiring Material Inputs

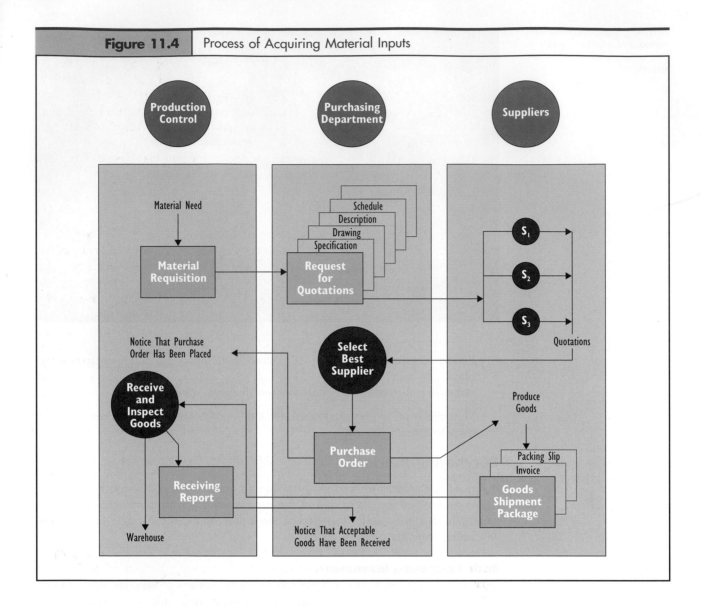

Requests for quotation are prepared by purchasing departments and sent to suppliers that are believed to be capable of meeting the cost, quality, and schedule requirements of the requesting departments. These instruments invite prospective suppliers to bid or quote on the goods or services. These forms usually include material specification, quantity of purchase, delivery date or schedule desired, where goods or services are to be delivered, and date that supplier selection will be completed. Requests for quotation usually request the following from each prospective supplier: price per unit and total price, information on whether the supplier pays the freight charges, cash discounts and other terms of payment, delivery date or schedule, and any special conditions of the supplier.

Purchase orders are the most important purchasing instruments. They are the basis of the suppliers' authority to produce the goods or services, and they represent the buyers' obligation to pay for the items. A legal commitment by the buyer is present when a purchase order is issued in response to a quotation from a supplier. When a

[handwritten annotation in left margin: most important ensures pmt.]

purchase order is issued in the absence of a request for a quotation, a legal commitment exists when a supplier acknowledges acceptance of the purchase order. These forms are usually designed to conform to the standards developed by the National Association of Purchasing Managers and the Division of Simplified Practice, National Bureau of Standards. Purchase order forms usually include purchase order number, quantity of the goods or services, material specifications, date and location for delivery, shipping and billing instructions, price per unit and total price, cash discount or other terms of payment, and any special terms of the purchase.

These instruments—specifications, requisitions, requests for quotation, and purchase orders—form the framework for buying goods or services.

Buyers and Their Duties

Buyers, as the name implies, do the buying in purchasing departments. They are typically specialized according to commodities. For example, one buyer may buy all ferrous metals, another may buy all nonferrous metals, and yet another may buy all machinery and tools. This specialization allows buyers to become experts at purchasing their particular commodities. To be effective, buyers must know both the manufacturing processes of their own companies and those of their supplier companies. This is typically possible only through specialization according to commodities. Buyers must know their markets—the going prices of commodities and their availability. Additionally, they must be cost and value conscious, strong negotiators who constantly push for the lowest prices possible with their suppliers. Knowledge of the laws that govern their areas of responsibility in purchasing is also a must. Contract law, misrepresentation and fraud, infringement of patent rights, damage claims against suppliers, and shipping regulations are only a few of the areas where laws and regulations must be understood by buyers. Buyers process purchase requisitions and requests for quotation, make supplier selections, place purchase orders, and follow up on purchase orders. Additionally, they negotiate prices and conditions of sale on open purchase orders, blanket purchase orders, adjustments to purchase orders, and all other purchasing contracts.

Make-or-Buy Analysis

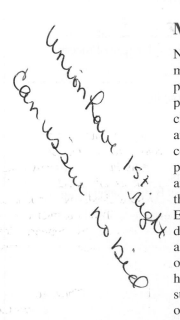

Not all requisitions for raw materials and parts that are received in purchasing departments are automatically ordered from suppliers. Production departments can often make parts in-house at lower cost, of higher quality, and with faster deliveries than would be possible in buying them from suppliers. On the other hand, because suppliers may specialize in certain types of production, some parts can be bought from these suppliers at lower cost, higher quality, and faster delivery times than would be possible if the company made them in-house. Buyers in purchasing departments, with assistance from production departments, routinely perform make-or-buy analyses for the raw materials and parts that go into existing products. In these instances, they must decide between the alternatives of making a part in-house or buying the parts from outside suppliers. Example 11.1 illustrates a make-or-buy analysis in which an operations manager must decide between two different in-house production processes and buying the part from a supplier. This example serves only one purpose—to determine if the purchase cost of the part from a supplier is less than the production cost if the part were made in-house. In practice, such analyses must be accompanied by other considerations. For instance, which alternative offers the best combination of part cost, product quality, and on-time deliveries? Additionally, there are strategic issues involved in outsourcing. For example, what degree of vertical integration is desirable, and should distinctive competencies be outsourced?

Example 11.1	A Make-or-Buy Decision

Drasco is a medium-size manufacturer of oil field pumps. The firm has developed a new model of its high-pressure, secondary-recovery purge pump with improved performance. Bonnie Nelson, manager of process engineering, is trying to decide whether Drasco should make or buy the electronically controlled input valve for the new pump. Her engineers have developed the following estimates:

	Make (Process A)	**Make (Process B)**	**Buy**
Annual volume	10,000 units	10,000 units	10,000 units
Fixed cost/year	$100,000	$300,000	—
Variable cost/unit	$75	$70	$80

a. Should Drasco make the valve using Process A, make the valve using Process B, or buy the valve?

b. At what annual volume should Drasco switch from buying to making the valve using Process A?

c. At what annual volume should Drasco switch from Process A to Process B?

Solution

a. Develop the annual cost of each alternative:

$$\text{Total annual costs} = \text{Fixed costs} + \text{Volume (variable cost)}$$
$$\text{Process A} = \$100,000 + 10,000\,(\$75) = \$850,000$$
$$\text{Process B} = \$300,000 + 10,000\,(\$70) = \$1,000,000$$
$$\text{Buy} = \$0 + 10,000\,(\$80) = \$800,000$$

If the annual volume is estimated to be stable at 10,000 units, Drasco should buy the valve.

b. At what annual volume should Drasco switch from buying to making the valve using Process A (Q = volume)?

$$\text{Total annual cost using Process A} = \text{Total annual cost of buying}$$
$$\$100,000 + Q(\$75) = Q(\$80)$$
$$\$5Q = \$100,000$$
$$Q = 20,000 \text{ units}$$

Drasco should switch when annual volume is greater than 20,000 units.

c. At what annual volume should Drasco switch from Process A to Process B (Q = annual volume, TC = total annual costs)?

$$TC_A = TC_B$$
$$\$100,000 + Q(\$75) = \$300,000 + Q(\$70)$$
$$\$5Q = \$200,000$$
$$Q = 40,000 \text{ units}$$

Drasco should switch when annual volume is greater than 40,000 units.

Ethics in Buying

A nagging problem within purchasing departments is the question of ethics in buying. Salespersons deluge buyers with offers of free lunches, free liquor, free tickets to professional ball games, free evenings on the town, free weekends at resorts, and occasionally even free summer homes in the Sierras. These attempts at offering gifts to buyers raise the question of how much is too much. At what point do gifts to buyers become unethical or even illegal? Buyers hold great power, sometimes even over the economic life or death of salespersons and their organizations. Furthermore, buyers are not always compensated equitably with their responsibilities. All the ingredients are present for temptation.

Some companies have laid down strict codes of conduct for buyers. Absolutely no gifts to buyers, no more than three bottles of liquor at Christmas, no gifts costing more than $25 per buyer per year from any one source, and no single gift exceeding $25 are examples of such rules of conduct. Policies covering gifts to company employees, whether they are buyers or not, certainly seem advisable. But perhaps more important is frequent communication within purchasing departments regarding what constitutes **ethical behavior.** The real worry here is that buyers may feel obligated to salespersons who have given them gifts and may not act in the best interests of their own organizations. Business Snapshot 11.1 illustrates that this is a knotty problem that can start out small and grow to huge proportions. There is no solution other than diligence in keeping open the channels of communication and staying on top of problems to head off undesirable trends before the problems become irreversible. Generally, most companies strive to eliminate kickbacks, out-and-out bribes, and excessive gifts, which are carefully defined. Another good practice is the use of internal audits to ensure continuing organizational control of the purchasing function.

BUSINESS SNAPSHOT 11.1

Allegations of Improper Behavior by Buyers

The New York Telephone Company disclosed that it had conducted an internal investigation into the purchasing practices of its construction department. As a result of the investigation, criminal charges were brought against some employees, several employees were dismissed, and some employees received lesser penalties. Employees were charged with:

1. In exchange for cash and gifts, allowing suppliers to store tools and park vehicles on company property and awarding contracts to suppliers without bidding.
2. Accepting gifts such as liquor or gift certificates during the holiday season.
3. Bid rigging, accepting bribes, theft and tax evasion, and accepting large sums of cash from five companies in exchange for awarding them overpriced contracts.[a]

And at Penney's, a top buyer has confessed that he accepted between $800,000 and $1.5 million in bribes and kickbacks from suppliers between 1988 and 1992.[b]

While charges such as these are subject to due process, organizational vigilance is necessary to avoid the kinds of unethical and illegal practices alleged in this disclosure.

Sources:
[a]Adapted from "28 Workers Depart New York Telephone." *New York Times*, November 16, 1990, C3; and "Inquiry Caused 15 to Depart at New York Telephone." *New York Times*, November 2, 1990, C4.
[b]"Ex-Penney's Rep Admits to Bribery." *San Antonio Express-News*, December 18, 1994, 32f.

BUSINESS SNAPSHOT 11.2

Guidelines for Ethical Behavior in Purchasing

The National Association for Purchasing Managers (NAPM) has developed a set of three principles and 12 standards to help guide ethical behavior in purchasing. These are the principles:

1. Loyalty to your organization
2. Justice to those with whom you deal
3. Faith in your profession

From these principles are derived the NAPM standards of purchasing practice (domestic and international).

1. Avoid the intent and appearance of unethical or compromising practice in relationships, actions, and communications.
2. Demonstrate loyalty to the employer by diligently following the lawful instructions of the employer, using reasonable care and only authority granted.
3. Refrain from any private business or professional activity that would create a conflict between personal interests and the interests of the employer.
4. Refrain from soliciting or accepting money, loans, credits, or prejudicial discounts, and the acceptance of gifts, entertainment, favors, or services from present or potential suppliers that might influence, or appear to influence, purchasing decisions.
5. Handle confidential or proprietary information belonging to employers or suppliers with due care and proper consideration of ethical and legal ramifications and governmental regulations.
6. Promote positive supplier relationships through courtesy and impartiality in all phases of the purchasing cycle.
7. Refrain from reciprocal agreements that restrain competition.
8. Know and obey the letter and spirit of laws governing the purchasing function and remain alert to the legal ramifications of purchasing decisions.
9. Encourage all segments of society to participate by demonstrating support for small, disadvantaged, and minority-owned businesses.
10. Discourage purchasing's involvement in employer-sponsored programs of personal purchases that are not business related.
11. Enhance the proficiency and stature of the purchasing profession by acquiring and maintaining current technical knowledge and the highest standards of ethical behavior.
12. Conduct international purchasing in accordance with the laws, customs, and practices of foreign countries, consistent with United States laws, your organization policies, and these Ethical Standards and Guidelines.

Source: **http://www.napm.org**. Reprinted with permission from the publisher, the National Association of Purchasing Management, *Principles & Standards of Purchasing Practice*, approved November 1992.

Other unethical, illegal, or questionable buying activities include taking advantage of obvious clerical or computational errors in quotations, fixing prices, collusion among bidders, playing favorites among suppliers in awarding orders, failing to respect personal obligations, and upgrading product samples with the intention of supplying lower-grade products. To help guide purchasing employees toward ethical behavior, the National Association for Purchasing Managers (NAPM) offers a set of principles and standards of purchasing practice, as listed in Business Snapshot 11.2.

Purchasing: The International Frontier

Increasingly, purchasing materials means shopping for materials in international markets. For example, U.S. manufacturers in the electronics/computer industry buy materials from all over the world. This means that purchasing agents must engage in negotiations with companies in other countries. The laws of foreign countries, currency exchange rates, cultural differences, and a host of other factors affect these purchases. Additionally, purchasing agents and other personnel routinely travel to foreign countries in the process of selecting vendors and awarding supply contracts. Because these purchases are complex and because much is riding on the success of these activities, organizations must select, develop, and reward purchasing personnel accordingly.

These and other developments make the field of purchasing a challenging one for professional managers to consider for future jobs.

Once the materials are bought, materials managers must then decide the least expensive and most effective method of shipping those materials to their organizations. Similarly, how to ship finished goods to customers is a critical question. These issues are central to the important materials management activity of logistics.

LOGISTICS

Although it is sometimes defined more broadly, logistics usually refers to the management of the movement of materials within the factory, the shipment of incoming materials from suppliers, and the shipment of outgoing products to customers.

Production Control: Movement of Materials within Factories

Production control includes such functions as assigning delivery due dates to orders, master production scheduling, shop-floor planning and control, and detailed production scheduling. While these and related topics are essential elements of materials management, they are discussed in some detail in later chapters of this text and thus are not discussed here. Production control also includes the movement of materials within factories, which consists of the following activities:

1. Removing materials from incoming vehicles and placing them on the receiving dock.
2. Moving materials from the receiving dock to inspection.
3. Moving materials from inspection to the warehouse and storing them until needed.
4. Retrieving materials from the warehouse and delivering them to production operations when needed.
5. Moving materials among production operations.
6. Moving finished products from final assembly and storing them in the finished-goods warehouse.
7. Retrieving finished goods from the finished-goods warehouse and delivering them to packaging and shipping.
8. Moving packaged finished goods to the shipping dock.
9. Loading finished goods into outgoing vehicles at the shipping dock.

The transportation of materials in services includes the type of movements described in Nos. 1–5 above, but usually not the type of movements described in Nos. 6–9. Materials are transported with all types of equipment from hand baskets to hand trucks to belt conveyors to forklift trucks to robotic carriers known as automated guided vehicle systems (AGVS).

The management of the movement of materials within the factory may involve decisions about how to route batches of materials among departments. All of these movements of materials are coordinated by production control and are critical to effective operations management.

more product in & out of factor

follow laws regulations ✗

Shipments to and from Factories

Traffic departments in organizations routinely examine shipping schedules and select shipping methods, timetables, and ways of expediting deliveries. The shipping costs to today's organizations represent such a huge proportion of costs that manufacturing plants, warehouses, and other facilities are often located with one overriding thought in mind: minimize incoming and outgoing shipping costs. In spite of these efforts, shipping costs alone can account for 50 percent or more of the sales price of some manufactured items.

The enormity of these expenditures has caused organizations to staff traffic departments with professional managers and operations analysts who continually search for better shipping techniques. Additionally, many companies have entered the transportation business (sometimes called **vertical backward and forward integration**) to reduce their freight bills.

Traffic management is a specialized field requiring intensive technical training in the Department of Transportation (DOT) and the Interstate Commerce Commission (ICC) regulations and freight rates. This patchwork of **regs and rates** forms the complex constraints with which logistics experts must work in attacking shipping costs. They must know the ins and outs of this complicated and changing field.

Distribution Management

Distribution, sometimes called physical distribution, is the shipment of finished goods through the distribution system to customers. A **distribution system** is the network of shipping and receiving points starting with the factory and ending with the customers. Shipments of goods through distribution systems may or may not be under the direct control of a materials manager. In some companies, the responsibility for managing the distribution system lies with the marketing function.

Distribution Requirements Planning

Material Requirement Planning

Distribution requirements planning (DRP) is the planning for the replenishment of regional warehouse inventories by using MRP-type logic to translate regional warehouse requirements into main-distribution-center requirements, which are then translated into gross requirements in the master production schedule at the factory. Example 11.2 illustrates the logic of distribution requirements planning.

a forecast of what you need

In Example 11.2, scheduled receipts represent orders that have previously been placed and are expected to arrive in a given week. These units can be used to fill future demand. The planned receipt of shipments row of the table represents orders that have not yet been placed but are planned in the future. Projected ending inventory is computed from the projected ending inventory in the previous week plus planned receipt of shipments and scheduled receipts in the current week minus forecasted demand in the current week.

Example 11.2	Distribution Requirements Planning (DRP)

A company has two regional warehouses that receive products from a main distribution center at the factory. The DRP time-phased order point records below illustrate how the planned order releases to the factory from the center are determined for a particular product. The planned order releases to the factory become the gross requirements in the master production schedule (MPS) of the factory.

Regional Warehouse #1

Lead time for shipping products from the main distribution center at the factory to Warehouse #1 is one week, the standard shipping quantity is 50 units, and the safety stock is 10 units.

	\-1	1	2	3	4	5
				Week		
Forecasted demand (units)		30	40	30	40	40
Scheduled receipts		50				
Projected ending inventory	60	80	40	10	20	30
Planned receipt of shipments					50	50
Planned orders for shipments				50	50	

Regional Warehouse #2

Lead time for shipping products from the main distribution center at the factory to Warehouse #2 is two weeks, the standard shipping quantity is 60 units, and the safety stock is 15 units.

	\-1	1	2	3	4	5
				Week		
Forecasted demand (units)		70	80	50	60	50
Scheduled receipts		60				
Projected ending inventory	110	100	20	30	30	40
Planned receipt of shipments				60	60	60
Planned orders for shipments		60	60	60		

Main Distribution Center at the Factory

Lead time for final assembly of products and moving them into the main distribution center is one week, the standard production lot size is 200 units, and the safety stock is 40 units.

	\-1	1	2	3	4	5
				Week		
Gross requirements (units)		60	60	110	50	
Scheduled receipts						
Projected ending inventory	110	50	190	80	230	230
Planned receipt of orders			200		200	
Planned order releases to factory		200		200		

Distribution resource planning extends distribution requirements planning so that the key resources of warehouse space, number of workers, cash, and shipping vehicles are provided in the right quantities and when needed to satisfy customers' demands.

Using Linear Programming to Analyze Shipping Decisions

Example 11.3 illustrates how to determine the monthly plan for shipping a product from several factories to several warehouses. The objective of the example is to minimize monthly shipping costs subject to the monthly plant capacities and the monthly requirements of the warehouses. Examples 4, 5, and 6 in the appendix on the CD accompanying this book illustrate how such transportation problems can be solved manually by using the transportation method of linear programming.

Example 11.3	Minimizing Shipping Costs at Star Computer Company

Star Computer Company produces personal computers at three factories and ships its products to five regional warehouses. The company wants to develop a plan for shipping products from its factories to its warehouses such that the monthly shipping costs are minimized. The shipping cost per computer is:

	Warehouse				
Factory	Wichita	Dallas	El Paso	Denver	Houston
Tulsa	$31	$39	$43	$41	$46
Austin	49	21	33	52	26
Denver	29	39	36	15	63

The factories have these monthly capacities of computers: Tulsa, 50,000; Austin, 60,000; and Denver, 40,000. The warehouses need at least these amounts of computers per month: Wichita, 30,000; Dallas, 40,000; El Paso, 20,000; Denver, 30,000; and Houston, 20,000. Use the *POM Software Library* that accompanies this book to solve this transportation problem.
a. How many computers should Star ship from each factory to each warehouse to minimize monthly shipping costs?
b. What will the total monthly shipping cost be if the shipping plan is followed?

Solution

a. Using the *POM Software Library*, we find that these monthly shipments should be made:

	Warehouse				
Factory	Wichita	Dallas	El Paso	Denver	Houston
Tulsa	30,000	0	10,000	0	0
Austin	0	40,000	0	0	20,000
Denver	0	0	10,000	30,000	0

b. The total monthly shipping cost will be $3,530,000.

Innovations in Logistics

New developments are continually affecting logistics. Piggyback rail shipments, truck trailers on ships, and other unique shipping methods are examples of hybrids that have resulted in great freight savings. Lighter-weight shipping containers, unitized loads, drop shipping, in-transit rates, consolidated shipments, deregulation of the trucking and air-freight industries, and fluctuating fuel costs are examples of developments that are affecting logistics today, and new ones are arising every day. Business Snapshot 11.3 discusses some interesting new concepts in shipping. With the prevalence of computers in today's organizations, up-to-the-minute information is available on the status of each shipment. Additionally, in complicated distribution problems, the computer can be used to plan better networks of shipping methods. Business Snapshot 11.4 discusses one computer software product that is helping companies with supply chain management.

BUSINESS SNAPSHOT 11.3

Trucking on the Web

The Internet has had an enormous impact on the way companies buy motor freight services, and the trucking industry has been moving quickly to offer a wide range of web-supported options and value-added services to buyers.

American Freightways, based in Harrison, Arkansas, recently redesigned its web site with input from its customers. One of its customers, Alro Specialty Metals of Tulsa, Oklahoma, now uses the site to look at inbound shipments 24 hours in advance so its receiving department knows what is en route. Alro also uses the web site to generate reports that show freight expenses.

UPS was one of the first logistics companies to offer tracking services using Palm VII organizers and other wireless devices. UPS customers have two-way, interactive access to UPS services from virtually any wireless device.

Keith Baddeley, traffic manager for Congoleum Corporation, a flooring products company headquartered in Mercerville, New Jersey, used to spend 30 minutes on the telephone giving New Penn Motor Express Inc. his pickup list. With New Penn's new web site, Baddeley now can accomplish the same task in half the time. Baddeley also uses the web site to receive on-line proofs of delivery, to look at the status of previously

picked-up shipments, and to see that New Penn has made the required delivery appointments.

Many transportation Internet portals and exchanges have been recently developed that allow customers to post shipments that need to be delivered or to find transportation companies that will deliver a particular shipment. Two such web sites that offer a variety of services to users are **http://www.transportation.com** and **http://www.gologistics.com**.

As the Internet continues to develop and more and more companies become involved in e-business, transportation services will continue to evolve on-line.

Source: Weart, Walter. "Trucking on the Web: Matching Demand with Supply." *Inbound Logistics*, September 2000, 30–42.

Integral to logistics are methods of warehousing materials and products once they are received from suppliers and before they are shipped to customers.

WAREHOUSING

Warehousing is the management of materials while they are in storage. It includes storing, dispersing, ordering, and accounting for all materials and finished goods from the beginning to the end of the production process. Warehousing facilities may range from small stockrooms to large, highly mechanized storage facilities.

Warehousing Operations

Warehousing deals with materials that directly support operations. The first problems that must be addressed are when to place an order for each material and how much to order. Orders are placed and shipments eventually appear in the receiving department, usually by either truck trailers or railroad cars.

Materials are routinely unloaded from delivery vehicles and held in temporary storage areas until quality control has tested them, confirmed their acceptability for use in operations, and released them. Materials-handling equipment such as forklift trucks, conveyors, straddle trucks, and pump-forced pipelines are used to place the materials

BUSINESS SNAPSHOT 11.4

Top-Selling Supply Chain Management Software

Running a modern factory requires complex decisions based on hundreds of variables. Prices for raw material may be in flux. Customer demand may shift from one product line to another.

In the late 1980s, a young Dallas engineer named Sanjiv Sidhu saw a business opportunity in the scientific observation that even the smartest people can only juggle as many as nine variables when making decisions. With that in mind, he developed computer software for shop-floor managers based on artificial intelligence and advanced simulation models. Founded in 1988, i2 Technologies, Inc., develops software for factories to manage the delivery of components and the shipment of products.

As the winner of *Information Week* magazine's 1999 Product of the Year award, i2 Technologies' *Rhythm* software owns 13 percent of the market for supply chain management software with more than 800 customer companies worldwide, including Compaq, Dell Computer, Ford, General Motors, Coca-Cola, Black and Decker, IBM, and Texas Instruments. The software helps companies to better manage inventories and manufacturing capacities by using simulation models instead of the rules of thumb that have traditionally been applied to managing plants. The *Rhythm* software also includes applications for product life-cycle management, supply planning, demand planning, demand fulfillment, financial and operations planning, and customer-relationship management.

A typical $1 billion-a-year manufacturer carrying $250 million in inventory can comfortably cut inventory to less than $100 million with better supply chain management, according to Mr. Sidhu. The savings come from reduced borrowing, lower storage costs, and reduced risk of damage or obsolescence. Companies can then reinvest much of the money in product development or building efficiencies. Gene Ramirez, an analyst at Southwest Securities in Dallas who follows i2, said, "The software offers companies a phenomenal return on their investment."

Sources: Goldstein, Alan. "Assembling Wealth: i2 Founder's Factory Software Fills High-Demand Niche." *Dallas Morning News*, October 6, 1997, 1D, 4D; Gilbert, Alorie. "i2 Technologies' Rhythm." *Information Week*, December 20, 1999, 56; and **http://www.i2.com**.

into **raw-materials inventory**. This inventory is stored on pallets (a small base frame on which bags and boxes of material are stacked), in high stacks, in storage tanks, or other means of holding raw materials.

In some firms, such as chemical-processing plants, bulk materials are used as needed by operations departments without asking warehousing. In other facilities, however, a **stock requisition** is prepared by production control and forwarded to warehousing, requesting that materials be delivered to specific locations within production departments. In production systems that use process layouts, where material moves intermittently through the facilities, **in-process inventories** are usually maintained. These partially completed products that are between processes are located at various designated locations throughout the production system.

Warehousing may or may not be responsible for accounting for these in-process inventories, managing their movement, receiving and disbursing them, and controlling what materials are put in and taken out. If the time that materials are in in-process inventory is short, production usually retains control. If the time delay is long, however, or if other prevailing reasons exist, such as safety, government regulation, and so on, warehousing takes charge and maintains storerooms at various points within the production system.

In systems that use product layouts, where material moves continuously through the facilities, storage of in-process inventories is rare, and therefore production maintains

Management of inventory depends on many factors, including how long materials are in process in the productive system.

control of the in-process materials until they become finished products. At that point, after the materials have been transformed into finished-goods inventory, they are relinquished to the finished-goods warehouse.

The record keeping within warehousing requires a **stock record** for each item that is carried in inventories. The individual item is called a **stock-keeping unit (SKU)**. Stock records are running accounts that show the on-hand balance, receipts, disbursements, and any other changes that actually affect the usable on-hand balance for each SKU. Additionally, stock records may show expected receipts, promises, or allocations of SKUs even though they are still in inventory. Computers have allowed managers to improve the accuracy of these records, post changes to records more frequently as they occur, and have on-hand balance information instantaneously.

Methods of Inventory Accounting

For hundreds of years inventory accounting was based on **periodic inventory accounting systems,** or periodic updating of manual stock records, and **physical inventory counts.** Stock records were updated by periodically (usually at the end of every workday) entering, by hand on cards filed in trays, the number of units added to and taken from inventory. If one wanted to know the number of units on hand of a particular material in inventory, one would go to the card tray, pull the material's stock record card, and see the inventory balance as of the last update. The accuracy of these systems depended on how often the stock records were updated and on how often the information on the stock records was verified or corrected through physical inventory counts. The more frequent the correction and the updating of the stock records, the more accurate was the information on the stock records. The annual or "end-of-the-year" physical inventory counts, in which all materials in the warehouses were physically counted, were traditional in many industries. Some companies today still use this type of inventory accounting because it is either more economical or the only feasible way to account for inventory.

Increasingly, however, firms are using **perpetual inventory accounting systems** in which stock records are maintained in computers. In such systems stock records, rather than being periodically updated, are updated at the time materials are received into or dispensed from inventory. The time lag between the last updating of the stock records and the time the records are accessed to determine the inventory balance is practically eliminated. These records are also subject to error, however, and they too must be verified or corrected. It is customary today to use cycle counting to maintain stock record accuracy in perpetual inventory accounting systems.

Cycle counting is an ongoing effort to physically count the number of units of each material in inventory, compare this number to the balance shown on stock records, and reconcile the difference. The twofold purpose of cycle counting is to correct the stock records and, more important, to identify shortcomings in all areas of the inventory system and initiate corrective actions. In cycle counting, *when* a material is counted is determined by a counting schedule for that material. A material may be counted when it reaches its reorder point, when a shipment of the material is received, or at a particular time interval.

High-value, fast-moving materials tend to be counted more frequently. *But how often we count an inventory item (monthly, quarterly, etc.) should depend on two factors: the history of the item's inaccuracies and the difficulties caused if an item's counts are inaccurate.* An item that has a history of inaccurate counts and one that will cause big problems in production if counts are inaccurate should be counted more frequently. Fast-moving items that have inaccurate counts usually cause great difficulties in production because they appear in production schedules more often. And when they do appear, the inaccuracy can cause major changes in the master production schedules, expediting, split orders, panic shipment procedures, extra transportation and production costs, and confusion on the shop floor.

In cycle counting, a specially trained crew of workers counts some materials every working day, and stock records are verified or corrected on an ongoing basis. The ultimate goal of cycle counting is to reduce the inaccuracy of stock records to a very small percentage. Since it is estimated that MRP (material requirements planning) systems require stock records that are accurate to within ±0.5 percent, cycle counting is an important part of MRP systems. Example 11.4 illustrates a common situation associated with cycle counting.

Example 11.4	Number of Cycle-Counting Personnel Required

A company wants to improve the accuracy of the stock records used in its MRP system. A consultant has recommended that all Class A (critical) materials be counted an average of 24 times per year, all Class B (important) materials be counted an average of 6 times per year, and all Class C (noncritical) materials be counted an average of 2 times per year. The consultant estimates that an experienced and well-trained cycle counter can count an average of 20 materials a day. A company works 260 days per year, and it has determined that it has 1,000 A materials, 3,000 B materials, and 6,000 C materials. How many workers would be required to perform cycle counting?

Solution			
Class of Materials	Number of Materials per Class	Number of Counts per Material per Year	Total Counts per Year
A	1,000	24	24,000
B	3,000	6	18,000
C	6,000	2	12,000
			Total 54,000

$$\text{Number of materials counted per day} = \frac{\text{Total counts per year}}{\text{Number of workdays per year}}$$

$$= \frac{54,000}{260} = 207.7$$

$$\text{Number of counters required} = \frac{\text{Number of materials counted per day}}{\text{Number of materials per day per counter}}$$

$$= \frac{207.7}{20} = 10.4, \text{ or } 11 \text{ counters}$$

Contemporary Developments in Warehousing

New developments are continuously modifying the management of warehousing systems. Advances in computing systems are allowing on-line instantaneous record-keeping transactions. The use of bar-coding systems is increasingly common as companies try to minimize data entry errors in inventory records. The automatic registering of products and prices at grocery stores is an example of these developments. Inventories are automatically adjusted as groceries are bought. Managers can remotely query the computing system and obtain instantaneous inventory balances. Motorola, Honeywell, Westinghouse, and other companies already have similar on-line systems for keeping stock records for all SKUs. Ralston Purina and Westinghouse have almost totally removed the human element from the physical movement and storage of materials at some of their newer locations. These automated storage and retrieval systems (ASRS) remove materials from raw-materials inventory, make up batches of complete material orders, and deliver them to the appropriate points within the production system, all without being touched by human hands. Other automated systems similarly assemble shipping orders and move them to shipping areas. These and other developments promise to make warehousing even more effective in the future in meeting the quantity and scheduling needs of customers and operations departments.

In spite of the advances made in computing systems, the establishment of materials manager positions, and centralization of materials management functions for greater control, occasional mistakes still occur. Materials are not where they should be when they are needed, a stockout occurs, or a stockout is anticipated. When these or similar situations arise, *and they do in all systems*, materials must be expedited.

EXPEDITING

Expediting is the focusing of one or more persons' attention on a particular order or batch of materials for the purpose of speeding up the order through all or part of the entire supply chain. **De-expediting** means slowing down an order. Expediting or de-expediting is necessary usually because unforeseen events have caused an order for materials or products to be late or early. Examples of some of these events are:

too when when's too much

- A customer increased the quantity of products ordered. The expanded order quantity now exceeds finished-goods inventory, and additional products must be quickly produced.
- A supplier fails to ship an order for materials when promised. Emergency shipping procedures must be employed in order to get the parts in-house in time to avoid a stockout or disruption of the production processes.
- Parts being processed in heat-treat have encountered technical difficulties. The batch must be quickly transferred ahead of other materials if the annealing process is not to be delayed.
- After a special order for an electric generator has been started in production, the customer calls and wants to delay the shipment for three weeks. The work in process should be slowed and rescheduled so that the product is completed when the customer wants it shipped.

Expediting most often is necessary because of the uncertainties present in production systems; customer demand, material delivery times, and in-house processing times are but a few of these uncertainties. Materials management must be flexible enough to accommodate these uncertainties by reacting quickly when the unexpected happens. Expediting is periodically performed by all materials management employees, and this activity helps make supply chains flexible.

Some managers and their organizations routinely operate by crisis management. *Every* activity is expedited. This approach to management is an excuse for poor planning, poor procedures, and poor management in general. When expediting becomes the dominant activity in materials management, something is wrong. Everyone and every production system makes mistakes, and these mistakes can create the need for expediting when materials managers, buyers, warehousing managers, logistics personnel, or others in the supply chain foul up. But expediting should be the exception to the rule, not the rule.

Expediting completes the materials cycle that proceeds from acquisition of materials to the delivery of finished goods into customers' hands. The means to change procedures, override policy, make telephone calls and collect past favors, devise quick solutions as they occur, and other tactics of expediting are some of the important ways that managers make materials systems work effectively and get the right quantity of the right material to the right place at the right time.

BENCHMARKING THE PERFORMANCE OF MATERIALS MANAGERS

Given the importance of materials management today, how do organizations measure how well materials managers are doing their jobs? Table 11.1 ranks several criteria, in order of their importance, that companies have traditionally used to evaluate materials managers. These criteria have been important, and will undoubtedly remain important, but the move toward global markets, time-based competition, and total quality man-

Table 11.1	Traditional Ranking of Performance Criteria in Materials Management

Rank	Performance Criteria
1	The level and value of in-house inventories
2	The percentage of orders that are delivered to customers on time
3	The number and severity of stockouts in in-house inventories
4	The annual costs of materials purchased from suppliers
5	The annual costs of transportation for materials from suppliers and for products to customers
6	The annual costs of operating warehouses
7	The number of customer complaints about poor service
8	Other factors such as profitability and manufacturing costs

Table 11.2	Materials Management Performance in World-Class Companies

Performance Criteria	All Companies	World-Class Companies
Number of suppliers for each purchasing agent	34	5
Number of purchasing agents per $100 million of purchases	5.4	2.2
Cost of purchasing as a percentage of purchases	3.3%	0.8%
Time required to perform an evaluation of a supplier	3 weeks	0.4 week
Time required to place an order with suppliers	6 weeks	2.4 minutes
Percentage of late deliveries	33%	2%
Percentage of defects	1.5%	0.0001%
Number of material stockouts per year	400	4

Source: Business Week, November 30, 1992, 72.

agement in U.S. companies has caused other important criteria to surface. Table 11.2 lists other factors being used by companies today to evaluate their materials management function.

THIRD-PARTY LOGISTICS MANAGEMENT PROVIDERS

A growing trend among world-class companies today is the reliance on third-party logistics management providers. As they try to focus more on their core competencies, many companies are outsourcing certain business functions such as warehousing and distribution. Companies such as Caliber Logistics (now FedEx Logistics) and United Parcel Service offer a variety of logistics services and expertise to other companies. As one example, Dell Computer Corporation recently contracted with FedEx Logistics to operate its finished-goods warehouse and distribution system near Austin, Texas.

A number of benefits can be realized from using third-party logistics management firms. These firms can provide state-of-the-art logistics information systems, lower negotiated prices for transportation carriers and warehouse space, and highly trained logistics personnel. They can also help design a logistics system that is most effective for a particular company.

E-BUSINESS AND SUPPLY CHAIN MANAGEMENT

As the Internet has grown and evolved, more and more companies have become involved in e-business. **E-business** *refers to using the Internet to conduct or facilitate business transactions, such as sales, purchasing, communication, inventory management, customer service, submitting orders, and checking the status of orders.* Examples of e-business also include selling directly to consumers via a web site and on-line auctions of products and services. E-business transactions among companies are referred to as **business-to-business (B2B) transactions** or **e-commerce**. As the Internet continues to evolve, more e-business applications will undoubtedly be developed.

In the last few years, e-business has had a significant impact on supply chain management activities. Business Snapshot 11.3 described examples of how the trucking industry is using the Internet to provide new services for transportation customers. Many other industries are also being impacted by e-business. A study published by Boston Consulting Group in January 2000 projected that Internet-based e-commerce among businesses will grow from $92 billion in 1999 to $2.0 trillion in 2003.[1] Today, Internet-based e-commerce is steadily replacing **Electronic Data Interchange (EDI)** systems that were popular in the 1980s and 1990s. EDI systems allow two companies to electronically conduct business transactions with each other, but they require special computer software and hardware and are typically much more expensive.

One of the most important impacts of the Internet and e-business in supply chain management is the availability of instantaneous information. Managers can immediately obtain information such as pricing, location of materials, status of shipments, and availability of parts throughout the supply chain. This access to information, along with e-mail, allows companies to closely coordinate their materials management activities with other companies in the supply chain, thereby avoiding many problems and creating a very efficient supply chain. This efficiency helps to reduce the operating costs of all companies in the supply chain.

A number of on-line auctions or exchange web sites have been developed in the last few years that are useful to supply chain managers. Some of these are for specific industries, such as **http://www.steelauction.com** for the steel industry. Others are more general, such as **http://www.verticalnet.com** for all types of industrial equipment and **http://www.transportation.com** for transportation equipment. Another example is the Automotive Network Exchange (ANX). ANX was originally developed by Daimler-Chrysler, Ford Motor Company, and General Motors Corporation to streamline automotive industry supplier communication efficiency. The goal for ANX was to develop a secure, high-performance, and highly reliable e-business system that members can use to exchange the large volumes of design data their computer-assisted design and manufacturing systems generate. According to high-ranking officials at Daimler-Chrysler, Ford, and GM, the ANX will be the crucial communication format for most engineering, purchasing, shipping, manufacturing, and materials handling functions. More of these on-line auction and exchange services will certainly be developed in the near future.

Enterprise resource planning (ERP) software systems such as *SAP*, *PeopleSoft*, and *Baan*, which became popular in the late 1990s, have recently incorporated features that facilitate e-business and coordination among companies. For example, *SAP*, the leading ERP software company, has created the web site **http://www.mysap.com** as a platform for companies to conduct e-business and to better coordinate their activities together. The mySAP web site offers companies a variety of services and tools to make their supply chain management activities and intercompany coordination easier.

Another way that e-business is affecting supply chain management results from companies selling directly to consumers over the Internet. Many companies that have sold their products through traditional marketing channels such as retail stores and distributors have also started selling directly to consumers on their web sites. This new marketing channel requires different approaches for getting products to customers. Instead of shipping large quantities of products to warehouses or retail stores using common trucking carriers, these companies now must also ship individual products directly to customers' homes. Selling directly to customers impacts the companies' finished-goods warehousing policies, transportation systems, distribution networks, packaging systems, and materials handling systems. Package carriers such as FedEx and UPS have experienced a substantial increase in the number of packages they deliver for companies due to the growth of e-business.

E-business and other information technologies have made for exciting times for supply chain managers. And the continuing advancement of these technologies will make for even more exciting times in the future.

Wrap-Up
WHAT WORLD-CLASS COMPANIES DO

World-class companies see supply chain management as a key element in capturing increased shares of world markets. They have given the executives in charge expanded and new responsibilities. These supply chain managers plan and control all the activities related to materials that move from suppliers, through the production processes, and to customers. The authority for the materials system residing in a single organizational function provides focus and avoids the former situation in which everyone blamed everyone else when difficulties related to materials developed. Whether or not world-class companies centralize materials management, the way that materials are managed has changed.

World-class companies are forming partnerships with suppliers to quickly produce products of near-perfect quality precisely when needed and with little inventory. Providing suppliers with information about when customer orders are needed and training them in quality control and manufacturing techniques are becoming more common. Suppliers are selected and developed with a long-term view toward improving product quality, fast deliveries, and responsiveness to customers' needs. Although price is important, being able to deliver enough materials when needed, producing materi-

als of exceptional quality, and being trustworthy and cooperative are even more important. Long-term, multiyear contracts are used to guarantee suppliers security and to provide incentives for developing trust and cooperation.

Nearby suppliers are preferred. Even if suppliers are located at great distances, they are often clustered together for combined shipments or are able to devise other innovative ways to deliver materials on a just-in-time basis. This may take some imagination because of great geographic distances, but the payoff is found in shorter and more dependable lead times and in reduced inventories. All materials in the system are geared to be produced and arrive just when needed by production so that products can be delivered just when needed by customers.

World-class companies use computers extensively to determine the most efficient routes for trucks, to find the best way to load and unload trucks, and to provide close communications between drivers and central offices. This use of computers not only holds down costs, but, of at least equal importance, it enables management to know where each order in the entire system is and when it is expected to arrive at its destination. World-class companies use computer models to develop shipping plans for manufacturing and service operations. Of particular value is linear programming. With this technique, shipping costs among many sources and many destinations can be minimized by developing shipping plans that require the least amount of travel.

Increasingly, some world-class companies are starting to rely on third-party logistics management firms as they outsource some of their business functions to become more focused on their core competencies.

World-class companies are also conducting B2B transactions with other companies via the Internet. This use of e-business helps to drive down costs, shorten procurement lead times, and improve communication throughout the supply chain.

REVIEW AND DISCUSSION QUESTIONS

1. Define these terms: *material, supply chain, supply chain management.*
2. What is the mission of purchasing? What factors are making purchasing more important today? Explain. In what activities does purchasing engage?
3. Define these terms: *material specification, purchase requisition, request for quotation, purchase order.*
4. Define *make-or-buy analysis.*
5. What practices of purchasing departments are considered unethical? How can companies prevent or control unethical purchasing practices?
6. List a few guidelines for ethical behavior in purchasing.
7. Define these terms: *logistics, distribution management, distribution requirements planning.*
8. List the activities included in logistics within a factory.
9. Define these terms: *warehousing, raw-materials inventory, stock requisition, in-process inventory, stock record, stock-keeping unit.*
10. Describe two methods of inventory accounting. Define *cycle counting* and explain its purpose. What factors would justify counting a material more frequently?
11. Why do firms occasionally have to expedite orders for materials? Does expediting occur only when materials managers foul up?
12. What are the most important criteria used in evaluating materials managers?
13. What benefits can be realized from using third-party logistics management firms?
14. Define *e-business.* How is e-business helping supply chain managers?

INTERNET ASSIGNMENTS

1. UPS Worldwide Logistics provides third-party logistics management services to companies. Visit the web site of UPS at **http://www.ups.com** and find the web pages for UPS Worldwide Logistics. Describe some of the services that are offered.
2. Varsity Logistics (**http://www.varsitynet.com**) offers software products to help companies better manage their logistics. Visit and explore the company's web site, and describe some of the software products offered.
3. i2 Technologies (**http://www.i2.com**) is a provider of planning and scheduling software for global supply chain management. Visit and explore i2's web site, and describe some of the features of its software.
4. Search the Internet for a warehousing company. Describe its facilities and the warehousing services it offers.
5. Search the Internet for a railroad company that offers freight transportation. Describe its facilities and the freight services it offers.
6. Search the Internet for a business-to-business auction or exchange. Describe the types of services offered and the types of products for auction or exchange.

FIELD PROJECTS IN MATERIALS MANAGEMENT

1. Make an appointment with a materials manager, an inventory manager, or a supply chain manager from one of these types of organizations:
   a. Manufacturing   d. Trucking
   b. Hospital   e. Warehousing
   c. Retailing

   Interview this manager, and describe in detail the three most important materials problems that plague his or her organization.

2. From any organization, interview one of these employees:
   a. Purchasing agent   d. Warehousing manager
   b. Purchasing buyer   e. Expediter
   c. Traffic or logistics manager

   Describe as completely as possible this person's duties as he or she perceives them.

3. Interview a purchasing buyer from any organization. Determine the buyer's idea of what is and what is not ethical buying behavior in regard to gifts. Do you agree or disagree with his or her point of view? Why?

4. From any organization, interview one of these employees:
   a. Purchasing agent   c. Warehouse manager
   b. Traffic or logistics manager   d. Expediter

   What new developments are expected to have an important effect on the performance of this employee's duties within the next five years? How will the person's duties be affected by these developments?

5. Investigate any manufacturing organization, and gather information about its materials system. Prepare a flowchart similar to Figure 11.2, but with more details, that depicts the organization's materials system.

6. Investigate any firm to determine how the materials management function fits into its organization. Prepare an organization chart similar to Figure 11.3 for the firm.

PROBLEMS

7. Spectragen Inc. is planning for production of a new product, and one necessary production process is to anneal the primary metal part. Because Spectragen does not currently have the annealing equipment, it can either purchase the equipment and anneal the parts itself or outsource this annealing process to a local subcontractor. Spectragen's purchasing department has developed the following estimates:

	Anneal In-House	Outsource Annealing
Number of parts per year	25,000	25,000
Fixed cost per year	$85,000	0
Variable cost per part	$32	$38

If product quality and delivery performance are about the same for the make-or-buy alternatives, should Spectragen purchase the annealing equipment or outsource the annealing process?

8. Susan Gilbert, a purchasing agent for Wisconsin Plastics Inc. (WSI), is reviewing quotations from suppliers for a new plastic gear. Susan plans to either place an order for 12,000 gears from a supplier with the least-cost quotation or recommend that WSI purchase the necessary equipment and make the gear itself. Relevant data for this make-or-buy decision are found below. What should Susan recommend?

	Make	**Buy**
Fixed cost of equipment	$60,000	0
Variable cost per part	$16	$20

9. The materials manager for K-Flex Corporation is analyzing how to produce a new part that will be needed for the next few years. K-Flex has manufacturing plants in Taiwan, Singapore, and India that could produce the part. The forecast calls for 20,000 units of the part each year. The materials manager has developed the following estimates for the three alternative locations:

Plant	**Type of Cost**	**Annual Fixed Cost**	**Variable Cost per Unit**
Taiwan	Annual tooling	$130,000	
	Inspection and rework		$ 1.30
	Shipping		3.20
	Production costs	4,500	23.50
Singapore	Annual tooling	$ 45,000	
	Inspection and rework		$ 2.55
	Shipping		3.90
	Production costs	9,500	26.20
India	Annual tooling	$ 65,000	
	Inspection and rework		$ 1.90
	Shipping		2.90
	Production costs	7,000	25.10

a. Which plant would provide the least cost?
b. How many units of the part would have to be produced and sold for each of the plants to be the least-cost alternative?

10. Neil Brockley, the purchasing manager at Agrifoods Processing Company, must decide on a purchasing strategy for this year's processing of broccoli. The regional harvest season will not begin for five months, and Neil is faced with three alternative purchasing strategies. One strategy is for Agrifoods to wait until the harvest has begun before trying to purchase broccoli. Many small farmers wait until harvest time to sell their crops. Another strategy is to wait three months until most farmers have planted their broccoli fields. At that time Agrifoods could negotiate contracts with several medium-sized farmers to purchase their crops. The third purchasing strategy is to immediately negotiate a contract with Northern California Growers Cooperative. Neil has estimated the following costs per pound and associated probabilities for each purchasing strategy:

	Probability	Cost per Pound
Small farmers	0.20	0.45
	0.25	0.60
	0.35	0.75
	0.20	0.95
Mid-sized farmers	0.25	0.55
	0.40	0.75
	0.35	0.85
Cooperative	0.40	0.70
	0.60	0.75

a. Use a decision tree to analyze the decision alternatives. (*Hint:* Review Example 5.1.)

b. How should Agrifoods purchase broccoli?

c. What will be the expected cost per pound for broccoli if Agrifoods follows your recommendation?

d. What other factors should be considered in this purchasing decision?

11. Nevada Cryogenics (NC) wants to submit one proposal to the National Science Foundation for a research contract to investigate cryogenics applications in agriculture. NC is considering three alternative levels of requested funding to bid. NC estimates the probability of winning a research contract and the net value to the organization as follows:

Level of Funding	Probability of Winning Research Contract	Net Research Contract Value
High	0.20	$750,000
Medium	0.50	375,000
Low	0.75	175,000

NC will lose $70,000 if it does not win a research contract. If a contract is received, NC expects that it may be able to then develop a commercial product based on the research. The net value of a successful commercial product is expected to be $400,000, but NC would need to spend about $200,000 to develop a commercial product based on the research. An unsuccessful commercial product would have no return. If NC decides to develop a commercial product, the probability that it would be successful in the marketplace is estimated at 40 percent. NC would only consider developing a commercial product if a research contract is received.

a. Use a decision tree to analyze the decision alternatives. (*Hint:* Review Example 5.1.)

b. What courses of action would you recommend to Nevada Cryogenics?

c. What is the expected value to Nevada Cryogenics if it follows your recommendations?

d. What other factors should be considered in this purchasing decision?

12. A purchasing agent at Bell Computers must award a video card supply contract to either Matrix or Advanced Video Graphics (AVG), two large manufacturers of computer video cards. Bell plans to use a new approach to assembling its computers, so the video card supplier must be able to make frequent, small deliveries of video cards. After evaluating the two potential vendors, the purchasing agent has prepared this information:

Performance Factor	Factor Weight	Rating	
		Matrix	AVG
Price	0.15	$68	$76
Delivery schedule	0.25	0.8	0.8
Schedule reliability	0.25	0.4	0.6
Video card quality	0.20	0.8	0.6
Video card features	0.15	0.5	0.9

Which vendor would you recommend? Why? (*Hint:* Look at Tables 5.5 and 6.4.) What other factors would be important in such a decision?

13. Yoshinori Otake is a purchasing agent at MicroAir, a manufacturer of microwave/convection oven units. MicroAir is about to change its production to a new approach, and Mr. Otake has been asked to reevaluate potential suppliers of a digital display module. After assessing the three potential vendors' likely performance on important factors, Mr. Otake has prepared the following information:

Performance Factor	Factor Weight	Rating		
		Sumsing	Parkasenic	Hatchui
Price	0.20	$13.60	$14.30	$13.20
Delivery schedule	0.20	0.8	0.7	0.9
Schedule reliability	0.25	0.8	0.6	0.7
Quality	0.20	0.6	0.8	0.6
Production capacity	0.10	0.5	0.6	0.8
Responsiveness	0.05	0.6	0.7	0.5

Which vendor would you recommend? Why? (*Hint:* Look at Tables 5.5 and 6.4.) What other factors would be important in such a decision?

14. Products are shipped from a company's main distribution center (adjacent to the factory) to two regional warehouses. The DRP records below indicate the forecasted demand, scheduled receipts, and the last period's projected ending inventory (in units) for a single product. The planned order releases to the factory become the gross requirements in the master production schedule (MPS) of the factory.
   a. Complete the DRP records below.
   b. From these records, what gross requirements will appear in the MPS at the factory?

Regional Warehouse #1

Lead time for shipping products from the main distribution center at the factory to Warehouse #1 is 1 week, the standard shipping quantity is 200 units, and the safety stock is 100 units.

	Week					
	−1	1	2	3	4	5
Forecasted demand		100	150	180	90	120
Scheduled receipts		200				
Projected ending inventory	300					
Planned receipt of shipments						
Planned orders for shipments						

Regional Warehouse #2

Lead time for shipping products from the main distribution center at the factory to Warehouse #2 is 2 weeks, the standard shipping quantity is 300 units, and the safety stock is 200 units.

		Week				
	−1	1	2	3	4	5
Forecasted demand		150	250	200	240	200
Scheduled receipts		300				
Projected ending inventory	350					
Planned receipt of shipments						
Planned orders for shipments						

Main Distribution Center at the Factory

Lead time for final assembling of products and moving them into the main distribution center is 1 week, the standard production lot size is 500 units, and the safety stock is 200 units.

		Week				
	−1	1	2	3	4	5
Gross requirements (units)						
Scheduled receipts		500				
Projected ending inventory	250					
Planned receipt of orders						
Planned order releases to factory						

15. Products are shipped from a company's factory warehouse to two regional warehouses. The DRP records below indicate the forecasted demand, scheduled receipts, and the last period's ending inventory in units for a single product. The planned order releases to the factory become the gross requirements in the master production schedule (MPS) of the factory.
    a. Complete the DRP records below.
    b. From these records, what gross requirements will show up in the MPS at the factory?

Regional Warehouse A

Lead time for shipping products from the warehouse at the factory to Warehouse A is 2 weeks, the standard shipping quantity is 250 units, and the safety stock is 150 units.

		Week				
	−1	1	2	3	4	5
Forecasted demand		130	190	280	150	310
Scheduled receipts		250				
Projected ending inventory	230					
Planned receipt of shipments						
Planned orders for shipments						

Regional Warehouse B

Lead time for shipping products from the warehouse at the factory to Warehouse B is 1 week, the standard shipping quantity is 150 units, and the safety stock is 80 units.

		Week					
	−1	1	2	3	4	5
Forecasted demand		210	140	180	150	140
Scheduled receipts		150				
Projected ending inventory	180					
Planned receipt of shipments						
Planned orders for shipments						

Warehouse at the Factory

Lead time for final assembly of products and moving them into the warehouse at the factory is 1 week, the standard production lot size is 500 units, and the safety stock is 150 units.

		Week					
	−1	1	2	3	4	5
Forecasted demand						
Scheduled receipts		500				
Projected ending inventory	100					
Planned receipt of shipments						
Planned orders for shipments						

16. A product is shipped from a main distribution center to three regional warehouses and directly to customers. The DRP records below indicate the forecasted demand, scheduled receipts, and the last period's projected ending inventory.
    a.   Complete the DRP records below.
    b.   From these records, what gross requirements will show up in the MPS at the factory?

	Warehouse A					Warehouse B				
	Week					Week				
	−1	1	2	3	4	−1	1	2	3	4
Forecasted demand		50	80	90	80		80	120	150	140
Scheduled receipts		100					150			
Projected ending inventory	160					200				
Planned receipt of shipments										
Planned orders for shipments										

	Warehouse C					Direct Customer Sales				
	Week					Week				
	−1	1	2	3	4	−1	1	2	3	4
Forecasted demand		30	80	90	50		150	200	100	160
Scheduled receipts		100								
Projected ending inventory	150									
Planned receipt of shipments										
Planned orders for shipments										

Main Distribution Center

	Week				
	−1	**1**	**2**	**3**	**4**
Gross requirements (units)					
Scheduled receipts		450			
Projected ending inventory	400				
Planned receipt of orders					
Planned order releases to factory					

The standard order quantities, lead times, and safety stocks for the warehouses are shown below:

	Order Quantity (units)	Lead Time (weeks)	Safety Stock (units)
Warehouse A	100	1	100
Warehouse B	150	2	150
Warehouse C	100	1	100
Main distribution center	450	1	400

17. A company ships products from three factories to six warehouses. The shipping cost per product, monthly capacity of each factory, and monthly demand at each warehouse are:

	Warehouse						
Factory	**A**	**B**	**C**	**D**	**E**	**F**	**Capacity**
1	$6.5	$4.2	$5.0	$1.9	$4.6	$7.1	25,000
2	3.8	2.8	5.1	6.8	3.5	4.0	40,000
3	4.6	4.4	4.1	3.5	6.4	5.2	20,000
Demand:	9,000	15,000	12,000	18,000	20,000	11,000	

Use the *POM Software Library* that accompanies this book to solve this transportation problem.
   a. How many products should the company ship from each factory to each warehouse to minimize monthly shipping costs?
   b. What will be the monthly shipping cost if the shipping plan is followed?

18. A company ships products from four factories to five warehouses. The shipping cost per product, monthly capacity of each factory, and monthly demand at each warehouse are:

	Warehouse					
Factory	**1**	**2**	**3**	**4**	**5**	**Capacity**
A	$12	$19	$10	$15	$15	10,000
B	17	23	15	19	10	15,000
C	21	20	14	12	11	8,000
D	13	17	11	22	16	7,000
Demand:	11,000	5,000	6,000	12,000	6,000	

Use the *POM Software Library* that accompanies this book to solve this transportation problem.
   a. How many products should the company ship from each factory to each warehouse to minimize monthly shipping costs?
   b. What will be the monthly shipping cost if the shipping plan is followed?

19. Use the *POM Software Library* that accompanies this book to solve these transportation problems from Chapter 8:
    a. LP-F
    b. LP-J
    c. Quality Pixels Inc. case

20. A company is implementing a cycle-counting system. Class A items would be counted monthly, Class B items would be counted quarterly, and Class C items would be counted annually. Sixty-five percent of the company's production items are Class C items, 25 percent are Class B items, and 10 percent are Class A items. If the firm has 30,000 different material and part numbers, how many items will need to be counted daily if there are 260 working days per year?

21. To improve its cycle-counting program, the manager of warehousing and inventory proposes to double the frequency of counting the B and C classes of materials. The present situation is:

Class of Material	Percentage of Items in Material Class	Frequency Counting
A	5%	Monthly
B	20	Quarterly
C	75	Annually

The company had 60,000 materials of all types. If a worker who does cycle counting costs $30,000 per year, can count an average of 25 items per day, and works 250 days per year:
    a. How many cycle counters does the present system require?
    b. How much does the present crew of cycle counters cost per year?
    c. How many cycle counters would the new system require?
    d. How much more would the improved accuracy cost per year?

CASES

Primo Clothing Manufacturing

Primo Clothing Manufacturing makes clothing at three factories in Mexico. The cases of clothing are shipped to four regional warehouses. The accompanying table shows the transportation cost per case from each factory to each regional warehouse, the minimum monthly warehouse requirements, and the maximum monthly capacities of each factory. The company wishes to ship cases of clothing from its factories to its regional warehouses so that the monthly total transportation cost is minimized.

	Destination				Maximum Factory Capacity (cases)
Source	Los Angeles	Dallas	Chicago	Atlanta	
Tijuana	$4.90	$5.25	$9.10	$5.90	35,500
Juarez	3.85	4.15	7.20	7.60	22,500
Matamoros	4.20	3.65	6.10	9.50	12,750
Minimum monthly warehouse capacity (cases)	19,500	15,750	16,500	18,500	

Assignment

1. Formulate the information in this case into an LP format. Define the decision variables, write the objective function, and write the constraint functions.
2. Using the LP computer program in the *POM Software Library* that accompanies this book, solve the problem that you have formulated in No. 1.
3. Fully interpret the meaning of the solution that you obtained in No. 2. In other words, what should the management at Primo Clothing do? Fully explain the meaning of the slack variable values.
4. If you could add production capacity at one of the factories, which one would you choose? How much could you afford to pay per case for additional factory capacity?
5. Is all factory capacity shipped? How much capacity is unshipped? If all factory capacity were shipped, how much additional cost would be incurred?
6. Explain the caution that must be observed in answering Nos. 4 and 5.

Acme Manufacturing

Acme has three fabrication departments (A, B, and C). Each fabrication department produces a single unique product with equipment that is dedicated solely to its product. The three products are moved to three assembly departments (1, 2, and 3), where they are assembled. Each fabrication and assembly department has a different monthly capacity, and it is desirable that each department operate at capacity. The monthly departmental capacities are:

Fabrication Department	Monthly Capacity (units)	Assembly Department	Monthly Capacity (units)
A	12,900	1	5,000
B	19,000	2	21,000
C	9,000	3	14,000

Any of the three products can be processed in any of the assembly departments, but the costs are different because of the varying distances between departments and the different equipment in each assembly department. The per unit production costs are:

Fabrication Department	Assembly Department	Total Cost ($/unit)
A	1	$16.20
	2	18.40
	3	21.30
B	1	$15.10
	2	12.80
	3	18.15
C	1	$12.50
	2	16.35
	3	17.89

The production control department at Acme is now trying to develop a plan for allocating the fabricated products to the three assembly departments for next month. This allocation amounts to a shipping plan that specifies how many of each product should be moved from each fabrication department to each assembly department for the month. If the company can sell all it produces of the three products, how many of each product should be moved from each fabrication department to each assembly department to minimize total monthly costs?

Assignment

1. Use the *POM Software Library* that accompanies this book to solve this transportation problem.
2. Fully explain the solution. How many products should be shipped from each of the fabrication departments to each of the assembly departments?
3. How much total monthly cost will result from your plan?
4. If you could choose a fabrication department to increase its capacity, which one would you choose? Why?
5. What factors other than those considered in this problem should be considered in determining such a shipping plan?

ENDNOTE

1. Cross, Gary J. "How E-Business Is Transforming Supply Chain Management." *Journal of Business Strategy* 21, no. 2 (March/April 2000): 36–39.

SELECTED BIBLIOGRAPHY

Adams, Nicholas D. *Warehouse and Distribution Automation Handbook.* New York: McGraw-Hill, 1996.

Arnold, J.R. Tony. *Introduction to Materials Management,* 4th ed. Upper Saddle River, NJ: Prentice Hall, 2001.

Ayers, James B., ed. *Handbook of Supply Chain Management.* Boca Raton, FL: St. Lucie Press, 2001.

Ballou, Ronald H. *Business Logistics Management,* 4th ed. Englewood Cliffs, NJ: Prentice Hall, 1999.

Banfield, Emiko. *Harnessing Value in the Supply Chain: Strategic Sourcing in Action.* New York: John Wiley & Sons, 1999.

Bayles, Deborah. *E-Commerce Logistics and Fullfillment: Delivering the Goods.* Upper Saddle River, NJ: Prentice Hall, 2001.

Brooks, Roger B., and Larry W. Wilson. *Inventory Record Accuracy: Unleashing the Power of Cycle Counting.* New York: John Wiley & Sons, 1995.

Carbone, James. "Web, Outsourcing Revolutionize Buying." *Purchasing* 129, no. 3 (August 24, 2000): 50–62.

Cavinato, Joseph L., and Ralph G. Kauffman, eds. *The Purchasing Handbook: A Guide for the Purchasing and Supply Professional,* 6th ed. New York: McGraw-Hill, 1999.

Chopra, Sunil, and Peter Meindl. *Supply Chain Management: Strategy, Planning, and Operation.* Upper Saddle River, NJ: Prentice Hall, 2001.

Cox, James F., III, and John H. Blackstone, eds. *APICS Dictionary,* 9th ed. Falls Church, VA: APICS—The Educational Society for Resource Management, 1998.

Coyle, John J., Edward J. Bardi, and C. John Langley, Jr. *Management of Business Logistics,* 6th ed. St. Paul, MN: West Publishing, 1996.

Coyle, John J., Edward J. Bardi, and Robert A. Novack. *Transportation.* Cincinnati, OH: South-Western College Publishing, 2000.

Cross, Gary J. "How E-Business Is Transforming Supply Chain Management." *Journal of Business Strategy* 21, no. 2 (March/April 2000): 36–39.

Grieco, Peter L. *Purchasing Ethics.* West Palm Beach, FL: PT Publications, 1997.

Handfield, Robert B., and Ernest L. Nichols. *Introduction to Supply Chain Management.* Upper Saddle River, NJ: Prentice Hall, 1999.

International Journal of Purchasing & Materials Management. Many related articles are found in this journal.

Jahn, Mary L. *Purchasing Transportation.* West Palm Beach, FL: PT Publications, 1997.

Lambert, Douglas, James R. Stock, and Lisa M. Ellram. *Fundamentals of Logistics.* New York: McGraw-Hill, 1998.

Lancioni, Richard A. "New Developments in Supply Chain Management for the Millennium." *Industrial Marketing Management* 29, no. 1 (January 2000): 1–6.

Leenders, Michael, and Harold E. Fearon. *Purchasing and Supply Management,* 11th ed. New York: McGraw-Hill, 1997.

Lowson, Bob. *Quick Response: Managing the Supply Chain to Meet Consumer Demand.* New York: John Wiley & Sons, 1999.

Peters, Le Roy R. "Is EDI Dead? The Future of the Internet in Supply Chain Management." *Hospital Materiel Management Quarterly* 22, no. 1 (August 2000): 42–47.

Pfohl, Hans-Christian. "Logistics: State of the Art." *Human Systems Management* 16, no. 3 (1997): 153–158.

Pilachowski, Mel. *Purchasing Performance Measurements: A Roadmap for Excellence.* West Palm Beach, FL: PT Publications, 1996.

Stimson, Judith A. *Supplier Selection.* West Palm Beach, FL: PT Publications, 1997.

Stuart, F. Ian, and David M. McCutcheon. "The Manager's Guide to Supply Chain Management." *Business Horizons* 43, no. 2 (March/April 2000): 35–44.

Transportation & Distribution. Many related articles are found in this journal.

12

Just-in-Time and Lean Manufacturing

Introduction

The Just-in-Time Manufacturing Philosophy

Prerequisites for JIT Manufacturing

Elements of JIT Manufacturing

- Eliminating Waste
- Enforced Problem Solving and Continuous Improvement
- People Make JIT Work
- Total Quality Management
- Parallel Processing
- Kanban Production Control
- JIT Purchasing
- E-Commerce and JIT Purchasing
- Reducing Inventories through Setup Reduction
- Working toward Repetitive Manufacturing

Benefits of JIT Manufacturing

Success and JIT Manufacturing

JIT in Service Companies

Wrap-Up: What World-Class Companies Do

Review and Discussion Questions

Internet Assignments

Problems

Case

- Utah Medical Instruments, Inc.

Endnotes

Selected Bibliography

IPS GOES JIT

Located in Everett, Washington, Intermec Printing Systems (IPS) is a manufacturer of bar-code printers, a fast-growing industry with a unit volume growth of 30 percent annually. Previously, IPS had a separate production line for each printer model it produced. With the growth the company was experiencing and with more new printer designs on the way, the company was running out of manufacturing space. In addition, frequent rework of printers to accommodate special configurations, excess finished-goods inventory, and slow response to customer demand were resulting from the company's approach to production.

To improve its competitiveness and profitability, and to reestablish itself as a world leader in the bar-code printing business, IPS management decided to adopt the techniques of JIT manufacturing. With the help of consultants, IPS embarked on a transformation to create a short–lead-time, low-inventory, high–product-quality, quick-response production system.

After sending all of its employees to training seminars, IPS collected data and thoroughly analyzed each production process necessary to produce its printers. Instead of using a separate production line for each printer model, IPS created a single, mixed-model production line to produce all of its printer models. The production sequence of its different models, the batch size for each model, and the number of kanban cards needed were then determined. Employees were cross-trained for multiple tasks, allowing employees to "flex" between workstations as demanded by the flow of products and also allowing management to dynamically change the capacity along the production line. Employee's pay rates were based in part on the number of tasks they were trained to perform.

Employees were also trained to perform quality inspections at each process, limiting the number of defects that were passed down the line. Raw materials storage areas were created at multiple locations near the production line, so that materials needed at each workstation were located very close to that station. These storage areas are frequently replenished from the main warehouse by materials handlers using a two-bin kanban system.

The results have been dramatic. IPS has experienced a 40 percent reduction in manufacturing space, even after two new models were introduced. Finished-goods inventory has been substantially reduced, with a goal of working toward zero finished-goods inventory with all products produced to order. Rework for special configurations has effectively been eliminated, because custom-ordered printers are initially built as ordered. Raw materials in the warehouse have been reduced, as IPS has worked to standardize the materials used and has worked with its suppliers to improve the quality of materials and have more frequent deliveries of smaller orders. IPS is now dedicated to continuous improvement of its operations.[1]

As the previous account illustrates, many companies are excited about **just-in-time (JIT) manufacturing**. In this chapter we will study the philosophy of JIT, when we can use JIT, the interworkings of JIT, and its benefits. The *APICS Dictionary* defines JIT as

A philosophy of manufacturing based on planned elimination of all waste and continuous improvement of productivity. It encompasses the successful execution of all manufacturing activities required to produce a final product, from

design engineering to delivery and including all states of conversion from raw material onward. The primary elements of Just-in-Time are to have only the required inventory when needed; to improve quality to zero defects; to reduce lead times by reducing setup times, queue lengths, and lot sizes; to incrementally revise the operations themselves; and to accomplish these things at minimum cost. In the broad sense, it applies to all forms of manufacturing—job shop, process, and repetitive—and to many service industries as well.[2]

Not all companies use the term *JIT*. IBM uses the term *continuous flow manufacture*, Hewlett-Packard calls it both *stockless production* and *the repetitive manufacturing system*, GE calls it *management by sight*, Motorola calls it *short cycle manufacturing*, and several Japanese firms simply use the term *The Toyota System*. Some companies are using the term *time-based competition (TBC)*.

Lean manufacturing, or lean production, is a popular term that many companies use today to refer to the philosophies and approaches embodied in JIT. For example, in the mid-1990s Boeing started implementing lean manufacturing in all of its manufacturing facilities. The various approaches adopted by Boeing include many of those that are part of the JIT philosophy. The *APICS Dictionary* defines lean manufacturing as

A philosophy of production that emphasizes the minimization of the amount of all the resources (including time) used in the various activities of the enterprise. It involves identifying and eliminating non-value-adding activities in design, production, supply chain management, and dealing with the customers. Lean producers employ teams of multiskilled workers at all levels of the organization and use highly flexible, increasingly automated machines to produce volumes of products in potentially enormous variety.[3]

Whether referred to as lean manufacturing, JIT, or some other name, we will study in this chapter those concepts and approaches that modern companies are adopting to become more streamlined and efficient. Though some people may distinguish slightly between the philosophies of JIT and lean manufacturing, we will use the term *JIT* to refer to the general set of concepts that are embodied in both. It is important to note that many of these approaches can also help service organizations become more efficient.

THE JUST-IN-TIME MANUFACTURING PHILOSOPHY

U.S. manufacturers are geographically located in the middle of the world's most lucrative market. This advantage should allow them to beat the competition in responding quickly to customer needs. The successes of foreign firms in U.S. markets compel U.S. firms to rearrange their business thinking to emphasize fast response to customers as a key weapon to win increased market share. U.S. firms also want to find ways of doing things quicker so that they can be successful in attractive foreign markets where they are at a geographic disadvantage. "For years manufacturing firms in the United States sought to provide products with the most value for the lowest cost. Now the leading firms provide products with the most value for the lowest cost with the fastest response time. Quick response to market demands provides a powerful, sustainable competitive advantage. Indeed, time has emerged as a dominant dimension of global competition, fundamentally changing the way organizations compete."[4] It is no longer good enough for firms to be high-quality and low-cost producers. To succeed today, they must also be first in getting products and services to the customer fast. Firms like Northern Telecom, Xerox, Hewlett-Packard, Motorola, General Electric, Honda, Toyota, Sony, and

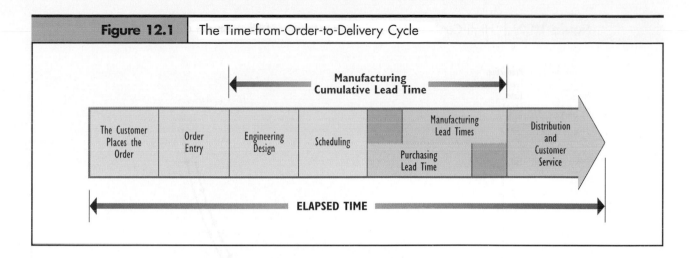

Figure 12.1 | The Time-from-Order-to-Delivery Cycle

Boeing are using JIT as a weapon in speeding market responsiveness. To compete in this new environment, the **order-to-delivery cycle** (the elapsed time between the moment that a customer places an order until the customer receives the order) must be drastically reduced. Figure 12.1 illustrates this important concept. JIT is the weapon of choice today in reducing the elapsed time of this cycle.

In the traditional view of manufacturing, a key objective was to fully utilize production capacity so that more products were produced with fewer workers and machines. This kind of thinking led to large queues of in-process inventory waiting at work centers in manufacturing. Large queues meant that machines and workers never had to wait on partially finished products to come to them; therefore, capacity utilization was very high and production costs were low. Unfortunately, large queues of in-process inventory also meant that products spent most of their time in manufacturing just waiting. With this arrangement, companies would be ill equipped to compete in today's time-based competition.

The just-in-time philosophy can eliminate large inventories in favor of producing just enough products to fill customers' orders.

| Figure 12.2 | High-Capacity Utilization: The Enemy of Time-Based Competition |

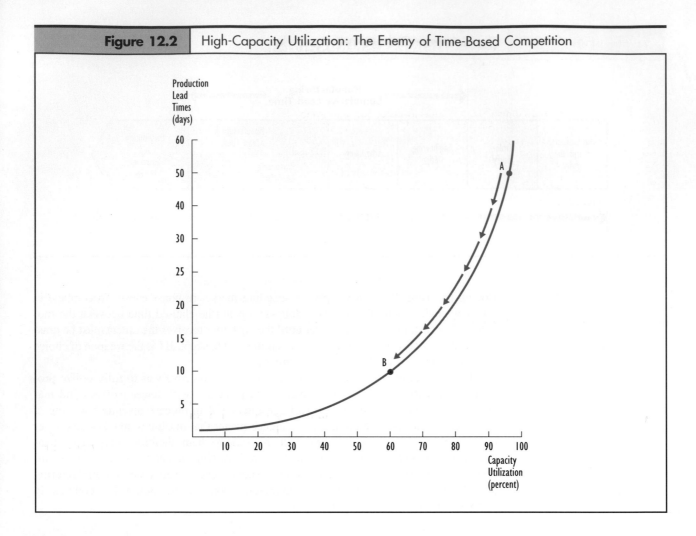

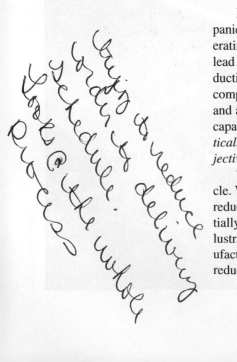

Figure 12.2 illustrates that this kind of traditional thinking can be deadly to companies that want to use speed as a weapon. In this figure, let us say that a firm is operating at Point A, with a 96 percent capacity utilization and a 50-day manufacturing lead time. One way to reduce manufacturing lead times is to find ways to increase production capacity. By studying the company's operations and increasing capacity, the company was able to move to Point B, with a manufacturing lead time of only 10 days and a 60 percent capacity utilization. To shorten production lead times, 100 percent of capacity utilization must not be the predominant objective. *In JIT manufacturing, drastically reducing the elapsed time of the order-to-delivery cycle has displaced the objective of 100 percent production capacity utilization in traditional manufacturing.*

There are many opportunities to speed up every step in the order-to-delivery cycle. We will discuss several of these opportunities in this chapter. An important way to reduce manufacturing lead times is to reduce queue lengths and waiting times of partially completed products at work centers in manufacturing. Business Snapshot 12.1 illustrates how one company used queuing theory and queuing software to reduce manufacturing lead times for its products. Example 12.1 also shows how the objective of reduced lead times can be achieved by using queuing theory to analyze waiting-line

BUSINESS SNAPSHOT 12.1

Using Queuing Theory to Achieve Time-Based Competition

Helkama Bica Oy is a Finnish company that manufactures communication cables in four factories. Annual sales are $50 million. The company has been successful competing with short delivery times and high quality. In 1988 the company ranked first among the 400 largest Finnish companies for profits and fifth in growth. But in 1990, the company was dealt two severe blows, a rapid increase in competition due to European integration and the loss of the Soviet Union as a customer. Helkama's response has been to increase its emphasis on time-based competition.

Queuing theory is being used throughout the company to calculate and reduce lead times, aid in capacity planning, and reduce lot sizes. MPX computer software (developed by Network Dynamics Inc., Burlington, Massachusetts) is being used within Helkama from shop floor to board room in a continuing attempt to reduce production lead times. Reductions of as much as 40 percent were accomplished over a few months. This substantial reduction in manufacturing lead times had positioned the company to use time-based competition as a weapon to secure present customers and obtain numerous new ones. Sales and profits have increased steadily.

Source: de Treville, Suzanne. "Time Is Money." *OR/MS Today,* October 1992, 30–34.

production problems. Further, Example 12.1 illustrates that drastic reduction of manufacturing lead times and work-in-process (WIP) inventory can often be achieved with only slight increases in production capacities. This is an important insight as we study the ways of positioning companies to survive in today's environment of time-based competition.

Example 12.1	Increasing Production Capacity Reduces Manufacturing Lead Times

A manufacturing operation wants to reduce its manufacturing lead time from 12 days to 4 days. If jobs are arriving at an average rate of 12 per day and the operation can produce an average of 12.083 jobs per day, what new production rate would allow a lead time of only 4 days? How much would work-in-process (WIP) inventory be reduced with the new production rate?

Solution

1. Use the formula for $\bar{t}_s$ from Model 1 in Table 9.6, Chapter 9:

$$\bar{t}_s = \frac{1}{(\mu - \lambda)}$$

2. Use the values of $\lambda = 12.000$ jobs per day and $\mu = 12.083$ jobs per day to verify that the lead time at the operation is in fact 12 days:

$$\bar{t}_s = \frac{1}{(\mu - \lambda)} = \frac{1}{(12.083 - 12.0)} = \frac{1}{0.083} = 12 \text{ days}$$

3. Next, let $\bar{t}_s = 4$ days and $\lambda = 12$ jobs per day, and solve for a new value of μ:

$$\bar{t}_s = \frac{1}{(\mu - \lambda)} = \frac{1}{(\mu - 12.0)} = 4$$

$$4(\mu - 12.0) = 1$$

$$4\mu - 48 = 1$$

$$4\mu = 1 + 48 = 49$$

$$\mu = 49/4 = 12.25 \text{ jobs per day}$$

By increasing the production rate from 12.083 jobs per day to only 12.25 jobs per day, the lead time is reduced from 12 days to only 4 days.

4. Compute $\bar{n}_s$ for $\mu = 12.083$ and for $\mu = 12.25$:

$$\bar{n}_{s_1} = \frac{\lambda}{(\mu_1 - \lambda)} = \frac{12}{(12.083 - 12.0)} = \frac{12}{0.083} = 144.6 \text{ jobs}$$

$$\bar{n}_{s_2} = \frac{\lambda}{(\mu_2 - \lambda)} = 1\frac{2}{(12.25 - 12.0)} = \frac{12}{0.25} = 48.0 \text{ jobs}$$

Reduction in $\bar{n}_s$ = 144.6 − 48.0 = 96.6 jobs

By increasing the production rate from 12.083 jobs per day to only 12.25 jobs per day, the WIP is reduced from 144.6 jobs to 48 jobs, a reduction of 96.6 jobs.

Today JIT is commonly viewed as a Japanese innovation, because Toyota popularized this approach two decades ago. However, you may find it interesting that most of the ideas embodied in JIT were combined and implemented successfully by an American company 50 years earlier. The Ford Motor Company implemented this approach at its Dearborn, Michigan, plant that produced Model T Fords. In his 1926 book entitled *Today and Tomorrow*, Henry Ford presents his approach to production, which is surprisingly similar to JIT.[5] Ford describes how raw iron ore was unloaded from a ship, transformed to steel, converted to finished automobiles, and shipped to the customer in a span of less than 48 hours. Regardless of the origin of JIT, this approach to production consists of a set of useful ideas that can help companies become more competitive. Now, let us consider the prerequisites for JIT manufacturing.

PREREQUISITES FOR JIT MANUFACTURING

The basic idea of JIT is rather simple—drastically reduce WIP inventories throughout the production system. In this way, products flow from suppliers to production to customers with little or no delays or interruptions beyond the amount of time they spend being produced at work centers in manufacturing. The main objective of JIT manufacturing is to reduce manufacturing lead times, and this is primarily achieved by drastic reductions in WIP. The result is a smooth, uninterrupted flow of small lots of products throughout production.

Most successful JIT applications have been in repetitive manufacturing, operations where batches of standard products are produced at high speeds and high volumes with materials moving in a continuous flow. The Toyota automobile factories, where the no-

JIT is ideal for use in repetitive manufacturing, such as in this paper mill.

© JUDY GRIESELIECK/CORBS

(handwritten margin notes, left side)

Japan contracts for life

Supplier contracts by the wide

Spent a long time sourcing work

Union dont want cross-trained they want the job

Tough

tion of JIT may have started, are perhaps the best example of the use of JIT in repetitive manufacturing. In these factories, the continuous flow of products makes planning and control rather simple, and JIT works best in these shop-floor situations. Successful use of JIT is rare in large, highly complex job shops where production planning and control is extremely complicated. Smaller, less complex job shops have used JIT, but these companies have taken many steps to change operations so that they behave somewhat like repetitive manufacturing. We will discuss more about this in the next section.

JIT does not come free—certain changes to the factory and the way it is managed must occur before the benefits can be realized. Among these changes are:

1. Stabilize production schedules. *Major piece.*
2. Increase production capacities of manufacturing work centers.
3. Improve product quality.
4. Cross-train workers so that they are multiskilled and competent in several jobs.
5. Reduce equipment breakdowns through preventive maintenance.
6. Develop long-term supplier relations that avoid interruptions to material flows.

At Toyota, for instance, there are both **stable** and **level production schedules**. The *doing same thing* master production schedule (MPS) is frozen for the first month, and the entire MPS covers one year. The production schedule is exactly the same for each day of the month. This means that the same products are produced in the same quantities in the same sequence every day of the month. Toyota divides the total number of each automobile model to be manufactured during a month by the number of workdays in the month to get the number of that model to be produced daily. Even if only a few of a particular model were needed in a month, some would be assembled in each day of the month. This provides the same daily production schedule throughout the month. This approach to the MPS simplifies parts explosions, material flows, and worker job assignments. If JIT is to work, stable and level production schedules are necessary.

A fundamental requirement for JIT is to *increase the production capacity* of manufacturing work centers. Figure 12.2 illustrated that by increasing production capacities, manufacturing lead times are reduced. Production capacities are usually increased in two ways, increasing production rates and reducing setup times at work centers. Example 12.1 illustrated that small increases in production rates of work centers can result in drastic reduction of manufacturing lead times. Production capacity can also be increased by reducing setup times at work centers. Setup time is the time it takes to adjust the machine settings, replace materials, change tools, and do everything it takes to change over from producing one product to a different one at a work center. Because production at work centers is shut down while the work centers are being changed over, reducing setup times will reduce down time and increase production capacity. As illustrated in Figure 12.2, increasing production capacities results in a faster and more continuous flow of products through manufacturing.

By improving product quality, cross-training workers, reducing equipment breakdowns through preventive maintenance, and establishing reliable material flows from suppliers, interruptions to production are minimized. We still study how to improve product quality in Chapter 17, Quality Control. And we will study about cross-training of workers in Chapter 18, Employee Productivity, and about preventive maintenance in Chapter 19, Maintenance Management. Because workers are trained on several jobs, they can be moved about to other jobs as needed to work off any imbalance in work flows that may be caused by either quality problems or machine breakdowns.

With these factors present in manufacturing, the ultimate success of JIT is vastly increased.

ELEMENTS OF JIT MANUFACTURING

We will discuss JIT by examining its important components: the underlying assumptions, its approach, its method of planning and controlling production, and several of its ongoing activities.

Eliminating Waste

Eliminating waste of all kinds is the deep-seated ideology behind JIT. Shigeo Shingo, a JIT authority at Toyota, identified seven wastes in production that should be eliminated. Table 12.1 lists and describes these wastes.

Table 12.1	Toward Eliminating Waste in Manufacturing

1. **Overproduction.** Make only what is needed now.
2. **Waiting.** Coordinate flows between operations, and balance load imbalances by flexible workers and equipment.
3. **Transportation.** Design facility layouts that reduce or eliminate materials handling and shipping.
4. **Unneeded production.** Eliminate all unneeded production steps.
5. **Work-in-process (WIP) inventories.** Eliminate by reducing setup times, increasing production rates, and better coordination of production rates between work centers.
6. **Motion and effort.** Improve productivity and quality by eliminating unnecessary human motions, make necessary motions more efficient, mechanize, then automate.
7. **Defective products.** Eliminate defects and inspection. Make perfect products.

Source: R. Hall. *Attaining Manufacturing Excellence,* p. 26. Homewood, IL: Dow Jones–Irwin, 1987.

Enforced Problem Solving and Continuous Improvement

In traditional manufacturing, in-process inventories allow production to continue even if production problems occur; thus, high machine and worker utilization is achieved. If defective products are discovered, machines malfunction, or material stockouts occur, in-process inventory can be used to feed what would otherwise be idle workers and machines. As Figure 12.3 illustrates, in-process inventory covers up production problems in traditional manufacturing. Behind JIT is the continuous drive to improve production processes and methods. Toward that end, JIT strives to reduce inventories because high inventory levels are thought to cover up production problems. By drastically reducing in-process inventories, production problems are uncovered and production stops until the causes of the production problems are solved. Only when the machine is fixed, the quality control problem is solved, or the cause behind the stockout is found and corrected—only then can production begin again.

JIT is really a system of enforced problem solving. There are few safety factors in JIT. Every material is expected to meet quality standards, every part is expected to arrive exactly at the time promised and precisely at the place it is supposed to be, every worker is expected to work productively, and every machine is expected to function as intended without breakdowns. Managers in JIT manufacturing have a choice. They can put a huge effort into finding and solving the causes of production problems, or they can live with an intolerable level of interruptions to production. One of the approaches to implementing a JIT program is to reduce in-process inventories incrementally in small steps. At each step, different production problems are uncovered, and the workers and their managers work to eliminate the problems. Then when there is almost no in-process inventory, the causes of most production problems have been removed.

But the job of eliminating production problems is not over. Vigilance in continuing to study potential problem areas is needed to ensure continuous improvement. Japanese manufacturers have long practiced what they called **kaizen**, the goal of continuous improvement in every phase of manufacturing. Managers may encourage workers to reduce in-process inventories a step further to see if any production problems occur, thus identifying a target for the workers to eliminate. Machine setups may be studied with workers and managers working to strip away the fat so that setups are almost instantaneous. Japanese manufacturers have long used the term *SMED*, which is an acronym for *single minute exchange of dies*, meaning that their goal is to have all setups take less than a minute.

Figure 12.3	Uncovering Production Problems by Reducing Inventories

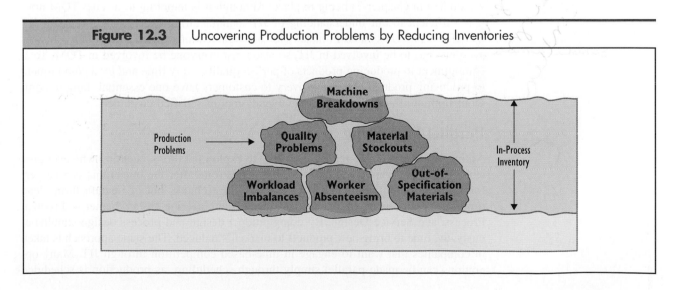

Continuous improvement is central to the philosophy of JIT and is a key reason for its success.

People Make JIT Work

Businesses ultimately succeed or fail because of their people. JIT is no exception to this rule. Because JIT is a system of enforced problem solving, having a dedicated workforce committed to working together to solve production problems is essential. JIT manufacturing, therefore, has a strong element of training and involvement of workers in all phases of manufacturing.

First, and foremost, a culture of mutual trust and teamwork must be developed in an organization. Managers and workers must see each other as coworkers committed to the company's success. Work teams are encouraged to meet together to search for long-term solutions to the causes of production problems. Workers are also encouraged to suggest better ways of doing things from small suggestions to strategic issues. Along with an open and trusting organizational culture, an attitude of loyalty to the team and self-discipline must also be developed. Because workers are committed to the success of the company, the work team—rather than the individual worker—becomes the focus. Workers are not free to go off on their own and try any method of doing their work according to any standard that they choose; rather, methods and standards agreed to by the team prevail.

Another important factor that is crucial to the success of JIT is the *empowerment of workers*. This means that workers are given the authority to take the initiative in solving production problems. Rather than waiting for guidance from above, workers have the authority to stop production at any time for such things as quality problems, machine malfunctions, or safety concerns. Groups of workers are then encouraged to work together to quickly get production going again. Once workers have identified problems, they are encouraged to meet during breaks, before work, or after work to discuss the problems while attempting to find solutions to the causes of the problems. Having workers actively involved in problem solving is the objective of worker empowerment.

People, suppliers, workers, managers, and customers must all be motivated and committed to teamwork for JIT manufacturing to be effective.

Total Quality Management

JIT manufacturing depends on a system of total quality management (TQM) (which we studied in Chapter 7) being in place. Although it is tempting to discuss TQM now, it is sufficient to our understanding of JIT manufacturing to say that successful JIT manufacturing goes hand-in-hand with an organization-wide TQM culture. Just as everyone has to be involved in JIT, so also must everyone be involved in TQM. Total commitment to producing products of perfect quality every time and total commitment to producing products for fast delivery to customers have one essential thing in common: Both are finely focused on the overall goal of satisfied customers.

Parallel Processing

An important part of JIT manufacturing is to exploit parallel processing wherever possible. Any operations being performed in series (one after the other) that can be performed in parallel (simultaneously) can take huge chunks out of manufacturing lead times. This concept is similar to simultaneous engineering from Chapter 4, Product, Process, and Service Design. By doing product design and process design simultaneously, the time to bring new products to market is reduced. The same approach is taken in companies that want to engage in time-based competition through JIT. Many operations can be made parallel simply through scheduling, as production is scheduled

[handwritten margin notes: JIT pull / pull / "push type operate / MRP material requirements planning]

to occur at the same time at one or more operations. In other cases, layout redesign and product redesign may be needed to achieve parallel processing. But the additional costs can usually be more than offset by significant reductions in manufacturing lead times.

Kanban Production Control

JIT manufacturing is considered to be a **pull system** of production planning and control. (This will be discussed more in Chapter 13.) In a **push system**, such as an MRP system (discussed in Chapter 15), we look at the schedule to determine what to produce next. In a pull system, we look only at the next stage of production and determine what is needed there, and then we produce only that. Thus, batches of products go directly from upstream stages of production to downstream stages without being stored in inventory. As Hall states, "You don't never make nothin' and *send* it no place. Somebody has got to come and get it."[6]

At the core of JIT manufacturing at Toyota is Kanban, an amazingly simple system of planning and controlling production. We will use Figures 12.4 and 12.5 to illustrate how Kanban plans and controls production between two adjacent work centers. **Kanban**, in Japanese, <u>means *card*</u> or *marquee* as on the front of a movie theater. In the context of JIT, Kanban is the means of signaling to the upstream workstation

[handwritten: on an assembly line the container of tire + a card, the card signals the need for more product also tells what goes on the car]

Figure 12.4	Kanban Cards

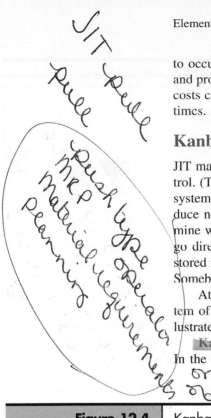

Conveyance Kanban Card

Part number to produce: M471-36	Part description: Valve housing
Lot size needed: 40	Container type: RED crate
Card number: 2 of 5	Retrieval storage location: NW53D
From work center: 22	To work center: 35

[handwritten margin note: packages instead of options]

Production Kanban Card

Part number to produce: M471-36	Part description: Valve housing
Lot size to produce: 40	Container type: RED crate
Card number: 4 of 5	Completed storage location: NW53D
From work center: 22	To work center: 35

Materials required:

Material no. 744B	Storage location: NW48C
Part no. B238-5	Storage location: NW47B

| **Figure 12.5** | Flow of Kanban Cards and Containers between Two Work Centers |

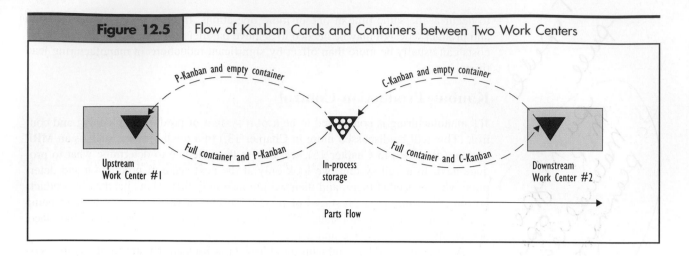

that the downstream workstation is ready for the upstream station to produce another batch of parts. In a simple shop environment with one or only a few products, signals such as an empty crate, an empty designated location on the floor (taped off or painted), or a colored golf ball rolled down a plastic pipe have been used by some companies. The most common signal, however, is a Kanban card. Much more information can be communicated by a card rather than a nonpaper signal.

There are two types of Kanban cards: a conveyance card (C-Kanban) and a production card (P-Kanban). Figure 12.4 shows examples of these types of cards. Basically these cards replace most of the other production control paper forms on the factory floor. It is important to note that with stable and level production schedules, priority decisions (which orders are released each day, when orders are released, and the sequence of the orders) are routine; thus, shop-floor planning and control are reduced to planning and controlling the movement of orders among work centers. In these simple scheduling situations, visual signals and Kanbans are the only devices needed.

Figure 12.5 illustrates how Kanban operates. When a worker on the shop floor at downstream Work Center #2 needs a container of parts for his operation, he does the following:

1. He finds the C-Kanban in the pocket on the side of the container that he has just emptied at his work center; this card is his authorization to replace the empty container with a full one from storage.
2. Next, he takes the C-Kanban and finds a full container of the needed parts in storage.
3. Then, he places the C-Kanban in the full container.
4. Next, he removes the P-Kanban from the full container and places it on a post or marquee at the upstream Work Center #1; this P-Kanban is the authorization for Work Center #1 to produce another container of the parts.
5. Finally, he takes the full container of parts with its C-Kanban to his downstream Work Center #2.

No parts can be produced or moved without a Kanban card. Kanban is based on the simple idea of replacement of containers of parts, one at a time. A container is not moved to a downstream production operation until it is needed, and a container of parts is not produced until it is needed. These containers are reserved for specific parts, are purposely kept small, and always contain the same standard number of parts for each part number. At Toyota the containers must not hold more than about 10 percent of a day's requirements. There is a minimum of two containers for each part number, one at the upstream producing work center and one at the downstream using work center. Example 12.2 illustrates how the number of containers between two adjacent work centers is calculated.

Example 12.2	Calculating the Number of Containers between Work Centers

There are two adjacent work centers, a downstream (using) work center and an upstream (producing) work center. The production rate of the using work center is 175 parts per hour. Each standard Kanban container holds 100 parts. It takes an average of 1.10 hours for a container to make the entire cycle from the time it leaves the upstream work center full until it is returned empty, filled with production, and leaves again. Compute the number of containers needed if the Kanban system is rated at a P of 0.25.

Solution

1. The formula and variable definitions used for this calculation are:

$$N = \frac{UT(1 + P)}{C}, \text{ where}$$

   N = total number of containers needed between the two work centers.
   U = the usage rate of the downstream work center, usually parts per hour.
   T = the average elapsed time required for a container to make the entire cycle from the time it leaves the upstream work center, is returned, is filled again with production, and leaves again. Measured in the same units of time as U.
   P = a policy variable that indicates the efficiency of the system. P can take on values from 0 to 1. A 0 would indicate perfect efficiency, a 1.0 would indicate perfect inefficiency.
   C = capacity of the standard container, number of parts.

2. Use the formula to calculate N, the number of containers:

$$N = \frac{UT(1 + P)}{C} = \frac{175(1.1)(1 + 0.25)}{100}$$

$$= \frac{240.6}{100} = 2.4, \text{ or } 3.0 \text{ containers}$$

Notice that by rounding 2.4 up to 3.0, some slack or safety stock is introduced in the system, but this is usually preferable to having too few containers.

More than the minimum number of containers may be used between two work centers because the upstream producing work center may not be able to fill the container right away. Such delays can result because other P-Kanbans were there first and their parts need to be produced first, and other complexities. Workers produce exactly the quantity listed on the recycling Kanban cards, no more and no less. Producing one part more than the standard amount for the container would be considered as bad as producing one part less. Producing one part more than needed would be wasteful because labor, materials, and machine capacity would be spent on producing the extra part that is not needed now and could not be used until later.

Some variation exists among Kanban systems. For example, at a Kawasaki motorcycle engine plant in Japan, workers communicate by means of painted golf balls that roll down pipes. At some Japanese plants, workers communicate with flashing lights, a system called *andon*. A green light means that there are no problems, an amber light means that production is falling behind, and a red light means that there is a serious problem. Workers and supervisors can tell the status of production at adjacent work centers just by glancing at the lights. Regardless of the variation in Kanban systems, workers must have cooperative attitudes for them to work. Similarly, programs to achieve excellence in preventive maintenance, product quality, and mutual trust with suppliers are musts.

Can Kanban and MRP coexist? Yes, they can, at least to a limited degree. MRP can be used in JIT manufacturing to obtain parts explosions and to order materials and parts from suppliers, but there is little influence of MRP within manufacturing. Suppliers use the MRP schedules as an overall plan for production and to determine the sequence of parts orders, but the actual production takes place by following the Kanban system of the customer. Likewise, production control within the customer's manufacturing is with Kanban. The excess in-process inventories that can result from the push approach of MRP is thus avoided in both the supplier's and customer's factories.

These versions of pull systems greatly reduce in-process inventory of parts between work centers on the shop floor, but JIT is also aimed at reducing raw-materials inventories.

JIT Purchasing

The same pull-type approach in JIT is applied to purchasing shipments of parts from suppliers. In JIT purchasing, suppliers use the replacement principle of Kanban by using small, standard-size containers and make several shipments daily to each customer. If Kanban is used by a supplier, Kanban cards authorize the movement of containers of parts between the supplier's shop and the customer. In such arrangements, suppliers are ordinarily located near their customers. JIT therefore not only reduces in-process inventories by using Kanban, but raw-materials inventories are also reduced by applying the same principles to suppliers.

The essential elements of JIT purchasing are as follows:

1. **Supplier development** and **supplier relations** undergo fundamental changes. The nature of the relationships between customers and suppliers shifts from being adversarial to being cooperative. The Japanese call these relationships subcontractor networks and refer to suppliers as co-producers. Sensitive information, assistance in reducing costs and improving quality, and even financing are often shared by customers and suppliers.
2. Purchasing departments develop long-term relationships with suppliers. The result is long-term supply contracts with a few suppliers rather than short-term supply contracts with many suppliers. Repeat business is awarded to the same suppliers, and competitive bidding is ordinarily limited to new parts.
3. Although price is important, delivery schedules, product quality, and mutual trust and cooperation become the primary basis for supplier selection.
4. Suppliers are encouraged to extend JIT methods to their own suppliers.
5. Suppliers are ordinarily located near the buying firm's factory, or if they are some distance from the factory, they are usually clustered together. This causes lead times to be shorter and more reliable.

[handwritten: Saturn plant suppliers put input on production line]

6. Shipments are delivered directly to the customer's production line. Because suppliers are encouraged to produce and supply parts at a steady rate that matches the use rate of the buying firm, company-owned hauling equipment tends to be preferred.
7. Parts are delivered in small, standard-size containers with a minimum of paperwork and in exact quantities.
8. Delivered material is of near-perfect quality. Because suppliers have a long-term relationship with the buying firms and because parts are delivered in small lot sizes, the quality of purchased materials tends to be higher.

Business Snapshot 12.2 illustrates how one firm is having success with JIT purchasing.

E-Commerce and JIT Purchasing

The continuing development of e-commerce is having a beneficial effect on JIT purchasing. Internet-based information systems allow companies to quickly place orders for materials with their suppliers. This eliminates wasted time dealing with paperwork and reduces the procurement lead time. The quality of the procurement process also improves because data entry errors created through the paperwork process are eliminated. Because e-commerce transactions with the supplier represent an automated process, labor costs are reduced as well. The bottom line is a more efficient and effective purchasing process.

BUSINESS SNAPSHOT 12.2

JIT Purchasing at Waterville TG, Inc.

Because so many automobile manufacturers have gone to a JIT manufacturing approach, increasing pressure has been placed on automotive suppliers to provide frequent, reliable deliveries. This in turn requires the automotive suppliers to work closely with their raw material suppliers to ensure reliable deliveries. Waterville TG, Inc. (WTG), located in Waterville, Quebec, specializes in designing and manufacturing top-quality weather strips for cars. Its product line includes close to 500 different models of weather strips, which it supplies to about a dozen automobile manufacturers.

To improve its purchasing performance, WTG undertook an effort to integrate its MRP system with a Kanban-type vendor-scheduling system. Master production scheduling is based on planned order releases supplied by customers and typically covering an 8- to 16-week horizon. Customer orders are firmed up weekly for the first week to 10 days. WTG's MRP system then computes the number of Kanban cards needed to cover the demand. Every Monday WTG faxes its gross requirements for the next 12 weeks to each of its suppliers. Updates are faxed to suppliers daily. A standard Kanban quantity is established for each material purchased from suppliers, and each week WTG faxes an order to each supplier for however many Kanbans are needed to replenish its inventory.

To help implement smaller and more frequent deliveries from suppliers, WTG established a daily milk–run–type of transportation schedule among its factory, its finished-goods warehouse, and 8 of its 12 suppliers of raw materials located in the area.

The results of these actions have been impressive. Total inventories have been reduced from 28 to 8.4 days supply. Average purchase lead times have been reduced from two weeks to one to two days. The average time to respond to changes has been reduced from four days to one day. And, the reduction of emergency situations (impending stockouts) has been reduced from 41 to 31 occurrences annually.

Source: Landry, Sylvain, Claude R. Duguay, Sylvain Chaussé, and Jean-Luc Themens. "Integrating MRP, Kanban and Bar-Coding Systems to Achieve JIT Procurement." *Production and Inventory Management Journal* 38, no. 1 (First Quarter 1997): 8–13.

E-commerce also facilitates the use of Kanbans between a manufacturer and its suppliers. Using its Internet-based system, a manufacturer can electronically send Kanbans to suppliers. These *e-Kanbans* have the same function as paper Kanbans, but they can be provided to suppliers more quickly.

Reducing Inventories through Setup Reduction

If it costs a lot to set up a machine to produce a part, it makes sense to produce many units of the part each time it is produced. For perhaps too long, U.S. manufacturers have held to this conventional wisdom and have neglected to work on reducing setup times and reducing production lot sizes. Central to JIT is an ongoing program aimed at the reduction of production lot sizes so that inventory levels are reduced. But doesn't it seem that very small production lot sizes would result in too many machine setups, increased production costs, and lost capacity because of idle machines during setups? JIT systems spend large sums of money to reduce setup times to avoid these negative consequences of small lot sizes. Engineers study the setups, automatic devices are attached to the machines, workers are trained in more efficient work methods, and the result is very short setup times. In some cases, computerized controls can make the new machine settings instantaneously, with the result that the setup time between different parts approaches zero. Figure 12.6 shows that economic production lot sizes (EOQ) approach zero as the setup costs approach zero. (The EOQ approach will be discussed in Chapter 14, Inventory Management.) JIT firms use the same EOQ formula to analyze lot sizes, but they turn it around. They treat a very small EOQ lot size as a given and then solve for the setup cost. In this way, production lot sizes can be set very low and the resulting setup times can be used for targets as engineers develop programs for reducing setup times.

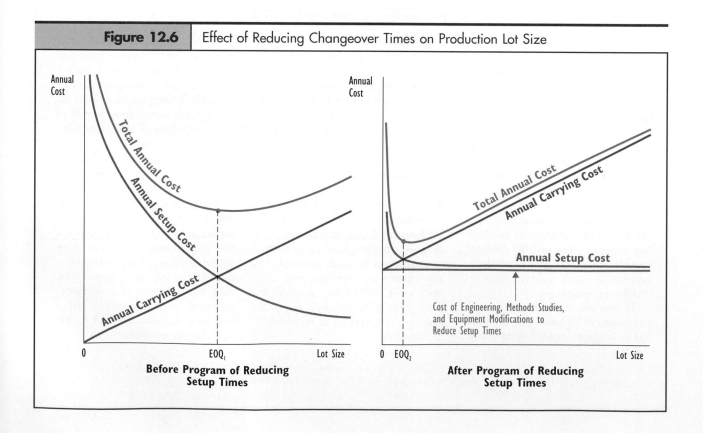

| **Figure 12.6** | Effect of Reducing Changeover Times on Production Lot Size |

Example 12.3 computes the setup time required to accommodate a small JIT production lot size. These types of computations could be used in a factory-wide program to reduce setup costs.

Example 12.3	Computing Setup Time When a Small JIT Production Lot Size Is Given

As part of a factory-wide JIT program to reduce setup times so that production lot sizes can be smaller, a firm wants to determine what the length of the setup time of a manufacturing operation should be in order to accommodate an economic production lot size (EOQ) of 20 units of a part. A production analyst has developed these data for the operation:

$$D = 20,000 \text{ units annual demand}$$
$$d = 80 \text{ units daily demand rate}$$
$$p = 200 \text{ units daily production rate}$$
$$EOQ = 20 \text{ units lot size for each production run}$$
$$C = \$15 \text{ per unit per year carrying cost}$$
$$S = \text{cost per setup, which is unknown—to be determined from the EOQ formula}$$
$$\quad\quad\text{for production lots}$$

If the labor rate for the operation is \$10 per hour, what setup time results in an economic production lot size of 20 units? (Refer to Chapter 14 for a discussion of the EOQ approach.)

Solution

$$EOQ = \sqrt{\frac{2DS}{C}\left(\frac{p}{p-d}\right)}$$

$$EOQ^2 = \frac{2DS}{C}\left(\frac{p}{p-d}\right)$$

$$S = \frac{C(EOQ)^2}{2D}\left(\frac{p-d}{p}\right) = \frac{\$15(20)^2}{2(20,000)}\left(\frac{200-80}{200}\right) = \$0.09$$

$$\text{Setup time} = \frac{S}{\text{Labor rate}} = \frac{\$0.09}{\$10/\text{hour}}$$

$$= 0.009 \text{ hour, or } 0.54 \text{ minute, or } 32.4 \text{ seconds}$$

Setup reduction is a continuing process in a JIT environment, and it is important to involve the workers at each workstation in this process. The best ideas for setup time reduction frequently come from the people who are most familiar with the machinery and equipment—the users. With encouragement from managers, workers can often come up with creative ideas for setup reduction that cost very little. One example of a low-cost setup improvement is to perform some of the setup tasks ahead of time, while the last part of the previous batch is still being processed on the machine. Depending on the technological requirements involved, the worker might be able to collect all the tools, jigs, fixtures, and the first part of the next batch together beside the machine, ready to go. She might even be able to load the first part into the new fixture that will be placed into the machine when it is free. These actions could substantially reduce the time the machine is nonproductive, during the changeover, with little additional cost.

Useful insights about setup reductions can be gained through studying companies that have implemented formal setup reduction programs. In one such research study, John Leschke at the University of Virginia analyzed the setup reduction programs at five companies, programs that ranged in duration from two months to five years. In a two-article series, Leschke provides details of the companies' setup reduction programs, and compares different approaches for allocating investments to setup reduction activities in order to gain the most benefits. The interested reader is referred to those articles.[7,8]

Not only do greatly reduced setup costs in JIT result in reduced inventory levels, but also the factory begins to act very much like a repetitive manufacturing system.

Working toward Repetitive Manufacturing

The *APICS Dictionary* defines **repetitive manufacturing** as

The repeated production of the same discrete products or families of products. Repetitive methodology minimizes setups, inventory, and manufacturing lead times by using production lines, assembly lines, or cells. Work orders are no longer necessary; production scheduling and control is based on production rates. Products may be standard or assembled from modules. Repetitive is not a function of speed or volume.[9]

This is product-focused production of batches of standardized products. These are systems in which products flow continuously along a direct route until they are finished and in which there is little in-process inventory and parts rarely stop moving. Repetitive manufacturing clearly does not refer to the process-focused production of custom products that occurs in job shops. Proponents of JIT would argue that even job shops can be made to behave more like repetitive manufacturing.

Some companies have worked hard to make their factories behave more like repetitive manufacturing. Among the things that can be done to modify a factory to be more repetitive in its production are:

- Reduce setup times and production lot sizes.
- Change the layout of the factory to allow streamlined product flows through the plant.
- Convert clusters of machines within process-focused layouts to cellular manufacturing (CM) centers or cells. In CM, groups of machines function as product-focused islands within the larger layout.
- Install flexible manufacturing systems (FMS). These groups of machines can accommodate product variety without the necessity of worker-performed machine changeovers.
- Standardize parts designs to reduce the number of parts and the number of changeovers.
- Train workers for several jobs. These flexible workers can move from work center to work center as necessary to balance the workload in the factory.
- Install effective preventive maintenance programs so that machine breakdowns do not interrupt product flows.
- Install effective quality control programs so that defective products do not interrupt product flows.
- Develop an effective subcontractor network so that materials flow into the factory smoothly to support the in-house production schedules, thereby allowing uninterrupted production.

Even if a firm cannot convert all of its operations to repetitive manufacturing, some sections of the system can be repetitive. For example, even if many custom-designed products are irregularly scheduled at final assembly, their component-part designs could be standardized, component-part production schedules could be made stable and level, and the component parts could be produced by repetitive manufacturing.

With such changes as these, many more factories that are not pure repetitive manufacturing may be able to implement JIT manufacturing systems and enjoy many of the same benefits.

BENEFITS OF JIT MANUFACTURING

Some of the benefits claimed for JIT systems are:

- Inventory levels are drastically reduced.
- The time it takes for products to get through the factory is greatly reduced, thus enabling factories to engage in time-based competition, using speed as a weapon to capture market share.
- Product quality is improved, and the cost of scrap is reduced. Product quality improves because of worker involvement in solving the causes of production problems; and with smaller lots, defective parts are discovered earlier.
- With less in-process inventory, less space is taken up with inventory and materials-handling equipment. Workers are closer together so that they can see each other, communicate more easily, work out problems more efficiently, learn each other's jobs, and switch jobs as needed. This promotes teamwork among workers and flexibility in work assignments.
- Because the focus in manufacturing is on finding and correcting the causes of production problems, manufacturing operations are streamlined and problem free.

Business Snapshot 12.3 illustrates how one company has successfully adopted JIT manufacturing. To obtain the benefits from JIT, however, companies have had to

---

BUSINESS SNAPSHOT 12.3

JIT at Perlos

Perlos (Texas), Inc., is a subsidiary of the Perlos Corporation, which is based in Nurmijärvi, Finland. Located in Fort Worth, Texas, the Perlos manufacturing facility produces a variety of plastic components for mobile phones. The Texas plant produces parts exclusively for Nokia, the world's leading producer of cell phones. Although some of the parts produced at the Perlos plant are shipped to Nokia plants around the world, most are sent to the Nokia plant just across the street from Perlos. With around 500 employees and 300 robots, Perlos's two-year-old plant is a state-of-the-

art facility for injection-molded plastic components. The plant operates 24 hours a day.

Perlos uses a JIT approach to production control, including Kanban cards. Nokia provides Perlos with forecasts for six months in the future and provides a blanket purchase order for plastic components. Production and delivery of components are controlled by Kanban cards. Perlos does not produce anything unless there is a Kanban card authorizing it to do so. If Nokia increases or decreases its production rate for cell phones during a week, then Perlos must also increase or de-

crease its production rate for plastic components.

Perlos makes frequent deliveries of parts to Nokia throughout each day to support Nokia's production plan. The parts delivered to Nokia are not packaged, which would slow Nokia's use of the parts, but rather they are placed on partitioned plastic trays holding a standard number of parts. After Nokia uses the parts, the empty trays are then returned to Perlos for reuse. There are no wasted packaging materials, such as cardboard boxes, with the parts provided to Nokia's Fort Worth plant.

invest heavily in engineering studies and equipment modifications to achieve drastically reduced setup times, establish training programs that train workers for several jobs, and develop different business strategies with narrower product lines that allow stable and level production schedules. Unless manufacturers are willing to commit to this new price instead of the old price of high inventory levels and low customer responsiveness, they cannot expect to reap the benefits of JIT.

SUCCESS AND JIT MANUFACTURING

Some of the success of companies that use JIT manufacturing may not be attributed only to JIT. Successful companies also have:

Business strategies based on producing standardized products that can be mass produced both at low cost and with outstanding product quality.

The latest production technology, including robotics, flexible manufacturing systems (FMS), group technology (GT), automatic storage and retrieval systems (ASRS), bar coding, computer-aided design/computer-aided manufacturing (CAD/CAM), and computer-integrated manufacturing (CIM).

Focused factories that are specialized in particular technologies or products. These factories are smaller, more compact, and require less capital investment.

Master production schedules that are stable and level. Not only do they not vary in level of load from month to month, they also freeze the early part of production schedules.

The economies of reduced setup times. Less labor is used to make the setups, and machines are not idle as long during the setups. This can contribute to lower labor cost and under certain conditions, higher machine capacity utilization.

Workers trained on many jobs. They can move from one job to another as needed to balance the workload, which contributes to high worker utilization and lower labor costs. In some companies, nonunion workers are uninhibited by restrictive union rules.

Job security programs for their workers. Less employee turnover results in a better-trained work force and reduced hiring and training costs.

A younger labor force. Health care and retirement costs are less.

Total quality management (TQM) programs. Every worker is involved and motivated to make the company a success through perfect product quality.

Subcontractor networks built on trust relationships between customers and suppliers. These long-term arrangements have resulted in constancy of supply, improved quality of supplied materials, and, in the long run, reduced cost of materials.

Participative management styles. The attitude of managers toward workers, and benevolent company personnel policies, have tended to develop cooperation between workers and management. Proponents of these management styles claim that these factors have resulted in more committed workers.

We probably shall never know which of these factors or combination of factors account for the success of today's businesses, because they all have been blended and integrated with JIT by the manufacturers and it is impossible to separate them. In the end, JIT and the other factors listed above comprise a total system and philosophy of manufacturing, and it is the whole rather than the parts that accounts for their success. Business Snapshot 12.4 describes how other approaches to manufacturing improvement can be integrated with JIT as the implementation of JIT matures in a company.

BUSINESS SNAPSHOT 12.4

Maturing JIT Implementation at Amadas

When JIT is first successfully implemented in a company, the benefits are usually clear and appear substantial. But as the years go by, the rate of improvements decreases. To continue improving the operations, companies may adopt other approaches to enhance their JIT manufacturing approach. The evolving operations at Amadas demonstrate such a strategy.

Amadas Industries of Suffolk, Virginia, manufactures agricultural machinery, including peanut combines and hard-hose irrigators, and industrial machinery, including equipment for processing horticultural mulches and for recycling organic waste products. With about 30 standard product models, agricultural machines are built in batches of 10 to 25 units, and industrial machines are built in batches of 1 to 3 units and are often custom designed.

In the 1990s, Amadas decided to implement JIT. Significant benefits were realized in labor cost and lead time improvements. After a couple of years, the improvement projects and successes continued, but it appeared that the number of successes and benefits were declining. Taking further steps to reduce setup times on machinery, for example, would be expensive and would result in only marginal improvements. At first this was a matter of concern to management, but it was later recognized as a normal part of the maturing process of JIT manufacturing. Amadas had "picked all the low hanging fruit." The company needed a means of determining which projects now had the greatest potential benefit and should be undertaken.

After studying different books on manufacturing, Amadas's management decided to adopt the the-

ory of constraints (TOC) approach to analyzing the production system. The general goal of TOC analysis is to identify bottlenecks in the production system that are currently limiting the amount or rate of production. The TOC analysis identified a CNC plasma torch as a constraint. Subsequently, a setup-reduction project was undertaken to change the materials-handling equipment being used.

Another constraint identified by TOC analysis was the purchasing department. To improve the timely availability of purchased parts, a Kanban system was then established for purchased parts. Arrangements were made with suppliers and Kanban cards were posted at the storage locations. Continuous improvement is still an ongoing effort at Amadas, and both JIT and TOC are playing important roles in this effort.

Source: Hobbs, Jr., O. Kermit. "Managing JIT toward Maturity." *Production and Inventory Management Journal* 38, no. 1 (First Quarter 1997): 47–50.

Whether most U.S. manufacturers should adopt JIT manufacturing is still an unanswered question. For some U.S. firms, the principal means of competing is not through short delivery times. For these firms, the cost and turmoil of implementing JIT may not be justified.

It can take many months and even years to change the fundamental culture of a company to one that is equipped to engage in time-based competition. The organization commitment from top to bottom is enormous, and such programs cannot be undertaken lightly with the idea of trying another new buzzword from the business press. Until small lot sizes are realized through factory-wide programs to reduce setup times, JIT just won't work. Also, unless product lines are narrowed through different business strategies, the nonrepetitive nature of production processes will work against JIT. Although MRP handles great product variety extremely well, JIT simply will not work as well under these conditions.

In their enthusiasm to gain the benefits of JIT manufacturing, U.S. manufacturers should not give up the positive features of their production systems without assurances that the new methods will achieve better results. Presently, some U.S. manufacturers accept high inventories as the price they must pay to achieve high worker and machine utilization. Although JIT manufacturers have achieved high worker and machine utilization without high inventories, they are paying a different price. These companies are investing heavily in automated equipment, cross-training of workers, engineering studies, and other improvements to achieve the benefits of JIT.

JIT IN SERVICE COMPANIES

The JIT goals of reduced waste, improved quality, and shorter lead times are attractive to all industries. In recent years, many service organizations have adopted some of the approaches and techniques of the JIT philosophy, in order to achieve some of these benefits. One such technique is **poka-yoke**, or mistake-proofing. **Mistake-proofing** refers to redesigning a process so that it is more difficult to make a mistake in the process.

As an example of mistake-proofing, consider an office worker that must put a check mark in eight specific boxes on a paper form that has dozens of boxes, and this process must be performed on hundreds of the forms. To prevent the wrong boxes from being checked by mistake, a template could be made that is overlaid on the paper form. The template would have only eight cutout holes in the precise locations of the correct boxes to be checked off. The worker would line up the template with the paper form and put check marks in all of the cutout locations. The process would be faster and no mistakes would be made. This technique is frequently used in JIT manufacturing and can be easily adopted in service organizations.

Another technique often used in JIT manufacturing is good housekeeping. The *APICS Dictionary* defines **housekeeping** as "the manufacturing activity of identifying and maintaining an orderly environment for preventing errors and contamination in the manufacturing process."[10] Both Lockheed Martin and Boeing have adopted good housekeeping rules as part of their lean manufacturing initiatives. Boeing even implemented these housekeeping rules in its service function departments, such as accounting, finance, and information systems.

These housekeeping rules are often referred to as the **5S process**, which originated from the five Japanese words *seiri* (sort), *seiton* (straighten), *seiso* (sweep, or spic and span), *seiketsu* (standardize), and *shitsuke* (self-discipline). These five housekeeping rules are:

- *Sort*—simplify what is kept or stored at each workstation.
- *Straighten*—keep every item in a designated place at each workstation.
- *Sweep*—keep each workstation clean.
- *Standardize*—set standards and require all employees to follow these rules as a habit.
- *Self-discipline*—instill the discipline in employees to keep their workstations organized.

These JIT approaches and many others are useful in service organizations as well as in manufacturing. And service operations managers can help to make their organizations more competitive by studying how manufacturing companies have implemented these JIT approaches.

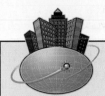

Wrap-Up

WHAT WORLD-CLASS COMPANIES DO

For many companies today, the name of the game is time-based competition. For them, the principal means of capturing market share is through finding ways to shrink the order-to-delivery cycle. Just-in-time (JIT) or lean manufacturing is a system that speeds production of products so much that no other form of production can compete. In JIT manufacturing, the fundamental culture of the organization must change from one of emphasizing labor and machine utilization to one that focuses on speed. And speed of production is achieved through drastically reducing manufacturing lead times.

Certain prerequisites must be present before JIT has a chance to succeed. Production must be repetitive manufacturing, or production must be changed to the extent that it behaves like repetitive manufacturing. Products must move through production in a continuous flow without waiting at any step. Schedules must be stabilized and leveled, and factories must become more specialized and focused. These changes make production planning and control simple enough to allow JIT to work. And costly programs must be implemented to increase production capacity by increasing production rates and reducing setup times. Additionally, programs must eliminate product defects and machine breakdowns as sources of interrupting production. To cope with unexpected events, workers must be cross-trained so that they can do several jobs.

All the elements of JIT are essential—eliminating waste, enforced problem solving, building teamwork, total quality management, parallel processing, Kanban production control, JIT purchasing, and ongoing programs that reduce inventories and bring about repetitive manufacturing.

For the companies that can implement a successful JIT manufacturing system, the rewards are enormous. Inventories will be drastically reduced, and the time from order to delivery is greatly reduced, allowing them to use speed as a weapon to capture market share. Product quality is improved, and the cost of scrap is reduced. Teamwork and organizational flexibility allow these companies to respond to all kinds of customer needs. And because JIT focuses on problem solving in production, manufacturing operations are streamlined and problem free.

Japanese and U.S. manufacturers in great numbers have switched their operations to JIT. But they have had to invest heavily in engineering studies and equipment modifications to drastically reduce setup times, training programs that train workers for several jobs, and new business strategies with narrower product lines that allow stable and level production schedules. Unless manufacturers are willing to make this kind of organization commitment, they cannot expect to reap the benefits of JIT.

Companies that have successful JIT programs in place are prepared to engage in time-based competition. Many believe that in JIT we have a glimpse of the future where speed will be the key factor in winning market share in global markets. Too many companies have switched to JIT to not pay attention.

Many JIT approaches can also be used in service organizations. Techniques such as mistake-proofing, housekeeping rules, cross-trained workers, rigorous preventive maintenance programs, and a strong focus on quality can help service operations to become more competitive.

REVIEW AND DISCUSSION QUESTIONS

1. List some other names for just-in-time manufacturing.
2. Explain the meaning of *time-based competition.*
3. What is the *order-to-delivery cycle?* What are its components?
4. Compare and contrast the philosophy of traditional and JIT manufacturing. What are their objectives? How do they achieve them?
5. Explain the relationship between capacity utilization and manufacturing lead times from Figure 12.2.
6. List and explain the prerequisites of JIT manufacturing. Briefly explain why each is a prerequisite.
7. Who is Shigeo Shingo? What are his contributions to JIT manufacturing?
8. Explain the meaning of Figure 12.3, Uncovering Production Problems.
9. Explain the roles of people in JIT. What is the meaning of *empowerment of workers* in JIT?

10. Why is total quality management (TQM) important in JIT?
11. What is *parallel processing?* Why is it desirable in JIT?
12. Briefly explain how Kanban works on the shop floor. What are *Kanban cards?* How are they used in Kanban?
13. List and explain the components of JIT purchasing.
14. Explain what companies can do to reduce inventories.
15. Explain some of the things that companies can do to make their operations behave more like repetitive manufacturing.
16. List and explain the benefits of JIT manufacturing.
17. Explain the difficulty of identifying the reasons for the successes of companies that use JIT manufacturing.
18. Explain the concepts of mistake-proofing and good housekeeping.

INTERNET ASSIGNMENTS

1. The Shingo Prize, named after Shigeo Shingo, recognizes world-class manufacturing excellence. Visit the web site **http://www.shingoprize.org** and describe what this award is intended to recognize. What companies are eligible to apply for this award?
2. Toyota is the company most credited with formalizing the JIT approach to manufacturing. Visit Toyota's web site at **http://www.global.toyota.com** and go to Corporate Info. Click on the label "Production & History," and then click on "making things." Step through Toyota's virtual tour of its manufacturing process and describe some of the interesting aspects you learned about Toyota's manufacturing approaches.
3. The Kaizen Institute was founded by Masaaki Imai, who helped make the term *Kaizen* popular in the 1980s. Visit the web site of the Kaizen Institute at **http://www.kaizen-institute.com**. What is the meaning of the word *Kaizen?* What are the 10 basic tips for Kaizen activities?
4. Search the Internet for a consulting company that assists firms in implementing JIT manufacturing or lean manufacturing. Describe the relevant services offered.

PROBLEMS

1. A production operation is a single-channel, single-phase, unlimited-queue-length queuing system. Products arrive at the operation at an average rate of 30 per hour, and the present average production rate is 33 products per hour. Management wants products to be at the operation an average of only 0.1 hour. What is the new average production rate at the operation?

2. In Problem 1, how much would the average work-in-progress (WIP) inventory be reduced with the new production rate?

3. A production operation is a single-channel, single-phase, unlimited-queue-length queuing system. Products arrive at the operation at an average rate of 90 per hour, and the automated operation produces products at a constant rate of 95 products per hour. Engineering can modify the machinery at the operation to increase the production capacity to a constant rate of 105 products per hour. How much would the average lead time be reduced?

4. In Problem 3, how much would the average WIP be reduced with the improvement in lead time?

5. A production operation is a single-channel, single-phase, limited-queue-length queuing system. Products arrive at the operation at an average rate of 35 per hour, and the average production rate is 40 products per hour. There can only be a maximum of 4 products in the system because of space limitations. Use the *POM Software Library* to answer these questions: What is the average WIP at the operation? What is the probability that the operation will not be idle?

6. A production operation is a multiple-channel, single-phase, unlimited-queue-length queuing system. Products arrive at the operation at an average rate of 70 per hour. Each of the three parallel channels has an average production rate of 25 products per hour. Use the *POM Software Library* to answer these questions: What is the average WIP at the operation? What is the average lead time at the operation?

7. If U = 250 parts per hour, T = 0.25 hour, P = 0.15, and C = 24 parts per container, how many Kanban containers are required?

8. There are two adjacent work centers, a downstream (using) work center and an upstream (producing) work center. The production rate of the using work center is 150 parts per hour. Each standard Kanban container holds 50 parts. It takes an average of 0.9 hour for a container to make the entire cycle from the time it leaves the upstream work center until it is returned, filled with production, and leaves again.
   a. Compute the number of containers needed if the Kanban system is rated at a P of 0.25.
   b. Would C ordinarily be rounded up or down? Why?

9. A company is using a Kanban system for production control between two adjacent work centers. The downstream work center has a production rate of 300 parts per hour. Management wants to have a P value of 0.1 and use three containers between the upstream and downstream work centers. If the desired time for a container to make the entire cycle from the time it leaves the upstream work center until it is returned, filled with parts, and leaves again is 30 minutes, how many parts should each container hold?

10. A production analyst and an industrial engineer are investigating potential setup time reductions at their plant to help make the production processes more efficient. A hydraulic stamping machine currently requires about 25 minutes for the machine operator to complete a changeover between different part types. Each part requires 2.75 minutes for the stamping process. Parts are currently produced in batches of 30 units. The labor rate is $15.75 per hour.
   a. What is the current average labor cost per part, including changeovers?
   b. If the changeover time could be reduced to 10 minutes, how much labor cost per part would be saved using the current batch size of 30 units?

c. If the changeover time could be reduced to 10 minutes, how much could the batch size be reduced in order to achieve the current average labor cost per unit?

11. A manufacturing engineering team is analyzing the changeover efficiency of a machine. The machine currently requires about 55 minutes for the machine operator to complete a changeover between different part types. Each part requires 7.5 minutes for processing. Parts are currently produced in batches of 40 units. The labor rate is $16.50 per hour.
    a. What is the current average labor cost per part, including changeovers?
    b. If the changeover time could be reduced to 30 minutes, how much labor cost per part would be saved using the current batch size of 40 units?
    c. If the changeover time could be reduced to 30 minutes, how much could the batch size be reduced in order to achieve the current average labor cost per unit?

12. A JIT implementation team is evaluating lot sizes and setup times throughout the factory. The first machine to be evaluated currently requires about 20 minutes for the machine operator to complete a changeover between different part types. Each part requires 1.2 minutes for processing. Parts are currently produced in batches of 60 units. The labor rate is $14.50 per hour.
    a. What is the current average labor cost per part, including changeovers?
    b. If the changeover time could be reduced to 10 minutes, how much labor cost per part would be saved using the current batch size of 60 units?
    c. If the changeover time could be reduced to 10 minutes, how much could the batch size be reduced in order to achieve the current average labor cost per unit?
    d. What changeover time would be required to produce in batches of 15 units and achieve the current average labor cost per part?

13. A production analyst and an industrial engineer have set a target batch size of 5 parts on the hydraulic stamping machine. The production rate is 18 parts per hour, the usage rate is 3 parts per hour, the carrying cost is $14.90 per unit per year, the labor rate is $15.75 per hour, and the annual demand is 3,000 per year. (The machine operator performs the setup.) (*Hint:* Use the EOQ model for production lots that is discussed in Chapter 14.)
    a. What must the setup time be for the hydraulic stamping machine?
    b. Compared to the current setup time of 25 minutes, is the setup time computed in Part a even possible? Discuss what could be done at the work center to achieve such a setup time.

CASE

Utah Medical Instruments Inc.

Utah Medical Instruments Inc. (UMI) manufactures precision equipment and parts for the laser eye surgery industry. UMI is implementing a JIT manufacturing system and is striving to reduce lead times throughout production. The production operation performed at work center #6 is the bottleneck operation for the entire production system. This means that the production rate at this operation is the slowest production rate in the factory. So in effect, the operation at work center #6 controls the production rate of the entire factory. The production rates at all other work centers are at least 10 percent greater than at work center #6, so improving the production rate at work center #6 will result in greater output for the entire factory.

Work center #6 is made up of five identical machines working in a parallel arrangement. Parts arrive at the work center at an average rate of 60 parts per hour and flow to the machine with the shortest waiting line. Each machine can process an average of 13 parts per hour.

UMI management is now studying two proposals for speeding the flow of parts through work center #6. Proposal A would install new variable-speed controllers on all the machines, average production rates would be increased to 15 parts per hour, and the total cost of equipment enhancements would be $80,000. Proposal B would add another identical machine to work center #6, and the cost would be $100,000. Use the *POM Software Library* to answer the following questions.

Assignment

1. What is the average lead time at work center #6 now?
2. What would be the average lead time at work center #6 with Proposal A?
3. What would be the average lead time at work center #6 with Proposal B?
4. Evaluate the two proposals. Which one would you recommend? Why?

ENDNOTES

1. Giles, Christopher A., James J. King, Ryan C. Murphy, and Paul J. Roney, "Meeting Customer Demand through Mixed-Model Manufacturing." *Production and Inventory Management Journal* 38, no. 2 (Second Quarter 1997): 82–87.
2. Cox, James F., III, and John H. Blackstone, eds. *APICS Dictionary*, 9th ed., p. 47. Falls Church, VA: APICS—The Educational Society for Resource Management, 1998.
3. Cox, James F., III, and John H. Blackstone, eds. *APICS Dictionary*, 9th ed., p. 49. Falls Church, VA: APICS—The Educational Society for Resource Management, 1998.
4. Blackburn, Joseph. "Time-Based Competition: JIT as a Weapon." *APICS: The Performance Advantage* (July 1991): 30–34.
5. Ford, Henry. *Today and Tomorrow*. London: William Heinemann, Ltd., 1926.
6. Hall, Robert W. *Zero Inventories*, p. 37. Homewood, IL: Dow Jones–Irwin, 1983.
7. Leschke, John P. "The Setup-Reduction Process: Part 1." *Production and Inventory Management Journal* 38, no. 1 (First Quarter 1997): 32–37.
8. Leschke, John P. "The Setup-Reduction Process: Part 2—Setting Reduction Priorities." *Production and Inventory Management Journal* 38, no. 1 (First Quarter 1997): 38–42.
9. Cox, James F., III, and John H. Blackstone, eds. *APICS Dictionary*, 9th ed., p. 82. Falls Church, VA: APICS—The Educational Society for Resource Management, 1998.
10. Cox, James F., III, and John H. Blackstone, eds. *APICS Dictionary*, 9th ed., p. 41. Falls Church, VA: APICS—The Educational Society for Resource Management, 1998.

SELECTED BIBLIOGRAPHY

Allen, John H. "Make Lean Manufacturing Work for You." *Manufacturing Engineering* 124, no. 6 (June 2000): 54–64.

Avery, Susan. "E-Procurement Is One Tool to Reduce Costs, Cycle Time." *Purchasing* 129, no. 5 (Sept. 2000): S15–S23.

Beard, Luciana, and Stephen A. Butler. "Introducing JIT Manufacturing: It's Easier Than You Think." *Business Horizons* 43, no. 5 (Sept./Oct. 2000): 61–64.

Blackburn, Joseph D. *Time-Based Competition*. Homewood, IL: Business One Irwin, 1991.

Cox, James F., III, and John H. Blackstone, eds. *APICS Dictionary*, 9th ed. Falls Church, VA: APICS—The Educational Society for Resource Management, 1998.

Eckes, George. *The Six Sigma Revolution: How General Electric and Others Turned Process into Profits*. New York: John Wiley & Sons, 2000.

Ford, Henry. *Today and Tomorrow*. London: William Heinemann, Ltd., 1926.

Hall, Robert W. *Zero Inventories*. Homewood, IL: Dow Jones–Irwin, 1983.

Klassen, Robert D. "Just-in-Time Manufacturing and Pollution Prevention Generate Mutual Benefits in the Furniture Industry." *Interfaces* 30, no. 3 (May/June 2000): 95–106.

Laraia, Anthony C., Patricia E. Moody, and Robert W. Hall. *The Kaizen Blitz: Accelerating Breakthroughs in Productivity and Performance.* New York: John Wiley & Sons, 1999.

Leschke, John P. "The Setup-Reduction Process: Part 1." *Production and Inventory Management Journal* 38, no. 1 (First Quarter 1997): 32–37.

Leschke, John P. "The Setup-Reduction Process: Part 2—Setting Reduction Priorities." *Production and Inventory Management Journal* 38, no. 1 (First Quarter 1997): 38–42.

McLachlin, Ron. "Management Initiatives and Just-In-Time Manufacturing." *Journal of Operations Management* 15, no. 4 (November 1997): 271–292.

Mia, Lokman. "Just-in-Time Manufacturing, Management Accounting Systems, and Profitability." *Accounting and Business Research* 30, no. 2 (Spring 2000): 137–151.

Minahan, Tim. "Dell Computer Sees Suppliers as Key to JIT." *Purchasing* 123, no. 3 (September 4, 1997): 43–48.

Monden, Yasuhiro. *Toyota Production System: An Integrated Approach to Just-In-Time,* 3rd ed. Norcross, GA: Engineering & Management Press, 1997.

Nicholas, John M. *Competitive Manufacturing Management: Continuous Improvement, Lean Production, Customer-Focused Quality.* Boston: Irwin/McGraw-Hill, 1998.

Ohno, Taiichi, and Setsuo Mito. *Just-in-Time for Today and Tomorrow.* Cambridge, MA: Productivity Press, 1988.

Pierce, F. David. "Applying Just in Time to Safety and Health." *Occupational Health & Safety* 66, no. 4 (April 1997): 65–69.

Power, Damien, and Amrik S. Sohal. "Human Resource Management Strategies and Practices in Just-in-Time Environments: Australian Case Study Evidence." *Technovation* 20, no. 7 (July 2000): 373–387.

Ruffa, Stephen A., and Michael J. Perozziello. *Breaking the Cost Barrier: A Proven Approach to Managing and Implementing Lean Manufacturing.* New York: John Wiley & Sons, 2000.

Sahin, Funda. "Manufacturing Competitiveness: Different Systems to Achieve the Same Results." *Production and Inventory Management Journal* 41, no. 1 (First Quarter 2000): 56–65.

Schniederjans, Marc J., and John R. Olson. *Advanced Topics in Just-In-Time Management.* Westport, CT: Quorum Books, 1999.

Schonberger, Richard J. *Japanese Manufacturing Techniques: Nine Hidden Lessons in Simplicity.* New York: Free Press, 1982.

Standard, Charles, and Dale Davis. *Running Today's Factory: A Proven Strategy for Lean Manufacturing.* Cincinnati, OH: Hanser Gardner Publications, 1999.

Wantuck, Kenneth A. *Just-In-Time for America.* Southfield, MI: KWA Media, 1989.

Whitson, Daniel. "Applying Just-In-Time Systems in Health Care." *IIE Solutions* 29, no. 8 (August 1997): 32–37.

Yasin, M. M., M. Small, and M. A. Wafa. "An Empirical Investigation of JIT Effectiveness: An Organizational Perspective." *Omega* 25, no. 4 (August 1997): 461–471.

13

Production Planning

Introduction

Production-Planning Hierarchy

Aggregate Planning
Aggregate Demand
Dimensions of Production Capacity
Sources of Medium-Range Production Capacity
Some Traditional Aggregate Plans
Criteria for Selecting Aggregate Plans
Aggregate Plans for Services
Mathematical Models for Aggregate Planning
Preemptive Tactics

Master Production Scheduling
Objectives of Master Production Scheduling
Time Fences in Master Production Schedules
Procedures for Developing Master Production
  Schedules
Demand Management
Weekly Updating of the MPS
MPS in Produce-to-Stock and Produce-to-Order
  Firms

Length of Planning Horizons
Computerized MPS

Types of Production-Planning and Control Systems
Pond-Draining Systems
Push Systems
Pull Systems
Focusing on Bottlenecks

Wrap-Up: What World-Class Companies Do

Review and Discussion Questions

Internet Assignments

Problems

Cases
Mrs. Massey's Master Mixers
British Aerocurrent, Ltd.
Cool Bevrich Company

Endnotes

Selected Bibliography

© SCOTT T. SMITH/CORBIS

AGGREGATE PLANNING AT NEW GENERATION COMPUTERS

The operations manager at New Generation Computers (NGC) is developing a six-month aggregate production plan for producing a family of computer printers. NGC's marketing department has estimated the demand for the printers for the six-month period. There are several printer models, and the amount of labor required to produce each printer depends on the characteristics of the model. Although overtime labor can be used, NGC has a policy that limits the amount of overtime labor in each month to 10 percent of the straight-time labor available. Overtime labor is more expensive than straight-time labor, and NGC's union has resisted the use of overtime. NGC has a no-layoff policy for its workers; thus, the same number of straight-time labor-hours is available for producing the printers in each month. The flow-soldering operation operates three shifts per day and can produce a maximum of only 2,000 printers per day. NGC incurs a carrying cost each time a printer is produced in one month and shipped in a later month. The objectives of the aggregate production plan are to fully utilize the workforce, not to exceed machine capacity, promptly ship customers' orders, and minimize the costs of overtime and of carrying inventory.

Effective production planning is the key to successful operations in a production system. The preceding account is an example of what is called **aggregate planning**. In such planning, operations managers develop medium-range plans of how they will produce products for the next several months. These plans specify the amount of labor, subcontracting, and other sources of capacity to be used. Operations managers also engage in **master production scheduling**, developing short-range production plans of which finished products to produce in the next several weeks. In this chapter, we study both medium- and short-range production planning.

PRODUCTION-PLANNING HIERARCHY

Figure 13.1 illustrates long-range, medium-range, and short-range production planning. We studied long-range capacity planning in Chapter 5; these plans are necessary to develop facilities and equipment, major suppliers, and production processes and become constraints on the medium- and short-range plans. Aggregate planning develops medium-range production plans concerning employment, aggregate inventory, utilities, facility modifications, and material-supply contracts. These aggregate plans impose constraints on the short-range production plans that follow. We study aggregate production planning next.

Master production schedules are short-range plans for producing finished goods or end items, which are used to drive production planning and control systems. These systems develop short-range production schedules of parts and assemblies, schedules of purchased materials, shop-floor schedules, and workforce schedules. The remaining chapters in Part 3 of this text, Chapters 14 through 16, are about these short-range production planning and control systems. Because master production scheduling drives these systems, this chapter is crucial to understanding the remaining chapters in Part 3. For this reason, we discuss master production scheduling later in this chapter.

Figure 13.1	Production Planning in Manufacturing

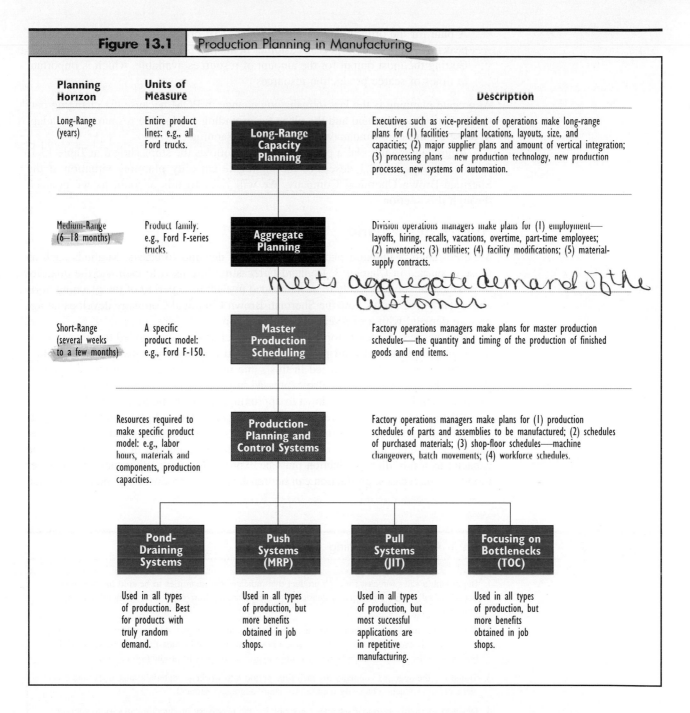

Planning Horizon	Units of Measure		Description
Long-Range (years)	Entire product lines: e.g., all Ford trucks.	**Long-Range Capacity Planning**	Executives such as vice-president of operations make long-range plans for (1) facilities—plant locations, layouts, size, and capacities; (2) major supplier plans and amount of vertical integration; (3) processing plans—new production technology, new production processes, new systems of automation.
Medium-Range (6–18 months)	Product family: e.g., Ford F-series trucks.	**Aggregate Planning**	Division operations managers make plans for (1) employment— layoffs, hiring, recalls, vacations, overtime, part-time employees; (2) inventories; (3) utilities; (4) facility modifications; (5) material-supply contracts.
Short-Range (several weeks to a few months)	A specific product model: e.g., Ford F-150.	**Master Production Scheduling**	Factory operations managers make plans for master production schedules—the quantity and timing of the production of finished goods and end items.
	Resources required to make specific product model: e.g., labor hours, materials and components, production capacities.	**Production-Planning and Control Systems**	Factory operations managers make plans for (1) production schedules of parts and assemblies to be manufactured; (2) schedules of purchased materials; (3) shop-floor schedules—machine changeovers, batch movements; (4) workforce schedules.

(handwritten annotation: meets aggregate demand of the customer)

Pond-Draining Systems	**Push Systems (MRP)**	**Pull Systems (JIT)**	**Focusing on Bottlenecks (TOC)**
Used in all types of production. Best for products with truly random demand.	Used in all types of production, but more benefits obtained in job shops.	Used in all types of production, but most successful applications are in repetitive manufacturing.	Used in all types of production, but more benefits obtained in job shops.

AGGREGATE PLANNING

Aggregate planning is necessary in operations management because it provides for:

- Fully loaded facilities and minimizes overloading and underloading, thus reducing production costs
- Adequate production capacity to meet expected aggregate demand

- A plan for the orderly and systematic change of production capacity to meet the peaks and valleys of expected customer demand
- Getting the most output for the amount of resources available, which is important in times of scarce production resources

Aggregate planning is the key to managing change in POM because the changing patterns of customer demand and the plans for providing production resources that adapt to those changes are fundamental to aggregate planning.

Aggregate planning as a process generally follows the steps shown in Table 13.1. Business Snapshot 13.1 describes the aggregate capacity planning situation at the Sherman-Brown Chemical Company. We will refer to this account as we proceed through this section.

Aggregate Demand

Medium-range production planning begins with demand forecasts. Methods such as those discussed in Chapter 3, Demand Forecasting, are used to estimate the quantity of products or services likely to be demanded in each time period of the planning horizon. Figure 13.2 shows how the Sherman-Brown Chemical Company develops an aggregate demand with a one-year planning horizon.

The quarterly forecasts for the three individual products are added together to form the aggregate demand for all products, expressed in gallons per quarter. The production capacities are also expressed in this same unit of measure—gallons per quarter. Because the aggregate plan is also expressed in gallons per quarter, production capacities can then be scaled up or down to approximately meet the aggregate demand.

When diverse products are produced, aggregating demand may not be so straightforward—for instance, for a firm that produces both lawn mowers and rototillers. Because it is unlikely that a lawn mower requires the same amount of labor and machine capacity as a rototiller, production must be expressed in units other than products per month. In such cases, production can be translated from products per month into such

Table 13.1	Steps in Aggregate Planning

1. Begin with a sales forecast for each product that indicates the quantities to be sold in each time period (usually weeks, months, or quarters) over the planning horizon (usually 6 months to 18 months).

2. Total all the individual product or service forecasts into one aggregate demand. If the products are not additive because of heterogeneous units, a homogeneous unit of measure must be selected that both allows the forecasts to be added and links aggregate outputs to production capacity.

3. Transform the aggregate demand for each time period into workers, materials, machines, and other elements of production capacity required to satisfy aggregate demand.

4. Develop alternative resource schemes for supplying the necessary production capacity to support the cumulative aggregate demand.

5. Select the capacity plan from among the alternatives considered that satisfies aggregate demand and best meets the objectives of the organization.

Note: Step 5 assumes that the production system is compelled by management policy to produce the sales forecast. There are occasions when capacity cannot be sufficiently increased or when it would be more profitable to produce less than the sales forecast. It is assumed, for the purposes of this chapter, that these issues have already been resolved and that the sales forecast is the production goal.

BUSINESS SNAPSHOT 13.1

Aggregate Planning at Sherman-Brown Chemical Company

The Sherman-Brown Chemical Company is about to finalize its aggregate capacity plan for next year. The company produces three paint products—latex interior, latex enamel, and latex stain—on a produce-to-stock basis. The production plant is located in Cleveland, Ohio, where there is an abundance of workers who perform the duties of material preparation, mixing, and canning—the principal operations of the production line.

The latex carrier, pigments, cans, boxes, and other materials required to produce Sherman-Brown's products are also readily available from tried and proven suppliers in abundant quantities. The processing equipment in the production departments is operated on only one shift because Sherman-Brown's management bought out a competitor last year, and so an excess of machine capacity is available. Similarly, ample warehouse space for holding finished-goods inventory is available.

The capacity situation at Sherman-Brown is this: Because the only limiting factor in capacity planning is the size of the work-force, the only production capacity issue to be resolved is determining the number of workers to be employed during each time period to support the sales forecasts of the three paint products.

Two plans for providing production capacity are currently being considered by Sherman-Brown's plant manager: (1) level capacity with inventory and (2) matching demand. These alternatives must be evaluated in terms of which plan results in the lowest total annual cost while considering three elements of cost: (1) cost of hiring workers from time period to time period over the entire year, (2) cost of laying off workers over the same period, (3) cost of carrying the finished-goods inventory for the entire year.

These are the pertinent data for this analysis: working days per quarter, 65; labor standard per gallon for all types of paint,

2.311 worker-hours per gallon; working hours per shift, 8 hours per shift per worker; maximum machine capacity on one shift, 100,000 gallons per quarter for all types of paint.

The key analyses that must be performed by Sherman-Brown in developing an aggregate capacity plan are:

1. Develop an aggregate demand forecast from the three individual product forecasts.
2. Compare the two alternatives for providing production capacity in the number of workers hired, the number of workers laid off, and the average finished-goods inventory levels for the entire year.
3. Develop an analysis of the two alternatives for providing production capacity in terms of their impact on worker employment levels and finished-goods inventories.
4. Select the capacity plan alternative with the lowest annual cost.

units as labor-hours, machine-hours, sales dollars, or other units that are a good measure of production capacity. Production of lawn mowers and rototillers could be translated to labor-hours by using a labor standard: One lawn mower requires 21 labor-hours, and one rototiller requires 17 labor-hours. The aggregate plan for the two products would be the total labor-hours for each time period required to produce the forecasted quantity of the two products.

Dimensions of Production Capacity

An essential part of aggregate planning is a comprehensive understanding of each production system's capacities. Of particular importance are the answers to the following questions:

1. **How much of each production resource is available?** Production capacity in each time period may be constrained by factors such as the number of workers or the number of machines.

Figure 13.2	Aggregating Individual Product Forecasts into Aggregate Demand: Sherman-Brown Chemical Company

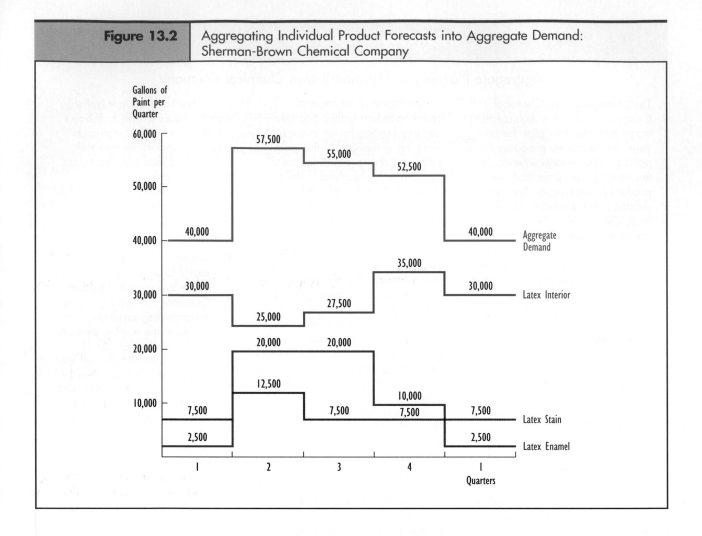

2. **How much capacity is provided by each type of resource?** The amount of resources required to produce a single product allows the translation of demand into production capacity needs. Labor standards (labor-hours per product) and machine standards (machine-hours per product) are commonly used to translate demand into the number of workers and machines needed.

3. **At what step in production do we determine capacity?** In product-focused production, capacity may be determined by the **gateway operation,** or the first operation in a production line. In process-focused production, capacity may be determined by a **bottleneck operation,** or an operation with the least capacity for a product. In other types of production, capacity may be determined by the number of labor-hours or machine-hours in a particular production department or an entire factory.

4. **How much does it cost to scale capacities up or down?** The cost of hiring, laying off, and recalling employees, for example, can affect plans for providing production capacity.

Such intricacies of production capacity have led production systems to identify several practical sources of providing medium-range production capacity.

Sources of Medium-Range Production Capacity

Because aggregate planning spans periods from only 6 to 18 months, not enough time is available to increase capacity by adding buildings, complex machines, and other capital goods. This shifts the focus to other sources of production capacity as plans are developed for supplying customer demand. Several variables can be altered to change medium-range production capacity from month to month. Among these variables are:

1. **Straight-time labor.** Production by workers paid straight-time labor rates, which usually means for 40 hours or less per week. The sources of labor are full-time and part-time present employees, new hires, and workers who have been laid off and can be recalled. The local labor market could be a limiting factor, and union contracts can limit management's flexibility in hiring new employees and laying off experienced workers.
2. **Overtime labor.** Production by workers paid overtime labor rates, which usually means for more than 40 hours per week. Overtime can be limited by union or company policies.
3. **Inventory.** Production in previous time periods that is held for shipment in later time periods.
4. **Subcontracting.** Production of products or services by suppliers.

Straight-time labor is the preferred source of production capacity and is used to provide a base production capacity. When demand exceeds the capacity of the existing workforce, new hires, overtime, inventory, and subcontracting can be used. But new hires, overtime, inventory, and subcontracting can cost more and cause other difficulties. Companies approach with caution the decision of how to best provide production capacity for the peaks of demand.

Some Traditional Aggregate Plans

Given the above sources of production capacity, certain traditional plans for providing production capacity to meet customer demand have evolved. The matching demand

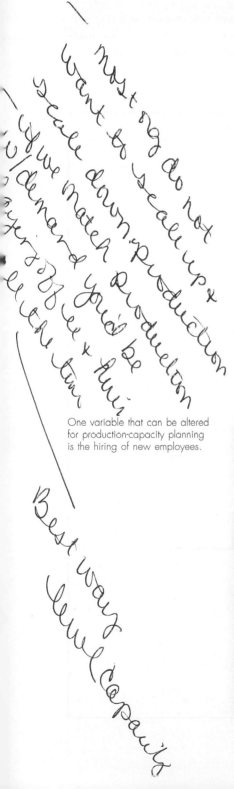

One variable that can be altered for production-capacity planning is the hiring of new employees.

Handwritten margin notes: most do not want to scale up & scale down production. if we match production w/ demand you'd be saying you can't level this. Best way level capacity

© PHOTODISC, INC.

plan and the level capacity plan used in conjunction with inventory, backlog, overtime, part-time labor, temporary employees, or subcontracting are commonly observed in POM practice.

Matching Demand

In the **matching demand** type of aggregate plan, production capacity in each time period is varied to exactly match the forecasted aggregate demand in that time period. Such an approach varies the level of the workforce in each time period by hiring new workers or laying off workers. Figure 13.3 shows how the workforce at the Sherman-Brown Chemical Company would fluctuate with this type of aggregate plan.

Figure 13.3	Matching Demand: Sherman-Brown Chemical Company

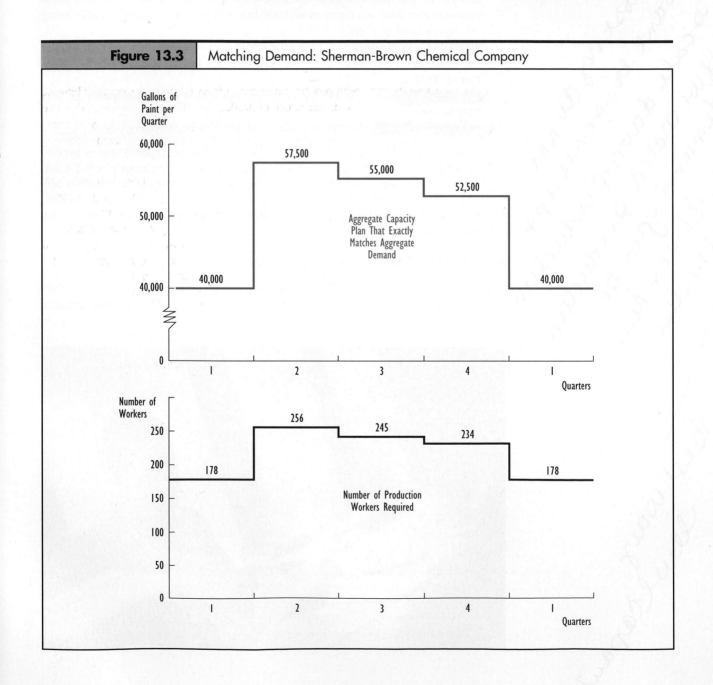

The labor standard at Sherman-Brown is 2.311 worker-hours per gallon of paint. The number of workers required in each quarter is therefore determined as follows:

$$\text{Workers} = \frac{\text{Gallons of paint per quarter} \times \text{Labor standard per gallon}}{\text{Working days per quarter per worker} \times \text{Hours per day}}$$

1st quarter $= (40{,}000 \times 2.311) \div (65 \times 8) = 178$ workers
2nd quarter $= (57{,}500 \times 2.311) \div (65 \times 8) = 256$ workers
3rd quarter $= (55{,}000 \times 2.311) \div (65 \times 8) = 245$ workers
4th quarter $= (52{,}500 \times 2.311) \div (65 \times 8) = 234$ workers

The chief advantage of this plan is that almost no finished-goods inventory is needed, and therefore much of the cost of holding or carrying inventory is avoided. However, labor and material costs tend to be higher because of the disruptions caused by frequently scaling the workforce and material-supplies capacities up and down.

Level Capacity

In the *level capacity* approach, production capacity is held constant over the planning horizon. The difference between the constant production rate and the varying demand rate is made up by inventory, backlog, overtime, part-time labor, temporary employees or subcontracting. Figure 13.4 illustrates how this difference is buffered with each of these sources of capacity.

Buffering with Inventory. If a firm is a produce-to-stock firm, finished-goods inventory buffers the difference between the varying demand and the constant production capacity. Figure 13.5 shows how this approach would operate if the Sherman-Brown Chemical Company were a produce-to-stock firm. The company would set its constant production capacity equal to the average quarterly demand of 51,250 gallons, and it would allow inventory to supply capacity in quarters when demand exceeds capacity.

The ending inventory of each quarter is computed by this formula:

$$EI_t = EI_{t-1} + (P_t - D_t)$$

where:

EI_t = ending inventory in Quarter t
EI_{t-1} = ending inventory in Quarter t − 1, the previous quarter
P_t = production in Quarter t
D_t = demand in Quarter t

If we assume that the inventory is zero at the beginning of Quarter 1, the ending inventory in each of the quarters is computed as follows:

$EI_1 = BI_0 + (P_1 - D_1)$ $EI_3 = EI_2 + (P_3 - D_3)$
$\quad\;\, = 0 + (51{,}250 - 40{,}000)$ $\quad\;\, = 5{,}000 + (51{,}250 - 55{,}000)$
$\quad\;\, = 11{,}250$ gallons $\quad\;\, = 1{,}250$ gallons

$EI_2 = EI_1 + (P_2 - D_2)$ $EI_4 = EI_3 + (P_4 - D_4)$
$\quad\;\, = 11{,}250 + (51{,}250 - 57{,}500)$ $\quad\;\, = 1{,}250 + (51{,}250 - 52{,}500)$
$\quad\;\, = 5{,}000$ gallons $\quad\;\, = 0$ gallons

Finished-goods inventory grows to a peak of 11,250 gallons at the end of the first quarter. In the second and third quarters, inventories fall because production is less than aggregate demand. In the fourth quarter, inventory declines further until it is entirely depleted because demand still exceeds production. With production levels held constant, finished-goods inventories rise and fall to buffer the differences between aggregate demand and production levels from time period to time period.

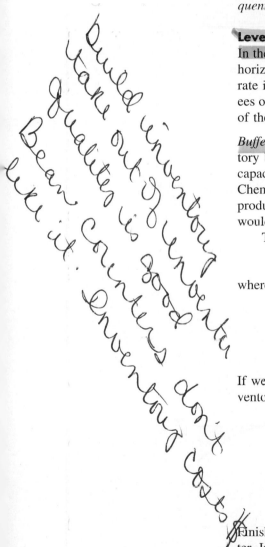

Figure 13.4	Level Capacity: With Inventory, with Backlog, and with Overtime or Subcontracting

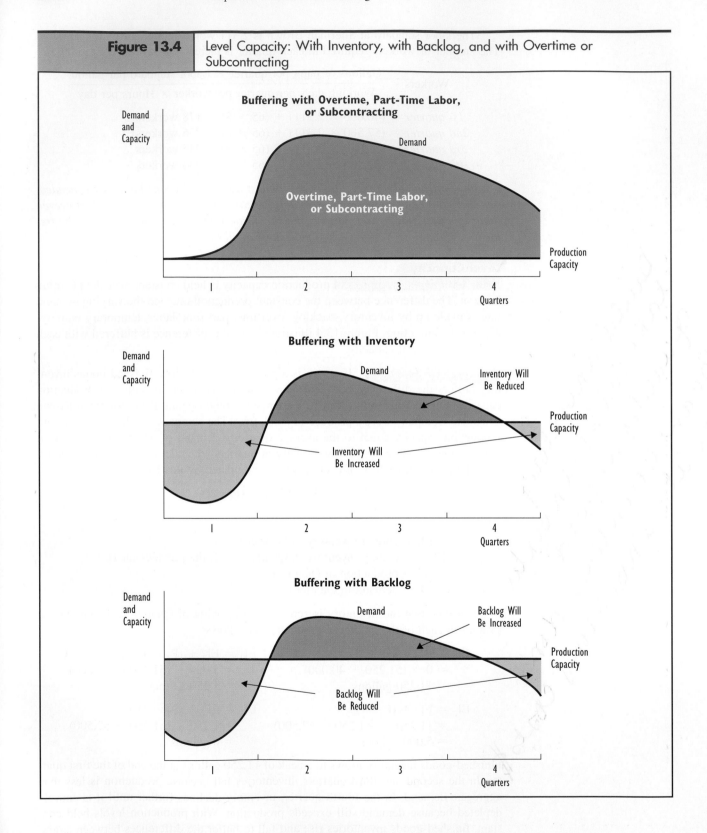

Figure 13.5	Level Capacity: Sherman-Brown Chemical Company—Produce-to-Stock

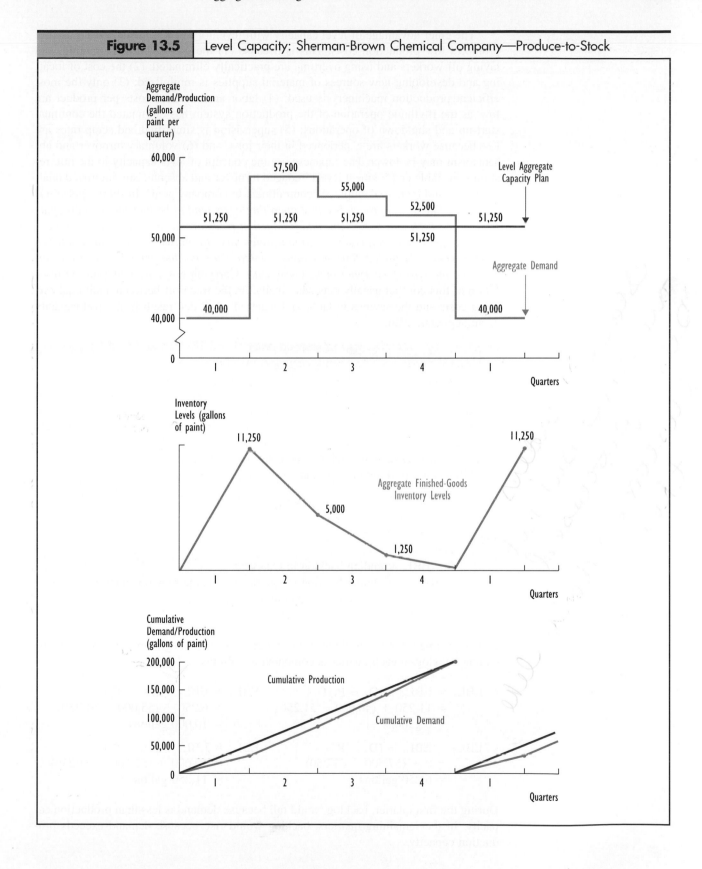

The chief advantage of level capacity with inventory is that this approach usually promotes low production costs. This is because (1) the costs of hiring, training, and laying off workers and using overtime are practically eliminated; (2) the cost of locating and developing new sources of material supplies is minimized; (3) only the most efficient production machinery is used; (4) labor and material costs per product are low, as the rhythmic operation of the production system has eliminated the continual start-up and shutdown of operations; (5) supervision is simplified and scrap rates are low because workers are experienced in their jobs; and (6) voluntary turnover and absenteeism may be lower. The Japanese use the concept of level capacity to the hilt, resulting in stable employment levels, reduced turnover and absenteeism, improved quality levels, and increased employee commitment to company goals. In short, *operations managers like this approach because operating costs tend to be low, quality of outputs tends to be high and consistent, and production rates are usually dependable. Financial managers, however, typically do not prefer this alternative because this approach usually results in higher finished-goods inventory levels, thus tying up cash and increasing the cost of carrying these inventories.* Carrying costs are real, and the resolution of this conflict usually depends, finally, on the trade-off between additional carrying costs and the savings in labor and material costs that result from level capacity as an aggregate plan.

Buffering with Backlog. In produce-to-order firms, backlog serves the purpose of buffering the difference between a varying demand rate and a constant production rate. A backlog of customer orders is simply a stack of customer orders that have been received but not yet produced or shipped. Figure 13.6 shows how a level capacity plan would operate if the Sherman-Brown Chemical Company were a produce-to-order firm. The company would set its constant production capacity equal to the average quarterly demand of 51,250 gallons, and it would allow backlog to make up the difference between the varying demand rate and the constant production rate.

The ending backlog of each quarter is computed by this formula:

$$EBL_t = EBL_{t-1} + (D_t - P_t)$$

where:

EBL_t = ending backlog in Quarter t
EBL_{t-1} = ending backlog in Quarter t − 1, the previous quarter
P_t = production in Quarter t
D_t = demand in Quarter t

If it is assumed that the backlog is 11,250 gallons at the beginning of Quarter 1, the ending backlog in each quarter is computed as follows:

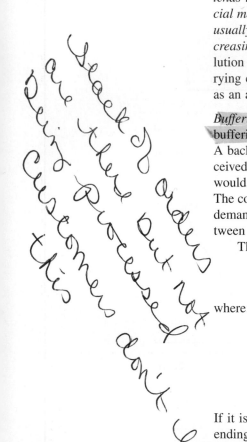

$$EBL_1 = EBL_0 + (D_1 - P_1)$$
$$= 11,250 + (40,000 - 51,250)$$
$$= 0 \text{ gallons}$$

$$EBL_2 = EBL_1 + (D_2 - P_2)$$
$$= 0 + (57,500 - 51,250)$$
$$= 6,250 \text{ gallons}$$

$$EBL_3 = EBL_2 + (D_3 - P_3)$$
$$= 6,250 + (55,000 - 51,250)$$
$$= 10,000 \text{ gallons}$$

$$EBL_4 = EBL_3 + (D_4 - P_4)$$
$$= 10,000 + (52,500 - 51,250)$$
$$= 11,250 \text{ gallons}$$

During the first quarter, backlog would fall because demand is less than production capacity. In the remaining quarters, backlog would rise because demand exceeds production capacity.

Figure 13.6	Level Capacity: Sherman-Brown Chemical Company—Produce-to-Order

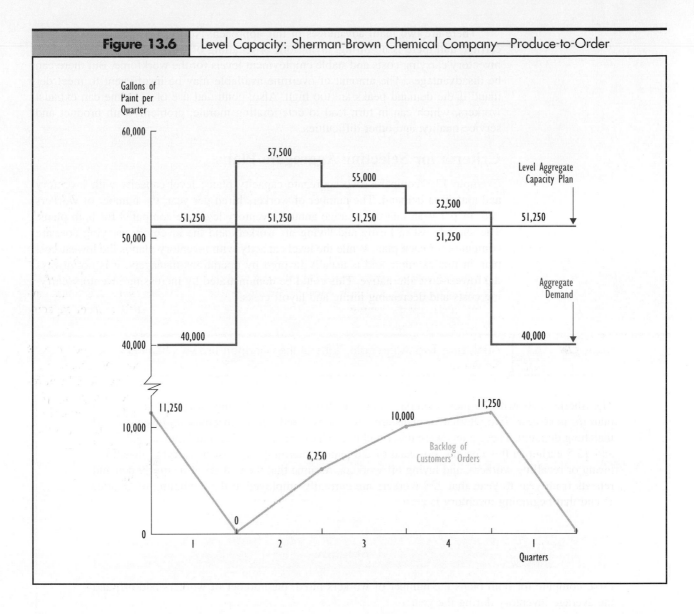

Level capacity with backlog is preferred by operations managers for the same reasons as level capacity with inventory—because low production costs, high and consistent product quality, and dependable production rates result. Produce-to-order firms ordinarily produce custom-designed products. Such firms may have difficulty in developing aggregate capacity plans because of product diversity. The problem is made a little easier if a firm has a large backlog of customer orders, because products can be designed and production can be planned far enough in advance that aggregate production capacity can be planned.

Buffering with Overtime or Subcontracting. Another approach to aggregate capacity planning is to use straight-time labor to provide a production capacity that equals the minimum forecasted demand rate during the planning horizon. Then overtime or subcontracting is used to supply any demand above the minimum. This approach to aggregate capacity planning can be used in either produce-to-stock or produce-to-order firms.

overtime is not cost effective

There are two main advantages of this approach: No finished-goods inventory is carried, and there is no hiring, laying off, or recalling of workers. This results in low inventory carrying costs and stable employment levels for the workforce. But there can be disadvantages. The amount of overtime available may be insufficient to meet demand if the demand peaks are too high. Also, continual use of overtime can exhaust workers, which can in turn lead to deteriorating morale, problems with product and service quality, and other difficulties.

Criteria for Selecting Aggregate Plans

Example 13.1 compares two aggregate capacity plans: level capacity with inventory and matching demand. The number of workers hired per year, the number of workers laid off per year, and the average annual inventory level are computed for both plans. The annual cost of hiring and laying off workers and the inventory carrying cost are computed for each plan. While the level capacity with inventory plan is the lowest-cost plan in this example and is usually favored by operations managers, it is not always the lowest-cost alternative. This could be demonstrated by increasing inventory carrying costs and decreasing hiring and layoff costs.

| **Example 13.1** | Analyzing Two Aggregate Plans at the Sherman-Brown Chemical Company |

The Sherman-Brown Chemical Company is in the process of developing an aggregate capacity plan for next year. Two alternative plans are being considered, level capacity with inventory and matching demand. These plans were described in Business Snapshot 13.1 and Figures 13.2, 13.3, and 13.5 earlier in this chapter. For each of the plans, determine the cost of carrying inventory, hiring or recalling workers, and laying off workers. Assume that the pattern of quarterly demand repeats from year to year, that 228 workers are currently employed at the beginning of Quarter 1, and that beginning inventory is zero.

Solution

First, compute for both plans the number of workers hired, the number of workers laid off, and the average inventory during the year:

(1) Aggregate Plan	(2) Quarter	(3) Aggregate Demand (gallons)	(4) Planned Outputs (gallons)	(5) Workers Required $\left[\dfrac{(4) \times 2.311}{8 \times 65}\right]$	(6) Workers Hired	(7) Workers Laid Off	(8) Inventory Addition or (Subtraction) [(4) − (3)]	(9) Beginning Inventory (gallons)	(10) Ending Inventory (gallons)	(11) Average Inventory per Quarter (gallons) $\left[\dfrac{(9) + (10)}{2}\right]$	(12) Average Inventory per Year (gallons) $\left[\dfrac{\Sigma(11)}{4}\right]$
Level capacity with inventory	1	40,000	51,250	228			11,250	0	11,250	5,625	
	2	57,500	51,250	228			(6,250)	11,250	5,000	8,125	4,375
	3	55,000	51,250	228			(3,750)	5,000	1,250	3,125	
	4	52,500	51,250	228			(1,250)	1,250	0	625	
Matching demand	1	40,000	40,000	178		56	0	0	0	0	
	2	57,500	57,500	256	78		0	0	0	0	0
	3	55,000	55,000	245		11	0	0	0	0	
	4	52,500	52,500	234		11	0	0	0	0	

Next, compute the annual costs for both plans:

(1) Aggregate Plan	(2) Total Annual Number of Workers Hired	(3) Total Annual Number of Workers Laid Off	(4) Average Annual Inventory (gallons)	(5) Annual Hiring Cost [(2) × $250]	(6) Annual Layoff Cost [(3) × $300]	(7) Annual Inventory Carrying Cost [(4) × $5.00]	(8) Total Annual Incremental Operating Cost [(5) + (6) + (7)]
Level capacity	0	0	4,375	$ 0	$ 0	$21,875	$21,875
Matching demand	78	78	0	19,500	23,400	0	42,900

Hiring costs typically include costs incurred in the hiring process, training of new workers, and the cost of products scrapped while workers are learning their jobs. **Lay-off costs** usually include termination pay, unemployment benefits, and so on.

Although Example 13.1 considers only two alternative aggregate plans, several other alternatives could exist in practice. For instance, extra days per week, extra shifts per day, shifts longer than eight hours, overtime, and subcontracting could supply the required capacity in each quarter. Example 13.2 compares two other alternative aggregate plans for Sherman-Brown. The two plans use either overtime or subcontracting to augment a constant straight-time workforce. As the example illustrates, many factors, some of whose effects on costs and profits are difficult to quantify, can be used to evaluate aggregate plans.

Example 13.2 | Level Capacity with Overtime or Subcontracting

The Sherman-Brown Chemical Company has been considering keeping only enough workers employed on straight time per quarter to produce 40,000 gallons. Either subcontracting or overtime would be used to supply the difference between the straight-time production capacity of 40,000 gallons per quarter and the highly variable quarterly demand. Sherman-Brown will furnish the materials and has a quote from a subcontractor for a price of $19.50 per gallon for each gallon supplied, and the subcontractor has guaranteed that it could supply up to 20,000 gallons a quarter. Sherman-Brown's labor union is willing to work as much overtime as necessary to avoid the use of the subcontractor. The cost of overtime pay is $9.50 per hour of overtime worked. **a.** Compute the overtime cost and the subcontracting cost per quarter for the two aggregate plans. **b.** Which factors would be important in deciding between the two plans?

Solution

a.   First, compute the amount of paint that would have to be supplied by either overtime or sub-contracting and determine the cost of each of the alternative plans:

(1) Quarter	(2) Aggregate Demand (gallons)	(3) Gallons to Be Supplied by Overtime or Subcontracting [(2) − 40,000]	(4) Cost of Overtime [(3) × 2.311 × 9.50]	(5) Cost of Subcontracting [(3) × 19.50]
1	40,000	0	$ 0	$ 0
2	57,500	17,500	384,204	341,250
3	55,000	15,000	329,318	292,500
4	52,500	12,500	274,431	243,750
			Total $987,953	$877,500

b. Which factors would be important in deciding between the two plans?

1. The costs developed in the table above are certainly an important factor.

2. Maintaining positive management–union relations is also important. If the workers say that they want to work the amount of overtime that would be necessary, then allowing them to work overtime could prove to be a positive factor in future dealings. The benefits of this factor would have to be weighed against the additional cost of overtime over subcontracting.

3. Fatigue, reduced morale, and increased costs could eventually result from working too much overtime on a continual basis. This factor would be an additional cost that would have to be added to Factor 2 above.

4. Product quality might or might not be better with the overtime plan because all production would be in-house and under the direct control of Sherman-Brown.

5. The flexibility of increasing or decreasing production levels in any quarter appears to be about the same with both alternatives. However, if the subcontracting alternative is selected, overtime could be used to increase production further. On the other hand, if the overtime alternative is selected, decreasing production levels could be made easier by simply reducing overtime.

Aggregate Plans for Services

Some service systems perform aggregate planning in almost the same way as in the Sherman-Brown case. In fact, in some service systems that supply standardized services to customers, aggregate planning may be even simpler than in systems that produce products. Examples of these straightforward aggregate-planning situations in service systems are restaurants, trucking firms, airlines, and banks. Example 13.3 illustrates aggregate capacity planning at an air freight company.

Example 13.3	Aggregate Capacity Planning at the Quick Cargo Air Freight Company

The central terminal at the Quick Cargo Air Freight Company receives air freight from aircraft arriving from all over the United States and redistributes it to aircraft for shipment to all U.S. destinations. The company guarantees overnight shipment of all parcels, so enough personnel must be available to process all cargo as it arrives. The company now has 24 employees working in the terminal. The forecasted demand for warehouse workers for the next seven months is 24, 26, 30, 28, 28, 24, and 24. It costs $2,000 to hire and $3,500 to lay off each worker. If overtime is used to supply labor beyond the present workforce straight-time capacity, it will cost the equivalent of $2,600 more for each additional worker needed. Should the company use a level capacity with overtime or a matching demand plan for the next six months?

Solution

The cost of straight-time labor may be disregarded for purposes of comparing the two plans because it would be included in both plans. The analysis hinges on the overtime cost of the level plan versus the cost of hiring and laying off workers in the matching plan.

First, determine the cost of overtime in the level capacity plan:

	(1)	(2) Number of Workers	(3) Overtime Labor Cost
	Month	Forecasted	[(2) − 24] × $2,600
	1	24	0
	2	26	$ 5,200
	3	30	15,600
	4	28	10,400
	5	28	10,400
	6	24	0
	7	24	0
		Overtime cost	$41,600

Next, determine the hiring and laying-off cost of the matching demand plan:

(1) Month	(2) Number of Workers Required	(3) Number of Workers Hired	(4) Number of Workers Laid Off	(5) Cost of Hired Workers [(3) × $2,000]	(6) Cost of Laid-Off Workers [(4) × $3,500]
0	24				
1	24	0	0	0	0
2	26	2		$ 4,000	
3	30	4		8,000	
4	28		2		$ 7,000
5	28	0	0	0	0
6	24		4		14,000
7	24				
				Cost $12,000	$21,000

The total cost of the matching demand plan is the cost of hiring and laying off workers, or $12,000 + $21,000 = $33,000. The cost of the matching demand plan is less than the level capacity plan with overtime and would be the preferred choice.

Some service systems that supply customized services to customers experience the same difficulty as job shops in specifying the nature and extent of services to be performed for each customer. Examples of these systems are hospitals, computer service centers, and automobile body repair shops. Another complicating factor with many of these customized service systems is that, unlike in job shops, the customer may be an integral part of the production system, and scaling production capacity up or down may directly alter the perceived quality of the delivered services. Examples of these services are small private colleges and universities, exclusive dinner clubs, private country clubs, and private health clinics.

Also particularly worrisome to managers who must plan capacity levels for service systems is the absence of finished-goods inventories as a buffer between system capacity and customer demand. But level capacity plans may still be used if overtime or part-time employees can be used to buffer the difference between the varying demand rate and the constant production rate. This is particularly true in direct worker-to-customer services where no products are processed, stored, or transferred. Examples of these systems are income tax services, legal services, and emergency ambulance and fire-fighting services. Other techniques also encourage the use of level capacity plans. For example, the use of appointment schedules tends to level the peaks and valleys of demand in medical clinics, thus facilitating level capacity plans. Similarly, after-hours windows at banks facilitate level capacity plans. In spite of these innovations, however, many of these systems must develop capacity plans that nearly match the expected aggregate demand.

In service systems that deliver standardized services, we would perform aggregate capacity planning as in Example 13.3. In custom-designed services, we suggest a two-step approach to aggregate planning. First, develop aggregate demand forecasts in some homogeneous units of measurement such as labor-hours, machine capacity, or sales dollars. Second, try to discover common-denominator units of capacity that are helpful in transforming aggregate demand into production resource requirements. Such experimentation may be necessary to develop these conversion factors. Next, particularly if the first suggestion is infeasible, develop alternative innovations for expanding the flexibility of production resource capacities. Examples of these innovations are standby workers who are on call for peak demand periods, machines and buildings that can be activated during peak demand periods, subcontractors who respond quickly, and retired supervisors who wish to work only part-time and can be recalled for short periods. These standby resources provide operations managers a near-level capacity aggregate plan with the extra capacity needed to respond to surges in demand.

Mathematical Models for Aggregate Planning

Several aggregate-planning methods have developed as the use of computers and the operations research discipline has grown. These methods seek to design capacity plans for production systems that achieve organizations' objectives within the availability of their production resources and aggregate demand constraints. Brief descriptions of three such methods are given Table 13.2. Example 13.4 illustrates the approach of linear programming to aggregate planning.

Mathematical models in aggregate planning do not dominate POM practice—not yet, anyway. But you should know about these techniques because their approaches are helpful in structuring the way we think about and approach these complex problems. And models may become more important in capacity planning in the future.

Table 13.2	Mathematical Models for Aggregate Planning

1. **Linear programming.** E. H. Bowman was one of the first to apply linear programming to aggregate planning.[a] Linear programming models seek to minimize total operating costs over the planning horizon and include such costs as straight-time labor costs, overtime costs, subcontracting costs, worker-hiring costs, worker-layoff costs, and inventory-carrying costs. The constraints of the models usually include such factors as the maximum capacity available in each time period from straight-time workers, overtime workers, subcontractors, and new workers, and the minimum cumulative aggregate demand over the planning horizon.

2. **Linear decision rules (LDRs).** Holt, Modigliani, Muth, and Simon of the Carnegie Institute of Technology were the first to use this approach.[b] LDRs develop a quadratic mathematical cost function that includes these costs: regular payroll, hiring, layoff, overtime, inventory carrying, back order or shortage, and setup. The quadratic composite mathematical cost function is solved by calculus or quadratic programming methods. The solution provides the number of workers to be hired or laid off, number of overtime hours required, expected fluctuations in inventories, and machine changeovers.

3. **Computer search.** This approach sequentially examines thousands of combinations of production resources (straight-time labor, overtime, layoffs, hiring, and subcontracting) in each time period to meet the cumulative aggregate demand over a planning horizon. This method uses preprogrammed rules that control the way resources can be combined to select a low-cost capacity plan for each time period.

[a]Bowman, E. H. "Production Planning by the Transportation Method of Linear Programming." *Journal of Operations Research Society* 4 (February 1956): 100–103.
[b]Holt, Charles C., Franco Modigliani, John F. Muth, and Herbert A. Simon. *Planning Production, Inventories, and Work Force.* Englewood Cliffs, NJ: Prentice Hall, 1960.

Example 13.4	Using Linear Programming to Analyze an Aggregate-Planning Problem

A production scheduler must develop an aggregate plan for the next two quarters of next year. The highly automated plant produces graphics terminals for the computer products market. The company estimates that 700 terminals will need to be shipped to customers in the first quarter and 3,200 in the second quarter. It takes an average of 5 hours of labor to produce each terminal, and only 9,000 hours of straight-time labor is available in each of the quarters. Overtime can be used, but the company has a policy of limiting the amount of overtime in each quarter to 10 percent of the straight-time labor available. Labor costs $12 per hour at the straight-time rate and $18 per hour at the overtime rate. If a terminal is produced in one quarter and shipped in the next quarter, a carrying cost of $50 is incurred. How many terminals should be produced on straight time and overtime in each of the first and second quarters to minimize straight-time labor, overtime labor, and carrying costs? **a.** Formulate this aggregate-planning problem as a linear programming problem. Define the decision variables, formulate the objective function, and formulate the constraint functions. **b.** Solve this problem using the *POM Software Library* that accompanies this book. What is the solution to the problem? What is the aggregate plan?

Solution

a. Formulate this aggregate-planning problem as a linear programming problem. Define the decision variables:

X_1 = number of terminals to be produced on straight time in the first quarter and shipped in the first quarter

X_2 = number of terminals to be produced on overtime in the first quarter and shipped in the first quarter

X_3 = number of terminals to be produced on straight time in the first quarter and shipped in the second quarter

X_4 = number of terminals to be produced on overtime in the first quarter and shipped in the second quarter

X_5 = number of terminals to be produced on straight time in the second quarter and shipped in the second quarter

X_6 = number of terminals to be produced on overtime in the second quarter and shipped in the second quarter

The coefficients of the objective function are computed as follows:

$$
\begin{array}{llll}
X_1: & 5 \times 12 = \$\,60 & X_4: & (5 \times 18) + 50 = \$140 \\
X_2: & 5 \times 18 = 90 & X_5: & 5 \times 12 = 60 \\
X_3: & (5 \times 12) + 50 = 110 & X_6: & 5 \times 18 = 90
\end{array}
$$

$$\text{Min } Z = 60X_1 + 90X_2 + 110X_3 + 140X_4 + 60X_5 + 90X_6$$

$$
\begin{array}{rll}
\text{Min } Z = \ \ X_1 + X_2 & \geq 700 & Q_1 \text{ demand} \\
X_3 + X_4 + X_5 + X_6 & \geq 3{,}200 & Q_2 \text{ demand} \\
5X_1 + 5X_3 & \leq 9{,}000 & Q_1 \text{ straight-time labor} \\
5X_5 & \leq 9{,}000 & Q_2 \text{ straight-time labor} \\
5X_2 + 5X_4 & \leq 900 & Q_1 \text{ overtime labor} \\
5X_6 & \leq 900 & Q_2 \text{ overtime labor}
\end{array}
$$

The solution to this linear programming problem is:

X_1 = 580 terminals to be produced on straight time in the first quarter and shipped during the first quarter

X_2 = 120 terminals to be produced on overtime in the first quarter and shipped during the first quarter

X_3 = 1,220 terminals to be produced on straight time in the first quarter and shipped during the second quarter

X_4 = 0 terminals to be produced on overtime in the first quarter and shipped during the second quarter

X_5 = 1,800 terminals to be produced on straight time in the second quarter and shipped during the second quarter

X_6 = 180 terminals to be produced on overtime in the second quarter and shipped in the second quarter

S_5 = 300 hours of unused overtime labor in the first quarter

Z = \$304,000 total cost of straight time and overtime labor and carrying cost for the aggregate plan

S_1, S_2, S_3, S_4, and S_6 = 0

Preemptive Tactics

From our discussion of aggregate planning, it may seem that management cannot affect the patterns of demand and that dealing with the peaks and valleys of demand is a necessary part of aggregate planning. While this is partially true, management can engage in activities that will reduce extreme peaks and valleys of demand. Companies often publish **discount prices** that are in effect during demand valleys and higher **peak-load prices** that are in effect for demand peaks. Such pricing tactics tend to motivate customers to place fewer orders during peak demand periods and more orders during periods with demand valleys. Similarly, companies can influence demand patterns with such tactics as baker's dozen promotions, delayed billings, and freight-free shipments during low demand periods. In these ways, customer demand becomes more uniform and aggregate planning becomes more straightforward.

We have discussed the major concepts, issues, and techniques of aggregate planning—the development of medium-range capacity plans for production systems. These plans directly impinge on the day-to-day scheduling of products and services. Master production scheduling is the starting point for these day-to-day schedules.

MASTER PRODUCTION SCHEDULING

Another important part of production planning is master production scheduling. The **master production schedule (MPS)** sets the quantity of each end item to be completed in each week of the short-range planning horizon. End items are finished products, or parts that are shipped as end items. End items may be shipped to customers or placed in inventory. *Operations managers weekly meet to review market forecasts, customer orders, inventory levels, facility loading, and capacity information so that master production schedules can be developed.* The MPS is a plan for future production of end items over a short-range planning horizon that usually spans from a few weeks to several months.

Objectives of Master Production Scheduling

As Figure 13.1 illustrated, short-range production capacity is constrained by the aggregate capacity plan. Master production scheduling takes this short-range production capacity that was determined by the aggregate plan and allocates it to orders for end items. The objectives of master production scheduling are twofold:

1. To schedule end items to be completed promptly and when promised to customers
2. To avoid overloading or underloading the production facility so that production capacity is efficiently utilized and low production costs result

Time Fences in Master Production Schedules

Master production schedules can be viewed as being divided into four sections, each section separated by a point in time that is called a **time fence**. The first section includes the first few weeks of the schedule and is referred to as frozen; the next section of a few weeks is referred to as firm; the next section of a few weeks is referred to as full; and the last section of a few weeks is referred to as open.

Frozen means that this early part of the MPS cannot be changed except under extraordinary circumstances and only with authorization from the highest levels in the organization. Change in this section of the schedule is ordinarily prohibited because it would be costly to reverse the plans to purchase materials and produce the parts that go into the products. Moreover, when we change the MPS, we move one order in ahead of another one—why make one customer happy at the expense of making another one unhappy? Firm means that changes can occur in this section of the schedule, but only in exceptional situations. Changes are resisted in this section of the schedule for the same reasons as in the frozen section. Full means that all the available production capacity has been allocated to orders. Changes in the full section of the schedule can be made and production costs will be only slightly affected, but the effect on customer satisfaction is uncertain. Open means that not all the production capacity has been allocated, and it is in this section of the schedule that new orders are ordinarily slotted.

Procedures for Developing Master Production Schedules

Figure 13.7 illustrates the process for developing the master production schedule. Working from customer orders, forecasts, inventory status reports, and production capacity information, schedulers place the most urgent orders in the earliest available open slot of the MPS. Several important activities occur at this point. First, the schedulers must estimate the total demand for products from all sources, assign orders to production slots, make delivery promises to customers, and make the detailed calculations for the MPS. Example 13.5 illustrates how a scheduler might total the demands and perform the detailed calculations for an MPS. The activities of order entry and order promising are discussed in the demand management section that follows.

Example 13.5	Developing a Master Production Schedule

A firm produces two products, A and B, on a produce-to-stock basis. The demands for the products come from many sources. The demand estimates for the two products over the next six weeks are given below.

Demands for Product A from All Sources

Sources of Demand	Weekly Demand (number of product A's)					
	1	**2**	**3**	**4**	**5**	**6**
Intercompany orders				20	10	10
Branch warehouse orders			20			
R&D orders			10	10		
Customer demand (forecasts and in-hand orders)	20	20	20	20	20	20
Total Demands for Product A	20	20	50	50	30	30

Demands for Product B from All Sources

Sources of Demand	Weekly Demand (number of product B's)					
	1	**2**	**3**	**4**	**5**	**6**
Intercompany orders			10		10	
Branch warehouse orders				20		
R&D orders					10	10
Customer demand (forecasts and in-hand orders)	30	30	30	20	20	20
Total Demands for Product B	30	30	40	40	40	30

The safety stock is the minimum level of planned inventory. The safety stock for A is 30 and for B it is 40. The fixed lot size (a *lot* means a batch, and the lot size is produced when production of the product occurs) for A is 50 and for B it is 60. The beginning inventory for A is 70 and for B it is 50. Prepare an MPS for these two products.

Solution

For each product, take the total demands, consider beginning inventory, determine in which weeks ending inventory would fall below the safety stock (SS) and thus require production, and schedule a lot of the product to be produced during those weeks.

| **Figure 13.7** | The Master Production Scheduling Process |

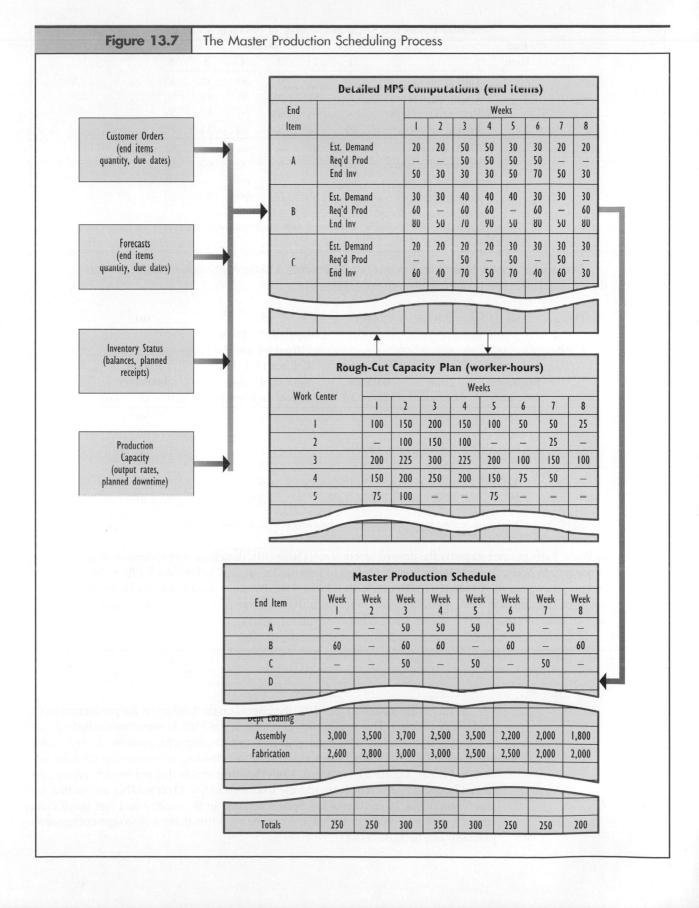

Customer Orders
(end items
quantity, due dates)

Forecasts
(end items
quantity, due dates)

Inventory Status
(balances, planned
receipts)

Production
Capacity
(output rates,
planned downtime)

Detailed MPS Computations (end items)

End Item		Weeks							
		1	2	3	4	5	6	7	8
A	Est. Demand	20	20	50	50	30	30	20	20
	Req'd Prod	—	—	50	50	50	50	—	—
	End Inv	50	30	30	30	50	70	50	30
B	Est. Demand	30	30	40	40	40	30	30	30
	Req'd Prod	60	—	60	60	—	60	—	60
	End Inv	80	50	70	90	50	80	50	80
C	Est. Demand	20	20	20	20	30	30	30	30
	Req'd Prod	—	—	50	—	50	—	50	—
	End Inv	60	40	70	50	70	40	60	30

Rough-Cut Capacity Plan (worker-hours)

Work Center	Weeks							
	1	2	3	4	5	6	7	8
1	100	150	200	150	100	50	50	25
2	—	100	150	100	—	—	25	—
3	200	225	300	225	200	100	150	100
4	150	200	250	200	150	75	50	—
5	75	100	—	—	75	—	—	—

Master Production Schedule

End Item	Week 1	Week 2	Week 3	Week 4	Week 5	Week 6	Week 7	Week 8
A	—	—	50	50	50	50		—
B	60	—	60	60	—	60	—	60
C	—	—	50	—	50	—	50	—
D								

Dept Loading								
Assembly	3,000	3,500	3,700	2,500	3,500	2,200	2,000	1,800
Fabrication	2,600	2,800	3,000	3,000	2,500	2,500	2,000	2,000

| Totals | 250 | 250 | 300 | 350 | 300 | 250 | 250 | 200 |

Master Production Schedule (Number of Products A and B)

End Item		Weeks					
		1	2	3	4	5	6
A	Total demand	20	20	50	50	30	30
	Beginning inventory	70	50	30	30	30	50
	Required production	—	—	50	50	50	50
	Ending inventory	50	30	30	30	50	70
B	Total demand	30	30	40	40	40	30
	Beginning inventory	50	80	50	70	90	50
	Required production	60	—	60	60	—	60
	Ending inventory	80	50	70	90	50	80

Note: Safety stocks are 30 for A and 40 for B, fixed lot sizes are 50 for A and 60 for B, and beginning inventory in Week 1 is 70 for A and 50 for B.

Let us take a closer look at the calculations for Product A in the MPS above. Follow through these computations and compare them to the MPS:

(1)	(2)	(3)	(4)	(5)	(6)
				Required Production [fixed lot size if Column (4) is less than safety stock; if not, then zero]	**Ending Inventory** [(2) + (5) − (3)]
Week	**Beginning Inventory**	**Total Demand**	**Balance** [(2) − (3)]		
1	70	20	50	—	50
2	50	20	30	—	30
3	30	50	(20)	50	30
4	30	50	(20)	50	30
5	30	30	0	50	50
6	50	30	20	50	70

Note: For Product A, safety stock is 30, fixed lot size is 50, and beginning inventory in Week 1 is 70.

In Week 1 the balance exceeds the desired safety stock (50 > 30); therefore, no production of A is needed. In Week 2 the balance is also enough to provide the desired safety stock (30 = 30) and no production of A is required. But in Weeks 3 and 4 the balances would actually be negative if production of A were not scheduled; therefore, a fixed lot size of 50 Product A's is scheduled in both of these weeks. Weeks 5 and 6 are computed similarly.

As orders are slotted in the MPS, the effects on the loading of the production work centers are checked. This preliminary checking of the MPS is sometimes called **rough-cut capacity planning**. The main goal in rough-cut capacity planning is to identify any week in the MPS where underloading or overloading of production capacity occurs and revise the MPS as required. **Underloading** means that not enough production of end items has been scheduled to fully load the facility. **Overloading** means that too much production of end items has been scheduled in the facility and that insufficient capacity exists to produce the MPS. Example 13.6 illustrates how rough-cut capacity planning can be carried out.

Example 13.6 | Rough-Cut Capacity Planning

The firm in Example 13.5 now wishes to determine if the MPS that was developed underloads or overloads the final assembly line that produces both Product A and Product B. The final assembly line has a weekly capacity of 100 hours available. Each Product A requires 0.9 hour and each Product B requires 1.6 hours of final assembly capacity. **a.** Compute the actual final assembly hours required to produce the MPS for both products; this is often referred to as the *load*. Compare the load to the final assembly capacity available in each week and for the total 6 weeks; this is often referred to as *rough-cut capacity planning*. **b.** Does sufficient final assembly capacity exist to produce the MPS? **c.** What changes to the MPS would you recommend?

Solution

a. Compute the load in each week and for the six weeks, and compare the load to the final assembly capacity:

End Item				Weekly Final Assembly Hours				
		1	2	3	4	5	6	Total
A	Production	—	—	(50)	(50)	(50)	(50)	
	Final assembly hours	—	—	45	45	45	45	
B	Production	(60)		(60)	(60)		(60)	
	Final assembly hours	96	—	96	96	—	96	
Load (hours)		96	—	141	141	45	141	564
Capacity (hours)		100	100	100	100	100	100	600

Note: The numbers in parentheses are the numbers of end items to be produced in each week. They come from the MPS in Example 13.5.

b. A total of 600 hours of final assembly capacity is available over the six-week schedule, and the MPS requires only a total of 564 hours. However, the MPS overloads final assembly in Weeks 3, 4, and 6, and it underloads final assembly in Weeks 1, 2, and 5.

c. A better balance of weekly final assembly capacity is possible if some of the production lots are moved into earlier weeks of the schedule. Move lots of Product A from Weeks 4 and 6 into Weeks 3 and 5, and move the lot of Product B from Week 3 into Week 2:

End Item				Weekly Final Assembly Hours				
		1	2	3	4	5	6	Total
A	Production	—	—	(100)	—	(100)	—	
	Final assembly hours	—	—	90	—	90	—	
B	Production	(60)	(60)	—	(60)	—	(60)	
	Final assembly hours	96	96	—	96	—	96	
Load (hours)		96	96	90	96	90	96	564
Capacity (hours)		100	100	100	100	100	100	600

Note: The numbers in parentheses are the numbers of end items to be produced in each week.

This revised MPS would better load the final assembly line, but some additional inventory would be created by producing these lots earlier.

Order entry is an important function in master production scheduling.

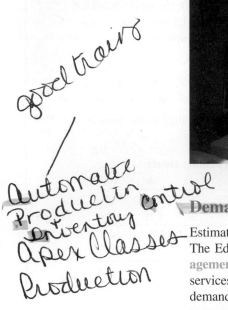

good trains

Automate Production Inventory control Systems Apex Classes Production

Demand Management

Estimating future demand is a crucial part of master production scheduling. APICS—The Educational Society for Resource Management—describes this as demand management, which is defined as "the function of recognizing all demands for goods and services to support the marketplace. It involves doing what is required to help make the demand happen and prioritizing demand when supply is lacking. Proper demand management facilitates the planning and use of resources for profitable business results. It encompasses the activities of forecasting, order entry, order promising, and determining branch warehouse requirements, interplant orders, and service parts requirements."[1] Demand management includes establishing an effective forecasting system for the end items, monitoring the forecasts, and changing the system as required to improve forecasts.

Order entry and order promising are important functions in master production scheduling. Master schedulers must review the customer orders, check the requested delivery dates against the open production slots in the MPS, determine the priority of the orders, assign production slots in the MPS to the orders, and communicate the promised dates to the customers. Each promised date guides an order through the production processes and becomes an important goal of operations managers until the order is delivered to the customer. Interplant orders come from inside the company. Marketing orders products as samples to give to customers for promotion, R&D orders products to be used in tests, and branch warehouses order products. Service parts are ordinarily ordered by distributors to be used in warranty or repair work. The orders for these parts are treated in master production scheduling like other customer orders except that the parts are treated as end items and thus become part of the MPS.

Weekly Updating of the MPS

To truly understand the nature of demand management, we must understand the dynamic nature of the MPS. The MPS is usually updated weekly, meaning that after one week has passed, one week is taken off the front end of the MPS, one week is added on to the back end, and the demands for the whole MPS are estimated anew. Because the demands that are far out in the later periods of the MPS are likely to be changed as they undergo many updates while moving toward the early, frozen part of the schedule, the accuracy of the forecasts in the latter part of the MPS are not as critical as in the earlier part. Also, the early part of the MPS tends to be dominated by actual in-hand customer orders, whereas the latter part of the schedule tends to be dominated by forecasts. Thus, the demand estimates of the early part of the MPS are by nature more accurate.

Figure 13.8 illustrates this principle. In Weeks 1 and 2 the demand estimate is made up entirely of orders. In Week 8 the demand estimate is made up entirely of forecasts. In the middle of the schedule the demand estimate is a combination of actual orders and forecasts, but forecasts become more predominant as we move into later periods. Through the weekly updating process, demand estimates in later periods of the MPS, which are based principally on forecasts, move forward in the MPS, and these demand estimates become more accurate for two reasons. First, much of the demand based on forecasts becomes based more on customer orders, and second, the forecasts become refined through the weekly updating process. Week after week as the MPS is updated, orders are flowing in and forecasts are being modified, and all of this is occurring before money must be committed to ordering materials, scheduling workers, and scheduling machine changeovers. By the time an order moves into the early, frozen portion of the MPS and money must be committed to the order, operations managers are able to place much confidence in the accuracy of the demand estimates.

MPS in Produce-to-Stock and Produce-to-Order Firms

Master production scheduling procedures differ according to whether a firm is a produce-to-stock or produce-to-order production system. The elements of the MPS that are affected most by the type of production system are **demand management,** lot-sizing, and **number of products to schedule.**

| Figure 13.8 | Demand Estimates: A Blend of Orders and Forecasts |

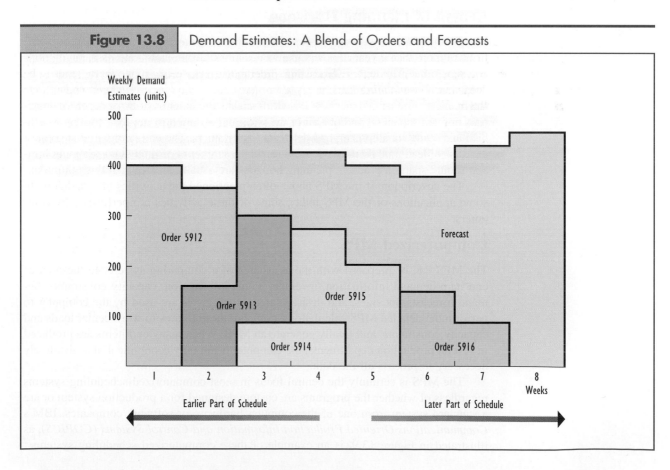

In produce-to-order systems, customer orders are the predominant focus in demand management. The master production scheduler usually works from a backlog of customer orders, and product demand forecasts may not be used. Customer orders in the backlog are assigned open production slots as we described earlier in the demand management section. The lot size, the number of products to produce on an order, is usually determined by the customer order. If a customer orders 500 of a particular product, ordinarily 500 of the products will be produced on the order. This approach to lot-sizing is called **lot-for-lot (LFL)**.

In produce-to-stock firms, the orders for products come principally from warehouse orders within the company. These orders are based on forecasts of future demand for products from many customers. Forecasts therefore tend to play a more important part in demand management in produce-to-stock firms. In the early part of the MPS, these warehouse orders that were based on forecasts may be backed up by actual customer orders. However, in produce-to-stock firms, customer orders only indirectly affect demand management by affecting warehouse orders.

The lot sizes of orders in produce-to-stock firms are a matter of economics. How many of a particular product should be produced, when we set up to produce the product, so that the average unit production cost is low? If we produce too few of the product, the fixed cost of getting ready to produce the order is spread over too few products and the average unit production cost is high. If we produce too many of the product, the inventory of the product will grow too large as we produce the order, the cost of carrying the inventory will be too high, and the average unit production cost will be too high also. A balance must be struck between these costs in determining economic lot sizes in produce-to-stock firms.

Length of Planning Horizons

The planning horizons in master scheduling may vary from just a few weeks in some firms to more than a year in others. How does a firm decide how long its planning horizon should be? Although several factors impinge on this decision, one factor tends to be dominant. *The planning horizon should at least equal the longest cumulative end item lead time.* Cumulative end item lead time means the amount of time to get the materials in from suppliers, produce all of the parts and assemblies, get the end item assembled and ready for shipment, and deliver it to customers. The end item with the greatest cumulative lead time therefore determines the least amount of time that a planning horizon should span. In practice, planning horizons are usually greater than this minimum.

The description of the MPS above often mentioned the activities of schedulers. In some applications of the MPS today, some of these activities are performed by computers.

Computerized MPS

The MPS can be prepared with the assistance of a computing system. In these cases end item demand information, inventory status information, capacity constraints, demand forecasts, lot sizes, and desired safety stock levels are used by the computer to perform the detailed MPS calculations, compare these figures to work center loads and capacity constraints, and finally generate an MPS. When many end items are produced in several production departments, the computer is not only economical, it is absolutely necessary to process all the data.

The MPS is certainly the central focus in most computerized scheduling systems regardless of whether the programs are custom designed for a production system or are a standard system from one of the computer hardware or software companies. IBM's *Communications Oriented Production Information and Control Systems (COPICS)*, as illustrated in Figure 13.9, is an example of these computerized scheduling systems.[2]

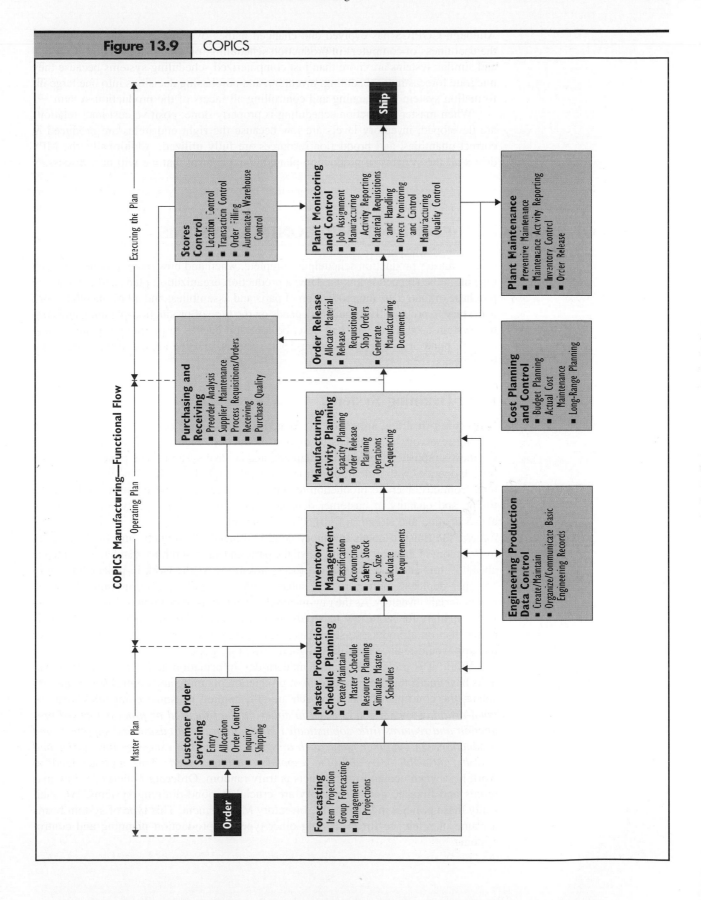

Figure 13.9 | COPICS

COPICS Manufacturing—Functional Flow

Master Plan — Operating Plan — Executing the Plan

Order

Customer Order Servicing
- Entry
- Allocation
- Order Control
- Inquiry
- Shipping

Forecasting
- Item Projection
- Group Forecasting
- Management Projections

Master Production Schedule Planning
- Create/Maintain Master Schedule
- Resource Planning
- Simulate Master Schedules

Inventory Management
- Classification
- Accounting
- Safety Stock
- Lot Size
- Calculate Requirements

Manufacturing Activity Planning
- Capacity Planning
- Order Release Planning
- Operations Sequencing

Purchasing and Receiving
- Preorder Analysis
- Supplier Maintenance
- Process Requisitions/Orders
- Receiving
- Purchase Quality

Order Release
- Allocate Material
- Release Requisitions/ Shop Orders
- Generate Manufacturing Documents

Stores Control
- Location Control
- Transaction Control
- Order Filling
- Automated Warehouse Control

Plant Monitoring and Control
- Job Assignment
- Manufacturing Activity Reporting
- Material Requisitions and Handling
- Direct Monitoring and Control
- Manufacturing Quality Control

Plant Maintenance
- Preventive Maintenance
- Maintenance Activity Reporting
- Inventory Control
- Order Release

Cost Planning and Control
- Budget Planning
- Actual Cost Maintenance
- Long-Range Planning

Engineering Production Data Control
- Create/Maintain
- Organize/Communicate Basic Engineering Records

Ship

Although COPICS has evolved and changed names over the years, it still illustrates the usefulness of computers in production scheduling, planning, and control. COPICS and similar systems are more than just computerized scheduling systems because they integrate forecasting, scheduling, inventory, and purchasing decisions into one large information system for planning and controlling all facets of the production system.

When master production scheduling is properly done, positive customer relations are developed, inventory levels are low because the right end items are produced in correct quantities, and production resources are fully utilized. Additionally, the MPS drives all the systems of production planning and control that we will now discuss.

TYPES OF PRODUCTION-PLANNING AND CONTROL SYSTEMS

Once a master production schedule is complete, when and how many products of each type are to be shipped is known. How a production organization plans and controls the purchase of materials, the production of parts and assemblies, and all of the other work necessary to produce the products depends on the type of production-planning and control system used. Here we shall describe four approaches to production planning and control: pond draining, push systems, pull systems, and the approach that focuses on bottlenecks.

Pond-Draining Systems

In the **pond-draining approach** to production planning and control, the emphasis is on holding reservoirs of materials to support production. Figure 13.10 describes perhaps the most simplistic of production planning and control systems. The pond-draining approach operates with little information passing through the chain of the production system, from customers to production to suppliers. Because producers may not know the timing and quantity of customer demand, many products of each type are produced ahead of time and stored in finished-goods inventory. As shipments are made to customers, the finished-goods inventory pond is drained of products, and final assembly makes more of them by draining down the parts and subassemblies that have been made ahead of time and held in work-in-process inventory. As the work-in-process inventory becomes depleted, more parts and subassemblies are produced by draining down the raw materials inventory. As the raw-materials inventory is drawn down, orders are placed with suppliers for more raw materials. If a firm operates on a produce-to-order basis rather than on a produce-to-stock basis as depicted in Figure 13.10, a customer order backlog would replace the finished-goods inventory pond.

While it is probably true that modern-day information and communication systems have made this simplistic form of production planning and control somewhat obsolete, the concepts of this approach are still applied by some companies today. *A pond-draining system can be used in either product-focused or process-focused production and requires little sophisticated information about customers, suppliers, and production. On the other hand, such a system may lead to excessive inventories and is rather inflexible in its ability to respond to customer needs.* This approach tends to work best when demand for products is truly random. Ordering policies for raw materials and finished-goods inventory are crucial to pond-draining systems. We shall study these policies in Chapter 14, Inventory Management. This type of system forms a frame of reference for discussing other types of production planning and control systems.

| Figure 13.10 | The Pond-Draining Approach to Production Planning and Control |

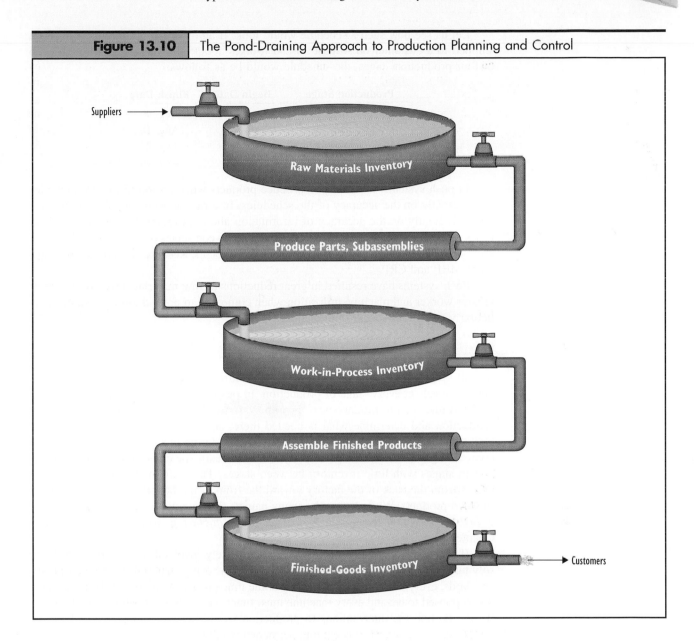

Push Systems

In a push system, the emphasis shifts to using information about customers, suppliers, and production to manage material flows. Batches of raw materials are planned to arrive at a factory about when needed to make batches of parts and subassemblies. Parts and subassemblies are made and delivered to final assembly about when needed, and finished products are assembled and shipped about when needed by customers. *Batches of materials are pushed into the back doors of factories one after the other, which in turn pushes other batches through all of the stages of production. These flows of materials are planned and controlled by a series of production schedules that state when batches of each particular product should come out of each stage of production.* "This is a push system: Make the parts and send them to where they are next needed, or to inventory, thus pushing material through production according to schedule."[3]

Let us see how such a schedule would look. If an order for 500 products must be shipped to a customer on August 30 and it takes about one week to go through each of four production stages, the schedule would be as follows:

Production Stage	Begin Date	Finish Date
Purchase material	Aug. 3	Aug. 9
Produce parts kit	Aug. 10	Aug. 16
Make subassemblies	Aug. 17	Aug. 23
Final assembly	Aug. 24	Aug. 30

In push systems, the ability to produce products when promised to customers depends greatly on the accuracy of the schedules. In turn, the accuracy of the schedules depends greatly on the accuracy of information about customer demand and on lead times—how long it will take for orders to move between stages of production. We study more about how to prepare such schedules in Chapter 15, Resource Requirements Planning: MRP and CRP.

Push systems have resulted in great reductions of raw-materials inventories and in greater worker and machine utilization when compared to pond-draining systems, particularly in process-focused production.

Pull Systems

In pull systems of production planning and control, the emphasis is on reducing inventory levels at every stage of production. In push systems, we look at the schedule to determine what to produce next. In **pull systems,** we look only at the next stage of production and determine what is needed there, and then we produce only that. As Hall states, "You don't never make nothin' and *send* it no place. Somebody has got to come and get it."[4] Products go directly from upstream stages of production to downstream stages with little inventory between stages. Thus, raw materials and parts are pulled from the back of the factory toward the front of the factory where they become finished products. While known by many names, the commonly accepted name today is *just-in-time (JIT) manufacturing*, or *lean manufacturing*, which was discussed in Chapter 12.

JIT requires operations managers to be intensely involved in shop-floor problem solving. With in-process inventories stripped away, every material must meet quality standards, every part must arrive exactly at the time promised and precisely at the place it is supposed to be, and every machine must function as intended without breakdowns. If they do not, the interruptions to production would be intolerable. In JIT systems, therefore, enormous effort is put into permanently eliminating each problem as it arises so that production is not interrupted again for that problem. For this reason, operations managers do not undertake JIT lightly.

Certain changes to the factory and the way it is managed must occur before JIT can be successful. To simplify production, production levels must remain relatively constant for long periods. This can be achieved by the use of inventory to buffer the difference between demand variability and level production capacity, or managers must engage in preemptive tactics to level out customer demand for products. We discussed these tactics earlier in this chapter. Also, the amount of work required to change over machines to other products must be drastically reduced. If this is not achieved, the great number of small batches of products required in JIT would result in exorbitant changeover costs.

The successful applications of JIT have been predominantly in smaller, more focused factories and in repetitive manufacturing. Repetitive manufacturing means producing standardized products along production lines. The complexity of job shops is an obstacle to the use of JIT. Proponents of JIT argue that JIT can be successful in job shops because many operations can be made to behave like repetitive manufacturing. The presence of successful JIT applications in job shops would seem to support this contention.

The benefits of JIT programs are so compelling that there is no wonder JIT is so popular today. Reduced inventories, faster delivery of products, improved product quality, and lower production costs are potent arguments for converting some push systems to pull systems.

Focusing on Bottlenecks

Some production-planning and control systems focus on production bottlenecks—operations, machines, or stages of production that impede production because they have less capacity than upstream or downstream stages. At bottleneck operations, batches of products arrive faster than they can be completed. Thus, these operations are binding capacity constraints that control the capacity of an entire factory.

Theory of Constraints (TOC)

The production control approach of managing bottlenecks, or constraint management, was popularized by Dr. Eliyahu Goldratt. He refers to this approach or philosophy as the **theory of constraints (TOC)**, and he has presented seminars on TOC around the world to all types of industry and academic groups. Some people refer to this philosophy of TOC as **synchronous manufacturing**, because all parts of the entire organization work together to achieve the organization's goals.

The concepts of TOC were developed by Dr. Goldratt into computer software called **optimized production technology (OPT)**. Today OPT continues to be improved and marketed by Scheduling Technology Group Ltd. (**http://www.stg.co.uk**), of London, England.

OPT is a complete production-planning and control information system that is particularly appropriate for complex job-shop environments. By developing the amount of work to be done at each work center, OPT, given a mix of products, finds the bottlenecks in the production processes. If a product must go through a series of operations, no matter how fast other operations in the series are, the capacity of the bottleneck determines the capacity of the series. It is at this point that OPT exhibits its advantage over other systems. Once the bottlenecks have been located, OPT uses a group of proprietary algorithms to schedule the workers, machines, and tools at the bottleneck work centers.

To illustrate the effects of TOC, Dr. Goldratt and Jeff Cox wrote *The Goal: A Process of Ongoing Improvement*, an intriguing and highly readable fictional work that dramatically illustrates the implementation of TOC in a factory.[5] Alex Rogo, a factory manager who is the main character in *The Goal*, searches for a way to save his factory, which is about to be deep-sixed by an uncaring and ignorant top management. By following the advice of Jonah, a consultant who continually asks easily understood questions that have very difficult answers, the factory survives. Dr. Goldratt later wrote *It's Not Luck*, another highly readable fictional work that is a companion book to *The Goal*.[6] He also wrote *Critical Chain*, which applies TOC concepts to project management,[7] and *Necessary But Not Sufficient*, which applies TOC concepts to high-tech and computer software companies.[8]

The process followed by the factory manager in *The Goal* is at the heart of TOC. First, the factory manager measures the production rates of the major operations in the factory. He discovers one operation that is much slower than all the others—a bottleneck.

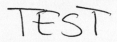

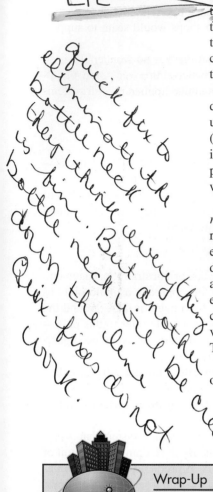

LIE

quick fix to eliminate the bottleneck. They think everything is fine. But another bottle neck will be created down the line. Quick fixes do not work.

Next, he asks a team of his best people to come up with ways to increase the production rate of the bottleneck operation. Then, after the production rate of the bottleneck operation is increased, the whole factory's production rate is observed to increase. The team then goes to the next slowest operation and repeats the process. The output of the factory increases as the production rate of each bottleneck operation is increased. This procedure results in the production rate of the factory being dramatically increased with little additional cost and with a consequent rise in profits.

A key aspect of the philosophy of TOC is the continuous improvement of production performance. Rather than using the traditional accounting measurements of unit cost and utilization of workers and equipment, the new measures of **throughput** (the rate that cash is generated by the sale of products), inventory (money invested in inventory), and **operating expenses** (money spent in converting inventory into throughput) are used to measure production performance. The idea is to increase throughput while reducing both inventory and operating expenses.

The system of production control is based on the concepts of *drum*, *buffer*, and *rope*. Production is controlled at control points or bottlenecks, which are collectively referred to as the **drum** because it establishes the beat to be followed by all other operations. The drum provides the MPS that is consistent with the bottlenecks of production. A time **buffer** in the form of inventory is kept before a bottleneck so that it always has material on which to work. These buffers provide the insurance that delivery promises to customers can be made with high reliability. A **rope** is some form of communication, such as a schedule, that is communicated back upstream to prevent inventory from building up and to coordinate the activities required to support the MPS. The rope ensures that every production stage is synchronized to the MPS.

The principles, theory, and philosophy of TOC provide an advance beyond the other forms of production planning and control systems.

Wrap-Up

WHAT WORLD-CLASS COMPANIES DO

World-class companies excel at business planning. With an eye on world markets, they develop strategies that enable them to capture increasing shares of those markets. Long-range capacity planning provides the production facilities, processes, and products to position production to become a competitive weapon in this effort. Medium-range production planning, or aggregate capacity planning as it is known, allows production to carry out its role in capturing increased shares of world markets over a 6-month to 18-month planning horizon. Aggregate planning provides the workforce, inventory, utilities, and material-supply contracts necessary to respond quickly to customer demand and at the same time produce high-quality and low-cost products and services.

Exceptional short-range production planning is also necessary to make increased market shares happen. Master production schedules, production schedules of components, schedules of purchased material, shop-floor schedules, and workforce schedules form an integrated system of production planning that covers a period ranging from a few weeks to a few months. These schedules are "where the rubber meets the road," or where customer satisfaction, high product quality, and low production costs occur. The ability of the production system to perform as necessary to achieve long-range plans boils down to the nitty-gritty of making it happen in the short run. These short-range plans hold the production system together and provide the detailed coordination of all elements of the production system as it moves toward its long-range goals.

The following statements describe the current trends among world-class companies in the use of the several approaches to short-range production planning:

1. Push systems dominate present use and can be applied to almost any type of production. In these systems, raw material and finished-goods inventories are reduced to manageable levels, customer orders are carefully tracked and delivered on time, and production costs are controlled. Push systems provide a comprehensive information system that supports improved short-run production performance and management decisions.

2. Pull systems are growing in use but are used more often in repetitive manufacturing. These systems, also known as just-in-time (JIT) or lean production systems, are spectacularly successful in some companies: Inventories are drastically reduced, production lead times fall precipitously, quality improves, workers become more involved, and production becomes relatively problem free. Perhaps more important than these direct benefits is the realization that JIT has become a mechanism for once again focusing on the improvement of production. Even in other types of production where pull systems are thought to be inappropriate, the philosophy that inventory is a form of waste has been adopted and applied with good results.

3. A few select companies are using the theory of constraints approach and focusing on bottlenecks to plan and control production. Systems like OPT provide the means to schedule production intelligently. Not only have phenomenal results occurred for these companies, but these systems have also given focus to production in a way that encourages everyone to get involved—a development that has reinvigorated some production organizations.

Taken together, long-, medium-, and short-range production planning and control provides production with the capability of being a competitive weapon to be used by businesses in capturing growing shares of world markets.

REVIEW AND DISCUSSION QUESTIONS

1. What long-range plans result from long-range capacity planning? Who prepares these plans?
2. What plans result from medium-range capacity planning? Who prepares these plans?
3. What are the main short-range production plans? How are they related? Who prepares these plans?
4. Explain the relationships among long-, medium-, and short-range production plans.
5. Define and describe *aggregate planning*.
6. Name and describe four sources of medium-range production capacity.
7. Describe how the following production resources can be increased or decreased to expand or contract production capacity: (a) workforce, (b) materials, and (c) machines.
8. List the advantages and disadvantages of these traditional aggregate plans: (a) matching demand, (b) level capacity with inventory, (c) level capacity with backlog, (d) level capacity with overtime, (e) level capacity with subcontracting, and (f) level capacity with part-time workers.
9. Why is aggregate planning in produce-to-order firms difficult? What can operations managers do to overcome these difficulties?
10. Give three reasons why aggregate planning in services is difficult. What can operations managers do to overcome these difficulties?
11. Explain how linear programming can be used in aggregate planning.
12. Explain how aggregate planning differs between produce-to-stock and produce-to-order firms.
13. What criteria would be used to decide between two aggregate plans?
14. What is a master production schedule? What inputs are needed? Describe the process of preparing a master production schedule.
15. Explain these master production scheduling terms: (a) frozen, (b) firm, (c) full, (d) open, (e) lot-sizing,

(f) rough-cut capacity planning, (g) updating, (h) demand management, (i) order entry, and (j) order promising.

16. Explain the process of weekly updating the master production schedule.

17. Explain why operations managers have confidence in the demand estimates included in the early part of the master production schedule. Why does the updating of the MPS tend to build this confidence?

18. Explain the differences in master production scheduling between produce-to-stock and produce-to-order firms.

19. What determines the length of planning horizons in master production scheduling?

20. Name and describe four types of production-planning and control systems.

21. Summarize what world-class companies do in their production-planning and control systems.

INTERNET ASSIGNMENTS

1. Visit the web site for the Optimized Production Technology (OPT) software (**http://www.stg.co.uk**). Find information on the latest version of the OPT software. Describe some of the features of OPT.

2. SAP is the leading provider of enterprise resource planning (ERP) software. Its software includes the *Advanced Planner and Optimizer* component, which helps companies with production planning. Visit SAP's web site at **http://www.mysap.com** and locate information on the *Advanced Planner and Optimizer* component. Describe some of the features related to production planning and detailed scheduling.

3. Search the Internet for software that will do *master production scheduling*. Describe some of the software features.

4. Companies sometimes hire temporary employees to help meet their peak capacity needs. Kelly Services Inc. is one of the largest providers of temporary employees to companies in the United States. Visit its web site at **http://www.kellyservices. com**. Explore Kelly's web pages for information on hiring temporary personnel in manufacturing. Summarize some of the stated advantages of using temporary manufacturing personnel from Kelly Services.

PROBLEMS

Aggregate Planning

1. QuickPlus is a software developer that produces software products for three markets: businesses, home consumers, and educational institutions. The company has a customer service operation that provides telephone support, and the number of customer service calls for each of the three markets varies throughout the year. The average time spent by a customer service representative on each call is 13 minutes. Each customer service representative works an average of 1,920 hours per year. The forecast for the number of calls from each market group for each quarter next year is:

Market Group	Number of Calls			
	1st Quarter	2nd Quarter	3rd Quarter	4th Quarter
Business	150,000	168,000	118,000	121,000
Home	101,000	109,000	92,000	83,000
Education	68,000	81,000	175,000	101,000

Compute the number of customer service representatives needed for each market group in each quarter, and compute the total number needed each quarter.

2. A company has these sales forecasts and labor and machine standards for its products:

	Quarterly Sales (products)				Labor Standard (labor-hours/product)	Machine Standard (machine-hours/product)
Product	1st Quarter	2nd Quarter	3rd Quarter	4th Quarter		
A	22,000	19,000	17,000	15,000	7.95	5.77
B	11,000	9,000	7,000	10,000	6.56	4.10
C	21,000	18,000	17,000	19,000	3.22	2.55
D	16,000	13,000	12,000	14,000	4.90	3.15
E	7,000	5,000	5,000	7,000	3.11	2.10

   a. Compute the labor-hours required for each quarter.
   b. Compute the machine-hours required for each quarter.
   c. Graph the information developed in Parts a and b.

3. A company is planning the aggregate production capacity required to produce the sales forecast in this table:

	Sales Forecast (thousands of tons)			
Resin	1st Quarter	2nd Quarter	3rd Quarter	4th Quarter
A	9.0	10.0	12.0	14.0
B	7.0	8.0	5.0	10.0
C	6.0	3.0	4.0	7.0

Ample machine capacity exists to produce the forecast and each ton of resin requires five labor-hours.
   a. Compute the aggregate demand for resin in each quarter.
   b. Compute the aggregate number of labor-hours in each quarter.
   c. If each worker works 520 hours per quarter, how many workers will be required in each quarter?

4. In Problem 3, it costs $2,000 to hire a worker and $1,000 to lay off a worker, and inventory carrying cost is $65 per ton of resin (this means that if one ton of resin were held in inventory for a year, it would cost $65 for finance charges, insurance, warehousing expense, etc.). The plant works the same number of days in each quarter, 13 five-day weeks. Evaluate two aggregate plans for next year: (a) matching demand and (b) level capacity with inventory. Which plan would you recommend? Why? Assume that the pattern of quarterly demand repeats from year to year and that beginning inventory is zero.

5. In Problem 1, suppose that after further investigation QuickPlus discovers that the time spent on customer service calls varies by market group. The average time spent by a customer service representative on each call is 7 minutes for business customers, 18 minutes for home customers, and 14 minutes for education customers. Compute the number of customer service representatives needed for each market group in each quarter, and compute the total number needed each quarter.

6. In Problem 2, if the machine-hours were sufficient and employees worked 13 weeks in each quarter and 40 hours in each week, determine how many employees the company would require in each quarter, using these aggregate plans: (a) level capacity and (b) matching demand.

7. A bowling ball manufacturer is considering two capacity plans for next year: level capacity with inventory and matching demand. The quarterly aggregate demand is shown below for the two plans. The labor standard is 1.6 hours per bowling ball, hiring cost is $600 per worker hired, layoff cost is $400 per worker laid off, carrying cost for finished goods is $5 per bowling ball per year, there is no beginning inventory for the first quarter, 83 workers are employed at the end of the fourth quarter of the previous year, and the company produces bowling balls 8 hours per day, 62 days per quarter.

Quarter	Aggregate Demand
1	14,500
2	22,800
3	34,600
4	30,200

Based on the information given, which capacity plan would you recommend? Assume that the quarterly demand pattern repeats from year to year.

8. A company is developing an aggregate capacity plan from the sales forecast below:

	Sales Forecasts (products)			
Product	1st Quarter	2nd Quarter	3rd Quarter	4th Quarter
1	2,000	1,500	1,600	1,800
2	1,200	1,000	800	1,000

Ample machine capacity exists to produce the forecast. Each Product 1 takes an average of 20 labor-hours and each Product 2 takes an average of 15 labor-hours.
a. Compute the aggregate number of labor-hours in each quarter.
b. If each worker works 520 hours per quarter, how many workers will be required in each quarter?

9. In Problem 8, it costs $1,000 to hire a worker and $500 to lay off a worker, and inventory carrying cost is $100 for each Product 1 and $100 for each Product 2 (this means that if one Product 1 were held in inventory for a year, it would cost $100 for finance charges, insurance, warehousing expense, etc.). The plant works the same number of days in each quarter, 13 five-day weeks. Evaluate two aggregate plans for next year: (a) level capacity with inventory and (b) matching demand. Beginning inventory is 275 for Product 1 and 200 for Product 2 in the level capacity plan and zero for both products in the matching demand plan. Assume that the quarterly demand pattern repeats from year to year.

10. Speed King Inc., a small aircraft company, manufactures four-seat airplanes that are customized for each individual customer. The company is currently assessing its manufacturing strategies, and two alternative aggregate capacity plans are being evaluated: level capacity with backlog and matching demand. Speed King estimates that it costs $1,850 for each airplane that is back-ordered in one quarter (and delivered in the next quarter). The cost to hire and train an employee is $4,100, and the cost to lay off an employee is $1,900. The labor standard is 158 hours per airplane, the company produces airplanes 8 hours per day, 62 days per quarter; 59 workers are employed at the end of the fourth quarter of the previous year, and the beginning backlog in the first quarter is zero. Here are the demand estimates for the next four quarters:

Quarter	Aggregate Demand
1	234
2	208
3	128
4	162

Based on the information given, which aggregate plan would you recommend? Assume that the quarterly demand pattern repeats from year to year.

11. Emerald Homes, a large home construction company in Seattle, builds custom homes for individuals. The company is reconsidering its construction strategies, and two alternative capacity plans are being evaluated: level capacity with backlog and matching demand. Emerald Homes estimates that it costs $1,400 for each home that is back-ordered in one quarter (and delivered in the next quarter). The cost to hire and train an employee is $1,600, and the cost to lay off an employee is $900. The average labor content for new homes is 775 hours per home, and the company builds homes 8 hours per day, 62 days per quarter. At the end of the fourth quarter of the previous year 31 workers are employed, and the beginning backlog in the first quarter is zero. Here are the demand estimates for the next four quarters:

Quarter	Aggregate Demand
1	38
2	46
3	25
4	21

Based on the information given, which aggregate plan would you recommend? Assume that the quarterly demand pattern repeats from year to year.

12. Amigos Mfg., located near the Mexico border in El Paso, Texas, supplies aluminum alloy parts to the automotive industry. The company is trying to decide between two aggregate capacity plans: level capacity with overtime and level capacity with subcontracting. Either overtime or subcontracting would supply all demand above what its current 183 employees can produce by working 8 hours per day, 62 days per quarter. The primary aluminum alloy used by Amigos costs $6.85 per pound. Each product requires an average of 2.4 labor-hours per unit. The aggregate product demand for the next four quarters is 47,500; 39,600; 36,400; and 42,100 units. A subcontractor can supply any quantity of the product for $24 per unit (raw materials would be provided by Amigos Mfg.). The straight-time labor cost of Amigos employees is $21 per hour, and the overtime cost rate is time and a half (150 percent).
    a. Compute the cost of each capacity plan.
    b. Which of the factors mentioned would be important in choosing between the two plans?

Master Production Scheduling

13. The White Company is a produce-to-stock firm that produces office products used by typists to correct typing mistakes. White develops master production schedules with 10-week planning horizons for its many products. One such product has a beginning inventory of 1,500 cases, a constant weekly demand of 1,000 cases, a fixed production lot size of 2,000 cases, and a minimum safety stock of 500 cases. Prepare the MPS detailed computations that result in the production schedule for the product under the assumption that ample production capacity exists.

14. A company manufactures a line of computer printers on a produce-to-order basis. Each printer requires an average of 30 labor-hours, and the manufacturing plant uses a backlog of orders to allow a level capacity aggregate plan. This plan provides a weekly capacity of 9,000 labor-hours. The company has prepared this five-week MPS:

	Weekly Production (printers)				
Product	**1**	**2**	**3**	**4**	**5**
Printers	200	275	275	300	360

    a. Compute the actual labor-hours required at the plant in each week and for the total five weeks to produce the MPS (this is often referred to as *load*). Compare the load to the labor-hours capacity in each week and for the total five weeks (this is often referred to as *rough-cut capacity planning*).

    b. Does enough production capacity exist to produce the MPS?

    c. What changes in the MPS would you recommend?

15. A company manufactures bar code scanners on a produce-to-order basis. The company manufactures three models of the scanners on the same final assembly line. The final assembly has 20,000 hours of weekly capacity. The six-week MPS and the final assembly standard for each model are:

	Final Assembly Standard	**Weekly Production (scanners)**					
Product	**(hours per scanner)**	**1**	**2**	**3**	**4**	**5**	**6**
A	25	200	150	200	250	150	250
B	30	100	200	350	250	150	250
C	35	150	150	150	200	250	250

    a. Compute the actual final assembly hours required at the plant in each week and for the total six weeks to produce the MPS (this is often referred to as *load*). Compare the load to the labor-hours capacity in each week and for the total six weeks (this is often referred to as *rough-cut capacity planning*).

    b. Does enough production capacity exist to produce the MPS?

    c. What changes to the MPS would you recommend?

16. A manufacturing plant is in the process of updating its master production schedule for its products. The plant produces a product on a produce-to-stock basis. The table below shows the estimates of demand for the product for the next six weeks.

	Week					
Type of Demand	**1**	**2**	**3**	**4**	**5**	**6**
Customers (forecasts and orders)	700	1,200	700	500	400	1,200
Branch warehouses	100	100	400	500	200	100
Market research		50			10	
Production research	10					

The safety stock level (inventory cannot fall below the safety stock level), minimum lot size (at least the minimum lot size must be produced when production of the product occurs), and beginning inventory level for the product are:

Minimum Lot Size	**Safety Stock**	**Beginning Inventory**
2,000	500	1,500

Prepare a six-week MPS for the product. Assume that there is ample production capacity at the plant.

17. A company produces three products on a produce-to-stock basis. The demands (in cases) for these products over the eight-week planning horizon are:

				Week				
Product Demand	1	2	3	4	5	6	7	8
Customers (Forecasts and Orders)								
A	1,000	2,000	2,000	500	1,000	2,000	1,500	500
B	3,000	2,000	2,000	5,000	7,000	6,000	4,000	4,000
C	1,500	500	500	1,500	1,000	500	500	500

				Week				
Product Demand	1	2	3	4	5	6	7	8
Branch Warehouses								
A	1,500		1,500			2,000		
B	1,500		2,000			3,000		
C		1,000					500	
Market Research								
A	50			50			50	
B		50			50			50
C			50		50			

The safety stock levels (inventory levels cannot fall below the safety stock level), minimum lot sizes (at least the minimum lot size must be produced when production of the product occurs), and beginning inventory levels for the products are:

Product	Minimum Lot Size (cases)	Safety Stock (cases)	Beginning Inventory (cases)
A	5,000	3,000	4,000
B	8,000	5,000	4,000
C	2,000	1,000	2,000

Prepare the next eight-week MPS. Assume that ample production capacity exists.

CASES

Mrs. Massey's Master Mixers

The Mrs. Massey's Master Mixers (4M) company, which was started 40 years ago by Mrs. Massey, designs and manufactures kitchen mixers and blenders. Today the 4M company is run by Jim Massey, who oversees demand management and production planning. The company's three product lines are commercial mixers (CM), commercial blenders (CB), and home blenders (HB). Jim is now planning how to best use the company's resources in the coming year. Based on past sales data and market trends, next quarter he expects to sell 8,400 CM products, 15,300 CB products, and 24,700 HB products. Jim's best estimates are that sales of CM products will decrease 3 percent per quarter after next quarter, sales of CB products will increase 2.5 percent per quarter, and sales of HB products will increase 9 percent per quarter.

Several product models are manufactured within each product line, but each model within a product line generally requires about the same amount of resources to produce. Each CM product requires about 23 minutes of labor time to produce, each CB requires 14 minutes, and each HB requires 9 minutes. Jim is considering whether to keep a labor force of 22 production workers each quarter in the next year. Employees work 8 hours (productive time) per day, Monday through Friday. Jim plans on each month having about 21 working days.

Assignment

1. Compute the forecasts for each product line for the next four quarters (round off).
2. Compute the total number of labor hours required for each product line in each quarter.
3. Generate a rough-cut capacity plan for a stable workforce of 22 employees for the next four quarters.
4. What are your suggestions to resolve any problems with your rough-cut capacity plan? Develop a labor plan (i.e., number of labor-hours planned each quarter) that allows for meeting demand and also minimizes inventory carrying costs.

British Aerocurrent Ltd.

British Aerocurrent Ltd. (BA), located outside of London, produces electrical generators for several European commercial aircraft manufacturers. One of the processes to build a generator involves assembling a wire coil assembly. Roger Bingham is the production planner responsible for this process, and he is currently planning the production needs for next quarter.

BA has 30 production employees that work on the wire coil assembly process. The productive time for each employee is 8 hours each day (straight time), and there will be 63 workdays next quarter. At Roger's discretion, employees can be required to work overtime each week. However, the union's contract restricts the amount of overtime to be at most 20 percent of the straight time worked. The average straight-time labor cost rate is $20 per hour, and the overtime cost rate is time and a half (i.e., 150 percent of straight-time cost). The labor standard is 2.5 hours per coil assembly.

In addition to using its own employees, BA has the option of outsourcing this process. BA supplies the materials and a subcontractor can perform the necessary tasks. Two subcontractors have been used before and both are available in the coming quarter if needed. Subcontractor A will perform the work at a cost of $80 per unit but only has the capacity to produce 1,500 wire coil assemblies next quarter. Subcontractor B will perform the work at a cost of $70 per unit and also has the capacity to produce only 1,500 assemblies.

The forecasted number of wire coil assemblies that will be needed next quarter is 8,200 units. Roger must now decide on a production plan for next quarter that will minimize the total cost of producing and obtaining the wire coil assemblies.

Assignment

1. Summarize the cost per unit and capacity for each of the four alternative means of getting the assemblies (i.e., straight-time labor, overtime labor, Subcontractor A, Subcontractor B).
2. Determine the most cost-effective production plan. How many units should be obtained from each alternative? What will be the total cost of labor and subcontracting? How much cost would be saved if Roger were to hire one additional employee?

Cool Bevrich Company

The Cool Bevrich Company manufactures carbonated beverage dispensing machines for the fast-food restaurant industry. Planning how to produce the machines to meet demand at the least cost is the responsibility of Anna Spencer, the company's top production planner. Anna has gathered all the necessary cost, demand, and capacity information to analyze the situation and develop a production plan for the next four months.

Drink machines can be produced each month using straight-time labor or overtime labor. The machines can also be produced in one month and then held in inventory until shipped in a later month. In this case a carrying cost of $25 per unit is incurred for each month that a unit is held in inventory. (No carrying cost is incurred if a machine is shipped in the same month it is produced.) The straight-time labor cost rate is $20 per hour, and the maximum available straight time labor is 31,000 hours each month. The overtime labor cost rate is time and a half (150 percent of straight-time cost), and the maximum available overtime labor is 20 percent of straight-time capacity each month. The labor standard is 6.2 hours per unit. The demand for the next four months is 5,500; 4,000; 5,200; and 5,700 units.

Assignment

1. Formulate a linear programming model to develop a production plan for the next four months that minimizes production costs and carrying costs. Clearly define your decision variables.
2. Solve this linear programming model using appropriate software. What is the solution, and what does the solution mean in terms of the original production-planning problem?

ENDNOTES

1. Cox, James F., III, and John H. Blackstone, eds. *APICS Dictionary*, 9th ed., p. 24. Falls Church, VA: APICS—The Educational Society for Resource Management, 1998.
2. *Communications Oriented Production Information and Control Systems (COPICS)*, Vol. 1, *Management Overview*, Publication G320-1974. White Plains, NY: International Business Machines, 1972.
3. Hall, Robert W. *Zero Inventories*, p. 37. Homewood, IL: Dow Jones–Irwin, 1983.
4. *Ibid.*

5. Goldratt, Eliyahu M., and Jeff Cox. *The Goal: A Process of Ongoing Improvement*, 2nd rev. ed. Croton-on-Hudson, NY: North River Press, 1992.
6. Goldratt, Eliyahu M. *It's Not Luck*. Croton-on-Hudson, NY: North River Press, 1994.
7. Goldratt, Eliyahu M. *Critical Chain*. Croton-on-Hudson, NY: North River Press, 1997.
8. Goldratt, Eliyahu M., Eli Schragenheim, and Carol A. Ptak. *Necessary But Not Sufficient*. Great Barrington, MA: North River Press, 2000.

SELECTED BIBLIOGRAPHY

Aggarwal, S. "MRP, JIT, OPT, FMS?" *Harvard Business Review* 66, no. 5 (September–October 1985): 8–16.

Bolander, Steven F., and Sam G. Taylor. "Scheduling Techniques: A Comparison of Logic." *Production and Inventory Management Journal* 41, no. 1 (1st Quarter 2000): 1–5.

Bowman, E. H. "Production Planning by the Transportation Method of Linear Programming." *Journal of Operations Research Society* 4 (February 1956): 100–103.

Brandimarte, Paolo, and A. Villa, eds. *Modeling Manufacturing Systems: From Aggregate Planning to Real-Time Control*. New York: Springer Verlag, 1999.

Buffa, E. S. "Aggregate Planning for Production." *Business Horizons* 10 (Fall 1967): 87–97.

Cox, James F., III, and John H. Blackstone, eds. *APICS Dictionary*, 9th ed. Falls Church, VA: APICS—The Educational Society for Resource Management, 1998.

Goldratt, Eliyahu M., and Jeff Cox. *The Goal: A Process of Ongoing Improvement*, 2nd rev. ed. Croton-on-Hudson, NY: North River Press, 1992.

LaForge, R. Lawrence, and Christopher W. Craighead. "Computer-Based Scheduling in Manufacturing Firms: Some Indicators of Successful Practice." *Production and Inventory Management Journal* 41, no. 1 (1st Quarter 2000): 29–34.

Landvater, Darryl V. *World Class Production and Inventory Management.* New York: John Wiley & Sons, 1997.

Miller, Tan C. *Hierarchical Operations and Supply Chain Planning.* New York: Springer Verlag, 2000.

Narasimhan, Seetharama L., Dennis W. McLeavey, and Peter J. Billington. *Production Planning and Inventory Control.* Englewood Cliffs, NJ: Prentice Hall, 1995.

Proud, John F. *Master Scheduling: A Practical Guide to Competitive Manufacturing.* New York: John Wiley & Sons, 1999.

Ptak, Carol A., and Eli Schragenheim. *ERP: Tools, Techniques, and Applications for Integrating the Supply Chain.* Boca Raton, FL: St. Lucie Press, 2000.

Sawik, Tadeusz. *Production Planning and Scheduling in Flexible Assembly Systems.* New York: Springer Verlag, 1999.

Schwarz, Leroy B., and Robert E. Johnson. "An Appraisal of the Empirical Performance of the Linear Decision Rule for Aggregate Planning." *Management Science* 24 (April 1978): 844–849.

Silver, Edward, David F. Pyke, Rein Peterson, and G. John Miltenburg. *Decision Systems for Inventory Management and Production Planning.* New York: John Wiley & Sons, 1998.

Sipper, Daniel, and Robert Bulfin. *Production: Planning, Control, and Integration.* New York: McGraw Hill, 1997.

Teufel, Thomas, Jurgen Robricht, and Peter Willems. *SAP Processes: Planning Procurement and Production.* Boston: Addison Wesley Professional, 2001.

Vollmann, Thomas E., William L. Berry, and D. Clay Whybark. *Manufacturing Planning and Control Systems.* New York: Irwin/McGraw-Hill, 1997.

Whacker, John G., and Malcolm Miller. "Configure-to-Order Planning Bill of Material: Simplifying a Complex Product Structure for Manufacturing Planning and Control." *Production and Inventory Management Journal* 41, no. 2 (2nd Quarter 2000): 21–26.

14

Inventory Management

Introduction

Opposing Views of Inventories
Why We Want to Hold Inventories
Why We Do Not Want to Hold Inventories

Nature of Inventories

Fixed Order Quantity Systems
Determining Order Quantities
Determining Order Points

Fixed Order Period Systems

Other Inventory Models
Hybrid Inventory Models
Single-Period Inventory Models

Some Realities of Inventory Planning
ABC Classification of Materials
EOQ and Uncertainty

Dynamics of Inventory Planning
Other Factors Affecting Inventory Planning
Vendor-Managed Inventories
Computers and Inventory Planning

Wrap-Up: What World-Class Companies Do

Review and Discussion Questions

Internet Assignments

Problems

Cases
Green Garden Products
Inventory Planning at Integrated Products
Corporation
Safety Stock Levels at Bell Computers

Selected Bibliography

SETTING INVENTORY POLICIES AT AIRCO DIVISION

The meeting was held at the Airco Division headquarters in St. Louis, and all of the division's plant and warehouse managers, its vice-president of operations, and its vice-president of marketing were present. Needless to say, the meeting was a command performance. Everyone was to be present so that an agreement could be reached on inventory policies for the division. The corporate vice-president and general manager of the division, Mr. Milligan, called the meeting to order and opened the discussion.

Mr. Milligan stated that inventory investment must be reduced, but that at the same time some customers had indicated in recent months that their orders could not be delivered immediately because Airco's warehouses were out of stock. The vice-president of marketing stated that the division had plenty of products in the warehouses but they were the wrong ones. Also, he felt that the division was cutting corners on the amount of safety stock in the warehouses. The vice-president of operations stated that the reason wrong products were in the warehouses was that marketing forecasts were always wrong. He asked the vice-president of marketing what percentage of the time the warehouses should be out of products when customer orders are received. The vice-president of marketing replied that enough inventory of products should always be on hand to fill customers' orders when they are received.

Inventory policies are important enough that production, marketing, and financial managers work together to reach agreement on these policies. That there are conflicting views concerning inventory policies underscores the balance that must be struck among conflicting goals—reduce production costs, reduce inventory investment, and increase customer responsiveness. This chapter concerns the integration of these seemingly irreconcilable views in setting inventory policies. We examine in this chapter the nature of inventories and the inner workings of inventory systems, build an understanding of the fundamental issues in inventory planning, and develop several techniques for analyzing inventory problems.

OPPOSING VIEWS OF INVENTORIES

Inventories today have a good-guy, bad-guy image. There are many reasons why we like to have inventories, but there are also reasons why holding inventories is considered to be unwise.

Why We Want to Hold Inventories

Inventories are necessary, but the important issue is how much inventory to hold. Table 14.1 summarizes the reasons for holding finished-goods, in-process, and raw-materials inventories.

In addition to the strategic importance in providing finished-goods inventory so that customer service is improved through fast shipment of customers' orders, we also hold inventories because by doing so certain costs are reduced:

Table 14.1	Why Do We Want to Hold Inventories?
Finished goods	1. Essential in produce-to-stock positioning strategies, of strategic importance. 2. Necessary in level aggregate capacity plans. 3. Products can be displayed to customers.
In process	1. Necessary in process-focused production; uncouples the stages of production; increases flexibility. 2. Producing and transporting larger batches of products creates more inventory but may reduce materials-handling and production costs.
Raw materials	1. Suppliers produce and ship some raw materials in batches. 2. Larger purchases result in more inventory, but quantity discounts and reduced freight and materials handling costs may result.

1. **Ordering costs.** Each time we purchase a batch of raw material from a supplier, a cost is incurred for processing the purchase order, expediting, record keeping, and receiving the order into the warehouse. Each time we produce a production lot, a changeover cost is incurred for changing production over from a previous product to the next one. The larger the lot sizes, the more inventory we hold, but we order fewer times during the year and annual ordering costs are lower.

2. **Stockout costs.** Each time we run out of raw materials or finished-goods inventory, costs may be incurred. In finished-goods inventory, stockout costs can include lost sales and dissatisfied customers. In raw-materials inventory, stockout costs can include the cost of disruptions to production and sometimes even lost sales and dissatisfied customers. Additional inventory, called safety stock, can be carried to provide insurance against excessive stockouts.

3. **Acquisition costs.** For purchased materials, ordering larger batches may increase raw-materials inventories, but unit costs may be lower because of quantity discounts and lower freight and materials-handling costs. For produced materials, larger lot sizes increase in-process or finished-goods inventories, but average unit costs may be lower because changeover costs are amortized over larger lots (see Figure 14.1).

4. **Start-up quality costs.** When we first begin a production lot, the risk of defectives is great. Workers may be learning, materials may not feed properly, machine settings may need adjusting, and a few products may need to be produced before conditions stabilize. Larger lot sizes mean fewer changeovers per year and less scrap.

Inventories can be indispensable to the efficient and effective operation of production systems. But there are good reasons why we do not want to hold inventory.

Why We Do Not Want to Hold Inventories

Certain costs increase with higher levels of inventories:

1. **Carrying costs.** Interest on debt, interest income foregone, warehouse rent, cooling, heating, lighting, cleaning, repairing, protecting, shipping, receiving, materials handling, taxes, insurance, and management are some of the costs incurred to insure, finance, store, handle, and manage larger inventories.

2. **Cost of customer responsiveness.** Large in-process inventories clog production systems. The time required to produce and deliver customer orders is increased, and our ability to respond to changes in customer orders diminishes.

Figure 14.1	Cost per Unit versus Size of Production Lot

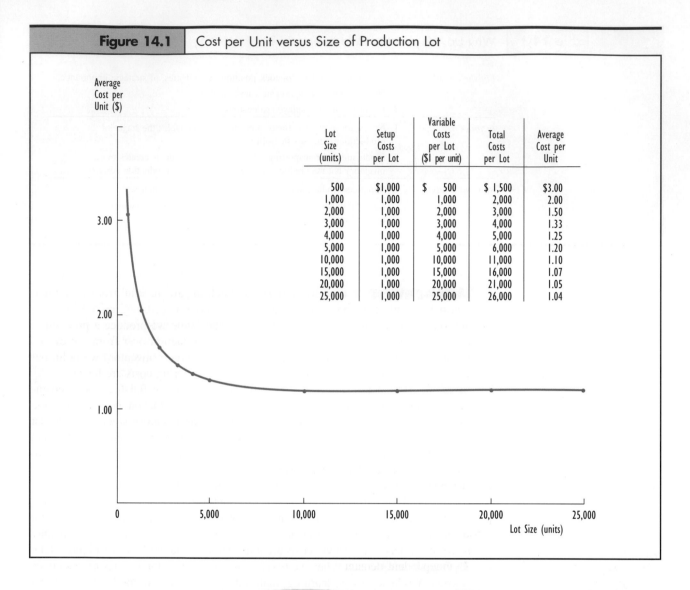

Lot Size (units)	Setup Costs per Lot	Variable Costs per Lot ($1 per unit)	Total Costs per Lot	Average Cost per Unit
500	$1,000	$ 500	$ 1,500	$3.00
1,000	1,000	1,000	2,000	2.00
2,000	1,000	2,000	3,000	1.50
3,000	1,000	3,000	4,000	1.33
4,000	1,000	4,000	5,000	1.25
5,000	1,000	5,000	6,000	1.20
10,000	1,000	10,000	11,000	1.10
15,000	1,000	15,000	16,000	1.07
20,000	1,000	20,000	21,000	1.05
25,000	1,000	25,000	26,000	1.04

3. **Cost of coordinating production.** Because large inventories clog the production process, more people are needed to unsnarl traffic jams, solve congestion-related production problems, and coordinate schedules.

4. **Cost of diluted return on investment (ROI).** Inventories are assets, and large inventories reduce return on investment. Reduced return on investment adds to the finance costs of the firm by increasing interest rates on debt and reducing stock prices.

5. **Reduced-capacity costs.** Inventory represents a form of waste. Materials that are ordered, held, and produced before they are needed waste production capacity.

6. **Large-lot quality cost.** Producing large production lots results in large inventories. On rare occasions, something goes wrong and a large part of a production lot is defective. In such situations, smaller lot sizes can reduce the number of defective products.

7. **Cost of production problems.** Higher in-process inventories camouflage underlying production problems. Problems like machine breakdowns, poor product quality, and material shortages never get solved.

At first, these costs may seem indirect, fuzzy, and even inconsequential, but reducing these costs by holding less inventory can be crucial in the struggle to compete for world markets.

NATURE OF INVENTORIES

Two fundamental issues underlie all inventory planning:

- How much to order of each material when orders are placed with either outside suppliers or production departments within organizations
- When to place the orders

Order quantities, sometimes also called **lot sizes,** and when to place these orders, called **order points,** determine in large measure the amount of materials in inventory at any given time.

The study of the inventory cycle—materials are ordered, received, used, and the process is repeated—uses a terminology all its own. These terms are included in the glossary at the end of this book.

Inventories may contain materials that have either dependent demand or independent demand. *In independent-demand inventories, the demand for an item carried in inventory is independent of the demand for any other item carried in inventory.* Finished goods shipped to customers is an example of independent-demand inventories. Demands for these items are estimated from forecasts or actual customer orders. The remainder of this chapter is aimed at the order quantity and order point decisions of independent-demand inventories. *Dependent-demand inventories consist of items whose demand depends on the demands for other items also held in inventory.* For example, the demand for a calculator case and shipping container, which are components, are both dependent on the demand for the calculator, a finished good. Typically, the demand for raw materials and components can be calculated if we can estimate the demand for the finished goods into which these materials go. Order quantity and order point decisions for dependent-demand inventories are therefore distinctly different from those of independent-demand inventories; these decisions will be treated in Chapter 15, Resource Requirements Planning: MRP and CRP.

In independent-demand inventories, how much should we order of a material when replenishing inventory? The answer depends on the costs of ordering too much and the costs of ordering too little. The costs of ordering too much are all the costs causing us to not want to hold inventory that were discussed earlier: carrying, customer responsiveness, coordinating production, diluted ROI, reduced capacity, large-lot quality, and production problems. The cost of ordering too little are all the costs causing us to want to hold inventory that were discussed earlier: ordering, stockout, acquisition, and start-up quality.

Materials are ordered so that the cost of ordering too little is balanced against the cost of ordering too much on each order. In Figure 14.2, two classes of costs are graphed. Carrying costs represent all the annual costs associated with ordering too much. These costs climb as order quantities rise because average inventory levels rise as order quantities rise. Ordering costs represent all the annual costs associated with ordering too little. These costs fall as order quantities rise because the number of annual orders falls and average inventory levels rise as order quantities rise.

As Figure 14.2 shows, when the annual carrying costs curve is added to the annual ordering costs curve, an annual total stocking costs curve results. *This total costs curve demonstrates an important concept in inventory planning: There exists for every*

| **Figure 14.2** | Balancing Carrying Costs against Ordering Costs |

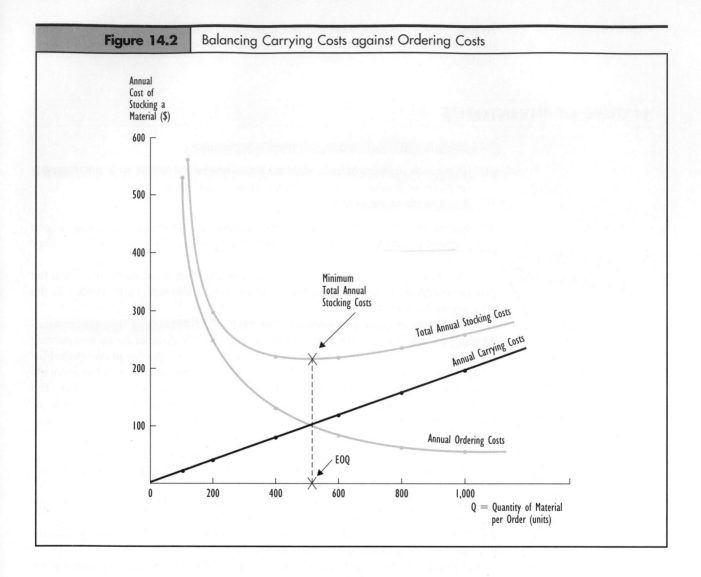

material held in inventory an optimal order quantity where total annual stocking costs are at a minimum. In this figure the optimal order quantity, traditionally called the **economic order quantity (EOQ)**, is approximately 524 units per order.

This concept is useful to operations managers, particularly if the fixed order quantity system is used.

FIXED ORDER QUANTITY SYSTEMS

Fixed order quantity systems place orders for the same quantity of a material each time that material is ordered. However, *when* the order is placed is allowed to vary. Inventory falls until a critical inventory level, the order point, triggers an order. The **order point (OP)** is determined by estimating how much we expect to use of a material between the time we order and receive another batch of that material. When the batch is received and inventory is replenished, the fixed order quantity is placed in inventory.

Inventory control systems are a vital component of production management.

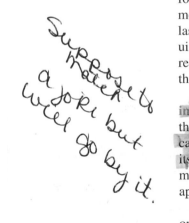

Suppose to materials a joke but will go by it.

The **two-bin system** of inventory control is a simple application of this type of system. In the two-bin system, each material has two bins that physically hold the material in a warehouse. As the material is used, material is withdrawn from a large bin until the large bin is empty. At the bottom of the large bin is a preprinted requisition for another order of the material. This replenishment requisition is sent out, and in the meantime materials are used out of the small bin, which holds just enough material to last until the next inventory replenishment. When the inventory is replenished, a requisition is placed in the bottom of the large bin, both bins are filled, and the cycle is repeated. The order quantity is the amount needed to fill both bins. The order point is the amount needed to fill the small bin.

In these systems, we usually assume perpetual inventory accounting. In **perpetual inventory accounting**, additions and subtractions from inventory records are made at the time that materials are added to or removed from inventory. With this method we can determine the amount of a material in inventory at any point in time by looking at its **inventory record**, a display of all the inventory transactions that have affected that material. Such displays today are usually a part of the company's computer system and appear on a computer terminal display when called.

Two decisions are essential to fixed order quantity systems: order quantities and order points.

Determining Order Quantities

When operations managers must decide the quantity of a material to order in fixed order quantity systems, no single formula applies to all situations. Each situation requires analysis based on the characteristics of that particular inventory system. We develop here estimates of optimal order quantities for three inventory models: Model I—basic economic order quantity (EOQ), Model II—EOQ for production lots, and Model III—EOQ with quantity discounts.

Model I—Basic Economic Order Quantity (EOQ)

Table 14.2 describes the assumptions, variable definitions, cost formulas, and derivation of the EOQ formula for Model I. The key question in applying this model is: Do

Table 14.2	Model I—Basic Economic Order Quantity (EOQ)

Assumptions

1. Annual demand, carrying cost, and ordering cost for a material can be estimated.
2. Average inventory level for a material is order quantity divided by 2. This implicitly assumes that no safety stock is utilized, orders are received all at once, materials are used at a uniform rate, and materials are entirely used up when the next order arrives.
3. Stockout, customer responsiveness, and other costs are inconsequential.
4. Quantity discounts do not exist.

Variable Definitions

D = annual demand for a material (units per year)*
Q = quantity of material ordered at each order point (units per order)
C = cost of carrying one unit in inventory for one year (dollars per unit per year)*
S = average cost of completing an order for a material (dollars per order)
TSC = total annual stocking costs for a material (dollars per year)

Cost Formulas

Annual carrying cost = Average inventory level × Carrying cost = $(Q/2)C$
Annual ordering cost = Orders per year × Ordering cost = $(D/Q)S$
Total annual stocking cost (TSC) = Annual carrying cost + Annual ordering cost
$$= (Q/2)C + (D/Q)S$$

Derivation of the Economic Order Quantity Formula

The optimal order quantity is found by setting the derivative of TSC with respect to Q equal to zero and solving for Q:

1. The formula for TSC is: $\qquad\qquad$ $TSC = (Q/2)C + (D/Q)S$
2. The derivative of TSC with respect to Q is: $\quad d(TSC)/d(Q) = C/2 + (-DS/Q^2)$
3. Set the derivative of TSC equal to zero and solve for Q:

$$C/2 + (-DS/Q^2) = 0$$

$$-DS/Q^2 = -C/2$$

$$Q^2 = 2DS/C$$

$$Q = \sqrt{2DS/C}$$

4. The EOQ is therefore: $\qquad\qquad$ $EOQ = \sqrt{2DS/C}$

*In cases where a material has a seasonal demand, D would represent quarterly demand and C would represent per-unit carrying cost for one quarter. Thus, the order policies would vary from quarter to quarter as the seasonal demand varies.

the assumptions fit our inventory situation, or are the deviations from these assumptions only minor?

As demonstrated in Figure 14.3, an average inventory of Q/2 implies that there is no safety stock, orders are received all at once, materials are used at a uniform rate, and materials are entirely used up when the next order arrives. The presence of all these characteristics is rare in practice; but in spite of minor deviations, Q/2 may still be a reasonable estimate of average inventory levels for some materials.

Example 14.1 applies the cost and EOQ formulas to one material purchased by a plumbing supply company.

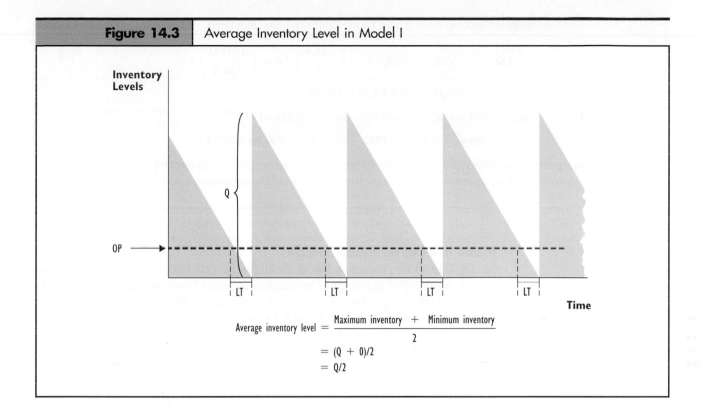

Figure 14.3 | Average Inventory Level in Model I

$$\text{Average inventory level} = \frac{\text{Maximum inventory} + \text{Minimum inventory}}{2}$$
$$= (Q + 0)/2$$
$$= Q/2$$

Example 14.1 | Use of Model I in a Plumbing Supply Company

The Call-Us Plumbing Supply Company stocks thousands of plumbing items sold to regional plumbers, contractors, and retailers. Mr. Swartz, the firm's general manager, wonders how much money could be saved annually if EOQ were used instead of the firm's present rules of thumb. He instructs Mary Ann Church, an inventory analyst, to conduct an analysis of one material only (Material #3925, a brass valve) to see if significant savings might result from using the EOQ. Mary Ann develops the following estimates from accounting information: D = 10,000 valves per year, Q = 400 valves per order (present order quantity), C = \$0.40 per valve per year, and S = \$5.50 per order.

Solution

1. Mary Ann calculates the present total annual stocking costs:

$$\text{TSC}_1 = (Q/2)C + (D/Q)S = \left(\frac{400}{2}\right)0.4 + \left(\frac{10,000}{400}\right)5.5 = 80 + 137.50 = \$217.50$$

2. The EOQ is calculated:

$$\text{EOQ} = \sqrt{\frac{2DS}{C}} = \sqrt{\frac{2(10,000)(5.5)}{0.4}} = \sqrt{275,000} = 524.4 \text{ valves}$$

3. The total annual stocking costs if EOQ were employed are calculated:

$$TSC_2 = (Q/2)C + (D/Q)\ S = \left(\frac{524.4}{2}\right)0.4 + \left(\frac{10,000}{524.4}\right)5.5$$

$$= 104.88 + 104.88 = \$209.76$$

4. The estimated annual savings in stocking costs is calculated:

$$\text{Savings} = TSC_1 - TSC_2 = 217.50 - 209.76 = \$7.74$$

5. Mary Ann concludes that if the annual savings on this one material were applied to the thousands of items in inventory, the savings from EOQ would be significant.

Model II—EOQ for Production Lots

Model II, EOQ for production lots, is useful for determining the size of orders if a material is produced at one stage of production, stored in inventory, and then sent along to the next stage in production or shipped to customers. Production occurs and flows into inventory at a rate (p) that is greater than the usage or demand rate (d) at which the material is flowing out of inventory. Therefore, this model is well suited for planning the size of production lots for in-house manufacture of products.

This model has only one slight modification to Model I: Orders are assumed to be supplied or produced at a uniform rate rather than all at once. Table 14.3 presents the assumptions, variable definitions, cost formulas, and derivation of the EOQ for Model II. Figure 14.4 shows that orders are produced at a uniform rate (p) during the early part of the inventory cycle and used at a uniform rate (d) throughout the cycle. Inventory levels build at a rate of (p − d) during production and never reach the level Q as in Model I. Example 14.2 illustrates the use of Model II in determining the size of production lots.

Example 14.2	Use of Model II in Determining the Size of Production Lots

The Call-Us Plumbing Supply Company has an adjacent production department that could produce the #3925 valve. If the valves were produced in-house in production lots, they would flow gradually into inventory at the main warehouse for use. The carrying cost, ordering or setup cost, and annual demand would remain about the same. Because the valves actually flow into inventory rather than being received all at once as a batch, Mr. Swartz wonders how this would affect the order quantity and annual stocking cost. Mary Ann Church develops these estimates: D = 10,000 valves per year, C = \$0.40 per valve per year, S = \$5.50 per order, d = 40 valves per day (10,000 valves per year ÷ 250 working days), and p = 120 valves per day.

Solution

1. Mary Ann calculates the EOQ:

$$EOQ = \sqrt{\frac{2DS}{C}\left(\frac{p}{p-d}\right)} = \sqrt{\frac{2(10,000)(5.5)}{0.4}\left(\frac{120}{120-40}\right)} = 642.26 \text{ valves}$$

Table 14.3	Model II—EOQ for Production Lots

Assumptions

1. Annual demand, carrying cost, and ordering cost for a material can be estimated.
2. No safety stock is utilized, materials are supplied at a uniform rate (p) and used at a uniform rate (d), and materials are entirely used up when the next order begins to arrive.
3. Stockout, customer responsiveness, and other costs are inconsequential.
4. Quantity discounts do not exist.
5. Supply rate (p) is greater than usage rate (d).

Variable Definitions

All the definitions in Model I apply also to Model II.* Additionally:

$$d = \text{rate at which units are used out of inventory (units per time period)}$$

$$p = \text{rate at which units are supplied to inventory (same units as d)}$$

Cost Formulas

Maximum inventory level = Inventory buildup rate × Period of delivery

$$= (p - d)(Q/p)$$

Minimum inventory level = 0

Average inventory level = ½(Maximum inventory level + Minimum inventory level)

$$= \tfrac{1}{2}[(p - d)(Q/p) + 0] = (Q/2)[(p - d)/p]$$

Annual carrying cost = Average inventory level × Carrying cost

$$= (Q/2)[(p - d)/p]C$$

Annual ordering cost = Orders per year × Ordering cost = (D/Q)S

Total annual stocking cost (TSC) = Annual carrying cost × Annual ordering cost

$$= (Q/2)[(p - d)/p]C + (D/Q)S$$

Derivation of the Economic Order Quantity Formula

Again, as in Model I, set the derivative of TSC with respect to Q equal to zero and solve for Q:

1. The formula for TSC is: $\text{TSC} = (Q/2)[(p - d)/p]C + (D/Q)S$
2. The derivative of TSC with respect to Q is: $d(\text{TSC})/d(Q) = [(p - d)/2p]C - DS/Q^2$
3. Set the derivative of TSC equal to zero and solve for Q:

$$[(p - d)/2p]C - DS/Q^2 = 0$$

$$Q^2 = (2DS/C)[p/(p - d)]$$

$$Q = \sqrt{(2DS/C)[p/(p - d)]}$$

4. The EOQ is therefore: $\text{EOQ} = \sqrt{(2DS/C)[p/(p - d)]}$

*See the note to Table 14.2.

2. The new total annual stocking costs are calculated:

$$\text{TSC}_3 = (Q/2)\left(\frac{p - d}{p}\right)C + (D/Q)S = \frac{642.26}{2}\left(\frac{120 - 40}{120}\right)0.4 + \left(\frac{10,000}{642.26}\right)5.5$$

$$= 85.63 + 85.63 = \$171.26 \text{ per year}$$

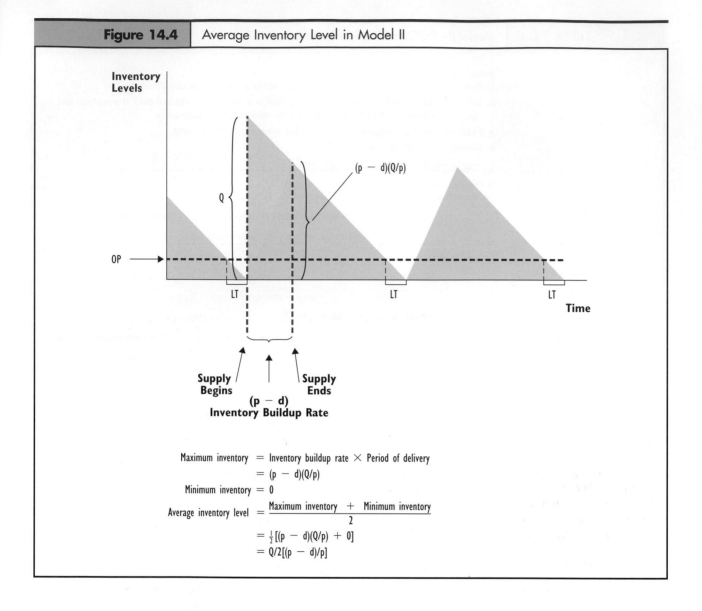

Figure 14.4 | Average Inventory Level in Model II

Maximum inventory = Inventory buildup rate $\times$ Period of delivery
$$= (p - d)(Q/p)$$
Minimum inventory = 0
Average inventory level = $\dfrac{\text{Maximum inventory} + \text{Minimum inventory}}{2}$
$$= \tfrac{1}{2}[(p - d)(Q/p) + 0]$$
$$= Q/2[(p - d)/p]$$

3. The EOQ and total annual stocking costs from Example 14.1, when the #3925 valves were delivered all at once, were EOQ = 524.4 and TSC_2 = \$209.76.

4. The estimated savings are calculated:

$$\text{Savings} = TSC_2 - TSC_3 = 209.76 - 171.26 = \$38.50 \text{ per year}$$

Model III—EOQ with Quantity Discounts

Suppliers may offer their goods at lower unit prices if larger quantities are ordered. This practice is referred to as **quantity discounting** and occurs because larger order quantities may be less expensive to produce and ship. A critical concern in most decisions of order quantities is ordering enough material on each order to qualify for the best price possible, but not buying so much that carrying costs consume the savings in purchase costs. Model III attempts to achieve this objective. The quantity purchased

| Table 14.4 | Model III—EOQ with Quantity Discounts |

Assumptions

1. Annual demand, carrying cost, and ordering cost for a material can be estimated.

2. Average inventory levels can be estimated at either:

> $Q/2$—if the assumptions of Model I prevail: no safety stock, orders are received all at once, materials are used at a uniform rate, and materials are entirely used up when the next order arrives.

> $Q/2[(p - d)/p]$—if the assumptions of Model II prevail: no safety stock, materials are supplied at a uniform rate (p) and used at a uniform rate (d), and materials are entirely used up when the next order arrives.

3. Stockout, customer responsiveness, and other costs are inconsequential.

4. Quantity discounts do exist. As larger quantities are ordered, price breaks apply to all units ordered.

Variable Definitions
All the definitions in previous models apply to Model III.* Additionally:

> TMC = total annual material costs (dollars per year)

> ac = acquisition cost of either purchasing or producing one unit of a material (dollars per unit)

Formulas
The EOQ and TSC formulas from either Model I or Model II are applied to Model III, depending on which assumptions best fit the inventory situation.

> Annual acquisition costs = Annual demand × Acquisition cost = (D)ac

> Total annual material costs (TMC) = Total annual stocking costs + Annual acquisition cost = TSC + (D)ac

Model I—Order Delivered All at One Time	Model II—Gradual Deliveries
$EOQ = \sqrt{2DS/C}$	$EOQ = \sqrt{(2DS/C)[p/(p - d)]}$
$TMC = (Q/2)C + (D/Q)S + (D)ac$	$TMC = (Q/2)[(p - d)/p]C + (D/Q)S + (D)ac$

Procedures

1. Compute the EOQ using each of the sales prices. Note that C is usually a function of sales price or production cost. For example, C may be defined as 20 percent of sales price. Therefore, EOQ will change as C and ac change.

2. Determine which EOQ from Step 1 above is feasible. In other words, is the computed EOQ in the quantity range for its price?

3. The total annual material cost (TMC) is computed for the feasible EOQ and the quantity at any price break with lower sales prices.

4. The order quantity with the lowest total annual material cost (TMC) is the economic order quantity for the material.

*See the note to Table 14.2.

does not necessarily have to be the EOQ amount as formulated from Model I or Model II; rather, it is the quantity that minimizes the sum of annual carrying, ordering, and acquisition costs. Table 14.4 lists the assumptions, variable definitions, formulas, and procedures of this model.

Model III utilizes either Model I or Model II formulas. If deliveries of orders occur all at once, Model I formulas are used. If deliveries are gradual, Model II formulas are used. It is particularly important to recognize that the key quantities to consider are any feasible EOQ (is the EOQ in the quantity range for its price?) and the quantity at any price break with lower prices. Table 14.5 gives four different quantity-discount/order-quantity decision situations to demonstrate the procedures for identifying the quantities to be investigated by comparing the total annual material costs (TMC).

Example 14.3 applies Model III to our old friends at the plumbing supply company. In this example, the manager must decide both the quantity and method of delivery—either gradual deliveries or orders received all at once—for one material. Follow through the steps of this example; it demonstrates the procedures of Model III.

Table 14.5	Identifying Key Quantities to Investigate When Quantity Discounts Exist

Quantity	Price	Feasible EOQ	Key Quantity to Investigate	Quantity	Price	Feasible EOQ	Key Quantity to Investigate
1–399	$2.20			1–499	$6.95		
400–699	2.00	524.4	524.4*	500–999	6.50		
700+	1.80		700*	1,000–1,999	6.25	1,700	1,700
				2,000+	6.10		2,000
1–699	$43.50	590	590	1–599	$10.50		
700–1,499	36.95		700	600–749	7.50		
1,500+	35.50		1,500	750–999	7.25		
				1,000+	7.15	1,200	1,200

*See Example 14.3 and Figure 14.5 on page 551.

Example 14.3	EOQ with Quantity Discounts in a Plumbing Supply Company

A supplier of the #3925 valve has offered Mr. Swartz quantity discounts if he will purchase more than his present order quantities. The new volumes and prices are:

Range of Order Quantities	Acquisition Cost per Valve (ac)
1–399	$2.20
400–699	2.00
700+	1.80

Mr. Swartz asks Mary Ann Church to investigate the new prices under two sets of assumptions: Orders are received all at once and deliveries are gradual.

Solution

Orders Received All at Once

1. Mary Ann has developed these estimates: D = 10,000 valves per year, C = 0.2(ac) dollars per valve per year, and S = $5.50 per order.
2. The EOQs are computed for each of the acquisition costs:

$$EOQ_{2.20} = \sqrt{\frac{2DS}{C}} = \sqrt{\frac{2(10,000)(5.5)}{0.2(2.2)}} = 500$$

$$EOQ_{2.00} = \sqrt{\frac{2DS}{C}} = \sqrt{\frac{2(10,000)(5.5)}{0.2(2.0)}} = 524.4$$

$$EOQ_{1.80} = \sqrt{\frac{2DS}{C}} = \sqrt{\frac{2(10,000)(5.5)}{0.2(1.8)}} = 552.8$$

3. Mary Ann graphs the TMC for each acquisition cost (see Figure 14.5). For instance, $TMC_{2.2}$ can be graphed by substituting several values for Q in this TMC formula:

$$TMC = \left(\frac{Q}{2}\right)C + \left(\frac{D}{Q}\right)S + (D)ac$$

$$TMC_{2.2} = \left(\frac{Q}{2}\right)(2.2)(0.2) + \left(\frac{10,000}{Q}\right)5.5 + (10,000)2.2$$

Mary Ann notes that only $EOQ_{2.00}$ is feasible because 524.4 valves per order can be purchased at \$2.00 per valve. The TMC at two quantities is therefore investigated: 524.4 units per order (each at \$2.00) and 700 units per order (each at \$1.80):

$$Q = 524.4: \quad TMC = \left(\frac{Q}{2}\right)C + \left(\frac{D}{Q}\right)S + (D)ac$$

$$= \left(\frac{524.4}{2}\right)0.4 + \left(\frac{10,000}{524.4}\right)5.5 + (10,000)2$$

$$= 104.88 + 104.88 + 20,000 = \$20,209.76 \text{ per year}$$

$$Q = 700: \quad TMC = \left(\frac{Q}{2}\right)C + \left(\frac{D}{Q}\right)S + (D)ac$$

$$TMC = \left(\frac{700}{2}\right)(0.2 \times 1.8) + \left(\frac{10,000}{700}\right)5.5 + (10,000)1.8$$

$$= 126.00 + 78.57 + 18,000 = \$18,204.57 \text{ per year}$$

4. Mary Ann concludes that if orders are delivered all at once, 700 valves should be ordered at each inventory replenishment.

Gradual Deliveries

1. Mary Ann has developed these estimates: D = 10,000 valves per year, S = \$5.50 per order, C = 0.2 (ac) dollars per valve per year, p = 120 valves per day, and d = 40 valves per day.
2. The EOQs are now computed:

$$EOQ_{2.20} = \sqrt{\frac{2DS}{C}\left(\frac{p}{p-d}\right)} = \sqrt{\frac{2(10,000)(5.5)}{0.2(2.2)}\left(\frac{120}{120-40}\right)} = 612.4$$

$$EOQ_{2.00} = \sqrt{\frac{2DS}{C}\left(\frac{p}{p-d}\right)} = \sqrt{\frac{2(10,000)(5.5)}{0.2(2.0)}\left(\frac{120}{120-40}\right)} = 642.3$$

$$EOQ_{1.80} = \sqrt{\frac{2DS}{C}\left(\frac{p}{p-d}\right)} = \sqrt{\frac{2(10,000)(5.5)}{0.2(1.8)}\left(\frac{120}{120-40}\right)} = 677.0$$

3. Mary Ann notes that only $EOQ_{2.00}$ is feasible because 642.3 valves per order can be purchased at \$2.00 per valve. Two quantities are investigated, 642.3 and 700 units per order:

$$Q = 642.3: \quad TMC = \frac{Q}{2}\left(\frac{p-d}{p}\right)C + \left(\frac{D}{Q}\right)S + (D)ac$$

$$= \frac{642.3}{2}\left(\frac{120-40}{120}\right)(0.2 \times 2.0) + \left(\frac{10,000}{642.3}\right)5.5 + (10,000)2.0$$

$$= 85.63 + 85.63 + 20,000 = \$20,171.26 \text{ per year}$$

$$Q = 700: \qquad \text{TMC} = \frac{Q}{2}\left(\frac{p-d}{p}\right)C + \left(\frac{D}{Q}\right)S + (D)ac$$

$$= \frac{700}{2}\left(\frac{120-40}{120}\right)(0.2 \times 1.8) + \left(\frac{10,000}{700}\right)5.5 + (10,000)1.8$$

$$= 84.00 + 78.57 + 18,000 = \$18,162.57 \text{ per year}$$

Mary Ann concludes that if gradual deliveries are used, 700 units per order should be purchased.

4. Given a choice, Mr. Swartz would prefer to have gradual deliveries of #3925 valves in quantities of 700 units per order because the TMC of gradual deliveries is slightly less than that for orders delivered all at once.

Quantity discounts, when used with the EOQ formulas, begin to build more realism into these methods of analysis. Although some restrictive assumptions are still present in Model III, enough real inventory decisions approach the assumptions of this model to make it a valuable technique in POM.

Determining Order Points

Table 14.6 contains many terms often used in setting order points. You may find it helpful to occasionally refer to the table as we progress through this section. When setting order points in a fixed order quantity inventory system, operations managers are confronted with an uncertain demand during lead time. **Demand during lead time (DDLT)** means the amount of a material that will be demanded while we are waiting for an order of a material to arrive and replenish inventory. The variation in demand during lead time comes from two sources. First, the lead time required to receive an order is subject to variation. For example, suppliers can encounter difficulty in processing orders, and trucking companies can have equipment failures or strikes that delay deliveries. Second, daily demand for the material is subject to variation. For example, customers' demands for finished products are known to be subject to great daily variation, and production departments' demands for raw materials can vary because of changes in production schedules. What makes this variation in demand during lead time particularly worrisome to operations managers is that this uncertainty hits them when they are most vulnerable—when they are waiting for an order of materials to arrive and inventory levels are low.

If orders arrive late or if demand for the materials is greater than expected while we are waiting for an order to come in, a stockout can occur. A **stockout** means that there is insufficient inventory to cover demands for a material during lead time. Operations managers carry safety stock so that stockouts will seldom occur. If we carry too much safety stock, the cost of carrying these materials becomes excessive; however, when too little safety stock is carried, the cost of stockouts becomes excessive. Operations managers want to balance these two costs as they set order points.

Figure 14.6 illustrates the relationships among the variables involved in setting order points and safety stock. The most important relationship for you to know is:

Order point = Expected demand during lead time + Safety stock

$$\text{OP} = \text{EDDLT} + \text{SS}$$

Figure 14.5	Quantity Discount TMC Curves

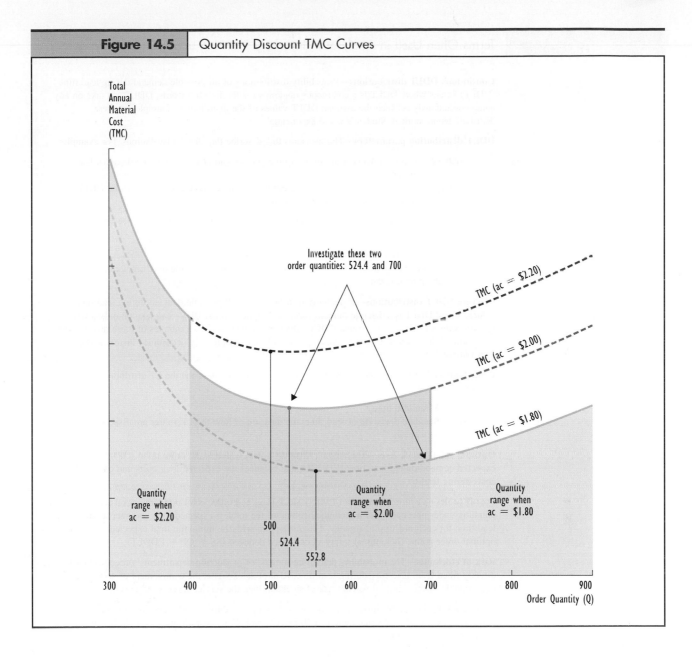

As you can see from the demand during lead-time distribution in Figure 14.6, safety stock is added to the expected demand during lead time to determine the order point. If we assume that we can accurately estimate the value of the expected demand during lead time from historical records or other sources, then setting the safety stock also sets the order point. So when we set the safety stock level for a material, we also simultaneously set the order point. As we can see from Figure 14.6, increasing the safety stock for a material reduces the probability of a stockout during lead time. This reduces the cost of stockouts but has the disadvantage of increasing carrying costs.

In attempting to balance the costs of carrying too much or too little safety stock for each material, analysts have searched for optimal solutions to this problem. The main obstacle to determining optimal safety stock levels is estimating the costs of stockouts. We know that stockouts cost, but how much? How much profit is lost when we

Table 14.6	Terms Often Used in Analyses in Inventory Planning under Uncertainty

Continuous DDLT distributions—Probability distributions of all possible demand during lead time (DDLT) values where DDLT is a continuous random variable. In other words, DDLT can take on any value continuously between the extreme DDLT values of the distribution. Examples of these distributions are normal, Student's t, and exponential.

DDLT distribution parameters—The measures that describe the DDLT distributions. For example:

> EDDLT—Expected demand during lead time is the mean of the DDLT distributions. For example:
> σ_{DDLT}—Standard deviation of demand during lead time, the measure of how the DDLT values are dispersed about their mean.

Demand per day (d) distribution parameters—The measures that describe the d distributions. For example:

> $\bar{d}$—Mean demand per day.
> σ_d—Standard deviation of demand per day, the measure of how the d values are dispersed about their mean.

Discrete DDLT distributions—Probability distributions of all possible demand during lead time values, where DDLT is a discrete random variable. In other words, DDLT can take on only a few specific values between the extreme DDLT values of the distribution. Examples of these distributions are binomial, hypergeometric, Poisson, and a host of other empirically determined historical data distributions.

Lead Time (LT) distribution parameters—The measures that describe the LT distributions. For example:

> $\overline{LT}$—Mean lead time.
> σ_{LT}—Standard deviation of lead time, the measure of how the LT values are dispersed about their mean.

Optimal safety stock level—The amount of safety stock, which is the order point (OP) minus the expected demand during lead time (EDDLT), that balances the expected long costs and expected short costs during lead time.

Payoff tables—A form of analysis of safety stock level and order point problems in inventory planning under uncertainty. This technique computes the total of expected long and short costs per lead time for each order point strategy. The order point with the minimum total expected cost is the optimal order point. The optimal safety stock is then deduced (SS = OP − EDDLT).

Risk of stockouts—The probability that all customers' or production departments' orders cannot be directly filled from inventory during lead time. Risk of stockouts is the complement of service level. For example, if there is a 10 percent risk of stockout, then the service level is 90 percent.

Service level—The probability that a stockout will not occur during lead time. For example, a 90 percent service level means that there is a 10 percent probability that *all* orders cannot be filled from inventory during lead time.

lose or disappoint customers because of stockouts? How much does it cost when production departments must change production schedules or shut down production when they experience stockouts of raw materials? Because of the difficulty in accurately determining the costs of stockouts, analysts have taken another approach to setting safety stocks—setting order points at service levels determined by management policy.

Setting Order Points at Service Levels

Service level refers to the probability that a stockout will not occur during lead time. Managers might say, for example, "We want a 90 percent probability that *all* customers' orders can be immediately filled out of inventory."

they want 98% [in?] book

| **Figure 14.6** | Relationships among DDLT, EDDLT, SS, OP, and Probability of Stockouts for Each Reorder Cycle |

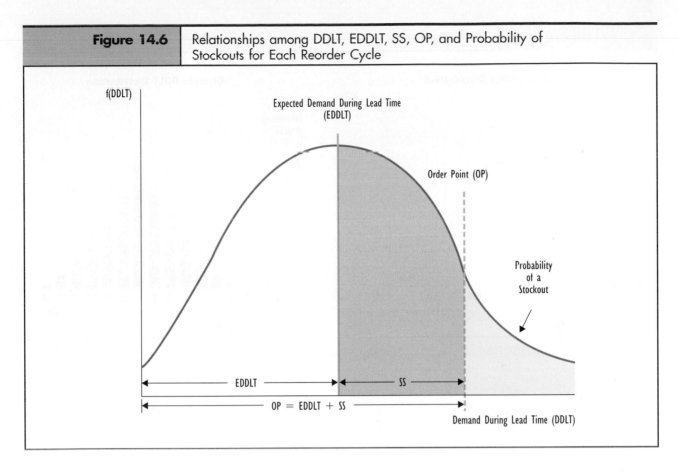

Discrete and Continuous DDLT Distributions. When DDLT ranges from 3 to 15 units as shown on the right side of Figure 14.7, a **discrete DDLT distribution** may more accurately describe the occurrence of DDLT since its values can only be integer values from 3 to 15 units. When the number of units in DDLT is very large, as shown on the left side of Figure 14.7, or when units are divisible, as in the case of barrels of crude oil, **continuous DDLT distributions** accurately describe the occurrence of DDLT. When enough historical data exist for the demand during lead time for a material, the setting of safety stock levels is straightforward. Example 14.4 sets the safety stock level for a material with a discrete DDLT distribution.

| **Example 14.4** | Setting Safety Stock at Service Levels for a Discrete DDLT Distribution |

Endless Road Honda (ERS) is a motorcycle dealership in Los Angeles that sells all models of Honda motorcycles. Sales manager Josh Morton is currently reevaluating the store's ordering policy for the Gold Wing model. ERS places an order with Honda each time its inventory of Gold Wings drops to the order point level. When ERS places an order, Honda's motorcycle manufacturing plant in Marysville, Ohio, ships the order in 7 days, and ERS receives the order 10 days after they place the order. Because it is expensive to hold inventories of the $20,000 Gold Wings, Josh Morton would like to set the order point so as to provide a 75 percent service level during the replenishment lead time. This would allow ERS to be able to provide Gold Wings from inventory on hand to 75 percent of customers who request one during the lead time. The frequency of demand levels during the lead times from the past 35 order cycles is:

Figure 14.7	DDLT Distribution

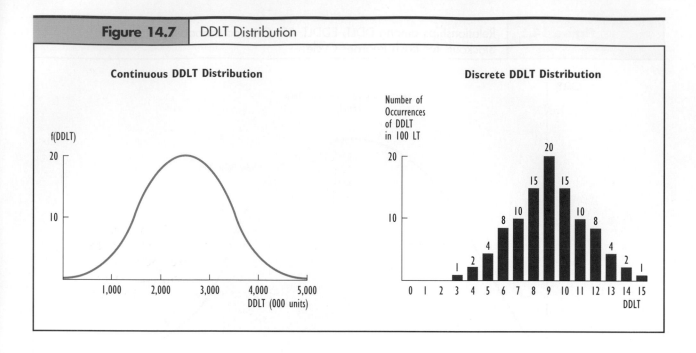

Actual DDLT	Frequency
2	2
3	6
4	11
5	8
6	4
7	2
8	1
9	1

Based on this historical demand data: **a.** What should be the order point? **b.** What is the expected demand during the lead time (EDDLT)? **c.** What is the effective level of safety stock that results?

Solution

a. First, use the DDLT data to develop a cumulative probability distribution of the service level:

Actual DDLT	Frequency	Probability of Occurrence	(Service Level) Cumulative Probability
2	2	0.057	0.057
3	6	0.171	0.228
4	11	0.314	0.542
5	8	0.229	0.771
6	4	0.114	0.885
7	2	0.057	0.942
8	1	0.029	0.971
9	1	0.029	1.000

Based on these cumulative probabilities, demand during the lead time has been 5 units or less for 77 percent of the time. So, to achieve a service level of 75 percent the order point should be set at 5 units.

b. To determine the expected demand during lead time we multiply the demand levels by the frequencies, sum the results, and divide by the number of observations:

$$\text{EDDLT} = (2*2 + 3*6 + 4*11 + 5*8 + 6*4 + 7*2 + 8*1 + 9*1)/35 = 4.60$$

c. Determine the effective safety stock that results:

$$\text{OP} = \text{EDDLT} + \text{Safety stock}$$

or

$$\text{Safety stock} = \text{OP} - \text{EDDLT} = 5 - 4.6 = 0.4 \text{ units}$$

How can ERS carry 0.4 motorcycles, since motorcycles must be whole units? When the number of Gold Wings drops down to the order point of 5 units left in the store an order will be placed. That is the only action that need be taken. The fact that the effective safety stock is a fraction of a motorcycle should not be of concern; it is merely the mathematical result of the difference between EDDLT and the order point. The 0.4 unit value is effectively the safety stock that results when the order point is set at 5 units.

Example 14.5 demonstrates how we would set safety stock levels when DDLT is depicted by a continuous distribution. This example assumes that the historical DDLT for a raw material is actually from a normal distribution. Remember that we earlier defined order point as:

$$\text{Order point} = \text{Expected demand during lead time} + \text{Safety stock}$$

Example 14.5	Setting Safety Stock at Service Levels for DDLT That Is Normally Distributed

Billie Jean Bray, the materials manager for INJECTO Wholesale Plastics, is attempting to set the safety stock level for resin #942. This material is sold to INJECTO's customers, and its demand during lead time is believed to be normally distributed with a mean of 693.7 pounds and a standard deviation of 139.27 pounds. **a.** What is the EDDLT for resin #942? **b.** What is the σ_{DDLT} for resin #942? **c.** If the production manager specifies a 95 percent service level for resin #942 during lead time, what safety stock should be maintained?

Solution

a. EDDLT is:

$$\text{EDDLT} = 693.7 \text{ pounds}$$

b. Standard deviation of DDLT is:

$$\sigma_{\text{DDLT}} = 139.27 \text{ pounds}$$

Therefore we have a normal distribution of DDLT with a mean of 693.7 pounds and a standard deviation of 139.27 pounds. (See figure below.)

c. Compute safety stock (SS) to provide a 95 percent service level; in other words, what is the DDLT level that has a probability of only 5 percent of being exceeded? This is the order point:

$$OP = EDDLT + Z(\sigma_{DDLT})$$

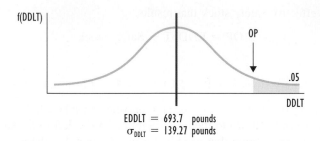

The Z value is read from Appendix A. Locate 0.95 (the area to the left of OP) in the body of the table, and read off the Z value of 1.64. This is the number of standard deviations that OP is away from EDDLT:

$$OP = 693.7 + 1.64\ (139.27) = 922.1 \text{ pounds}$$

The safety stock is then deduced:

$$SS = OP - EDDLT = 922.1 - 693.7 = 228.4 \text{ pounds}$$

Constant Lead Time and Normally Distributed Demand per Day. There are times when it is difficult to obtain DDLT data. In these instances, it is often satisfactory to obtain demand-per-day data and assume a constant lead time. Because historical demand-per-day data are usually abundantly available and lead time is ordinarily subject to less variation than the daily demand, this approach can be useful.

Example 14.6 develops safety stock levels for a material while assuming constant lead time and a normally distributed demand per day. A normal DDLT distribution is developed by computing the expected demand during lead time (EDDLT) and standard deviation of demand during lead time (σ_{DDLT}):

$$EDDLT = LT(\bar{d}) \qquad \text{and} \qquad \sigma_{DDLT} = \sqrt{LT(\sigma_d)^2}$$

The resulting DDLT normal distribution is then analyzed to calculate the DDLT value that provides the specified service level, and this value is the order point (OP).

Example 14.6	Setting Safety Stock Levels at Service Levels for Constant Lead Time and Normally Distributed Demand per Day

Bob Fero is an operations analyst for Sell-Rite Discount Stores of Washington, D.C. He is currently studying the ordering and stocking policies at Sell-Rite's central warehouse for one of its best-moving items, a child's toy. An examination of historical supply and demand data for this item indicated an almost constant lead time (LT) of 10 days, and abundant production capacity allowed very consistent production and delivery times. Bob also discovered that the demand per day (d) was nearly normally distributed with a mean ($\bar{d}$) of 1,250 toys per day with a standard deviation (σ_d) of 375 toys per day. **a.** Compute the order point for the toy if the service level is specified at 90 percent during lead time. **b.** How much safety stock is provided in your answer in Part a?

Solution

a.   Compute the order point:
  1.   First, compute the EDDLT and σ_{DDLT}:

$$\text{EDDLT} = \text{Lead time} \times \text{Average demand per day} = \text{LT}(\bar{d}) = 10(1,250)$$

$$= 12,500 \text{ toys during lead time}$$

$$\sigma_{DDLT} = \sqrt{\text{LT}(\sigma_d)^2} = \sqrt{10(375)^2} = 1,185.85 \text{ toys during lead time}$$

  2.   EDDLT and σ_{DDLT} totally describe the DDLT distribution:

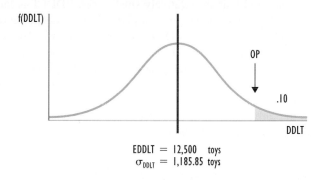

  3.   Next, we must determine Z, the number of standard deviations that OP is from EDDLT. Look up 0.900 in the body of the table in Appendix A, and read off the corresponding Z value of 1.28.
  4.   Next, compute the order point:

$$\text{OP} = \text{EDDLT} + Z(\sigma_{DDLT}) = 12,500 + 1.28(1,185.85) = 12,500 + 1,517.89$$

$$= 14,017.89 \text{ toys}$$

  Orders for the toy would be placed when the inventory level falls to 14,018 toys.
b.   Compute the safety stock (SS):

$$\text{SS} = \text{OP} - \text{EDDLT} = 14,018 - 12,500 = 1,518 \text{ toys}$$

All of these approaches to dealing explicitly with uncertainty in inventory planning have relied on managers to specify service levels to comply with either manufacturing policy or marketing policy. Let us now examine some rules of thumb for determining order points and safety stock levels.

Some Rules of Thumb in Setting Order Points

Perhaps the most common rule of thumb involves setting safety stock levels at a **percentage of EDDLT:**

Order point = EDDLT + j(EDDLT), where j = a factor that varies from 0 to 3.00

Materials are usually categorized according to classifications such as these:

Class	Description	j
1	Uncritical	0.10
2	Uncertain-uncritical	0.20
3	Critical	0.30
4	Uncertain-critical	0.50
5	Supercritical	1.00
6	Uncertain-supercritical	3.00

These classifications would be custom designed for a firm's inventory system and uniformly applied to most materials in finished-goods and raw-materials inventories.

Another approach sets safety stock at **square root of EDDLT:**

$$\textbf{Order point} = \textbf{EDDLT} + \sqrt{\textbf{EDDLT}}$$

This method selects safety stock levels that are large relative to EDDLT when EDDLT is small and that are relatively small when EDDLT is large. This approach is usually applied when stockouts are not particularly undesirable or costly.

The percentage of EDDLT and square root of EDDLT methods for setting order points are demonstrated in Example 14.7. In this example, the two methods of computing order points develop safety stocks of 12 and 8 castings. Which one is correct? Both are mathematically correct, but the correctness of each order point can be tested only by experimentation—choose one and keep records on DDLT as time passes. This is the only true test of an order point: Does the safety stock give the desired level of protection against stockouts?

Example 14.7	Using Rules of Thumb to Set Order Points

Dapple Manufacturing Company produces bronze castings. One type of casting, #699, is held in inventory until customers order it from Dapple. George Dapple, Dapple's materials manager, is dabbling with various approaches to setting order points for materials. The #699 casting is selected as the material for investigation. The following data were collected on #699: Average demand per day is six castings, and average lead time is 10 days, the time needed to produce a lot of castings. George's study requires the following: **a.** If safety stock is set at 20 percent of EDDLT, what is the order point? **b.** If safety stock is set at square root of EDDLT, what is the order point?

Solution

a. Order point = EDDLT + 0.2 (EDDLT)

= Average demand per day × Average lead time + 0.2 (EDDLT)

= 6.0(10) + 0.2(6.0 × 10) = 60 + 12 = 72 castings

b. Order point = EDDLT + $\sqrt{\text{EDDLT}}$ = 60 + $\sqrt{60}$ = 60 + 7.75 = 67.75, or 68 castings

How does the use of safety stocks affect the order quantity (EOQ) in a fixed order quantity inventory system? Minimally, if at all! However, total annual stocking costs are affected because safety stocks cause these developments:

- **Increased annual carrying costs.** This results from the fact that safety stocks are considered dead stock: On the average they are never used. The additional inventory therefore results in higher annual carrying costs.
- **Lower annual stockout costs.** The basic EOQ models do not include stockout costs, and for good reason: They are difficult to estimate. But conceptually we know that the cost of stockouts are real, and these would be reduced by safety stocks.

We have considered the determination of order quantities and order points in fixed order quantity inventory systems. Let us now consider fixed order period inventory systems.

FIXED ORDER PERIOD SYSTEMS

EDDLT

Expected demand during lead time

Fixed order period systems review inventory levels at fixed time intervals, and orders are placed for enough material to bring inventory levels back up to some predetermined level. Orders are placed at equally spaced time intervals, and the amount ordered in each cycle is computed with this formula:

Order quantity = Upper inventory target − Inventory level + EDDLT

Upper inventory target is usually determined by the amount of space allocated to a material either in a warehouse or on store shelves. If at the time of review the inventory level is relatively low, larger order quantities are placed. If, on the other hand, inventories are high when reviewed, smaller quantities are ordered.

The fixed order period system lends itself to inventories where it is desirable to physically count inventory on a regular periodic basis, as in some retail stores. In these situations, particularly with goods that are in displays where perpetual inventory accounting may not be feasible, periodic counts of materials on hand may be the most practical system to use, and the fixed order period system would be appropriate.

Once the order interval has been set and we know the dates of inventory reviews, the inventory level need not be monitored until the next review. Between these reviews, the uncertainties of both demand and lead time combine to make this system at greater risk of stockouts than the fixed order quantity system. In fixed order period systems, with no perpetual review of inventory levels, stockouts can occur at almost any time. The fixed order period system therefore usually requires more safety stock to accommodate this increased risk of stockouts.

Selecting an order period for materials is the key decision in fixed order period systems. If materials are reviewed too often, annual ordering costs will be excessive. But if they are reviewed too infrequently, order quantities and inventory levels will be too high and the probability of stockouts will be increased. Therefore the time interval between reviews should be such that the annual carrying costs are balanced against the annual ordering costs. Table 14.7 presents the assumptions and variable definitions and formulas for Model IV—fixed order period.

Example 14.8 applies the formulas for optimal order period and order quantity of this model to one material in a wholesaling company. Note that T, the optimal time

Table 14.7	Model IV—Economic Order Period

Assumptions
1. Annual demand, carrying cost, and ordering cost for a material can be estimated.
2. Average inventory is average order size divided by 2. This implicitly assumes no safety stock, orders are received all at once, materials are used at a uniform rate, and materials are used up on the average when the next order is received.
3. Stockout, customer responsiveness, and other costs are inconsequential.
4. Quantity discounts do not exist.

Variable Definitions
The variable definitions in Model I apply here.* Additionally:

$$T = \text{Time between orders in fraction of a year}$$

Cost Formulas

$$\text{Annual carrying costs} = \text{Average inventory} \times \text{Carrying cost} = (DT/2)C$$

$$\text{Annual ordering costs} = \text{Number of orders per year} \times \text{Cost per order}$$

$$= (D/DT)S = S/T$$

$$\text{Total annual stocking cost (TSC)} = \text{Annual carrying costs} + \text{Annual ordering costs}$$

$$= (DT/2)C + S/T$$

Derivation of the Optimal Order Period Formula
Set the derivative of TSC with respect to T equal to zero and solve for T:

1. The formula for TSC is: $\qquad\qquad\qquad\qquad$ $TSC = (DT/2)C + S/T$
2. The derivative of TSC with respect to T is: $\quad$ $d(TSC)/d(T) = (D/2)C - (S/T^2)$
3. Set the derivative of TSC with respect to T equal to zero and solve for T: $\qquad$ $(D/2)C - (S/T^2) = 0$
   $$T^2 = 2S/DC$$
4. The optimal T is therefore: $\qquad\qquad\qquad$ $T = \sqrt{2S/DC}$

*See the note to Table 14.2.

interval for reviewing the status of a material and placing a material order, is expressed as a fraction of a year. Note also that T is a computation that would be made only about once a year, whereas order quantity computations must be made for each order. In other words, T remains fixed for a long time and Q is allowed to vary from order to order.

Example 14.8	Optimal Order Period in a Fixed Order Period Inventory System

The C, D, & F Retailing Company routinely reviews the inventory levels of its products on display monthly and places orders for these products, if needed, from its suppliers. The regional manager wonders if monthly reviews are optimal when considering both carrying costs and order costs.

One product is selected to be the focus of investigation—Goo-Goo, a jarred baby-food cereal. The following information was developed for Goo-Goo: D = 29,385 jars per year, C = 30 percent of acquisition cost, ac = \$.29 per jar, and S = \$10.90 per order. **a.** How often should Goo-Goo be ordered? **b.** At the first review after T has been computed in Part a, if inventory level

= 985 jars, upper inventory target (including safety stock) = 3,220 jars, and expected demand during lead time = 805 jars, how many jars should be ordered?

Solution

a. $C = 0.3 \times 0.29$

$$T = \sqrt{\frac{2S}{DC}} = \sqrt{\frac{2(10.9)}{(29,385)(0.3 \times 0.29)}} = 0.0923 \text{ years} = 33.7 \text{ days}$$

b. Order quantity = Upper inventory target − Inventory level + EDDLT

   = 3,220 − 985 + 805 = 3,040 jars

The following generalizations can be deduced from the formula for T:

1. More expensive materials are reviewed more frequently.
2. Materials with higher usage rates are reviewed more frequently.
3. Materials with higher ordering costs are ordered less frequently.

These seem to be rational criteria for determining order intervals for materials.

OTHER INVENTORY MODELS

While the models of fixed order quantity and fixed order period systems are well known, other inventory models are also in use. Among these, hybrid models and single-period models are noteworthy.

Hybrid Inventory Models

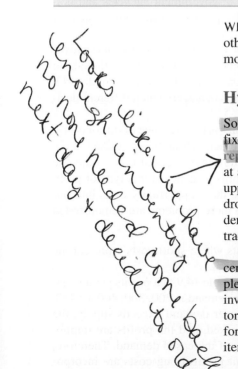

Some inventory models include some but not all of the features of the models of the fixed order quantity and fixed order period systems. One such model is the optional replenishment model. Like the fixed order period system, inventory levels are reviewed at a fixed time interval and a large enough order is placed to bring inventory up to an upper inventory target. But unlike fixed order period systems, unless inventory has dropped below a certain minimum level at the time of a review, no replenishment order is placed. This model protects against placing very small orders and would be attractive when review and ordering costs are large.

A base stock model is a very simple inventory planning system. It begins with a certain inventory level and then whenever a withdrawal is made from inventory, a replenishment order is placed that is equal to the withdrawal. This model ensures that inventory will be maintained at an approximately constant level. The beginning inventory is usually equal to EDDLT plus safety stock, and many replenishments are placed for relatively small orders. Such a system would be appropriate for very expensive items with small ordering costs.

Some companies are known to use more than one of the optional replenishment, base stock, fixed order quantity, and fixed order period models at the same time, but in different production departments. For example, a retailer might use fixed order period in the front end of the business on the display floor, where doing physical counts is the only way to determine accurate inventory levels. But fixed order quantity could be used in the back end of the business at the warehouse, where a computerized perpetual inventory accounting system might be in operation. Thus, several inventory models could be used at the same time, each best suited to its particular application.

Single-Period Inventory Models

Some inventory problems involve determining an order quantity for an item to cover the demand for only a single period. This type of problem is common for short-lived materials such as fashion goods, perishable foods, and published matter such as magazines and newspapers. Such inventory problems have traditionally been called newsboy problems. The structure of these problems is particularly well suited for the use of payoff tables.

Payoff tables are applied to a broad range of stocking problems when operations managers face an uncertain demand and it costs to stock too many or too few. For example, retailers must decide how many units of a particular product to stock for the next week, given the many possible levels of demand for the product. In such situations, operations managers must evaluate the many alternatives available for meeting the uncertain states of nature.

How do operations managers choose among the alternatives? They usually use one of these rules or criteria: (1) Choose the alternative with the greatest expected profits. (2) Choose the alternative with the least total expected long and short costs. (3) Choose the alternative with the least total expected costs. Because operations managers ordinarily prefer to maximize expected profits, Rule 1 is usually preferred. Rule 2 is also often used by operations managers, and if profits are involved it gives results equivalent to Rule 1. When revenues are not involved, as in government agencies and not-for-profit organizations, or when revenues cannot be precisely attributed to specific products or units being stocked, Rule 3 is frequently used.

Because the choice of rule or criterion used for deciding among the alternatives can affect the alternative eventually selected, it is important to give careful thought to the most appropriate rule for the decision situation under analysis. Example 14.9 demonstrates how payoff tables are used by operations managers when different decision criteria are used.

One complication that students regularly encounter is the presence of opportunity costs. Such costs are incurred when, for example, not enough units are stocked at the beginning of the period and demand exceeds the number of stocked units sometime during the period. These costs are in the form of profits forgone. In this type of problem we are often confused about how to incorporate these opportunity costs into our payoff tables. Two equally acceptable approaches to these problems are demonstrated in Example 14.9:

1. Minimize the total expected long and short costs where short costs represent the profit per unit. Long costs are incorporated as usual.
2. Maximize the total expected profits. Notice in Example 14.9 that profits per unit are $5 and that for Stocking Strategy 200, whenever demand is 200, 300, 400, or 450, the profits are $1,000. In this treatment, whenever demand exceeds supply, the number of units sold is the number of units stocked, and the profits are implicitly penalized by remaining the same regardless of increased demand. Therefore, the implicit unit short cost is the entire per-unit profit. Long costs are incorporated as usual.

| **Example 14.9** | Payoff Tables: A Retail Stocking Decision |

Fashion Retailers Inc. is trying to decide how many #325 silk scarves to stock for sale next season. The sales history of this item is as follows:

Number of Seasons	Scarves Demanded (SN)	Probability of Scarves Demanded P(SN)
1	100	0.1
1	200	0.1
4	300	0.4
3	400	0.3
1	450	0.1
Total 10		1.0

The #325 scarf sells for $15 per unit and has a cost of goods sold of $10 per unit. If one of these scarves is stocked for sale but is not sold during the season, it costs $2 to discount it next season, or long cost. **a.** Use payoff tables to minimize the total expected long and short costs. What is the expected value of perfect information (EVPI)? Explain its meaning. **b.** Use payoff tables to maximize the total expected profits. Compute the EVPI. **c.** Which stocking strategy is best for the #325 scarf? Explain the equivalence of the solutions of Parts a and b above.

Solution

a. Use payoff tables to minimize the total expected long and short costs. What is the EVPI? Explain its meaning.

First, complete a payoff table that minimizes the total expected long and short costs where long costs are $2 per unit and short costs are $5 per unit, the lost profit on sales forgone.

	SN_i		States of Nature				Total Expected Long and Short Costs
	S_j	100	200	300	400	450	$EC = \Sigma[P(SN_i)c_{ij}]$
	100	$ 0	$500	$1,000	$1,500	$1,750	$1,075
	200	200	0	500	**1,000**	1,250	645
Strategies	300	400	200	**0**	500	750	285
	400	**600**	400	200	0	250	205
	450	700	500	300	100	0	270
	$P(SN_i)$	0.1	0.1	0.4	0.3	0.1	

The procedures of payoff tables can be illustrated by explaining the three colored elements of the table in detail, using S_j to mean *stocking strategies* and SN_i to mean *states of nature*, or uncertain levels of demand:

- **S of 200 and SN of 400:** The $1,000 found in this position means that if a stocking strategy of 200 units is selected and a demand of 400 units is experienced, this would put the firm 200 units short during the season. Since short costs are $5 per unit, the period short costs are $5 per unit times 200 units, which equals $1,000.

- **S of 300 and SN of 300:** The zero found in this position means that since the strategy exactly meets the state of nature, there are neither short nor long costs.
- **S of 400 and SN of 100:** The \$600 found in this position means that if a stocking strategy of 400 units is selected and a demand of 100 units is experienced, this will yield an excess in inventory of 300 units at the end of the season. The season long cost is 300 units times \$2 per unit, which equals \$600.

All other elements of the payoff table are computed similarly. The expected cost column (EC) of the table is completed by summing along each strategy row (S_j) the products of the probability of the states of nature $P(SN_i)$ and their C_{ij}. For instance, the EC of $S_j = 400$ units is computed this way:

$$EC = 0.1(600) + 0.1(400) + 0.4(200) + 0.3(0) + 0.1(250)$$
$$= 60 + 40 + 80 + 0 + 25 = 205$$

Now, what is the EVPI and what is its meaning? The EVPI is \$205, the value of the minimum total expected long and short costs derived from the payoff table above. The EVPI means that if all of the uncertainty from the problem could be removed through perfect market research or some other means, an average of \$205 per season could be saved by eliminating long and short costs altogether. In other words, as much as \$205 per season could be spent for perfect market information to remove the uncertainty. The long and short costs for each level of demand under the perfect information condition are found on the diagonal of the payoff table. Because all of these values on the diagonal are zero, the total expected long and short costs are also zero. The difference between the total expected long and short costs under conditions of perfect information (\$0) and under conditions of imperfect information or uncertainty (\$205) is the EVPI.

b. Use payoff tables to maximize the total expected profits. Compute the EVPI.

First, complete a payoff table that maximizes the total expected profits (see the accompanying payoff table). The colored elements of the table are explained as follows:

- **S of 200 and SN of 400:** The \$1,000 found in this position means that if a strategy of 200 units is selected and a demand of 400 units is experienced, revenues would equal \$15(200), or \$3,000, and cost of goods sold would be \$10(200), or \$2,000, for a profit of \$1,000 for the season.
- **S of 300 and SN of 300:** The \$1,500 found in this position means that the strategy exactly meets the state of nature; revenues would be \$15(300), or \$4,500, and cost of goods sold would be \$10(300), or \$3,000, for a profit of \$1,500 for the season.

States of Nature

	SN_i / S_j	100	200	300	400	450	Total Expected Profits $EP = \Sigma[P(SN_i) \times \pi_{ij}]$
	100	\$ 500	\$ 500	\$ 500	\$ 500	\$ 500	\$ 500
Strategies	200	300	1,000	1,000	**1,000**	1,000	930
	300	100	800	**1,500**	1,500	1,500	1,290
	400	(100)	600	1,300	2,000	2,000	1,370 ←
	450	(200)	500	1,200	1,900	2,250	1,305
	$P(SN_i)$	0.1	0.1	0.4	0.3	0.1	

Note: π_{ij} is the profits of S_j and SN_i.

- **S of 400 and SN of 100:** The ($100) means that if a strategy of 400 units is selected and a demand of 100 units is experienced, revenues would be $15(100), or $1,500; cost of goods sold would be $10(100), or $1,000; and long costs would be $2(300), or $600. Profits would then be ($100) for the season.

All other elements of the payoff table are computed similarly. The expected profit column (EP) is completed by summing along each strategy row (S_j) the products of the probability of the states of nature $P(SN_i)$ and their π_{ij}. For instance, the EP of $S_j = 400$ units is computed this way:

$$EP = 0.1(-100) + 0.1(600) + 0.4(1,300) + 0.3(2,000) + 0.1(2,000)$$

$$= -10 + 60 + 520 + 600 + 200 = 1,370$$

Now compute the EVPI:

$$EVPI = [0.1(500) + 0.1(1,000) + 0.4(1,500) + 0.3(2,000) + 0.1(2,250)] - 1,370 = \$205$$

The profits for each level of demand under conditions of perfect information are found on the diagonal of the payoff table. The total expected profits under conditions of perfect information minus the maximum total expected profits under conditions of imperfect information or uncertainty is the value of EVPI.

c. Which stocking strategy is best for the #325 scarf? Explain the equivalence of the solutions of Parts a and b above.

The best stocking strategy is 400 units of the #325 scarves. This alternative is preferred regardless of whether the total expected profits or the total expected long and short costs criterion is used. The equivalence of the two analyses is evident from a comparison of their payoff tables. For instance, it can be seen that the difference between the optimal strategy of 400 units and any other stocking strategy is the same in both analyses: For a strategy of 200 units, costs increase ($645 − $205 = $440) and profits decrease ($1,370 − $930 = $440) by the same amount. The criterion of minimizing the total expected costs (cost of goods sold, long costs, and short costs) would be inappropriate in this example because of the presence of revenues.

Payoff tables are an effective tool for analyzing single-period decisions under conditions of uncertainty. Their flexibility in evaluating a multitude of POM stocking decisions is perhaps their greatest strength. Cash, maintenance parts, workers, inventory items, production capacity, standby machines, and service capacity are all single-period stocking decisions that can be analyzed by payoff tables when demand levels or states of nature are uncertain.

SOME REALITIES OF INVENTORY PLANNING

We have discussed several analytical approaches to inventory planning. Now we need to consider the magnitude of the problem and some of the practical difficulties that operations managers have in making these decisions.

ABC Classification of Materials

Because of the large number of materials used in production at many manufacturing plants, it can be desirable to classify materials according to the amount of analysis that can be justified. One scheme for classifying materials is the ABC method, which is based on the idea that only a small percentage of materials represents the majority of inventory value. Figure 14.8 illustrates the ABC method of classifying materials.

These observations about the ABC classification explain the interpretation of Figure 14.8:

1. The A materials represent only 20 percent of the materials in inventory and 75 percent of the inventory value.
2. The B materials represent 30 percent of the materials in inventory and 20 percent of the inventory value.
3. The C materials represent 50 percent of the materials in inventory and only 5 percent of the inventory value.

This classification suggests that the higher the inventory value of a material, the more analysis that should be applied to the material. Ordinarily, Class A materials would be analyzed extensively and Class C materials would be analyzed little.

However, judgment must be used in applying this approach or any of the inventory models of this chapter because other practical factors can be crucial in inventory decisions. Exceptions must be made for certain types of materials:

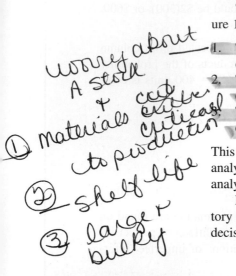

worry about A stock
1) materials critical to production
2) shelf life
3) large + bulky

Figure 14.8 | ABC Classification of Materials

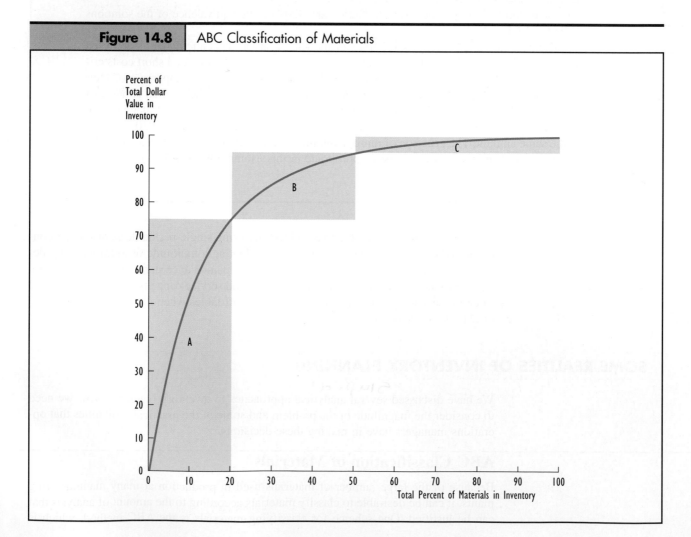

- **Materials critical to production.** Because stockouts of these materials can shut down entire production lines, larger inventories may be justified.
- **Materials with short shelf lives.** Because these materials may be subject to very fast obsolescence or deterioration, smaller inventories may be justified.
- **Materials that are very large and bulky.** Because these materials require so much storage space, smaller inventories may be justified.
- **Valuable materials subject to pilferage.** To reduce risk of loss, smaller inventories may be justified.
- **Materials with highly erratic lead times.** Larger orders for these materials reduce the number of orders during the year and mitigate the uncertainty of supply.
- **Materials with highly erratic demand.** Large order quantities and order points may be justified for materials with unpredictable demands.
- **Standard packaging, shipping container, or vehicle size.** Quantities other than the EOQ may be justified because of extra costs if order size departs from the norm.

big motors

EOQ and Uncertainty

Order quantities and order points require the use of information subject to uncertainty. Look at Figure 14.2 again. Note that estimation errors in demand (D), carrying cost (C), or ordering cost (S) would move us to the right or left of EOQ along the total annual stocking costs curve for a material. Moving in either direction increases our annual costs for stocking a material. Notice, however, that this curve tends to be rather flat near the EOQ; this is thought to be typical. The total impact of errors in estimating quantity for one material is usually not significant. However, when tens of thousands of items are carried in inventory, the impact of estimation errors expands tremendously.

Many factors must be considered in inventory decisions, such as size, value, and demand for materials.

© PREMIUM STOCK/CORBIS

Of perhaps greater concern to inventory decisions in POM are the costs that are not included in the EOQ formulas. Stockout, start-up quality, customer responsiveness, coordinating production, diluted ROI, reduced capacity, large lot quality, and production problem costs are real and substantial and should affect ordering decisions. But the EOQ models do not directly incorporate these costs. In practice, when these costs are important factors, ordering decisions are adjusted accordingly. For example, if stockout costs are predominant, order quantities and order points will be made large. The EOQ philosophy still applies in these situations, but more types of costs can implicitly be included in the models.

Another pragmatic POM tactic for all types of production is to establish emergency procedures to replenish inventories quickly. These emergency procedures are aimed at avoiding stockouts and permitting lower levels of safety stocks. One good example of the use of emergency replenishment procedures is found in hospitals, many of which have helicopters available to supply critical materials as needed from other hospitals or hospital supply warehouses.

Dynamics of Inventory Planning

Almost all inventory systems continually review their ordering practices and modify their order quantities, order points, and time intervals as required to give the kind of inventory performance desired. When we view inventory planning as a dynamic system that is continually modified as needed, less emphasis must be placed on any one computation. Actually, rather than using the EOQ, many firms set *initial* order quantities based on tradition, rough estimates, or other factors. Then they increase or decrease order quantities to fit their demand and supply patterns. Thus, the inventory systems empirically develop order quantities and order points so that neither excessive stockouts nor excessive inventories result.

Other Factors Affecting Inventory Planning

The quantity of a material that *can* be ordered may be constrained. For example, warehouse capacity may limit the order quantity of a material. Also, the production capacity and the production schedules for other products may limit the size of order quantities.

Special buys on materials is a factor that causes order quantities to be greater than the EOQ. When purchasing discovers a special buy, the savings from quantity discounts may be so spectacular that a company will buy all it can get of that material. Although this tends to play havoc with warehousing and increases other costs, the savings in purchase costs may be so great that firms occasionally make these special buys.

Vendor-Managed Inventories

One inventory management approach that has become popular in recent years is **vendor-managed inventories**. Many companies today are outsourcing the management of some of the materials that they use or sell. With this approach, a vendor will stock supplies of a material in the customer's manufacturing facility or retail store. The vendor will frequently monitor the inventory level of that material, and when the level gets low the vendor will replenish that material. The customer company is charged for the material only when it is used, so the vendor incurs the carrying cost of stocking the material in the customer's facility.

For this approach to be effective, the customer must have a high level of confidence in the vendor's ability to always keep plenty of the material in stock. And the vendor must have confidence that the customer will accurately record usage of the material. Long-term contracts are typically used with vendor-managed inventories. This provides the vendor with stable customer demand and frees the customer from the hassles of managing the inventory. Wal-Mart is one example of a company that uses the vendor-managed inventory approach with many of the products it sells. Wal-Mart provides vendors with point-of-sale demand data so that vendors can better anticipate demand and develop more accurate forecasts.

Given the benefits to the customer company, vendor-managed inventories will undoubtedly continue to increase in popularity.

Computers and Inventory Planning

One of the first areas in business to benefit from computerization was inventory planning. Business Snapshot 14.1 illustrates that today, inventory stock records are routinely maintained with the use of computers. As changes in inventory levels occur, the computer files are modified to reflect the latest inventory transactions. Managers can query these files and instantaneously determine how much of a material is in inventory, how much of a material is on order, when certain orders are expected to be received, and other information critical to inventory management. Computing order quantities, determining when orders should be placed, and printing purchase requisitions and purchase orders are routinely performed by computers. A few examples of management

---

BUSINESS SNAPSHOT 14.1

Improved Inventory Management at 3M

Minnesota Mining & Manufacturing Co. (3M) has recently modernized its finished-goods inventory management system and now uses the Internet to provide better customer service. 3M, with more than 70,000 employees, produces a wide variety of paper and tape office supplies such as Post-It notes and Scotch tape, selling more than 50,000 different products in 200 countries. Before the modernization, many customers had difficulty getting everything they ordered. One such customer was Staples, a large chain of office supply stores. According to Staples' vice-president for supply-chain management, David Crosier, Staples would order 10,000 rolls of Scotch tape and get 8,000. Worse, 3M couldn't

be counted on to get products to Staples' stores on time. The problem was causing stockouts of popular 3M office products.

To address these inventory problems, 3M developed its Global Enterprise Data Warehouse (GEDW) database of product, inventory, and customer information, and made it accessible over the Internet. Customers can now see what is in stock and order on-line. In the past three years 3M has invested $30 million in the database, while ongoing maintenance costs have been $2.6 million per year. However, savings in maintenance, reporting, and customer service costs have been $12.5 million per year.

The new GEDW system has allowed 3M to better anticipate cus-

tomer demands and substantially reduce its inventories of finished products. 3M now places detailed product descriptions and pictures on its web site (**http://www.3m.com**), and allows customers to download these descriptions for their own catalogs and web sites. This has reduced misinformation about its products.

3M's new inventory management system has done away with the frustration of paper forms and countless phone calls by customers concerning their orders. According to Crosier, in the first 18 months of using the system, 3M's product fill rate improved 20 percent, and its on-time performance almost doubled. "The technology takes a lot of inefficiencies out of the supply-chain process," he says.

Source: Little, Darnell. "3M: Glued to the Web." *Business Week E.Biz,* November 20, 2000, EB63–EB70.

information systems with embedded inventory management software are iCollaboration (**http://www.adexa.com**), SKEP (**http://www.dynasys.tm.fr**), Glovia (**http://www.glovia.com**), Macola (**http://www.macola.com**), SAP (**http://www.sap.com**), and Baan (**http://www.baan.com**).

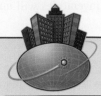

Wrap-Up

WHAT WORLD-CLASS COMPANIES DO

The inventory cycle is the central focus of independent demand inventory systems. Materials are ordered, received, and used, and the cycle is then repeated. The key decisions are how much to order of each material and when to place the orders. The formulas and variable definitions for the inventory models of this chapter are given in Table 14.8.

Under what circumstances would these models be appropriate? Many retailing, wholesaling, and warehousing operations routinely use the models. Inventories provide the means of meeting highly variable demand for their products and the need for instantaneous delivery. If a manufacturer uses the pond-draining method of production planning and control, as described in Chapter 13, the inventory models would be used throughout the production system. If push-type production planning and control is used, however, the models would not be used for most materials in raw-materials inventory, but they could be used for determining sizes of production lots and finished-goods inventories in produce-to-stock production. In pull-type production planning and control, given small and predetermined production lot sizes, the models could be used to determine setup times. *But today, all types of world-class companies are striving to be more inventory lean.*

Toward this end, the types of production planning and control systems that companies use are changing. The basic fact about the order quantity and order point systems of inventory planning is that they are based on the absence of accurate information about how many of each product is going to be demanded and how fast suppliers can supply materials. World-class companies have established information systems that electronically link the companies with their suppliers and customers. The availability of real-time information about orders from customers and deliveries from suppliers has allowed these companies to move from pond-draining to push systems to pull systems to focusing on bottlenecks. Although some companies are still using pond-draining approaches, most companies are using push systems, many companies have adopted pull systems, and some companies are focusing on bottleneck approaches.

Many world-class companies today are using vendor-managed inventories. Vendors are responsible for monitoring the inventory levels in the company's facility, and when the inventory gets low the vendor replenishes the stock. This outsourcing of inventory management allows world-class companies to focus more of their attention on their core business competencies.

The combination of improved information about future customer demand and an inventory-lean production system has allowed some companies to change from produce-to-stock to produce-to-order production. With less in-process inventory, orders can be produced so fast that finished-goods inventory is unnecessary for fast delivery of orders to customers. Business Snapshot 14.2 illustrates how some computer manufacturers are changing to produce-to-order production to remain competitive. For some world-class companies, the reduction of inventory levels throughout the production system is cited as a key factor in their success. Being inventory lean has reduced production and other costs, and it has improved product quality and customer responsiveness.

Table 14.8	Summary of Inventory-Planning Models

Variable Definitions

ac = acquisition cost—cost of producing or purchasing one unit of a material (dollars per unit)

C = carrying cost—cost of carrying one unit in inventory for one year (dollars per unit per year); proportion of value that is carrying cost times ac

D = annual demand for a material (units per year)

d = rate at which materials are used out of inventory (units per time period)

$\bar{d}$ = mean of d, demand per time period (units per time period)

DDLT = demand during lead time (units)

EDDLT = expected demand during lead time (units)

EOQ = economic order quantity—optimal quantity of material to order (units per order)

j = percentage of EDDLT as safety stock

LT = lead time (number of time periods)

OP = order point—point at which materials should be ordered (units or point in time)

p = rate at which materials are supplied to inventory (same units as d)

Q = quantity of material ordered at each order point (units per order)

σ_{DDLT} = standard deviation of DDLT

σ_d = standard deviation of d

S = average cost of completing an order for a material (dollars per order)

SS = safety stock (units)

T = order period—time interval between orders for a material (fraction of a year)

TMC = total annual material costs—total annual costs of stocking and acquiring a material (dollars per year)

TSC = total annual stocking costs—total annual carrying and annual ordering costs for a material (dollars per year)

Z = value from Appendix A, number of standard deviations that OP is from EDDLT

Formulas

Fixed Order Quantity Inventory Systems

Model I—Basic EOQ (see Example 14.1)

$EOQ = \sqrt{2DS/C}$ $TSC = (Q/2)C + (D/Q)S$

Model II—EOQ for Production Lots (see Example 14.2)

$EOQ = \sqrt{(2DS/C)[p/(p - d)]}$

$TSC = (Q/2)[(p - d)/p]C + (D/Q)S$

Order points (see Examples 14.4, 14.5, 14.6, and 14.7)

$OP = EDDLT + SS$

$OP = EDDLT + j(EDDLT)$ Percentage of EDDLT

$OP = EDDLT + \sqrt{EDDLT}$ Square root of EDDLT

$OP = EDDLT + Z(\sigma_{DDLT})$ Normal DDLT

$OP = LT(\bar{d}) + Z\sqrt{LT(\sigma_d)^2}$ Constant LT and normal d

Model III—EOQ with Quantity Discounts (see Example 14.3)

When assumptions of Model I apply:

$EOQ = \sqrt{2DS/C}$ $TMC = (Q/2)C + (D/Q)S + (D)ac$

When assumptions of Model II apply:

$EOQ = \sqrt{(2DS/C)[p/(p - d)]}$

$TMC = (Q/2)[(p - d)/p]C + (D/Q)S + (D)ac$

In either case, the procedures of Table 14.4 must be followed.

Fixed Order Period System

Model IV—Economic Order Period (see Example 14.8)

$T = \sqrt{2S/DC}$ $TSC = (DT/2)C + S/T$

$Q = $ Upper inventory target − Inventory level + EDDLT

BUSINESS SNAPSHOT 14.2

Computer Manufacturers Adopt Produce-to-Order Strategies

Want to know why every major manufacturer of personal computers is rushing to be like Dell Computer, the high-flying outfit that invented direct selling of PCs? Just ask a competitor. "In the ideal world," says Jim McDonnell, top marketer for Hewlett-Packard's PC group, "your customer wants to buy a PC, you source all the parts that day, ship it that day, and get it to the customer that day. There's no price protection. There's no inventory. Michael Dell is probably as close to that as anybody."

Dell Computer Corporation's build-to-order strategy has made Dell the industry's hottest and fastest-growing company. Its formula: Bypass distributors and other resellers and sell directly to customers. That enables Dell to build a customized configuration for every buyer and sell its PCs at below retailer prices. Compaq, Hewlett-Packard, IBM, and Packard Bell NEC have all been tweaking their strategies to include some form of build-to-order production.

At Dell, the entire process from the time the customer's phone call order is received to loading the finished PC onto a delivery truck takes just 36 hours. Orders are instantly relayed to one of Dell's three plants—in Austin, Texas; Penang, Malaysia; or Limerick, Ireland. You won't find any inventory there, though. "All our suppliers know that our components must be delivered within an hour," says Austin plant manager John Varol. Chips, boards, and drives are kept in trucks backed up into bays 50 feet from the beginning of the production line. There's no inventory of finished goods either. For large customers, Dell has a quick-ship plan where computers are delivered to the customer's door within 48 hours of an order.

Sources: "And Give Me an Extra-Fast Modem with That, Please." *Business Week*, September 29, 1997, 38; Serwer, Andrew E., "Michael Dell Turns the PC World Inside Out." *Fortune*, September 8, 1997, 76–86; Kirkpatrick, David, "Now Everyone in PCs Wants to Be Like Mike." *Fortune*, September 8, 1997, 91–92.

REVIEW AND DISCUSSION QUESTIONS

1. Name two purposes of carrying these inventories: (a) finished goods, (b) in-process, and (c) raw materials.

2. Define these terms: *backlogging, produce-to-order, produce-to-stock, order quantity, order point, inventory cycle, machine changeover, lot size, order period, two-bin system, vendor-managed inventory.*

3. Name and describe four costs that are reduced by holding inventories.

4. Name and describe seven costs that are increased by holding inventories.

5. Explain what is meant by a material with independent demand. Give an example, and explain why its demand is independent.

6. Explain what is meant by a material with dependent demand. Give an example, and explain why its demand is dependent.

7. Compare and contrast fixed order quantity inventory systems with fixed order period inventory systems.

8. Define these terms: *carrying costs, ordering costs, stockout costs, annual carrying costs, annual ordering costs, total annual stocking costs.*

9. List the costs included in annual carrying costs in Figure 14.2.

10. List the costs included in annual ordering costs in Figure 14.2.

11. Name four assumptions of the basic EOQ—Model I.

12. Name five assumptions of the EOQ for production lots—Model II.

13. In what units are these variables: D, S, C, Q, EOQ, p, and d?

14. Explain why the maximum inventory level of a material is greater when orders are received all at once than when orders are received gradually.

15. What are the purposes of safety stock? How will the use of safety stock affect the EOQ? How will the use of safety stock affect the TSC?

16. Explain what is meant by this statement: "The un-

certainties of inventory planning almost always affect operations managers when they are most vulnerable—when inventory levels are at their lowest points."

17. Give a brief explanation for each of the following: (a) DDLT, (b) EDDLT, (c) σ_{DDLT}, (d) discrete DDLT distributions, (e) continuous DDLT distributions, (f) LT, (g) σ_{LT}.

18. Define *service levels*.

19. Assuming the DDLT distribution is normal, write the formula for computing (a) EDDLT and (b) σ_{DDLT}.

20. Explain the relationship among these variables: order point, safety stock, and EDDLT.

21. What factors other than total annual stocking costs typically affect Q and T in practice?

22. Explain what world-class companies are doing in regard to inventory management.

INTERNET ASSIGNMENTS

1. Search the Internet for a producer of inventory control software. Describe what the software can do.

2. Search the Internet for a company that offers a quantity discount (or volume discount) on its products. Describe the pricing discounts.

3. Marcola produces software for manufacturing and distribution applications, among others. Visit Marcola's web site at **http://www.marcola.com** and locate information on its *Progression Series ERP* software. Describe some of the software features related to inventory management.

4. *MAPICS XA* is the most widely used manufacturing software worldwide and was first developed by IBM more than 20 years ago. Visit the web site of MAPICS at **http://www.mapics.com** and locate information on the *MAPICS XA* software. Describe some of the software features related to inventory management.

PROBLEMS

1. If the annual demand for a product is 350,000 units, then the annual carrying cost rate is 25 percent of the cost of the unit, the product costs $14.75 per unit to purchase, and each time the product is ordered the related ordering cost is $53.00.
   a. What is the EOQ?
   b. What is the TSC at the EOQ?
   c. How much would the TSC increase if the order quantity must be 2,500 units because of a standard shipping-container size?

2. If the annual demand for a product is 200,000 units, then the annual carrying cost rate is 30 percent of the cost of the unit, the product costs $37.50 per unit to purchase, and each time the product is ordered the related ordering cost is $96.00.
   a. What is the EOQ?
   b. What is the TSC at the EOQ?
   c. How much would the TSC increase if the order quantity must be 2,500 units because of a standard shipping-container size?

3. The information systems department of a local university buys paper for its copier machine frequently. Andrea Webb, the office manager, would like to determine the best quantity to order each time an order is placed. She has estimated that the ordering cost is $12 each time an order is placed. The monthly demand for paper is 135 reams (500 sheets to a ream). The cost of paper is $6.50 per ream, and the carrying cost is 25 percent of the paper cost per month. How many reams should be ordered at a time, and what is the expected average inventory level for copier paper?

4. First City Bank orders cash from the Federal Reserve Board to meet daily transaction needs. Linda Davis, the operations manager, estimates that $5,000,000 in cash will be needed next month. She has estimated that the cost to order, receive, and store each shipment of cash from the Federal Reserve Board will be $675 per shipment. First City Bank is open for business 250 days each year. The bank's related carrying cost for cash is 0.65 percent per month. (That is, each dollar held in the bank's vault costs $0.0065 per month in foregone profits.)

   a. How much should Linda order from the Federal Reserve Board each time a cash order is placed?
   b. What is the expected total annual carrying cost plus ordering cost?
   c. How many working days should one shipment of cash last First City Bank?

5. The Peace Care Hospital uses about 3,500 boxes of sterile bandages per month. The annual carrying cost rate is $2.90 per box per year. A typical box of sterile bandages costs $14.50 to purchase. The ordering cost is $25 each time an order is placed, regardless of the order quantity. There is storage space for at most 1,500 boxes of bandages at any time. The hospital operates 365 days per year. Peace Care Hospital would like to use the EOQ model.

   a. How many boxes of sterile bandages should be ordered each time an order is placed?
   b. How many orders per year should be expected?
   c. What is the expected TSC per year?
   d. How many days should one order last, on average?

6. The production rate of final assembly is 2,400 digital video discs (DVDs) per day. After DVDs are assembled, they go directly to finished-goods inventory. Customer demand averages 1,300 DVDs per day, or about 325,000 per year. It costs $700 to set up the assembly line for the DVDs, the cost per DVD is $2.30, and the carrying cost rate is 30 percent of product cost per year.

   a. How many DVDs should be in a production batch at final assembly?
   b. What is the annual TSC at the EOQ?

7. Louisiana Oil Refining buys crude oil on a long-term supply contract for $38 per barrel. When shipments of crude oil are made to the refinery, they arrive at the rate of 12,000 barrels per day. Louisiana Oil uses the oil at a rate of 5,000 barrels per day and plans to purchase 600,000 barrels of crude oil next year. If the carrying cost is 30 percent of acquisition cost per unit per year and the ordering cost is $11,600 per order:

   a. What is the EOQ for the crude oil?
   b. What is the TSC at the EOQ?
   c. How many days' worth of demand are supported by each order of crude oil?
   d. How much needed storage capacity is expected for the crude oil?

8. The Ohio Electric generating plant in Cincinnati buys coal to generate electricity. Coal is supplied by rail cars at the rate of 9,000 tons per day at a price of $16.50 per ton and is used at a rate of 1,400 tons per day. The plant operates 365 days per year, and its annual carrying cost for the coal is 28 percent of the average value of its inventory of coal. The ordering cost for a shipment of coal is $675. Ohio Electric would like to use the EOQ model.

   a. What quantity of coal should Ohio Electric order each time it places an order?
   b. What is the annual TSC that Ohio Electric should expect?
   c. How many days should it take to receive one shipment after it starts arriving?
   d. What is the maximum inventory level of coal that should be expected?

9. E Office Supplies, Inc., sells discounted office supplies over the Internet. One popular product sold is legal-size notepads, which are ordered by many law firms. E Office Supplies offers the following quantity discount structure, based on how many dozen notepads are ordered: 1–19 dozen, $21.95 per dozen; 20–99, $19.95 per dozen; 100–199, $18.95 per dozen; 200+, $17.95 per dozen. The law firm of Sanders, Taylor, Hernandez, Donahue and Smith (STHDS) would like to decide how many legal notepads to order using the EOQ model for quantity discounts. Its ordering cost is $35 per order, its anticipated need in the coming year is for 1,500 dozen notepads, and its annual carrying cost rate is 40 percent of acquisition cost.
   a. How many dozen notepads should STHDS order each time?
   b. What would be the resulting total inventory cost per year (ordering plus carrying plus materials)?
   c. How many orders per year should be expected?
   d. What is the expected maximum inventory level of notepads?
   e. If STHDS has only enough storage space for 150 dozen notepads, how many should it order each time?

10. A grocery store orders paper grocery bags from a distributor. The store uses about 2,300 cases of bags per year, and its ordering cost is $65 per order. The store's carrying cost rate is 35 percent of acquisition cost. The distributor has the following pricing structure for cases of bags: 1–49 cases, $129.95 per case; 50–249, $127.95 per case; 250–999, $126.95 per case; 1000+, $125.95 per case.
   a. How many cases of bags should the store order each time?
   b. What would be the resulting total inventory cost per year (ordering plus carrying plus materials)?
   c. How many orders per year should be expected?
   d. What is the expected maximum inventory level of paper bags (in cases)?
   e. If the store has only enough storage space for 200 cases of bags, how many should it order each time?

11. A fuel distributor near the Toledo airport is the sole vendor of jet fuel at the airport. Annual demand for jet fuel is 5,202,000 gallons, and daily demand averages 17,000 gallons. The distributor operates 306 days per year. The distributor orders jet fuel from a refinery that is several hundred miles away. The refinery will deliver fuel to the distributor at the rate of 44,000 gallons per day, although a smaller quantity can be delivered to complete an order. The distributor's ordering cost is $1,500 per order, and the annual carrying cost rate is 30 percent of the acquisition cost. The refinery has the following pricing structure: 10,000–44,000 gallons is $3.40 per gallon; 44,001–88,000 gallons is $3.30 per gallon; 88,000+ is $3.20 per gallon. Orders of less than 10,000 gallons are not accepted.
   a. How many gallons of jet fuel should the distributor order each time?
   b. What would be the resulting total inventory cost per year (ordering plus carrying plus materials)?
   c. How many orders per year should be expected?
   d. How many days will it take to receive the entire order if the first shipment arrives the day after the order is placed?
   e. What should be the maximum inventory level that is expected?

12. An auto dealership has experienced the following historical demands during lead times for Ford half-ton pickup trucks:

Actual DDLT	# of Occurrences	Actual DDLT	# of Occurrences
7	2	12	6
8	6	13	11
9	4	14	9
10	8	15	3
11	7	16	1

This data covers the dealership's past 57 orders to Ford. The replenishment lead time is five days to receive an order of trucks.
a. Compute the order point using a 90 percent service level.
b. Compute the expected demand during lead time.
c. What is the effective level of safety stock resulting from this order point?

13. The University of Madrid Computer Services Center orders cases of blank CDs, which university departments then order from the center. The center wants to determine the order point to use so that a 75 percent service level is provided to departments during the replenishment periods. The following historical demand during lead time data for the center has been collected:

Actual DDLT	# of Occurrences	Actual DDLT	# of Occurrences
3	2	8	7
4	3	9	4
5	6	10	2
6	8	11	1
7	11	12	1

This data covers the center's past 45 orders to its supplier. The replenishment lead time is four days to receive an order of CDs.
a. Compute the order point.
b. Compute the expected demand during lead time.
c. What is the effective level of safety stock resulting from this order point?

14. If EDDLT = 65.5 units, σ_{DDLT} = 10.5 units, DDLT is normally distributed, and service level is 95 percent:
a. What is the order point?
b. What is the safety stock level?

15. A bank wants to know how low it should let the level of cash fall before ordering more cash from its parent bank. If the demand during lead time for cash is normally distributed with a mean of $160,000 and a standard deviation of $20,000 and the service level is 85 percent:
a. What is the order point?
b. What is the safety stock level?

16. A part used to repair machines has a normally distributed monthly demand with a mean of 65.0 and a standard deviation of 5.2. If lead time is so predictable that it can be considered a constant 0.25 month and the service level is 90 percent:
a. What is the order point?
b. What is the safety stock level?

17. If j = 30 percent and EDDLT = 740 units:
a. Compute the safety stock using the percentage of EDDLT method.
b. Compute the order point using the percentage of EDDLT method.
c. Compute the safety stock using the square root of EDDLT method.
d. Compute the order point using the square root of EDDLT method.

18. The maintenance manager of a local manufacturing company wants to decide on a safety stock level and order point for a machine lubricating oil used by many of the company's machines. The typical usage of lubricating oil is 65 quarts per week. The oil is ordered from a company in Mexico and the replenishment lead time is 2.6 weeks to receive a shipment of oil. The company's policy is to carry 40 percent of EDDLT as safety stock for consumable supplies.
    a.   What is the expected demand during lead time for this lubricating oil?
    b.   How many quarts of oil should be carried as safety stock?
    c.   How many quarts of oil should be left when a replenishment order is placed?

19. A company wants to use a fixed order period for ordering a particular inventory item that is purchased for $180 per unit. The annual demand for the product is 15,000 units. The ordering cost is $800 per order. The annual carrying cost rate is 35 percent of the acquisition cost. The expected demand during lead time is 200 units, and the upper inventory target is 700 units.
    a.   How often should the product be ordered?
    b.   What is the annual total inventory cost that should be expected?
    c.   If the company is going to place an order now and the current inventory level is 248 units, what should be the order quantity?

20. Supplies-To-Go is an office supplies warehouse that is reviewing its ordering policies for its inventory items. The warehouse takes periodic inventory counts of its stock and places orders for materials needed. One of its items is a stapler, stock number BA550b. Inventory counts were taken today, and the inventory level was 1,216 units of the BA550b stapler. The upper inventory target is 4,800 units, and EDDLT is 745. Annual demand for this item is 82,000 units, ordering cost is $120 per order, acquisition cost is $4.85, and the annual carrying cost rate is 30 percent of acquisition cost.
    a.   When should the physical inventory count be taken next (i.e., how many calendar days)?
    b.   How many BA550b staplers should be ordered today?

21. An electronics manufacturer uses a gold alloy for plating. When a stockout occurs, it costs $60 to rush in an order. Any gold not used in any week costs $30 an ounce to finance, secure, and insure. The weekly demand pattern for gold has been determined by studying recent production records at the plant:

Weekly Demand for Gold (ounces)	Probability of Weekly Demand
100	0.1
150	0.2
200	0.3
300	0.3
500	0.1

    a.   How many ounces of gold should be stocked in each week with the objective of minimizing the total expected long and short costs for the material?
    b.   What is the EVPI?

22. An auto parts store sells automobile batteries. Batteries are ordered weekly for delivery on Monday morning. The sales price for an A50 is $85 and its cost for Big Store is $55. If too many batteries are ordered and stock must be carried over the weekend, corporate headquarters charges the store $10 per battery for increased

insurance, finance, and warehouse occupation costs. If the store is out of stock, it forgoes the profits from missed sales. How many A50 batteries should Big Store order each week if the weekly sales pattern is as shown below?

Number of Batteries Demanded	Probability
20	0.1
30	0.2
40	0.4
45	0.3

a. Work this problem by first minimizing the weekly total expected long and short costs (carrying and opportunity costs).

b. Next, work the problem by maximizing the total expected profits, and compute the EVPI.

c. Show the equivalence of your solutions in Parts a and b.

23. A bank keeps cash on hand to meet daily needs. If too much cash is on hand, the bank foregoes some interest income that it could have earned in alternative investments; that is, idle cash has an opportunity, or long cost. If the bank keeps too little cash on hand, it must go to other lending institutions for cash, and this results in extra operating costs (short costs). The estimates of demand for the next period are:

Demand or SN (thousands)	Frequency	P(SN)
$100	1/10	0.1
200	1/10	0.1
250	2/10	0.2
300	3/10	0.3
400	3/10	0.3

The firm's estimates of long and short costs are:

$$SC = \$1,000 + 0.8X \qquad LC = \$500 + 1.0Y$$

where:

SC = total period short costs

LC = total period long costs

X = total number of units (thousands of dollars) short during the period

Y = total number of units (thousands of dollars) long during the period

How much cash should the bank keep on hand for the next period to minimize total expected long and short costs?

CASES

Green Garden Products

Christina Phillips is the inventory manager at Green Garden Products, a large home gardening store. The store's owners have recently initiated a directive to reduce the store's operating costs and also improve customer service. As inventory manager, Christina would like to find ways to reduce inventory costs. She would also like to help improve customer service by better managing potential stockout situations.

Last semester Christina took a course on operations management at the local university and became familiar with simple inventory models. Now she would like to investigate the use of the EOQ model for the store's products. Christina has selected one popular product to start with: peat moss. Peat moss is sold in two-cubic-foot cubes, which cost the store $6.20 each to purchase from a vendor. Last year the average monthly sales volume of peat moss was 1,040 cubes and average daily sales volume was 40 cubes. The store is open about 26 days per month. This year Christina expects sales volume to be 10 percent greater than last year.

Stan Harrison, the store's cost accountant, has determined that the annual carrying cost rate should be 35 percent of the cost of a product. Stan also determined that the average cost of placing and receiving an order from a vendor is $80 per order, regardless of order quantity.

Based on her experience with the vendor for peat moss, Christina knows that the vendor has been very consistent in delivering a new order of peat moss four days after an order is placed. Christina also expects that the standard deviation of demand during lead time next year should be about 60 cubes, and she believes that actual demand during lead time is close to normally distributed. To try to improve customer service, Christina wants to have enough cubes of peat moss on hand so that no more than 1 out of 10 customers who want to buy a cube leaves empty-handed during the replenishment lead time.

Assignment

1. Using the EOQ model, how many cubes of peat moss should be ordered each time?
2. What is the expected annual inventory cost (carrying plus ordering plus material costs)?
3. How many orders should be expected next year, and how many working days should one order last?
4. What level of safety stock should be used, and what should be the order point?
5. If the order point were set at 200 cubes, what service level would this provide during the replenishment lead time?

Inventory Planning at Integrated Products Corporation

The Integrated Products Corporation (IPC) is developing ordering policies for its materials that it stocks for resale to its customers. The materials have been classified into three classes:

Class of Material	Description of Material Class
A *(Example: TS500)*	Materials that are of high cost, high volume, or otherwise of critical importance to customers. While these materials represent only about 20 percent of the *number* of materials, they represent about 80 percent of material *value*.
B	Materials that are of moderate cost, moderate volume, or otherwise moderately important to customers. These materials represent about 30 percent of the *number* of materials and about 15 percent of material *value*.
C *(Example: S80)*	Materials that are of low cost, low volume, or otherwise of low importance to customers. They can usually be obtained on short notice or other materials can be substituted. They represent about 50 percent of the *number* of materials and only about 5 percent of material *value*.

Assignment

1. The TS500 costs $24.95; IPC is forecasting that 10,000 of the parts will be needed annually; IPC estimates a 40 percent carrying cost for its inventory per year; it costs approximately $100 to process, receive, and inspect an order for these parts; IPC uses a fixed order quantity inventory system for Class A materials. How many of the parts should be ordered when the material is replenished?

2. The supplier of the TS500 has offered to ship the part at a rate of 100 per day during shipping periods via the supplier's own truck and IPC's plant works 300 days per year. If all other data in No. 1 above remain the same: a. How many parts should be ordered when the TS500 is replenished? b. What annual savings will come to IPC if the new shipping policy is enacted?

3. The supplier of the TS500 has agreed to give IPC a quantity discount. The cost to IPC will be:

Parts Ordered per Order	Cost per Part
1–999	$24.95
1,000–4,999	24.85
5,000+	24.80

If all other data in No. 1 above remain the same: a. How many parts should be ordered when the TS500 is replenished? b. What annual savings will come to IPC because of quantity discounts?

4. The supplier of the TS500 has offered to combine its offer of gradual supply during shipping periods of No. 2 above and the quantity discount offer of No. 3. How many parts should be ordered when the material is replenished if all other data remain the same as in Nos. 2 and 3?

5. The S80 costs $3.40 per pound; IPC is forecasting that 8,000 pounds will be needed annually; it costs approximately $25 to process, receive, and inspect an order for the material; and IPC uses a fixed order period inventory system for Class C materials. a. How often should the material be ordered? b. If the upper inventory target for S80 is to be 1,000 pounds, the present inventory level is 540 pounds, and the EDDLT is 300 pounds, how many pounds of the S80 should be ordered?

6. The expected demand during lead time (EDDLT) for the TS500 is 6,000 parts.
   a. Compute the order point for the TS500 by using a 20 percent of EDDLT method for computing safety stock.
   b. Compute the order point for the TS500 by using the square root of EDDLT method of computing safety stock.

Safety Stock Levels at Bell Computers

Bell Computers produces and stocks computer printers in its finished-goods warehouse. These DDLT historical data are believed to be representative of future demand for one printer model.

Actual DDLT	Frequency	Actual DDLT	Frequency
0–29	0	70–79	0.25
30–39	0.10	80–89	0.10
40–49	0.10	90–99	0.05
50–59	0.15	100–109	0.05
60–69	0.20	110–120	0

Assignment

1. If at least a 90 percent service level is to be provided for these printers: a. What is the order point? b. What is the safety stock?
2. If the DDLT for the printer is actually normally distributed with a mean of 65 and a standard deviation of 10, and a 90 percent service level is to be provided for these printers: a. What is the order point? b. What is the safety stock?
3. If the lead time for these printers is so stable that the lead time can be assumed to be a constant 6.5 days, the demand per day is normally distributed with a mean of 10 and a standard deviation of 2, and at least a 90 percent service level is to be provided for these printers: a. What is the order point? b. What is the safety stock?

SELECTED BIBLIOGRAPHY

Abernathy, Frederick H., John T. Dunlop, Janice H. Hammond, and David Weil. "Control Your Inventory in a World of Lean Retailing." *Harvard Business Review* 78, no. 6 (November/December 2000): 169–176.

Blatherwick, Andrew. "Inventory Management—The State of the Art." *Logistics Focus* 5, no. 8 (October 1997): 2–5.

Broeckelmann, Russ. *Inventory Classification Innovation: Paving the Way for Electronic Commerce and Vendor Managed Inventory.* Boca Raton, FL: St. Lucie Press, 1999.

Cox, James F., III, and John H. Blackstone, eds. *APICS Dictionary*, 9th ed. Falls Church, VA: APICS—The Educational Society for Resource Management, 1998.

Greene, James H., ed. *Production and Inventory Control Handbook.* Falls Church, VA: American Production and Inventory Control Society, 1997.

Henderson, Timothy P. "Software Helps Retailers Remove Millions of Dollars in Inventory from the Supply Chain." *Stores* 82, no. 10 (October 2000): 50–54.

Ketzenberg, Michael, Richard Metters, and Vicente Vargas. "Inventory Policy for Dense Retail Outlets." *Journal of Operations Management* 18, no. 3 (April 2000): 303–316.

Krupp, James A. G. "Managing Demand Variations with Safety Stock." *Journal of Business Forecasting* 16, no. 2 (Summer 1997): 8–13.

Luciano, Elisa, and Lorenzo Peccati. "Some Basic Problems in Inventory Theory: The Financial Perspective." *European Journal of Operational Research* 114, no. 2 (April 16, 1999): 294–303.

Rummel, Jeffrey L. "An Empirical Investigation of Costs in Batching Decisions." *Decision Sciences* 31, no. 1 (Winter 2000): 79–103.

Silver, Edward, David F. Pyke, and Rein Peterson. *Inventory Management and Production Planning and Scheduling*, 3rd ed. New York: John Wiley & Sons, 1998.

Smith, Stephen A., and Narendra Agrawal. "Management of Multi-Item Retail Inventory Systems with Demand Substitution." *Operations Research* 48, no. 1 (January/February 2000): 50–64.

Sox, Charles R., L. Joseph Thomas, and John O. McClain. "Coordinating Production and Inventory to Improve Service." *Management Science* 43, no. 9 (September 1997): 1189–1197.

Spedding, Paul. "Time-Phased Order Points." *Hospital Materiel Management Quarterly* 19, no. 2 (November 1997): 59–63.

Toomey, John W. *Inventory Management: Principles, Concepts, and Techniques.* Boston: Kluwer Academic Publishers, 2000.

Viale, J. David. *Inventory Management: From Warehouse to Distribution Center.* Menlo Park, CA: Crisp Publications, 1996.

Wild, Tony. *Best Practices in Inventory Control.* New York: John Wiley & Sons, 1998.

Zipkin, Paul H. *Foundations of Inventory Management.* Boston: McGraw-Hill, 2000.

15

Resource Requirements Planning: MRP and CRP

Introduction

Material Requirements Planning (MRP)
Objectives of MRP
Elements of MRP
Green Thumb Water Sprinkler Company
Lot-Sizing in MRP
Issues in MRP
From MRP I to MRP II to ERP
How MRP Adapts to Change
Evaluation of MRP

Capacity Requirements Planning (CRP)
Load Schedules

Wrap-Up: What World-Class Companies Do

Review and Discussion Questions

Internet Assignments

Problems

Cases
Integrated Products Corporation
Bank Sort International
Blanco Foods

Endnotes

Selected Bibliography

REDUCING INVENTORIES AT SC CORPORATION THROUGH MRP

At SC Corporation, the world's largest producer of evaporative coolers, sales had grown from $5 million to $20 million during the previous 15 years. This growth had resulted from the efficiency that evaporative coolers have over conventional refrigeration systems as the cost of electricity escalated. Mr. Gentry had owned SC for more than 30 years, but he recently sold the company to a large, diversified electrical machinery manufacturer. The new owner sent in a team of young, aggressive operations managers to take over the factory, and its initial impression was not favorable. The factory was overloaded with inventory: $20 million in raw materials inventory to support $20 million in sales per year seemed out of line. Inventory occupied so much space in the factory that production capacity was being curtailed. With sales forecasted to be $30 million next year, it was clear that something had to be done to increase production capacity. The team of operations managers initiated material requirements planning (MRP) to reduce inventory levels. It was also hoped that by freeing up factory space through reduction of inventories, another assembly line could be installed without increasing the size of the physical plant. After two years, the results of the MRP project are spectacular. Annual sales are $40 million, total materials inventory is $9.8 million, profits have increased fivefold, and the factory now has enough capacity to support sales of about $50 million. All of this was accomplished with less investment. The machinery needed for the new assembly line required less investment than the reduction in inventory levels attributed to MRP.

As the success story above indicates, material requirements planning (MRP) is being used increasingly as manufacturers strive to reduce inventory levels, increase production capacity, and increase profits. This chapter is about resource requirements planning systems, and MRP is an important part of these systems.

In Chapter 13 we studied aggregate capacity plans, master production schedules, and push-type production-planning and control systems. In these systems, the emphasis shifts to using information about customers, suppliers, and production to manage material flows. Batches of raw materials are planned to arrive at a factory about when needed to make batches of parts and subassemblies. Parts and subassemblies are made and delivered to final assembly about when needed, and finished products are assembled and shipped about when needed by customers. Batches of materials are pushed into the back of factories one after the other, which in turn push other batches through all the stages of production. These flows of materials are planned and controlled by a series of production schedules. These schedules state when batches of each particular product should come out of each stage of production.

Resource requirements planning has a language that has evolved with its growing use in industry. The terms and their definitions that are a part of this language are found in the glossary at the end of this book. Figure 15.1 illustrates how the functional areas of a business work together to plan and control a firm's resource requirements. All of these functions supply information that makes the resource requirements planning system work, and then each of the functions receives information back so that it can do its job better. Figure 15.2 illustrates the major elements of resource requirements planning systems. Estimated end-item demands, inventory status of end items, lot-sizing and safety stock policies of end items, and rough-cut capac-

Figure 15.1	Inputs and Outputs of a Resource Requirements Planning System

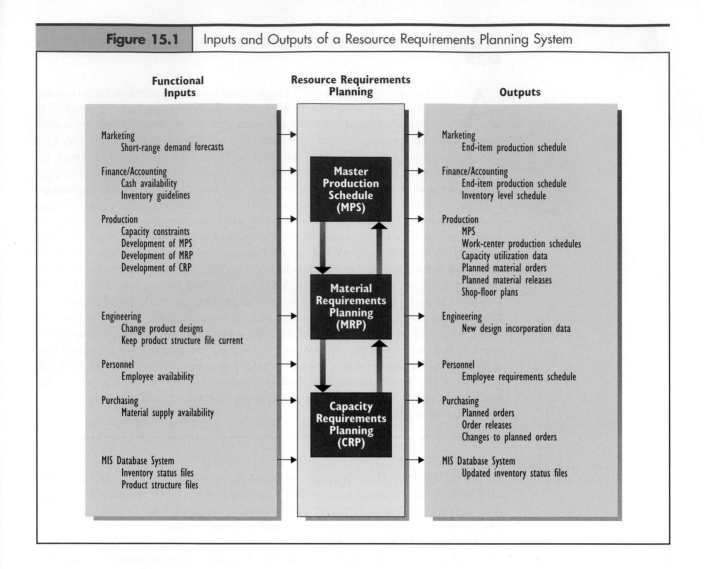

ity planning are integrated into a trial master production schedule (MPS). This trial MPS is tested by materials requirements planning and capacity requirements planning (CRP). In other words, can enough materials be purchased and does enough production capacity exist to produce the end items in the MPS? If either purchased materials or production capacity is not economically available, the MPS must be changed. After MRP and CRP determine that a MPS is feasible, the MPS becomes the nucleus of a short-range production plan.

In the remainder of this chapter, we study the two main elements of resource requirements planning systems: material requirements planning and capacity requirements planning.

MATERIAL REQUIREMENTS PLANNING (MRP)

Material requirements planning (MRP) begins with the principle that many materials held in inventory have dependent demands, a concept introduced in Chapter 14. Materials in raw-materials inventory and partially completed products held in in-process

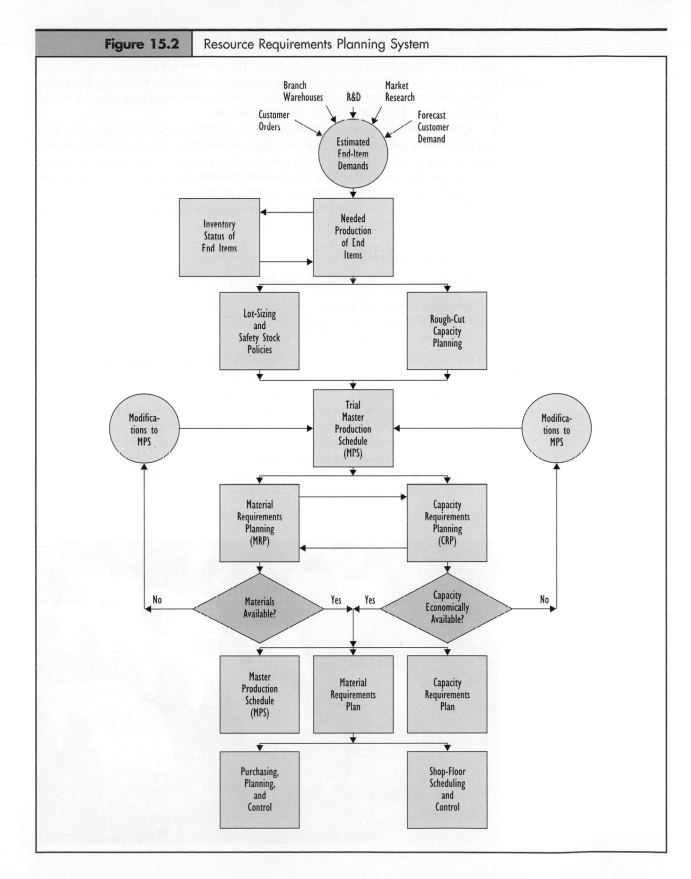

Figure 15.2 Resource Requirements Planning System

inventory are materials with dependent demand. The amount of a particular material with dependent demand that is needed in any week depends on the number of products to be produced that require the material. The demand for raw materials and partially completed products does not have to be forecast, therefore, because if it is known what finished products must be produced in a week, the amount of each material needed to produce these finished products can be calculated.

MRP is a computer-based system that takes the MPS as given; explodes the MPS into the required amount of raw materials, parts, subassemblies, and assemblies needed in each week of the planning horizon; reduces these material requirements to account for materials that are in inventory or on order; and develops a schedule of orders for purchased materials and produced parts over the planning horizon.

Why have so many production organizations today adopted MRP systems? The objectives of MRP help explain why its use has mushroomed.

Objectives of MRP

Operations managers adopt MRP for these reasons:

- To improve customer service.
- To reduce inventory investment.
- To improve plant operating efficiency.

Improving customer service means more than just having products on hand when customer orders are received. To have satisfied customers also means meeting delivery promises and shortening delivery times. Not only does MRP provide the necessary management information to make delivery promises that can be kept, but also the promises are locked into the MRP control system that guides production. Therefore, promised delivery dates become goals to be met by the organization, and the probability of meeting promised delivery dates is improved.

Figure 15.3 illustrates why MRP tends to reduce inventory levels. When fixed order quantity, order point systems are used to plan orders for a raw material, the order

The managers of this steel plant must consider material requirements planning to ensure the overall success of the enterprise.

© CORBIS

Figure 15.3	Raw-Materials Inventory Levels in MRP versus Fixed Order Quantity, Order Point Systems

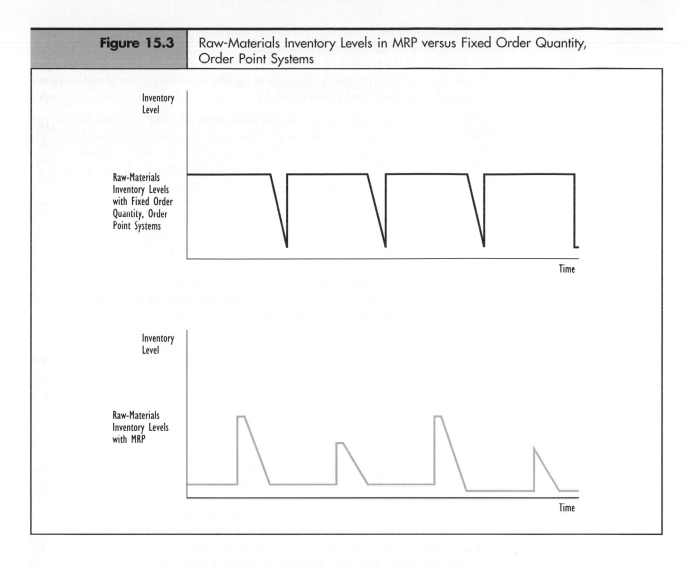

quantity plus safety stock remains in inventory until the raw material's end item appears in the master production schedule (MPS). Because these appearances may be several weeks apart, the pattern of inventory levels is long periods of full inventories interspersed with brief periods of low levels. In MRP, on the other hand, orders for raw materials are timed to arrive at approximately the time that the raw material's end item appears in the MPS. The pattern of inventory levels in MRP is long periods of low levels of inventory interspersed with brief periods of full inventories. The impact of MRP on raw-materials inventory levels is therefore dramatically reduced average inventory levels.

Because MRP better controls the quantity and timing of deliveries of raw materials, parts, subassemblies, and assemblies to production operations, the right materials are delivered to production at the right time. Additionally, inflows can be slowed or accelerated in response to changes in production schedules. These controls of MRP result in reduced labor, material, and variable overhead costs for the following reasons:

- Reduced numbers of stockouts and material delivery delays result in more production without increases in the number of employees and machines.

- Reduction of the incidence of scrapped subassemblies, assemblies, and products resulting from the use of incorrect parts.
- Capacity of the production departments is increased as a result of decreased production idle time, increased efficiency of the physical movements of materials, and reduced confusion and planning delays.

All of these benefits result mainly from the **philosophy of MRP systems.** Simply put, MRP systems are based on the philosophy that each raw material, part, and assembly needed in production should arrive simultaneously at the right time to produce the end items in the MPS. This philosophy results in expediting materials that are going to be late and slowing down the delivery of materials that are going to be early. For example, if one material is going to be late and nothing can be done about it, the other materials needed to assemble the end item will not be needed until the one late material arrives. The MRP system changes the due dates of all the materials so that materials arrive simultaneously to assemble the end item. A chief benefit of MRP systems is that production operations work on parts that are really needed on their due dates so that production capacity is being used to directly support the MPS. This avoids expediting the production of parts through the factory so that they arrive at final assembly to find that the parts' end items are not being assembled this week.

MRP has become a valuable planning tool for thousands of manufacturing facilities around the world. After implementing MRP, common benefits are increased inventory turns, more delivery promises met, fewer orders that need to be split because of material shortages, fewer expediters required, and shorter lead times from customer order to delivery of finished products. Let us now examine the features of MRP systems.

Elements of MRP

Figure 15.4 describes the operation of the MRP system. The master production schedule drives the entire MRP system. It is accepted as given. The inventory status file and bills of material file supply additional information about products included in the master production schedule. These inputs are fed into the MRP computer program, which generates the outputs. The inventory transactions resulting from the MRP actions are put back into the inventory status file so that current inventory records are maintained. The planned order schedule and changes to planned orders are the primary outputs of MRP. Exception, performance, and planning reports are also generated for management's use.

Master Production Schedule

A master production schedule (MPS) is devised to either replenish finished-goods inventories or to fill customer orders. An MPS begins as a trial schedule to be tested for feasibility through MRP and CRP. As these schedules are proved feasible, they become the MPS that is put into action. MRP cannot distinguish between feasible and infeasible master production schedules. That is to say, MRP assumes that the MPS can be produced within the production capacity constraints. MRP explodes the master schedule into material requirements. If these requirements cannot be met by the materials available from inventory or from materials on order, or if insufficient time is available for new orders, then the MPS will need to be modified to a new MPS.

The MPS drives the MRP system, and as the MPS is updated, the MRP results are also modified. Material orders are speeded up or slowed down or canceled. When the MPS is frozen, the plan for the inflow of materials emanating from MRP is also frozen.

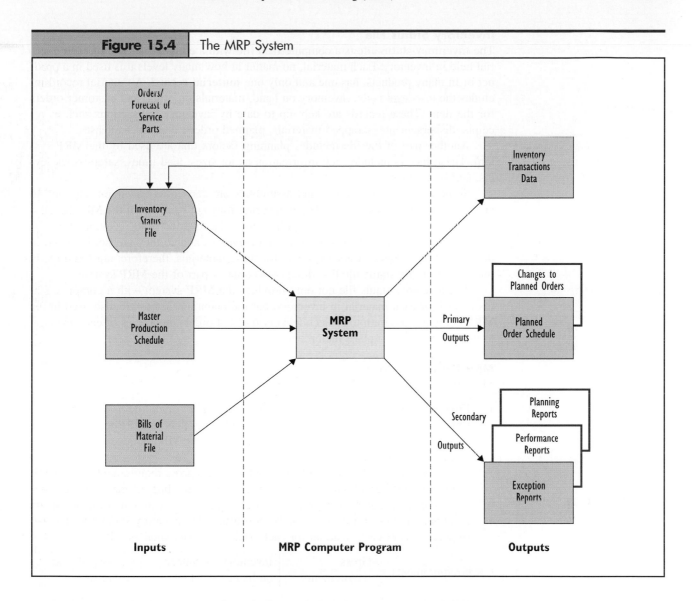

Figure 15.4 | The MRP System

Inputs   **MRP Computer Program**   **Outputs**

Bills of Material File

A bill of material is a list of the materials and their quantities required to produce one unit of a product, or end item. Each product therefore has a bill of material. A bills of material file, or **product structure file** as it is sometimes called, is a complete list of all finished products, the quantity of each material in each product, and the structure (assemblies, subassemblies, parts, and raw materials and their relationships) of products. Another term for a bill of material is **indented bill of material,** a list in which the parent is in the margin and its components are indented to show structure. (See Table 15.3 on page 594.)

The bills of material file is an up-to-date computerized file that must be revised as products are redesigned. Accuracy of the bills of material file is a major hurdle that must be overcome in most MRP applications. With the confidence that the file is current, once the MPS is prepared, end items in the MPS can be *exploded* into the assemblies, subassemblies, parts, and raw materials required. These units may be either purchased from outside suppliers or produced in in-house production departments.

Inventory Status File

The inventory status file is a computerized file with a complete record of each material held in inventory. Each material, no matter at how many levels it is used in a product or in many products, has one and only one **material record.** A material record includes the low-level code, inventory on hand, materials on order, and customer orders for the item. These records are kept up to date by inventory transactions such as receipts, disbursements, scrapped materials, planned orders, and order releases.

Another part of the file includes planning factors that are used by the MRP system. These factors include such information as lot sizes, lead times, safety stock levels, and scrap rates.

Some parts, subassemblies, and assemblies are carried as end items supplied to customers as replacement parts. These materials may not be a part of the MPS because they are purchased directly from suppliers and placed directly in inventory for customer demand; in other words, they are not *produced* and so they are not included in the MPS. The orders or forecast orders for these materials, therefore, are fed directly into the inventory status file that directly becomes a part of the MRP system.

The inventory status file not only provides the MRP system with a complete status record for each material in inventory, but the planning factors are also used in the MRP computer program to project delivery dates of orders, quantities of each material to order, and when to place the orders.

MRP Computer Program

The MRP computer program operates this way:

1. First, with the MPS it begins to determine the number of end items needed in each time period. Time periods are sometimes called buckets in MRP terminology.
2. Next, the numbers of service parts not included in the MPS but deduced from customer orders are included as end items.
3. Next, the MPS and service parts are exploded into gross requirements for all materials by time period into the future by consulting the bills of material file.
4. Next, the gross materials requirements are modified by the amount of materials on hand and on order for each period by consulting the inventory status file. The net requirements of each material for each bucket are computed as follows:

$$\text{Net requirements} = \frac{\text{Gross}}{\text{requirements}} - \left[\frac{\text{Inventory}}{\text{on hand}} - \frac{\text{Safety}}{\text{stock}} - \frac{\text{Inventory allocated}}{\text{to other uses}} \right]$$

   If the net requirements are greater than zero, orders for the material must be placed.
5. Finally, the orders are offset to earlier time periods to allow for lead times at each step in the production process and supplier lead times.

This procedure results in inventory transactions data (orders released, changes in orders, and so on), which are used to update the inventory status file, the primary output reports, and secondary output reports.

Outputs of MRP

The outputs of MRP systems dynamically provide the schedule of materials for the future—amount of each material required in each time period to support the MPS. Two primary outputs result:

1. **Planned order schedule**—a plan of the quantity of each material to be ordered in each time period. This schedule is used by purchasing to place orders with suppliers and by production to order parts, subassemblies, or assemblies from upstream production departments. The planned orders become a guide for future production at suppliers and for in-house production schedules.

2. **Change in planned orders**—modification of previous planned orders. Quantities of orders can be changed, orders can be canceled, or the orders can be delayed or advanced to different time periods through the updating process.

The secondary MRP outputs provide this information:

1. **Exception reports**—reports that flag items requiring management attention in order to provide the right quantity of materials in each time period. Typical exceptions noted are reporting errors, late orders, and excessive scrap.
2. **Performance reports**—reports that indicate how well the system is operating. Examples of performance measures utilized are inventory turns, percentage of delivery promises kept, and stockout incidences.
3. **Planning reports**—reports to be used in future inventory-planning activities. Examples of such planning information are inventory forecasts, purchase commitment reports, traces to demand sources (pegging), and long-range material requirements planning.

These are the major elements of MRP—the inputs, the MRP computer program, and the outputs. Let us now work through an example to see how inventory planning can be affected by the use of MRP.

Green Thumb Water Sprinkler Company

Business Snapshot 15.1 demonstrates how MRP can be applied to one product, a water sprinkler. Figure 15.5 illustrates this product. Read the account and work your way through Figure 15.7, the MRP schedule. Make sure you understand how each piece of information is taken from the MPS (Table 15.1), the bill of material (Table 15.2), and the inventory status report (Table 15.4) to be used in the calculations of the MRP schedule.

BUSINESS SNAPSHOT 15.1

Green Thumb Water Sprinkler Company

James Verde, president of Green Thumb Water Sprinkler Company, has just called a meeting of his key personnel to discuss new approaches to inventory planning at Green Thumb. Mr. Verde starts the meeting:

Mr. Verde: I've called this meeting to explore new avenues for inventory planning in our organization. The incidences of stockouts in our raw-materials inventory have led to lost business to the point that we just can't tolerate them anymore. And the answer is not larger order quantities and higher safety stocks, because the interest charges for carrying our

inventory are eating us alive. Somehow we've got to plan our acquisition of materials to mesh more closely with our customers' orders for finished products.
Bonnie Buck: I heartily agree, Mr. Verde. As production manager, may I say that when we in production place orders for materials from the warehouse, it seems they're out of stock as often as not. The warehouses are full—but of the wrong materials. Something has got to to be done.
Bill Compton: Well, as materials manager, I'm obviously on the hot seat here. We've already concluded that our traditional system of fixed order quantities and order

points is just not doing the job. Our individual customer orders are simply too large and too far apart to fit the assumptions of our present system. In anticipation of this problem, Joe Johnson, our inventory system analyst, has been attending a night class in material requirements planning (MRP) over at the university. Joe has selected the #377 lawn sprinkler (Figure 15.5) to demonstrate the MRP technique. Joe, will you show us the results of your analysis?
Joe Johnson: Thank you, Mr. Compton. I've prepared an MRP schedule for the #377 based on our most recent master production schedule, #377 bill of material,

| Figure 15.5 | #377 Lawn Sprinkler |

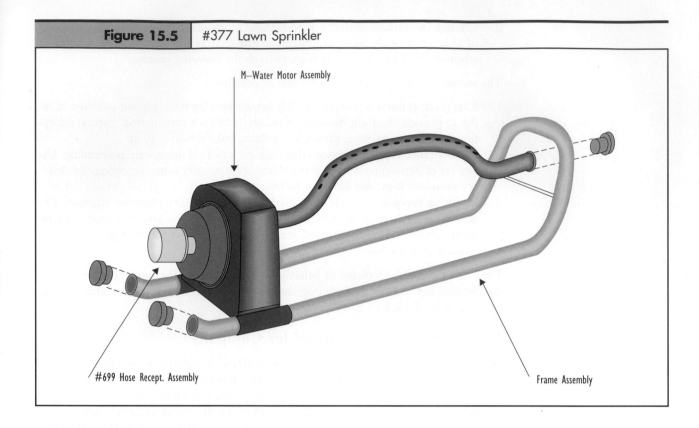

M—Water Motor Assembly

#699 Hose Recept. Assembly

Frame Assembly

and the inventory status of #377 and its components. The planned order schedule summarizes the recommended timing and size of orders of #377 components.

After the group studies the results of the MRP analysis, Bonnie Buck has some clarifying questions:

Bonnie Buck: Joe, so I'll understand the mechanics of MRP, could you take just one component in the MRP schedule and explain your calculations?

Joe Johnson: Sure, Bonnie. Let's concentrate on Component C—the

water motor. First, notice that our analysis of customer orders and forecasts of orders has resulted in Table 15.1, the master production schedule for the #377 lawn sprinkler. One thousand units are needed in Week 4 and 2,000 units are needed in Week 8. Next, from the bill of material for the #377 (Table 15.2), we can see that one unit of Component C goes into each unit of Component M (water motor assembly) and one unit of Component M goes into each #377. This relationship can perhaps be seen more clearly

in Figure 15.6—Product Structure: #377 Lawn Sprinkler—and Table 15.3—Indented Bill of Material: #377 Lawn Sprinkler. Next, looking at the MRP schedule for the #377 in Figure 15.7, note that the number of #377 units available going into Week 4 is 200 units (the difference between the on-hand inventory balance and the safety stock). Because we need 1,000 #377 units in Week 4 and 200 units are available from inventory, we have a net requirement of 800 units in Week 4. Because it takes one week to

| Table 15.1 | Master Production Schedule: #377 Lawn Sprinkler |

						WEEK			
	1	2	3	4	5	6	7	8
Gross requirement				1,000				2,000

Table 15.2	Bill of Material: #377 Lawn Sprinkler

Parent Code	Component Code	Level Code	Description	Components Required per Parent
	377	0	#377 Lawn Sprinkler	
377	M	1	Water motor assembly	1
	F	1	Frame assembly	1
	H	1	#699 hose recept. assembly	1
M	A	2	$\frac{1}{2}''$ dia. $\frac{1}{32}''$ alum. tube	10
	B	2	$\frac{1}{2}'' \times \frac{1}{16}''$ metal screws	3
	C	2	Water motor	1
F	A	2	$\frac{1}{2}''$ dia. $\frac{1}{32}''$ alum. tube	40
	D	2	$\frac{1}{2}'' \times \frac{1}{2}''$ #115 plastic cup	3
	B	2	$\frac{1}{2}'' \times \frac{1}{16}''$ metal screws	3

Figure 15.6	Product Structure: #377 Lawn Sprinkler

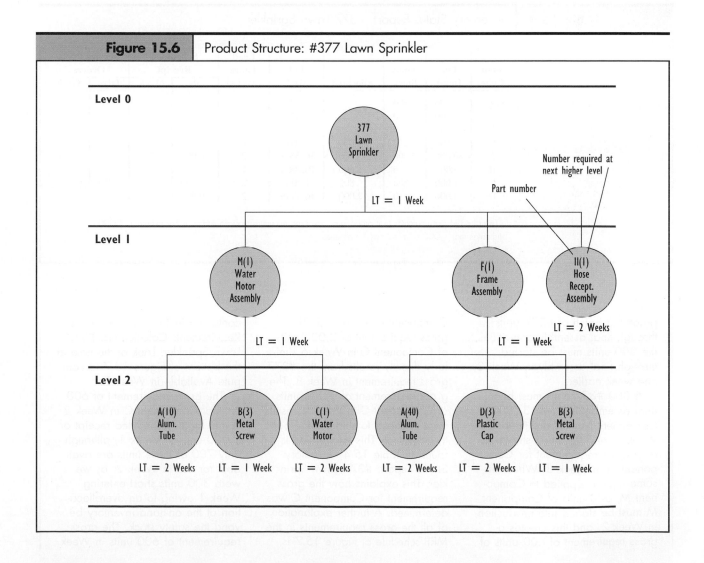

Table 15.3	Indented Bill of Material: #377 Lawn Sprinkler

LEVEL			
0	**1**	**2**	**Quantity**
377			1
	M		1
		A	10
		B	3
		C	1
	F		1
		A	40
		D	3
		B	3
	H		1

Table 15.4	Inventory Status Report: #377 Lawn Sprinkler

Item Code	On Hand	Safety Stock	Allocated	Lot Size*	Lead Times (weeks)	Scheduled Receipt		Service Parts Orders	
						Qty.	Week	Qty.	Week
377	500	300		LFL	1				
M	200	0		LFL	1				
F	300	0		LFL	1				
H	1,500	200	1,000	1,000+	2				
A	30,000	5,000	15,000	50,000+	2	50,000	1		
B	5,000	0	2,500	10,000+	1				
C	1,000	500	800	1,000+	2	1,000	1	1,000	4
D	3,000	0	2,000	10,000+	2	10,000	1		

*The plus (+) sign indicates that any quantity over the minimum may be ordered. For example, 1,000+ indicates that 1,000 or more may be ordered.

process a batch of #377 units through final assembly operations, the 800 units must be started through final assembly in Week 3, one week earlier.

If 800 #377 units must begin final assembly in Week 3, 800 Component M units are needed in Week 3, and this need shows up as a gross requirement for Component M in Week 3. When this same logic is applied to Component M, 600 units of Component M must be started into production in Week 2, and this creates a gross requirement of 600 units of Component C in Week 2. The gross requirement of 2,000 units of Component C in Week 6 similarly directly results from the #377 gross requirement in Week 8. The gross requirement of 1,000 units of Component C in Week 4 results from the need to ship service parts to customers. This information is found in Table 15.4—Inventory Status Report: #377 Lawn Sprinkler. This explains how the gross requirement for Component C was determined. A further explanation of all the gross requirements in the MRP schedule of Figure 15.7 is

contained in Table 15.5—Gross Requirements Calculations: #377 Lawn Sprinkler. Look at the note at the bottom of Figure 15.7 to compute Available in Week 1.

The gross requirement of 600 units of Component C in Week 2 is met by the scheduled receipt of 1,000 units in Week 1, although only 700 of these units are available for use in Week 2, as we were 300 units short entering Week 1 owing to an overallocation of the on-hand inventory beyond the safety stock. The gross requirement of 600 units in Week

Figure 15.7 | MRP Schedule: #377 Lawn Sprinkler

Item Code	Level Code	Lot Size	Lead Time Weeks	On Hand	Safety Stock	Allo-cated		1	2	3	4	5	6	7	8
															Week Number
377	0	LFL	1	500	300		Gross Requirements				1,000				2,000
							Scheduled Receipts								
							Available	200	200	200	200				
							Net Requirements				800				2,000
							Planned Order Receipts				800				2,000
							Planned Order Releases			800				2,000	
M	1	LFL	1	200			Gross Requirements			800				2,000	
							Scheduled Receipts								
							Available	200	200	200					
							Net Requirements			600				2,000	
							Planned Order Receipts			600				2,000	
							Planned Order Releases		600				2,000		
F	1	LFL	1	300			Gross Requirements			800				2,000	
							Scheduled Receipts								
							Available	300	300	300					
							Net Requirements			500				2,000	
							Planned Order Receipts			500				2,000	
							Planned Order Releases		500				2,000		
H	1	1,000+	2	1,500	200	1,000	Gross Requirements			800				2,000	
							Scheduled Receipts								
							Available	300	300	300	500	500	500	500	
							Net Requirements			500				1,500	
							Planned Order Receipts			1,000				1,500	
							Planned Order Releases	1,000				1,500			
A	2	50,000+	2	30,000	5,000	15,000	Gross Requirements		26,000				100,000		
							Scheduled Receipts	50,000							
							Available	60,000	60,000	34,000	34,000	34,000	34,000		
							Net Requirements						66,000		
							Planned Order Receipts						66,000		
							Planned Order Releases				66,000				
B	2	10,000+	1	5,000		2,500	Gross Requirements		3,300				12,000		
							Scheduled Receipts								
							Available	2,500	2,500	9,200	9,200	9,200	9,200	7,200	7,200
							Net Requirements		800				2,800		
							Planned Order Receipts		10,000				10,000		
							Planned Order Releases	10,000				10,000			
C	2	1,000+	2	1,000	500	800	Gross Requirements		600		1,000		2,000		
							Scheduled Receipts	1,000							
							Available	700	700	100	100	100	100		
							Net Requirements				900		1,900		
							Planned Order Receipts				1,000		1,900		
							Planned Order Releases		1,000		1,900				
D	2	10,000+	2	3,000		2,000	Gross Requirements		1,500				6,000		
							Scheduled Receipts	10,000							
							Available	11,000	11,000	9,500	9,500	9,500	9,500	3,500	3,500
							Net Requirements								
							Planned Order Receipts								
							Planned Order Releases								

Notes: (1) Any Scheduled Receipt is included in the Available row for that week; (2) Net Requirements = Gross Requirements − Available; (3) Week 1 Available = On Hand − Safety Stock − Allocated + Scheduled Receipts; (4) (Available for all other weeks) Week 4 Available = Week 3 Available − Week 3 Gross Requirements + Week 3 Planned Order Receipts + Week 4 Scheduled Receipts.

Table 15.5	Gross Requirements Calculations: #377 Lawn Sprinkler

Component Code	Parent Code	Components Required per Parent	Components Required for Parents' Production		Service Parts Required		Total Gross Requirement	
			Quantity	Week	Quantity	Week	Quantity	Week
M	377	1	800	3			800	3
M	377	1	2,000	7			2,000	7
F	377	1	800	3			800	3
F	377	1	2,000	7			2,000	7
H	377	1	800	3			800	3
H	377	1	2,000	7			2,000	7
A	M	10	6,000	2				
A	F	40	20,000	2			26,000	2
A	M	10	20,000	6				
A	F	40	80,000	6			100,000	6
B	M	3	1,800	2				
B	F	3	1,500	2			3,300	2
B	M	3	6,000	6				
B	F	3	6,000	6			12,000	6
C	M	1	600	2			600	2
C	—	—			1,000	4	1,000	4
C	M	1	2,000	6			2,000	6
D	F	3	1,500	2			1,500	2
D	F	3	6,000	6			6,000	6

2 combined with the 700 units available in Week 2 results in 100 units available to meet the gross requirement of 1,000 units in Week 4. This leaves a net requirement of 900 units in Week 4 and 1,000 units, the minimum lot size, are planned to be received in Week 4. After offsetting for the two weeks of lead time to receive the shipment of Component C, we should release the order for 1,000 units in Week 2.

The gross requirement of 2,000 units in Week 6 is similarly computed. Now do you see how we work our way through Figure 15.7, the MRP schedule?

Bonnie Buck: Yes. How do you know that the MPS and the planned order schedule are feasible? In other words, how do you know that we have the production capacity to produce the MPS, and how do you know that the materi-

als will be available in time to allow us to produce the MPS?

Joe Johnson: That's a good question, Bonnie. We know that purchased materials will be available in sufficient quantities and in time to satisfy the planned order schedule (Table 15.6) because we have double-checked with our suppliers. This method of checking whether materials can be supplied in time to make the production of the MPS feasible will be a continuing requirement in MRP. If we discovered that a material could not be supplied in time or in sufficient quantities to conform to the planned order schedule, we would have only two alternatives: expedite the order and perhaps pay extra to have the order processed on an overtime basis at our suppliers, or change the MPS and go through the MRP process again. If the MPS is changed, the

affected end item would have to be moved outward to later periods in the MPS.

The MPS has also been checked for production capacity feasibility. Load schedules were developed for each production department at the plant. All the products in the MPS were included, and it was clear that sufficient production capacity exists in each department to allow us to produce the MPS. This brings up an interesting point: How do we develop detailed weekly production schedules from the MRP schedule that is shown in Figure 15.7? Only items 377, M, and F, which are higher-level items, require in-house production. All other items are purchased from our suppliers.

The production departments where the 377, M, and F items will be produced include the

Table 15.6	Planned Order Schedule: #377 Lawn Sprinkler

Item Code	WEEK							
	1	2	3	4	5	6	7	8
377			800				2,000	
M		600				2,000		
F		500				2,000		
H	1,000				1,500			
A				66,000				
B	10,000				10,000			
C		1,000		1,900				
D								

planned order releases for these items in their load schedules. For example, 600 and 2,000 units of Component M must enter production in the Mechanical Fabrication and Assembly Department in Weeks 2 and 6, respectively. The amount of labor per unit and the amount of machine-hours per unit are multiplied by these quantities, and the result is the amount of production capacity required in the department for Component M. When this same process is followed for all our products, the loading can be compared to the labor and machine capacity of the department. The same loading analysis would also be applied to the Final Assembly Department and the Metal Fabrication and Assembly Department.

As you can see, capacity requirements planning (CRP), as this analysis is called, is a required part of the overall production and inventory-planning process. Additionally, the detailed production schedules of the production departments are picked off the MRP schedules. When all the planned order releases are picked off all the components of the MRP schedule that are to be produced in-house and classified according to their production departments, the result is departmental production schedules.

Do you see the connection between MRP and the departmental production schedules?

Bonnie Buck: Yes. Now would you summarize how MRP would be applied to all of our products in practice?

Joe Johnson: The procedure for our six major products would mechanically be the same as we demonstrated for #377. The big difference would be in computerizing the whole process. The figures that we've seen here today were all manually calculated. These could be the major tasks for us to get an MRP system operative: (1) Build an accurate computerized inventory status file for all of our products. (2) Improve our forecasting methods so that we can combine forecasts with in-hand customer orders to form a reliable basis for an accurate master pro-

duction schedule. (3) Build an up-to-date computerized bills of material file for all our products. (4) Buy the services of ABM Computer Services to assist us in installing the MRP computer program and debugging the MRP system after it's installed. I would estimate that we could have an MRP system operating for all our products in about six months.

Mr. Verde: Joe, what are the major advantages of MRP over our present inventory-planning system, which is tied to economic order quantities and order points?

Joe Johnson: (1) Better customer service, (2) lower inventory levels, and (3) higher operating efficiency in our production departments.

The group members all agreed to give MRP a try by running the new system parallel with the present system for six months. They thought that this approach should give a practical comparison of the results of MRP and the present inventory-planning system.

The planned order schedule (Table 15.6) is the primary output of MRP. The **planned order schedule** is a schedule of planned future order releases over the entire planning horizon. This report indicates to purchasing and production schedulers what materials to order, what quantities of materials to order, and when to place the orders for every material in the production system.

Lot-Sizing in MRP

In MRP, whenever there is a net requirement for a material, a decision must be made concerning how much of the material to order. These decisions are commonly called **lot-sizing decisions**. In produce-to-order firms, the size of the customer's order is usually the lot size that will be produced because it cannot be assumed that there will be other orders for the custom-designed product in the future. On the other hand, in produce-to-stock firms, because only a few standard product designs are produced for inventory, the size of production lots is primarily a question of economics. Operations managers would ordinarily like to order and produce large lots of materials for these reasons:

1. The annual cost of changing over machines between production lots is less and production capacity is greater because of less downtime caused by machine changeovers.
2. The annual cost of placing purchase orders is less because only a few orders for large lots of materials are placed with suppliers.
3. By ordering large lots of materials from suppliers, price breaks and transportation cost breaks can be taken advantage of, resulting in lower purchasing costs of the materials.

On the other hand, operations managers would ordinarily like to produce small lots of materials for these reasons:

1. Smaller lots of materials result in lower average inventory levels and the annual cost of carrying inventories is less.
2. Lower inventory levels can reduce the risk of obsolescence when product designs are changed.
3. Smaller lots result in less in-process inventory and customers' orders can be produced faster.

Operations managers cannot have the benefits of both small and large lots. They must strike a balance between lots that are not too small and lots that are not too large. Much research has been conducted in developing methods of determining lot sizes. For example, in Chapter 14, the EOQ was used to compute lot sizes, but two restrictive assumptions of the EOQ make its use in MPS and MRP costly.

First, the basic EOQ assumes that the per-unit cost does not depend on the quantity of a material ordered, but we know that suppliers often offer quantity discounts for purchased materials. Likewise, for materials produced in-house, as illustrated in Figure 14.1 in Chapter 14, the size of the lot affects the unit cost of the material. Operations managers therefore either use the EOQ with quantity discounts or, perhaps more commonly, specify **minimum lot sizes.** For purchased materials these minimum lot sizes are typically at price breaks, and for materials produced in-house the minimum lot size is at a point like 5,000 units in Figure 14.1, where the unit cost goes up sharply when fewer than this number of units are produced. For instance, a minimum lot size of 5,000 units means that any quantity greater than or equal to 5,000 units may be ordered, but never less than 5,000 units. If there were a net requirement of 2,000 units of this material, a lot size of 5,000 units would be ordered. On the other hand, if there were a net requirement of 9,999 units, a lot size of 9,999 units would be ordered.

Second, the EOQ assumes that the demand for a material is uniform from week to week. *In MRP and MPS, the net requirements for materials have been described as lumpy demands. Lumpy demand means that demand varies greatly from week to week.* In the presence of lumpy demands, other lot-sizing methods often exhibit lower costs than the EOQ. Two additional lot-sizing methods are the **lot-for-lot method** and the **period order quantity (POQ) method.** Example 15.1 demonstrates the use of these methods when applied to a net requirements schedule. Other approaches have also been experimented with. The methods of least total cost, least unit cost, and part-period balancing are discussed and described in Orlicky's book.[1] Heuristic methods of Gaither,[2] Groff,[3] and Silver and Meal[4] provide good cost performance and are very efficient to use. The Wagner and Whitin method yields optimal results, but it is based on dynamic programming and is difficult to understand and may not exhibit good cost performance when many changes to net requirements occur weekly.[5]

It is important to understand that the lot-sizing method resulting in the least cost depends on the data—costs and demand patterns. Experimentation is advised before a method is selected for specific production systems.

Example 15.1	Lot-Sizing Decisions for Materials with Lumpy Demands

The net requirements for a material from an MRP schedule are:

	Week							
	1	2	3	4	5	6	7	8
Net requirements	300	500	1,000	600	300	300	300	1,500

The annual demand for this end item is estimated to be 30,000 units over a 50-week-per-year schedule, or an average of 600 units per week. It costs $500 to change over the machines in the final assembly department to this end item when a production lot is begun. It costs $0.50 per unit when one unit of this product must be carried in inventory from one week to another; therefore, when one unit of this product is in ending inventory, it must be carried over as beginning inventory in the next week and incurs the $0.50 per-unit carrying cost. Determine which of these lot-sizing methods results in the least carrying and changeover (or ordering) costs for the eight-week schedule: **(a)** lot-for-lot (LFL), **(b)** economic order quantity (EOQ), or **(c)** period order quantity (POQ).

Solution

a. Develop the total carrying and ordering costs over the eight-week schedule for the lot-for-lot method. *Lot-for-lot (LFL) production lots equal the net requirements in each period.*

	Week								Costs		
	1	2	3	4	5	6	7	8	Carrying	Ordering	Total
Net requirements	300	500	1,000	600	300	300	300	1,500			
Beginning inventory	0	0	0	0	0	0	0	0			
Production lots	300	500	1,000	600	300	300	300	1,500	$0	$4,000	$4,000
Ending inventory	0	0	0	0	0	0	0	0			

Ordering costs = Numbers of orders × $500 = 8 × $500 = $4,000

b. Develop the total carrying and ordering costs over the eight-week schedule for the EOQ lot-sizing method. *EOQ production lots equal the computed EOQ.*

First, compute the EOQ. [Annual carrying cost is computed as C = ($0.50 per unit per week) × (50 weeks per year).]

$$EOQ = \sqrt{2DS/C} = \sqrt{2(30,000)(500)/[(0.50)(50)]} = 1,095.4, \text{ or } 1,095 \text{ units}$$

| | Week | | | | | | | | Costs | | |
	1	2	3	4	5	6	7	8	Carrying	Ordering	Total
Net requirements	300	500	1,000	600	300	300	300	1,500			
Beginning inventory	0	795	295	390	885	585	285	1,080			
Production lots	1,095	—	1,095	1,095	—	—	1,095	1,095	$2,495	$2,500	$4,995
Ending inventory	795	295	390	885	585	285	1,080	675			

Carrying costs = Sum of ending inventories × $0.50 = 4,990 × $0.50 = $2,495
Ordering costs = Number of orders × $500 = 5 × $500 = $2,500

c. Develop the total carrying and ordering costs over the eight-week schedule for the POQ lot-sizing method. *POQ production lots equal the net requirements for POQ computed periods.*
First, compute the POQ:

$$POQ = \frac{\text{Number of weeks per year}}{\text{Number of orders per year}} = \frac{50}{D/EOQ} = \frac{50}{30,000/1,095.4}$$

$$= 1.83, \text{ or } 2 \text{ weeks per order}$$

| | Week | | | | | | | | Costs | | |
	1	2	3	4	5	6	7	8	Carrying	Ordering	Total
Net requirements	300	500	1,000	600	300	300	300	1,500			
Beginning inventory	0	500	0	600	0	300	0	1,500			
Production lots	800	—	1,600	—	600	—	1,800	—	$1,450	$2,000	$3,450
Ending inventory	500	0	600	0	300	0	1,500	0			

Carrying costs = Sum of ending inventories × $0.50 = 2,900 × $0.50 = $1,450
Ordering costs = Number of orders × $500 = 4 × $500 = $2,000

Among the lot-sizing methods considered for this data, the POQ method exhibits the least carrying and ordering costs for the eight-week net requirements schedule.

The net requirements line in the MRP schedule for each component is analyzed to determine the timing and size of production lots or purchased lots by using one of the lot-sizing techniques mentioned earlier. The Planned Order Receipt line in the MRP schedule is the end result of these lot-sizing decisions.

Issues in MRP

Any treatment of MRP should include a discussion of important issues yet to be resolved.

Lot-Sizing

One potential problem is said to exist when lot-sizing techniques are applied at every level in the product structure. Using lot-sizing in lower-level components (raw materials and parts) poses no serious problems, but with economic lot sizes for higher-level components (end items and assemblies), some MRP users believe that excessive inventory buildups in lower-level components can result. For example, three components are related as follows:

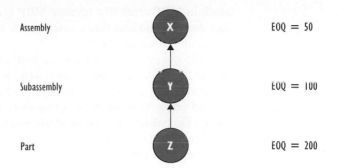

If a customer order of 25 units of Part X is received, if no inventory is on hand for Parts X, Y, and Z, and if orders equal to EOQ are ordered, then the inventory available for use immediately after shipping the customer order is:

$$\text{Inventory of Part X} = \;\; 25 \text{ units}$$
$$\text{Inventory of Part Y} = \;\; 75 \text{ units}$$
$$\text{Inventory of Part Z} = 175 \text{ units}$$

Some MRP users argue, however, that excessive inventory levels are not reached. The lower per-unit cost of lower level components leads to larger lot sizes and consequently higher inventory levels. These MRP users contend that higher inventory levels of lower level components should not be surprising or disturbing; the economic lot-sizing of all levels of components is therefore recommended.

The tendency in practice is to use lot-for-lot (LFL) at all levels for produce-to-order firms. Also, LFL is commonly used in produce-to-stock firms for end items and assemblies, and minimum lot sizes are used for lower-level components such as raw materials and parts. The use of LFL in end items and assemblies avoids the large inventory buildups in lower-level components described above. In the factories of tomorrow, operations will be leaner, more flexible, and more automated. In such environments, the use of LFL would be expected to become more common for all materials.

Net Change versus Regenerative MRP Systems

Some organizations use what is called **net change MRP**. These systems update the master production schedule as changes in the MPS occur. The MRP system is then activated to generate one set of MRP outputs. These outputs, however, are only the net changes to past MRP runs and not an entire set of MRP outputs. The planned order schedule report, for example, would indicate only changes to previous planned order schedules, not a completely new schedule. Although this concept is tempting in theory, its incidence of application has been disappointing because it tends to generate too many action notices.

Many organizations continue to use what is called **regenerative MRP**. In these systems, a complete MRP run is processed periodically, usually every week. At these times a new MPS, an updated inventory status file, and an up-to-date bills of material file are fed into the MRP computer program, which generates a complete set of outputs. Although regenerative MRP systems are slightly more costly to prepare and process, they also apparently are easier to implement and manage.

Safety Stock

MRP users do not agree on whether safety stock should be used in MRP. Proponents for using safety stock in MRP argue that safety stock performs the same function in MRP systems as in other inventory-planning systems—avoiding excessive stockouts caused by uncertain lead times and daily demands. Those who oppose the use of safety stock in MRP argue that because MRP systems adapt to changing conditions that affect demand and lead times, safety stock will not actually be used under the majority of circumstances in MRP.

The use of safety stock can be justified only by the sources of uncertainty present during lead times. For higher level items such as end items, the uncertainty of demand compares with any other inventory item having independent demand. The uncertainty of lead times for these items seems more controllable if these items are produced in-house. On balance, the use of safety stock for end items in MRP systems can be justified on the same basis as in any other system—the presence of uncertain demand and uncertain lead times.

For lower-level items such as raw materials and parts, the uncertainty of demand is more controlled because the demand is a dependent demand. The MPS sets the weekly demand for these items. The only major uncertainties present during lead times are scrap and the uncertainty of lead time and demand that occurs because of changes in the MPS. It appears that some safety stock can certainly be justified, even in raw materials, parts, and other lower-level items, although at significantly reduced levels.

MRP in Assemble-to-Order Firms

The **assemble-to-order firm** is a special type of produce-to-order firm. In these firms there can be millions of possible unique end items because customers have their choice of options and accessories. An automobile manufacturer is an example of an assemble-to-order firm. While only a few standard models are offered to customers, dealers can specify colors, engine types, transmission types, trim options, air-conditioning, power windows and door locks, cruise control, and a host of other options. In these cases there are only a few options and basic product models, but there are literally thousands of possible unique finished products. An MRP system that attempted to develop an MPS for such unique end items would be swamped with the burden of trying to explode millions of bills of material for end items into the resources necessary to produce the MPS.

In assemble-to-order firms, therefore, the MPS and MRP are treated separately from the **final assembly schedule (FAS)**. The FAS is usually prepared only a week or two ahead, and it schedules the unique products ordered by customers. This is necessary because the customers must be shipped products that include the specific options that they have ordered. But the MPS, MRP, and all other elements of the resource requirements planning system require a much longer lead time and are not based on unique customer orders. Instead, the MPS explodes modular bills of material, which can be thought of as families of products. A **modular bill of material** for a particular product family will list the forecasted percentage of customer orders that require each option along with the kit of parts that is common to all customer orders. These unassembled families of products with all of their options and kits of common parts are scheduled through the production operations such that the product families arrive at final assembly ready to be assembled into the specific products for customer orders. This greatly reduces the computational burden in the MRP system, although it creates the need to modify the way that final assembly schedules (FAS) and the bills of material are prepared.

From MRP I to MRP II to ERP

Resource requirements planning systems are in a continuous state of evolution. The earlier systems were quite simple and unsophisticated, and the value of the information that was generated for operations was limited. In its most primitive form, MRP simply exploded the MPS into the required materials.

Then in the late 1970s Oliver Wight, George Plossl, and others began to talk about closing the loop in MRP systems. The term **closed-loop MRP** means:

A system built around material requirements planning that includes the additional planning functions of sales and operations planning (production planning), master production scheduling, and capacity requirements planning. Once this planning phase is complete and the plans have been accepted as realistic and attainable, the execution functions come into play. These include the manufacturing control functions of input–output (capacity) measurement, detailed scheduling and dispatching, plus anticipated delay reports from both the plant and suppliers, supplier scheduling, etc. The term "closed loop" implies that not only are these elements included in the overall system but also that there is feedback from the execution functions so that the planning can be kept valid at all times.[6]

Later the need for more sophisticated MRP systems led Wight, Plossl, and others to call for a move from MRP I to manufacturing resource planning (MRP II). The term **manufacturing resource planning** means:

A method for the effective planning of all resources of a manufacturing company. Ideally, it addresses operational planning in units, financial planning in dollars, and has a simulation capability to answer "what if" questions. It is made up of a variety of functions, each linked together: business planning, sales and operations planning, production planning, master production scheduling, material requirements planning, capacity requirements planning, and the execution support systems for capacity and material. Output from these systems is integrated with financial reports such as the business plan, purchase commitment report, shipping budget, and inventory projections in dollars. Manufacturing Resource Planning is a direct outgrowth and extension of closed-loop MRP.[7]

The evolution of resource requirements planning systems is continuing today. The latest in this evolution is referred to as enterprise resources planning (ERP), which is even more comprehensive than MRP II is. The term **enterprise resources planning** means:

An accounting-oriented information system for identifying and planning the enterprisewide resources needed to take, make, ship, and account for customer orders. An ERP system differs from the typical MRP II system in technical requirements such as graphical user interface, relational database, use of fourth-generation language, and computer-aided software engineering tools in development, client/server architecture, and open-system portability.[8]

ERP systems consist of many software modules that can be separately purchased to help manage many different activities in different functional areas of a business. For example, SAP's R/3 software, the largest-selling ERP software, offers modules for sales and distribution, financial accounting, financial controlling, fixed assets management, human resources, work flow, industry solutions, materials management, production planning (including MRP and CRP), quality management, plant maintenance, and project systems. ERP systems require a major commitment and investment, often require companies to modify some of their processes to accommodate the software, and can take many years to implement. Three of the top-selling ERP software systems are SAP's R/3 (**http://www.sap.com**), Baan (**http://www.baan.com**), and PeopleSoft (**http://www.peoplesoft.com**).

How MRP Adapts to Change

You may have the impression that once an MRP system is in place it would be difficult to change the system. On the contrary, one of the cornerstones of MRP is that it must be a dynamic system and that it must adapt to change. By its very nature, MRP reflects the latest information in its planned order releases. In the updating procedures of the MPS, one week is added to the back end of the schedule and one week is taken off the front end, and all the weekly demands are again estimated. This updating of the MPS is aimed at making the MRP system adaptive to changes in demands for the end items.

As the MPS is updated weekly, the MRP schedules are also updated weekly. Another reason for updating MRP schedules weekly is to allow any changes to the inputs to MRP to be reflected in the schedules. Since the inventory status file and its material records could have been changed since the last updating, the MRP schedules pick up these changes. For example, let us say that we have changed suppliers for a certain material and the purchasing lead time for the material has changed. The next updating of the MRP schedules will reflect this change. Similarly, if engineering were to change the bills of material file to effect product design changes, after the next updating the MRP schedules would reflect these changes.

One of the great improvements of MRP systems over the traditional order quantity, order point methods of planning material requirements is its dynamic nature. MRP effectively adapts to change, and operations managers are provided with information based on present conditions rather than on what conditions were several weeks or months ago.

Evaluation of MRP

The advantages claimed for MRP over more conventional inventory-planning approaches such as fixed order quantities and order points have been demonstrated here and elsewhere in POM—improved customer service, reduced inventory levels, and improved operating efficiency of production departments. This sounds so good that we wonder why the whole world has not been "MRP'ed." There are good reasons why this isn't the case.

Table 15.7 lists the characteristics of production systems that support the successful implementation of MRP. The presence of an effective computer system is an absolute must. Two other characteristics that similarly seem almost automatic are accurate bills of material and inventory status files. The absence of these files and an ineffective computer system often pose the largest headaches for the implementation of MRP in practice. Correcting deficiencies such as these may take the bulk of implementation time.

MRP is conventionally applied only to manufacturing systems. These organizations process discrete products for which bills of material are possible, a requirement of MRP. This means that MRP is seldom applied to service systems, petroleum refineries, retailing systems, transportation firms, and other nonmanufacturing systems. Many believe that MRP can be successfully applied to some of these nonmanufacturing systems. When service systems require sets of raw materials to deliver one unit of service (a pseudo bill of material), MRP potentially can be applied. Surgical opera-

Table 15.7	Desirable Characteristics of Production Systems Suitable for MRP

1. An effective computer system.
2. Accurate computerized bills of material and inventory status files for all end items and materials.
3. A production system that manufactures discrete products made up of raw materials, parts, subassemblies, and assemblies that are processed through many production steps.
4. Production processes requiring long processing times.
5. Relatively reliable lead times.
6. The master schedule frozen for a period of time sufficient to procure materials without excessive expediting and confusion.
7. Top management support and commitment.

tions in large hospitals, high-volume professional services, and other processes are likely to use MRP systems in the future.

MRP delivers the most benefits to process-focused systems that have long processing times and complex multistage production steps because inventory and production planning are more complex. Picture a hypothetical production system that converts raw materials into finished goods instantaneously, as is the case in some simple product-focused systems. Raw materials would be ordered in to *exactly* match finished-goods requirements. In most process-focused systems, however, the in-house processing lead times can exceed the lead times required to obtain the raw materials from suppliers. MRP's ability to offset planned order receipts to planned order releases to account for long lead times and complex production processing steps greatly simplifies production and inventory planning.

In order for MRP to be effective, lead times must be reliable. Also, the MPS must be *frozen* for a time before actual production to the MPS is begun, meaning that what is to be produced, the MPS, must be known with certainty and the timing and quantity of raw material receipts must be dependable. When lot sizes of raw materials are large and variability in demand is small, the conventional economic lot size and order point inventory-planning systems tend to work quite well because their assumptions of uniform demand apply. MRP therefore offers more improvement in inventory planning when lot sizes are small and demand variability is large.

MRP has not been and will not be applied to all production systems. In some POM applications, MRP is either unnecessary or economically unjustifiable. The frequency of MRP usage is, however, definitely on a dramatic upward trend. As we gain more experience with MRP, we realize that it is not a panacea. It doesn't solve all our inventory-planning problems. Basically, MRP is a POM computerized information system. When computer systems are ineffective, inventory status and bills of material files are inaccurate, master production schedules are undependable, and when the remainder of the organization is otherwise mismanaged, MRP—or any other technique—will not be of much help. It will generate greater volumes of inaccurate and unused information than previously thought possible. MRP is best applied when production systems are basically well managed and a more comprehensive production and inventory planning system is needed.

Implementation of an MRP system is not a painless process. Because MRP is an information system that is driven by information, merely buying software and maybe some hardware does not guarantee a successful MRP system. Some significant start-up costs and some ongoing costs are involved when implementing an MRP system. Many of these costs are associated with rectifying poor or inadequate information as well as instituting system discipline to ensure that correct information continues to flow into the MRP system. These are usually hidden costs that are often not formally recognized when the proposal for an MRP system is presented.

CAPACITY REQUIREMENTS PLANNING (CRP)

Capacity requirements planning (CRP) is that part of the resource requirements planning that tests the master production schedule (MPS) for capacity feasibility. In the process of this testing, a plan is developed for the assignment of orders to work centers, the use of overtime, standby equipment, and subcontracting. Figure 15.8 illustrates this process. CRP takes the **planned order releases** off the MRP schedules and assigns the orders to work centers by consulting the routing plans. **Routing plans** specify the sequence of production processes required for each order. Next, the lots of materials are converted to capacity load data by using labor and machine standards, and then weekly load schedules are prepared for each work center that includes all orders.

Figure 15.8   The Capacity Requirements Planning Process

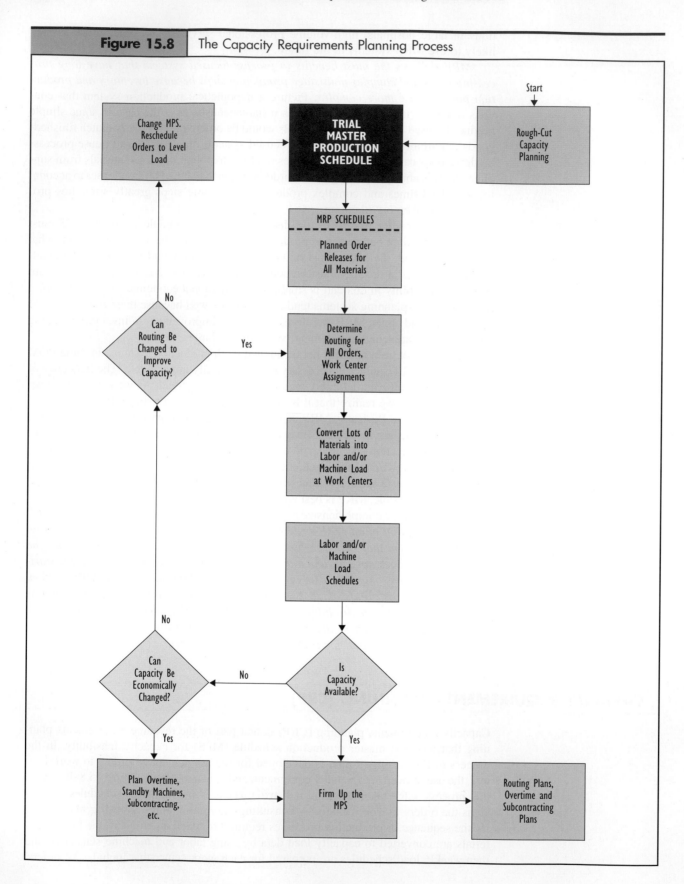

This transmission-production work center is the starting point for the hierarchy used to develop a load schedule.

© DANNY LEHMAN/CORBIS

If enough capacity is available at all the work centers in all weeks, then the MPS is firmed up. If not, then it must be determined if the capacity can be economically changed. If overtime, subcontracting, standby machines, or other means can be used to augment capacity, then the MPS can be firmed up. If capacity cannot be economically changed, then either the routing or assignment of orders to work centers must be changed to improve capacity, or the MPS must be changed by rescheduling orders to better level capacity, and the process is repeated.

The principal means of testing the feasibility of the MPS is through work-center load schedules.

Load Schedules

A load schedule is a device for comparing the actual labor-hours and machine-hours required to produce the MPS against the available labor-hours and machine hours in each week. Load schedules are usually prepared in a hierarchy from work centers at the beginning of the manufacturing system through successive stages to the end of the manufacturing system.

Figure 15.9 demonstrates that when end items are included in the MPS, this inclusion causes activities to be undertaken at successively earlier stages in the production system. MRP schedules determine the planned order releases, and these releases are the basis for production in all work centers. Beginning at the top of the figure in Week 5 in the Final Assembly work center, we find that 600 units must be finished in Final Assembly in Week 5. One week earlier, in Week 4, 600 units must be finished in the Assemble Frame work center. The one-week lead time is required to perform the operations in the Assemble Frame work center and transport the units to Final Assembly.

In Week 3, 1,800 #115 parts must be ordered from the supplier. Although ordering parts may not require any production capacity, the activity must begin in Week 3, thus demonstrating the need to offset the ordering activity by a lead time of one week from Assemble Frame. Offsetting for lead times between successive stages of the production system is fundamental to resource requirements planning.

Notice in Figure 15.9 that we can determine the actual number of labor- and machine-hours that the MPS will require weekly in each work center for this product.

| **Figure 15.9** | Loading Effects of MPS on Work-Center Capacities |

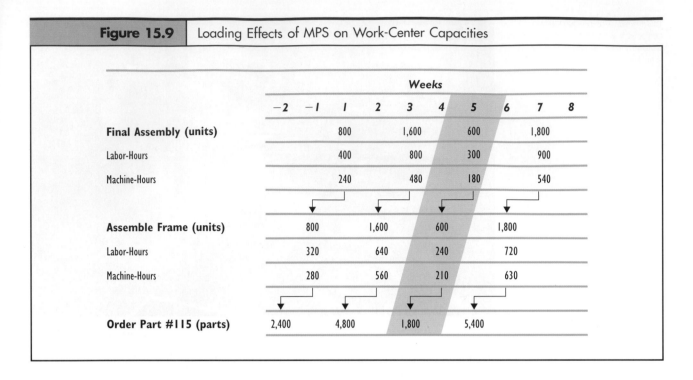

When all end items from the MPS are included, the total labor- and machine-hours required weekly in each work center can be compared to the number available. Such comparisons allow operations managers to determine the feasibility of the MPS in each work center weekly and also answer operating questions about overtime, standby machines, subcontracting, and other overloading and underloading issues.

Let us suppose that we have a trial MPS and we wish to test its feasibility through CRP. Load schedules such as the ones illustrated in Figure 15.10 can be used for this purpose. From such schedules we can determine the following:

1. The labor-hours loading is out of balance in the Fabrication Department. It appears that some fabrication work needs to be shifted from Weeks 3, 4, and 8 into Weeks 5, 6, and 7. A review of the machine loading in the Fabrication Department in these weeks indicates that such a shift would not cause machine overloading.

2. The change suggested in Fabrication above would not adversely affect Final Assembly because all units in Fabrication move to Final Assembly one week later and overtime could be used to alleviate the labor hours overloading in Weeks 6, 7, and 8 in Final Assembly. The machine-hour loading in all weeks in Final Assembly is not a limiting factor.

3. At the plant level, the later part of the schedule is overloaded on both machine-hours and labor-hours. Overtime could be used to relieve the labor-hours overloading, and subcontracting or the use of standby machines could reduce the machine-hour overloading. Another alternative is always present, however, and that is to modify the MPS to shift end items from the later part of the schedule to the earlier weeks.

If the MPS is modified, then the logic of the CRP would be applied again through a revised set of load schedules. In this process we develop a trial MPS and then modify it through CRP until not only is the MPS feasible, but also the work centers are economically loaded. This promotes internal operating efficiency and low unit costs throughout the entire manufacturing system.

| **Figure 15.10** | The Capacity Loading Hierarchy |

	Labor-Hours (000)	Machine-Hours (000)

Knoxville Plant

Labor-Hours chart: y-axis 10, 20, 30, 40, 50; x-axis Weeks 1 2 3 4 5 6 7 8

Machine-Hours chart: y-axis 10, 20, 30, 40, 50; x-axis Weeks 1 2 3 4 5 6 7 8

Final Assembly Department

Labor-Hours chart: y-axis 2, 4, 6, 8; x-axis Weeks 1 2 3 4 5 6 7 8

Machine-Hours chart: y-axis 1, 2, 3, 4; x-axis Weeks 1 2 3 4 5 6 7 8

Fabrication Department

Labor-Hours chart: y-axis 3, 6, 9, 12; x-axis Weeks 1 2 3 4 5 6 7 8

Machine-Hours chart: y-axis 6, 12, 18, 24; x-axis Weeks 1 2 3 4 5 6 7 8

Underloading   Overloading

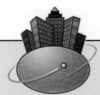

Wrap-Up

WHAT WORLD-CLASS COMPANIES DO

World-class companies long ago moved away from using the pond-draining type of production-planning and control systems to MRP and CRP systems. They probably began as Class D MRP users: those that used simple parts explosions to order materials. Then, as these manufacturers learned, they incorporated more and more features of MRP until they became Class A users, those that have adopted manufacturing resource planning (MRP II) or enterprise resources planning (ERP). For these users, their MRP systems are complete and comprehensive production information systems. These organization-wide information systems provide short-range plans that guide companies toward improved productivity, lower costs, and better customer service.

World-class producers are continually improving their MRP systems. Here are some examples of interesting features that are being included:

- They have developed a system of setting lead times that respond to operating and economic conditions. If backlog is high and in-process inventory is high, longer lead times are used and vice versa. Also, if the economy is booming and suppliers' shops are full, longer delivery lead times are used, and the reverse is also true.
- Compaq Computer Corporation has a very effective MRP system that is conventional in many respects. The system covers 18 months in one-week buckets with a 30-day frozen time fence. What sets Compaq's system apart, however, is that the activities required to develop new products are included as levels in the product structure tree for planning when to launch development projects for the new products. The activities are offset for lead times so that man-

agers know when each activity must begin and end for the required introduction of the new products to occur on schedule. Such an approach would be helpful in industries with very short product life cycles and rapidly changing product designs.

- Sophisticated algorithms are used to adjust lead times to take into account the load at bottleneck operations and the impact that these operations will have on the lead times of the products.
- The reports generated from MRP systems are shared with suppliers and customers to inform them about when materials will be needed and when orders will be finished and shipped.
- By improving communication with suppliers and customers and having lead times that are adaptive to operating conditions, a general bias toward smaller batches and shorter lead times has resulted in less in-process inventory and faster production of customer orders.

Such improvements as these set world-class companies apart from their competition because their production-planning and control systems are in large measure responsible for the higher product quality, lower production costs, and greater responsiveness to customer needs that have allowed these firms to increase market share even in an environment of fierce international competition.

REVIEW AND DISCUSSION QUESTIONS

1. What is resource requirements planning?
2. Identify the major elements of resource requirements planning.
3. Describe the role of MPS, MRP, and CRP in resource requirements planning.
4. Describe the relationships among MPS, MRP, and CRP.
5. Describe the process of MRP.
6. Define these terms: *bills of material file, inventory status file, master production schedule, planned order schedule, changes to planned orders, MRP schedules, offsetting for lead time.*
7. What are the objectives of MRP? Explain how each of these objectives is achieved.
8. What is lumpy demand? Name three methods of lot-

sizing that are used when demand is lumpy. How does a minimum lot size work?
9. Explain how net requirements for a material in a bucket are computed.
10. Explain the differences between regenerative and net change MRP systems. What are the advantages and disadvantages of each type of MRP system?
11. Explain these terms: *MRP I, closed-loop MRP, MRP II, ERP.*
12. Describe the process of CRP.
13. Name the characteristics of production systems that are suitable for MRP.
14. Summarize what world-class companies are doing in their MRP systems.

INTERNET ASSIGNMENTS

1. PeopleSoft is one of the leading producers of enterprise resource planning (ERP) software. Visit and explore PeopleSoft's Internet site at **http://www.peoplesoft. com**. Briefly describe the software modules that are part of PeopleSoft's Enterprise Solutions ERP software.

2. Search the Internet to find a company that produces MRP II software. Describe the features of the MRP II software.

3. GRMS, Inc., was organized in 1981 to develop a fully integrated, closed-loop MRP system for its parent organization. This software has continued to evolve and now is marketed as an ERP system. Visit the company's web site at **http://www. grms.com** and locate information about its capacity requirements planning module. Describe the features of the CRP software module.

4. Search the Internet for a consulting firm that helps companies implement MRP or ERP software. Briefly describe the services it offers.

PROBLEMS

Material Requirements Planning (MRP)

1. If the beginning inventory for a product is 500 units, safety stock is 200 units, and estimated weekly demand is 300, 400, 300, 800, 1,000, and 500 units over a six-week planning horizon, develop a net requirements schedule for the product.

2. If the beginning inventory for a product is 600 units, safety stock is 200 units, and the estimated weekly demand is 355, 800, 910, 500, 600, and 500 over a six-week planning horizon, develop a net requirements schedule for the product.

3. Product A is assembled from two B assemblies, one C assembly, and three D assemblies. Each B assembly is made from two E components and three F components. Each C assembly is made from four G subassemblies and three I components. Each D assembly is made from one E component, two I components, and one H component. Each G subassembly is made from two H components.
   a. Construct a product structure tree for Product A.
   b. Prepare an indented bill of materials for Product A.

4. Product A is assembled from one B assembly, three C assemblies, two D assemblies, and four H components. Each B assembly is made from two F subassemblies. Each C assembly is made from one G component and one H component. Each D assembly is made from two I subassemblies and three G components. Each F subassembly is made from three H components. Each I subassembly is made from one H component.
   a. Construct a product structure tree for Product A.
   b. Prepare an indented bill of materials for Product A.

5. Complete the MRP schedule for the part below.

Lot size = 1,200+	Safety stock = 300
Lead time = 2 weeks	Allocated = 150
On hand = 850	

	Week					
	1	**2**	**3**	**4**	**5**	**6**
Gross requirements	100	600	400	900	1,350	700
Scheduled receipts	500					
Available						
Net requirements						
Planned order receipts						
Planned order releases						

6. Complete the MRP schedule for the part below.

Lot size = 2,000+   Safety stock = 400
Lead time = 1 week   Allocated = 300
On hand = 1,300

	Week					
	1	**2**	**3**	**4**	**5**	**6**
Gross requirements	1,100	700	1,500	900	1,850	1,400
Scheduled receipts	2,000					
Available						
Net requirements						
Planned order receipts						
Planned order releases						

7. Given the following product structure tree and inventory information, complete the MRP schedule below.

Level Code   **Product Structure Tree**

0   A

I   B(2)   C(4)

2   D(3)

Product A		Week					
		1	**2**	**3**	**4**	**5**	**6**
Lot size = LFL	Gross requirements	120	340	310	530	410	380
Lead time = 1	Scheduled receipts	275					
On hand = 650	Available						
Safety stock = 100	Net requirements						
Allocated = 75	Planned order receipts						
	Planned order releases						

Product B		**1**	**2**	**3**	**4**	**5**	**6**
Lot size = LFL	Gross requirements						
Lead time = 1	Scheduled receipts	400					
On hand = 430	Available						
Safety stock = 120	Net requirements						
Allocated = 80	Planned order receipts						
	Planned order releases						

Product C		Week					
		1	**2**	**3**	**4**	**5**	**6**
Lot size = 1500+	Gross requirements						
Lead time = 2	Scheduled receipts		1,500				
On hand = 460	Available						
Safety stock = 140	Net requirements						
Allocated = 160	Planned order receipts						
	Planned order releases						

Product D		**1**	**2**	**3**	**4**	**5**	**6**
Lot size = 1000+	Gross requirements						
Lead time − 1	Scheduled receipts						
On hand = 1,100	Available						
Safety stock = 200	Net requirements						
Allocated = 60	Planned order receipts						
	Planned order releases						

8. Each E subassembly is made up of two G parts, one H part, and one I part. Complete an MRP schedule for the E subassembly and all of its components:

	E Subassembly	G Part	H Part	I Part
Lot size	900+	1,500+	1,500+	2,000+
Lead time	1 week	1 week	1 week	2 weeks
On hand	500	400	800	800
Safety stock	200	—	—	500
Allocated	500	—	600	500

Component		Week				
		1	**2**	**3**	**4**	**5**
E	Gross requirements		1,000	700	900	800
E	Scheduled receipts	1,000				
G	Scheduled receipts	700				
H	Scheduled receipts	1,000				
I	Scheduled receipts	2,000				

9. A product has this indented bill of materials:

	Level			Quantity
0	**1**	**2**	**3**	
B353				1
	R25			4
		B5		2
		F3		1
	N35			2
		L7		3
		F3		2
	K45			3
		D9		5

This inventory status report has just been issued for the project:

Item Code	On Hand	Safety Stock	Allocated	Lot Size	Lead Time (weeks)
B353	340	100	50	LFL	1
R25	2,500	200	0	LFL	1
N35	1,500	200	15	LFL	1
K45	2,000	200	80	LFL	1
B5	750	300	250	10,000+	1
F3	7,600	300	100	8,000+	1
L7	11,000	1,000	175	1,000+	2
D9	25,000	1,000	200	2,000+	2

a. Prepare an MRP schedule for all the items to cover a six-week planning horizon if the MPS for product B353 shows an estimated demand or gross requirement of 750 units in Week 2, 1,800 units in Week 4, and 1,500 units in Week 6.

b. Are the MRP schedules for all items feasible from a material supply perspective? If not, what might be done?

10. A product has this indented bill of materials:

Level				Quantity
0	**1**	**2**	**3**	
X285				1
	A10			3
		T3		1
			Z7	2
		V1		2
	J20			2
		H8		1
		U4		2
	M30			3
		P2		2
			V1	1

This inventory status report has just been issued for the project:

Item Code	On Hand	Safety Stock	Allocated	Lot Size	Lead Time (weeks)
X285	250	50	0	LFL	1
A10	900	100	0	LFL	1
J20	850	100	10	LFL	1
M30	1,100	100	35	LFL	1
T3	750	300	60	LFL	1
V1	2,000	500	110	2,000+	1
H8	500	300	90	750+	2
U4	500	300	0	1,000+	1
P2	1,000	300	105	500+	1
Z7	2,500	500	250	2,000+	2

a. Prepare an MRP schedule for all the items to cover a six-week planning horizon if the MPS for product X285 shows an estimated demand or gross requirement of 80, 135, 280, 155, 210, and 275 units in Weeks 1 through 6, respectively.

b. Are the MRP schedules for all items feasible from a material supply perspective? If not, what might be done?

11. A product has this product structure tree:

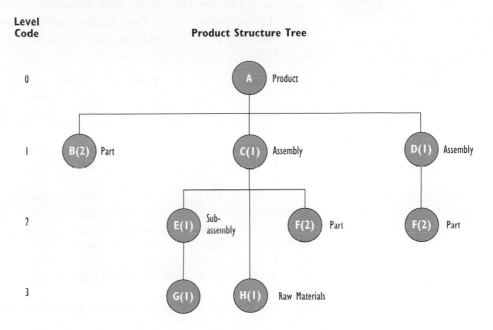

Level Code	Product Structure Tree
0	A — Product
1	B(2) Part C(1) Assembly D(1) Assembly
2	E(1) Sub-assembly F(2) Part F(2) Part
3	G(1) H(1) Raw Materials

This inventory status report has just been issued for the product:

Item Code	On Hand	Safety Stock	Allocated	Lot Size	Lead Time (weeks)	Scheduled Receipts Quantity	Scheduled Receipts Week	Service Parts Orders Quantity	Service Parts Orders Week
A	1,500	500	800	LFL	1	1,000	1		
B	1,500	200	700	LFL	1	1,000	2	1,000	3
C	1,500	500	500	LFL	1				
D	1,000	500	500	500+	1				
E	1,000	500	0	5,000+	1				
F	2,500	500	500	5,000+	3				
G	3,500	1,000	500	6,000+	2	6,000	1		
H	2,500	500	1,200	4,000+	2	4,000	2	5,000	6

a. Prepare an MRP schedule for all the components in the product to cover a six-week planning horizon if the MPS for the product shows an estimated demand or gross requirements of 2,000 units in Week 5 and 2,500 units in Week 6.

b. Is the MPS feasible from a material supply perspective?

c. If the MPS is not feasible, what actions could be taken to make it feasible?

12. In the Green Thumb Water Sprinkler Company example in this chapter, the MPS is changed from 1,000 units in Week 4 and 2,000 units in Week 8 to 2,500 units in Weeks 4, 5, and 7. If all other data in the case remain unchanged:

a. Prepare an MRP schedule.

b. Is the MPS feasible from a material supply (purchased or produced components) perspective?

c. What actions could be taken to allow Green Thumb to meet the material supply requirements of the MPS?

13. A manufacturer produces product Q44. The Q44 part is made of one B assembly, one A part, and two C parts. Each B assembly is made of one E subassembly, two D parts, and one F part. Each E subassembly is made of two G parts, one H part, and one I part. The inventory status report exhibits this information for the Q44 unit:

Component	Lot Size	Lead Time (weeks)	On Hand	Safety Stock	Allocated	Scheduled Receipts Quantity	Week
Q44	LFL	—	100	—	—	—	—
A	1,500+	2	1,500	200	200	1,500	1
B	LFL	—	500	200	100	1,000	1
C	2,000+	1	1,000	300	300	1,000	1
D	1,500+	1	1,500	100	200	1,000	1
E	1,000+	1	2,000	500	500	3,000	1
F	2,000+	1	1,200	500	—	700	1
G	3,000+	1	1,600	500	300	1,000	1
H	2,000+	2	1,600	500	100	2,000	1
I	2,000+	2	1,800	500	300		

The MPS for the plant shows these quantities of the Q44 unit to be produced:

Product	Week				
	1	2	3	4	5
Q44 unit		2,500	1,700	1,900	1,800

a. Construct a product structure tree for the Q44 unit.
b. Complete an MRP schedule for the Q44 unit and all of its components.

14. If the weekly net requirements for a product are 700, 800, 900, 500, 1,000, and 800 units over a six-week planning horizon, carrying cost per unit per week is $1 whenever a unit must be carried over into the next week, there are 52 workweeks per year, and ordering cost is $500 per order, develop a schedule of completed production lots and calculate the cost of your schedule by using these methods:
a. Lot-for-lot (LFL).
b. Economic order quantity (EOQ).
c. Period order quantity (POQ).

You may disregard the effects of initial inventory and safety stock on your calculations.

15. You are given this net requirements schedule:

	Week							
	1	2	3	4	5	6	7	8
Net requirements (units)	500	500	1,000	3,000	1,500	2,500	2,000	1,000

If it costs $6,000 to get the final assembly department ready to assemble batches of this product, it costs $30 to carry one unit in inventory for a year, and 52 weeks per year are worked by the final assembly department, develop a schedule of completed production lots for the product and calculate the cost of your schedule by using these methods:

a. Lot-for-lot (LFL).
b. Economic order quantity (EOQ).
c. Period order quantity (POQ).

You may disregard the effects of initial inventory and safety stock on your calculations.

16. Given this net requirements schedule for a product for the next six weeks, if it costs $3,000 to set up the production line to produce this product and it costs $6 to carry one unit of the product in inventory for one week, develop a schedule of completed production lots for the product and compute the cost of your schedule by using these methods:

	Week					
	1	**2**	**3**	**4**	**5**	**6**
Net requirements	500	700	500	700	400	600

a. Lot-for-lot (LFL).
b. Economic order quantity (EOQ).
c. Period order quantity (POQ).

You may disregard the effects of initial inventory and safety stock on your calculations.

Capacity Requirements Planning (CRP)

17. The Track Right Company produces track balls for desktop computers. The master production schedule developed for the next six weeks is:

	Week					
	1	**2**	**3**	**4**	**5**	**6**
Track balls	24,000	29,000	43,000	35,000	26,000	28,000

Track Right's labor- and machine-hours available and its production standards are:

	Labor	**Machine**
Weekly capacity available (hours)	6,600	1,650
Production standard (hours/unit)	0.20	0.05

a. Determine the percent utilization of the labor and machine capacity in each week.
b. What suggestions would you make to Track Right's management concerning its MPS?

18. The PetroFlow Company produces three different models of oil well valves for the oil-producing industry. Each valve must be processed through three production departments in this sequence: foundry, fabrication, and assembly. Approximately one week is required for a valve to be completely processed through each department. PetroFlow is now in the process of capacity requirements planning (CRP) and has just developed this MPS:

Model	Week							
	1	**2**	**3**	**4**	**5**	**6**	**7**	**8**
A25	400	300	600	300	200	400	500	300
B34	200	500	300	200	400	600	500	400
C71	500	700	400	600	500	400	600	600

Weekly labor and machine standards for the three production departments are:

| | Foundry | | Fabrication | | Assembly | |
| | Labor Standard (hrs/unit) | Machine Standard (hrs/unit) | Labor Standard (hrs/unit) | Machine Standard (hrs/unit) | Labor Standard (hrs/unit) | Machine Standard (hrs/unit) |
Model						
A25	3.5	2.9	3.0	2.1	2.1	1.4
B34	1.8	2.6	2.8	1.7	3.0	2.5
C71	2.2	1.8	1.5	3.2	2.9	2.2

a. Determine the labor and machine loads for each department and for all departments combined for the first six weeks of the MPS (remember to offset for lead times between departments).

b. What do you conclude and suggest about the loadings of the three departments?

CASES

Integrated Products Corporation

Integrated Products Corporation (IPC) produces graphic boards and internal modems for personal and small-business computers. Each of these products must be processed through two manufacturing departments: first through Component Fabrication and then through Assembly. Approximately one week is required to process one graphic board or modem through each of the two manufacturing departments. Here is the six-week master production schedule (MPS) for the products:

| | Week | | | | | |
	1	2	3	4	5	6
Graphic board	500	600	700	900	1,000	800
Modem	290	900	810	600	600	600

The weekly labor and machine capacities for the production departments are:

Department	Labor-Hour Capacity (labor-hours per week)	Machine-Hour Capacity (machine-hours per week)
Fabrication	16,000	9,000
Assembly	10,000	3,000

The labor and machine standards for each of the products in the manufacturing departments are:

| | Fabrication | | Assembly | |
Product	Labor Standard (hours/unit)	Machine Standard (hours/unit)	Labor Standard (hours/unit)	Machine Standard (hours/unit)
Graphics board	9.0	5.0	8.0	2.0
Modem	8.0	6.0	6.0	2.0

The plant's personnel policy does not allow transfer of personnel between departments, and overtime hours may not exceed 10 percent of the straight-time hours.

Assignment

1. Develop labor and machine load schedules for each department for the first five weeks of the master production schedule (remember to offset for lead times between departments).

2. Interpret the meaning of your load schedule: Is the MPS feasible? Can you make suggestions for changing the MPS to improve loading?
3. Evaluate your proposal in No. 2.

Bank Sort International

Bank Sort International Ltd. (BSI) is a Canadian manufacturer of check sorting machines for the banking industry. BSI has just received a Request for Proposal from a large banking firm in Mexico. The Mexican firm is interested in a total of 300 check sorting machines (model BS740). They would like to have 100 machines shipped from BSI in each of Weeks 6, 7, and 8, but they are open to slight modifications of this shipping schedule to accommodate any manufacturing constraints. The indented bill of materials and inventory status report are shown below.

		Level				
0	**1**	**2**	**3**	**4**		**Quantity**
BS740						1
	A48					3
		D5				2
		E22				2
			L1			1
				M3		1
	B13					2
		F43				1
		G7				1
			D5			3
		H6N				2
	C56					1
		I8				2
			D5			1
		J14				3
			K6			1
				K6		4

Item Code	On Hand	Safety Stock	Allocated	Lot Size	Lead Time (weeks)
BS740	0	0	0	LFL	1
A48	30	0	30	LFL	1
B13	20	0	20	LFL	1
C56	10	0	10	LFL	1
D5	400	100	85	LFL	1
E22	130	50	60	500+	1
F43	90	50	20	250+	3
G7	100	50	20	100+	2
H6N	120	50	40	LFL	1
I8	90	30	20	LFL	3
J14	100	30	30	1,000+	2
K6	400	200	80	LFL	2
L1	150	30	60	750+	1
M3	150	30	60	1,000+	1

Assignment

1. Prepare MRP schedules for all items to cover an eight-week planning horizon.
2. Are the MRP schedules feasible from a materials-planning perspective?
3. If the MRP schedules are not feasible, what actions would you recommend to make them feasible?

Blanco Foods: Material Requirements Planning in the Processing Industry

Blanco Foods manufactures food products. Among its many products is a very popular bread loaf used for breakfast toast, Bright & Early. The company uses a six-week planning horizon in its marketing and production plans and is now in the process of developing a material requirements plan. Its production-planning department has just gathered this information to be used in these plans:

1. Estimated weekly demands or gross requirements for the Bright & Early product are 1,200; 1,500; 900; 1,800; 2,000; and 1,500.
2. The bill of material for the Bright & Early product is:

Parent Code	Component Code	Level Code	Description	Amount of Component per Unit of Parent
	B&E	0	Breakfast toast bread loaf	
B&E	A	1	Batter mix	1.0 pound
B&E	B	1	Icing	0.1 pound
B&E	C	1	Raisins	0.2 pound
A	D	2	Flour	0.60 pound
A	E	2	Yeast, salt, sugar package	0.15 pound
A	F	2	Milk and egg package	0.35 pound

3. The present production capacity is adequate to produce the Bright & Early product.
4. The purchasing lead times for purchased materials are: B = 1 week, C = 1 week, D = 2 weeks, E = 2 weeks, and F = 2 weeks. D, E, and F can be shortened to 1 week with expediting and additional freight costs.
5. The inventory status report for the Bright & Early product is:

Item Code	On Hand	Safety Stock	Allocated	Lot Size	Scheduled Receipts Quantity	Week
B&E	500	250		LFL		
A	1,600#		1,500#	LFL		
B	1,050#		1,000#	LFL	1,500#	1
C	1,200#		2,000#	LFL	1,000#	1
D	1,900#	1,000#	2,000#	2,000#+	2,000#	1
E	1,500#	1,000#	1,000#	1,000#+	1,000#	1
F	1,800#	1,000#	1,000#	1,000#+	1,000#	1

Assignment

1. Prepare an MRP schedule for the Bright & Early product. Is the plan feasible from the perspective of availability of materials? What expediting, if any, is required to allow Blanco Foods to meet the material requirements of the MPS?
2. Summarize your material requirements plan for the Bright & Early product, and outline any extraordinary measures required to render the plan feasible.

ENDNOTES

1. Orlicky, Joseph. *Material Requirements Planning*, pp. 120–138. New York: McGraw-Hill, 1975.
2. Gaither, Norman. "A Near-Optimal Lot-Sizing Model for Material Requirements Planning Systems." *Production and Inventory Management* 22 (Fourth Quarter 1981): 75–89.
3. Groff, G. K. "A Lot-Sizing Rule for Time Phased Component Demand." *Production and Inventory Management* 20 (First Quarter 1979): 47–53.
4. Silver, E. A., and H. C. Meal. "A Heuristic for Selecting Lot Size Quantities for the Case of a Deterministic Time-Varying Demand Rate and Discrete Opportunities for Replenishment." *Production and Inventory Management* 14 (Second Quarter 1973): 64–75.
5. Wagner, H. M., and T. M. Whitin. "Dynamic Version of the Economic Lot Size Model." *Management Science* 5, no. 1 (October 1958): 89–96.
6. Cox, James F., III, and John H. Blackstone, eds. *APICS Dictionary*, 9th ed., p. 15. Falls Church, VA: APICS—The Educational Society for Resource Management, 1998.
7. *Ibid.,* 54.
8. *Ibid.,* 30.

SELECTED BIBLIOGRAPHY

Benton, W. C., and Hojung Shin. "Manufacturing Planning and Control: The Evolution of MRP and JIT Integration." *European Journal of Operational Research* 110, no. 3 (November 1, 1999): 411–440.

Berry, W. L. "Lot-Sizing Procedures for Requirements Planning Systems: A Framework for Analysis." *Production and Inventory Management* 13 (Second Quarter 1972): 19–34.

Cox, James F., III, and John H. Blackstone, eds. *APICS Dictionary*, 9th ed. Falls Church, VA: APICS—The Educational Society for Resource Management, 1998.

Drexl, Andreas, and Alf Kimms, eds. *Beyond Manufacturing Resource Planning (MRP II): Advanced Models and Methods for Production Planning.* New York: Springer Verlag, 1998.

Enns, S. T. "The Effect of Batch Size Selection on MRP Performance." *Computers and Industrial Engineering* 37, nos. 1, 2 (October 1999): 15–19.

Gaither, Norman. "A Near-Optimal Lot-Sizing Model for Material Requirements Planning Systems." *Production and Inventory Management* 22 (Fourth Quarter 1981): 75–89.

Gambrel, Bryan, and Angela Kozlowski, eds. *Special Edition Using Baan IV.* Indianapolis, IN: Que, 1998.

Gray, Christopher D., and Darryl V. Landvater. *MRP II Standard System: A Handbook for Manufacturing Software Survival.* New York: John Wiley & Sons, 1995.

Groff, G. K. "A Lot-Sizing Rule for Time Phased Component Demand." *Production and Inventory Management* 20 (First Quarter 1979): 47–53.

Haddock, Jorge, and Donald E. Hubicki. "Which Lot Sizing Techniques Are Used in MRP?" *Production and Inventory Management* 30, no. 3 (Third Quarter 1989): 57.

Hernandez, Jose Antonio. *The SAP R/3 Handbook.* New York: McGraw-Hill, 1997.

Miller, Jeffrey G., and Linda G. Sprague. "Behind the Growth in Material Requirements Planning." *Harvard Business Review* 53 (September–October 1975): 83–91.

Orlicky, Joseph, and George W. Plossl. *Orlicky's Material Requirements Planning.* New York: McGraw-Hill, 1994.

Perreault, Yves, and Tom Vlasic. *Implementing Baan IV.* Indianapolis, IN: Que, 1998.

Plenert, Gerhard. "Focusing Material Requirements Planning (MRP) towards Performance." *European Journal of Operational Research* 119, no. 1 (November 16, 1999): 91–99.

Ptak, Carol A. *MRP and Beyond: A Toolbox for Integrating People and Systems.* Chicago: Irwin Professional Publishing, 1997.

Ptak, Carol A., and Eli Schragenheim. *ERP: Tools, Techniques, and Applications for Integrating the Supply Chain.* Boca Raton, FL: St. Lucie Press, 2000.

Rowell, Michael. *SAP R/3 Consultant's Bible.* Foster City, CA: IDG Books Worldwide, 2000.

Schroeder, Roger G., et al. "A Study of MRP Benefits and Costs." *Journal of Operations Management* 2, no. 1 (October 1981): 1–9.

Segerstedt, Anders. "Formulas of MRP." *International Journal of Production Economics* 46–47 (December 1996): 127–136.

Sharpe, Simon. *10 Minute Guide to SAP R/3.* Indianapolis, IN: Que, 1997.

Silver, E. A., and H. C. Meal. "A Heuristic for Selecting Lot Size Quantities for the Case of a Deterministic Time-Varying Demand Rate and Discrete Opportunities for Replenishment." *Production and Inventory Management* 14 (Second Quarter 1973): 64–75.

Wagner, H. M., and T. M. Whitin. "Dynamic Version of the Economic Lot Size Model." *Management Science* 5, no. 1 (October 1958): 89–96.

Wallace, Thomas F. *MRP II: Making It Happen: The Implementers' Guide to Success with Manufacturing Resource Planning.* Essex Junction, VT: O. Wight Limited Publications, 1994.

16

Manufacturing Operations Scheduling

Introduction

Scheduling Process-Focused Manufacturing
Shop-Floor Planning and Control
Order-Sequencing Problems
Assignment Problems

Scheduling Product-Focused Manufacturing
Batch Scheduling
Delivery Schedules: Line-of-Balance Method

Computerized Scheduling Systems

Wrap-Up: What World-Class Companies Do

Review and Discussion Questions

Internet Assignments

Problems

Cases
Star DigiVideo Inc.
Integrated Products Corporation
NewWood Ltd.

Endnote

Selected Bibliography

PRODUCTION SCHEDULING DECISIONS AT MICRO-SCANNERS CORPORATION

It was Monday morning five minutes into the day shift at Micro-Scanners Corporation and Lisa Johnson was looking over the orders waiting to be worked on at her machine. She and her foreman studied the six waiting orders, trying to decide in what sequence Lisa should produce the orders. First, they looked at the planned order releases on the latest MRP schedule. One order had arrived early and was not scheduled to be released to (started through) the work center until next week; that order was placed at the back of the waiting line. Another order was past due because it was scheduled to have been released to the work center last week; that order was put at the front of the line. Now Lisa and her foreman had to decide in what sequence to produce the four remaining orders. The foreman knew that such things as production costs, capacity utilization, and delivery promises to customers could be affected by their decision. While the four orders could be produced on a first-come first-served basis, Lisa preferred to work on the orders that could be finished the fastest because more orders could then be finished per shift, and that would make her look good. The foreman believed that the orders with the earliest promised delivery date and the most work remaining should be produced first. They turned to page 5 of the MRP report to find the critical ratios for the four orders: 0.95, 1.05, 1.25, and 1.30. The foreman explained to Lisa that these ratios had been computed by dividing the time remaining to due date by the production time remaining; therefore, those orders with low critical ratios should be produced first. Lisa now had her instructions and the sequence in which to produce the orders. The foreman wondered what effects his decision would have on production cost and capacity utilization.

In the last three chapters we have studied aggregate planning, master production scheduling (MPS), independent demand inventory systems, and material requirements planning (MRP). These elements of production planning provide information about which products and components are to be produced in each week of the planning horizon. But the nitty-gritty, day-to-day shop-floor issues described in the account above remain unresolved.

In this chapter we shall consider shop-floor issues by discussing scheduling in process-focused and product-focused manufacturing.

SCHEDULING PROCESS-FOCUSED MANUFACTURING

Process-focused factories are often called *job shops*. A **job shop** is an organization in which the work centers or departments are organized around similar types of functions or departmental specialties, such as forging, milling, turning, heat treating, drilling, and assembly. Jobs are usually processed in batches, with the batch size based either on the customer order size or some economical quantity. Each job or order follows a distinct route through various work centers, and typically many different routings exist in a job shop because of the wide variety of jobs processed.

| Figure 16.1 | Scheduling and Shop-Floor Decisions in Process-Focused Operations |

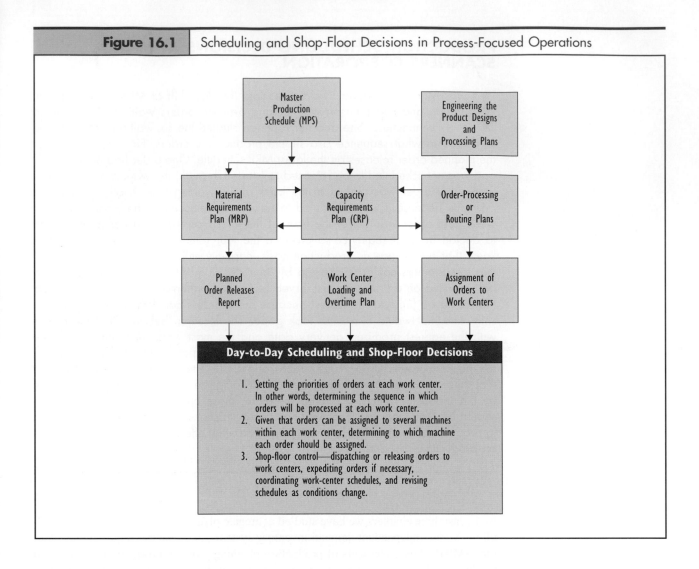

Job shops ordinarily use push systems of production planning and control, and MRP is a central part of these systems. Figure 16.1 illustrates that scheduling and shop-floor decisions in process-focused operations or job shops ordinarily begin with the planned order releases report from an MRP system. An order is defined as the quantity of a unique part number. Because a part takes on a different part number as it passes through successive stages of production, an order for a unique part number can be tied to specific work centers within the factory. From the planned order releases report of the MRP system, it can be determined when orders for each part number must be released (production is authorized), and from the CRP system it can be determined to which work center each order must go. Armed with this information, operations managers can make the day-to-day scheduling and shop-floor decisions, which include deciding in what sequence orders should be produced at work centers, assigning orders to machines within work centers, and making shop-floor control decisions.

Table 16.1 describes some of the characteristics of process-focused manufacturing and their scheduling implications. One thing should be clear from studying this table:

| Table 16.1 | Process-Focused Manufacturing: Characteristics and Their Scheduling Implications |

Characteristics	Scheduling Implications
Similar operations are grouped with common supervision.	Numerous individual work-center schedules must be developed and coordinated within production departments.
Products are diverse and sometimes custom designed.	Much preproduction planning is necessary to establish routing, job instructions, processing plans, and product designs.
Processing steps are uncoupled, and orders can follow a multitude of paths through production systems.	A complex production control system must plan and control the movement of orders through the production system.
In-process inventories build up between processing steps. Workers possess a variety of skills. Machines can adapt to a variety of products and operations.	There is great flexibility in shifting workers and machines from order to order.
Workloads are typically unbalanced between processing steps.	An extra burden is put on schedulers to fully load the facility and minimize idle time and underloading.
When equipment breakdowns, material delivery delays, and other interruptions occur, downstream operations typically are not immediately affected.	Fewer allowances for idle time need to be included in schedules.
Numerous orders can build up at each processing step.	A system of priorities must be established that determines which order should be scheduled first at each work center.
Products are typically of the produce-to-order type.	Long lead times are necessary for manufacture and material deliveries. Raw-material input schedules (MRP) and output schedules (MPS) are used.

These characteristics make job shops complex to schedule. Since job shops ordinarily produce orders for customers who have been given promised delivery dates, customers are directly affected by production. Also, because production lots in job shops tend to be small, numerous machine changeovers are required. The network of work centers to which an order is assigned determines the routing plan for the order, and the number of possible networks for an order can be large. *Workers and machines are so flexible that they are capable of being assigned and reassigned to many different orders. In such a flexible, variable, and changing environment, schedules must be specific and detailed in each work center to bring orderliness to a potentially hectic situation.*

Perhaps if you have an idea about how orders are actually moved around a job shop, it will be easier to understand how work-center schedules fit into the overall scheme of shop floor management. In job shops, the following two types of **preproduction planning** may have to occur before production of an order can begin:

1. Designing the product in a customer's order.
2. Planning the network of work centers through which the order must pass before it is completed; this is an order's **routing plan**.

Production control departments then guide the movement of the order among the work centers on the routing plan. Material handlers are notified to move the order to the next work center by a **move ticket.** The order may be accompanied by engineering drawings, specifications, or job instructions so that workers at a work center have the necessary information about how to do their work on the order. A detailed schedule gives information to the production supervisor about which order should be produced first at each work center and when each order should be finished. As an order is completed, the worker notifies the production planning and control department, a move ticket is issued for the next work center on the order's routing plan, and the detailed schedules are updated. It is apparent, then, that work-center schedules are an important part of shop-floor management.

With this description of the environment of scheduling in job shops as a background, we now discuss shop-floor planning and control.

Shop-Floor Planning and Control

Shop-floor control includes these activities:

1. Assigning a **priority** to each order, a measure of the relative importance of each order. This aids in setting the sequence of producing orders at work centers.
2. Issuing **dispatching lists** to each work center. These lists let production supervisors know which orders are to be produced at a work center, their priorities, and when each order should be completed.
3. Keeping the work-in-process (WIP) inventory updated. This includes knowing the location of each order and the quantity of parts in each order in the system; tracking the movement of orders between work centers when move tickets are used; and knowing the number of good parts that survive each production step, the amount of scrap, the amount of rework required, and the number of units short on each order.
4. Providing input–output control on all work centers. This means developing information about how jobs are flowing among work centers.
5. Measuring the efficiency, utilization, and productivity of workers and machines at each work center.

Production-planning and control departments perform these activities and report the results to operations managers so that corrective actions can be taken when orders are going to be late or when capacity or workload problems occur at work centers.

Input–Output Control

Input–output control is a key activity that allows operations managers to identify such problems as insufficient capacity, excessive capacity, and production difficulties among a group of connected workstations. Example 16.1 presents an analysis of an input–output control report. From such reports, operations managers can determine if the amount of work flowing to a work center is the planned amount and if the capacity of the work center is according to plan. If too much work is flowing to a work center compared to its capacity, then excessive WIP inventory will occur preceding the work center. When jobs pile up at work centers, not only does the work center become cluttered and crowded, but also downstream work centers may become starved for jobs. If, on the other hand, too little work is flowing to a work center compared to its capacity, the work center will be underutilized and idle machines and workers could result. Business Snapshot 16.1 describes how Boeing used computer simulation analysis to improve input–output control.

Example 16.1	Analyzing Input–Output Reports

Input–Output Report at the End of Week 5 for Work Center 240

			Week			
	−1	1	2	3	4	5
Planned input—labor-hours		300	300	300	300	300
Actual input—labor-hours		250	220	260	180	150
Cumulative deviation		−50	−130	−170	−290	−440
Planned output—labor-hours		300	300	300	300	300
Actual output—labor-hours		300	270	260	180	150
Cumulative deviation		0	−30	−70	−190	−340
Planned ending WIP—labor hours		50	50	50	50	50
Actual ending WIP—labor-hours	100	50	0	0	0	0

Shown above is an input–output report for Work Center 240 as of the end of the fifth week. All the values in the report are labor-hours. The jobs coming into the work center (input) have been converted to labor-hours, and the jobs coming from the work center (output) have also been converted to labor-hours with the use of labor standards. This conversion lets us compare different jobs using a common measure that directly relates to capacity.

Notice that the planned input to the work center (jobs coming to the work center) is 300 labor-hours in each of the past five weeks, which is the same as the planned output (jobs coming from the work center). The actual output from the work center is far less than planned, which ordinarily might indicate that production problems have caused the capacity of the work center to be insufficient. A closer look at the input part of the report, however, tells a different story. Not enough jobs are coming from the upstream work centers to keep the work center fully utilized. The WIP at the work center was 100 labor-hours at the end of Week −1 or at the beginning of Week 1, but this was depleted by the end of the second week to make up for the insufficient input to the work center.

The cause of the production problems at the upstream work centers must be found and corrected so that an increased flow of jobs can come into Work Center 240 to balance with the capacity of the work center.

The coordination of work-center schedules aids in the orderly flow of jobs between work centers, and Gantt charts are useful for this purpose.

Gantt Charts

Gantt charts can be used to visually display the workloads in each work center in a department. Figure 16.2 is an example of a Gantt chart used to compare the weekly schedule for five work centers in a model shop (a shop used to produce experimental products). The jobs scheduled to be worked on during the week are displayed with their code names or numbers (A, B, C, etc.), beginning times, and ending times, which are represented by an open bar. As work progresses on a job, a solid bar shows how the work center is performing to the schedule. The time of the review is indicated by a vertical arrow.

Machine changeovers, machine maintenance, and other planned nonproduction work are indicated by an X. Blank spaces indicate planned idle time at the work center; work crews are not required during these periods and may be shifted to other work

BUSINESS SNAPSHOT 16.1

Input–Output Control at Boeing

The Boeing Company produces between 300 and 500 commercial airplanes each year, ranging from 185-passenger 737s to 400-plus-passenger 747s. One of the major production steps in making airplane wings is the shot peening process, in which streams of metal pellets are shot at parts for shaping, work hardening, crack prevention, and surface defect prevention. Five gigantic machines at Boeing's Everett, Washington, facility perform shot peening on the various parts. These machines are tied together by an overhead rail system, consisting of cranes, transfer bridges, and load bars.

Historically, the shot peening process had gained a reputation as a problem area in the production process. In an effort to improve this operation, computer simulation was used to analyze how many parts were coming into and leaving from this operation. Using the simulation model, the number of load bars in the materials-handling system was varied to find the best level. Based on the simulation analysis, a decision was made to reduce the number of load bars on the overhead rail system from 22 down to 14 load bars. With the 22 load bars previously used there were too many parts in the shot peening operation, causing slower part flow times and higher work-in-process inventories. Reducing the number of load bars reduced the number of parts going into the shot peening operation and also reduced the part flow time, or the amount of time a part spent in the operation. It also made the operation easier to manage because less material was in the system.

Using computer simulation for input–output analysis of the shot peening process resulted in improved cycle time, improved performance, reduced inventory holding costs, and increased worker satisfaction. Such actions that reduce production costs and improve the production process help to make Boeing more competitive in the commercial aircraft industry.

Source: Gilbert, Dave. "Winging It." *APICS—The Performance Advantage* (December 2000): 40–41.

---

centers, or other jobs may be scheduled into these time slots later. Supervisors and production planners can see with a glance at the Gantt chart the progress of the work centers toward their schedules. For instance, Figure 16.2 shows that the time of the review is midafternoon on Wednesday. At this time the machining work center is ahead of schedule by about half a day on Job E because its shaded bar extends to the right of the vertical arrow, the packaging work center is ahead of schedule by about three hours on Job B, the test and assembly work centers are on schedule, and the fabrication work center is about two hours behind schedule on Job D. *Gantt charts are found in most factories and service operations, and they are very useful for coordinating a diversity of schedules of work teams, work centers, and activities of projects.*

Finite and Infinite Loading

Two approaches to how jobs are assigned to work centers are sometimes used—finite and infinite loading.

The **infinite loading** approach is used when jobs are assigned to work centers without considering the capacities of the work centers. Such an approach abandons capacity requirements planning (CRP) and its loading schedules. Unless a company has excessive production capacity, unacceptable queues of waiting jobs occur at work centers.

The **finite loading** approach is used when the capacities of work centers are allocated among a list of jobs. By using a computer simulation model or other means, each work center's capacity is allocated to jobs hour-by-hour by varying the start and completion times of the jobs. The end result of this approach is that no more work is sched-

| Figure 16.2 | Gantt Chart for Coordinating Work Centers' Schedules |

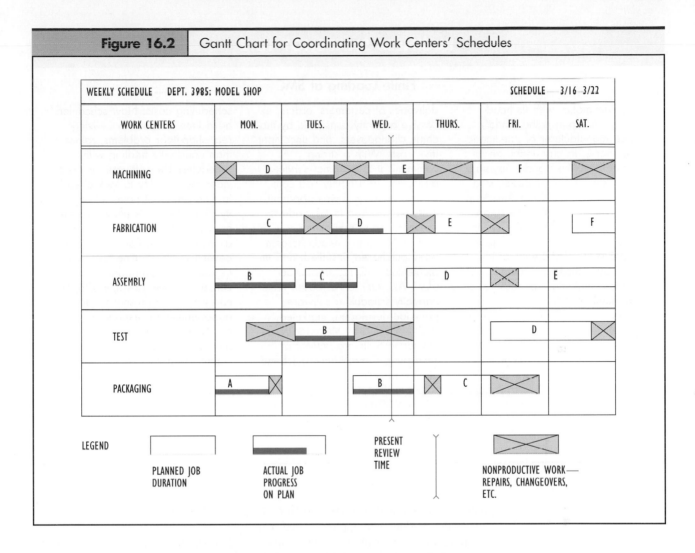

uled to a work center during any hour than the capacity of the work center. This approach is integral to CRP and is used by many companies today. See Business Snapshot 16.2 for a discussion of this approach.

Forward and Backward Scheduling

In preparing Gantt charts as in Figure 16.2 or loading schedules as in Figure 15.10 in Chapter 15, there are two ways to determine to which time slots jobs are assigned within work centers: forward scheduling and backward scheduling.

In forward scheduling, jobs are assigned to the earliest unassigned time slots in work centers. This approach assumes that customers want their jobs delivered as soon as possible. Although simple to use, excessive in-process inventories usually result because jobs tend to sit and wait for their next work-center assignments.

In backward scheduling, the starting point for planning is a promised delivery date to the customer. This date is then taken as given, and schedulers work backward through the factory using lead times to determine when jobs should pass through each stage of production. Jobs are assigned to latest possible time slots in work centers to meet the promised delivery date. Although this approach requires accurate lead times, it tends to reduce in-process inventories because jobs are not completed until they are

BUSINESS SNAPSHOT 16.2

Finite Loading at SMC

SMC Pneumatics with its headquarters in Japan is the world's largest manufacturer of pneumatic components. Its customers are industrial firms like Honda, Toyota, Sony, TRW, Anheuser-Busch, and Eli Lilly. SMC has North American plants at Indianapolis, Los Angeles, Toronto, and Mexico City. Its products at the Indianapolis plant number 6,000, and with variations they number 50,000. Scheduling is a nightmare because of a huge number of make-to-order jobs in very small batches. SMC's scheduling software used an infinite loading approach where jobs were assigned to work centers without considering work centers' capacities. This resulted in continuous hassles in dealing with late

deliveries of customers' orders, excessive capacity consumed by machine changeovers, and uncompetitive costs. With a strong commitment to customer service and being in a highly cost competitive industry, it was apparent that changes had to be made to its approach to scheduling.

To address this need, the company purchased, installed, and implemented *TACTIC: The Scheduler's Assistant*, a PC–based finite capacity scheduling software package developed, marketed, and supported by Waterloo Manufacturing Software (WMS) of Twinsburg, Ohio. Numerous benefits have resulted from the new software. Perhaps the most obvious is a 50 percent reduction in

scheduling costs. Now schedulers have time to spend on solving real shop-floor problems, rather than constantly fiddling with schedules. The software also provides the visibility to look ahead in time and spot potential capacity difficulties. This allows the necessary changes to be made to avoid problems. For example, the better use of overtime and reducing excessive overloading of machines are now possible. Opportunities are now present to identify opportunities for expanding capacity at some work centers at relatively low costs. The company claims great improvements in costs, profits, quality, and customer service because of its shift to the finite loading approach.

Source: "Finite Capacity Scheduling Helps SMC Improve Delivery, Control Costs." APICS—The Performance Advantage (February 1993): 24–27.

needed at the next work centers on their routing plans. For this reason, backward scheduling is the predominant approach used by progressive companies today.

Input–output control and Gantt charts provide operations managers with systematic ways of coordinating the flow of jobs among work centers. Let us now consider ways of setting priorities for jobs at work centers.

Order-Sequencing Problems

In order-sequencing problems we want to determine the sequence in which we will produce a group of waiting orders at a work center. We analyze these problems by discussing the various sequencing rules, the criteria for evaluating the sequencing rules, a comparison of sequencing rules, the control of changeover costs, and the minimization of production costs.

Sequencing Rules

Many rules can be followed in setting the priorities among orders or jobs waiting at work centers. Among the most common are:

- **First-come first-served (FCFS)**—The next job to be produced is the one that arrived first among the waiting jobs.
- **Shortest processing time (SPT)**—The next job to be produced is the one with the shortest processing time among the waiting jobs.

- **Earliest due date (EDD)**—The next job to be produced is the one with the earliest due date (the date promised to the customer) among the waiting jobs.
- **Least slack (LS)**—The next job to be produced is the one with the least slack (time to due date minus total remaining production time) among the waiting jobs.
- **Critical ratio (CR)**—The next job to be produced is the one with the least critical ratio (time to due date divided by total remaining production time) among the waiting jobs.
- **Least changeover cost (LCC)**—Since some jobs logically follow each other because of ease of changeovers, the sequence of waiting jobs is determined by analyzing the total cost of making all of the machine changeovers between jobs.

Other rules such as most valued customer, most profitable job, and shortest waiting line at the next operation can also be applied.

Criteria for Evaluating Sequencing Rules

In deciding which sequencing rule performs best for a group of waiting jobs, several criteria are commonly used:

- **Average flow time**—The average amount of time jobs spend in the shop.
- **Average number of jobs in the system**—The average number of jobs in the shop.
- **Average job lateness**—The average amount of time that a job's completion date exceeds its promised delivery date.
- **Changeover cost**—The total cost of making all the machine changeovers in a group of jobs.

A Comparison of Sequencing Rules

Let us demonstrate the use of sequencing rules and evaluation criteria in a one-work-center production system. Example 16.2 compares the shortest processing time and the critical ratio sequencing rules with the first-come first-served policy presently in use at the company.

Example 16.2	Evaluating Sequencing Rules

Precision Machining provides custom machining for its customers. The company presently uses a first-come first-served sequencing rule for customer jobs. Because the company wants to finish customers' jobs faster, it is considering two other rules: shortest processing time and critical ratio. The company thinks that these criteria are important in choosing a sequencing rule: average flow time, average number of jobs in the system, and average job lateness. Study Precision's situation and recommend a sequencing rule.

Solution

Six jobs are received at Precision, and their production times are estimated and delivery dates are promised to customers. Use the three rules to set the sequence of the jobs, and evaluate the rules according to the three criteria.

1. For the first-come first-served rule, the sequence for the jobs is A, B, C, D, E, and F, the sequence in which the jobs were received at Precision. The production time and time to promised delivery are given below. The flow time is computed by summing the flow time for the

preceding job and the production time for the present job. If a job is late, its lateness is the difference between its flow time and its time to promised delivery.

First-Come First-Served (FCFS)

(1) Job Sequence	(2) Production Time (hours)	(3) Time to Promised Delivery (hours)	(4) Flow Time (hours)	(5) Lateness (hours) [(4) − (3)]
A	2	4	2	0
B	5	18	7	0
C	3	8	10	2
D	4	4	14	10
E	6	20	20	0
F	4	24	24	0

2. For the shortest processing time rule, the sequence is determined by the jobs' production times: The job to be produced next is the one with the shortest processing time among the waiting jobs. The production time and time to promised delivery are given below. The flow time and lateness are computed as described in Step 1.

Shortest Processing Time (SPT)

(1) Job Sequence	(2) Production Time (hours)	(3) Time to Promised Delivery (hours)	(4) Flow Time (hours)	(5) Lateness (hours) [(4) − (3)]
A	2	4	2	0
C	3	8	5	0
D	4	4	9	5
F	4	24	13	0
B	5	18	18	0
E	6	20	24	4

3. For the critical ratio rule, the sequence is determined by computing the critical ratios for all the jobs: The job to be produced next is the one with the least critical ratio (time to promised delivery divided by production time) among the waiting jobs. The production time and time to promised delivery are given below. The flow time and lateness are computed as described in Step 1.

Critical Ratio (CR)

(1) Job Sequence	(2) Production Time (hours)	(3) Time to Promised Delivery (hours)	(4) Critical Ratio [(3)/(2)]	(5) Flow Time (hours)	(6) Lateness (hours) [(5) − (3)]
D	4	4	1.00	4	0
A	2	4	2.00	6	2
C	3	8	2.67	9	1
E	6	20	3.33	15	0
B	5	18	3.60	20	2
F	4	24	6.00	24	0

Evaluate the three rules by using these criteria: average flow time, average number of jobs in the system, and average job lateness.

1. Average flow time is computed by summing the flow times for the jobs and dividing by the number of jobs.

Sequencing Rule	Average Flow Time	Rank
FCFS	(2 + 7 + 10 + 14 + 20 + 24)/6 = 12.83 hours	2
SPT	(2 + 5 + 9 + 13 + 18 + 24)/6 = 11.83 hours	1
CR	(4 + 6 + 9 + 15 + 20 + 24)/6 = 13.00 hours	3

2. Average number of jobs in the system is computed by taking a weighted average of the number of jobs in the system where the weights are the production times for the jobs. For instance, the average number of jobs in the system for the first-come first-served rule is determined by: six jobs are in the system while job A is produced for 2 hours, five jobs are in the system while job B is produced for 5 hours, four jobs are in the system while job C is produced for 3 hours, three jobs are in the system while job D is produced for 4 hours, two jobs are in the system while job E is produced for 6 hours, and one job is in the system while job F is produced for 4 hours. Job F is the last job out, and it is in the system for a total of 24 hours.

Sequencing Rule	Average Number of Jobs in the System	Rank
FCFS	[2(6) + 5(5) + 3(4) + 4(3) + 6(2) + 4(1)]/24 = 3.21 jobs	2
SPT	[2(6) + 3(5) + 4(4) + 4(3) + 5(2) + 6(1)]/24 = 2.96 jobs	1
CR	[4(6) + 2(5) + 3(4) + 6(3) + 5(2) + 4(1)]/24 = 3.25 jobs	3

3. The average job lateness is computed by summing the lateness for all the jobs and dividing by the number of jobs.

Sequencing Rule	Average Job Lateness	Rank
FCFS	(0 + 0 + 2 + 10 + 0 + 0)/6 = 2.00 hours	3
SPT	(0 + 0 + 0 + 5 + 4 + 0)/6 = 1.50 hours	2
CR	(2 + 2 + 1 + 0 + 0 + 0)/6 = 0.83 hour	1

The sequencing rule that should be selected in this example depends on the type of performance that is most important to Precision Machining. If meeting customers' due dates is most important, then critical ratio would be the preferred rule. On the other hand, if keeping work-in-process inventories low is most important, then shortest processing time would be the preferred rule.

In the Precision Machining example, no single sequencing rule ranks first on all the evaluation criteria. This is what we find in real-world applications. We know from experience that:

1. **First-come first-served does not perform particularly well on most commonly used evaluation criteria.** It does, however, give customers a sense of fair play, and this can be an important consideration with customers.

Managers must assess a variety of evaluation criteria to decide on sequencing rules for manufacturing, such as in this paper mill.

© SALLY A. MORGAN; ECOSCENE/CORBIS

2. **Shortest processing time does perform well on most evaluation criteria.** It is optimal on average flow time and tends to perform well on average number of jobs in the system. But it may not perform as well as critical ratio on average job lateness. One shortcoming of the shortest processing time rule is that long-duration jobs are continuously pushed back in the schedule. The rule must, therefore, be overridden periodically so that long-duration jobs can be moved ahead and worked on.

3. **Critical ratio usually performs well only on the average job lateness criterion.** Critical ratio is intrinsically appealing: We want to first work on jobs that are most likely to be required before they can be finished.

Scheduling departments usually analyze the performance of different sequencing rules on representative groups of jobs, as in the Precision Machining example. Once they have selected the rule that tends to perform best for them on the most important criteria, it is made a part of their scheduling and shop-floor system but is reviewed at intervals.

Controlling Changeover Costs

Changeover costs are the costs of changing a processing step in a production system over from one job to another. They include costs for such things as changing machine settings, getting job instructions, and changing materials and tools. Usually, jobs should be produced in the sequence that minimizes the cost of these changeovers. For example, when two jobs use almost the same machine settings, tools, and materials, changing over from the first job to the second is very quick and inexpensive. Example 16.3 demonstrates a simple rule for determining a job sequence that will hold down the cost of changeovers among a group of waiting jobs. The procedure selects the first and second jobs in the sequence by finding the lowest changeover cost among all the possible changeovers. From the second job on, the next job is always determined by selecting the lowest changeover cost from among the remaining jobs. This rule may not be optimal, but it usually performs well in practice.

Example 16.3	Changeover Costs and Job Sequence

The Sure Print Company does custom printing jobs for local firms, political candidates, and schools. Sure Print is in the middle of an election year boom, and numerous political poster jobs are waiting to be processed at the offset press. Alicia Smith, who does Sure Print's job planning, is currently developing a weekly printing schedule for the offset press. She has developed these changeover costs for the six waiting jobs. All jobs carry equal priority, so the deciding factor in selecting a job sequence is the total changeover cost for the six jobs.

Jobs That Precede

		A	B	C	D	E	F
Jobs That Follow	A	—	$12	$15	$10	$35	$20
	B	$25	—	20	20	25	20
	C	27	15	—	12	20	15
	D	16	30	10	—	25	30
	E	35	20	25	30	—	30
	F	20	25	15	25	30	—

Alicia uses this rule to develop a low-cost job sequence: *First, select the lowest changeover cost among all the changeovers. The next job to be selected will have the lowest changeover cost among the remaining jobs that follow the previously selected job.* Since there is a tie for the starting jobs (D–A and C–D), Alicia develops two sequences:

1. A follows D ($10 is the minimum changeover cost, D is first and A is next).
    F follows A (read down A column; Job F has lowest changeover cost among the remaining jobs).
    C follows F (read down F column; Job C has lowest changeover cost among the remaining jobs).
    B follows C (read down C column; Job B has lowest changeover cost among the remaining jobs).
    E follows B (read down B column; Job E has lowest changeover cost among the remaining jobs).
    The job sequence is DAFCBE; its total changeover cost is 10 + 20 + 15 + 20 + 20 = $85.
2. Because there was a tie for the starting jobs above, the second job sequence is now developed: D follows C, A follows D, F follows A, B follows F, and E follows B. The job sequence is CDAFBE; its total changeover cost is 10 + 10 + 20 + 20 + 20 = $80.

Of the two sequences, CDAFBE is preferred because its total changeover cost is lower.

Now, Alicia knows that this is not necessarily the lowest possible total changeover cost for the six jobs. In other words, the method does not guarantee an optimal solution. But the simple rule is easy to understand and it gives satisfactory results.

Other more mathematically sophisticated procedures can achieve optimal results. **Integer linear programming** has been used to minimize changeover costs within a set of constraints that require all jobs to be assigned to the sequence once and only once.

Minimizing Total Production Time

We may want to determine a job sequence that minimizes the total time for producing a group of jobs. This objective would ordinarily result in low production costs and high worker and machine utilization.

Sequencing n *Jobs through Two Work Centers*   When several jobs must be sequenced through two work centers, we often want to select a job sequence that must hold for both work centers. This situation can be effectively analyzed by using Johnson's rule.[1]

Example 16.4 demonstrates the use of Johnson's rule in a two–work-center production system—Precision Machining. Customers' jobs must pass through machining (Work Center 1) and finishing (Work Center 2) *in the same job sequence*. The job sequence that results has the minimum total production time through both work centers for all the jobs.

Example 16.4	Sequencing Jobs through Two Work Centers with Johnson's Rule

There are two work centers at Precision Machining, machining and finishing. Precision's management wishes to adopt a procedure that would routinely set the sequence in which jobs would go through both work centers. Jane Bergland has been experimenting with Johnson's rule; she believes that Precision's situation can be effectively analyzed with this technique. Precision's management wants both work centers to change over to new jobs at the same time. In other words, if Work Center 1 completes its work on a job, it must wait until Work Center 2 has completed the job that it has been working on so that both work centers can begin new jobs simultaneously. The reason for this requirement is that supervisors can give job instructions to both work centers at the same time about how to do the jobs.

Jane visits the computer center, noting that six jobs are waiting.

a.   These data are developed for the six jobs:

	Estimated Processing Time (hours)	
Computer Job	**Work Center 1, Machining**	**Work Center 2, Finishing**
A	1.50	0.50
B	4.00	1.00
C	0.75	2.25
D	1.00	3.00
E	2.00	4.00
F	1.80	2.20

b.   Johnson's rule is:
1.   Select the shortest processing time in either work center.
2.   If the shortest time is at the first work center, do the job first in the schedule. If it is at the second work center, do the job last in the schedule.
3.   Eliminate the job assigned in Step 2.
4.   Repeat Steps 1, 2, and 3, filling in the schedule from the front and back until all jobs have been assigned a position in the schedule.

Jane then begins to follow the steps of the rule:

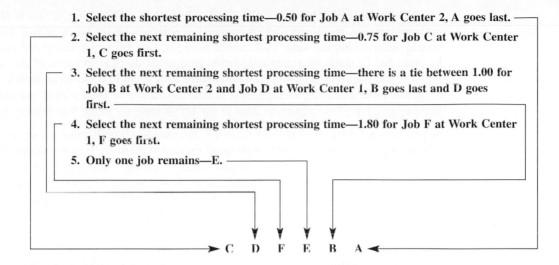

1. **Select the shortest processing time—0.50 for Job A at Work Center 2, A goes last.**
2. **Select the next remaining shortest processing time—0.75 for Job C at Work Center 1, C goes first.**
3. **Select the next remaining shortest processing time—there is a tie between 1.00 for Job B at Work Center 2 and Job D at Work Center 1, B goes last and D goes first.**
4. **Select the next remaining shortest processing time—1.80 for Job F at Work Center 1, F goes first.**
5. **Only one job remains—E.**

C D F E B A

c. This CDFEBA job sequence is further studied by developing the cumulative time to do all six jobs in both work centers. Jane knows that Precision's management wants the jobs to begin at the same time in both work centers:

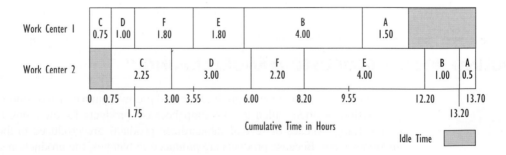

Cumulative Time in Hours

Idle Time

d. Jane can see that the CDFEBA job sequence allows both work centers to do all the jobs in 14.20 hours. She wonders how much this cumulative time could be reduced if Precision's management would relax the requirement that the jobs must begin at the same time in both work centers.

Cumulative Time in Hours

Idle Time

e. When jobs need not begin at the same time in both work centers, the cumulative time is 13.70 hours.
f. Jane will use this example to demonstrate to Precision's management the application of Johnson's rule.

Note in Example 16.4 that if a tie for the shortest processing time occurs in different work centers, no difficulty is encountered in determining the job sequence. If a tie should occur within the same work center, however, two job sequences would need to be evaluated by comparing their cumulative production times as in Part c of the example. The job sequence with the least cumulative time would be the recommended job sequence. Note also in the example that Johnson's rule can be used with or without the requirement that job changeovers must occur simultaneously in the two work centers.

Sequencing n *Jobs through* m *Work Centers*   Job shops ordinarily must sequence many jobs through many work centers, a problem for which there are no easy analytical solutions. And yet operations managers and schedulers make these types of sequencing decisions daily; how do they go about making these complex decisions? Ordinarily, a sequencing rule such as shortest processing time, critical ratio, or earliest due date is uniformly applied. The job sequences are then modified to take advantage of economies in changeovers. If some jobs are particularly late, changeover economies may have to be forgone in order to meet customer due-date commitments. Because sequencing decisions are increasingly an integral part of computerized scheduling systems, the sequencing procedures must be formalized and programmed into computers.

Research is continuing to explore mathematical methods for optimal solutions to these complex sequencing problems. Queuing theory, computer simulation, and computer search algorithms have all been used to study sequencing problems.

Assignment Problems

When many jobs are arriving in job shops that need to be assigned to work centers or machines within work centers, determining which jobs should be assigned to which work centers or machines is an important part of scheduling. These problems are commonly referred to as **assignment problems.**

The assignment method of linear programming is discussed and demonstrated in Example 7 in the Linear Programming Solution Methods appendix located on the CD accompanying this textbook. In that example, five jobs at the Mercury Electric Motor Company are assigned to five rewinding work centers. When *n* jobs must be assigned to *n* work centers at only one production stage, as in the rewinding step at Mercury Electric, then the assignment method is an appropriate technique for analyzing the problem. The assignment method is, however, impractical to use when *n* jobs must be assigned to *n* work centers in two or more downstream stages of production.

This concludes our discussion of shop-floor planning and control in job shops. Let us now turn to the study of shop-floor planning in product-focused factories.

SCHEDULING PRODUCT-FOCUSED MANUFACTURING

There are two general types of product-focused production: batch and continuous. **Batch production** is often called a **flow shop** because products follow along direct linear routes. Large batches of several standardized products are produced in the same production system. Because products are produced in batches, the production system must be changed over when a different product is to be produced. Many discrete-product manufacturers use this type of production. In **continuous production**, a few highly standardized products are produced continuously in very large volumes and changeovers are rare. The products may be discrete, such as plastic molded products, or they may be continuous, such as gasoline. Table 16.2 lists some characteristics of product-focused manufacturing and their scheduling implications.

| Table 16.2 | Product-Focused Manufacturing: Characteristics and Their Scheduling Implications |

Characteristics	Scheduling Implications
Products are standard designs. The parts and raw materials, required processing steps, and sequence of operations are known.	Little preproduction planning concerning routing of products, job instructions, processing plans, and product designs is necessary.
Products may be produced for inventory rather than to customer order.	Schedules can be based on economic production lots for products without pressure for deliveries to customers.
Production steps are coupled together in product layouts.	Production is scheduled much like a pipeline, concentrating on raw-material input schedules (MRP) and output schedules (MPS).
Production rates are greater than demand rates for products.	The predominant scheduling concerns are timing of production line changeovers and production lot sizes.
Because operations are coupled together, material supply delays, equipment breakdowns, scrap, and other factors that cause one operation to become idle also cause downstream operations to shut down.	Production schedules must have safety factors built in to allow for periodic idle time, must have preventive maintenance programs, and must have effective quality control programs.
The pipeline nature of the production line results in materials, once they have entered the line, flowing continuously from operation to operation until emitted at the end.	Production control may not need to keep complex records of in-process material movements, authorize in-process material movements, or otherwise plan for the timing of in-process material movements along the line. The key planning and materials movement authorization activities concern the supply of materials to the line and removal of finished units from the line.

These are the most common scheduling decisions for these factories:

1. If products are produced in batches and multiple products are produced on the same production lines, how large should the production lot size be for each product and when should machine changeovers be scheduled?
2. If products are produced to a specific delivery schedule, at any point in time how many products should have passed each upstream production operation if future deliveries are to be on schedule?

We now develop some techniques to assist managers in resolving these scheduling-related problems—batch scheduling, and scheduling and controlling production for delivery schedules.

Batch Scheduling

In product-focused systems that produce products in batches, a key issue is the size of batches. Two approaches to this issue will be discussed here: EOQ for production lots and the run-out method.

EOQ for Production Lots

In Chapter 14 we discussed the concept of an economic order quantity (EOQ) for production lots. Picture yourself in a production department looking toward the finished-goods warehouse. How many units of a product should we include in each production lot of a product to minimize annual inventory carrying costs and annual ordering costs (including machine changeover costs in production)? The production lot size problem is solved using the following formula:

$$EOQ = \sqrt{(2DS/C)[p/(p - d)]}$$

Table 14.3 in Chapter 14 contains the assumptions, variable definitions, and derivation of the formula. When using this formula to determine the number of products to produce in a batch, managers can be assured that annual cost of carrying in-process inventories equals the annual cost of setting up to run the batches. While appealing, this approach to setting batch size does not consider production capacity.

Run-Out Method

The EOQ formula discussed above is used to determine the size of a production lot or batch for a single product. As a comprehensive scheduling technique in batch scheduling, therefore, the EOQ is not entirely satisfactory because it fails to account for these facts:

1. Only so much production capacity is available in each week, and products share the same scarce production capacity. The size of production lots, therefore, should be determined simultaneously for all products within the capacity constraints for each week.
2. Decisions about production lot sizes should be based on the most current information about demand rates and production rates and not on annual ballpark demand estimates as in EOQ.

These deficiencies of the EOQ in planning production lot sizes have led to the development of the **run-out method** in capacity-constrained production operations when batches of products are produced on the same production lines. *This method attempts to use the total production capacity available in each time period to produce just enough of each product so that if all production stops, the finished-goods inventory for each product runs out at the same time.*

Example 16.5 uses the run-out method to develop a production schedule for five products of a wood putty company. Notice in this example that the run-out method is deficient in one respect. It does not attempt to set economic production lot sizes for products. But the run-out method does overcome a key weakness of the EOQ as a method of determining the size of production lots: It recognizes that products share production capacity and allocates the available capacity among products. In this example, all 1,600 hours of extruder time per week are allocated among the five products so that if the weekly forecast demand actually happens, the company would run out of each of the five products at exactly the same time.

Example 16.5	Run-Out Method of Production Scheduling

The Rock-Hard Wood Putty Company is planning its production for next week. All wood putty products at Rock-Hard must be processed through 20 mixer-extruders at its Peoria, Illinois, plant. Rock-Hard has a total of 1,600 extruder-hours per week of production capacity based on its six-month aggregate capacity plan. Rock-Hard's scheduling department is reviewing the inventory levels, machine-hours required per 1,000 pounds, and forecasted usage for its five principal products. Develop a production schedule for the extruders by using the run-out method.

Solution

1. First, convert inventory on hand and the forecasts into extruder hours:

(1) Product	(2) Finished-Goods Inventory (000 pounds)	(3) Extruder Time Required (hours per 000 pounds)	(4) Forecasted Demand for Next Week (000 pounds)	(5) Inventory in Extruder-Hours [(2) × (3)]	(6) Forecasted Demand for Next Week in Extruder-Hours [(4) × (3)]
A	160.0	1.0	100.0	160.00	100.00
B	210.0	2.0	200.0	420.00	400.00
C	200.5	2.5	200.0	501.25	500.00
D	150.6	1.5	160.0	225.90	240.00
E	170.2	1.5	100.0	255.30	150.00
			Totals	1,562.45	1,390.00

2. Next, compute the aggregate run-out time (in weeks). This value represents the amount of time that the last unit of an item would remain in inventory *beyond the week being planned, assuming that future weekly demands are the same as the forecasted demand for next week.* This value is computed by dividing the inventory balance at the end of the week being planned (which is the numerator of the fraction that follows) by the demand per week:

$$\text{Aggregate run-out time} = \frac{\begin{bmatrix}\textbf{(5)} \text{ Total} \\ \text{inventory on hand} \\ \text{(in extruder-hours)}\end{bmatrix} + \begin{bmatrix}\text{Total extruder} \\ \text{hours available} \\ \text{per week}\end{bmatrix} - \begin{bmatrix}\textbf{(6)} \text{ Forecasted demand} \\ \text{for next week} \\ \text{(in extruder-hours)}\end{bmatrix}}{\begin{bmatrix}\textbf{(6)} \text{ Forecasted demand} \\ \text{for next week} \\ \text{(in extruder-hours)}\end{bmatrix}}$$

$$= \frac{1,562.45 + 1,600.00 - 1,390.00}{1,390.00} = 1.275 \text{ weeks}$$

3. Next, develop a weekly production schedule that uses the 1,600 hours of extruder time:

     Product	(7) Desired Ending Inventory at End of Next Week (000 pounds) [(4) × 1.275]	(8) Desired Ending Inventory and Forecast (000 pounds) [(7) + (4)]	(9) Required Production (000 pounds) [(8) − (2)]	(10) Extruder-Hours Allocated to Products [(9) × (3)]
A	127.5	227.5	67.5	67.50
B	255.0	455.0	245.0	490.00
C	255.0	455.0	254.5	636.25
D	204.0	364.0	213.4	320.10
E	127.5	227.5	57.3	85.95
			Total	1,599.80

The line of balance (LOB) method is one way delivery schedules could be controlled in this warehouse.

© KEITH WOOD/CORBIS

Delivery Schedules: Line-of-Balance Method

Some production systems often commit to delivery schedules for their products that stipulate how many products must be delivered to customers in each future week. If it is important that actual product deliveries match with the planned delivery schedule, a system must be devised to schedule and control all the production steps. All too often, the production of a customer's order seems to be on schedule because deliveries are and have been on schedule. But things may already be happening in production that will result in late deliveries in the future. And corrective action may be impossible after deliveries are late, because the production pipeline may have run dry. In such instances, **line of balance (LOB)** has been used to schedule and control upstream production steps. Example 16.6 illustrates how a company uses LOB analysis to establish and control a delivery plan to a customer.

Example 16.6	Line of Balance (LOB) in the Snowball Snowblower Company

The Snowball Snowblower Company produces riding snowblowers in its manufacturing plant. Snowball has just signed a contract for its total output to be sold to one of the giant retailing chains. One of the stipulations of the contract was an ironclad delivery schedule:

Month	Units to Be Delivered	Month	Units to Be Delivered	Month	Units to Be Delivered
January	1,000	May	1,000	September	2,000
February	1,000	June	2,000	October	2,000
March	1,000	July	2,000	November	2,000
April	1,000	August	2,000	December	2,000

The production-processing steps, the relationships among the steps, and the lead times are shown on the following flowchart:

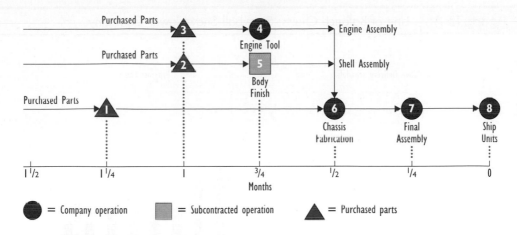

= Company operation ◼ = Subcontracted operation ▲ = Purchased parts

After eight months into the shipping schedule, these cumulative quantities of units have passed these processing steps in the production process:

Processing Step	Cumulative Production Quantity	Processing Step	Cumulative Production Quantity
⑧ Ship units	11,000	④ Engine test	12,000
⑦ Final assembly	11,000	△3 Receive purchased parts	12,000
⑥ Chassis fabrication	11,500	△2 Receive purchased parts	14,000
⑤ Body finish	12,000	△1 Receive purchased parts	15,000

Develop an LOB chart and evaluate the status of production at each processing step.

Solution

1. First, construct a cumulative delivery schedule as shown in Figure 16.3.
2. Next, locate the review point on the cumulative delivery schedule in Figure 16.3. The review point is at eight months. Proceed vertically upward until the cumulative delivery schedule curve is reached; proceed horizontally to the right until the last processing step, ⑧, on the progress chart is reached. Draw a short horizontal line across the Processing Step ⑧ column at this level. This is the *line of balance* for Processing Step ⑧. To locate the line of balance for Step ⑦, go *forward* (to the right) a quarter-month from the previous review point on the cumulative delivery schedule to 8¼ months and repeat the procedure. Why go forward in a schedule a quarter-month when Step ⑦ is back upstream in the production process? Because the units that are at Processing Step ⑦ now should be shipped a quarter-month (the amount of lead time between Steps ⑦ and ⑧) from now in the future, or 8¼ months in the schedule. The line of balance is similarly drawn for all processing steps.
3. Next, draw a vertical bar for each processing step on the progress chart to indicate the cumulative number of units that have passed each step.
4. Next, evaluate the progress chart: (a) Snowball is on its delivery schedule; the vertical bar for units shipped ⑧ exactly meets the line of balance. However, trouble looms ahead. (b) Processing Steps △2 and △1 are on schedule or ahead of schedule; that is, their bars either meet or exceed the line of balance. (c) Processing Steps ⑦, final assembly, and ⑥, chassis fabrication, are both 500 units behind schedule, probably because of engine assemblies and shell assemblies deficiencies. (d) Processing Step ⑤, subcontracted body finish, is 500

| Figure 16.3 | Line-of-Balance Charts: Snowball Snowblower Company |

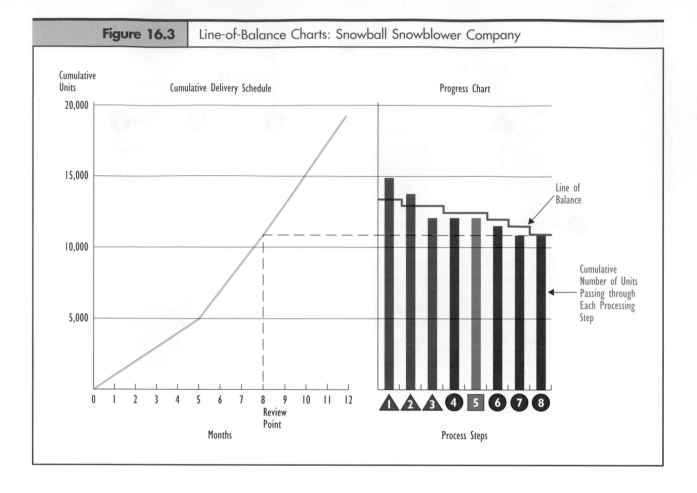

units behind schedule. The fault lies with the subcontractor and not purchased parts. (e) Processing Steps ④ and ⑤, engine assemblies, are 500 and 1,000 units behind schedule, respectively. Purchased parts is holding up engine test operation.

This evaluation suggests that management should immediately take corrective steps to accelerate purchase engines, engine test, and subcontracted body finish processing steps. Deliveries will be deficient by 500 units during the next review period (a quarter-month). Unless progress is made to accelerate ⑤ and ⑤, more serious delinquencies can be expected in the coming periods.

Periodically a new line of balance is drawn on the progress chart and vertical bars are extended to reflect additional units passing each production step since the last review. Thus, a snapshot evaluation of each production step is taken at regular intervals. These periodic evaluations provide operations managers with information about the performance of each step in relation to the schedule. This information is known before any production difficulties actually affect delivery schedules. Therefore, corrective action may be taken to avoid late deliveries. LOB achieves its greatest benefits when products or services are produced to specific delivery schedules, when production involves many production steps, and when production lead times are long.

Computer packages for scheduling are growing in both number and frequency of application in today's production systems.

COMPUTERIZED SCHEDULING SYSTEMS

Computer software packages are available to help companies develop detailed schedules for each work center and macro schedules that help coordinate all the jobs to be produced. Increasingly, these scheduling programs are an integral part of larger manufacturing planning software systems, such as *WinMagi* (**http://www.magimfg.com**) and *Macola* (**http://www.macola.com**), or even larger enterprise resources planning (ERP) systems. Three popular examples of these integrated ERP software systems are *SAP's R/3* (**http://www.sap.com**), *Baan* (**http://www.baan.com**), and *Peoplesoft* (**http://www.peoplesoft.com**). Another popular software system that includes sophisticated shop-floor control and scheduling components is *i2 TradeMatrix* by i2 Technologies (**http://www.i2.com**). There is no denying that these computer packages are appealing, but don't jump to the conclusion that they can be adapted to a particular production system quickly or easily just because the programs are already written and debugged. Many companies have found, much to their disappointment, that it often takes years to effectively implement the information systems.

Regardless of the scope of these packages, the scheduling portion of the programs ordinarily must perform these functions:

1. Develop for each work center daily detailed schedules that indicate beginning and ending times for each order.
2. Develop departmental daily and weekly detailed schedules that are used to coordinate work centers.
3. Generate modified schedules as new customer or work-center progress information surfaces.

Before these programs can be used, priority rules for determining the sequence of jobs at work centers must be developed, the necessary set of rules for determining which jobs will be assigned to which work centers must be established, and a system of follow-up and feedback within the facility for modifying schedules must be developed.

Computer software packages are available to help develop detailed work schedules for use in large production operations such as this one, but implementing and incorporating them are not always easy.

These are not easy tasks. When computerized systems are installed, managers cannot play fast and loose with their scheduling decisions. One of the most common complaints from schedulers is that managers always seem to be changing the rules to save them from the latest customer's telephone call. Schedulers seem to be whipsawed among the changing orders from the top concerning which jobs are the hot ones in the current period. Computerized systems require that consistent rules must be developed and followed, rational approaches to routing and production must be planned, and schedules must be followed if meaningful production-planning information is to be delivered.

These requirements are often forced on some managers by the necessity of installing a computerized scheduling system. In short, *a structure is forced on scheduling decisions when computers are used to develop detailed schedules.* Substantial improvements in customer service and internal operating efficiency are possible in these production systems only if sequencing rules, routing plans, and other inputs are realistic and if schedules are followed.

Some computerized scheduling systems focus on managing the schedules of bottleneck operations. With this approach, all other work-center schedules are controlled by the schedules of the bottleneck operations. Eli Goldratt popularized this approach, which he calls the **theory of constraints** (discussed in Chapter 13). Others have called this approach **synchronous manufacturing** or the **drum–buffer–rope** approach. Goldratt's original software was called *Optimized Production Technology (OPT)* and is currently maintained and marketed by Scheduling Technology Group,

---

BUSINESS SNAPSHOT 16.3

One Company's Experience with *OPT* Software

Guest & Chrimes Ltd. is the leading manufacturer of waterworks valves in the United Kingdom. Its manufacturing process takes scrap and pig iron into a foundry at one end of the operation and eventually produces finished valves at the other end. It employs 400 people at its 14-acre manufacturing site, and annually sells around 100,000 valves of vastly differing sizes and values.

In an effort to improve customer service levels and ensure continued profit growth into the future, Guest & Chrimes decided to adopt and implement *Optimized Production Technology (OPT)* from Scheduling Technology Group Ltd.

The entire implementation was completed within six months.

Today, work schedules are run once a week. In addition, many simulations are run for general forecasting purposes as well as measuring the effect of handling rush orders or subcontracting out certain processes. In this way, close control of the whole operation is maintained to minimize overdue orders. Typically, a simulation run takes only a few minutes.

Stuart Wilson, production director at Guest & Chrimes, is clear on the results so far: "The benefits of the project have been enormous for Guest & Chrimes. Lead times have been reduced to 6

weeks on most of our products, down on some from 36 weeks. In addition, customer service levels have improved, with the backlog of orders reduced to 2–3 days from 3–4 weeks, a fantastic achievement if one considers that throughput has increased meanwhile.

"There has been a 20% overall increase in turnover and profit levels while employee costs have remained stable. The whole company has benefited from this improvement due to our Value Added Bonus improving from 8% to over 13%—a true measure of our profitability."

Source: OPT software informational brochure. Scheduling Technology Group Ltd., Hounslow, U.K.

BUSINESS SNAPSHOT 16.4

OPT—The Logical Solution

*OPT*21 applies a simple but extremely powerful approach to scheduling a business: First, the process is scheduled to produce at the rate of the major constraints whether fixed or moving. This schedule is the "drum" beating out the pace at which the whole process will produce across time (Figure 16.4).

Next, the constraints are protected from the inevitable up-stream problems caused by statistical fluctuations by creating time buffers (not inventory buffers) in front of them. Due date performance is protected with buffers at key assembly points to ensure smooth flow beyond the constraints.

Last, all nonconstraining resources are synchronized to a rate at which the constraints can produce, like a "rope" linked to the constraint, opening and closing the gating operation.

This "drum–buffer–rope" concept is the core of *OPT*21's planning and scheduling mechanism and can be globally applied to any number of linked facilities. In this way the constraints inherent in a multiplant organization and its supply chain can be synchronized.

Source: Reprinted with permission from *OPT*21 software informational brochure. Scheduling Technologies Group Ltd., Hounslow, U.K.

Ltd. (**http://www.stg.co.uk**). Another software product utilizing this approach is *Manufacturing 5* by Thru-Put Technologies (**http://www.thru-put.com**). Business Snapshot 16.3 describes one company's experience with *OPT* software. Business Snapshot 16.4 illustrates the logic behind synchronous manufacturing, and Figure 16.5 illustrates the information inputs and outputs of the *OPT* software. These and similar types of scheduling software are most beneficial for the complex scheduling environment found in large job shops.

Figure 16.4	Synchronous Manufacturing the "Drum–Buffer–Rope" Way

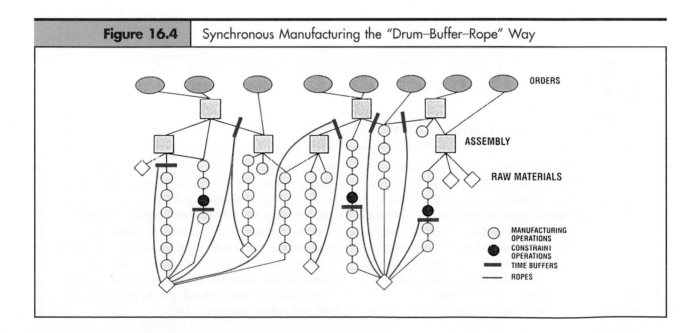

| Figure 16.5 | Information Inputs and Outputs for *OPT* |

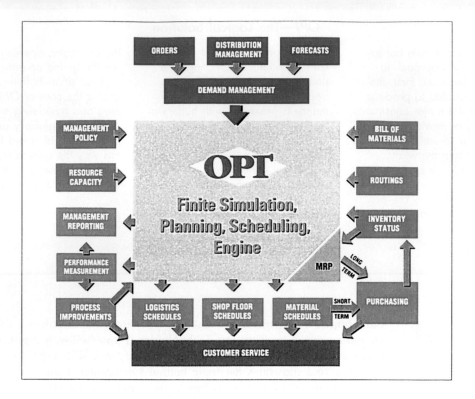

Source: Reprinted with permission from *OPT*21 software informational brochure. Scheduling Technologies Group Ltd., Hounslow, U.K.

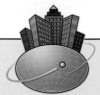

Wrap-Up
WHAT WORLD-CLASS COMPANIES DO

The nature of scheduling decisions varies among the types of production systems. In process-focused factories, priorities must be set for each order at each work center, orders must be assigned to machines within work centers, and shop-floor control must be applied to orders. Shop-floor planning and control in process-focused factories includes setting priorities for orders, issuing dispatching lists to work centers, keeping work-in-process (WIP) updated, providing input–output control for work centers, and measuring and reporting the performance of work centers. In this type of production, world-class companies have effective MRP II systems in place that provide near-real-time information for companies, their suppliers, and their customers about the status of orders. These systems have been continuously refined so that customer delivery promises are met, shop loading is near optimal, production costs are low, and product quality is high.

In scheduling product-focused factories, production lot sizes, the timing of machine changeovers, and the planning and control of production for delivery schedules are important scheduling problems. Production lot sizes may be determined by EOQ, but in world-class companies, the EOQ is set to fit standard parts containers and the setup cost, S, is computed. Then shop-floor studies are conducted to attain this level of S. In this way, lot sizes are drastically reduced, in-process inventories are slashed, and customer responsiveness is greatly improved.

In world-class companies, scheduling information and scheduling decisions are part of a computer information system. *SAP's R/3, Macola, OPT,* and other computerized information systems impose structure on scheduling decisions. In this way, delivery times are more predictable and production performance is more uniform. These systems not only can provide information on the status of orders but also can provide answers to "what if" questions about orders from suppliers and customers.

REVIEW AND DISCUSSION QUESTIONS

1. Explain the relationship between material requirements planning and scheduling decisions. From where in the MRP system does the information for making shop-floor scheduling decisions come?
2. Describe a process-focused factory. What are the implications of the characteristics of such a factory for scheduling decisions?
3. What are two key scheduling problems in job shops?
4. Explain how an operations manager would select and use a sequencing rule in practice.
5. Define these terms: a. *infinite loading*, b. *finite loading*, c. *forward scheduling*, d. *backward scheduling*.
6. Explain the advantages of backward scheduling over forward scheduling.
7. What is the objective of Johnson's rule? Under what conditions would it be used?
8. What scheduling decisions must operations managers resolve in product-focused factories?
9. Evaluate EOQ as a method of setting production lot sizes. What are its strengths and weaknesses?
10. Explain how the run-out method improves on the EOQ. What are its disadvantages?
11. What is input–output analysis? What information does it provide operations managers? What is its main purpose?
12. Explain what world-class companies are doing in their production scheduling.

INTERNET ASSIGNMENTS

1. Visit and explore the Internet site of Macola Software (**http://www.macola.com**). Under Macola's manufacturing software (ERP), find its *Shop Floor Control* module. Describe the features of the *Shop Floor Control* software module.
2. Search the Internet for a consulting firm that offers services to help companies with shop-floor control or production control in manufacturing. Describe the services that are offered.
3. Visit and explore the web site of SAP at **http://www.sap.com**. Find information on SAP's *Supply Chain Management* software and describe features of the software related to production scheduling.
4. Search the Internet for a producer of shop-floor control software. Describe the features of this software.

PROBLEMS

1. Given this input–output report at the end of Week 4:
   a. What production difficulties does the report indicate?
   b. What corrective actions do you recommend?

| | | Week | | | |
	−1	1	2	3	4
Planned input (labor-hours)		200	300	300	200
Actual input (labor-hours)		200	250	275	175
Cumulative deviation		0	−50	−75	−100
Planned output (labor-hours)		200	300	300	200
Actual output (labor-hours)		200	250	275	175
Cumulative deviation		0	−50	−75	−100
Planned ending WIP (labor-hours)		200	200	200	200
Actual ending WIP (labor-hours)	200	200	200	200	200

2. Given this input–output report at the end of Week 4:
   a. What production difficulties does the report indicate?
   b. What corrective actions do you recommend?

| | | Week | | | |
	−1	1	2	3	4
Planned input (labor-hours)		100	50	20	100
Actual input (labor-hours)		150	75	30	120
Cumulative deviation		50	75	85	105
Planned output (labor-hours)		100	50	20	100
Actual output (labor-hours)		90	50	15	100
Cumulative deviation		−10	−10	−15	−15
Planned ending WIP (labor-hours)		20	30	20	20
Actual ending WIP (labor-hours)	70	130	155	170	190

3. Ace Machine Shop processes custom metal parts for customers. Ace operates Monday through Friday, eight hours per day. A production schedule has been prepared for next week. The jobs, estimated production times, estimated changeover times, and the progress as of the end of Wednesday are shown below.

Work Center	Job Production Time (hours)				Changeover Time (hours)	Wednesday Progress [hours ahead or (behind)]
	A	B	C	D		
Turning	4	8	4	8	1	(2)
Milling	8	4	4	8	2	—
Heat Treating	4	4	8	4	1	2
Finish	8	4	4	4	2	(4)

The four jobs are being produced in this sequence: A, B, C, and D. Prepare a Gantt chart that shows how the work centers must be coordinated and shows the end-of-Wednesday progress.

4. An electronic manufacturer produces assemblies on a produce-to-order basis for other manufacturers. The plant now has accepted customer orders for the next

workweek, Monday through Friday, eight hours per day. The customer orders, estimated production times, estimated changeover times, and the Wednesday 5:00 p.m. progress are shown in the following table:

Work Center	Order Numbers and Production Time (hours)				Changeover Time (hours)	Wednesday Progress [hours ahead or (behind)]
	14	98	55	49		
Inspection	4	4	6	4	1	—
Fabrication	8	8	12	8	2	2
Assembly	8	12	8	12	2	(4)
Packaging	4	2	4	2	2	—

The orders will be produced in this sequence: 14, 98, 55, and 49. Prepare a Gantt chart for one workweek that shows how the work centers must be coordinated.

5. Six jobs are waiting to be processed at a workstation. Their job code numbers, estimated production times, and promised delivery times are given in the following table:

Job Code Number	Production Time (hours)	Time to Promised Delivery (hours)
161	3.8	6.0
162	2.1	3.0
163	4.5	14.0
164	3.0	10.0
165	4.2	20.0
166	2.9	19.0

Determine the sequence of producing the jobs using the following rules:
a. shortest processing time rule
b. least slack rule
c. critical ratio rule

6. Seven jobs are waiting to be processed at a workstation. Their job code numbers, estimated production times, and promised delivery times are given below.

Job Code Number	Production Time (hours)	Time to Promised Delivery (hours)
241	2.4	31.0
242	3.7	12.0
243	5.2	19.0
244	3.3	14.0
245	5.6	10.0
246	6.1	27.0
247	4.0	24.0

Determine the sequence of producing the jobs using the following rules:
a. shortest processing time rule
b. least slack rule
c. critical ratio rule

7. A company does heat-treating for industrial customers on a first-come first-served basis, but wonders if shortest processing time would be better. The jobs that are now waiting to be produced are listed in the order in which they arrived, with their estimated production times, time to promised delivery, and the necessary computations:

Job	Estimated Production Time (days)	Job Sequence	Flow Time (days)	Job Sequence	Flow Time (days)
A	6	1	6	4	16
B	3	2	9	2	5
C	2	3	11	1	2
D	5	4	16	3	10

    a. Rank the two sequencing rules on two evaluation criteria: average flow time and average number of jobs in the system.

    b. Which sequencing rule would you recommend? Why?

8. A production planner must decide the sequence in which to produce four customer orders.

Customer Order	Estimated Production Time (days)	Time to Promised Delivery (days)	First-Come First-Served Order Sequence	Flow Time (days)	Lateness (days)
A	10	15	1	10	0
B	21	30	2	31	1
C	26	60	3	57	0
D	19	77	4	76	1

Rank the first-come first-served, shortest processing time, and critical ratio sequencing rules on three evaluation criteria: average flow time, average number of jobs in the system, and average job lateness.

9. A company does heat-treating (annealing, case hardening, water plunge, oil plunge, etc.) jobs for customers. Each job usually requires a different setup, and these changeovers have different costs. Today the company must decide the job sequence for five jobs to minimize changeover costs. Below are the changeover costs between jobs.

Jobs That Precede

		A	B	C	D	E
	A	—	$53	$47	$67	$59
	B	$57	—	55	61	43
Jobs That Follow	C	40	49	—	48	42
	D	62	46	51	—	63
	E	50	64	41	55	—

    a. Use this rule to develop a job sequence: First, select the lowest changeover cost among all changeovers; this sets the first and second jobs. The next job to be selected will have the lowest changeover cost among the remaining jobs that follow the previously selected job.

    b. What is the total changeover cost for all five jobs?

10. The production planner in Problem 8 is taking another look at the four customer orders. It appears that the sequence in which the orders are produced affects the setup costs. These setup cost estimates have been developed:

Order That Follows	Order That Precedes			
	A	B	C	D
A	—	$4,290	$1,800	$3,500
B	$3,500	—	2,900	2,600
C	4,450	3,960	—	2,900
D	5,400	1,970	1,900	—

   a. Use this rule to develop a job sequence: First, select the lowest setup cost among all setups; this sets the first and second orders. The next order to be selected will have the lowest setup cost among the remaining orders that follow the previously selected orders.
   b. What is the total setup cost for all four orders?

11. A company receives parts from suppliers to be used in its manufacturing departments. The quality control department must perform two operations when shipments are received: Operation A—draw a random sample, package, and deliver to testing, and Operation B—test the materials and issue a disposition report. The time estimates for processing six shipments through quality control are:

Shipment	Operation A (hours)	Operation B (hours)
1	1.3	0.9
2	1.3	1.1
3	0.8	1.5
4	1.6	1.4
5	1.5	1.0
6	1.2	1.9

   a. Use Johnson's rule to set the sequence of processing the shipments through quality control. (Operations need not change over to new jobs at the same time.)
   b. How much total time is required to process the six shipments through quality control?

12. A production scheduler must determine the sequence in which to process four customer orders. Each of the orders must go through two principal operations: insertion and soldering. The scheduler has developed these production time estimates for the four orders:

Customer Order Number	Component Insertion (hours)	Flow Soldering (hours)
A	6.9	5.9
B	7.3	6.1
C	5.7	4.9
D	2.6	3.6

If the operations need not change over to new jobs at the same time:
   a. Use Johnson's rule to set the sequence of producing the orders in the two operations.
   b. How many hours will be required to produce all the orders through both operations?

13. These five jobs must be assigned to five work centers. The job codes and the production time in hours at each work center are given below.

Job	Work Center				
Code	1	2	3	4	5
A	4.3	3.5	3.3	4.0	4.1
B	2.9	4.0	4.5	3.2	3.8
C	1.9	2.7	3.0	4.5	3.1
D	4.8	3.9	2.9	3.7	3.0
E	3.5	4.4	4.1	4.7	3.9

   a. Use the assignment LP program in the *POM Software Library* to determine the assignment that minimizes the total production time required to produce all five jobs.

   b. Fully interpret the meaning of the solution. How much production time will the solution require for all five jobs?

   c. What factors should be considered in making this assignment?

14. These five jobs must be assigned to five work centers. The job codes and the profits in dollars for the jobs at the work centers are given below.

Job	Work Center				
Code	1	2	3	4	5
A	270	280	310	340	290
B	320	380	290	300	330
C	390	360	290	370	310
D	350	370	330	340	360
E	290	350	320	330	300

   a. Use the assignment LP program in the *POM Software Library* to determine the assignment that maximizes total profits for producing all five jobs.

   b. Fully interpret the meaning of the solution. How much total profit will the solution provide for all five jobs?

   c. What factors should be considered in making this assignment?

15. A manufacturer produces several electronic assemblies on a produce-to-stock basis. The annual demand, setup or ordering costs, carrying costs, demand rates, and production rates for the assemblies are shown below.

Assembly	Annual Demand (000 units)	Setup or Ordering Cost ($/lot)	Carrying Cost ($/unit/year)	Demand Rate (units/day)	Production Rate (units/day)
A	10	$1,500	$ 8	100	300
B	12	900	6	300	500
C	8	2,000	10	100	200
D	5	1,200	5	200	400

   a. Using the EOQ model, compute the production lot size for each assembly.

   b. What percentage of the batch of A assemblies is being used during production?

   c. For the A assembly, how much time will pass between setups?

16. Qualiscan Inc. produces five models of high-quality scanners for computer systems. The annual demands, setup or ordering costs, carrying costs, demand rates, and production rates for the final assembly of the scanners are given as follow.

Scanner Model	Annual Demand (scanners)	Setup or Ordering Cost ($/lot)	Carrying Cost ($/scanner/year)	Demand Rate (scanners/day)	Production Rate (scanners/day)
SC1	18,000	$4,000	$107	72	225
SC2	15,000	3,000	148	60	200
SC3	12,000	3,500	175	48	180
SC4	9,000	3,000	210	36	150
SC5	6,000	2,500	250	24	150

a. Using the EOQ for production lots model, compute the production lot size for each scanner model.

b. Assuming that there are 250 working days per year and that the final assembly department produces only these scanner models, what percentage of the year's capacity is required for Model SC1?

17. Qualiscan Inc. produces five models of high-quality scanners for computer systems. It is now June 15, and Qualiscan is planning its final assembly department schedule for the fall quarter—July, August, and September. The inventory on hand, final assembly hours required per scanner, and forecasted demand are shown in the following table:

Scanner Model	Inventory on Hand or in Production (scanners)	Final Assembly Time Required (hours/scanners)	Forecasted Demand for Fall Quarter (scanners)
SC1	1,000	0.03	4,500
SC2	1,800	0.04	3,750
SC3	900	0.05	3,000
SC4	750	0.06	2,250
SC5	600	0.07	1,500

The winter quarter demand forecast is the same as that for the fall quarter. If there are 800 final assembly hours available in each quarter, use the run-out method to develop a final assembly production schedule for the fall quarter.

18. A manufacturer must develop a production schedule for March, the upcoming month, for producing electronic assemblies. The electronic assemblies are standard designs that are produced to stock. The information below applies:

Assembly	Inventory on Hand (units)	Flow-Soldering Time Required (hours/unit)	March Forecasted Demand (units)	April Forecasted Demand (units)
A	200	0.3	500	500
B	800	0.2	1,000	1,000
C	600	0.5	1,500	1,500
D	500	0.4	900	900

The soldering operation is the bottleneck operation. If there are 1,000 soldering hours available per month to produce these assemblies, use the run-out method to develop a schedule for March for the production of these assemblies.

19. A company has a contractual delivery schedule for its products. The delivery schedule calls for 10,000 products to be delivered each week for 30 weeks. The

production process for the products has the lead times shown in the accompanying illustration. Ten weeks into the delivery schedule, production records indicate that these cumulative quantities have passed the production steps:

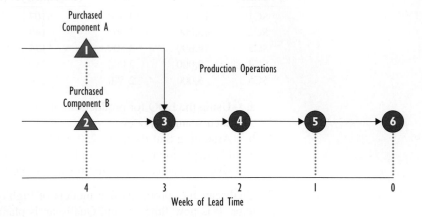

Processing Step	Cumulative Production (products)	Processing Step	Cumulative Production (products)
1	120,000	4	120,000
2	150,000	5	115,000
3	120,000	6	105,000

a. Prepare a cumulative delivery schedule chart, a progress chart, and a line of balance.
b. Evaluate the prospects for future deliveries. Do there appear to be any delivery difficulties in the future?

CASES

Star DigiVideo Inc.

Star DigiVideo Inc. produces five models of DVD players. The annual demands, setup or ordering costs, carrying costs, demand rates, and production rates for the final assembly of the DVD players are given below.

Player Model	Annual Demand (players)	Setup or Ordering Cost ($/lot)	Carrying Cost ($/players/year)	Demand Rate (players/day)	Production Rate (players/day)
D1	54,000	$3,000	$65	180	850
D2	36,000	1,500	40	120	750
D3	81,000	4,500	35	270	1200
D4	48,000	2,000	56	160	700
D5	24,000	2,500	80	80	600

It is now June 15, and Star DigiVideo is planning its final assembly department schedule for the fall quarter—July, August, and September. The inventory on hand, final assembly hours required per DVD player, and forecasted demand are given below.

Player Model	Inventory on Hand or in Production (players)	Final Assembly Time Required (hours/players)	Forecasted Demand for Fall Quarter (players)
D1	10,000	0.012	13,500
D2	7,000	0.013	9,000
D3	15,000	0.008	20,250
D4	21,000	0.014	12,000
D5	3,000	0.017	6,000

The winter quarter demand forecast is the same as that for the fall quarter.

Assignment

1. Using the EOQ for production lots model, compute the production lot size for each model.
2. Assuming that there are 300 working days per year and that the final assembly department produces only these DVD player models, what percentage of the year's capacity is required for Model D1?
3. If there are 640 final assembly hours available in each quarter, use the run-out method to develop a final assembly production schedule for the fall quarter.
4. What are the advantages of the EOQ as a way of computing production lot sizes in this case? What are the disadvantages?
5. What are the advantages of the run-out method as a way of computing production lot sizes in this case? What are the disadvantages?
6. Which approach to lot-sizing—EOQ or run-out method—would you recommend for Star DigiVideo?

Integrated Products Corporation

The Integrated Products Corporation (IPC) has contracted to supply a customer with IPC's T40 unit on a strict shipping schedule. The agreed-to schedule is shown below:

Month	Units to Be Delivered	Month	Units to Be Delivered
January	2,000	April	3,000
February	2,000	May	3,000
March	2,000	June	3,000

The production-processing steps, the relationships among the steps, and the lead times are shown on the following flowchart:

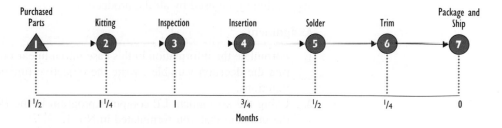

At the end of March these cumulative quantities of units have passed these production-processing steps:

Processing Step	Cumulative Units	Processing Step	Cumulative Units
1. Purchased parts	9,000	5. Soldering	6,500
2. Kitting	9,000	6. Trimming	5,250
3. Inspection	9,000	7. Package and ship	5,000
4. Insertion	9,000		

Assignment

1. Construct a cumulative shipping chart, a progress chart, and a line of balance as of the end of March.
2. What is the status of IPC's progress to the present?
3. What is the future status of IPC's progress likely to be? What corrective actions are likely to be required by IPC's operations managers if they are to meet their shipping schedule?
4. Discuss the usefulness of LOB in planning and controlling IPC's shipments. How would an MRP system compare with LOB in this application? Defend your answer.

NewWood Ltd.

NewWood Ltd. produces several types of wood filler for repairing dents and holes in hardwoods. NewWood's manufacturing plant just north of Montreal produces wood filler products that are sold throughout the eastern part of Canada and the northeastern part of the United States. Pierre LeBlanc, the production analyst at the plant, must decide which mixing machine should be used for each of the five products that are to be produced tomorrow morning. Each of NewWood's five mixing machines was acquired at a different time and has different characteristics, so the mixing time for each product is different on each machine. Three of the products can be produced on any of the five machines, one product must be produced on one of four machines, and one product must be produced on one of three machines. Mr. LeBlanc has estimated the production time for each product on each machine, as shown below. An "X" indicates that the product cannot be produced on that machine.

	Mixing Machine				
Product	1	2	3	4	5
QuickDry	3.4	3.1	4.1	3.9	3.5
RockHard	5.2	5.0	4.5	4.9	4.2
SandEZ	X	4.0	5.3	X	5.1
Nail-It	2.5	3.7	2.4	3.3	3.0
RealWood	6.1	5.0	X	5.5	4.8

Which product should be assigned to each mixing machine to minimize the total mixing machine time used by all the products?

Assignment

1. Formulate the information in this case into a linear programming (LP) model. Define the decision variables, write the objective function, and write the constraint functions.
2. Using the assignment LP computer program in the *POM Software Library*, solve the problem that you formulated in No. 1.
3. Fully interpret the meaning of the solution you obtain in No. 2. In other words, which products should be assigned to which mixing machines? How much total machine time will be required to produce all the products?

4. Suppose now that Mr. LeBlanc has just found out that Machine 2 has malfunctioned and will not be available for two days. This means that only four of the five products can be produced tomorrow morning. Modify your LP formulation in No. 1 to reflect this new situation. Use the *POM Software Library* to solve this new problem. (You can modify the LP model generated by the assignment LP program.)

5. Fully interpret the meaning of the solution you obtained in No. 4.

ENDNOTE

1. Johnson, S. M. "Optimal Two-Stage and Three-Stage Production Schedules with Setup Times Included." *Naval Research Logistics Quarterly* 1 (March 1954): 61–68.

SELECTED BIBLIOGRAPHY

Bagchi, Tapan P. *Multiobjective Scheduling by Genetic Algorithms.* Boston: Kluwer Academic Publishers, 1999.

Bolander, Steven F., and Sam G. Taylor. "Scheduling Techniques: A Comparison of Logic." *Production and Inventory Management Journal* 41, no. 1 (First Quarter 2000): 1–5.

Clark, Wallace. *The Gantt Chart: A Working Tool of Management.* New York: Ronald Press, 1922.

Correll, James G., and Norris W. Edson. *Gaining Control. Capacity Management and Scheduling.* New York: John Wiley & Sons, 1999.

Goldratt, Eliyahu M., and Jeff Cox. *The Goal: A Process of Ongoing Improvement,* 2nd rev. ed. Croton-on-Hudson, NY: North River Press, 1992.

Johnson, S. M. "Optimal Two-Stage and Three-Stage Production Schedules with Setup Times Included." *Naval Research Logistics Quarterly* 1 (March 1954): 61–68.

Kempf, Karl, Reha Uzsoy, Stephen Smith, and Kevin Gary. "Evaluation and Comparison of Production Schedules." *Computers in Industry* 42, nos. 2, 3 (July 2000): 203–220.

McKay, Kenneth N., and John A. Buzacott. "The Application of Computerized Production Control Systems in Job Shop Environments." *Computers in Industry* 42, nos. 2, 3 (July 2000): 79–97.

Melnyk, Steven. *Shop Floor Control.* Homewood, IL: Irwin Professional, 1985.

Michel, Roberto. "The Tools to Improve." *Manufacturing Systems* 17, no. 8 (August 1999): 86–87.

Mishina, Mayu. "The New Face of Scheduling." *American Printer* 224, no. 6 (March 2000): 36–42.

Moss, Steven, Cheryl Dale, and Glenn Brame. "Sequence-Dependent Scheduling at Baxter International." *Interfaces* 30, no. 2 (March–April 2000): 70–80.

Pinedo, Michael. *Scheduling: Theory, Algorithms, and Systems.* Upper Saddle River, NJ: Prentice Hall, 1995.

Plenert, Gehard J., and Bill Kirchmier. *Finite Capacity Scheduling: Management, Selection, and Implementation.* New York: John Wiley & Sons, 2000.

Salegna, Gary. "Integrating the Planning and Scheduling Systems in a Job Shop." *Production & Inventory Management Journal* 37, no. 4 (1996): 1–7.

Schaap, Dave. "Scheduling Repetitive Production." *Manufacturing Systems* 15, no. 6 (June 1997): 46–50.

Scherer, Eric, ed. *Shop Floor Control—A Systems Perspective: From Deterministic Models Towards Agile Operations Management.* New York: Springer Verlag, 1998.

Silver, Edward A., David F. Pyke, and Rein Peterson. *Inventory Management and Production Planning and Scheduling.* New York: John Wiley & Sons, 1997.

Taylor, Sam G., and Steven F. Bolander. "Process Flow Scheduling: Past, Present, and Future." *Production & Inventory Management Journal* 38, no. 2 (1997): 21–25.

Vollmann, Thomas E., William L. Berry, and D. Clay Whybark. *Manufacturing Planning and Control Systems,* 4th ed. New York: McGraw-Hill, 1997.

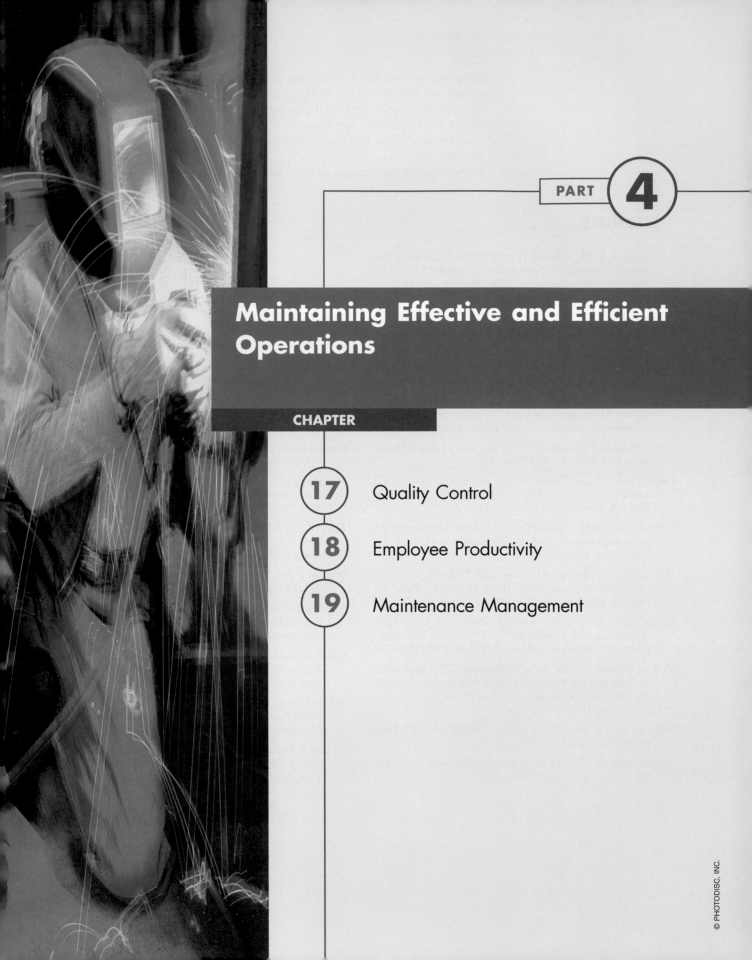

PART 4

Maintaining Effective and Efficient Operations

CHAPTER

17 Quality Control

18 Employee Productivity

19 Maintenance Management

In Part 4 of this text we examine many of the decisions involved in maintaining effective operations and improving the efficiency of operations. By their very nature, there is a sense of urgency about these decisions because they have an immediate impact on the short-term performance of operations. On the other hand, *the issues discussed in this part of the text are also of strategic importance because the long-term survival of businesses in global competition depends on the ability of companies to excel in delivering products of the highest quality and fast and on-time deliveries, with the overall goal of satisfied customers.* And so it is that the topics of this part of the text play two roles: one is short-term planning and control, but because global competition has elevated these topics to strategic importance, they also hold the key to long-term survival. Operations managers, therefore, are key players on the field of global competition.

These are some of the things for which operations managers are responsible: producing products fast and keeping delivery promises to customers, high productivity and low production costs, workers' safety, producing products of the highest quality, and keeping customer satisfaction high.

More than any other factor, people—the employees in production systems—directly affect costs, timely production, quality, and customer satisfaction. Because of employees' great impact, their jobs must be carefully planned, they must work together, and they must be empowered to take on more active roles. Employees have many of the answers to questions about how to improve productivity, and operations managers must draw out these ideas and assist employees in implementing them.

Programs of total quality management (TQM) and their implementation are crucial to long-term survival. And the day-to-day quality control must be managed so that the organization will produce products or services that meet its predetermined quality standards and are continuously improving. Setting these standards, inspecting outputs and comparing the actual product or service characteristics to these standards, and taking corrective actions as required are important aspects of operations managers' daily jobs.

Maintaining the machines of production is another important aspect of controlling costs and quality. Exercising preventive maintenance helps ensure that machines will not interfere with operations managers' cost, timely production, and quality objectives.

If our industries are to survive global competition in the long run, they must improve the ways that they are planning and controlling their day-to-day operations. What this means to us is that the topics in Part 4—quality control, employee productivity, and maintenance management—when taken together are crucial to the success and survival of our organizations.

17

Quality Control

Introduction
Statistical Concepts in Quality Control
  Sampling
  Central Limit Theorem and Quality Control
Control Charts
  Control Charts for Attributes
  Control Charts for Variables
Acceptance Plans
  Single, Double, and Sequential Samples
  Single-Sample Acceptance Plans for Attributes
  Estimating Acceptance Criteria
  Single-Sample Acceptance Plans for Variables

Computers in Quality Control
Quality Control in Services
Wrap-Up: What World-Class Companies Do
Review and Discussion Questions
Internet Assignments
Problems
Cases
  Five Star Fasteners Inc.
  Integrated Products Corporation
Endnotes
Selected Bibliography

QUALITY CONTROL AT TEXAS TELECOM

Texas Telecom produces a variety of set-top TV converter boxes for the cable TV and satellite TV industries. Established in the late 1980s, Texas Telecom initially focused on low-cost products. But in recent years, the company has refocused its operations to provide dependable, high-performance products. In the effort to refocus on higher-end products, Texas Telecom implemented a total quality management (TQM) program and has been pleased with the results. One aspect of TQM that has been particularly helpful in improving product quality and gaining new business is the use of control charts.

Before control charts were used, many of the company's products did not consistently conform to customer specifications. Even though the products were designed to be superior, there was too much variation in product performance. To address this problem, production manager Mary Boone introduced control charting throughout the production process. The key elements of this initiative were self-charting by workers, small group meetings to analyze quality control, and management's recognition of high-quality performance. Work teams meet at the beginning of each shift to review their most recent eight-hour control charts, detect any undesirable trends, and discuss any needed corrections in the production processes. Then during his or her shift, each worker plots the measure of quality of products at his or her operation every 30 minutes. Any trend that a worker thinks is getting out of control is reported immediately to the team leader. If serious enough, production is stopped until the problem is corrected.

Employee training was a critical part of Texas Telecom's control chart program. Before using control charts, each worker underwent two weeks of training on the fundamentals of quality management and control charts. With the help of control charts, product performance is now at extremely high levels. Defect rates (out-of-specification products) are running only 0.01 percent, or about 1 defect in 10,000 units, which is about one-tenth of the industry average.

The preceding account describes a program to improve conformance of product quality to customer specifications. That is what this chapter is mainly about, developing control chart programs to monitor the performance of production processes so as to produce products that meet customer expectations. We also discuss acceptance plans for special situations where they are appropriate.

As discussed in Chapter 7, Operations Quality Management, the customers determine the quality of products and services. Customer expectations are the basis for determining if products and services are of superior quality. Table 17.1 lists some products and services and their customer expectations. It is customer expectations that must be translated into standards for controlling the quality of goods and services in production.

But quality control begins long before products and services are delivered to customers. As Figure 17.1 shows, early in the production system raw materials, parts, and supplies must be of high quality before they are used. Materials are examined to make sure that they meet the appropriate specifications—strength, size, color, finish, appearance, chemical content, weight, and other characteristics. As the materials proceed through production, the quality of partially completed products is analyzed to determine whether the production processes are operating as intended. This monitoring is aimed at improving product quality and identifying undesirable trends that

Table 17.1	Some Products and Services and Their Customer Expectations

Product/Service Organization	Customer Expectations
Commercial chemical fertilizer manufacturer	Does the product contain the correct amount of each chemical? Does the packaging avoid the absorption of excess moisture under ordinary conditions of use? Is particle sizing correct?
Hospital	Is the patient treated courteously by all hospital personnel? Does each patient receive the correct treatments at the correct times? Is each treatment administered with precision? Does the entire hospital environment support patient recovery?
University	Does each student take the prescribed courses? Is each student achieving acceptable performance in courses? Is each faculty member contributing to the growth and development of students? Does the university environment support high scholarship?
Automaker	Does the auto perform as intended? Is its appearance pleasing? Is each part of the auto within the manufacturing tolerances? Is the design safe to operate? Does the auto have the intended reliability? Is the auto's gas mileage, pollution control, and safety equipment within government guidelines?
Bank	Is each customer treated courteously? Are each customer's transactions completed with precision? Do customers' statements accurately reflect their transactions? Does the bank comply with government regulations? Is the physical environment pleasing to customers?
Lumber mill	Is the lumber properly graded? Is the lumber within moisture content tolerances? Are knotholes, splits, surface blemishes, and other defects excessive? Is lumber properly packaged for shipment? Does the lumber comply with strength specifications?

Figure 17.1	Quality Control throughout Production Systems

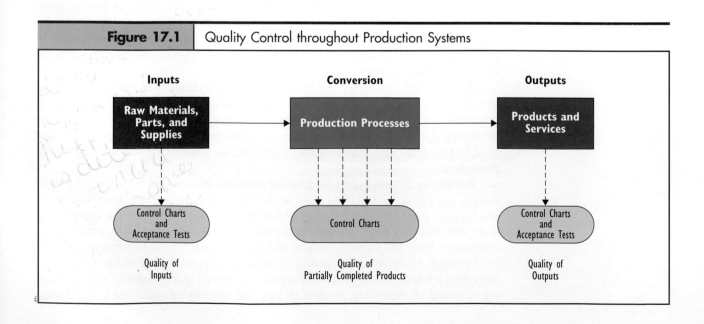

indicate needed corrective actions. Then finished products and services are studied to determine if they meet customer expectations. Quality control includes the activities from the suppliers, through production, and to the customers.

STATISTICAL CONCEPTS IN QUALITY CONTROL

The statistical underpinnings of today's quality control practices stem from the work of Shewhart, Dodge, and Romig at the Bell Telephone Laboratories during the 1920s. Sampling methods, control charts, and acceptance plans were developed by these men during that period.

Sampling

The flow of products is broken into discrete batches called lots. A quality control lot is produced under the same operating conditions. Lots of materials, parts, assemblies, and products are sampled to determine if the lots meet quality standards. Random samples are removed from these lots and measured against certain standards. *A random sample is one in which each unit in the lot has an equal chance of being included in the sample;* thus the sample is likely to be **representative** of the lot. Either attributes or variables can be measured and compared to standards.

Attributes are characteristics that are classified into one of two categories. In quality control, the two categories are usually **defective** and **nondefective.** For example, the lamp either lights up when connected to electrical current or it does not. Variables are characteristics that can be measured on a continuous scale. Employees who are inspecting for variables must measure the amount of a characteristic that is present and then determine if that amount is within the acceptable range. For example, the diameter of a motor shaft can be measured in thousandths of an inch.

What percentage of lots should be included in samples? Put another way, what should be the size and frequency of samples? Generally, one argument is that as the percentage of lots in samples is increased, there are two effects: (1) The sampling and testing costs increase and (2) the quality of products going to customers increases. Sampling and testing costs do increase as the percentage of lots sampled and tested increases. And if only good products survive testing, the quality of products going to customers would increase with the greater percentage of lots being sampled and tested. In an era of companies that are trying to become first-in-class in product quality, you might conclude that large percentages of lots should be included in samples. This is true for many products and certainly true for most products that must be very reliable. For example, a computer manufacturer runs 100 percent of production or every single personal computer for about 24 hours and inspects, tests, and compares all the computers to quality standards. To avoid the very high costs of testing such a high percentage of its production, the testing has been completely automated. *For companies that aspire to be first-in-class in product quality, it seems to be a good tactic, for some products, to increase the quality of products by significantly reducing the costs of sampling and testing so that almost all the products can be economically tested.*

For other products, a relatively small percentage of lots are sampled and tested because testing costs cannot be significantly reduced. In these cases, very large samples are too costly and are avoided, and extremely small samples may suffer from statistical imprecision and are also avoided. Between these extremes, larger samples are ordinarily used when sampling for attributes rather than for variables. Sample sizes for attributes must ordinarily be large enough to detect at least one defective on the average. For example, if a lot had 2 percent defectives, we would need a sample of at least

50 to capture an average of 1 defective. Sample sizes for variables are typically in the range of 4 to 20.

When to inspect during production processes can usually be determined by following these general principles: (1) Inspect *after* operations that are likely to produce faulty items. (2) Inspect *before* costly operations. (3) Inspect *before* operations that cover up defects. (4) Inspect *before* assembly operations that cannot be undone. (5) On automatic machines, inspect first and last pieces of production runs but few in-between pieces. (6) Inspect finished products. The reasoning behind these principles is largely economic.

A concept that is important in inspection is the central limit theorem.

Central Limit Theorem and Quality Control

The central limit theorem may well be the most important single statistical concept in POM. Stated simply, this theorem is: *Sampling distributions can be assumed to be normally distributed even though the population distributions are not normal.* The only exception to this theorem occurs when sample sizes are extremely small. Computer studies show that in some cases even when sample sizes are as small as five, however, their **sampling distributions** are very close to normal distributions.[1]

Figure 17.2 compares a population distribution with its sampling distribution of sample means. This sampling distribution includes all the possible measures of sample means ($\bar{x}$). We can make the following generalizations about this sampling distribution:

1. The sampling distribution can be assumed to be normally distributed unless sample size (n) is extremely small.
2. The mean of the sampling distribution ($\bar{\bar{x}}$) is equal to the population mean (μ).
3. The standard error of the sampling distribution ($\sigma_{\bar{x}}$) is smaller than the population standard deviation (σ_x) by a factor of $1/\sqrt{n}$.

The power of the central limit theorem in quality control lies in its ability to allow use of the normal distribution to easily set limits for control charts and acceptance plans for both attributes and variables.

CONTROL CHARTS

[handwritten margin note: all get together & figure out why product has deteriorated but we need to look @ improve to do it again]

For the continual improvement of product quality, it is essential to study closely the quality of products coming from each production operation. Control charts assist in achieving this purpose. For each production operation, periodic sample data are posted on a control chart and compared to standards. If the sample data are close to the standards, the operation is in control and no action is needed. If the data are far from the standards or if unexpected trends are present, however, then the operation should be investigated. *The primary purpose of control charts is to indicate when production processes may have changed sufficiently to affect product quality. An investigation would then be conducted into the causes of the change. If the indication is that product quality has deteriorated or is likely to deteriorate in the future, then the problem would be corrected by taking actions such as replacing worn tools, making machine adjustments, or training and instructing workers. If the indication is that product quality is better than expected, then it is important to find out why so that the high quality can be maintained.* Investigation of the quality problem may reveal that no corrective action is needed, that the data variation was only an anomaly. The beauty of control charts is that managers and workers can quickly glance at them and determine if quality standards are being met and if unusual trends should be investigated. Because of

| **Figure 17.2** | Comparison of Population and Sampling Distributions |

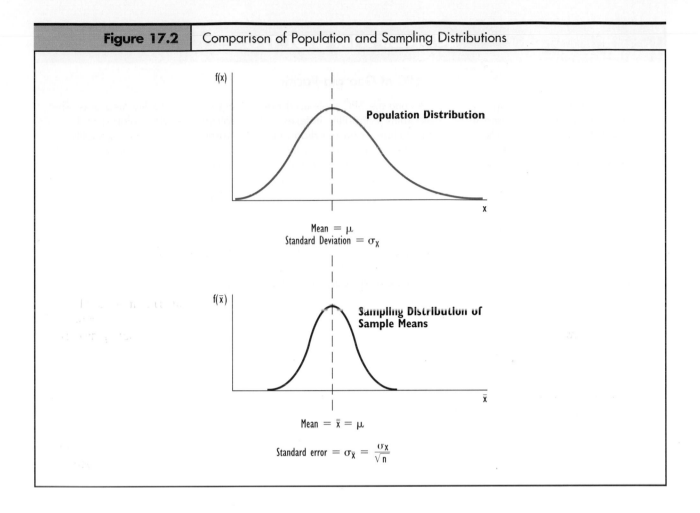

the flexibility of application of these tools, control charts are used in all types of businesses and government organizations today.

The use of control charts is often referred to as **statistical process control (SPC)** Business Snapshot 17.1 discusses SPC at Georgia-Pacific.

Control Charts for Attributes

Constructing control charts involves three determinations: (1) center line, (2) upper control limit, and (3) lower control limit. Once these three values are established, they become the standards or benchmarks against which to compare future samples. Figure 17.3 is a p chart used to plot the percent defectives in daily samples in the month of March. The upper control limit is slightly over 10 percent, the center line is 5 percent, and the lower control limit is 0 percent. As the daily sample percent defectives are plotted on this control chart, we can see that all the points are within the upper and lower control limits and no unusual trends are present. Therefore, no investigation of product quality at the operation is warranted at this time.

Table 17.2 displays the formulas and variable definitions for the necessary calculations in control charts. Example 17.1 presents the preparation of a p chart for monitoring the percent defectives for capacitors produced by machine operators. The center line of a control chart is ideally determined from observing the capability of the

SPC at Georgia-Pacific

Georgia-Pacific (GP) is a large forest products company based in Atlanta, Georgia. One of GP's many manufacturing facilities, located in Eugene, Oregon, produces resins for manufacturers of plywood, particle board, OSB, and other similar wood products that require adhesives. As part of a company-wide quality management program, statistical process control (SPC) was adopted at the Eugene resin plant.

Among the SPC tools used are histograms, capability indexes, control charts, and run diagrams. Some of the process performance measures, or quality measures, that are monitored with SPT tools are viscosity, temperature, pH level, heating time, refractive index, percent caustic, pump time, and load time.

SPC software was installed to automate some of the SPC tools and to allow for real-time monitoring of some quality measures. The software provides alarms and warnings when process quality levels fluctuate. Computer printouts of control charts and run diagrams for certain quality measures are routinely provided to customers. This lets customers know that GP is serious about quality and is using the latest SPC tools to control quality.

| **Figure 17.3** | *p* Chart for Controlling Percent Defectives in Samples |

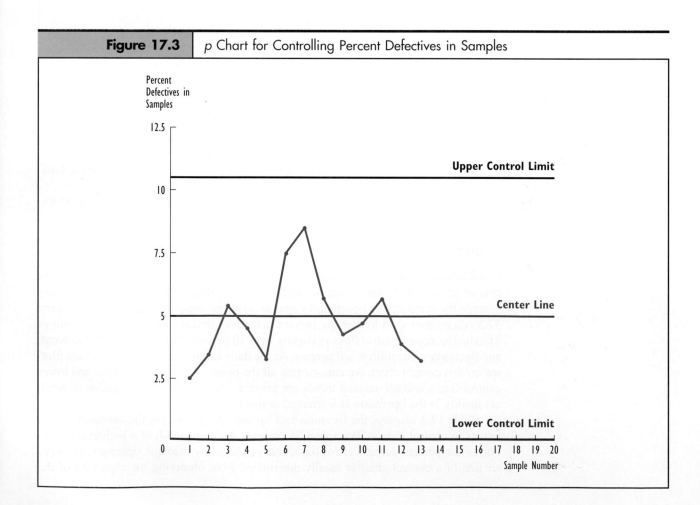

Table 17.2		Formulas and Variable Definitions for Computing 3σ Control Limits for Control Charts		

Type of Control Chart	Center Line	3σ Lower Control Limit	3σ Upper Control Limit
p	$\bar{p}$	$\bar{p} - \sqrt{3\bar{p}(100 - \bar{p})/n}$	$\bar{p} + \sqrt{3\bar{p}(100 - \bar{p})/n}$
x	$\bar{\bar{x}}$	$\bar{\bar{x}} - A\bar{R}$	$\bar{\bar{x}} + A\bar{R}$
R	$\bar{R}$	$D_1\bar{R}$	$D_2\bar{R}$

p = percent defectives in a sample
$\bar{p}$ = average percent defectives across many samples
n = sample size—number of observations in a sample
$\bar{x}$ = a sample mean
$\bar{\bar{x}}$ = mean of many sample means
R = a sample range
$\bar{R}$ = mean of many sample ranges
A, D_1, D_2 = factors from Table 17.3

process. But in some instances, particularly in new processes, center lines may be determined from the expert knowledge of a supervisor, a target that we want to attain, the average number over some trial period, or the data provided by the supplier of a key machine about its capability.

Example 17.1		Constructing Control Charts for Attributes

Pedro Reyes operates a machine that makes capacitors. Pedro's company is implementing a self-charting program, and he wants to begin keeping track of the percent defectives at his operation. He knows that with this type of process, about 4 percent defectives are expected plus or minus some chance variation. Pedro wishes to initially construct a p chart with three standard deviation control limits, and he has prepared 10 daily samples of 100 capacitors each.

Sample Number	Percent Defectives	Sample Number	Percent Defectives	Sample Number	Percent Defectives
1	4	5	1	8	12
2	3	6	9	9	4
3	3	7	5	10	3
4	6				

Solution

1. Compute 3σ control limits for p:
   First, from Table 17.2 observe the control limits for p charts:

   $$\text{Upper control limit} = \bar{p} + 3\sqrt{\bar{p}(100 - \bar{p})/n} = 4 + 3\sqrt{4(96)/100} = 4 + 3(1.9596)$$
   $$= 4 + 5.8788 = 9.88 \text{ percent}$$

   $$\text{Lower control limit} = \bar{p} - 3\sqrt{\bar{p}(100 - \bar{p})/n} = 4 - 3\sqrt{4(96)/100} = 4 - 3(1.9596)$$
   $$= 4 - 5.8788 = -1.88 \text{ percent, or } 0 \text{ percent}$$

2. Construct a p chart, and plot the 10 data points that Pedro has collected:

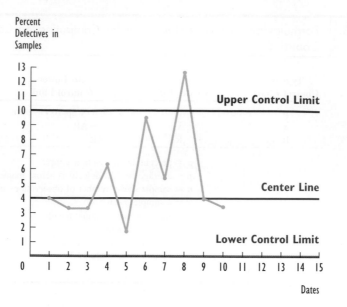

3. Although most of the samples are within the control limits, Pedro intends to investigate the conditions surrounding Samples 6 and 8.

The control limits in Table 17.2 are 3σ control limits. This means that the control limits are three standard deviations from the center line. Control charts are really sampling distributions because we are plotting sample statistics, and from the central limit theorem we know that sampling distributions are normally distributed. In normal distributions, three standard deviations either side of the mean include 99.7 percent of the total observations. Therefore, there is a 99.7 percent probability that sample data points will fall within the 3σ upper and lower control limits of control charts if the center line of the process being monitored has not changed. When data points are trending outside the control limits, the underlying process is changing and management investigation is in order. Control limits for attributes could similarly be set at 95 percent, 90 percent, or any other confidence interval by substituting the appropriate Z scores from the normal distribution for the 3 in the formulas for p charts in Table 17.2. For example, 95 percent Z score = 1.96, 90 percent Z score = 1.64, and so on (found in Appendix A).

Because the lower control limit in Example 17.1 is negative, we set the limit at 0 percent defectives. Lower control limits do not have to be negative or zero; they can also be positive values. If the percent defectives in samples goes below the lower limit of a control chart, what is indicated? Just that fewer defectives than expected are in the samples. This does not indicate that anything is wrong. But it does indicate that something may have changed in production, and we would therefore want to investigate to find out why so that we could continue producing such high product quality. Why? Because a major objective of the use of control charts is to *improve* quality.

Control Charts for Variables

Control charts are constructed for monitoring the variables $\bar{x}$ and R. An $\bar{x}$ chart and an R chart are frequently used together to monitor the quality of products and services. The $\bar{x}$ chart monitors the average value of the variable being measured. The R chart monitors the variation among the items within samples. This dual monitoring therefore controls both average values and variation of values from their mean. Take, for exam-

Using a control chart to monitor production involves considering both the average values as well as variation among items to maintain product quality.

© PHILIP GOULD/CORBIS

ple, the weights of boxes of cornflakes from a production line. An $\bar{x}$ chart may indicate that the sample average box weights are on target, but without an R chart to monitor variation, box weights could range from 0 to 10 pounds (assuming that a box would hold that much) within samples. This example demonstrates that we usually cannot conclude that a process is in control just by monitoring sample means and that variation within samples must also be monitored.

Table 17.3 lists the control chart factors A, D_1, and D_2 for variables. Example 17.2, which demonstrates the construction of $\bar{x}$ and R charts in monitoring fill weights of boxes of cornflakes, illustrates an important truth in interpreting the information from control charts. Sometimes, data trends are more important than the absolute values of the data. Unfavorable trends can indicate the need for corrective action *before* products and services of substandard quality are actually produced. And favorable trends can indicate that changes need to be made in production to lock in the improved

Table 17.3	3σ Control Chart Factors for Variables

Sample Size n	Control Limit Factor for Sample Mean	Control Limit Factor for Sample Range	
	A	D_1	D_2
2	1.880	0	3.267
3	1.023	0	2.575
4	0.729	0	2.282
5	0.577	0	2.116
10	0.308	0.223	1.777
15	0.223	0.348	1.652
20	0.180	0.414	1.586
25	0.153	0.459	1.541
Over 25	$0.75(1/\sqrt{n})$*	$0.45 + 0.001(n)$*	$1.55 - 0.0015(n)$*

*These values are linear approximations for student use in constructing control charts.

Source: Economics Control of Manufactured Products. New York: Litton Educational Publishing, Van Nostrand Reinhold Co., 1931. Copyright 1931, Bell Telephone Laboratories. Reprinted by permission.

product quality. Thus, managers and workers carefully monitor the trends of control charts with the objective of making changes in production processes that will result in a continual improvement in product quality.

Example 17.2	Constructing Control Charts for Variables

As part of a self-charting program at his company, Joe Wilson wants to construct $\bar{x}$ and R charts at the filling operation for the 16-ounce cornflakes product. Engineers have studied the filling operation and have determined that when operating properly, boxes average 16.1 ounces and hourly samples of 20 boxes each have sample ranges that average 2.22 ounces. Here are the data from 12 hourly samples that Joe has taken:

Sample Number	Sample Mean (ounces)	Sample Range (ounces)	Sample Number	Sample Mean (ounces)	Sample Range (ounces)
1	16.2	2.0	7	16.0	2.9
2	15.9	2.1	8	16.1	1.8
3	16.3	1.8	9	16.3	1.5
4	16.4	3.0	10	16.3	1.0
5	15.8	3.5	11	16.4	1.0
6	15.9	3.1	12	16.5	0.9

Solution

1. Compute the upper and lower control limits for the $\bar{x}$ and R charts:

First, from Table 17.2 observe the control limits for an $\bar{x}$ chart ($\bar{\bar{x}}$ is the center line and equals 16.1 ounces; A is found in Table 17.3, A = 0.180 when n = 20):

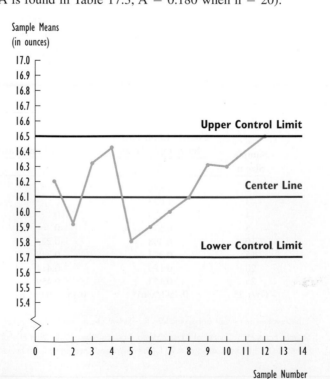

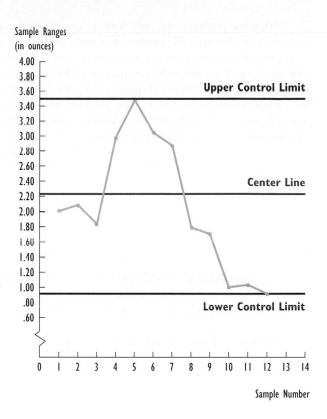

Sample Ranges (in ounces)

Upper Control Limit

Center Line

Lower Control Limit

Sample Number

Upper control limit $= \bar{\bar{x}} + A\bar{R} = 16.1 + 0.180(2.22) = 16.1 + 0.400 = 16.500$ ounces

Lower control limit $= \bar{\bar{x}} - AR = 16.1 - 0.180(2.22) = 16.1 - 0.400 = 15.700$ ounces

Next, from Table 17.2 observe the control limits for an R chart (D_2 is found in Table 17.3, $D_2 = 1.586$ when n = 20; D_1 is found in Table 17.3, $D_1 = 0.414$ when n = 20):

Upper control limit $D_2\bar{R} = 1.586(2.22) = 3.521$ ounces

Lower control limit $D_1\bar{R} = 0.414(2.22) = 0.919$ ounce

2. Plot the sample means and ranges on the $\bar{x}$ and R control charts.
3. What can Joe conclude about the filling operation?

Although none of the sample means exceeded the control limits, the trend of the last eight hours indicates a definite out-of-control situation. Unless this trend is reversed by corrective action, excessive numbers of overfilled boxes probably will result. The R chart indicates that the sample ranges do not exceed the control limits. Curiously, however, the sample ranges of the last eight hours have narrowed. This trend could be associated with the out-of-control situation of the sample means and should be investigated.

ACCEPTANCE PLANS

For most products today, the trend is toward developing testing methods that are so quick and effective that products are submitted to *100 percent inspection and testing, which means that every product shipped to customers is inspected and tested to determine if it meets customer specifications.* But there are situations where it is either impossible or uneconomical to inspect and test each and every product.

With some products, the only way we can determine if they perform satisfactorily is to conduct what are called *destructive tests, tests where no products survive the tests.* Examples of such products are ammunition that is tested by being shot in guns, concrete blocks that are tested by crushing in hydraulic presses, missiles that put satellites in orbit which are fired on test ranges, and a host of tests performed on chemicals, paper, metals, and other materials. And yet with other products, the cost of sampling, inspecting, and testing each and every product is not warranted. For these products, where 100 percent inspection and testing is uneconomical, impractical, or impossible, acceptance plans are the only sensible basis for inspecting and testing.

An **acceptance plan** is the overall scheme for either accepting or rejecting a lot based on information gained from samples. The acceptance plan identifies both the size and type of samples and the criteria to be used to either accept or reject the lot. Samples may be either single, double, or sequential.

Single, Double, and Sequential Samples

In a **single-sampling plan,** an acceptance or rejection decision is made after drawing only one sample from the lot. If the same data do not exceed the acceptance criteria (c), the lot is accepted. Figure 17.4 illustrates how single-sampling plans operate.

Figure 17.5 illustrates how a **double-sampling plan** for attributes operates. One small sample is drawn initially. If the number of defectives is less than or equal to some lower limit, the lot is accepted. If the number of defectives is greater than some upper limit, the lot is rejected. If the number of defectives is neither, a second larger sample is drawn. The lot is either accepted or rejected on the basis of the information from both of the samples. Although the first sample in double samples is smaller than

Figure 17.4	Single-Sampling Plans

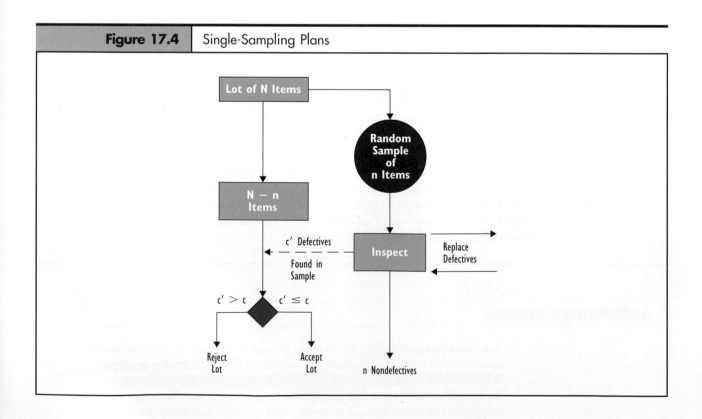

Figure 17.5	Double-Sampling Plans

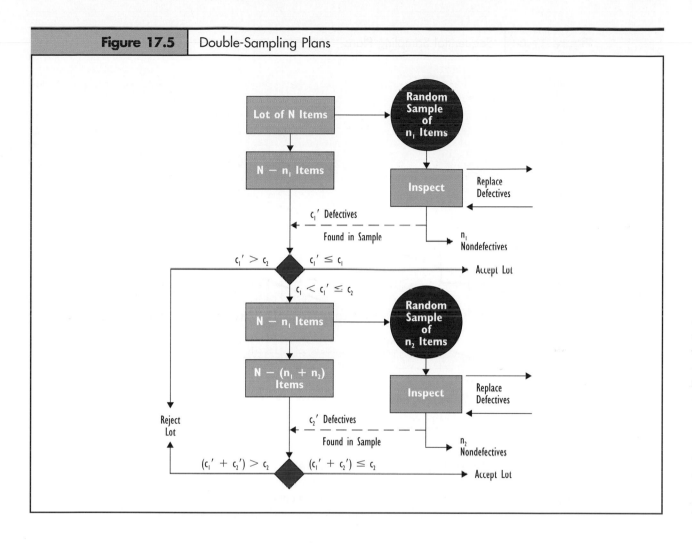

the sample in single samples, double samples overall tend to require a greater inspection load.

In a sequential-sampling plan, units are randomly selected from the lot and tested one by one. After each one has been tested, a reject, accept, or continue-sampling decision is made. This process continues until the lot is accepted or rejected. Figure 17.6 illustrates how such plans operate with attributes. In this figure, units are randomly drawn from a lot and tested. The first defective is the 15th unit, putting us in the **continue-sampling zone,** and so we continue to sample units from the lot. The second defective is the 25th unit, and we still must continue sampling. The third defective is the 30th unit, and we continue sampling. The fourth defective is the 40th unit, and thus puts us in the **reject-lot zone;** therefore the lot is rejected. Conceivably, the whole lot could be tested unit by unit.

Let us now discuss how to establish acceptance plans for attributes.

Single-Sample Acceptance Plans for Attributes

Table 17.4 defines several terms used in connection with acceptance plans for attributes. Two important concepts are needed to understand acceptance plans for attributes: operating characteristic curves and average outgoing quality curves.

Figure 17.6	Sequential-Sampling Plans

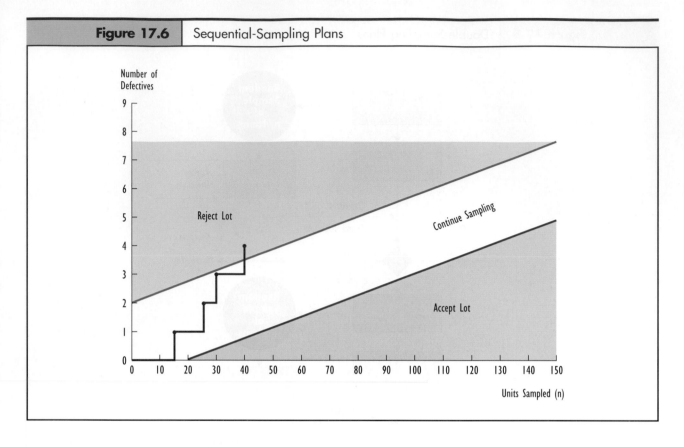

Operating Characteristic Curves

An **operating characteristic (OC) curve** is a graph of the performance of an acceptance plan. It shows how well an acceptance plan discriminates between good and bad lots. Figure 17.7 is an example of an OC curve for an acceptance plan with n = 50

Table 17.4	Terms Used in Acceptance Plans for Attributes

Acceptance plan—The sample size (n) and the maximum number of defectives (c) that can be found in a sample to accept a lot.

Acceptable quality level (AQL)—Used to define good lots. If lots have no more than AQL percent defectives, they are considered good lots.

Average outgoing quality (AOQ)—Given the actual percentage of defectives in lots and a particular acceptance plan, the AOQ is the average percentage of defectives in lots leaving an inspection station.

Average outgoing quality limit (AOQL)—Given a particular sampling plan, the AOQL is the maximum AOQ that can occur as the actual percent defectives in lots varies.

Consumer's risk (β)—Given a particular acceptance plan, the percent probability of accepting a bad lot. The probability that a lot with LTPD will be accepted with a particular acceptance plan.

Lot tolerance percent defective (LTPD)—Used to define bad lots. If lots have greater than LTPD, they are considered bad lots.

Producer's risk (α)—The percent probability of rejecting a good lot. The probability of rejecting a lot with AQL percentage defectives.

| **Figure 17.7** | Operating Characteristic (OC) Curve |

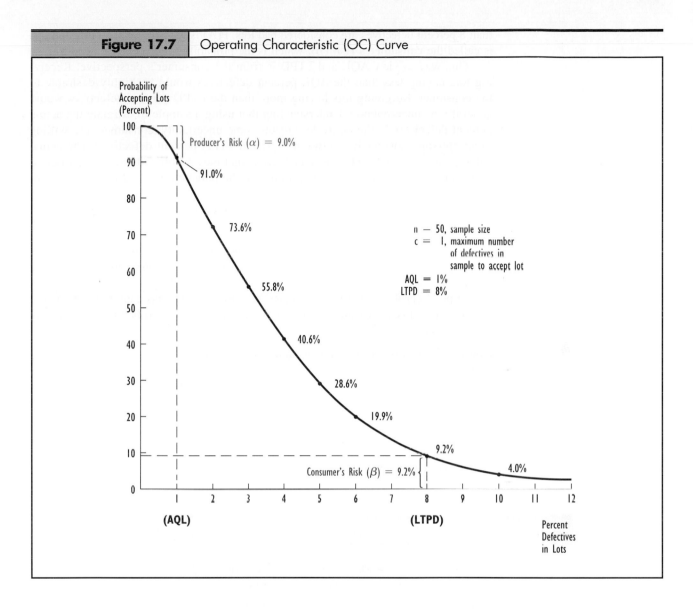

and c = 1, where n is a sample size and c is the maximum number of defectives that can be found in a sample to accept a lot—in other words, if two or more defectives are in a sample, then the lot must be rejected. Along the horizontal axis of Figure 17.7 is the actual percent defectives in lots coming into inspection, which is generally unknown, from 0 to 12 percent. On the vertical axis is the probability of accepting lots. Along the OC curve in Figure 17.7 are the probabilities of accepting lots at several levels of actual percent defectives in lots.

We can see from Figure 17.7 that as the percent defectives in lots increases, the probability of accepting the lots decreases. In this figure, the **acceptable quality level (AQL)** is 1 percent; this means that lots with 1 percent defectives or less are considered to be good lots. P(A), the probability of accepting a lot, is 91.0 percent at AQL. P(R) = 100% − P(A), the probability of rejecting a lot, is 9.0 percent at AQL, and this is called the **producer's risk (α)**, which is the probability of rejecting a good lot. The **lot tolerance percent defective (LTPD)** is 8 percent, meaning that lots with more than 8 percent defectives are considered bad lots. P(A) is 9.2 percent at LTPD, and this is called the **consumer's risk (β)**, which is the probability of accepting a bad lot.

One way to view AQL and LTPD is from the consumer's perspective. Receiving lots having less than the AQL percent defectives would be highly desirable to the consumer. Receiving lots having more than the LTPD percent defectives would generally be unacceptable. Understanding that using a sample to estimate the actual percent defectives in the entire lot creates some uncertainty, consumers are willing to accept some lots having between AQL and LTPD percent defectives. The actual values used for AQL, LTPD, α, and β are sometimes negotiated between particular producers and consumers, and help to define the parameters n and c for the acceptance plan to be used.

We would like to have acceptance plans that always pass good lots and always fail bad lots, but this objective may not be achieved because of two types of sampling errors:

- **Type I errors.** A good lot is rejected because a sample has captured too many defectives. This is measured by the producer's risk (α), the probability of rejecting a good lot.
- **Type II errors.** A bad lot is accepted because a sample has captured too few defectives. This is measured by the consumer's risk (β), the probability of accepting a bad lot.

How can managers avoid or reduce these errors? First, samples must be taken in ways that allow them to be truly random, thus improving the likelihood that samples will be representative of lots. Another way to reduce these errors is to increase the sample size. To better understand why sample size affects the discriminating power of acceptance plans, let us see how OC curves are constructed.

Table 17.5 contains all the probabilities for graphing the three OC curves in Figure 17.8. The Poisson probability distribution can be used to find the probability of x defectives in a sample:

Table 17.5	Probabilities for Three Operating Characteristic Curves (percent)

	n = 50, c = 1		n = 100, c = 2		n = N	
π	P(A)	P(R)	P(A)	P(R)	P(A)	P(R)
0	100.0	0	100.0	0	100.0	0
AQL = 1	91.0	$\alpha = 9.0$	92.0	$\alpha = 8.0$	100.0	$\alpha = 0$
2	73.6	26.4	67.7	32.3	0	100.0
3	55.8	44.2	42.3	57.7	0	100.0
4	40.6	59.4	23.8	76.2	0	100.0
5	28.6	71.3	12.5	87.5	0	100.0
6	19.9	80.1	6.2	93.8	0	100.0
LTPD = 8	$\beta = 9.2$	90.8	$\beta = 1.4$	98.6	$\beta = 0$	100.0
10	4.0	96.0	0.3	99.7	0	100.0

n = sample size
c = largest number of defectives per sample to accept the lot
π = percent defectives in a lot coming into inspection
P(A) = probability of accepting the lot
P(R) = probability of rejecting the lot
α = producer's risk, P(R) at AQL
β = consumer's risk, P(A) at LTPD

| Figure 17.8 | OC Curve for Different Sample Sizes |

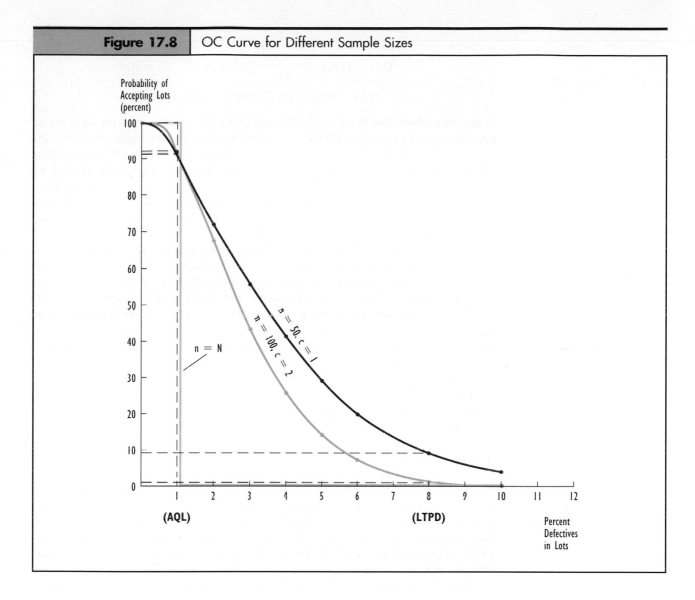

$$P(x) = (100) \frac{\left(n\frac{\pi}{100}\right)^x}{x!} \ e^{-n(\pi/100)}$$

where:

    x = number of defectives for which we want to find the probability
    n = sample size
    π = actual percent defectives in a lot coming into inspection
    c = basc of natural logarithms = 2.71828

For example, to obtain the P(A) = 91.0 percent in the n = 50, c = 1 acceptance plan for π = AQL = 1 percent in Table 17.5, use the formula above to find:

$$P(0) = (100) \frac{\left(50\frac{1}{100}\right)^0}{0!} \ 2.71828^{-50(1/100)} = 60.7$$

$$P(1) = (100) \frac{\left(50 \frac{1}{100}\right)^1}{1!} \, 2.71828^{-50(1/100)} = 30.3$$

$$P(A) = P(0) + P(1) = 60.7 + 30.3 = 91.0\%$$

Using the probabilities in Table 17.5, Figure 17.8 exhibits OC curves for three acceptance plans. Let us compare the OC curves for two of these acceptance plans: n = 50, c = 1; and n = 100, c = 2. Notice that by doubling n from 50 to 100 and doubling c from 1 to 2, we have kept the c/n ratio the same, but α has been reduced from 9.0 percent to 8.0 percent and β has been reduced from 9.2 percent to 1.4 percent. Thus, the ability of acceptance plans to discriminate between good and bad lots is enhanced by increasing sample size. This means that we would then reject fewer good lots and accept fewer bad lots. To further demonstrate this point, consider the OC curve of the acceptance plan of n = N in Figure 17.8. This plan perfectly discriminates between good and bad lots because $\alpha = 0$ and $\beta = 0$. The probability of accepting a lot with 1 percent or less defectives is 100 percent, and the probability of rejecting a lot with more than 8 percent defectives is 100 percent. But in this plan, the sample size would be the same as the lot size; in other words, every unit in the lot would have to be included in our sample. And so it is that *managers can reduce producer's risk (α) and consumer's risk (β), but at the extra cost of taking larger samples.*

Average Outgoing Quality Curves

Acceptance plans provide managers with the assurance that the percent defectives actually leaving an inspection station will not exceed a certain limit. Figure 17.9 illustrates this concept. The probabilities in Table 17.6 are used to prepare Figure 17.9, the **average outgoing quality (AOQ)** curve. This figure illustrates that as the percentage of defectives in lots coming into inspection increases, the percentage of defectives in lots leaving inspection deteriorates at first, then peaks at the **average outgoing quality limit (AOQL)**, and then improves. The improvement in quality occurs because as the acceptance plan rejects lots, the rejected lots are 100 percent inspected and the defectives are replaced with nondefectives. The net effect of rejecting lots is therefore an improvement in the quality of lots leaving inspection. The extreme condition exists when all lots are rejected and the percent defectives leaving an inspection station approaches zero.

Now let us see how to estimate the acceptance criteria in single-sample acceptance plans for attributes.

Estimating Acceptance Criteria

In practice, what operations managers must know to make accept-or-reject decisions about attributes in lots of materials are the sample size (n) and the maximum number of defectives in a sample to accept the lot (c). We shall use two approaches to making these decisions: Dodge-Romig tables and statistics.

Using Dodge-Romig Tables

One of the most common ways to set n and c is to use what are often referred to as **QC tables.** The two most common sets of these tables are:

- **Military Standard MIL-STD-105D tables.** These attribute acceptance plans set n and c for a specified AQL. Rejected lots are 100 percent inspected.
- **Dodge-Romig tables.** These attribute acceptance plans set n and c while assuming that rejected lots are 100 percent inspected and defectives are replaced with

| **Figure 17.9** | Average Outgoing Quality (AOQ) Curve |

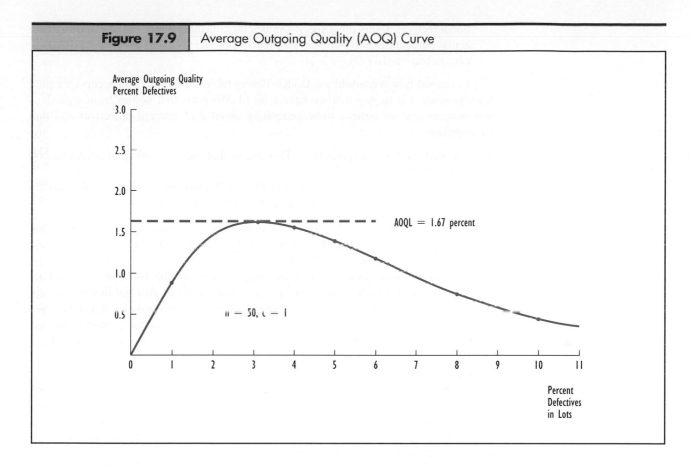

Average Outgoing Quality Percent Defectives

AOQL = 1.67 percent

n = 50, c = 1

Percent Defectives in Lots

| **Table 17.6** | Probabilities for an Average Outgoing Quality Curve for an Acceptance Plan with n = 50, c = 1 (percent) |

π	P(A)	AOQ = π[P(A)]/100
0%	100.0%	0%
1	91.0	0.91
2	73.6	1.47
3	55.8	AOQL = 1.67
4	40.6	1.62
5	28.7	1.44
6	19.9	1.19
8	9.2	0.74
10	4.0	0.40

π = percent defectives in a lot coming into inspection
P(A) = probability of accepting a lot
AOQ = percent defectives in a lot leaving inspection
AOQL = maximum AOQ

nondefectives. Users must specify values for consumer's risk (β), the approximate actual percent defectives in lots (π), the size of lots (N), and the lot tolerance percent defective (LTPD).

Let us see how we would use Dodge-Romig tables to establish an acceptance plan for a product. Let us say that we have a lot of 350 parts that comes from a production process that we believe to be generating about 2.25 percent defectives and that we stipulate:

1.   The consumer's risk (β) is 0.10. This means that the probability of accepting bad lots is 0.10.
2.   The lot tolerance percent defective (LTPD) is 5.0 percent. This means that we are defining bad lots as those with more than 5.0 percent defectives.

Table 17.7 is a section of a Dodge-Romig table. This section would be found in a book of Dodge-Romig tables where β = 0.10, LTPD = 5.0 percent, and π is between 2.01 percent and 2.50 percent.[2]

We can see from Table 17.7 that the sample size would be 145 and we would accept any lots with 4 or fewer defectives in a sample. We can also see that this acceptance plan would provide an average outgoing quality limit (AOQL) of 1.10 percent. Notice that this acceptance plan of n = 145 and c = 4 reduces the actual percent defectives in lots from 2.25 percent coming into inspection to 1.10 percent leaving inspection.

Using Statistics

In this approach, we are testing a hypothesis that a sample comes from a population with a certain percent defectives. The purpose of the analysis is to set an accept rule, which is also called an acceptance criterion, against which sample percent defectives are compared. A lot is accepted if a sample percent defectives does not exceed the acceptance criterion, or it is rejected if it does.

Table 17.8 exhibits the formulas and variable definitions for computing acceptance criteria. Example 17.3 demonstrates how we would use statistics to formulate an ac-

Table 17.7	Section of a Dodge-Romig Table When β Is 10 Percent, LTPD Is 5.0 Percent, and Process Average (π) Is 2.01–2.50 Percent		

Lot Size	n	c	AOQL (%)
101–200	40	0	0.74
201–300	95	2	0.99
301–400	145	4	1.10
401–500	150	4	1.20
501–600	175	5	1.30
601–800	200	6	1.40
801–1,000	225	7	1.50
1,001–2,000	280	9	1.80
2,001–3,000	370	13	2.10

n = sample size
c = largest number of defectives per sample to accept the lot
AOQL = average outgoing quality limit

Source: Harold F. Dodge and Harry G. Romig, *Sampling Inspection Tables—Single and Double Sampling,* 2nd ed. Copyright © 1959 John Wiley & Sons, Inc. Reprinted by permission of John Wiley & Sons, Inc.

Table 17.8	Formulas and Variable Definitions for Computing Acceptance Criteria for Acceptance Plans	

Characteristic Being Measured	Sample Measure	Acceptance Criteria
Attribute	Percent defectives (p)	$\bar{p} + Z\sqrt{\bar{p}(100 - \bar{p})/n}$
Variable	Sample mean (x)	$\bar{\bar{x}} \pm Z\sigma_{\bar{x}}$

α = significance level; the area in a single tail if a one-tailed α, or the area in both tails if a two-tailed α. Unlike the producer's risk, which is expressed in percent, the significance level is a proportion.

p = percent defectives in a sample

$\bar{p}$ = average percent defectives of the process

n = sample size

$\bar{x}$ = a sample mean

$\bar{\bar{x}}$ = mean of many sample means

Z = Z scores. These values from the normal distribution depend on the significance level.

$\sigma_{\bar{x}}$ = standard error of the mean of the sampling distribution. $\sigma_{\bar{x}} = \sigma_x/\sqrt{n}$, where σ_x is the population standard deviation.

ceptance plan. In this example, we must stipulate the values of p, the average percent defectives in lots; n, the sample size; and the significance level α. In thinking about and selecting values of α, understand these concepts:

Example 17.3	Setting an Acceptance Criterion for Attributes

The Precision Bearing Company in Toledo, Ohio, produces ball and roller bearings of various sizes for automobile manufacturers. One such ball bearing, the ½″ 5525 Chrome Polished Bearing—No. 3580—has been the subject of numerous customer complaints in recent months because of surface defects. Marsha Pool, the director of Precision's quality control department, has decided that an acceptance plan based on random samples should be established for this product. Marsha carefully researches records of past periods when the surface-polishing operation was known to be functioning properly and finds that 2 percent of the No. 3580 ball bearings were defective. If a sample size of 200 bearings and a one-tailed significance level of 0.025 is to be used: **a.** Set the acceptance criterion for the percent defectives in a sample. **b.** If a sample is drawn that has seven defective ball bearings, should the lot be accepted?

Solution

a. Set the acceptance criterion for the percent defectives in a sample:
First, refer to Table 17.8 and observe that the acceptance criterion formula for the percent defectives is:

$$\bar{p} + Z\sqrt{\bar{p}(100 - \bar{p})/n}$$

where $\bar{p}$ is the average percent defectives for the process and equals 2 percent in this example.

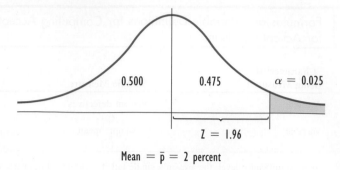

Mean = p̄ = 2 percent

Because $\alpha = 0.025$, this fixes Z at 1.96 in the normal sampling distribution (see Appendix A). Therefore, the acceptance criterion for p is:

$$\bar{p} + Z\sqrt{p(100 - \bar{p})/n} = 2 + 1.96\sqrt{2(98)/200} = 2 + 1.96(0.9899) = 2 + 1.9403$$
$$= 3.9403, \text{ or } 3.94 \text{ percent}$$

b.   A sample of 200 ball bearings has 7 defectives. Should the sample be accepted?

Yes, because 7/200 = 3.5 percent, which falls within the acceptance criterion of 3.94 percent defectives. We would reject any lots with greater than 3.94 percent defectives in a sample.

- α is the significance level, the probability of a sample percent defectives exceeding the acceptance criterion just due to chance.
- α is commonly specified as a management policy that is a statement about the preference for Type I and Type II errors.
- In setting the acceptance criterion for percent defectives, α is a one-tailed test. In other words, we are interested in determining if a sample percent defectives is *too large* to accept the hypothesis that the sample comes from a population with a certain percent defectives.
- In setting the value α, the rules in Table 17.9 are commonly used, although there are exceptions.
- α is the producer's risk that we discussed earlier—the probability of rejecting a good lot, and the significance level.

Acceptance plans for variables are not as commonly found in books of tables as are those for attributes. Statistical computations therefore tend to be used in establishing these acceptance plans.

Table 17.9	Rules Commonly Used to Set Values of α		
		VALUE OF α	
Error Preference		**One-Tailed**	**Two-Tailed**
Prefer to err on the side of rejecting good lots		0.050	0.100
Prefer to err on the side of accepting bad lots		0.005	0.010
Middle ground		0.025	0.050

Single-Sample Acceptance Plans for Variables

In using statistics to establish an acceptance plan for variables, we are testing a hypothesis that a sample comes from a population with certain variable characteristics. The purpose of the analysis is to set accept and reject rules, which are also called acceptance criteria, against which sample characteristics are compared. A lot is accepted if a sample from the lot meets the acceptance criteria; it is rejected if it does not.

Example 17.4 shows how to set the acceptance criteria for sample means. Setting acceptance criteria in this example requires that the mean of sample means $\bar{\bar{x}}$, significance level (α), and the standard error of the mean of the sampling distribution ($\sigma_{\bar{x}}$) must be known. In acceptance plans for variables, α has the same meanings as discussed before in relation to acceptance plans for attributes, with one important exception: α may apply to either a one-tailed or a two-tailed test. In other words, we may be interested in knowing whether $\bar{x}$ or R or both are too small or too large to accept the hypothesis that the sample comes from a certain population. In setting the value α for the variables, the rules in Table 17.9 are commonly used.

Practically speaking, we seldom know the values of $\bar{\bar{x}}$ and ($\sigma_{\bar{x}}$); rather, we must usually estimate their values through field research. Although no one way is perfect, there are several ways to estimate these values. The $\bar{\bar{x}}$ could be estimated by averaging many sample means ($\bar{x}$) from good highway sections or by using a target, goal, or customer specification value as in Example 17.4. The $\sigma_{\bar{x}}$ could be estimated by computing the standard deviation of sample means from good highway sections about $\bar{\bar{x}}$. Or σ_x could be estimated by computing the standard deviation of many cores from good highway sections about their mean. Or s_x^2, the variances of many samples from good sections of highway, could be averaged and this would be an estimate of the population variance σ_x^2. Then $\sigma_{\bar{x}}$ could be computed by dividing σ_x by $\sqrt{n}$.

| **Example 17.4** | Setting Acceptance Criteria for Variables |

The U.S. Department of Transportation (DOT) must accept sections of paving constructed by private contractors in the interstate highway system. These sections are usually 10 miles long, and they are accepted based on cores drilled from the concrete pavement at random intervals. DOT specifications require a compression strength in the roadway of 12,500 pounds per square inch.

Luis Gentry, head testing engineer for the third district, wishes to establish a statistical acceptance plan wherein sections of pavement would be accepted based on the mean compression strength of a sample of 50 cores removed from each section. Luis knows from experience that the standard deviation of compression strength for thousands of cores from hundreds of miles of pavement is 1,625 pounds per square inch. **a.** Set the acceptance criteria of DOT's acceptance plan if a one-tailed $\alpha = 0.005$. **b.** Fifty cores are pulled from a 10-mile section. The mean compression strength of the sample is 11,500 pounds per square inch. Should the section of pavement be accepted?

Solution

a. Set the acceptance criteria:
    Refer to Table 17.8 and observe that the acceptance criteria formula for sample means ($\bar{x}$) is:

Acceptance criteria = $\bar{\bar{x}} - Z\sigma_{\bar{x}}$, because of a one-tailed α

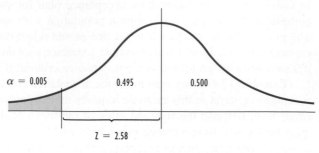

Because $\alpha = 0.005$, the Z score is 2.58 (see Appendix A). Because $\sigma_x = 1,625$ from the problem,

$$\sigma_{\bar{x}} = \sigma_x/\sqrt{n} = 1,625/\sqrt{50} = 229.81 \text{ pounds per square inch}$$

Therefore, the acceptance criterion is:

$$\text{Acceptance criterion} = \bar{\bar{x}} - Z\sigma_{\bar{x}} = 12,500 - 2.58(229.81) = 12,500 - 592.91$$
$$= 11,907.09 \text{ pounds per square inch}$$

Luis Gentry is not concerned that a section of pavement might have a compression strength that is too high.

b. Should a section with a sample mean compression strength of 11,500 pounds per square inch be accepted?

No, because 11,500 falls outside the minimum sample mean acceptance criterion of 11,907.09 pounds per square inch.

COMPUTERS IN QUALITY CONTROL

The use of computers is extensive in quality control. Industries such as the automobile, pharmaceutical, food, and specialty-chemicals industries are required under federal and state government regulations to be able to trace defects through the entire production and distribution systems. Even if an industry is not closely regulated by government agencies, however, such records are kept in order to limit a firm's exposure in the event of a product liability suit or the threat of such an action. Besides, it's just good business for a company to be able to track its products from production through consumer use, and this tracking is becoming feasible and economical with the use of computers. Highly publicized product recall programs in recent years highlight the importance of these computer systems. Such recall programs require that manufacturers (1) know the lot numbers of the raw materials, assemblies, and parts that are responsible for the potential defects; (2) have an information storage system that can tie the lot numbers of the suspected raw materials, assemblies, and parts to the final product model numbers; and (3) have an information system that can track the model numbers of final products to customers.

Using computers to regulate quality, production, and processing can improve both speed and quality of goods and services.

© ED KASHI/CORBIS

Computers also provide more timely and economical information to managers about the quality of products and services. Because control charts can be quickly prepared, the time lag is reduced between the time when materials, assemblies, parts, or products are inspected and the time when the results are posted on control charts. Computer programs are also used in lot acceptance decisions. *With automation, inspection and testing can be so inexpensive and quick that companies may be able to increase sample sizes and the frequency of samples, thus attaining more precision in both control charts and acceptance plans.* In some cases, acceptance plans may be abandoned altogether and replaced with 100 percent inspection and testing. For example, at Garret Pneumatic Systems in Phoenix, computers are used to test products as they come off the assembly line. These tests are so fast that 100 percent inspection is now economical. Also, the tests are so thorough that every single function of the product can be quickly tested.[3]

In addition to automatic inspections in which computers are used to check the quality of products after they are made, computers are also being used to directly control the quality of products *while* they are being made. As discussed in Chapter 6, automated process controls measure the performance of production processes during production and automatically make corrections to the process settings to avoid producing defective products. Business Snapshot 17.1 described how SPC software is used at Georgia-Pacific to help control quality.

Service systems must also be concerned with the quality of their services.

QUALITY CONTROL IN SERVICES

In Chapter 7, Operations Quality Management, we discussed TQM in services. Business Snapshot 7.6 gave examples of how TQM is applied in banks, hospitals, universities, law offices, and insurance companies. In all of these applications, there is a continuing need to monitor the progress of quality. Control charts are ideal for this purpose.

An example in Chapter 7 explained how American Express, a financial services company, uses control charts to monitor such things as the amount of time required to process a customer's application for an American Express card. Because of the flexibility of control charts, they are used extensively in services.

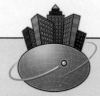

Wrap-Up
WHAT WORLD-CLASS COMPANIES DO

World-class companies understand that quality cannot be inspected into products. They also understand that the management of product and service quality is much broader than quality control. These companies have comprehensive proactive total quality management (TQM) programs with specific projects aimed at improving product quality to meet customer expectations. But this does not mean that they have abandoned quality control. Once production processes have been designed and built that have the capability of producing products that meet customer expectations, these processes must be operated to achieve quality conformance. And quality control is the way that product quality is made to conform to customer expectations.

Several techniques aid in achieving effective quality control. Statistical control charts are used extensively to provide feedback to everyone about quality performance. These charts can be prepared by workers themselves so that workers assume the responsibility for product quality in production. Being so flexible, control charts can be used in just about any application, from automated manufacturing to service operations, that is based on personal service. And in certain special situations where 100 percent inspection and testing are impractical, uneconomical, or impossible, acceptance plans may be used to determine if lots of products are likely to meet customer expectations. For most world-class companies, however, the trend is toward 100 percent inspection and testing. Automating inspection and testing has made such an approach both effective and economical.

REVIEW AND DISCUSSION QUESTIONS

1. Explain the relationship between total quality management (TQM) and quality control.
2. What are some customer expectations for these organizations? (a) commercial chemical fertilizer manufacturer, (b) hospital, (c) university, (d) automaker, (e) bank, (f) lumber mill.
3. Define these terms: (a) *random sample*, (b) *attribute*, (c) *variable*, (d) *single sample*, (e) *double sample*, (f) *sequential sample*.
4. Are p, x, and R variables or attributes?
5. What is the *central limit theorem?* What is its significance to quality control?
6. What is the purpose of control charts? Explain how this purpose is achieved.
7. What is statistical process control (SPC)?
8. Explain why $\bar{x}$ and R charts are used together.
9. What is an *OC curve?* Explain its purpose.
10. Explain the meaning of this statement: "An OC curve explains how an acceptance plan discriminates between good and bad lots."
11. Explain what an AOQ curve indicates.
12. Define these terms: (a) n, (b) c, (c) AQL, (d) AOQ, (e) AOQL, (f) LTPD, (g) α, (h) β.
13. What are Type I and Type II errors? How may we avoid or reduce these errors?
14. Discuss and evaluate this statement: "The time is fast approaching when there will be no place for acceptance plans in manufacturing."
15. Discuss the role of computers in quality control.
16. Discuss quality control in services.
17. What factors make quality management more difficult in services than in manufacturing?

INTERNET ASSIGNMENTS

1. Northwest Analytical, Inc., produces a quality control software package called *Quality Analyst*. Visit the web site of Northwest Analytical at **http://www.nwasoft.com** and find information on the *Quality Analyst* software. Describe the features and capabilities of this software.

2. Search the Internet for a company that produces statistical process control (SPC) software. Describe the features of this software.

3. *Quality Digest* is a magazine that focuses on quality management. Visit the magazine's web site at **http://www.qualitydigest.com**. Find and summarize a company application of quality management tools or principles.

4. Search the Internet for a consulting company that provides consulting services for quality control. Describe the related services offered.

PROBLEMS

Control Charts

1. An automated production process consists of assembling four components to make a 5-amp fuse. Every two hours a sample of 75 fuses is collected and each fuse is tested. Typically in the past, 1.8 fuses on average have failed the test. Compute 3σ control limits for a p chart.

2. A robotic welder spot-welds a bracket onto a metal frame. The weld should be able to support 350 pounds applied to the bracket. Every four hours a sample of 50 welded frames is taken, and a 350-pound weight is attached to the bracket. Typically in the past, 2.2 brackets on average have broken loose from the frame when the test weight was applied. If a control chart is to be used to monitor the consistency of the welding process, what control limits should be used?

3. In a manufacturing operation, the percentage defective averages 2.5 percent and sample size is 200.
   a. Compute the center line for the p chart.
   b. Compute the 3σ control limits for the chart.
   c. Plot these recent data collected from daily samples and decide if the operation is in control: Number of defectives per sample = 2, 9, 7, 5, 0, 3, 8, 7, 2, 5, 3, 2.

4. The control chart program at a soldering operation specified a sample size of 300, a target of 1.0 percent defective, and control limits of 2σ. Recent samples had these number of defectives: 1, 0, 4, 3, 6, 2, 0, 5, 7, 3.
   a. Compute the center line and the upper and lower control limits for the chart.
   b. Plot the data from the 10 samples, and decide if the soldering operation is in control.

5. A university with 15,000 students should average about 750 academic drops per semester. A control chart program is undertaken to track the academic drop situation. Random samples of 100 students are taken each semester. The last 10 semesters' records show these numbers of academic drops in random samples: 5, 6, 8, 4, 2, 4, 3, 4, 3, 2.

a. Compute the 95 percent control limits.
b. Plot the 10 semesters of sample data on a control chart.
c. Has there been a change in the percentage of academic drops per semester?

6. An insurance company tracks absenteeism by weekly random samples. The company expects about 250 employees to be absent from its workforce of 5,000 on the average. These sample sizes and number of absences are recorded:

Sample Number	Sample Size	Number Absent	Sample Number	Sample Size	Number Absent
1	100	5	6	100	7
2	120	6	7	110	8
3	90	6	8	90	10
4	95	7	9	130	11
5	110	7	10	120	10

a. Construct a 3σ control chart for p and plot the sample data points. (*Hint:* The upper and lower control limits vary with sample size.)
b. Has there been a change in the absenteeism rate?

7. If $\bar{\bar{x}}$ = 12 inches, $\bar{R}$ = 3 inches, and n = 20:
a. Compute 3σ control limits for x.
b. Plot these sample means on an $\bar{x}$ control chart: 12.1, 12.5, 12.7, 12.2, 12.8, 12.7, 12.1, 11.8, 11.7, 12.0.
c. Decide if the process is in control.

8. If $\bar{R}$ = 3.0 inches and n = 20:
a. Compute 3σ control limits for R.
b. Plot these sample ranges on a 3σ control chart for R: 0.9, 2.6, 4.9, 3.4, 0.6, 0.7, 4.8, 4.5, 4.1, 1.6.
c. Is the process in control?

9. A trucking company has had several complaints about late deliveries. The company tries to deliver all of its freight in 12 hours on average. Weekly samples of 25 customers are taken and exhibit an average range of 2.5 hours. The company thinks this is about right.
a. Compute 3σ control limits for $\bar{x}$.
b. Plot these sample means on a 3σ control chart for $\bar{x}$: 11.4, 12.2, 12.0, 11.9, 12.6, 12.4, 12.1, 11.8, 11.5, 12.4.
c. Is management's target of an average 12-hour delivery being met?

10. A company manufactures an electrical cooling fan. When the fans are performing properly, samples of 200 fans average 12.5 watts with an average range of 1.2 watts. A 3σ control chart program is being used to monitor the performance of the fans, and these data from the 10 most recent samples were collected:

Sample Number	Sample Mean (watts)	Sample Range (watts)	Sample Number	Sample Mean (watts)	Sample Range (watts)
1	12.50	1.1	6	12.60	1.0
2	12.45	1.2	7	12.48	1.4
3	12.55	0.9	8	12.46	1.1
4	12.50	0.8	9	12.56	0.9
5	12.45	0.9	10	12.48	0.8

a. Compute the 3σ control limits and center line for an $\bar{x}$ chart.

b. Compute the 3σ control limits and center line for an R chart.
c. Plot the sample data on the $\bar{x}$ and R charts, and decide if the performance of the fan is in control.

11. A company bottles soft drinks. The bottles come in only one flavor and only one size (16 ounces). The first daily samples of fill weights of 20 bottles are:

Sample	$\bar{x}$	R	Sample	$\bar{x}$	R
1	16.05	0.20	6	16.09	0.37
2	16.04	0.25	7	15.95	0.35
3	15.98	0.62	8	16.06	0.21
4	15.91	0.71	9	15.94	0.29
5	16.02	0.58	10	15.97	0.46

If sample ranges ordinarily average 0.5 ounces:
a. Compute 3σ control limits for sample means.
b. Compute 3σ control limits for sample ranges.
c. What would you conclude about the fill weights?

12. A company has just set up a single-sample acceptance plan for attributes using n = 80 and c = 0. Review the discussion material surrounding Table 17.5 and Figure 17.7. What is the probability of accepting a lot if the percent defectives in the lot is 2 percent?

13. A company has just set up a single-sample acceptance plan for attributes using n = 80 and c = 1. Review the discussion material surrounding Table 17.5 and Figure 17.7. If AQL = 1 percent and LTPD = 5 percent:
a. Compute α.
b. Compute β.
c. Explain the meaning of your answers in Parts a and b.

14. If the section of a Dodge-Romig table shown in Table 17.7 is used to establish a single-sample acceptance plan for attributes and if lot size = 700, β = 10 percent, LTPD = 5 percent, and π = 2.2 percent:
a. What are the appropriate values for n, C, and AOQL?
b. Explain the meaning of your answers in Part a.

15. A company wants to establish a single-sample acceptance plan for attributes. It believes that the percent defectives in lots coming into inspection is about 2.2 percent. Any lots with more than 5 percent defectives are unacceptable to the company's customers. The company knows that acceptance plans will sometimes accept a bad lot, but it wants this to occur no more than about 1 time in 10. The standard lot size for a particular product is 280 units. Using the discussion material surrounding Table 17.7, design an acceptance plan for the firm.
a. What are the appropriate values for n, c, and AOQL?
b. Explain the meaning of your answers in Part a.

Acceptance Plans

16. $\bar{p}$ = 1.5 percent, n = 300, one-tailed α = 0.02, and c = number of defectives in a sample from a lot is 7 units. Is the sample percent defectives large enough to reject the lot?

17. Customer surveys indicate that customers expect about 0.8 percent defectives in a particular product. A sample of 600 cartons from a lot of 50,000 cartons had 6 defective units. If a one-tailed α of 0.05 is used, should the lot be accepted?

18. A manufacturer purchases a component from a supplier. The component ordinarily averages about 2 percent defectives. The company wishes to establish an acceptance plan for percent defectives for the component to control the quality level going to production. If the sample size is 200 and one-tailed $\alpha = 0.05$, what acceptance criteria would you recommend?

19. A destructive test is used to test the tensile strength of bolts. Random samples of bolts are subjected to tensile force until they fail. If they fail after the force reaches 35,000 pounds, they pass. If they fail before the force reaches 35,000 pounds, they don't pass. Good lots of bolts average about 0.5 percent defectives. A sample of 400 bolts from a lot has just been tested with 395 passing. If, given the choice, you would rather err on the side of rejecting good lots, should you accept the lot?

20. If $\mu = 20$ ounces, $\sigma_x = 1.5$ ounces, n = 80, $\bar{x} = 20.23$ ounces, and two-tailed $\alpha = 0.10$, determine whether to accept or reject the lot.

21. Wyoming Trail Coal Company sells its coal to a steel mill in Iowa. The mill's records show that when Wyoming Trail is attentive, its cars of coal average 55 tons, with a standard deviation of 2 tons. But when Wyoming Trail is not attentive, the mill must unload the cars, weigh out exactly 55-ton charges of coal, and then load the coke ovens. The mill wants to take daily samples of car weights and determine whether unloading and weighing the entire daily shipment is necessary. Fifteen cars are randomly selected from a day's shipment, and the mean car weight is 53.9 tons. If the mill would rather err on the side of accepting out-of-weight cars, should it accept the day's shipment from Wyoming Trail directly into the coke ovens?

22. Educational Testing Services (ETS) offers the Graduate Management Admissions Test (GMAT) for people who want to attend graduate business schools. ETS gives about 175,000 GMAT exams each year and is concerned about the scores of a recent sample of exams. The average score during the last five years is 510, with a standard deviation of 75 for individual exams. The recent sample of 450 exams had an average score of 492. Using a two-tailed $\alpha = 0.01$, determine whether the sample should be considered as typical or whether it should be viewed as unusual and investigated further.

CASES

Five Star Fasteners Inc.

Five Star Fasteners Inc. (FSF) produces millions of aluminum rivets each year for the aircraft manufacturing industry. One type of rivet produced is model R44A, an aluminum alloy rivet that is 6 mm in diameter and 14 mm in length. In the past, FSF's quality assurance (QA) department has taken random samples at random time intervals to test the tensile (breaking) strength of the rivets. When samples have failed to meet tensile strength standards, all rivets produced since the previous quality test were discarded to avoid sending substandard rivets to the aircraft manufacturers.

Chris Meyers, the production manager at FSF, feels frustrated by having to waste so many rivets when a poor-quality sample is found. To remedy this situation, Chris has decided to start using a control chart at the machine that produces these rivets. Sharon Gray is the operator at the machine. Since the machine is mostly automated, Sharon's primary responsibilities are monitoring and adjusting the machine settings and characteristics on the computer display attached to the machine, and making sure the machine stays running. Chris feels that Sharon has ample time to take routine sample measurements and plot these on a control chart.

Bob Davis in the QA department has been asked by Chris to develop appropriate control chart limits for this process and to provide Sharon with a printed control chart. Bob first determines that since tensile strength is measured on a continuous scale, an x̄ chart and an R chart should be used. Next, he gathers tensile strength data from all the past samples the QA department has taken from the machine. He decides that the same sample size that has been used in the past, 15 rivets, should be used for the control chart. Bob determines that the mean tensile strength from all the past samples is 1,027 pounds, and the average range of samples is 286.

From this information, Bob develops two 3σ control charts (an x̄ chart and an R chart) and takes them to Sharon. Chris directs the QA department to take one of its spare tensile strength testing machines to Sharon's workstation and show her how to use it. Bob explains that each hour Sharon should take a random sample of 15 rivets produced by the machine and test each one. Using a calculator she should average the tensile strength measurements of the sample and compute the sample range. These values are to then be plotted on the two control charts. Any values that fall outside the control limits or any unusual trends in the sample measurements are to be immediately reported to the QA department, which will then thoroughly investigate the production process.

The following day Sharon, who works a 10-hour shift, takes hourly samples and plots these on the control charts. At the end of the day, the following data has been recorded:

Sample Number	Mean x̄	Range R	Sample Number	Mean x̄	Range R
1	1,004	357	6	988	280
2	1,094	295	7	1,015	344
3	1,045	215	8	1,050	368
4	1,020	318	9	1,025	427
5	1,039	252	10	1,055	460

Assignment

1. Compute the control limits and draw the x̄ and R control charts.
2. Plot the 10 sample observations on the control charts.
3. Discuss whether the production process appears to be in control.
4. Should any action be taken by the QA department? If so, what should be done?
5. Discuss the benefits of using control charts at this operation versus the QA department taking random samples to assess the quality of the production process.

Integrated Products Corporation

The Integrated Products Corporation (IPC) manufactures resins. The company installed what it called *Total Quality Management (TQM)* last year. The purpose of the new program was to involve everyone from the plant manager to the shop-floor workers in achieving excellent product quality. This program would feature *quality at the source* concepts and *quality circles*. A new resin has been developed and IPC's quality control department is now developing a quality plan for the new product. Of particular importance is an acceptance plan for the finished resin before it is shipped to IPC's customers. The key performance characteristic for the resin is its "pot life," the amount of time it takes for the resin to be converted to its finished form after it is mixed with plasticizers. The "nominal pot life" of the resin is 2.5 minutes at room temperature with a standard deviation of 0.2 minutes. The customary shipping unit of the resin is a 10-pound bag, and the quality plan calls for random samples of 200 bags drawn from finished production lots of 10,000 bags.

Assignment

1. What acceptance criteria for production lots would you recommend for the means of samples at a two-tailed significance level of 0.01?
2. If a two-tailed significance level of 0.01 is used, what does this say about management's attitude toward accepting bad lots as opposed to rejecting good lots? Does this attitude seem reasonable, considering the nature of the product?
3. Explain what total quality management means. What are the major elements of TQM? What are the major benefits of TQM?
4. Explain the meaning of quality at the source. On what principles is it based? What are its major benefits?
5. Describe quality circles. What are their major benefits?
6. If TQM aims for perfect product quality, why should an acceptance plan be required for the new resin? Does not this violate a major principle of TQM—to produce products of high quality and not try to inspect quality into the products later? What is the appropriate role of acceptance sampling in a TQM environment?

ENDNOTES

1. Buffa, Elwood S. *Operations Management: Problems and Models*, 3rd ed. New York: Wiley, 1972.
2. Dodge, H. F., and H. G. Romig. *Sampling Inspection Tables*, Table I(SL-5), cols. 1, 7, rows 4–12, p. 72. New York: Wiley, 1959.
3. "Computer Aids Firm's Quality Checks." *Arizona Republic*, December 20, 1985, D1.

SELECTED BIBLIOGRAPHY

Asaka, Tetsuichi and Kazuo Ozeki. *Handbook of Quality Tools: The Japanese Approach*. Cambridge, MA: Productivity Press, 1997.

Besterfield, Dale H. *Quality Control*. Upper Saddle River, NJ: Prentice Hall, 1997.

Burr, Adrian, and Malcolm Owen. *Statistical Methods for Software Quality: Using Metrics to Control Process and Product Quality*. Cincinnati, OH: International Thomson Publishing, 1996.

Carlyle, W. Matthew, Douglas C. Montgomery, and George C. Runger. "Optimization Problems and Methods in Quality Control and Improvement." *Journal of Quality Technology* 32, no. 1 (January 2000): 1–17.

Deming, W. Edwards. "On Some Statistical Aids toward Economic Production." *Interfaces* 5, no. 5 (August 1975): 1–15.

Deming, W. Edwards. *Out of Crisis*. Cambridge, MA: Center for Advanced Engineering Study, 1986.

Dietrich, Edgar. "SPC or Statistics?" *Quality* 39, no. 8 (August 2000): 40–45.

Dodge, H. F., and H. G. Romig. *Sampling Inspection Tables— Single and Double Sampling*, 2nd ed. New York: Wiley, 1959.

Evans, James R. *The Management and Control of Quality*. Cincinnati, OH: South-Western College Publishing, 1999.

Gryna, Frank M. *Quality Planning and Analysis*. Boston: McGraw-Hill, 2001.

Harrington, H. James. *Statistical Process Control Explained: The Easy-to-Understand Guide to SPC*. New York: McGraw-Hill, 1998.

Hostage, G. M. "Quality Control in a Service Business." *Harvard Business Review* 53, no. 4 (July–August 1975): 98–106.

Ishikawa, Kaoru. *What Is Total Quality Control?* Translated by David J. Lu. Upper Saddle River, NJ: Prentice-Hall, 1985.

Juran, Joseph M., and A. Blanton Godfrey, eds. *Juran's Quality Handbook*, 5th ed. New York: McGraw-Hill, 1999.

Kelley, D. Lynn. *How to Use Control Charts for Healthcare*. Milwaukee, WI: ASQ Quality Press, 1999.

Kessler, Sheila. *Total Quality Service.* Milwaukee, WI: ASQ Quality Press, 1995.

Montgomery, Douglas C. *Introduction to Statistical Quality Control,* 4th ed. New York: John Wiley & Sons, 2001.

Moses, Timothy P., Anthony J. Stahelski, and Gary R. Knapp. "Effects of Attribute Control Charts on Organizational Performance." *Journal of Organizational Behavior Management* 20, no. 1 (2000): 69–90.

Pyzdek, Thomas. *The Six Sigma Handbook: A Complete Guide for Greenbelts, Blackbelts, and Managers at All Levels.* New York: McGraw-Hill, 2001.

Townsend, Patrick L., and Joan E. Gebhardt. *Quality Is Everybody's Business.* Boca Raton, FL: St. Lucie Press, 2000.

U.S. Department of Defense. *Military Standard (MIL-STD-105), Sampling Procedures and Tables for Inspection for Attributes.* Washington DC: U.S. Government Printing Office, 1963.

Wise, Stephen A., and Douglas C. Fair. *Innovative Control Charting: Practical SPC Solutions for Today's Manufacturing Environment.* Milwaukee, WI: ASQ Quality Press, 1998.

Woodall, William H., and Douglas C. Montgomery. "Research Issues and Ideas in Statistical Process Control." *Journal of Quality Technology* 31, no. 4 (October 1999): 376–386.

18

Employee Productivity

Introduction

Productivity and Human Behavior
Multifactor Approach to Measuring Productivity
Labor Productivity

Designing Workers' Jobs

Empowering Workers

Work Methods Analysis
How to Do Methods Analysis

Work Measurement
Labor Standards
Time Study
Work Sampling
Predetermined Time Standards

Learning Curves
Arithmetic Analysis
Logarithmic Analysis

Learning-Curve Tables
Selecting a Learning Rate
Uses and Limitations of Learning Curves

Employees' Health and Safety

Wrap-Up: What World-Class Companies Do

Review and Discussion Questions

Internet Assignments

Problems

Cases
Caliber Bar Code Company
Integrated Products Corporation
Springfield Motors

Endnotes

Selected Bibliography

U.S. COMPANIES FOCUS ON PRODUCTIVITY

When Federal Reserve Board Chairman Alan Greenspan addressed Congress in early 1998 he stressed two key areas of importance to U.S. companies: productivity and foreign trade. At the national level, foreign trade affects the U.S. trade deficit and productivity gains help to maintain a delicate balance between economic growth and inflation. But at the company level, productivity gains are important as companies strive to reduce costs and become more competitive.

All across America, managers are burning the midnight oil to figure out how to wring further productivity gains from their businesses. Because U.S. unemployment is at a quarter-century low, wages are on the rise. But companies cannot afford to raise the prices of their products in response because of stiff competition. This situation makes potential worker productivity improvements look very attractive. According to Greenspan, "The threat of rising costs in tight labor markets has imparted a substantial impetus to efforts to take advantage of possible efficiencies."

With an eye toward productivity gains, U.S. businesses continue to invest heavily in technology. Many companies are particularly interested in new computer information systems, with the goal of replacing human capital with information technology capital. For example, St. Paul Co., a giant insurance company based in Minnesota, is aiming for productivity gains of 5 percent annually by increasing its information technology spending some 10 to 15 percent a year.

Aside from investing in technology, boosting productivity frequently comes just from thinking a little smarter. At Dallas-based Southland Corp., parent of the 7-Eleven convenience store chain, a recent increase in the minimum wage combined with a tight labor market forced the company to think creatively to improve productivity. To better utilize its employees, Southland developed a worksheet for store managers to help them match such tasks as stocking shelves to employees' hours worked.

Companies have found another source of productivity improvements through increased employee training. Allied Signal is aiming for 6 percent productivity gains a year by training all of its manufacturing employees on principles of quality control and quality management. Fewer mistakes throughout the production process mean improved productivity per employee.[1]

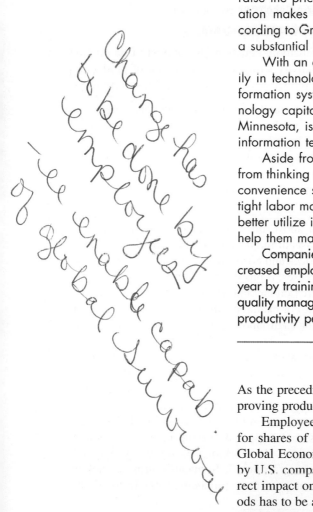

As the preceding account indicates, the attention of U.S. companies is focused on improving productivity. The growth of U.S. productivity is an increasing national concern.

Employees are of both strategic and tactical importance as U.S. companies strive for shares of world markets. As mentioned in Chapter 2, Operations Strategies in a Global Economy, the major factors that determine how much market can be captured by U.S. companies today are productivity, cost, and quality, and employees have a direct impact on these factors. Likewise, implementation of high-tech production methods has to be accomplished by employees. In fact, *all the strategic initiatives that U.S. companies must undertake to be more competitive must be carried out by their employees. So in this respect, employees represent an asset of strategic importance.* And yet, employees are managed every day to get customers' orders shipped and so the actions of employees have short-run impact. Thus, a discussion of the short-run impact of employees naturally falls into this section of the book about planning and controlling operations for productivity, quality, and reliability.

In this chapter we first develop an understanding of what productivity is and how human behavior is related to productivity. Next, we study how operations managers design employees' jobs so that the workers can be more productive. Finally, we examine the methods of measuring employees' work with a view to setting labor standards. The overall purpose of this chapter is to explore the setting in which operations managers today must achieve productivity and to develop some techniques that can be used to improve productivity.

PRODUCTIVITY AND HUMAN BEHAVIOR

Productivity means the amount of products or services produced with the resources used. Productivity in a time period is usually measured with this formula:

$$\text{Productivity} = \frac{\text{Quantity of products or services produced}}{\text{Amount of resources used}}$$

Notice that there are two sides to the productivity equation: the amount of production and the amount of resources used. Productivity varies with the amount of production relative to the amount of resources used. Productivity can be increased in several ways:

- Increase production using the same or a smaller amount of resources.
- Reduce the amount of resources used while keeping the same production or increasing it.
- Allow the amount of resources used to increase as long as production increases more.
- Allow production to decrease as long as the amount of resources used decreases more.

Notice that the productivity formula above does not include provisions for the prices of the products or services or the costs of the resources. There are, however, important implications in this formula for prices and costs. We can observe from the formula that when the cost of a resource increases, if profits are to remain the same, some combination of increased production, decreased amount of resources used, or price increases of products or services must occur. For example, when wage rates increase, either more production must be realized for each labor-hour or product/service prices must increase if profits are not to fall.

The proportion of the U.S. population working on farms shrank from 39 percent in 1900, to 30 percent in 1920, to 23 percent in 1940, to 8 percent in 1960, to 3 percent in 1980, and to less than 2 percent in 2000. But the output of U.S. farms has never been greater. This transformation of U.S. agriculture occurred because of rapidly rising labor productivity resulting from mechanization of farms, agricultural chemicals, improved strains of agricultural products, and improved farming methods. A similar transformation is occurring in manufacturing—the workforce is shrinking, output is growing steadily, and productivity is climbing. In fact, U.S. manufacturing is looking a lot like U.S. agriculture, with only a small workforce producing from 15 to 20 percent of GDP.

The substitution of capital equipment for labor in manufacturing has been going on for many decades. Then in the 1980s, there was a dramatic shift to automation in manufacturing and services.[2] This shift to automation in many industries today is dramatically changing the mix of their costs. For some firms, production workers, or **touch labor**, represent such a small part of the firms' total costs that product quality, inventories, engineering, materials, shipping, knowledge workers, and other overhead costs hold more promise for reducing costs and increasing productivity. Failing to recognize this fact can be a major pitfall in productivity improvement programs. "American manufacturers have boosted productivity for several years now, largely by closing old plants and laying off workers. But some U.S. companies focus too much on capital investment as a way to reduce labor—ignoring the huge benefits to be gained from improved quality, reduced inventories, and faster introduction of new products."[3] For most U.S. businesses today, the productivity picture is brighter. Information technology, CAD/CAM, computer-integrated manufacturing (CIM), all kinds of automated systems, innovative product designs, and advances in product quality are profoundly changing the nature of operations in both manufacturing and services. The result is fewer staff employees, middle managers, and blue-collar workers, while organizations are made smaller, more flexible, leaner, and more productive.

Multifactor Approach to Measuring Productivity

Productivity of a resource is the amount of products or services produced in a time period divided by the amount of that resource required. The productivity of each resource can and should be measured. For example, measures such as the following could be used to determine productivity in a time period:

- **Capital:** Number of products produced divided by asset value.
- **Materials:** Number of products produced divided by dollars spent on materials.
- **Direct labor:** Number of products produced divided by direct labor-hours.
- **Overhead:** Number of products produced divided by dollars spent on overhead.

Such measures are not perfect. For example, the measure for materials productivity includes price. This is generally undesirable, but there is no other practical way to combine the many different units of measurement for the diverse materials used in production. Although such measures of productivity have their shortcomings, they do provide a starting point for tracking productivity so that managers can be aware of productivity trends. In decades past when labor cost was the predominant cost of production, productivity was measured only by the output per hour of direct labor. Today, however, there is a need to look beyond direct labor costs and develop a multifactor perspective.

The problem with focusing on the productivity of only one type of resource, or factor, is that the productivity of this resource can be increased simply by replacing some of this resource with a different type of resource. For example, consider an automobile manufacturer that formerly purchased the components of a water pump and assembled these into a completed water pump for a car. Suppose that it now decides to purchase preassembled water pumps, thereby reducing the number of employees and equipment needed in-house. Consider what happens to the productivity of different factors because of this change. Production output remains constant, but the type of resources used changes. Direct labor productivity increases, because fewer employees are needed for in-house assembly. Capital productivity increases, because the assembly equipment and machines are no longer needed and can be sold. However, materials productivity declines, because the purchased cost of preassembled water pumps is higher than the cost of water pump components. This example illustrates the importance of examining the productivity of multiple factors in assessing the efficiency of a production system. The Bureau of Labor Statistics (**http://stats.bls.gov**) publishes statistics on multifactor productivity, which is a composite measure of labor, capital, energy, and materials resources.

To understand the present status of labor productivity in the United States, we must examine two concepts: labor productivity and rate of change of productivity. Let us first consider labor productivity, the absolute level of U.S. labor productivity.

(handwritten margin note: used to machine produces of building)

Table 18.1	Real Gross Domestic Product per Employed Person by Country

	1978	1983	1988	1993	1998
United States	100.0	100.0	100.0	100.0	100.0
Canada	86.5	84.5	83.6	80.8	81.5
Japan	61.5	66.3	71.5	74.0	71.7
Korea	23.8	28.5	35.9	44.6	51.4
Austria	71.0	78.7	78.6	83.3	86.8
Belgium	84.1	89.9	89.8	97.2	97.4
Denmark	68.4	71.3	69.6	74.4	78.0
France	81.5	87.1	89.4	89.8	86.1
Germany	81.1	83.0	82.6	85.7	90.2
Italy	n/a	84.8	89.1	90.0	93.7
Netherlands	86.9	84.5	81.9	78.0	77.5
Norway	68.8	72.7	72.0	83.2	82.0
Sweden	65.7	67.2	67.1	66.6	70.0
United Kingdom	67.6	71.8	72.8	71.9	70.9

Note: Each country's GDP per employed person value is shown as a percentage of the value for the U.S. that year.

Source: Bureau of Labor Statistics report "Comparative Real Gross Domestic Product Per Capita and Per Employed Person, January 2001" (**http://stats.bls.gov**).

The Bureau of Labor Statistics publishes statistics on labor productivity that are computed by dividing the real dollar value of all goods and services produced in the United States in a given year by the direct labor-hours used in producing those goods and services. For many decades, the United States has led the world in labor productivity. Another measure that reflects productivity differences between countries is gross domestic product per employed person. Table 18.1 shows this comparison for 14 countries over two decades, with the value for each country shown as a percentage of the U.S. value. Although our international trading partners lag behind the United States on this measure, Table 18.1 shows that many are catching up.

Next, let us consider the second concept: the rate of change of labor productivity. This measure is also commonly referred to as the rate of growth of labor productivity, which implies that labor productivity is increasing. The Bureau of Labor Statistics also publishes statistics for the rate of growth of U.S. labor productivity, the percentage of change from the previous year. In the decades of the 1960s, 1970s, and 1980s, the U.S. rate of growth of labor productivity increased at these average rates: 2.5, 1.2, and 1.0 percent. Over the same period, the rate of growth of labor productivity in the United Kingdom, Canada, France, Italy, West Germany, and Japan was much higher than that in the United States. In fact, the rate of growth of labor productivity in Japan was in the double-digit range. With the globalization of business, it was probably inevitable that our foreign competitors began to catch up in labor productivity.

On a positive note for U.S. companies, labor productivity growth increased in the 1990s. According to Bureau of Labor Statistics figures, the productivity growth in 1998–1999 was 3.1 percent for the business sector of the economy and 2.9 percent for the nonfarm business sector. But for manufacturing, the productivity growth was 6.3 percent, including 9.3 percent for durable goods manufacturing and 2.7 percent for nondurable goods manufacturing.[4]

If U.S. businesses are to remain number one in labor productivity, they must renew their efforts to increase the rate of growth of labor productivity. And our view of productivity today must be toward improving the productivity of all the factors of production—labor, capital, materials, and overhead.

Many companies today are pushing hard to improve their labor productivity. Business Snapshot 18.1 discusses recent productivity improvements in U.S. companies. The day may come when the productivity of direct labor will receive only a cursory discussion in textbooks such as this, but that day is not yet here. For many U.S. manufacturers, direct labor cost remains a significant expense. Some manufacturing operations are not yet automated and never will be because either it is not cost effective or insufficient capital is available. Moreover, many services remain direct-labor intensive. For these reasons, the cost of labor and the need to improve the productivity of labor continues to receive management attention. In the remainder of this chapter, therefore, we focus on labor productivity.

Labor Productivity

What causes employees to be more productive? Figure 18.1 shows the major factors that affect labor productivity. This illustration demonstrates an important truth: The causes of productivity are many. We have not yet developed a set of formulas that

---

BUSINESS SNAPSHOT 18.1

Productivity Improvements in the United States

Automakers have learned to build cars using robotic welding machines run by computers that are precise and consistent—and don't charge overtime. Warehouses have computerized tracking systems that reduce or eliminate the need for manual inventory counts, saving hundreds of worker-hours. Grocery and convenience stores have computerized cash registers that track inventory through every sale and that can automatically order the exact amount of merchandise needed. Even the smallest businesses have computerized payroll and inventory systems, which means that a higher percentage of employees are focused on the company's primary business.

These innovative technologies and information systems have enabled U.S. companies to improve output per worker by 21.5 percent in the 1990s, according to figures provided by the U.S. Department of Labor. "You have to

go back to the British Industrial Revolution to see the kind of change that we are undergoing now," says economist Ray Perryman of the Perryman Group in Waco, Texas. And the advent of the Internet and e-commerce promises even further efficiencies.

Productivity in manufacturing, where many technical innovations got an early start and where their output is most easily measured, has grown even faster: increasing by 47 percent, or almost half again from what a company produced per worker in 1990.

At paper products giant Kimberly Clark, based in Irving, Texas, added precision from technological advances helped the company make significant productivity gains. "There is less waste and less downtime," says Craig Price, a company spokesman. This has allowed the company to enjoy a growth in operating profit of 18 percent per employee in 1999

over 1998. "That came at a time when we increased our workforce from 54,700 to about 54,800 employees," Price says. "So we didn't get the increase by cutting workers."

The gains in productivity have created a macroeconomic model that has never been observed in modern times. Economic growth of the kind tabulated in recent years has historically been accompanied by inflation because of higher wages paid to attract workers in tightening labor markets. But the recent productivity increases have been able to create a rise in GDP without significant increases in labor cost, resulting in a long period of sustained economic growth, even with unemployment at one of the lowest rates in history. "If you have growth in productivity you can have higher wages and higher standards of living without inflation," Perryman says.

Source: Bowen, Bill. "Computerized Innovations: Technology Improved U.S. Worker Output by 21.5 Percent in the 1990s." *Arlington Star-Telegram*, May 22, 2000, 27–28, All Stars section.

Figure 18.1   Variables Affecting Labor Productivity

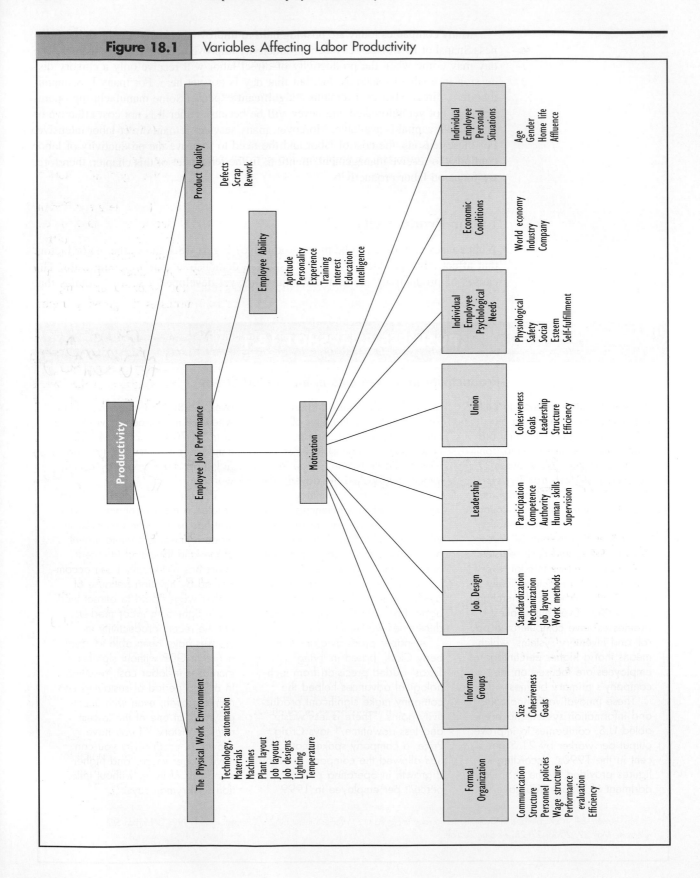

precisely predicts human behavior in general and productivity in particular. We have, however, begun to understand enough about employee behavior to remove some of the uncertainty about why employees are productive.

Three major factors affect labor productivity: employees' job performance; technology, machines, tools, and work methods that support and assist their work; and product quality. Staff groups such as industrial, process, product, and systems engineering strive to develop better automation, machines, tools, and work methods to enhance labor productivity. Increasing productivity through technological developments is at least as important as employee job performance in increasing productivity. And reducing defects, scrap, and rework directly increases the productivity of all factors of production.

Employee job performance is a complex topic because all people are different. Abilities, personalities, interests, ambitions, energy levels, education, training, and experience vary widely. It is important for operations managers to consider these differences because blanket or universal approaches to improving job performance may not be effective for all employees. Personnel departments recognize these differences and attempt to select employees who have the desired abilities to develop training programs to improve employees' skills. Business Snapshot 18.2 discusses the growing importance of employee training and education.

Motivation is perhaps the most complex variable in the equation of productivity. Motivation is what prompts a person to act in a certain way. Abraham Maslow identified five levels of needs that prompt people to act: physiological, safety, social, esteem, and self-fulfillment.[5] These needs are arranged in a hierarchy from physiological at the lowest level to self-fulfillment at the highest level. Only unsatisfied needs are **motivators,** or

BUSINESS SNAPSHOT 18.2

Smarter and Better-Trained Employees

Northeast Tool & Manufacturing Co., located outside of Charlotte, North Carolina, is requiring all of its 43 employees to take aptitude exams, measuring everything from math and mechanical skills to leadership and adaptability. Test results are analyzed by the North Carolina Labor Department in Raleigh and then returned to Northeast Tool with a prescription for each worker. Based on the results, the company will develop customized training for each worker. Some will enroll at a nearby community college. Others will take remote courses via computers set up at the plant. A few

will attend afternoon classes with professors brought right to the site of the plant.

The trend toward high-skills manufacturing began in the mid-1980s, when many companies began replacing low-skill assembly line work with computer-controlled equipment that required skilled and nimble workers to think while they work. In the 1990s, companies learned the lesson that investments in training boost productivity, often at less cost than capital investments. Now even small manufacturers like Northeast Tool see high skills as essential to remain competitive.

According to surveys of large companies by the University of California's Center for Effective Organizations, the number of companies that have put a majority of their workers through different types of training have doubled or tripled in the past decade. Between 1985 and 1995 the percentage of manufacturing workers with at least some college education increased from 33 to 44 percent. "There's a real rise in companies' willingness to invest in their workforces," says Pamela J. Tate, president of the Council for Adult & Experiential Learning, a Chicago consulting group.

Source: "Special Report: The New Factory Worker." *Business Week,* September 30, 1996, 59–68.

Understanding employees' higher-level needs for esteem and self-fulfillment can help managers motivate them to greater productivity.

cause people to act, and as each lower-level need becomes relatively satisfied, higher-level needs emerge as motivators. Today, many employees' lower-level needs (physiological and safety) are mostly taken care of by the economic packages at work. The higher- level needs (social, esteem, and self-fulfillment) may hold more promise for managers in their attempts to motivate employees.

How does an understanding of employees' needs help us to design a work environment that encourages productivity? If we can determine what class of needs is important to our employees, we can apply this framework. *If productivity is seen by employees as a means of satisfying their needs, high productivity is likely to result. Once employees have their needs satisfied through rewards that have been conditional upon productivity, the process is likely to be repeated.* Figure 18.2 illustrates this concept.

Figure 18.2	The Productivity Pathway to Satisfy Workers' Needs

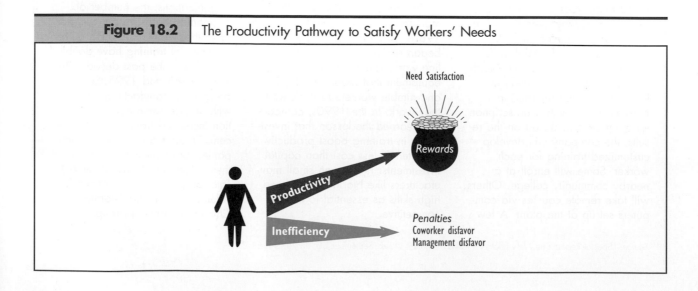

Labor unions and work groups can influence employees to be either productive or unproductive. If employees think that their work groups may treat them as outcasts because they have been productive, they may not cooperate with management in this productivity–reward–productivity cycle. Operations managers should recognize the influence that work groups have on labor productivity and develop cooperative work groups by carefully selecting employees for these groups and by influencing group norms through effective cooperation and communication.

Why worry about satisfaction of employees' needs? What's in it for the organization? The obvious answer is an improvement in productivity, as we have discussed. Another equally important answer is that satisfied employees are less likely to be absent from work, less likely to leave their jobs for other ones, and more likely to produce high-quality goods and services. In today's working environment where absenteeism, turnover, and low quality of products and services are staggering problems, this reason alone seems sufficient to get operations managers interested in designing jobs in ways that provide for a broader range of employees' need satisfaction.

DESIGNING WORKERS' JOBS

Some behavioral scientists argue that assembly line jobs are boring and monotonous and that workers are not satisfying their needs for socialization, self-esteem, and self-fulfillment on these jobs. The high rates of absenteeism and turnover among our workers seem to validate these contentions. This criticism of assembly line jobs is aimed at the high degree of labor specialization in these jobs. **Labor specialization** refers to the number of tasks that a worker performs. A highly specialized job is one in which the worker repetitively performs only a narrow range of activities, such as folding a sheet of paper and placing it in an envelope. On the other hand, a job that is not very specialized would be one in which the worker does a variety of tasks during the day. Table 18.2 lists some advantages and disadvantages of labor specialization.

Several proposals for modifying specialized jobs to provide for a broader range of needs satisfaction are:

- **Cross-training**—Training workers to perform several jobs so that they can be moved about from job to job as needed.

Table 18.2	Some Advantages and Disadvantages of Labor Specialization

Advantages
1. Because of the repetitive work, production rates are high.
2. Because skill requirements of jobs are low:
   a. Wage rates are low.
   b. Workers can be trained quickly.
   c. Workers can be recruited easily.

Disadvantages
1. Worker dissatisfaction can cause total costs to be excessive because of high rates of turnover, absenteeism, tardiness, union grievances, job-related sicknesses, and sabotage.
2. Production quality can be low because:
   a. Workers are not motivated to produce high-quality products.
   b. Since workers make only a small part of a product, no single worker is accountable for the quality of the whole product.

- **Job enlargement**—Adding additional similar tasks to workers' jobs; this is referred to as *horizontal job enlargement*.
- **Job enrichment**—Adding more planning, inspecting, and other management functions to workers' jobs; this is referred to as *vertical job enlargement*.
- **Team production**—Organizing workers into work teams; selecting workers and training them to work in teams; assigning some responsibility for management of production to teams.

Building effective work teams means more than just grouping workers into work groups—much more is required. Team building requires training in team effectiveness, conflict resolution, team measurement, and motivation systems. A powerful feature of effective work teams is that they can focus on processes rather than departments. For example, if a team is to design and develop a new product, the team can focus on the process of designing and developing the new product and not be constrained by departmental boundaries and responsibilities. These remedies have been experimentally applied with varying degrees of success and failure.

A burning issue remains: *Can we simultaneously give workers the satisfaction they want from their work and still give the organization the productivity and efficiency it needs to survive economically?* Is such a blend possible? How do we design jobs so that we integrate organizations' needs for high productivity and employees' needs for interesting work, self-direction, self-control, socialization, participation, and achievement? Are there practical guidelines that engineers and other technical specialists who design workers' jobs can follow to accomplish both of these necessary and worthwhile goals? Table 18.3 suggests several such guidelines for designing workers' job tasks, workers' immediate job settings, and the larger work environment.

Table 18.3 was developed with the assumption that individual worker jobs have first been designed to be technically efficient and productive. These suggestions for modifying worker tasks have been practically applied in real-world organizations to provide workers with opportunities for self-control, self-direction, and socialization. The remainder of this table offers other suggestions for modifying in positive ways both the immediate job setting and the larger work environment.

Labor unions are a strong force in affecting workers' attitudes toward work. Unions have been suspicious of managements' actions to make work more satisfying; thus, workers and unions usually have not cooperated in implementing job design modification proposals. Also, over the years unions have negotiated labor agreements containing restrictive work rules. These rules control such things as pay, hours of work, overtime, seniority in filling vacancies, scope of jobs, incentive pay, layoff and recall procedures, and transfer between jobs. One common work rule inhibits a worker in one labor classification from doing work in another classification, as, for example, when a production worker is not allowed to do any maintenance work. Such rules restrict management flexibility and reduce productivity.

In recent years, however, the loss of union jobs because of foreign competition has put great pressure on unions to change restrictive work rules in union contracts. These changes included eliminating unneeded jobs, more flexibility in moving workers around from job to job, modifications in seniority rules, and changing crew structure to be more appropriate for high-technology production equipment. Such changes have improved productivity in many industries. Not only do work rule changes improve productivity by eliminating waste, but they also allow the formation of motivated work teams that were formerly impossible.

Although obstacles do exist to designing workers' jobs that are both efficient and satisfying, experience shows that these obstacles can be overcome through education, cooperation, and persistence.

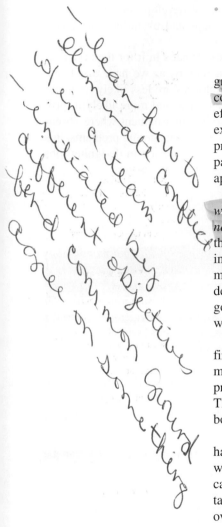

Table 18.3	Some Practical Guidelines for Designing Workers' Jobs and Work Environments That Accommodate Workers' Needs	

Elements of Workers' Jobs	Suggested Design Guidelines	Workers' Needs Affected
Worker's job tasks (the work itself—arrangement of machines, workplace layouts, work methods, and sequence of work tasks)	1. Avoid machine pacing of workers. Workers should determine, when possible, rates of output.	Self-control
	2. When practical, combine inspection tasks into jobs so that workers inspect their own output.	Self-control
	3. Design work areas to allow open communication and visual contact with other workers in adjacent operations.	Socialization, team building
	4. When economically feasible and generally desired by workers, combine machine changeover, new job layouts, setups, and other elements of immediate job planning into workers' jobs.	Self-direction/control
	5. Replace workers with automated equipment on boring, uncomfortable, or unsafe jobs.	Dissatisfaction
Immediate job setting (the management policies and procedures that directly impinge on workers' jobs)	1. Rotate workers where practical between jobs that are repetitive, monotonous, boring, and short cycled.	Variety and relief of boredom and monotony
	2. Assign new workers to undesirable jobs for fixed periods of time, then transfer them to more preferred jobs.	Equity
	3. Recruit mentally or physically challenged, hard-core unemployed, or otherwise disadvantaged persons for jobs with high absenteeism and high turnover.	Interesting work and basic needs
	4. To relieve monotony, provide workers with periodic rest periods away from repetitive jobs.	Relief of boredom and socialization
	5. Set higher pay rates for undesirable jobs.	Physiological, security, equity, and achievement
Larger work environment (organization-wide policies, climate, management philosophy, structure, facilities, and programs)	1. Select and train supervisors who openly communicate on most issues that affect workers.	Recognition and socialization
	2. Develop supervisors who are comfortable with a participative team environment, both with their superiors and with workers.	Participation, recognition, socialization, and achievement
	3. Remove barriers between management and other employees, such as separate dining or washroom facilities.	Equity and recognition
	4. Create an organizational climate and management philosophy that recognizes workers and work teams as important elements of the organization. This tends to give workers a sense of personal worth.	Recognition and achievement
	5. Develop formal and informal channels of communication among workers, work teams, and all levels of management. These channels function best when used often, in all directions, and on a wide range of topics.	Participation, self-control, and recognition

EMPOWERING WORKERS

For U.S. companies to compete and survive in global competition, it is mandatory that they draw out and apply all the ability and energy of their employees. As we have discussed at several places in this text, continuing improvement of production costs, product quality, delivery times, and customer satisfaction are the means by which companies today will gain market share. Employees—blue-collar workers, office workers, managers, engineers, and scientists, all of them together—form the core resource that is the power for achieving excellence in production and in gaining market share.

How do companies draw out and apply this powerful resource to achieve excellence? The guidelines for change suggested in Table 18.3 represent important basics,

[handwritten margin notes: "Ownership relates to more productivity"]

[handwritten margin notes: "Empowered workers accept charge if they are involved in the change."]

but more must be done. As companies undertake continuous improvement programs of total quality management (TQM), just-in-time (JIT) manufacturing, and other radically different programs of excellence, employees must step forward and accept responsibility for every facet of production. Managers for some time now have realized that they can't control everything in production; it is the employees who have control of and know the most about the details of production. How do managers get employees to accept this responsibility? *Managers must first give employees the authority to act.*

One word for the process of conveying authority from management to workers is **worker empowerment.** To see how empowerment works, let us say that a manager tells workers that they have the authority to stop production lines if they see that product quality is beginning to deteriorate. In this situation, workers tend to accept responsibility for product quality and shut down production and work together to correct the cause of low product quality. Worker safety, maintenance problems, material shortages, and other occurrences can cause the need for production to be stopped. Giving workers the authority to stop production for these and other causes is perhaps the most visible conveyance of authority to workers. Workers accepting responsibility for production can lead to what is called **internal ownership,** where workers feel that the production line belongs to them, and they are responsible for everything that occurs in production. But a key to achieving internal ownership is to first give workers the authority to act.

Empowering workers is management's way of unleashing a powerful force for continuously working toward excellence in production. And excellence in production is needed by U.S. companies if they are to succeed in global competition.

WORK METHODS ANALYSIS

From Figure 18.1 we can see that the machines, tools, materials, and work methods used by workers directly affect labor productivity. How do we go about improving work methods? One of the first places to start is with the workers themselves. They do their jobs daily, and on some things related to their jobs, they are the experts. Besides offering some valuable suggestions, workers who are empowered to improve their own jobs will be more likely to make and accept changes.

Ordinarily, the objective of improving work methods is to increase productivity by increasing the production capacity of an operation or group of operations, reducing the cost of the operations, or improving product quality. One key to successful methods analysis is the development of a questioning attitude about every facet of the job being studied. Is every part of the job necessary? Why is it done that way? Who could do it better? Questions such as these ensure that analysts accept nothing in an operation as sacred; everything about the job will be meticulously scrutinized. With this questioning attitude, analysts can develop improved work methods.

How to Do Methods Analysis

How do we go about analyzing work methods? Table 18.4 lists 10 steps that are generally followed by methods analysts. In performing work methods analysis, certain diagrams and charts can be useful.

Diagrams and Charts

Flow diagrams and **process charts** are perhaps the most versatile techniques available for analyzing work methods. They are usually used together to eliminate or reduce delays, eliminate or combine tasks, or reduce travel time or distance. At FedEx,

Table 18.4	Procedures of Methods Analysis

1. Make an initial investigation of the operation under consideration.
2. Decide what level of analysis is appropriate.
3. Talk with workers, supervisors, and others who are familiar with the operation. Get their suggestions for better ways to do the work.
4. Study the present method. Use process charts, time study, and other appropriate techniques of analysis. (These techniques are discussed later in this section.) Thoroughly describe and evaluate the present method.
5. Apply the questioning attitude and the suggestions of others. Devise a new proposed method by using process charts and other appropriate techniques of analysis.
6. Use time study if necessary. Compare new and present methods. Obtain supervisors' approval to proceed.
7. Modify the proposed method as required after reviewing the details with workers and supervisors.
8. Train one or more workers to perform the proposed method on a trial basis. Evaluate the proposed method. Modify the method as required.
9. Train workers and install the proposed method.
10. Check periodically to ensure that the expected savings are being realized.

flow diagrams and process charts were used to reduce the time required to settle customers' claims from six weeks on average to only one day. Example 18.1 illustrates how a large insurance company uses flow diagrams and process charts to improve the work methods of clerks who repetitively prepare a certain type of form. Read the example and notice that first the present method is studied, then a new and improved method is developed, the two methods are compared, and the best one is selected.

Example 18.1	Methods Analysis at the American Insurance Company

Work was piling up in the claims department of the American Insurance Company because so many authorization-to-investigate forms had to be processed. It was thought that the workload could be reduced if the methods of processing the forms through the department could be streamlined.

Solution

1. Prepare a flow diagram and a process chart of the present method. (See Figure 18.3.)
2. Develop an improved method and prepare a flow diagram and a process chart of the proposed new method. (See Figure 18.4.)
3. Compare the two methods and select the best method. What are the main improvements in the new method? (See Table 18.5.)

What are the principal improvements of the proposed method?

1. It eliminates retrievals of client's file by attaching claim department's claim form to request. All necessary client information is contained on this previously completed form.
2. It eliminates the necessity for clerk to obtain section leader's approval by utilizing existing interoffice mail service.

Figure 18.3 | Flow Diagram and Process Chart: Present Method for Completing Authorization-to-Investigate Form

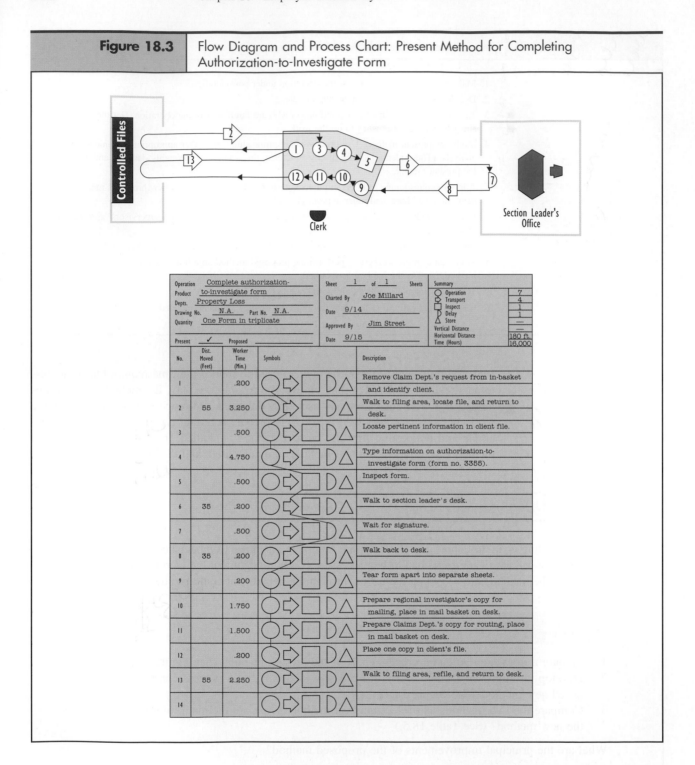

There are several forms of **multiactivity charts**, but they all have one thing in common: They show how one or more workers work together and/or with machines. A **worker and machine chart,** for example, could show how a clerk in a grocery store works with a customer and with a coffee-grinding machine to produce ground coffee

Figure 18.4 Flow Diagram and Process Chart: Proposed Method for Completing Authorization-to-Investigate Form

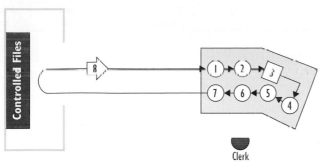

Controlled Files

Clerk

Section Leader's Office

Operation	Complete authorization-
Product	to-investigate form
Depts.	Property Loss
Drawing No.	N.A. Part No. N.A.
Quantity	One Form in triplicate

Sheet	1	of	1	Sheets
Charted By	Joe Millard			
Date	9/20			
Approved By	Jim Street			
Date	9/21			

Summary	
◯ Operation	6
⇨ Transport	1
▢ Inspect	1
D Delay	
△ Store	—
Vertical Distance	—
Horizontal Distance	55 ft.
Time (Hours)	12.250

Present _____ Proposed ✓

No.	Dist. Moved (Feet)	Worker Time (Min.)	Symbols	Description
1		.200	◯ ⇨ ▢ D △	Remove Claim Dept.'s request with client's claim form attached from in-basket.
2		4.750	◯ ⇨ ▢ D △	Type information on authorization-to-investigate form.
3		.500	◯ ⇨ ▢ D △	Inspect form.
4		.100	◯ ⇨ ▢ D △	Attach routing slip to the completed form and place in mail basket on desk.
5		.200	◯ ⇨ ▢ D △	Remove approved form from in-basket and tear apart into separate sheets.
6		1.750	◯ ⇨ ▢ D △	Prepare regional investigator's copy for mailing, place in mail basket on desk.
7		1.500	◯ ⇨ ▢ D △	Prepare Claim Dept.'s copy for routing, place in mail basket on desk.
8	55	3.250	◯ ⇨ ▢ D △	Walk to filing area, locate client's file, place copy of form in file, and return to desk.
9			◯ ⇨ ▢ D △	
10			◯ ⇨ ▢ D △	
11			◯ ⇨ ▢ D △	
12			◯ ⇨ ▢ D △	
13			◯ ⇨ ▢ D △	
14			◯ ⇨ ▢ D △	

Table 18.5	Comparison of Present and Proposed Methods of Completing Authorization-to-Investigate Form—Property Loss Department

Comparison Factor	Present Method	Proposed Method	Estimated Savings
Feet traveled per form	180	55	125
Number of operations per form	7	6	1
Number of inspections per form	1	1	—
Number of delays per form	1	—	1
Minutes per form	16.000	12.250	3.750
Labor cost per form ($10 per hour)	$2.667	$2.042	$0.624
Annual labor cost (300,000 forms per year)	$800,100	$612,600	$187,200

for the customer. These charts are helpful for minimizing worker and machine delay and for determining the optimal number of machines per worker.

Although methods analysis is an important element in achieving high labor productivity, work measurement is also helpful.

WORK MEASUREMENT

What units of measurement shall we use to measure human work? Foot-pounds, calories per minute, and other units have been used in the physical sciences to measure work. But in operations, a unit of work that is both easily measured and easily understood must be used. The unit of measure that has evolved is **worker-minutes per unit of output.** In other words, how many minutes does it ordinarily take a well-trained worker, on the average, to produce one component, subassembly, product, or service? **Work measurement** therefore refers to the process of estimating the amount of worker time required to generate one unit of output. The ultimate goal of work measurement is usually to develop labor standards that will be used for planning and controlling operations, thereby achieving high labor productivity.

Labor Standards

A **labor standard** is the number of worker-minutes required to complete an element, operation, or product under ordinary operating conditions. The term **ordinary operating conditions** refers to a hypothetical *average* situation—workers' ability, workers' working speed, condition of machines, supply of materials, availability of information, presence of physiological or psychological stress, and all other aspects of workers' jobs.

Labor standards are used to plan and control operations. For example, when we know the amount of worker-minutes required for each product, we can estimate the number of workers needed in a production department. Also, labor standards can be used to determine if a production department's labor is performing above, below, or at standard. Moreover, labor standards are used in developing accounting labor cost standards. These cost standards are particularly useful in cost estimates, labor cost variance reports, and in the pricing of new products.

Another use of labor standards is in incentive pay systems.

Incentive Pay Systems

An **incentive pay system** makes the amount of workers' pay conditional upon job performance. For example, with a piece-rate pay plan a worker would receive a specific dollar amount for each unit of product produced. Alternatively, with a gain-sharing pay plan a worker's hourly base rate of pay would be adjusted upward proportional to his or her amount of performance above the standard. Profit-sharing bonuses are another form of incentive pay.

Although incentive pay systems have diminished in popularity in the United States, their use is still common, particularly in mature firms and industries where tradition dictates incentive pay. In Japanese firms such as Toyota, workers' paychecks are affected by "production allowances." These allowances are based on the production of the work team during a month. In the United States, enormous variety exists in incentive pay systems, and as union–management contract negotiations evolve, so also do these systems. Increasingly today, companies are using team-oriented incentive pay systems. Such systems stress teamwork by rewarding individuals based on their contribution to team goals through peer reviews.

Three approaches are used to set labor standards: time study, work sampling, and predetermined time methods.

Time Study

In time study, analysts use stopwatches to time the operation being performed by workers. These observed times are then converted into labor standards that are expressed in minutes per unit of output for the operation. Table 18.6 lists the steps employed by analysts in determining labor standards based on time study. Example 18.2 demonstrates the steps in computing a labor standard from a time study.

Table 18.6	Steps in Determining Labor Standards from Time Studies

1. Make sure that the correct method is being used to perform the operation being studied.
2. Determine how many cycles to time. A **cycle** is one complete set of the elemental tasks included in the operation. Generally, more cycles must be timed when cycle times are short, when cycle times are highly variable, and when the annual production of the product is high.
3. Break the operation down into basic tasks, which are also called **elements** (get part, hold against grinder, adjust machine, etc.).
4. Observe the operation and use a stopwatch to record the elapsed time for each element for the number of required cycles. The **observed element times** are recorded in minutes.
5. For each elemental task, estimate the speed that the worker is working. A **performance rating** of 1.00 indicates that the worker is working at normal speed, the speed at which a well-trained worker would work under ordinary operating conditions. A performance rating of 1.20 indicates 20 percent faster than normal, and a performance rating of 0.80 indicates 20 percent slower than normal.
6. Compute an **allowance fraction** for the operation. The allowance fraction is the fraction of the time that workers cannot work through no fault of their own. For example, if workers cannot work 15 percent of the time because of cleanup work, rest periods, company meetings, etc., the allowance fraction would be 0.15.
7. Determine the **mean observed time** for each element by dividing the sum of the observed element times for each element by the number of cycles timed.
8. Compute the **element normal time** for each element:

$$\text{Element normal time} = \text{Mean observed time} \times \text{Performance rating}$$

9. Compute the **total normal time** for the entire operation by summing the element normal times for all elements.
10. Compute the **labor standard** for the operation:

$$\text{Labor standard} = \text{Total normal time} \div (1 - \text{Allowance fraction})$$

Example 18.2	Setting Labor Standards with Time Study

A new *Guide to Registration*, to be given to all new students, is proposed for Metro University. The dean of student services wonders what the labor cost would be for 30,000 of the 12-page handouts.

The dean asked a business student to investigate the problem and report the results. The student thought that a good way to estimate the labor cost would be to:

1. Train a worker to collate the handouts.
2. Conduct a time study of the worker as a few of the handouts were collated.
3. Use the results of the time study to compute a labor standard for collating the handout.
4. Use the labor standard to estimate the labor cost of the entire project.

Solution

The student followed the steps of Table 18.6 and conducted a time study of the worker as the handouts were collated. The results of the time study are found in Figure 18.5. From the time study, the student knew that each handout would require 0.4482 minute of a worker's time. Also, the labor cost of workers in the work pool is $8 per hour, and about 15 percent of each worker's time is spent in cleaning up the work pool area, personal time, unavoidable delays, and other unproductive activities.

1. Compute the labor cost per handout:

$$\text{Labor cost per unit} = \text{Labor standard} \times \text{Labor cost per minute}$$
$$= 0.4482 \text{ minute} \times (\$8 \text{ per hour} \div 60 \text{ minutes per hour})$$
$$= \$0.05976 \text{ per handout}$$

2. Compute the total labor cost for the project:

$$\text{Total-project labor cost} = \text{Number of handouts} \times \text{Labor cost per unit}$$
$$= 30,000 \times \$0.05976 = \$1,792.80$$

Although time study offers precision in determining labor standards, in most situations it requires a competent staff of analysts. Another difficulty is that the labor standard cannot be determined before the operation is actually performed. These disadvantages have led to the development of other work measurement techniques.

Work Sampling

Work sampling is a work measurement technique that randomly samples the work of one or more employees at periodic intervals to determine the proportion of the total operation that is accounted for in one particular activity. These studies are frequently used to estimate the percentage of employees' time spent in such activities as these: unavoidable delays, which are commonly called ratio-delay studies; repairing finished products from an operation; or supplying material to an operation. The results of these studies are commonly used to set allowances used in computing labor standards, in estimating costs of certain activities, and in investigating work methods.

Work sampling is also used to set labor standards. Example 18.3 uses a work-sampling study to set a labor standard for billing clerks to conduct credit checks on

Figure 18.5	The Study for Collating Handouts

Time Study

Operation Collate Materials for University Handouts

Dept. University Work Pool	Start 12:10	Date 8/15	Operator Suzanne Ogden
Part	Stop 13:14	Shift 2	M. F. ✓
Size 12-page 8.5"x11" handout	Diff. (Elapsed Time) 4 min.	Study 1	Analyst Mary Delaney
	Production 10 handouts	Sheet 1	
	Est. Time .400 min. per handout		

Remarks 12 stacks are arranged in two rows of 6 stacks each on a large table

Elements		Cycles																Summary			
		1	2	3	4	5	6	7	8	9	10	11	12	13	14	15	Sum	Mean	Rating	Normal
1. Collate Row #1		.10	.09	.09	.08	.08	.09	.07	.10	.08	.09						.87	.087	1.00	.087
2. Tap handout on edge		.04	.03	.04	.05	.03	.04	.04	.04	.03	.05						.39	.039	.90	.035
3. Collate Row #2		.12	.09	.10	.09	.10	.10	.09	.08	.11	.10						.98	.098	1.00	.098
4. Tap handout on edge		.04	.02	.03	.05	.03	.04	.04	.03	.05	.04						.37	.037	.90	.033
5. Staple handout		.06	.06	.07	.05	.07	.06	.06	.06	.08	.05						.62	.062	1.10	.068
6. Aside		.02	.03	.04	.04	.03	.03	.03	.04	.04	.03						.33	.033	1.00	.033
7. Miscellaneous elements																				
a. Apply "stickum" to fingers						.06											.06	.006	1.00	.006
b. Straighten stacks									.21								.21	.021	1.00	.021
																			Total	.381

Labor standard = Total Normal time ÷ (1 − Allowance fraction) = .381 ÷ (1 − .15) = .4482 minutes per handout

prospective customers. In this instance, the purpose of the labor standard is to estimate the number of billing clerks that would be required if a new credit check department were established.

Example 18.3	Setting Labor Standards with Work Sampling

The billing department at Gasco, the natural gas utility for the metropolitan Los Angeles, California, area, has clerks who perform these activities: (1) audit customers' bills, (2) make corrections to customers' bills, and (3) perform credit checks on prospective customers. Gasco has grown so rapidly in recent years that the credit-checking workload is mushrooming. The manager of the billing department forecasts that 150,000 credit checks will have to be made by the department next year and wonders how many clerks will be required to perform these credit checks. An analyst is assigned the job of estimating the number of clerks that would be required. This procedure is to be followed in the investigation:

1. Perform a work-sampling study to determine the proportion of time that a clerk does credit checks.
2. Compute a labor standard for each credit check based on the work-sampling study.
3. Compute the number of clerks required to perform credit checks next year.

Solution

1. Determine how many work-sampling observations are required:

   Departmental personnel estimated that credit checks represented about 25 percent of clerks' jobs. The analyst referred to Table 18.7 and determined that a 95 percent confidence interval and ±3 percent absolute error would require 833 work-sampling observations. This means that the analyst would be 95 percent confident that between 22 and 28 percent of a clerk's job was credit checks.

2. Determine the time interval between work-sampling observations and the total time of the study:

   The analyst planned to study a single clerk for 2.5 hours with work-sampling snapshots every 10 seconds for a total of 900 observations (6/minute × 60 minutes/hour × 2.5 hours = 900). At each snapshot, the analyst would record whether the clerk was doing credit checks.

3. Perform the work-sampling study and compute the labor standard for a credit check:

Type of Data	Data
Elapsed time of study (2.5 × 60 minutes/hour)	150 minutes
Total number of observations during study	900
Number of credit-check observations during study	211
Proportion of clerk's work that was credit checks	0.234
Number of credit checks completed during study	10
Performance rating of the clerk	1.10
Allowance fraction	0.20

$$\begin{array}{c}\text{Time per}\\\text{credit check}\end{array} = \left(\begin{array}{c}\text{Elapsed time}\\\text{of study}\end{array}\right) \times \left(\begin{array}{c}\text{Proportion of work}\\\text{that was credit checks}\end{array}\right) \div \left(\begin{array}{c}\text{Number of credit}\\\text{checks completed}\end{array}\right)$$

$$= 150 \times 0.234 \div 10 = 3.51$$

$$\text{Total normal time} = \text{Time per credit check} \times \text{Performance rating}$$
$$= 3.51 \times 1.10 = 3.861 \text{ minutes}$$
$$\text{Labor standard} = (\text{Total normal time}) \div (1 - \text{Allowance fraction})$$
$$= 3.861 \div (1 - 0.20)$$
$$= 4.82625 \text{ minutes per credit check}$$

4. Compute the number of clerks required for credit checks next year:

$$\begin{array}{c}\text{Number of}\\\text{clerks per year}\end{array} = \left(\begin{array}{c}\text{Number of checks}\\\text{forecasted next year}\end{array}\right) \times \left(\begin{array}{c}\text{Labor standard}\\\text{for credit checks}\end{array}\right) \div \left(\begin{array}{c}\text{Minutes/year}\\\text{that clerks work}\end{array}\right)$$

$$= (150{,}000 \times 4.82625) \div (50 \text{ weeks/year} \times 2{,}400 \text{ minutes/week})$$
$$= 6.03, \text{ or slightly more than 6 clerks}$$

Work sampling is less expensive than time study, but it usually offers less precision. Work sampling is usually preferred when many workers perform a single operation that is spread out over a large geographic area. In these cases, a single analyst could observe all workers at fixed time intervals, say, taking a snapshot every 10 seconds. This "sampling" of employees' activities allows analysts to break an operation into elements and to record which element each employee is performing when the work-sampling snapshot is taken. The number of times that each element is performed in an eight-hour shift becomes the basis for the labor standard.

Table 18.7	A Guide to Minimum Number of Work-Sampling Observations

| Activity Percentage [p or (1 − p)] | ABSOLUTE ERROR | | |
	±1%	±2%	±3%
1 or 99	396	99	44
5 or 95	1,900	475	211
10 or 90	3,600	900	400
15 or 85	5,100	1,275	567
20 or 80	6,400	1,600	711
25 or 75	7,500	1,875	833
30 or 70	8,400	2,100	933
35 or 65	9,100	2,275	1,011
40 or 60	9,600	2,400	1,067
45 or 55	9,900	2,475	1,099
50	10,000	2,500	1,111

Note: This table is based on a 95 percent confidence interval. Absolute error means the actual range of observations of *p*, the percentage of the total job devoted to a particular activity. For example, if *p* = 25 percent and the ±2 percent column were used, we could say that we were 95 percent confident that *p* ranged between 23 and 27 percent. Smaller absolute errors require larger numbers of work-sampling observations.

Predetermined Time Standards

When labor standards must be determined in advance of performing an operation, predetermined time standards can be used. These standards utilize data that have been historically developed for basic body movements, elements of operations, and entire operations. When cost estimates or pricing information is required for new operations or new products, these standards are commonly used.

Many predetermined time standard systems are used today—work factor, methods–time measurement (MTM), basic motion time (BMT) study, and a host of systems custom designed for individual companies. To demonstrate the use of these systems, we examine the development of MTM labor standards in Example 18.4. In this example, a manager must estimate the labor cost for a newly imposed inspection and cleaning of electrical diodes. MTM is an excellent choice when ultralight assembly work must be performed in a small geographic area and when quick, accurate, low-cost labor standards are required.

Example 18.4	Developing Labor Standards with MTM

Carlos Sanchez, production superintendent for Diocom, which manufactures diodes for the electronics industry, has just requested an estimate of additional labor costs if the company's XG1500 diode were to be inspected and cleaned. This request resulted from a few recent component failures in the field. Amanda Jones, an industrial engineer, is briefed on how the new inspection operation would be performed. She tells Carlos that she will have an estimate for him in an hour and disappears to her office.

Amanda knows that although Diocom personnel had never performed the inspection and cleaning operation, a good labor estimate could be developed by using methods–time measurement (MTM). She got out her MTM manual, wrote down the right- and left-hand activities, estimated distances to be traveled, described the nature of the hand motions, and looked up the TMUs (time measurement units) for each activity. One TMU equals 1/100,000 of an hour. The results of this analysis are found in Table 18.8.

Because Amanda estimates that 80 minutes per shift will be unavoidably nonproductive, she calculates the following:

Allowance fraction = (Minutes of allowance) ÷ Minutes per shift
= 80 minutes ÷ 480 minutes = 0.1667

Labor standard = Normal time ÷ (1 − Allowance fraction)
= 0.0629 minute ÷ (1 − 0.1667) = 0.0755 minute per XG1500 diode

Standard cost = Labor standard × Labor cost per minute
= 0.0755 minute × $0.129 per minute = $0.0097 per XG1500 diode

Amanda returned to the meeting and told Carlos the results of her MTM analysis: The estimated labor standard for the proposed inspection and cleaning operation was 0.0755 minute per diode, and the estimated labor cost was $0.0097 per diode. She took along the MTM table for the basic *Move* motion (Table 18.9) to demonstrate how the standard was estimated. She explained the third left-hand activity, M10A. To find this, look up the distance moved of 10 inches, go across to Column A, and read the TMU—11.3, which is in 100,000ths of an hour. This is converted to hours and minutes by dividing by 100,000 and multiplying the result by 60.

Table 18.8	MTM Labor Standard Calculation for XG1500 Diode Inspection and Cleaning Operation

Left Hand	MTM Code	TMU (1/100,000 hour)	MTM Code	Right Hand
1. Reach to bin of electrical components.	R10C	12.9		
2. Grasp component to be tested.	G4B	9.1		
3. Move component to exposed inspection meter stop (10 inches).	M10A*	11.3		
4. Position component on test meter.	P2SS	19.7		
5. Observe electrical continuity light.	EF	7.3		
6. Transfer component to other hand.	G3	5.6	G3	Grasp component.
		9.2	M5C	7. Move component to abrasion wheel.
		19.7	P2SS	8. Position component on abrasion wheel.
		8.0	M5B	9. Move component to bin.
		2.0	RL1	10. Release component.

Total TMU = 104.8 units
= 104.8 ÷ 100,000 = 0.001048 hour
= 0.001048 × 60 = 0.0629 minute

*Look up this TMU in Table 18.9.

Table 18.9	MTM—TMUs for Moving Objects with Hands and Arms (Move—M)

Distance Moved (inches)	TIME TMU				WT. ALLOWANCE			Case and Description
	A	B	C	Hand in Motion B	Wt. (lb) Up to	Dynamic Factor	Static Constant TMU	
−1 or less	2.0	2.0	2.0	1.7				
1	2.5	2.9	3.4	2.3	2.5	1.00	0	
2	3.6	4.6	5.2	2.9				A. Move object to
3	4.9	5.7	6.7	3.6	7.5	1.06	2.2	other hand or
4	6.1	6.9	8.0	4.3				against stop.
5	7.3	8.0	9.2	5.0	12.5	1.11	3.9	
6	8.1	8.9	10.3	5.7				
7	8.9	9.7	11.1	6.5	17.5	1.17	5.6	
8	9.7	10.6	11.8	7.2				
9	10.5	11.5	12.7	7.9	22.5	1.22	7.4	B. Move object to
10	11.3	12.2	13.5	8.6				approximate or
12	12.9	13.4	15.2	10.0	27.5	1.28	9.1	indefinite
14	14.4	14.6	16.9	11.4				location.
16	16.0	15.8	18.7	12.8	32.5	1.33	10.8	
18	17.6	17.0	20.4	14.2				
20	19.2	18.2	22.1	15.6	37.5	1.39	12.5	
22	20.8	19.4	23.8	17.0				
24	22.4	20.6	25.5	18.4	42.5	1.44	14.3	C. Move object to
26	24.0	21.8	27.3	19.8				exact location.
28	25.5	23.1	29.0	21.2	47.5	1.50	16.0	
30	27.1	24.3	30.7	22.7				
Additional	0.8	0.6	0.85		TMU per inch over 30 inches			

Source: Copyrighted by the MTM Association for Standards and Research. No reprint permission without written consent from the MTM Association, 1111 East Touhy Avenue, Des Plaines, IL 60018.

Labor standards may also be estimated subjectively. For instance, historical labor standards are determined by using historical data from the actual performance of the operation. Although this procedure is low cost, quick, and easy to understand, it has a fundamental flaw: Because no attempt to improve work methods is involved, use of the labor standards is likely to perpetuate sloppy work methods. Crew size standards are determined by estimating the total number of workers required to produce the necessary output per shift. This total number of worker-minutes per shift is then divided by the required output per shift. Supervisor estimates are also occasionally used. These standards are based on supervisors' intimate knowledge of the operations for which they are responsible. These and other subjectively estimated labor standards are known to be used in industry. Their uses are, however, limited to those situations where more expensive techniques cannot be economically justified.

Time study, work sampling, predetermined time standards, and subjectively set labor standards may all be appropriate work measurement techniques, depending on the nature of the job being considered. Table 18.10 describes some jobs for which each of

Table 18.10	Appropriate Work Measurement Techniques for Some Jobs

Job	Appropriate Work Measurement Technique
1. A job performed by a single worker in a fixed location. The job involves repetitive short cycles and is expected to continue relatively unchanged for long periods while producing large quantities of outputs. The resulting labor standards must be very accurate.	Time study
2. A job performed by a single worker in a fixed location. The job involves repetitive short cycles and will be changed periodically as customer orders for relatively small quantities of products change. The labor standards are used for accounting cost standards, pricing analyses, and production planning.	Predetermined time standards
3. A job performed by many workers over a compact area. The tasks may involve little repetition; but if repetitious, the cycles are usually very long. Workers must be observed by a single analyst. Although a moderate degree of accuracy in the labor standards is desired, time study would be too costly. Only large elements of work need to be observed; little detail is needed in setting the labor standards.	Work sampling
4. Any job or group of jobs in which very accurate labor standards are not required or in which the cost of time study, predetermined time standards, and work sampling is prohibitive.	Subjectively set labor standards

these techniques is appropriate. Regardless of the work measurement techniques employed to develop labor standards, their ultimate goals are the same:

1. To set benchmarks or standards against which to measure the actual performance of operations. The objective is to improve labor productivity.
2. To establish estimates of labor content in operations as planning aids for operations managers. Such estimates can be used to compare production methods, make cost estimates, determine product prices, and set incentive pay rates.

Labor standards are dynamic and must change as job conditions change. The dynamic nature of labor standards is important because as firms strive for continuous improvement, standards must adjust to the new and improved work methods. One type of change that affects all jobs is that workers learn, and as they learn, production times decrease.

LEARNING CURVES

In 1925 the commander of the Wright-Patterson Air Force Base in Dayton, Ohio, observed that workers exhibited definite learning patterns in manufacturing operations.[6] Since these first studies, we have learned that most aircraft-manufacturing tasks experience an 80 percent learning rate. In other words, the labor-hours required to assemble an aircraft is reduced by a factor of 0.8 as the production quantity is doubled. Figure 18.6 shows how the learning of workers causes the labor-hours per unit to fall as the number of units produced increases. If the first aircraft assembled requires 100 labor-hours, the second aircraft would require $0.8 \times 100 = 80$ labor-hours, the fourth would require $0.8 \times 80 = 64$ labor-hours, the eighth would require $0.8 \times 64 = 51.2$ labor-hours, and so on.

| **Figure 18.6** | Aircraft Assembly 80 Percent Learning Curve |

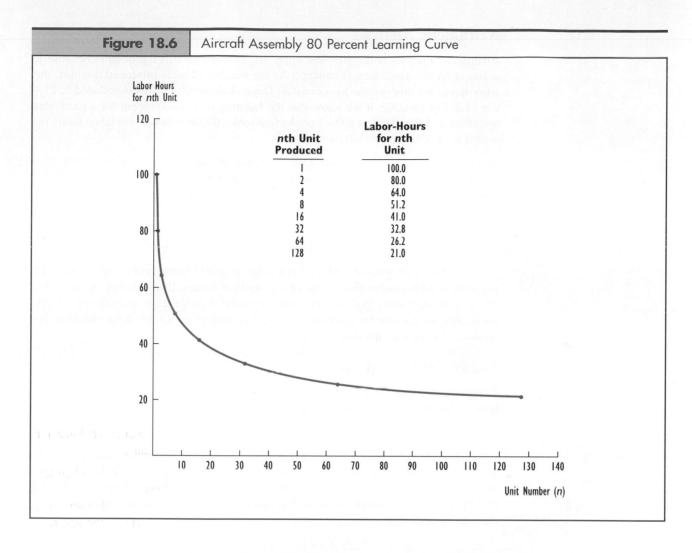

nth Unit Produced	Labor-Hours for nth Unit
1	100.0
2	80.0
4	64.0
8	51.2
16	41.0
32	32.8
64	26.2
128	21.0

The concept of the learning curve rests well with operations managers because they know through experience that in the beginning of production runs workers are unfamiliar with their tasks and the amount of time required to produce the first few units is high. But as the workers learn their tasks, their output per day increases up to a point and then levels off to a rather constant output rate. Additionally, learning curve concepts are based on these underpinnings: (1) Where there is life, there can be learning. (2) The more complex the life, the greater the rate of learning. Worker-paced operations are more susceptible to learning or can give greater rates of progress than machine-paced operations. (3) The rate of learning can be sufficiently regular to be predictive. Operations can develop trends that are characteristic of themselves.[7] Workers are thus observed to improve eye and hand coordination, learn to perform tasks, and develop technical skills as they gain more experience in performing certain operations. It is helpful to be able to analyze these workers' learning situations and to be able to estimate: (1) the average number of labor-hours required per unit for N units in a production run, (2) the total number of labor-hours required to produce N units in a production run, and (3) the exact number of labor-hours required to produce the *n*th unit of a production run.

There are three approaches to learning-curve problems: arithmetic analysis, logarithmic analysis, and learning-curve tables.

Arithmetic Analysis

Arithmetic analysis is the simplest approach to learning-curve problems because it is based on this fundamental concept: As the number of units produced doubles, the labor-hours per unit decline by a constant factor. This approach was introduced in Figure 18.6. For instance, if we know that the learning rate is 80 percent for a particular operation and that the first unit of production took 100 labor-hours, the labor-hours required to produce the eighth unit are:

nth Unit Produced	Labor-Hours for nth Unit
1	100.0
2	80.0
4	64.0
8	51.2

As long as we wish to find the labor-hours required to produce n units and n just happens to be a number that is one of the doubled values, then this approach works. But what if we want to find the labor-hours required to produce the seventh unit? Arithmetic analysis does not let us answer this question with precision, but logarithmic analysis does answer such questions.

Logarithmic Analysis

In logarithmic analysis this relationship allows us to compute T_n, which is the labor-hours required to produce the nth unit:

$$T_n = T_1(n^b) \quad \text{and} \quad b = \log r/\log 2$$

where T_1 is the labor-hours to produce the first unit, b is the slope of the learning curve, and r is the learning rate percentage. The values of b are found in Table 18.11. For instance, if we know that the learning rate for a particular operation is 80 percent and that the first unit of production took 100 labor-hours, the labor-hours required to produce the seventh unit are:

$$T_n = T_1(n^b)$$
$$T_7 = 100(7^{-0.322}) = 53.4 \text{ labor-hours}$$

The learning-curve table approach allows us to answer such questions as the one posed above. We can also answer other important questions.

Table 18.11	Learning-Curve Values of b

Learning Rate	b
70%	−0.515
75%	−0.415
80%	−0.322
85%	−0.234
90%	−0.152

Note: $b = (\log r)/(\log 2)$, where r is the learning rate. For example, with a 70 percent learning rate $b = (\log 0.7)/(\log 2) = -0.515$.

Learning-Curve Tables

Table 18.12 gives us learning-curve coefficients that allow us to compute not only the labor-hours for the *n*th unit in a production run but also the total labor-hours for the entire production run where the *n*th unit is the last unit in the production run. Example 18.5 illustrates the use of the coefficients in the table.

Example 18.5 | Using Learning-Curve Tables

A manufacturing plant must develop a cost estimate for a customer's order for eight large turbine shafts. It is estimated that the first shaft will take 100 hours of shop time, and an 80 percent learning curve is expected. **a.** How many labor-hours should the eighth shaft require? **b.** How many labor-hours should the whole order for eight shafts require? **c.** If the labor rate is $19.00 per hour and the pricing policy of the company is to double the labor cost of the order, what is the customer price for each shaft? **d.** Trouble is encountered on the order, and it is obvious that the original estimate was too low because it took 90 labor-hours for the third shaft. The company wants to approach the customer with a revised price for the order. What should the new customer price be for the whole order?

Solution

a. How many labor-hours should the eighth shaft require?
First, look up the unit time for Unit No. 8 in Table 18.12. This value is 0.512, and the labor-hours for the eighth shaft are:

$$\text{Labor-hours for eighth unit} = \left(\begin{array}{c}\text{Labor-hours} \\ \text{for first} \\ \text{unit}\end{array}\right) \times \left(\begin{array}{c}\text{Unit time} \\ \text{for Unit} \\ \text{No. 8}\end{array}\right)$$

$$= 100 \times 0.512 = 51.2 \text{ labor-hours}$$

b. How many labor-hours should the whole order for eight shafts require?
First, look up the total time for Unit No. 8 in Table 18.12. This value is 5.346, and the labor-hours for the whole order are:

$$\text{Labor-hours for whole order} = \left(\begin{array}{c}\text{Labor-hours} \\ \text{for first} \\ \text{unit}\end{array}\right) \times \left(\begin{array}{c}\text{Total time} \\ \text{for Unit} \\ \text{No. 8}\end{array}\right)$$

$$= 100 \times 5.346 = 534.6 \text{ labor-hours.}$$

c. If the labor rate is $19.00 per hour and the pricing policy of the company is to double the labor cost of the order, what is the customer price for each shaft?

$$\text{Labor cost for order} = \left(\begin{array}{c}\text{Labor-hours} \\ \text{for order}\end{array}\right) \times \left(\begin{array}{c}\text{Labor} \\ \text{rate per} \\ \text{hour}\end{array}\right)$$

$$= 534.6 \times \$19.00 = \$10,157.40$$

Next, double the labor cost to obtain the customer price for the whole order:

$$\text{Price for order} = 2 \times \text{Labor cost for order}$$
$$= 2 \times \$10,157.40 = \$20,314.80$$

Table 18.12 | Learning-Curve Coefficients

	75%		80%		85%		90%	
Unit No.	Unit Time	Total Time	Unit Time	Total Time	Unit Time	Total Time	Unit Time	Total Time
1	1.000	1.000	1.000	1.000	1.000	1.000	1.000	1.000
2	.750	1.750	.800	1.800	.850	1.850	.900	1.900
3	.634	2.384	.702	2.502	.773	2.623	.846	2.746
4	.562	2.946	.640	3.142	.723	3.345	.810	3.556
5	.513	3.459	.596	3.738	.686	4.031	.783	4.339
6	.475	3.934	.562	4.229	.657	4.688	.762	5.101
7	.446	4.380	.534	4.834	.634	5.322	.744	5.845
8	.422	4.802	.512	5.346	.614	5.936	.729	6.574
9	.402	5.204	.493	5.839	.597	6.533	.716	7.290
10	.385	5.589	.477	6.315	.583	7.116	.705	7.994
11	.370	5.958	.462	6.777	.570	7.686	.695	8.689
12	.357	6.315	.449	7.227	.558	8.244	.685	9.374
13	.345	6.660	.438	7.665	.548	8.792	.677	10.05
14	.334	6.994	.428	8.092	.539	9.331	.670	10.72
15	.325	7.319	.418	8.511	.530	9.861	.663	11.38
16	.316	7.635	.410	8.920	.522	10.38	.656	12.04
17	.309	7.944	.402	9.322	.515	10.90	.650	12.69
18	.301	8.245	.394	9.716	.508	11.41	.644	13.33
19	.295	8.540	.387	10.10	.501	11.91	.639	13.97
20	.288	8.828	.381	10.49	.495	12.40	.634	14.61
21	.283	9.111	.375	10.86	.490	12.89	.630	15.24
22	.277	9.388	.370	11.23	.484	13.38	.625	15.86
23	.272	9.660	.364	11.59	.479	13.86	.621	16.48
24	.267	9.928	.359	11.95	.475	14.33	.617	17.10
25	.263	10.19	.355	12.31	.470	14.80	.613	17.71
30	.244	11.45	.335	14.02	.450	17.09	.596	20.73
35	.229	12.62	.318	15.64	.434	19.29	.583	23.67
40	.216	13.72	.305	17.19	.421	21.43	.571	26.54
45	.206	14.77	.294	18.68	.410	23.50	.561	29.37
50	.197	15.78	.284	20.12	.400	25.51	.552	32.14
60	.183	17.67	.268	22.89	.383	29.41	.537	37.57
70	.172	19.43	.255	25.47	.369	33.17	.524	42.87
80	.162	21.09	.244	27.96	.358	36.80	.514	48.05
90	.155	22.67	.235	30.35	.348	40.32	.505	53.14
100	.148	24.18	.227	32.65	.340	43.75	.497	58.14
120	.137	27.02	.214	37.05	.326	50.39	.483	67.93
140	.129	29.67	.204	41.22	.314	56.78	.472	77.46
160	.122	32.17	.195	45.20	.304	62.95	.462	86.80
180	.116	34.54	.188	49.03	.296	68.95	.454	95.96
200	.111	36.80	.182	52.72	.289	74.79	.447	105.0
250	.101	42.08	.169	61.47	.274	88.83	.432	126.9
300	.094	46.94	.159	69.66	.263	102.2	.420	148.2
350	.088	51.48	.152	77.43	.253	115.1	.411	169.0
400	.083	55.75	.145	84.85	.245	127.6	.402	189.3
450	.079	59.80	.140	91.97	.239	139.7	.395	209.2
500	.076	63.68	.135	98.85	.233	151.5	.389	228.8
600	.070	70.97	.128	112.0	.223	174.2	.378	267.1
700	.066	77.77	.121	124.4	.215	196.1	.369	304.5
800	.062	84.18	.116	136.3	.209	217.3	.362	341.0
900	.059	90.26	.112	147.7	.203	237.9	.356	376.9
1,000	.057	96.07	.108	158.7	.198	257.9	.350	412.2
1,200	.053	107.0	.102	179.7	.190	296.6	.340	481.2
1,400	.050	117.2	.097	199.6	.183	333.9	.333	548.4
1,600	.047	126.8	.093	218.6	.177	369.9	.326	614.2
1,800	.045	135.9	.090	236.8	.173	404.9	.320	678.8
2,000	.043	144.7	.087	254.4	.168	438.9	.315	742.3
2,500	.039	165.0	.081	296.1	.160	520.8	.304	897.0
3,000	.036	183.7	.076	335.2	.153	598.9	.296	1,047.0

Next, divide the customer price for the whole order by the number of units in the order to obtain a per-unit price:

$$\text{Price per shaft} = (\text{Price for order}) \div (\text{Units in order})$$
$$= \$20,314.80 \div 8 = \$2,539.35$$

d. What should the customer price be for the whole order if the third unit took 90 labor-hours? First, compute a revised value for the first unit. The unit time for Unit No. 3 in Table 18.12 is 0.702:

$$\text{Labor-hours for third unit} = \begin{pmatrix} \text{Labor-hours} \\ \text{for first} \\ \text{unit} \end{pmatrix} \times \begin{pmatrix} \text{Unit time} \\ \text{for Unit} \\ \text{No. 3} \end{pmatrix} = 90$$

$$= \begin{pmatrix} \text{Labor-hours} \\ \text{for first} \\ \text{unit} \end{pmatrix} \times 0.702 = 90$$

Labor-hours for first unit = 90/0.702 = 128.21 labor-hours

Next, compute the labor-hours for the whole order by using the new 128.21 estimate for the labor-hours for the first unit:

$$\text{Labor-hours for whole unit} = \begin{pmatrix} \text{Labor-hours} \\ \text{for first} \\ \text{unit} \end{pmatrix} \times \begin{pmatrix} \text{Total time} \\ \text{at No. 8} \\ \text{Unit} \end{pmatrix}$$

$$= 128.21 \times 5.346 = 685.41 \text{ labor-hours}$$

Next, compute the new customer price on the whole order by doubling the labor cost for the whole order:

$$\text{Customer price for order} = 2 \times 685.41 \text{ labor-hours} \times \$19.00 = \$26,045.58$$

Selecting a Learning Rate

How does a firm select a learning rate for a particular operation? In many firms, production analysts are trained to analyze an operation and fit a learning rate to that operation. They read trade journals that publish industry-wide data on specific types of operations and their learning rates. Also, they compare historical records with learning rates within their own companies and categorize their operations according to established learning rates. When new operations require learning-rate estimates, the analysts can compare these operations to existing operations with known learning rates within their own companies, or they can fit the new operations to industry standards.

Uses and Limitations of Learning Curves

Experienced operations managers know that as production personnel gain experience with a new product/service or operation, the labor-hours per unit fall. Consequently, labor standards are expected to decline on many products and operations, and cost standards, budgets, production scheduling, staffing plans, and prices are necessarily affected.

In job shops and custom service operations, learning-curve theory is very important because:

1. Products and services tend to be custom designs that require workers to start near the beginning of small batches.
2. Batches tend to be small; thus, labor-hours per unit improve dramatically from the first to the last unit.
3. Product/service designs tend to be complex; thus labor-hours per unit improve quickly.

The application of learning curves to mass production and standard service operations is less significant because entirely new products or services are rare, and long production runs and simplified tasks combine to cause labor-hours per unit to improve only slightly.

Staff specialists routinely use learning-curve theory to develop labor cost estimates for new products and services. For example, for companies that produce products for the U.S. military, NASA, and companies outside their own firms, learning curves are routinely used to estimate the amount of labor that will be required on each contract. This use allows the companies to prepare cost estimates and product prices for bidding purposes.

Applying learning curves in practice can be difficult because:

1. It may be impossible either to develop precise labor-hour estimates for the first unit or to determine the appropriate learning rate. Large unique projects exhibit both of these difficulties.
2. Different workers have different learning rates. In a pure sense, learning theory applies only to individual workers, but little difficulty is encountered in applying learning curves to groups of workers by developing an **average learning rate.** But we can get into trouble when we apply learning curves to further aggregations such as direct labor cost per unit, indirect labor cost per unit, material cost per unit, or even the labor-hours in a production department. Although these aggregations may be observed to improve as output increases, we must remember that individual workers learn and materials and machines do not. Application of learning curves to these aggregate measures must therefore be based on substantial evidence of improvement.
3. Few products are completely unique. Workers are usually well trained in the completion of tasks within their skill classifications. Past performance on related tasks therefore results in latent learning that is transferred to new products and services. As lot sizes are reduced through JIT programs, workers will produce about the same number of parts annually, but in many more and smaller lots. How much learning is carried over from lot to lot, and what does the concept of a first unit mean in this setting?

These and other difficulties cause us to use great care in applying learning curves.

EMPLOYEES' HEALTH AND SAFETY

Hazards are inherent in most jobs. Employees can fall on slippery floors; fall from ladders; walk into protrusions; get parts of their clothing or bodies caught in belts, gears, cutting tools, dies, and drill presses; be hit by flying pieces from grinding wheels and metal chips from lathes; and so on. Elevator shafts, stairs, balconies, heavy moving equipment, trucks, fires, explosions, high-voltage electricity, molten metals, toxic chem-

Many government laws and regulations exist to protect employees from workplace hazards, and managers must be careful that operations are in compliance with these statutes.

© DAVID H. WELLS/CORBIS

icals, noxious fumes, dust, and noise—all pose dangers to employees. These and other hazards have always been around. They are not new. What perhaps is new is the growing body of government laws and regulations intended to provide employees with uniformly safe working conditions across all states, industries, and companies.

In modern times, management has been concerned about the safety and health of employees. This concern was evident in the establishment of safety and loss prevention departments early in this century before laws rigidly forced employers to comply with government-imposed safety standards. The personnel management movement in the early 1900s and the human relations movement in the 1940s both contributed to this development. These movements emphasized the necessity to protect employees on the job and directly contributed to the growing number of formal safety programs in government and industry.

Two sets of laws have also critically affected employees' health and safety: the workers' compensation laws and the Occupational Safety and Health Administration Act (OSHA). During the early 1900s, states gradually passed workers' compensation laws. These laws provided for specific compensation amounts going to employees for various types of injuries incurred on the job. Employees no longer were required to bring suit through the courts and prove negligence by employers. Additionally, employers were protected by the maximum limitation on these settlements, and the number of court suits was reduced.

Although workers' compensation laws went a long way toward compensating employees after they were injured on the job, three facts detracted from their effectiveness in ensuring safe working conditions:

1. Because the laws varied greatly among states and industries, this patchwork of regulations created great gaps in coverage and extreme variation in compensation for similar injuries.
2. Inflation and the enormous rise in the cost of health care have made compensation amounts of most of these laws inadequate.
3. The laws do not strike directly at the heart of the worker health and safety problem— creating a safe work environment for employees.

These and other deficiencies of the workers' compensation laws and other contemporary developments led to the passage in 1971 of the **Occupational Safety and Health Administration (OSHA) Act.** OSHA established a federal agency whose primary functions were to set safety standards for all areas of the work environment for all industries and to enforce these standards through an inspection and reporting system. This law officially recognized, perhaps for the first time, the basic right of all employees to a safe working environment regardless of the state, industry, or firm in which they worked.

No company is beyond the reach of OSHA. Its inspectors routinely call on employers, conduct inspections, identify unsafe working conditions or violations of OSHA standards, and require employer corrective actions, and the law can force compliance through the courts with fines and even criminal prosecution. OSHA is indeed a potential force with which management must deal.

OSHA is charged with trying to protect the safety and health of 105 million U.S. workers at 6.9 million work sites. During the three decades OSHA has been in existence, job-related deaths have decreased by half. According to a recent study, in the three years following an OSHA inspection that results in penalties, the number of injuries and illnesses drops on average by 22 percent. Overall injury and illness rates have declined in the industries where OSHA has concentrated its attention—yet have remained unchanged or have actually increased in the industries where OSHA has had less presence. Despite OSHA's efforts, every year more than 6,000 Americans die from workplace injuries, an estimated 50,000 people die from illnesses caused by workplace chemical exposures, and 6 million people suffer nonfatal workplace injuries. According to OSHA, injuries alone cost the U.S. economy more than $110 billion a year.[8]

Cities, counties, and states also participate in regulating and/or inspecting the safety of working conditions of operations. In California, for example, a manufactur-

---

BUSINESS SNAPSHOT 18.3

Dramatic Safety Improvements at Georgia-Pacific

At one time, you weren't considered a real Georgia-Pacific mill employee unless you were missing a few fingers. Now, after a corporate makeover, safety comes first.

The forest products industry has historically experienced a high rate of employee accidents, partly due to the use of cutting tools, heavy equipment, and the heavy weight of logs and some wood products. Seven years ago the 241 plants and mills operated by Georgia-Pacific had a terrible safety record. With more than 47,000 employees, each year there were 9 serious injuries per 100 employees, and during the previous five years 26 employees lost their lives on the job.

The safety situation began to change, however, when Pete Correll took over as president and chief operating officer of Georgia-Pacific (GP). After a six-year company-wide safety crusade, GP has recorded the best safety record in the industry for the past four years. Last year, 80 percent of its plants operated without any injuries, and best of all, nobody died anywhere. GP's serious injury accident rate last year was less than 3 injuries per 100 employees, after decreasing in each of the previous six years.

With a goal of zero accidents, GP continues to train its employees about safe practices and is trying to find new ways to provide a safer working environment.

Source: Fisher, Anne. "Danger Zone." *Fortune,* September 8, 1997, 165–167.

ing plant can expect inspections concerning fire hazards on a regular basis from these sources: (1) in-plant inspectors, (2) division and corporate inspectors, (3) city fire marshal, (4) county fire marshal, (5) state fire marshal, (6) OSHA, (7) insurance carriers, and (8) union inspectors. These and other sources of regulation of operations form a network of worker safety protection that should provide continual diligence in designing jobs that are safe for employees.

Experienced managers know, however, that employees can still be injured and their health damaged. Managers therefore establish **safety and loss prevention departments.** Not only do these departments interface with all the sources of safety inspections, but these specialists also design safety devices and procedures aimed at protecting employees, raise employee awareness, and design advertising programs to minimize hazards resulting from human error. These and other activities are undertaken not just because it is the law, but because it is also the right and ethical thing to do. And besides—it is good business. When working conditions are safe, employee morale and labor productivity tend to be higher and the direct costs of accidents tend to be lower. Therefore, management has a large stake in maintaining a safe working environment for employees. Business Snapshot 18.3 describes safety improvements at Georgia-Pacific.

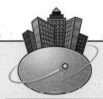

Wrap-Up
WHAT WORLD-CLASS COMPANIES DO

As they strive to capture world markets, world-class companies recognize that their employees are of both strategic and tactical importance. Employees are of strategic importance because they directly affect product costs, product quality, customer satisfaction, and the successful implementation of such strategic initiatives as installing high-tech productions systems, JIT, and TQM. In fact, business strategies are carried out *by* employees. But employees are also of tactical importance: The everyday activities of getting customers' orders out on time within cost and quality standards must be done by employees.

Mass production has traditionally meant that production workers did tiny bits of work that was so specialized that little mental ability or training was needed. For a long time the system of mass production worked: Costs were low and quality was acceptable. But these systems were so inflexible that customers were neglected and worker attitudes deteriorated until costs shot up and product quality was no longer good enough.

World-class companies have taken a different approach. Now workers are hired who have problem-solving abilities and they are trained, cross-trained, educated, and empowered so that they can work in teams to solve production problems and be ready to change things to respond to customers' needs. These companies may apply 5 to 10 percent of their total labor expenditures to training and educating employees. Additionally, an organizational structure and climate are developed that encourage the full use of employees. The payoff is increased productivity, improved product quality, and increased responsiveness to customer needs—all essential for companies that aspire to be world class.

To attain significant improvements in labor productivity takes more than motivated workers. Quality must be improved, and they must have the latest machines, tools, and production technology with which to work. Also, products must be designed for manufacturability. World-class companies have invested heavily in state-of-the-art manufacturing technology. Employees are the key to successful introduction of this advanced technology, and their skills and education must be upgraded if these advanced production systems are to be effective. This underscores the necessity of training, communication, and the creation of a collaborative organizational climate in which individual and group initiative is encouraged. In this way, advanced production technology creates the need for innovative ways of developing and managing employees.

For world-class companies, information is the main medium of management. All intelligent managerial action is based on information. Scientifically developed labor standards are used to great advantage as production is planned and controlled, costs are estimated, accounting labor standards are set, and prices of products are established. In their crusade to continuously improve every facet of their operations, world-class companies use accurate labor standards as one of the benchmarks to gauge their progress.

REVIEW AND DISCUSSION QUESTIONS

1. Describe the general attitudes of employees in industry toward their work. What explanation can you give for these attitudes?
2. Define *productivity*. How should we measure productivity? Why should companies today be particularly concerned with productivity?
3. Given the makeup of production costs of U.S. manufacturers today, which resources should receive the focus of productivity improvement programs? Why?
4. Explain why a multifactor approach to measuring productivity is needed.
5. What three variables affect labor productivity? Under what conditions should we expect employees whose needs are satisfied to be productive?
6. Describe Maslow's hierarchy of needs. What meaning does the hierarchy have for today's operations managers?
7. Make three suggestions for each of these:
   a. Modifying employees' job tasks to improve employees' needs for self-control.
   b. Modifying employees' immediate job settings to make jobs more satisfying.
   c. Modifying employees' larger work environments to make jobs more satisfying.
8. Define *job design*.
9. What two criteria must be used to evaluate proposals to remedy job design?

10. Name three key obstacles to achieving the integration of employees' needs with productivity in job design.
11. What are union work rules? Give examples of work rules, and explain how they affect productivity.
12. What is *worker empowerment?* What is *internal ownership?* What role do these two concepts play in today's world-class companies?
13. Define and explain the questioning attitude of methods analysis.
14. Name three techniques of methods analysis.
15. Define *work measurement*. What is the universal unit of measure in work measurement?
16. Name three uses of work sampling.
17. Discuss the role of time study, work sampling, and other techniques in designing jobs.
18. As the number of aircraft doubles in production runs, what happens to the labor-hours per unit?
19. Why are learning curves perhaps more beneficial in job shops, custom services, and other intermittent production systems?
20. Give three reasons why problems can be encountered in using learning curves. Explain why care must be taken in applying learning curves to material costs, overhead costs, and departmental labor costs.
21. Describe the role of OSHA.

INTERNET ASSIGNMENTS

1. Visit and explore the Internet site for the Bureau of Labor Statistics (**http://stats.bls.gov**). Find and discuss the most recent quarterly and annual productivity growth rates for different sectors of the U.S. economy.

2. For many decades, Massachusetts Institute of Technology (MIT) has operated the Laboratory for Manufacturing and Productivity (LMP). One area of research within this laboratory is Design and Operation of Manufacturing Systems. Visit and explore MIT's web site for its LMP (**http://web.mit.edu/lmp/www/**). Briefly describe one of the research projects currently under way in the research area of Design and Operation of Manufacturing Systems.

3. Founded in 1977, the American Productivity & Quality Center (APQC) is a nonprofit education and research organization supported by hundreds of organizations. Its purpose is to help enterprises manage change, improve processes, leverage knowledge, and increase performance by becoming more agile, creative, and competitive. Visit and explore APQC's Internet site (**http://www.apqc.org**). List several large companies that are members/supporters of APQC. Explain how benchmarking might help companies to increase their productivity.

4. Visit and explore the Internet site of the Occupational Safety and Health Administration (OSHA) at **http://www.osha.gov**. Find and summarize OSHA's mission. Locate and explore information on the OSHA Act of 1970. How many sections are there in this congressional act?

PROBLEMS

1. Sandi Castillo is Superesearch Pharmaceuticals's sales manager for the western region. Thirty-four salespersons report to Sandi and sell pharmaceuticals to retail chains and stores throughout 11 western states. During the past five years, Sandi has put together a team of salespersons that is second to none in its ability to cooperate. These salespersons appear to be happy with their jobs in all respects, including pay, supervision, attitude toward the company, and morale. Sandi feels that she has done everything in her power to make each salesperson in her group happy with his or her particular job.

    In recent months, Superesearch's sales in the western region have declined 10 percent when compared to comparable periods in the past. Sandi has racked her brain to come up with some reason, such as decline in the overall economy or competitor activity, to explain the sales decline. After much investigation, however, Sandi has concluded that there has been a drop-off in productivity among the salespersons because of lack of motivation.

    a. Use motivation theory to explain how employees who are happy with their jobs could be unproductive.

    b. What was Sandi doing wrong?

    c. What should Sandi do to correct this situation? Give the specific steps that she should follow in improving the productivity of the western region sales staff.

2. Force One Inc. manufactures hydraulic valve assemblies in Lexington, Kentucky. Force One's industrial engineering department has been successful in designing assembly line jobs that are highly specialized and technically efficient. The assembly line at Force One is so refined, in fact, that its labor cost per unit is lower than that of any of its competitors in spite of its workers receiving the highest average annual pay in the industry. When Force One's workers were recently interviewed by a national television commentator, their comments were:

- We like working at Force One; we wouldn't work anywhere else.
- The pay is good, and besides we like the way management treats us.
- Our foremen are great guys; you know we work hard, but you can depend on them giving you a square deal and they stick up for you.
- If you screw up, they don't crucify you; sure, they point out what we did wrong and tell us to avoid the problem in the future, but they don't make a federal case out of it.
- When we do a good job, they're down here in a hurry to let us know that they appreciate the good work.
- If we've got a problem, we can walk right in to the boss's office and level with him. That gets results around here. And if he's got a rush order that needs to be produced and shipped quick, he'll come right down on the line and talk to us about it. We appreciate the way we can talk openly around here. It's a two-way street, you know?
- Sure, the work on the assembly line can get monotonous, but taking everything into consideration, this is the best job I've ever had.
- Quality is good, absenteeism is low, and turnover is low around here. Why not? It's a good place to work.

a. Are these workers satisfied with their jobs? Explain how these workers are satisfying their physiological, safety, social, esteem, and self-fulfillment needs.

b. Why haven't the monotonous assembly line jobs at Force One resulted in high absenteeism, high turnover, and low product quality?

c. A new personnel manager at Force One insists that he expects absenteeism and turnover to increase as new, younger workers with a lower tolerance for job boredom are gradually hired into the plant. What job-design remedies should be tested at Force One? Justify your proposals.

3. Vince Lundberg manages a medium-size garment factory in San Diego, California. Worker turnover and absenteeism have plagued his operation during the two years he has been plant manager. The cost of hiring new workers and having standby workers to fill in for absent workers is excessive. With the help of some personnel and engineering persons from the home office in Gary, Indiana, the following estimates of cost savings and cost increases from alternative job-design remedies were made:

Job-Design Remedy	Average Per-Unit Cost Increase Due to Reduced Technical Efficiency	Average Per-Unit Cost Savings Due to Reduced Turnover and Absenteeism
Job rotation	$0.081	$0.105
Job enrichment	0.072	0.112
Time away from jobs	0.058	0.097
Supervisor training	0.095	0.116

a. If only one of the proposals can be accepted, rank the remedies in order of desirability.

b. Should Vince reassign his industrial engineers to another plant because time studies will no longer be needed?

c. Are the above remedies mutually exclusive; that is, in practice can only one of the remedies be applied at a time? What are some likely combinations?

4. Prepare a flow diagram for going to your dentist for a checkup, including x-rays and cleaning.

5. Prepare a flow diagram for going to a Christmas tree lot, buying a tree, bringing it home, and decorating it.

6. Prepare a process chart for going to your dentist for a checkup, including x-rays and cleaning.

7. Prepare a process chart for going to a Christmas tree lot, buying a tree, bringing it home, and decorating it.

8. Prepare a flow diagram and process chart for making a pot of coffee in your kitchen.

9. Examine your school's procedures for registering and paying for classes. Prepare a process chart for the present method and one for an improved method. Discuss the advantages and disadvantages of your improved method, for both students and the school.

Time Study

10. In a time study of a manufacturing operation, the average time to complete a product was 36.5 minutes, the performance rating was 1.20, and the allowances were 60 minutes per eight-hour shift.
    a. Compute a labor standard for the operation.
    b. How many products per eight-hour shift should an experienced operator be expected to produce under ordinary operating conditions?
    c. If the labor rate is $15 per hour, what should the accounting department use as the standard labor cost per product?

11. A time study of a postal sorting operation yielded an average time of 4.75 minutes per hundred letters sorted, a performance rating of 1.1, and allowances of 80 minutes per 8-hour shift.
    a. Compute a labor standard for the letter sorting operation.
    b. If a postal employee performed only this operation, how many hundreds of letters per eight-hour shift could be sorted under ordinary operating conditions?
    c. If the labor rate is $15 per hour, what should the accounting department use as the standard labor cost per hundred letters?

12. A worker on an assembly line performs a certain task on products several times each hour. A time study shows that the average time spent by the worker on each product is 7.80 minutes per product. The performance rating is 1.35, and allowances are 53 minutes per eight-hour shift.
    a. Compute the labor standard for the operation.
    b. If the worker performed only this task repeatedly, how many products per eight-hour shift could be completed under ordinary operating conditions?
    c. If the worker's labor rate is $14.75 per hour, what should the accounting department use as the standard labor cost per product?

13. A time study is performed on an operation, resulting in the data following (in minutes).

Element	Cycle 1	2	3	4	5	6	7	8	Performance Rating
1. Get and position unit	0.22	0.27	0.19	0.24	0.17	0.24	0.21	0.18	1.10
2. Perform calibration	2.20	2.70	2.50	3.10	2.80	2.40	3.20	2.70	1.30
3. Perform standard tests	4.60	4.00	4.50	3.80	4.30	4.50	3.90	4.40	0.85
4. Update card and remove unit	0.50	0.50	0.70	0.60	0.80	0.40	0.50	0.60	1.20

Allowance per Eight-Hour Shift:

Clothes change	15 minutes
Unavoidable delay	35
Lunch	30
Shower and change	30
Total	110 minutes

a. Compute the mean observed time for each element in minutes.
b. Compute the normal time for each element and total normal time in minutes.
c. Compute the allowance fraction for the operation. Assume 480 minutes per shift.
d. Compute the labor standard for the operation.

14. A production operation is repeated three times for each product by a worker. The data below came from a time study of the operations.

Element	Cycle 1	2	3	4	5	6	7	8	9	10	Performance Rating
1	0.13	0.09	0.10	0.13	0.11	0.08	0.12	0.14	0.11	0.10	1.15
2	0.38	0.29	0.31	0.27	0.35	0.33	0.28	0.29	0.34	0.30	0.95
3	0.21	0.20	0.26	0.22	0.19	0.18	0.24	0.23	0.20	0.24	1.20
4	0.45	0.57	0.50	0.54	0.46	0.49	0.44	0.55	0.52	0.48	1.05
5		0.52		0.59		0.50		0.48		0.53	0.90
6	0.32	0.38	0.42	0.37	0.40	0.35	0.39	0.33	0.42	0.38	1.00

Allowance per Eight-Hour Shift:

Clothes change	10 minutes
Unavoidable delay	30
Rest periods	20
Area cleanup	10
Change	10
Total	80 minutes

a. Compute the labor standard for this operation.
b. If the labor rate is $16.55 an hour, what is the accounting standard labor cost per product for the operations?
c. How many times should the worker be expected to perform the operation during each eight-hour shift?

Work Sampling

15. The allowances at a manufacturing operation are 60 minutes per 10-hour shift. If a work sampling study of the allowances is to be performed with a 95 percent confidence interval and a ±3 percent absolute error is acceptable, how many work-sampling observations are required?

16. Currently a production operation has 108 minutes of allowances during each 12-hour shift. A work-sampling study of the allowances for the operation is to be conducted. If a 95 percent confidence interval and a ± 2 percent absolute error are acceptable, how many work-sampling observations are required?

17. An industrial engineer is performing a time study and knows that 70 minutes are normally devoted to rest periods and lunch, but an allowance for unavoidable delay must be estimated. A ratio-delay work-sampling study was conducted, with the following results:

Activity	Number of Observations
Unavoidable delay	38
Avoidable delay	66
Other	446
Total:	550

What allowance fraction should be used in setting the labor standard if allowances include unavoidable delay, lunch, and rest periods? Assume 480 minutes per shift.

18. A work-sampling study was conducted of an assembly operation. The results of the study are:

Activity	Percentage of Workers' Time
Assemble products	85%
Allowances	15

If the workers who were performing the operation during the study each produced an average of 100 products per eight-hour shift and received a performance rating of 1.15, what is the labor standard per product?

19. A work-sampling study was conducted for a production operation over a 40-hour week. During the study the operator completed 580 finished products and was assessed a 0.90 performance rating while working. The results of the study were:

Activity	Number of Observations
Production	492
Avoidable delay*	63
Rest periods*	45

*Included in allowances.

a. Determine the total normal time per product.
b. Determine the labor standard per product.

Incentive Pay Systems

20. An employee in an incentive plan has just completed a one-week pay period. The information on her time card is:

Total hours worked = 44 hours
Total production = 340 units
Labor standard per unit = 8.15 minutes
Hourly base pay = $15.60 per hour

If the company uses the following formula to compute actual hourly pay, what is the employee's pay for the period?

$$\text{Actual hourly pay} = \frac{\text{(Hourly base pay)(Units produced)(Labor standard)}}{\text{Minutes worked}}$$

21. A new employee is a machinist in a machine shop. The company has installed a straight piece-rate incentive pay system for its employees. A two-week pay period has just ended, and the employee is estimating her pay for the period from this information:

    Total production = 155 units
    Labor standard per unit = 29.75 minutes
    Hourly base pay = $15.60 per hour

    a. Compute the employee's piece rate for this product.
    b. Compute her pay for the period.

22. A production worker has finished a week of assembling products at a manufacturing plant. The operation that he performs is included in a piece-rate compensation plan at the plant. He has just completed his production and time record to be turned in to his supervisor, and he wants to determine what his pay is for the week. His production and time record includes this information:

    Production for week = 595 products
    Labor standard per product = 5.52 minutes
    Hourly base pay = $15 per hour

    a. Compute the worker's piece rate per product.
    b. Compute the worker's pay for the week.

23. The first product through a production operation takes 24 minutes, and an 85 percent learning rate is expected.
    a. Estimate the time it will take to produce the third product.
    b. Estimate the total time it will take to produce the first 20 products.

24. It takes a manufacturer 120 hours to produce the first product in a batch of 15 products, and a 75 percent learning rate is expected.
    a. Estimate the time it will take to produce the fourth product.
    b. Estimate the total time it will take to produce the entire batch.

25. A ceiling fan business just received a contract to install 70 ceiling fans in a new apartment complex. In his bid for the contract, the store owner estimated that the first ceiling fan would take 110 minutes to install. The owner also expected a 90 percent learning rate.
    a. How long should the owner have expected it would take to install the 10th ceiling fan only?
    b. How long should the owner have expected it would take to install all 70 ceiling fans?
    c. The first 10 ceiling fans have now been installed, and the owner wants to reevaluate how long the job will take. As it turned out, the first ceiling fan required 130 minutes to install and the 10th fan required 75.8 minutes to install. What is the actual learning rate that has been experienced? Using this actual learning rate, estimate the total time required for all 70 ceiling fans.

26. A machine shop has received an order to manufacture 10 large drum rollers. After examining the design of the rollers, the production engineer expects 55 labor-

hours to be required for the first drum roller and a learning rate of 75 percent. The shop's standard charge (including overhead and profit) for this type of job is $60 per labor-hour required.

a. How many total labor-hours should this job require?

b. How much should the machine shop charge the customer for this order?

c. The customer has just called and would like to know how much it would be charged for an additional five drum rollers. How many additional labor-hours should this require? What should be the additional charge to the customer?

CASES

Caliber Bar Code Company

Caliber Bar Code Company manufactures a high-volume bar code printer that is sold all over the world. Caliber's U.S. production facility is located in Boise, Idaho, and serves all of the Americas and East Asia. Ben Sharma is the new plant manager at the Boise plant and is now confronted with a problem left over from his predecessor—low productivity within the shell finishing operation. This operation removes excess plastic material from the outer shell of the bar code printers so that the units can be properly assembled. It is imperative to increase the output of this operation because it is the bottleneck operation for the entire assembly line of the plant. In fact, the shell finishing operation's present production level is 25 percent below the capacity of all other operations on the assembly line. The excessive labor costs that result from underutilized personnel have caused the plant to operate in the red for several months and, furthermore, the plant's production level is inadequate to satisfy the demand of its customers.

Twelve employees per shift now staff this operation. In the distant past, the operation was performed totally by hand and the workers' pay was based on the number of pieces produced by the group per shift. The workers now say that they never liked the incentive pay system. About a year ago, some machines were installed in the operation as part of a plantwide program aimed at increasing plant capacity. It was estimated at the time that the production level of the operation would be increased by 30 percent. The number of employees in the group was reduced according to plan, the machines were installed, and the production levels did increase, but only by about 10 percent. About three months ago, when Mr. Sharma took over as plant manager, one of his first duties was to negotiate with the union representatives concerning the incentive pay system of the shell finishing operation, the only such system in the plant. The system was done away with, and the employees were placed on hourly rates in line with similar work in other areas of the plant. The negotiations went well, and all parties seemed satisfied with the outcome.

Mr. Sharma thought the change in the pay system would trigger higher production levels in the shell finishing operation, but the output remained below that of the other operations. Mr. Sharma met with the operation's employees as a group and individually to discuss the situation. Phyllis Jennings, the union steward for the plant and a member of the shell finishing group, candidly indicated that the working relations between the former plant manager and the group had been strained. She seemed open and cooperative, not at all the troublemaker described by the previous plant manager. Mr. Sharma spoke plainly to the group. "The plant is in trouble in terms of our profits. We can't produce enough products to satisfy our customers, and they are beginning to turn to our competitors. As I see it, the output of the shell finishing operations is presently at the center of our difficulties. Time studies indicate that we should be able to get another 25 percent of production per shift out of the operation with just a fair day's work for a fair day's pay. Can't we work together to get the production level of your operation up? If I can assist you in any way, my door is open. Just walk across and tell me your needs and we'll get going." The group did not deny that production levels of the operation could be substantially improved. No immediate response came from the group, but during the next two weeks several personal contacts were made between individuals and Mr. Sharma.

1. Timothy Grubbs walked into Mr. Sharma's office during an afternoon break and said that the shell finishing room was so hot the employees were all wrung out by the end of the shift. He thought that two or three fans would solve the problem. Mr. Sharma believed that the room was warm, perhaps a little warmer than some of the other operations' locations.
2. Hashem Assadullahi walked up to Mr. Sharma in the parking lot before work one morning and showed him his hands. His fingernails were torn and broken, and his hands had several nicks, scratches, and scrapes. He said that the new machines were chewing up the workers' hands. He felt that some of the new-type gloves that he had seen at a local store would solve the problem and asked Mr. Sharma if he would supply the gloves to the group.
3. Toya Banks came into the main office during an afternoon break and asked Mr. Sharma if he would come over to the shell finishing room. He accompanied her to a window on the west side of the room. She told him that the sun glared directly into the workers' eyes during the late afternoon and wondered if he would have a sunshade, blind, or awning installed.
4. Phyllis Jennings, the plant's union steward, entered Mr. Sharma's office during a morning break and asked him if he would support a plantwide Christmas party.

Assignment

1. Why is the production level depressed at the shell finishing operation? Discuss the possible reasons for the development of the problem.
2. What should Mr. Sharma do about the requests from the shell finishing group? Discuss the pros and cons of following your recommendations for responding to the requests. How are your recommendations directed toward the underlying problem?
3. What course of action should Mr. Sharma take to solve the problem of low productivity and to avoid its recurrence?

Integrated Products Corporation

A production analyst at Integrated Products Corporation (IPC) has just completed a time study of a quality control test. Here are the results of the study (in minutes):

			Cycle				Performance
Element	1	2	3	4	5	6	Rating
1. Get and place	0.25	0.19	0.18	0.21	0.24	0.20	1.20
2. Connect probes	0.40	0.45	0.36	0.34	0.41	0.43	1.10
3. Computer test	3.50	3.50	3.50	3.50	3.50	3.50	1.00
4. Record results	0.70	0.69	0.69	0.65	0.68	0.66	0.90

The analyst has determined that for an eight-hour shift the nonproductive time for the operation should be 20 minutes for unavoidable delay, 15 minutes for starting up the operation at the beginning of the shift, and 15 minutes for cleaning up and straightening up around the operation.

Assignment

1. Compute the labor standard for the operation.
2. How many tests should an experienced worker perform in an eight-hour shift under ordinary operating conditions?
3. If you were the operations manager in charge of this operation and the workers performing the test did fewer tests per shift than your answer to No. 2 above, what would you do?
4. How are the concepts of *normal speed* and *ordinary operating conditions* used in time studies? How do these concepts affect how you would use the labor standard developed in No. 1 above?
5. What is it about time studies that leaves workers and even some business students with a bad feeling? What could you as an operations manager do to help alleviate these feelings?

Springfield Motors

Springfield Motors specializes in maintaining vehicle fleets for organizations. Susan Barnes, the operations manager, just received word that Springfield Motors has been awarded a large contract to perform engine overhauls on 60 state highway department trucks. All trucks will be delivered tomorrow, and the entire job must be completed 40 working days later. Due to a no overtime policy, a lunch break, and a coffee break, a mechanic will be productive only 7.25 hours each day. A mechanic must individually perform a complete overhaul on a truck, without assistance from other mechanics. Ms. Barnes estimates that each mechanic assigned to the overhauls will require 22 hours for his or her first overhaul, with a 90% learning rate thereafter. A mechanic's labor rate is $25 per hour.

Assignment

1. Disregarding the 40-day time limit, how many working days would it take one mechanic to perform the engine overhauls for all 60 trucks?
2. How many completed overhauls can one mechanic perform in 40 working days?
3. How many mechanics should be required to complete all 60 overhauls in 40 working days? How many total labor-hours would be used? What would be the total labor cost?
4. If the state highway department would extend the job due date from 40 working days to 52 working days, how much should be the new total labor cost? Should Springfield Motors request this 12-day due date extension? How could Springfield Motors justify or negotiate this extension with the state highway department?

ENDNOTES

1. "The Promise of Productivity." *Business Week*, March 9, 1998, 28–30.
2. Ayres, Robert U. "Future Trends in Factory Automation." *Manufacturing Review* 1, no. 2 (June 1988): 96.
3. Pennar, Karen. "The Productivity Paradox." *Business Week*, June 6, 1988, 100–102.
4. **http://stats.bls.gov**.
5. Maslow, A. H. "A Theory of Human Motivation." *Psychological Review* (July 1943): 370–396.
6. Reguero, Miguel A. *An Economic Study of the Military Airframe Industry*, p. 213. Wright-Patterson Air Force Base, OH: Department of the Air Force, October 1957.
7. Hirschmann, Winfred B. "Profit from the Learning Curve." *Harvard Business Review* 42 (February 1964): 118.
8. **http://www.osha.gov**.

SELECTED BIBLIOGRAPHY

Abernathy, W. J. "The Limits of the Learning Curve." *Harvard Business Review* 52 (September–October 1974): 109–119.

Aft, Lawrence S. "The Need for Work Measurement: Some Observations on the Current State of Affairs in the Business World." *IIE Solutions* 29, no. 12 (December 1997): 16–19.

Aft, Lawrence S. *Work Measurement and Methods Improvement.* New York: John Wiley & Sons, 2000.

Andress, Frank J. "The Learning Curve as a Production Tool." *Harvard Business Review* 32 (January–February 1954): 87–95.

Atkinson, William. "The Impact of OSHA's New Ergonomics Standard." *Transportation and Distribution* 41, no. 8 (August 2000): 103–110.

Cascio, Wayne F. *Managing Human Resources: Productivity, Quality of Work Life, Profits.* New York: McGraw-Hill, 1995.

Dar-El, Ezey M. *Human Learning: From Learning Curves to Learning Organization.* Boston: Kluwer Academic Publishers, 2000.

DeNisi, Angelo S., and Ricky W. Griffin. *Human Resource Management.* Boston: Houghton Mifflin, 2001.

Gagnon, Eugene J. "How to Measure Work." *Material Handling Management* 55, no. 2 (February 2000): 71–77.

Goldsmith, Arthur H., Jonathan R. Veum, and William Darity, Jr. "Working Hard for the Money? Efficiency Wages and Worker Effort." *Journal of Economic Psychology* 21, no. 4 (August 2000): 351–385.

Hirschmann, Winfred B. "Profit from the Learning Curve." *Harvard Business Review* 42 (February 1964): 118.

Jorgensen, Karen. *Pay for Results: A Practical Guide to Effective Employee Compensation.* Santa Monica, CA: Merrit Publishing, 1996.

MacLeod, Dan. *The Ergonomics Edge: Improving Safety, Quality, and Productivity.* New York: John Wiley & Sons, 1997.

Martocchio, Joseph J. *Strategic Compensation: A Human Resource Management Approach*, 2nd ed. Upper Saddle River, NJ: Prentice Hall, 2000.

Meyers, Fred E., and James R. Stewart. *Motion and Time Study for Lean Manufacturing*, 3rd ed. Upper Saddle River, NJ: Prentice Hall, 2002.

Niebel, Benjamin W., and Andris Freivalds. *Methods, Standards, and Work Design*, 10th ed. Boston: WCB/McGraw-Hill, 1999.

Ost, Edward J. "Team-Based Pay: New Wave Strategic Incentives." *Sloan Management Review* (Spring 1990): 19–27.

Perry, Ian. "Creating & Empowering Effective Work Teams." *Management Services* 41, no. 7 (July 1997): 8–11.

Reguero, Miguel A. *An Economic Study of the Military Airframe Industry.* Wright-Patterson Air Force Base, OH: Department of the Air Force, October 1957.

Sarkis, Karen. "Safety in the Union Shop." *Occupational Hazards* 62, no. 3 (March 2000): 45–50.

Scott, Miriam B. "Ergonomic Evaluations Yield Happier, Healthier, More Productive Employees at Low Cost." *Employee Benefit Plan Review* 54, no. 9 (March 2000): 25–27.

Smith, Elizabeth A. *The Productivity Manual: Methods and Activities for Involving Employees in Productivity Improvement.* Houston, TX: Gulf Publishing, 1995.

Taylor, Tom. "How to Pay and Reward Multidiscipline Work Teams." *Journal of Compensation & Benefits* 12, no. 6 (May/June 1997): 30–33.

Topolosky, Paula S. *Linking Employee Satisfaction to Business Results.* New York: Garland Publishing, 2000.

U.S. Department of Labor, Occupational Health and Safety Administration. *All About OSHA.* OSHA publication No. 2056.

Yelle, Louis E. "The Learning Curve: Historical Review and Comprehensive Survey." *Decision Sciences* 10, no. 2 (April 1979): 302–328.

19

Maintenance Management

Introduction

Repair Programs
  Repair Crews, Standby Machines, and Repair Shops
  Breakdowns Trigger Repairs and Corrective Actions
  Early Parts-Replacement Policies
  Letting Workers Repair Their Own Machines

Preventive Maintenance (PM) Programs
  PM and Operations Strategies
  Automation and the Prominence of PM
  Scheduling PM Activities
  PM Database Requirements
  Modern Approaches to PM

Machine Reliability

Secondary Maintenance Department Responsibilities

Trends in Maintenance

Maintenance Issues in Service Organizations

Wrap-Up: What World-Class Companies Do

Review and Discussion Questions

Internet Assignments

Problems

Cases
  Integrated Products Corporation
  Roadrunner Coach

Endnote

Selected Bibliography

LEADING MANUFACTURERS ADOPT TOTAL PREVENTIVE MAINTENANCE

Today's leading manufacturers take a serious view toward preventive maintenance. They absolutely detest interruptions to production, so they adopt total preventive maintenance programs to try to avoid this problem. When a machine breaks down, a flashing red light goes off at the machine and production workers and repair specialists from maintenance departments work side by side to fix the machine fast so that production can resume. The breakdown also triggers another action: Coworkers meet after work to study the problem and devise a program for eliminating the malfunction as a cause of future breakdowns. Also, as workers change over their own machines to other products, they repair the machines or assist repair specialists in repairs. Workers perform preventive maintenance on their own machines as a morning ritual. They methodically run down checklists for their machines much as pilots and flight crews check out aircraft before taking off. They pay close attention as they operate the machines during the day, carefully listening for any hint of an impending malfunction. Machines are adjusted, serviced, and repaired before minor problems develop into larger problems that could interrupt production. This compulsion to avoid interruptions to production is shared by management and workers alike. The cornerstone of their total preventive maintenance programs is worker involvement.

The preceding account illustrates the importance of keeping production equipment adjusted, repaired, and in good operating condition. The reasons for this compulsion to have equipment in perfect operating condition are not only to avoid interruptions to production but also to keep production costs low, keep product quality high, maintain safe working conditions, and avoid late shipments to customers.

Equipment malfunctions in manufacturing and service industries have a direct impact on:

- **Production capacity.** Machines idled by breakdowns cannot produce; thus, the capacity of the system is reduced.
- **Production costs.** Workers idled by machine breakdowns cause labor costs per unit to climb. When machine malfunctions cause scrap products to be produced, unit labor and material costs increase. Also, maintenance department budgets include such costs as the costs of providing repair facilities, repair crews, preventive maintenance inspections, standby machines, and spare parts.
- **Product and service quality.** Poorly maintained equipment produces low-quality products.
- **Employee or customer safety.** Worn-out equipment is likely to fail at any moment, and these failures can cause injuries to workers.
- **Customer satisfaction.** When production equipment breaks down, products often cannot be produced according to the master production schedules. This means that customers may not receive products when promised.

To ensure better maintenance management, maintenance departments are developed within organizations. A maintenance manager typically is a plant engineer who reports to either a plant manager or a manufacturing manager. The organizational level of the department depends on the importance of maintenance to the organization. Maintenance departments are usually split into two groups: buildings and grounds, and equipment maintenance. Buildings and grounds can include workers such as electricians, welders, pipefitters, steamfitters, painters, glaziers, carpenters, millwrights, janitors, and groundskeepers. It is the responsibility of the building and grounds group to maintain the appearance and functional utility of all buildings, lawns, planting areas, parking lots, fences, and all other facilities from the interior of the buildings to the perimeter of the grounds. The equipment maintenance group can include such workers as mechanics, machinists, welders, oilers, electricians, instrument calibrators, and electronic technicians. It is the responsibility of the equipment maintenance group to provide equipment repair crews, shops for repairing equipment, and the appropriate level of preventive maintenance for the equipment.

The degree of technology of the production processes, the amount of investment in plant and equipment, the age of the buildings and equipment, and other factors will affect how maintenance departments are organized, the required worker skills, and the overall mission of maintenance departments.

For most organizations, maintenance activities are directed at both repairs and preventive maintenance. The scope of these maintenance activities is as follows:

- **Repairs.** When buildings and equipment break down, malfunction, or are otherwise damaged so that normal operations are hindered, they are repaired, mended, overhauled, and put back into operating condition. Repair activities are reactive; that is, they are performed *after* a malfunction has occurred. A malfunction is indicated when a piece of equipment will not operate, operates at a less than normal speed, produces products below quality standards, or when workers think that the equipment is about to malfunction. Repair crews and repair shops work together with production workers to get the machine or building back into operation as fast as possible so that the interruption to production is minimized. Standby machines and spare parts are often used to speed this process.

- **Preventive maintenance (PM).** Regularly scheduled inspections of buildings and all pieces of equipment are performed. At these times, machine adjustments, lubrication, cleaning, parts replacement, painting, and any needed repairs or overhauls are done. These activities are performed *before* the buildings or machines malfunction. The inspections and the needed repairs are usually performed during periods when the buildings and equipment are not needed for production. The inspection for a piece of equipment could be scheduled at a regular time interval, say, once a month, or after a certain number of operating hours, miles, or another measure of usage.

Operations managers make a trade-off between the amount of effort to expend on repairs and PM. As Figure 19.1 shows, some minimum amount of PM is necessary to provide the minimal amount of lubrication and adjustments to avoid a complete and imminent collapse of the production system. At this minimal level of PM, the cost of breakdowns, interruptions to production, and repairs is so high that total maintenance cost is beyond practical limits. Such a policy is simply a remedial policy: Fix the machines only when they break or will not operate any longer. As the PM effort is increased, breakdown and repair costs are reduced. The total maintenance cost is the sum of the PM and the breakdown and repair costs. At some point for each piece of equipment, additional spending for PM is uneconomical because PM costs climb faster than breakdown and repair costs fall. Conceptually, operations managers seek to find the optimal level of PM where total maintenance costs are at a minimum both for each piece of equipment and for the entire production system.

The trade-off between PM and repairs is not simple because more than just production costs are involved in the decision. Production capacity, product quality, employee and customer safety, and customer satisfaction are also involved. The more money spent on PM, the higher we would expect production capacity, product quality,

Figure 19.1	Total Maintenance Cost as a Function of Repair Cost and Preventive Maintenance Cost

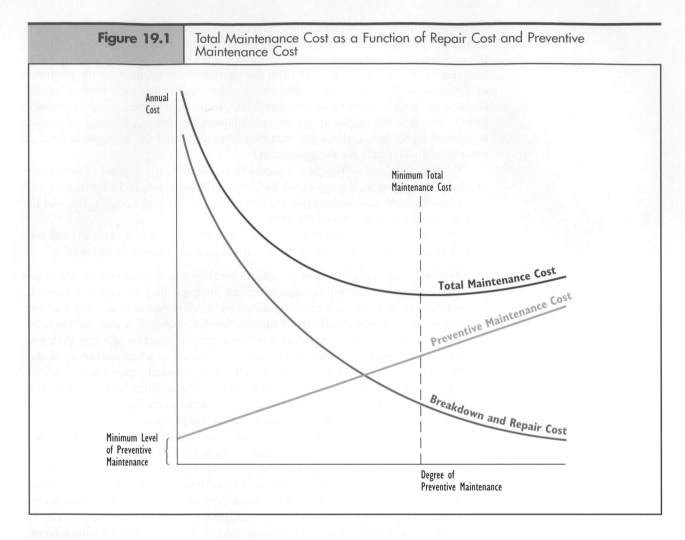

employee safety, and customer satisfaction to be. Moreover, the amount of PM effort expended may be fundamental to a company's operating strategies and the positioning strategies selected. For example, in product-focused firms or in firms that are highly automated, the breakdown of one piece of equipment can idle an entire production system. It is important to note that even in firms with flexible automation such as FMS, a single machine breakdown can shut down all or a major part of the production system. Also, cellular manufacturing layouts experience similar problems. Such firms may emphasize preventive maintenance to avoid frequent breakdowns.

Process-focused firms, however, may have an abundance of in-process inventories, and work centers are buffered from interruptions of production at upstream work centers. Such firms may emphasize efficient and prompt repair programs to avoid the severity of breakdowns. The choice of the appropriate mix of emphasis on repairs and preventive maintenance is, therefore, a function of a number of factors, and this decision has strategic implications for the firm.

As an overview of maintenance management, Table 19.1 describes some maintenance policies often used by operations managers to reduce both the frequency and the severity of malfunctions in buildings and equipment.

Enhancing preventive maintenance, providing extra machines so that all machines wear more slowly, replacing parts early, training operators in machine care, enhancing

| Table 19.1 | Maintenance Policies That Reduce Frequency and Severity of Malfunctions |

Maintenance Policies	Reduces Frequency of Malfunctions	Reduces Severity of Malfunctions
Emphasize preventive maintenance.	✓	✓
Provide extra machines, reduce utilization to reduce wear rate.	✓	
Replace parts early to reduce number of breakdowns.	✓	
Train operators and involve them in machine care.	✓	✓
Overdesign machines for durability, precision, and redundancy so that likelihood of breakdowns is reduced.	✓	
Design machines for maintainability, emphasizing modular designs, quick-change parts, and accessibility so that repairs can be made faster.		✓
Enhance maintenance department's capability: crew sizes, capacity of repair facilities, cross-training for personnel, flexibility, etc.	✓	✓
Increase supply of spare parts so that repairs can be made faster.		✓
Increase supply of standby or backup machines, devise alternative product routings, or arrange parallel production lines so that lost production is avoided in case of breakdowns.		✓
Increase in-process inventories.		✓

the maintenance department's capability, and overdesigning production machines are alternative policies to reduce the frequency of malfunctions. Preventive maintenance, involving operators in repairs, simplifying repairs through innovative machine designs, enhancing the maintenance department's capability, increasing the supply of spare parts and standby machines, and increasing in-process inventories are alternative policies used by operations managers to reduce the severity of malfunctions.

In the remainder of this chapter we explore repair programs and PM programs in more detail. We also learn about reliability, secondary maintenance department responsibilities, and trends in maintenance.

REPAIR PROGRAMS

Operations managers implement repair programs to achieve the following objectives:

1. To get equipment back into operation as quickly as possible in order to minimize interruptions to production. This objective can directly affect production capacity, production costs, product quality, and customer satisfaction.

Maintenance management considerations include both preventive and repair functions.

© ROGER RESSMEYER/CORBIS

2. To control the cost of repair crews, including straight-time and overtime labor costs.
3. To control the cost of the operation of repair shops.
4. To control the investment in replacement spare parts that are used when machines are repaired.
5. To control the investment in replacement spare machines, which are also called **standby** or **backup machines**. These replace malfunctioning machines until the needed repairs are completed.
6. To perform the appropriate amount of repairs at each malfunction. The decision about how far to go with a repair ranges from a "Band-Aid and bubble gum" fix to a complete overhaul. Some parts can be replaced early to extend the time until the next repair is required.

Repair Crews, Standby Machines, and Repair Shops

Production workers, repair specialists, spare parts and supplies, specialized tools and machines, repair shops, and standby machines are used to repair production equipment and buildings *after* malfunctions have occurred or when malfunctions are imminent. Repairs can be performed on an emergency basis to minimize interruptions to production, to correct unsafe working conditions, and to improve product quality. In these emergency situations, production workers and repair specialists may work overtime or they may be shifted from other, less critical projects. Maintenance supervisors and engineers are close at hand to collaborate with workers to make decisions as the repairs proceed. Malfunctioning machines may be quickly replaced by standby machines. The fundamental goal in repairs is to minimize the length of the interruption to production. Quick response times and fast repair jobs are therefore required.

Figure 19.2 illustrates how operations managers must trade off the cost of making repairs against the cost of interruptions to production. Large repair crews, the use of overtime to make repairs, maintaining large-capacity repair shops, and large supplies of spare parts and standby machines all work together to speed up repairs and reduce the cost of interruptions to production. As Figure 19.2 shows, however, a point is reached where the cost of speedy repairs is not offset by savings in interruptions to production. The fundamental challenge in managing repair programs is to balance the cost of repair crews, repair shops, spare parts, and standby machines against the need for speedy repairs.

Breakdowns Trigger Repairs and Corrective Actions

Ideally, an equipment malfunction should trigger two actions: first, a fast repair of the malfunction to get the equipment back into production as fast as possible, and second, and perhaps more important, the development of a program to eliminate the cause of

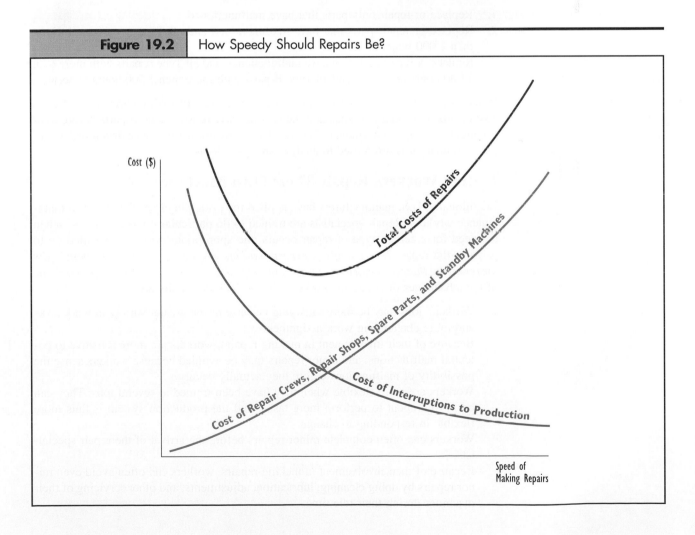

Figure 19.2 | How Speedy Should Repairs Be?

the malfunction and the need for such repairs in the future. Such a program could include redesign and modification of the machine that malfunctioned, modification and redesign of the part or product being processed, training of the production workers to improve machine care, and more frequent adjustments, lubrication, and preventive maintenance inspections.

Early Parts-Replacement Policies

When repairs to production machines are to be made, maintenance supervisors must decide how extensive the repairs should be. The extent of repairs can span this range:

- Do just enough minor repairs to get the machine going again.
- Repair the malfunction and replace some parts that are worn but have not yet malfunctioned.
- Perform a major overhaul of the machine.
- Replace the old machine with a newer one.

Operations managers should establish policies for how extensive repairs for each type of machine should be. For example, let us assume that a particular production machine has malfunctioned. Workers who are to perform repairs on the machine could follow one of these policies:

1. Replace or repair only parts that have malfunctioned.
2. Replace or repair parts that have malfunctioned and all Type A parts with more than 1,000 hours of service.
3. Replace or repair parts that have malfunctioned and all Type A parts with more than 1,000 hours of service and all Type B parts with more than 1,500 hours of service.

When operations managers have data on the frequency of malfunctions of parts, the cost of repairs or malfunctions, and the cost of early replacement of parts before malfunctioning, early replacement policies such as those discussed can be developed. Computer simulation is often used to analyze such problems.

Letting Workers Repair Their Own Machines

Traditionally, U.S. manufacturers have applied the principle of specialization to maintenance workers. Repair specialists are trained to do particular kinds of repairs. When the need for a certain type of repair occurs, the appropriate specialist is called on to perform the repair. *Increasingly, however, workers are being given the responsibility for repairing their own machines or assisting repair specialists in making repairs.* Some of the advantages of enlarging workers' jobs to include repairs are:

- Workers' jobs may be more satisfying because of the greater variety in work tasks and more challenging work assignments.
- Because of their involvement in making repairs, workers are more sensitive to potential malfunctions, and major repairs may be avoided because workers sense the possibility of malfunctions before they actually occur.
- Workers are more flexible when they have been trained at several jobs. They can be moved about to perform more tasks, and the production system is thus more flexible in responding to change.
- Workers can often complete minor repairs before the arrival of the repair specialists.
- Because of their involvement in making repairs, workers can often avoid even minor repairs by doing cleaning, lubrication, adjustments, and other servicing of their machines during their idle time.

- Because of their involvement in making repairs, workers tend to operate their machines more carefully, thus avoiding the need for even minor repairs. For example, when excessive chip buildups are avoided, fewer cutting tools are broken.

Robert W. Hall makes a good case for workers' involvement in doing their own repairs:

> *It creates more pride in the machine, and it requires closer observation than if the operator merely watches it run. This also helps dispel the propensity for equipment abuse—the feeling that "I can operate it as I please, and someone else will figure out if something is wrong. The company has more than enough money for repairs anyway." (The author has watched operators deliberately jam machines just to take a break while someone else repaired them. That might not have happened had the operators felt that a machine breakdown was their responsibility and breakdowns caused them more work.)*[1]

The trend toward more direct worker involvement in maintenance activities in U.S. manufacturing firms may be a key factor in reducing production costs and in improving product quality and customer satisfaction.

Examples 19.1 and 19.2 are illustrations of how operations managers can analyze some important issues in repair programs. In Example 19.1 an operations manager uses queuing analysis to determine the size of repair crews that repair machines in a production department. You may want to review the queuing analysis section in Chapter 9 before reading this example. This type of problem occurs when operations managers must estimate the amount of repair capacity to provide. Such problems ordinarily involve two types of repair capacity issues: size of repair crews and capacity of repair shops. Either of these issues can conveniently be analyzed by using queuing formulas. Care should be taken, however, to review the assumptions of the queuing formulas and make sure that they fit the problem being analyzed. Computer simulation is often used to analyze repair capacity problems when the assumptions of queuing formulas do not fit the maintenance problem.

Example 19.1	Determining the Size of Repair Crews

Bill Willis is the maintenance supervisor at an automobile tire factory. Several years ago the plant installed over 200 tire-building machines of the same design, and Bill is the manager responsible for seeing that the machines are repaired when they break down. He supervises repair specialists who repair malfunctioning machines on the shop floor. Bill has been instructed by the plant manager that when the tire machines break down, they should be back in service in 2 hours on the average. Bill has collected data from historical records and has found that the machines break down at an average rate of 3.5 per hour and that each repair specialist can repair a machine in 4 hours on the average. Thus each repair specialist can repair 0.25 machine per hour on the average. How many repair specialists are required?

Solution

1. First, look at Table 9.6 in Chapter 9. If we assume that machine repairs are made according to the assumptions of Model 1, the formula for finding the value of the average repair rate (μ) is:

$$t_s = \frac{1}{\mu - \lambda}$$

2. Next, manipulate the formula so that the average repair rate (μ) is on the left-hand side of the expression:

$$t_s = \frac{1}{\mu - \lambda}, \quad (\mu - \lambda)t_s = 1, \quad \mu = \lambda + 1/t_s$$

3. Next, given that the average breakdown rate (λ) is 3.5 and the average time required for machines to be repaired (t_s) is 2, compute the required average repair rate (μ):

$$\mu = \lambda + 1/t_s = 3.5 + 1/2 = 4 \text{ machines per hour}$$

4. Next, since we now know the average repair rate (μ) and that each repair specialist requires 4 hours on the average to repair a machine, compute the number of repair specialists required:

$$\text{Number of specialists} = \mu \div \text{Machines per hour a specialist can repair}$$
$$= 4 \div 0.25 = 16 \text{ repair specialists}$$

In Example 19.2, a payoff table is used to determine the number of standby machines to provide in order to minimize the cost of making repairs to machines that malfunction in a production department. This type of problem occurs when operations managers must provide:

1. A stock of spare parts for repairing machines *after* breakdowns.
2. A stock of spare parts for making unanticipated repairs during PM inspections.
3. A stock of standby machines for replacing machines *after* breakdowns.

In these problems, operations managers do not know how many of each part will be needed in each week. In the face of this uncertainty, they do not want to stock too many parts because it is expensive to store, insure, finance, maintain, and handle the stock. Similarly, they do not want to stock too few because of production downtime and other costs. When faced with such decisions, operations managers therefore attempt to provide the level of stock that balances the cost of stocking too few parts against the cost of stocking too many parts, given an uncertain demand for the stock.

Example 19.2	Determining the Number of Standby Machines

Bill Willis from Example 19.1 is the manager responsible for the repair of 200 identical tire-building machines. When one of the machines breaks down, Bill's repair specialists replace the malfunctioning machine with a standby machine if one is available. When a standby machine is available, the length of time that the operation is out of production is greatly reduced. The plant manager has recently asked Bill to review the number of standby machines available and to recommend whether the number should be increased. Bill studies the historical records of breakdowns among the tire-building machines and finds this information:

Number of Machines Malfunctioning per Hour	Occurrence	Relative Frequency (fraction and proportion)
6	25	25/500 = 0.05
5	75	75/500 = 0.15
4	125	125/500 = 0.25
3	175	175/500 = 0.35
2	100	100/500 = 0.20
Total	500	1.00

Bill collaborates with the accounting and industrial engineering departments to develop cost estimates. When too few standby machines are provided, each breakdown for which a standby machine is not available costs the company $150 in lost production time and increased repair costs because of the emergency conditions. When too many standby machines are provided, each standby machine not in use costs the company $80 per hour in storage, special handling, and other costs. How many standby machines should be provided to minimize the total expected cost?

Solution

1. First, turn to Example 14.9 in Chapter 14 and review how to solve payoff table problems.
2. Next, set up the payoff table and complete the calculations:

Number of Standby Machines Required per Hour

Number of Standby Machines Provided S_j \ SN_i	6	5	4	3	2	Total Expected Costs per Hour $EC = \Sigma[P(SN_i)C_{ij}]$
6	$ 0	$ 80	$160	$240	$320	$200.00
5	150	0	80	160	240	131.50
4	300	150	0	80	160	97.50 ←
3	450	300	150	0	80	121.00
2	600	450	300	150	0	225.00
$P(SN_i)$	0.05	0.15	0.25	0.35	0.20	

Note: C_{ij} is the costs of S_j and SN_i.

3. Next, recommend the number of standby machines to be provided.

The payoff table analysis indicates that four standby machines should be provided. Bill Willis recognizes, however, that costs are but one factor to be considered in his recommendation. He also has to consider the impact on production capacity (production capacity is reduced when machine repairs take longer owing to unavailability of standby machines) and on customer satisfaction (delivery promises to customers are broken when machine repairs take longer owing to unavailability of standby machines). Both of these factors argue for a larger number of standby machines. By looking at the payoff table, Bill can see that if he recommended five standby machines, hourly expected costs would increase by only $34. Bill believes that production capacity and customer satisfaction would be greatly improved if five standby machines are provided.

These examples are common types of decisions that must be analyzed by operations managers as they strive to achieve the objectives of repair programs.

Let us now turn to a discussion of preventive maintenance issues.

PREVENTIVE MAINTENANCE (PM) PROGRAMS

*In the case of machine breakdowns, operations managers have no choice—repairs must be made. On the other hand, the decision to have regularly scheduled inspections, machine adjustments, lubrication, and parts replacement as a part of a **preventive maintenance (PM)** program is discretionary.* Operations managers do not *have* to have PM programs, but most do have them because they want to:

- Reduce the frequency and severity of interruptions to production caused by machine malfunctions. This objective can directly affect production capacity, production costs, product quality, employee and customer safety, and customer satisfaction.
- Extend the useful life of production machinery.
- Reduce the total cost of maintenance by substituting PM costs for repair costs.
- Provide a safe working environment for workers. Worn-out machines in poor operating condition create safety hazards for workers.
- Improve product quality by keeping equipment in proper adjustment, well serviced, and in good operating condition.

PM and Operations Strategies

PM can be an important factor in achieving operations strategies. For example, a PM program can be essential to the success of a product-focused positioning strategy. In product-focused positioning strategies, standardized product designs are produced along production lines where there are little if any in-process inventories between adjacent operations. If a machine breaks down at one operation, all other downstream operations will soon run out of parts on which to work. An extensive PM program in such systems will reduce the frequency and severity of machine breakdowns.

Automation and the Prominence of PM

In automated factories, PM programs are essential. Consider the concept of *workerless factories*. In this concept, systems of automated machines operate continuously without the need for production workers. In such an environment, a large number of maintenance workers would be needed to keep the machines adjusted, lubricated, and in good operating condition. Although many of our factories will never become workerless, they will become more automated and we shall see a shift from large to smaller production workforces, but we shall also see a shift from small to larger PM workforces. Some of the production workers who will be displaced by automation will need to be retrained to become a part of the growing maintenance workforce.

Scheduling PM Activities

At some Ford, Toyota, General Motors, and other plants, production is scheduled on two eight-hour shifts per day along with one four-hour minishift for PM activities. At other factories that produce on three shifts per day, the capacity of each machine used for production-planning purposes (master production scheduling and capacity requirements planning) is reduced to allow time for each machine to undergo its regular PM inspection, adjustment, lubrication, and parts replacement. Regardless of the arrangement devised to schedule PM activities, PM and production are increasingly viewed as being equally important, and therefore PM and production must be regularly scheduled on each machine.

PM Database Requirements

For an effective PM program, detailed records must be maintained on each machine. An ongoing history of the dates and frequency of breakdowns, descriptions of malfunctions, and costs of repairs is fundamental to determining how often to schedule PM for each machine. Equipment specifications and checklists are needed for PM inspections and early parts-replacement decisions. These records form the basis for improving PM programs, and the amount of data for a large factory can be great. Computers are generally used to maintain a database for maintenance departments to access as needed. Also, much of the data can be kept in a plastic pocket on each machine; then, as repairs or preventive maintenance is performed, the cards in the pocket can be updated.

Modern Approaches to PM

A discussion of just-in-time (JIT) manufacturing was included in Chapter 12 of this book. In JIT, in-process inventories and production lot sizes are reduced to very low levels. This forces the attention of workers and managers to be focused on machine breakdowns. If a machine breaks down, all downstream machines will soon be out of parts and the whole production system will soon stop. Machine breakdowns simply cannot be tolerated in JIT systems; this is why manufacturers strive for *perfect machine maintenance*. We have discussed earlier how these manufacturers speed up repairs so that interruptions to production are minimized. The account at the beginning of this chapter described the concept of total preventive maintenance, which is being adopted by leading manufacturers. Here we want to emphasize how they strive to *eliminate* machine breakdowns through PM.

A cornerstone of PM programs is worker involvement. Just as in the concept of **quality at the source** *(placing the responsibility for product quality on the production worker), U.S. producers must also similarly apply the concept of **PM at the source**. In this approach, workers have the fundamental responsibility for preventing machine breakdowns by conducting preventive maintenance on their own machines.* Workers must develop an aircraft mentality toward PM. You know how pilots and air crews go down checklists before an aircraft can take off? This meticulous attention to each small detail of the performance of the aircraft is to avoid the unthinkable—an air crash. Workers must also go down a PM checklist every morning, inspecting, lubricating, and adjusting their own machines with the same dread of the unthinkable—a machine breakdown. Business Snapshot 19.1 illustrates the concepts of PM at the source and total preventive (or productive) maintenance.

As workers operate their machines throughout the day, they listen intently as the machines operate, hoping to pick up any hints of machine irregularities so that they can correct the problem before a machine malfunction occurs. They fill out cards, which are kept in pockets attached to their machines, indicating PM, repair, and service data. If, during these PM inspections, parts replacement or other repairs are called for, the production workers assist repair specialists in this work. After a time these production workers are trained not only in several production jobs but also in the maintenance of the machines of several jobs. Because workers know more than one job and can do more than one job, they are more valuable to the company and the company is more flexible in responding to change.

BUSINESS SNAPSHOT 19.1

Total Productive Maintenance at Asten, Inc.

Asten, Inc., is a South Carolina company that produces press fabrics for the paper industry. Its plant in Clinton, South Carolina, manufactures combined woven and nonwoven press fabrics, which are used in the production of paper. As part of an effort to compete for the Malcolm Baldrige National Quality Award in the early 1990s, Asten reviewed its maintenance practices and decided to improve these by introducing total productive maintenance (TPM) in the plant.

As part of the TPM initiative, maintenance associates were trained in TPM by outside consultants. The maintenance associates then train the machine operators. A cross-departmental TPM implementation team was formed to promote and champion TPM. Each production department is required to create a maintenance schedule and develop its own TPM operating policies. Machine operators are trained to perform preventive maintenance on their machines and are given a certification for each maintenance task they are capable of performing. Also, ammeters have been installed on some machines so that the need for maintenance can be predicted in advance by analyzing the amount of current a machine uses over time. On some machines, the lubricating oil is regularly analyzed to predict breakdowns.

Over a six-year period, beginning shortly after TPM was introduced, the impacts of machine breakdowns improved substantially. The number of breakdowns per month decreased from 158 to 95, and the resulting man-hours of downtime per month decreased from 4,043 to 342. Also, the amount of maintenance department man-hours spent on machine breakdowns decreased by about 60 percent, and total maintenance department man-hours spent on preventive maintenance and breakdowns decreased by about one-third.

Source: Patterson, J. Wayne, Lawrence D. Fredendall, William J. Kennedy, and Allen McGee. "Adapting Total Productive Maintenance to Asten, Inc." *Production and Inventory Management Journal* 37, no. 4 (Fourth Quarter 1996): 32–37.

In Chapter 7, we discussed the use of quality circles to solve production problems. One of the production problems commonly attacked by these circles is the avoidance of machine breakdowns. PM activities are studied by coworkers to decide how often each machine should receive its PM inspection and to identify other PM activities that should be performed at these times. The use of worker study teams to solve maintenance problems is a key element of the PM programs.

A major obstacle to more worker involvement in PM at U.S. manufacturers is labor union work rules that restrict the kinds of tasks that each worker can do. For example, such rules may not allow production workers to change over their own machines or to perform maintenance on their machines. These rules evolved because of unions' interests in job protection, job security, and pay rate differences and have become traditional even in nonunion shops in the United States. Recent company–union negotiations have focused on eliminating many of these restrictive work rules. The General Motors Saturn assembly plant in Spring Hill, Tennessee, for instance, made sweeping changes to the traditional United Auto Workers (UAW) work rules.

Three examples illustrating the analysis of some common decisions in preventive maintenance are now presented. In Example 19.3, the problem of determining how many spare parts to stock for replacement parts during PM inspections is studied and discussed. This type of problem is perhaps unique to PM because the demand for replacement parts comes from two sources and the appropriate ways to estimate the two types of demands differ. Of particular interest in this example is the description of a system for scheduling orders for the planned replacement parts for PM inspections. This system utilizes logic that is similar to that used in material requirements planning (MRP).

Example 19.3	Determining the Number of Spare Parts to Carry for PM

Bill Willis from Example 19.2 supervises the preventive maintenance program for 200 tire-building machines. The plant manager stopped by Bill's office the other day and asked how Bill's staff determined the number of spare parts to be used in PM inspections of tire-building machines. There seemed to be too much money tied up in spare parts used for PM, according to the plant manager, and he wondered if this inventory could be reduced somewhat without hindering the PM program overall. He was emphatic that he did not want the frequency of machine breakdowns to increase beyond present levels. Admitting that he did not fully understand how the appropriate number of spare parts for PM should be determined, he asked Bill to look into the matter, discuss it with his staff, and then report back to him. The plant manager wanted Bill to recommend a process for determining the appropriate number of spare parts for PM.

Solution

1. First, Bill called a meeting of his key people to discuss the problem. These basic points were established by the group:

   a. The need for each spare part originates from two types of demand. One type of demand is uncertain because the need for spare parts is not known until discovered during PM inspections. Another type of demand is certain and can be easily calculated because the spare parts scheduled to be replaced during PM inspections can be anticipated.

   b. The type of demand that is uncertain is created when, during a regularly scheduled PM inspection of a machine, it is determined that a particular part is wearing faster than expected or is otherwise not expected to last until the next scheduled inspection. An inventory of the part is stocked to meet this uncertain demand. Determining how much of this type of inventory of the part to hold is similar to determining how much inventory of a part to hold to make repairs during equipment breakdowns or computing the number of standby machines as in Example 19.1. In this approach, the cost of stocking too few parts must be balanced against the cost of stocking too many parts while considering the uncertain demand for the part.

   c. The type of demand that is certain is created by regularly scheduled PM inspections of machines. For instance, if a particular part is to be replaced at every PM machine inspection, we know that one of the parts will be needed at every inspection, and orders for the part can be placed so that parts arrive when the PM inspections are scheduled. This type of demand can be satisfied by applying MRP–type logic.

   d. The number of each type of spare part in inventory at any point in time will be made up of two components. The first will be inventory stocked to meet uncertain demand during PM inspections. The second will be a transient inventory of parts flowing in as needed to be used in scheduled installations at regular PM inspections.

2. Next, Bill prepared an example of how the number of spare parts to hold for PM would be computed to meet the uncertain portion of demand.

   a. First, Bill prepared these data for the example: Cost of stocking too many parts (the part is stocked, but not used during the week) is $20 per part to cover carrying, extra handling, and other costs. Cost of stocking too few parts (the part is needed but not stocked) is $50 per part to cover emergency supply of the part, extra production downtime, and other costs. The demand pattern for the part is:

Number of Parts Demanded per Week	Occurrence	Relative Frequency (fraction and proportion)
10	15	15/100 = 0.15
20	25	25/100 = 0.25
30	35	35/100 = 0.35
35	25	25/100 = 0.25
Total	100	1.00

b. Next, Bill prepared a payoff table analysis of the data of the example:

Number of Spare Parts Required per Week

		SN_i				Weekly Expected Costs
S_j		10	20	30	35	$EC = \Sigma[P(SN_i) \times C_{ij}]$
Number of Spare Parts Stocked per Week	10	$ 0	$500	$1,000	$1,250	$787.50
	20	200	0	500	750	392.50
	30	400	200	0	250	172.50 ←
	35	500	300	100	0	185.00
	$P(SN_i)$	0.15	0.25	0.35	0.25	

Note: C_{ij} is the costs of S_j and SN_i.

c. Next, Bill summarized the payoff analysis: The number of spare parts to be stocked per week is 30 because this number provides the best balance between the cost of stocking too few and stocking too many. However, Bill pointed out that other factors such as production capacity and customer satisfaction would encourage a larger stock. In this example, it can be seen that if 35 of the spare parts were carried, weekly expected costs would go up by only $12.50. Therefore, Bill would recommend stocking 35 of the parts per week.

3. Next, Bill explained how a system could be developed for ordering spare parts so that they would arrive for installation at regularly scheduled PM inspections.

   a. First, all the PM inspections to be made in each week of the planning horizon would be picked off the master production schedule and MRP records. Then these inspections would be classified according to the type of machines to be inspected in each week. This master PM schedule (MPMS) would be analogous to the master production schedule in MRP systems, and each type of PM machine inspection in the MPMS would be analogous to a product in the master production schedule.

   b. Next, a bill of spare parts would be prepared and kept up to date for each type of machine that receives a PM inspection. This bill is analogous to a bill of material in MRP systems. Although each spare part may not be replaced at each PM inspection, the planned frequency of replacement could be taken into account in the bill.

   c. Next, the bill of PM spare parts would be exploded by the MPMS into weekly PM demand for each type of spare part.

   d. Next, the parts explosion would be offset for lead time required to order and receive each type of spare part. The result would be a schedule for placing orders for each type of spare part for PM.

4. Finally, Bill prepared a summary of his recommendations. The demand for PM spare parts is made up of two components. The uncertain type can be estimated for each type of part based on the example prepared above. This analysis should take into account all the factors affected by stocking too many or too few spare parts for unanticipated demand during PM inspections. Also, a system similar to an MRP system could be developed in which a weekly schedule would be prepared for placing orders for each type of spare part to be used in regularly scheduled PM inspections.

In Example 19.4, the problem of determining how often to perform PM on a group of machines is analyzed. Such decisions are important because if PM inspections occur too frequently, the additional maintenance expense is not justified by the reduced frequency of breakdowns. On the other hand, if PM inspections occur too infrequently, too many breakdowns occur and production costs, production capacity, product quality, worker safety, and customer satisfaction suffer.

Example 19.4	Determining the Frequency of Performing PM

It costs $2,000 to perform PM on a group of five machines. If one of the machines malfunctions between PM inspections, it costs $4,000. Records indicate this breakdown history on the machines:

Weeks between PM	Probability That a Machine Will Malfunction
1	0.1
2	0.2
3	0.3
4	0.4

If only costs are considered, how often should PM be performed to minimize the expected cost of malfunctions and the cost of PM?

Solution

1. First, compute the expected number of breakdowns for each PM policy. The formula for the expected number of breakdowns is:

$$B_n = N\left(\sum_{1}^{n} p_n\right) + B_{(n-1)}p_1 + B_{(n-2)}p_2 + B_{(n-3)}p_3 + \cdots + B_1 p_{(n-1)}$$

where:

B_n = expected number of breakdowns for each of the PM policies
p_n = probability that a breakdown will occur between PM inspections when PM is performed every n period
N = number of machines in group.

Therefore:

$$B_1 = N(p_1) = 5(0.1) = 0.500$$
$$B_2 = N(p_1 + p_2) + B_1(p_1) = 5(0.1 + 0.2) + 0.5(0.1) = 1.550$$
$$B_3 = N(p_1 + p_2 + p_3) + B_2(p_1) + B_1(p_2)$$
$$= 5(0.1 + 0.2 + 0.3) + 1.55(0.1) + 0.5(0.2) = 3.000 + 0.155 + 0.100$$
$$= 3.255$$
$$B_4 = N(p_1 + p_2 + p_3 + p_4) + B_3(p_1) + B_2(p_2) + B_1(p_3)$$
$$= 5(0.1 + 0.2 + 0.3 + 0.4) + 3.255(0.1) + 1.550(0.2) + 0.5(0.3)$$
$$= 5.000 + 0.326 + 0.310 + 0.150$$
$$= 5.786$$

2. Next, compute the expected breakdown cost, preventive maintenance cost, and total cost for each PM policy:

(1) PM Every n Weeks	(2) Expected Number of Breakdowns	(3) Expected Number of Breakdowns per Week [(2) ÷ (1)]	(4) Weekly Expected Cost of Breakdowns [(3) × \$4,000]	(5) Weekly Cost of PM [\$2,000 ÷ (1)]	(6) Total Weekly Cost [(4) + (5)]
1	0.500	0.500	\$2,000	\$2,000	\$4,000
2	1.550	0.775	3,100	1,000	4,100
3	3.255	1.085	4,340	667	5,007
4	5.786	1.447	5,788	500	6,288

3. The policy that minimizes weekly costs is to perform PM every week.

In Example 19.5, planning and controlling a large-scale PM project is studied. Large-scale projects occur commonly in maintenance departments. In fact, Chapter 10 indicated that one of the most common applications of CPM/PERT and other project management approaches is in maintenance. In many maintenance departments, banks of machines, whole production departments, and even entire factories are shut down periodically to perform PM. In such shutdowns, the number and diversity of the PM tasks that must be performed is so great that some means is needed to plan and control the projects. As Example 19.5 illustrates, CPM is a useful way to plan and control large-scale maintenance projects.

Examples 19.3, 19.4, and 19.5 concern decisions about major issues in PM. Because PM is growing in importance today, an understanding of these examples is also important.

Example 19.5	Planning and Controlling Large-Scale PM Projects

Natasha Jackson is a maintenance planner at Cajun Oil's refinery in Lafayette, Louisiana. She is developing a plan for the refinery's annual PM shutdown. She had identified these major PM activities, estimated their durations, and determined the precedence relationships among the activities:

Activity	Immediate Predecessor Activities	Activity Duration (days)
a. Award subcontractor contracts	—	5
b. Call in Cajun Oil workers for PM	—	10
c. Drain storage tanks	—	8
d. Tear down cracking unit	b	7
e. Subcontract cracking unit work	a	10
f. Subcontract painting work	a	20
g. Clean and repair storage tanks	b,c	20
h. Reassemble cracking unit	d,e	12

Develop a CPM analysis of the PM project. Compute the critical path, the duration of the project, and the slack for each activity.

Solution

1. First, turn to Examples 10.1 through 10.4 in Chapter 10 and review the procedures for a CPM analysis.
2. Next, draw the CPM network diagram for the project. Compute the LS, LF, and S for each activity in the diagram.
3. Next, determine the critical path, the duration of the project, and the slack for each activity.

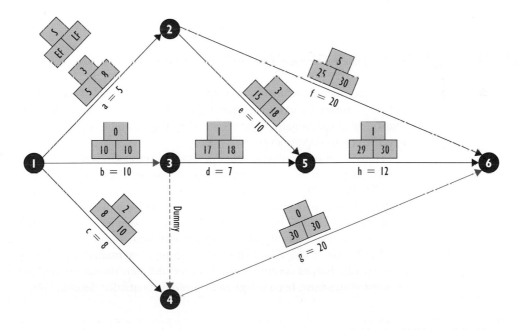

The critical path is Path b–g. The PM project should require 30 days for completion. The slack for each activity is found in the top box over each activity arrow. All the activities with zero slack are on the critical path.

Let us now discuss the concepts of reliability and their relationship to maintenance management.

MACHINE RELIABILITY

Our interest here is in **machine reliability,** *the likelihood of a machine not breaking down, malfunctioning, or needing repairs in a given time period or number of hours of use.* If machine reliability can be increased, the incidence of machine breakdowns and the cost of the havoc caused in production by breakdowns can also be reduced. In Chapter 7, Operations Quality Management, we discussed the concepts and issues related to designing products for reliability. That discussion in Chapter 7 exactly applies here with the exception that the word *machine* is substituted for *product*. For you see, our machine that we want to be more reliable was another department's or another company's product when it was designed and produced.

As discussed in Chapter 7, there are three approaches to improving machine reliability—overdesign, design simplification, and redundant components—and all three take place when a machine is designed. *Overdesign means enhancing a design to avoid a particular type of failure.* If a machine has only a few independent critical interacting parts, then overdesign may be an effective way to increase machine reliability. *Design simplification means reducing the number of interacting parts in a machine.* Because there are fewer parts that can fail, machine reliability increases when the number of interacting parts is reduced. *Redundant components means building backup components right into the machine so that if one part fails, its backup is automatically substituted.* These approaches can be used together or separately to design more reliable machines.

SECONDARY MAINTENANCE DEPARTMENT RESPONSIBILITIES

All maintenance departments are responsible for the repair of buildings and equipment and for performing certain preventive maintenance inspections, repairs, lubrication, and adjustments. Additionally, certain secondary responsibilities have traditionally been assigned to these departments.

Housekeeping, janitorial, window washing, groundskeeping, and painting services are usually performed by maintenance departments. These activities usually include all areas of the facility, from rest rooms to offices to production departments to warehouses. In some plants, however, the area around each production worker's immediate workstation is cleaned by the worker, and the appearance and cleanliness of all other areas are the responsibility of the maintenance department.

New construction, remodeling, safety equipment maintenance, loss prevention, security, public hazard control, waste disposal and transformation, and pollution control responsibilities have been assigned to some maintenance departments.

TRENDS IN MAINTENANCE

Production machinery today is far more complex than it was a decade or two ago. Computerized controls, robotics, new technology in metallurgy, more sophisticated electronic controls, new methods in lubrication technology, and other developments have resulted in many changes in the way complex machines are maintained.

Special training programs have sprung up to give maintenance workers the skills necessary to service and repair today's specialized equipment. An example of this training is found in the field of life-support systems in hospitals. The engineers and technicians who design and perform maintenance programs for this sophisticated medical equipment must be involved in continuous training programs to stay abreast of new equipment developments. These training programs are conducted by individual hospitals, by cooperative health care groups, and by public and private educational institutions.

Subcontracting service companies have developed to supply specialized maintenance services. Computers, automobiles, office machines, and other products are increasingly serviced by outside subcontracting companies. Their specialized technical training and their fee structure, which is usually based on an as-needed basis, combine to offer competent service at reasonable cost.

Other technologies are developing that promise to reduce the cost of maintenance while improving the performance of production machines. An example is the network of computerized temperature-sensing probes connected to all key bearings in a machine system. When bearings begin to fail, they overheat and vibrate, causing these sensing systems to indicate that a failure is imminent. The massive damage to machines that can happen when bearings fail—snapped shafts, stripped gears, and so on—can thus be avoided.

Because computers have been almost universally absorbed into management information systems in all types of organizations, maintenance departments have also been affected by this development. Five general areas in maintenance commonly use computer assistance today: (1) scheduling maintenance projects; (2) maintenance cost reports by production department, cost category, and other classifications; (3) inventory status reports for maintenance parts and supplies; (4) parts failure data; and (5) operations analysis studies, which may include computer simulation, waiting lines (queuing theory), and other analytical programs. Information from these uses of computers can provide managers in maintenance with the necessary failure patterns, cost data, and other information fundamental to the key maintenance decisions discussed in this section. Business Snapshot 19.2 illustrates the use of computers in scheduling maintenance projects.

Although computers, robotics, and high-tech machinery are important concerns in maintenance management today, people concerns may be at the heart of better maintenance. One important trend is the involvement of production workers in repairing their own machines and performing PM on their own machines. By enlarging production workers' jobs to include maintenance of their machines, not only is maintenance likely to improve, but many side benefits open up as well. Restrictive union work rules seem to be falling away at a record pace.

MAINTENANCE ISSUES IN SERVICE ORGANIZATIONS

In this chapter we focused mainly on maintenance issues in manufacturing, but maintenance is also an important concern to service organizations. Airlines, package delivery companies like FedEx, and trucking companies all must establish preventive maintenance programs to keep their aircraft and trucks in top operating condition. They also must make repairs to correct unexpected failures, so spare parts inventories have to be managed. State highway departments must maintain roads and highways. Decisions have to be made about how much to spend on preventive maintenance for roadways, such as recoating or resurfacing, versus how much to spend on making repairs, such as filling potholes and fixing cracks and sinkholes. Office managers in all organizations have to deal with occasional malfunctioning of copy machines, fax machines,

BUSINESS SNAPSHOT 19.2

Decision Support System for Aircraft Maintenance Planning at American Airlines

American Airlines has two huge overhaul and maintenance (OM) facilities at Tulsa and Fort Worth. American's fleet of Boeing 727, 737, 747, 757, 767; McDonnell Douglas Super 80, DC-10, MD-11; Airbus 300; and Fokker 100 aircraft are scheduled for over 30 different types of maintenance visits through the OM facilities. The most costly of these visits is the MBV, in which the entire aircraft is rebuilt; this can cost from $250,000 to $1 million depending on the type of aircraft. The frequency of MBVs ranges from one every 18 months for a DC-10 to one every 5 years for a 727.

American develops and maintains a 5-year planning horizon maintenance schedule for the fleet. This schedule tracks when aircraft maintenance will be performed and includes MBVs, component removals (landing gears, flaps, etc.),

and special visits. American used to do this 5-year planning with paper and pencil, but the rapid growth of American's fleet and the growing complexity associated with new aircraft coming into the fleet and old aircraft being phased out of the fleet made this approach impractical.

American's Decision Technologies (AADT) developed and implemented a decision support system for generating and updating the 5-year aircraft overhaul and maintenance plans. The system uses an Apple Macintosh IIcx platform and is written in the C++ language. The benefits from the decision support system have been astounding:

- The fleet 5-year plans can be generated in these times: DC-10 fleet in about 1 minute, 727 fleet in about 5 minutes,

Super 80 fleet in about 8 minutes.
- Planners can now quickly generate tentative plans by asking "what if" questions.
- Overhaul and maintenance costs have been drastically reduced. With increased hours between overhauls, $454 million has been saved over the active life of the 227 widebody aircraft in the fleet.
- Because of more efficient scheduling of facilities, reduced required capacity of facilities, and overhaul avoidance, $3 million has been saved.
- The reduced downtime on aircraft equates to giving an aircraft back to the airline for an entire year over its expected life, which provides considerable increased revenue.

© DAVE BARTRUFF/CORBIS

Source: Gray, Douglas A. "Airworthy." *OR/MS Today,* December 1992, 24–29.

Maintenance management is an important consideration in service organizations as well as production.

© MARK GIBSON/CORBIS

computers, printers, and other office equipment. Secondary maintenance is necessary in all organizations as well. In fact, nearly all of the ideas discussed in this chapter can be applied to maintenance management in both service and manufacturing organizations.

Maintenance today in POM means more than simply maintaining the machines of production. As POM has broadened its perspectives from minimizing short-range costs to other, long-range performance measures such as customer service, return on investment, product and service quality, and providing for workers' needs, so also has maintenance broadened its perspectives. Today maintenance means that the prompt supply of quality products and services is what is maintained, and not merely machines.

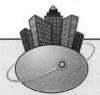

Wrap-Up

WHAT WORLD-CLASS COMPANIES DO

World-class companies give much of the responsibility for repairs and preventive maintenance to workers. Workers are made to feel that they *own* their machines when it comes to maintenance. Being alert to potential malfunctions, workers avoid major equipment breakdowns by making minor repairs themselves, by meticulously cleaning, lubricating, and adjusting their own machines, and by operating their machines more carefully. Additionally, because workers are more flexible, the production systems are more responsive to customer needs. For world-class companies, greater involvement of workers in maintenance is a key factor in

reducing production costs, improving product quality, and increasing customer satisfaction.

Toward increasing the flexibility of production, some world-class companies have implemented just-in-time (JIT) systems. This approach increases flexibility by removing a key cause of inflexibility—bloated inventories. By removing inventories, particularly in-process inventories, production systems become more vulnerable to machine breakdowns. A cornerstone of JIT is therefore to implement a sophisticated preventive maintenance program to reduce the frequency of machine malfunctions. For world-class companies, the involvement of workers in quality circles provides the opportunity for these groups to study maintenance problems. Because an effective preventive maintenance program is essential to JIT, having quality circles study maintenance problems is a natural result of implementing a JIT system.

World-class companies have invested heavily in factory and service operation automation projects and in training and educating personnel to use automated equipment. The widespread use of automation has made these systems more vulnerable to equipment breakdowns. Sophisticated systems of automation have therefore, like JIT systems, created the need for improved preventive maintenance programs. And as production equipment has become more sophisticated and complex, maintaining the equipment has also become more difficult. World-class companies have intensive training programs for maintenance workers so that they can keep up with ongoing technological advances.

Preventive maintenance has also been aided by technological developments. World-class companies have added automated process sensing and control systems to production equipment to give warning before machines fail or are damaged by vibration or heat. In this way, failure of seals, bearings, gears, shafts, or electronic components can be avoided by shutting down machines and performing preventive maintenance before they are damaged.

World-class companies make extensive use of computers in maintenance management. Scheduling maintenance projects, inventory systems for spare parts, and parts failure data are examples of this use of computers.

Because world-class companies know that customer service, production capacity, production costs and productivity, and product quality are all affected by it, effective maintenance management carries a high priority.

REVIEW AND DISCUSSION QUESTIONS

1. Identify five factors or performance measures of production that are affected by maintenance management and equipment malfunctions.
2. Define the terms *repairs* and *preventive maintenance*. Describe the relationship between repairs and preventive maintenance.
3. Name five ways in which the frequency of equipment malfunctions can be reduced.
4. Name three ways in which the severity of equipment malfunctions can be reduced.
5. Identify and explain five objectives of repair programs.
6. Explain the relationship between the costs of interruptions to production and the costs of making repairs.
7. What actions are triggered by a machine breakdown? Describe and discuss the actions and their role in maintenance management.

8. Explain the meaning and significance of early parts-replacement policies in a repair program.
9. Identify and discuss the advantages of letting production workers repair their own machines.
10. What are the objectives of PM programs?
11. Explain and discuss how PM can be an important factor in achieving operations strategies.
12. Explain why the trend toward automation has increased the importance of PM.
13. Explain and discuss the modern approaches to PM.
14. Explain how an operations manager might determine how many spare parts to order for a PM program.
15. Define and explain the meaning of *overdesign, simplification,* and *redundancy*. Discuss their roles in maintenance management.
16. What are some secondary responsibilities that are assigned to maintenance departments?
17. What are the trends in maintenance management?

INTERNET ASSIGNMENTS

1. Search the Internet for two companies that offer preventive maintenance products or services. Describe what they offer, related to preventive maintenance.
2. VehiCare is a company based in Richmond, Virginia, that provides on-site preventive maintenance and repairs for fleets of trucks, trailers, forklifts, and utility

and construction vehicles. Visit and explore VehiCare's web site at **http://www.vehicare.com**. Describe more about the services provided by VehiCare. List the current locations of VehiCare facilities.

3. Heat Seekers Infrared Imaging is a company based in Bellevue, Washington, that specializes in providing infrared thermal imaging systems for predictive maintenance and repair troubleshooting. Visit and explore the company's web site at **http://www.heatseekr.com**. Describe some of the potential benefits of infrared imaging for maintenance management. Describe some of the applications of this technology.

4. Search the Internet for a software product that assists with maintenance management. Describe the features of this software related to maintenance management.

PROBLEMS

1. A certain type of machine in a manufacturing plant breaks down at the rate of three machines per hour on average, and the Model 1 queuing formulas apply. If the production manager specifies that machines should be out of production for no more than an average of three hours, how many machines on average must the maintenance department be able to repair per hour?

2. Machines break down at a rate of eight per hour on average, and each repair technician can repair a machine in 1.5 hours on average. Management states that each malfunctioned machine should be out of production for no more than 2 hours on average. If Model 1 queuing formulas apply, how many repair technicians are needed to repair the machines?

3. A repair shop has three identical repair centers that repair machines independently. Machines arrive according to a Poisson distribution with a mean rate of 20 per hour. Each center repairs machines according to a Poisson distribution with a mean rate of 8 per hour. The space needed for waiting machines is considered to be adequate.

   a. How long will machines be out of production on the average?
   b. If each machine occupies 40 square feet of floor space, how much floor space should be occupied by waiting machines on the average?

4. A bushing is stocked as a spare part to repair machines when they break down. If not enough bushings are on hand when needed, the production downtime, emergency supply procedures, and other short costs are $100 per bushing short. If too many of these bushings are stocked, it costs $40 per bushing per week for carrying, handling, and storage costs. The expected demand for these bushings is:

Demand per Week	Occurrence	Relative Frequency (fraction and proportion)
80	30	30/165 = 0.182
90	45	45/165 = 0.273
100	55	55/165 = 0.333
105	35	35/165 = 0.212
Total	165	1.000

How many bushings should be stocked per week to minimize the total expected costs?

5. A repair shop uses seals to repair machines. If the shop needs a seal and it is out of stock, it costs $50 to get one quickly from a local supplier. If a seal is stocked on Monday but not needed during the week, it costs $75 because the seals deteriorate so fast that they must be cleaned and treated if they are not used in five days. The demand history for the seals is:

Weekly Demand	Occurrence
50	5
60	10
70	25
75	25
80	15
Total	80

How many seals should be stocked per week to minimize the total expected costs?

6. A standby testing machine is stocked and used to replace testing machines that malfunction anywhere in the factory. If one of the standby testing machines is not available when a malfunction occurs, it costs the company $350 in lost productivity. On the other hand, if one of the standby testing machines is not used, it costs $180 per week for extra handling, storage, carrying, and other costs. The demand for these standby testing machines is:

Weekly Demand	Occurrence
4	15
5	28
6	22
7	9
8	3
Total	77

How many standby testing machines should be stocked by the company to minimize expected costs?

7. For a mainframe computer, a preventive maintenance inspection and repair cycle costs a total of $2,000 on the average. If the computer breaks down, an average cost of $5,000 is incurred. The historical breakdown pattern for the computer is:

Months between PM	Average Number of Breakdowns between PM Cycles
1	0.2
2	0.6
3	1.8
4	3.6
5	7.0

Recommend how often preventive maintenance should be performed.

8. It costs a total of $2,000 to perform preventive maintenance (PM) on five identical production machines. If one of the machines malfunctions between PM inspections, the cost averages $5,000. Here is the historical breakdown data for the machines:

Months between PM	Average Number of Breakdowns between PM Inspections
2	0.1
3	0.5
4	1.6
5	3.2

What interval between PM inspections minimizes the total expected repair costs and PM costs?

9. It costs $1,000 for an automobile engine repair, and the probabilities of an engine failure with varying intervals between oil changes are:

Thousands of Miles between Oil Changes	Probability of Engine Failure
60	0.05
70	0.10
80	0.20
90	0.30
100	0.35

If a custom oil change with filters, long-wearing oil, and careful adjustments costs $200 at each oil change for each automobile, which interval between oil changes would you select for a fleet of five automobiles? (*Hint:* Base your analysis on cost per 1,000 miles.)

10. Preventive maintenance (PM) can be performed on six identical production machines for a total cost of $6,000. If one of the machines malfunctions between PM inspections, it can be repaired for an average cost of $3,000. The probability of a machine malfunctioning between PM inspections is:

Weeks between PM	Probability of a Breakdown for Each Machine
1	0.05
2	0.15
3	0.20
4	0.25
5	0.35

How often should PM be performed to minimize the total expected repair costs and PM costs?

11. Suppose your car has an eight-cylinder engine with eight spark plugs. Each spark plug has a probability of failure of 0.003 for a period of 7,000 operating hours.

   a. What is the reliability level of each spark plug?
   b. What is the reliability of the spark plug system of your car?

12. Eighty units of a component for a machine are tested for 780 hours and three units fail.

   a. What is the reliability of the component?
   b. What is the mean time between failures for the component?
   c. How would you explain to a manager the meaning of your answers to Parts a and b?

13. A machine has three critical component parts. If any of these three component parts fails, the machine cannot operate. The three parts have component reliabilities of 0.98, 0.93, and 0.99.

    a. Compute the system reliability of the machine.

    b. If the machine could be redesigned to allow redundancy for the part that presently has a reliability of 0.93, what would be the new system reliability of the machine?

14. A plant will close soon for its annual PM shutdown. The PM activities, their durations, and their immediate predecessor activities are:

Activity	Immediate Predecessor Activities	Activity Duration (days)
a. Instruct electrical repair team	—	3
b. Instruct mechanical repair team	—	5
c. Disassemble electronic controls	a	9
d. Modify computerized scale monitors	a	4
e. Disassemble and repair scales	b	3
f. Repair hopper vibrator mechanisms	b	9
g. Repair electronic controls	c	9
h. Reassemble automatic hoppers	f	6
i. Calibrate and adjust scales	d,e	3

Using the CPM program in the *POM Software Library:*

    a. Compute the EF, LF, and slack for each activity.

    b. What is the critical path?

    c. What is the project's estimated duration?

15. A factory is scheduled to have a plantwide PM shutdown soon. The PM activities, their durations, and their immediate predecessor activities are:

Activity	Immediate Predecessor Activities	Activity Duration (days)
a. Train and instruct workers	—	12
b. Disassemble electronic controls	a	10
c. Disassemble curing molds	a	15
d. Modify mold tooling	a	9
e. Repair mold control panels	b	7
f. Repair defective molds	c,e	11
g. Repair electronic controls	b	13
h. Install mold tooling	b,d	21
i. Calibrate and adjust mold tooling	b,d	15
j. Reassemble curing molds	f,g,h	9

Using the *POM Software Library:*

    a. Compute the EF, LF, and slack for each activity.

    b. What is the critical path?

    c. What is the project's estimated duration?

CASES

Integrated Products Corporation

Integrated Products Corporation (IPC) manufactures resins and molded plastic products. One production department has 10 injection-molding machines. The maintenance manager at the plant is studying this group of machines to determine how often the department should shut down all of the machines and perform preventive maintenance (PM). The nature of the department and its processes causes PM to be performed on all the machines at one time at a cost of $10,000 for the entire group of machines. When a single machine breaks down, it costs about $2,000, on the average, to repair it. These data from production records about machine breakdowns between PM have been gathered:

Months between PM	Probability of a Breakdown for Each Machine	Cumulative Probability of Breakdown
1	0.10	0.10
2	0.15	0.25
3	0.20	0.45
4	0.25	0.70
5	0.30	1.00

The probability that each machine will break down before the next PM inspection is 1.00 if there are five months between PM. This means that each machine is certain to break down before the next PM if there are five months between PM.

Assignment

1. Compute the expected number of breakdowns between PM with each of the PM policies.
2. Which PM policy minimizes the expected repair costs and PM costs?
3. What other factors would affect the choice of a PM policy?
4. Explain the relationship between the choice of PM policy and its effect on: (a) production capacity, (b) product quality, (c) customer satisfaction, and (d) worker safety.
5. How much would an improvement in the factors listed in No. 4 have to be worth to justify changing the PM policy that minimized costs in No. 2?
6. Recommend the PM policy that should be adopted. Justify your recommendation.

Roadrunner Coach

Roadrunner Coach operates a fleet of 150 buses that serves commuters going into New York City from outlying communities, with service only on Monday through Friday. Roadrunner's maintenance department has been troubled by frequent failures of the fuel system microprocessors on the buses. Vinni Lambrito, the maintenance manager, wants to determine the most cost-effective number of microprocessors to stock as spares at the beginning of each week.

Roadrunner's contract with a microprocessor manufacturer in Malaysia provides that Roadrunner will place an order for this part late each Friday afternoon, and the order will be airmailed to arrive the following Monday morning. If the maintenance department runs out of the part during the week the additional cost to purchase the part from a different manufacturer in the U.S. is $60, and the part will arrive early the next morning. Because each microprocessor is expensive, the carrying cost for each part not needed during a week has been established at $25 per week. Mr. Lambrito has summarized maintenance records for the past 40 weeks to show the failure pattern for the fuel system microprocessor as follows:

Failures Per Week	Number of Past Weeks
2	5
3	11
4	13
5	6
6	4
7	1

Assignment

1. How many spare microprocessors should Mr. Lambrito plan to stock at the beginning of each week in order to minimize the combined carrying cost and additional purchasing cost from the U.S. manufacturer? What would be the expected cost each week?
2. Based on your recommendation in No. 1, what is the likelihood of a stockout next week?
3. Next month the contract with the Malaysian supplier will be up for renegotiation. What changes to the supply arrangement would you encourage Mr. Lambrito to try to make?
4. What other factors should be considered in the decision of how many spare microprocessors to stock? How would these factors change your recommendation in No. 1?

ENDNOTE

1. Hall, Robert W. *Zero Inventories*, pp. 134–135. Homewood, IL: Dow Jones–Irwin, 1983.

SELECTED BIBLIOGRAPHY

Birkland, Carol. "Maintaining Shop Equipment." *Fleet Equipment* 24, no. 2 (February 1998): 64–69.

Bloch, Heinz P., and Fred K. Geitner. *Machinery Failure Analysis and Troubleshooting*. Houston, TX: Gulf Publishing, 1997.

Cooke, Fang Lee. "Implementing TPM in Plant Maintenance: Some Organizational Barriers." *International Journal of Quality and Reliability Management* 17, no. 8 (2000): 1003–1016.

Fredendall, Lawrence D., J. Wayne Patterson, William J. Kennedy, and Tom Griffin. "Maintenance: Modeling Its Strategic Impact." *Journal of Managerial Issues* 9, no. 4 (Winter 1997): 440–453.

Gertsbakh, Ilya. *Reliability Theory: With Applications to Preventive Maintenance*. New York: Springer-Verlag, 2001.

Hipkin, I. B., and C. D. Cock. "TQM and BPR: Lessons for Maintenance Management." *Omega* 28, no. 3 (2000): 277–292.

Lee, Reginald, and Paul Wordsworth. *Building Maintenance Management*. Malden, MA: Blackwell Science, 2000.

Levitt, Joel. *Managing Factory Maintenance*. New York: Industrial Press, 1996.

Lewis, Bernard T. *Facility Manager's Operation and Maintenance Handbook*. New York: McGraw-Hill, 1998.

Luxhoj, James T., Jens O. Riis, and Uffe Thorsteinsson. "Trends and Perspectives in Industrial Maintenance Management." *Journal of Manufacturing Systems* 16, no. 6 (1997): 437–453.

Malm, Howard, and Fernando Halpern. "Using Ultrasonic Instrumentation to Enhance Plant Maintenance." *Plant Engineering* 52, no. 2 (February 1998): 75–77.

Nakajima, Seiichi. *Introduction to TPM: Total Productive Maintenance.* Cambridge, MA: Productivity Press, 1994.

Patrick, Ken L. "Renewed Focus on Maintenance Basics Can Put Mill Programs Back on Track." *Pulp & Paper* 72, no. 2 (February 1998): 45–51.

Patton, Joseph D., Jr. *Preventive Maintenance.* Research Triangle Park, NC: International Society for Measurement and Control, 1995.

Percy, David F., and Khairy A. H. Kobbacy. "Determining Economical Maintenance Intervals." *International Journal of Production Economics* 67, no. 1 (2000): 87–94.

Robinson, Charles J., and Andrew P. Ginder. *Implementing TPM: The North American Experience.* Portland, OR: Productivity Press, 1995.

Schimmoller, Brian K. "Outsourcing Plant Maintenance." *Power Engineering* 102, no. 2 (February 1998): 16–22.

Swanson, Laura. "Empirical Study of the Relationship between Production Technology and Maintenance Management." *International Journal of Production Economics* 53, no. 2 (November 20, 1997): 191–207.

Tajiri, Masaji, and Fumio Gotoh. *Autonomous Maintenance in Seven Steps: Implementing TPM on the Shop Floor.* Portland, OR: Productivity Press, 1999.

Taylor, J. C. "The Evolution and Effectiveness of Maintenance Resource Management (MRM)." *International Journal of Industrial Ergonomics* 26, no. 2 (2000): 201–216.

Wilkinson, John J. "How to Manage Maintenance." *Harvard Business Review* 46 (March–April 1968): 191–205.

Willmott, Peter, and Dennis McCarthy. *TPM: A Route to World Class Performance.* Boston: Butterworth-Heinemann, 2000.

Appendixes*

Appendix A
Normal Probability Distribution

Appendix B
Student's t Probability Distribution

Appendix C
Answers to Odd-Numbered Problems

*Refer to the enclosed CD for the Linear Programming Solution Methods Appendix

Appendix A: Normal Probability Distribution

Z	.00	.01	.02	.03	.04	.05	.06	.07	.08	.09
.0	.50000	.50399	.50798	.51197	.51595	.51994	.52392	.52790	.53188	.53586
.1	.53983	.54380	.54776	.55172	.55567	.55962	.56356	.56749	.57142	.57535
.2	.57926	.58317	.58706	.59095	.59483	.59871	.60257	.60642	.61026	.61409
.3	.61791	.62172	.62552	.62930	.63307	.63683	.64058	.64431	.64803	.65173
.4	.65542	.65910	.66276	.66640	.67003	.67364	.67724	.68082	.68439	.68793
.5	.69146	.69497	.69847	.70194	.70540	.70884	.71226	.71566	.71904	.72240
.6	.72575	.72907	.73237	.73536	.73891	.74215	.74537	.74857	.75175	.75490
.7	.75804	.76115	.76424	.76730	.77035	.77337	.77637	.77935	.78230	.78524
.8	.78814	.79103	.79389	.79673	.79955	.80234	.80511	.80785	.81057	.81327
.9	.81594	.81859	.82121	.82381	.82639	.82894	.83147	.83398	.83646	.83891
1.0	.84134	.84375	.84614	.84849	.85083	.85314	.85543	.85769	.85993	.86214
1.1	.86433	.86650	.86864	.87076	.87286	.87493	.87698	.87900	.88100	.88298
1.2	.88493	.88686	.88877	.89065	.89251	.89435	.89617	.89796	.89973	.90147
1.3	.90320	.90490	.90658	.90824	.90988	.91149	.91309	.91466	.91621	.91774
1.4	.91924	.92073	.92220	.92364	.92507	.92647	.92785	.92922	.93056	.93189
1.5	.93319	.93448	.93574	.93699	.93822	.93943	.94062	.94179	.94295	.94408
1.6	.94520	.94630	.94738	.94845	.94950	.95053	.95154	.95254	.95352	.95449
1.7	.95543	.95637	.95728	.95818	.95907	.95994	.96080	.96164	.96246	.96327
1.8	.96407	.96485	.96562	.96638	.96712	.96784	.96856	.96926	.96995	.97062
1.9	.97128	.97193	.97257	.97320	.97381	.97441	.97500	.97558	.97615	.97670
2.0	.97725	.97784	.97831	.97882	.97932	.97982	.98030	.98077	.98124	.98169
2.1	.98214	.98257	.98300	.98341	.98382	.98422	.98461	.98500	.98537	.98574
2.2	.98610	.98645	.98679	.98713	.98745	.98778	.98809	.98840	.98870	.98899
2.3	.98928	.98956	.98983	.99010	.99036	.99061	.99086	.99111	.99134	.99158
2.4	.99180	.99202	.99224	.99245	.99266	.99286	.99305	.99324	.99343	.99361
2.5	.99379	.99396	.99413	.99430	.99446	.99461	.99477	.99492	.99506	.99520
2.6	.99534	.99547	.99560	.99573	.99585	.99598	.99606	.99621	.99632	.99643
2.7	.99653	.99664	.99674	.99683	.99693	.99702	.99711	.99720	.99728	.99736
2.8	.99744	.99752	.99760	.99767	.99774	.99781	.99788	.99795	.99801	.99807
2.9	.99813	.99819	.99825	.99831	.99836	.99841	.99846	.99851	.99856	.99861
3.0	.99865	.99869	.99874	.99878	.99882	.99886	.99889	.99893	.99896	.99900
3.1	.99903	.99906	.99910	.99913	.99916	.99918	.99921	.99924	.99926	.99929
3.2	.99931	.99934	.99936	.99938	.99940	.99942	.99944	.99946	.99948	.99950
3.3	.99952	.99953	.99955	.99957	.99958	.99960	.99961	.99962	.99964	.99965
3.4	.99966	.99968	.99969	.99970	.99971	.99972	.99973	.99974	.99975	.99976
3.5	.99977	.99978	.99978	.99979	.99980	.99981	.99981	.99982	.99983	.99983
3.6	.99984	.99985	.99985	.99986	.99986	.99987	.99987	.99988	.99988	.99989
3.7	.99989	.99990	.99990	.99990	.99991	.99991	.99992	.99992	.99992	.99992
3.8	.99993	.99993	.99993	.99994	.99994	.99994	.99994	.99995	.99995	.99995
3.9	.99995	.99995	.99996	.99996	.99996	.99996	.99996	.99996	.99997	.99997

Table A.1, Areas under the Normal Curve, gives the Z scores, or number of standard deviations from the mean, for each value of x and the area under the curve to the left of x. For example, in Figure A.1, if Z = 1.96, the 0.9750 value found in the body of the table is the total unshaded area to the left of x.

Figure A.1

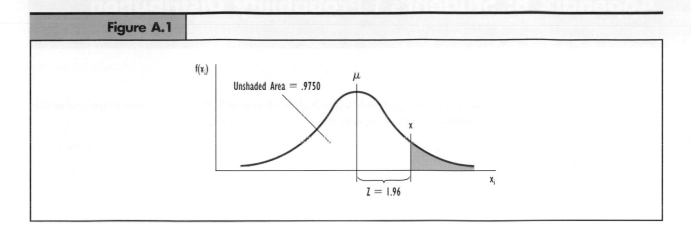

Figure A.2

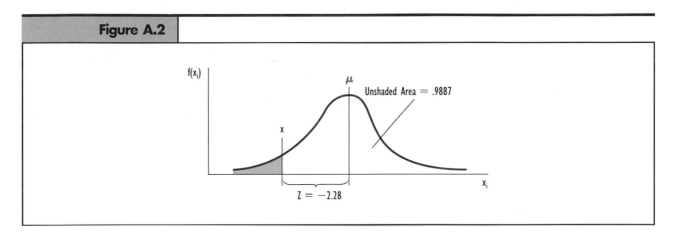

The Z scores in Table A.1 are signless; that is, the Z scores can be either negative (−) or positive (+). We determine the sign of Z in each problem. In Figure A.1, Z is positive because x falls to the right of the mean (μ). In Figure A.2, x falls to the left of the mean (μ), and the area found in the body of the table lies to the right of x. In this figure, Z = −2.28 because x falls to the left of the mean.

In these examples, Z scores of 1.96 and −2.28 were specified and the unshaded area to the left of x (positive Z scores) or to the right of x (negative Z scores) was read from the body of the table. The reverse process is often used: Either the shaded area or the unshaded area is specified and the Z score is read from the Z score column. For example, if the unshaded area = 0.90, the Z score is read from the table, Z = 1.28.

The shaded area is α, the significance level, if a one-tailed α is used. If a two-tailed α is used, however, the shaded area is $\alpha/2$. In some applications, such as control charts in quality control, a two-tailed α is almost always used. In other applications, such as setting acceptance criteria in quality control, however, either a one-tailed or a two-tailed α may be used.

Appendix B: Student's t Probability Distribution

The Student's t probability distribution shown in Table B.1 is a two-tailed probability distribution. Follow these rules to use the table to set confidence limits:

1. Select the desired confidence interval. Subtract this confidence interval from 1. This will give the area in both tails outside the confidence interval. This area in the tails is shown in Figure B.1 as the shaded area and is often referred to as the level of significance (α).

Figure B.1

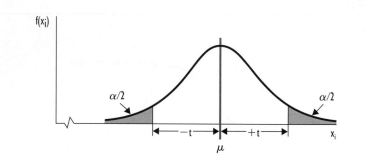

2. Find the column in Table B.1 with the appropriate level of significance heading.
3. Determine the degrees of freedom (d.f.). The d.f. usually equal $n - 1$ or $n - 2$, depending on the formula used, where n is the sample size or the number of observations. Find the row in the table with the appropriate d.f.
4. The intersection of the level of significance column and the d.f. row is the t value. This t value means the number of standard deviations from the mean out to the shaded areas or the outer limits of the confidence interval.
5. The upper limit is computed by adding the product of the t value and the standard deviation to the mean. The lower limit is computed by subtracting this product from the mean.

Example B.1

You have 25 observations with a mean of 32 and a standard deviation of 4.2. What are the upper and lower limits of a 90 percent confidence interval: $\alpha = 0.10$, n = 25, $\mu = 32$, and $\sigma_x = 4.2$?

1. Level of significance = 0.10.
2. d.f. = $n - 2 = 25 - 2 = 23$.
3. t = 1.714.
4. Upper limit = $\mu + t(\sigma_x) = 32 + 1.714(4.2) = 39.20$.
5. Lower limit = $\mu - t(\sigma_x) = 32 - 1.714(4.2) = 24.80$.

Table B.1	Student's t Probability Distribution

d.f.	.9	.8	.7	.6	.5	.4	∝ .3	.2	.1	.05	.02	.01	.001
1	.158	.325	.510	.727	1.000	1.376	1.963	3.078	6.314	12.706	31.821	63.657	636.619
2	.142	.289	.445	.617	.816	1.061	1.386	1.886	2.910	4.303	6.965	9.925	31.598
3	.137	.277	.424	.584	.765	.978	1.250	1.638	2.353	3.182	4.541	5.841	12.941
4	.134	.271	.414	.569	.741	.941	1.190	1.533	2.132	2.776	3.747	4.604	8.610
5	.132	.267	.408	.559	.727	.920	1.156	1.476	2.015	2.571	3.365	4.032	6.859
6	.131	.265	.404	.553	.718	.906	1.134	1.440	1.943	2.447	3.143	3.707	5.959
7	.130	.263	.402	.549	.711	.896	1.119	1.415	1.895	2.365	2.998	3.499	5.405
8	.130	.262	.399	.546	.706	.889	1.108	1.397	1.860	2.306	2.896	3.355	5.041
9	.129	.261	.398	.543	.703	.883	1.100	1.383	1.833	2.262	2.821	3.250	4.781
10	.129	.260	.397	.542	.700	.879	1.093	1.372	1.812	2.228	2.764	3.169	4.587
11	.129	.260	.396	.540	.697	.876	1.088	1.363	1.796	2.201	2.718	3.106	4.437
12	.128	.259	.395	.539	.695	.873	1.083	1.356	1.782	2.179	2.681	3.055	4.318
13	.128	.259	.394	.538	.694	.870	1.079	1.350	1.771	2.160	2.650	3.012	4.221
14	.128	.258	.393	.537	.692	.868	1.076	1.345	1.761	2.145	2.624	2.977	4.140
15	.128	.258	.393	.536	.691	.866	1.074	1.341	1.753	2.131	2.602	2.947	4.073
16	.128	.258	.392	.535	.690	.865	1.071	1.337	1.746	2.120	2.583	2.921	4.015
17	.128	.257	.392	.534	.689	.863	1.069	1.333	1.740	2.110	2.567	2.898	3.965
18	.127	.257	.392	.534	.688	.862	1.067	1.330	1.734	2.101	2.552	2.878	3.922
19	.127	.257	.391	.533	.688	.861	1.066	1.328	1.729	2.093	2.539	2.861	3.883
20	.127	.257	.391	.533	.687	.860	1.064	1.325	1.725	2.086	2.528	2.845	3.850
21	.127	.257	.391	.532	.686	.859	1.063	1.323	1.721	2.080	2.518	2.831	3.819
22	.127	.256	.390	.532	.686	.858	1.061	1.321	1.717	2.074	2.508	2.819	3.792
23	.127	.256	.390	.532	.685	.858	1.060	1.319	1.714	2.069	2.500	2.807	3.767
24	.127	.256	.390	.531	.685	.857	1.059	1.318	1.711	2.064	2.492	2.797	3.745
25	.127	.256	.390	.531	.684	.856	1.058	1.316	1.708	2.060	2.485	2.787	3.725
26	.127	.256	.390	.531	.684	.856	1.058	1.315	1.706	2.056	2.479	2.779	3.707
27	.127	.256	.389	.531	.684	.855	1.057	1.314	1.703	2.052	2.473	2.771	3.690
28	.127	.256	.389	.530	.683	.855	1.056	1.313	1.701	2.048	2.467	2.763	3.674
29	.127	.256	.389	.530	.683	.854	1.055	1.311	1.699	2.045	2.462	2.756	3.659
30	.127	.256	.389	.530	.683	.854	1.055	1.310	1.697	2.042	2.457	2.750	3.646
40	.126	.255	.388	.529	.681	.851	1.050	1.303	1.684	2.021	2.423	2.704	3.551
60	.126	.254	.387	.527	.679	.848	1.046	1.296	1.671	2.000	2.390	2.660	3.460
128	.126	.254	.386	.526	.677	.845	1.041	1.289	1.658	1.980	2.358	2.617	3.373
∞	.126	.253	.385	.524	.674	.842	1.036	1.282	1.645	1.960	2.326	2.576	3.291

Source: Table III of Fisher and Yates: *Statistical Tables for Biological, Agricultural, and Medical Research,* published by Longman Group Ltd., London (previously published by Oliver and Boyd, Edinburgh), by permission of the authors and Addison Wesley Longman Ltd.

Two situations usually occur in using the Student's t distribution table (Table B.1):

1. You specify α and d.f. and you read t (the number of standard deviations to the right and left of the mean that spans the confidence interval or the unshaded area in the figure) from the body of the table.
2. You specify d.f. and t and read α from the top of the table.

Appendix C: Answers to Odd-Numbered Problems

CHAPTER 3

(1) $a = 34.8$, $b = -1.8$, $Y_7 = 22.2$. • **(3)** $a = 39.773$, $b = 9.646$, $Y_7 = 107.293$. • **(5)** $a = 17.799$, $b = 4.743$, $Y_7 = 88.001$. • **(7)** a. $a = -196.381$, $b = 67.238$, $Y_9 = 247.4$; $r^2 = 0.927$. • **(9)** a. Forecasts for month 24: $F_{AP=2} = 53.50$, $F_{AP=4} = 55.75$, $F_{AP=6} = 54.67$, $F_{AP=8} = 57.50$; b. $MAD_{AP=2} = 5.45$, $MAD_{AP=4} = 5.73$, $MAD_{AP=6} = 4.70$, $MAD_{AP=8} = 5.06$; c. $F_{25} = 54.00$. • **(11)** a. $F_{AP=2} = 140.0$, $F_{AP=4} = 138.0$, $F_{AP=6} = 138.5$; b. $MAD_{AP=2} = 2.417$, $MAD_{AP=4} = 2.083$, $MAD_{AP=6} = 1.944$. • **(13)** Forecasts for month 16: $F_{\alpha=0.1} = 0.388$, $F_{\alpha=0.3} = 0.378$, $F_{\alpha=0.5} = 0.372$; b. $\alpha = 0.1$; c. $F_{17} = 0.388$. • **(15)** $F_{13} = 173.55$ units. • **(17)** MAD is least when $\alpha = 0.9$. • **(19)** $F_7 = 109.15$. • **(21)** 23.738 engineers. • **(23)** a. $s_{yx} = 8.094$; b. 616.3 and 676.3. • **(25)** a. $Y_7 = 88.001$; b. $s_{yx} = 10.6305$, Range = 48.169 to 127.833. • **(27)** $F_{Q1} = \$11.08$ million, $F_{Q2} = \$6.88$ million, $F_{Q3} = \$5.81$ million, $F_{Q4} = \$18.46$ million. • **(29)** a. $Y_{18} = 24.877$; b. $SI_{Fall} = 0.849$; c. $UL_{18} = 30.895$.

CHAPTER 4

(9) A: 1306.8 units, B: 1437.5 units, C: 1312.5 units. • **(11)** a. $TC_{Manual} = \$3,358,750$; b. $Q = 372,340$; c. $Q = 1,230,000$. • **(13)** a. depends on annual quantity; b. $Q = 2,246$; c. Low-Tech: $Q = 0$ to 2,246, High-Tech: $Q = 2,246+$. • **(15)** a. $Z_{425} = 0.75$; b. \$30 per month per customer.

CHAPTER 5

(1) a. 8,044 helmets; b. \$796,356; c. \$160,000; d. \$108.34. • **(3)** b. Expand old store; c. \$1,400,000, \$800,000, or \$(400,000). • **(5)** b. Build small plant now; c. \$12,000,000, \$4,000,000, or \$3,000,000. • **(7)** b. 3.7 years. • **(9)** a. 31.065 years; b. lease existing building. • **(11)** a. San Antonio in Year 1, Dallas in Year 3 and beyond; b. San Antonio: $Q = 0$ to 6,500, Dallas: $Q = 6,500+$. • **(13)** Location scores: Hartford = 0.815, Philadelphia = 0.787, Baltimore = 0.793. • **(15)** b. 0.045 minutes; c. 31.1 workstations. • **(17)** b. 0.500 minutes; c. 10.1 workstations; d. (A), (B,C,D,E,F), (G,H,I), (J), (K), (L), 12 workstations, utilization = 84%. • **(19)** b. 0.250 minutes; c. 5.28 workstations; d. (A,B), (C,D,G), (E,G), (H,I), (J,K), (L), 6 workstations, utilization = 88%. • **(21)** a. (A,B), (C,D,E,F,G), (H,I), (J,K,L), 4 work centers and 6 workstations; b. (A,B), (C,D,F), (E,G), (H,I), (J,K), (L), 6 work centers and 6 workstations. • **(23)** Cell 1: machines A, D, F and parts 2, 5, 6; Cell 2: machines B, C, E and parts 1, 3, 4. • **(25)** Cell 1: machines B, C, F and parts 3, 5, 6, 8; Cell 2: machines D, G, I and parts 1, 4; Cell 3: machines A, E, G and parts 2, 6, 7.

CHAPTER 6

(5) a. Vandine: \$17,180, and Murcheck: \$20,640; b. 75 sorts per year. • **(7)** a. semiautomated: 0–1,707, and fully automated: 1,708+; b. 1,600 units; c. semiautomated:

$184,250, and fully automated: $275,000. • **(9)** a. CM and N/C: 3,928.6 units, and N/C and FMS: 19,571 units; b. CM: 2,893,000 and 3,838,000, N/C: 2,738,000 and 3,613,000, and FMS: 2,770,000 and 3,610,000. • **(11)** a. Machine A: 3.389 years, and Machine B: 2.923 years; b. Machine A: $2,700, and Machine B: $1,600. • **(15)** Gamma: 0.69, and Omega: 0.79. • **(17)** Alternative 1: 0.81, and Alternative 2: 0.73.

CHAPTER 7

(1) a. 0.993; b. 0.972. • **(3)** a. 0.8658; b. 0.9351. • **(5)** a. No, PCI must be ≥ 1.00 for production processes to have the capability of meeting customer expectations; b. σ must be reduced to allow PCI to be ≥ 1.00. • **(7)** 0.0833 ounces.

CHAPTER 8

(1) a. No; b. No, there are two managerial objectives. • **(3)** Max $Z = 15X_1 + 21X_2$; $4X_1 + 3X_2 \leq 920$; $8X_1 + 12X_2 \leq 2,400$; $X_1 \geq 100$; $X_2 \geq 100$; $X_1 =$ number of chairs to produce next week; $X_2 =$ number of bookshelf units to produce next week. • **(5)** Max $Z = 250X_1 + 200X_2$; $200X_1 + 150X_2 \leq 80,000$; $4X_1 + 2X_2 \leq 1,200$; $3X_1 + 5X_2 \leq 2,000$; $X_1 =$ number of relays to produce next quarter; $X_2 =$ number of capacitors to produce next quarter. • **(7)** Min $Z = 0.12X_1 + 0.07X_2$; $200X_1 + 100X_2 \geq 3,000$; $200X_1 + 300X_2 \geq 4,000$; $100X_1 + 200X_2 \geq 2,000$; $X_1 =$ pounds of oats per day; $X_2 =$ pounds of corn per day. • **(9)** Max $Z = 64X_1 + 87X_2$; $2.5X_1 + 3.2X_2 \leq 80$; $4X_1 + 2X_2 \leq 80$; $8X_2 \leq 80$; $X_1 =$ number of cases of Product A per week; $X_2 =$ number of cases of Product B per week. • **(11)** Min $Z = 0.5X_1 + 0.4X_2 + 0.8X_3$; $-X_1 + 5X_3 \geq 0$; $X_2 \leq 100,000$; $X_1 + X_2 + X_3 \geq 700,000$; $X_1 =$ number of pounds of carrier to include in glue next year; $X_2 =$ number of pounds of filler/color to include in glue next year; $X_3 =$ number of pounds of adhesive to include in glue next year. • **(13)** $X_1 = 150$, $X_2 = 100$, $Z = \$4,350$. • **(15)** $X_1 = 142.86$, $X_2 = 314.29$, $Z = \$98,571$. • **(17)** $X_1 = 12.5$, $X_2 = 5.0$, $Z = \$1.85$. • **(19)** $X_1 = 1,200$, $X_2 = 1,300$, $Z = \$30,300,000$.

CHAPTER 9

(1) a. 12.25 or 13 cashiers; c. Yes, the schedule is optimal, 13 cashiers are required, three shifts have an extra cashier. • **(3)** a. 1.63 units in line; b. 2.33 units in system; c. 14.0 minutes; d. 20.0 minutes; e. 0.300. • **(5)** Present: 0.083 student in line, 0.167 minute, and 0.250; proposed: 1.63 students in line, 3.27 minutes, and 0.700. • **(7)** a. 1.60 units in line; b. 2.4 units in system; c. 4.80 minutes; d. 7.20 minutes. • **(9)** Annual savings is $7,981.50, the savings can pay for the device in 1.25 years, buy the device. • **(11)** 1.868 units. • **(13)** a. 0.0895; b. 7.706 units in line. • **(15)** N = 4: unstable; N = 5: 0.2182 hours or 13.09 minutes in line; N = 6: 0.0499 hours or 2.99 minutes in line. • **(17)** a. Number of students arriving in five periods: 5, 4, 4, 6, 5; b. Number of minutes required to service students in five periods: 51.92, 43.68, 36.86, 61.64, 50.36.

CHAPTER 10

(1) Activity F, field test, is 1 month behind schedule; Activity G, production design, is 1 month ahead of schedule. • **(3)** Production transistor sets were begun 1 month late and are approximately 1.5 months behind schedule; the production chassis were begun 1 month early and are 0.5 month ahead of schedule; instrumentation sets and production packaging are 0.5 months behind schedule. • **(5)** 10 weeks. • **(7)** c. Path b–e–h–j–k, 30 days. • **(9)** d. Path b–d–g–i, 42 days. • **(11)** d. Path b–d–f–g–j–k, 32 days. • **(13)** a. 14.167; b. 1.361. • **(15)** Path duration = 53.66, path variance = 2.610. • **(17)** e. Path b–d–g–i, 42.00 days; f. 0.00539 or 0.539%. • **(19)** Path 1. • **(21)** b. Crash activities b, g, and i; 38 days, $5,300.

CHAPTER 11

(7) Make; TC_{Buy} = $950,000; TC_{Make} = $880,000. • **(9)** a. India, TC_{India} = $670,000; b. Taiwan: 32,895+, Singapore: 0–6,363, India: 6,364–32,894. • **(11)** b. Submit proposal for medium level of funding; if they win the contract, they should develop a commercial product; c. EV = $172,000. • **(13)** Scores: Sumsing = 0.754, Parkasenic = 0.730, Hatchui = 0.780; Hatchui is the preferred vendor. • **(15)** b. 500 units in Week 1 and Week 2. • **(17)** a. 18,000 units from 1 to D; 7,000 units from 1 to E; 1,000 units from 2 to A; 15,000 units from 2 to B; 13,000 units from 2 to E; 11,000 units from 2 to F; 8,000 units from 3 to A; 12,000 units from 3 to C; b. $287,700. • **(21)** a. 20.64 or 21 counters; b. $630,000; c. 35.52 or 36 counters; d. $450,000.

CHAPTER 12

(1) 40 products per hour. • **(3)** Lead time would be reduced from 6.316 to 2.286, or 4.03 minutes. • **(5)** WIP = 1.735; probability of system not idle = 0.7434. • **(7)** 2.995 or 3 containers. • **(9)** 55 parts. • **(11)** a. $2.441; b. $0.172 savings; c. New Q = 21.797 or 22 units per batch. • **(13)** a. 0.197 minute, or 11.8 seconds.

CHAPTER 13

(1) Business: Q_1 = 16.93, Q_2 = 18.96, Q_3 = 13.32, Q_4 = 13.65; Home: Q_1 = 11.40, Q_2 = 12.30, Q_3 = 10.38, Q_4 = 9.37; Education: Q_1 = 7.67, Q_2 = 9.14, Q_3 = 19.75, Q_4 = 11.40. • **(3)** a. Q_1 = 22.0, Q_2 = 21.0, Q_3 = 21.0, Q_4 = 31.0; b. Q_1 = 110, Q_2 = 105, Q_3 = 105, Q_4 = 155; c. Q_1 = 211.5, Q_2 = 201.9, Q_3 = 201.9, Q_4 = 298.1. • **(5)** Business: Q_1 = 9.11, Q_2 = 10.21, Q_3 = 7.17, Q_4 = 7.35; Home: Q_1 = 15.78, Q_2 = 17.03, Q_3 = 14.38, Q_4 = 12.97; Education: Q_1 = 8.26, Q_2 = 9.84, Q_3 = 21.27, Q_4 = 12.27. • **(7)** Level costs $36,812.50 and matching costs $59,000. • **(9)** Level costs $31,250 and matching costs $40,500. • **(11)** Level costs $50,400 and matching costs $68,700. • **(13)** MPS ending inventory in weeks 1–10: 500; 1,500; 500; 1,500; 500; 1,500; 500; 1,500; 500; 1,500. • **(15)** a. Total load = 109,250 hours, total capacity = 120,000 hours; b. Yes, but underloading exists in Weeks 1, 2, 5 and overloading exists in Weeks 3, 4, 6; c. Move some production from Weeks 3, 4, 6 to Weeks 1, 2, 5. • **(17)** A: 5,000 cases in Weeks 1, 3, 6; B: 8,000 cases in Weeks 1, 3, 4, 7, 8 and 8,600 cases in Week 6; C: 2,000 cases in Weeks 1, 3, 4, 7.

CHAPTER 14

(1) a. 3,172; b. $11,696.42; c. $332.96. • **(3)** 45 reams, 22.5 reams. • **(5)** a. 851 boxes; b. 49.35 orders per year; c. $2,467.79; d. 7.4 days per order. • **(7)** a. 45,752 barrels; b. $304,249.90; c. 9.15 days; d. 26,688.7 barrels. • **(9)** a. 200 dozen; b. $27,895.50; c. 7.5 orders per year; d. 200 dozen; c. 118 dozen. • **(11)** a. 200,000 gallons; b. $17,263,968.60; c. 26.01 orders per year; d. 4.545 or 5 days; e. 122,727 gallons. • **(13)**

a. 8 cases; b. 6.844; c. 1.156. • **(15)** a. $180,800; b. $20,800. • **(17)** a. 222; b. 962; c. 27.2; d. 767. • **(19)** a. Every 15 days; b. $2,738,884.45; c. 652. • **(21)** a. 300 ounces; b. EVPI = $3,600. • **(23)** $400,000.

CHAPTER 15

(1) Net requirements: 0, 400, 300, 800, 1000, 500. • **(5)** Planned order releases: 1200, 0, 1250, 1200, 0, 0. • **(7)** Planned order releases—A: 0, 20, 530, 410, 380, 0; B: 0, 470, 820, 760, 0, 0; C: 1,500, 1,500, 1,500, 0, 0, 0; D: 1,000, 2,030, 2,280, 0, 0, 0. • **(9)** Planned order releases—B353: 560, 0, 1,800, 0, 1,500, 0; R25: 0, 7,140, 0, 6,000, 0, 0; N35: 0, 3,435, 0, 3,000, 0, 0; K45: 0, 5,360, 0, 4,500, 0, 0; B5: 14,080, 0, 12,000, 0, 0, 0; F3: 8,000, 0, 10,810, 0, 0, 0; L7: 1,000 (rush), 0, 8,480, 0, 0, 0; D9: 3,000 (rush), 22,500, 0, 0, 0, 0. • **(11)** Planned order releases—A: 0, 0, 0, 800, 2,500, 0; B: 0, 0, 1,000, 5,000, 0, 0; C: 0, 0, 300, 2,500, 0, 0; D: 0, 0, 800, 2,500, 0, 0; E: 0, 0, 5,000, 0, 0, 0; F: 9,300, 0, 0, 0, 0, 0; G: 0, 0, 0, 0, 0, 0; H: 0, 0, 0, 4,000, 0, 0. • **(13)** Planned order releases—Q44: 0, 2,400, 1,700, 1,900, 1,800; A: 1,500, 1,900, 1,800, 0, 0; B: 0, 1,200, 1,700, 1,900, 1,800; C: 3,400, 3,400, 3,800, 3,600, 0; D: 1,500, 2,100, 3,800, 3,600, 0; E: 0, 0, 1,000, 1,600, 0; F: 0, 2,000, 2,000, 2,000, 0; G: 0, 3,000, 3,000, 0, 0; H: 0, 0, 0, 0, 0; I: 0, 2,000, 0, 0, 0. • **(15)** a. $48,000; b. Lots of 5,586 in Weeks 1, 5, 8, cost = $32,780; c. 5,000 units in Week 1 and 7,000 units in Week 5, cost = $24,115.39. • **(17)** a. Labor: 72.7, 87.9, 130.3, 106.1, 78.8, and 84.8%; machine: 72.7, 87.9, 130.3, 106.1, 78.8, and 84.8%.

CHAPTER 16

(1) a. Not enough input to the work center; b. Increase upstream capacities. • **(5)** a. 162, 166, 164, 161, 165, 163; b. 162, 161, 164, 163, 165, 166; c. 162, 161, 163, 164, 165, 166. • **(7)** a. Shortest processing time ranks first on both criteria; b. Shortest processing time, but must deal with long jobs. • **(9)** a. A–C–E–B–D; b. $170. • **(11)** a. 3–6–4–2–5–1; b. 8.6 hours. • **(13)** a. A–2, B–4, C–1, D–3, E–5; b. 15.4 hours. • **(15)** a. $EOQ_1 = 2,371.7$, $EOQ_2 = 3,000.0$, $EOQ_3 = 2,529.8$, $EOQ_4 = 2,109.9$; b. 33%; c. 23.7 days. • **(17)** Aggregate runout time = 0.532 quarters, final assembly hours for each scanner—SC1: 176.82, SC2: 157.80, SC3: 184.80, SC4: 161.82, SC5: 118.86. • **(19)** b. All steps are on schedule except 1 and 3; delivery of component A seems to be the cause of the difficulty.

CHAPTER 17

(1) 0 and 7.70%. • **(3)** a. 2.5%; b. 0 and 5.812%. • **(5)** a. 0.728 and 9.272%; c. Number of academic drops is falling. • **(7)** a. 11.46 and 12.54 inches; c. No, the sample means in inches are erratic and the process is out of control on the upward side. • **(9)** a. 11.617 and 12.383 hours; c. Yes, the process seems to be in control; while some samples are beyond the limits, no out-of-control situation seems to exist. • **(11)** a. 15.91 and 16.09 ounces; b. 0.793 and 0.207 ounce; c. The charts indicate that the between-sample variation and within-sample variation are in control. • **(13)** a. α = 19.12%; b. β = 9.16%. • **(15)** a. n = 95, c = 2, AOQL = 0.99%. • **(17)** Reject the lot, p = 1.0% and acceptance criterion = 0.86%. • **(19)** Reject the lot, p = 1.25% and acceptance criterion = 1.078%. • **(21)** Do not reject the lot, 53.9 tons falls within the acceptance criteria of 53.669 and 56.331 tons.

CHAPTER 18

(3) Remedies rank in this order: time away from job, job enrichment, job rotation, and supervisor training. • **(11)** a. 6.270 minutes per hundred letters; b. 76.56 hundred letters per shift; c. $1.568 per hundred letters. • **(13)** a. 1: 0.215 minute, 2: 2.700, 3: 4.250, 4: 0.575; b. 1: 0.2365 minute, 2: 3.5100, 3: 3.6125, 4: 0.6900; c. 0.2292; d. 10.442 minutes. • **(15)** 400. • **(17)** 0.2149. • **(19)** a. 3.054 minutes per product; b. 3.724 minutes per product. • **(21)** a. $7.735 per unit; b. $1,198.93. • **(23)** a. 18.55 minutes; b. 297.6 minutes, or 4.96 hours. • **(25)** a. 77.55 minutes; b. 4,715.7 minutes, or 78.595 hours; c. 85%, and 4,312.1 minutes, or 71.868 hours.

CHAPTER 19

(1) 3.333 machines per hour. • **(3)** a. 18.02 minutes; b. 140.4 square feet. • **(5)** 70 seals, $360.50. • **(7)** Perform PM every two months; expected cost of this policy is $2,500 per month. • **(9)** Perform PM every 60,000 miles; expected cost of this policy is $20.87 per 1,000 miles. • **(11)** a. 99.7%; b. 97.6%. • **(13)** a. 0.902; b. 0.965. • **(15)** b. Path a–b–h–j; c. 52 days.

A

Acceptable quality level (AQL) In quality control, level used to define good lots.

Acceptance plan In quality control, the overall scheme for accepting or rejecting a product lot based on information gained from samples.

Acquisition cost Cost of purchasing or producing a unit of a material or product.

Activity In project management, a task or a certain amount of work required in a project.

Aggregate planning Process of providing an intermediate-term production capacity scheme to support a sales forecast for a product.

Aggregate unit of capacity Measure that allows rates of various outputs to be converted to a common unit of output measure.

Arrival One unit of the arrival rate distribution. Occurs when one person, machine, part, etc., arrives and demands service. Each unit may continue to be called an arrival while in the service system.

Arrival rate The rate at which things or persons arrive, in arrivals per unit of time (e.g., persons per hour). Arrival rate is usually normal or Poisson distributed.

Assemble-to-order firm Firm that assembles, from a relatively few major assemblies or components, customer-ordered end items having many options.

Assembly chart Macroview chart listing all major materials, components, subassembly and assembly operations, and inspections for a product.

Assignment method Linear programming solution method used to assign jobs or personnel to machines or departments.

Attributes In quality control, product characteristics that are classified into one of two categories: defective or nondefective.

Automated assembly system System of automated assembly machines linked by automated materials-handling equipment; used to produce major assemblies or completed products.

Automated flow line Production line that includes several automated machines linked by automated parts transfer and handling machines; designed to produce one type of component or product.

Automated guided vehicle system (AGVS) System that uses powered and computer-controlled conveyors such as driverless trains, pallet trucks, and unit load carriers to deliver orders to workstations in operations.

Automated process controls system System that uses sensors to obtain measures of the performance of industrial processes, compare them to predetermined standards, and then automatically signal changes in the settings of those processes.

Automated quality control inspection system System utilizing machines that have been integrated into the inspection of products for quality control purposes.

Automated storage and retrieval system (ASRS) System for receiving orders for materials, collecting the materials, and delivering them to work stations in operations.

Automatic identification system (AIS) System that uses bar codes, radio frequencies, magnetic strips, optical character recognition, and machine vision to sense and input data into computers.

Automation Integrating a full range of advanced scientific and engineering discoveries into production processes for strategic purposes.

Average outgoing quality (AOQ) Average percentage of defectives in lots leaving an inspection station.

Average outgoing quality limit (AOQL) Maximum average outgoing quality that can occur as the actual percent defectives in lots varies.

B

Backward integration Expansion of the ownership of a company's production and distribution chain backward toward the sources of supply.

Backward scheduling Scheduling jobs at work centers starting backwards in time from the customer due date, so that jobs start as late as possible at each work center and still meet the due dates.

Base stock model Simple inventory-planning system that replenishes inventory only in the amount of each withdrawal, thereby maintaining inventory at a constant level.

Batch production Product-focused production in which large batches of standardized products follow direct linear routes in the same production system.

Benchmarking The practice of establishing internal standards of performance by looking at how world-class companies run their businesses.

Best-in-class Being the best product or service in a particular class of products or services.

Bill of material List of the materials and their quantities required to produce one unit of a product, or end item.

Bills of material file Complete list of all finished products, quantity of each material in each product, and the structure of all products; may also be called an *indented parts list.*

Break-even analysis Process of determining the production volume needed to make revenues equal to costs.

Bucket Principal unit of time measurement in a material requirements planning system; usually one week.

Buffer Work in process inventory that is kept in front of the bottleneck machine so that it does not run out of work. Used in theory of constraints approach.

Business strategy Long-range plan of an organization and the methods to be used to achieve its corporate objectives.

Business-to-business (B2B) transactions E-business transactions between companies; also called e-commerce.

C

Capacity cushion Additional amount of production capacity added on to the expected demand.

Capacity utilization percentage The percentage of capacity that is used during a time period.

Capital-intensive Depending on capital rather than labor as the predominant resource in an operation.

Carrying cost Total cost of holding a material in inventory; expressed in dollars per unit per year.

Causal forecasting model Model that develops forecasts after establishing and measuring an association between the dependent variable and one or more independent variables; used to predict turning points in sales.

Cellular manufacturing (CM) Grouping of machines into cells that function like a product layout island within a larger job shop or process layout.

Central limit theorem Theorem that states that sampling distributions can be assumed to be normally distributed even though the population distributions are not normal.

Changes to planned orders Reports that show how planned order schedules should be changed to allow for earlier or later delivery, for cancellation, or for change in quantity.

Channels The number of waiting lines in a service system. A single-channel system has only one line, and a multichannel system has two or more lines.

Closed-loop MRP System built around material requirements planning and also including production planning, master production scheduling, capacity requirements planning, and various execution functions.

Closeness ratings Used to reflect the desirability of having one department near another.

Coefficient of correlation Measure that explains the relative importance of the relationship between two variables.

Coefficient of determination Measure of the expected precision of a forecast, explaining the amount of variation in one variable that is explained by another variable.

Component reliability Probability that a type of part will not fail in a given time period or in a number of trials under ordinary conditions of use.

Computer-aided design (CAD) Computerized process for designing new products or modifying existing ones.

Computer-aided manufacturing (CAM) Use of computers to plan and program production equipment in the production of manufactured items.

Computer-integrated manufacturing (CIM) Total integration of all business functions associated with production through computer systems.

Consumer's risk In quality control, the probability of accepting a bad lot.

Continuous production Product-focused production in which a few highly standardized products are produced continuously in very large volumes.

Control chart Chart used to routinely monitor a production operation to determine if its outputs meet quality standards.

Control decision Short-range, relatively simple decision about the planning and controlling of day-to-day operations.

Control subsystem Subsystem of a larger production system in which a portion of the outputs is monitored for feedback signals to provide corrective action if required.

Continuous improvement Allows companies to accept modest beginnings and make small incremental improvements toward excellence.

Controllable factors Machine malfunctions, bad materials, and incorrect work methods.

Conversion subsystem Subsystem of a larger production system in which inputs are converted into outputs.

Co-producers What the Japanese call suppliers.

Corporate mission A set of long range goals unique to an organization and including statements about the kind of business the company wants to be in, who its customers are, its basic beliefs about business, and it goals of survival, growth, and profitability.

Crashing Accelerating or speeding up an activity by adding resources; reducing the time required for a project.

Crew size standard Labor standard determined by estimating the total number of workers required to produce the necessary output per shift.

Critical activity In project management, an activity that has no room for schedule slippage; an activity with zero slack.

Critical path In project management, a chain of critical activities for a project; the longest path through a network.

Critical path method (CPM) Network-based project management initially used in maintenance and defense projects; nearly identical to PERT.

Cumulative end item lead time Amount of time required to obtain materials from suppliers, produce and assemble all parts of a product, and deliver the product to the customer.

Custom product Product designed to meet the needs of individual customers.

Customer-as-participant There is a high degree of customer involvement in this type of service operation. Physical goods may or may not be a significant part of the service, and the services may be either custom or standard. Retailing is an example of this type of service operation.

Customer-as-product In this type of service operation, customers are so involved that the service is actually performed on the customer. Physical goods may or may not be a significant part of the service, and the services are usually custom. Examples of this type of service operation are hair salons, medical clinics and hospitals, and tailors.

Customer satisfaction Determination of customer requirements and demonstrated success in meeting them.

Customer surveys Allow customers to fill out survey questionnaires or participate in interviews that are aimed at determining the customers' perceptions about several quality-related issues.

Cycle counting Verifying the accuracy of inventory records by periodically counting the number of units of each material in inventory.

D

Decision tree analysis Graphic aid in making multiphase decisions that shows the sequence and interdependence of decisions.

De-expediting Slowing down a job order in the production system that is ahead of schedule.

Delphi method Qualitative forecasting method used to achieve consensus within a committee.

Demand during lead time (DDLT) Number of units of a material demanded during the inventory replenishment process or lead time.

Demand management Recognizing and managing all demands for products and services to ensure that the master scheduler is aware of them.

Deming Prize Established in 1951 for innovation in quality management to be awarded annually to a company that has distinguished itself in quality management programs.

Dependent demand Demand for an item that depends on the demands for other inventory items.

Design simplification In product and machine reliability, the reduction of the number of interacting parts in a machine or product.

Discrete unit manufacturing Manufacturing distinct or separate products such as automobiles or dishwashers.

Diseconomies of scale Increase in unit cost caused by additional volume of outputs past the point of best operating level for a facility.

Dispatching list A list showing the sequence in which a set of jobs at a work center should be processed.

Distinctive competencies Competitive advantages of a firm that can be used in capturing markets.

Distribution requirements planning (DRP) Planning for the replenishment of regional warehouse inventories.

Distribution resource planning Planning for the provision of the key resources of warehouse space—number of workers, cash, shipping vehicles, etc.—in the right quantities and when needed.

Distribution system Network of shipping and receiving points starting with the factory and ending with the customers.

Dodge-Romig tables In quality control, attribute acceptance plans that set sample size and maximum number of defectives in a sample to accept the lot.

Double-sampling plan In quality control, an acceptance sampling plan in which an accept or reject decision can be made on the first sample drawn, but if it is not, a second sample is taken and a decision is made on the basis of the combined samples.

Drum The bottleneck process that sets the pace of the entire production system. Used in theory of constraints approach.

Dummy activity In project management, a CPM network device that simply indicates precedence relationships.

E

Earliest finish (EF) In project management, the earliest that an activity can finish.

Earliest start (ES) In project management, the earliest time that an activity can start.

E-business Use of the Internet to conduct or facilitate business transactions, such as sales, purchasing, communication, inventory management, customer service, submitting orders, and checking the status of orders.

E-commerce E-business transactions between companies.

Economic order quantity (EOQ) Optimal order quantity that minimizes total annual stocking costs.

Economies of scale Reduction in unit cost as fixed costs are spread over increasingly more units.

Economies of scope Production of many product models in one highly flexible production facility more cheaply than in separate production facilities.

Electronic Data Interchange (EDI) A dedicated computer hardware and software system that allows two companies to electronically conduct business transactions with each other.

End item Product, service, or other output that has a demand independent of the demands for other components or end items.

Enterprise resource planning (ERP) systems Comprehensive software packages that companies use to help automate a variety of business processes. ERP systems integrate most of the business functions in an organization.

Event In project management, a signal that an activity has either begun or ended.

Expediting Speeding up an order through all or part of the entire materials system.

Exponential smoothing Short-range forecasting model that takes the forecast for the preceding period and adds an adjustment to obtain the forecast for the next period.

F

5S process Another name for housekeeping. Five housekeeping rules include sort, straighten, sweep, standardize, and self-discipline.

Facility layout Plan for the location of all machines and utilities and for the physical arrangement within facilities of all manufacturing processes and their support functions.

Facility planning Determination of how much long-range production capacity is needed, when it is needed, where production facilities should be located, and the layout and characteristics of the facilities.

Final-assembly schedule (FAS) Schedule for assembling unique products ordered by customers.

Finite loading Assigning jobs to work centers so that the capacities of the work centers are not exceeded.

Fishbone diagram Diagram used to trace back a customer complaint about a quality problem to the responsible production operation.

Fixed order quantity system System of inventory planning that places fixed quantity orders for a material when the inventory level falls to a predetermined critical level.

Fixed-position layout Layout that locates the product in a fixed position and transports workers, materials, machines, and subcontractors to and from the product.

Flexible automation Use of computer-driven automated machines that are easily reprogrammed for other products.

Flexible manufacturing system (FMS) System in which groups of production machines are sequentially connected by automated materials-handling and transferring machines and integrated into a computer system.

Flow diagram Diagram of the flow of workers, equipment, or materials through a process.

Flow shop Type of product-focused factory in which large batches of standardized products are produced in the same production system.

Focus groups Groups of customers brought together to discuss and evaluate quality with executives and engineers.

Forecasting Estimating the future demand for products/services and the resources necessary to produce them.

Forward integration Expansion of the ownership of a company's production and distribution chain forward toward the market.

Forward scheduling Scheduling jobs to start as early as possible at each work center, without considering the due dates of the jobs.

G

Gantt chart Chart that coordinates work center schedules by showing the progress of each job in relation to its scheduled finish date.

Group technology Form of production based on a coding system for parts that allows families of parts to be assigned to manufacturing cells for production.

Group technology coding system A coding system that is developed for parts in a factory. A code describes physical characteristics, processing characteristics, and other information about a part.

H

Hard automation Use of automatic machinery that is difficult to change over to other products.

Heuristics Simple rules or guides to action.

Historical labor standard Labor standard determined by using historical data from the actual performance of the operation being studied.

Housekeeping Maintaining an orderly environment at a workstation in order to avoid confusion and errors.

Human relations movement Early twentieth-century development of a philosophy among managers that workers are human beings and should be treated with dignity in the workplace.

Hybrid layout Layout that uses a combination of layout types, as an assembly line combined with a process layout.

I

Impulse response In forecasting, the speed at which forecasts reflect changes in underlying data.

Incentive pay system Pay system that makes the amount of workers' pay conditional upon job performance.

Incremental utilization (IU) heuristic Adding tasks to a workstation one at a time in order of precedence until the worker utilization is either 100 percent or observed to fall, then repeating the process for the remaining tasks.

Independent demand Demand for an item that is independent of the demand for any other item carried in inventory.

Industrial revolution Widespread substitution of machine power and the establishment of the factory system.

Infinite loading Assigning jobs to work centers without considering the capacities of the work centers.

In-process inventory Inventory of partially completed products that are between processing steps.

Input rate capacity Measure that allows rates of various inputs to be converted to a common unit of input measure.

Inputs Any raw material, personnel, capital, utilities, or information that is entered into a conversion system.

Intermittent production Production performed on products on a start-and-stop basis.

Internal customer The next production operation.

International company Company that engages in production sharing and sells its products in world markets.

Inventory cycle Activities of sensing a need for a material, placing an order, waiting for the material to be delivered, receiving the material, and using the material.

Inventory record Display of all of the inventory transactions that have affected a material.

Inventory status file Computerized file with a complete record of each material held in inventory.

J

Job shop Factory whose departments of work centers are organized around particular types of equipment or operations; products flow through departments in batches corresponding to stock orders or customer orders.

Just-in-time (JIT) manufacturing system Production and inventory control system based on small lot sizes, stable and level production schedules, and a pull system of production; system of enforced problem solving.

K

Kaizen The goal of continuous improvement in every phase of manufacturing.

Kanban Production system based on conveyance and production cards that determine the movement of production orders between work stations.

L

Labor intensive Depending on labor rather than capital as the predominant resource in an operation.

Labor standard Number of worker-minutes required to complete an element, operation, or product under ordinary operating conditions.

Latest finish (LF) In project management, the latest time that an activity can finish without delaying the entire project.

Latest start (LS) In project management, the latest time that an activity can start without delaying the entire project.

Lean manufacturing Production and inventory control system that emphasizes the minimization of the amount of all the resources used (including time).

Level production Stabilized production output levels from time period to time period.

Line balancing Allocating the various work tasks among all work stations on a production line in order to equally divide, or balance, the work effort.

Line of balance (LOB) Method of scheduling and controlling upstream production steps to ensure deliveries to customers.

Linear programming (LP) Technique for applying scarce resources optimally to competing demands.

Linear regression analysis Forecast model that establishes a relationship between a dependent variable and one or more independent variables.

Load schedule Comparison of the labor- and machine-hours needed to produce the master production schedule with the labor- and machine-hours actually available in each week.

Longest-task-time (LTT) heuristic Adding tasks to a work station one at a time in the order of precedence.

Lot Discrete group of products that have been produced under the same conditions.

Lot-for-lot (LFL) A lot-sizing approach in which there are no restrictions on the order quantity allowed.

Lot size decisions Given a net requirements schedule, decisions on how to group these requirements into production lots or purchase lots. The decisions usually include both the size and timing of the lots.

Lot-sizing Determining how many units of a product to produce to minimize unit cost.

Lot tolerance percent defective (LTPD) In quality control, term used to define bad lots; if lots have greater than LTPD, they are considered bad lots.

Low-level coding Coding of a material at the lowest level that the material appears in any product structure.

Lumpy demand Demand for a material that has an irregular period-to-period pattern.

M

Machine attachments Add-ons to machines that reduce the amount of human effort and time required to perform an operation.

Manufacturing resource planning Process of planning all resources of a firm, including business planning, production planning, master production scheduling, material requirements planning, and capacity requirements planning.

Master production schedule (MPS) Schedule of the amount and timing of all end items to be produced over a specific planning horizon.

Matching demand plan Aggregate production plan in which production capacity in each time period is varied to exactly match the forecasted aggregate demand in that time period.

Material specification Detailed description of a good to be purchased; can include engineering drawings, chemical analysis, and a list of physical characteristics.

Materials Any commodities used directly or indirectly in producing a product or service, such as raw materials, component parts, assemblies, and supplies.

Materials-handling system Entire network of transportation that receives, sorts, moves, and delivers materials within a production facility.

Materials management Management of all of the functions related to the complete cycle of materials flows, including the purchase and internal control of materials, the planning and control of work in process, and the warehousing, shipping, and distribution of end items.

Mistake-proofing Redesigning a process so that it is more difficult to make a mistake.

Modular bill of material In assemble-to-order firms, a bill of material that lists the forecasted percentage of customer orders that require each option together with the kit of parts common to all of the customer orders.

Monte Carlo In computer simulation, a technique for generating random values from discrete distributions.

Most likely time The time duration estimate for an activity in a project if the activity were to occur normally or typically.

Moving average method Short-range forecasting method that averages the data from a few recent past periods to form the forecast for the next period.

Multiactivity chart Chart showing how one or more workers work together and/or with machines.

Multiple regression analysis Forecasting model used when there are two or more independent variables.

Mystery shoppers Employees who pretend to be customers but who actually monitor the quality of services worldwide.

N

Net change material requirements planning system MRP system in which changes to the master production schedule initiate an updating of only the affected inventory records.

Newsboy problem The problem of determining the order quantity of an item to cover the demand for only a single time period.

Numerically controlled (N/C) machines Machines preprogrammed through magnetic tape or computers to perform a cycle of operations repeatedly.

O

Offsetting for lead time Accounting for the time required to produce a production lot in-house or to receive a lot purchased from a supplier. A requirement in one time period will necessitate the release of the order in some earlier time period; the number of periods between the requirement and the release is the offset and is equal to the lead time.

Operating characteristic (OC) curve In quality control, a graph of the performance of an acceptance plan.

Operating decision Short-range or intermediate-range decision about planning production to meet demand.

Operating expense Money spent in converting inventory into throughput. Used in theory of constraints approach.

Operations management The management of an organization's productive resources or its production system, which converts inputs into the organization's products and services.

Operations research World War II term for scientific investigations; sought to replace intuitive decision making with an analytical, systematic, and interdisciplinary approach.

Operations strategy Plan for achieving the operations objective for a major product line.

Opportunity cost Cost in the form of profits forgone.

Optimistic time The best case time duration estimate for an activity in a project if all goes as well as possible.

Optimized production technology (OPT) A production planning and control information system that finds the bottlenecks in a production process.

Optional replenishment model System of inventory planning that reviews inventory levels at fixed time intervals but replaces the inventory only if levels have dropped below a certain minimum level.

Order backlog A set of job orders that have been received but that have not yet been started in production.

Order entry Acceptance of an order into the master production schedule; includes check of delivery date, assignment of production slot in the MPS, and communicating the promised date to the customer.

Order point (OP) Point when an order is placed for a material in a fixed order period inventory system; expected demand during lead time plus safety stock.

Order promising Setting a date on which a product is to be delivered to the customer.

Order quantity Quantity of a material ordered each time inventory is replenished.

Order-to-delivery-cycle The elapsed time between the moment that a customer places an order until the customer receives the order.

Ordering cost Average cost of each inventory replenishment for a material (excluding material cost); includes such costs as processing purchasing requisitions, purchase order, machine changeovers, postage, telephone calls, quality inspections, and receiving.

Output End product or service of a conversion system.

Output rate capacity Companies having a small variety of products can measure their capacity based on units of output, such as automobiles per month, tons of coal per day, or barrels of beer per week.

Outsourcing Hiring out or subcontracting some of the work that a company needs to do.

Overdesign Enhancement of a machine design to avoid a particular type of failure during production.

P

Parameter design Determining product specifications and production process settings that will permit satisfactory product performance in spite of undesirable production and field conditions.

Perpetual inventory accounting System in which stock records are continually updated as materials are received into or dispensed from inventory.

Pessimistic time The worst case time duration estimate for an activity in a project if all goes poorly.

Plan-do-check-act (PDCA) cycle Concept of continuous improvement as an endless cycle.

Planned order release Quantity of a material to be ordered in each time period of the planning horizon.

Planned order schedule Schedule of planned future order releases over the entire planning horizon.

Poka-yoke Redesigning a process so that it is more difficult to make a mistake. Japanese term used in JIT manufacturing; also called mistake-proofing.

Pond draining approach A production planning and control system that uses large amounts of raw materials, work in process, and finished goods inventories. Large inventories allow production and purchasing activities to be decoupled from customer demand.

Predetermined time standards Work measurement technique that uses historically developed data to determine labor standards before an operation is performed.

Preproduction planning Developing the technical designs of products and the processing plans for how a product will be produced.

Present-value analysis Process of determining the amount of money that must be invested now at a specified rate of interest to accumulate to a certain amount in the future.

Preventive maintenance (PM) Activities, such as machine adjustments, lubrication, cleaning, parts replacement, painting, and needed repairs and overhauls, that are performed before malfunction of facilities or machines occurs.

Process capability Production process's ability to produce products within the desired expectations of customers.

Process capability index (PCI) Determining if a production process has the ability to produce products within the desired expectations of customers.

Process chart Chart documenting the elemental steps in one of the several operations in producing a product.

Process layout Layout for the production of a variety of nonstandard products in relatively small batches, as in a custom machine shop.

Process life cycle As a product moves through its product life cycle, the way it is processed often changes from low volume, small batch, process-focused production early in its life to high volume, large batch, product-focused production later in its life.

Process-focused production Factory operation that produces many unique products in relatively small batches flowing along different paths through the factory and requiring frequent machine changeover; also called a *job shop*.

Process reengineering Drastically redesigning a process to achieve substantial improvements.

Produce-to-order Produce products only after customers' orders are in hand.

Produce-to-stock Produce products ahead of time and place them in inventory until customers demand them.

Producer's risk In quality control, the probability of rejecting a good lot.

Product flexibility Ability of the production system to quickly change from producing one product/service to producing another.

Product-focused production Factory or service operation in which there are only a few standardized product/service designs, the product/services are usually produced for finished-goods inventory, and the production rates of individual products and services are usually greater than their demand rates.

Product layout Layout designed to accommodate only a few product designs, as in product-focused production.

Product life cycle After a new product is developed it moves through several demand stages during its life, from introduction to growth to maturity and then to decline.

Production capacity Maximum production rate of an organization.

Production lot A quantity of material produced at one stage of production, stored in inventory, and then sent to the next stage in production or shipped to customers.

Production sharing Participation of several companies from various countries in the design, financing, production, assembly, shipment, and sale of a product.

Productivity Amount of products or services produced with the resources used.

Program evaluation and review technique (PERT) Project-planning method that uses multiple activity time estimates.

Project organization A separate organizational unit or division is created for a project within the organization's management reporting structure. Personnel are temporarily assigned to this new unit for the duration of the project, and the project manager reports directly to a high-level executive.

Prototype design Initial product design exhibiting the basic characteristics of a product's form, fit, and function that will be required of the final design.

Pull system System of production planning and control in which the next stage of production is looked at, determined what is needed, and that only is produced.

Purchase requisition Authorization to purchase a good or service.

Push system System of production planning and control in which products are moved forward through production by the preceding step in the process.

Q

Q-1 list List of suppliers with which Ford is willing to have long-term (usually three-year) supply contracts in order to achieve highest quality at competitive costs.

Quality at the source Assignment of responsibility for product quality to production workers, who are expected to produce parts of perfect quality before those parts are passed on to the next production operation.

Quality circle (QC circle) Small group of employees who voluntarily and regularly meet to analyze and solve production and quality problems.

Quality function deployment (QFD)   A formal system for identifying customer wants and eliminating wasteful product features and activities that do not contribute.

Quantity discount   Decrease in unit price as larger quantities are ordered.

Quasi-manufacturing   In this type of service operation, production occurs much as in manufacturing. The emphasis is on production costs, technology, physical materials and products, product quality, and prompt delivery. Physical goods are dominant over intangible services, products may be either standard or custom, and there is little customer contact or involvement. The back-room operations at banks, industrial heat-treating services, and aircraft maintenance operations are examples of this type of service operation.

Queue   Waiting line.

Queue discipline   The rules that determine the order in which arrivals are sequenced through service systems. Some common queue disciplines are first-come first-served, shortest processing time, critical ratio, and most valuable customers served first.

Queue length   The number of arrivals waiting to be serviced.

Queuing theory   Body of knowledge about waiting lines.

R

Random sample   Sample of a product in which each unit in the product lot has an equal chance of being included in the sample.

Raw-materials inventory   The reservoir of raw materials held in warehouses until demanded by production.

Redundant component   Backup component built into a machine or product.

Regenerative MRP system   Material requirements planning system in which a complete MRP is processed periodically, resulting in a new MPS, an updated inventory status file, and an updated bills of material file that generates a complete set of outputs in the MRP computer program.

Repairs   The activity of fixing or correcting malfunctioned machines, equipment, or facilities.

Request for quotation   Form inviting prospective suppliers to bid or quote on a good or service.

Robust design   Design that will perform as intended even if undesirable conditions occur either in production or in the field.

Robot   Reprogrammable, multifunctional manipulator designed to move materials, parts, tools, or specialized devices through variable programmed motions for the performance of a variety of tasks.

Rope   The form of communication to upstream work stations to ensure that every production stage is synchronized with the bottleneck machine. Used in theory of constraints approach.

Rough-cut capacity planning   Preliminary checking of the master production schedule that identifies any week in the MPS where underloading or overloading of production capacity occurs and then revises the MPS as required.

Routing plan   Network of work centers through which an order must pass before it is completed.

Run-out method   Method for planning production and delivery schedules that allocates production capacity to products in proportion to their demand and their inventory levels.

S

Safety stock   Quantity of a material held in inventory to be used in time periods when demand is greater than expected or when supply is less than expected.

Scientific management   Application of scientific principles to the management of production systems.

Seasonality   Seasonal patterns that are fluctuations, usually within one year, and that tend to be repeated annually.

Sequential-sampling plan   In quality control, an acceptance sampling plan in which each time a unit is tested, an accept, reject, or continue-sampling decision is made.

Service level   Probability that a stockout will not occur during lead time.

Service phases   The number of steps in servicing arrivals. A single-phase service system has only one service step, whereas a multiphase system has two or more service steps.

Service rate   The rate that arrivals are serviced, in arrivals per unit of time (e.g., per hour). Service rate is usually constant, normal, or Poisson distributed.

Service recovery   Involves all actions taken to resolve customer problems, alter negative attitudes, and ultimately to retain customers who are dissatisfied with the quality of service they received.

Service time   The time it takes to service an arrival, expressed in minutes (or hours, days, etc.) per arrival. The measure does not include waiting time.

Shop system   Systematic approach to improving labor efficiency, introduced by Frederick Winslow Taylor in the late nineteenth century.

Simplex method   Linear programming solution method that provides precise solutions to complex problems that have many variables and constraints.

Simplification   Elimination of complex features in a product or service so that costs are reduced and quality is improved.

Simultaneous engineering   Concept of product/service design proceeding at the same time as process design, with continuous interaction between the two.

Slack   In project management, an amount of time that an activity or group of activities can slip without causing delay in the completion of the project.

Specification   Detailed description of a material, part, or product that gives all of the physical measurements needed for its design.

Standard error of the forecast   In time series regression, a measure of how historical data points have been dispersed about the trend line. Generally, a standard measure of how close past forecasts were to past actual demand.

Standardization   Reduction of variety among a group of products or parts.

Standard product   Product produced either continuously or in very large batches; implies only a few product designs.

Standby machine   Spare machines that are used when primary machines malfunction and are being repaired.

Statistical control charts   A quality management tool used to frequently monitor different aspects of product or service quality over time.

Statistical process control (SPC)   Use of control charts to determine if quality standards are being met.

Stock-keeping unit (SKU)   Any item that is carried in inventory.

Stockout   Reduction of a material's usable inventory level to zero.

Stockout cost   The cost of stockouts. It includes such costs as profits forgone through lost sales, cost of reclaiming disappointed customers, special expediting, special handling of backlogged orders, and additional production costs.

Strategic decision   Long-range, one-time, complex decision about a product, process, or facility.

Strategic outsourcing   Subcontracting particular processes for the purpose of being able to react more quickly to changes in customer demands, competitor actions, and new technologies.

Subcontractor and supplier networks   Arrangements in which a manufacturer develops long-range contractual relationships with several suppliers of parts, components, and subassemblies.

Successor activity   In project management, an activity that must occur after another activity.

Supervisor estimate   Labor standard based on a supervisor's intimate knowledge of the operation for which he or she is responsible.

Supply chain   The flow of materials through different organizations, starting with basic raw materials and ending with finished products delivered to the ultimate consumer.

Sustainable practical capacity   The greatest level of output that a plant can maintain within the framework of a realistic work schedule, taking account of normal downtime, and assuming sufficient availability of inputs to operate the machinery and equipment in place.

Synchronous manufacturing   System of production planning and control in which all parts of an organization work together to achieve the organization's goal. Also called Theory of Constraints.

System reliability (SR)   Combined reliability of all of the interacting components of a machine.

T

Theory of constraints (TOC)   The philosophy and production control approach of managing bottlenecks, or capacity constraints, that was popularized by Eliyahu Goldratt. Also called synchronous manufacturing.

Throughput   Rate that cash is generated by the sale of products.

Time fence   A point in time that separates sections of the master production schedule. For example, the first three weeks of the schedule may be considered frozen with no changes allowed. The next section may be considered firm, with only important changes allowed.

Time in system   The total time that arrivals spend in the system, including both waiting time and service time.

Time series   Set of observed values, usually sales, measured over successive periods of time.

Time study   Method of establishing time standards by using stopwatches to time operations being performed by workers.

Tolerance   Specification for each dimension of a physical product in a range from minimum to maximum.

Total quality management (TQM)   System of producing high-quality products and services initially rather than depending on detecting defects later through inspection.

Touch labor   Labor expended by human production workers.

Tracking signal   Measurement showing whether a forecast has had any built-in biases over a period of time.

Traffic department   Division of an organization that routinely examines shipping schedules and selects shipping methods, time tables, and ways of expediting deliveries.

Transportation method   Linear programming solution method used to find the minimal cost of shipping products from several sources to several destinations.

Two-bin system   Simple, fixed-order quantity inventory control system that uses two bins to hold a material in inventory; orders are triggered when one bin becomes empty, and both bins are filled when inventory is replenished.

U

Uncontrollable factors   Temperature, friction, vibration, chance variation, natural causes.

Utilization   The degree to which any part of a service system is occupied by an arrival. Usually expressed as the probability that n arrivals are in the system.

V

Variables   In quality control, product characteristics that can be measured on a continuous scale.

Vendor managed inventories   A parts supplier monitors and restocks inventory items in a customer's facility.

Vertical integration   Amount of the production and distribution chain brought under the ownership of a company.

Volume flexibility   Ability to quickly increase or reduce the volume of products/services produced.

W

Waiting time   The amount of time an arrival spends in queue.

Warehousing   Management of materials while they are in storage.

Work measurement   Process of estimating the amount of worker time required to generate one unit of output.

Work sampling   Work measurement technique that randomly samples the work of one or more persons at periodic intervals to determine the proportion of the total operation that is accounted for by one particular activity.

Worker's compensation laws   Laws providing for specific compensation amounts to be given to employees for various types of injuries incurred on the job.

World-class company   Each product and service would be considered best-in-class by its customers.

A

Abernathy, Frederick H., 581
Abernathy, W. J., 740
Abromovitz, Hedy, 296
Abromovitz, Les, 296
Ackoff, Russell L., 24
Adams, Nicholas D., 460
Aft, Lawrence S., 740
Aggarwal, S., 533
Agrawal, Narendra, 581
Ahles, Andrea, 170n, 183n
AIPCS, 630n
Allen, John H., 489
Al-Shammari, Minwir, 331
Ambs, Ken, 331
Anderson, David R., 24, 331
Anderson, Randy I., 331
Andress, Frank J., 740
Andrew, C. G., 24
Andrews, Bruce H., 79n
Apte, Uday M., 263, 295
Arditi, David, 296
Arizona Republic, 694
Arlington Morning News, 57
Arlington Star-Telegram, 33n, 41n, 173n, 228, 701
Arnold, J.R. Tony, 460
Arnold, Matthew B., 58
Arntzen, Bruce C., 179n
Asaka, Tetsuichi, 694
Asarmi, Nader, 374
Atkinson, William, 740
Avery, Susan, 489
Aviel, David, 374
Ayers, James B., 460
Ayres, Robert U., 739

B

Bagchi, Tapan P., 659
Ballou, Ronald H., 460
Banfield, Emiko, 460
Banks, Jerry, 374
Bardi, Edward J., 460
Bayles, Deborah, 460
Beard, Luciana, 489
Beck, Robert E., 332
Bennatan, Edwin M., 420
Benton, W. C., 621
Berry, Leonard L., 296

Berry, William L., 534, 621, 659
Besterfield, Dale H., 694
Billington, Peter J., 534
Birkland, Carol, 770
Bistritz, Nancy, 358n
Blackburn, Joseph D., 489
Blackstone, John H., 162, 263, 460, 489, 533, 581, 621
Blackstone, William H., Jr., 228
Blank, Dennis, 111
Blatherwick, Andrew, 581
Bloch, Heinz P., 770
Bolander, Steven F., 533, 659
Boronico, Jess, 374
Boston Globe, 58
Bowen, Bill, 701
Bowman, E. H., 533
Box, George E. P., 111
Brame, Glenn, 659
Brandimarte, Paolo, 533
Brandon, John A., 228
Brausch, John M., 228
Broeckelmann, Russ, 581
Brooks, Roger B., 460
Brown, Eryn, 263
Brown, Gerald G., 179n
Browne, Jim, 228, 374
Buffa, Elwood S., 533, 694
Bulfin, Robert, 534
Bullen, George N., 231n
Burr, Adrian, 694
Burrows, Peter, 58
Business Horizons, 162
Business Week, 33n, 34n, 36n, 41n, 58, 93n, 115n, 124n, 162, 169n, 228, 241n, 263, 264, 295, 569n, 572n, 703, 739
Butler, Stephen A., 489
Buzacott, John A., 659

C

Caldwell, Ronald D., 228
Cameron, Bonnie, 420
Camm, Jeff, 332

Canary, Patrick H., 228
Cannon, Terry, 58
Carbone, James, 460
Carey, M., 374
Carlson, Walter, 332
Carlyle, W. Matthew, 694
Carr, David K., 162
Carson, John S., 374
Carville, S., 374
Cascio, Wayne F., 740
Cashin, Jerry, 162
Cattanach, Robert E., 58
Cavinato, Joseph L., 460
Chakravarti, Nilotpal, 332
Chambers, J. C., 111
Chan, Yupo, 228
Chase, Richard B., 24
Chatfield, Carl, 420
Chaussé, Sylvain, 477n
Chen, Mark T., 420
Chicago Tribune, 57, 58, 117n
Chopra, Sunil, 460
Clark, Wallace, 659
Clausing, Don, 296
Clements, James P., 420
Cock, C. D., 770
Cohen, Morris A., 263
Cohen, Stephen S., 57
Cohn, David S., 263
Colley, John L., 374
Collier, David A., 296
Cook, Nathan H., 237n
Cooke, Fang Lee, 770
Copeland, Duncan, 332
Copely, F. B., 24
Correll, James G., 659
Cox, Charles A., 295
Cox, James F., III, 31n, 162, 263, 460, 489, 533, 581, 621
Cox, Jeff, 533, 534, 659
Coyle, John J., 460
Craighead, Christopher W., 296, 534
Crosby, Philip B., 295, 296
Cross, Gary J., 460
Cunningham, Shawn M., 79n
Cwilich, Sebastian, 331

D

Dale, Cheryl, 659
Dallas Morning News, 41n, 170n, 228
Dar-El, Ezey M., 740
Darity, William, Jr., 740
Davis, Dale, 490
Dawood, Isaam, 331
de Treville, Suzanne, 467n
Dell, Kris A., 263
DeLurgio, Stephen A., 111
Deming, W. Edwards, 296, 694
Deng, Mei, 331
DeNisi, Angelo S., 740
Dietrich, Edgar, 694
Dillon, Jeffrey E., 374
Dodge, Harold F., 682n, 684, 694
Domanski, Bernard, 228
Drexl, Andreas, 621
Drucker, Peter F., 24
Duguay, Claude R., 477n
Duncan, William R., 420
Dunlop, John T., 581
Dyson, Esther, 24

E

Eckes, George, 489
Edson, Norris W., 659
Edum-Fotwe, F. T., 420
Ellram, Lisa M., 460
Englund, Randall L., 420
Enns, S. T., 621
Etienne-Hamilton, E. C., 25, 58
Evans, James R., 332, 694

F

Fair, Douglas C., 695
Fearon, Harold E., 460
Federal Reserve Statistical Release, 228
Feeney, Anne-Marie, 296
Feigenbaum, Armand V., 295, 296
Feitzinger, Edward, 162
Ferrell, Linda, 58

Ferrell, O. C., 58
Fisher, Anne, 728n
Fisher, Marshall L., 111
Fitzsimmons, James A., 58, 263, 374
Fitzsimmons, Mona J., 58, 263, 374
Flattery, M. Thérèse, 58
Fok, Robert, 331
Ford, Henry, 24, 25, 489
Fort Worth Star-Telegram, 170n, 183n
Fortune, 263
Fortune 500 Industry List, 15n
Fortune Global 500, 31n
Fraedrich, John, 58
Frazier, Gregory V., 162, 228
Fredendall, Lawrence D., 754n, 770
Freivalds, Andris, 740
Friedman, Hershey H., 374
Friedman, Linda W., 374
Frigon, Normand L., 228
Frontline Solutions, 286n
Fuquay, Jim, 173n

G

Gagnon, Eugene J., 740
Gaither, Norman, 162, 228, 621
Galbraith, Craig S., 111
Gambrel, Bryan, 621
Garcia, Luis, 374
Gardner, Everette S., 111
Gary, Kevin, 659
Gau, Kai-Yin, 228
Gebhardt, Joan E., 296, 695
Geitner, Fred K., 770
Georgoff, David M., 111
Gertsbakh, Ilya, 770
Gido, Jack, 420
Gilbert, Alorie, 442n
Gilbert, Dave, 628n
Giles, Christopher A., 489
Gill, Mark Stuart, 295
Gilmore, James H., 162
Ginder, Andrew P., 771
Godfrey, A. Blanton, 296, 694
Godfrey, Graham, 296
Goldratt, Eliyahu M., 533, 534, 659
Goldsmith, Arthur H., 740
Goldstein, Alan, 170n, 442n
Goover, Mikell P., 263

Gotlob, David, 332
Gotoh, Fumio, 771
Graham, Robert J., 420
Gray, Christopher D., 621
Gray, Clifford F., 420
Gray, Douglas A., 762n
Greene, James H., 581
Greenwald, Bruce, 58
Grieco, Peter L., 460
Griffin, Ricky W., 740
Griffin, Tom, 770
Groff, G. K., 621
Groover, Mikell P., 263
Gross, Neil, 115n
Gryna, Frank M., 694
Gunaydin, H. Murat, 296
Gurin, Rick, 263
Guven, S., 332

H

Haddock, Jorge, 621
Haksever, Cengiz, 162, 228, 374
Halberstam, David, 12n, 25
Hall, Ernest L., 264
Hall, R., 470n
Hall, Randolph W., 374
Hall, Robert W., 489, 533, 770
Hallows, Jolyon E., 420
Halpern, Fernando, 770
Halvey, John K., 162
Hammer, Michael, 162
Hammond, Janice H., 111, 581
Handfield, Robert B., 460
Handy, Charles, 24
Hansell, Saul, 228
Harrington, H. James, 694
Harrison, Terry P., 179n
Hart, Stuart L., 58
Harvard Business Review, 24, 57, 58, 111, 162, 228, 581, 621, 739, 740
Hauser, John R., 296
Hayes, Robert H., 25, 57, 58, 162
Henderson, Timothy P., 581
Hendricks, Devin B., 296
Hernandez, Jose Antonio, 621
Hillier, Frederick S., 332
Hipkin, I. B., 770
Hirschmann, Winfred B., 739, 740
Hobbs, O. Kermit, Jr., 483n
Holdreith, Jake M., 58

Hooker, J. N., 332
Hope, Christine, 162
Hostage, G. M., 694
Houck, David J., 331
Houshyar, Azim, 228
Houston Chronicle, 41n, 57, 98n, 169n, 291n, 295
Hubicki, Donald E., 621
Huffman, Jack L., 296
Hurter, Arthur P., Jr., 228
Hyer, N. L., 162
Hyer, Nancy Lea, 228
Hyndman, Rob J., 112

I

Industry Week, 58
International Journal of Purchasing & Materials Management, 460
Ishikawa, Kaoru, 295, 296, 694

J

Jackson, Harry K., 228
Jacobs, F. Robert, 263
Jacobs, Timothy L., 301n
Jahn, Mary L., 460
Jain, Chaman L., 111
Jenkins, Gwilym M., 111
Jennings, Peter, 287n
Johansson, Henry J., 162, 295
Johnson, Robert E., 534
Johnson, S. M., 659
Johnson, Tim, 420
Jorgensen, Karen, 740
Juran, Joseph M., 295, 296, 694

K

Karwan, Dirk R., 296
Kauffman, Ralph G., 460
Kay, John M., 228
Kelley, D. Lynn, 694
Kelton, W. D., 374
Kempf, Karl, 659
Kennedy, William J., 754n, 770
Kerzner, Harold, 420
Kessler, Sheila, 296, 695
Ketzenberg, Michael, 581
Kimms, Alf, 621
King, James J., 489
Kirchmier, Bill, 659
Kirkpatrick, David, 572n
Klafehn, Keith, 374

Klammer, Thomas P., 228
Klassen, Robert D., 490
Knapp, Gary R., 695
Knouse, Stephen B., 296
Kobbacy, Khairy A. H., 771
Koehler, Jerry W., 296
Kolman, Bernard, 332
Kontogiorgis, Spyros, 374
Kozlowski, Angela, 621
Kraebber, Henry W., 264
Kruglianskas, Isak, 420
Krupp, James A. G., 581

L

Lacity, Mary C., 162
LaForge, R. Lawrence, 534
Lambert, Douglas, 460
Lampel, Joseph, 162
Lancioni, Richard A., 460
Landry, Sylvain, 477n
Landvater, Darryl V., 534, 621
Langley, C. John, 460
Laraia, Anthony C., 490
Larson, Erik W., 420
LaVal, David K., 374
Law, A. M., 374
Lee, Hau L., 162
Lee, Reginald, 770
Lee, Steven H., 228
Leenders, Michael, 460
Lesaint, David, 374
Leschke, John P., 489, 490
Levitt, Joel, 770
Levitt, T., 162
Lewis, Bernard T., 770
Lewis, Colin D., 111
Lewis, James P., 420
Lieberman, Gerald J., 332
Little, Darnell, 569n
Lock, Dennis, 420
Long, Frederick J., 58
Los Angeles Times, 245n
Lovelock, Christopher H., 58
Lowson, Bob, 460
Luciano, Elisa, 581
Luxhoj, James T., 770

M

Macadam, Stephen E., 162
MacHover, Carl, 263
MacLeod, Dan, 740
Mahoney, Francis X., 296
Makridakis, Spyros G., 111, 112

Malm, Howard, 770
Maney, Kevin, 245n
Mantel, Samuel J., 420
Marchington, Mick, 296
Marchman, David A., 420
Martin, James, 420
Martinich, Joseph S., 228
Martocchio, Joseph J., 740
Maslow, A. H., 739
Mason, Richard O., 332
Maynard, H. B., 233n
McCarthy, Dennis, 771
McClain, John O., 581
McCutcheon, David M., 461
McGee, Allen, 754n
McGregor, Wes, 228
McKay, Kenneth N., 659
McKenney, James L., 332
McLachlin, Ron, 490
McLeavey, Dennis W., 534
McMahon, Chris, 228
Meal, H. C., 621
Meindl, Peter, 460
Melby, Barbara M., 162
Meller, Russell D., 228
Melnyk, Steven, 659
Meredith, Jack R., 420
Meredith, Robyn, 167n
Merrill, Gregory B., 111
Metters, Richard, 581
Meyers, Fred E., 228, 740
Mia, Lokman, 490
Michalski, Liz, 420
Michel, Roberto, 659
Milakovich, Michael E., 296
Milas, Gene H., 296
Miller, Janis L., 296
Miller, Jeffrey G., 621
Miller, Malcolm, 534
Miller, Tan C., 534
Miltenburg, G. John, 534
Minahan, Tim, 490
Mintzberg, Henry, 162
Mishina, Mayu, 659
Mito, Setsuo, 490
Mitrofanov, S. P., 162
Monden, Yasuhiro, 490
Monroe, Joseph, 264
Montgomery, Douglas C.,
    694, 695
Moody, Patricia E., 490
Moore, James S., 332
Moore, Jeffrey H., 332
Moore, Kim S., 332
Moran, John W., 295
Moritz, John, 183n

Moses, Timothy P., 695
Moss, Steven, 659
MTM Association, 719n
Muhlemann, Alan, 25, 58, 162
Murdick, Robert G., 111,
    162, 228
Murphy, Ryan C., 489

N

Nakajima, Seiichi, 771
Narasimhan, Seetharama L.,
    534
Narayanan, V. K., 264
Naylor, Henry F. W., 420
Nelson, Barry L., 374
New York Times, 33n, 132n,
    167n, 228, 263, 435n
Newmark, Henry R., 420
Nicholas, John M., 420, 490
Nichols, Ernest L., 460
Nicol, David, 374
Niebel, Benjamin W., 740
Ninemeier, Jack D., 374
Novack, Robert A., 460

O

O'Reilly, Jean J., 374
Obermeyer, Walter R., 111
Ohno, Taiichi, 490
Orlicky, Joseph, 621
Ost, Edward J., 740
Owen, Malcolm, 694
Ozeki, Kazuo, 694

P

Palmer, Roger C., 264
Parasuraman, A., 296
Patillo, Linda, 287n
Patrick, Ken L., 771
Patterson, J. Wayne, 754n,
    770
Patton, Joseph D., Jr., 771
Peccati, Lorenzo, 581
Pennar, Karen, 739
Percy, David F., 771
Peroziello, Michael J., 490
Perreault, Yves, 621
Perry, Ian, 740
Persentili, E., 332
Peters, Le Roy R., 461
Peterson, Rein, 534, 581, 659
Pfohl, Hans-Christian, 461
Pierce, F. David, 490
Pilachowski, Mel, 461

Piller, Dan, 170n
Pine, B. Joseph, II, 162
Pinedo, Michael, 659
Pisano, Gary P., 57, 58
Plenert, Gerhard, 621, 659
Plossi, George W., 621
Porter, Michael E., 57, 58
Power, Damien, 490
Powers, Vicki J., 289n
Prabhu, N. U., 374
Prasad, Biren, 162
Prentis, Eric L., 24
Price, Robert M., 264
Pringle, Lew, 299n
Pritsker, A. Alan B., 374
Project Management Institute
    Headquarters, 380n
Proud, John F., 534
Ptak, Carol A., 533, 534, 621
Purha, Sanjiv, 420
Pyke, David F., 534, 581, 659
Pyzdek, Thomas, 695

R

Ragsdale, Cliff, 332
Raman, Ananth, 111
Ramaswamy, Rohit, 162
Ratliff, Richard M., 301n
Reguero, Miguel A., 739, 740
Rehg, James A., 264
Reider, Rob, 296
Reinke, Daniel P., 58
Reinsel, Gregory C., 111
Render, Barry, 162, 228, 374
ReVelle, Jack B., 295
Reynolds, Charles C., 295
Ribbens, Jack, 162
Riis, Jens O., 770
Robertazzi, Thomas G., 374
Robinson, Charles J., 771
Robricht, Jurgen, 264, 534
Romig, Harry G., 682n, 694
Roney, Paul J., 489
Rowell, Michael, 621
Roy, Ranjit K., 296
Royer, Paul S., 420
Ruffa, Stephen A., 490
Rummel, Jeffrey L., 581
Runger, George C., 694
Russell, Roberta S., 162, 228,
    374

S

Sadowski, Deborah, 374
Sadowski, Randall, 374

Saffo, Paul, 24
Sahin, Funda, 490
Salegna, Gary, 659
San Antonio Express-News,
    40n, 41n, 239n, 435n
Sanders, Edmund, 245n
Sanders, Nada R., 112
Sarkis, Karen, 740
Sawik, Tadeusz, 534
Saylor, James H., 296
Sayre, Don, 58
Schaap, Dave, 659
Scheduling Technologies
    Group Ltd., 646n, 647n,
    648n
Scherer, Eric, 659
Schimmoller, Brian K., 771
Schmele, June A., 296
Schmenner, Roger W., 25, 58,
    374
Schniederjans, Marc J., 228,
    490
Schonberger, Richard J., 25,
    58, 490
Schragenheim, Eli, 533, 534,
    621
Schroeder, Roger G., 621
Schwarz, Leroy B., 534
Scott, John, 331
Scott, Miriam B., 740
Segerstedt, Anders, 621
Senge, Peter M., 24
Serwer, Andrew E., 572n
Shah, Bharat, 420
Sharpe, Simon, 621
Shell, Richard L., 264
Shiem-Shin, Danny, 228
Shim, Jae K., 112
Shin, Hojung, 621
Shostack, G. Lynn, 58, 162
Sibbet, David, 24
Sibik, Larry K., 58
Silos, Irene M., 296
Silver, Edward A., 534, 581,
    621, 659
Singhal, Vinod R., 296
Sipper, Daniel, 534
Skinner, Wickham, 25
Small, M., 490
Smith, Barry C., 301n
Smith, Bernard T., 95n, 112
Smith, Elizabeth A., 740
Smith, Stephen A., 581, 659
Sohal, Amrik S., 490
Sox, Charles R., 581
Spedding, Paul, 581

Sprague, Linda G., 621
Spriggs, Mark T., 162, 228
St. Vincent, Jim, 291n
Stahelski, Anthony J., 695
Stamatis, Dean H., 296
Standard, Charles, 490
Stephens, Matthew P., 228
Stewart, James R., 740
Stimson, Judith A., 461
Stock, James R., 460
Stuart, F. Ian, 461
Suresh, Nallan C., 228
Swain, James J., 374
Swamidass, P. M., 228
Swanson, Laura, 771
Sweeney, Dennis J., 24, 331

T

Taha, Hamdy A., 25
Tajiri, Masaji, 771
Taylor, Frederick Winslow, 25
Taylor, J. C., 771
Taylor, Sam G., 538, 659
Taylor, Thomas C., 228
Taylor, Tom, 740
Teufel, Thomas, 264, 534
Thamhain, Hans J., 420
Themens, Jean-Luc, 477n
Thomas, L. Joseph, 581

Thor, Carl G., 296
Thorsteinsson, Uffe, 770
Toomey, John W., 581
Topolosky, Paula S., 740
Townsend, Patrick L., 296, 695
Trafton, Linda L., 179n
*Transportation &
    Distribution,* 461
Tryfos, Peter, 112

U

U.S. Department of Defense,
    695
U.S. Department of Labor, 740
Upton, David M., 162
Urli, Bruno, 420
Urli, Didier, 420
USA Today, 41n, 57, 58, 111,
    169n, 245n
Uzsoy, Reha, 659

V

Van Biema, Michael, 58
Vanderbei, Robert J., 332
Vargas, Vicente, 581
Verma, Vijay K., 420
Veum, Jonathan R., 740
Viale, J. David, 581

Villa, A., 533
Vlasic, Tom, 621
Vollmann, Thomas E., 534,
    659
Voudouris, Christos, 374

W

Wafa, M. A., 490
Wagner, H. M., 621
Wall Street Journal, 33n, 263,
    291n
Wallace, Thomas F., 621
Walley, Noah, 58
Wantuck, Kenneth A., 490
Weart, Walter, 441n
Weatherford, Larry R., 332
Wei, Jerry C., 162, 228
Weil, David, 581
Weinroth, Jay, 374
Wemmerlov, U., 162, 228
Whacker, John G., 534
Wheelwright, Steven C., 58,
    112, 162
White, Bob, 228
Whitehead, Bradley, 58
Whitin, T. M., 621
Whitson, Daniel, 490
Whybark, D. Clay, 263, 534,
    659

Wild, Tony, 581
Wilkinson, Adrian, 296
Wilkinson, John J., 771
Willcocks, Leslie, 162
Willems, Peter, 264, 534
Williams, Thomas A., 24, 331
Willmott, Peter, 771
Wilson, Darryl D., 296
Wilson, Larry W., 460
Winarchick, Charles, 228
Winston, Wayne L., 374
Wise, Stephen A., 695
Witt, Chris, 25, 58, 162
Woodall, William H., 695
Wordsworth, Paul, 770
Wu, Alan, 296
Wu, Yuin, 296

Y

Yasin, Mahmoud M., 420, 490
Yelle, Louis E., 740
Yip, George S., 58

Z

Zairi, Mohamed, 296
Zeithaml, Valarie A., 296
Zipkin, Paul H., 581
Zysman, John, 57

A

ABC classification of materials, 565-567
Absolute measures, 174
Accelerating, 400
Acceptable quality level (AQL), 676, 677
Acceptance criteria, estimating, 680
Acceptance plans, 673-686
  for attributes, single-sample, 675-680
  for variables, single-sample, 685
Accuracy, cost and, 92-93
Ackoff, Russell, 17
Acquisition costs, 537
Activity, 381, 385
  and events of the RAMOV project, 387
  cost-time trade-offs, 400
  duration, 381
Actual cash demand
  exponential smoothing forecasts versus, 88
  moving average forecast versus, 85
Adequate quality, 35
Advanced Management Solutions, 404
Advanced technologies, 37, 231
AEC Software Inc., 404
Aggregate capacity planning at the Quick Cargo Air Freight Company, 506-507
Aggregate demand, 494-495
  aggregating individual product forecasts into, 496
Aggregate planning, 492, 493-511
  mathematical models for, 508-510
  steps in, 494
  using linear programming to analyze problems, 509-510

Aggregate plans
  analyzing, 504-505
  criteria for selecting, 504-506
  for services, 506-508
  some traditional, 497-504
Aggregate unit of capacity, 166
Allowance fraction, 713
Amadas Industries, 483
American Airlines, 301, 762
American Bar Association, 98
American Hardware Supply, 95
American Manufacturers Association, 98
American's Decision Technologies (AADT), 762
AMS REALTIME Projects, 404
Andersen Consulting, 98
Andom, 476
AO Moskvich, 33
APICS Dictionary, 463, 464, 480, 484
Apple Computer, Inc., 45-46
Applied research, 115
ArchiCAD, 194
Arena, 360
Arithmetic analysis, 722
Artemis Management Systems, 404
Artemis Views, 404
Assemble-to-order firms, MRP in, 602
Assembly charts, 140, 141
Assembly lines, 125, 189
Assignment method, 318
Assignment problems, 318, 638
ASTA Development Inc., 405
Asten, Inc., 754
Attributes, 665, 683-684
  control charts for, 667-670
  single-sample acceptance plans for, 675-680
  terms used in acceptance plans for, 676
AutoCAD Architectural Desktop, 194

Automated assembly system, 236-237
Automated equipment, 274
  degree of customer contact in services and the use of, 244
Automated flow line, 236
Automated guided vehicle systems (AGVS), 238
Automated process controls, 235
Automated production systems, 235-239
Automated quality control inspection systems, 234
Automated storage and retrieval systems (ASRS), 238-239, 445
Automated technologies, 245
Automatic identification systems (AIS), 235
Automation, 231
  and prominence of PM, 752
  degree of, 124
  fixed, 236
  flexible, 247
  hard, 236, 247
  in services, 242-246
  issues, 246-250
  projects, justifying, 248
  software systems for, 239-242
  types of manufacturing, 231-235
  use of, 246-247
Automation alternatives
  deciding among, 250-253
  rating scale approach to comparing, 252
  relative-aggregate-scores approach to comparing, 252
Automotive Network Exchange (ANX), 448
AutoSketch, 194
Average flow time, 631
Average inventory level in Model II, 546
Average job lateness, 631

Average learning rate, 726
Average number of jobs in the system, 631
Average outgoing quality (AOQ), 676, 680
Average outgoing quality curves, 680, 681
Average outgoing quality limit (AOQL), 676, 680

B

Baan, 241, 448, 570, 603, 645
Backlog, buffering with, 502
Backup or standby machines, 746
Backward scheduling, 629
Barnard, Chester, 13
Barth, Carl G., 11
Base stock model, 561
Basic economic order quantity (EOQ)
  Model I, 541-544
  Model II, 544
Basic research, 115
Basis, 320
Batch production, 638
Batch scheduling, 639-641
Batch size and product variety, 134-135
Behavioralists, 13
Benchmarking, 288
  and continuous improvement, 288-289
  the performance of materials managers, 446-447
Best operating level, 168
Bill of material, 589, 593
Bills of material file, 589
Binding, 150
Boeing Company, 43, 118, 169, 193, 628
Booz, Allen & Hamilton, 98
Bottleneck operation, 496
Bottlenecks, focusing on, 523-524
Breakdowns trigger repairs and corrective actions, 747-748

Break-even analysis, 137-139, 173
  graphical approach to, 139
  selecting a production process, 138
  variable definitions and formulas for, 137
Bridgestone/Firestone, 43
Buckets, 590
Buffer, 524
Buffering
  with backlog, 502
  with inventory, 499
  with overtime or subcontracting, 503
Bureau of Labor Statistics, 699
Business conditions, factors affecting today's global, 29
Business planning, forecasting as an integral part of, 65
Business Site/Construction Planner, 182
Business strategy, 43, 143-144
Business-to-business (B2B) transactions, 429, 448
Buyers, 433
  allegations of improper behavior by, 435
Buying, ethics in, 435-436

C

CAD/CAM, 239-240
Capacity
  aggregate unit of, 166
  excess, 247
  increases in incremental facility, 171
  input rate, 166
  measurements of, 166
  output rate, 166
  outsourcing provided additional, 173
  production, 165
  sustainable practical, 165
  too little and too much, 169
  ways of changing long-range, 168
Capacity cushion, 167
Capacity demand, forecasting, 166-168

Capacity loading hierarchy, 609
Capacity planning, long-range, 165-175
Capacity requirements planning (CRP), 605-609
Capacity utilization percentage, 166
Capacity-planning decisions, analyzing, 173-174
Capital, 699
Capital intensive, 124, 180
Capital requirements for process designs, 136
Carrying costs, 537
  balancing against ordering costs, 540
  increased annual, 559
Casual forecasting models, 72
Cell formation decision, 191, 204-205
Cellular manufacturing, 128, 130
Cellular manufacturing layouts, 190-191
  cell formation decisions in, 204-205
  planning, 204-207
Central limit theorem, 666
Centralized supply chain management at Motoarc, 425
Changeover cost, 631
  and job sequence, 635
  controlling, 634-635
Charts
  assembly, 140, 141
  diagrams and, 708-712
  gozinto, 140
  process, 140, 142
Chlorofluorocarbons (CFCs), 40
Chrysler, 33
Classes, 267
Clean Air Act of 1990, 39
Closed-loop MRP, 602
Closeness ratings, 209
  procedure for using, 210
  using to develop service facility layouts, 209-210
Coefficient of correlation (r), 74
Coefficient of determination, 75

Cohen, Stephen, 38
Collins & Aikman Floorcoverings, 41
Communications Oriented Production Information and Control Systems (COPICS), 518, 519
Communications technology demolishes time and distance, 245
Community decision, 177
Compaq Computer Corporation, 42, 132
Competitive priorities, 45-46
  for services, 51
Complex mathematical techniques, 14
Computer Associates International, 405
Computer revolution, 16
Computer simulation, 173
  analysis, characteristics of POM problems that are appropriate for, 359
  evaluation of, 366
  of an outpatient clinic, 360-366
  problems, characteristics of, 359
  procedures of, 359, 360
Computer software
  for forecasting, 97
  for project management, 404-406
Computer-aided design. *See* CAD
Computer-aided manufacturing. *See* CAM
Computer-integrated manufacturing (CIM), 240
Computerized scheduling systems, 645-648
Computers
  and inventory planning, 569-570
  in quality control, 686-687
Concurrent engineering, 117
Conference Board, 98
Conservation and recycling in industry, 41
Constant lead time and normally distributed demand per day, 556-557
Consumer attitudes, 39
Consumer's risk (β), 676, 678

Continue-sampling zone, 675
Continuous DDLT distributions, 552, 553-556
Continuous flow manufacture, 464
Continuous improvement, 288
  benchmarking and, 288-289
  enforced problem solving and, 471-472
Continuous production, 125, 638
Control charts, 666-673
  for attributes, 667-670
  for variables, 670-673
  scheduling and, 379-384
Control decisions, 21, 22
Control systems, types of production-planning and, 520-524
Controllable factors, 279
Conventional cost analysis, 184
Conversion subsystem, 17
Conveyance card (C-Kanban), 474
Conveyor/sorts system, 153
Cooke, Morris L., 11
Co-producers, 476
Corporate mission, 43
Corporations, world's 20 largest, 31
Correlation
  linear regression and, 69-76
  partial and multiple coefficients, 76
Cost
  and accuracy, 92-93
  comparisons, alternative manufacturing locations, 185
  functions of processing alternatives, 136-137
  of coordinating production, 538
  of customer responsiveness, 537
  of diluted return on investment (ROI), 538
  of production problems, 538
  per unit versus size of production lot, 538
Cost-time trade-offs in the RAMOV project, 400-404

Cottage systems, 8
Countrywide Home Loans, Inc., 245
Cox, Jeff, 523
CPM. *See* Critical path method
CPM/PERT
  an evaluation of, 406-408
  in practice, 400-404
Crashing, 400
Crew size standards, 719
Critical activities, 381, 393
Critical Chain, 523
Critical path, 381, 393
Critical path method, 384-394
  analysis, steps in, 386
  management information system, 386
  network conventions, 389
  network of the RAMOV project, 387-388
  manager's view of, 385
Critical ratio (CR), 631, 634
Crosby, Philip B., 272
Cross-training, 705
Cumulative end item lead time, 518
Custom products, 46
Customer demand patterns, 342
Customer involvement, 278-279
Customer satisfaction, 742
Customer service, distribution, and installation, 285
Customer-as-participant, 133, 337
  service operations, 345-355
Customer-as-product, 133, 337
  service operations, 355-366
Cycle, 68, 713
Cycle counting, 444
  personnel required, number of, 444-445

D

Daimler Benz, 33
DaimlerChrysler, 33
Data
  available, 93
  politics, incentives and preemptive tactics, 182-184

DDLT. *See* Demand during lead time
Decision support system for aircraft maintenance planning at American Airlines, 762
Decision tree analysis, 174-176
  to manufacture or not to manufacture, 174-176
Decline stage, 47
Dedicated factory, 145
De-expediting, 446
Defective products, 665
  detecting, 269
  in the hands of customers, 268
  preventing, 268
Delivery schedules, 642
Dell Computer Corporation, 27-28
Delphi method, 66
Demand during lead time (DDLT), 550
Demand during lead time (DDLT) distributions, 554
  discrete and continuous, 553-556
  parameters, 552
Demand estimates: a blend of orders and forecasts, 517
Demand management, 516, 517
Demand per day (d) distribution parameters, 552
Deming Prize, 270, 275-277
Deming, W. Edwards, 270-272, 275
Deming's 14 points, 271
Department of Defense (DOD), 398
Department of Transportation (DOT), 438
Dependent demand, 539
Dependent variable (y), variation of, 75
Deposit point, 238
Design simplification, 280, 760
Design system and process planning, 122
Designing workers' jobs, 705-707
Destructive tests, 674
Diagrams and charts, 708-712
Dickson, W. J., 13

Digital Equipment Corporation (DEC), 179
Direct labor, 699
Direct outputs, 18
Discount prices, 511
Discrete DDLT distribution, 552, 553-556
  setting safety stock at service levels for, 553-555
Discrete unit manufacturing, 125
Diseconomies of scale, 170, 171
Dispatching lists, 626
Distinctive competencies, 44
Distribution
  customer service, and installation, 285
  management, 438
  resource planning, 439
  system, 438
Distribution requirements planning (DRP), 438-439
Division of labor, 9
Dodge-Romig tables, 680-682
Dollar versus the yen and the mark, 34
Double exponential smoothing, 88
Double-sampling plan, 674-675
Drucker, Peter, 13, 32
Drum, 524
Drum-buffer-rope, 646
Dummy activity, 381, 388
Dun's Review, 182
DuPont, 41

E

Earliest due date (EDD), 631
Earliest finish (EF), 381, 390
  for the RAMOV project's activities, computing, 390-391
Earliest start (ES), 381, 393
  and latest start (LS) for the RAMOV project's activities, 393-394
Early part-replacement policies, 748
E-business, 241, 448
  and supply chain management, 448-449
E-commerce, 448
  and JIT purchasing, 477-478

Economic analysis, 136-140
Economic evaluation of the prototype design, 116
Economic order period–Model IV, 560
Economic order quantity (EOQ), 540
  and uncertainty, 567-568
  for production lots, 639-640
    Model II, 544-546
  with quantity discounts, 548-550
    Model III, 546-550
Economies
  and diseconomies of scale, 170
  of scale, 168-173
  of scope, 173
Educated guess, 66
Efficiency, 13
  engineers, 11
  experts, 11
E-Kanbans, 478
Electronic Data Interchange (EDI), 448
Electro-Thermal-Deactivation (ETD), 40
Element normal time, 713
Elements, 713
  of operations strategy, 46-49
Emerson, Harrington, 11
Employee(s)
  building teams of empowered, 285-288
  health and safety, 726-729
  impact, 43
  or customer safety, 742
  schedules, using simulation to develop, 358
  scheduling, 334, 342-345
  smarter and better trained, 703
  training programs, 285-286
Empowerment
  of workers, 472, 707-708
  work teams and, 286-287
End item, 589
Enterprise resource planning (ERP), 16, 37, 240-242, 603
  MRP I to MRP II to, 602-603
  software, 241

Environmental efforts at Compaq, 42
Environmental impact, 39-41
Environmental Protection Agency (EPA), 39
EOQ. *See* Economic order quantity
EPA (Environmental Protection Agency), 39
Erlang, A. K., 348
ERP. *See* Enterprise resource planning
Errors in forecasting, 77
Ethical behavior, 435
  in purchasing, guidelines for, 436
Ethics in buying, 435-436
European Union (EU), 30
Event, 381, 385
  of the RAMOV project, activities and, 387
Exception reports, 591
Excess capacity, 247
Executive committee consensus, 66
Expected value (EV), 174
  as a decision criterion, 174
Expediting, 446
Expenditures chart, 410
  RATS project expenditures plan/status report, 383
Explained variation, 75
Exponential smoothing, 86
  forecasts, formulas and variable definition for, 86
  forecasts versus actual cash demand, 88
  method, 86-88
  short-range forecast, 86-87
  weighting of past data in, 89
  with trend, 88-92
Exponentially weighted moving average, 87
External inputs, 17

F

Facility layout, 186
  manufacturing, 187-207
  service, 207-210
  some objectives of, 187
  traditional versus modern, 193

types of service, 207-208
using closeness ratings to develop service, 209-210
Facility location, 176-186
  analyzing industrial, 184
  decision, 178
Facility planning, 49, 164
Factors affecting location decisions, 177
Factory, 145-147
Factory-within-a-factory, 287
Family Leave Act of 1993, 39
FastTrack Schedule, 404
Feigenbaum, Armand V., 272
Final assembly schedule (FAS), 602
Financial analysis, 140
Finite loading, 628
  and infinite loading, 628-629
  at SMC, 630
First-come first-served (FCFS), 630, 633
Fishbone diagrams, 272
  for tread blisters on automobile tires, 273
5S process, 484
Fixed automation, 236
Fixed manufacturing system, 247
Fixed order period systems, 559-561
  optimal order period in, 560-561
Fixed order quantity systems, 540-559
  versus raw-materials inventory levels in MRP, order point systems, 587
Fixed-position layouts, 191
Flame mix, 144
Flare sales, Olin Corporation's railroad, 94
Flexible automation, 247
Flexible manufacturing systems (FMS), 237-238
Flow diagram and process chart, 710, 711
Flow of printing jobs at R. R. Donnelley & Sons, 148
Flow shop, 638
Focus forecasting at American Hardware Supply, 95

Focus groups, 278
Ford, Henry, 11-13, 468
Ford Motor Company, 11, 12, 117
Forecast
  long-range, 68-81
  naive, 82-83
  ranging, 76
  seasonality in time series, 79
  short-range, 81-92
  standard deviation of, 77
  standard error of, 77, 82
Forecast accuracy, 67-68
  measures of, 82
Forecast error, 68
Forecasting, 63
  as an integral part of business planning, 65
  capacity demand, 166-168
  computer software for, 97
  errors in, 77
  expert system at Xerox, 93
  flare sales at Olin Corporation, 94
  in small businesses and start-up ventures, 97
  meals on airline flights, 63
  method, selecting, 92-95
  reasons for ineffective, 92
  some reasons why it is essential in operations management, 64
  sources of data, 98
  system, 92-97
  telephone calls at L. L. Bean, 79
Forecasting model
  evaluating performance, 82
  how to monitor and control, 95-97
  quantitative, 67-92
Forks, 175
Forward scheduling, 629
  and backward scheduling, 629-630

G

Gantt chart, 627-628
  for coordinating work centers' schedules, 629
  for the RAMOV project, Microsoft project, 406

Gantt, Henry L., 11
Gateway operation, 496
General Agreement of Tariffs and Trade (GATT), 29
General Motors Corp. (GM), 30, 33, 36
Georgia-Pacific (GP), 668, 728
Gilbreth, Frank B., 11
Gilbreth, Lillian M., 11
Global business conditions
  factors affecting today's, 29
  today's, 29-43
Global competition, reality of, 29-35
Global facility location at DEC, 179
Global village, 30
Globalization, pros and cons of, 34
GlobaLogic Inc., 405
GlobaLogic Projects, 405
Glovia, 570
Goldratt, Dr. Eliyahu, 523, 646
Government regulation, 39
Gozinto charts, 140
Grades, 267
Graphical LP solutions, 307
  steps in, 308
Graphical solution, 307
Grasso, Richard A., 164
Green Thumb Water Sprinkler Company, 591-597
Gross domestic product (GDP), 15, 29
Gross requirements calculations, 596
Group technology, 128
  cellular manufacturing (GT/CM), 128-131
  coding example, 129
Growth stage, 47
Guide to Quality Control, 272

H

Hard automation, 236, 247
Harvard Business Review, 16
Hawthorne studies, 13
Hayes, Robert, 52
Herzberg, Frederick, 13
Hewlett-Packard Corporation, 278, 299
High accuracy, 68

High impulse response, 82
High-capacity utilization, 466
Highway flare, 15-minute, 144
Hiring costs, 505
Historical analogy, 66, 67
Historical labor standards, 719
Horizontal bar chart–RATS project schedule plan/status report summary, 382
Housekeeping, 484
Human behavior, productivity and, 698-705
Human relations movement, 13
Hybrid inventory models, 561-562
Hybrid layouts, 192

I

i2 TradeMatrix, 645
iCollaboration, 570
Ignitor button, 144
Impulse response
    and noise dampening, 95
    versus noise-dampening ability, 82
IMSI, 405
Inbound merchandise, 152
Incentive pay systems, 712-713
Incremental utilization heuristic, 197
    line balancing with, 198-201
    steps in, 198
Indented bill of material, 589, 594
Independent demand, 539
Indirect outputs, 18
Industrial engineers, 11
Industrial facility locations, analyzing, 184
Industrial revolution, 8-10
Industry, recycling and conservation in, 41
Infinite loading, 628
In-process inventories, 442
Input rate capacity, 166
Input-output control, 626-627
    at Boeing, 628
Input-output reports, analyzing, 627

Inputs
    and outputs for OPT, information, 648
    and outputs of a resource requirements planning system, 584
    external, 17
    market, 17
Installation, customer service, and distribution, 285
Intangible, 50
    outputs, 18
Integer linear programming, 635
Intel, 278
    delays opening of new plant, 170
    Texas incentives not enough for, 183
Interchangeable parts, 9
    system of, 119
Interdisciplinary teams, 14
Intermec Printing Systems (IPS), 463
Intermittent production, 127
Internal ownership, 708
International Benchmarking Clearinghouse (IBC), 288
International companies, 31-32
International financial conditions, fluctuation of, 32-35
International Organization for Standardization, 40, 277
Internet, 3
Interrelationships among product design, process design, and inventory policy, 131-132
Interstate Commerce Commission (ICC), 438
Introduction stage, 47
Inventory(ies), 497
    average level in Model I, 543
    average level in Model II, 546
    buffering with, 499
    cycle, 539
    management at 3M, 569
    nature of, 539-540
    opposing views of, 536-539
    record, 541
    reducing through MRP, 583

reducing through setup reduction, 478-480
    setting policies at Airco Division, 536
    status file, 590
    status report, 594
    uncovering production problems by reducing, 471
    vendor-managed, 568-569
    why hold, 536-537
    why we do not want to hold, 537-539
Inventory accounting, methods of, 443-445
    periodic systems, 443
    perpetual systems, 444
Inventory policy, interrelationships among product design and process design, 131-132
Inventory models, other, 561-565
Inventory planning
    computers and, 569-570
    dynamics of, 568
    models, summary of, 571
    other factors affecting, 568
    some realities of, 565-570
    under uncertainty, terms often used in analyses in, 552
Ishikawa, Kaoru, 272
ISO 14000, 40
ISO 9000 Standards, 277

J

J. D. Edwards, 241
Job enlargement, 706
Job enrichment, 706
Job sequence and changeover costs, 635
Job shops, 127, 623
Jobs, designing workers', 705-707
Jobs, Steve, 45
Johnson's rule, sequencing jobs through two work centers with, 636-638
Juran, Joseph M., 272
Just-in-time (JIT) implementation at Amadas, 483
Just-in-time (JIT) in service companies, 484

Just-in-time (JIT) manufacturing, 273, 463-464, 522
    benefits of, 481-482
    elements of, 470-481
    people make it work, 472
    philosophy, 464-468
    prerequisites for, 468-470
    success and, 482-484
Just-in-time (JIT) purchasing, 476-477
    e-commerce and, 477-478

K

Kaizen, 471
Kanban, 473
Kanban cards, 473-474
Kanban production control, 473-476
Keiretsu, 32
Kelly, J. E., 384
Kentucky Fried Chicken (KFC) Corporation, 266
Kia Motor Corp., 33, 42
Kroger Company, 244

L

L. L. Bean, 79
Labor, division of, 9
Labor intensive, 37
Labor productivity, 701
    variables affecting, 702
Labor specialization, 705
    some advantages and disadvantages of, 705
Labor standards, 712-713
Large-lot quality cost, 538
Largest EF, 391
Latest finish (LF), 381, 391
    and slack (S) for the RAMOV project's activities, computing, 391-393
Latest start (LS), 381, 393
    for the RAMOV project's activities, earliest start (ES) and, 393-394
Layoff costs, 505
Lead time (LT)
    cumulative end item, 518
    distribution parameters, 552
Leadership through Quality, 277-278
Leading indicator, 76

Lean manufacturing, 273, 464, 522
Learning curves, 720-726
    coefficients, 724
    tables, 723-725
    uses and limitations of, 725-726
    values of *b*, 722
Learning rate, selecting, 725
Least changeover cost (LCC), 631
Least slack (LS), 631
Level capacity, 499
    produce-to-order, 503
    produce-to-stock, 501
    with backlog, 500
    with inventory, 500
    with overtime or subcontracting, 500, 505-506
Level production schedules, 470
Life cycle, stages in a product's, 48
Line balancing, 195-204
    with the incremental utilization heuristic, 198-201
    with the longest-task-time heuristic, 201-203
Line of balance (LOB), 642
Linear programming (LP), 173, 299
    cutting costs at American Airlines, 301
    solution methods, overview of other, 312-318
    using to analyze an aggregate-planning problem, 509-510
    using to analyze shipping decisions, 439
Linear programming problems
    characteristics of in POM, 302
    formulating, 303-307
    in POM, five common types of, 300
    interpreting computer solutions of, 320-323
    real, 318-320
    recognizing, 302-303
    solving, 307-318
Linear regression analysis, 69

Linear regression and correlation, 69-76
Line-balancing heuristics, 197
Line-balancing issues, 203
Line-balancing procedure, 196
Line-of-balance charts, 644
Load schedule, 607-609
Lobaccaro, Nicholas, 36
Location decisions, integrating quantitative and qualitative factors into, 185
Locational factors in types of facilities, relative importance of, 181
Logarithmic analysis, 722
Logistics, 437-441
    innovations in, 440-441
    management, 426
Longest-task-time heuristic, 197
    line balancing with, 201-203
    steps in, 201
Long-range capacity planning, 165-176
    ways of changing, 168
Long-range forecasts, 68-81
    data patterns in, 69
Lot sizes, 539
Lot tolerance percent defective (LTPD), 676, 677
Lot-for-lot (LFL), 518, 599
Lot-sizing, 517, 600-601
    in MRP, 598
Lot-sizing decisions, 598
    for materials with lumpy demands, 599-600
Lots, 665
Low impulse response, 82
Low-level code, 590
Lumpy demand, 598
    lot-sizing decisions for materials with, 599-600

M

Machine attachments, 232
Machine power, 9
Machine reliability, 760
Machine vision and optical sensors, 234
Macola, 570, 645
MacroSonix Corp., 115
Maintenance
    issues in service organizations, 761-763

policies that reduce frequency and severity of malfunctions, 745
    secondary department responsibilities, 760
    trends in, 760-761
Make-or-buy analysis, 433
Make-or-buy decision, 434
Malcolm Baldrige National Quality Award, 274-275, 276, 754
Management
    adding value by improving operations, 6-8
    by sight, 464
    demand, 516, 517
    logistics, 426
    modern quality, 270-274
    production and operations, 6
    providers, third-party logistics, 447
    scientific, 10-13
    supply chain, 425-427
    traditional quality, 269
Manager
    of purchasing, 430
    operations, 7
Manufactured products, characteristics of, 50-51
Manufacturers adopt total preventive maintenance, 742
Manufacturing
    and service jobs in the U.S., percentage of, 335
    cellular, 128
    discrete unit, 125
    eliminating waste in, 470
    JIT, 273, 463-464, 522
    lean, 273, 464, 522
    process, 125
    production planning in, 493
    supply chain management in, 428
    synchronous, 523
Manufacturing automation, types of, 231-235
Manufacturing facility layouts, 187-207
    analyzing, 194
Manufacturing 5, 647
Manufacturing flexibility, 247
    building, 247-248

Manufacturing layouts
    cellular, 190-191
    new trends in, 192-193
    planning cellular, 204-207
Manufacturing lead times, increasing production capacity reduces, 467-468
Manufacturing locations, rankings of U.S. regions and states as, 179
Manufacturing Matters: The Myth of the Post-Industrial Economy, 38
Manufacturing philosophy, JIT, 464-468
Manufacturing resource planning, 603
Manufacturing system, fixed, 247
Market inputs, 17
Market sensing and evaluation, 115-116
Market strategies, linking positioning strategies with, 54
Market surveys, 66, 67
Marketing and operations strategies, linking, 52-53
Maslow, Abraham, 13
Mass production, 13
Master production scheduling (MPS), 492, 511-520, 588
    computerized, 518-520
    in produce-to-stock and produce-to-order firms, 517-518
    objectives of, 511
    procedures for developing, 512-516
    process, 513
    time fences in, 511-512
    weekly updating of, 516-517
Matching demand, 498
Material inputs, process of acquiring, 432
Material record, 590
Material requirements planning (MRP), 584-605
    adapts to change, 603-604
    computer program, 590
    desirable characteristics of production systems suitable for, 604
    elements of, 588-591
    evaluation of, 604-605

in assemble-to-order firms, 602
issues in, 600-602
loading effects on work-center capacities, 608
lot-sizing in, 598
objectives of, 586-588
outputs of, 590-591
reducing inventories through, 583
schedule, 595
system, 589
systems, net change versus regenerative, 601
Material specification, 431
Materials, 425, 699
ABC classification of, 565-567
movement of within factories, 437
vice-president of, 426
with lumpy demands, lot-sizing decisions for, 599-600
Materials chart, 411
RATS project key materials acquisition plan/status report, 383
Materials management performance in world-class companies, 447
traditional ranking of performance criteria in, 447
Materials manager, 426
benchmarking the performance of, 446-447
Materials-handling, 187-188
equipment, 189
principles, 188
system, 188
Mathematical models for aggregate planning, 508-510
Mathematical programming, 307
Maturity stage, 47
Mayo, Elton, 13
McDonald's, 41
McGregor, Douglas, 13
MPS. See Master production scheduling
MRP. See Material requirements planning
Mean absolute deviation (MAD), 82
Mean observed time, 713
Mean squared error (MSE), 82

Measurements of capacity, 166
Measures of forecast accuracy, 82
Medical waste, cleaning up, 40
Methods analysis, 708-712
procedures of, 709
Methods-time measurement (MTM), 719
developing labor standards with, 717-718
labor standard calculation, 718
Microsoft Corp., 405
Microsoft Project, 405
data entry for the RAMOV project, 405
Gantt chart for the RAMOV project, 406
network diagram for the RAMOV project, 407
Military standard MIL-STD-105D tables, 680
Minimization problem, 306
Minimum lot sizes, 598
Minnesota Mining & Manufacturing Co. (3M), 41, 569
Mistake-proofing, 484
Mixed positioning strategies, 52
Modern quality management, 270-274
Modular bill of materials, 602
Moh, Laurence, 33
Monte Carlo, 362
Most likely time (t_m), 381, 394
Motivators, 703
Motoarc, 425
Motorola, 277
Move ticket, 626
Moving average forecasts versus actual cash demand, 85
Moving average method, 83-85
Moving average short-range forecasting, 83-84
Multiactivity charts, 710
Multiphase decisions, 174

Multiple regression analysis, 76

N

Nabisco, 230
Naive forecasts, 82-83
National Aeronautics and Space Administration (NASA), 398
National Association for Purchasing Managers (NAPM), 436
National Highway Traffic Safety Administration, 43
National Home Builders Association, 98
Necessary But Not Sufficient, 523
Net change MRP, 601
New Generation Computers (NGC), 492
New York Stock Exchange and a hog farm, 164
News-boy problems, 562
Nodes, 175
Noise, 68
Noise dampening, 82
impulse response and, 95
impulse response versus, 82
Nondefective, 665
Nonlinear multiple regression analysis, 76
Nonuniform demand, dealing with, 338
North American Free Trade Agreement (NAFTA), 30
Northeast Tool & Manufacturing Co., 703
Northrop Grumman, 231
Number of products to schedule, 517
Numerically controlled (N/C) machines, 232-233

O

Observed element times, 713
Occupational Safety and Health Administration (OSHA) Act, 39, 727, 728
Office of the President, 98
Offsetting for lead times, 607
Olin Corporation, 94
Operating characteristic (OC) curve, 676-680

for different sample sizes, 679
probabilities for, 678
Operating decisions, 21, 22
Operating expenses, 524
Operational effectiveness, 28
Operations, 17
and marketing strategies, linking, 52-53
and production functions and jobs in diverse organizations, 21
as a system, 17-20
managers, 7
nature of, 345-346
scarcity of resources, 38
systems, 19
Operations management, 6
adding value by improving, 6-8
entry-level jobs in, 7
factors affecting today, 16-17
some reason why forecasting is essential in, 64
studying, 17-22
Operations research, 13-14, 298
characteristics of, 14
in U.S. corporations, 299
Operations strategy, 43-51
developing, 44
elements of, 46-49
for services, 336
for the twenty-first century, 114
forming, 52-55
in services, 50-51
Opportunity costs, 562
Optimal safety stock level, 552
Optimistic time (t_o), 381, 394
Optimized Production Technology (OPT), 523, 646, 647
Optional replenishment model, 561
Oracle, 16, 241
Oracle Corporation, 405
Oracle Projects, 405
Order backlog, 132
Order entry, 516
Order filling, 152
Order point (OP), 539, 540
determining, 550-559
setting at service levels, 552

some rules of thumb in setting, 557-559

Order point systems, raw-materials inventory levels in MRP versus fixed order quantity, 587

Order promising, 516

Order quantities, 539
determining, 541-550

Ordering costs, 537
balancing against carrying costs, 540

Orders from the stores, 151-152

Order-sequencing problems, 630-638

Order-to-delivery cycle, 465

Ordinary operating conditions, 712

Organization chart showing supply chain management, 428

OSHA. *See* Occupational Safety & Health Act

Outbound merchandise, 153

Output rate capacity, 166

Outputs, 17
and inputs of a resource requirements planning system, 584
direct, 18
indirect, 18
intangible, 18
of MRP, 590-591

Outsourcing, 48
plans, 48-49
provided additional capacity, 173

Overcapacity, 167

Overdesign, 280, 760
and redundancy, improving product reliability with, 281-282

Overhead, 699

Overloading, 514

Overtime labor, 497

Overtime or subcontracting, buffering with, 503

P

Parallel processing, 472-473

Part families, 128

Partial and multiple correlation coefficients, 76

Partnership for a New Generation of Vehicles (PNGV), 117

Partnerships, developing supplier, 284-285

Parts family, 190

Payoff tables, 552
a retail stocking decision, 563-565

*(PDQ)*², 278

Peak-load prices, 511

PeopleSoft, 16, 241, 448, 603, 645

Percentage of EDDLT, 557

Perfect Design Quality, Pretty Darn Quick, 278

Perfect product and service quality, 35

Performance rating, 713

Performance reports, 591

Period order quantity (POQ) method, 599

Periodic inventory accounting systems, 443

Perlos Corporation, 481

Perpetual inventory accounting, 541
systems, 444

PERT, 384, 394-398
analysis of the RAMOV project, 395-396
critical paths, closer look at, 397-398

Pessimistic time (t_p), 381, 394

Philosophy of MRP systems, 588

Physical inventory counts, 443

Pickup point, 238

Plan-do-check-act (PDCA) cycle, 270, 271

Planned order
change in, 591
releases, 605
schedule, 590, 597

Planning horizons, length of, 518

Planning process and warehouse layouts, 194-195

Planning reports, 591

Planning, scheduling, and controlling projects, 378

Plant tours, 140-153

Plantation Timber Products (PTP), 33

Plate making, 149

Plate proofing, 149

Poka-yoke, 484

POM. *See* Production and operations management

Pond-draining approach, 520
to production planning and control, 521

Pond-draining systems, 520

Porter, Michael, 28

Positioning strategies
evolution of, 52
for a product life cycle, evolution of, 53
for services, 51
linking with market strategies, 54
pure and mixed, 52

Post-Civil War period, 10

PowerProject, 405

Predecessor activity, 381

Predetermined time standards, 717-720

Preemptive tactics, 183, 510-511

Preproduction planning, 131, 625

Present and proposed methods of completing authorization-to-investigate form, 712

Present-value analysis, 173

Preventive maintenance (PM), 274, 743
activities, 752-753
at the source, 753
database requirements, 753
determining the frequency of performing, 757-758
determining the number of spare parts to carry for, 755-757
modern approaches to, 753-760
programs, 752-760
projects, planning and controlling large-scale, 758-759

Primary resources, 18

Primavera Project Planner, 405

Primavera Systems Inc., 405

Printing and drying, 149

Priority, 626

Process and product/service design, simultaneous engineering, 118

Process and technology plans, 49

Process capability, 284

Process capability index (PCI), 284
three examples of, 285

Process chart, 140
for mixing aspirin, 142
flow diagram and, 710, 711

Process controls, automated, 235

Process design(s), 125-131
capital requirements for, 136
decisions, major factors affecting, 122-125
in services, 132-134
interrelationships among product design and inventory policy, 131-132
major factors affecting choice of, 123
type of depends on product diversity and batch size, 135

Process layouts, 188-189

Process life cycle, 135

Process manufacturing, 125

Process planning and design, 121-122

Process reengineering, 134

Process-focused, 127-128
factory, 147-150
production, 46, 127

Process-focused manufacturing, 625
scheduling, 623-638

Process-focused operations, 340-341
scheduling and shop-floor decisions in, 624

Processing alternatives
cost functions of, 136-137
deciding among, 134-140

Procter and Gamble Company (P&G), 299

Producer's risk (α), 676, 677

Produce-to-order, 47
Compaq changes to, 132
strategies, computer manufacturers adopt, 572

Produce-to-stock, 47
and produce-to-order firms MPS in, 517-518

Product design process at Boeing, virtual reality simulations in, 118
Product design, interrelationships among process design and inventory policy, 131-132
Product diversity and batch size, type of process design depends on, 135
Product flexibility, 123
Product flow at Safety Products Corporation, 146
Product forecasts into aggregate demand, 496
Product innovation, sources of, 115
Product layouts, 189-190
    planning, 195-204
Product life cycles, 135
    evolution of positioning strategies for, 53
    stages in, 48
Product quality, dimensions of, 267
Product standardization, 274
Product structure, 593
    file, 589
Product variety and batch size, 134-135
Products, 144-145
    designing and developing, 114-120
    designing for quality, 279
    developing new, 115-116
    getting new products to market faster, 116-118
    improving the designs of existing, 119
    to schedule, number of, 517
Products and services
    and their customer expectations, 664
    nature of, 93
    quality, 742
Product-focused, 125-127
    dedicated factory, 140-147
    manufacturing, scheduling, 638-644
    operations, 340
    production, 46, 126
Product/service
    demand, nature of, 122-123

design, simultaneous engineering: process and, 118
    plans, 47-48
    quality, 125
Production
    and operations functions and jobs in diverse organizations, 21
    designing for, 119, 279
    intermittent, 127
    process-focused, 127
    product-focused, 126
Production and operations management (POM), 6
    an evaluation of waiting-line analysis in, 355
    decision making in, 20-22
    evolution of, 9
    examples of things that must be forecasted in, 64
    five common types of LP problems in, 300
    historical milestone in, 8, 16
    problems that are appropriate for computer simulation analysis, characteristics of, 359
Production capacity, 165, 742
    dimensions of, 495-496
    increasing reduces manufacturing lead times, 467-468
    sources of medium-range, 497
Production card (P-Kanban), 474
Production control, 437
Production costs, 742
Production design, 116
Production flexibility, 123-124
Production line, 125, 189
    analysis, terminology of, 196
    rebalancing, 204
Production lots, 544
    effect of reducing changeover times on size, 478
    EOQ for, 639-640
    Model II–economic order quantity (EOQ) for, 544-546

use of Model II in determining the size of, 544-546
Production planning
    and control, pond draining approach to, 521
    and control systems, types of, 520-524
    hierarchy, 492
    in manufacturing, 493
Production problems, uncovering by reducing inventories, 471
Production process, 121
    break-even analysis, 138
    designing and controlling, 283
    type of, 51, 336
Production rates, variable, 247
Production scheduling
    decisions at Micro Scanners Corporation, 623
    run-out method of, 640-641
Production sharing, 32
Production system, 6, 17, 19
    automated, 235-239
    model, 18
    positioning, 46-47
    quality control throughout, 664
Production technology, 231
Production time, minimizing total, 636-638
Productive maintenance at Asten, Inc., 754
Productivity
    and human behavior, 698-705
    improvements in the United States, 701
    multifactor approach to measuring, 699-701
    pathway to satisfy workers' needs, 704
    U.S. companies focus on, 697
Program evaluation and review technique. See PERT
Project cost control systems, 398-400
Project Management Institute (PMI), 380
Project Management Professional (PMP), 380

Project management, 376-378
    computer software for, 404-406
    professionals, 380
    terms used in, 381
Project organization, 376, 377
Project schedule, 410
Project slack versus target slack, 400
Project teams, scheduling and controlling projects with, 379
Project-planning and control techniques, 379-404
ProModel, 194, 360
Proximity sensors, 234
Pull systems, 473, 522-523
Purchase orders, 432
Purchase requisitions, 431
Purchasing, 427-437
    agent, 430
    basic instruments, 431
    departments, 427, 430-431
    guidelines for ethical behavior in, 436
    manager of, 430
    mission of, 429-430
    processes, 431-433
    the international frontier, 436-437
Pure positioning strategies, 52
Push systems, 473, 521-522

Q

Q-1 list, 284
Qualitative forecasting methods, 66-67
Quality
    at the source, 272, 287, 753
    costs of, 268-269
    customer service, and cost challenges, 35-37
    designing for, 120, 279-283
    determinants of, 267-268
    dimensions of, 267
    drives the productivity machine, 272-273
    nature of, 267-269
    other aspects of the picture, 273
Quality circles (QC), 272, 287, 288

Quality control
 at Texas Telecom, 663
 computers in, 686-687
 in services, 687-688
 statistical concepts in,
  665-666
 throughout production
  systems, 664
Quality Control Handbook,
 272
Quality function deployment
 (QFD), 279
Quality gurus, 270-272
Quality Is Free, 272
Quality management
 at KFC, 266
 in services, 289-291
 modern, 270-274
 recognition, 274-277
 traditional, 269
Quality of design, 267
Quantitative forecasting models, 67-92
Quantity discount TMC
 curves, 551
Quantity discounting, 546
Quantity discounts
 economic order quantity
  (EOQ) with, 548-550
 identifying key quantities
  to investigate when
  quantity discounts ex-
  ist, 548
 Model III–EOQ with,
  546-550
Quasi-manufacturing, 133,
 337
 service operations, scheduling, 340-345
Queues, 348
 terminology of, 349
Queuing models
 and their formulas, 348-
  354
 definitions of variables
  for, 350
Queuing system structures,
 349
Queuing theory, 348
 using to achieve time-
  based competition, 467

R

R. R. Donnelley & Sons, 147-
 150

R/3. See Sap's R/3
RAMOV (Random Access
 Mobile Orthogonal Vi-
 sion), 387
RAMOV project, 388-390
 activities and event of, 387
 cost-time trade-offs in,
  400-404
 drawing the CPM net-
  work, 387-388
 Microsoft project data entry for, 405
 Microsoft project Gantt
  chart for, 406
 Microsoft project network
  diagram for, 407
 PERT analysis of, 395-
  396
RAMOV project's activities
 computing earliest finish
  (EF) for, 390-391
 computing latest finish
  (LF) and slack (S) for,
  391-393
 earliest start (ES) and latest start (LS) for, 393-
  394
Random Access Mobile Or-
 thogonal Vision. *See*
 RAMOV
Random fluctuation, 68
Random number ranges, 363
Random samples, 665
Ranging forecasts, 76
Ranging time series forecasts,
 77-78
Rating scale approach, 251-
 252
 to comparing automation
  alternatives, 252
RATS project
 expenditures plan/status
  report-expenditures
  chart, 383
 key materials acquisition
  plan/status report-
  materials chart, 383
 managing, 376
 schedule plan/status report
  summary-horizontal
  bar chart, 382
 time/cost plan versus actual performance chart,
  399
RATS time/cost status report,
 398

Raw-materials inventory, 442
 levels in MRP versus
  fixed order quantity,
  order point systems,
  587
Real gross domestic product
 per employed person by
 country, 700
Rebalancing a production
 line, 204
Receiving, 149
Reckitt & Colman, Inc., 42
Recycling and conservation in
 industry, 41
Reduced-capacity costs, 538
Redundant components, 281,
 760
Regenerative MRP, 601
Regional decision, 177
Regression equation, 70
Regs and rates, 438
Reject-lot zone, 675
Relative measures, 174
Relative-aggregate-scores ap-
 proach, 252-253
 to comparing alternative
  locations, 186
 to comparing automation
  alternatives, 252
Relative-aggregate-scores,
 252
Reliability, designing for,
 280-283
Renault SA, 33
Reorder cycle, relationships
 among DDT, EDDLT, SS,
 OP, and probability of
 stockouts for each, 553
Repair crews
 determining the size of,
  749-750
 standby machines, and repair shops, 746-747
Repair programs, 745-752
Repairs, 743
Repetitive manufacturing,
 480-481
 system, 464
Representative, 665
Requests for quotation, 432
Resource requirements planning system, 585
 inputs and outputs of, 584
Resources
 efficient use of at Tristar,
  298

strategic allocation of, 49
Retailing and other service
 locations, analyzing, 184
Returns, 248
Rework, 268
Risk of stockouts, 552
Robotry, 233
Robots, 233-234
Robust, 272
Robust design, 279
Rocket Aerial Target System.
 See RATS
Roethlisberger, F. J., 13
Rope, 524
Rough-cut capacity planning,
 514, 515
Routing plan, 605, 625
Rules commonly used to set
 values of •, 684
Run-out method, 640
 of production scheduling,
  640-641

S

S. C. Johnson, 41
S8 Architectural and Building
 Design Software, 194
Safety and loss prevention de-
 partments, 729
Safety impact, 41-43
Safety improvements at
 Georgia-Pacific, 728
Safety Products Corporation,
 140-147
Safety stock, 601-602
Safety stock at service levels
 for a discrete DDLT distri-
  bution, 553-555
 for constant lead time and
  normally distributed
  demand per day, 556-
  557
 for DDLT that is normally
  distributed, 555-556
Sales forecasts, 63
Sampling, 665-666
Sampling distributions, 666,
 667
SAP, 16, 241, 448, 570
SAP's R/3, 241, 603, 645
SC Corporation, 583
Scheduling Technologies
 Group Ltd., 523
Scientific management, 10-13
 at Ford's Rouge plant, 12

the players and their parts, 11

Scrap, 268

Scratch mix, 144

Sears, Roebuck and Company, 299

Seasonal patterns, 79

Seasonality, 68
in time series forecasts, 79

Seasonalized time series forecasts, 80-81

Secondary maintenance department responsibilities, 760

Seiketsu (standardize), 484

Seiri (sort), 484

Seiso (sweep, or spic and span), 484

Seiton (straighten), 484

Self-discipline (shitsuke), 484

Self-interests, 39

Sequencing jobs through two work centers with Johnson's rule, 636-638

Sequencing rules, 630-631
comparison of, 631-634
criteria for evaluating, 631
evaluating, 631

Sequential-sampling plan, 674-675, 676

Service and manufacturing jobs in the U.S., percentage of, 335

Service companies, JIT in, 484

Service design
simultaneous engineering: process and product/, 118
type of, 51, 336

Service economy, 38

Service facility layouts, 207-210
analyzing, 208-210
types of, 207-208
using closeness ratings to develop, 209-210

Service facility location decisions, steps in analyzing, 184

Service industries and companies, 15

Service levels, 552
for a discrete DDLT distribution, setting safety stock at, 553-555

for constant lead time and normally distributed demand per day, setting safety stock levels at, 556-557
for DDLT that is normally distributed, setting safety stock at, 555-556
setting order points at, 552-557

Service locations, analyzing retailing and other, 184

Service operations, 150-153
nature of customer-as-product, 356-358
scheduling customer-as-participant, 345-355
scheduling customer-as-product, 355-366
scheduling quasi-manufacturing, 340-345
types of, 337
using computer simulation in, 358-366
waiting lines in, 346-355
work-shift scheduling in, 341-345

Service organizations, maintenance issues in, 761-763

Service recovery, 290

Service revolution, 15

Service sector, continued growth of, 37-38

Service times, normally distributed, 364

Service/product demand, nature of, 122-123

Service/product quality, 125

ServiceModel, 360

Services
aggregate plans for, 506-508
and the use of automated equipment, degree of customer contact in, 244
automation in, 242-246
characteristics of, 50-51
competitive priorities for, 51
designing and developing, 114-120
examples of total quality management in, 291
nature of products and, 93

operations strategies for, 336
operations strategy in, 50-51
positioning strategies for, 51
process design in, 132-134
quality control in, 687-688
quality management in, 289
revisited, nature of, 334-336
scheduling challenges in, 337-340
some common misconceptions about, 335

Shewart, Walter, 270

Shipments to and from factories, 438-440

Shipping, 150

Shipping costs, minimizing, 440

Shitsuke (self-discipline), 484

Shop system, 10

Shop-floor planning and control, 626-630

Short cycle manufacturing, 464

Shortest processing time (SPT), 630, 634

Short-range forecasting, moving average, 83-84

Short-range forecasts, 81-92
exponential smoothing, 86-87

Signatures, 149

Simple linear regression
analysis, 69, 72-74
a time series, 71-72
variable definitions and formulas for, 70

Simplex method, 313

Simplification, 119

SIMPROCESS, 194, 360

SIMSCRIPT, 360

Simultaneous engineering, 117, 121
process and product/service design, 118

Single-period inventory models, 562-565

Single-sample acceptance plans
for attributes, 675-680
for variables, 685

Single-sampling plan, 674-675

Sino Aerospace Investment Corporation, 33

Site selection, 177

Six Sigma, 277

SKEP, 570

Slack (S), 381, 391
for the RAMOV project's activities, computing latest finish (LF) and, 391-393
target versus project, 400
variable, 320

Slitting and collating, 149

Small Business Administration, 250

Small businesses, forecasting in, 97

Smallest LF – D, 392

SMART (Scheduling Management And Restaurant Tool) Labor Management System, 358

SMC Pneumatics, 630

SMED (single minute exchange of dies), 471

Smith, Adam, 9

Smoothing constant, 86
one company's rules for changing, 96

Social-responsibility issues, 39-43

Software for analyzing facility layouts, 194

Software systems for automation, 239-242

Software, top-selling supply chain management, 442

Sonoco, 41

Sort (seiri), 484

Specification, 119

Spitzer, Daniel, 33

Sprint, 289

Square D Corporation, 287

Stable, 470

Standard deviation of the forecast, 77

Standard error of the forecast, 77, 82

Standard products, 46

Standardization, 119

Standardize (seiketsu), 484

Standby machines, determining the number of, 750-751

Standby or back up machines, 746

Start-up quality costs, 537

Start-up ventures, forecasting in, 97

Statistical control, 290

Statistical process control (SPC), 667
  at Georgia-Pacific, 668

Statistics, using, 682-684

Stepwise regression, 76

Stock record, 443

Stock requisition, 442

Stock-keeping unit (SKU), 443

Stockless production, 464

Stockout costs, 537
  lower annual, 559

Storage and retrieval (S/R) machine, 238

Straighten (seiton), 484

Straight-line labor, 497

Strategic alliances, 32, 33

Strategic allocation of resources, 49

Strategic decisions, 21-22

Strategic outsourcing, 123
  from vertical to virtual integration, 124

Strategies
  a variety can be successful, 53-55
  at the U.S. Postal Service and Dell, 27-28
  linking operations and marketing, 52-53
  linking positioning with market, 54

Study for collating handouts, 715

Subcontracting, 497
  or overtime, buffering with, 503

Subcontractor and supplier networks, 172-173

Subcontractor networks, 172, 476

Successor activity, 381

SuperProject, 405

Supervisor estimates, 719

Supplier development, 476

Supplier partnerships, developing, 284-285

Supplier relations, 476

Supply chain, 426
  for steel in an automobile door, 427

Supply chain management, 425-427
  e-business and, 448-449
  in manufacturing, 428
  organization chart showing, 428
  software, 442

Supply chain manager, 426

Survey of customers, 66, 67

Survey of sales force, 66, 67

Sustainable practical capacity, 165

Swearingen Aircraft Co., 33

Sweep, or spic and span (seiso), 484

Synchronous manufacturing, 523, 646
  the "drum-buffer-rope" way, 647

System, 17
  of interchangeable parts, 119
  operations as, 17-20
  production, 17, 19

System reliability (SR), 280
  as a function of component part reliability and number of component parts, 281

T

Taco Bell Corporation, 299, 358

Tactile sensors, 233

Taguchi, Genichi, 272

Tangible goods, 18, 50

Target slack versus project slack, 400

Taylor, Frederick Winslow, 10-11

Team production, 706

Technical and economic feasibility studies, 115

Technological change, managing, 248-249

Technology
  advanced, 37, 231
  and process plans, 49
  automated, 245
  communications, 245
  group, 128
  production, 231
  radio and laser, 286
  strategic use of at Nabisco, 230

Terms used in project management, 381

The Goal: A Process of Ongoing Improvement, 523

Theory of constraints (TOC), 523, 646

Time fence, 511
  in master production scheduling (MPS), 511-512

Time series, 67
  simple linear regression, 71-72

Time series forecasts
  seasonality in, 79
  seasonalized, 80-81

Time span, 93

Time study, 713-714
  setting labor standards with, 714
  steps in determining labor standards from, 713

Time-based competition (TBC), 355, 464, 466
  using queuing theory to achieve, 467

Time-from-order-to-delivery cycle, 465

Time-phasing products, effects of on facility capacity utilization, 169

Today and Tomorrow, 12, 468

Tolerances, 119

Top management commitment and involvement, 278

Total normal time, 713

Total quality control (TQC), 272, 278

Total quality management (TQM), 277, 472
  in services, examples of, 291
  programs, 277-289

Total systems approach, 14

Total variation, 75

Toyota System, The, 464

Tracking signal, 95

Trade-off decision, 176

Traditional quality management, 269

Traditional view of how much to inspect, 270

Traffic departments, 438

Traffic management, 438

Transportation LP problem, 315

Transportation method, 315

Trends, 68
  exponential smoothing with, 88-92
  in maintenance, 760-761
  in manufacturing layouts, new, 192-193

Tristar Pet Food Company, 298

Trucking on the web, 441

TurboProject, 405

Turning points, 72

Two-bin system, 541

U

U.S. Department of Commerce, 98, 250

U.S. Department of Labor, 98, 250

U.S. export growth, 30

Uncertainty and EOQ, 567-568

Uncontrollable factors, 279

Underloading, 514

Unexplained variation, 75

United Auto Workers (UAW), 754

United States Postal Service, 27

V

Value analysis, 119

Variable production rates, 247

Variables, 665
  affecting labor productivity, 702
  setting acceptance criteria for, 685-686
  single-sample acceptance plans for, 685

Variation of dependent variable (y), 75

Vendor-managed inventories, 568-569

Vertical backward and forward integration, 438

Vertical integration, 123
  degree of, 123

Vice-president of materials, 426

VisFactory, 194

Visual Basic, 360

Volume flexibility, 124

W

Waiting line analysis, 173
Waiting lines
   analyzing, 351
   characteristics of, 348
Waiting-line analysis in POM,
   evaluation of, 355
Walker, M. R., 384
Wal-Mart Regional Distribution Center , 150-153
Walton, Bud, 150
Walton, Sam, 150
Warehouse layouts and planning process, 194-195
Warehousing, 441-445
   contemporary develop-
      ments in, 445
   operations, 441-443
Waste
   cleaning up medical, 40
   eliminating, 470

Watt, James, 9
Wealth of Nations, The, 9
Weighted moving average
   method, 85
Wheelwright, Steven, 52
Whitehead, T. N., 13
Whitney, Eli, 9
WinMagi, 645
Work measurement, 712-720
   techniques for some jobs,
      720
Work methods analysis, 708-
   712
Work sampling, 714-717
   setting labor standards
      with, 715-716
Work teams and empower-
   ment, 286-287
Worker and machine chart,
   710
Worker displacement, train-
   ing, and retraining, 249

Worker empowerment, 708
Workerless factories, 752
Worker-minutes per unit of
   output, 712
Workers repair their own ma-
   chines, 748-752
Workers, empowerment of,
   472, 707-708
Workers' compensation laws,
   727
Workers' jobs, designing,
   705-707
Work-sampling observations,
   guide to minimum number
   of, 717
Work-shift heuristic rule, 344
Work-shift scheduling in ser-
   vice operations, 341-345
World business, changing na-
   ture of, 29-30
World Trade Organization
   (WTO), 31

World-class companies, 23

X

Xerox Corporation, 41, 93,
   277

Z

Z scores, 364
Zero defects, 272
Zysman, John, 38

Photo Credits

Page 2   © PhotoDisc, Inc.
Page 5   © Ed Kashi/Corbis
Page 15   © Susan Van Etten
Page 15   © Susan Van Etten
Page 15   © South-Western Publishing
Page 20   © Pablo Corral V/Corbis
Page 26   © Steve Chenn/Corbis
Page 32   © Susan Van Etten
Page 39   © Corbis
Page 60   © PhotoDisc, Inc.
Page 62   Courtesy © Southwest Airlines
Page 70   © R.W. Jones/Corbis
Page 96   © Susan Van Etten
Page 113   Courtesy © Boeing Company
Page 126   © Paul A. Souders/Corbis
Page 143   © Doug Wilson/Corbis
Page 163   © Ronnen Eshel/Corbis
Page 180   © Susan Van Etten
Page 208   © Reinhard Eisele/Corbis
Page 229   © Corbis
Page 234   © Charles O'Rear/Corbis
Page 242   © PhotoDisc, Inc.
Page 265   Courtesy © Southwest Airlines
Page 268   © Ed Young/Corbis
Page 283   © Adamsmith Productions/Corbis
Page 297   © Danny Lehman/Corbis
Page 301   Courtesy © Southwest Airlines
Page 308   © AFP/Corbis
Page 333   © Susan Van Etten
Page 347   © Mark Richards/PhotoEdit
Page 356   © PhotoDisc, Inc.
Page 375   © Bob Rowan; Progressive Image/Corbis
Page 384   © Corbis

Page 395   © Susan Van Etten
Page 422   © PhotoDisc, Inc.
Page 424   © Reuters Newmedia, Inc./Corbis
Page 431   © Charles O'Rear/Corbis
Page 443   © Charles E. Rotkin/Corbis
Page 462   © Charles O'Rear/ Corbis
Page 465   © Keith Wood/Corbis
Page 469   © Judy Griesedieck/Corbis
Page 491   © Scott T. Smith/Corbis
Page 497   © PhotoDisc, Inc.
Page 516   © Ed Kashi/Corbis
Page 535   © Kenneth Rogers/Corbis
Page 541   © PhotoDisc, Inc.
Page 567   © Premium Stock/Corbis
Page 582   © Kevin Fleming/Corbis
Page 586   © Corbis
Page 607   © Danny Lehman/Corbis
Page 622   © Wally McNamee/Corbis
Page 634   © Sally A. Morgan; Ecoscene/Corbis
Page 642   © Keith Wood/Corbis
Page 645   © Paul A. Souders/Corbis
Page 660   © PhotoDisc, Inc.
Page 662   © Tim Wright/Corbis
Page 671   © Philip Gould/Corbis
Page 687   © Ed Kashi/Corbis
Page 696   © James A. Sugar/Corbis
Page 704   © Reuters Newmedia, Inc./Corbis
Page 727   © David H. Wells/Corbis
Page 741   © PhotoDisc, Inc.
Page 746   © Roger Ressmeyer/Corbis
Page 762   © Dave Bartruff/Corbis
Page 763   © Mark Gibson/Corbis